The Handbook of Homicide

Wiley Handbooks in Criminology and Criminal Justice

Series Editor: Charles F. Wellford, University of Maryland College Park.

The handbooks in this series will be comprehensive, academic reference works on leading topics in criminology and criminal justice.

The Handbook of Law and Society
Edited by Austin Sarat and Patricia Ewick

The Handbook of Juvenile Delinquency and Juvenile Justice
Edited by Marvin D. Krohn and Jodi Lane

The Handbook of Deviance
Edited by Erich Goode

The Handbook of Gangs
Edited by Scott H. Decker and David C. Pyrooz

The Handbook of Criminological Theory
Edited by Alex R. Piquero

The Handbook of Drugs and Society
Edited by Henry H. Brownstein

The Handbook of the Criminology of Terrorism
Edited by Gary LaFree and Joshua D. Freilich

The Handbook of Homicide
Edited by Fiona Brookman, Edward R. Maguire, and Mike Maguire

The Handbook of Homicide

Edited by

Fiona Brookman, Edward R. Maguire,
and Mike Maguire

WILEY Blackwell

This edition first published 2017

Registered Office
John Wiley & Sons Ltd, The Atrium, Southern Gate, Chichester, West Sussex, PO19 8SQ, UK

Editorial Offices
350 Main Street, Malden, MA 02148-5020, USA
9600 Garsington Road, Oxford, OX4 2DQ, UK
The Atrium, Southern Gate, Chichester, West Sussex, PO19 8SQ, UK

For details of our global editorial offices, for customer services, and for information about how to apply for permission to reuse the copyright material in this book please see our website at www.wiley.com/wiley-blackwell.

Library of Congress Cataloging-in-Publication Data

Names: Brookman, Fiona, editor. | Maguire, Edward R., editor. | Maguire, Mike, 1945– editor.
Title: The handbook of homicide / edited by Fiona Brookman, Edward R. Maguire, and Mike Maguire.
Description: Chichester, West Sussex, UK : John Wiley & Sons, 2017. | Includes bibliographical references and index.
Identifiers: LCCN 2016044491 | ISBN 9781118924471 (cloth) | ISBN 9781118924495 (epub) | ISBN 9781118924488 (ePDF)
Subjects: LCSH: Homicide.
Classification: LCC HV6515 .H3547 2017 | DDC 364.152–dc23
LC record available at https://lccn.loc.gov/2016044491

A catalogue record for this book is available from the British Library.

Cover image: ©Betty Fernandes
Cover design by Wiley

Set in 10.5/13pt Minion by SPi Global, Pondicherry, India
Printed and bound in Malaysia by Vivar Printing Sdn Bhd

10 9 8 7 6 5 4 3 2 1

Contents

Notes on Contributors

Erik Alda is a PhD candidate in justice, law, and criminology at American University, Washington, DC. Erik has conducted extensive research and published peer-reviewed articles on Latin America, the Caribbean and sub-Saharan Africa on issues related to crime and violence, policing, and related issues. Erik's main interest lies in the measurement of efficiency of criminal justice institutions and differences in crime and security in developing countries.

Thomas S. Alexander is Lieutenant of Police with the Hagerstown, MD, police department and the Director of Grants and Research. He is also an adjunct faculty member in the University of Maryland's Department of Criminology and Criminal Justice and in the graduate Criminal Justice Management program. His current research interests are in homicide clearance, race and policing, and evidence-based policing strategies. He received his PhD from the University of Maryland.

Olivia R. Allen is a graduate student at the University of Missouri-Kansas City, where she graduated with her bachelor's degree. She is currently the principal investigator of an evaluation of a summer jobs and life-skills program designed to prevent gang membership and violence among high-risk youth in Kansas City, Missouri. Her research interests include juvenile justice, gangs, and pretrial services.

Cheryl Allsop is Senior Lecturer at the University of South Wales, UK. In 2012 she completed a PhD on cold case investigations, looking at how the police seek to solve long-term unsolved major crimes, drawing on eight months spent with a major crime review team and interviews with UK Home Office, policing officials, and experts frequently involved in the investigation of hard to solve crimes.

Andy Aydın-Aitchison is Senior Lecturer in Criminology and Postgraduate Research Director at the University of Edinburgh School of Law. He researches and writes on the criminology of atrocity, with a primary focus on the former Yugoslavia, and on criminal justice reform in states in transition. He directed the MSc program in global crime, justice and security from 2009 to 2016 and he continues to teach and supervise on this program.

Alfred Blumstein is the J. Erik Jonsson University Professor of Urban Systems and Operations Research and former Dean of Carnegie Mellon's Heinz College of Public Policy and Information Systems. He has had extensive experience in both research and policy with the criminal justice system since serving as Director of Science and Technology for the President's Crime Commission (1966–1967). He was Chair of the Pennsylvania Commission on Crime and Delinquency and was a member of the Pennsylvania Commission on Sentencing. He was awarded the Stockholm Prize in Criminology in 2007.

Patrick Q. Brady is a doctoral student in the Department of Criminal Justice and Criminology at Sam Houston State University. His research interests focus on campus crime, burnout, and decision-making practices among investigators of interpersonal violence. His work has appeared in the *Journal of Interpersonal Violence*, the *Journal of Contemporary Criminal Justice*, and the *Journal of Criminal Justice Education*.

Anthony A. Braga is Distinguished Professor and Director of the School of Criminology and Criminal Justice at Northeastern University. Dr. Braga's research involves collaborating with criminal justice, social service, and community-based organizations to address illegal access to firearms, reduce gang and group-involved violence, and control crime hot spots.

Fiona Brookman is Professor of Criminology at the University of South Wales (UK) and Chair of the Criminal Investigation Research Network (CIRN) that she established in 2011. She received her PhD from Cardiff University in 2000. Fiona's research focuses on various aspects of violence and homicide and she is currently leading a British ethnographic study (funded by the Leverhulme Trust) exploring the role of science and technology in homicide investigation.

Timothy S. Bynum, PhD, is Professor in the School of Criminal Justice at Michigan State University. His research focuses on public policy evaluation in the area of crime and justice. He directed numerous projects evaluating criminal justice interventions and was a member of the evaluation team for the Weed and Seed Program, the Youth Firearms Violence Initiative, the Transition from Prison to Community Initiative, School Resource Officer Programs, and the Juvenile Accountability Block Grant Program.

Liqun Cao is Professor of Sociology and Criminology at the University of Ontario Institute of Technology, Canada. He is also an Adjunct Professor at Queensland University of Technology, Australia. His research essays have appeared in numerous professional journals. He is the author of *Major Criminological Theories: Concepts and Measurement* (2004) and the lead author of *Policing in Taiwan: From Authoritarianism to Democracy* (2014). He is also the lead editor of *The Routledge Handbook of Chinese Criminology* (2014).

Heng Choon (Oliver) Chan, PhD, is Assistant Professor of Criminology at City University of Hong Kong. His academic background is in criminology and forensic psychology. Oliver's research focuses on sexual homicide, offender profiling, sex offending, homicide, stalking behavior, and criminological issues related to the Asian population. He has published extensively in the area of sexual homicide, with his most recent research monograph, *Understanding Sexual Homicide Offenders: An Integrated Approach,* being published by Palgrave Macmillan (2015).

Mark Cooney is Professor of Sociology and Adjunct Professor of Law at the University of Georgia, USA. His work addresses various aspects of conflict and its management including the role of third parties in homicide, the long-term decline of lethal conflict among elites, and, most recently, family honor killing. His publications include a theoretical study of responses to homicide in human societies, *Is Killing Wrong? A Study in Pure Sociology* (University of Virginia Press, 2009).

Deborah Davis is Professor of Psychology at the University of Nevada, Reno, and a member of the faculty of the National Judicial College. She has published widely in the areas of witness memory, police interrogation and confessions, and communicating and understanding sexual intentions. She worked for more than 20 years as a trial consultant, has testified as an expert witness in close to 150 trials, and is a frequent speaker at CLE seminars across the country.

Myrna Dawson is Professor of Sociology, Canada Research Chair in Public Policy in Criminal Justice, and Director of the Centre for the Study of Social and Legal Responses to Violence, University of Guelph, Canada. Her current research examines intimacy, violence, and law as well as the rise and impact of domestic violence death review committees. Recent articles appear in *Trauma Violence & Abuse, Child Abuse & Neglect*, and *Journal of Research in Crime and Delinquency.*

Russell P. Dobash and R. Emerson Dobash (Emeritus Professors) Criminology, School of Law, University of Manchester, UK, have conducted groundbreaking research on violence against women and published award-winning publications including: *Violence Against Wives* (Free Press, 1979); *Women, Violence and Social Change* (Routledge, 1992); *Rethinking Violence Against Women* (Sage, 1998); *Changing Violent Men* (Sage, 2000); and *When Men Murder Women* (Oxford University Press, 2015).

Tom Ellis is Principal Lecturer in the Institute of Criminal Justice Studies, University of Portsmouth, UK. He has published extensively on Japanese criminal justice, often with Koichi Hamai, and also in a number of other areas, including gambling in Japan. His current research interests and activities are comparative youth justice, police use of body worn video cameras, and combat sports.

Li Eriksson is Lecturer with the School of Criminology and Criminal Justice at Griffith University. Her research forms part of the Australian Homicide Project, which is a national ARC Discovery project examining developmental and situational pathways to homicide. Her research interests include violence, intimate partner homicide, filicide, and criminological theory. Before joining Griffith University, Li worked as a research analyst for the Swedish National Council of Crime Prevention.

Andrew M. Fox is Assistant Professor in the Department of Criminology at California State University, Fresno. He received his PhD from Arizona State University in criminology and criminal justice. His research interests include social network analysis, gangs, crime prevention, mental health, and communities. His work has been published in the *Pan American Journal of Public Health, Crime and Delinquency, Justice Quarterly*, and the *American Sociological Review.*

James Alan Fox is the Lipman Family Professor of Criminology, Law, and Public Policy at Northeastern University. With specializations in homicide and statistical methods, he has written 18 books, including *Extreme Killing, The Will to Kill*, and *Violence and Security on Campus*. He has published widely in both scholarly and popular outlets, and, as a member of its board of contributors, his column appears regularly in *USA Today*.

Soenita M. Ganpat is Lecturer and post-doctoral fellow in criminology at Nottingham Trent University, UK. She played an active role in maintaining and further expanding the Dutch Homicide Monitor to provide the most reliable overview of homicide in the Netherlands. Ganpat furthermore contributed to building the first joint database on homicide in Europe: the European Homicide Monitor. Her research focuses on homicide, violence, interaction between offenders, victims, and third parties, personal characteristics of offenders and victims, and immediate situational factors.

Aisha K. Gill, PhD, is Professor of Criminology at University of Roehampton, UK. Her main areas of interest and research are health and criminal justice responses to violence against black, minority, ethnic, and refugee women in the UK, Iraqi Kurdistan, and India. She has been involved in addressing the problem of violence against women and girls/"honor" crimes and forced marriage at the grassroots level for the past seventeen years and has published widely in refereed journals.

Eric Grommon is Assistant Professor in the School of Public and Environmental Affairs at Indiana University-Purdue University Indianapolis. His research interests include community crime prevention, research methods, and the evaluation of criminal justice programs and policies. His work has been published in *Criminology & Public Policy, Evaluation Review, Journal of Experimental Criminology, Justice Quarterly, Police Quarterly*, and *Policing and Society.*

Debarati Halder, PhD, is an Advocate and legal researcher. She is the Managing Director of the Centre for Cyber Victim Counselling, India. She received her LLB from the University of Calcutta, her master's degree in international and constitutional law from the University of Madras, and PhD degree from the National Law School of India University (NLSIU), Bengaluru, India. She has published many articles in peer-reviewed journals including the *British Journal of Criminology* and *Victims and Offenders.*

Nathan Hall is Associate Head of Department at the Institute of Criminal Justice Studies at the University of Portsmouth, UK. He has published widely in the field of hate crime, and is a member of the Cross-Government Hate Crime Independent Advisory Group, the National Police Chief's Council Hate Crime Working Group, and the Crown Prosecution Service's Hate Crime Scrutiny Panel.

Koichi Hamai graduated from Waseda University, Japan. He worked in the area of offender rehabilitation in the Ministry of Justice of Japan including a secondment to UNICRI until 2003. His research focus has been in criminal justice statistics and the rehabilitation of offenders. He is the author of about ninety national and international publications. He currently holds a position as Professor of the Law School at Ryukoku University in Kyoto.

Kathleen M. Heide, PhD, is Professor of Criminology at the University of South Florida, Tampa. Professor Heide is an internationally recognized consultant and lecturer on homicide, particularly as it pertains to juvenile defendants and individuals who kill parents (parricide). She is the author or co-author of four books and approximately 100 other scholarly publications. Dr Heide, a licensed mental health professional and a court-appointed expert, has evaluated adolescents and adults charged with murder in 13 US states and Canada.

Helen Innes is a research associate at the Crime and Security Research Institute at Cardiff University specializing in the analysis of social survey and police data. Recent projects have reported on anti-social behavior (2013–2014, Her Majesty's Inspectorate of Constabulary), community support officers in Wales (2014, Welsh Government) and victims of crime (2014, OPCC South Wales). Her current research interests focus on the application of nudge theory to preventative crime behaviors.

Martin Innes is Director of the Crime and Security Research Institute, Universities' Police Science Institute, and the Open Source Communications Analytics Research (OSCAR) Development Centre, all at Cardiff University. He is author of the books *Signal Crimes* (Oxford University Press, 2014), *Investigating Murder* (Oxford University Press, 2003), and *Understanding Social Control* (Open University Press, 2003).

K. Jaishankar is presently the Professor and Head of the Department of Criminology, Raksha Shakti University, Ahmedabad, Gujarat, India. He is the recipient of the National Academy of Sciences, India (NASI) - SCOPUS Young Scientist Award (2012)—Social Sciences. He is the founding president of the South Asian Society of Criminology and Victimology (SASCV) and an international ambassador of the British Society of Criminology (BSC).

Holly Johnson has been engaged in research on violence against women for 30 years, first at Statistics Canada and more recently as Professor of Criminology at the University of Ottawa. Her research interests center on primary prevention, improving societal responses to crimes of violence against women, and improving research methodologies for measuring women's experiences of violence. She has been a visiting fellow at Griffith University and the Australian Institute of Criminology.

Helen Jones, PhD, is a research fellow at the University of South Wales, UK, and is working with Fiona Brookman on a British study exploring the role of forensic and digital technologies in homicide investigation. Prior to this, Helen worked for an English police force for over 12 years, which included roles as the protecting vulnerable people intelligence analyst and a review officer, reviewing undetected homicides, stranger rapes, missing persons, and "cold cases."

Erin M. Kearns is a postdoctoral research fellow in the Global Studies Institute at Georgia State University. Her primary research seeks to understand the relationships among terrorism, counterterrorism, and security policy. Her publications include articles on why groups lie about terrorism, conditions that impact perceptions of counterterrorism practices, and relationships between communities and law enforcement. Her work has been funded through a number of sources, including the National Consortium for the Study of and Responses to Terrorism (START).

William R. King is a Professor and Associate Dean of Research in the College of Criminal Justice at Sam Houston State University in Texas, USA. He received his PhD in criminal justice from the University of Cincinnati in 1998. His research interests include the study of police and forensic evidence processing organizations from a theoretical perspective. He also studies the investigation of homicides and the operation and utility of ballistics imaging systems.

Joseph B. Kuhns is Professor in the Department of Criminal Justice and Criminology at the University of North Carolina, Charlotte. He previously worked for the Office of Community Oriented Policing Services in the US Department of Justice. Joe has managed a number of research and evaluation projects that have focused on lethal violence against the police, adaption to residential burglary, reducing harms associated with prostitution, the impact of community policing, and the linkages between alcohol and drug use and violent crime.

Richard A. Leo, PhD, JD, is the Hamill Family Professor of Law and Psychology at the University of San Francisco. He is one of the leading experts in the world on police interrogation practices, psychological coercion, false confessions, and the wrongful conviction of the innocent. He has won numerous individual and career achievement awards for research excellence and distinction. His research has been cited by numerous appellate courts, including the United States Supreme Court, on multiple occasions.

Jack Levin is Professor Emeritus and Co-director of Northeastern University's Center on Violence and Conflict. He has authored or co-authored more than 30 books, including *Mass Murder: America's Growing Menace, Extreme Killing, and Serial Killers and Sadistic Murderers* as well as more than 150 articles in professional journals and major newspapers. Levin has received awards from the American Sociological Association, Eastern Sociological Society, Association of Clinical and Applied Sociology, and Society for the Study of Social Problems.

Marieke Liem is a Marie Curie fellow at the Kennedy School for Government at Harvard University and holds a position as Associate Professor at the Department of

Governance and Global Affairs at Leiden University, the Netherlands. She is chairing the European Homicide Research Group and is the coordinator of the European Homicide Monitor. Her work focuses on the causes and correlates of homicide as well as on the effects of long-term incarceration among those sentenced for homicide.

Marie Rosenkrantz Lindegaard is anthropologist, criminologist, and senior researcher at the Netherlands Institute for the Study of Crime and Law Enforcement (NSCR). Her work focuses on the social mechanisms behind violent acts and victimization, cultural explanations for crime, and micro-sociological approaches to violence. She did ethnographic fieldwork in South Africa and currently analyzes CCTV camera footage of robberies and street fights in the Netherlands and Denmark.

Alexandra Lysova, PhD, is Assistant Professor in the School of Criminology at Simon Fraser University, Canada. Her research interests focus on intimate partner violence, homicide in Russia, and international homicide statistics. She has received her Doctor of Sciences degree from the Russian Academy of Sciences and her PhD in criminology from the University of Toronto. Her recent publications appear in the *Handbook of European Homicide Research*, *Theoretical Criminology*, *Aggressive Behaviour*, and the *Journal of Interpersonal Violence*.

Edward R. Maguire is Professor in the School of Criminology and Criminal Justice and Associate Director in the Center for Violence Prevention and Community Safety at Arizona State University. His professional interests focus on policing, violence, research methods, and comparative criminology. His current research focuses on procedural justice and legitimacy in policing and corrections and on gangs and violence in the United States, the Caribbean, and Latin America.

Mike Maguire is part-time Professor of Criminology at the University of South Wales and Professor Emeritus at Cardiff University, UK. His work has covered many areas of crime and justice, including burglary, violence, criminal statistics, victims, policing, crime reduction, and offender rehabilitation. He co-edited five editions of the *Oxford Handbook of Criminology*. His current research concerns prisoner resettlement and the role of voluntary agencies in criminal justice. He is a long-standing member of the Correctional Services Accreditation and Advice Panel.

Carl P. Malmquist, MD, MS, is Professor of Social/Forensic Psychiatry at the University of Minnesota and board-certified in adult/child-adolescent and forensic psychiatry. Dr Malmquist teaches courses entitled "Killing" and "Criminal Psychopathology." He also co-teaches a law school course on "Law, Society & Mental Health System." Apart from this academic work, he consults on court cases with law firms or court-ordered cases. He has personally evaluated over 500 homicide cases.

Christopher D. Maxwell received his PhD from Rutgers in 1998 and is currently Professor in the School of Criminal Justice at Michigan State University, faculty associate at the University of Michigan's Institute for Social Research, and honorary senior research fellow at Cardiff University. Dr Maxwell formerly served as the director of the US Department of Justice's National Archive of Criminal Justice Data.

Paul Mazerolle is Professor and Pro Vice Chancellor at Griffith University, Australia. He also directs the Violence Research Program at Griffith and is co-editor of the *Journal of Developmental and Life-Course Criminology*. He undertakes research on the processes that shape criminal offending across the life course. Most recently, he led the Australian Homicide Project in collaboration with Li Eriksson, Richard Wortley, and Holly Johnson.

John D. McCluskey is Professor in the Department of Criminal Justice at the Rochester Institute of Technology. His current research projects involve evaluations of body-worn video in several departments and assessing the extent and causes of teacher victimization in San Antonio, TX.

Sophie Pike is a doctoral student and lecturer at the University of South Wales. Sophie's research explores changes to the investigation of homicide in England and Wales from the 1980s to the present day. During her fieldwork, she interviewed former and serving homicide detectives, analyzed homicide case files, and observed investigations and detective training. Her publications include an article for *Sage Research Methods Cases* detailing her fieldwork experiences.

Jesenia M. Pizarro is Associate Professor in the School of Criminology and Criminal Justice at Arizona State University. Professor Pizarro has worked with various police departments throughout the United States in joint efforts to curb violence. Her work focuses on the social ecology and social reaction of homicide. Her work has appeared in the *American Journal of Public Health*, *Justice Quarterly*, *Criminal Justice and Behavior*, and *Homicide Studies*.

William Alex Pridemore is Dean of and Professor in the School of Criminal Justice at the University at Albany, State University of New York. His primary criminological research interests include social structure and homicide, alcohol and violence, cross-national homicide rates, and rural criminology. He also carries out research on alcohol epidemiology, the Russian mortality crisis, and the sociology of health and illness.

Charles Ransford, MPP, is the Director of Science and Policy for Cure Violence where he leads the campaign to make violence a health issue, oversees all research, and plays a central role in the development of the organization's strategic and operational plans. At Cure Violence, he previously served as Director of Communications, responsible for leading the overall communication strategy, and as senior researcher, producing research, reports, and papers on the program.

Amanda L. Robinson received her PhD from Michigan State University and has worked as a criminologist at Cardiff University since 2001. She has undertaken qualitative and quantitative research in the United States and the United Kingdom focused on violence, policing, specialist courts, and multi-agency approaches.

Dr Robinson has served as an expert advisor on several UK committees that have shaped professional practice in responding to violent crime. She is currently an editor of the *British Journal of Criminology*.

Meghan L. Rogers is a postdoctoral research associate in the School of Criminal Justice at the University at Albany, State University of New York. Her research interests include cross-national research, violence, quantitative research methods, criminological theory, social structures and crime, and measurement of crime.

Nikolay Shchitov, PhD, is affiliated with the School of Criminology at Simon Fraser University, Canada. His main research interests include sociology of punishment, deviant behavior, and sexual violence. His recent publications appear in the *Handbook of European Homicide Research* and *Theoretical Criminology*.

Gary Slapper, LLM, LLB, PhD, was Global Professor at New York University, a legal consultant at the London barristers' chambers, 36 Bedford Row, and director of New York University in London until his death in December 2016. He was educated at University College London and the London School of Economics. He has published 20 academic legal books, including *How the Law Works*, and written prolifically on corporate crime. The philosopher Noam Chomsky described his work on corporate manslaughter as "path-breaking."

Gary Slutkin, MD, is a physician and Professor of Global Health and Epidemiology at the University of Illinois at Chicago School of Public Health and founder and CEO of Cure Violence, a scientifically demonstrated health approach to violence reduction using behavior change and epidemic control methods. In 2016, Cure Violence was ranked fourteenth in the Top 500 nongovernmental organizations (NGOs) in the world by NGO Advisor and listed as the top NGO dedicated to reducing violence.

Sarah Tucker was formerly a research associate at the Universities' Police Science Institute, Cardiff University, UK, having previously served as a police officer for over a decade. Sarah gained experience in policing working as both a uniformed officer and a detective. This experience is now being applied to academic interests focusing on policing research, specifically in the areas of operational policing and investigation of serious crimes.

Sean P. Varano is Associate Professor in the School of Justice Studies at Roger Williams University. His research interests include juvenile justice policy, violent crime reduction strategies, gang violence, police technology, and program evaluation. Dr. Varano earned his BA from the Pennsylvania State University, and his Masters and Doctorate degrees from Michigan State University.

Charles F. Wellford is Professor Emeritus in the Department of Criminology and Criminal Justice at the University of Maryland. He is past Chair of the Department, President of the American Society of Criminology, and Chair of the Committee on Law and Justice of the National Research Council. His current research focuses on patterns of crime clearance and on the epidemiology of gun crime. He received his PhD from the University of Pennsylvania.

Robin Williams is Professor Emeritus at Durham University, Professor of Forensic Science Studies at Northumbria University, and a Visiting Professor at the Policy, Ethics and Life Sciences Research Centre at Newcastle University. He is the NUCFS (Northumbria University Centre for Forensic Science) lead researcher on EUROFORGEN, a FP7 "Network of Excellence" in forensic genetics, and is actively engaged in several empirical studies of the investigative uses of forensic science in the United Kingdom and the United States.

Richard Wortley has been Director of the Jill Dando Institute for Security and Crime Science at University College London (UCL) since 2010. A psychologist by discipline he began his career as a prison psychologist and he is a past national chair of the Australian College of Forensic Psychologists. His research interests center on the role that immediate environments play in criminal behavior and how such behavior may be altered through situational crime prevention.

Joseph K. Young is Associate Professor with appointments in the School of Public Affairs and School of International Service at American University. He is an expert on terrorism and political violence. His work has been published in journals across scholarly disciplines, including political science, criminology, economics, and international studies. His research has been funded by the National Science Foundation and the National Consortium for the Study of and Responses to Terrorism (START).

Introduction
Homicide in Global Perspective

Fiona Brookman, Edward R. Maguire, and Mike Maguire

Homicide—the killing of one human being by another—captures the public imagination like little else. Homicide ignites widespread curiosity and dominates popular novels, television shows, and movies. It makes headlines and takes over the evening news. People are simultaneously disturbed and fascinated by the idea that some human beings are willing and capable to taking the lives of others, sometimes in a distant or impersonal manner and other times in an up-close and personal manner. The impacts of homicide are far reaching. As well as the loss of a life and the obviously devastating consequences for the victim's family, the ripples spread throughout the local community and beyond.

A strong yearning to understand the nature and causes of homicide, and to find ways of preventing it, has led to a considerable body of research and scholarship on the topic. Unfortunately, the vast majority of such evidence comes from just a handful of developed nations. Ironically, in the nations with the highest homicide rates in the world, the topic is often relatively unstudied. The *Handbook of Homicide* is the first genuinely international sourcebook of information and scholarship on the nature, causes, and patterns of homicide, as well as policies and practices for investigating and preventing it. The volume was carefully prepared with an international readership in mind. The contributors come from all over the globe and bring with them a variety of unique experiences and vantage points through which to think about homicide.

In addition to its international focus, the *Handbook* aims to capture the significant range and complexity of homicide in its many different forms. The kinds of cases featured on the evening news and in popular "whodunits" provide a very narrow perspective on homicide and its causes. Homicide is a multifaceted phenomenon. Moreover, certain aspects of this crime have been widely studied while little is known about others. The work included in the *Handbook* was purposely selected to illustrate the many complexities of homicide, including types of cases and regions of the world that are often overlooked.

The *Handbook* was compiled at a time when homicide rates in many regions of the world had been declining, and scholars continue to debate why this is the case. In the United States, for instance, homicide rates in 2014 (the latest full year available) were the lowest they had been in more than fifty years. By contrast, particularly in certain parts of the developing world, some nations continue to experience epidemic levels of violence, including homicide, associated with street gangs, illegal guns, and the distribution of illegal drugs.

Outline of the *Handbook*

We cannot hope to summarize every chapter of such a lengthy volume in a short introduction. Our aim here is simply to provide an overview of the main themes and arguments to be found in each of the five parts into which it is divided. In doing so, we outline the contents of a number of individual chapters, principally as illustrative examples of common themes; there is of course no suggestion that those we specifically discuss are any more important than others we do not.

Part I, Homicide in Context, provides some broad theoretical and research-based insights into how we may begin to explain homicide, account for its changing patterns and trends, and assess social and legal responses. In the first chapter, Innes and co-authors outline the main theoretical frameworks that social scientists have used to understand homicide and its consequences. While acknowledging the value of both macro and micro frameworks, they argue that scholars would benefit from a greater focus on the "momentary"—the "specific spatial-temporal intersections when significant events take place"—which has been relatively neglected.

Chapters 2 and 3 look at patterns and trends. Rogers and Pridemore (Chapter 2) outline key features of global homicide victimization rates, introducing a theme that reappears many times in this volume: the huge variations in crime rates—and in the characteristics of victims and perpetrators—that are found across the globe and over time. Blumstein (Chapter 3) identifies some interesting patterns in homicide rates in the United States associated with the rapid increase that occurred between 1985 and 1993 and subsequent substantial falls. He shows that the rise was largely accounted for by increases in homicides by people under 20. Indeed, he goes as far as to say that "by 1993 murder had become almost exclusively a crime of the young," identifying the key factors as the growth of lucrative and highly competitive crack cocaine markets combined with the recruitment of younger, more reckless dealers to replace older offenders removed from the scene through the mass incarceration resulting from the "war on drugs." His analysis underlines important general messages for understanding crime patterns, particularly around the role of markets and the unintended consequences of social policies. Finally, Cooney (Chapter 4) draws attention to the fact that, like the crime itself, social and legal responses to homicide (and to individual kinds of homicide) vary widely across space and time. He puts forward a theoretical framework, based on "pure sociology," for beginning to understand and explain this variation.

Part II, Understanding Different Forms of Homicide, features 12 chapters that explore some of the most important types of homicide. These include gang homicides, drug-related homicides, sexual homicides, the killing of women, honor killings, hate killings, the killing of children by parents, the killing of parents by children, corporate homicide, terrorism, multiple homicide (including mass, spree, and serial killing), and genocide and state-sponsored killings. A number of common themes emerge from these chapters. Several authors note that the precise causes of particular forms of homicide are still unclear. For example, Varano and Kuhns (Chapter 6) acknowledge that the causal linkages between drugs and homicide are not fully understood. Similarly Pizarro (Chapter 5) observes that it is still unclear how the various individual, situational, and structural factors interact to culminate in gang homicide. Moreover, even within particular subcategories of homicide there is significant variation in the circumstances and causes of these events. For example, as Malmquist (Chapter 11) recognizes, some cases of infanticide are heavily driven by the psychopathology of the offender, while others have a clearer socioeconomic basis. It is for such reasons that some of our contributors have highlighted the importance of disaggregating homicide into ever more refined categories. For example, Dobash and Dobash (Chapter 8) suggest that within the category of femicide, a further disaggregation into three main types is required: the murder of intimate partners, sexual murders, and the murder of older women. Similar arguments are put forward by Young and Kearns (Chapter 14) with respect to terrorism and by Heide (Chapter 12) about parricide. Heide adds that the gathering of more detailed insights from working with different kinds of parricide offenders may provide a blueprint for preventing these events.

Aydın-Aitchison (Chapter 16) and Slapper (Chapter 13) discuss some of the difficulties in prosecuting the perpetrators of genocide and corporate homicide respectively, noting that this is often due to a lack of political will or institutionalized coercive power to back up the law. It is notable that disproportionately little attention is given to these important forms of homicide. This contrasts, most notably, with the excessive and undue attention given to serial and mass murder (see Chapter 15).

Finally several contributors to this part of the *Handbook* (and in fact other parts of the *Handbook* too) set out their ideas for further research. These include more cross-national and comparative studies, more mixed-method approaches to gathering data and evidence, and improvements in the quality of and access to official homicide data.

Overall, the chapters in this section show that homicide is a complex and heterogeneous phenomenon driven by a wide variety of motivations, and that the forces or conditions that foster it operate at many levels including the individual, situational, community, societal, and even global. This point is perhaps made most graphically in Chapter 10 where Hall sets out some of the many causal explanations that have been put forward for "hate homicide." These include: reactions to social strain and relative deprivation, expressions of relative power and dominance, thrill, retaliation, territoriality, xenophobia, fundamentalism, anger, fear, inadequate self-control, mental disorder, social learning, social identity, in-group loyalty, cultural norms, conformity, and persuasion.

Part III, Homicide around the Globe: International Perspectives, contains 12 chapters that chronicle the nature and predominant causes of homicide in different parts of the world. All but one of the world's continents are represented in this section (Antarctica is the exception). Eight of the chapters focus on individual nations, namely Britain, Canada, the United States, Japan, Russia, China, India, and South Africa. The remaining four chapters cover either a whole continent or regions within particular continents. The chapters in this section illustrate the wide variation in the nature and extent of the homicide problem across the globe, from countries with very low homicide rates like Japan, Australia, Britain, and Canada, to those whose rates reach epidemic proportions—notably Russia, South Africa, and many nations in Latin America. In fact, nearly half of all homicides take place in countries with only 10 percent of the planet's population (UNODC 2014: 11).

Just as homicide is unevenly distributed across the globe, it is also unequally distributed among citizens within particular countries. Hence, one of the key messages to emerge from the chapters in this part of the *Handbook* is the extent to which the risk of falling victim to homicide varies persistently along sociodemographic lines, most notably gender, race, and age. For example, the homicide rate for Aboriginal Canadians is almost seven times higher than it is for non-Aboriginal peoples (Chapter 20). Similar disturbing disparities are found in the United States between black and white citizens (see Chapter 21) and between indigenous populations of Australia (Aboriginal and Torres Strait Islanders) and New Zealand (Maori) as compared to Caucasians/Europeans (see Chapter 23). In terms of age, the youthfulness of homicide victims and offenders is a pattern replicated across most parts of the world, yet there are some interesting exceptions. For example, in Japan, older people (aged 40 or over) are now committing a much larger share of homicides than was previously the case. Perhaps most unusually in comparison with other countries, people aged 60 or over commit 22 percent of all homicides. This is partly a consequence of a dramatic (and as yet unexplained) decline in homicide among young Japanese males since the 1970s (see Chapter 22).

Part IV, Investigating Homicide, contains five chapters that examine some of the approaches used by police agencies and forensic science/crime laboratories to investigate homicide cases. The chapters in this section examine the role of technology in homicide investigations, the factors that influence investigative success, the use of DNA as an investigative tool, the investigation of "cold case" homicides, and factors that contribute to investigative errors and miscarriages of justice. While homicide investigation is a common theme in popular television shows and movies, much of what is portrayed in the popular media is misleading. These pervasive depictions can have important impacts in the real world where justice is at stake. For example, the notion that DNA can and should solve crime has led to the so-called "CSI effect," whereby the public and jurors expect DNA evidence to be a pivotal part of evidence in homicide cases and may be hesitant to convict in its absence.

Importantly, too, the five chapters in this section provide empirically informed discussion of homicide investigation as it is actually practiced. A number of common themes emerge, including the rhetoric and reality of the value and impact of science and technology, the (sometimes forgotten) role of human factors in such investigations, and, perhaps most importantly, the dearth of empirical evidence regarding the effectiveness of science and technology in homicide investigations. For example, in Chapter 29, Brady and King explore the use of various technologies in homicide investigations (including DNA and ballistic databases, cell tower and location data, and social networking sites) and discover a lack of clear evidence available on the impact of most technologies on homicide investigations. Nevertheless, they demonstrate that training in the use of technology and legislation surrounding its use often lag behind advances in (and use of) such technologies, and that this can pose challenges to individual civil liberties and the legitimacy of policing. They also suggest that in order to be effective, technology must be part of a three-pronged process that also includes people and processes. The importance of the human factor in the investigative process is a theme elaborated upon by Alexander and Wellford (Chapter 30) in their consideration of the factors that contribute to homicide cases being solved. It is once again striking that the evidence base for understanding homicide closure is limited. In Chapter 31, Williams examines the 30 year history of developments in forensic DNA analysis as well as the available evidence of its impacts in homicide investigations. Once again, a stark conclusion from this chapter is the need for more intensive and detailed research in order to establish the effectiveness of DNA evidence within homicide investigation. In Chapter 32, Allsop discusses the importance of advances in forensic techniques and technologies in enabling cold case homicides to be progressed. She considers the cost implications of such investigations during times of austerity and highlights how cold case homicides are not easily detected, despite how they are portrayed in the media and in fictional accounts. Bringing this section to a close, Davis and Leo (Chapter 33) examine wrongful convictions and demonstrate how they often flow from a cascade of investigative errors. They discuss, among other things, the role of heuristics, bias, and stereotyping in the misidentification of homicide suspects; coercion in suspect interrogations; and forensic science errors. Moreover, they conclude that little has been done (in the United States) to address the various problems that can lead to miscarriages of justice. Clearly this is not an issue unique to the United States and there is a long way to go in terms of improving criminal justice systems around the world, protecting suspects' rights and, ultimately, ensuring that innocent people are not convicted.

Part V, Reducing and Preventing Homicide, features five chapters that cover state-of-the-art research on what can be done to reduce and prevent homicide. The chapters in this section cover public health approaches to homicide prevention, the use of network theory and social network analysis to intervene in violent social networks, the use of focused deterrence strategies for reducing urban homicides, the role of gun-related initiatives in reducing homicides, and a final chapter that provides an overview of the available research evidence on how to prevent homicides. Taken together, these chapters illustrate a number of novel and evidence-informed strategies and practices that can be adopted by jurisdictions seeking to lower their homicide rates. These chapters also demonstrate where there remain significant gaps in our knowledge about how to reduce and prevent homicide.

In Chapter 34, Ransford and Slutkin suggest that violence should be viewed as a health issue and that public health methods should be used to prevent or "interrupt" violence. A key aspect of a public health approach to violence is the use of data to improve understanding about the nature of the problem. Data also play a central role in Chapter 35 in which Fox and Allen discuss the role of social network analysis in "identifying and intervening in" networks of people with a heightened risk of either committing murder or being murdered. Social network analysis is being used not only to improve scholarly knowledge about violence, but also in a practical sense to help develop more targeted interventions. In Chapter 36, Braga discusses a specific type of targeted intervention called *focused deterrence* which is often used to address gang homicides (though it can also be adapted for use with other types of violence). There is strong scientific evidence to support the conclusion that focused deterrence reduces homicide and saves lives. Other violence reduction initiatives focus on the role of guns. In Chapter 37, Grommon, McCluskey, and Bynum discuss a gun violence reduction initiative that was implemented in Detroit. Making sense of the many approaches to reducing violence can be very challenging, particularly when considering the wide variability in both the availability and quality of evidence on how to prevent homicide.

In conclusion, we hope that this *Handbook* is not only interesting and informative for the general reader, but provides a valuable resource for scholars, researchers, and students with an interest in homicide and for policymakers and practitioners involved in responding to it. We also hope that it will stimulate others to undertake further research. Finally, we would like to take this opportunity to thank each of the contributors to this volume. We are delighted to have been able to include such an impressive range of experts from across the world and are hugely grateful to them for sharing their unique research and insights with us all.

Reference

UNODC (United Nations Office on Drugs and Crime) (2014) *Global Study on Homicide 2013*. Vienna: United Nations.

Note of Condolence

The editors are sad to report that Professor Slapper passed away in December 2016. We extend our sincere condolences to his family.

Part I

Homicide in Context

1

Murderous Thoughts

The Macro, Micro, and Momentary in Theorizing the Causes and Consequences of Criminal Homicide

Helen Innes, Sarah Tucker, and Martin Innes

Introduction

"Who shall heal murder? What is done, is done."

Lord Byron, "Cain: A Mystery" (1826: 433)

Our culture is replete with representations of murder as the prototypical crime. For as captured in the above quotation, there is an intrinsic, irrevocable, and irreversible sense of harm involved in the act of one person deliberately killing another. Stories of the causes and consequences of murder provide the basic ingredients for the kind of morality tales that anthropologists suggest are necessary conditions for the production of a sense of collective identity and belonging. Following Mary Douglas (1966), such narratives function as social devices through which "the pure" and "dangerous" are delineated, providing resources for many of the stories that we tell ourselves about ourselves in the ordering of social reality (Geertz 1973).

In contra-distinction to these cultural representations of criminal homicide, social research has consistently evidenced that the modal homicide is not the "cold-blooded" calculated act so beloved of fiction writers, but rather a "hot blooded" conflict most often involving protagonists well known to each other (e.g., Polk 1994; Collins 2008). In this sense, such incidents are the epitome of C. Wright-Mills's (1959) private troubles that travel to become public issues.

Our aim in this chapter is to discuss how social and criminological theory can help to illuminate and interpret such issues, explaining both how and why criminal homicides happen and the social implications that flow from these patterns.

The Handbook of Homicide, First Edition. Edited by Fiona Brookman, Edward R. Maguire, and Mike Maguire.

To frame and organize this discussion, we draw a distinction between theoretical accounts that focus upon the causes of criminal homicides and those that attend more to the consequences of such actions. Cutting across this meta-distinction we argue that broadly speaking there are three principal theoretical frames applicable to such an endeavor: the macro, the micro, and the momentary.

The distinction between macro- and micro-theoretical approaches is well rehearsed across the social sciences (Giddens 1984). The former focus upon how structural forces shape and influence patterns of human behavior and action. Micro-accounts privilege and emphasize the ability of individuals and groups to exercise agency, power, and a degree of self-determination. One of the most influential movements in late twentieth- and early twenty-first-century social theory was the derivation of positions that, in different ways, sought to bridge macro and microexplanations (Parker 2000; Mouzelis 2008). Following this lead, in this chapter we seek to advance the view that attending to key "moments" in a case of criminal homicide can shed unique insights that are unobtainable when the issues are perceived from either a "pure" macro or micro vantage point. The concept of the "moment" seeks to recognize that there are specific intersecting points in space and time where especially influential and consequential processes occur to construct and define the situation as homicide. Such processes directly configure how the events and situations associated with a specific case come to be constructed and reconstructed through sequences of differently oriented actions and reactions. Attending to these moments, where structure and agency intersect in interesting ways, can be extremely useful in distilling forms of cause and consequence that are of interest to the student of society.

Table 1.1 summarizes how we adopt these frames to organize our discussion of social theory and criminal homicide, enabling a structured analysis of a large amount of potentially relevant material according to whether their primary accent is upon accounting for the causes or consequences of murder. The cells in the table list the "headline" themes and issues to be addressed by the sections of this chapter.

Before expanding upon these issues, the chapter commences with a brief commentary on the status of theory in the social sciences. This is to recognize a range of different theoretical standpoints that can be, and have been, used to think about murder and criminal homicide. These are founded upon different epistemological foundations and values, and their very different disciplinary backgrounds need to be taken into account. The discussion then progresses on to consider several influential macrostructural positions on criminal homicide before attention then switches to the more "high resolution" focus of microsocial theories. The penultimate section turns to consider what unique insights can be obtained by attending to key moments.

Thinking about Theory

In seeking to account for how people think about and understand criminal homicide as a social problem, there is a critical point of separation in the literature between the more descriptive and more explanatory approaches. There are many

Table 1.1 Theoretical approaches applied to the causes and consequences of criminal homicide.

	Causes	*Consequences*
Macro "structural" How social forces structure situations	The civilizing process; Socioeconomic inequality and poverty; Gangs and gun culture; Anomie.	Crime Drop; Concentrated risk; Legislative and policing reform; Cultures of control and governing through crime.
Micro "processual" How individual-level processes are framed by situations to produce patterns of harmful behavior that can be generalized ("types of homicide")	Emotion and "forward panic"; Honor/respect; Interaction dynamics of types of homicide.	Aftermath and secondary victims; Shaming and perpetrator's families.
Momentary "post-event accounting processes" How post-event accounting processes applied in time and space to specific case studies construct and reconstruct its contributing factors	Police murder investigations; Retroactive social control; Legal scrutiny and definitional processes.	Moral panics; Signal crimes; Miscarriages of justice.

fine journalistic accounts of murder that shine lights on its causes and conditions, but remain in a more descriptive register (e.g., Simon 1991). What these do not possess is a theoretical imperative to reason from the particular to the general in some fashion. Other kinds of approaches do seek to engage with theoretical issues in more explicit ways and here we can distinguish between those where theory is an "input" and those where it is an "output"—and of course some studies seek to do both (Collins 2008).

Cast as an "input" to the study of criminal homicide, theory is used to frame and configure the epistemological standpoint that is adopted in approaching the subject itself. Different academic disciplines evidence different predilections in terms of the ways that they define the key issues to be investigated, interpreted, and explained. For example, studies emanating from a psychology background are more likely to focus upon individual behaviors as the key unit of analysis, where sociologists would tend to emphasize the collective components of behavior and action. Layered across these disciplinary frames, there are positions that key into particular social mechanics and dynamics. For example, feminist theory has insightfully looked at how patriarchal gender relations in society shape the prevalence and distribution of fatal violence (e.g., Hester, Kelly, and Radford 1996). Likewise, Marxist and neo-Marxist accounts have sought to show how the structures of political economy manifest in the social distribution of higher rates of participation in criminal homicide among certain social classes (Taylor 1999). New theory and theoretical revisions have also been "products" of studying criminal homicide.

Acknowledging the role played by theory as both an input and output certainly aids the student of society to navigate between the perils of Mills's (1959) famous two poles of "abstracted empiricism" and "grand theory." The former focusing exclusively on describing patterns in data with no attempt to generalize and the latter reserved for theory that is constructed with no reference to data. Becker (2014) makes the case that careful description of *how* something happens is one of the principal ways in which social analysts can generate new conceptual and theoretical ideas; a move away from the dominant use of theory to engage with "why" something happens. He articulates this with reference to murder and the implications it has for labeling theory in criminology, of which he was a principal architect. Becker shows how the application of labeling processes shape how some acts come to be defined as murders, which is consequential for their processing by the criminal justice system, while others are classified in other ways—for example, as terrorism or acts of war—altering the societal reactions and responses to them. Becker's is a position that exemplifies how theoretical innovations can both inform and result from the study of criminal homicide.

We will return to some of these issues about definitions and classifications in the later phases of this chapter. For now, we can conclude that there are a variety of different theoretical positions that have been engaged in different ways to study the causes and consequences of murder and manslaughter. For any given aspect of homicidal violence, being able to state how it happens, why it happens like this, and what implications flow from such patterns, is critical to improving our understandings.

Macrostructural Accounts of Murder

Macrostructural accounts attend to the ways large-scale social forces shape risk, choices, and ultimately behavior. We can distinguish between longitudinal structural theories and cross-sectional or comparative structural theories in terms of how they explain trends in murder. The former focus on changing levels of murder over time, while the latter are more concerned with different patterns that emerge across varying geographical areas, contexts, and situations in contemporary society.

Longitudinal structural theories

Daly and Wilson's (1988) influential book *Homicide* was quite explicit in advocating a social-Darwinist position to explain violent impulses and homicide. Theoretically, patterns in the etiology of homicide are cast as evolutionary shadows of sexual selection processes whereby individuals compete and pursue their own interests. The adaptive logic of human desires, motives, and emotions is to propagate our "selfish genes" to future generations. Accordingly, masculine competitiveness and risk taking explains why men kill women in far greater number than women kill men, and the large number of homicides involving young men known to each other which erupt and escalate over seeming trivialities (Wilson and Daly,1985).

Contrary to the popular notion that homicide is more commonplace today than ever before, long-term historical data shows that levels of lethal violence have declined with the evolution and advancement of human society. Pinker (2012) meticulously traces levels of violence through the historical and cultural transitions of human society, from small nomadic, egalitarian bands of hunters and gatherers to settled communities and the gradual emergence of a state society. The first major historical decline in violence at the end of the Middle Ages coincided with the beginnings of more formalized and centralized governance structures (Eisner 2001). Drawing on forensic and ethnographic data to compare the rate of violence in early non-state with post-state or civilized societies, Pinker reports that the latter suffered no more than one-quarter of the average death rate of non-state societies, even at their most violent.

Norbert Elias (1978) introduced the idea of a "civilizing process" to explain the widespread uniformity and scale of the historical decline in lethal violence. The emergence of states and the monopolization of violence by powerful central authorities were the impetus for changes in psychological traits and modes of behavior among the populace, most notably greater individual self-control. This prompted the pacification of everyday interactions and fewer violent altercations, initially among the nobility and subsequently other social strata.

Emile Durkheim's theory of homicide also links declining rates of fatal violence to societal advancement, evidenced by a growing division of labor (Dicristina 2004). The causal mechanism for the decline is held to be the waning significance of collective bonds in society as the prevailing social order transitions toward more individual sentiments. This "moral individualism" is commensurate with a greater respect for human life, tough legal sanctions, and an associated decline in the homicide rate. Durkheim asserts that collective states of consciousness, such as religious beliefs and group practices, are more characteristic of "lower societies" and can act as "stimulants to murder" with such forces overriding individual pity or empathy for the value of a human life (Durkheim 1957[1900]: 115). However, periods of rapid social change and economic development can elevate levels of "anomie" whereby individuals feel unable to satisfy their desires. Anomie can foster lethal emotions that "turn against the self" resulting in suicide, or "turn against another," according to circumstances, resulting in homicide.

Cross-sectional comparative theories of homicide

Contemporary rates of homicide, although not comparable with premodern societies because of advancements in medicine and increased life expectancy, place the global intentional homicide rate at 7.6 per 100,000 population in 2004, although this conceals considerable variation between countries and in recording practices (UNODC 2008). In more recent decades, individual countries have experienced periods where the homicide rate has increased. Most European countries saw increases between the early 1960s and mid-1990s (Eisner 2001) and the United States experienced a well-documented sharp rise in homicide in the latter half of the 1980s, peaking in the 1990s before declining rapidly (Blumstein, Rivara, and Rosenfeld 2000). Britain's homicide rate is in the lower half of the distribution for European countries, but the homicide index for England and Wales showed an increase in the number of police recorded homicides between the 1960s and the early years of the 2000s, followed by a downward trajectory from 2002/2003 to a current low of 9.7 per million in 2011/2012 (ONS 2013).

Some macro-theories have engaged with how the hierarchical organization of a society and the degree of structural inequality therein can account for rates of violent crime and homicide. Focus is given to the negative effects of inequality on interpersonal relationships and to how the social patterning of homicide shapes the risk of mortality from lethal violence for particular social groups or neighborhoods. A statistical correlation between the scale of income inequality and the homicide rate within states, countries, and communities underpins the theory that more egalitarian societies will have a lower rate of homicide than those that are more hierarchical in structure. It is hypothesized that inequities have a detrimental and divisive impact on social relationships, including trust and social capital (Putnam 2000), and as societies become less equal, so hostility and discrimination within them increase. Wilkinson (2004) draws attention to individuals' inherited attentiveness and sensitivity to their social status relative to others within the broader social structure as a trigger to acts of violence.

The over-representation of particular social groups as victims (in homicide mortality statistics) and as perpetrators of lethal violence has led theorists to argue that large-scale changes in the homicide rate can only be understood from how various sociodemographic and socioeconomic factors interact with each other and with structural factors in society. For example, homicide research from the United States finds that victims are disproportionately male, from minority ethnic populations, have low income, and are poorly educated, out of work or in manual occupations. Blumstein, Rivara, and Rosenfeld (2000) attribute the homicide peak in America to the excess victimization of young adults, with the risk concentrated among black men.

Today, when the main trajectory of criminal homicide is downward in England and Wales, social and spatial inequalities in homicide rates are reportedly widening (Shaw, Tunstall, and Dorling 2005). The homicide death rate among Scottish adults in routine occupations was nearly twelve times that of those in the managerial and professional class, far greater than for all-cause mortality (Leyland and Dunas 2009). Both studies show that murders are disproportionately concentrated in poor areas of the United Kingdom based on relative income or poverty.

Multiple processes are proposed to underlie the links between poverty, inequality, and the homicide rate—chief among these being illegal drugs markets and the availability of guns (Bowling 1999). The rapid escalation in US homicide in the late 1980s and into the 1990s coincided with the emergence of crack cocaine drug markets in impoverished inner cities and a time of lessening economic opportunity. This was a period of growing unemployment and anomie in poor racially segregated neighborhoods where the choices and life chances faced by individuals therein were constrained by wider social forces. Illegal drug markets are generative of violence through territorial gang-related activities where conflict between rivals is often resolved through the use of firearms. The United States has a high rate of gun ownership and is set apart from other countries by the large proportion of its homicide attributable to the use of firearms (Brookman and Maguire 2003). Drugs and guns framed an informal economy regulated by gang-based norms and codes of honor. In this social situation, aggressive and violent behavior became a rational response to hostilities, discrimination, and disrespect in the environment, an environment where police were not viewed as a legitimate presence. This had, and continues to have, profound ramifications for policing and the delivery of policing interventions and these are considered in the next section.

Structural consequences of murder

The weight of attention among structural theories is undoubtedly upon explaining the causes of murder. That said, important contributions have been made in terms of the consequences that patterns and trends in criminal homicide have for social structures and the ordering of social reality.

Kubrin and Weitzer (2003), for instance, argue that a major consequence of the high rates of gang-related homicide in many North American cities is to cause more violence and murder. Their work unpicks how a principal motivation is retaliation for prior killings, which in turn pushes young men toward further involvement in gang structures (Papachristos 2009). The wider availability of guns arguably sets in motion an escalating process whereby others in the community feel that they too must take up arms in order to protect themselves and their families. However, the high toll of street violence on families may make gang life less appealing to younger people—what Currie (2013) terms "the little brother effect." This may be one explanation for the decline in homicidal violence in recent years.

Comparatively high rates of murder and violent crime in the 1980s and 1990s, embedded within rises in criminal offending more generally, were responsible for triggering a profound re-engineering of key social institutions to focus their attention on crime and offender management tasks. Garland (2001) posits that at the time he was writing, the whole culture of neoliberal states had come to be defined by the preeminent task of controlling crime. Similar themes can be detected in Simon's (2007) contention that by the 2000s state institutions were "governing through crime." Discourses of welfare and social protection had been supplanted and replaced by a rhetoric of "a war on crime." Institutions and interventions that in previous generations would have been intended to provide social support to vulnerable and deprived individuals and communities were increasingly directed toward controlling crime risks. According to Simon, these rhetorical devices were not just expressive, but induced specific material effects and consequences.

These impacts were evident, for example, in the changes wrought to the conduct of policing in cities like New York. High rates of homicide in such urban areas in the 1980s created a climate of political permission for police to adopt more aggressive and interventionist strategies and tactics (Zimring 2012). The most infamous of these was the NYPD's (New York Police Department) implementation of "broken windows" policing, derived from a short article penned by Wilson and Kelling (1982). Precisely what such approaches did, or did not, achieve has been widely debated across the academic and policy literatures and lies beyond the scope of this chapter. The key point is that high rates of murder shaped the trajectory of criminal justice policy development with the consequence that the conduct of policing and the use of incarceration was drastically re-engineered to craft a response to high levels of fatal violence. In the early 1990s, zero-tolerance policing strategies were widely credited with ending the peak in New York homicide, neglecting to mention a longer-term downward trend in homicide that preceded its enforcement in the city (Bowling 1999).

In her ethnographic account of life in a deprived Philadelphia neighborhood, Alice Goffman (2014) focuses upon the lives of young black men "on the run" from the criminal justice system. She carefully documents how crime control imperatives have taken over from other social functions of the state and its relationships with its citizens. Although not a structuralist account, her book gives a compelling and tragic account of how social-structural forces influence and determine the biographies and identities of many marginalized young men and the communities of which they are a part.

Microsocial Interactions and Emotions

Where macrostructural theories focus on abstract social forces, microsocial perspectives attend more to actions and behaviors performed in particular social situations as contributors to fatal interactions. Departing from the primary focus of much homicide analysis upon statistics or a post-incident narrative, the most important elements of homicide are cast as the "pre-" and "during" stages of the act itself (Collins 2008). This is on the grounds that the "foreground" of the act can shine a light on the behavioral, cognitive, and affective social dynamics that propel a person to engage in fatal violence. As previously, we distinguish between theories disposed toward causes and those concerned with consequences.

Emotional causes

In a major contribution to the field, Randall Collins (2008) proposes a general theory of violence that concentrates upon the "situational processes" taking place within the violent encounter, sometimes culminating in a killing. Within its purview his theory spans police violence, riots, war, and intimate partner violence as well as murder and criminal homicide.

Where traditional psychological perspectives attend to the "hardwiring" of "violent individuals," Collins explores the situational dynamics of violence through individuals' emotional reactions to conflictual confrontations, and how they negotiate barriers of tension and fear. Collins accepts that social, psychological, and physiological factors play an important part in the move to violence, but emphasizes how the emotional dynamics are positioned at the center of the violent situation. Domestic violence is used as one example where stress, poverty, life transitions, and social isolation can be important, but not sufficient, for individuals in these situations to behave violently (Straus 1990). Collins proposes that it takes a further situational process to create actual incidents of violence in this context.

Arguably the signature innovation of Collins's theory is his description of the ways situational emotional tension and rage can ignite into "forward panic." The concept of "forward panic" begins with tension and fear in a conflict situation, moving an individual from a passive to an action state of mind, where there is "an emotional rush"—an overpowering emotional rhythm carrying them to actions that they would not normally commit in a calm reflective moment. The onset of forward panic leads to individuals overriding emotional and psychological barriers that in other circumstances would prevent violence from occurring, such as fear of retaliation. Developing these insights through a diverse array of empirical evidence, it is identified that a power asymmetry between parties to a violent situation renders physical attack more likely.

Collins acknowledges that not all violence occurs in a hot emotional rush, allowing for a more cold and calculated mode of execution. But he provides compelling evidence that, in contrast to many fictional and nonfictional representations, it is a relative rarity. Coldblooded killing exists at the "apex of violence" in a hierarchy of competent performance. Most people, including those in professions trained to legally enact it, are not good at violence. They are not able to suppress the emotional and physiological states of acting violently, which typically results in greater levels of harm and damage being caused.

This emphasis on the role of emotions can be traced back to Katz's (1988) work on the "seductions of crime." Controversially, Katz seeks to both differentiate and integrate the "situational emotional" and the "personal emotional" facets of criminal conduct. He focuses upon the "positive," and often "wonderful attraction" within the lived experience of crime that seduces individuals and groups to be involved in potentially fatal violence. As with Collins, Katz explores the "foreground" of homicide in order to understand what it feels, means, tastes, and sounds like to commit homicide.

Many theories of violence, whether micro or macro in focus, have failed to understand how and why some murderers can rationalize it as a sensible and justifiable act. Katz approaches this with an intimate view of the emotions of the criminal act—the sensual dynamics of what happens just prior to a crime being committed. From enticement to fury and how individuals conjure up the "magic" to conduct the required action to commit a crime, Katz proposes a distinct set of individually necessary conditions required to commit homicide: a path of action, a line of interpretation, and an emotional process. These conditions typically require additional elements to ignite the emotional trigger, such as humiliation, ridicule, and arrogance to name a few. This resonates with other contributions to the literature, such as Polk's (1994) focus on the "defense of masculine honor" as a "justifiable" cause for murder.[1] He notes how personal slights and insults become more pronounced and more acutely felt in the presence of a social audience, amplifying the risk of conflict. Examining homicide, Katz explores how individuals move through these conditions to negotiate what he terms the act of "righteous slaughter."

Ideas such as these resonate with a long-established finding of social research into the interactional dynamics of criminal homicide and the extent to which the identities of who kills and who dies is often not clearly evident at the outset of a fatal encounter (Wolfgang 1958). In emotionally fraught and often confused interpersonal conflicts in public spaces involving young men, who will transpire to be the victim and who the perpetrator is not easily predictable (Luckenbill 1977). The introduction of theories of affect and emotion into our understandings of how and why criminal homicides arise is then potentially the most significant contribution of micro-theoretical perspectives to explaining the causes of such violent acts. Concepts of the sensual dynamic, righteous slaughter and forward panic give theoretical form to the emotional forces that propel the moves to murder.

Micro-consequences of homicide

Mirroring structural accounts, micro-theories of murder again display a disposition to identify causes. That said, some of the most compelling studies emanate from broadly phenomenological and interactionist approaches and provide "high resolution" pictures of the aftermath of homicidal acts. These include: accounts of the secondary victims of such crimes and their trauma, grief, and experiences of the criminal justice process (Rock 1998); how some of these individuals mount moral entrepreneurship campaigns leading to changes in law (Rock 2004); the stigma and shame borne by families and friends of offenders (Condry 2007); the work of criminal justice agencies in marshaling a response to such acts (Innes 2003); and those who are "victimized" when the criminal justice process "miscarries" (Naughton 2007).

Extending and elaborating the reach of the affective phenomenology that has proven so productive in unpicking the causes of homicides, Howarth and Rock (2000) apply similar ideas to framing an analysis of the aftermaths of such incidents. They identify how, following a murder, a complex blend of emotional and physical labor performed by a range of actors is enacted with the intent that it should dispel chaos and alienation while affording recognition of the harms suffered. In certain circumstances these affective responses are translated into a political imperative, such as occurred in the Stephen Lawrence case.

Mirroring the interchangeability between eventual victims and perpetrators discussed earlier, Burgess and Holstrom (1974) found that the parents of the murdered and the parents of the murderer experience many of the same problems and symptoms following the death. These are themes developed by Condry (2007) in her account of how families of serious offenders seek to negotiate public opprobrium and stigma. As Howarth and Rock (2000: 59.) state, there is much still to explore in order to understand how homicide and its aftermath can assist in "illuminating the complexity of crime, the abundance of the group which it creates and effects, the multiple consequences that it inflicts, the diversity of the responses that it elicits and concomitant intricacy and scale of the social structures that it generates."

Toward a "Momentary" Sociology of Criminal Homicide

> Not then, men and their moments. Rather, moments and their men. (Goffman 1967: 3)

Erving Goffman suggests that even students of society attracted to microsocial perspectives must be appreciative that how people act is not unconstrained, but rather strongly conditioned by the norms and conventions of the particular social situations in which they are located. Although he never really worked through the full implications of the concept of the "moment" that he introduced, Goffman was subtly gesturing to something rather different to that which is typically emphasized by macrostructural accounts. For a "moment" is a particular point in space and time where something significant happens, with causal consequences for what follows after. This focus upon specific spatial-temporal intersections when significant events take place is, we want to argue, potentially profoundly useful in providing a new theoretical lens to unpack some neglected dimensions of criminal homicide cases.

Moments, definitions, and causes

We now return to the issue of how fatal situations are defined. How an incident is labeled and officially categorized is freighted with several significant implications. Not least, for the statistical data that are the raw ingredients for many social-structural analyses, which are aggregated artifacts of such decisions. Whether an incident of fatal violence is treated as potentially criminal or not determines how it will be treated by the institutions whose work comprises the criminal justice process, as well as the wider public. As long ago as 1960, Havard noted the potential for "hidden" homicides to occur. His work pointed to significant numbers of undetected criminal acts occurring in cases that were being classified as "sudden deaths," especially where the deceased was very young or very old. In subsequent years, with cases such as those involving the serial killer Dr Harold Shipman, Havard's conclusions appear to have been exceedingly prescient.

Important variants of these definitional processes relate to the category of cases and incidents that come to be revealed as miscarriages of justice. The public stories about these cases pivot around the moments where cases were originally defined as homicides, the wrongful assigning of blame, and the subsequent moments where the original definition is revealed as erroneous and consequently must be publicly redefined in consequential ways (Naughton 2007).

Innes's (2003) ethnographic study of police murder investigation expends considerable effort upon deconstructing how and why police detectives come to define the circumstances of suspicious deaths in particular ways, and their work to try and ensure that these are authorized by the judicial process. He details the contingencies of such processes and how the art and craft of the police murder squad detective pivots around synthesizing and blending different pieces of information to construct a narrative of the event, setting out "who did what to whom and why." In so doing, police detectives working a case must contend with partial and incomplete data, all of which have to be reconciled with each other to some degree in order to tell a coherent story. Any police definitions will be scrutinized and tested during subsequent legal proceedings such as coroner's inquests or criminal trials, but the police investigative function possesses particular influence upon how a cause of death is established and any blame assigned.

This "narrative reasoning" is an intrinsic part of the sense-making process police investigators employ. It is transformative in the status of an event, but it also inflects how the incident is subsequently projected publicly in journalists' reporting. In the production of these definitions of the situation, police (and later criminal trials) attend to particular moments in the story such as the fatal interaction. In respect of this chapter, the point is that practitioners have a particular focus on retrospectively unpacking and understanding key moments, rather than structural forces that would be the principal issue of interest to a sociologist. The investigation of a murder is literally "a defining moment" in how a fatal interaction is to be publicly understood and treated—it is the point in time where a public definition of the situation is worked up and adversarially tested.

The significance of understanding the work of police investigators and their auxiliaries in the criminal justice process in this light is exemplified by cold case review (CCR) conferences of long-term unsolved homicides. These innovations in policing were "invented" by a number of policing agencies in the United Kingdom and United States in the 1990s as a methodology for revisiting past cases where a suspect had not been successfully prosecuted. As Allsop (2013; see also Chapter 32, this volume) reports, they have come to be defined by an increasing "reliance on science," particularly DNA analysis. Allsop's empirics suggest the application of such methods has produced relatively few case "solutions," but enough for CCRs to be strategically important as "symbols" of integrating "high science" into police work. Innes and Clarke (2009) posit that CCRs are emblematic of wider and deeper trajectories in the conduct of social control. CCRs are imbued with the logics of "retroactive social control," where past events are placed under new descriptions that change, or radically revise, what is held to have happened in the past. Here, thinking in terms of key "moments" becomes profoundly insightful. Potentially, a past incident that may not even have been categorized as a crime, is redefined; what is understood to have happened is substantively reconfigured. These kinds of development pose deep questions for our ideas about justice and social order: are there any temporal limits in terms of how long an individual should be accountable to justice, especially if they are responsible for taking the life of another? They also establish connections to new theoretical traditions. For example, the concept of retroactive social control keys into the ways that collective memories are constructed and CCRs potentially identify moments when established collective memories, in terms of how a murder has previously been publicly defined, are disturbed and redefined.

Consequential Moments

The principal theme of the preceding section has been how the criminal justice process works to define incidents and cases in ways that profoundly shape the ways they are treated and processed. In this penultimate section, we focus upon the social consequences that these definitional moments have.

When Stan Cohen (1972) developed his processual model of moral panics, he was concerned to show how a small number of social problems are able to trigger profound institutional consequences that reshape culture and the ordering of reality. It is an approach that has been subsequently picked up and applied widely in respect of a range of issues and problems. There are certainly a small number of murders that have provided the raw ingredients for setting off moral panics over the past couple of decades. For example, the killing of the toddler Jamie Bulger in Liverpool in 1993 by two other young boys played directly into a wider environment of concern about the safety of children.

In his original formulation, Cohen was careful to detail how key social institutions (including the magistracy, media, and criminal justice system) were both *agents* of consequential social change, amplifying concern about a social problem condensed by the incident in question into a highly memorable form, and *reactors* to the changes that they induced. Positioned in a chapter on theorizing the causes and consequences of murder, moral panic theory keys into how a small subset of murders have been responsible for wide and deep cultural transformation.

Picking up on this issue, Innes (2014) has argued that most murders do not induce the institutional ramifications associated with moral panics and are better conceptualized as "signal crimes"—infractions of the criminal law that send a signal to the public about the distribution of risk and threat across social space. Based upon a study of collective reactions to six high-profile murders in England and Wales, he models the consequences of these incidents in terms of "how fear travels" in the aftermath of such crimes. Informed by detailed empirical data collected through interviewing a sample of community representatives living near to where the crimes occurred, he derives several key reaction patterns in terms of how particular behavioral, cognitive, and affective responses flow out from the crime incident (Table 1.2). Appropriating aspects of Albert Hunter's (1985) conceptual differentiation between public, parochial, and private social orders, he shows how collective reactions to murders follow particular trajectories.

Table 1.2 Reaction patterns emanating from incidents of homicide.

Reaction pattern	*Consequences of the crime*
Private	Restricted to those known to the victim or offender in some way.
Parochial	Travel across a neighborhood or defined community, but do not extend beyond these boundaries.
Public	The effects of the signal crime influence a lot of people in terms of how they think, feel, or act in relation to their safety and security (tend to be high-profile cases).
Public with parochial counter-reaction	In a small number of cases where a high-profile crime captures the public imagination and the area where the crime occurred starts to be stigmatized, local communities sometimes "push back" against the reputational consequences.

This approach starts to open up new ways of theorizing how particular moments of fatal violence are responsible for inducing social impacts and consequences that touch people in a range of different ways. In due course, they may provide an evidence base for conducting community impact assessments and consequent management strategies, both of which have become an increasingly important aspect of how police and other agencies respond to murders and other instances of serious violence.

Conclusion

Drawing back from the detail of individual theoretical contributions, it can be observed that most attention has focused on trying to explain the causes of murder and homicidal violence. More recently, however, as exemplified by an increasing focus on issues of victimology and consequence management, effort has attended to explaining and interpreting the effects that travel out in the aftermath of such incidents. To make sense of such developments we have devised a "meta-frame" that distinguishes between "causal" and "consequentialist" accounts. We have also sought to outline a new conceptual "space" that is delineated by attending to a sociology of "moments"—points in social space and time where things change markedly in the accounting and construction of a homicide.

This chapter started by setting out how murder as a social problem attains its particular status and symbolic power through its finality and irreversibility. We have concluded with reference to the ways murder can be defined and redefined by accounting processes applied after the event that frame and influence the social meaning and consequences that become attached to a specific incident or case. In so doing, the discussion has illustrated the ways that extant theoretical perspectives, such as notions of "collective memory," can be deployed as inputs to produce new insights into why murder matters so much to the stories our culture tells us about ourselves. At the same time, we have also outlined some of the new insights into social life that are being generated through the study of homicidal violence.

Notes

1 We use "justifiable" here in the sense of something for which an act of justification can plausibly be made as opposed to it being considered legitimate.

References

Allsop, C. (2013) A reliance on science: DNA, detective work and cold case major crime reviews. Unpublished PhD, University of Cardiff.

Becker, H. (2014) *What about Mozart? What about Murder?* Chicago: University of Chicago Press.

Blumstein, A., Rivara, F., and Rosenfeld, R. (2000) The rise and decline of homicide and why. *Annual Review of Public Health*, 21: 505–541.

Bowling, B. (1999) The rise and fall of New York murder. *British Journal of Criminology*, 39(4): 531–554.

Brookman, F. and Maguire, M. (2003) Reducing homicide: Summary of a review of the possibilities. Home Office Research and Development Directorate, Occasional Paper no. 84, London.

Burgess, A. and Holstrom, L. (1974) Rape trauma syndrome. *American Journal of Psychiatry*, 131(9): 981–986.

Byron, G. (1826) *The Works of Lord Byron: Complete in One Volume*. Frankfurt: H.L. Broenner.

Cohen, S. (1972) *Folk Devils and Moral Panics*. London: MacGibbon and Kee.

Collins, R. (2008) *Violence: A Micro-sociological Theory*. Princeton, NJ: Princeton University Press.

Condry, R. (2007) *Families Shamed: The Consequences of Crime for Relatives of Serious Offenders*. Portland, OR: Willan.

Currie, E. (2013) *Crime and Punishment in America*. New York: Picador.

Daly, M. and Wilson, M. (1988) *Homicide*. New Brunswick, NJ: Transaction.

Dicristina, B. (2004) Durkheim's theory of homicide and the confusion of the empirical literature. *Theoretical Criminology*, 8(1): 57–91.

Douglas, M. (1966) *Purity and Danger*. London: Routledge & Kegan Paul.

Durkheim, E. (1957[1900]) *Professional Ethics and Civic Morals* (trans. C. Brookfield). New York: Routledge.

Eisner, M. (2001) Modernization, self-control and lethal violence: The long-term dynamics of European homicide rates in theoretical perspective. *British Journal of Criminology*, 41(4): 618–638.

Elias, N. (1978) *The History of Manners: The Civilizing Process* (vol. 1). New York: Pantheon.

Garland, D. (2001) *The Culture of Control: Crime and Social Control in Contemporary Society*. Oxford: Oxford University Press.

Geertz, C. (1973) *The Interpretation of Cultures*. New York: Basic Books.

Giddens, A. (1984) *The Constitution of Society: Outline of the Theory of Structuration*. Cambridge: Cambridge University Press.

Goffman, A. (2014) *On the Run: Fugitive Life in an American City*. Chicago: University of Chicago Press.

Goffman, E. (1967) *Interaction Ritual: Essays on Face-to-Face Behavior*. Garden City, NY: Doubleday.

Havard, J. (1960) *The Detection of Secret Homicide*. Basingstoke, UK: Macmillan.
Hester, M., Kelly, L., and Radford, J. (1996) *Women, Violence and Male Power*. Buckingham, UK: Open University Press.
Howarth, G. and Rock, P. (2000) Aftermath and the construction of victimisation: "The other victims of crime." *The Howard Journal*, 39(1): 58–78.
Hunter, A. (1985) Private, parochial and public social orders: The problem of crime and incivility in urban communities. In M. Janowitz, G.D. Suttles, and M.N. Zald (eds), *The Challenge of Social Control: Citizenship and Institution Building in Modern Society* (pp. 230–242). Norwood, NJ: Ablex.
Innes, M. (2003) *Investigating Murder: Detective Work and the Police Response to Criminal Homicide*. Oxford: Clarendon Press.
Innes, M. (2014) *Signal Crimes: Social Reactions To Crime, Disorder and Control*. Oxford: Oxford University Press.
Innes, M. and Clarke, A. (2009) Policing the past: Cold case studies, forensic evidence and retroactive social control. *British Journal of Sociology*, 60(3): 543–563.
Katz, J. (1988) *Seductions of Crime: Moral and Sensual Attractions in Doing Evil*. New York: Basic Books.
Kubrin, C.E. and Weitzer, R. (2003) Retaliatory homicide: Concentrated disadvantage and neighborhood culture. *Social Problems*, 50(2): 157–180.
Leyland, A.H. and Dunas, R. (2009) The social patterning of deaths due to assault in Scotland, 1980–2005: Population-based study. *Journal of Epidemiology and Community Health*, 64(5): 432–439.
Luckenbill, D. (1977) Criminal homicide as a situated transaction. *Social Problems*, 25: 176–186.
Mills, C. Wright (1959) *The Sociological Imagination*. Oxford: Oxford University Press.
Mouzelis, N. (2008) *Modern and Postmodern Social Theorising: Bridging the Divide*. Cambridge: Cambridge University Press.
Naughton, M. (2007) *Rethinking Miscarriages of Justice*. New York: Palgrave Macmillan.
ONS (Office for National Statistics) (2013) Focus on: Violent crime and sexual offences, 2011/12. Statistical Bulletin. Available online at http://webarchive.nationalarchives.gov.uk/20160105160709/http://www.ons.gov.uk/ons/dcp171778_298904.pdf (accessed August 1, 2016).
Papachristos, A. (2009) Murder by structure: Dominance relations and the social structure of gang homicide. *American Journal of Sociology*, 115(1): 74–128.
Parker, J. (2000) *Structuration*. Milton Keynes: Open University Press.
Pinker, S. (2012) *The Better Angels of Our Nature: The Decline of Violence in History and its Causes*. London: Penguin Books.
Polk, K. (1994) *When Men Kill*. Cambridge: Cambridge University Press.
Putnam, R. (2000) *Bowling Alone: The Collapse and Revival of American Community*. New York: Simon & Schuster.
Rock, P. (1998) *After Homicide: Practical and Political Responses to Bereavement*. Oxford: Oxford University Press.
Rock, P. (2004) *Constructing Victims' Rights: The Home Office, New Labour, and Victims*. Oxford: Oxford University Press.
Shaw, M., Tunstall, H., and Dorling, D. (2005) Increasing inequalities in risk of murder in Britain: trends in the demographic and spatial distribution of murder 1981–2000. *Health and Place*, 11: 45–54.

Simon, D. (1991) *Homicide: A Year on the Killing Streets*. Boston: Houghton Mifflin.
Simon, J. (2007) *Governing Through Crime*. New York: Oxford University Press.
Strauss, M.A. (1990) Social stress and marital violence in a national sample of American families. In M.A. Strauss and R.J. Gelles (eds), *Physical Violence in American Families: Risk Factors and Adaptations to Violence in 8,145 Families* (pp. 181–201). New Brunswick, NJ: Transaction.
Taylor, I. (1999) *Crime in Context: A Critical Criminology of Market Societies*. Cambridge: Polity Press.
UNODC (United Nations Office on Drugs and Crime) (2008) International homicide statistics (IHS), 2004. Available online at https://www.unodc.org/documents/data-and-analysis/IHS-rates-05012009.pdf (accessed August 1, 2016).
Wilkinson, R. (2004) Why is violence more common where inequality is greater? *Annals of the New York Academy of Sciences*, 1036(1): 1–12.
Wilson, J. and Kelling, G. (1982) Broken windows. *Atlantic Monthly*, 249(3): 29–38.
Wilson, M. and Daly, M. (1985) Competitiveness, risk taking and violence: The young male syndrome. *Ethology and Sociobiology*, 6: 59–73.
Wolfgang, M.E. (1958) *Patterns in Criminal Homicide*. Philadelphia: University of Pennsylvania Press.
Zimring, F. (2012) *The City That Became Safe: New York's Lessons for Urban Crime and Its Control*. New York: Oxford University Press.

Further Reading

Innes, M. (2010) Criminal legacies: Community impact assessments and defining success and harm in police homicide investigations. *Journal of Contemporary Criminal Justice*, 26(4): 367–381.
Lane, R. (1997) *Murder in America*. Chicago: Ohio State University Press.

2

Geographic and Temporal Variation in Cross-National Homicide Victimization Rates

Meghan L. Rogers and William Alex Pridemore

Introduction

The goal of this chapter is to describe geographic and temporal variation in regional and national homicide rates around the world. We begin with a brief description of two main sources of cross-national homicide data, the United Nations and the World Health Organization. We then employ data from the latter to describe regional and national total and sex-specific homicide victimization rates between 1979 and 2010 in Africa, Asia, Europe, North America, and South America. We then briefly compare homicide victimization rates between these regions. Our aim is purely descriptive in nature and thus we refrain from speculating about the reasons for (1) higher or lower homicide rates in regions or nations relative to others and (2) changes in homicide rates over time in regions or nations. Substantively, the causes of such variation are empirical questions. Our goal in this chapter is not to attempt to answer those questions (and practically, such speculation would be distracting given the large number of nations we cover in this chapter) but instead simply to provide the initial observations of geographic and temporal variation that will allow others to generate and test hypotheses meant to explain this variation. To facilitate cross-national homicide research by our colleagues across multiple disciplines we provide a persistent link to a website containing our dataset.

The Handbook of Homicide, First Edition. Edited by Fiona Brookman,
Edward R. Maguire, and Mike Maguire.

Sources of Homicide Data

The description of these sources of cross-national homicide offending and victimization data is meant only as a brief and general summary. Other publications contain more detailed descriptions of these and related sources of cross-national homicide data, including their strengths and limitations (see Marshall and Block 2004; Smit, De Jong, and Bijleveld 2012). Further, one general limitation exists no matter the data source. Many places throughout the world remain unstable and in turmoil with terrorist events, nation-sponsored violence, civil war, and corrupt regimes. It is especially difficult to obtain an accurate reflection of homicide in these nations and caution is required when interpreting data from them as they may inaccurately reflect homicide rates within these nations (Smit, De Jong, and Bijleveld 2012).

Homicide offense data

The central source of homicide offending data cross-nationally is the United Nations, which collects these data by surveys. The "United Nations Survey on Crime Trends and the Operations of Criminal Justice Systems (CTS)" is sent to all member nations. There have been multiple versions of the questionnaire with the latest revision occurring with the 2014 fielding of the survey (United Nations Office on Drugs and Crime 2015). Member states typically have a United Nations correspondent who works with relevant agencies within their nation to complete the survey (Stamatel 2006). Intentional homicide is defined by the CTS as "unlawful death inflicted upon a person with the intent to cause death or serious injury" (United Nations Office on Drugs and Crime 2014: 20).

Police-reported data like those provided by the UN possess numerous limitations. This is especially true when testing hypotheses because some of these limitations may be confounded with common theoretical indicators examined in cross-national homicide research. While the United Nations provides a uniform definition of homicide it does not enforce this definition and has little oversight over nations to determine if they are using the provided definitions (Smit, De Jong, and Bijleveld 2012) or simply depending upon their own local definitions. Many researchers assume the definition of homicide is uniform across nations but there is evidence that what constitutes homicide varies across the nations reporting their homicide offending data to the United Nations. For instance, something as simple as the counting unit (does a nation count one victim as one homicide despite the number of offenders, or are multiple offenders counted separately despite one victim?) can change across nations and even within nations based on how local practices vary within the nation (Smit, De Jong, and Bijleveld 2012). There is little oversight by the UN to ensure that data reported to it accurately reflect the definitions they provide nations.

Another limitation with the homicide offending data collected by the United Nations is that not all crime is reported to police, and police do not always record crimes reported to them. Goudriaan, Lynch, and Nieuwbeerta (2004) found significant differences in the proportion of various crimes reported to police across nations (see also Lynch and Pridemore 2011). While it is commonly believed that the police record most homicides, there has been little research on this topic and it is not possible to ascertain from the UN data if the differences in reporting to the police and police recording of homicides are uniform across nations. In one large industrialized nation, for example, research on Russia showed substantial underenumeration of homicides by the police and that this underenumeration varies over time by region of the country (Pridemore 2003). In the likely event that homicide reporting and recording are not uniform across nations it would make comparing rates and trends difficult. This might also bias arguments about the causes of cross-national variation because homicide reporting and recording could be associated with concepts of interest to cross-national crime and homicide scholars, such as level of development, poverty (Pridemore 2008, 2011), resources available to the police, police professionalism and effectiveness (Paré 2014), and trust in the government and police.

Homicide victimization data

The World Health Organization (WHO) provides yearly counts and rates of causes of death across nations. Approximately 200 nations are included with the WHO data collection. For homicide, current data availability ranges from 1979 to approximately 2012, though data are not available on all nations for all years. Information is gathered using vital statistics data through death report registries within each nation. WHO uses two methods—household surveys and census data—to estimate vital statistics for nations that may have unreliable death report registries, thereby creating more reliable counts of deaths within nations (World Health Organization 2014).

The main WHO information of interest for criminological research is the homicide victimization data. Unlike the United Nations' data on homicide offending, WHO enforces a uniform definition of homicide across nations. They do this by utilizing the International Classification of Diseases (ICD) coding system for death classification. This is important to researchers as it helps prevent one of the key limitations within cross-national research, definitional differences of homicide across nations (Smit, De Jong, and Bijleveld 2012). This facilitates the use of these data for cross-national comparisons and for tests of theory. Vital statistics registration systems also record a higher proportion of all deaths compared to homicides that are recorded by the police.

One limitation of vital statistics registration systems at the national level is classification error (Wiersema, Loftin, and McDowall 2000), which occurs when deaths are recorded in the incorrect category or when precise cause of death is unknown. As an example of the latter, recent research shows that use of the ICD code "event of undetermined intent" (EUI) is not uncommon in some nations when recording deaths due to external causes (EUI deaths are 7–15% of all deaths due to external causes in Germany, Poland, Russia, Sweden, and the United Kingdom) and reclassification of these deaths into known causes based on data available on the death certificate can result in homicide rates that are substantially higher than those based only on the ICD homicide category (Andreev *et al.* 2015). Missing observations are the strongest limitation of the WHO homicide victimization data. For most nations there are missing data for multiple years. In cross-national studies of homicide missing data often result in limited and homogeneous samples. For instance, WHO only provides consistent data for four African nations, a handful of Asian nations, and only a few nations in the South Pacific. If researchers were simply interested in comparing nations in North America or Europe (Messner, Raffalovich, and Sutton 2010), then they would be able to obtain an adequate sample over a number of years, but scholars interested in expanding beyond these nations are often frustrated by missing data for many nation-years.

Regional and National Homicide Patterns and Trends

Our main task in this chapter is to describe geographic and temporal variation in homicide rates. In doing so, our description is not based on reviews of others' prior work but instead on our own data collection and analysis of patterns and trends. Our description is based on the WHO homicide victimization data described above. We included nations in our sample if they reported a non-zero homicide rate to WHO for any year between 1979 and 2010. For each global region—Africa, Asia, Europe, North America, and South America—we describe total and sex-specific homicide rates. See Rogers (2014) for a recent description of cross-national age-specific homicide victimization rates. As a service to our colleagues and for the sake of transparency and replication, the database we compiled is permanently available online at https://sites.google.com/site/homicidedata/home. We are happy to make these data available to other scholars for their use and ask only that those employing our data cite to the World Health Organization and to our specific dataset. The link above contains not only the data used here but also additional figures that we do not have the space to include in this chapter.

As with all discussion of crime and victimization rates, readers should use caution when interpreting the information provided below. While the WHO homicide victimization data are considered the most valid and reliable measures of homicide, for reasons discussed above there is no such thing as perfect crime data. WHO goes to great lengths to ensure the validity of the mortality data reported to them, and thus greater faith can be placed in these data even in some nations that may have questionable recording practices. However, complete faith in the homicide estimates is unwise. Still, the reader should be comforted because WHO is unlikely to report an estimate if they have little or no confidence in its accuracy.

Comparing regional homicide trends

Figure 2.1, Figure 2.2, and Figure 2.3 show regional total and male- and female-specific homicide victimization rates between 1979 and 2010. Given the sample of nations for which data are available from WHO, there appear to be a few general trends in homicide victimization rates across the globe. The first trend is that in Western developed nations homicide victimization has been declining since at least the beginning of the 2000s. In Latin American nations, however, homicide victimization rates have been mostly increasing in recent years. There are of course a few exceptions to each of these observations. Second, East European nations have higher homicide rates than West European nations and other developed nations (excluding Latin America). The exception to this is the higher homicide rate in the United States relative to most other Western nations. Finally, male homicide victimization rates are much higher across all nations compared to female homicide victimization rates.

These regional comparisons should not be substituted for a more in-depth discussion of cross-national homicide. A regional trend may not reflect within-nation trends and so these are meant only as a general summary of what is occurring with homicide across nations in a region. In the next few pages we systematically explore national differences in overall, male-, and female-specific national trends in homicide victimization. Due to space limitations we cannot provide here all the figures for these nations, total, male-, and female-specific homicide victimization trends, but again we do provide them in the website mentioned above.

Table 2.1 summarizes these data and shows (1) the highest and lowest total and male- and female-specific nation-year homicide victimization rates for each region

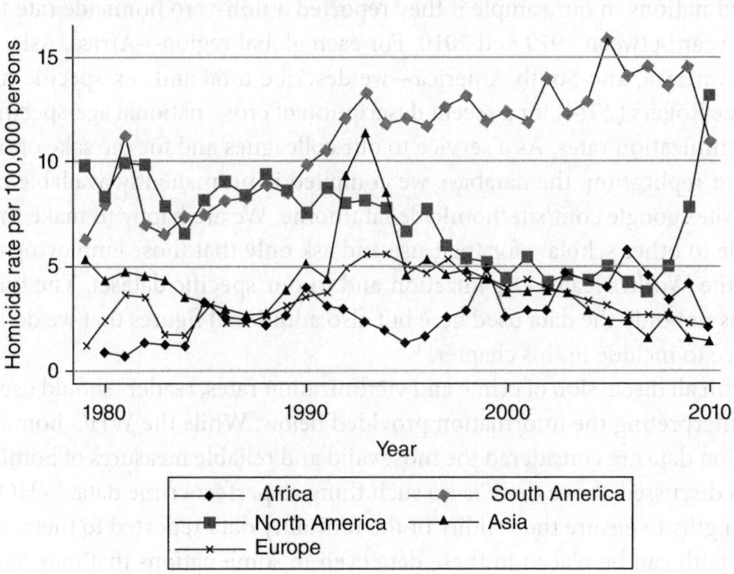

Figure 2.1 Regional total homicide victimization rate trends.
Note: Regional trends should not be relied upon to make strong conclusions regarding homicide victimization rates, especially for regions like Africa where there is little homicide victimization data available.

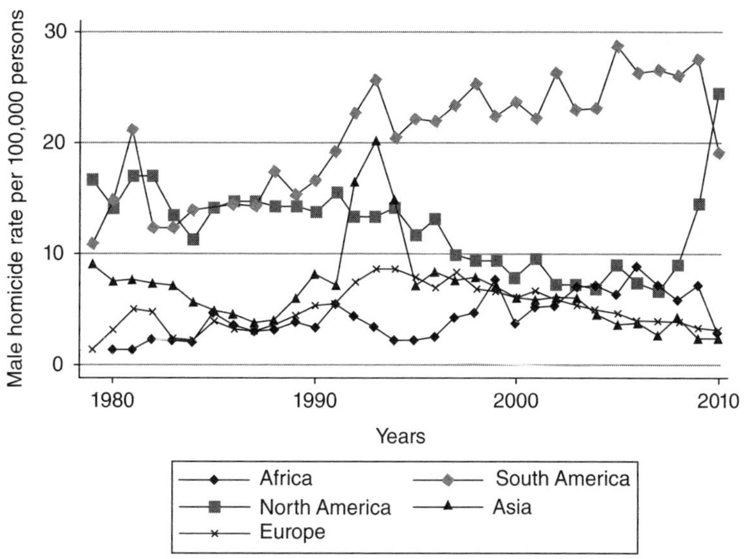

Figure 2.2 Regional male homicide victimization rate trends.

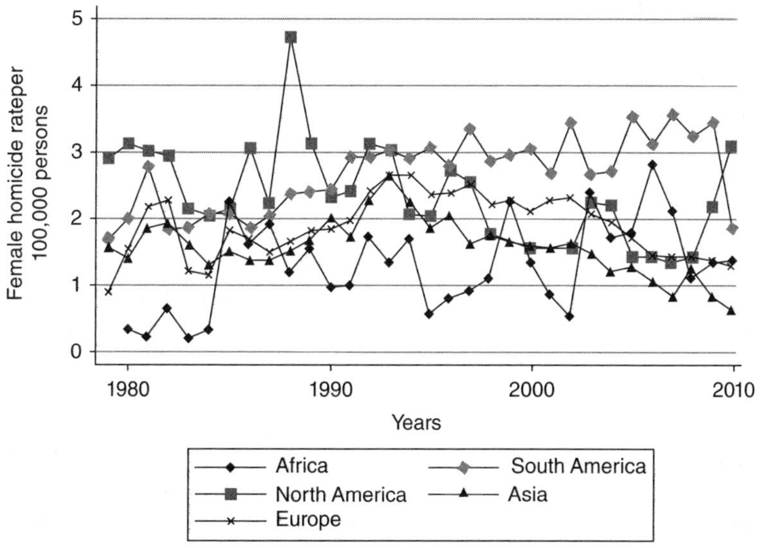

Figure 2.3 Regional female homicide victimization rate trends.

and (2) the most recent total and male- and female-specific homicide victimization rates and the mean rates for each nation for those years between 1979 and 2010 for which data were available for each nation. The following subsections discuss the results presented in the table by region.

Table 2.1 Regional and national homicide victimization rates per 100,000 residents.

		Most recent homicide rate (year)	*Most recent male homicide rate (year)*	*Most recent female homicide rate (year)*
Africa				
Mean regional homicide rate	—			
Mean regional male homicide rate	—			
Mean regional female homicide rate	—			
Highest total nation-year homicide rate (nation, year)	12.1 (Seychelles, 2003)			
Lowest total nation-year homicide rate (nation, year)	0.08 (Egypt, 2000)			
Highest total nation-year male homicide rate (nation, year)	21.1 (South Africa, 2007)			
Lowest total nation-year male homicide rate (nation, year)	0.1 (Egypt, 2000)			
Highest total nation-year female homicide rate (nation, year)	3.0 (Mauritius, 2008)			
Lowest total nation-year female homicide rate (nation, year)	0.02 (Egypt, 2001)			
Egypt		0.10 (2010)	0.2 (2010)	0.03 (2010)
Mauritius		3.9 (2010)	6.0 (2010)	1.9 (2010)
Morocco		0.2 (2008)	0.3 (2008)	0.04 (2008)
Reunion		2.2 (2009)	2.7 (2009)	1.7 (2009)
São Tomé and Príncipe		2.7 (1987)	1.9 (1987)	3.6 (1987)
Seychelles		2.2 (2010)	2.2 (2010)	2.3 (2010)
South Africa		10.1 (2009)	18.4 (2009)	2.6 (2009)
Zimbabwe		5.6 (1990)	NA	NA
Asia				
Mean regional homicide rate	4.2			
Mean regional male homicide rate	7.2			

Table 2.1 (Continued)

		Most recent homicide rate (year)	*Most recent male homicide rate (year)*	*Most recent female homicide rate (year)*
Mean regional female homicide rate	1.7			
Highest total nation-year homicide rate (nation, year)	60.8 (Azerbaijan, 1994)			
Lowest total nation-year homicide rate (nation, year)	0.2 (Georgia, 1994)			
Highest total nation-year male homicide rate (nation, year)	118.8 (Azerbaijan, 1994)			
Lowest total nation-year male homicide rate (nation, year)	0.2 (Hong Kong SAR, 2008)			
Highest total nation-year female homicide rate (nation, year)	8.2 (Kazakhstan, 1998)			
Lowest total nation-year female homicide rate (nation, year)	0.04 (Georgia, 1994)			
Armenia		1.5 (2010)	2.1 (2010)	0.6 (2010)
Azerbaijan		0.2 (2007)	0.4 (2007)	0.1 (2007)
Bahrain		0.6 (2001)	0.8 (2001)	0.4 (2001)
Brunei Darussalam		0.5 (2007)	0.5 (2007)	0.6 (2007)
Cyprus		1.6 (2009)	3.0 (2009)	1.2 (2009)
Georgia		0.3 (2010)	0.5 (2010)	0.2 (2010)
Hong Kong SAR		0.5 (2010)	0.5 (2010)	0.5 (2010)
Israel		2.07 (2010)	3.26 (2010)	0.9 (2010)
Japan		0.3 (2010)	0.4 (2010)	0.3 (2010)
Jordan		2.3 (2009)	3.4 (2009)	1.0 (2009)
Kazakhstan		9.0 (2010)	15.0 (2010)	3.4 (2010)
Kuwait		0.7 (2010)	1.1 (2010)	0.2 (2010)
Kyrgyzstan		6.2 (2010)	10.1 (2010)	2.4 (2010)
Malaysia		0.9 (2008)	1.35 (2008)	0.3 (2008)
Philippines		13.9 (2008)	25.2 (2008)	2.3 (2008)
Qatar		0.5 (2009)	0.5 (2009)	0.5 (2009)
South Korea		1.3 (2010)	1.4 (2010)	1.1 (2010)
Singapore		0.3 (2010)	0.6 (2010)	0.1 (2010)
Sri Lanka		3.3 (2006)	5.5 (2006)	1.1 (2006)
Tajikistan		1.8 (2005)	2.7 (2005)	0.9 (2005)
Thailand		5.1 (2006)	9.5 (2006)	1.3 (2006)
Turkey		1.5 (2010)	2.4 (2010)	0.6 (2010)

(Continued)

Table 2.1 (Continued)

		Most recent homicide rate (year)	*Most recent male homicide rate (year)*	*Most recent female homicide rate (year)*
Turkmenistan		7.6 (1998)	11.9 (1998)	2.3 (1998)
United Arab Emirates		0.3 (2010)	0.4 (2010)	0.2 (2010)
Uzbekistan		2.8 (2005)	4.4 (2005)	1.2 (2005)
Europe				
Mean regional homicide rate	3.8			
Mean regional male homicide rate	5.6			
Mean regional female homicide rate	2.0			
Highest total nation-year homicide rate (nation, year)	42.4 (Albania, 1997)			
Lowest total nation-year homicide rate (nation, year)	0.3 (United Kingdom, 2010)			
Highest total nation-year male homicide rate (nation, year)	71.0 (Albania, 1997)			
Lowest total nation-year male homicide rate (nation, year)	0. 4 (Austria, 2010, Switzerland, 2006; United Kingdom, 2009; and United Kingdom, 2010)			
Highest total nation-year female homicide rate (nation, year)	14.4 (Russia, 1994)			
Lowest total nation-year female homicide rate (nation, year)	0.2 (Ireland-1982; Ireland, 1989; Ireland, 1990; and United Kingdom, 2010)			
Albania		4.4 (2004)	7.4 (2004)	1.3 (2004)

Table 2.1 (Continued)

		Most recent homicide rate (year)	*Most recent male homicide rate (year)*	*Most recent female homicide rate (year)*
Austria		0.5 (2010)	0.4 (2010)	0.7 (2010)
Belarus		6.3 (2009)	8.8 (2009)	4.1 (2009)
Belgium		1.1 (2010)	1.4 (2010)	0.8 (2010)
Bulgaria		1.5 (2010)	2.2 (2010)	0.9 (2010)
Croatia		1.3 (2010)	1.5 (2010)	1.2 (2010)
Czech Republic		0.8 (2010)	0.9 (2010)	0.8 (2010)
Denmark		0.8 (2010)	0.8 (2010)	0.7 (2010)
Estonia		4.7 (2010)	7.8 (2010)	1.9 (2010)
Finland		1.9 (2010)	3.1 (2010)	0.8 (2010)
France		0.6 (2010)	0.8 (2010)	0.5 (2010)
Germany		0.6 (2010)	0.6 (2010)	0.6 (2010)
Greece		1.5 (2010)	2.4 (2010)	0.6 (2010)
Hungary		1.5 (2010)	2.0 (2010)	1.1 (2010)
Iceland		1.4 (2004)	0.7 (2004)	2.1 (2004)
Ireland		0.8 (2010)	1.5 (2010)	0.2 (2010)
Italy		0.8 (2010)	1.1 (2010)	0.4 (2010)
Latvia		6.6 (2010)	9.5 (2010)	3.4 (2010)
Lithuania		5.6 (2010)	7.9 (2010)	2.9 (2010)
Luxembourg		2.2 (2010)	2.4 (2010)	2.0 (2010)
Malta		1.0 (2010)	1.5 (2010)	0.5 (2010)
Montenegro		2.3 (2009)	3.2 (2009)	1.3 (2009)
Netherlands		0.9 (2010)	1.1 (2010)	0.7 (2010)
Norway		0.7 (2010)	0.7 (2010)	0.7 (2010)
Poland		0.9 (2010)	1.3 (2010)	0.6 (2010)
Portugal		1.2 (2010)	1.7 (2010)	0.8 (2010)
Republic of Moldova		7.0 (2010)	10.0 (2010)	4.2 (2010)
Romania		2.5 (2010)	3.3 (2010)	1.5 (2010)
Russia		13.3 (2010)	21.5 (2010)	6.2 (2010)
Serbia		1.8 (2010)	2.5 (2010)	1.1 (2010)
Slovakia		1.2 (2010)	1.4 (2010)	1.0 (2010)
Slovenia		0.5 (2010)	0.5 (2010)	0.5 (2010)
Spain		0.7 (2010)	0.9 (2010)	0.5 (2010)
Sweden		0.9 (2010)	1.3 (2010)	0.6 (2010)
Switzerland		0.5 (2010)	0.5 (2010)	0.5 (2010)
TFYR Macedonia		2.1 (2010)	3.0 (2010)	1.3 (2010)
Ukraine		6.0 (2010)	9.2 (2010)	3.4 (2010)
United Kingdom		0.3 (2010)	0.4 (2010)	0.2 (2010)
North America				
Mean regional homicide rate	8.1			

(Continued)

Table 2.1 (Continued)

		Most recent homicide rate (year)	Most recent male homicide rate (year)	Most recent female homicide rate (year)
Mean regional male homicide rate	14.0			
Mean regional female homicide rate	2.7			
Highest total nation-year homicide rate (nation, year)	21.0 (Mexico, 2010)			
Lowest total nation-year homicide rate (nation, year)	1.4 (Canada, 2003)			
Highest total nation-year male homicide rate (nation, year)	41.0 (Mexico, 2010)			
Lowest total nation-year male homicide rate (nation, year)	1.9 (Canada, 1997)			
Highest total nation-year female homicide rate (nation, year)	4.4 (United States, 1980 and United States, 1991)			
Lowest total nation-year female homicide rate (nation, year)	0.7 (Canada, 2008)			
Bermuda		6.7 (1996)	10.0 (1996)	3.2 (1996)
Canada		1.7 (2009)	2.6 (2009)	0.9 (2009)
Mexico		21.0 (2010)	41.0 (2010)	4.0 (2010)
United States		5.3 (2010)	8.4 (2010)	2.2 (2010)
South America				
Mean regional homicide rate	12.9			
Mean regional male homicide rate	23.8			
Mean regional female homicide rate	3.1			
Highest total nation-year homicide rate (nation, year)	112.6 (Guatemala, 1981)			
Lowest total nation-year homicide rate (nation, year)	0.02 (Haiti, 1980)			

Table 2.1 (Continued)

		Most recent homicide rate (year)	*Most recent male homicide rate (year)*	*Most recent female homicide rate (year)*
Highest total nation-year male homicide rate (nation, year)	210.5 (Guatemala, 1981)			
Lowest total nation-year male homicide rate (nation, year)	0.4 (Jamaica, 1982 and Jamaica, 1988)			
Highest total nation-year female homicide rate (nation, year)	18.1 (Guatemala, 1981)			
Lowest total nation-year female homicide rate (nation, year)	0.08 (Jamaica-2002 and Jamaica-2003)			
Antigua and Barbuda		4.8 (2006)	7.6 (2006)	2.2 (2006)
Argentina		4.5 (2010)	7.7 (2010)	1.4 (2010)
Aruba		3.9 (2009)	5.9 (2009)	1.8 (2009)
Bahamas		21.8 (2008)	40.5 (2008)	3.9 (2008)
Barbados		17.65 (2008)	31.62 (2008)	4.9 (2008)
Belize		27.9 (2009)	44.4 (2009)	6.0 (2009)
Bolivia		0.2 (2003)	NA	NA
Brazil		26.8 (2010)	50.4 (2010)	4.6 (2010)
Cayman Islands		14.7 (2009)	26.7 (2009)	3.8 (2009)
Chile		5.3 (2009)	9.6 (2009)	1.1 (2009)
Colombia		43.0 (2009)	81.3 (2009)	7.2 (2009)
Costa Rica		10.4 (2010)	18.8 (2010)	2.3 (2010)
Cuba		4.5 (2010)	6.7 (2010)	2.3 (2010)
Dominica		22.48 (2010)	2.8 (2006)	2.9 (2006)
Dominican Republic		9.1 (2010)	17.4 (2010)	1.8 (2010)
Ecuador		15.5 (2010)	28.7 (2010)	2.6 (2010)
El Salvador		60.9 (2009)	113.4 (2009)	14.4 (2009)
French Guiana		9.8 (2009)	6.0 (2009)	3.6 (2009)
Grenada		3.0 (1996)	2.0 (1996)	4.0 (1996)
Guadeloupe		4.4 (2009)	7.9 (2009)	1.3 (2009)
Guatemala		43.2 (2009)	78.3 (2009)	9.6 (2009)
Guyana		8.7 (2009)	13.9 (2009)	3.6 (2009)
Haiti		0.6 (2004)	1.0 (2004)	0.1 (2004)
Honduras		23.2 (1990)	41.1 (1988)	5.3 (1988)
Jamaica		0.7 (2006)	1.1 (2006)	0.3 (2006)
Martinique		2.8 (2009)	4.3 (2009)	1.4 (2009)
Nicaragua		6.1 (2010)	15.7 (2009)	1.8 (2009)
Panama		22.0 (2009)	41.6 (2009)	4.2 (2009)
Paraguay		9.8 (2010)	17.4 (2010)	2.1 (2010)

(Continued)

Table 2.1 (Continued)

	Most recent homicide rate (year)	*Most recent male homicide rate (year)*	*Most recent female homicide rate (year)*
Peru	1.4 (2010)	2.4 (2010)	0.5 (2010)
Puerto Rico	25.7 (2010)	50.5 (2010)	3.0 (2010)
Saint Lucia	2.3 (2008)	3.5 (2008)	1.1 (2008)
Saint Vincent and Grenadines	12.0 (2010)	21.7 (2010)	1.9 (2010)
Suriname	6.9 (2009)	11.1 (2009)	2.7 (2009)
Trinidad and Tobago	43.2 (2008)	78.0 (2008)	8.6 (2008)
Turks and Caicos Islands	6.6 (2009)	5.6 (2007)	5.9 (2007)
Uruguay	5.1 (2009)	8.7 (2009)	1.8 (2009)
Venezuela	33.6 (2009)	63.3 (2009)	3.7 (2009)
Virgin Islands (USA)	40.0 (2007)	78.0 (2007)	5.4 (2007)

Notes: NA = Not available. Mean regional homicide rates are simple unweighted averages for the nation-years on which data were available. Male- and female-specific rates are per 100,000 males and 100,000 females.

Europe

Overall homicide victimization Figure 2.4 shows annual total homicide victimization rates for some of the European nations we examined in our analysis. For many years homicide victimization rates have been decreasing across most regions of Europe. For most East European nations the declines that occurred after the peaks in the mid-1990s have generally extended to recent years. One exception to the overall trend is Greece in recent years.

Table 2.1 shows that the average national European homicide victimization rate was 3.8 per 100,000 residents between 1979 and 2010. There is some variation within Europe. For example, East European nations had an average homicide rate of 5.9, North European nations had an average rate of 4.2, South European nations had an average rate of 2.0, and West European nations had an average homicide victimization rate of 1.7 per 100,000 residents. On average, Eastern Europe had higher homicide rates than Western Europe and had a slower decline in homicide victimization rates compared to Western Europe. At 42.4 homicides per 100,000 residents, Albania in 1997 had the highest nation-year homicide rate in Europe during this period, and United Kingdom in 2010 had the lowest nation-year rate with 0.3 homicides per 100,000 residents. Several European nations had high average homicide rates, including Russia (18.8 homicide victimizations per 100,000 residents), Estonia (12.1), Latvia (10.4), Moldova (10.3), Albania (9.6), Ukraine (8.7), Lithuania (7.6), and Belarus (7.1). Nations with the highest average homicide rates in the region tend to be in Eastern Europe and many of the nations with lower homicide rates are in Western Europe (e.g., France, Germany, Netherlands, Norway, and Switzerland).

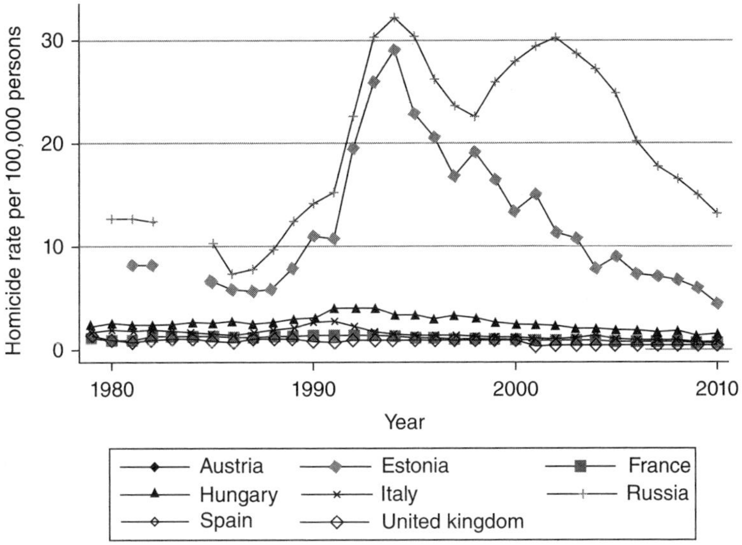

Figure 2.4 European total homicide victimization rate trends.

Male homicide victimization Male-specific national homicide victimization rates in Europe have been declining in many nations. For some nations (i.e., Austria, Italy, and the United Kingdom) the decrease started in the 1990s. In several other nations, however, the decrease in male homicide victimization did not start until the 2000s. The latter includes Belarus, Belgium, the Netherlands, Romania, Russia, Slovenia, and Spain. Two exceptions to this general pattern were Greece and Malta, which both experienced an increase in male homicide victimization rates over the period under observation. Finally, Iceland, Luxembourg, and Sweden had more erratic male homicide rates that increased and decreased over time with less of a clear pattern.

The average male-specific national homicide victimization rate in Europe during this period was 5.6 homicides per 100,000 males. Eastern Europe had a higher average male homicide victimization rate at 9.8, followed by Northern Europe at 6.5, Southern Europe at 3.1, and Western Europe at 1.4. Nations with especially high average male homicide victimization rates between 1979 and 2010 were Russia (32.2), Estonia (20.5), Latvia (16.0), Albania (15.2), Ukraine (14.5), Moldova (14.1), Lithuania (12.4), and Belarus (12.1).

The lowest nation-year male homicide victimization rate was 0.4 male homicides per 100,000 males in Switzerland (2006), the United Kingdom (2009 and 2010), and Austria (2010). Albania in 1997 had the highest nation-year male homicide rate at 71.0 per 100,000 males. This was an unusual year in Albania, however, as it appeared to be an extreme spike in male homicide victimization.

Female homicide victimization Female homicide victimization rates in Europe have generally been decreasing since the 2000s. There are a few exceptions. For example, Macedonia's female homicide victimization has been increasing. Other exceptions, all of which had similar trends, experienced decreasing female homicide victimization rates during the early 2000s but closer to 2010 there were increases in female homicide victimization rates. These nations included Denmark, Germany, Malta, Norway, Poland, the Republic of Moldova, and Slovakia.

The overall average national female homicide victimization rate in Europe between 1979 and 2010 was 2.0 homicides per 100,000 females. Average female homicide victimization rates were the lowest in Western and Southern Europe, at 1.0 per 100,000 females, with rates of 2.3 in Northern Europe and 3.6 in Eastern Europe. Nations with higher average female homicide victimization rates were Russia (9.5), Latvia (5.8), Ukraine (5.3), Belarus (5.1), Estonia (5.1), and Lithuania (4.3). Russia in 1994 had the highest nation-year female homicide victimization rate with a rate of 14.39 female homicides per 100,000 females. Ireland had the lowest average female homicide victimization rate during this period with a rate of 0.4, and in 1982, 1989, and 1990 Ireland also had the lowest nation-year female homicide victimization rate of 0.2 homicides per 100,000 females. The United Kingdom also observed a female homicide victimization rate of 0.2 homicides per 100,000 females in 2010.

North America

Overall homicide victimization Figure 2.5 shows annual total homicide victimization rates for the North American nations we examined in our analysis. The four nations in North America for which we had consistent homicide victimization data from WHO were Bermuda, Canada, Mexico, and the United States. The overall homicide victimization rates for North America generally declined during the mid- to late 1990s for these nations. For the United States this decline continued throughout the period under observation, though beginning in 2003 in Canada and 2007 in Mexico homicide victimization rates began to increase. Mexico experienced the most dramatic change during this period, increasing from 7.4 homicides per 100,000 residents in 2007 to 19.9 homicides per 100,000 residents in 2010.

Table 2.1 shows that the average regional homicide rate in North America between 1979 and 2010 was 8.1 homicides per 100,000 residents. Mexico had the highest average national homicide rates during this period at 15.0 per 100,000 residents, and Canada the lowest with 1.8. The average annual homicide rate in the United States during this period was 7.9 per 100,000 residents.

Male homicide victimization Male-specific homicide victimization rates in North American nations exhibited a consistent pattern across each nation from approximately the 1990s until the 2000s with general declines. However, in the 2000s Canada's male homicide victimization rate increased (though from a low baseline) and in 2007 Mexico's male homicide victimization rates began a dramatic

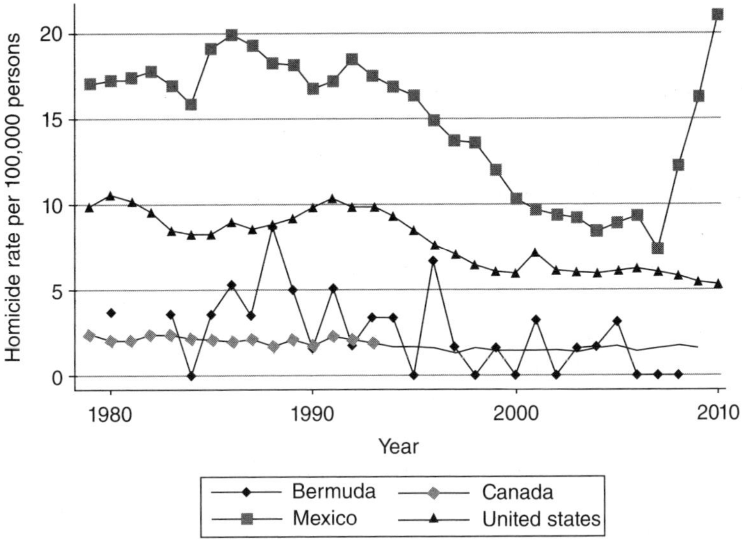

Figure 2.5 North American total homicide victimization rate trends.

increase. The United States is the only nation that observed consistent declines in male homicide victimization since the early to mid-1990s. On average, Mexico had the highest average male homicide victimization rates in North America between 1979 and 2010 with a rate of 27.9 per 100,000 males. The lowest average male homicide rates in the region were observed in Canada at 3.2 per 100,000. The average male homicide victimization rate in the United States between 1979 and 2010 was 13.4 per 100,000 males. Mexico in 2010 had the highest nation-year male homicide rate at 41.0 per 100,000 males and Canada in 1997 had the lowest nation-year male homicide rate at 1.9. For the United States the average male homicide victimization rate during this time was 12.5 per 100,000 residents and its highest male rate was 17.0 in 1980.

Female homicide victimization Female homicide victimization rates in North America have been declining since the 1990s, though in Mexico female rates began to increase again in 2007. The average national female homicide victimization rate for North American nations was 2.7 homicides per 100,000 females between 1979 and 2010. The United States had both the highest average female homicide victimization rate during this period at 3.5 and the highest nation-year female homicide victimization rate at 4.4 in 1980 and 1991. Canada experienced both the lowest average female homicide victimization rate at 1.2 and the lowest nation-year female rate of 0.7 in 2008.

South America

Overall homicide victimization Figure 2.6 shows annual total homicide victimization rates for the South American nations we examined in our analysis. In general, overall homicide victimization rates have been increasing in South American nations since the beginning of the 2000s. The Bahamas, Barbados, Belize, Brazil, Cayman Islands, Chile, Costa Rica, Ecuador, El Salvador, Guatemala, Puerto Rico, Trinidad and Tobago, and Venezuela all experienced increases in homicide victimization rates during this period. On the other hand, Antigua and Barbuda, Argentina, Aruba, Colombia, Cuba, Guyana, Jamaica, Nicaragua, Paraguay, Peru, and Uruguay all observed decreased homicide victimization rates during this time.

Table 2.1 shows that South America's average national homicide rate between 1979 and 2010 for the nations for which we had consistent data was 12.9 per 100,000 residents. Colombia had the highest average homicide rate in South America over these years with a rate of 59.8 per 100,000 residents. Other nations with high average homicide rates included El Salvador (42.2), Guatemala (25.2), Brazil (20.6), Puerto Rico (19.8), and Venezuela (18.7). Guatemala in 1981 had the highest nation-year homicide rate at 112.6 homicides per 100,000 residents.

Peru had the lowest average homicide rates in the region between 1979 and 2010 with a mean annual rate of 2.5 homicides per 100,000 residents. Other nations with low average homicide rates were Aruba (4.3), Suriname (4.2), Uruguay (4.1), and Chile (3.7). Haiti in 1980 had the lowest nation-year homicide rate in the region at 0.02 homicides per 100,000 residents.

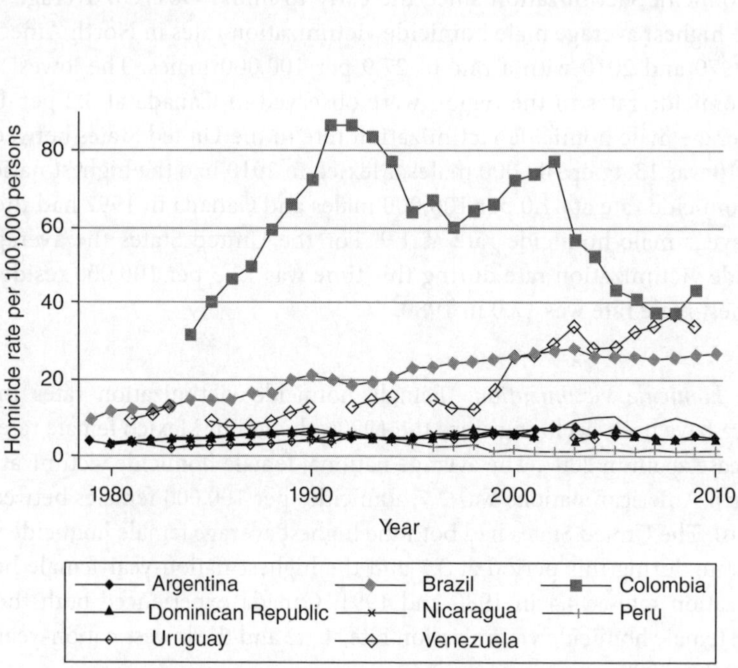

Figure 2.6 South American total homicide victimization trends.

Male homicide victimization South American nations have mostly experienced increases in male homicide victimization rates since the beginning of the 2000s. Nations that saw increases in male homicide rates during this period were Barbados, Belize, Brazil, Chile, Costa Rica, Ecuador, El Salvador, Guatemala, Nicaragua, Panama, Puerto Rico, and Venezuela. On the other hand, some nations in this region experienced decreasing male homicide rates since 2000, including Argentina, Colombia, Cuba, Dominica, Paraguay, Peru, and Uruguay.

The average national male homicide victimization rate for South American nations between 1979 and 2010 was 23.8 per 100,000 males. Guatemala's male homicide victimization rate in 1982 of 210.5 per 100,000 males was the highest nation-year rate. The lowest nation-year rate was 0.4 per 100,000 males in Jamaica in 1982 and 1988.

While Colombia's annual male homicide victimization rates generally decreased between 1979 and 2010 it still had the highest average rate of 111.6 per 100,000 males. Other nations with high average male homicide victimization rates in the region included El Salvador (78.8), Guatemala (51.8), Brazil (39.3), Bahamas (27.2), Puerto Rico (36.6), and Venezuela (34.8). The lowest average male homicide victimization rate in South America during this period was 4.2 per 100,000 males in Peru.

Female homicide victimization South American nations experienced mixed trends for female homicide victimization rates between 1979 and 2010. In recent years Brazil, Colombia, Cuba, Peru, and Puerto Rico all had decreases in female homicide victimization rates. Belize, Chile, Costa Rica, Ecuador, El Salvador, Guatemala, Nicaragua, Panama, Paraguay, and Venezuela all experienced general increases in female homicide victimization rates. Jamaica in 2002 and 2003 had the lowest nation-year female homicide victimization rate at 0.1 homicides per 100,000 females. Guatemala in 1981 had the highest nation-year female homicide victimization rate at 18.1 homicides per 100,000 females.

Between 1979 and 2010 the average annual national female homicide victimization rate for South American nations was 3.1 homicides per 100,000 females. Colombia had the highest average annual female homicide victimization rate during this period with a mean rate of 8.9 homicides per 100,000 females. Other nations with high average female homicide victimization rates included El Salvador (7.4), Guatemala (5.4), the Bahamas (4.2), Belize (4.0), Puerto Rico (3.7), Brazil (3.6), Guyana (3.6), and Antigua and Barbuda (3.4). Peru had the lowest average annual female homicide victimization rates in the region during this period with a mean rate of 0.7 homicides per 100,000 females.

Asia

Overall homicide victimization Figure 2.7 shows annual total homicide victimization rates for the Asian nations we examined in our analysis. National homicide rates in Asia have been decreasing in recent years with the exceptions of Tajikistan

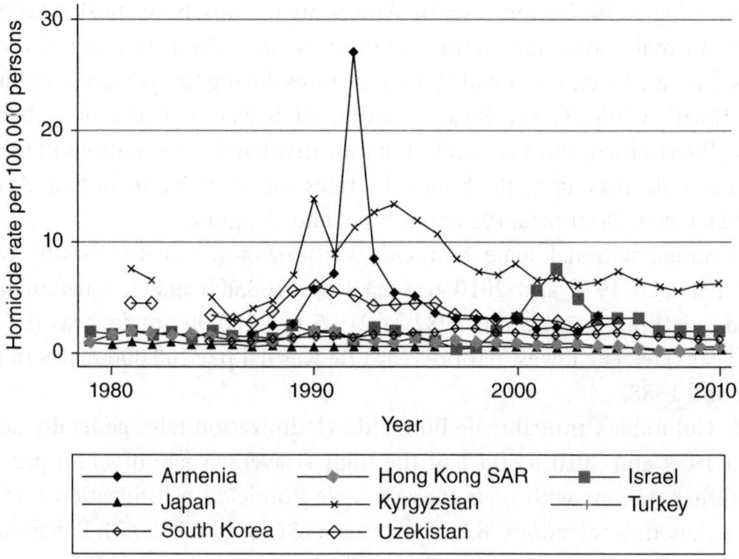

Figure 2.7 Asian total homicide victimization rate trends.

and Malaysia which experienced increases. For some nations (e.g., Israel) the decline began around 2000, while for others (e.g., South Korea) the decline began in the mid-1990s.

Table 2.1 shows that the average homicide rate during the period under review for the Asian nations on which we had data was 4.2 homicides per 100,000 residents. Azerbaijan in 1994 had the highest nation-year homicide victimization rate in Asia during this period. This high homicide rate was part of a large increase in the nation's rate from 1991 to 1994. In 1991, the homicide rate in Azerbaijan was 4.8 and increased tenfold in 1992 to 51.0 per 100,000 residents. By 1995 the rate decreased to 8.7 per 100,000 residents. Georgia in 1994 had the lowest nation-year homicide rate at 0.2 per 100,000 residents. On average, Japan had the lowest homicide victimization rates among these Asian nations with an average rate of 0.6 homicides per 100,000 residents. The Philippines had the highest average homicide rate at 13.4 homicides per 100,000 residents.

Male homicide victimization Male homicide victimization rates have been declining in most Asian nations since the 1990s. In Bahrain, Georgia, and Israel, male homicide victimization rates started to decline in the 2000s. The average male homicide victimization rate between 1979 and 2010 for these Asian nations for which we had data was 7.2 per 100,000 males. Bahrain had the lowest average male homicide victimization rates with 0.7 homicides per 100,000 residents during this period. Japan had a similarly low mean male homicide victimization rate of 0.8 male homicides per 100,000 males. The Philippines had the highest mean male homicide victimization rates with 24.8 male homicides per 100,000 males. Other nations with high average male homicide victimization rates in the region included Kazakhstan (20.9 homicides per 100,000 males), Thailand (19.5), Azerbaijan (18.2), Kyrgyzstan

(12.1), Tajikistan (11.2), and Sri Lanka (8.1). Hong Kong SAR in 2008 had the lowest nation-year male homicide victimization rates in the region at 0.2 per 100,000 males. Azerbaijan in 1994 had the highest nation-year male homicide victimization rate at 118.8 homicides per 100,000 males.

Female homicide victimization Female homicide victimization rates in Asian nations have generally been declining since the 2000s, with the exception of Turkmenistan and Hong Kong SAR. Turkmenistan female homicide victimization rates are increasing. Hong Kong SAR had been decreasing but recently increased sharply. The average female homicide victimization rate in Asia between 1979 and 2010 was 1.7 homicides per 100,000 females. Kazakhstan had the highest average female homicide victimization rate with 5.9 homicides per 100,000 females. Other nations with high average female homicide victimization rates included Kyrgyzstan (an average of 3.5 homicides per 100,000 females), Thailand (2.8), Turkmenistan (2.4), and Azerbaijan (2.0). Japan had the lowest average female homicide victimization rate in Asia with 0.5 homicides per 100,000 females. Georgia in 1992 had the lowest nation-year female homicide victimization rate in Asia between 1979 and 2010 with 0.04 homicides per 100,000 females. Kazakhstan in 1998 had the highest nation-year female homicide rate with 8.2 homicides per 100,000 females.

Africa

Overall homicide victimization The data presented for Africa should be interpreted with even more caution given the instability of some of these nations and the lack of information provided by WHO for most African nations. Figure 2.8 shows annual total homicide victimization rates for the African nations we examined in our analysis. There are only four African nations with consistently available homicide victimization data, two of which are island states in the Indian Ocean. Among the last two, homicide rates have generally declined since the beginning of the 2000s while rates in South Africa (increasing victimization) and Egypt (relatively stable trend with exception of 2003) have recently departed from this trend. Mauritius observed an increase in homicide until the late 2000s and since then homicide rates declined. Seychelles has had erratic homicide trends, but overall homicide rates decreased since 2000. South Africa experienced an increase in homicide throughout the time that homicide data were available.

For those few African nations for which recent and regular homicide data are available the average annual homicide victimization rate was 3.3 per 100,000 residents. Both Seychelles (an average of 5.7 homicides per 100,000 residents) and South Africa (an average of 7.2 homicides per 100,000 residents) had higher homicide rates than the sample average. Egypt had the lowest average at 0.2 homicides per 100,000 residents. Seychelles (12.07) in 2003 and Egypt (0.08) in 2000 had the highest and lowest nation-year homicide victimization rates, respectively.

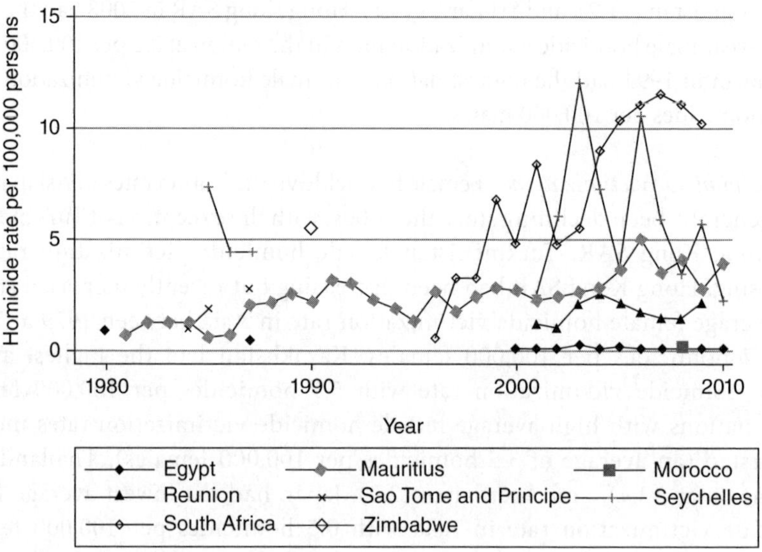

Figure 2.8 African total homicide victimization rate trends.

Male homicide victimization There is not a consistent trend in male homicide victimization rates for the four African nations for which victimization data were available for a number of years. Egypt and Seychelles both appear to have declining male homicide victimization rates in recent years. Mauritius and South Africa both appear to have increasing rates of male homicide victimization. The average male homicide victimization rate for the four African nations was 5.2 homicides per 100,000 males. Egypt reported the lowest average male homicide victimization rate at 0.3 male homicides per 100,000 males. Egypt also had the lowest regional nation-year homicide rate in 2000 with 0.1 male homicides per 100,000 males in 2000. South Africa had the highest average male homicide victimization rate at 12.8 male homicide victimizations per 100,000 males and it had the highest nation-year homicide rate with 21.1 male homicides per 100,000 males in 2007. Seychelles also observed an average male homicide rate greater than the regional average with an average of 8.7 male homicides per 100,000 males.

Female homicide victimization There are even less data available from Africa for female homicide victimization as only three nations—Egypt, Mauritius, and South Africa—had female homicide victimization data available for over a 10 year period between 1979 and 2010. Egypt appears to have consistently low female homicide victimization rates. Mauritius and South Africa both appear to have increasing female homicide victimization over time. The average female homicide victimization rate for these three nations during this period was 1.5 homicides per 100,000 females. The nation with the highest average was South Africa, with 2.0 female homicide victimizations per 100,000 females. Egypt had the lowest average female homicide victimization rate, with 0.1 female homicides per 100,000 females. Egypt also had the lowest nation-year female homicide victimization rate with 0.02 female homicides per 100,000 females in 2001. Mauritius had the highest nation-year female homicide victimization rate, with 3.0 female homicides per 100,000 females in 2008.

Conclusion

Our description reveals considerable geographic and temporal variation in total and sex-specific national homicide victimization rates both in recent years and over the last three to four decades. This up-to-date description is valuable because regional and national homicide rates change in absolute terms and relative to other regions and nations. Thus, a basic understanding of these patterns and trends is a necessary first step in determining the efficacy of existing theories attempting to explain cross-national homicide rates and when considering new hypotheses about the causes of the geographic and temporal variation we reveal here.

Research on cross-national homicide rates is growing. We believe this to be an underappreciated topic because homicide rates respond to national characteristics and thus help to tell us something about the characteristics of social structure, culture, and criminal justice within a nation. There is already a decades-long empirical literature examining the impact on cross-national homicide rates of social forces, such as poverty (Paré and Felson 2014; Pridemore 2008, 2011), economic inequality (Fajnzylber, Lederman, and Loayza 2002; Messner, Raffalovich, and Sutton 2010), economic development (Bennett 1991; Kick and LaFree 1985), ethnic and linguistic heterogeneity (Avison and Loring 1986), social support (Altheimer 2008; Savolainen 2000), and policing effectiveness (Paré 2014), and how characteristics like institutional imbalance (Messner and Rosenfeld 1997) and social protection (Rogers and Pridemore 2013) may moderate the deleterious effects of some of these characteristics on homicide rates. We are still at the very beginning of our understanding of the causes driving geographic and temporal variation in cross-national homicide rates, however, and there remains much to learn.

The patterns and trends described here offer many things to consider. Why the generally increasing and high homicide rates in Latin America? What is happening in the United States to bring its traditionally higher homicide rate closer to that of other Western nations? What explains the intra-European variation in homicide rates? Do specific nations follow a more general global homicide trend in the same way that cities may partially follow a national homicide trend (McDowall and Loftin 2009)? These are just a few of the many intriguing questions derived from the updated patterns and trends in homicide victimization rates we describe here. We hope our description will help to generate many more research questions and to inspire scholars to undertake increasingly sophisticated research to understand better the causes of geographic and temporal variation in cross-national homicide victimization rates.

References

Altheimer, I. (2008) Social support, ethnic heterogeneity, and homicide: A cross-national approach. *Journal of Criminal Justice*, 36: 103–114.

Andreev, E.M., Shkolnikov, V.M., Pridemore, W.A., and Nikitina, S.Y. (2015) A method for reclassifying cause of death in cases categorized as "event of undetermined intent." *Population Health Metrics*, 13: 23.

Avison, W.R. and Loring, P.L. (1986) Population diversity and cross-national homicide: The effects of inequality and heterogeneity. *Criminology*, 24: 733–749.

Bennett, R.R. (1991) Development and crime: A cross-national time series analysis of competing models. *Sociological Quarterly*, 32: 343–363.

Fajnzylber, P., Lederman, D., and Loayza, N. (2002) Inequality and violent crime. *Journal of Law and Economics*, 45: 1–40.

Goudriaan, H., Lynch, J.P., and Nieuwbeerta, P. (2004) Reporting to the police in Western nations: The effect of country characteristics. *Justice Quarterly*, 21: 933–969.

Kick, E.L. and LaFree, G. (1985) Development and the social context of murder and theft. *Comparative Social Research*, 8: 37–58.

Lynch, J. and Pridemore, W.A. (2011). Crime in international perspective. In J.Q. Wilson and J. Petersilia (eds), *Crime and Public Policy* (pp. 5–52). New York: Oxford University Press.

Marshall, I.H. and Block, C.R. (2004) Maximizing the availability of cross-national data on homicide. *Homicide Studies*, 8: 267–310.

McDowall, D. and Loftin, C. (2009) Do US city crime rates follow a national trend? The influence of nationwide conditions on local crime patterns. *Journal of Quantitative Criminology*, 25: 307–324.

Messner, S.F., Raffalovich, L.E., and Sutton, G.G. (2010) Poverty, infant mortality, and homicide rates in cross-national perspective: Assessments of criterion and construct validity. *Criminology*, 48: 509–537.

Messner, S.F. and Rosenfeld, R. (1997) Political restraint of the market and levels of criminal homicide: A cross-national application of institutional-anomie theory. *Social Forces*, 75: 1393–1416.

Paré, P.-P. (2014) Indicators of police performance and their relationships with homicide rates across 77 nations. *International Criminal Justice Review*, 24: 254–270.

Paré, P.-P. and Felson, R. (2014) Income inequality, poverty, and crime across nations. *British Journal of Sociology*, 65: 434–458.

Pridemore, W.A. (2003) Measuring homicide in Russia: A comparison of estimates from the crime and vital statistics reporting systems. *Social Science & Medicine*, 57: 1343–1354.

Pridemore, W.A. (2008) A methodological addition to the cross-national empirical literature on social structure and homicide: A first test of the poverty–homicide thesis. *Criminology*, 46: 133–154.

Pridemore, W.A. (2011) Poverty matters: A reassessment of the inequality–homicide relationship in cross-national studies. *British Journal of Criminology*, 51: 739–772.

Rogers, M.L. (2014) A descriptive and graphical analysis of the (lack of) association between age and homicide cross-nationally. *International Criminal Justice Review*, 24: 235–253.

Rogers, M.L. and Pridemore, W.A. (2013) Poverty, social protection, and cross-national homicide rates: direct and moderating effects. *Social Science Research*, 42: 584–595.

Savolainen, J. (2000) Inequality, welfare state, and homicide: Further support for the institutional anomie theory. *Criminology*, 38: 1021–1042.

Smit, P.R., De Jong, R.R., and Bijleveld, C.J. (2012) Homicide data in Europe: Definitions, sources, and statistics. In M. Liem and W.A. Pridemore (eds), *Handbook on European Homicide Research: Patterns, Explanations, and Country Studies* (5–24). New York: Springer.

Stamatel, J.P. (2006) An overview of publicly available quantitative cross-national crime data. *IASSIST Quarterly*, 30: 16–20.

United Nations Office on Drugs and Crime (2015) United Nations surveys on crime trends and the operations of criminal justice systems (CTS). Available online at https://www.unodc.org/unodc/en/data-and-analysis/United-Nations-Surveys-on-Crime-Trends-and-the-Operations-of-Criminal-Justice-Systems.html (accessed January 6, 2016).

United Nations Office on Drugs and Crime (2014) International classification of crimes for statistical purposes. Available online at https://www.unodc.org/documents/data-and-analysis/statistics/crime/ICCS/ICCS_Draft_for_consultation_August_2014.pdf (accessed January 6, 2016).

Wiersema, B., Loftin, C., and McDowall, D. (2000) A comparison of supplementary homicide reports and national vital statistics systems homicide estimates for US counties. *Homicide Studies*, 4: 317–340.

World Health Organization (2014) WHO Statistical information system (Global Health Observatory). Available online at http://www.who.int/whosis/en/(Accessed January 6, 2016).

3

Some Trends in Homicide and Its Age-Crime Curves

Alfred Blumstein

Homicide, the crime widely recognized as being of most serious concern in any community, is the crime that is most well-reported and recorded and most aggressively studied by criminologists. In criminology, the changing patterns of homicide are clearly of interest to criminologists as well as to policy officials.

An issue of continuing widespread interest and controversy among criminologists is the impressive drop in the US homicide rate between 1993 and 2000. In 1993, the US homicide rate was 9.5 per 100,000 population and it declined to a level of 5.5 in 2000, an impressive drop of 42 percent over those seven years. This drop followed a strong rise of 23 percent from a level of 8.0 in 1985 to 9.8 in 1991, so the drop was partly an undoing of the rise (FBI 2014).

In this chapter, I explore the ups and downs of the US homicide rate in that period, invoking not only the data on the homicide rate itself, but also invoking the age-crime curve as an indicator of changing patterns in the ages of those committing homicide.

We will also look at the similarities and contrasts between homicide and robbery, the two best defined and reliably reported "violent" crimes. We will see that homicide and robbery have followed rather similar paths over the past 40 years. But we will also see some deviations because robbery, a "violent" crime from the perspective of the victim, is certainly a property crime from the perspective of the perpetrator, and that important distinction could well account for important differences in the details of their trajectories, even if not in their basic trends.

The Handbook of Homicide, First Edition. Edited by Fiona Brookman, Edward R. Maguire, and Mike Maguire.

Trends Over the Past 40 Years

The past 40 years have seen considerable fluctuation in the rates of homicide as well as robbery. This pattern can be seen in Figure 3.1, which provides a graph of the rates reported by the FBI's Uniform Crime Reports (UCR) (FBI 2014) on US homicide and robbery (with robbery scaled-down by a factor of 25 to put it on a similar scale to that of homicide) between 1975 and 2013. The turning points or peaks and valleys of the graphs are of particular interest to generate insight into the factors contributing to those turns.

We will focus here on homicide, which is of primary interest, as well as robbery, a different crime that does display similar peaks and valleys at about the same time. They are well defined and reasonably well reported to local police departments, well recorded by those sources of UCR information, and they are well reported to the UCR.

They are the two more interesting of the four "violent" crimes classified in the FBI's UCR. The other two are "aggravated assault," which raises concern about subjective variation in separating "aggravated" from "simple" assault, and "forcible rape," which is subject to considerable variation in victims' willingness to report the rape as well as in the police departments' willingness to record it, perhaps because of prosecutors' reluctance to charge when there are often important evidentiary problems when there are no witnesses other than the victim and the accused.

The first interesting turning point in Figure 3.1 occurs at a peak in about 1980. That peak is readily attributable to the aging of the post-World War II "baby boomer" generation, which started in 1946, shortly after the end of the war, peaked in 1960, and demographers define the end of that generation in 1964. As that generation moved into its teenage years, it engaged in the crime initiation commonly associated with teenagers, which typically peaks at about ages 18 to 20. The largest cohort of

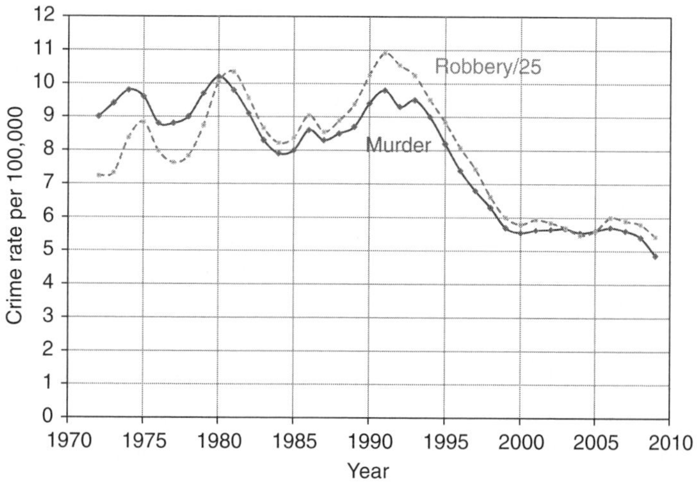

Figure 3.1 UCR murder and robbery rates, 1972–2013.

that generation was born in about 1960, and so, about 20 years later, in 1980, we expect to see the numbers in those high-crime ages start to decline. These demographic trends have been examined by Blumstein, Cohen, and Miller (1980), who anticipated the 1980 crime peak, but also suggested an incarceration peak about ten years later, reflecting the fact that it will take about a decade of recidivist offending, several rounds of probation, perhaps jail, and eventually those still criminally active having an impact on a prison population peak.

As the number of baby boom teenagers diminished after 1980, crime rates declined until the next turning point, the trough in 1985. The sharp rise after that trough has been largely attributable to the recruitment of young people into the crack market. Crack was an interesting technological innovation that made the "pleasures" of cocaine available at a much lower price than the powder version. Crack was introduced into the United States in the early 1980s at a time when drug enforcement was becoming most intense. It also happened that crack markets were typically open-air markets operated primarily by African Americans in their neighborhoods, and so the competition for those lucrative markets became intense and gave rise to considerable violence as the form of dispute resolution between competitors as well as between sellers and buyers when one or the other failed to deliver on the presumed deal. Those markets then became primary targets for drug enforcement, primarily because they were easily accessible (compared to the powder cocaine markets which were typically operated by whites and Hispanics behind closed doors) and because the violence they engendered was an issue of major public concern. This led to major growth in prison populations in the 1980s to the point where drug-related offenses (including possession as well as trafficking) became the modal prison offense, reaching 20 percent of state prison populations and 50 percent of federal prison populations.

One of the inherent problems in the incarceration of offenders who function through a market, as opposed to individually, is that the intended incapacitation effect is largely nullified through the recruitment of replacements to meet the market demand. This could be true of burglars who work through a fence and certainly true of drug sellers. This was the theme of Blumstein's ASC presidential address (1993) in late November of 1992, shortly after the newly elected US president, Bill Clinton, raised the hope that the leadership change might give rise to a rethinking of the then intense "drug war."

A key problem that contributed to the rise of homicide after 1985 was the nature of the recruits brought into the drug markets as replacements: they were predominantly young, about 15 to 25. Arrests of adults for drug offenses rose rather sharply in the early 1980s, but arrests of juveniles did not begin to rise until 1985, and then they too rose rather sharply.

Thus, young people became major participants in the crack markets beginning in about 1985. The sellers in those street markets were vulnerable to street robbers and had to carry guns to protect themselves. Unfortunately, the young people were far less restrained in their use of their guns than were their older predecessors and so there was a widespread rise in gun homicides by young people, an issue we will explore in more detail below. That rise began in 1985 and reached a peak in about 1993, the start of the major decline of about 42 percent in both murder and robbery until 2000.

Then there was a flat period followed by a much slower decline that began in about 2008 and continued fairly slowly until 2013. But it is the rise and the subsequent fall that is our primary interest here.

Figure 3.1 also displays the robbery trend, which follows the homicide pattern fairly closely. The 1980 peak, driven by demographics, is reasonably understandable because robbery could well be affected by the same age patterns affecting homicide. The rise after 1985 could well be attributable to the growing demand for drugs, especially crack, and the associated need for money to buy the drugs, and the availability of robbery providing "one-stop-shopping" for the money, in contrast to burglary, which could provide property that would then have be fenced to yield the money.

The Age-Crime Curve for Homicide

One important approach to examining these patterns in greater detail is captured by the age-crime curve, a graph of the ratio of the number of arrests for a particular kind of crime by age divided by the population of that age, or A(a)/N(a). This pattern could well vary across communities and over time.

The general shape of the pattern, illustrated in Figure 3.2 for homicide in 1985, is fairly typical, starting at an early teen age, rising fairly rapidly to a peak at about age 18–20, and then declining more slowly at older ages. This general pattern is typical at most times, but occasionally we find a particularly anomalous pattern that warrants considerable probing to discern what factors in the social environment contributed to those anomalies. The 1985 pattern, with a fairly flat peak from 18 to 21, was quite representative of prior years.

The rise in the homicide rate from 1985 to 1993 is dramatically reflected in the two age-crime curves displayed in Figure 3.3. The period from 1985 to 1993 saw a

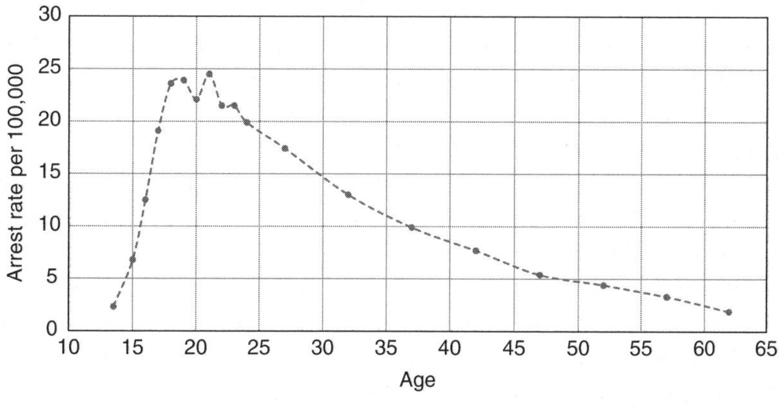

Figure 3.2 Age-crime curve for murder for 1985 and previous years.

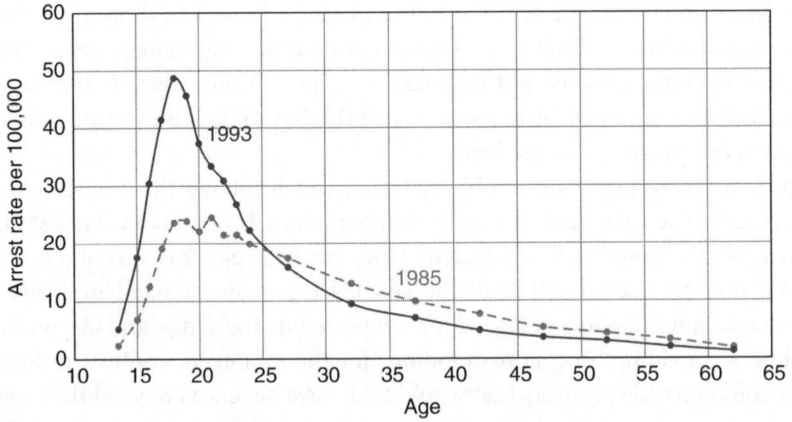

Figure 3.3 Age-crime curves for murder for 1985 and 1993.

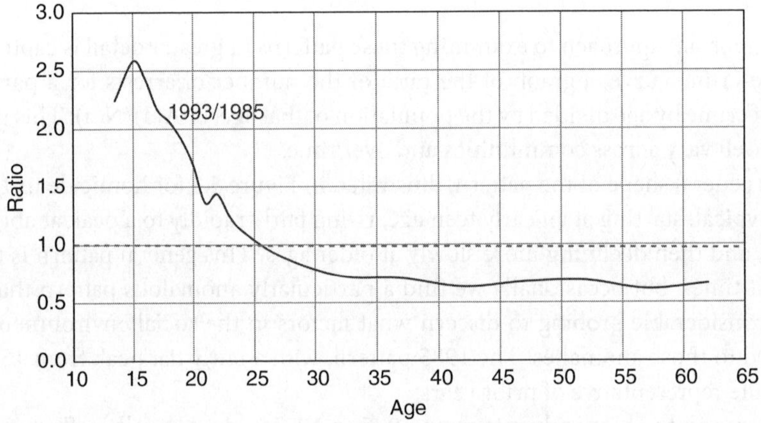

Figure 3.4 Murder age-crime curve for 1993 relative to 1985.

dramatic growth in the involvement of young people in homicide. The peak is still at age 18, but at more than twice the rate that prevailed in 1985.

One can get a better sense of the magnitude of the change by examining Figure 3.4, the ratio of the 1993 to 1985 age-specific murder arrest rate. That ratio peaks at a value of 2.5 for age 15 and then comes down for older ages, but for all ages below 20, the 1993 rate is still more than 1.5 times that of 1985.

It is interesting to note that for ages of 30 and above, the ratio falls to about three-quarters that of 1985, suggesting even more strongly that by 1993 murder had become almost exclusively a crime of the young, and that these older people were now less significant factors in homicide into the early 1990s, their role in that regard having been taken over by the younger people. It is reasonable to presume that the older people were removed from the marketplace through incarceration. This highlights the possibility that the massive growth of incarceration during the 1980s, however much it failed in incapacitating drug sales because of the recruitment of younger sellers as replacements, could well have contributed to incapacitation for murder of one population subgroup, but it also suggests that their replacements—the young people—could well have been a more aggressive and problematic contributor to that homicide (Blumstein 1995).

It is also interesting to note that if we enter a more recent 2000 age-crime curve for murder onto Figure 3.3 (as shown in Figure 3.5), most of its range comes well below that of 1985, but the value for the young people until age 24 is reasonably close. The largest drop occurs at age 25 and beyond. Indeed, if we add 2013 to Figure 3.3 (in Figure 3.5), we see that the murder arrest rate for the over-30 population is still lower than it was previously. Figure 3.6 shows that it has dropped below *half* that of 1985, a reflection that a large contributor to the 42 percent decrease in the homicide rate between 1993 and 2001 was the decreasing involvement in

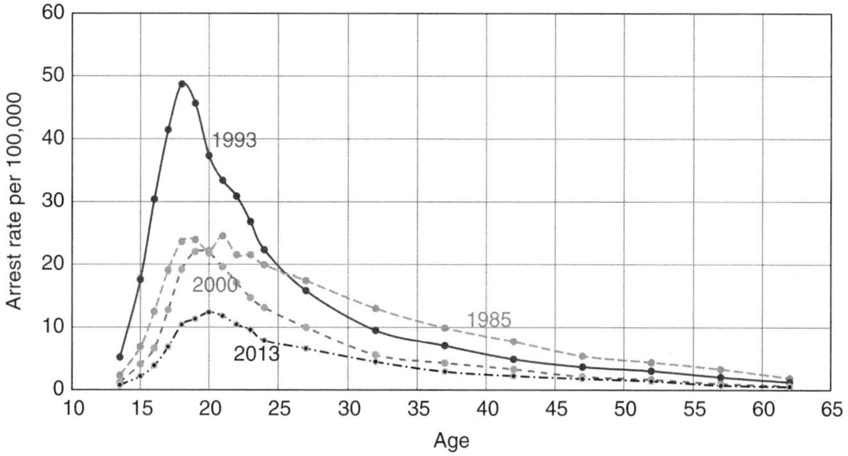

Figure 3.5 Age-crime curve for murder for 1985, 1993, 2000, 2013.

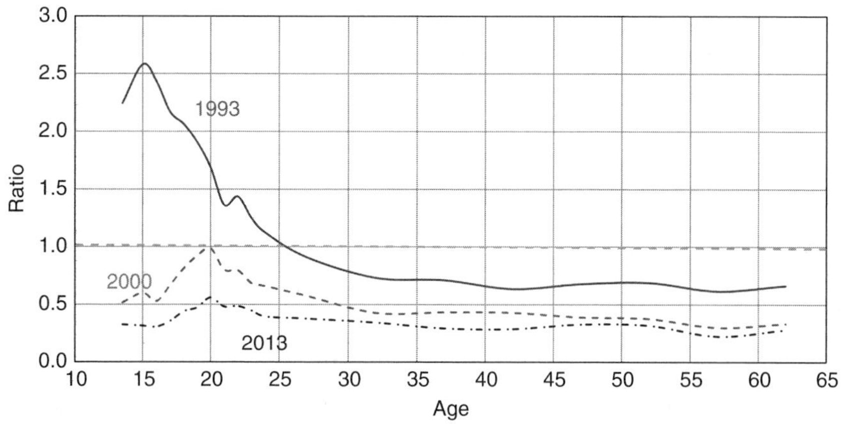

Figure 3.6 Age-crime curves for murder relative to 1985.

homicide by the older population, much more so than any reduction by the younger people under 25.

These insights deriving from these unusual changes in the shape of the age-crime curves for homicide highlight the importance of linking participant information with the raw data to reflect the changes, not only in the homicide rates but in the composition of who is doing the homicides.

It also highlights the degree to which the criminal justice system can be counterproductive in blindly pursuing the simplistic policy that all incarceration "works" because the individual offender is locked away. But it is clearly important to consider the systemic consequences of that incarceration, and especially so when dealing with offenses involving markets that can react to that incarceration by undoing the intended effect of the incarceration.

The Age-Crime Curve for Robbery

Since robbery was seen to track homicides so closely in Figure 3.1, it would be useful to examine the degree to which its age-crime curve tracks that of homicide or possibly follows a very different course.

Figure 3.7 provides the age-crime curves for robbery for 1985, the starting point of the rise in homicide–robbery violence rise; 1993, the peak of the violence rise; 2000, the end of the violence drop; and 2013, a recent year. At first glance, the curves do not look much different, with a rapid rise to a peak at about 17–18, but with a somewhat faster drop after the peak. The striking difference is that the sharp anomaly we saw in the rapid rise of youth homicide in 1993 does not show in robbery.

We can examine more of this subtlety by comparing the robbery age-crime curves in relation to the one that prevailed in 1985. As seen in Figure 3.8, the relative robbery age-crime curve for 1993/1985 is strikingly different from the comparable graph in Figure 3.4 for homicide. For the younger ages, 15 to 19, the robbery curve

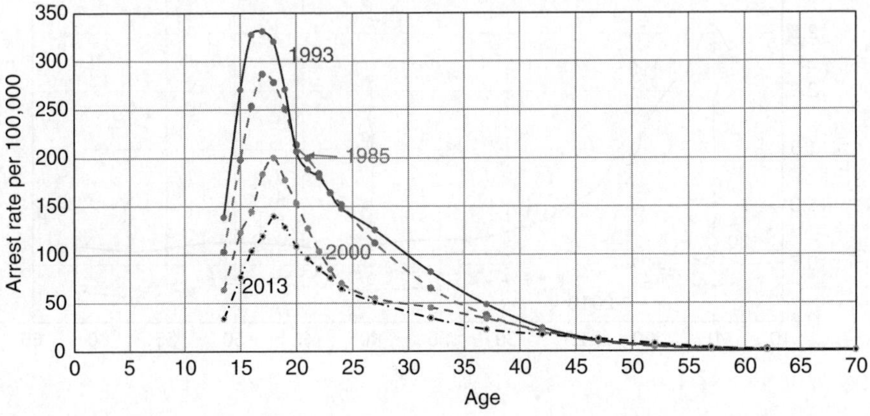

Figure 3.7 Age-crime curves for robbery for 1985, 1993, 2000, and 2013.

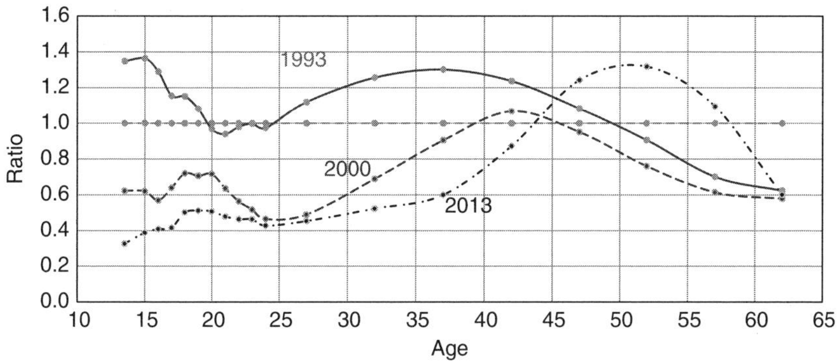

Figure 3.8 Age-crime curves for robbery relative to 1985.

starts at 40 percent above 1985 at age 15 and then declines rapidly to the 1985 rate by age 20. For ages 20 to 24, the rate is no different from that of 1985, perhaps a reflection of the fact that the young cohorts who contributed so dramatically to the rise in homicide were also involved as recruits into the drug markets, and that provided them with funding, thereby replacing any need they may have had for robbery. The more recent curves for the more tranquil years of 2000 and 2013 start at a level about half that of 1985 until about age 25. In 2000, the older people show a slow rise to little more than the 1985 level at age 42 and then decline. In 2013, when the nation's robbery rate is 25 percent below that of 2000, these older people have become even more obstreperous; their rate at age 50 is about 30 percent higher than that of their 1985 predecessors.

These trends raise the perplexing question of what changes were going on recently that reduced both homicide and robbery by the young people at the peak of the age-crime curve. At the same time, homicide by older people was probably reduced through incapacitation. The dilemma is what accounts for the more recent growth in robbery by older people as reflected in the growth of the numbers of newly admitted prisoners in their 50s and beyond.

Our previous discussion focused primarily on age, but it is well known that gender, race, and ethnicity are also important factors contributing to criminal involvement. Figure 3.9 invokes the interaction between age and ethnicity by examining the victims of homicide, at least in part because the UCR does not provide adequate details on the interaction between age and race and provides no information on Hispanic ethnicity (see also FBI: UCR, n.d.). We also know that the victims of homicide look very similar to the perpetrators. We partition between young (15–24) and old (25–44) for three groups (white, black, and Hispanic). It is clear from Figure 3.9 that the dramatic rise of homicide between 1985 and 1993 was attributable predominantly to young black males. Their rate more than doubled between 1985 and 1993, with the only other discernible growth being of young Hispanics, who may have filled their functional niche in predominantly Hispanic communities.

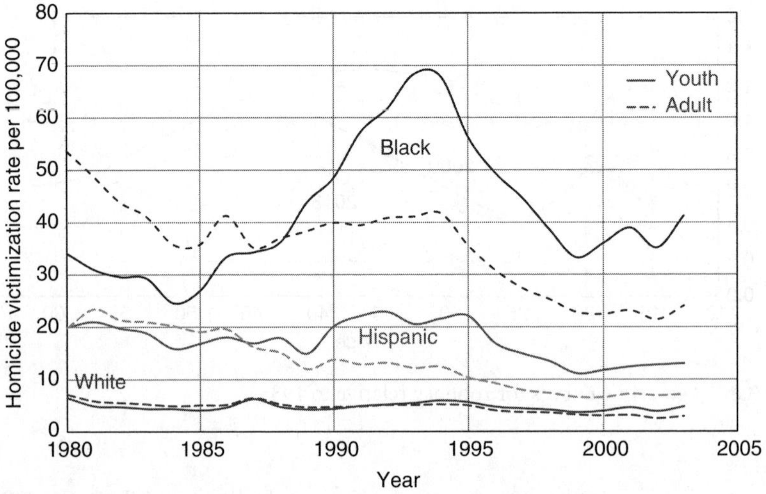

Figure 3.9 SHR homicide victimization rates youth (18–24) versus adult (25–44) by race and ethnicity.

This race/ethnicity perspective is an important further indication of the profound effect of crack markets as a major contributor to that 1985–1993 homicide increase, as the young blacks replaced their older predecessors who were shipped off to prison. The sharpness of the decline after the 1993 peak is a reflection of the intensity of police efforts at cracking down on guns as well as the declining demand for crack as its physiological consequences to older users became apparent (Curtis 1998).

Discussion

In this chapter, we have been particularly concerned with addressing the problem of homicide and its ups and downs in the United States over the past 40 years. To do so, we have introduced a diversity of perspectives, particularly the age-crime curve and the diversity of information it provides. We have also examined the relationship between homicide and its violent-crime partner, robbery, and have seen how well the two crimes rates track each other, and even how their respective age-crime curves look somewhat similar in their rapid rise to a peak at about age 18 and their slower decline. But we have certainly seen some important differences as we get into the fine structure of which age groups are doing what.

In the process, we have also seen the important influence of illicit drug markets, and particularly of the open-air crack markets, as major contributors to homicide as well as to robbery, but in very different ways. We have also seen ways in which the political responses to the horrors associated with those markets have resulted in actions ostensibly taken to address the problems the markets create, but end up creating their own problems that can be profoundly counterproductive. Further examination of those effects will hopefully help inform the shaping of future policies.

References

Blumstein, A. (1993) Making rationality relevant—the American Society of Criminology presidential address. *Criminology*, 31(1): 1–16.

Blumstein, A. (1995) Youth violence, guns, and the illicit-drug industry. *Journal of Criminal Law and Criminology*, 86(4): 10–36.

Blumstein, A., Cohen, J., and Miller, H. (1980) Demographically disaggregated projections of prison populations. *Journal of Criminal Justice*, 8(1): 1–25.

Curtis, R. (1998) The improbable transformation of inner-city neighborhoods: crime, violence, drugs, and youth in the 1990s. *Journal of Criminal Law and Criminology*, 88(4): 1233–1276.

FBI (Federal Bureau of investigation) (2014) Uniform crime reports 2013. Available online at http://www.ucrdatatool.gov/Search/Crime/State/RunCrimeStatebyState.cfm (accessed August 8, 2016).

FBI: UCR (n.d.) Supplementary homicide reports. Available online at https://www.fbi.gov/about-us/cjis/ucr (accessed August 8, 2016).

4

Social and Legal Responses to Homicide

Mark Cooney

Homicide (killing within a society) is one of the most immoral acts a person or group can commit. Robbery, rape, fraud, and theft all commonly evoke strong disproval in human societies, but homicide consistently elicits stronger condemnation. Even so, not all homicides attract the same level of censure. Some even evoke a measure of praise. The response to any given homicide, then, is a complex matter warranting closer scrutiny.

Since most homicides are defined and treated as deviant acts, the typical response to them is a penalty or sanction. Sanctions are of two main types—those imposed by society (popular sanctions) and those imposed by the state (legal sanctions).[1] Consider each.

Popular and Legal Sanctions

Popular sanctions

Information on popular sanctions is found primarily in the work of historians and, especially, anthropologists (see, e.g., Llewellyn and Hoebel 1940: ch. 6; Colson 1953; Boehm 1984). Varied though they are, popular sanctions can be arrayed on a single scale of severity/leniency. The most severe category of sanction is death, which may be of two main types: *vengeance* or *lynching*. Vengeance is typically exacted by the victim's intimates against the killer or his associates; lynching is perpetrated by the community of which the victim is part. (Since men commit the great majority of homicides in modern and premodern societies alike, I use the male pronoun to refer

The Handbook of Homicide, First Edition. Edited by Fiona Brookman, Edward R. Maguire, and Mike Maguire.

to the killer unless the facts of a case dictate otherwise.) Vengeance and lynching alike are more severe when they are accompanied by torture and mutilation or when more than one person is killed. *Compensation* is next in severity since in the premodern societies in which it is primarily levied compensation tends to place grave financial burdens on those who agree to pay it. After compensation comes *shunning*—individual or collective avoidance of the killer and, perhaps, his associates and *criticism* (including behind-the-back gossip). Next comes *toleration*—which may signify approval of the killing or may not (e.g., inability to penalize). The most lenient response is something not conventionally considered to be a sanction at all: *praise*—when the killer is defined and treated as a hero. People who kill group enemies, for instance, are sometimes lauded for their actions. Thus, in rural Laos, he who kills a village leader who has abused his position of power is "often admired, occasionally even revered" (Westermeyer 1973: 123).[2]

The waning of popular justice; the ascent of law

In stateless settings, all sanctions are by definition popular (though not everybody might agree with them). The gradual emergence of state structures some 5,000 years ago and their eventual diffusion across the globe thereafter resulted in a long-term decline in the role of popular justice and a concomitant rise in law. Early states often had to tolerate traditional forms of popular justice such as vengeance or negotiated compensation (e.g., Rousseaux 1999). Only gradually did they amass the capital, staff, weapons, jails, and other resources to establish effective control over violence within their territory. Their intervention was often resented and rejected at the local level where violence was seen as a private wrong to be remedied directly by the parties concerned and law an alien force imposed by outsiders. The long history of the struggle between law and popular justice for control over homicide was often highly contentious, even violent. The struggle played out differently in different places at different times. But the end result hardly varied—the state prevailed and homicide became a punishable crime. Typically it did so in a centrifugal manner—establishing its rule from the center to the periphery: first in urban centers, then in rural areas, and, finally, in more remote regions. In England, for example, the Crown had established a high measure of effective and exclusive control over homicide cases by the thirteenth century. Scotland and Wales, however, were slower to submit to royal authority (e.g., Davies 1969; Wormald 1980).

A relatively recent and well-documented example of the struggle between law and popular justice is the campaign against lynching in the United States, particularly in the South, from about 1900 onwards. People who killed or committed other deviant acts in southern states following the Civil War were liable to be captured by members of the local community and killed, sometimes in excruciatingly painful ways, before a large and approving crowd. Black people who offended white people were particularly vulnerable to this severe form of popular justice. In a good number of cases, the deviant was seized from the custody of the police; occasionally, the police colluded in the seizure. Over time, however, state officials began to treat lynching as itself deviant and take measures to prevent and punish it. As opponents became more vocal and influential, lynching became more furtive and smaller in scale. Like most social change, progress was not linear: two steps forward and one step back was a common pattern. But by the 1950s, lynching had largely died out. Even in isolated rural areas, the state had assumed effective jurisdiction over homicide (see, e.g., Brundage 1993: 161–259).

Popular sanctions remain the primary means of handling homicide in societies with weak legal systems, especially in more remote regions such as deserts, mountains, and jungles. In addition, popular justice continues to loom large today in the criminal underworld where the victim's associates may prefer to avenge the killing rather than have the state prosecute the killer. But what role do popular sanctions play among the generally law-abiding members of societies with developed legal systems?

Popular sanctions today

Relatively little systematic information exists on popular sanctions for homicide in modern state societies. Seeking to discover what, if anything, lies in law's shadow, I undertook a study of the popular response to killers and killing in the American state of Virginia. I interviewed 63 men and 12 women randomly selected from all those admitted to the Virginia prison system for homicide (murder and manslaughter) in 1988. All 75 participants (52% of whom were black) were currently incarcerated and interviewed at their assigned institution. Part of the interview focused on how people responded to the killer and his or her family as a result of the arrest and conviction for homicide. In addition, I conducted 42 telephone interviews with members of the participant's family (most often the mother) (Cooney 1994a).

The study has limitations: the sample is relatively small, confined to one state, only includes cases that resulted in a conviction, does not cover the post-release period, and provides no information on any responses of which the defendant or the family were unaware (e.g., the dissemination of gossip). Even so, it remains the only systematic investigation of the extra-legal sanctions triggered by modern homicide.

Popular penalties turned out to be relatively common but comparatively mild in the great majority of cases. The most frequent sanction was avoidance or shunning—the curtailment or elimination of interaction. Forty-five of the 75 participants reported some form of shunning that they attributed to the homicide (e.g., a man whose son was killed by his girlfriend did not respond to her phone calls or letters from jail and would not talk to her at the trial). Most of the participants (24) were shunned by one or two people but as many as nine were shunned by more than ten people.

The second most frequent sanction was aggression. Threats of violence were more common than actual violence (perhaps because none of the sample were members of organized gangs). In 22 cases out of 69 for which information could be obtained, the participant or a member of his or her family was threatened with violence. Usually, the threats were issued by the victim's kin. In one case, the victim's brother and some friends drove up to the participant's house. When his sister opened the door, the victim's brother took a gun from beneath his coat and told her to tell the participant that he was a wanted man. However, nothing further ensued. Some threats were issued by self-appointed representatives of the community. These were often anonymous (e.g., a phone caller saying, "I hope they fry you"). In the most severe case, the participant's family were threatened and had their house vandalized to the point that his mother felt compelled to leave the neighborhood altogether.

Important as popular responses are, however, it is clear that the most salient and impactful sanctions are legal in nature.

Legal sanctions

In modern legal systems, homicide can typically give rise to both civil and criminal cases. Civil cases are brought to obtain monetary compensation from the killer for wrongfully causing death. Criminal cases are brought to punish the killer for committing the crime of homicide. While civil cases require the deceased's next of kin to file and pursue a law suit, criminal cases are initiated by state agencies that specialize in prosecuting crimes. Consequently, criminal cases are vastly more common than civil cases.

Like their popular counterparts, criminal sanctions exhibit a continuum of severity. Each stage of the criminal justice system—*investigation*, *arrest*, *prosecution*, *conviction*, and *sentence*—represents an increase in severity. Thus, to be arrested is a more severe sanction than to be not arrested and to be convicted is more severe than to be acquitted. Custodial sentences are more severe than noncustodial sentences (e.g., fines, probation). And longer prison terms are clearly more severe than shorter terms. The most severe penalty of all is *death* (in jurisdictions that permit it), particularly when accompanied by torture prior to death and mutilation of the corpse after death.

Legal leniency is represented by *toleration*—no legal penalty. An even more lenient response is praise—the killer, far from being punished, receives an award from the state. Official praise is relatively rare for homicide (as distinct from other forms of killing such as those committed during warfare). Still, praise is not unknown as attested, for example, by the awarding of promotions, pay increases, and commendations to Brazilian police officers who kill multiple criminal suspects (see, e.g., Cavallaro 1997).

Jurisdictions exhibit considerable aggregate differences in the proportion of their homicides that result in conviction and punishment. More developed countries, those with lower homicide rates and those in which most homicides occur between intimates (rather than gangs or other criminal organizations), generally are more successful in apprehending, prosecuting, and punishing offenders. A recent United Nations report provides data from three regions of the world: Asia, the Americas, and Europe (insufficient information was available for Africa and Oceania). The homicide clearance rate (essentially a measure of arrest) is higher in Europe (85 percent) and Asia (80 percent) than in the Americas (about 50 percent).[3] The conviction rate shows even greater variation: the number of persons convicted per 100 victims is 81 in Europe, 48 in Asia and just 24 in the Americas (UNODC 2013: 91–95).

In short, legal and popular sanctions both exist on a continuum of severity. Any given homicide will come to occupy a place on each continuum. The critical question is: what explains this variation?

Explaining sanction severity

Traditional moral and legal theory attributes variation in severity of legal and popular sanctions to the thoughts and deeds of the actor (known in common law as the *mens rea* and *actus reus* of a crime). Thus, intentional deviance is more blameworthy than careless or negligent deviance which is more blameworthy than accidental deviance. Deviance freely chosen is more blameworthy than deviance committed under compulsion (provided the compulsion was not freely chosen, e.g., drunkenness). And aggressive deviance (to attack another) is more blameworthy than defensive deviance (to protect life or property).

These traditional variables are undoubtedly important in determining the severity of sanctioning that killers will receive. However, they do not provide a complete explanation. The empirical literature is rife with examples of people who killed intentionally, freely, and aggressively and yet were penalized minimally or not at all. Consider, for instance, a case from Houston, Texas, in which a woman tried to persuade her husband to leave a bar. When he refused, she left but returned minutes later with a pistol. She then shot her husband and shot at the bartender, narrowly missing him. Her husband died shortly afterwards. Despite the damning circumstances she was acquitted at the trial (Lundsgaarde 1977: 70–71). Conversely, those who kill accidentally may be held fully responsible as when killers among the nomadic Bedouin traditionally had to pay compensation for homicide or suffer vengeance, regardless of their intent (Ginat 1997).

Traditional legal and moral theory, then, is unable to explain fully variation in legal or popular sanctions. But so, too, is conventional sociological theory. The classical theories of Marx, Weber, and Durkheim each provide important insights into legal sanctions but they all do so at the macro or aggregate level: they explain variation over time or across place. Marx (and Engels) proposed that law reflects the interests of the dominant class but provided no testable propositions as to how law responds to particular cases within social classes (the modal type). Similarly, neither Weber's argument that law reflects long-term rationalization nor Durkheim's hypothesis that law reflects the division of labor provides any grounds for predicting why, for example, a judge or jury might sentence one murder defendant to the maximum allowed by the law while another receives but a nominal penalty.

Equally unhelpful is modern sociological theory. A slew of theories predict criminality—the disposition to commit some crime against some victim at some time (see, e.g., Akers and Sellers 2012). But there is only one general theory of social control at the case level—of the sanctions that wrongdoers attract for particular acts of wrongdoing. That is the body of ideas developed by Donald Black and elaborated by him and others since the publication of his seminal work, *The Behavior of Law* (1976). Blackian theory is formulated within a larger theoretical paradigm known as pure sociology (Black 1995, 2000; see also Campbell 2011).

Pure Sociology

Pure sociology begins from a simple yet far-reaching assumption: social life is a distinct realm of reality. As such, social life obeys laws of its own that are independent of the laws of the mind or the body; these general laws are not limited by time or place.

Pure sociology therefore eschews biological (e.g., genes) or psychological (e.g., motivations) variables. It neither asserts nor assumes that people's conduct is driven by a desire to maximize their genetic fitness or personal preferences, or is motivated by anger, fear, love, or any other emotion. Instead, pure sociology explains behavior with its social geometry—its location, direction, and distance in social space. Social space has multiple dimensions, including the vertical (the distribution of wealth), horizontal (the distribution of relationships), organizational (the distribution of groups), cultural (the distribution of symbols), and the normative (the distribution of morality). How each dimension predicts sanctions for homicide is elaborated in Cooney (2009). Here I combine the dimensions and draw upon just a portion of the evidence to illustrate how, holding constant the homicidal conduct, the location, direction, and distance of the case predict the severity of sanctions—legal or popular—it will attract.

Social location

Location refers to the relative elevation of the homicide in social space: whether it occurs among high, medium, or low status actors. Blackian theory predicts that the higher the elevation of the homicide, the more severity it will attract. Thus, homicides among the members of cultural majorities, the wealthy, socially integrated (e.g., employed, married), and the morally respectable are more likely to be investigated thoroughly, prosecuted more fully, and lead to more severe dispositions. This leads to what is for many people a counter-intuitive prediction: lower status defendants do not invariably receive greater severity. Lower status defendants are only treated more severely when they offend higher status victims.[4] If they offend lower status victims, they will generally be treated less severely than a high status defendant accused of offending a high status victim.

Consider, for example, the fate of black people—a racial minority that continues to possess less wealth and power than white people—in the US system of capital punishment. A large Georgia study, for instance, found that in cases involving black defendants convicted of murdering black victims prosecutors were less likely to seek the death sentence (15% vs 38%) and juries were less likely to impose the death sentence (40% vs 56%) than in cases involving white defendants convicted of murdering white victims (Baldus, Woodworth, and Pulaski 1990: 162). The pattern held up after controlling for the legal seriousness of the murder: for the same level of culpability, prosecutors were more likely to seek and juries to impose a sentence of death in white–white cases than black–black cases (1990: 163, fig. 23, 164, fig. 24).

Among homicides at high elevations of social space those that are higher attract the most severity. An experimental study presented mock jurors with a hypothetical case in which a man was accused of killing his wife under ambiguous circumstances (Rosoff 1989). One version identified the accused as "Dr Williams"; the other version identified him as "Mr Williams," a member of a less prestigious profession. Since most people marry within their own social class and spouses share, at least to some degree, their wealth and social standing, husbands and wives are typically of the same social status. Hence, the study was, in effect, comparing cases at different, though both relatively high, social elevations. Consistent with Blackian theory, Dr Williams was more likely to be convicted (39% vs 11%), and more likely to be convicted of first-degree murder. Going a step further, the researcher compared the response to the killing of a wife by a surgeon and by a dermatologist, medical specialties representing the "alpha and omega in the status hierarchy of medicine." Once again, mock jurors responded to the higher status defendant with greater severity, assigning higher culpability to the surgeon.

Popular sanctions manifest the same pattern. Murders between high status families traditionally elicit more severity than murders between low status families. At the top of social hierarchies, killings are likely to be avenged, sometimes more than one victim being sought. Lower down the status hierarchy, families tend to be more willing to forgo vengeance and accept compensation (Cooney 2009: 58). For example, in Lebanon, the son, his wife, and daughter of a leading politician were assassinated. The family believed that the killings were carried out by or on the orders of J., another leading politician. J. was himself later assassinated. The original victims' father expressed unhappiness that he had not killed J. himself and vowed not to rest until he had exacted revenge by killing other members of the J. family. No other solution seemed possible:

> Because of their high status the two families cannot allow themselves to settle their dispute through a *sulha* (peace agreement) and payment of *diyya* (compensation). If they take money, it will affect their long-term status—people will use it against them in other disputes and will be wary of entering alliances with them (Ginat 1997: 49–50).

Social direction

Homicide has a direction when it occurs between parties at different elevations in social space. An upward homicide is committed by a lower status actor against a higher status victim; a downward homicide is committed by a higher status actor against a lower status victim. Blackian theory proposes that upward offenses attract greater penalties than downward offenses. Thus, poor-on-wealthy killings tend to result in legally more serious convictions and more severe sentences than wealthy-on-poor killings (see, e.g., Farrell and Swigert 1978; Baldus, Woodworth, and Pulaski 1990: 157–160, 588–590).

The many studies of race and the American death penalty illustrate the same pattern (Dodge 1990). The most rigorous such study was conducted by David Baldus and colleagues in Georgia. They found that black offenders convicted of murdering white people were two and a half times more likely to be sentenced to death than white offenders convicted of murdering black people (35% vs 14%). This was not because black–white murders are, on average, more legally aggravated (e.g., committed more often in the course of a robbery) than white–black murders: even adjusting for the defendant's level of legal culpability, black people convicted of murdering white people had an elevated probability of being sentenced to death (Baldus, Woodworth, and Pulaski 1990: 150–151).

The impact of social direction is further evident in the differential response to civilian–police homicide and police–civilian homicide. As agents of the state—typically the most powerful and wealthiest corporate entity in a society—police officers enjoy organizational status not shared by citizens. Civilian–police homicides are therefore committed upwardly in social, specifically organizational, space, while police–civilian homicides occur in the opposite direction.

Civilian–police homicides are among the most serious of all crimes. If the killer is unknown, the police will go to great lengths to find the suspect, often cordoning off large areas, conducting extensive door-to-door inquiries, posting road blocks, and exerting pressure on informants. Should an arrest be made, bail is likely to be refused and charges laid will be serious. The case will be prosecuted vigorously and have a high probability of conviction. Sentencing will be severe. In jurisdictions that have capital punishment, the murder of a police officer is commonly an aggravating factor that the court can legitimately consider in deciding whether to impose the ultimate penalty. Not surprisingly, research reveals that killings of police officers have a considerably higher probability of receiving a death sentence than other killings (see, e.g., Baldus, Woodworth, and Pulaski 1990: 157, 657).

Police–civilian homicides, by contrast, attract much less severity. Police tend to get the benefit of the doubt from the initial assessment by the coroner and the investigation by fellow officers. As an observer of Baltimore detectives noted: "inside every major police department, the initial investigation of any officer-involved shooting begins as an attempt to make the incident look as clean and professional as possible" (Simon 1991: 377). Grand juries are slow to indict police officers (e.g., McKinley and Baker 2014). Prosecutors, judges, and juries are generally sympathetic to the officer as well, so that only the most damning cases result in a criminal conviction. Convictions for murder are especially rare (Bulwa 2009).

Popular sanctions are more severe too in upward homicides. In many premodern societies, the killing of a wealthy victim by a poor perpetrator is more likely to lead to vengeance by the victim's kin than the killing of a poor victim by a wealthy perpetrator (e.g., Oberg 1934: 146–147). Higher status victims also tend to generate greater popular revulsion than their lower status counterparts. For instance, in the American South after the Civil War, the killing of a police officer raised the odds of a lynching (Brundage 1993: 76–77). In addition, the lynching was often especially violent, accompanied by torture before death and/or mutilation following it (Senechal de la Roche 1997: 57). Lynching of police officers for killing citizens were unknown, however. Such homicides may not always have been welcomed, but they rarely elicited group violence against the officer.

Social distance

The distance of the homicide refers to how proximate or remote the parties are in social space. Distance is of two types: vertical and horizontal.

Vertical distance is the breadth of social space that a case spans in an upward or downward direction—the magnitude of the status differential between the parties. Upward homicide becomes more serious with vertical distance; downward homicides become less serious with vertical distance. Consider just one example: police–citizen killings. As mentioned, these cases rarely generate much severity. Still, police officers in Western, democratic countries do not a have a license to kill. Should they aggressively kill multiple citizens in the presence of multiple witnesses they run a grave risk of being punished. That is much less true of their counterparts in more centralized states. There, the power or status of the state vis-à-vis civilians is much greater: more organizational distance separates police and civilians. Consequently, police officers who kill civilians enjoy an extensive degree of legal immunity. In Brazil, for example, where the military police operate under a hierarchical model subject to little citizen oversight, police homicides often involve multiple victims, overkill, and apparent premeditation (as evidenced by, for example, the frequency of close-range, head bullet wounds in cases that are occasionally investigated). Yet prosecutions, let alone convictions, are rare (Delgado 2009).

Popular sanctions tend to be equally lenient for Brazilian police. Brazil has high rates of violent crime and officers who kill are often the object of popular admiration. For example, an officer who commanded a raid on a prison in 1992 in which 111 prisoners were killed, most after already surrendering to the police, later stood for political office. He chose the number 111 as his electoral ticket, and was elected (Amnesty International 1999, 2001).

Horizontal distance is the span of a case in relational or cultural space. Consider, for example, relational distance—the degree of involvement in the life of another. Relationally distant homicides are handled more severely than relationally close homicides. The US death penalty, for instance, is largely reserved for the killing of strangers, rarely being imposed in cases involving spouses or close relatives (e.g., Baldus, Woodworth, and Pulaski 1990: 319–320, 588–590). Intimate homicides consistently attracted less severity in nineteenth-century England, France, and Ireland, and continue to do so today (e.g., Cooney 2009: 163–165; Lundsgaarde 1977).

Among intimates, a Canadian study shows that killings occurring between those who are closer (e.g., in ongoing marriages) are handled more leniently than killings occurring between those who are somewhat less close (e.g., ex-partners) (Dawson 2003). The most intimate homicide is suicide, and it attracts least severity of all (death does not preclude sanctions being imposed on the killer's corpse or estate).

Popular sanctions are likewise less severe in intimate homicides. People often describe the killing of an intimate such as a parent or sibling as the worst thing a human can do. The Bedouin of North Africa, for example, consider a man who kills a member of his own family to be an animal, "for no human being would do this," and they refer to him with a term that means "one who defecates in the tent" (Peters 1967: 264). Yet the actual sanctions imposed in these cases are virtually always lenient. Intimate killers in stateless societies may be roundly criticized or avoided but they are rarely themselves killed in retaliation (e.g., Lindholm 1982: 66). By contrast, stranger killings are much more likely to be avenged and avenged more severely. For instance, among the Jivaro Indians of South America, vengeance within the tribe is limited to killing enemies; between tribes, the heads of slain victims can be severed, taken home, and shrunk as trophies (Karsten 1923).

Third Parties

The social geometry of a case extends beyond the principal parties to include all others who have knowledge of it. These "third parties" are of two main types: partisans and settlement agents. Partisans enter cases on one side (e.g., lawyers, witnesses); settlement agents enter cases neutrally, though they may exit them by siding with one principal (e.g., judges, jurors). Although the information is less abundant than for the principal parties, a variety of empirical evidence supports the claims of Blackian theory that both partisanship and settlement vary with their direction and distance in social space.

Partisanship

Partisanship confers a significant advantage in most conflicts. In stateless societies, the party with the most and most powerful supporters generally prevails. A killer from a large and important clan may face few consequences if his victim is from a smaller and less powerful clan. On the other hand, the penalties may be very serious when the killing occurs in the opposite direction. In Montenegro, for example, the smaller clan might have to abandon its land and flee in order to avoid being massacred (Boehm 1984: 107–108).

When both sides have partisans of approximately equal might, much hinges on the social distance between them. The more polarized the two sides, and the greater their internal solidarity, the more likely homicide is to be avenged and to lead to reciprocal feuding (Otterbein and Otterbein 1965; Peters 1967). Conversely, when the two sides have ties to one another those caught in the middle of the conflict tend to urge a peaceful resolution, such as a compensation payment (Colson 1953). Modern urban inter-gang homicides exhibit the same patterns: polarized ties across coupled with solidary ties within the opposing sides increase the risk of vengeance while ties that cross-cut the conflict enhance the probability of a nonviolent outcome (Cooney 1998: 73–79, 95–96).

Partisanship is important in legal conflicts as well. On paper, a homicide may present as an open and shut case of intentional killing. However, without lawyers to prosecute it and, more commonly, witnesses to support it, the case may founder. The facts do not speak for themselves (Innes 2003). Thus, when homicides are committed in low income and minority neighborhoods few or no witnesses may be prepared to testify, even when the incident occurred in broad daylight in front of many people. In a case from my Virginia study, for instance, a man was killed in a dispute over a bicycle in a crowded public park on a Saturday afternoon. Only one witness was prepared to come forward—the victim's girlfriend.

Partisanship in general increases with the third party's social closeness to one side and distance from the other (Black 1993: 127). Thus, family members and friends will generally show up in court and support their relative provided they are distant from the other party. Witnesses who are close to both sides, however, are often reluctant to provide evidence and, if they do, will tend to hedge their testimony. Stranger witnesses are more unreliable, often being slow to get involved ("it's not my concern"). But stranger witnesses are more credible than intimate witnesses ("of course, his brother would say he did not do it") (Cooney 1994b).

Blackian theory also predicts that partisanship flows upward in social space—from lower status toward higher status actors. Higher status litigants attract more and higher status lawyers and witnesses. Consider, for example, the "dream team" of renowned lawyers, investigators, and expert witnesses that the celebrity, O.J. Simpson, attracted to his case compared to the haphazard platoon of partisans the ordinary criminal defendant can muster (Toobin 1996).

Settlement

Settlement agents include mediators, arbitrators, and judges. Settlement virtually always has a downward direction in social space: parties rarely cede control of their conflict to lower status actors. Even so, settlement behavior differs across cases in at least three important ways (Black 1993: 145–149). Settlement varies in *decisiveness* or authoritativeness. Is the decision an all-or-nothing victory for one side or a compromise between both sides? It varies, too, in *severity*. Was the defendant convicted and, if so, sentenced stiffly? Finally, settlement varies in its degree of *formalism*. Was the outcome based on explicit rules of procedure and substance or on unstructured notions of fairness?

All three forms of variation increase with the social distance—vertical and horizontal—of the case. Judges, for example, as affluent, highly educated, state officials usually decide cases more authoritatively, severely, and formalistically than do the respected community members usually chosen to be tribal mediators. Typically, mediators are unfettered by precedent, uninterested in punishment, and much given to compromise (as a Montenegran mediator stated, "it would be an evil thing if one party to a legal case were to go home singing and the other lamenting"; Boehm 1984: 127). Judges, by contrast, will often decide for one side only, sentence a convicted defendant to punishment, and justify the decision by reference to written rules. Moreover, within modern societies, judges are generally both of higher status than jurors and more authoritative, strict, and formalistic. In their famous study, Kalven and Zeisel (1966) asked judges whether they would have reached the same decision as had the jury. They found that the judge disagreed with the jury in about 40 percent of homicide cases. In virtually all of those cases, the jury was more lenient than the judge would have been (e.g., acquitting rather than convicting). Juries were also less authoritative, more likely to render the compromise decision of manslaughter than the all-or-nothing decision of murder. And juries were less formalistic, particularly in self-defense cases where they often did not require the defendant to have been in imminent danger and to use only the amount of force necessary to repel the attack.

In sum, legal and popular sanctions for homicide conform closely to the predictions of pure sociology. The elevation, direction, and distance of the case in social space explain a wide range of facts about the handling of homicides in different societies at different times, whether governed by a state or not. When a case has the same legal and popular geometry, the same degree of legal and popular severity can be expected; when their case geometries diverge, legal sanctions will be more or less severe than popular sanction. Even so, the response to homicide does not depend only on the social geometry of the case. Something else matters. The missing element is precisely that part of the case that lawyers and moral philosophers are concerned with: the nature of the killing itself.

In *Moral Time* (2011), Black advanced an empirical explanation of the wrongfulness of wrongful conduct, including homicide. The explanation is embedded within a general theory of human conflict.

Social Time

The fundamental cause of conflict, Black (2011) proposes, is not divergent values, competition for scarce resources, or conflicting preferences, but the *movement of social time*. Just as physical time is a change in physical space (e.g., the movement of the sun) social time is a change in social space. "Time is the dynamic dimension of reality, and social time is the dynamic dimension of social reality" (Black 2011: 4). Movements of social time are of three main types: relational, vertical, and cultural. *Relational time* is any change in intimacy (involvement in the life of another). An increase in intimacy is overintimacy; a decrease is underintimacy. *Vertical time* is any change in inequality (e.g., wealth, power, reputation). An increase in inequality is overstratification; a decrease is understratification. *Cultural time* is any increase or decrease in (or rejection of) diversity (e.g., in ethnicity, ideas, art). An increase in diversity is overdiversity; a decrease is underdiversity. Larger and faster movements of social time cause more conflict—are more serious—than smaller and slower movements. And multidimensional movements are more serious than unidimensional ones. Since conflict is itself a movement of social time, social time explains moral time.

Homicide is a multidimensional movement of social time. All violence is a movement of relational time, an intrusion into the life of another through physical contact. As Black (2011: 23) notes:

> Violence is a form of intimacy, and all the more when it inflicts pain. Spanking a child is a form of intimacy and so is slapping a wife, beating a prisoner, or whipping a slave. So is torture, which might include additional increases in intimacy, such as stripping or raping the prisoner.

Homicide is a sizable movement of vertical time because it both destroys the foundation of all wealth—the human body—and subordinates the victim (and since self-defense is a response to subordination, it is a lesser movement of social time). When homicide is perpetrated across racial, religious, or linguistic boundaries, it is a movement of cultural time, too. In short, homicide is deviant—always and everywhere attracting sanctions—because it is a large movement of relational, vertical, and, sometimes, cultural time.

Not all homicides are equal movements of social time, however. The speed and size of the movement helps to explain many of the geometrical patterns noted previously. For instance, the killing of a stranger is a greater increase in physical intimacy than the killing of an intimate—and hence is more serious. The killing of a high status person is a greater drop in status for the victim and his or her dependents than the killing of a low status person—and is also more serious (see, e.g., Phillips 2009).

Crime and punishment are reciprocal movements of social time: the greater the former, the greater the latter. Imprisonment, for example, is both triggered by large movements of social time and is itself a large movement of social time, severing relationships and reducing social standing. Since imprisonment generally results in less loss of wealth and prestige for a low status offender than a high status offender the same prison term is a small movement of social time for that offender. Consequently, holding the victim's status constant, penalties tend to be more severe for the poor, the deviant, minorities, and the marginal.

Social time predicts, then, many of the same facts as social geometry. But social time additionally explains why homicide is wrong at all and why some homicidal acts are more serious—those that are aggressive, involve multiple victims or torture, or are committed in the course of another criminal movement of social time (e.g., robbery, rape). However, social time does not predict third-party behavior—who supports whom and how settlement agents settle cases. For that important component, social geometry is still required. Think, then, of the relationship between social time and social geometry as being represented by a Venn diagram with a considerable area of overlap yet with significant independent domains.

Conclusion

Legal and popular responses to homicide exhibit enormous variation, ranging from praising the murderer to killing him and others in excruciatingly painful ways. Traditional legal and moral variables based on the conduct of the parties cannot explain all the observed variation. Some people kill intentionally, aggressively, and freely yet are punished only lightly or not at all. Others kill accidentally, defensively, and under compulsion but are not spared. Yet the nature of the killing clearly matters.

Pure sociology unites social and legal variables into a single, logically coherent theory. The theory provides a general yet parsimonious explanation of the myriad facts discovered by anthropologists, historians, criminologists, sociologists, human rights workers, law professors, and others. More remains to be discovered and explained. But it is clear that penalties for homicide vary systematically with the location, direction, and movement of the killing in social space. Homicides that are larger movements of social time—including those committed upwardly and distantly—attract more severity. They attract especial severity when they are the subject of downward and distant settlement. In short, regardless of time or place, legal and popular responses to homicide depend on who kills whom and how, and who else participates in the case.

Notes

1 Two additional sources of sanctions not addressed here are the self (e.g., guilt) and the supernatural (e.g., sin).
2 Note that I use the "ethnographic present tense" to refer to behavior reported by anthropologists regardless of whether that behavior is currently found in the setting.
3 To "clear" a case generally means identifying and charging a suspect. In exceptional cases (e.g., death of the suspect) the case may be recorded as cleared without an arrest.
4 Or when there is no identifiable victim, as in most drug cases.

References

Akers, R.L. and Sellers, C. (2012) *Criminological Theories: Introduction, Evaluation, and Application*, 6th edn. New York: Oxford University Press.

Amnesty International (1999) Brazil—7th anniversary of Carandiru massacre: Contempt and neglect for 111 lives. Amnesty International Index: AMR 19/25/99.

Amnesty International (2001) A victory for Brazilian justice: Carandiru prison massacre police colonel convicted. Amnesty International Index: NWS 21/007/200.

Baldus, D.C., Woodworth, G., and Pulaski, C.A., Jr (1990) *Equal Justice and the Death Penalty: A Legal and Empirical Analysis*. Boston: Northeastern University Press.

Black, D. (1976) *The Behavior of Law*. New York: Academic Press.

Black, D. (1993) *The Social Structure of Right and Wrong*. San Diego, CA: Academic Press.

Black, D. (1995) The epistemology of pure sociology. *Law and Social Inquiry*, 20(3): 829–870. doi: 10.1111/j.1747-4469.1995.tb00693.x.

Black, D. (2000) Dreams of pure sociology. *Sociological Theory*, 18(3): 343–367. doi: 10.1111/0735-2751.00105.

Black, D. (2011) *Moral Time*. New York: Oxford University Press.

Boehm, C. (1984) *Blood Revenge: The Enactment and Management of Conflict in Montenegro and Other Tribal Societies*. Philadelphia: University of Pennsylvania Press.

Brundage, W.F. (1993) *Lynching in the New South: Georgia and Virginia, 1880–1930*. Urbana: University of Illinois Press.

Bulwa, D. (2009) Ex BART cop is accused of murder in rare group. *San Francisco Chronicle*, February 15: A-1. Available online at http://articles.sfgate.com/2009-02-15/news/17187934_1_police-officers-bart-police-dangerous-job (accessed August 8, 2015)

Campbell, B. (2011) Black's theory of law and social control. In R. Rosenfeld (ed.), *Oxford Bibliographies Online: Criminology*. Oxford: Oxford University Press. doi: 10.1093/obo/9780195396607-0067.

Cavallaro, J. (1997) *Police Brutality in Urban Brazil*. New York: Human Rights Watch.

Colson, E. (1953) Social control and vengeance in Plateau Tonga society. *Africa*, 23(3): 199–212. doi: 10.2307/1156280.

Cooney, M. (1994a) The informal social control of homicide. *Journal of Legal Pluralism*, 34: 31–59. doi: 10.1080/07329113.1994.10756454.

Cooney, M. (1994b) Evidence as partisanship. *Law and Society Review*, 28(4): 833–858. doi: 10.2307/3053999.

Cooney, M. (1998) *Warriors and Peacemakers: How Third Parties Shape Violence*. New York: NYU Press.

Cooney, M. (2009) *Is Killing Wrong? A Study in Pure Sociology*. Charlottesville: University of Virginia Press.

Davies, R.R. (1969) The survival of the bloodfeud in medieval Wales. *History*, 54: 338–357. doi: 10.1111/j.1468-229X.1969.tb02328.x.

Dawson, M. (2003) The cost of "lost" intimacy: The effect of relationship state on criminal justice decision making. *British Journal of Criminology*, 43(4): 689–709. doi: 10.1093/bjc/43.4.689.

Delgado, F.R. (2009) *Lethal Force: Police Violence and Public Security in Rio de Janeiro and São Paolo*. New York: Human Rights Watch.

Dodge, L. (1990) *Death Penalty Sentencing: Research Indicates Pattern of Racial Disparities*. Report T-GGD-90-37. Washington DC: US General Accounting Office.

Farrell, R. and Swigert, V. (1978) Legal dispositions of inter-group and intra-group homicides. *Sociological Quarterly*, 19(4): 565–576. doi: 10.1111/j.1533-8525.1978.tb01200.x.

Ginat, J. (1997) *Blood Revenge: Family Honor, Mediation, and Outcasting*. Brighton, UK: Sussex Academic Press.

Innes, M. (2003) *Investigating Murder: Detective Work and the Police Response to Criminal Homicide*. Oxford: Oxford University Press.

Kalven, H., Jr, and Zeisel, H. (1966) *The American Jury*. Boston: Little, Brown.

Karsten, R. (1923) *Blood Revenge, War, and Victory Feasts among the Jibaro Indians of Eastern Ecuador*. Washington DC: Government Printing Office.

Lindholm, C. (1982) *Generosity and Jealousy: The Swat Pukhtun of Northern Pakistan.* New York: Columbia University Press.

Llewellyn, K.N. and Adamson Hoebel, E. (1940) *The Cheyenne Way: Conflict and Case Law in Primitive Jurisprudence.* Norman: University of Oklahoma Press.

Lundsgaarde, H.P. (1977) *Murder in Space City: A Cultural Analysis of Houston Homicide Patterns.* New York: Oxford University Press.

McKinley, J.C. and Baker, A. (2014) Grand jury system, with exceptions, favors the police in fatalities. *New York Times,* December 7.

Oberg, K. (1934) Crime and punishment in Tlingit society. *American Anthropologist,* 36(2): 146–152. doi: 10.1525/aa.1934.36.2.02a00010.

Otterbein, K.F. and Otterbein, C.S. (1965) An eye for an eye, a tooth for a tooth: A cross-cultural study of feuding. *American Anthropologist,* 67(6): 1470–1482. doi: 10.1525/aa.1965.67.6.02a00070.

Peters, E.L. (1967) Some structural aspects of the feud among the camel-herding Bedouin of Cyrenaica. *Africa,* 37(3): 261–282. doi: 10.2307/1158150.

Phillips, S. (2009) Status disparities in the capital of capital punishment. *Law and Society Review,* 43(4): 807–838. doi: 10.1111/j.1540-5893.2009.00389.x.

Rosoff, S.M. (1989) Physicians as criminal defendants: Specialty, sanctions, and status liability. *Law and Human Behavior,* 13(2): 231–236. doi: 10.1007/BF01055925.

Rousseaux, X. (1999) From case to crime: homicide regulation in medieval and modern Europe. In D. Willoweit (ed.), *Die Entstehung des öffentlichen Strafrechts: Bestandsaufnahme Eines Europäischen Forschungsproblems.* Cologne: Böhlau Verlag.

Senechal de la Roche, R. (1997) The sociogenesis of lynching. In W.F. Brundage (ed.), *Under Sentence of Death: Lynching in the New South* (pp. 48–76). Chapel Hill: University of North Carolina Press.

Simon, D. (1991) *Homicide: A Year on the Killing Streets.* New York: Fawcett Columbine.

Toobin, J. (1996) *The Run of His Life: The People vs. O.J. Simpson.* New York: Random House.

UNODC (United Nations Office on Drugs and Crime) (2013) *Global Study on Homicide: Trends, Context, Data.* Vienna: United Nations Office on Drugs and Crime.

Westermeyer, J.A. (1973) Assassination and conflict resolution in Laos. *American Anthropologist,* 75(1): 123–131. doi: 10.1525/aa.1973.75.1.02a00070.

Wormald, J. (1980) Bloodfeud, kindred and government in early modern Scotland. *Past and Present,* 87(May): 54–97.

Part II

Understanding Different Forms of Homicide

5

Gang Homicide in the United States
What We Know and Future Research Directions

Jesenia M. Pizarro

Gangs and the violence that accompanies them affect various countries throughout the world. Research suggests that gangs are present in over thirty countries spanning almost every continent (Gatti, Haymoz, and Schadee 2011) and that they contribute to the homicide and violence rate worldwide (Decker and Pyrooz 2010). Recently, criminologists have increased their efforts to understand the prevalence of, and violence associated with, gangs outside the United States. For example, the research of European and Latin American gangs has expanded over the past decade (Decker and Pyrooz 2010). Despite these efforts, the knowledge base on gangs outside the United States is relatively scant. The study of gangs and their accompanying violence has mostly been an American phenomenon.

This chapter examines the current state of knowledge regarding the etiology and prevalence of gang homicides in the United States. Homicides in the United States began steadily declining in the 1990s. The homicide rate reached an all-time low of 4.6 per 100,000 citizens in 2013—a decline from 9.8 in 1991. Although overall homicide rates nationwide have been trending downwards, gang homicide rates appear to be on the rise. The National Gang Intelligence Center (NGIC) estimates that nearly half of all violent crime in the nation's large cities are gang related (NGIC 2011). An examination of homicides by Pyrooz (2012) found that the gang homicide rate is approximately 12 per 100,000 citizens in the top 88 most populated cities in the United States. Hence, it is clear that gang members significantly contribute to the homicide problem.

The Handbook of Homicide, First Edition. Edited by Fiona Brookman,
Edward R. Maguire, and Mike Maguire.

Defining Gangs and their Etiology

Before discussing gang homicides, it is important to first define gangs, their prevalence, and etiology. Thrasher (1927) introduced the first comprehensive definition of a gang in his book *The Gang: A Study of 1313 Gangs in Chicago*. He defined a gang as:

> an interstitial group originally formed spontaneously and then integrated through conflict … characterized by the following types of behavior: meeting face to face, milling, movement through space as a unit, conflict, and planning. (Trasher 1927: 46)

Since Thrasher's study, scholars have debated how to define "gang," and various frameworks have emerged (see Klein 1971; and Miller 1980), with some arguing that gangs cannot be defined (see Horowitz 1990). The Department of Homeland Security's Immigration and Customs Enforcement has set forth the most commonly used definition of gang in recent research. They define a gang as

> An association of three or more individuals; whose members collectively identify themselves by adopting a group identity, which they use to create an atmosphere of fear or intimidations, frequently by employing one or more of the following: a common name, slogan, identifying sign, symbol, tattoo, or other physical marking, style or color of clothing, hairstyle, hand sign or graffiti; whose purpose is part to engage in criminal activity and which uses violence or intimidation to further its criminal objectives, whose members engage in criminal activity or acts of juvenile delinquency … with the intent to enhance or preserve the association's power, reputation, or economic resources. (National Institute of Justice 2011)

The latest census of gangs in the United States, which was published in 2011, suggests that there are approximately 1.4 million gang members in the country; an increase from an estimate of 800,000 in 2005 (NGIC 2009, 2011).[1] According to the NGIC (2011), these gang members are active in over 33,000 gangs throughout the United States. Hispanics make up the largest portion of gang members, followed by African American, white, and other ethnicities. The vast majority of gang members are males, although female membership has become more prominent. Gang members tend to be adolescents and teens; however, recent figures suggest that gangs have a growing percentage of adult members over the age of eighteen (Adams and Pizarro 2014).

Gang membership, crime, and violence

A common theme among gang definitions centers on their involvement in criminal and delinquent behaviors. To date, the bulk of studies suggest that gang members are disproportionally involved in criminal activities (NGIC 2011), with some studies suggesting that over half of delinquent acts can be attributed to gang membership (Thornberry and Burch 1997). Decker (1996) found that one of the defining features of gang members is their involvement in and willingness to use violence. Gang members are also more likely to carry firearms and be involved in firearm-related crime (Decker and Van Winkle 1996) and experience higher incidents of serious and fatal firearm injuries (Loeber *et al.* 1999).

Although gang members engage in higher levels of violent behavior, they do not appear to specialize in violence (Armstrong and Britt 2004; Esbensen and Huizinga 1993; Maxson and Klein 2006). Armstrong and Britt (2004) found that gang association had mixed minimal effects on most offense types with the strongest effect being drug offenses. Adams and Pizarro (2014) confirmed these findings by showing that gang members who offended in a homicide were most often arrested for drug crimes before a homicide incident, and that involvement in drug trafficking poses the highest risk for offending in a homicide act. Their findings also suggest that gang members were likely to escalate into other violent crimes after a history of drug offense arrests. A possible explanation of this could be related to the changing nature of gangs, as Decker, Katz, and Webb (2008) found that increases in gang organization are related to increases in gang member involvement in drug sales. Given the prevalence of involvement of gang members in drug trafficking it is no surprise that there is a relationship between gang membership and homicide.

Theories of gang formation

Scholars have proposed various explanations as to why and how gangs form. Among the first explanations, Thrasher (1927) proposed that gangs are a product of their social environment due to their emergence and growth in geographic areas characterized by lack of social cohesion and organization. A decade later, Shaw and McKay (1942) developed this idea into social disorganization theory. Social disorganization theory posits that factors such as economic deprivation, ethnic composition, and residential mobility affect the levels of cohesion and informal control within neighborhoods; thus, starting a spiral of deterioration that can result in youth adopting deviant subcultures such as gangs.

Cohen (1955) elaborated on this theory by positing that youth who reside in socially disorganized areas are socialized differently so they cannot measure up to middle class standards. As a result, these youth become frustrated and may respond by either striving to achieve the success, accepting the working class ideals and settle for menial jobs, or with reaction formation where they reject the middle class values and develop their own. These values may be deviant in nature and may result in the emergence of gangs in distressed communities.

Cloward and Ohlin (1960) integrated the social disorganization framework with the aforementioned structural theory proposed by Cohen to explain factors that influence the emergence of distinct types of gangs. They posited that level of organization in a neighborhood would influence the type of delinquent subculture (i.e., gang) that emerges. Specifically, delinquent gangs, which make a living from involvement in criminal markets, emerge in neighborhoods where there is an integration of legitimate and illegitimate businesses and opportunities. Members of these gangs are able to obtain status and success with the money and funds they earn though illicit means. On the other hand, areas characterized with pervasive social disorganization and, thus, the lack of legitimate and illegitimate opportunity structures, breed violent and conflict gang subcultures. The only means by which youth in these gangs can attain status is through toughness and willingness to use violence. As a result, geographic areas characterized by conflict gangs are expected to exhibit higher rates of violent crime. Finally, a retreatist subculture in which members are characterized by drug consumption emerges among youth who do not succeed in the delinquent or conflict groups.

The common thread among early explanations of gang formation centers on how social structure pushes individuals to adopt gangs. Recent explanations have also focused on social structural conditions. Vigil's (2002) research on Latino gangs posits that the strains related to living in economically disadvantaged communities with weakened institutions of social control and poor police–community relations breed gang membership and proliferation. His research suggests that immigrant youth often feel socially, culturally, and economically marginalized. These conditions lead youth to band together based on their ethnicity and nationality (Vigil 2002), resulting in the emergence and proliferation of Latino gangs. Similar perspectives have emerged to explain African America gang violence in inner cities (Matsuda *et al.* 2013).

Overall, current explanations on gang formation are mostly rooted in the works of Anderson (1999) and Wilson (1996) who suggest that violence and other social problems in inner cities, such as the prevalence of gangs, are a direct result of the disappearance of work. Specifically, they posit that the outmigration of industries increased economic deprivation in these areas. As a result, social institutions, such as schools and other organizations, that provide pro-social activities and informal social controls to youth were not present or could not provide proper services. This was coupled by lack of supervision of youth by parents due to having to work longer hours or resorting to illegal markets owing to the family's economic condition. The loss of work industries resulted not only in increased economic deprivation, but also in the loss of "better-off" residents who served as role models and had the social capital to mobilize their peers for the betterment of the community. As a result, these communities experienced an increase in deviant subcultures and, thus, crime.

The crime increase in turn led to more formal social control on the part of law enforcement resulting in a spiral of decay in many communities. Indeed, research suggests that this increase had detrimental consequences for communities due to the actual or perceived negative experiences by citizens in their interactions with law enforcement officers (Terrill and Reisig 2003; Weitzer 1999) and the consequent increase in incarceration (Rose and Clear 1998). To be clear, policing research suggests that officers typically behave differently across neighborhoods, and that officers employ more force and unprofessional behaviors in areas that are considered "bad" (Terrill and Reisig 2003; Weitzer 1999). This problem was exacerbated by perceived, or real, under-policing with officers failing to respond quickly to calls for police assistance, investigate crimes, and provide assistance to crime victims. Additionally, increased incarceration of residents further weakened informal social control by disrupting families, friendships, and other informal networks (Rose and Clear 1998).

According to Sampson and Jeglum-Bartusch (1998), in the United States the sum of these structural problems left inner-city residents feeling vulnerable and unprotected, resulting in the emergence of delinquent/criminal subcultures and the proliferation of illegal behaviors. These subcultures increase the risk of joining gangs as they serve to not only provide an identity to residents in the area, but also offer protection. According to Decker and Van Winkle (1996), fear of crime and violent victimization is an important covariate of gang formation and continuation. Fear of victimization and violence also serves as a tool for expansion and recruitment, and increases cohesiveness among the group (Decker and Van Winkle 1996).

Interestingly, emerging international studies on gangs suggest similar structural dynamics have sparked the emergence and proliferation of gangs in other countries. A recent survey conducted in 30 countries with youth by Gatti and colleagues (2011) suggests that the children of immigrants and youth living in poverty and in single-parent households are more likely to join gangs than those not experiencing such structural conditions. Rodgers and Baird (2015) found that similar to the United States, gangs in Latin American provide security (real and/or perceived) to youth who reside in poor communities and lack trust for state institutions. Overall, the emerging literature of gangs outside the United States suggests that the proliferation of gangs worldwide is rooted in the increase of urban slums, a decrease in social controls, income inequality, and the marginalization of some groups (Hagedorn 2005).

Gang Homicides

Gang members are up to one hundred times more likely than non-gang members to be involved in homicides as victims or offenders (Decker and Pyrooz 2011). Gang homicides have traditionally been defined one of two ways (Maxson and Klein 1990). The first definition is person-based and classifies an incident as a gang homicide if either the victim and/or offender were gang members at the time of the incident. In these incidents a gang member can commit a homicide for a host of reasons that are not related to their group status or membership. The second definition is more restrictive and only classifies an incident as a gang homicide if it was a result of furthering the economic, social, or territorial interests of a gang, including internal conflict within a gang. Homicides that fall under the purview of the first definition are referred to as gang related, while those that are consistent with the second definition are often referred to as gang motivated. The bulk of gang homicides are gang related.

The varying definitions of gang homicides pose two limitations to this line of research. First, it impedes the ability to compare the rate and proportion of gang homicides across cities, since some studies focus on gang-related homicides while others on gang-motivated incidents. Second, there is a possibility that scholars are not accurately capturing the processes and dynamics that result in gang violence. Given the lower number of gang-motivated cases, researchers most often employ the gang-related definition when examining these homicides. The reliance on a gang-related definition limits the examination of the actual processes that spark gang violence, since gang-related homicides could occur for a host of reasons and not necessarily due to gang dynamics.

Maxson and Klein (1990) revisited data on gang homicides in Los Angeles in an effort to examine the definitional limitation. Their analyses found that employing the gang-motivated operationalization reduced the rate of gang homicides by approximately one half. However, they found minimal differences between gang-motivated and gang-related homicides. As a result, Maxson and Klein (1990) concluded: "the choice of motive or member definition would make little difference empirically, conceptually, or in policy relevance" (p. 83). Almost a decade later, Rosenfeld, Bray, and Egley (1999), disagreed due to their finding that gang-related and gang-motivated homicides in St Louis significantly differed. Given these diverging findings, gang researchers should be cautious in the interpretation of findings and ensure that the definition employed in their studies is clear to the consumers of their research.

Individual and situational characteristics

Research suggests that gang homicides (both gang-related and gang-motivated) have individual and situational characteristics that distinguish them from non-gang incidents. For example, the average gang homicide victim and offender is a young, minority male who resides in an inner city. Research has demonstrated that the victims and offenders of gang homicides are on average younger than those of non-gang incidents (Decker and Curry 2002; Pizarro and McGloin 2006), which is expected given that gang members often range from adolescents to young adults. Additionally, these incidents often involve males and occur in inner cities (NGIC 2011). Gang members who are offenders in a homicide are also more likely to have a history of drug-related crimes, which often escalates into violence (Adams and Pizarro 2014).

Gang members are often killed by members of their own gang (Decker and Curry 2002). These incidents are also more likely to be carried out with a firearm, occur in public settings, and involve co-offending (Decker and Curry 2002; Pizarro and McGloin 2006; Rosenfeld, Bray, and Egley 1999). Finally, they tend to be intra-racial and intra-gender (Klein and Maxson 1989) involving individuals who knew each other at the time of the homicide.

The majority of gang homicides are spontaneous retaliatory expressive events. They are often the result of retaliation that was initiated by a perceived threat against an individual or his gang (Decker 1996; Pizarro and McGloin 2006) and are not necessarily intended to further the gang's interests. Papachristos's (2009) study in

Chicago suggests that these events are the culmination of altercations that result from dominance disputes and symbolic threats to manhood. Recent research also supports previous works in showing that these homicides are the result of escalating disputes and are not specifically a result of gang activities (DeLisi *et al.* 2014).

Decker's (1996) study explains these findings. He posited that gang violence, including homicide, is an expressive result of the gang's collective behavior response to a real or perceived threat. He defined threat as "the potential for transgressions against or physical harm to the gang, represented by the acts or presence of a rival group" (Decker 1996: 244). Based on recent research (e.g., Papachristos 2009; Zeoli *et al.* 2014) this definition can be expanded to include not only rival groups that are members of other gangs, but also rival individuals from within their gang and non-gang members. The retaliatory nature of these incidents also results in the "contagion" of violence in which subsequent acts of violence occur because of previous incidents. Zeoli and colleagues (2014) offer support to the hypothesis that gang homicides may result in contagion. Specifically, they found evidence of expansion diffusion where homicides spread from their point of origin to other areas in the city while remaining at its origin. Their findings suggest that social structural variables, such as economic disadvantage and racial isolation, foster and contribute to the spread of homicides. Interestingly, a follow up study examining the diffusion patterns based on homicide motive type show that the only homicide types that diffused in both space and time were gang-motivated incidents, suggesting that the group dynamics of these incident types influence the spread of homicide in cities (Zeoli *et al.* 2015).

Structural characteristics

Research on the spatial concentration of gang homicides confirms what scholars have found regarding the proliferation and concentration of gangs in specific areas. Confirming the work of Cloward and Ohlin (1960), which theorized that the most violent gangs would emerge in areas with higher rates of social disorganization, the bulk of studies to date suggest that gang homicides concentrate in areas characterized by social disorganization and economic disadvantage. In one of the first studies to examine the structural covariates of gang homicides, Curry and Spergel (1988) found that gang homicides in Chicago concentrate in areas with a high percentage of Hispanic residents and poverty. Similarly, Rosenfeld and colleagues (1999) found that neighborhood disadvantage was a significant predictor of both gang-motivated and gang-affiliated homicides in St Louis. It is important to note, however, that these structural factors are not only related to gang homicides, but that they are important in the explanation of the overall occurrence of homicide (Pyrooz 2012).

In an effort to uncover the structural covariates of gang homicides, Pyrooz (2012) examined whether there are differences between gang and non-gang incidents in terms of their relationship with common economic and disorganization measures. He found that while economic deprivation and social disorganization measures were significant in predicting both gang and non-gang incidents, their effects differed. Specifically, socioeconomic deprivation had a stronger effect on non-gang incidents, leading Pyrooz to hypothesize that this effect may be due to unmeasured important factors related to group process. This finding is in line with previous work by Decker (1996) and Pizarro and McGloin (2006), which suggest cultural and group processes are more robust in the explanation of gang homicides. Pyrooz (2012) also found that population density had a stronger effect on gang homicides when compared to non-gang incidents. He hypothesized that this finding may be a function of the territoriality of gangs and the fact that they may have more competition for space in densely populated areas. The most important finding of his work, however, may be the indirect relationship of social structure on gang homicides. To be clear, social structure is related to gang formation; hence, the more structural problems (i.e., poverty, single-parent households, unemployment, etc.), the more individuals join gangs. Consequently, as the number of gang members increases so does the number of gang homicides.

Theories of gang homicides

Scholars have employed one of three theoretical models in the explanation of delinquent/criminal involvement among gang members—*selection model, facilitation model, and enhancement model* (Thornberry *et al.* 1993). The *selection model* is related to theories of continuity, such as the general theory of crime (Gottfredson and Hirschi 1990), which posits that criminal propensity is stable across the life course. That is, some individuals develop a criminal propensity during their childhood and this propensity does not change with adulthood or life circumstances. An individual is consequently prone to offend given the opportunity regardless of group involvement and other life events (Gottfredson and Hirschi 1990). As a result, this model posits that the relationship between gang membership and criminal offending is spurious and that criminal offending among this group is a result of other underlying factors that occurred during childhood.

The *facilitation model* is rooted in social learning theory (Akers 1998). This model posits that gang members are not inherently violent, but that violence is learned via socializing processes that occur within the gang. The differential associations with other gang members and reinforcements that reward violence employed by the group serve as a form of learning conducive toward the acceptance of crime and violence. Therefore, gang members engage in more crime and violence because they learn from other group members (Thornberry *et al.* 1993).

The *enhancement model*, on the other hand, combines key elements of the selection and facilitation models. According to this model, gang members are likely more delinquent than non-gang youth even before gang involvement due to an inherent criminal propensity; however, the gang context further exacerbates violent traits via learning (Thornberry *et al.* 1993). Thus, this model suggests individuals join gangs due to underlying individual risk factors, however, once in the gang, individuals learn behaviors that are likely to enmesh them in criminal and delinquent activities. To date, studies suggest this model is the most robust of the three (Gatti *et al.* 2005).

The aforementioned models can be employed in the explanation of gang homicides. Using the *selection model,* one could posit that individuals who ultimately engage in a gang homicide are inherently more violent. The *facilitation model* can also explain gang violence due to evidence that gang homicides are a product of learned behaviors and codes, which push gang members to react with violence that can turn lethal (Matsuda *et al.* 2013). Finally, the *enhancement model* can also serve to explain these homicides as it is plausible to hypothesize that violence-prone individuals are more likely to join gangs where they then learn codes and behaviors that exacerbate preexisting tendencies which culminate in a homicide.

What is missing from these explanations is the integration of social structural factors. Research suggests that explanations of gang homicides must rely on both structural and social processes (McGloin and Decker 2010). As discussed above, there is a strong and consistent relationship between the prevalence of gangs and gang violence with the social structural characteristics of places. Furthermore, there is evidence indicating the existence of group processes that push individuals toward violence. A comprehensive explanation of gang homicides should then combine these two frameworks.

An integrated framework

As illustrated in Figure 5.1, an integrated framework explaining the occurrence of gang homicides begins with the assumption that structural conditions breed individual level propensities and cultural processes that encourage gang formation

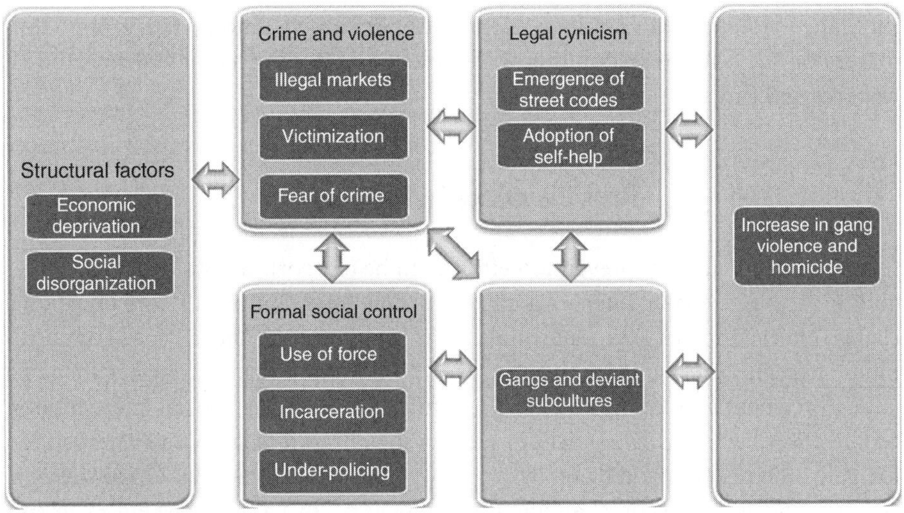

Figure 5.1 Integrated model of gang homicide and violence.

and consequent acts of lethal violence. As indicated by Thrasher (1927), Shaw and McKay (1942), Cohen (1955), and others, the breakdown of social control results in the emergence of deviant groups in geographic areas. Specifically, the lack of informal social control from parents results in the maladjustment of children, leading them to develop low self-control and violent tendencies (Pratt, Turner, and Piquero 2004) while at the same time facilitating the emergence of illegal markets. This in turn results in an increase in crime and risk of victimization. Related to this, the availability of illegal markets serves to exacerbate the already existing criminal propensities among individuals by offering opportunities to offend.

Given the increase in crime and risk of victimization, levels of formal social control on the part of law enforcement also increase and become distinct in these areas resulting in legal cynicism among residents. Over time, the cumulative effect of these conditions results in the adoption of attitudes and behaviors consistent with Black's (1983) notion of self-help to ensure survival in these areas. These tactics for survival include aggressive behavior and joining a gang for self-protection among some of the area's residents (Anderson 1999; Matsuda *et al.* 2013; Vigil 2002; Wilson 1996). Once adopted, the street code intensifies already existing behaviors and tendencies that increase the risk of homicide victimization and offending among gang members. For example, in an effort to save face, gang members may be more willing and ready to respond with violence. The threat of victimization may cause gang members to carry a firearm for self-protection, and they may be more willing to use it in occasions where they perceive it necessary.

In summary, poverty and social disorganization may cause the development of criminal propensities and the emergence of illegal markets and crime. Increased crime rates result in changes in levels of social control that result in detrimental consequences such as the loss of trust in the police and family disruption. This in turn gives rise to the adoption of alternate norms and values that solidify and further support the formation and proliferation of gangs. Once individuals join the gang, violent and criminal norms are reinforced among the group, thus increasing the odds of responding with violence, including lethal violence, to real or perceived threats.

Best Practices in Prevention

Gang and gang violence prevention efforts can be categorized into one of five categories: (1) suppression interventions, (2) social intervention, (3) organizational change interventions, (4) fundamental causes interventions, and (5) social opportunities strategies (Fearn, Decker, and Curry 2006). Suppression strategies focus on law enforcement identifying and incapacitating gang members. Social interventions, on the other hand, involve practices such as social services and crisis intervention for gang members carried out by non-law enforcement groups. Organizational change strategies focus on changing the practices of formal (i.e., law enforcement) and informal social (i.e., families, neighbors) control agencies in an effort to address the root causes that give rise to the formation of gangs and their involvement in crime. These types of programs require law enforcement to change their day-to-day work habits and to join forces with social agencies that can provide services to youths. Organizational change strategies also require changes in legislation and policy. Similarly, fundamental cause interventions focus on community mobilization and the residents changing the manner in which they do business. These strategies differ from organizational change efforts in that community members are the ones spearheading the efforts. Finally, social opportunities strategies require providing gang and would-be members with social opportunities, such as education and job prospects, that would allow them to gain status in legitimate ways and bond them with pro-social agents.

Studies suggest that the most promising gang violence prevention approaches involve a combination of all the aforementioned tactics (Fearn, Decker, and Curry 2006), which should be no surprise given the multilevel processes that result in gang violence. The Ceasefire Boston intervention is the best example of how these strategies, when combined, can be effective. Ceasefire Boston involves an interagency collaboration that requires organizational change, while employing a "pulling levers strategy" in which gang members are threatened with sanctions in an effort to deter them from engaging in violence (Braga *et al.* 2001). Chapter 36 (this volume) presents a description and discussion about this strategy. The Ceasefire Chicago or Cure Violence approach, which is characterized by the mobilization of community members and the use of outreach workers, who are often ex-gang members, to intervene in instances when violence can erupt, has also shown promise (see Chapter 34, this volume).

Interventions that focus on the root causes of gang formation by improving the structural and cultural conditions that result in the emergence of gangs can also be successful in the prevention of gang violence and homicide. Although highly debated in criminology, recent evaluations of the Gang Resistance and Education Training (G.R.E.A.T) program show promising results in the reduction of gang membership (Esbensen *et al.* 2013). The G.R.E.A.T program focuses on providing youth (middle and elementary school age) a curriculum that teaches them about the dangers of gang involvement while offering cognitive behavior training, social skill development, and conflict resolution training. In doing this, the program also familiarizes youth with police officers in the area because a local police officer is responsible for carrying out the curriculum. Related programs such as Big Brother/Sister that match at-risk youth with positive role models can also be useful in the prevention of gang involvement. Research suggests that youths involved in Big Brother/Sister mentoring programs are more likely to develop a strong self-concept and are thus less likely to engage in violence and use drugs (Tierney, Grossman, and Resch 2000).

Programs that focus on alleviating the structural strains that push youth to life in a gang can also be beneficial. These programs can include job and vocational training and other scholastic opportunities. Another valuable intervention would focus on improving police–community relations since residents who feel they can count on the police and agents of formal social control may be less resistant to rely on them when problems arise within their neighborhoods. Finally, programs that limit access to gang homicide facilitators, such as firearms (the most common used weapon in gang homicides), may also limit the spread and increase of these homicide types.

Zeoli and colleagues (2014) note that the most successful homicide prevention strategy might be one that not only targets the root causes of the violence, but also simultaneously focuses on problematic groups such as gangs. While studies suggest that programs that focus on preventing youth from joining gangs such as G.R.E.A.T and the Boys/Girls Club are promising in reducing gang violence via the mechanism of decreasing gang membership, research has also documented the effect of focused deterrence interventions, such as Ceasefire, that focus directly on gang members. Consequently, jurisdictions experiencing gang violence problems should employ a two-pronged approach consisting of gang membership prevention while at the same time attempting to decrease the violence via a program such as Ceasefire.

Conclusion and Direction for Future Research

The relationship between gangs and homicide is significant. This chapter examined the current state of knowledge on this homicide type in the United States. In doing so, a discussion of the etiology of gangs was presented followed by a review of the gang homicide literature. As evidenced by the review, the state of knowledge on gang homicides has grown exponentially in recent years. To date, scholars have uncovered multiple individual, situational, and structural factors that are conducive toward gang homicides. This growing body of literature, however, still has questions that merit future inquiry.

It is still unclear how the various individual, situational, and structural factors interact to culminate in violence. That is, what are the processes that breed gang homicides, and what is their relation to structural and situational conditions? In this chapter, I expanded on this work by presenting an integrated framework of the conditions that breed this homicide type. Future research should further explore this framework and test its validity. Specifically, more longitudinal studies examining neighborhoods and how they breed the formation of gangs and violence should be further explored. Relatedly, longitudinal studies focusing on the criminal career of gang members would also serve to answer this question. More in depth ethnographic studies with violent gangs in inner cities can also shed light onto the group processes that result in lethal violence.

Perhaps the most pressing question for researchers today is the extent of gang homicide and violence throughout the world and whether similar dynamics to those seen in the United States breed violence in other countries. While this chapter focused primarily on gang violence and homicide in the United States, many other countries around the world are facing similar problems. Indeed, gang violence is a worldwide phenomenon (Decker and Pyrooz 2010). As a result, researchers should continue examining the prevalence of gangs and their accompanying violence in other countries. Although researchers have begun exploring gangs outside the

United States, most notably in Europe via the Eurogang network, this line of international research is still in its infancy. Therefore, it is pivotal for gang researchers to extend their studies to other countries in an effort to understand better the gang phenomena and its relation to worldwide homicide patterns.

Note

1 This increase should be interpreted with caution given that it may be a reflection of increased awareness of gangs and changes in the identification methodology adopted by law enforcement and academics.

References

Adams, J.J. and Pizarro, J.M. (2014) Patterns of specialization and escalation in the criminal careers of gang and non-gang homicide offenders. *Criminal Justice and Behavior*, 41: 237–255. doi: 10.1177/0093854813503637.

Akers, R.L. (1998) *Social Learning and Social Structure: A General Theory of Crime and Deviance*. Boston: Northeastern University Press.

Anderson, E. (1999) *Code of the Street: Decency, Violence, and the Moral Life of the Inner City*. New York: W.W. Norton.

Armstrong, T.A. and Britt, C.L. (2004) The effect of offender characteristics on offense specialization and escalation. *Justice Quarterly*, 21: 843–876. doi: 10.1080/07418820400096011.

Black, D. (1983) Crime as social control. *American Sociological Review*, 48: 34–45.

Braga, A.A., Kennedy, D.M., Piehl, A.M., and Waring, E.J. (2001) Measuring the impact of Operation Ceasefire. In National Institute of Justice, *Reducing Gun Violence: The Boston Gun Project's Operation Ceasefire* (Part II, pp. 55–71). National Institute of Justice Research Report.

Braga, A.A. and Weisburd, D.L. (2012) The effects of focused deterrence strategies on crime: A systematic review and meta-analysis of the empirical evidence. *Journal of Research in Crime and Delinquency*, 49: 323–358. doi: 10.1177/0022427811419368.

Cloward, R.A. and Ohlin, L.E. (1960) *Delinquency and Opportunity: A Theory of Delinquent Gangs*. New York: Free Press.

Cohen, A.K. (1955) *Delinquent Boys: The Culture of the Gang*. Glencoe, IL: Free Press.

Curry, G.D. and Spergel, I.A. (1988) Gang homicide, delinquency, and community. *Criminology*, 26: 381–403. doi: 10.1111/j.1745-9125.1988.tb00847.x.

Decker, S.H. (1996) Collective and normative features of gang violence. *Justice Quarterly*, 13: 243–264. doi: 10.1080/07418829600092931.

Decker, S.H. and Curry, G.D. (2002) Gangs, gang homicides, and gang loyalty: Organized crimes or disorganized criminals. *Journal of Criminal Justice*, 30: 343–352. doi: 10.1016/S0047-2352(02)00134-4.

Decker, S.H., Katz, C.M., and Webb, V.J. (2008) Understanding the black box of gang organization: Implications for involvement in violent crime, drug sales, and violent victimization. *Crime and Delinquency*, 54: 153–172. doi: 10.1177/0011128706296664.

Decker, S. and Pyrooz, D. (2010) *Gang Violence Worldwide: Context, Culture, and Country in Small Arms Survey* (pp. 128–155). Cambridge: Cambridge University Press.

Decker, S.H. and Pyrooz, D.C. (2011) On the validity and reliability of gang homicide: A comparison of disparate sources. *Homicide Studies*, 14: 359–376. doi: 10.1177/1088767910385400.

Decker, S.H. and Van Winkle, B. (1996) *Life in the Gang*. New York: Cambridge University Press.

DeLisi, M., Spruill, J.O., Vaughn, M.G., and Trulson, C.R. (2014) Do gang members commit abnormal homicide? *American Journal of Criminal Justice*, 39: 125–138. doi: 10.1007/s12103-013-9201-y.

Esbensen, F.-A. and Huizinga, D. (1993) Gangs, drugs, and delinquency in a survey of urban youth. *Criminology*, 31: 565–589. doi: 10.1111/j.1745-9125.1993.tb01142.x.

Esbensen, F.-A., Osgood, D.W., Peterson, D., *et al.* (2013) Short- and long-term outcome results from a multisite evaluation of the G.R.E.A.T. program. *Criminology & Public Policy*, 12: 375–411. doi: 10.1111/1745-9133.12048.

Fearn, N., Decker, S.H., and Curry, G.D. (2000) Public policy responses to gangs: Evaluating the outcomes. In J. Miller, C.L. Maxson, and M.W. Klein (eds), *The Modern Gang Reader* (2nd edn, pp. 330–343). Los Angeles: Roxbury.

Fox, A.M., Katz, C.M., Choate, D.E., and Hedberg, E.C. (2015) Evaluation of the Phoenix Truce project: A replication of Chicago ceasefire. *Justice Quarterly*, 32: 85–115. doi: 10.1080/07418825.2014.902092.

Gatti, U., Haymoz, S., and Schadee, H.M.A. (2011) Deviant youth groups in 30 countries: Results from the Second International Self-Report Delinquency Study. *International Criminal Justice Review*, 21: 208–224. doi: 10.1177/1057567711418500.

Gatti, U., Tremblay, R.E., Vitaro, F., and McDuff, P. (2005) Youth gangs, delinquency and drug use: A test of the selection, facilitation, and enhancement hypotheses. *Journal of Child Psychology and Psychiatry*, 46: 1178–1190. doi: 10.1111/j.1469-7610.2005.00423.x.

Gottfredson, M.R. and Hirschi, T. (1990) *A General Theory of Crime*. Stanford, CA: Stanford University Press.

Hagedorn, J.M. (2005) The global impact of gangs. *Journal of Contemporary Criminal Justice*, 21: 153–169. doi: 10.1177/1043986204273390.

Horowitz, R. (1990) Sociological perspectives on gangs. In C.R. Huff (ed.), *Gangs in America* (1st edn, pp. 37–54). Thousand Oaks, CA: SAGE.

Klein, M.W. (1971) *Street Gangs and Street Workers*. Englewood Cliffs, NJ: Prentice-Hall.

Klein, M.W. and Maxson, C.L. (1989) Street gang violence. In M.E. Wolfgang and N. Weiner (eds), *Violent Crime, Violent Criminals* (pp. 198–234). Beverly Hills: SAGE.

Loeber, R., DeLamatre, M., Tita, G., *et al.* (1999) Gun injury and mortality: The delinquent backgrounds of juvenile victims. *Violence and Victims*, 14: 339–352.

Matsuda, K.N., Melde, C., Taylor, T.J., *et al.* (2013) Gang membership and adherence to the code of the street. *Justice Quarterly*, 30: 440–468. doi: 10.1080/07418825.2012.684432.

Maxson, C.L. and Klein, M.W. (1990) Street gang violence: Twice as great, or half as great? In C.R. Huff (ed.), *Gangs in America* (1st edn, pp. 71–100). Newbury Park, CA: SAGE.

Maxson, C.L. and Klein, M.W. (2006) Defining gang homicide: An updated look at member and motive approaches. In A. Egley Jr., C.L. Maxson, J. Miller, and M.W. Klein (eds),*The Modern Gang Reader* (3rd edn, pp. 30–42). Los Angeles, CA: Roxbury.

McGloin, J.M. and Decker, S.H. (2010) Theories of gang behavior and public policy. In H. Barlow and S.H. Decker (eds), *Criminology and Public Policy: Putting Theory to Work* (pp. 150–165). Philadelphia, PA: Temple University Press.

Miller, W.B. (1980) Gangs, groups, and serious youth crime. In D. Schichor and D.H. Kelly (eds), *Critical Issues in Juvenile Delinquency* (pp. 115–138). Lexington, MA: DC Health.

National Gang Intelligence Center (NGIC). (2009) National gang threat assessment 2009. Available online at http://www.justice.gov/ndic/pubs32/32146/32146p.pdf (accessed January 20, 2015).

National Gang Intelligence Center (NGIC). (2011) National gang threat assessment 2011: Emerging trends. Available online at http://www.fbi.gov/stats-services/publications/2011-national-gang-threat-assessment (accessed January 20, 2015).

National Institute of Justice. (2011) What is a gang: Definitions. Available online at http://www.nij.gov/topics/crime/gangs/Pages/definitions.aspx#note1 (accessed January 20, 2015).

Papachristos, A.V. (2009) Murder by structure: Dominance relations and the social structure of gang homicide. *American Journal of Sociology*, 115: 74–128. doi: 10.1086/597791.

Pizarro, J.M. and McGloin, J.M. (2006) Explaining gang homicides in Newark, New Jersey: Collective behavior or social disorganization? *Journal of Criminal Justice*, 34: 195–207. doi: 10.1016/j.jcrimjus.2006.01.002.

Pratt, T.C., Turner, M.G., and Piquero, A.R. (2004) Parental socialization and community context: A longitudinal analysis of the structural sources of low self-control. *Journal of Research in Crime and Delinquency*, 41: 219–243. doi: 10.1177/0022427803260270.

Pyrooz, D.C. (2012) Structural covariates of gang homicide in large cities. *Journal of Research in Crime and Delinquency*, 49: 489–518. doi: 10.1177/0022427811415535.

Rodgers, D. and Baird, A. (2015) Understanding gangs in contemporary Latin America. In S.H. Decker and D.C. Pyrooz (eds), *The Handbook of Gangs*. New York: Wiley-Blackwell.

Rose, D.R. and Clear, T.R. (1998) Incarceration, social capital, and crime: Implications for social disorganization theory. *Criminology*, 36: 441–479. doi: 10.1111/j.1745-9125.1998.tb01255.x.

Rosenfeld, R.B., Bray, T., and Egley, A.H. (1999) Facilitating violence: A comparison of gang-motivated, gang-affiliated, and non-gang youth homicides. *Journal of Quantitative Criminology*, 15: 495–516. doi: 10.1023/A:1007548309620.

Sampson, R.J. and Jeglum-Bartusch, D. (1998) Legal cynicism and (subcultural) tolerance of deviance: The neighborhood context of racial differences. *Law and Society Review*, 32: 777–804. doi: 10.2307/827739.

Shaw, C.R. and McKay, H.D. (1942) *Juvenile Delinquency and Urban Areas*. Chicago: University of Chicago Press.

Terrill, W.C. and Reisig, M.D. (2003) Neighborhood context and police use of force. *Journal of Research in Crime and Delinquency*, 40: 291–321. doi: 10.1177/0022427803253800.

Thornberry, T.P. and Burch, J.H. (1997) *Gang Members and Delinquent Behavior*. Washington, DC: Office of Juvenile Justice and Delinquency Prevention.

Thornberry, T.P., Krohn, M.D., Lizotte, A.J., and Chard-Wierschem, D. (1993) The role of juvenile gangs in facilitating delinquent behavior. *Journal of Research in Crime and Delinquency*, 30: 55–87. doi: 10.2307/827739.

Thrasher, F.M. (1927) *The Gang: A Study of 1313 Gangs in Chicago*. Chicago: University of Chicago Press.

Tierney, J.P., Grossman, J.B., and Resch, N.L. (2000) Making a difference: An impact study of big brothers big sisters. Public/Private Ventures. Available online at http://ppv.issuelab.org/resources/11972/11972.pdf (Accessed January 20, 2015).

Vigil, J.D. (2002) A multiple marginality framework of gangs. In A. Egley Jr., C.L. Maxson, J. Miller, and M.W. Klein (eds), *The Modern Gang Reader* (3rd edn, pp. 20–29). Los Angeles: Roxbury.

Weitzer, R. (1999) Citizen perceptions of police misconduct: Race and neighborhood context. *Justice Quarterly*, 16: 819–846. doi: 10.1080/07418829900094381.

Wilson, W.J. (1996) *When Work Disappears: The World of the New Urban Poor*. New York: Vintage Books.

Zeoli, A.M., Grady, S., Pizarro, J.M., and Melde, C. (2015) Modeling the movement of homicide by type to inform public health prevention efforts. *American Journal of Public Health*, 105(10): 2035–2041. doi: 10.2105/AJPH.2015.302732.

Zeoli, A.M., Pizarro, J.M., Grady, S., and Melde, C. (2014) Homicide as infectious disease: Using public health methods to investigate the diffusion of homicide. *Justice Quarterly*, 31: 609–632. doi: 10.1080/07418825.2012.732100.

6

Drug-Related Homicide

Sean P. Varano and Joseph B. Kuhns

Introduction

An inextricable link between drugs and lethal violence has been part of the backdrop of the discourse on drug policy for generations. News stories about the emergence of marijuana into American communities during the early twentieth century, for example, fueled public fears of an impending disaster in neighborhoods already distressed by sharp increases in poverty, disease, and social disorder. As one example, in their influential account of the "growing marijuana" problem in the United States during this period, Anslinger and Cooper's (1937) characterized marijuana as the "assassin of youth" that would lead young people into violent, unpredictable behavior.

These early linkages between drug use and violent behavior extend well beyond marijuana and included "hardcore" drugs such as heroin and cocaine during the 1970s and 1980s (Baumer *et al.* 1998; Cook and Laub 2002; Fagan and Chin 1989), and more contemporary synthetic "designer" drugs such as bath salts (a term used to describe recreational drugs which often resemble true bath salts, but contain one or more synthetic amphetamines) more recently (Schaller 2013). Synthetic drugs, for example, are often intentionally used for reasons other than intended purposes, produce pharmacological effects similar to cocaine, LSD, or methamphetamine, and have been known to contribute to excessive and unpredictable violence. The potential for explosive violence associated with synthetic drugs was evident in the case of Randy Eugene, a homeless 31-year old man in Miami whose vicious attack on another homeless man included savagely "eating his face," and plucking out and eating his eyeballs (*The Huffington Post* 2012).

The Handbook of Homicide, First Edition. Edited by Fiona Brookman,
Edward R. Maguire, and Mike Maguire.

Although the precise causal links between drug use and violence are not fully clear (Kuhns and Clodfelter 2009), evidence clearly indicates that drugs and drug markets are both related to crime trends, including homicide trends (Baumer *et al.* 1998; Blumstein, Rivara, and Rosenfeld 2000; Cook and Laub 2002; Riley 1997). This chapter will specifically consider and explore this relationship between drug use and homicide victimization and offending. We begin with some historical observations regarding how drug use and drug markets empirically linked to violent behavior and violence rates. We next consider the empirical relationships between drug and alcohol use and violent crime, including homicide rates and trends. We follow with some observations of the drug use–violence relationship within the context of Goldstein's (1985) tripartite framework. We conclude with some suggestions for how we might further study and understand precisely how drug use contributes to and, in some cases, facilitates lethal offending and victimization within and outside of illicit drug markets.

Drugs and Lethal Violence

Connections between drug use and violence, including homicide, have been observed for much of modern history. Historically, drug abuse, immigration, and violence were viewed as aspects of the growing squalor in newly developing United States cities. Reinarman (1994), for example, documents how the interrelationships between drugs and violence facilitated a moral panic that played on the fears of the growing middle and upper classes. The temperance movement of the early twentieth century in the United States, for example, was explicitly connected to perceptions that alcohol and drugs contributed to violence and other negative behaviors. Stories of horrific violence associated with drug and alcohol use were common and enhanced efforts toward firmer regulation and prohibition. Anslinger and Cooper's (1937) vivid descriptions of the drug-induced psychoses related to marijuana use, included one example which allegedly led a young person in Florida to murder his entire family with an ax. When asked about the circumstances by a responding police officer, the offender recalled "I've had a terrible dream. People tried to hack off my arms" (Anslinger and Cooper 1937: 19). Having no recollection of the horrific crime he had just committed, the police attempted to piece together how an otherwise "sane" person had turned "pitifully crazed." Further, the link between drugs and unpredictable behavior, including homicide, is well-entrenched in the folklore of crime control policy.

While the connection between the use of drugs and violent crime lingered in the public discourse for decades, the crack cocaine "epidemic" of the 1980s moved this discussion into the national conversation. During the early to mid-1980s communities across the United States began to experience sharp and sustained increases in violence and homicide. National arrest rates for aggravated assault, for example, nearly doubled from approximately 125 per 100,000 in 1980 to more than 200 per 100,000 by 1995 (Snyder 2011). Of particular concern was the sharp increase in violent crime arrest rates for juveniles, which increased from approximately 300 per 100,000 in 1980 to about 500 per 100,000 in 1995 (Puzzanchera 2013: 6). Around the same time, the United States experienced almost a 25 percent increase in arrest rates for homicide, from approximately 8 per 100,000 in 1985 to almost 10 per 100,000 in 1995. However, drug-related deaths are certainly not restricted to the United States (United Nations Office on Drugs and Crime 2011).

A notable and particularly alarming aspect of the changing crime levels was a sharp increase in the arrest rates for juveniles, for both aggravated assault and murder. By the early 1990s, it was suggested a generation of "super-predators," who were scouring American streets and engaging in heightened levels of violence, never previously seen (see Fox 1996). Seemingly overnight, many large urban jurisdictions experienced significant increases in lethal violence among young people. As one example, the number of murder victims age 24 and younger in Boston increased by more than 350 percent between 1987 and 1990 (from 20 to more than 70) (McDevitt *et al.* 2003: 57). The trends observed in cities like Boston were replicated across many parts of the United States during those timeframes. Homicide victimization rates for victims between the ages of 18 and 24 also increased significantly, from approximately 14 per 100,000 in 1985 to 25 per 100,000 by the mid-1990s (Blumstein, Rivara, and Rosenfeld 2000: 508). Again, these patterns extend to many countries and cultures (World Health Organization, 2015).

The sharp increase in serious violent crime during the 1980s was quickly associated with the emergence of crack cocaine, a freebase form of cocaine that could be smoked. Although freebasing cocaine was known among some users prior to the emergence of crack (Inciardi 1987), it was not widely used or available because production required large amounts of raw product which made it cost-prohibitive for most typical users (Fagan and Chin 1989). The drop in costs for the raw materials during the 1980s, combined with an increase in the purity of cocaine during the same period, made modified or "cooked" versions of cocaine highly profitable.

The drop in prices and an increase in purity, coupled with the ability to transform an otherwise expensive drug into "affordable" single doses, facilitated a "perfect" drug market storm that expanded access for a wide cross-section of users. By the 1980s, crack cocaine was identified as one of the most significant public safety threats facing communities in the United States. In a 1986 report to the US Congress, for instance, the National Drug Enforcement Policy Board identified cocaine as "the drug that now poses the greatest threat to the physical, emotional and social well-being of this nation," and crack cocaine as an "extremely destructive" version of the larger cocaine problem (1986: 22). This new drug, hardly known in the early 1980s, quickly spread across the United States and became a drug of choice among many street addicts by the mid-1980s. A study of 600 "seriously delinquent" adolescents in Miami indicated that nearly 95 percent reported having used crack cocaine at least once (Inciardi and Pottieger 1995: 245).

Almost from the beginning, crack cocaine was clearly linked to crime, particularly serious violent crimes. Major cities experiencing some of the sharpest increases in crack cocaine sales were simultaneously experiencing notable increases in homicide.

New York City, for example, experienced a 13 percent increase in homicides between 1987 and 1988 (Goldstein *et al.* 1989). Similar increases were noted in other large cities and observers quickly began to associate these increases to shifts and destabilizations in local drug markets coincided with crack cocaine (Blumstein and Rosenfeld 1998; Molotsky 1988; Wolff 1988). Blumstein and Rosenfeld (1998) conducted an analysis of changes in homicide levels in both large and small cities and argued such shifts accompanied the rise and decline of the crack cocaine markets. Their analyses support the conclusion crack cocaine was of "central importance" to variations in homicide levels during the 1980s and early 1990s (Blumstein and Rosenfeld 1998: 1206). Dealers involved in the crack cocaine industry self-reported higher levels of involvement in serious felony crimes including robbery and assaultive violence (Inciardi and Pottieger 1995). However, Johnson, Golub, and Fagan (1995) reported that crack users who had not demonstrated violent behavior before initiation did not report significant increases in violence after initiation. Thus, the crack–violence relationship is likely more nuanced with prior history, crack use, and features of lifestyles intersecting in important ways.

The crack cocaine market was arguably different from other traditional drug markets in several ways. First, in contrast to prior heroin and cocaine markets, crack cocaine was "marketed" as a drug that was readily available in smaller doses, often single "hits," that were more easily packaged and affordable to the average user (Curtis 2003; Johnson, Golub, and Fagan 1995). This created an economy of scale which opened the marketplace to a more diverse clientele from a broad socioeconomic spectrum. The availability of crack in small doses not only made it more accessible to a broader cross-section of users, but also created a busier marketplace as consumers needed to purchase the product on a more frequent basis. This moved both dimensions of the crack market, the *consumption* and *purchase* segments, to public streets and alleyways. To fill the demands of the expanding street marketplace, traffickers and distributors required a network of smalltime, street corner dealers to handle the market demands. Juveniles and younger dealers, many of whom were in gangs, filled this void (Cook and Laub 1998). More prone to resort to violence as a primary mechanism for settling illicit business disputes, and as a strategy for increasing status on the street (Cook and Laub 2002; Fagan and Chin 1989), levels of lethal and nonlethal violence among juveniles increased. The perception that the crack cocaine market was a distinctive type of drug market associated with heightened levels of violence subsequently facilitated enhanced federal penalties for crack-related crimes (United States Sentencing Commission 2002).

Alcohol and Drug Use and Homicide Offending and Victimization

The challenges of the crack cocaine market were further exacerbated by the observed relationship between cocaine consumption and frequent alcohol consumption (Gossop, Manning, and Ridge 2006; Magura and Rosenblum 2000). While much of the historical discourse on the drugs–homicide connection typically focuses on harder drugs, alcohol, as a primary drug associated with violence behavior and homicide, necessarily becomes a part of this research process. Alcohol use is clearly linked to violent behavior (Chermack and Giancola 1997; Felson and Staff 2010), whether the behavior in question is assaultive crime (Ladouceur and Temple 1985), assaultive crime on college campuses (West, Drummond, and Eames 1990), sexual assault (Ullman and Najdowski 2010; Brecklin and Ullman 2002; see Roizen 1993 for a review of rape studies prior to 1979), violence within families (Hastings and Hamberger 1988; Roberts 1988; Rath, Jarratt, and Leonardson 1989), sexual violence within families (Barnard 1990) or, more directly, homicide (Rossow 2001; Forrest and Gordon 1990; Holcomb and Anderson 1983; Wieczorek, Welte, and Abel 1990). Alcohol use has been demonstrated to have immediate effects on aggressive behavior under controlled experimental conditions (Taylor and Leonard 1983; Exum 2006), though obviously not all alcohol users will become aggressive while intoxicated. Many illicit drug users simultaneously use and abuse alcohol. As one example, heroin addicts were more likely under the influence of alcohol than any other drug during the commission of a crime, including heroin, their primary drug of addiction (Strug *et al.* 1984). Further, the extent and pattern of alcohol use is also related to violence; specifically acuteness and chronicity of alcohol abuse were found to be related to severity of violence, though not related to frequency of violence (Hillbrand, Foster, and Hirt 1991). Additional empirical evidence linking alcohol consumption and intoxication to homicide victimization and offending will be discussed below (see Bye 2008).

Exploring Drug-Related Homicide within the Tripartite Framework

From both a theoretical and policy perspective, it is important to understand the prevalence, characteristics, and causal factors associated with all drug-related homicide events. Although popular opinion has generally drawn linkages between drugs (including alcohol) and homicide, the exact role drugs play is not fully clear. Goldstein, Brownstein, and Ryan (1992: 465) relied on a content analysis of homicide case files to determine the actual role of drugs and drug-related behavior in precipitating lethal encounters. The study found approximately 24 percent of all homicides in New York State and 42 percent of all homicides in New York City were drug-related in 1984, and the prevalence of drug-related homicides in New York City increased by over 20 percent by 1988. In their analysis of 175 homicide cases in Detroit, MI, between the years 1999 and 2002, Varano, McCluskey, and Bynum (2004: 378) reported approximately 50 percent involved drug circumstances. Of those found to be drug-related, drugs played a relatively benign role, with little direct involvement beyond the mere possession of drugs or paraphernalia (victim or offender) or the mere use of drugs within some temporal proximity to the lethal encounter. Drug possession by the victim or offender was the most prevalent

(27 percent) drug circumstance, followed by the presence of drugs or drug paraphernalia (25 percent) and drug consumption by the victim or offender (14 percent). In approximately 40 percent of homicide events, the victim or offender were in the process of selling drugs at the time of the encounter, but circumstances where the sale or use of drugs was the *motivation* for the lethal encounter were relatively rare (19 percent).

Goldstein's (1985) tripartite framework offers a conceptual and practical basis for organizing and understanding drug-related violence and homicide. Psychopharmacological violence includes violence associated with the pharmacological properties of a consumed substance which affects or possibly triggers the user's aggressive or violent behavior (e.g., a man gets drunk and assaults his wife in a domestic violence dispute). Economic-compulsive violence includes violence that occurs as a result of a chronic user's need to acquire more drugs (e.g., a crack user robs someone and the citizen or user is killed during the robbery). Systematic violence includes violence that occurs within the context of the illicit drug trade (e.g., one gang member murders another in an effort to protect or expand street drug dealing territory). Various studies have attempted to measure each of these relationships using a range of methodologies, although the strength of these relationships varies considerably depending on the definitions used, the subjects and settings examined, and the methodologies employed (Goldstein 1985). Some of these studies have examined violence, more generally, although the tripartite framework might easily be applied within the context of homicide victimization and offending as well.

Psychopharmacologically related homicide

A proportion of homicides are undoubtedly psychopharmacologically related to alcohol and drug use, which suggests the use of alcohol and other drugs has a direct or indirect physiological impact on a given homicide event (victimization and/or offending). This might occur as a result of a potential homicide offender ingesting a substance and subsequently committing a homicide, perhaps in part because of the psychoactive influence of the substance on their decisions and behavior. As one common example, an alcohol-fueled disagreement in a bar or pub might escalate into a homicide event and alcohol may serve as a trigger for the offender, the victim, or both. Alternatively, a potential victim might consume another drug and the substance might contribute to victimization vulnerability. For example, use of the substance might unintentionally expose them to robbery or to sexual victimization, which might then result in a lethal outcome. Regardless of the exact causal mechanisms, cross-cultural studies indicate a strong and likely universal association. Bye (2008), for example, noted that across Eastern European countries such as Russia, Bulgaria, and Hungary, homicide and alcohol consumption patterns were strongly related to one another (see also Pridemore 2002).

Copes, Hochstetler, and Sandberg's (2015) narrative accounts of incarcerated felons provide a vivid understanding of how drugs alter the cognitive and emotional frameworks of users. Subjects, for example, spoke of how drug use turned them into another person that even they did not recognize. One subject reported, "When I was on drugs I was just deranged and crazy … [I was] not in my own mind. I just blanked out from normal, you know what I'm saying. Nothing about it was normal." Another stated "I guess I just had the demon in me, you know, that's all I can say …. My mind wasn't right, you know. I can look back today and know my mind wasn't right" (Copes, Hochstetler, and Sandberg 2015: 37). The authors suggest drug use results in "fundamental transformations of character" that changes abusers in critical ways.

One way in which these relationships can be examined is through the use of toxicology testing. Toxicology tests are often routinely conducted on homicide victims and, less often, among some homicide offenders. Importantly, toxicology testing is scientifically standardized, used in many different countries, and are readily available for analysis in many communities. On the other hand, the types of drugs examined may vary, drug positive thresholds have changed over time, and drug testing protocols have also changed. Drug toxicology test results for homicide offenders are not routinely gathered in any country or jurisdiction and are, in fact, extremely limited given the logistical uncertainties associated with testing offenders at or near the time of a homicide. However, two meta-analyses of alcohol toxicology test results among homicide offenders and homicide victims provide some useful insights and estimates regarding the extent of alcohol use and alcohol intoxication during or immediately prior to homicide events. A third meta-analysis of drug toxicology test results among homicide victims provides some drug-related insights and estimates among victims.

First, Kuhns *et al.* (2014) meta-analyzed 23 independent studies across nine countries (including Australia, England, England and Wales, Finland, Ireland, Scotland, Sweden, Russia, and the United States) that reported alcohol use status among 28,265 homicide *offenders*. In this study, alcohol use status was documented through self-reports, extraction from case file information, and/or urinalysis results (in only one study). The meta-analytic results suggested an average of 48 percent of homicide offenders tested positive for alcohol at the time of the offense, with 37 percent reportedly intoxicated. In this offender-based study, there were no differences in the percent positive across age, gender, or race; however, percent positive was lower among offenders who used a firearm as opposed to some other weapon (e.g., blunt object, or knife). Exploratory analyses suggested the prevalence of homicide offenders who were positive for alcohol has declined over a select period of time within the United States. This pattern corresponds with observed decreases in homicides in the United States over the past three decades (Cooper and Smith 2011). In this study, the authors were unable to explore patterns or draw meaningful conclusions from other countries given the limited number of studies that were available.

Second, Kuhns *et al.* (2011) meta-analyzed 61 independent studies from 57 published manuscripts, which reported alcohol toxicology test results for homicide *victims*. A total of 71,031 toxicology test results, derived from 78,265 homicide victims across 10 countries (including Australia, Canada, Denmark, Finland, Norway, South Africa, Sweden, Thailand, Turkey, and the United States) were analyzed. The results suggested an average of 48 percent of homicide victims tested positive for alcohol and 33 percent (using the 0.08 threshold) or 35 percent (using the 0.10 threshold) were determined to be intoxicated at the time of death. These studies reported using a wide range of units of measurement (e.g., milligrams per milliliter, grams per milliliter). Interestingly, these proportions are nearly identical to the estimates from a meta-analysis of alcohol use by homicide offenders (Kuhns *et al.* 2014). The proportion of homicide victims testing positive for alcohol also appeared to be decreasing over time. Further, the proportion testing positive increased with age, was higher for female than for male victims, and differed by race. The overall estimates were relatively stable across study sites.

Finally, Kuhns *et al.* (2009) meta-analyzed 18 independent studies that reported marijuana, cocaine, and/or opiate toxicology test results for 30,482 homicide victims from five countries (Canada, Denmark, Norway, Sweden, and the United States). The results revealed an average of six percent of homicide victims tested positive for marijuana, 11 percent tested positive for cocaine, and five percent tested positive for opiates. However, the proportion of homicide victims testing positive for these three illicit drugs has increased over time. Age had a strong curvilinear relationship with toxicology test results but gender differences were not observed. On the other hand, across these 18 studies Hispanic and African American homicide victims were more likely to test positive for cocaine (among US studies only), while Caucasians were most likely to test positive for opiates. Cocaine use appeared to be related to increased risk of death from a firearm and was a greater risk factor for lethal victimization in the United States than in Newfoundland and Scandinavia. However, few cross-cultural comparisons were available in this drug-based meta-analysis.

Considered collectively, these three meta-analyses provide some useful insights and mean estimates regarding the extent and possible psychopharmacological role of drugs and alcohol in contributing to homicide offending and victimization. These studies also offer points of comparison for other cities, counties, and countries that may need a point of comparison for their local toxicology test results. However, one cannot conclude from these studies a positive toxicology test result is causally related to homicide offending or victimization.

Economic-compulsive homicide

Economic-compulsive homicide may include situations where chronic or persistent drug users feel compelled to commit violent acts, which may result in homicide, in order to acquire money for continued drug use. Robbery is a typical example, as it provides immediate financial rewards that can be quickly traded for additional drugs. Robbery also involves the use of force and increases the potential for violence, which may result in a homicide. Evidence from one Caribbean-based study suggested robbery-related homicide victims were more likely to test positive for marijuana than other homicide victims (Pierce and Kuhns 2012; Kuhns *et al.* 2009), thus suggesting a linkage between instrumental motives, drug use, and lethal violence (robbery and/or homicide), perhaps as a result of daily hand-to-hand drug purchases.

Economic-compulsive homicides associated with alcohol are rare. Possible exceptions might include violence committed by alcoholic homeless persons or by alcoholics who are violent during attempts to burglarize, rob, or directly steal alcohol or money for alcohol. However, sufficient research exists to conclude economically motivated violent crime (and property crime) is more common among narcotic users than previously thought (Blumstein, Cohen, and Visher 1986; M.R. Chaiken and J.M. Chaiken 1990; Goldstein 1989; also see Nurco, Hanlon, and Kinlock 1991 for a review). Economic-compulsive violence, including homicide, is also common among heavy adolescent and adult users of other drugs (M.R. Chaiken and J.M. Chaiken 1990; Chaiken and Chaiken 1982; Inciardi 1980, 1986, 1990). Reports suggest crack addicts will sometimes resort to violence for financial gain in order to procure more drugs. Inciardi (1990) found youths more involved in crack distribution markets (using and dealing) were more likely to commit robberies and assaults, some of which resulted in homicides. Interestingly, Goldstein, Brownstein, and Ryan (1992: 466) reported only between three and four percent of all drug-related homicides were economically compulsive events.

Economically motivated homicide, compared with psychopharmacologically induced homicide, (overwhelmingly alcohol-related) and systemically related homicide (discussed below), were very rare within a small sample of drug-related murder cases in New York (Goldstein, Brownstein, and Ryan 1992; Brownstein *et al.* 1992). There may be clear reasons for these differences. For example, many heavy drug users are primarily concerned with continued drug use. Recognition and realization that a homicide will result in extensive police investigation (possibly resulting in capture and eventual involuntary withdrawal from a drug) is a sufficient motivator for many to avoid these situations. In this context, Miron (2001) argued the connection between drug marketplaces and violence/homicide is not universal but is instead related to larger enforcement practices that are country specific. The drug–violence nexus, for example, is less apparent in many places in Europe due to a much more tempered approach to enforcement practices. The presence of extensive drug marketplaces, for example, does not necessarily equate to higher levels of lethal or nonlethal violence. Prohibition efforts (e.g., enforcement practices) ratchet up or down the level of violence associated with illicit marketplaces by places external pressure on those who operate within the market.

Systemic homicide

Systemic violence, which is associated with the distribution of illicit drugs, accounts for a substantial proportion of drug-related homicides. Some examples include a sanctioned execution of a competitor who might be selling drugs within established territory; violent enforcement of drug organizational rules of conduct and business; and lethal encounters with drug enforcement personnel, informants, and competitors who might interfere with the distribution of illicit drugs. Reuter (2009), for example, observes "managers have reason to fear subordinates who can provide evidence against them; the longer the relationship, the greater the potential for harm from informing" (2009: 277). Violence is an inherent and acceptable behavior within the system of distribution of illicit substances. Drug traffickers, users, and sellers cannot rely on the police and other legitimate channels for assistance in facilitating and protecting their illicit business interests. Therefore, systemic violence is often unreported or misreported and subsequently it is more difficult to measure accurately. Homicide is perhaps an exception, given most homicides are investigated and typically investigated thoroughly in many, although not all, countries. However, consistently and accurately defining a homicide as "drug-related" is not always easy given that gangs often distribute drugs (and therefore the homicide may be characterized as "gang-related") and that gangs often fight (meaning the homicide may be characterized as an altercation or dispute). Regardless, the extent of systemic violence associated with the trafficking and dealing of illicit drugs is substantial. Systemic violence has also been associated with the marijuana business, the heroin business, and the cocaine and crack business (see various studies cited in Fagan and Chin 1990). Such violence is likely common in any new, emerging, or changing drug market. Methamphetamine distribution, for example, has generated substantial violence (Kuhns 2005; Blumstein and Rosenfeld 1998).

The "it's just business" mentality, arguably part of street culture that is sometimes associated with people fully engrained in the "code of the street" (Anderson 1999; Brookman *et al.* 2011), plays a powerful force in certain neighborhoods. The "code" discussed by Anderson (1999), represents cultural frameworks that provide informal cues about how conflict and disputes should be resolved. Copes, Hochstetler, and Sandberg (2015: 38) present observations from one subject who offered:

> Everything revolves around money and business. It's business. When we go to war with people over there, if we go to war with them, that shit's just business. They got to do it. They going to kill beaucoup [many] people, but it's just business.

The inevitability of violence and presumption that all are aware of the street code not only leads some to minimize the harm associated with their destructive behavior, but can even further lead toward the belief that some, particularly addicts, actually deserve their victimization.

Goldstein *et al.* (1989) determined New York City drug-related homicide events from 1988 were predominately systemic in nature, although another study indicated the psychopharmacological association between alcohol and homicides was more prevalent four years earlier (Goldstein, Brownstein, and Ryan 1992). Systemic homicides at the time were predominately associated with crack cocaine markets. These associations would be expected to fluctuate depending on availability, popularity, and predominance of other drug markets (e.g., heroin, marijuana, PCP, methamphetamine). It is possible the role of systemic violence was particularly important to the crack cocaine market as dealers tried to assume ownership of this new, quickly emerging drug market. Many methodological shortcomings were acknowledged by Goldstein, Brownstein, and Ryan (1992) including the difficulties associated with utilizing police data for assessment of drug-relatedness in homicides, difficulties assigning precise motives to some homicides, and confusion and inconsistency regarding what constitutes a drug-related homicide. Therefore, conclusions regarding the percentages of systemic homicides (and psychopharmacological and economic, for that matter) must be considered in light of these limitations. In this particular study, 24 percent (in 1984) and 53 percent (in 1988) of the homicides for a given year were characterized as drug-related based on available case file information. Meanwhile, Varano, McCluskey, and Bynum (2004) reported the prevalence of systemic violence was relatively rare among drug-related homicide events in Detroit. The authors, for example, found only 19 percent of drug-related homicides were motivated by the sale or use of drugs. However, these kinds of studies are relatively rare, and more studies which closely examine the drug-related circumstances associated with homicides are clearly needed within and outside of the United States.

Conclusion

There is little doubt alcohol and other drugs play an important role in facilitating violence, particularly lethal violence, although the exact prevalence of alcohol and drugs in lethal violence varies considerably across studies. It is difficult to imagine a period in the past century or more where drugs were not perceived as playing an important role in facilitating many forms of violence. The evidence presented here, however, makes it clear drugs not only play roles in the production of violence *within* any given time period, but may also partially explain dramatic shifts in crime rates *between* time periods. While the causal link between crack cocaine and violence is not altogether clear, there is strong evidence it was an important contributor to sharp increases in homicide in the United States during the 1980s, particularly in large urban centers where the crack trade was most prominent (Blumstein, Rivara, and Rosenfeld 2000; Fagan and Chin 1989; Fagan, Zimring, and Kim 1998; Goldstein *et al.* 1989).

It is equally as important to note that, although the drug–homicide connection is deeply ingrained in the psyche of policymakers, the exact causal linkages between these two phenomena are *not* fully clear. First, according to several of the studies cited here, it is fair to conclude drugs are not the driving force behind all homicides. That is, while alcohol and drug use is common in lethal encounters, a sizable proportion of homicides may not be linked to drug use or dealing. Varano, McCluskey, and Bynum (2004), for example, reported approximately 50 percent of all homicides in Detroit had no drug involvement at all. In this study, when drugs were linked to lethal encounters, drugs were generally only peripherally involved (e.g., drugs or drug paraphernalia were present at the scene), and only rarely played a direct causal role in events. In her analysis of homicide events in both England and Wales, Brookman (2003) reported in more than half of the cases either the victim or offender (or both) had consumed excessive amounts of alcohol prior to the event. Here alcohol, while not causally connected to homicide events, played an important role.

Similarly, Dobash *et al.* (2002) reported approximately 38 percent of all homicides in England involved excessive alcohol use by either the victims or offenders, and that co-occurring drug use was also typical. Thus, drugs and alcohol seem to play an important but secondary role in lethal encounters.

There does, however, appear to be a *time period* effect at work where the drug–crime nexus plays itself out depending on larger market and cultural dynamics. For example, Goldstein, Brownstein, and Ryan (1992) found the percentage of "drug-related" homicides in New York City increased from approximately 42 percent in 1984 to 51 percent in 1988. It also remains unclear whether the estimates of the prevalence of alcohol and drug-related homicides are a function of the quality of surveillance/detection systems used to track these specific problems.

Future research needs to focus in more discrete ways on the causal dynamics by which alcohol and drugs influence violence. Drug and alcohol use are common behaviors across many cultures and societies. Therefore, it is difficult to determine causality based on mere presence or use of substances in close temporal proximity to violent encounters. Researchers focus on the intersections of drugs and violence have relied heavily on Goldstein's (1995) conceptual framework that classifies drug-related events according to the psychopharmacological, economical, or systemic models. There are both conceptual and empirical reasons to believe this approach is useful for understanding the linkages between drugs and violence.

Few researchers, however, have attempted systematically to apply this framework to lethal encounters on a larger scale. This is likely due in part to the reality that such information is difficult to gather. Even in the unlikely situation in which police departments or prosecutors' offices maintain automated data systems that permit such examinations, it is likely internal data collection efforts would reflect bureaucratic, as opposed to theoretically driven, data collection priorities. Researchers need access to raw investigative files that include social artifacts such as autopsy reports (including toxicology test results), suspect/witness interviews, and analyses of crime scenes. Being granted full access to complete investigative files of this sort is relatively rare for researchers. This said, researchers are encouraged to take such tangible steps to further our understanding of how, and to what extent, drugs and homicide intersect, so that we may better inform local intervention and crime prevention efforts. With the considerations of the limitations to official data sources in mind, researchers are further encouraged to give more attention to this substantive area but also adopt mixed-method approaches that provide more in-depth understandings of these complex relationships. Findings from Copes, Hochstetler, and Sandberg (2015), for example, provide rich details about how street culture, drugs, and violence intersect in powerful ways. The authors document, for instance, how subjects' own accounts of their behaviors while under the influence of narcotics resulted in behaviors that even they did not and could not understand. These and similar types of qualitative approaches provide a contextual understanding to how alcohol, drugs, and violence intersect in ways not always possible with more typical data sources.

References

Anderson, E. (1999) *Code of the Street*. New York: W.W. Norton.

Anslinger, H.J. and Cooper, C.R. (1937) Marihuana: Assassin of youth. *American Magazine*, 124: 19.

Barnard, C. (1990) Alcoholism and sex abuse in the family: Incest and marital rape. *Journal of Chemical Dependency Treatment*, 3(1): 131–144.

Baumer, E., Lauritsen, J.L., Rosenfeld, R., and Wright, R. (1998) The influence of crack cocaine on robbery, burglary, and homicide rates: A cross-city, longitudinal analysis. *Journal of Research in Crime and Delinquency*, 35(3): 316–340. doi: 10.1177/0022427898035003004.

Blumstein, A., Cohen, J., and Visher, C. (1986) *Criminal Careers and Career Criminals*. Washington, DC: National Academy Press.

Blumstein, A., Rivara, F.P., and Rosenfeld, R. (2000) The rise and decline of homicide—and why. *Annual Review of Public Health*, 21(1): 505–541.

Blumstein, A. and Rosenfeld, R. (1998) Explaining recent trends in US homicide rates. *Journal of Criminal Law and Criminology*, 88(4): 1175–1216.

Brecklin, L.R. and Ullman, S. (2002) The roles of victim and offender alcohol use in sexual assaults: Results from the National Violence Against Women Survey. *Journal of Studies on Alcohol and Drugs*, 63(1): 57.

Brookman, F. (2003) Confrontational and grudge revenge homicides in England and Wales. *Australian & New Zealand Journal of Criminology*, 36 (1): 34–59.

Brookman, F., Bennett, T., Hochstetler, A., and Copes, H. (2011). The "code of the street" and the generation of street violence in the UK. *European Journal of Criminology*, 8(1): 17–31.

Brownstein, H., Shiledar Baxi, H., Goldstein, P., and Ryan, P. (1992) The relationship of drugs, drug trafficking, and drug trafficker to homicide. *Journal of Crime and Justice*, 15(1): 25–44.

Bye, E.K. (2008) Alcohol and homicide in Eastern Europe: A time series analysis of six countries. *Homicide Studies*, 12(1): 7–27.

Chaiken, J.M. and Chaiken, M.R. (1982) *Varieties of Criminal Behavior*. Santa Monica, CA: Rand.

Chaiken, J.M. and Chaiken, M.R. (1990) Drugs and predatory crime. In M. Tonry, and J. Wilson (eds), *Drugs and Crime* (vol. 13, pp. 203–239). Chicago: University of Chicago Press.

Chaiken, M. and Chaiken, J. (1990) Offender types and public policy. In N. Weiner, M. Zahn, and R. Sagi (eds), *Violence: Patterns, Causes, and Public Policy* (pp. 351–367). New York: Harcourt Brace Jovanovich.

Chermack, S.T. and Giancola, P. (1997) The relation between alcohol and aggression: An integrated biopsychosocial conceptualization. *Clinical Psychology Review*, 17(6): 621–649.

Cook, P.J. and Laub, J.H. (1998) The unprecedented epidemic in youth violence. In M. Tonry and M. Moore (eds), *Youth Violence* (pp. 27–64). Chicago: University of Chicago Press.

Cook, P.J. and Laub, J.H. (2002) After the epidemic: Recent trends in youth violence in the United States. *Crime and Justice*, 29: 1–37.

Cooper, A. and Smith, E. (2011) *Homicide Trends in the United States: 1980–2008*. Washington DC: Bureau of Justice Statistics, US Department of Justice.

Copes, H., Hochstetler, A., and Sandberg, S. (2015) Using a narrative framework to understand the drugs and violence nexus. *Criminal Justice Review*, 40(1): 32–46.

Curtis, R. (2003) Mike Agar: The story of crack. *Addiction Research and Theory*, 11(1): 39–42.

Dobash, R.P., Dobash, R.E., Cavanagh, K., and Lewis, R. (2002) *Homicide in Britain: Risk Factors, Situational Contexts and Lethal Intentions*. Swindon, UK: Economic and Social Research Council.

Exum, M.L. (2006) Alcohol and aggression: An integration of findings from experimental studies. *Journal of Criminal Justice*, 34: 131–145.

Fagan, J. and Chin, K.-L. (1989) Initiation into crack and cocaine: A tale of two epidemics. *Contemporary Drug Problems*, 16(4): 579–617.

Fagan, J. and Chin, K.-L. (1990) Violence as regulation and social control in the distribution of crack. In M. de la Rosa, E.Y. Lambert and B. Gropper (eds), *Drugs and Violence: Causes, Correlates and Consequences*. Rockville, MD: US Department of Health and Human Services, National Institute on Drug Abuse.

Fagan, J., Zimring, F.E., and Kim, J. (1998) Declining homicide in New York: a tale of two trends. *Journal of Criminal Law and Criminology*, 88(4): 1277–1323.

Felson, R.B. and Staff, J. (2010) The effects of alcohol intoxication on violent versus other offending. *Criminal Justice and Behavior*, 37(12): 1343–1360.

Forrest, G.G. and Gordon, R.H. (1990) Alcoholism, homicide, and violent behavior: The research evidence. In *Substance Abuse, Homicide, and Violent Behavior* (pp. 6–49). New York: Gardner Press.

Fox, J.A. (1996) *Trends in Juvenile Violence: A Report to the United States Attorney General on Current and Future Rates of Juvenile Offending*. Washington, DC: US Department of Justice, Bureau of Justice Statistics.

Goldstein, P.J. (1985) The drugs/violence nexus: A tripartite conceptual framework. *Journal of Drug Issues*, 15: 493–506.

Goldstein, P. (1989) Drugs and violent crime. In N. Weiner and W. Marvin (eds), *Pathways to Criminal Violence*. Newbury Park, CA: Sage.

Goldstein, P.J., Brownstein, H.H., and Ryan, P.J. (1992) Drug related homicide in New York: 1984 and 1988. *Crime and Delinquency*, 38(4): 459–476.

Goldstein, P., Brownstein, H., Ryan, P., and Bellucci, P. (1989) Crack and homicide in New York City, 1988: A conceptually based event analysis. *Contemporary Drug Problems*, 16: 651–687.

Gossop, M., Manning, V., and Ridge, G. (2006) Concurrent use and order of cocaine and alcohol: Behavioral differences between users of crack cocaine and cocaine powder. *Addiction*, 101(9): 1292–1298.

Hastings, J.E. and Hamberger, L.K. (1988) Personality characteristics of spouse abusers: A controlled comparison. *Violence and Victims*, 3: 31–48.

Hillbrand, M., Foster, H., and Hirt, M. (1991) Alcohol abuse, violence, and neurological impairment: A forensic study. *Journal of Interpersonal Violence*, 6(4): 411–422.

Holcomb, W.R. and Anderson, W.P. (1983) Alcohol and multiple drug abuse in accused murders. *Psychological Reports*, 52: 159–164.

Huffington Post, The (2012) Ronald Poppo tapes: face-eating victim says Rudy Eugene just ripped me to ribbons. Available online at http://www.huffingtonpost.com/2012/08/08/ronald-poppo-speaks-police-interview-tapes-face-eating_n_1758216.html (accessed February 11, 2015).

Inciardi, J. (1980) Youth, drugs and street crime. In F. Scarpitti and S. Datesman (eds), *Drugs and the Youth Culture*. Springfield, IL: Thomas.

Inciardi, J. (1986) *The War on Drugs: Heroin, Cocaine and Public Policy*. Palo Alto, CA: Mayfield.
Inciardi, J.A. (1987) Beyond cocaine: Basuco, crack, and other coca products. *Contemporary Drug Problems*, 14: 461.
Inciardi, J.A. (1990) The crack–violence connection within a population of hard-core adolescent offenders. In M. de la Rosa, E. Y. Lambert and B. Gropper (eds), *Drugs and Violence: Causes, Correlates and Consequences*. Rockville, MD: US Department of Health and Human Services, National Institute on Drug Abuse.
Inciardi, J.A. and Pottieger, A.E. (1995) Kids, crack, and crime. In J. Inciardi and K. McElrath (eds), *The American Drug Scene: An Anthology* (pp. 245–264). Los Angeles: Roxbury.
Johnson, B.D., Golub, A., and Fagan, J. (1995) Careers in crack, drug use, drug distribution, and nondrug criminality. *Crime and Delinquency*, 41(3): 275–295.
Kuhns, J.B. (2005) The dynamic nature of the drug use/serious violence relationship: A multi-causal approach. *Violence and Victims*, 20(4): 433–454.
Kuhns, J.B. and Clodfelter, T.A. (2009) Illicit drug related psychopharmacological violence: The current understanding within a causal context. *Aggression and Violent Behavior*, 14(1): 69–78.
Kuhns, J.B., Exum, M.L., Clodfelter, T.A., and Bottia, M. (2014) The prevalence of alcohol-involved homicide offending: A meta analytic review. *Homicide Studies*, 18(3): 251–270.
Kuhns, J.B., Wilson, D.B., Clodfelter, T.A., *et al.* (2011) A meta-analysis of alcohol toxicology study findings among homicide victims. *Addiction*, 106(1): 62–72.
Kuhns, J.B., Wilson, D.B., Maguire, E.R., *et al.* (2009) A meta-analysis of marijuana, cocaine and opiate toxicology study findings among homicide victims. *Addiction*, 104(7): 1122–1131.
Ladouceur, P. and Temple, M. (1985) Substance use among rapists: A comparison with other serious felons. *Crime and Delinquency*, 31(2): 269–294.
Magura, S. and Rosenblum, A. (2000) Modulating effect of alcohol use on cocaine use. *Addictive Behaviors*, 25(1): 117–122.
McDevitt, J., Braga, A., Nurge, D., and Buerger, M. (2003) Boston's youth violence prevention program: A comprehensive community-wide approach. In S.H. Decker (ed.), *Policing Gangs and Youth Violence* (pp. 53–76). Belmont, CA: Wadsworth.
Miron, J.A. (2001) Violence, guns, and drugs: A cross-country analysis. *Journal of Law and Economics*, 44(S2): 615–633.
Molotsky, I. (1988) Capital's homicide rate is at a record. *New York Times*, 14.
National Drug Enforcement Policy Board (1986) *Report to Congress on Crack Cocaine*. Washington, DC: National Institute of Justice.
Nurco, D.N., Hanlon, T.E., and Kinlock, T.W. (1991) Recent research on the relationship between illicit drug use and crime. *Behavioral Sciences and the Law*, 9: 221–242.
Pierce, R.J. and Kuhns, J.B. (2012) Alcohol and drug use among robbery-based homicide victims in Trinidad and Tobago. *Criminal Justice Policy Review*, 23(2): 211–230.
Pridemore, W.A. (2002) Vodka and violence: Alcohol consumption and homicide rates in Russia. *American Journal of Public Health*, 92(12): 1921–1930.
Puzzanchera, C. (2013) *Juvenile Arrests 2011*. Washington, DC: Office of Juvenile Justice and Delinquency Prevention.
Rath, D.G., Jarratt, L.G., and Leonardson, G. (1989) Rates of domestic violence against adult women by men partners. *Journal of the American Board of Family Practice*, 2(4): 227–233.
Reinarman, C. (1994) The social construction of drug scares. In P.A. Adler and P. Adler (eds), *Constructions of Deviance: Social Power, Context, and Interaction* (pp. 92–105). Belmont, CA: Wadsworth.

Reuter, P. (2009) Systemic violence in drug markets. *Crime, Law and Social Change*, 52(3), 275–284.

Riley, K.J. (1997) *Crack, Powder Cocaine, and Heroin: Drug Purchase and Use Patterns in Six Cities*. Washington, DC: National Institute of Justice.

Roberts, A. (1988) Substance abuse among men who batter their mates: The dangerous mix. *Journal of Substance Abuse Treatment*, 5: 83–87.

Roizen, J. (1993) Issues in the epidemiology of alcohol and violence. In S. Martin (ed.), *Alcohol and Interpersonal Violence: Fostering Multidisciplinary Perspectives*. Research Monograph #24. Rockville, MD: US Department of Health and Human Services.

Rossow, I. (2001) Alcohol and homicide: A cross-cultural comparison of the relationship in 14 European countries. *Addiction*, 96(S1): 77–92.

Schaller, J. (2013) Not for bathing: Bath salts and the new menace of synthetic drugs. *Journal Health Care, Law, and Policy*, 16: 245.

Snyder, H.N. (2011) *Arrest in the United States*, 1980–2009. Washington: Bureau of Justice Statistics.

Strug, D., Wish, E., Johnson, B., *et al.* (1984) The role of alcohol in the crimes of active heroin users. *Crime and Delinquency*, 30(4): 551–567.

Taylor, S. and Leonard, K. (1983) Alcohol and human physical aggression. In R.G. Geen and E.I. Donnerstein (eds), *Aggression: Theoretical and Empirical Reviews* (vol. 2, pp. 77–101). New York: Academic Press.

Ullman, S.E. and Najdowski, C. (2010) Understanding alcohol-related sexual assaults: Characteristics and consequences. *Violence and Victims*, 25(1): 29–44.

United Nations Office on Drugs and Crime (2011) *World Drug Report: 2011*. Vienna: United Nations.

United States Sentencing Commission (2002) *Cocaine and Federal Sentencing Policy*. Washington, DC: US Sentencing Commission.

Varano, S.P., McCluskey, J.D., and Bynum, T.S. (2004) Exploring the drugs-homicide connection. *Journal of Contemporary Criminal Justice*, 20(4): 369–392.

West, R., Drummond, C., and Eames, K. (1990) Alcohol consumption, problem drinking and antisocial behavior in a sample of college students. *British Journal of Addiction*, 85: 479–486.

Wieczorek, W.F., Welte, J.W., and Abel, E.L. (1990) Alcohol, drugs and murder: A study of convicted homicide offenders. *Journal of Criminal Justice*, 18: 217–227.

Wolff, C. (1988) As drug trade rises in Hartford, so does violent crime. *New York Times*, A1.

World Health Organization. (2015) Global status report on violence prevention 2014. Available online at at http://www.who.int/violence_injury_prevention/violence/en/ (accessed April 2015).

Further Reading

Baumer, E. (1994) Poverty, crack, and crime: A cross-city analysis. *Journal of Research in Crime and Delinquency*, 31(3): 311–327.

Goldstein, P.J., Brownstein, H.H., Ryan, P.J., and Bellucci, P.A. (1990) Crack and homicide in New York City, 1988: A conceptually based event analysis. *Contemporary Drug Problems*, 16: 651–687.

Nurco, D.N., Hanlon, T.E., Kinlock, T.W., and Duszynski, K.R. (1989) The consistency of types of criminal behavior over preaddiction and nonaddiction status periods. *Comprehensive Psychiatry*, 30(5): 391–340.

7

Sexual Homicide

A Review of Recent Empirical Evidence (2008 to 2015)

Heng Choon (Oliver) Chan

Introduction

The occurrence of sexual homicides is rare yet public interest and media attention paid to this form of homicide never ceases. In the United States, sexual homicide accounts for approximately 1 percent of all reported homicides annually (Chan and Heide 2009). Based on a 36-year period (1976–2011), Chan and Beauregard (2016a) found that only 0.86 percent of all reported homicide cases in the United States could be classified as having a sexual element. However, the prevalence of sexual homicides is reported to be much higher in some European nations. For instance, a 10-year study (1985–1994) conducted by Francis and Soothill (2000) found that 3.7 percent ($N = 178$), out of 4,860 individuals in England and Wales, were convicted of a homicide that occurred in sexual circumstances. In a 62-year period of study (1948–2010) conducted by Beauregard and Martineau (2013), about 600 potential sexual homicide cases were investigated by the Royal Canadian Mounted Police (Beauregard and Martineau 2013).

The discrepancy in sexual homicide reported rates could partly be due to the inconsistent criteria used to define sexual homicides. Law enforcement's unawareness of the underlying sexual dynamics in homicides may be a reason for the difficulty in the classification (Ressler, Burgess, and Douglas 1988). According to the US Federal Bureau of Investigation (FBI), in order for a homicide to be classified as sexual in nature, the index offense has to meet at least one criterion in addition to the death of the victim: (a) victim naked; (b) exposure of the sexual parts of the victim's body; (c) sexual positioning of the victim's body; (d) insertion of foreign objects into the victim's body cavities; (e) evidence of sexual intercourse; or

The Handbook of Homicide, First Edition. Edited by Fiona Brookman, Edward R. Maguire, and Mike Maguire.

(f) evidence of substitute sexual activity, sexual interest, or sadistic fantasy, such as victim genitalia mutilation (Ressler, Burgess, and Douglas 1988). Although the criteria suggested by the FBI are widely adopted, there exist many other definitions proposed by various researchers and practitioners in classifying sexual homicides (see Chan 2015; Chan and Heide 2009). Thus, the lack of a standardized definition or classification criteria is argued to be a key challenge to accurately classifying sexual homicides.

In view of this problem, Chan (2015) has recently proposed a revised definition of sexual homicide, with the aim of providing standardization in classifying sexual homicide. To rule a homicide as sexual, one of the following criteria has to be met: (a) physical evidence of pre-, peri-, and/or postmortem sexual assault (vaginal, oral, or anal) against the victim; (b) physical evidence of substitute sexual activity against the victim (e.g., exposure of the sexual parts or sexual positioning of the victim's body, insertion of foreign objects into the victim's body cavities, and genitalia mutilation) or in the immediate area of the victim's body (e.g., masturbation) reflecting the deviant or sadistic sexual fantasy of the offender; (c) a legally admissible offender confession of the sexual motive of the offense that intentionally or unintentionally results in a homicide; and (d) an indication of the sexual element(s) of the offense from the offender's personal belonging (e.g., journal entries and/or home computer).

Another potential byproduct of the lack of a standardized definition of sexual homicide is the relatively fewer numbers of published empirical studies prior to 2008. For example, for the 22-year period (1986–2007), there are only about 32 empirically informed published studies on sexual homicides (Chan and Heide 2009). The FBI was first to publish several studies on sexual homicides in the late 1980s. Most of these studies are conducted on North American samples and many of them are published in the early 2000s (i.e., 19 studies published between 2000 and 2007, 11 studies published in the 1990s, and only two studies published in the late 1980s).

It is the key aim of this chapter to extend the effort of Chan and Heide (2009) to synthesize the findings of the sexual homicide empirical studies published between 2008 and 2015. In this eight-year review period, 47 empirical studies have been published. Clearly, the number of empirical studies published per year has increased tremendously compared with the period prior to the 2000s. Specifically, five studies were published in 2008, two in 2009, eight in 2010, two in 2011, four in 2012, nine in 2013, seven in 2014, and ten in 2015[1]. The majority of these 47 studies were based on North America samples (i.e., 16 from the United States and 15 from Canada). The rest of the studies sampled offender populations from Germany (six studies), the United Kingdom (five studies), Finland (one study), and South Africa (one study). One study sampled offenders from both Canada and the United Kingdom, and the remaining two studies lack sampling specifics. Key findings from these 47 empirical studies are synthesized in five sections: (a) the sociodemographic characteristics of sexual homicide offenders (SHOs), (b) the developmental phase, (c) the pre-crime phase, (d) the crime phase, and (e) the post-crime phase.

Table 7.1 Empirical studies of sexual homicide offenders (SHOs) in review, 2008–2015 ($N = 47$).

Study (year published)	*Country of study*	*Number of SHO subjects*	*Gender of SHO subjects*	*Types of victims*	*Data source(s)*	*Year(s) of sample*	*Variable(s) of analysis*	*Crime stage(s) of analysis*
Year 2008 ($N = 5$)								
Abrahams *et al.* (2008)	South Africa	561	Not specified	Females	Medicolegal laboratory records	1999	Offender and victim demographics, modus operandi, crime scene profiles, and legal outcome	Crime and post-crime phases
Beauregard and Field (2008)	Canada	85	Males	Mixed (male and female child, adolescent, adult, and elderly victims)	Official records and psychological interview	1998–2005	Offender and victim demographics, psychiatric diagnostic features, modus operandi, and crime scene profiles	Pre-crime, crime, and post-crime phases
Beauregard *et al.* (2008)	Canada	77	Males	Mixed (male and female child, adolescent, adult, and elderly victims)	Official records and psychological interview	1998–2005	Offender demographics, developmental profiles, modus operandi, and crime scene profiles	Developmental, pre-crime, crime, and post-crime phases
Chan and Heide (2008)	United States	3,845	Males and females	Mixed (male and female child, adolescent, adult, and elderly victims)	FBI's official arrest data (UCR-SHR)	1976–2004	Offender and victim demographics and modus operandi	Crime phase
Hill *et al.* (2008)	Germany	139	Males	Not specified	Psychiatric and forensic reports and federal criminal records	1945–1991	Criminal histories, psychiatric diagnostic features, legal outcome, risk assessment results, and post-incarceration record	Post-crime phase

(*Continued*)

Table 7.1 (Contiuned)

Study (year published)	*Country of study*	*Number of SHO subjects*	*Gender of SHO subjects*	*Types of victims*	*Data source(s)*	*Year(s) of sample*	*Variable(s) of analysis*	*Crime stage(s) of analysis*
Year 2009 ($N=2$)								
Häkkänen-Nyholm *et al.* (2009)	Finland	18	Not specified	Not specified	Criminal reports from the Finnish Police Computerized Criminal Index File and Forensic psychiatric records from the Finnish National Authority for Medicolegal Affairs (NAMA)	1995–2004	Offender demographics, criminal histories, psychiatric diagnostic features, crime scene profiles	Developmental, pre-crime and crime phases
Juodis *et al.* (2009)	Canada	Not specified	Males	Mixed (male and female child, adolescent, adult, and elderly victims)	Official records and psychological assessment reports	Not specified	Offender and victim demographics, psychiatric diagnostic features, modus operandi, and crime scene profiles	Crime phase
Year 2010 ($N=8$)								
Myers *et al.* (2010)	United States	22	Juvenile males	Not specified	Official records, psychiatric interview, and medical reports	Not specified	Offender and victim demographics, psychiatric diagnostic features, legal outcome, and post-incarceration record	Developmental, pre-crime, crime, and post-crime phases

Briken *et al.* (2010)	Germany	166	Males	Not specified	Psychiatric and forensic reports, and federal criminal records	1945–1991	Psychological and psychiatric diagnostic features, and legal outcome	Pre-crime phase
Chan, Myers, and Heide (2010)	United States	3,868	Males and females	Mixed (male and female child, adolescent, adult, and elderly victims)	FBI's official arrest data (UCR-SHR)	1976–2005	Offender and victim demographics	Crime phase
Henry (2010)	United States	50	Not specified	Females	Forensic nursing postmortem medical-forensic records	1999–2007	Victim demographics, offense location, victim physical, and injury conditions	Crime phase
Mieczkowski and Beauregard (2010)	Canada	83	Males	Mixed (male and female child, adolescent, adult, and elderly victims)	Official records and psychological interview	1994–2005	Offender and victim demographics, modus operandi, and crime scene profiles	Pre-crime and crime phases
Schlesinger *et al.* (2010)	United States	38	Males	Mixed (male and female child, adolescent, adult, and elderly victims)	FBI Behavioral Science Unit's cases	1990s	Offender and victim demographics, and crime scene profiles	Crime phase

(*Continued*)

Table 7.1 (Contiuned)

Study (year published)	*Country of study*	*Number of SHO subjects*	*Gender of SHO subjects*	*Types of victims*	*Data source(s)*	*Year(s) of sample*	*Variable(s) of analysis*	*Crime stage(s) of analysis*
Spehr *et al.* (2010)	Germany	135	Males	Mixed (male and female child, adult, and elderly victims)	Psychiatric court reports	1945–1991	Offender demographics, developmental profiles, criminal histories, and psychological and psychiatric diagnostic features	Developmental and pre-crime phases
Stein, Schlesinger, and Pinizzotto (2010)	United States	16	Males	Mixed (male and female child, adolescent, adult, and elderly victims)	FBI Behavioral Science Unit's cases	Not specified	Crime scene profiles	Crime and post-crime phases
Year 2011 ($N = 2$)								
Koch *et al.* (2011)	Germany	166	Males	Mixed (male and female child, adolescent, adult, and elderly victims)	Forensic psychiatric court reports	1945–1991	Psychological and psychiatric diagnostic features	Pre-crime phase
Smith, Basile, and Karch (2011)	United States	Not specified	Not specified	Mixed (male and female child, adolescent, adult, and elderly victims)	Official data from the National Violent Death Reporting System (NVDRS)	2003–2007	Victim demographics and crime scene profiles	Crime phase

Year 2012 ($N=4$)								
Beauregard and Mieczkowski (2012)	Canada	Not specified	Males	Mixed (male and female child, adolescent, adult, and elderly victims)	Official records and psychological interview	1994–2005	Victim demographics, modus operandi, and crime scene profiles	Pre-crime and crime phases
Hill *et al.* (2012)	Germany	90	Males	Not specified	Forensic psychiatric court reports	1945–1991	Psychiatric diagnostic features, legal outcome, risk assessment results, and post-incarceration record	Post-crime phase
Mieczkowski and Beauregard (2012)	Canada	83	Males	Mixed (male and female child, adolescent, adult, and elderly victims)	Official records and psychological interview	1994–2005	Offender demographics, modus operandi, and crime scene profiles	Crime phase
Myers and Chan (2012)	United States	445	Juvenile males and females	Mixed (male and female child, adolescent, adult, and elderly victims on homosexual-oriented killings)	FBI's official arrest data (UCR-SHR)	1976–2005	Offender and victim demographics and modus operandi	Crime phase
Year 2013 ($N=9$)								
Beauregard and Martineau (2013)	Canada	350	Males	Mixed (male and female child, adolescent, adult, and elderly victims)	Official data from the Royal Canadian Mounted Police (RCMP)	1948–2010	Offender and victim demographics, modus operandi, and crime scene profiles	Pre-crime, crime, and post-crime phases

(*Continued*)

Table 7.1 (Contiuned)

Study (year published)	*Country of study*	*Number of SHO subjects*	*Gender of SHO subjects*	*Types of victims*	*Data source(s)*	*Year(s) of sample*	*Variable(s) of analysis*	*Crime stage(s) of analysis*
Bennell *et al.* (2013)	United States	53	Males	Not specified	Homicide Investigation and Tracking System (HITS) and Violent Criminal Apprehension Program (ViCAP) databases	Not specified	Offender demographics, criminal histories, psychological features, and crime scene profiles	Pre-crime, crime, and post-crime phases
Chan and Frei (2013)	United States	204	Females	Mixed (male and female child, adolescent, adult, and elderly victims)	FBI's official arrest data (UCR-SHR)	1976–2007	Offender and victim demographics and modus operandi	Crime phase
Chan, Frei, and Myers (2013)	United States	204	Females	Mixed (male and female child, adolescent, adult, and elderly victims)	FBI's official arrest data (UCR-SHR)	1976–2007	Offender and victim demographics, offense location, and modus operandi	Crime phase
Chan, Heide, and Myers (2013)	United States	3,868	Males and females	Mixed (male and female child, adolescent, adult, and elderly victims)	FBI's official arrest data (UCR-SHR)	1976–2005	Offender and victim demographics and modus operandi	Crime phase
Healey, Lussier, and Beauregard (2013)	Canada	86	Males	Females	Official records and psychological interview	1994–2000	Offender demographics, modus operandi, and crime scene profiles	Pre-crime and crime phases
Radojević *et al.* (2013)	Not specified	60	Not specified	Mixed (male and female child, adolescent, adult, and elderly victims)	Autopsy reports	Not specified	Crime scene profiles	Crime phase

Rettenberger *et al.* (2013)	Germany	163	Males	Not specified	Psychiatric and forensic reports, and federal criminal records	1945–1991	Psychological and psychiatric diagnostic features	Developmental and pre-crime phases
Sewall, Krupp, and Lalumière (2013)	Not specified	82	Males	No specified	Biographies available from the TruTV website	Not specified	Offender demographics, psychosocial developmental background, psychological and psychiatric diagnostic features, and crime scene profiles	Developmental, pre-crime, and crime phases
Year 2014 ($N = 7$)								
Balemba, Beauregard, and Martineau (2014)	Canada	350	Males	Mixed (male and female child, adolescent, adult, and elderly victims)	Official data from the Royal Canadian Mounted Police (RCMP)	1948–2010	Crime scene profiles	Crime phase
Chan and Beauregard (2014; * published in print in 2016)	United States	2,472	Males	Mixed (male and female child, adolescent, adult, and elderly victims)	FBI's official arrest data (UCR-SHR)	1976–2011	Offender and victim demographics, offense location, and modus operandi	Crime phase
DeLisi (2014)	United States	618	Males	Not specified	Official data on arrest, conviction, incarceration	2004	Offender criminal histories	Pre-crime and crime phases
Healey *et al.* (2014)	Canada and United Kingdom	131	Males	Not specified	Official records and psychological interview	1994–2000 (Canada) 1998–2000 (United Kingdom)	Modus operandi, crime scene profiles	Pre-crime and crime phases

(Continued)

Table 7.1 (Contiuned)

Study (year published)	*Country of study*	*Number of SHO subjects*	*Gender of SHO subjects*	*Types of victims*	*Data source(s)*	*Year(s) of sample*	*Variable(s) of analysis*	*Crime stage(s) of analysis*
Khachatryan *et al.* (2014)	United States	59	Juvenile males	Not specified	Official records and psychosocial interview	1982–2012	Legal outcome and post-incarceration record	Post-crime phase
Myers, Chan, and Mariano (2014)	United States	3,848	Males and females	Mixed (male and female child, adolescent, adult, and elderly victims)	FBI's official arrest data (UCR-SHR)	1976–2007	Offender demographics	Crime phase
Vettor, Beech, and Woodhams (2014)	United Kingdom	38	Not specified	Mixed (male and female child, adolescent, adult, and elderly victims)	Prison records, and psychological and psychiatric reports	1998–2002	Offender and victim demographics, developmental profiles, modus operandi, and crime scene profiles	Developmental, pre-crime, and crime phases
Year 2015 ($N = 10$)								
Beauregard and Martineau (2015)	Canada	350	Males	Mixed (male and female child and adult victims)	Official data from the Royal Canadian Mounted Police (RCMP)	1948–2010	Offender and victim demographics, modus operandi, and crime scene profiles	Pre-crime, crime, and post-crime phases
Chan (2015)	Canada	55	Males	Mixed (male and female child, adolescent, adult, and elderly victims)	Official records and psychological interview	1995–2005	Offender and victim demographics, developmental profiles, and modus operandi	Developmental, pre-crime, and crime phases
Chan and Beauregard (2015*; published in print in 2016)	Canada	74	Males	Mixed (male and female child, adolescent, adult, and elderly victims)	Official records and psychological interview	1994–2005	Offender and victim demographics, modus operandi, crime scene profiles, and psychiatric diagnostic features	Pre-crime and crime phases

Chan, Beauregard, and Myers (2015)	Canada	86	Males	Mixed (male and female child, adolescent, adult, and elderly victims)	Official records and psychological interview	1994–2005	Offender and victim demographics, modus operandi, crime scene profiles, and psychiatric diagnostic features	Pre-crime and crime phases
Greenall and Richardson (2015)	Great Britain	81	Adult males	Stranger females	Official data from the National Crime Agency (NCA)	1970–2010	Offender and victim demographics, criminal histories, offense location, and modus operandi	Crime phase
Greenall and Wright (2015)	Great Britain	81	Adult males	Stranger adult females	Official data from the National Crime Agency (NCA)	1970–2010	Offender demographics and criminal histories	Crime phase
Healey and Beauregard (2015)	Canada	83	Adult males	Not specified	Official records and psychological interview	Not specified	Offender and victim demographics, developmental profiles, modus operandi, and crime scene profiles	Developmental, pre-crime, and crime phases
Kerr and Beech (2015)	United Kingdom	14	Adult males	Mixed	Prison records, and psychological and psychiatric reports	Not specified	Offender and victim demographics, modus operandi, and crime scene profiles	Pre-crime and crime phases
Martineau and Beauregard (2015)	Canada	350	Males	Mixed (male and female child, adolescent, adult, and elderly victims)	Official data from the Royal Canadian Mounted Police (RCMP)	1948–2010	Offender and victim demographics, modus operandi, and crime scene profiles	Pre-crime, crime, and post-crime phases
Stefanska *et al.* (2015)	United Kingdom	129	Adult males	Mixed (female adolescent, adult, and elderly victims)	Prison records, and psychological and psychiatric reports	1954–2012	Offender and victim demographics, modus operandi, and crime scene profiles	Pre-crime, crime, and post-crime phases

The Sociodemographic Characteristics of SHOs

Most sexual homicides are committed by males (95%; Chan, Myers, and Heide 2010; Myers and Chan 2012) with less than 5 percent of those arrested are females (Chan and Frei 2013; Chan, Frei, and Myers 2013). Approximately 88 percent of SHOs are adults while the remaining 12 percent are juveniles under 18 (Chan, Heide, and Myers 2013; Chan, Myers, and Heide 2010). Relative to juveniles, more adult SHOs are found in single-victim males (92% versus 8%; Chan and Beauregard 2016a). The offenders' mean age at arrest is between 25 and 34 years, depending on samples recruited in different countries ($N = 18$ to 2,472; e.g., Beauregard and Martineau 2013; Chan 2015; Chan and Beauregard 2016a, 2016b; Greenall and Richardson 2015; Rettenberger *et al.* 2013; Stefanska *et al.* 2015). The most likely age at arrest for sexual homicide is 21 years, with two-thirds of the offenders committing sexual homicide between 18 and 35 years (Myers, Chan, and Mariano 2014).

Research indicates that most victims are females (Beauregard and Martineau 2013; Chan and Beauregard 2016a; Chan, Beauregard, and Myers 2015; Smith, Basile, and Karch 2011) and a large proportion of the female victims (70% to 80%) are at least 18 years old (e.g., Chan, Myers, and Heide 2010, Chan, Beauregard, and Myers 2015; Greenall and Richardson 2015). These victims are, on average, aged between 27 and 37 years, depending on the samples recruited (e.g., Chan 2015; Greenall and Richardson 2015; Myers, Chan, and Mariano 2014). The mean age for victims of serial SHOs (23 years) is significantly younger than victims of nonserial SHOs (29 years; Chan, Beauregard, and Myers 2015). Similarly, the majority of female offenders' victims (74%) are males (Chan and Frei 2013; Chan, Frei, and Myers 2013).

Although most offenders (59% to 95%) and victims (63% to 93%) are whites (e.g., Chan 2015; Chan, Beauregard, and Myers 2015; Greenall and Richardson 2015; Stefanska *et al.* 2015), black offenders in the United States are disproportionately overrepresented in the SHO population (41%) given their relatively low representation in the overall US population (13%; Chan, Myers, and Heide 2010). Similar trends in offenders' racial background are also observed in female sexual killers (Chan, Frei, and Myers 2013). In the United States, white SHOs are highly likely to kill within their own race (i.e., intra-racial killing), whereas black SHOs murdered both intra-racially and inter-racially (i.e., outside of their race) with the propensity of their killing inter-racially increasing as the age of their victim increased (Chan, Myers, and Heide 2010). Although opposite-sex sexual murders are also common among female SHOs, American white females are found to engage in more same-sex killings (32%) than their black counterparts (19%; Chan, Frei, and Myers 2013).

Findings of previous school performance among sexual killers in recent studies are mixed; with some studies reporting that their sample of sexual killers are either under-educated or school dropouts (Rettenberger *et al.* 2013;

Spehr *et al.* 2010), while others found that SHOs are educated to at least secondary or high school (Healey, Lussier, and Beauregard 2013). Average to slightly above average mean scores on intelligence tests (mean IQ ranges from approximately 99 to 103) is reported in several studies (Häkkänen-Nyholm *et al.* 2009; Myers *et al.* 2010; Spehr *et al.* 2010). Many SHOs are reported to be single (e.g., unmarried, divorced, and widowed) at the time of offense, with a range of 69 percent to 87 percent (e.g., Beauregard and Field 2008; Beauregard and Martineau 2013; Chan 2015; Chan, Beauregard, and Myers 2015; Martineau and Beauregard 2015).

Greenall and Richardson (2015) found that although the majority of British adult male SHOs who perpetrated female stranger homicides were employed at the time of offense (64%), most of their employment is either static (i.e., the nature of work does not require the worker to travel during work, e.g., factory worker) or mobile in nature (i.e., the nature of work requires the worker to travel during work, e.g., taxi driver, construction worker). Nearly half (46%) of Stefanska and colleagues' (2015) sample of nonserial sexual killers were reported to either holding full-time (41.3%) or part-time (4.7%) employment at the time of offense. The remaining offenders were unemployed (36%). Unemployment among sexual killers is commonly observed in Häkkänen-Nyholm *et al.*'s (2009) sample of Finnish offenders (50%), Rettenberger *et al.* (2013) and Spehr *et al.*'s (2010) sample of German offenders (30%), Healey, Lussier, and Beauregard's (2013) sample of Canadian offenders (19%), and Abrahams *et al.*'s (2008) sample of South African offenders (18%). Even if these offenders are employed at the time of offense, their status of employment is relatively low and the work nature does not require high technological skills (e.g., farm worker, blue-collar worker).

Criminal histories are common among sexual murderers. In Greenall and Richardson's (2015) study, about two-thirds (64%) of British adult male SHOs are reported to have previous criminal convictions, with theft being the most common offense (87%) among recidivists. An average of 26 past convictions is found in Greenall and Wright's (2015) sample of British male SHOs. Sexual murderers in Beauregard and Martineau's (2013) Canadian sample also have a diverse criminal history, with an average of 1.7 violent offense convictions, 0.4 sexual offense convictions, and 7.3 property offense convictions. In another sample of Canadian SHOs, Beauregard *et al.* (2008) found that 68 percent of their sample who victimized children and adult females had prior convictions in nonsexual nonviolent offenses (e.g., drug offenses), nonsexual violent offenses (e.g., physical assault), or sexual offenses with or without contacts (e.g., indecent exposure, voyeurism, and obscene phone calls). Nearly 89 percent of Häkkänen-Nyholm *et al.*'s (2009) sample of Finnish SHOs were found to have a criminal history prior to their index offense; with 56 percent, 25 percent, and 19 percent found to have at least one prior conviction for violent, sexual, and homicidal offenses, respectively. Moreover, relative to nonhomicidal counterparts, sexual murderers are reported to have a higher prevalence of previous sexual offense.

A brief summary

The following are the major highlights with regards to the sociodemographic characteristics of SHOs.

- Most sexual homicides are committed by adult male offenders, with the mean age at arrest between 25 and 34 years.
- Most victims are female adults and the mean age is between 27 and 37 years. Victims of serial SHOs (23 years) are on average much younger than victims of nonserial SHOs (29 years). Female offenders also reported to murder predominantly males.
- Most SHOs and their victims are whites. In the United States, intra-racial killings are more often among white SHOs, while black SHOs killed both inter- and intra-racially.
- Most SHOs are reported to be single (e.g., unmarried, divorced, and widowed) at the time of offense, with a criminal history background. Unemployment is also common among SHOs. Even if they are employed, their work status is relatively low with a job nature that does not require high technological skills.

The Offending Patterns and Process of SHOs

The process of an offender to commit a sexual murder does not begin when the victim is identified and end when the victim is killed. Instead, the process of becoming a sexual killer starts much earlier in life during his/her physical, psychological, and sociological development stages (i.e., the developmental phase). A psychologically damaging childhood and adolescent development seems to be a major factor in shaping an individual to commit violent sexual offenses (Chan, Heide, and Beauregard 2011). Consequent to the defects in psychological development, predisposing factors (e.g., indulgence in deviant fantasies is insufficient to produced expected sexual euphoria, social loneliness) often occur prior to the offense commission (i.e., the pre-crime phase). Once the individual is substantially determined to carry out the offense, he/she would begin the process of hunting for a victim and subsequently assaulting and murdering the victim (i.e., the crime phase). The killing process does not end when the victim is sexually murdered. Post-offense behaviors (e.g., victim's body disposal and police arrest avoidance method to be employed) are typically performed during this phase (i.e., post-crime phase). Other related topics (e.g., risk and rate of recidivism) are also pertinent issues that are categorized under this phase of offense.

The developmental phase of sexual homicide

Consistent with previous studies (see Chan and Heide 2009), recent research has consistently reported that sexual murderers suffer from problems experienced in their childhood and adolescence. Factors leading to unhealthy development may include physical, psychological, and sexual abuse, physical neglect, and emotional deprivation by parents or primary caregivers (Beauregard *et al.* 2008; Spehr *et al.* 2010). Relative to nonsexual killers, some studies have found that SHOs have experienced higher childhood sexual and physical abuse and have suffered from childhood mental health problems (e.g., Häkkänen-Nyholm *et al.*'s (2009) Finnish study and Koch *et al.*'s (2011) German study). However, a low base rate of sexual abuse (9%) among juvenile SHOs is evident in Myers *et al.*'s (2010) study of American juveniles.

The developmental breakdown, as an outcome of the failure to develop secure attachment with parents or primary caregivers, can lead to psychosocial deficits such as low self-esteem or self-image and lack of skills necessary to establish and maintain prosocial relationship with peers (Chan and Heide 2009; Healey and Beauregard 2015; Reckdenwald, Mancini, and Beauregard 2014). Childhood behavioral problems, such as enuresis or encopresis, chronic lying, animal cruelty, fire setting, and school problems are frequently observed in sexual murderers (Beauregard *et al.* 2008; Spehr *et al.* 2010). Negative childhood experiences, particularly sexual abuse, may be seen as a risk factor leading to the development of deviant and/or sadistic sexual fantasies. With limited exposure to quality relationships with prosocial peers, these socially isolated individuals may intensify their engagement and reliance in deviant sexual fantasies that may provide them with a sense of personal relief and achievement, which seems otherwise unachievable in real life (Chan and Heide 2009). Recent studies again confirmed that problems with social and interpersonal skills are generally observed in the early years of SHOs. This issue is more apparent in Beauregard *et al.*'s (2008) sample of Canadian SHOs who victimized children compared to those who assaulted adult females. Similarly, German SHOs who victimized only child victims are found to report a higher level of social isolation as a child than those who assaulted only adult victims (Spehr *et al.* 2010). Healey and Beauregard (2015) found that both persistent low self-esteem and deviant sexual interests are important predictors of subsequent commission of a sexual homicide.

Some interesting findings emerged from the study by Rettenberger *et al.* (2013) of sexual murderers' early childhood genital-related physical problems and abnormalities. Notably, nearly one-fifth of the 163 German SHOs described symptoms and indicators of genital abnormalities in early childhood and/or reported having at least one of the relevant diagnoses (e.g., phimosis, cryptorchidism, inguinal or scrotal hernia, and hypospadias). Relative to those without genital abnormalities, sexual killers with genital abnormalities are found to show indicators for more sexual dysfunctions (e.g., erectile dysfunction) and a significantly higher tendency toward masochistic sexual interests in their later life.

A brief summary The following are the major highlights with regards to the developmental phase of sexual homicide:

- Developmental issues during childhood and adolescence are common among SHOs, with physical and sexual abuse as a child being more prevalent. Childhood behavioral problems (e.g., enuresis or encopresis, chronic lying, animal cruelty, fire setting, and school problems) are frequently observed in SHOs. Early childhood genital-related physical problems and abnormalities are also reported among SHOs.

- Consequent to the failure to develop secure attachment with parents or primary caregivers, psychosocial deficits, such as low self-esteem or self-image and the lack of social skills to establish and maintain prosocial peer relationship, are evident.
- These negative childhood and/or adolescence experiences may be seen as a risk factor leading to the development of deviant and/or sadistic sexual fantasies, which may subsequently intensify from the lack of exposure to quality relationships with prosocial peers. The engagement and reliance in deviant sexual fantasies could offer a sense of personal relief and achievement that seems otherwise unachievable in real life.

The pre-crime phase of sexual homicide

The extant literature indicates that psychopathology is common among sexual murderers. Personality disorders (or maladaptive traits) and paraphilias (or paraphilic behaviors) are consistently diagnosed in SHOs (Chan and Heide 2009). Other offender psychopathologies, such as mood disorder, schizophrenia, psychosis, and impulsive disorder, are also reported in recent research (Koch *et al.* 2011).

Antisocial personality disorder (PD) or traits are the most common PD diagnosis, with the prevalence ranging from 25 percent to 58 percent in recent studies (e.g., Briken *et al.* 2010; Chan and Beauregard 2016b; Chan, Beauregard, and Myers 2015; Koch *et al.* 2011). Schizoid, borderline, narcissistic, dependent, and obsessive-compulsive personality traits and disorders have also been frequently observed, especially among those who have killed in a serial manner (Chan, Beauregard, and Myers 2015) and those who are also diagnosed with paraphilias or paraphilia-related disorders (Briken *et al.* 2010). The diagnosis of psychopathy or psychopathic traits is also prevalent among SHOs (e.g., Hill *et al.* 2012; Juodis *et al.* 2009), particularly when comparing with nonsexual killers (Häkkänen-Nyholm *et al.* 2009).

In terms of paraphilias, sexual sadism is reported to be the most common paraphilia among SHOs (Healey, Lussier, and Beauregard 2013). The prevalence rate of sexual sadism or sadistic behaviors varies from 18 percent to 73 percent in recent studies (e.g., Chan and Beauregard 2016b; Chan, Beauregard, and Myers 2015; Myers *et al.* 2010). Diagnosis of other paraphilias and/or the co-occurrence of multiple paraphilias are possible; with fetishism, tranvestism, exhibitionism, and voyeurism often co-occurring (Myers *et al.* 2008). Other commonly observed paraphilias or paraphilic behaviors among SHOs include heterosexual and/or homosexual pedophilia, partialism, sexual masochism, and necrophilia (e.g., Chan and Beauregard 2016b; Chan, Beauregard, and Myers 2015; Stein, Schlesinger, and Pinizzotto 2010). In the study of Canadian serial and nonserial sexual murderers by Chan and colleagues (2015), serial offenders are found to display significantly more paraphilic behaviors (e.g., exhibitionism, homosexual pedophilia, sexual masochism, voyeurism, and partialism) than their nonserial counterparts. In another study, Chan and Beauregard (2016b) indicate that Canadian sexual killers reported significantly more paraphilic behaviors (e.g., exhibitionism, fetishism, frotteurism, homosexual pedophilia, sexual masochism, and partialism) than nonhomicidal sexual offenders. Briken and colleagues (2010), conversely, reported that paraphilia-related disorders, such as compulsive masturbation, promiscuity, pornography or telephone sex dependence, and severe desire incompatibility, are also frequently observed in their sample of German SHOs.

Several recent studies have also examined various precipitating factors that led sexual murderers to commit their offense. Among others, offenders' indulgence in deviant sexual fantasies prior to offending is frequently reported (e.g., Beauregard and Field 2008; Chan 2015; Chan and Beauregard 2016b). Deviant sexual fantasies typically serve as the offenders' gateway to control and sexual euphoria. When the mere indulgence in deviant sexual fantasies is insufficient to produce expected sexual euphoria, offenders may begin to seek alternatives and act out their deviant sexual fantasies to achieve psychological gratification (Chan, Heide, and Beauregard 2011). Relative to SHOs of adult females, those who victimized children are reported to indulge in more frequent deviant sexual fantasies (Beauregard *et al.* 2008). Chan and Beauregard (2015) found that significantly more sexual killers reported to have indulged in deviant sexual fantasies 48 hours prior to their offense than nonhomicidal sexual offenders.

The use of drugs and/or alcohol prior to the commission of sexual homicide or with problems of substance dependence is not uncommon among SHOs (e.g., Abrahams *et al.* 2008; Chan 2015; Martineau and Beauregard 2015). Findings on the influence of substance use on the offense execution are yet inconclusive as some studies found support of such effects (e.g., Beauregard *et al.* 2008; Mieczkowski and Beauregard 2012), while others failed to find any connections (e.g., Beauregard and Mieczkowski 2012; Mieczkowski and Beauregard 2010). Furthermore, the use of pornographic materials has also been cited as a precipitator of sexual murder (Beauregard *et al.* 2008; Chan 2015; Mieczkowski and Beauregard 2010, 2012). Other reported precipitators include prior contacts with the victim; victim under the influence of drugs and/or alcohol; and unemployment, relational/interpersonal issues, and accelerating sexual problems occurred immediately prior to the offense (Beauregard and Field 2008; Beauregard *et al.* 2008; Chan 2015).

A brief summary The following are the major highlights with regards to the precrime phase of sexual homicide.

- Psychopathology is common, with PDs (or maladaptive traits) and paraphilias (or paraphilic behaviors) consistently diagnosed in SHOs.
- Antisocial PDs or traits are the most commonly diagnosed PD in SHOs. The diagnosis of psychopathy or psychopathic traits is also prevalent among SHOs.

- Sexual sadism is reported to be the most common paraphilia among SHOs, with the co-occurrence of multiple paraphilias also possible. Other common diagnoses of paraphilia or paraphilic behaviors include heterosexual and/or homosexual pedophilia, partialism, sexual masochism, and necrophilia.
- The major precipitating factors that led to the commission of sexual homicide include the offenders' indulgence in deviant sexual fantasies, the use of drugs and/or alcohol or with problems of substance dependence, and the use of pornographic materials prior to their offense.

The crime phase of sexual homicide

Crime characteristics or crime scene behaviors are the most widely examined aspect in recent empirical studies. Nearly 83 percent ($N = 39$) of the listed recent studies have analyzed crime scene variables. SHOs are found to engage in at least a minimal level of premeditation prior to their criminal attack (Chan and Heide 2009); and this practice is again demonstrated in recent studies, with the prevalence ranging from 19 percent to 77 percent (e.g., Beauregard and Martineau 2015; Chan and Beauregard 2016b; Chan, Beauregard, and Myers 2015; Healey, Lussier, and Beauregard 2013; Healey *et al.* 2014; Stefanska *et al.* 2015). As part of the offending plan, victims are typically carefully selected by SHOs for distinctive physical and/or personality characteristics. The rate ranging from 19 percent to 47 percent (e.g., Chan and Beauregard 2016b; Chan, Beauregard, and Myers 2015; Healey *et al.* 2014; Martineau and Beauregard 2015), with the con approach (i.e., to use ruse or ploy to gain the victim's trust or to lower their guard) more frequently observed (Beauregard and Martineau 2013; Martineau and Beauregard 2015). Although most offenders are known to their victim (Chan and Beauregard 2016b; Martineau and Beauregard 2015), strangers are also targeted especially by serial SHOs (Chan, Beauregard, and Myers 2015). Random victim selection is less often described in recent research. Most offenses are committed at night, with indoor and outdoor crime scenes equally prevalent (e.g., Greenall and Richardson 2015; Healey *et al.* 2014; Mieczkowski and Beauregard 2010). SHOs committed their offense for different motivations. Sexual murderers could kill following negative emotions (i.e., anger), deviant urges (i.e., sadism), sexual pleasure, or situational precipitation (e.g., Balemba, Beauregard, and Martineau 2014; Bennell *et al.* 2013; Healey *et al.* 2014; Kerr and Beech 2015). Outcomes of these different motivations often could lead to either instrumental or expressive aggression. Instrumental aggression is typically invoked when the offender is interested in possessing something that he/she currently lack but which is possessed by the victim; while expressive aggression often occurs as a reaction to provocation or anger and the ultimate intention is to cause harm to the victim (see Adjorlolo and Chan 2015). Hence, different offender typologies have been developed over the years to explicate the distinctiveness of each sexual murderer type (see Chan 2015).

Weapon use in sexual homicides is common, with the prevalence rate ranging from 54 percent to 78 percent in recent studies (e.g., Beauregard and Martineau 2013, 2015;

Chan and Beauregard 2016b; Martineau and Beauregard 2015). Although the dominant cause of death among victims differed in recent studies, killing by personal weapons (e.g., strangulation, beating, asphyxiation, drowning, and other methods with bare hands and feet) and edged weapons (e.g., stabbing and cutting with knife) remain the most commonly employed methods across studies (e.g., Beauregard and Martineau 2013; Chan and Beauregard 2016a; Chan, Heide, and Myers 2013; Greenall and Richardson 2015; Radojević *et al.* 2013). The use of firearms in sexual homicides is less common. However, studies conducted on female and juvenile SHOs found that firearms are more often used in killing their victim than their male and adult counterparts (Chan and Frei 2013; Chan, Frei, and Myers 2013; Myers and Chan 2012). Clearly, the choice of weapon used is partly dictated by the offender–victim differential in physical strength.

However, the possibility to "enjoy" the killing process by using a more intimate method—personal weapons—cannot be denied among SHOs (Chan and Heide 2009). Ritualistic and signature behaviors (e.g., binding, torturing, posing, humiliation, mutilation, overkill, dismemberment, foreign object insertion, and necrophilic acts) that are used to satisfy the offenders' deviant sexual fantasies and urges are often evident in sexual homicides (e.g., Beauregard and Martineau 2013; Chan, Beauregard, and Myers 2015; Radojević *et al.* 2013). Sadistic acts, arguably a type of ritualistic behavior, may be performed on the victim, especially for SHOs who are sadists and have innate sadistic urges (Healey, Lussier, and Beauregard 2013). Physical restraints are often used on the victim by sexual murderers (Beauregard and Martineau 2013; Martineau and Beauregard 2015; Stefanska *et al.* 2015) for purposes of either practicality or to satisfy their deviant urges. Sexual killers are also reported to have spent more time with their victim compared to nonhomicidal sexual offenders (Mieczkowski and Beauregard 2010). Sexual murderers who killed only children are also found to spend more time at the crime scene with their victim than those who victimized only adult females (Beauregard *et al.* 2008; Spehr *et al.* 2010).

A brief summary The following are the major highlights with regards to the crime phase of sexual homicide:

- Most SHOs engaged in at least a minimal level of premeditation prior to their criminal offense. Victims are often carefully selected for their distinctive physical and/or personality characteristics. The con approach is more frequently used by offenders and most offenses are committed at night.
- Weapon use in sexual homicides is common, with killing by personal weapons (e.g., strangulation, beating, asphyxiation, drowning, and other methods with bare hands and feet) and edged weapons (e.g., stabbing and cutting with knife) the most commonly employed methods by SHOs.
- Ritualistic and signature behaviors (e.g., binding, torturing, posing, humiliation, mutilation, overkill, dismemberment, foreign object insertion, and necrophilic acts) intended to satiate the offenders' deviant sexual fantasies and urges are often evident in sexual homicides.

The post-crime phase of sexual homicide

Sexual murderers, after committing the crime and depending on the nature of their offense, may or may not adopt any strategy to avoid detection. Sexual killers who are forensically aware are less likely to penetrate their victim vaginally, leave any semen, or steal or remove items from the crime scene. Conversely, SHOs who are sloppy or reckless are more likely to be apprehended much earlier as their semen is more likely to be detected at the crime scene (Balemba, Beauregard, and Martineau 2014). Besides, the condition of the victim's body after the killing is likely to suggest not only the SHO's modus operandi (i.e., method of operation) but also the likelihood of the victim's body to be recovered. In turn, it also suggests the tendency of the offender to be apprehended. Sexual murderers who are forensically aware or more organized in their psychological characteristics are more likely to conceal or move their victim to another location after killing the victim, whereas those who are less forensically aware or who are disorganized/sloppy are more likely to leave their victim at the crime scene without expending additional effort to delay the victim's recovery (Beauregard and Field 2008). Beauregard and colleagues (2008) found that SHOs who only victimized children are more likely to conceal their victim's corpse than those who murdered only adult females.

On the criminal mobility aspect of the offending process, Martineau and Beauregard (2015) observed that sexual killers who left their victim's corpse at the scene are less likely to travel at any point during their offense. Beauregard and colleagues (2008) found that a large majority (61%) of their sample admitted all acts committed during their offense. Relative to those who only victimized adult females, more SHOs of children are arrested because of police investigation, admitting their offense when arrested, and admitting the harm they have done to the victim. Similar trends were also observed in Spehr *et al.*'s (2010) sample of German SHOs where sexual killers of children more readily admitted responsibility upon arrest than sexual murderers of adults.

Several recent studies have examined the recidivism rate of SHOs upon their incarceration (Khachatryan *et al.* 2014; Hill *et al.* 2008; Myers *et al.* 2010). The use of Psychopathy Checklist-Revised (PCL-R), Historical-Clinical-Risk Management-20 (HCR-20), Sexual Violence Risk-20 (SVR-20), and Static-99 in predicting recidivism risk among sexual murderers has demonstrated to be valid predicting tools in Hill *et al.*'s (2012) sample of 90 German offenders. The first follow-up study on SHOs was conducted by Hill *et al.* (2008) on their sample of 90 German offenders for a 10-year period. The time at risk of 20 years in their study are 23 percent for sexual offenses, 18 percent for nonsexual offenses, 35 percent for any violent offenses, and 58 percent for nonviolent offenses. An estimated 12 percent sexual recidivism rate is found after six years' time at risk, with the majority of any violent reoffending occurred during the first five years after release. Myers and colleagues (2010) conducted the first follow-up study that focused solely on juvenile SHOs. With 11 offenders, five juveniles remained free from any additional convictions for an average of nine years, while the remaining six juveniles reoffended within an average of 4.4 years. Out of the six recidivists, three evolved into serial SHOs. These serial SHOs survived an average of 5.5 years before committing another sexual homicide. The other three recidivists had remained conviction-free for an average of 3.6 years in the community prior to committing a new nonsexual offense. Khachatryan and colleagues (2014) conducted the most recent and longest follow-up recidivism study on juvenile sexual murderers. Six out of eight juvenile SHOs are release from prison during the 30-year follow-up period, with four out of six released juveniles subsequently rearrested for offenses related to violence, drugs, property, and possession of a firearm. None of them were rearrested for serious violent offenses such as homicide and sexual assault.

A brief summary The following are the major highlights with regards to the post-crime phase of sexual homicide.

- Sexual murderers who are forensically aware are more likely to adopt strategies to avoid detection (e.g., not to penetrate their victim vaginally, not to leave any semen, not to steal or remove items from the crime scene, and to conceal or move the victim's body to another location after the murder), while those who are sloppy or reckless are most likely to be arrested much earlier. SHOs who left their victim's corpse at the scene are less likely to travel at any point during their offense.
- Most SHOs are found to confess to their offense after being apprehended. This pattern is especially prominent among offenders who killed children compared to those who only victimized adult females.
- SHOs are more likely to recidivate in sexual and/or violent offenses upon release from the prison.

Conclusion

This review of 47 empirically published sexual homicide studies for the period of 2008 to 2015 sets out to synthesize the most recent findings in order to understand better not only the psychological dynamics of sexual murderers, but also to comprehend the overall offending patterns and processes. This review does not aim to provide an exhaustive list of the offending background and characteristics of SHOs, but, instead, to offer a glimpse of key findings derived from the recent empirical research on the topic. Bearing in mind the diverse sampling methodologies used in these studies, such as the defining criteria of sexual homicide, convenience sampling, and sampling of arrested offenders, it is not possible to "accurately" and consistently compare studies of sexual murderers and sexual homicide.

Regardless of these limitations, the recent empirical studies undoubtedly extend knowledge in this underresearched topic area, particularly in some unexplored parts (e.g., offender's early genitalia abnormalities, psychopathologies, criminal histories, criminal mobility, choice of weapon, or the lethality outcome of a sexual assault, the offender's body disposal patterns, and criminal recidivism in sexual murderers). To some extent, some of the findings confirmed what have already been known from past studies, which further strengthen the validity and accuracy of these findings. Taken together, this review may have implications not only from the theoretical standpoint to advance the research on sexual homicide and SHOs, but also have practical values in terms of suspect prioritization in police investigations of such offense and crime preventive strategies.

Nevertheless, more is to be learned about sexual homicide and sexual murderers; and more research is needed. For instance, a large majority of the studies sampled only male offenders or without any indication of the male–female offenders ratio. Thus, little is known on whether gender differences exist and to what extent, if any, these differences are important. Additionally, although comparative studies on serial and nonserial sexual offenders and nonsexual murderers are more frequently conducted (e.g., Kraemer, Lord, and Heilbrun 2004; Salfati and Bateman 2005; Slater, Woodhams, and Hamilton-Giachritsis 2014), studies on serial and nonserial SHOs are relatively scarce. Clearly more comparative studies are desirable, not only for theoretical purposes, but also for practical implications in the area of criminal investigation. Efforts and resources could then be strategized effectively to expedite the investigation and offender apprehension process. However, a uniform definition for the term "serial" is currently lacking (e.g., three or more forensically linked murders, the unlawful killing of two or more victims) in the scientific community (see Adjorlolo and Chan 2014), whereas such a term ought to be standardized in these comparative studies as findings could be considerably affected by the use of different defining criteria. More importantly, most studies, if not all, examined a specific group of SHOs. The lack of a control group (e.g., non-SHOs), the offender stratification by offense type (e.g., rapists and child molesters), and violence risk levels (e.g., low, medium, and high) may hinder the generalizability of the findings. Therefore, future research on sexual homicides may consider using a control group, stratifying the offenders by their offense type, and classifying their violence risk level to enhance the robustness of findings. By improving the research design, the police could be provided with a better empirically supported guidance in strategizing their investigative efforts.

Note

1 Bearing in mind that some of these studies are currently published in an Online First version (i.e., advance online version), and the finalized version is only likely to be published "in print" in the subsequent year or so.

References

Abrahams, N., Martin, L.J., Jewkes, R., *et al.* (2008) The epidemiology and the pathology of suspected rape homicide in South Africa. *Forensic Science International*, 178(2–3): 132–138. doi: 10.1016/j.forsciint.2008.03.006.

Adjorlolo, S. and Chan, H.C.O. (2014) The controversy of defining serial murder: Revisited. *Aggression and Violent Behavior*, 19(5): 486–491. doi: 10.1016/j.avb.2014.07.003.

Adjorlolo, S. and Chan, H.C.O. (2015) The nature of instrumentality and expressiveness of homicide crime scene behaviors: A review. *Trauma, Violence, & Abuse*. Advance online publication. doi: 10.1177/1524838015596528.

Balemba, S., Beauregard, E., and Martineau, M. (2014) Getting away with murder: A thematic approach to solved and unsolved sexual homicides using crime scene factors. *Police Practice and Research*, 15(3): 221–233. doi: 10.1080/15614263.2013.846548.

Beauregard, E. and Field, J. (2008) Body disposal patterns of sexual murderers: Implications for offender profiling. *Journal of Police and Criminal Psychology*, 23(2): 81–89. doi: 10.1007/s11896-008-9027-6.

Beauregard, E. and Martineau, M. (2013) A descriptive study of sexual homicide in Canada: Implications for police investigation. *International Journal of Offender Therapy and Comparative Criminology*, 57(12): 1454–1476. doi: 10.1177/0306624X 12456682.

Beauregard, E. and Martineau, M. (2015) An application of CRAVED to the choice of victim in sexual homicide: A routine activity approach. *Crime Science*, 4: 24. doi: 10.1186/ s40163-015-0036-3.

Beauregard, E. and Mieczkowski, T. (2012) Risk estimations of the conjunction of victim and crime event characteristics on the lethal outcome of sexual assaults. *Violence and Victims*, 27(4): 470–486. doi: 10.1891/0886-6708.27.4.470.

Beauregard, E., Stone, M.R., Proulx, J., and Michaud, P. (2008) Sexual murderers of children: Developmental, precrime, crime, and postcrime factors. *International Journal of Offender Therapy and Comparative Criminology*, 52(3): 253–269. doi: 10.1177/0306624 X07303907.

Bennell, C., Bloomfield, S., Emeno, K., and Musolino, E. (2013) Classifying serial sexual murder/murderers: An attempt to validate Keppel and Walter's (1999) model. *Criminal Justice and Behavior*, 40(1): 5–25. doi: 101177/0093854812460489.

Briken, P., Hill, A., Habermann, N., *et al.* (2010) Paraphilia-related disorders and personality disorders in sexual homicide perpetrators. *Sexual Offender Treatment*, 5(1): 1–7.

Chan, H.C.O. (2015) *Understanding Sexual Homicide Offenders: An Integrated Approach*. Basingstoke, UK: Palgrave Macmillan.

Chan, H.C.O. and Beauregard, E. (2016a) Choice of weapon or weapon of choice? Examining the interactions between victim characteristics in single-victim male sexual homicide offenders. *Journal of Investigative Psychology and Offender Profiling*, 13(1): 70–88. doi: 10.1002/jip.1432.

Chan, H.C.O. and Beauregard, E. (2016b) Nonhomicidal and homicidal sexual offenders: Prevalence of maladaptive personality traits and paraphilic behaviors. *Journal of Interpersonal Violence*, 31(13): 2259–2290. doi: 10.1177/0886260515575606.

Chan, H.C.O., Beauregard, E., and Myers, W.C. (2015) Single-victim and serial sexual homicide offenders: Differences in crime, paraphilias, and personality traits. *Criminal Behaviour and Mental Health*, 25(1): 66–78. doi: 10.1002/cbm.1925.

Chan, H.C.O. and Frei, A. (2013) Female sexual homicide offenders: An examination of an underresearched offender population. *Homicide Studies*, 17(1): 95–118. doi: 10.11 77/1088767912449625.

Chan, H.C.O., Frei, A.M., and Myers, W.C. (2013) Female sexual homicide offenders: An analysis of the offender racial profiles in offending process. *Forensic Science International*, 233(1–3): 265–272. doi: 10.1016/j.forsciint.2013.09.011.

Chan, H.C.O. and Heide, K.M. (2008) Weapons used by juveniles and adult offenders in sexual homicides: An empirical analysis of 29 years of US data. *Journal of Investigative Psychology and Offender Profiling*, 5(3): 189–208. doi: 10.1002/jip.87.

Chan, H.C.O. and Heide, K.M. (2009) Sexual homicide: A synthesis of the literature. *Trauma, Violence, & Abuse*, 10(1): 31–54. doi: 10.1177/1524838008326478.

Chan, H.C.O., Heide, K.M., and Beauregard, E. (2011) What propels sexual murderers: A proposed integrated theory of social learning and routine activities theories. *International Journal of Offender Therapy and Comparative Criminology*, 55(2): 228–250. doi: 10.1177/0306624X10261317.

Chan, H.C.O., Heide, K.M., and Myers, W.C. (2013) Juvenile and adult offenders arrested for sexual homicide: An analysis of victim–offender relationship and weapon used by race. *Journal of Forensic Sciences*, 58(1): 85–89. doi: 10.1111/j.1556-4029.2012.02188.x.

Chan, H.C.O., Myers, W.C., and Heide, K.M. (2010) An empirical analysis of 30 years of US juvenile and adult sexual homicide offender data: Race and age differences in the victim–offender relationship. *Journal of Forensic Sciences*, 55(5): 1282–1290. doi: 10.1111/j.1556-4029.2010.01448.x.

DeLisi, M. (2014) An empirical study of rape in the context of multiple murder. *Journal of Forensic Sciences*, 59(2): 420–424. doi: 10.1111/1556-4029.12335.

Francis, B. and Soothill, K. (2000) Does sex offending lead to homicide? *Journal of Forensic Psychiatry*, 11(1): 49–61.

Greenall, P.V. and Richardson, C. (2015) Adult male-on-female stranger sexual homicide: A descriptive (baseline) study from Great Britain. *Homicide Studies*, 19(3): 237–256. doi: 10.1177/1088767914530555.

Greenall, P.V. and Wright, M. (2015) Exploring the criminal histories of stranger sexual killers. *The Journal of Forensic Psychiatry and Psychology*, 26(2): 242–259. doi: 10.1080/14789949.2014.999105.

Häkkänen-Nyholm, H., Repo-Tiihonen, E., Lindberg, N., *et al.* (2009) Finnish sexual homicides: Offence and offender characteristics. *Forensic Science International*, 188: 125–130. doi: 10.1016/j.forsciint.2009.03.030.

Healey, J. and Beauregard, E. (2015) The impact of persistent deviant sexual interests and persistent low self-esteem on sexual homicide. *Criminal Justice and Behavior*, 42(12): 1225–1242. doi: 10.1177/0093854815605874.

Healey, J., Beauregard, E., Beech, A., and Vettor, S. (2014) Is the sexual murderer a unique type of offender? A typology of violent sexual offenders using crime scene behaviors. *Sexual Abuse: Journal of Research and Treatment*, 28(6): 512–533. doi: 10.1177/1079063214547583.

Healey, J., Lussier, P., and Beauregard, E. (2013) Sexual sadism in the context of rape and sexual homicide: An examination of crime scene indicators. *International Journal of Offender Therapy and Comparative Criminology*, 57(4): 402–424. doi: 10.1177/0306624X12437536.

Henry, T. (2010) Characteristics of sex-related homicides in Alaska. *Journal of Forensic Nursing*, 6(2): 57–65. doi: 10.1111/j.1939-3938.2010.01069.x.

Hill, A., Habermann, N., Klusmann, D., *et al.* (2008) Criminal recidivism in sexual homicide perpetrators. *International Journal of Offender Therapy and Comparative Criminology*, 52(1): 5–20. doi: 10.1177/0306624X07307450.

Hill, A., Rettenberger, M., Habermann, N., *et al.* (2012) The utility of risk assessment instruments for the prediction of recidivism in sexual homicide perpetrators. *Journal of Interpersonal Violence*, 27(18): 3553–3578. doi: 10.1177/0886260512447570.

Juodis, M., Woodworth, M., Porter, S., and Ten Brinke, L. (2009) Partners in crime: A comparison of individual and multi-perpetrator homicides. *Criminal Justice and Behavior*, 36(8): 824–839. doi: 10.1177/0093854809337822.

Kerr, K.J. and Beech, A.R. (2015) A thematic analysis of the motivation behind sexual homicide from the perspective of the killer. *Journal of Interpersonal Violence*. Advance online publication. doi: 10.1177/0886260515585529.

Khachatryan, N., Heide, K.M., Hummel, E.V., and Chan, H.C.O. (2014) Juvenile sexual homicide offenders: Thirty-year follow-up investigation. *International Journal of Offender Therapy and Comparative Criminology*, 60(3): 247–264. doi: 10.1177/0306624X14552062.

Koch, J., Berner, W., Hill, A., and Briken, P. (2011) Sociodemographic and diagnostic characteristics of homicidal and nonhomicidal sexual offenders. *Journal of Forensic Sciences*, 56(6): 1626–1631. doi: 10.1111/j.1556-4029.2011.01933.x.

Kraemer, G.W., Lord, W.D., and Heilbrun, K. (2004) Comparing single and serial homicide offenses. *Behavioral Sciences and the Law*, 22: 325–343. doi: 10.1002/bsl.581.

Martineau, M. and Beauregard, E. (2015) Journey to murder: Examining the correlates of criminal mobility in sexual homicide. *Police Practice and Research*, 17(1): 68–83. doi: 10.1080/15614263.2014.994215.

Mieczkowski, T. and Beauregard, E. (2010) Lethal outcome in sexual assault events: A conjunctive analysis. *Justice Quarterly*, 27(3): 332–361. doi: 10.1080/07418820902960105.

Mieczkowski, T. and Beauregard, E. (2012) Interactions between disinhibitors in sexual crimes: Additive or counteracting effects? *Journal of Crime and Justice*, 35(3): 395–411. doi: 10.1080/0735648X.2012.666408.

Myers, W.C., Bukhanovskiy, A., Justen, E., *et al.* (2008) The relationship between serial sexual murder and autoerotic asphyxiation. *Forensic Science International*, 176: 187–195. doi: 10.1016/j.forsciint.2007.09.005.

Myers, W.C. and Chan, H.C.O. (2012) Juvenile homosexual homicide. *Behavioral Sciences and the Law*, 30(2): 90–102. doi: 10.1002/bsl.2000.

Myers, W.C., Chan, H.C.O., and Mariano, T. (2014) Sexual homicide in the USA committed by juveniles and adults, 1976–2007: Age of arrest and incidence trends over 32 years. *Criminal Behaviour and Mental Health*, 26(1): 38–49. doi: 10.1002/cbm.1947.

Myers, W.C., Chan, H.C.O., Vo, E.J., and Lazarou, E. (2010) Sexual sadism, psychopathy, and recidivism in juvenile sexual murderers. *Journal of Investigative Psychology and Offender Profiling*, 7(1): 49–58. doi: 10.1002/jip.113.

Radojević, N., Radnić, B., Petković, *et al.* (2013) Multiple stabbing in sex-related homicides. *Journal of Forensic and Legal Medicine*, 20: 502–507. doi: 10.1016/j.jflm.2013.03.005.

Reckdenwald, A., Mancini, C., and Beauregard, E. (2014) Adolescent self-image as a mediator between childhood maltreatment and adult sexual offending. *Journal of Criminal Justice*, 42: 85–94. doi: 10.1016/j.jcrimjus.2013.12.007.

Ressler, R.K., Burgess, A.W., and Douglas, J.E. (1988) *Sexual Homicide: Patterns and Motive.* New York: Free Press.

Rettenberger, M., Hill, A., Dekker, A., *et al.* (2013) Genital abnormalities in early childhood in sexual homicide perpetrators. *Journal of Sexual Medicine*, 10(4): 972–980. doi: 10.1111/jsm.12051.

Salfati, C.G. and Bateman, A.L. (2005) Serial homicide: An investigation of behavioural consistency. *Journal of Investigative Psychology and Offender Profiling*, 2: 87–103. doi: 10.1002/jip.26.

Schlesinger, L.B., Kassen, M., Mesa, V.B., and Pinizzotto, A.J. (2010) Ritual and signature in serial sexual homicide. *The Journal of the American Academy of Psychiatry and the Law*, 38(2): 239–246.

Sewall, L.A., Krupp, D.B., and Lalumière, M.L. (2013) A test of two typologies of sexual homicide. *Sexual Abuse: A Journal of Research and Treatment*, 25(1): 82–100. doi: 10.1177/1079063212452617.

Slater, C., Woodhams, J., and Hamilton-Giachritsis, C. (2014) Can serial rapists be distinguished from one-off rapists. *Behavioral Sciences and the Law*, 32(2): 220–239. doi: 10.1002/bsl.2096.

Smith, S.G., Basile, K., and Karch, D. (2011) Sexual homicide and sexual violence-associated homicide: Findings from the National Violent Death Reporting System. *Homicide Studies*, 15(2): 132–153. doi: 10.1177/1088767911406236.

Spehr, A., Hill, A., Habermann, N., *et al.* (2010) Sexual murderers with adult or child victims: Are they different? *Sexual Abuse: A Journal of Research and Treatment*, 22(3): 290–314. doi: 10.1177/1079063210374346.

Stefanska, E.B., Carter, A.J., Higgs, T., *et al.* (2015) Offense pathway of non-serial sexual killers. *Journal of Criminal Justice*, 43(2): 99–107. doi: 10.1016/j.jcrimjus.2015.01.001.

Stein, M., Schlesinger, L.B., and Pinizzotto, A.J. (2010) Necrophilia and sexual homicide. *Journal of Forensic Sciences*, 55(2): 443–446. doi: 10.1111/j.1556-4029.2009.01282.x.

Vettor, S., Beech, A.R., Woodhams, J. (2014) Rapist and sexual murderers: Combined pathways to offending. In J. Proulx, E. Beauregard, P. Lussier, and B. Leclerc (eds), *Pathways to Sexual Aggression* (pp. 285–315). New York: Routledge.

8

When Women are Murdered

R. Emerson Dobash and Russell P. Dobash

Worldwide, the vast majority of murders are committed by men who murder other men, followed by murders in which men murder women. By comparison, women commit very few murders and are not discussed here. In countries with very high rates of homicide per 100,000 members of the population, such as some countries in Africa and South and Central America, the high rate is mostly accounted for by large numbers of male-male murders (MMmurder) involving young men engaged in war, civil conflicts, or various illegal activities like drug dealing, smuggling, gambling, and/or human trafficking where violence and murder form a part of the management and control of these affairs (Smith and Zahn 1999; Liem and Pridemore 2013; UNODC 2013: 13). Although high rates of homicide are driven by large numbers of murders between men, this does not mean that few women are killed. On the contrary, many women may also be killed in countries with very high rates of homicide but those numbers are overwhelmed by the even greater number of male-male murders. Unless the murders of women are examined separately from the murders of men, that is, disaggregated by gender, little can be known about this type of murder which is otherwise lost within the larger number of male-male homicides.

Even in countries with low rates of homicide, such as Britain, most European countries, Canada, and Australia, the majority of cases still involve men killing other men. In short, male-male murders drive the homicide rate, shape the resulting findings, and obscure what can be known about the killing of women unless the data are disaggregated by gender. This has long been known and sometimes commented upon, but often forgotten or ignored. Based on extensive statistical research in Finland from the 1920s–1950s, Veli Verkko was an early proponent of disaggregating homicides by gender and noted that, "the proportion of female homicide victims

The Handbook of Homicide, First Edition. Edited by Fiona Brookman, Edward R. Maguire, and Mike Maguire.

was higher when the overall homicide rate was low, and vice versa" (Verkko 1951, cited in Kivivuori, Savolainen, and Danielson 2013: 96). This and other statistical patterns in homicide became known as "Verkko's laws" (Verkko 1951), which still applies and can be illustrated using data from various regions around the world. For example, in countries with low homicide rates, such as France from the 1970s onwards, about 40 percent of all victims of homicide were women (Mucchielli 2013) and in England/Wales, from 1998 to 2008, women represented 31 percent of all homicide victims (Soothill and Francis 2013). Across various European countries with relatively low rates of homicide, 28 percent of the victims of homicide are women. In the United States, with a somewhat higher homicide rate, in 2010 women represented 22 percent of all victims of homicide (VPC 2011; FBI 2012) while in some Latin and Central American countries and some African countries, with very high rates of homicide, only about 12 percent of all victims of homicide are women (UNODC 2013: 13). As early as 1957, Wolfgang emphasized that, although most homicides were committed by men against other men, the murder of women was also an important part of the overall examination of and concern about homicide (Wolfgang 1957; Wolfgang and Ferracuti 1967). Although issues relating to the murder of women were noted by Verkko in the 1930s and Wolfgang in the 1950s, they were mostly forgotten or ignored by statisticians and researchers until the 1980s and 1990s when some researchers began to focus on the murder of women.

Knowledge about Homicide: National Datasets, Case Reviews, Academic Research, and the Popular Media

What is known about homicide comes from many different sources, and each may be more or less reliable and generalizable to all homicides, to a particular type of homicide, or to only a single case. Each source provides different types and levels of information and is directed to different audiences including national agencies, academic researchers, and the general public.

National datasets on homicide

National datasets contain a limited amount of information about every homicide, murder, or manslaughter known to have been committed during a specific period of time. Findings are reported to the public and/or official bodies on a regular or periodic basis and include national statistics, homicide rates, and other information. For each case, a limited amount of descriptive information is recorded, often by the police, such as the age, race, education, occupation, and gender of perpetrators and victims, and summary information about the homicide such as time, location, circumstances, and injuries. These data provide an overview of general patterns but the limited amount of information about each case restricts what can be known about homicide in general and about different types of homicide including those that involve women either as victims or as offenders (Dobash and Dobash 2015: 4–6).

In the United States, Gartner (1990) provided an early overview, and examples of national datasets include the US Homicide Reports (SHRs) gathered through the Uniform Crime Reporting program of the FBI (Riedel 1999), the Centers for Disease Control and Prevention, and CDC's National Violent Death Reporting System (NVDRS) reported by Paulozzi *et al.* (2004). Findings for England/Wales and for Scotland have been reported by Brookman (2005, 2010), Miles (2012), and Soothill and Francis (2013). For various European countries, see Liem and Pridemore (2013). National datasets yield a small amount of data about a large number of cases that can show general patterns but are too restricted to provide extensive details about the circumstances of murder events or the dynamic processes involved. This requires much more information about each case than can possibly be gathered within a dataset that must include information about every case of homicide across the entire population. Of necessity, the purpose is delimited to general patterns of homicides and cannot be extended to more detailed aspects of these events, the dynamic elements within them, or later reflections upon them.

Case reviews of a single homicide

By contrast, "case reviews" or "fatality reviews" contain extensive details about a single case, usually one that went wrong, in order that various agencies may learn lessons about their policies and practices and make relevant changes in light of exhaustive information from one case (Websdale 1999, 2010). The focus is on intervention, interagency coordination, information sharing, or other activities prior to the homicide. Although the extensive amount of information gathered on a single case of homicide can be invaluable to the various agencies, and may also be suggestive of relevant factors to be included in research that extends beyond a single case of homicide, it cannot be used to provide overall generalizations and is not intended to do so.

Academic research

The research of many academic scholars stands somewhere between the large numbers but limited content of national datasets and the limited number but exhaustive content of case reviews. Academic research is often funded by scientific bodies and foundations that support researchers for a limited period of time which limits the number of cases that can be studied to a sample rather than to the whole population and to a specific period of study. However, academic studies that are well-constructed have the advantage of being able to gather much more information about each case than is possible within national datasets. This may include more quantitative details about perpetrators, victims, murder events, and the contexts in which they occur as well as qualitative evidence that adds further depth and detail about the dynamic aspects of murder events that are often very complex and difficult to understand fully without such information.

Popular media

Finally, the source of information about homicide that is most accessible to the general population and likely to receive the widest exposure comes from the popular media including newspapers, radio, television, the Internet, and social media. Within these formats, the coverage of homicide in general, as well as specific cases of murder, frequently focuses on the most unusual or extreme examples, and may contain details that are more or less complete or accurate. While some of this coverage is relatively thorough and accurate, much is more speculative and sensational. Despite these weaknesses, the information presented in the popular media is often the primary or sole source of knowledge about homicide available to most members of the public, and it thus has an inordinate influence on what is "known" or believed about homicide. For example, cases of serial killings, which are extremely rare, are often given air time and column space that far outweigh the frequency of their occurrence, while those that are more "ordinary" and occur more frequently may receive far less coverage or be ignored. This has a distorting effect on what is "known" or believed about murder in general and about the murder of women in particular, and especially cases that also involve sex.

Disaggregating Homicide by Gender of Victims

While it is necessary to disaggregate homicide data by gender in order to differentiate the murders of men from those of women (Flewelling and Williams 1999), this may not be enough. Simply disaggregating victims by gender into those who are men and those who are women, "femicide" (Russell 1992; Radford and Russell 1992; Russell and Harmes 2001), may not yield sufficient knowledge about the nature and dynamics of each type. It may be necessary to divide the murders of women still further in order to refine what can be known about the different situations and circumstances in which men murder women and the nature and dynamics of these murders. Finally, and of equal importance, findings about the murder of women need to be compared to those about the murder of men in order to provide evidence about the differences between them but also to shed light on those factors that are similar.

The Murder of Women—Three Types

In one study of murder in Britain, the double disaggregation of the murders of women by men resulted in three main types: intimate partner murder (IPM), sexual murder (SexM), and the murder of older women (OWoM) (Dobash and Dobash 2015). At present, most research on the murder of women does not disaggregate them but either examines all cases together, often described as "femicide," or focuses solely on one type, usually the murder of intimate partners, or murders that involve sex. Comparisons with male-male murders are not usually made and little research has focused on the life course of the men who commit murder, whether their victims are other men, women, or children. Although findings about each of these three types of murder of women often draw on different bodies of research, the focus is usually on similar factors relating to the murder event, the relationship between perpetrators and their victims, and the situations and circumstances in which the murders occur.

Intimate Partner Murder

Women are most likely to be killed in their own home and in the context of an intimate relationship, a pattern that differs dramatically for men who are rarely killed by a woman partner. In an analysis of global data from 66 countries, the World Health Organization reported that intimate partner homicides accounted for about 40 percent of all killings of women but only 6 percent of the murders of men (Stockl *et al.* 2013). For murders between intimate partners, the ratio of male to female victims is about 1 to 5 or 6, that is, for every six women killed by a male intimate partner only one man is killed by a woman intimate partner (Daly and Wilson 1988), and this pattern of gender asymmetry is duplicated throughout most of the world. Figures for England/Wales from 1998 to 2008 indicate that 54 percent of all women victims were murdered by an intimate partner, usually in their own home, while only 5 percent of all men who were murdered were killed by a woman partner (Cooper and Smith 2011; Soothill and Francis 2013; Dobash and Dobash 2015: 24). For many European countries, figures are not available or are unclear because of definitions that combine all murders under a single category such as "domestic" or "family" homicide that may include parents, siblings, or other relatives who may be male or female and young or old. However, countries such as the Netherlands, Finland, Germany, Sweden, and Switzerland have well-developed national figures on homicide, including information about different types, and report that women are the victims in nearly one-third of all homicides, and that nearly half to three-quarters of these are intimate partners (for specific countries, see Liem and Pridemore 2013). Figures from the Unites States for 2009, reveal that most female victims were over the age of 18, the vast majority were murdered by a man known to them, usually an intimate partner or ex-partner, half of them involved a firearm usually a handgun, and that African American women were over twice as likely as white women to be murdered (FBI 2012; Violence Policy Center 2011: 6; for trends from 1976 to 1987, see Browne and Williams 1993).

IPM: lethal, nonlethal comparisons of intimate partner violence and murder

Some studies have focused solely on intimate partner murder while others compare lethal and nonlethal violence against women intimate partners in order to identify similarities and differences between those that end in a death and those that do not. The comparisons are quite diverse but an overall view highlights many similar issues that differentiate outcomes that become lethal from those that do not. These include the nature of the relationship between victims and perpetrators with particular risks in relationships that are less permanent and/or in the process of breaking or separating, the importance of possessiveness and jealousy, previous violence to women, and the excessive use of alcohol (Johnson and Chisholm 1989; Carcach and James 1998; Moracco, Runyan, and Butts, 1998; Smith, Moracco, and Butts 1998; Campbell, *et al.* 2003, 2007; Dobash *et al.* 2007; Thomas, Dichter, and Matejkowski 2011: 302; Bye 2013; Dobash and Dobash 2015: 26–30).

IPM: the nature of the intimate relationship

Although women are placed in danger of being killed by virtue of being in an intimate relationship with a man, the evidence suggests that the nature of the relationship between them, whether married, cohabiting or boyfriend/girlfriend, may somehow be related to differing levels of danger and the prospects of violence with a lethal outcome. Early studies comparing nonlethal physical abuse and violence among couples who were married with those who were cohabiting found more violence among cohabitants, but it was debated whether this was related to the different types of relationship (married or cohabiting), or to the different types of individuals living within each type (younger, undereducated, unemployed). That is, whether older, more educated, middle-class conforming individuals with fewer personal difficulties were more likely to be married compared to those who were cohabiting, and these issues, rather than the status of the relationship, was more likely to be related to men's use of violence against their women partners (Daly and Wilson 1988; Wilson, Johnson, and Daly 1995; Dawson and Gartner 1998; Shackelford and Mouzos 2005). With changing patterns of intimate relationships, more couples cohabiting, and a greater acceptance of such relationships, James and Daly (2012) found that cohabitation was no longer associated with elevated spousal homicide rates in the United States, but this remains debatable. Other findings from Australia, Canada, the United Kingdom, Europe, and the Unites States suggest that the nature of the relationship still matters, with boyfriends/girlfriends more likely than cohabiting or marital relationships to be associated with intimate partner homicides (Dawson and Gartner 1998; Johnson and Hotton 2003; Miethe and Regoeczi 2004; Shackelford and Mouzos 2005; Dobash *et al.* 2007; Liem and Pridemore 2013; Dobash and Dobash 2015). The question may have moved on and been modified, and the answer may still be unsettled, but both the earlier and later findings and the evolving debates highlight the continuing importance of examining the nature of intimate relationships and the prospects of violence and murder within them.

IPM: the context of murder—possessiveness, jealousy, separation, previous violence to the victim

Using Canadian data, Johnson and Hotton (2003) compared the risk of homicide in estranged and intact intimate relationships and highlighted the importance of separation in the increased risk to women of being murdered during the process of leaving or after separation from their male partner. Separation, possessiveness, and jealousy have long been highlighted as potent risk factors when men murder women. Extreme possessiveness and jealousy mean that men define numerous daily activities as signs of dishonesty or disloyalty on the part of the woman partner and, armed with such views, behave with a violent ferocity ranging from nonlethal violence to a deliberate act to kill (Daly and Wilson 1988; Polk and Ranson 1991; Campbell 1992; Wilson, Johnson, and Daly 1995; Dawson and Gartner 1998; Dobash, *et al.* 2004; Shackelford and Mouzos 2005; Adams 2007; Websdale 2010; James and Daly 2012; Dobash and Dobash 2015).

IPM: previous violence to the victim, alcohol, and weapons

The previous use of violence by men against the women they kill or against previous women partners or women outside of an intimate relationship have been found to be risk factors for the intimate partner murder. In their multisite case control study, Campbell and colleagues (Campbell 1992; Campbell *et al.* 2003, 2007, 2014) assessed risk factors for intimate partner homicide and highlighted the importance of previous violence to the victim, alcohol, and other factors including the presence of firearms in the home which is of particular importance in the United States where gun ownership is very high. The abuse of alcohol and drunkenness have repeatedly been found to be of relevance in the murders of women partners. Also of particular importance are orientations to women in general and to women partners in particular that are highly gendered in nature and include notions of the power of men over women and the importance of control and punishment for real or perceived departures from men's expectations and demands. Overall, these and other findings reflect on gender and gender relations between men and women partners, the conflicts associated with them, the sense of entitlement that men often bring to such relationships, and their willingness to use physical violence, including murder, in efforts to assert their will, enforce their authority, and mete out punishment for perceived wrongdoings (Daly and Wilson 1988; Wilson, Johnson, and Daly 1995; Dawson and Gartner 1998; Shackelford and Mouzos 2005; Adams 2007; Websdale 2010; James and Daly 2012; Campbell, *et al.* 2003, 2007, 2014; Dobash and Dobash 2011, 2015; Dobash *et al.* 2004).

IPM: collateral murders related to intimate partner conflict

Finally, some men murder others in the context of conflicts with women partners. In such cases, the woman partner does not become the victim of murder but the intimate relationship needs to be viewed as the context in which the murder of children, new partners, or protectors such as parents, relatives, friends, or neighbors occurs. As such, the collateral murders of children, protectors, and new partners must be considered in the context of intimate partner conflict if the dynamics associated with them are to be understood (Dobash and Dobash 2012, 2015: 58–62).

Sexual Murder

The long-standing media and public interest in sexual murder has had the dual effect of elevating general interest in this type of murder but, at the same time, has distorted notions about the nature of these murders and the characteristics of the perpetrators and victims. Although serial murders represent only a microdot of all murders and of all sexual murders, the public and popular interest in them is phenomenal, and this has also had an effect on the study of sexual murder and sexual murderers. It is sufficient to note the enduring interest in "Jack the Ripper," the nineteenth-century serial killer in London, the countless books, television series, and movies on the topic, as well as the wholesale coverage of the few cases of serial murder that have occurred anywhere in the world in order to appreciate the tremendous interest in the topic and the powerful imagery of serial murder and the serial murderer. Such cases have everything: sex, violence, mystery about who committed the crime; tension about if/when another murder will be committed; widespread public alarm; unknown danger; and the hunt for a killer.

Serial sexual murders

In the 1990s, the FBI estimated that there were about 35 serial killers across the whole of the United States (Myers *et al.* 1993), and another estimate in 2005 suggested that about 2 percent of all sexual murders in the United States and about 3 percent in Canada might be at the hands of serial murderers (Cusson 2007; Oliver *et al.* 2007). Despite the infrequency of serial murders, the interest in them is intense, and the alarm far outreaches the likelihood of their occurrence. In 1993, Myers and colleagues examined 36 "motiveless" cases of murder initially investigated by the FBI, described the crime scenes, and speculated about the backgrounds and sexual orientations of the perpetrators. This laid the foundation for much of the imagery of the serial killer as a man who not only sexually assaults and kills several women but mutilates and dismembers their bodies, retains trophies, has fantasies that fuse sex and sadistic violence, and, beginning in childhood, is socially and psychologically set apart from others. This imagery distorted perceptions about the vast majority of sexual murders which were assumed to fit a similar profile although they were less likely to be studied than serial sexual murders. After a systematic review of 32 reports of research on sexual murder, Chan and Heide (2009: 31–54) concluded that "Studies of sexual homicides are still in their preliminary stages and research procedures do not generally lead to 'reliable' results." Carter and Hollin (2010) drew similar conclusions from their comprehensive review of ten studies of sexual murder (for a discussion, see Dobash and Dobash 2015: 105–107, 118–120; see also Chapter 7 in this volume).

SexM: comparisons of sexual assaults and sexual murders

Some studies have compared lethal and nonlethal sexual assaults against women in an effort to identify similarities and differences between sexual assaults/rape that end in a death and those that do not. These and other findings suggest that men who commit sexual assault/rape are generally quite similar to those who commit a sexual murder, with both groups experiencing numerous problems in childhood and adulthood. These range from early problems among parents or caretakers to disruptive behavior and physical and sexual abuse as children, and unemployment, substance abuse, and offending, including sexual offenses, as adults. However, sexual murderers appeared to differ in adolescence in terms of various indicators of social isolation and loneliness. Based on their review of literature about rapists and sexual murderers, Birkel and Dern (2013: 323) note that there is a huge variation in sexual murders that make them difficult to classify but note the relevance of situational factors such as intoxication, resistance from the victim, and the presence of witnesses in whether a sexual assault will end fatally. They stress that it is difficult to answer the question of whether there is a difference between sexual murderers and rapists but state that there is both evidence and widely held assumptions that "sexual murderers are in principle merely rapists who kill" (for comparisons of sexual assault and sexual murder, see Langevin *et al.* 1988; Grubin 1994: 626–627; Meloy 2000; Langevin 2003; Salfati and Taylor 2006; Oliver *et al.* 2007: 162–166; Nicole and Proulx 2007; Chan and Heide 2009; Carter and Hollin 2010; Dobash and Dobash 2015: 107–114).

SexM: the nature of the relationship between sexual murderers and their victims

Sexual attack and murder at the hands of a stranger is a powerful imagery that often overshadows the reality of most sexual murders that are more usually committed by men known to the women they kill. The relationship between male perpetrators and the women they murder mediates the kind of access the man has to the woman and the level of caution the woman may have about a man who is a stranger compared to one with whom she is acquainted. For strangers, the man has no "legitimate" social access to the woman and the woman is likely to be cautious or guarded about any form of contact or approach from a man she does not know. For those who are strangers, the murder event is more likely to begin either as the man tricks the woman into contact such as pretending to be a taxi driver or by a surprise direct physical attack in a place out of sight of others who might intervene. For those who are acquainted or related, men have differing levels of social access to the woman and the woman's level of caution about the man is, to some extent, mediated by the nature of their relationship to one another. Although some may have been acquainted only briefly, such as meeting at a club or pub, but of a sufficient duration to move from a "complete stranger" to someone who might be allowed to provide a lift home or be invited in for a coffee or a drink, where the sexual attack and murder then occurs. Notions about men's access to women and their levels of caution differ for women who are sex workers. Although women's caution about the male stranger still exists, the nature of their relationship is such that the man who is a stranger nonetheless has a form of access to the woman and the purpose is to negotiate a sexual act with her. Here, the woman must undertake this negotiation with a concern about her own safety albeit within the context of having sex with a stranger. This can, of course, be very dangerous for women who work on the streets and must make quick judgments about the men who seek to buy sex from them.

SexM: the murder event—context, situations, and circumstances

The contexts of sexual murders vary but generally involve men who seek to have sex with or without the consent of the woman concerned and are willing to use extreme force in doing so. Some men fail to perform sexually, blame the woman for their own failure, and make her pay with her life. Some men are angry at women in general or at a particular woman and sexually assault and murder another woman in a proxy act of revenge. As early as the 1970s, sexual assault and rape were associated with power, control, anger, and sexuality (Groth, Burgess, and Holmstrom 1977), and in the 1990s Grubin (1994) found little or no difference between men who committed rape and those who committed a sexual murder except that "loneliness" was more likely among sexual murderers.

The Murder Study (Dobash and Dobash 2015) contained 98 cases of sexual murder of women under the age of 65, and an additional 21 cases involved women over age 65 that are examined separately in relation to the murders of older women. For the 98 cases of women under 65 years of age, 37 percent were committed by a stranger and 63 percent by men acquainted with the woman for a period as brief as one day to long-term neighbors, friends, or relatives. Most (58%) of the women were murdered in or near their own home and the remainder were killed in public places that were dark or deserted where the man was unlikely to be observed and the lone woman was unlikely to be able to call for assistance. Alcohol was often involved, with most offenders in various stages of drunkenness and, in some cases, the man and woman had been drinking together. Strangling and choking, the use of clubs or other instruments, and the infliction of five or more injuries were the most common pattern, although some men mutilated the woman, particularly her face and sexual parts of the body, and a few committed sexual acts against the woman's body after death (Dobash and Dobash 2015: 122–138, 142–146, 202, 290–298).

Murder of Older Women

In their 15-year review of homicide of the elderly, Falzon and Davis (1998) note that there is much less research on this type of murder and stress the pressing need for more knowledge particularly in societies with an aging population. Existing findings indicate that those who are older are less likely to be murdered than those who are younger, that the majority of perpetrators are men, and that the elderly are often murdered in their place of residence. However, in the United States, a few are murdered in their place of employment such as late-night convenience stores or gas stations. Some research suggests a greater risk to older women than to older men, while other research does not. Using the entire Chicago Homicide Dataset of 27,345 cases gathered over 45 years beginning in 1965, Block (2013: 174) found 1,486 cases with victims age 60 or older and noted gender asymmetry among victims (30% women and 70% men). By contrast, Abrams *et al.* (2007) examined all 11,850 homicides in New York City from 1990 to 1998 and found near parity between the genders of those murders that involved the elderly (43% women and 57% men). Citing several studies, Chu and Kraus (2004) reported that women accounted for anywhere from 32 percent to 51 percent of all older victims. Overall, the preponderance of evidence so far is suggestive of near parity between men and women victims in murders of the elderly, and this is in contrast to gender asymmetry among younger victims.

Using the same database of homicides in Chicago from 1965 to 1981, Nelson and Huff-Corzine (1998) compared victims under and over the age of 65, and found that older men and women were more likely than younger victims to be killed in their own home by a stranger in theft-related homicides that involve little or no conflict (16% vs 53%). Kennedy and Silverman (1990) found a similar pattern in Canada. In Chicago, older victims were more likely than younger victims to be strangled/suffocated, clubbed with a blunt instrument, or beaten with fists and feet than to be killed with a firearm (Block 2013: 177), and Fox and Levin (1991) noted that while older people were less likely to be assaulted than those in other age groups, they were more likely to die during such attacks.

Among the European countries examined, Liem and Oberwittler (2013: 201, 209) found that women aged 65 and over represented about 15 percent of all victims of homicide–suicide, that many of these involved a firearm and were committed by husbands against wives which might suggest that they were actually intimate partner murders. In Britain, Dobash and Dobash found that only 8 percent (n = 36) of the victims among the 424 male-male murders were men over age 65, while 17 percent (n = 40) of the women victims among the 243 male-female murders were over that age. Of the 40 murders of women over the age of 65, the vast majority of older women (88%) were killed in their own home or place of residence for the elderly, and most received five or more injuries during the murder, with some of the oldest of the old suffering the greatest number of injuries. The 40 murders of older women were divided between 19 theft/murders (mostly committed by men known to the woman) and 21 sex/murders (divided almost equally between strangers and those known to the woman) (Dobash and Dobash 2015: 202–209, 260, 298).

Overall, findings from several countries indicate that elderly victims, both men and women, are most likely to be killed by a man during a theft in their own home or place of residence; and in the United States some are also killed during a robbery of their place of work at late-night convenience stores or gas stations. Most perpetrators are men who are strangers or someone minimally acquainted through the delivery of goods, work in the house or garden, or who live nearby. Some are killed by spouses, usually husbands who kill wives, and a few are killed by their own children or caretakers. Older victims are more likely to be strangled or beaten to death rather than killed with a firearm, and some older women are also subjected to a sexual attack in the context of the murder (Safarik, Jarvis, and Nussbaum 2002: 515–516; Block 2013: 174; Riedel 2013; Dobash and Dobash 2015: 197–200, 206–211, 219).

Life Course of Men Who Murder Women and Men Who Murder Men—Four Types of Murder Compared

Very little research focuses on the life course of men who commit crimes of violence and even less on those who commit murder whether their victims are men, women, or children. Although the primary focus of the field of developmental criminology is the life course of offenders and criminal careers from the onset of offending in childhood to life thereafter, most of these studies focus on the lives of nonviolent offenders, few on those who commit crimes of violence, and even fewer on those who commit murder. While nearly a dozen academic books have focused on the few women who kill men, albeit often sympathetic treatments of women victims of violence who eventually defend themselves by using lethal force against a male abuser, there is little work on the life course of the many men who kill women. See Polk (1994) and Adams (2007) on men who murder woman intimate partners, and the Murder Study that covers the life course of a total of 866 murderers (786 men and 80 women) from childhood, to adulthood, and in prison (Dobash and Dobash 2015).

Evidence from the casefiles of all of the 786 male murders in the Murder Study revealed that 20 percent were early onset offenders who committed an offense before the age of 13 (which compares to wider population-based studies that report that no more than 5 percent of the male population offend before age 13), 67 percent were "late-onset offenders" who committed their first criminal offense after age 13, and 13 percent had no known history of offending prior to committing murder (Dobash *et al.* 2007; Dobash and Dobash 2011, 2015: 9).

In the absence of a larger body of research about the life course of men who commit murder, a summary of some of the findings from the Murder Study are presented here. This includes only the life course of men who murdered other men (MMmurder, n = 424) and of men who murdered women: intimate partners (IPM, n = 105), sexual murders (SexM, n = 98), and older women (OWoM, n = 40), and excludes 28 cases that did not fit within the three types as well as the murders of children and those committed by women. Data from the casefiles of the 667 adult male murderers indicates that despite the type of murder they eventually commit, most of the men experienced numerous problems as children, including broken families, alcohol abuse, violence, and offending by parents, particularly fathers, as well as their own problematic behaviors as children, including problems and failure at school, disruptive behavior, alcohol and drug abuse before age 16, and the early onset of offending and convictions before the age of 16. Across the many comparisons in childhood, the group of men who later murder an intimate partner stand apart as the least likely to experience each of the issues examined. As adults, the majority of men who committed homicide had had numerous contacts with the police, engaged in persistent criminal behavior, and had broken and problematic intimate relationships, although one-quarter of the IPMs differed from the other men by having no histories of previous offending and were more likely to be employed and to exhibit other more conventional lifestyles.

Across all four types of murder, the adult lives of men differed in the proportion of those with sexual problems (most frequent among sexual murderers), broken relationships, violence in previous intimate relationships, convictions for assaulting a woman (most among IPMs), contact with the police, persistent criminal behavior, alcohol abuse (most among MMmurderers and men who murdered older women), and previous imprisonment (most likely for men who murdered older women and least likely for those who murdered an intimate partner). In prison, men who murdered older women were least likely and IPMs the most likely to be defined as model prisoners. The men who murdered older women and sexual murderers were most likely to be uncooperative with prison professionals, and 10+ disciplines reports occurred most frequently among men who murdered older women and MMmurderers. Prison professionals defined SexMs and IPMs as most likely, and MMmurderers as least likely, to have problems with women. For these and other comparisons of the life course of men who committed one of these four types of murder, see Dobash and Dobash (2015: 262 for childhood, 263 for adulthood, and 264 for assessments in prison).

Conclusions

There is a vast body of literature on homicide in general and on nonlethal forms of violence against women, particularly intimate partner violence, sexual assault, and rape, but far less research focused specifically on the murder of women and even less on the life course of the men who kill women. Although further research will continue to advance understanding of the complex and dynamic nature of the murders of women, existing evidence about each of the three main types (intimate partner murder, sexual murder and the murder of older women), whether studied separately or combined in a larger overview, all indicate the overwhelming importance of gender and gender relations in the wider understanding of when and why men murder women.

The limited amount of research on the life course of men who murder women strongly suggests the importance not only of focusing on the lives of the men who murder women, but of doing so in ways that delineate the different types of murder, differentiate one from another, and provide a fuller and deeper understanding of the dynamics involved in each. The broadest of generalizations suggests that, as a group, men who murder older women experienced the widest range of problems across the life course and were the least capable of functioning either socially or economically. Men who committed sexual murders were focused on obtaining sex at any cost, were willing to use violence in doing so, and were indifferent to the consequences even if that involved murder. Finally, the life course of the group of men who murdered intimate partners were divided as three-quarters of the men had a history of previous offending including violence to women and other problems, while one-quarter of IPMs had no history of previous offending and, in that sense, the murder appeared to "come out of the blue." However, despite the difference in the background of previous offending among men who murdered an intimate partner, they were alike in their attitudes to women and were among the most focused on the act of killing.

Overall, men who murder women often "specialize" in using violence against women, and the majority have a history of physical and/or sexual violence against women. In order to obtain a better understanding of the nature and dynamics of when men murder women, it is not only necessary to disaggregate homicide data by the gender of perpetrators and victims, but to divide them still further into the different types of homicide that allow for a much closer examination of the nature of each type that are distinguished by the relationship between the perpetrators and their victims, the dynamic nature of the murder events, and the life course of the men who murder women compared to those who murder other men.

References

Abrams, R.C., Leon, A.C., Tardiff, K., *et al.* (2007) "Gray murder": Characteristics of elderly compared with nonelderly homicide victims in New York City. *American Journal of Public Health*, 97: 1666–1670.

Adams, D. (2007) *Why Do They Kill? Men Who Murder Their Intimate Partners*. Nashville, TN: Vanderbilt University Press.

Birkel, C. and Dern, H. (2013) Homicide in Germany. In M.C.A. Liem and W.A. Pridemore (eds), *Handbook of European Homicide Research: Patterns, Explanations and Country Studies* (pp. 313–328.). New York: Springer Science.

Block, C.R. (2013) Homicide against or by the elderly in Chicago, 1965–2000. *Homicide Studies*, 17: 154–183.

Brookman, F. (2005) *Understanding Homicide*. Thousand Oaks, CA: SAGE.

Brookman, F. (2010) Homicide. In F. Brookman, M. Maguire, H. Pierpoint, and T. Bennett (eds), *Handbook on Crime*. Devon, UK: Willan.

Browne, A. and Williams, K.R. (1993) Gender, intimacy, and lethal violence: Trends from 1976 through 1987. *Gender and Society*, 7: 78–98.

Bye, E.K. (2013) Alcohol and homicide in Europe. In M.C.A. Liem and W.A. Pridemore (eds), *Handbook of European Homicide Research: Patterns, Explanations, and Country Studies* (pp. 231–246). New York: Springer Science.

Campbell, J.C. (1992) "If I can't have you, no one can": Power and control in homicide of female partners. In J. Radford and D.E.H. Russell (eds), *Femicide: The Politics of Woman Killing* (pp. 99–113). New York: Twayne.

Campbell, J.C., Glass, N., Sharps, P.W., *et al.* (2007) Intimate partner homicide: Review and implications of research and policy. *Trauma, Violence, & Abuse*, 8: 246–269.

Campbell, J.C., Webster, D., Koziol-McLain, J., *et al.* (2003) Risk factors for femicide in abusive relationships: Results from a multisite case control study. *American Journal of Public Health*, 93: 139–152.

Campbell, J.C., Webster, D., Koziol-McLain, J., *et al.* (2014) Assessing risk factors for intimate partner homicide. *National Institute of Justice Journal*, 250: 14–19.

Carcach, C. and James, M. (1998) Homicide between intimate partners in Australia. Trends and Issues in Crime and Criminal Justice, no. 90. Canberra: Australian Institute of Criminology. Available online at http://www.aic.gov.au/media_library/publications/tandi_pdf/tandi090.pdf (accessed September 29, 2016).

Carter, A.J. and Hollin, C.R. (2010) Characteristics of non-serial sexual homicide offenders: A review. *Psychology, Crime & Law*, 16: 25–45.

Chan, H.C. and Heide, K.M. (2009) Sexual homicide: A synthesis of the literature. *Trauma, Violence, & Abuse*, 10: 31–54.

Chu, L.D. and Kraus, J.F. (2004) Predicting fatal assault among the elderly using the national incident-based reporting system crime data. *Homicide Studies*, 8: 71–95.

Cooper, A. and Smith, E.L. (2011) Homicide trends in the United States, 1980–2008. US Department of Justice, Bureau of Justice Statistics. Available online at www.bjs.gov/content/pub/pdf/htus8008.pdf (accessed September 29, 2016).

Cusson, M. (2007) Introduction. In J. Proulx, E. Beauregard, M. Cusson, and A. Nicole (eds), *Sexual Murderers: A Comparative Analysis and New Perspectives* (pp. 1–5). Chichester, UK: John Wiley & Sons.

Daly, M. and Wilson, M. (1988) *Homicide*. New York: Aldine de Gruyter.

Dawson, R. and Gartner, R. (1998) Differences in the characteristics of intimate femicides: The role of relationship state and relationship status. *Homicide Studies*, 2: 378–399.

Dobash, R.E. and Dobash, R.P. (2011) What were they thinking? Men who murder an intimate partner. *Violence Against Women*, 17: 111–134.

Dobash, R.E. and Dobash, R.P. (2012) Who died? Murder of others in the context of intimate partner conflict. *Violence Against Women*, 18: 662–671.

Dobash, R.E. and Dobash, R.P. (2015) *When Men Murder Women*. Oxford: Oxford University Press.

Dobash, R.P., Dobash, R.E., Cavanagh, K., and Lewis, R. (2004) Not an ordinary killer—just an ordinary guy: When men murder an intimate woman partner. *Violence Against Women*, 10: 577–605.

Dobash, R.E., Dobash, R.P., Cavanagh, K., and Medina-Ariza, J.J. (2007) Lethal and non-lethal violence against an intimate partner: Comparing male murderers with non-lethal abusers. *Violence Against Women*, 13(4): 1–27.

Falzon, A.L. and Davis, G.G. (1998) A 15 year retrospective review of homicide in the elderly. *Journal of Forensic Sciences*, 43(2): 371–374.

FBI (Federal Bureau of Investigation) (2012) Table 13: Murder circumstances. In *Crime in the United States: Uniform Crime Reports, Supplemental Homicide Reports*. Washington, DC: Government Printing Office.

Flewelling, R.L. and Williams, K.R. (1999) Categorizing homicides: The use of disaggregated data in homicide research. In M.W. Smith and M.A. Zahn (eds), *Homicide: A Sourcebook of Social Research* (pp. 96–106). Thousand Oaks, CA: SAGE.

Fox, J.A. and Levin, J. (1991) Homicide against the elderly: A research note. *Criminology*, 29: 317–329.

Gartner, R. (1990) The victims of homicide: A temporal and cross-national comparison. *American Sociological Review*, 55: 92–106.

Groth, A.N., Burgess, A.W., and Holmstrom, L.L. (1977) Rape: Power, anger, and sexuality. *American Journal of Psychiatry*, 134: 1239–1243.

Grubin, D. (1994) Sexual murder. *British Journal of Psychiatry*, 165: 624–629.

James, B. and Daly, M. (2012) Cohabitation is no longer associated with elevated spousal homicide rates in the United States. *Homicide Studies*, 16(4): 393–403.

Johnson, H. and Chisholm, P. (1989) Family homicide. Statistics Canada. *Canadian Social Trends*, 14: 17–28.

Johnson, H. and Hotton, T. (2003) Losing control: Homicide risk in estranged and intact intimate relationships. *Homicide Studies*, 7: 58–84.

Kennedy, L.W. and Silverman, R.A. (1990) The elderly victim of homicide: An application of routine activity theory. *Sociological Quarterly*, 31: 305–317.

Kivivuori, J., Savolainen, J., and Danielson, P. (2013) Theory and explanation in contemporary European homicide research. In M.C.A. Liem and W.A. Pridemore (eds), *Handbook of European Homicide Research* (p. 96). New York: Springer Science.

Langevin, R. (2003) A study of the psychosexual characteristics of sex killers: Can we identify them before it is too late? *International Journal of Offender Therapy and Comparative Criminology*, 47, 366–382.

Langevin, R., Ben-Aron, M.H., Wright, P., et al. (1988) The sex killer. *Annals of Sex Research*, 1: 263–301.

Liem, M.C.A. and Oberwittler, D. (2013) Homicide followed by suicide in Europe. In M.C.A. Liem and W.A. Pridemore (eds), *Handbook of European Homicide Research: Patterns, Explanations, and Country Studies* (pp. 197–215). New York: Springer Science.

Liem, M.C.A. and Pridemore, W.A. (eds) (2013) *Handbook of European Homicide Research: Patterns, Explanations and Country Studies*. New York: Springer Science.

Meloy, J.R. (2000) The nature and dynamics of sexual homicide. *Aggression and Violent Behavior*, 5: 1–22.

Miethe, T.D. and Regoeczi, W.C. (2004) *Rethinking Homicide: Exploring the Structure and Process Underlying Deadly Situations*. New York: Cambridge University Press.

Miles, C. (2012) Intoxication and homicide: A context-specific approach. *British Journal of Criminology*, 52: 870–888.

Moracco, K.E., Runyan, C.W., and Butts, J.D. (1998) Femicide in North Carolina, 1991–1993: A statewide study of patterns and precursors. *Homicide Studies*, 2: 422–446.

Mucchielli, L. (2013) Homicides in contemporary France. In Liem, M.C.A. and Pridemore, W.A. (eds), *Handbook of European Homicide Research: Patterns, Explanations and Country Studies* (pp. 301–312), New York: Springer Science.

Myers, W.C., Reccoppa, L., Burton, K., and McElory, R. (1993) Malignant sex and aggression: An overview of serial sexual homicide. *Bulletin of the American Academy of Psychiatry Law*, 21: 435–451.

Nelson, C. and Huff-Corzine, L. (1998) Strangers in the night: An application of the life-style routine activities approach to elderly homicide victimization. *Homicide Studies*, 2(2): 130–159.

Nicole, A. and Proulx, J. (2007) Sexual murderer and sexual aggressors: Developmental paths and criminal history. In J. Proulx, E. Beauregard, M. Cusson, and A. Nicole (eds), *Sexual*

Murderers: A Comparative Analysis and New Perspectives (pp. 29–50). Chichester, UK: John Wiley & Sons.

Oliver, C.J., Beech, A.R., Fisher, D., and Beckett, R. (2007) A comparison of rapists and sexual murderers on demographic and selected psychometric measures. In J. Proulx, E. Beauregard, M. Cusson, and A. Nicole (eds), *Sexual Murderers: A Comparative Analysis and New Perspectives* (pp. 159–173). Chichester, UK: John Wiley & Sons.

Paulozzi, L.J., Mercy, J., Frazier, L., and Annest, J.L. (2004) CDC's national violent death reporting system (NVDRS): Background and methodology. *Injury Prevention*, 10: 47–52.

Polk, K. (1994) *When Men Kill: Scenarios of Masculine Violence*. New York: Cambridge University Press.

Polk, K. and Ranson, D. (1991) The role of gender in intimate homicide. *Australian and New Zealand Journal of Criminology*, 24: 15–24.

Radford, J. and Russell, D.E.H. (eds) (1992) *Femicide: The Politics of Woman Killing*. New York: Twayne.

Riedel, M. (1999) Sources of homicide data: A review and comparison. In M.D. Smith and M.A. Zahn (eds), *Homicide: A Sourcebook of Social Research* (pp. 75–95). Thousand Oaks, CA: SAGE.

Riedel, M. (2013) Special issue on elderly homicide: An introduction. *Homicide Studies*, 17: 123–133.

Russell, D.E.H. (1992) Femicide: The murder of wives. In J. Radford and D.E.H. Russell (eds), *Femicide: The Politics of Woman Killing* (pp. 286–299). New York: Twayne.

Russell, D.E.H. and Harmes, R.A. (eds) (2001) *Femicide in Global Perspective*. New York: Teachers College Press.

Safarik, M.E., Jarvis, J.P., and Nussbaum, K.E. (2002) Sexual homicide of elderly females: Linking offender characteristics to victim and crime scene attributes. *Journal of Interpersonal Violence*, 17: 500–525.

Salfati, C.G. and Taylor, P. (2006) Differentiating sexual violence: A comparison of sexual homicide and rape. *Psychology, Crime & Law*, 12: 107–126.

Shackelford, T.K. and Mouzos, J. (2005) Partner killing by men in cohabiting and marital relationships: A comparative, cross-national analysis of data from Australia and the United States. *Journal of Interpersonal Violence*, 20: 1310–1324.

Smith, M.D. and Zahn, M.A. (eds) (1999) *Homicide: A Sourcebook of Social Research*. Thousand Oaks, CA: SAGE.

Smith, P.H., Moracco, K.E., and Butts, J.D. (1998) Partner homicide in context: A population based perspective. *Homicide Studies*, 2: 400–421.

Soothill, K. and Francis, B. (2013) Homicide in England and Wales. In M.C.A. Liem and W.A. Pridemore (eds), *Handbook of European Homicide Research: Patterns, Explanations, and Country Studies* (pp. 287–300). New York: Springer Science.

Stockl, H., Devries, K., Rotstein, A., *et al.* (2013) The global prevalence of intimate partner homicide: A systematic review. *Lancet*, 282: 859–865.

Thomas, A., Dichter, M.E., and Matejkowski, J. (2011) Intimate versus non-intimate partner murder: A comparison of offender and situational characteristics. *Homicide Studies*, 15: 291–311.

UNODC (United Nations Office of Drugs and Crime) (2013) *Global Study on Homicide 2013: Trends Contexts and Data*. Vienna: UNODC.

Verkko, V. (1951) *Homicides and Suicides in Finland and Their Dependence on National Character*. Copenhagen: G.F.C. Gad.

VPC (Violence Policy Center) (2011) When men murder women: An analysis of 2009 homicide data. Available online at http://www.vpc.org/studies/wmmw2011.pdf (accessed September 29, 2016).

Websdale, N. (1999) *Understanding Domestic Homicide*. Boston: Northeastern University Press.

Websdale, N. (2010) *Familicidal hearts: The emotional styles of 211 killers*. New York: Oxford University Press.

Wilson, M., Johnson, H., and Daly, M. (1995) Lethal and non-lethal violence against wives. *Canadian Journal of Criminology*, 37: 331–362.

Wolfgang, M. (1957) Victim precipitated criminal homicide. *Journal of Criminal Law, Criminology, and Police Science*, 48: 1–11.

Wolfgang, M.E. and Ferracuti, F. (1967) *The Subculture of Violence*. London: Tavistock.

Further Reading

Dobash, R.E. and Dobash, R.P. (2009) Out of the blue: Men who murder an intimate partner. *Feminist Criminology*, 4: 194–225.

Dobash, R.E. and Dobash, R.P. (2015) When men murder Women. New York and Oxford: Oxford University Press.

Wilson, M. and Daly, M. (1992) Till death us do part. In J. Radford and D.E.H. Russell (eds), *Femicide: The Politics of Woman Killing*. New York: Twayne.

Wilson, M. and Daly, M. (1993) Spousal homicide risk and estrangement. *Violence and Victims*, 8: 3–16.

Wilson, M. and Daly, M. (1995) Familicide: The killing of spouses and children. *Aggressive Behavior*, 21: 275–291.

Wilson, M. and Daly, M. (1998) Lethal and nonlethal violence against wives and the evolutionary psychology of male sexual proprietariness. In R.E. Dobash and R.P. Dobash (eds), *Rethinking Violence Against Women* (pp. 199–230). Thousand Oaks, CA: SAGE.

9

Women Murdered in the Name of "Honor"

Aisha K. Gill

Introduction

For decades, anthropologists and sociologists have developed a rich body of research on the complex, multifaceted concept of honor. In his influential article, Pitt-Rivers (1966) describes honor as an individual's claim to pride, as well as his or her right to be granted it by others (Pitt-Rivers 1966)—realized through a system of symbols, values, and rules of conduct. Although this socially constructed system, known as the "honor code," varies between cultures (Gill 2014), it does nonetheless share a number of common elements across cultures. While not usually considered cultures of honor, contemporary Western cultures value honor in relation to a person's integrity, pride, and self-worth. Individuals view themselves as honorable to the extent that they feel pride as a result of their own actions and beliefs. Western societies tend to consider cultures of honor as those that place honor above all else, including the lives of female family members who are perceived to have committed actions of shame and dishonor, typically through sexual or other forms of disobedience. Drawing on the specific case of Shafilea Ahmed, a UK-born woman of Pakistani origin who was murdered by her parents, this chapter presents a critical analysis of how the prosecution as well as the media identified a culture of honor as the primary explanation for her murder without adequately exploring other contributing factors, perpetuating harmful generalizations about ethnic minority groups in Britain.

The Handbook of Homicide, First Edition. Edited by Fiona Brookman, Edward R. Maguire, and Mike Maguire.

The Face of "Honor"-Based Violence

The United Nations (UN) Population Fund estimates that between 5,000 and 12,000 women are murdered in the name of honor each year, primarily in the Middle East and Asia (Manjoo 2011; Gill 2014).[1] It is impossible to determine the true number of honor killings or the true incidence of "honor"-based violence (HBV) more generally: reports to the police are rare and sporadic, not least because both male and female family members often try to conceal honor-related crimes; many victims of HBV are abducted and never reported missing (Manjoo 2011).

Western countries with large multi-ethnic immigrant communities, such as Britain, began recognizing HBV as a significant and growing domestic issue in the late twentieth century. Understandings and awareness of HBV shifted accordingly, prompting the initiation of concerted national and international counter-efforts. In Europe, most reported honor killings occur in South Asian, Turkish, or Kurdish migrant communities; however, there have also been cases in Brazil, Italy, and the United States involving Roman Catholic perpetrators with varied ethnic backgrounds (Chesler 2010).

Perpetrators are often part of minority groups, even in countries where HBV is prevalent, a fact that underlines the significance of economic and social marginalization as aggravating factors (Kulczycki and Windle 2011). For example, Sheeley (2007) surveyed a stratified convenience sample from Jordan—a nation with a strong tradition of honor. A third of respondents knew someone who had been threatened with HBV, and 28 percent knew someone who had died as a result of it, suggesting the vast majority of people were unacquainted with anyone who had been threatened with or victimized by HBV. While incidence data do not explain the mechanisms through which cultural concerns with honor or male dominance come to motivate HBV, media reporting of HBV cases all too often treats such data as explanatory, attributing responsibility for HBV to specific cultures and minority groups.

What Is Honor?

Honor is characterized in various ways. In a broad sense, it is perceived as a social process that determines and designates social value to an individual or subgroup. When viewed as a whole, it contains distinct primary and secondary concepts, referred to both within the literature and in common use (Stewart 1994). Honoring is an action involving two or more parties, occurring between individuals, and within subgroups and groups. Any examination of this concept thus requires a broad analysis extending from individual to state levels. This internally integrative process of socialization defines the formation and dynamics of relationships among individuals within subgroups and groups. It establishes norms for behavior as well as disciplinary action to be taken against transgressors, such as expulsion from the group. Prestige, shame, face, esteem, and affiliated honor are the primary characteristics of honor. *Prestige* is the process whereby a group bestows honor on an individual or subgroup for attributes, characteristics and actions the group values as "good," elevating the hierarchal standing of an individual in relation to others in the group as a reward for demonstrating a standard of excellence though his or her deeds and attributes (Stewart 1994).

Conversely, *shame* lowers the standing of an individual or subgroup within the group, because of attributes, characteristics, and actions that are deemed "bad," or antithetical to excellence. Shame and prestige are not mutually exclusive. One may be shamed without a loss of prestige or gain prestige without a loss of shame. Stewart (1994), however, identifies an inverse relationship between shame and prestige, which together form the process of vertical honoring. Whereas prestige increases the social value of an individual, shame decreases it. Shame has an absolute characteristic; it can be lost, but will never be less than zero. The more shame a person has, the lower his or her social value to the group. When an individual is shamed, the group lowers his or her value without necessitating separation from the group. A shamed individual maintains utility within the group as an exemplar of how not to act, serving as a warning to other members to avoid departing from group values.

To maximize prestige and minimize shame, individuals or subgroups strive to maintain a position of honor in the group through *face* to preserve social identity and determine who is "first among equals" in the group hierarchy. "Saving face" refers to maintaining one's claim to membership in a particular group by resisting either the loss of a particular identity or a less-valued position within the group. An individual or group gains *esteem* by excelling in an honor system, even when the system is not necessarily agreed upon by both parties. The group bestowing esteem does not need to accept the values by which the individual is judged, but recognizes that the group judging the individual follows a comprehensible honor system. Esteem acknowledges the social value an individual contributes as a member of the group (Stewart 1994).

When a group member assumes an honorable status, based upon the reputation of the group with which he or she is associated, it is known as *affiliated honor*. The individual needs to do nothing more than maintain his or her status as a member by appearing to uphold the values of the group. Deriving social value from groups is a double-edged sword. Association with desirable parties can raise one's status, while membership within disreputable or unacceptable groups can result in dishonor and shame. Stewart (1994) articulates the division of honor into vertical and horizontal forms, described below.

Although respect gained through possessing horizontal honor can be lost, it cannot be increased. "Negative honor" is not considered to be respect that is due an equal, as one person has a right to more respect than others. According to Stewart (1994), horizontal honor is akin to shame, forming a base from which one can only lose honor. This idea has been likened to female chastity as a source of potential negative value to families (Oner-Ozkan and Gencoz 2006). It represents inclusion in a group with a particular standard of conduct that affords a distinction both within the group and with outsiders. In contrast with horizontal honor, vertical or positive honor is the right to special respect enjoyed by those with superior status in the group, whether by virtue of their ability, rank, community service, sex, kin relationship, office, or other factors. Class, rank, caste, or other overt distinctions of position are the most evident forms of vertical honor along a continuum, with corresponding rights and obligations both up and down the group hierarchy (Stewart 1994).

Consequences of Losing Honor

In honor cultures, aggression is an acceptable reaction to insults and threats to honor. Ethnographic and sociological research on diverse honor cultures, such as Iraqi Kurdistan (Begikhani, Gill, and Hague 2015), Spain (Gilmore 1987), rural Greece (Safilios-Rothschild 1969) and Turkey (Oner-Ozkan and Gencoz 2006), suggests that members of honor cultures consider retaliation to be a duty when a particular individual or family is insulted. Failure to retaliate connotes acceptance of the insult and admission of being unworthy of honor. The most effective way to restore tarnished honor is to repudiate the insult by demonstrating a willingness to engage in physical aggression when necessary. Under certain circumstances, when the accusation or insult is perceived as justified, such as when a female member of the family engages in a premarital or extramarital sexual affair, aggression is directed toward the "wrongdoer," rather than the insulting party.

Intra-familial honor killings embody the most extreme form of such aggression (Faqir 2001; Gill 2014). The willingness of people in honor cultures to take such radical measures, however painful and self-destructive, provides insights into the gravity of the consequences if action is not taken as perceived by members of the group, actions including shame, ridicule, loss of respect and social resources, and even complete ostracism (Gill 2014). In traditional societies where social mobility is limited, and where individuals' social, psychological and material prospects are closely interwoven with those of their family, tribe, or clan members, ostracism would mean the loss of not only social support, but also the material resources necessary for survival. A group's projection of aggression against the offender or wrongdoer highlights the necessity of addressing problems of honor directly rather than peripherally.

According to Pitt-Rivers (1966), losing honor by accepting humiliation cannot be repaired by demonstrating excellence. When someone has neither the ability nor the opportunity to take appropriate action, he or she will be shamed by the group, acknowledged as the strongest emotional reaction to the loss of honor in honor cultures. A susceptibility to shame is considered to be a positive quality, illustrated by phrases such as "having a sense of shame," popular among cultures of honor (Abu-Lughod 2011). In this respect, shame is not only an emotional consequence of losing honor, but also an important regulator of behavior.

In such societies, words corresponding to shame are used in a way that makes them synonymous with dishonor (Abu-Lughod 2011). Dishonor differs from shame, because it is antithetical to the values of the group, affecting the individual who commits the deed and threatening the foundation of the values upon which the entire system rests. Dealing with dishonored members differs from one honor group to another. Some honor cultures allow an individual to atone for "bad" deeds, while others allow for grace depending upon the severity of the dishonorable action (Casimir and Jung 2009). More extreme honor cultures actively rid the group of dishonored individuals by means of ostracism, exile, and capital punishment.

Honor Killing

Gendered violence encompasses HBV, "crimes of honor," "crimes related to honor conflict," "crimes of tradition," and "culture-based violence." The terms "honor killing" and "honor murder" are typically used interchangeably to refer to situations where violence results in a woman's death. Some scholars and activists reject the use of these designations altogether, categorizing such crimes as "domestic violence" (Terman 2010), while others place the various types of "honor violence" under the umbrella of "violence against women" (VAW).

Although most victims of HBV are female, there is also evidence of victimization among young men. According to Chesler (2010), 7 percent of victims in a sample of 230 honor killings examined worldwide between 1989 and 2009 were male. A German study on the prevalence of honor killings during 1996–2005 found that, of the 20 cases unequivocally classified as honor killings, 43 percent of victims were male (Oberwittler and Kasselt 2011). Like women, young men must respect and heed the wishes of more senior, usually older, male relatives (Abu-Lughod 2011). Subordinate men are most likely to cause dishonor as a result of (1) their choice of dating or sexual partners, (2) refusing an arranged marriage, (3) coming out as gay, bisexual or transgender (Ozturk 2011), and/or (4) refusing to commit an act of HBV (Roberts, Campbell, and Lloyd 2014).

Nevertheless, the majority of victims are female and the majority of perpetrators male. Eisner and Ghuneim (2013) examined the attitudes of fifteen-year-olds in Amman, Jordan, demonstrating that the practice of brutal vigilante justice, predominantly against young women perceived to have committed slights against family "honor," finds favor with a significant proportion of adolescents. The study revealed that almost half of boys and one in five girls believed that killing a daughter, sister, or wife who has "dishonored" or shamed her family is justified. A third of all teenagers involved in the research supported honor killings. These disturbing attitudes were connected more closely to patriarchal and traditional worldviews, including "moral" justification of violence, and the importance of female "virtue," rather than stemming from religious beliefs. Women's victimization is thus an outgrowth of broad cultural norms that legitimize gendered violence (Ertürk 2012).

An honor killing is a murder committed against a woman for actual or perceived immoral behavior deemed to be in breach of a household or community's honor (Gill 2014), most commonly for intimate relations between a woman and a man, whether that involves (alleged) adultery, sex outside marriage, or simply close companionship. Even women who have been victims of rape and sexual assault become targets for honor killing. Honor killings also take place because a woman or girl is in the presence of a male who is not a relative, refuses to agree to an arranged marriage, falls in love with someone who is unacceptable to the family, seeks a divorce, tries to escape marital violence, or appears Western. In some cases, the mere perception that a woman has behaved disobediently, thus shaming her father, brother, uncle, or cousin, has been reason enough to motivate an attack on her life. The norms of honor societies exist to maintain the sexual "purity" of women and to ensure that only certain bloodlines are allowed to blend, preventing wealth from becoming diluted by a woman from the landed class through marrying or consorting with someone of lower status in the social hierarchy. Rumors and gossip serve as society's greatest weapons for instilling shame in male members of society who cannot preserve the purity and chastity of female family members (Shalhoub-Kevorkian and Daher-Nashef 2013).

Honor killings form part of a larger category of violence against women, though violence against women generally takes many different forms and names. Bride burning in India (Ahmad 2008), crimes of passion in Latin America (Brinks 2008), and honor killings in Islamic nations (Hellgren and Hobson 2008), for example, all share the same dynamic: women are killed by male family members, an act which is deemed as socially acceptable, "understandable," or "excusable." Although crimes of passion, bride burning, and honor killings share this dynamic, there are key distinctions. In a crime of passion, it is the woman's husband or lover who commits the murder in heated reaction to a sense of personal betrayal or anger (Sen 2005), whereas an honor killing is carried out by a male family member on a premeditated basis as a symbol of rejecting a perceived dishonorable action to prevent the family from being shamed by the group (Sen 2005).

This chapter applies these concepts to the murder of Shafilea Ahmed, a young British woman of Pakistani origin, and examines how the prosecution and the mainstream British media presented culture as the overriding explanation for this crime. A critical analysis of racialized interpretations of such murder cases is presented to advance an appeal for greater vigilance against the acceptance of "honor" used as a justification for brutally murdering young women perceived to have shamed family members (Gill 2014).

The Murder of Shafilea Ahmed

The eldest of five children, Shafilea Ahmed was born in Bradford on July 14, 1986, shortly after her parents emigrated from Pakistan. Shafilea attended Great Sankey High School in Warrington until her father removed her from school in February 2003 for a trip to Pakistan. She was murdered later that year. In the year prior to Shafilea's death, tension over clashing "traditional" and "Western" values intensified between Shafilea and her parents, Farzana and Iftikhar. For instance, one of her parents' complaints was that Shafilea's wide circle of friends mostly consisted of Caucasian peers from school, with only a small percentage from minority ethnic backgrounds.

Shafilea's case was first referred to Warrington social services on October 3, 2002, after another pupil told teachers that Shafilea's parents had physically assaulted her and prevented her from attending school. Shafilea's social services file notes a mark on her face and the fact that she believed she was going to be sent to Pakistan for an arranged marriage. When Shafilea returned to school five days later, she revealed to her best friend that her mother, Farzana, had threatened a forced marriage. According to the friend, Shafilea's mother said "I can't wait till you go to Pakistan to teach you a lesson" (Gill 2014), prompting school staff to refer Shafilea to social services again several weeks later. This time, Shafilea's social services file noted that her father, Iftikhar, forced Shafilea to withdraw savings from her bank account, evidencing an attempt to exert control over his daughter.

Late in November 2002, one of Shafilea's friends saw her in a park, carrying her belongings wearing only a "thin sari." Shafilea indicated she was running away from home "because her parents would not let her be." Although the school reported the incident to social services, there is no record on file. In a meeting subsequently arranged by her teacher, Joanna Code, between Shafilea and her parents, Shafilea spoke "quite openly" about wanting "to be able to work and have money and go out." By the end of the meeting, Mr Ahmed had agreed that Shafilea would be allowed more freedom. However, things did not improve and teachers continued to refer Shafilea to social services and suggested that she should contact Childline (author's personal notes related to court attendance of this case in 2012 at Chester Crown Court—May 21, 2013–August 3, 2012). From the age of 15, Shafilea frequently reported suffering from domestic violence.

On February 18, 2003, her parents drugged her and took her to Pakistan. The trip was cut short in May of that year, when Shafilea swallowed bleach, or a similar caustic liquid, and required treatment at a local hospital. Her mother later told the police that Shafilea had accidentally ingested the bleach, mistaking it for mouthwash. Medical practitioners reported that the mouth injury was inconsistent with the action of gargling mouthwash, yet was consistent with a deliberate act of swallowing. The most likely explanation is that this was a deliberate act of self-harm by Shafilea to frustrate her parents' plans of forced marriage in Pakistan. As a result of this injury, she was no longer considered "marriageable," thus shaming her family.

Despite her illness, Shafilea was determined to continue her education and become a lawyer. In September 2003, Shafilea commenced a series of courses at Warrington's Priestly College. On the evening of September 11, 2003, she worked at her part-time job until 9.00 p.m. when another employee observed her leaving at the end of her shift. She spent the evening at her family home in Warrington with her parents and four siblings. Her father claims that she was alive though asleep when he and the rest of the family went to bed at 11.00 p.m. Although Shafilea was due for treatment at the hospital the following day, she was not seen alive again after that night.

Shafilea's former teacher reported her missing on September 18, 2003, prompting an extensive police investigation into her disappearance. At the time, the primary sources of information were Shafilea's family, friends, and teachers. Significant inconsistencies soon emerged, casting suspicion over her disappearance. The investigation also revealed the history of school, social services, and law enforcement involvement with Shafilea and her family as early as her entry into secondary school and continuing until her disappearance. In December 2003, Shafilea's parents were arrested on suspicion of abduction. They denied any involvement in their daughter's disappearance and were released on police bail.

Shafilea's parents gave a number of press interviews in March 2004, including one broadcasted on *Newsnight* on March 2, 2004. Whereas Mrs Ahmed remained silent throughout the interview, Mr Ahmed appeared attentive and focused, distancing himself from Shafilea by referring to her as "the daughter" or "the girl." When asked about Shafilea's suicide attempt, he contradicted the medical evidence, stating that his daughter "took a sip" of poisonous liquid. Mr Ahmed claimed "I'm not a strict parent in any way … I'm as English as anybody can picture me, right. But obviously the police portrayal of me is different … we have not been treated fairly" (Gill 2014). He complained that his family was misunderstood by the police and the public and feigned being hurt by suspicion of him and his family's responsibility for the death of "the girl."

His response focused less on the loss of his daughter and more on what he perceived as unfair treatment directed at him and his family. Rather than making a plea to those responsible for his daughter's death, he defended his "Englishness," illustrating the importance he placed on saving face and maintaining honor in the eyes of others. Mr Ahmed used the word "normal" many times in the *Newsnight* interview when describing Shafilea, his family, the "holiday" to Pakistan during which Shafilea swallowed bleach, and the night of her disappearance (Gill 2014). He continuously sought to present his family in a positive light.

R v Iftikhar Ahmed and Farzana Ahmed 2012

In September 2004, the police submitted a file of evidence to the Crown Prosecution Service to determine whether to pursue a case against Shafilea's parents. Six months later, Mr Robin Spencer QC advised the police there was insufficient evidence to demonstrate guilt beyond a reasonable doubt and secure a conviction. On January 11, 2008, a coroner's inquest into the circumstances of Shafilea's death found that she had been "unlawfully killed" (*Warrington Guardian* 2009). The situation changed in August 2010 when "Alesha" (a pseudonym) Ahmed was taken into custody on suspicion of having arranged a robbery at her parents' home. Having requested to speak to officers about another matter, she was interviewed in the presence of her solicitor. During the interview, Alesha claimed that, as a 15-year-old, she and her three surviving siblings had witnessed their parents killing Shafilea on the night of September 11, 2003. "Both of my parents were very controlling and tried to bring us up in the

Pakistani Muslim way," she said, before going on to explain that Shafilea was the one who was "picked on" most by their parents (Gill 2014: 185).

One of Alesha's earliest childhood memories was of seeing her mother hitting Shafilea. She stated that her parents attacked her and her sisters countless times, both verbally and physically. According to Alesha, her parents' abuse of Shafilea escalated over time. Between the ages of 14 and 17, her sister was attacked virtually every day for the most trifling reasons. If Shafilea received a text message or phone call from a boy, wore "inappropriate" clothes, or associated with white friends at school, her mother would claim that Shafilea had shamed the family. Alesha described one incident in which her mother hit Shafilea and then shut her in a room without food for two days, only allowing her out to use the toilet. "They knew that they could control us completely through fear" (Gill 2014: 186). Alesha's testimony presented the "missing piece" of evidence, allowing the Crown Prosecution Service to advance a convincing case against Shafilea's parents. In September 2011, both parents were charged with murder. Their trial commenced on May 21, 2012 at Chester Crown Court.

The trial of "normal" parents

As a witness for the prosecution, Alesha was called on to describe the night of Shafilea's disappearance. She recalled going with her mother and brother to collect Shafilea from work just after 9.00 p.m. on September 11, 2003. When Shafilea reached the car, they saw that she was wearing a lilac t-shirt and white trousers made from stretchy material, with ties at each side on her hips. As soon as her mother saw Shafilea, she complained that her clothes were too revealing.

Alesha stated that when they arrived home, the whole family assembled together in the kitchen, her mother demanding that the family collectively search Shafilea's bags. This practice was not unusual. Finding some money in Shafilea's handbag increased her mother's anger and she accused her of hiding the money. She pushed Shafilea with both hands on her chest and shoulders on to the settee. Alesha stated that Shafilea, still weak from her illness, had a small frame of not much more than five or six stone (31–38 kg). Alesha then heard her mother say "*Etay khatam kar saro*," Punjabi for "just finish it here." Iftikhar went to Shafilea and pulled her into a lying position on the settee. Shafilea began to struggle as both parents hit her and held her down. One of them said, "Get the bag." Alesha saw her mother grab a thin white carrier bag from the stool next to the settee. Then they both forced the entire bag into Shafilea's mouth. Each placed a hand over her mouth and nose. Her legs kicked, but Iftikhar put his knee up on the settee to pin her down until she stopped struggling (Gill 2014: 186–187).

Alesha went on to explain that, despite having seen her sister die the night before, the following morning she asked her mother where Shafilea was. The children were sternly instructed that if anyone asked, they were to say that Shafilea came home from work, went to bed, then ran away in the night. The day after Shafilea's murder all the children were sent to school. Alesha recalled breaking down and telling some friends what had occurred. She described being very upset and confused at the time and, as a result, spontaneously blurted out that her father had killed her sister. When her teachers asked her about this, she recanted from fear of reprisal from her parents and the matter was not pursued until later. Questions remain as to why those who had witnessed Alesha's breakdown at school did not take further action to investigate the disappearance of her sister. Why did the teachers only contact the police on September 18, 2003?

During the trial, both of Shafilea's parents insisted that they had not been involved in their daughter's disappearance. They also denied claims that they had repeatedly beaten her over a prolonged period. Eight weeks into the trial, Shafilea's mother, Farzana Ahmed, changed her defense in what the judge described as a "significant" development (Gill 2014: 187). On July 8, 2012, she admitted that an incident of "violence" involving Shafilea took place on September 11, 2003 (Gill 2014: 187). Shafilea had confided in her friends that her mother was particularly abusive toward her while she was growing up. Perhaps the most damning evidence for Farzana's complicity in her daughter's murder came from the installation of a covert listening device in the Ahmed home in November 2003. In conversations with her other children, Shafilea's mother can be heard warning them not to say anything at school. She was also recorded saying to her son: "If the slightest thing comes out of your mouth, we will be stuck in real trouble. Remember that." These covert recorded conversations further suggest that Farzana may have had knowledge of what happened to Shafilea. She exclaims to Iftikhar: "You're a pimp. You're shameless. I'm going to say it to you clearly, I swear to Allah, everything happened because of you" (Bhagdin 2012).

In other recorded conversations she remarks on the mileage of their family car: " … Yeah, so this means they will look at the mileage of our car as well to see how much it is" (Bhagdin 2012).

In the year of Shafilea's "disappearance," Farzana scolded her children:

> That's what I'm saying. That slut is acting as if she is relieved. The face is getting puffed up. And you behave *bandeh di ti ban* ["become the daughter of a human"] yourself, as well. Today is not a day to be beaten up, okay. Are you listening to me? I'm talking to you ….

Farzana's treatment of her daughter could be explained using Kandiyoti's seminal 1988 study, describing the phenomenon of abuse by women against daughters as a culturally specific form of "patriarchal bargain" between the mother and the extended household. Her discussion of "classic patriarchy" sets out how family dynamics between younger and older women in the South Asian familial systems are structured by a model of patriarchy that stresses "corporate male-headed entities rather than more autonomous mother and child units" (Kandiyoti 1988: 275). Kandiyoti further explains:

> Different forms of patriarchy present women with distinct "rules of the game" and call for different strategies to maximize security and optimize life options with varying potential for active or passive resistance in the face of oppression. (1988: 275)

Ultimately, the men make the rules, but if women are able to play by those rules, they gain for themselves a form of symbolic capital. Specifically, they can present themselves as conforming women, enabling their survival in the field of patriarchy (Kandiyoti 1988). With the honor schema, misbehavior by one woman dishonors the entire patriarchal familial unit, male and female; to ensure their survival and security, women monitor the behavior of their kinswomen as much as men.

Up until the trial in May 2012, Shafilea's mother denied that she had any knowledge of what happened to her daughter. The defense counsel stated that, on the night in question, Iftikhar was

> very angry ... hitting [Shafilea], slapping her with his hands towards the facial area and punching her two to three times to the upper part of her body. [Shafilea's mother] tried to intervene but she was told to go away. (author's personal notes, 2012)

When she tried again to help her daughter, she was "pushed away by both hands and also punched with a clenched fist" (Gill 2014: 187). Contrary to Alesha's account, Shafilea's mother claimed that only her third eldest daughter, "M" (then aged 12), was present. "Extremely scared" and fearing for M's safety, Shafilea's mother took her upstairs. Some 20 minutes later, she heard a car leave and came downstairs to find Shafilea and her husband gone, along with her car. At 6:30 a.m. the next day, her husband returned without Shafilea (author's personal notes, 2012). In response to these allegations, Shafilea's brother, who was 13 at the time of her disappearance, told the jury: "I think it's a lie what she's saying but that's her account to give." He also said: "It's a whole pack of lies that [Alesha's] told and I don't believe a word of what she's saying" (see Gill 2014: 187). He described the Ahmed household as a "happy family" before Shafilea disappeared and told the jury that "nothing out of the ordinary" happened on September 11, 2003. He claimed that he only knew his sister was missing the next morning (author's personal notes, 2012).

Ultimately, the jury accepted Alesha's version of events and on August 3, 2012, Shafilea's parents were convicted of her murder. Both received life sentences. While the true facts of the case may never be known, all the accounts of what happened on September 11, 2003, circle back to the key role of "honor." They also simultaneously demonstrate how cultural explanations for Shafilea's death are insufficient; it was a product of many factors, including the relationship between "honor," gender, and power inequalities within the Ahmed household.

Cultural Predicaments

The Ahmed family lived in a context that was simultaneously British and Pakistani, in what Homi Bhabha (1994) refers to as a "third space." This applies to both generations, albeit in different ways. Shafilea's social location was determined partly by her being born in the 1980s in postcolonial Britain and partly by the fact that her parents had migrated from a rural area of Pakistan. The patriarchal gender system that Shafilea was ensnared in did not derive simply from the Ahmeds' "backward" rural roots standing in opposition to the enlightened culture of British society outside the Ahmed home. Instead, Shafilea lived her life in and through both the British patriarchal values to which all women in Britain are subject and the patriarchal values of her parents' rural Pakistani upbringing.

Mr Ahmed's defense of his "Englishness" is particularly interesting in this context. It reveals how his own implicit claims that he was sufficiently influenced by local cultural practices to consider himself English indicate that his actions were not simply the result of cultural conflict (Brah 1996). Indeed, Mr Ahmed had been married before to a Danish woman with whom he had a child (Keaveny 2012) and with whom he had led a "creolized-Western" lifestyle (Grillo 2003). It is not only immigrant parents, but also their children, who must negotiate their intersectionally configured location. Thus, while families may share a common ethos, individual members often express and experience this ethos differently. The fact that the different members of the Ahmed family did not occupy a single, shared intersectionally configured location helps to explain why the Ahmed children reacted in different ways to Shafilea's murder.

Jacqueline Rose (2012), writing in *The Guardian* about the Ahmed trial, argued that

> Missing in the court room, in pretty much any court room, is the idea of fantasy, of how we make our lives bearable by elaborating stories about ourselves. For both Alesha and [her sister] lying was a way to survive. If, in the judges [*sic*] own words, this case has been "extraordinary," it is not least by bringing these contortions of the inner world, the agonies of attachment and belonging, so painful [*sic*] to life.

As a victim of domestic violence herself, Shafilea's sister, Alesha, had nowhere to go when, in August 2010, she disclosed to the police that her parents were responsible for her sister's murder. Her situation was complicated by the fact that giving evidence against her parents had serious repercussions for her within Warrington's tight-knit Pakistani community. Alesha told the police that for many years she had been too afraid to discuss Shafilea's disappearance. Although her testimony proved crucial in securing her parents' conviction, Alesha was too afraid to attend court again afterwards and was not present to hear the verdict on August 3, 2012.

In comparison to their white counterparts, for whom shame tends to take on a more personal character, black and minority ethnic victims often see themselves as responsible for their families' as well as their own "honor," causing them to experience heightened feelings of shame (Feldman 2010). South Asian women are socialized to believe that they are primarily to blame for any violence they experience, especially when it is triggered by dishonor perceived to stem from their own actions. In struggling to make their own life choices, both Alesha and Shafilea were continuously confronted with the internalized need to conform to their family's values and, in doing so, to avoid bringing "shame" upon them. Shame creates feelings of humiliation, indignity, and exposure to debasement in the eyes of others.

This, in turn, increases victims' sense of vulnerability (Gill 2009); the wish to conceal this lies at the heart of many women's silence about the violence they have experienced.

South Asian women are socialized not to discuss private matters with outsiders, seeing this, in itself, as shameful, often encountering difficulty with talking about their experiences of violence, even with trained professionals. Further complicating the situation is the emphasis Pakistani society places on behavior that encourages harmony in the home, rendering many women reluctant to complain for fear of being perceived as "trouble-makers." Just as negative family and community responses encourage women to remain silent about abuse, positive responses often play a crucial role in enabling women from ethnic minorities to discuss their experiences of violence (Gill 2014).

The Wider Implications of Shafilea Ahmed's Case

The violence that Shafilea suffered within the confines of her private home, which ultimately ended beside the River Kent in Sedgwick, Cumbria, serves as a metaphor for how Western nations point to domestic cases of crimes related to "honor" as illustrative of a growing threat to dominant cultural norms and, by extension, maintaining security within society. Consequently, the discourse surrounding Shafilea's murder supports Hellgren and Hobson's (2008) contention that:

> honour killings are boundary-making arenas … intended to be public statements, to restore honour to a family … [but] are also public dramas re-enacted in the courts and media … arenas for boundary marking beyond the family and local community. (Hellgren and Hobson 2008: 386)

Media coverage of Shafilea's "honor killing," and the actors involved, provides a convenient opportunity to make sweeping generalizations about the Muslim, South Asian migrant population, and the implications of their presence for the British nation, drawing from the experience of a single Muslim/Pakistani family. Shafilea's death embodies a complicated, symbolic battlefield for an entire discourse about national inclusion and exclusion. She becomes what Reimers identifies as the "other but with us." Shafilea is "othered" as a victim to be saved by Western culture, while the act of claiming Shafilea as "Western" makes her a "worthy" victim. On a secondary level, Shafilea is also sacrificed for her family's "honor," thus her "Westernization" also makes her a martyr for the British nation and the ideal migrant citizen. We must not overlook, however, the extreme costs that such news has upon the lives of Shafilea and women like her. These women vacillate between cultures within the discursive no-man's land described in Anzaldúa's (2007) concept of borderlands.

Representations of honor killings that construct South Asian culture as the key causal factor are permeated with discursive strategies associated with moral panics.

The perpetrators of these crimes are labeled "deviant" with the problem of HBV seen as pervasive among such deviants—in this case, among all Muslims. Specific forms of domestic violence common in minority communities tend to be depicted as the norm in these "deviant" communities. Whereas "mainstream" forms of domestic violence are generally represented through rhetoric focused on the individuals involved, the majority of news stories about HBV employ framing devices centered on the cultural differences of perpetrators of this form of violence. As such, the media's framing of honor killings contributes to the perception that culturally specific forms of violence are more abhorrent than "normal" domestic violence and that they are rightfully subject to media-driven moral crusades (Anitha and Gill 2011).

Conclusion

The police refused to call Shafilea's murder an "honor killing" precisely because they wanted to stress that no license should be granted to those who claim that their cultural rights excuse acts of brutality, marking a step in the right direction. At the same time, those charged with protecting the public must be able to identify and understand the risk factors associated with all forms of VAW in order to respond effectively. Such an understanding is only possible if, instead of talking purely about culture, debates about HBV and VAW explore the intersection of culture with gender and other axes of differentiation; it is a question of equity, not just of culture. In sentencing Shafilea Ahmed's parents to life imprisonment on August 3, 2012, the judge, Mr Justice Roderick Evans, described Shafilea as a determined, able, and ambitious girl "squeezed between two cultures, the culture and way of life that she saw around her and wanted to embrace and the culture and way of life her parents wanted to impose upon her" (Gill 2014: 195). However, the causal factors behind Shafilea's murder were far more complex than was suggested by the judge and also by the British media's tale of backward parents acting against the backdrop of modern Britain's progressive society. Understanding the forms of violence experienced by minority ethnic women in Britain requires an approach that takes account of the continuities between different forms of gender-based violence, while addressing the specificity of particular forms, such as HBV. A distinction must be drawn between the wholesale condemnation of the culture of a specific social group and condemnation of a particular cultural practice.

Note

1 According to women's advocacy groups the figure could be around 20,000. In general, given the difficulty surrounding the reporting of these crimes, official statistics are understood to be grossly underreported (see Manjoo 2012).

References

Abu-Lughod, L. (2011) Seductions of honor crime. *Differences: A Journal of Feminist Cultural Studies*, 22(1): 17–63.

Ahmad, N. (2008) Dowry deaths in India and abetment of suicide: A socio-legal appraisal. *Journal of East Asia International Law*, 1(2): 275–289.

Anitha, S. and Gill, A. (2011) The social construction of forced marriage and its "victim" in media coverage and crime policy discourses. In A. Gill and S. Anitha (eds), *Forced Marriage: Introducing a Social Justice and Human Rights Perspective*. London: Zed Books.

Anzaldúa, G. (2007) *Borderlands/La Frontera: The New Mestiza*. San Francisco: Aunt Lute.

Begikhani, N., Gill, A., and Hague, G. (2015) *"Honour"-based Violence: Experiences and Counter Strategies in Iraqi Kurdistan and the UK Kurdish Diaspora*. Aldershot, UK: Ashgate.

Bhabha, H. (1994) *The Location of Culture*. London: Routledge.

Bhagdin, A. (2012) Transcript of sections of audio from covert recordings with audio file and real timings. Available online at http://docslide.us/documents/shafilea-ahmed-murder-intestigation-covert-recording-from-inside-the-ahmed-house.html http://docslide.us/documents/shafilea-ahmed-murder-intestigation-covert-recording-from-inside-the-ahmed-house.html (accessed August 8, 2015).

Brah, A. (1996) *Cartographies of Diaspora/Contesting Identities*. New York: Routledge.

Brinks, D. (2008) *The Judicial Response to Police Killings in Latin America: Inequality and the Rule of Law*. New York: Cambridge University Press.

Casimir, M. and Jung, S. (2009) "Honor and dishonor": Connotations of a socio-symbolic category in cross-cultural perspective. In B. Röttger-Rössler and H. Markowitsch (eds), *Emotions as Bio-Cultural Processes* (pp.281–316). New York: Springer.

Chesler, P. (2010) Worldwide trends in honor killings. *Middle East Quarterly*, Spring: 3–11.

Eisner, M. and Ghuneim, L. (2013) Honor killing attitudes amongst adolescents in Amman, Jordan. *Aggressive Behavior*, 39(5): 405–417.

Ertürk, Y. (2012) Culture versus rights dualism: A myth or a reality? *Development*, 55(3): 273–276.

Faqir, F. (2001) Intrafamily femicide in defence of honour: The case of Jordan. *Third World Quarterly*, 22(1): 65–82.

Feldman, S. (2010) Shame and honour: The violence of gendered norms under conditions of global crisis. *Women's Studies International Forum*, 33(4): 305–315.

Gill, A. (2009) "Honour" killings and the quest for justice in black and minority ethnic communities in the UK. *Criminal Justice Policy Review*, 20(4): 475–494.

Gill, A. (2014) "All they think about is honour": The murder of Shafilea Ahmed. In A. Gill, K. Roberts, and C. Strange (eds), *"Honour" Killing and Violence: Theory, Policy and Practice*. London: Palgrave Macmillan.

Gilmore, D. (1987) *Aggression and Community: Paradoxes of Andalusian Culture*. New Haven, CT: Yale University Press.

Grillo, R. (2003) Cultural essentialism and cultural anxiety. *Anthropological Theory*, 3(2): 157–173.

Hellgren, Z. and Hobson, B. (2008) Cultural dialogues in the good society: The case of honour killings in Sweden. *Ethnicities*, 8(3): 385–400.

Kandiyoti, D. (1988) Bargaining with patriarchy. *Gender and Society*, 2(3): 274–290.

Keaveny, P. (2012) Murderer Iftikhar Ahmed abandoned son and Danish first wife to follow through with arranged marriage to Shafilea's mother Farzana. *Independent*, August 3. Available online at http://www.independent.co.uk/news/uk/crime/murderer-iftikhar-ahmed-abandoned-son-and-danish-first-wife-to-follow-through-with-arranged-marriage-to-shafileas-mother-farzana-8005441.html (accessed August 8, 2015).

Kulczycki, A. and Windle, S. (2011) Honor killings in the Middle East and North Africa: A systematic review of the literature. *Violence Against Women*, 17(11): 1442–1464.

Manjoo, R. (2011) *Report of the Special Rapporteur on Violence against Women, Its Causes and Consequences*, UN Doc. A/HRC/17/26 (May 2). Geneva: United Nations.

Manjoo, R. (2012) *Report of the Special Rapporteur on Violence against Women, Its Causes and Consequences*, UN Doc A/HRC/20/16 (May 23). Geneva: United Nations.

Oberwittler, D. and Kasselt, J. (2011) *Ehrenmorde in Deutschland: Eine Untersuchung auf der Basis von Prozessakten* [Honor killings in Germany: A study based on prosecution files] (Polizei + Forschung, Bd. 42, hrsg. vom Bundeskriminalamt). Cologne, Germany: Wolters Kluwer.

Oner-Ozkan, B., and Gencoz, T. (2006) Gurur toplumu bakis acisiyla Turk kulturunun incelenmesi [The importance of investigation of Turkish culture from the point of view of cultural pride]. *Kriz Dergisi*, 14: 19–25.

Ozturk, S. (2011) Sydney's killer: The gay-hate epidemic that claimed 80 men. *Star Observer*, August. Available online at http://www.starobserver.com.au/news/local-news/new-south-wales-news/sydneys-killer-the-gay-hate-epidemic-that-claimed-80-men/107657 (accessed September 29, 2013).

Pitt-Rivers, J. (1966) *Honour and Social Status. Honour and Shame: The Values of Mediterranean Society*. Cambridge: Cambridge University Press.

Roberts, K., Campbell, G., and Lloyd, G. (2014) *Honor-Based Violence: Policing and Prevention, Advances in Police Theory and Practice*. London: Routledge.

Rose, J. (2012) Shafilea Ahmed's murder is a crime meshed in migration and modernity. *The Guardian*, August 6: 22. Available online at http://www.guardian.co.uk/commentisfree/2012/aug/05/shafilea-ahmed-murder-migration-modernity (accessed August 8, 2015).

Safilios-Rothschild, C. (1969) Honour crimes in contemporary Greece. *British Journal of Sociology*, 20: 205–218.

Sen, P. (2005) Crimes of honour: Value and meaning. In L. Welchman and S. Hossain (eds), *Honour: Crimes, Paradigms and Violence against Women*. London: Zed Books.

Shalhoub-Kevorkian, N., and Daher-Nashef, S. (2013) Femicide and colonization between the politics of exclusion and the culture of control. *Violence against Women*, 19(3): 295–315.

Sheeley, E. (2007) *Reclaiming Honor in Jordan: A National Public Opinion Survey on "Honor" Killings*. Amman, Jordan: Black Iris.

Stewart, F. (1994) *Honour*. Chicago: Chicago University Press.

Terman, R. (2010) To specify or single out: Should we use the term "honour killing"? *Muslim World Journal of Human Rights*, 7(2): 1.

Warrington Guardian (2009) Shafilea Ahmed's father fails to overturn verdict that she was "unlawfully killed." Available online at http://www.warringtonguardian.co.uk/news/4436238.print/(accessed August 8, 2015).

10

Hate and Homicide
Exploring the Extremes of Prejudice-Motivated Violence

Nathan Hall

As I sit here writing this introduction,[1] the BBC breaking news ticker scrolling across the bottom of my laptop is reporting a series of almost simultaneous but seemingly unconnected murderous attacks in different parts of the world—at least 38 people, mostly British holidaymakers, it seems have been killed and 36 injured in an apparent extremist attack on a beach in the Tunisian resort town of Sousse; a man has been found decapitated, and an explosion has occurred, at a gas factory near Lyon in France after an attack allegedly perpetrated by a suspect with apparent links to radical Islam; a sectarian attack on a Shia mosque during Friday prayers in the Kuwaiti capital has killed at least 27 people with another 227 wounded, with an Islamic State-affiliated group claiming responsibility; and emerging reports are suggesting that Islamic State (IS) militants have killed more than 120 civilians during an attack on the Syrian border town of Kobane.

Also on this day, Queen Elizabeth has visited the site of the World War II concentration camp at Bergen-Belsen, where the Nazis killed more than 50,000 people, while in the United States the US Supreme Court has ruled that same-sex marriage is a legal right across the United States, meaning that the 14 states with bans on same-sex marriage will no longer be able to enforce them. In his speech on the issue, President Obama has lauded the ruling as a "*victory for America*," and the White House has used all its social media pages to declare, "*today love wins in America*." On a quite extraordinary day of *targeted* violence and murder, many outside of America would perhaps be forgiven for thinking that hate, and not love, has won today.

But of course all of these events come just nine days after the murder of nine people, all African American, during a Bible study group at Emanuel African

The Handbook of Homicide, First Edition. Edited by Fiona Brookman, Edward R. Maguire, and Mike Maguire.

Methodist Episcopal Church in Charleston, South Carolina. In seeking to provide "justification" for his alleged actions, Dylann Roof, the 21-year-old white man charged with perpetrating the massacre, published an online hate-filled "manifesto." Within this document, Roof identifies himself as a white nationalist whose extreme racist views were shaped by, for example, online material from websites belonging to groups such as the Council of Conservative Citizens. As the Southern Poverty Law Center (SPLC 2015b) note:

> Roof fits the profile of the lone wolf terrorist radicalized in the echo chamber of racist websites that increasingly promote a global white nationalist agenda. In his manifesto, Roof wrote that he began researching "black [sic] on White" crime after the Trayvon Martin incident and found "pages upon pages of these brutal black [sic] on White murders," then discovered the "same things were happening" in Western European countries.

As a result, it seems that Roof felt compelled to take matters into his own hands to redress this "injustice," as he perceived it. While we shall consider the accuracy of Roof's assumptions concerning the volume of homicides in due course, it is worth noting here that in two separate studies considering the influence of online racist propaganda and the activities of "lone wolf terrorists," the SPLC (2014, 2015a) suggests that members of Stormfront—the world's largest white supremacist website with 300,000 registered users—have murdered around 100 people in the past five years, and that a domestic terror attack or foiled plot occurred on average every 34 days over the last six years.

On May 24, 2014, in another example of hate-motivated homicide, Elliot Rodger repeatedly stabbed three men to death in his apartment, before killing two women and another man, and wounding several others, before committing suicide, during a shooting spree across ten locations in Isla Vista, close to the University of California, Santa Barbara. Rodger, it seems, had been diagnosed with Asperger's Syndrome. He had certainly been receiving psychiatric care from multiple therapists. Like Dylann Roof, he had published a 141-page manifesto entitled "My Twisted World" on the Internet, and posted a number of videos on You Tube in which his hatred of others, particularly in the form of misogyny, was explicit.

As we have seen in the examples mentioned here, Rodger is not alone. Human history is littered with incidents of extreme hate-motivated violence and murder. One need only think of the countless examples of genocide and mass murder that have occurred around the world (an issue to which we shall return), or indeed any of the seemingly nameless suicide bombers that we have now sadly become so accustomed to hearing about in the news. Or, like Elliot Rodger and Dylann Roof, the similar actions of other individuals such as Timothy McVeigh, John William King, Benjamin Smith, Buford Furrow, David Copeland, Anders Breivik, Michael Adebowale or (Michael Adebolajo), to name but a few whose hatred of "the Other" has, for whatever reason and to differing degrees, led them to murder.

In this chapter, then, we shall explore some of the issues surrounding hate-motivated homicide. This, however, is a far from straightforward task, and the various examples referred to above encapsulate many of the complex issues associated with our understanding of "hate" and in particular the role it might play (whether exclusively or in conjunction with other motivating factors) in the perpetration of homicide. Moreover, it is important to acknowledge the expansive nature of the subject in hand because, as the cases referred to above imply, "hatred," or more accurately "prejudice," as a motivation for murder can and does transcend the somewhat conceptually blurred lines between more traditional notions of hate crime and extremism, terrorism (both domestic and international), sectarianism, and genocide. Clearly, then, a comprehensive discussion of the role that hate plays in each of these arenas is beyond the scope of a chapter of this size, so we shall necessarily limit ourselves here to a more general exploration of what we know about the nature of hatred as a motivation for homicide, while drawing upon relevant examples where appropriate. In particular, we shall explore the meaning of "hate" within the context of hate crime, attempt to establish the extent and nature of hate-motivated homicide, and consider issues of causation.

Understanding "Hate" Crime

Although there is not the space here to fully examine all of the issues in hand, the reader should be aware from the outset that hate and hate crime are complex phenomena, characterized by scholarly, political, and legal debates and controversies at almost every level. Within the literature, a lack of clarity surrounds aspects such as how to define and conceptualize the problem; how it has come to be formally acknowledged, or not, as a contemporary socio-legal issue; how much of it exists around the world; who should be recognized as victims and what impacts it can have on those who experience it; and how the problem should be responded to both via the criminal justice system and through other preventive and reformative methods. More pertinently for our purposes here, as Sullivan (1999) points out (and as we shall see in more detail later), hatred remains something of a psychological mystery and consequently anything that might even closely resemble a comprehensive or holistic explanation of how and why hatred becomes the motivation for criminal behavior, in this case murder, remains elusive.

So what, then, is "hate crime"? And what, in the context of hate crime, is "hate"? Barbara Perry (2001) suggests that, as is the case with crime in general, it is very difficult to construct an exhaustive definition of "hate crime" that is able to take account of all of its facets. Crime is of course socially constructed and means different things to different people, different things at different times, and what constitutes a crime in one place may not in another. As Perry suggests, crime is therefore relative and historically and culturally contingent, and this is particularly true of hate crime, and these facets are reflected in the variation to be found in how the concept is defined and how much of it exists, at least on paper, in different parts of the world.

As Barbara Perry implies, hate crime is therefore not a universally accepted or adopted concept. Indeed there are plenty of critics who, for a host of legal, practical, and moral reasons (see Hall 2013 for a wider discussion of these) argue that the concept should be abolished altogether, and plenty of countries that do not, or will not, acknowledge it as a problem in need of attention. But in the jurisdictions where it is formally recognized as a distinct criminal act, and indeed in the vast majority of scholarly interpretations, what might appear to the lay person as a rather curious common theme emerges, namely that in contemporary constructions of the problem, hate crime isn't really about hate at all. Rather, the definitions commonly employed today speak of crimes and incidents aggravated or motivated by *prejudice* and *bias* and *hostility*, and few (if any) refer solely to *hatred* as a causal factor.

As such, American legal scholars Jacobs and Potter (1998) suggest that hate crime, as a contemporary social construct, is therefore a potentially expansive concept that covers a great many offenders and situations. This, they note, incorporates clear-cut hate crimes where there is little doubt that the offender *hates* his or her victim in the truest sense of the word (such as, for example, some of those identified at the start of this chapter) and where such individuals are totally committed to their hate and view the objects of this hate as an evil that must be removed from the world, through to those incidents or offenses that are described as being "situational" in that they arise from ad hoc disputes or short tempers, but are neither products of strong prejudicial attitudes nor are they strongly causally related to the incident in question.

Jacobs and Potter (1998) argue, therefore, that if contemporary conceptualizations of hate crime included only these more extreme examples, the concept would not be ambiguous, difficult to understand, or controversial, nor would there be many hate crimes occurring because cases like these, generally, are rare. The problem is that the definitions currently in use in many jurisdictions around the world ensure that the majority of offenses officially labeled as hate crimes are not motivated by hate at all, but by prejudice, which is often an entirely different thing. The number of hate crimes in society is therefore entirely determined by how hate crime is defined, conceptualized, and interpreted, as is our interpretation of what "hate" is, or might be.

In terms of understanding "hate" as a motivation for violence, a central problem clearly relates to the word "hate" and what, exactly, is meant by it. Despite the frequency with which the term is used, for the purpose of furthering our understanding of hate crime, the word hate is distinctly unhelpful. As Sullivan (1999) points out in a dated but nonetheless still relevant observation, for all our zeal to attack hate we still have a remarkably vague idea of what hate actually is, and despite the powerful and emotional images that it invokes it is still far less nuanced an idea than prejudice, bias, bigotry, hostility, anger, or just a mere aversion to others.

The question is, then, when we talk about "hate," do we mean all of these things or just the extremes of them? In contemporary explanations of hate crime,[2] it is often the former (see Hall 2013 for a wider discussion of definitions of hate crime). Few speak of "hate" as a causal factor. Rather, as noted above, the definitions refer to prejudice, hostility or bias, or *-isms* (racism, disablism, and so on). Clearly, then, hate crime thus defined is not really about hate, but about criminal behavior motivated by prejudice, of which hate is just one small and extreme part. But as Sullivan

(1999) rightly suggests, if "hate" is to stand for all of these varieties of human experience, and everything in between, then the war against it will likely be so vast as to be quixotic.

In short, Jacobs and Potter's point serves to illustrate that hate crimes, and the "hates" that underpin them, are in effect a social construction, and, as Sullivan (1999) puts it, the transformation of a "psychological mystery" into a "facile political artefact," often far removed from what we might consider "true hatred" has served to considerably complicate our understanding of hatred. Sullivan (1999: 54) further laments this "watering down" of the concept of hate, stating that:

> Hate used to be easier to understand. When Sartre described anti-Semitism in his 1964 essay "Anti-Semite and Jew," he meant a very specific array of firmly held prejudices, with a history, an ideology and even a pseudo-science to back them up. He meant a systematic attempt to demonize and eradicate an entire race ... And when we talk about hate, we often mean this kind of phenomenon. But this brand of hatred is mercifully rare ... These professional maniacs are to hate crime what serial killers are to murder. They should certainly not be ignored but they represent ... "niche haters": cold-blooded, somewhat deranged, often poorly socialized psychopaths ... But their menace is a limited one, and their hatred is hardly typical of anything widespread.

Measuring Hate Homicide

Perry (2001) suggests that there are few endeavors so frustrating as trying to estimate and establish the extent of hate crime. Part of the reason for this, as we have alluded to above, is that hate crime is essentially a social construction and that the size of the problem depends almost entirely on how we define and conceptualize it, which of course will vary from place to place, and from time to time. As such, hate crime statistics should be treated with extreme caution, particularly when used comparatively. Nevertheless, various attempts have been made, both at domestic and international levels, by a range of bodies, both formal (such as state agencies) and informal (such as NGOs and advocacy groups), to measure the extent and nature of the hate crime "problem" in different parts of the world.

The official data that are collected generally reflect only traditional conceptualizations of "hate crime," and hence take little or no account of events involving terrorism, extremism, or genocide. As such, they tend to support Sullivan's point above. In short, hate homicide is rare. Using the United States as an illustrative example, the latest official FBI figures at the time of writing show that of the 4,430 victims of hate crimes against the person in 2013, five were murdered (FBI 2014). Elsewhere, official statistics on the numbers of hate-motivated murders are hard to come by. One of the key sources of information of this type is published annually by the Organization for Security and Cooperation in Europe (OSCE)—the world's largest regional security organization with members from 57 countries across Europe, Central Asia, and North America. Although the data collected represents something of a "patchwork quilt," the various annual reports of the OSCE suggest that around 40 of the 57 participating countries regularly and as a matter of course collect data on the number of hate-motivated homicides that occur in their jurisdiction. But few of these homicides seem to occur, at least officially.

For example, the latest OSCE report (2014), which refers to 2013, illustrates the number of officially recorded hate-motivated homicides in the region, by victim category: Bulgaria—2 (unspecified victim category); Greece—2 (unspecified); Italy—1 (LGBT); Latvia—1 (racism/xenophobia); and Poland—1 (unspecified). Much of the data from other countries, however, remains disaggregated leaving us with some sense of, for example, how many racist or homophobic crimes occurred, but not what those crimes were. It may well be, of course, that homicides are indeed buried within these statistics. And of course, given the discussion above, it is also the case that some countries do not recognize nor record hate homicides, or indeed hate crimes per se, at all. In order to try filling some of these gaps, useful information can be gleaned from NGOs and other advocacy groups. Unsurprisingly perhaps, these tend to show higher volumes of homicide than the official data, although once again these should be treated with caution, not least because of the subjectivity associated with the interpretation of motivation.

The case of the Russian Federation serves as a useful example in this regard. No racist or xenophobic crimes were reported by the Russian Federation to the OSCE for the year 2011 (OSCE 2012). However, a number of relevant and independent organizations reported starkly different findings. For example, for the same year, the SOVA Center for Information and Analysis (2012) recorded 22 racist murders and 128 racist physical assaults. For the previous year, another Moscow-based NGO reported 3 murders and 22 physical assaults (Moscow Protestant Task Force on Racial Violence 2011), while another reported 19 murders and 89 physical assaults (Moscow Bureau for Human Rights 2010: http://antirasizm.ru). More recently, Human Rights Watch (2012) stated that although racist murders in Russia declined in 2011, aggressive racism and xenophobia continued to rise.

Elsewhere, using the issue of lesbian, gay, bisexual and transgender (LGBT) hate crime as a framework, the advocacy group Transgender, Europe's Trans Murder Monitoring project report (Transgender Europe 2015), found that 1,731 transgender and gender diverse people were murdered in 44 countries between 2008 and 2014, although (to illustrate the issue of subjectivity) it is not clear how many of these were specifically hate motivated. Similarly, the Inter-American Commission on Human Rights documented 770 killings and serious violent attacks against LGBT people between January 2013 and March 2014 (Organization of American States 2014), and the advocacy group Erasing 76 Crimes (a reference to the number of countries with antigay laws still in place) reported that in Brazil, 1,431 LGBT were reported murdered between 2007 and 2012, with 249 murdered in Peru in a similar timeframe (Erasing 76 Crimes, https://76crimes.com). And in the United States, the National Coalition of Anti-Violence Programs (NCAVP 2015) reported a record 14 homicides of LGBT people in the first three months of 2015, with at least half seemingly hate motivated.

Of course, if we move away from traditional notions of hate crime, and consider the broader context of hatred as a motivation for murder, then the figures change dramatically. Take a moment to think about these troubling numbers from James Waller's book, *Extraordinary Evil* (2002). Since the Napoleonic Wars there have been an average of six international and six civil wars each decade, and from the end of World War II to the end of the twentieth century there have been approximately 150 wars and just 26 days of world peace. In the twentieth century alone more than 100 million people were killed by their fellow human beings.

While war is tragic enough, Waller suggests that the greatest catastrophes occur when the distinctions between war and crime fade and the line between military and criminal conduct disappear. During the twentieth century, he suggests, more than 60 million people were victims of mass killing and genocide (see also Chapter 16, this volume). In other words, 60 percent of the people killed during the various conflicts of the twentieth century were the victims of criminal, and not "legitimate" military, conduct. Specific examples that Waller cites include the near-complete annihilation of the Hereros by the Germans in South-West Africa in 1904, the Turkish assault on the Armenian population between 1915 and 1923, the Soviet manmade famine in the Ukraine in 1932, the Nazi extermination of two-thirds of Europe's Jews (along with others) during World War II, the massacre in Indonesia in 1965, and mass killings and genocide in Bangladesh (1971), Burundi (1972), Cambodia and East Timor (1975–1979), Rwanda (1994), and the Sudan (present).

As Waller (2002: xi) points out, mass killing is the killing of members of a group without the intention to eliminate the whole group, or killing large numbers of people without a precise definition of group membership. Collective violence, he explains, becomes genocide when a specific group is systematically and intentionally targeted for destruction. For an ordinary crime to become a *hate crime* necessarily requires the intentional and prejudicial selection of a victim on the basis of some group affiliation. Given this necessity, to my mind, mass killing, and in particular genocide, undoubtedly represent the most extreme examples of hate-motivated crime, and as such we shall consider the motivations of the perpetrators of genocide in due course.

Explaining Hate-Motivated Homicide

The various definitions of hate crime in existence around the world illustrate, as we have noted, that hate crime is not always about *hate*, but rather it is predominantly about *prejudice* of which hate is just a small part. It follows then that if we want to understand hate crime, and thus the causes of hate-motivated homicide, then we should explore the nature of prejudice. Fortunately, as Stangor (2000) points out, there are few if any topics that have engaged the interests of social psychologists as much as those of *prejudice, stereotypes*, and *discrimination* where, as Paluck and Green (2009) note, the "remarkable volume" of literature on prejudice ranks among the most impressive in all of social science. And as Perry (2009) suggests, these concepts mark the starting point for theorizing about the perpetrators of hate crime. Indeed, she notes that the literature has been dominated by psychological and social-psychological accounts that necessarily emphasize individual-level analyses (Paluck and Green 2009: 56), including significant contributions from Allport on the nature of prejudice as well as a seminal model of the five stages of prejudice that culminate in the extermination of a "hated group" (1954); Adorno *et al.* (1950); Tajfel and Turner on social identity (1979); Sherif and Sherif on realistic conflict (1953); Bandura on social learning (1977), and Stephan and Stephan (1996) on integrated threat, to name but a few (see Hall 2013 for a broader discussion of psychological theorizing in relation to hate crime).

However, for all our theorizing about these concepts, the existing literature tells us remarkably little about *how* prejudice transforms into actions that would constitute hate crimes. Indeed, there is little consensus for theories that seek to explain this phenomenon. It is also clear that there are many kinds of prejudice that vary greatly and have different psychological dynamics underpinning them, and this can have important implications for understanding hate as a motivation for criminal behavior. Furthermore, because prejudices are independent psychological responses they can be expressed, as Allport illustrates, in a bewildering number of ways, ranging from a mild dislike or general aversion to others to extreme acts of violence, including murder. But (and this is crucial for our understanding of hate-motivated offending) as Green, McFalls, and Smith (2003: 27) suggest in a position that still holds true today:

> It might take the better part of a lifetime to read the prodigious research literature on prejudice … yet scarcely any of this research examines directly and systematically the question of why prejudice erupts into violence.

Stern (2005) reiterates this point. While *psychology* informs us that most people are capable of hatred and gives us some insights into the relationship between identity and hate, its rather narrow focus on the individual as an explanation is necessarily limited and needs, if it is to provide more comprehensive answers, to be integrated into a larger framework. The broader approach taken by *social psychology*, which considers the individual in social situations where certain attributes may come to the fore, offers arguably greater insight into intergroup conflict. As we shall see below, this is particularly true of those who participate in acts of genocide. Nevertheless, while collectively psychology has some important contributions to make to our understanding of hate, it does not provide the complete explanation of hate-motivated offending that we might hope for.

Moreover, the psychological literature is clear that the holding of prejudices, both positive and negative, is an inevitable part of human nature. But, as Gaylin (2003) argues, to suggest that *hatred* is normal to the human condition is too simplistic an argument to sustain. After all, he suggests, even given the opportunity and freedom to hate or express hatred without obstruction or sanction, most of us would still not choose to do so. So while prejudice might be normal, hatred, it would seem, is not—a point arguably lost in the contemporary social construction of hate crime.

A significant contributor to this lack of distinction between prejudice and hatred within the literature, it seems, has been psychology's preoccupation with prejudice and its normality to the human condition as an aspect of personality, rather than a specific focus on hatred as an "abnormal" psychological disorder. Indeed, even Allport's (1954) seminal text, *The Nature of Prejudice*, which ran to 519 pages and is considered to be the departure point for most, if not all, subsequent research into prejudice, dedicated just three pages directly to hatred (Allport 1954: 363–365; although as Gaylin points out, Allport was a psychologist studying normal personality, not a psychiatrist involved with mental illness). Gaylin, however, emphasizes the importance of distinguishing between prejudice and bigotry and hatred, describing the former as a way-station on the road to the latter, and argues that there is indeed an important role for psychiatry in the understanding of pathological hatred:

> To understand hatred … we must get into the head of the hater. We now have a psychological framework for doing this. We must apply modern psychological understanding of perception, motivation, and behavior to discover what hatred is. Only when we have identified the nature of the beast can we properly address the environmental conditions that support it … Hatred is severe psychological disorder. The pathological haters … externalis[e] their internal frustrations and conflicts on a hapless scapegoat population. They are "deluded," and their self-serving and distorted perceptions allow them to justify their acts of hatred against the enemy they have created. We must start our investigation, therefore, with an examination of the hater's mind rather than his milieu … To date there has been little call for such information, and little volunteered from the psychological community (Gaylin 2003: 14–15).[3]

So while psychology and psychiatry offer plenty of insights into hate-motivated offending, they do not provide comprehensive answers. And nor, unfortunately, do any of the other social sciences. It is worth noting at this juncture, though, that hate crime is still relatively new to the criminological lexicon. Its origins are traceable to the late 1970s and early 1980s, and its emergence as a contemporary social problem, particularly in the United Kingdom and the United States, has been largely driven by concerns relating to the disproportionate victimization of certain groups based on various inherent personal characteristics (initially race) and by a number of causes célèbres, most notably homicides (see Hall 2013). In England and Wales, for example, one can readily identify causal links between interest in racist hate crime and the murder of Stephen Lawrence (1993); homophobia and the murder of Jodi Dobrowski (2005); alternative subcultures and the murder of Sophie Lancaster (2007); disability and the murder of (among others) Brent Martin (2008); and the deaths of Fiona Pilkington and Francecca Hardwick (2007), to name but a few. Likewise, in the United States key federal legislation is named after the victims of two of America's most notorious hate murders—Matthew Sheppard (1998; homophobia) and James Byrd Jr (1998; racism).

Consequently, Perry (2009) has suggested that research on, and theorizing about, *perpetrators* and their *motivations* has been scant partially because hate crime is "new" to the criminological horizon, partially because it has predominantly concentrated on issues of victimization, and also because of a lack of agreement about how exactly we should define "hate crime" and, of course, the implications that necessarily follow for the production of reliable data upon which to base research and to construct conceptual frameworks. Indeed, writing in 1999, Bowling suggested that research into perpetrators was so scarce that they represented a "devilish effigy" within the criminological literature (1999: 305). Although progress in this area has since been made, Bowling's statement remains uncomfortably close to the truth.

Perhaps unsurprisingly given the often-secular nature of the social sciences, explanations of hate and hate crime offending have been proffered in a rather disparate and often isolated manner, and often in silos, leaving us with a somewhat disjointed framework of analysis. Indeed, explanations of hate-motivated offending can be found within, as we have seen, psychology and psychiatry, but within also economics, political science, cultural studies, history, geography, religious studies, sociology, and, of course, criminology. Within these various disciplines, possible explanations for hate crimes include, but are not limited to, reactions to social strain and relative depravation, expressions of relative power and dominance, difference, thrill, retaliation, territoriality, xenophobia, scapegoating, dehumanization, ideological belief, fundamentalism, religious interpretation, anger, frustration, inadequate self-control, mental disorder, personality, social learning, social identity, in-group loyalty, subcultures, conformity, persuasion, realistic conflict, threat, fear, choice, cultural norms, historical interpretation, and demonization. The list goes on.

From this brief overview then, it should at least be clear that, notwithstanding both Bowling and Perry's concerns, potential explanations for hate and hate offending are many and varied, and come from a range of disciplines. But they too are inconclusive and disparate. Moreover, Gaylin (2003: 14) argues that socioeconomic and political explanations are insufficient because they assume a rational basis for hatred and suggest a direct link between the hater's needs and the selection of their victims, and in so doing deny the pathological core of hatred. In addition, explanations of offending have tended to be both specific (in the sense that they are located within silos that concentrate on either race, or homophobia, or some other category) and generic (in the sense that they focus on broad notions of offending behavior, rather than on those who kill, or those who assault, and so on).

New Directions

This lack of specific research on those who commit hate-motivated homicide has, however, recently started to be addressed, albeit still within the framework of silos. For example, Gruenewald and Kelley (2014), in highlighting the reality that our understanding of hate crime has been largely shaped by general typologies[4] that concentrate on differences in offender motives, similarly note that these typologies, while significant in advancing our understanding, are necessarily limited because it is difficult to determine the actual motives of offenders, and because they do not explicitly discern between crime types. As such, they argue that such typologies implicitly assume homogeneity across forms of hate crime and, consequently, little is known about the specific circumstances under which specific types of hate crime are initiated and performed.

In seeking to remedy these limitations, Gruenewald and Kelley's (2014) research has produced a typology of anti-LGBT homicide consisting of two categories—predatory and responsive—with a number of associated subcategories, the main thrusts of which are briefly summarized below:

The first category, *predatory homicide*, they suggest, consists of planned acts of violence against members of the LGBT community, where offenders took time to orchestrate a plan for perpetrating the homicide prior to encountering victims, typically during the precursor phase of the criminal event. Two variants, they suggest, are present within this category. First, predatory *representative* offenders appeared to select victims whose deaths would communicate symbolic messages regarding the social standing of the LGBT community.[5] That is to say that the victim was representative of the LGBT community and attacks were unprovoked. Second, predatory *instrumental* attacks occurred where offenders selected victims based on their sexual orientation or gender identity primarily to rob them and, as such, attacks were considered instrumental because anti-LGBT homicide victims were selected as a means to another end, rather than some deep-seated hatred of LGBT people.

The second category, *responsive homicide*, refers to expressive violent acts with little rational planning where offenders typically did not take care to plan the offense prior to the homicide transaction and offenders selected victims in response to real or perceived affronts. The affront, Gruenewald and Kelley suggest, was usually perceived by the offender as a personal attack related to their sexual orientation or gender identity or, less commonly, as a general affront to traditional norms of sexual behavior. Within this category are three variants. First, *gay bash offenses* where offenders selected victims who they believed to have insulted or disrespected them in some way. Second, *undesired romantic or sexual advance offenses*, where attacks occurred when offenders selected victims in response to a real or perceived sexual (or romantic) advance made by the victim toward the offender. Finally, *mistaken identity offenses*, which occurred following cases of offenders mistaking the sex of victims, most often as part of a sexual encounter.

Gruenewald and Kelley's new typology therefore advances our understanding of anti-LGBT homicide cases by shedding light on a range of issues relating to the incident, the victim, and the motivations of the offender. As they themselves acknowledge, however, the task now is to replicate and expand studies such as these to other forms of hate crime.

The complexities of seeking to understand hate-motivated homicide are, however, perhaps best illustrated by research conducted into the perpetrators of genocide. While we may be tempted to draw a distinction between "ordinary" and "extraordinary" offenders when we think of genocide, the distinction is perhaps more appropriate for the *crimes* than for the *criminals*. Killing on a genocidal scale is clearly extraordinary, but Waller (2002) suggests that in order to understand "extraordinary evil" we in fact have to understand its "ordinariness." In other words, the perpetrators of mass killing and genocide are extraordinary because of what they do, not who they are. According to Waller, to consider the perpetrators of mass killing and genocide simply as psychopaths or monsters (that is, by employing individual-level analyses) is not sufficient to account for all the examples throughout human history. For example, Waller points out that up to 500,000 people took part in the Holocaust, and that up to 150,000 Hutus took part in the killing of at least 800,000 Tutsis in Rwanda in 1994. Not all of these perpetrators can be psychotic, or sadistic, or attributed to some other extreme psychological label. Rather, Waller contends, it is more fruitful to holistically understand the ways in which *ordinary* people come to commit *extraordinary* acts.

To this end Waller suggests a synthesis of a number of factors that he combines to produce a unified theory of offender behavior, and one that makes for rather uncomfortable reading. The first prong of Waller's model focuses on three tendencies of human behavior; *ethnocentrism* (the belief that one's in-group is superior to other groups), *xenophobia* (the fear of outsiders and members of "out-groups"), and the desire for *social dominance*. These factors are universal and, given the nature of prejudice, both normal and unavoidable. However, while these form the foundations of hatred, we have already noted that this is not enough, and that not everyone expresses these natural tendencies in a violent way.

The second part of Waller's theory therefore focuses on the factors that shape the identities of the individual perpetrators. Here three factors are held to be particularly significant; *cultural belief systems* (external, controlling influences; authority orientation; ideological commitment), *moral disengagement* of the perpetrator from the victim (facilitated by moral justification, euphemistic labeling of evil actions, and exonerating comparisons), and *rational self-interest* (professional and personal).

The third strand of Waller's theory considers the role of the social context in influencing individuals. Of particular significance is the role of *professional socialization* (built on escalating commitments, ritual conduct, and the repression of conscience), the *binding factors of the group* (including diffusion of responsibility, deindividuation, and conformity to peer pressure), and the *merger of role and person* (the significance of an organization in changing a person within it). The final strand of the theory relates to the victims, or more accurately, how the victims are perceived. In this regard three further factors are significant; *us–them thinking*, *dehumanization of the victim*, and *blaming of the victim*.

Waller points out that his theoretical model is not an invocation of a single psychological state or event. Rather it represents an analysis of the process through which perpetrators are changed from an ordinary person to an individual for whom committing extraordinarily evil acts becomes a part of their new self. The model, he suggests, specifically explicates the forces that shape human responses to authority by looking at who the perpetrators are, the situational framework they are in, and how they see "outsiders." By considering those factors that make humans the same (the nature of prejudice), those factors that make humans different (thoughts, feelings, and behaviors), contextualizing these within cultural and situational influences, and by considering the psychological processes by which victims are excluded, Waller provides a framework which facilitates the commission of extraordinary evil by ordinary people. In other words, under Waller's model, the nature of prejudice leaves all humans capable of extreme hatred and extraordinary evil, and therefore murder, when activated by appropriate cues contained within the identities of the perpetrators, the social context, and the perception of victims.

Rather than provide a definitive and conclusive account of why people commit acts of mass killing and genocide, Waller's model instead presents an account of the conditions under which such acts can take place. It is a complex interplay of a number of factors and as such is similar to accounts of "ordinary" hate crime. Simply, there is no single factor that causes people to commit crimes against "the Other," regardless of the scale of those crimes. What is certain, however, is that prejudice plays a central role as the underlying facilitator that is triggered by other factors.

Concluding Comments

This chapter has sought to explore some of the issues surrounding hate-motivated homicide. At the start, the reader was made aware that this was a far from straightforward task. On reflection, you may think this was an impossible task, not just for a chapter of this size, but also in general given the inherent complexities of the subject area that I hope, if nothing else, will now be apparent. To illustrate these complexities, but also the inherent and overlapping similarities, the chapter purposefully leaned toward what one might refer to as two ends of a "spectrum of hate" in terms of what one might reluctantly describe as more "ordinary" hate-motivated homicides on the one hand, and more "extraordinary" homicides, in the form of genocide, on the other. While plenty of potential explanations exist concerning the role that prejudice and hatred might play in a variety of murderous situations, there are still far too many gaps in our knowledge in this area. And given the examples that this chapter began with, arguably the need to fill those gaps has never been greater.

Notes

1 The date is Friday, June 26, 2015.

2 Let's take the situation in England and Wales as an example. Here, the Crown Prosecution Service (CPS) and the Association of Chief Police Officers (ACPO—now the National Police Chiefs' Council) have agreed the following common operational definition of hate crime: "Any criminal offence which is perceived by the victim or any other person to be *motivated* by *hostility* or *prejudice* based on a person's race or perceived race; religion or perceived religion; sexual orientation or perceived sexual orientation; disability or perceived disability and any crime motivated by hostility or prejudice against a person who is transgender or perceived to be transgender" (ACPO 2013; emphasis added).

3 A situation that remains largely valid today. See Tyson and Hall (2015) for a wider discussion of hatred as a mental disorder.

4 Within the criminological literature, a typology produced by McDevitt, Levin, and Bennett (2002) is the most often cited. Their research in Boston revealed four categories of offending motivation—thrill seeking, retaliation, defensive, and mission.
5 This is in keeping with other literature in the field that identifies hate crime as having an *in terrorum* effect on the wider community to which the victim belongs.

References

Allport, G.W. (1954) *The Nature of Prejudice*. Cambridge, MA: Addison-Wesley.

ACPO (2013) *Hate Crime Manual and Tactical Guidance*. London: ACPO.

Bowling, B. (1999) *Violent Racism: Victimization, Policing and Social Context*. New York: Oxford University Press.

FBI (Federal Bureau of Investigation) (2014) *2013 Hate Crime Statistics*. Washington DC: US Department of Justice.

Gaylin, W. (2003) *Hatred: The Psychological Descent into Violence*. New York: Public Affairs.

Green, D.P., McFalls, L.H., and Smith, J.K. (2003) Hate crime: An emergent research agenda. In B. Perry (ed.), *Hate and Bias Crime: A Reader* (pp. 27–48). New York: Routledge.

Gruenewald, J. and Kelley, K. (2014) Exploring anti-LGBT homicide by mode of victim selection. *Criminal Justice and Behavior*, 41(9): 1130–1152. doi: 10.1177/0093854814541259.

Hall, N. (2013) *Hate Crime* (2nd edn). Abingdon: Routledge.

Human Rights Watch (2012) *World Report*. Available online at http://www.hrw.org/world-report-2012 (accessed March 17, 2016).

Jacobs, J.B. and Potter, K. (1998) *Hate Crimes: Criminal Law and Identity Politics*. New York: Oxford University Press.

McDevitt, J., Levin, J., and Bennett, S. (2002) Hate crime offenders: An expanded typology. *Journal of Social Issues*, 58: 303–317.

Moscow Protestant Chaplaincy Task Force on Racial Violence (2011) *Quarterly Statistical Reports*. Moscow: MPCTFRV.

NCAVP (2015) An open letter from LGBTQ organizations in the United States regarding the epidemic violence that LGBTQ people, particularly transgender women of color, have experienced in 2015. Available online at http://avp.org/storage/documents/webversion_ncavp_ma_national2015.pdf (accessed August 24, 2016).

Organization of American States (2014) *An Overview of Violence Against LGBTI Persons*. Washington, DC: Inter-American Commission on Human Rights.

OSCE (2012) *Hate Crimes in the OSCE Region: Incidents and Responses. Annual Report for 2011*. Warsaw: OSCE.

OSCE (2014) *Hate Crimes in the OSCE Region: Incidents and Responses. Annual Report for 2013*. Warsaw: OSCE.

Paluck, E.L. and Green, D. (2009) Prejudice reduction: What works? A review and assessment of research and practice. *Annual Review of Psychology*, 60: 339–367.

Perry, B. (2001) *In the Name of Hate: Understanding Hate Crimes*. New York: Routledge.

Perry, B. (2009) The sociology of hate: Theoretical approaches. In B. Perry (ed.), *Hate Crimes* (vol. 1, pp. 55–76). Westport, CT: Praeger.

SOVA Center for Information and Analysis (2012) Between Manezhnaya and Bolotnaya: Xenophobia and radical nationalism in Russia, and efforts to counteract them in 2011.

Available online at http://www.sova-center.ru/en/xenophobia/reports-analyses/2012/04/d24088/(accessed February 23, 2016).

SPLC (Southern Poverty Law Center) (2014) White homicide worldwide. Available online at http://www.splcenter.org/sites/default/files/downloads/publication/white-homicide-worldwide.pdf (accessed May 15, 2016).

SPLC (Southern Poverty Law Center) (2015a) Age of the wolf. Lone Wolf Report. Available online at http://www.splcenter.org/lone-wolf (accessed May 30, 2016).

SPLC (Southern Poverty Law Center) (2015b) Charleston shooter's manifesto reveals hate group helped to radicalize him. Available online at http://www.splcenter.org/get-informed/news/charleston-shooter-s-manifesto-reveals-hate-group-helped-to-radicalize-him (accessed May 30, 2016).

Stangor, C. (ed.) (2000) *Stereotypes and Prejudice*. Philadelphia: Psychology Press.

Stern, K. (2005) *Hate Matters: The Need for an Interdisciplinary Field of Hate Studies*. New York: American Jewish Committee.

Sullivan, A. (1999) What's so bad about hate? The illogic and illiberalism behind hate crime laws. *New York Times Magazine*, September 26.

Transgender Europe (2015) Trans Murder Monitoring 2015. Available online at http://tgeu.org/tmm-idahot-update-2015/(accessed October 4, 2016).

Tyson, J. and Hall, N. (2015) Medicalising hatred? Exploring the sense and sensitivities of classifying prejudice and bigotry as mental disorders in hate crime perpetrators. In J. Winstone (ed.), *Mental Health, Crime and Criminal Justice*. Oxford, Palgrave.

Waller, J. (2002) *Becoming Evil: How Ordinary People Commit Genocide and Mass Killing*. New York: Oxford University Press.

11

Infanticide

Carl P. Malmquist

Introduction

Constructing a typology of infanticides and neonaticides has unfolded over time in social, cultural, legal, and clinical settings. Since the killing of newborns and infants has existed throughout history, perspectives have varied. More recently attempts evolved to classify such behavior. After reviewing hundreds of accounts, one approach delineated five categories of infanticide: neonaticide, assisted/coerced (in conjunction with a male partner), neglect related, abuse related, and mental illness related (Meyer and Oberman 2001). Legal settings use their own definitions. Although the focus in this chapter is often on the individual mother, especially for neonaticides, fathers may also be the perpetrators or participants.

Data on homicides of children often lump victims as under age five. However, data from the US Department of Justice from 1980 to 2008 tracked child homicides yearly from under one year up to age five (Cooper and Smith 2011). It found that infants under one year of age had the highest homicide victimization rate of all children under age five. Summary data for the under age five group showed the following: parents were responsible for the deaths in 63 percent of cases (33 and 30 percent respectively for fathers and mothers), other family members 7 percent, friend/acquaintance 28 percent, and strangers 3 percent. The data were unfortunately not broken down yearly up to age five. Other studies have found that mothers are the majority perpetrators only in the first week which would usually be neonaticides (Kunz and Bahr 1996).

Infanticides, neonaticides, feticides, and filicides are basic terms which vary in their usage depending on the setting and presumably in different countries. The following are commonly used definitions.

The Handbook of Homicide, First Edition. Edited by Fiona Brookman,
Edward R. Maguire, and Mike Maguire.

The term *infanticide* is used in somewhat different ways. For example, it is sometimes (arguably mistakenly) applied to any young child killed by a biological or adoptive parent. More often, the term is restricted to parental killing of an infant up to 12 months in keeping with medical viewpoints of infants meaning the first year. In this chapter the term is used with that meaning of a killing in the first 12 months.

Neonaticide is described as the killing by a parent of the newborn in the first 24 hours after birth. This distinction emerged psychiatrically from observations of differences between perpetrators who killed on the first day and those who killed later (Resnick 1970). For example, a pedantic debate might arise over whether a killing which occurred at 48 or 72 hours after birth is a neonaticide but in actual situations this type of debate is bypassed.

What if the victim is still in a fetal state in utero when killed? Examples are a mother who overdoses on drugs which kills the fetus or who is the object of a traumatic incident leading to the death of the fetus. Such *feticides* are distinguished from acts of abortion.

Filicide is a generic term for parents murdering their offspring. It can be confusing since filicide is not restricted to the victim being a child. The perpetrator and victim could both be adults, such as an adult parent murdering his or her adult child.

These terms are descriptive and not explanatory. First, they are not medico-psychiatric terms although they frequently appear in articles and texts. They are not part of psychiatric diagnostic nomenclature. Second, the terms are used in legal contexts, with or without having a statutory status. The acts may simply be subsumed under some level of legal homicide, such as murder or manslaughter. Third, the terms are used by criminologists or social scientists in their studies on types of murders. Lastly, the media use these terms in reporting (television, radio, the Internet, etc.) in an overlapping manner. Whatever the context, these homicides engender powerful public emotions.

Different Perspectives

Over time diverse groups have taken an interest in parents who kill their infants. There is a good deal of historical material on this matter. In the period 4000–2000 BCE Babylonian and Chaldean civilizations reported infanticides (Oberman 2003). Sparta noted infants being abandoned in outside settings (Pomeroy 2002). Judaic tradition differed since it was opposed to child sacrifice although there was some backsliding (Schwartz and Isser 2001). Greek and Roman societies differed on whether infanticides could be legal acts. The decision was left to the father as head of the household until Constantine declared it to be a crime in 318 CE (Noonan 1986).

European church records from the Middle Ages list infanticide as a venial sin, not a mortal sin, with a penance of three years to live on bread and water (Kellum 1974). Levels of penance were based on desire, fruition of desire, the will to act, or the act itself and involved degrees of fasting (Meens 2014). By the sixteenth century infanticide had become a criminal offense listed in the penal code used in most of Europe (Schwartz and Isser 2001).

Unfolding Perspectives

Diverse groups early took an interest in how societies should deal with infanticides. One group involved an erratic blending of *moral and welfare approaches* which became a dominant theme paralleling legal interests. Some of these concerns were preventive, such as developing foundling homes.[1] The idea was that this would prevent infanticides among those in poverty. Community intervention with unwed mothers later had a similar goal. By the nineteenth century in Europe welfare approaches were directed at vulnerable women. Debates arose as to whether charitable interventions perpetuated sinful and licentious behavior (Fuchs 2001). Religious charities and welfare institutions tried to stem infanticides, abortions, and out-of-wedlock births with minimal success.

Statutes eventually emerged in various countries to deal with infanticide and neonaticide. This is discussed in detail in a comparative study of the United States with 50 other countries where many created special statutes differentiating neonaticide from infanticide (Malmquist 2013).

Physicians and midwives were a second group who later became involved with infanticides. Stillborns or deaths in those born with deformities unavoidably led to inquiries. Over the last century psychiatric specialists entered the picture in diverse ways. One was by recognizing that some of the women who killed their infants were mentally ill which was labeled postpartum psychosis. This approach emphasized a diagnostic framework and possible legal involvement as "alienists."[2] Another perspective focused on the psychopathology of such acts. The latter focus was not primarily to diagnose whether a psychosis was present or not, but to unravel what had transpired in the minds of mothers who killed their newborns.

The *legal profession and law enforcement* were a third group with an ongoing interest. A death necessitates a legal inquiry. Neonaticides have always had a low level of discovery (Overpeck 2003). Even when discovered, and a coroner examination performed, diverse causes of death needed to be ruled out, such as a stillborn, malnutrition, diverse medical conditions, and so on. These challenges persist into the contemporary era where prosecutors play key roles in decision-making. The approach developed in the United States was a legal one involving murder/manslaughter with a plea bargain possibility. This is not the typical path taken in many other countries. Prosecutions vary widely from country to country, within a country, and between jurisdictions. Few cases raise an insanity defense (Yang 2009). The medico-psychiatric focus has often been on postpartum psychosis even though this explains a small minority of infanticide/neonaticide cases that occur in the United States and elsewhere (Oberman 2003). A 40 year review of the literature on infanticide/neonaticide concluded that the majority do not involve a maternal mental illness (Porter and Gavin 2010). A British study found only 26 percent of 89 women who had committed infanticide suffered with a mental illness (D'Orban 1979).

By the twentieth century many countries enacted legislation to deal with infanticides and neonaticides (Malmquist 2013). Some differentiated neonaticides from infanticides. The statutes often put infanticides into a different legal category than routine murder-manslaughter cases. The United States has not developed any special categories for infanticides and most cases are charged as a murder or manslaughter which may result in long sentences (Lang 2005). Prosecutorial discretion in these cases looms large.

Case Characteristics Related to Infanticides/Neonaticides

Clinicians realized that females who commit neonaticides have different clinical and social features from those who commit infanticides. One complexity is that such differences may not be the same for women in different countries and cultural settings. Whatever these differentials may be, it is important in the assessment of women within the broad spectrum of postpartum disturbances who develop homicidal tendencies. Predisposing factors should have a bearing on legal outcomes although some jurisdictions ignore them.

Many studies have concluded that women who commit *neonaticides* are younger than those who commit infanticides or filicides. One found the median age for neonaticide was 17 years (Oberman 2003). These findings stress that neonaticidal mothers are mid- to late adolescents not only biologically but also cognitively (Kaye, Berenstein, and Donnelly 1990). Yet, there are frequently contradictory findings. Thus, a French study concluded that more than half of neonaticidal mothers already had other children and were living with a partner (Vellut, Cook, and Tursz 2012). India illustrates the practice of female infants being murdered at birth either by mothers or someone arranged to do the killing. This is not attributed to psychopathology but the low value of a female child despite denial by the government (Oberman 2003). It would take a volume to compare and contrast every country just on the variable of socioeconomic causation. Hence, the "classic" picture presented is often based on data from the United States and England and Wales, unless otherwise noted.

The frequent picture of the neonaticidal mother, as an adolescent or early adult, is that she is living with a parent with whom she shares no knowledge of the pregnancy even if she admits it to herself. Many live in a milieu of denial to themselves and others, which may literally be a denial of pregnancy. The male involved is also often an adolescent and, if informed, feels as powerless as the girl. The socioeconomic status results in a parental dependency or poverty if living alone. Such situations create a sense of powerlessness. Whatever the level of denial, the result is an affective flatness, emotional isolation, and detachment until delivery (Resnick 1970).

While writings focus on postpartum psychoses, studies of neonaticidal mothers indicate that the majority do not suffer from a psychotic condition or preexisting mental illness (Macfarlane 2003). In a study of 45 cases only one mother was found to be psychotic at the time of the offense (Shelton, Muirhead, and Canning 2010). This does not mean an absence of emotional conflicts or symptoms, but rather a lack of overt psychotic symptoms. Legal dilemmas arise if a mental illness defense is contemplated, or some type of plea bargaining is ongoing. This is especially relevant in the United States with its long sentences for all criminal homicides, and lack of differentiation of neonaticide convictions from other types of homicides (Malmquist 2013).

Patterns of delivery for neonaticides have an amazingly similar script. Since many of them have been in some level of denial, with anxiety or depression being held in abeyance, the delivery is often a jolt—a real happening—which breaks through the denial. It may initially be misinterpreted as a gastro-intestinal disturbance or flu. Steps may be taken to treat these supposed conditions, such as medications or bowel movements, which may precipitate a birth. If the labor goes on for hours, the denial may break down, but for some it continues through to the delivery.

Once a neonate emerges, the response is to undo it—to get rid of it promptly. Life is to proceed as though the event never occurred by simply going to school or a job. Actions vary from flushing newborns down a toilet, drowning them in bath tubs or toilets, bashing their heads with an object, or grabbing knives and repetitively stabbing. Typical disposals of the body include putting the baby in a garbage bin, wrapping it up and leaving it in some convenient location, or throwing the newborn into a pond or lake (Meyer and Oberman 2001).

A caveat often ignored in neonaticide and infanticide is the "dark figure." Whatever the official statistics given by governmental agencies, the incidence is at best an underestimate. "Successful" neonaticides are not discovered and are obviously not on official registries. Infanticide is complicated by the necessity of ruling out sudden infant death syndrome (SIDS) from a smothered or neglected infant (Brookman and Nolan 2006). Official figures represent women who at the time of the act have come to the attention either of law enforcement or health care personnel. The problem of undetected cases is rarely noted (Gartner and McCarthy 2006). Clinicians of different specialties have related that they had woman patients in the past who stated that they once carried out a neonaticide which they haven't told to anyone before.

Infanticides, in contrast to neonaticides, occur throughout the first year and present a different picture and mental elements. These women are often older, married, or in some type of relationship. Financial considerations may govern the act, but they are more likely to have had an antecedent history of mental problems, perhaps after a previous pregnancy, or independent of a pregnancy. A history of a serious mental disorder may be present or a psychotic reoccurrence. This group is more likely to go beyond transient mood swings after a delivery into a more entrenched type of emotional disturbance. Some of these merge into a postpartum psychosis with delusions and hallucinations. If some of these symptoms involve thoughts of killing the infant, it is a medical emergency. The symptoms may mimic those seen in other types of psychotic breakdowns. Debate continues as to whether postpartum psychoses is a distinct diagnostic entity, an affective illness, or a schizoaffective illness (O'Hara and McCabe 2013).

Whatever diagnosis is emphasized, the delusional pictures encountered by clinicians are those of unworthiness to be a mother, an altruistic idea of sparing the infant living in a terrible world, the belief that outside forces are controlling her thoughts or actions, or pseudorational explanations of why the infant needs to die such as "the devil being in the child" (Meyer and Spinelli 2003).

Hallucinations may be frequent in these psychotic states. The most ominous are commands to kill the child and/or herself. Highly labile mood fluctuations occur from deep despair in a depressed state to agitation in which the mother experiences an impulsive need to act. A rapid onset may occur with expansive progression from within the first week. For example, in one study psychotic symptoms emerged in 79 percent of the sample studied[3] within 30 days and in 94 percent within 60 days (Kendell, Chalmers, and Platz 1987). The situations are treacherous since the symptoms may wax and wane abruptly with the mother not revealing her frightening or confusing experiences. The secrecy may later emerge and cloud the pursuit of certain legal defenses since periods of lucidity may be elicited from those in contact with her during the postpartum period.

However, it should not be assumed that every infanticidal mother has a psychosis. Some of these mothers have had maltreatment in their backgrounds or do not want another child for financial reasons. Others are "accidental" in the sense of a battering mother who went too far which often connects with their earlier abuse. Rarer motivations include Munchausen syndrome or by proxy, or revenge on a spouse.

While neonaticides are predominantly by biological mothers, this is not so for infanticides where fathers or partners may be the perpetrators. Similar motives may operate with males and females for infanticides, but a wider spectrum exists. Factors such as rivalries between the male and newborn, another male being the biological father, and impulsivity and anger may lead to assaultive and child maltreatment and eventuate in infanticides. At the extreme it leads to a family annihilation where the mother and infant are killed and the father commits suicide (O'Hagan 2014).

Unfortunately, official data often lack specificity. Thus, the Uniform Crime Reports list homicide victims under one year but lacks neonaticide data, and we are also left without knowledge of the male–female division. The infanticide by a male might be recorded as a death by accident or SIDS (Sudden Infant Death Syndrome) rather than a smothering. Information is often problematic, such as a US Department of Health and Human Services estimate that 2,000 "children" are killed annually in the United States with 1,100 by a biological mother during the first year of life (Kohm and Liverman 2002). Another study concludes that infants are more likely to be killed by their mother during the first week of life, but thereafter more likely to be killed by a father or stepfather (Overpeck *et al.* 1998). A relatively safe conclusion would be that the majority of infanticides in the United States are by male caretakers (fathers or mothers' intimate partners) who have acted impulsively (Fujiwara *et al.* 2009). However, such a conclusion might vary widely in different countries.

The Legal Context

Legal proceedings commence at various levels.[4] Cases which eventuate in trials are often the easiest to apprehend. The dichotomy between the detected and undetected might reveal a striking contrast as well as cases where prosecutors decide not to bring criminal charges. In American jurisprudence a crucial junction is whether an adolescent will be handled by juvenile procedures or certified into adult criminal proceedings. The certification could be by a judicial decision, by legislation based on age, or a prosecutor's option. If certified into criminal proceedings, the juvenile is dealt with like any charged adult in criminal court since there are no separate infanticide statutes. Countries vary in how they handle adolescents who have committed an infanticide.

With adults, preliminary questions arise, such as competency to proceed to trial, to plead guilty or not to some offense, or to be sentenced for a crime. If the mental state at the time of the offense seems aberrant, an insanity or mental illness defense is considered. Mental illness defenses again vary in different countries. In the United States it is complicated by 50 states having their own definitions and precedents with most infanticides simply being charged under regular homicide statutes (Malmquist 2013).

The proceedings in the United States are limited by the diagnostic options available in the manual of the American Psychiatric Association DSM-5 (APA 2013). Infanticide is discussed within major depressive disorders where a "specifier," "noting a peripartum onset," can be added if mood symptoms occurred during pregnancy or within four weeks following delivery, with or without a psychosis. Fifty percent of postpartum depressive episodes are noted to begin before delivery in the peripartum period. If a psychotic postpartum episode occurred, the risk of recurrence is between 30 and 50 percent with each subsequent pregnancy. No reference is made to neonaticide, or other types of mental disorders which can occur. The International Classification of Diseases (ICD-10-CM) has a code, "Postpartum mood disturbance," listing conditions varying from "blues" to psychosis which may also bypass other conditions (2015).

Forensic Cases

The following are from cases on which I have consulted. They illustrate diversity from a young mother with overt messianic delusions to an adolescent with blank denial and secrecy about her pregnancy.

Case 1 A woman of 20 with twins aged one year old developed the delusion that she was the "female messiah." She told a few people in her religio-cultural group about this belief which they did not take seriously. This did not pose a problem until her beliefs consolidated into the next step of testing her messiahship. The test was to drop one infant off a bridge into a river. If she was in fact the messiah, God would not let the child drown, but would raise him. She brought the twins to a bridge and dropped one over the edge. The failure convinced her it was time to die with the other twin, and she jumped with him. People on shore saw the events and jumped in to rescue. One twin was rescued but the other drowned; the mother was rescued and found guilty of second degree murder despite a mental illness defense.

Case 2 A 16 year old, pregnant by her boyfriend, developed gastrointestinal problems. Her mother took her to a pediatrician who prescribed antispasmodics.

A friend suggested she might be pregnant, and a walk-in-center told her she might be, but later blood "spotting" led her to conclude she was not. Months later, at a family gathering, she believed she was coming down with flu and excused herself to go home. Attempts to have a bowel movement led to a birth. She immediately grabbed a knife, stabbed the newborn multiple times, and placed the body in a garbage bin. She described witnessing the birth as though from an elevated distance in a dissociative state. Testimony about a neonaticidal syndrome was not allowed, and testimony centered on whether the infant's lungs had inflated or not. She was found guilty and sentenced to life for first degree murder. An appeal ordered a new trial and the trial judge found her guilty of second degree murder.

These types of cases raise multiple questions. One is the reluctance of prosecutors to accept an insanity plea, or juries to render an insanity verdict. For some, it results in punishing someone who was clearly psychotic at the time of a criminal act. A second is whether the jury system is adequate to handle such cases. The situation of multiple experts testifying for a mental illness verdict which the jury does not accept is troublesome. Does this impute inadequacy of such testimony, or that for these type of acts the criminal justice system does not work? Perhaps jurors simply fear such individuals will get released from hospitals while still dangerous. Questions about insanity tests have been raised for centuries, but in Anglo-American jurisdictions the McNaughton test is the most difficult for the defense since it has the burden to prove that the defendant did not know the nature and quality of the act or that it was wrong. Among the questions that persist are: is civil commitment the best option, should the woman remain in a hospital, will she follow medical advice on medications, has she received adequate treatment, will she follow medical advice on medications, and is she at high risk for subsequent pregnancies.

Diversity among Countries

The United States can be used for comparative purposes with other countries on how mothers who kill their newborns or infants are handled. In contrast to other countries the United States has 50 separate legal jurisdictions with diverse statutes.

First, none of them single out the situation of neonaticide as requiring separate legal handling in terms of a homicide; most do not even distinguish infanticides from other homicides. Second, legal complaints are brought within the regular homicide statutes. Given this situation and the awareness that these cases might not be the same as other homicides, decisions often rest with prosecutorial discretion about disposition. Some are prosecuted for murder while others are dismissed; some are put on a miscellaneous court calendar for prolonged periods of negotiation or stalling. Third, although all participants in the system are aware that psychosocial conflicts and stresses have been operating in these women that may be different than other homicides, it is problematic whether such factors emerge. Fourth, states differ as to the cutoff age for certifying a juvenile; some maintain juvenile jurisdiction up to the age of 18, others place it at 15 years or younger. Unpredictability enters as to whether the case will be certified to adult court for prosecution. Inconsistency permeates decisions in dispositions of cases. Fifth, developmental phenomena of adolescence with respect to physiological and cognitive functioning may play a role or be totally ignored. It is not only the usual hormonal changes accompanying pregnancy, but the hormonal changes of puberty and the adolescent time period which get ignored (see also Chapter 12 in this volume for further discussion on the issue of carefully determining, through forensic assessment, the mental functioning of juveniles who kill and the appropriate processing of these cases in the criminal justice processing).

A comparison of the United States with the statutes and criminal codes of 50 different countries reveals striking differences (Malmquist 2013[5]). These countries represent widely different parts of the globe with varying cultures. A significant finding was that these diverse countries customarily distinguish infanticides from other types of homicides and carry lesser sentences upon a conviction. Even more significant, the statutes often differentiate, in some form, the killings of newborns.

The approach to infanticide in England and Wales

Cultural and legal shifts in England and Wales illustrate a different pathway to legislating for infanticide than that which emerged in the United States. A 1623 statute was directed against infanticides of bastards which was subsequently adopted in Canada and New England (Ayres 2007). The burden was placed on the defendant mother to prove the baby was stillborn. Since this was difficult, it led to an increase in the number of prosecutions (Hoffer and Hull 1981). Over time the approach had little impact on the prevalence of infanticide and public opinion changed as witnessed in more jury acquittals. Diverse legal defenses arose, such as women claiming they had sought assistance for the delivery but help had not arrived, or a "benefit of linen" defense where the woman claimed she had been making linen in preparation for childbirth (Zunshine 2005: 119).[6]

An 1803 statute was a punitive revision. Infanticides of illegitimate children were to be handled like other homicides. However, the prosecution had the burden of showing a live birth had occurred. In response, a legal defense called "concealment" arose where a woman had hidden her pregnancy, but a live birth could not be determined. By 1828 the statute was expanded to any pregnant female who concealed a birth. In time the idea arose that women who concealed might be suffering from "temporary insanity." This was the gateway for medical testimony on the question of whether the mental effects of a delivery could lead to an infanticide. As with most medical "discoveries" a diagnosis was produced and "puerperal mania" and "lactational insanity" were coined (Behlmer 1979).

The English Infanticide Law of 1922 made a direct connection between childbirth and infanticide by the phrase "the balance of her mind was disturbed by reason of her not having fully recovered from the effect of birth and lactation" (Ward 1999: 170).

It initially applied only to the newly born, but the Infanticide Act of 1938 amended it to include any child under 12 months which allowed a conviction for infanticide, rather than murder or manslaughter. The Act still allowed a partial defense to a homicide charge of murder or manslaughter. While imprisonment was possible, probation or a limited sentence was typical. However, by 1998 no woman found guilty of infanticide had been incarcerated in England and Wales for over fifty years (Barton 1998).

Responsibility Questions

Cases of infanticide and neonaticide raise unique questions about the mental capacity of those committing such acts. A recurrent question is what makes these homicides different from other homicides? (1) It is the only homicide in which women have a higher incidence than men among perpetrators; (2) Clinically neonaticide has different features than infanticides, let alone the general run of homicides. (3) Many perpetrators are adolescents. This means not only the psychosocial milieu and identity struggles, but hormonal and physiological changes from that developmental stage; (4) It seems indisputable that physiological changes occurring during the perinatal period, and after a delivery, place females in a different category than during the commission of other homicides. The persistent question is why some women have mild mood disturbances along a spectrum, while a small number proceed to show more serious effects in their mental functioning and impulse control.

Postpartum psychotic mothers raise different questions than other mothers who commit an infant homicide. It seems axiomatic, even in jurisdictions which do not give special legal consideration to these homicides, that a mental illness type of defense or insanity defense needs consideration. Two caveats arise in the forensic setting. First, such a defense is not routinely raised, and even if it is, it may not be successful. Prosecutors may wish to avoid trials for psychotic women who might win an insanity defense because of the image that it conveys about their office. Hence, they will try and negotiate pleas for a lesser offense with the threat of seeking a maximum sentence if it proceeds to trial and the defense fails. Questions also arise about the quality of legal representation available to defendants. Second, the disagreements among forensic experts, not only on diagnoses, but on answers to legal questions, create skepticism about accepting testimony regarding legal insanity. The expansion of diverse experts[7] allowed to testify may also be confusing since it further confuses which opinion to accept or reject.

Even more challenging than women who were psychotic at the time of the neonaticide are the majority who carry out the act but were not psychotic at the time. Many of them have a variety of personality disorders and/or come from disturbed or abusive social backgrounds, but the family is seemingly intact (Spinelli 2003). As noted earlier, the phenomena of denial, avoidance, and dissociation are frequent. Social background may show minimal support with families disavowing any knowledge of the pregnancy with typical disclaimers of, "If we'd only known, we would have gladly helped." Paradoxically, some woman might end up being more harshly criticized for not taking advantage of community agencies that are allegedly available.

Agency

Agency is a key component for responsibility since it raises clinical, legal, and moral issues. Assumptions about responsibility from these different perspectives arise and influence how a particular society deals with infanticides/neonaticides. The United States differs from most other countries in terms of how infanticides and neonaticides are dealt with legally (Malmquist 2013). A primary reason is the absence of any special statutes in the 50 states to handle these cases. Another is the long imprisonment carried out upon a plea or conviction of guilt (Stuntz 2011). Since many of the defendants are adolescents, they may not be confined within the juvenile justice system but certified to adult courts. The question is whether perpetrators of infanticide/neonaticide have the capacity to be viewed as responsible agents; if responsible, to what degree? One viewpoint sees infanticides as simply another act of killing that the criminal law should handle like any other homicide. They do not see any problems with pursuing regular criminal trials, and occasionally dealing with a few who raise an insanity defense.

Some feminist jurisprudence has taken issue with viewing infanticidal mothers as different from others who commit a homicide. They argue that women, like men, possess agency, and therefore should not be placed in a separate category simply because they experienced postpartum effects. It is an argument to avoid placing infanticidal mothers into special categories of victimhood because of the effects of pregnancy and birth (Morrissey 2003). Thus, carrying out a neonaticide would not justify viewing the woman as a passive victim. However, the dispositional issues actually focus on the status of the post-delivery mother, since she is no longer pregnant, and what relationship the pregnancy may have had on her behavior subsequent to the birth of the child.

Similar arguments have been raised for other "syndromes" such as battered women or rape trauma (Slobogin 2010). Assertion of a neonatal syndrome may not meet criteria for a clinical diagnosis, or legal standards for admission as evidence to mitigate the offense. Biological changes in pregnancy per se do not classify a woman as a victim alleged to be suffering from a neonaticidal syndrome. In fact, actions of concealing the pregnancy, hiding the delivery, and later disposing of the corpse can be seen as evidence of active agency serving one's own interests. These acts may be viewed as depraved, from a "bad" woman, but they do not reflect a lack of agency.

Agency viewpoints bear on criteria for criminal responsibility. While the neonaticidal mother may have a plethora of diverse symptoms in the perinatal period, often associated with diverse personality disorders, the absence of psychotic symptoms is relevant if an insanity defense is considered. Since the majority of these women do not have a psychotic diagnosis, it is difficult to establish that *mens rea* was lacking at the time of the killing. Establishing limitations on the capacity of these women to challenge their active agency for the criminal act of killing an infant, or newborn, leads to the relevancy of a "neonatal syndrome."

Syndrome Issues

The clinical use of the term "syndrome" as defined in the American Psychiatric Diagnostic Manual (APA 2013: 830) is "a grouping of signs and symptoms, based on their frequent co-occurrence, that suggest a common underlying pathogenesis, course, familial pattern or treatment selection." Significantly, a syndrome is not equivalent to a mental disorder or illness. Advocates urge its use in trials of infanticide arguing that it would be useful to the finders of fact to explain more about the behavior in question; those opposed to its introduction hold that juries can decide the issues without getting into the complexities of assessing experts testifying on syndromes.

For courts to admit syndrome evidence, they must examine the materiality of the evidence, its probative value, helpfulness, and whether the testimony will be distracting or confusing to the fact finder (Slobogin 2010). Materiality is whether the testimony about a neonaticide syndrome will be recognized by the law. The question is whether such testimony will be helpful, or distract the jury from its independent verdict. The probative value of testimony involves the screening of expert testimony. In the United States such screening is governed by two evidentiary tests. The Frye test (1923) aims to determine whether the expert testimony has a general acceptance among experts in the field; the other is the Daubert test (1993) based on a verification process to assess (1) whether the proffered testimony has been tested to see if it can be falsified, (2) the error rate, (3) peer review, and (4) general acceptance.

Testimony about a neonaticidal syndrome would require testimony under one of these standards. A Frye test would require that the psychiatric profession agree on whether a neonaticidal syndrome is validated—that is, if it is accepted as a clinical entity by the majority of the profession. Since the American Psychiatric Association does not list it as a diagnosis, acceptance is questionable. If the Daubert test is used, the issue is not only the reliability of using such a syndrome, but its relevance. While it could be argued that it is relevant to elaborate about psychiatric symptoms, the reliability question would arise, such as how testing could be used to establish the syndrome as a scientifically accepted clinical entity. Inquiry would also be made into the error rate of the diagnosis. The methodology used for its testing and why it has not been accepted by the psychiatric community as a diagnosis become issues. Whether these types of evidentiary issues are relevant to countries other than the United States is questionable given that most other jurisdictions appear to have handled the problem legislatively by changing the sentencing structures, or creating definitions of the offenses of infanticide or neonaticide.

The legal "infanticide doctrine" has as a correlate the social idea of an "infanticidal woman" (Loughnan 2012). It leads to the "instantiation" of abnormality in the criminal law sustained by nonexpert or lay ideas from the realms of gender, birth, and madness. The vulnerability of the infanticidal woman is related to a conception of responsibility based on character and reputation (Lacey 2001). Such a vacuum originated in the absence of an expert medical consensus about the concept of infanticide. When medical opinion did emerge, it blended with community ideas about why a "bad woman" killed her offspring (Ward 1999). The outcome was a blurring between unfortunate circumstances in a woman's life and legitimate biological or mental disturbances.

Prevention Possibilities

In thinking about preventing neonaticide, a critical avenue relates to the alertness of clinical and social agencies to relevant features or risk factors; for example, a young, single woman denying she is pregnant, living alone, suffering from deprived socioeconomic conditions, and feeling powerless. However, the number of false positives from such a picture to assess neonaticides would be high. Even with this hypothesized young woman, the assumptions are often unrealistic—that she would be in touch with professionals, not concealing her status, pursuing prenatal care, and open about her dilemma.

Historically, neonaticides worldwide were often ascribed to young women in economic difficulties or whose newborns had congenital abnormalities (Craig 2004). These are often in the background but another key variable for neonaticides is the primiparous state.[8] Beyond being single and living alone, there is often poor communication with her mother and family, personality traits of immaturity and passivity, and perhaps limited education. As noted, the denial present in adolescents may have persisted to the point of commencing labor. Cultural issues such as the devaluation and killing of female infants in some societies raise a broader topic.

The embarrassment of having an illegitimate child has often been voiced. Its current cogency is questionable. A married woman with an extramarital pregnancy may still raise the risk. However, given the context associated with a neonaticidal mother, the idea for detection of a homicidal state ahead of the delivery seems optimistic since these mothers are usually not seeking assistance. Even with postpartum depressions, the effects of preventive interventions are limited (O'Hara and McCabe 2013). The key is detecting the stresses in a pregnant female. The Centers for Disease Control and Prevention in the United States, with data from 27 states, found 70.2 percent of women reported a stressful life event in the year before giving birth (CDC 2015). This would seem relevant to prevention efforts.

Countries have tried different approaches to limit neonaticides with questionable success. Safe haven laws may offer some prevention, but the question is how many young women can be made aware of such possibilities. The idea of anonymously giving up the newborn, labeled in France as "accouchement soux X," and dating to the French Revolution, has its appeal (Lefaucher 2004). Questions arise about the absence of a medical history if the infant is adopted. The practice of arranging anonymously to leave the newborn and nothing more dating from the Middle Ages seems to point out the lack of newer approaches. Perhaps the best prevention is getting more young women into family planning and preventing pregnancies rather than pinning hopes on later discovering the potentially neonaticidal mother.

Infanticide prevention,[9] in contrast to neonaticide, has other opportunities. Again, attention needs to be paid to diverse cultural situations. The women are more often married, older, and living with a partner. A psychosis in the mother following a delivery is an important sign regarding increased risk potential, as is an unremitting depression during the first year. Some of these cases have a background of physical abuse by the mother of the infant or by her partner. Alcohol or substance abuse may be playing a significant role. These figure in evaluating the status of the mother, especially if there is a sense of increased irritability and aggression. Males may also suffer from postpartum disturbances as separate from impulsive young males who physically assault infants. Previous episodes of postpartum psychosis raise the infanticidal risk for any subsequent delivery. Munchausen by proxy can also heighten the risk utilizing miscarried drug dosages to the infant or suffocation. Many of these cases do not appear related to psychoses but aberrant personality disorders. Among various preventive proposals mandated state policies for home visits by nurses may be an effective process (Rowan, Duckett, and Wang 2015).

Conclusion

Infanticide and neonaticide have existed since *homo sapiens* emerged and probably earlier. As different cultures developed, and in different historical periods, societies and legal systems varied in how they dealt with such behavior. The United States and England have been used to illustrate some of these changes. Explanations also continue to vary, which correlates with different bases for the acts. Some cases have a primary socioeconomic basis while others show different degrees of psychopathology. The role of partners, male and female, is another variable. Prevention as a public health problem always looms. At this point a comprehensive grasp of the diversity of biopsychosocial variables is the hope for understanding and prevention.

Notes

1 These were usually homes created by charitable organizations where newborns and abandoned children could be placed.

2 This refers to physicians who would testify in courts on such cases.

3 These figures indicate the high incidence of psychotic symptoms within 30–60 days when they occur.

4 Some cases may directly be charged as a felony murder on some level, others may be kept in a juvenile proceeding, and others may be kept in a miscellaneous filing for an indefinite period before a resolution. Those working in this area, but from different professions, often find this uncertainty confusing and frustrating.

5 This article illustrates the diversity among different countries in how cases of infanticide and neonaticide are handled and how they differ in their approaches to such problems. These vary, from a punitive emphasis as in the United States, to more leniency with others if not welfare oriented.
6 This was a defense used to try and show a lack of intent to commit an infanticide since she was preparing linen to use with her newborn.
7 Courts may have expanded who is qualified to testify to include not only physicians of different specialties (obstetricians, pediatricians, psychiatrists, child psychiatrists) but psychologists (clinical psychologists, social psychologists, school psychologists), social workers, clinical social workers, teachers, and so on.
8 This refers to a female with her first pregnancy.
9 Preventive efforts might vary widely depending on the culture in question. India is often used as an example with different cultural norms, as well as some cultures placing an emphasis on males, and so on. This perspective would require a chapter by itself but it is important and needs to be kept in mind. The focus in this chapter has been primarily on Western culture with some differences within.

References

APA (American Psychiatric Association) (2013) *Diagnostic and Statistical Manual of Mental Disorders* (5th edn). Washington, DC: American Psychiatric Association.

Ayres, S. (2007) Who Is to shame? Narratives of neonaticide. *William & Mary Journal of Women & Law*, 14: 55–105.

Barton, B. (1998) When murdering hands rock the cradle: An overview of America's incoherent treatment of infanticidal mothers. *Southern Methodist University Law Review*, 51: 591–619.

Behlmer, G.K. (1979) Deadly motherhood: Infanticide and the medical opinion in mid-Victorian England. *Journal of the History of Medicine and Allied Sciences*, 34: 403–427.

Brookman, F. and Nolan, J. (2006) The dark figure of infanticide in England and Wales. *Journal of Interpersonal Violence*, 21:869–889.

CDC (Centers for Disease Control and Prevention) (2015) Stressful life events experienced by women in the year before their infants' births—United States, 2000–2010. *Morbidity and Mortality Weekly Report*, 64: 247–251.

Cooper, A. and Smith, E.L. (2011) *Patterns & Trends: Homicide Trends in the United States, 1980–2008*. Washington, DC: US Department of Justice, Bureau of Justice Statistics.

Craig, M. (2004) Perinatal risk factors for neonaticide and infant homicide: Can we identify the risk? *Journal of the Royal Society of Medicine*, 97: 57–61.

Daubert v Merrell Dow Pharmaceuticals, Inc. (1993) 509 US 579.

D'Orban, P.T. (1979) Women Who Kill Their Children. *The British Journal of Psychiatry*, 134:560–571.

Frye v United States (1923) 293 F 1013, DC Cir 1923.

Fuchs, R.G. (2001) Charity and welfare. In D.I. Kirtzer and M. Barbagl (eds), *Family Life in the Nineteenth Century* (pp. 154–194). New Haven, CT: Yale University Press.

Fujiwara, T., Barber, C., Schaecter, J., and Hemenway, D. (2009) Characteristics of infant homicide: Findings from a US multisite reporting system. *Pediatrics*, 124: 210–217.

Gartner, R. and McCarthy, B. (2006) Killing one's children/maternal infanticide and the dark figure of homicide. In K. Heimer and C. Kruttschnitt (eds), *Gender and Crime* (pp. 91–114). New York: NYU Press.

Hoffer, P.C. and Hull, N.E.H. (1981) *Murdering Mothers: Infanticide in England and New England 1558–1803*. New York: NYU Press.

International Classification of Diseases (2015) Postpartum mood disturbance. ICD-10-CM Code 090.6. IC10Data.com

Kaye, N.S., Berenstein, N.M., and Donnelly, S.M. (1990) Families, murder and insanity: A psychiatric review of paternal infanticide. *Journal of Forensic Sciences*, 35: 133–139.

Kellum, B.A. (1974) Infanticide in England and the later Middle Ages. *History of Child Quarterly*, 1: 367–389.

Kendell, R.E., Chalmers, L.C., and Platz, C. (1987) Epidemiology of puerperal psychoses. *British Journal of Psychiatry*, 150: 662–673.

Kohm, L. and Liverman, T. (2002) Prom mom killers: The impact of blame shift and distorted statistics on punishment for neonaticides. *William and Mary Journal of Women and the Law*, 9: 43–71.

Kunz, J. and Bahr, S. (1996) A profile of parental homicide against children. *Journal of Family Violence*, 11: 347–362.

Lacey, N. (2001) Responsibility and modernity in criminal law. *The Journal of Political Philosophy*, 9: 249–276.

Lang, L.J. (2005) To love the babe that milks me: Infanticide and reconceiving the mother. *Columbia Journal of Gender & Law*, 14: 114–141.

Lefaucher, N. (2004) The French tradition of anonymous birth: The lines of argument. *International Journal of Policy and Family*, 18: 319–342.

Loughnan, A. (2012) The "Strange" case of the infanticide doctrine. *Oxford Journal of Legal Studies*, 32: 685–711.

Macfarlane, J. (2003) Criminal defense in cases of infanticide and neonaticide. In M.G. Spinelli (ed.), *Infanticide/Psychosocial and Legal Perspectives on Mothers Who Kill* (pp. 133–166). Washington, DC: American Psychiatric Publishing.

Malmquist, C. (2013) Infanticide/neonaticide: The outlier situation in the United States. *Aggression and Violent Behavior*, 18: 399–408.

Meens, R. (2014) *Penance in Medieval Europe, 600–1200*. New York: Cambridge University Press.

Meyer, C. and Oberman, C. (2001) *Mothers Who Kill Their Children: Understanding the Acts of Moms from Susan Smith to the "Prom Mom."* New York: NYU Press.

Meyer, C. and Spinelli, M.G. (2003) Medical and legal dilemmas of postpartum psychiatric disorders. In M.G. Spinelli (ed.), *Infanticide/Psychosocial and Legal Perspective on Mothers Who Kill* (pp. 167–183). Washington, DC: American Psychiatric Publishing.

Morrissey, B. (2003) *When Women Kill: Questions of Agency and Subjectivity*. New York: Routledge.

Noonan, J.T. (1986) *Contraception: A History of Its Treatment by the Catholic Canonists*. Cambridge, MA: Harvard University Press.

Oberman, M. (2003) Mothers who kill: Cross-cultural patterns in and perspectives on contemporary maternal filicide. *International Journal of Law and Psychiatry*, 26: 493–514.

O'Hagan, K. (2014) *The Killing of Children in the Context of Separation, Divorce and Custody Disputes*. New York: Palgrave Macmillan.

O'Hara, M.W. and McCabe, J.E. (2013) Postpartum depression: Current status and future directions. *Annual Review of Clinical Psychology*, 9: 379–407.

Overpeck, M. (2003) Epidemiology of infanticide. In M.G. Spinelli (ed.), *Infanticide/Psychosocial and Legal Perspectives on Mothers Who Kill* (pp. 19–34). Washington, DC: American Psychiatric Publishing.

Overpeck, M., Brenner, R.A., Trumble, A.C., *et al.* (1998) Risk factors for infant homicide in the United States. *New England Journal of Medicine*, 339: 272–275.

Pomeroy, S.P. (2002) *Spartan Women*. New York: Oxford University Press.

Porter, T. and Gavin, H. (2010) Infanticide and neonaticide: A review of 40 years of research literature on incidence and causes. *Trauma, Violence, & Abuse*, 11: 99–112.

Resnick, P.J. (1970) Murder of the newborn: A psychiatric view of neonaticide. *American Journal of Psychiatry*, 126: 1414–1420.

Rowan, P.J., Duckett, S.A., and Wang, J.E. (2015) State mandates regarding postpartum depression. *Psychiatric Services*, 66: 324–328.

Schwartz, L.L. and Isser, N.K. (2001) Neonaticide: An appropriate application for therapeutic jurisprudence? *Behavioral Sciences & the Law*, 19: 703–719.

Shelton, J.L.E., Muirhead, Y., and Canning, K.E. (2010) Ambivalence toward mothers who kill: An Examination of 45 US cases of maternal neonaticide. *Behavioral Sciences and the Law*, 28: 812–831.

Slobogin, C. (2010) Psychological syndrome and criminal responsibility. *Annual Review of Law and Social Science*, 6: 109–127.

Spinelli, M.G. (2003) Neonaticide. In M.G. Spinelli (ed.), *Infanticide/Psychosocial and Legal Perspectives on Mothers Who Kill* (pp. 105–118). Washington, DC: American Psychiatric Publishing.

Stuntz, W.J. (2011) *The Collapse of American Criminal Justice*. Cambridge, MA. Harvard University Press.

Vellut, N., Cook, J.M., and Tursz, A. (2012) Analysis of the relationship between neonaticide and denial of pregnancy using data from judicial files. *Child Abuse & Neglect*, 36: 553–563.

Ward, T. (1999) The sad subject of infanticide: Law, medicine and child murder, 1860–1938. *Social & Legal Studies*, 8: 163–180.

Yang, B. (2009) Postpartum depression and the insanity defense: A poor mother's two worst nightmares. *Wisconsin Journal of Law, Gender & Society*, 24: 229–253.

Zunshine, L. (2005) *Bastards and Foundlings: Illegitimacy in Eighteenth-Century England*. Columbus: Ohio State University Press.

Further Reading

Gunn, J., Joseph, P., MacKay, R.D., and Denyer, T. (2014) Criminal and civil law for the psychiatrist in England and Wales. In J. Gunn and P.J. Taylor (eds), *Forensic Psychiatry/Clinical, Legal and Ethical Issues* (2nd edn, pp. 18–55). Boca Raton, FL: CRC Press.

Overpeck, M.D., Brenner, R.A., Cosgrove, C., *et al.* (2002) National underascertainment of sudden unexpected infant deaths associated with deaths of unknown cause. *Pediatrics*, 109: 274–283.

12

Parricide Encapsulated

Kathleen M. Heide

The killing of a parent by a child, often referred to as parricide, is a shocking event that occurs worldwide. Studies and clinical reports document the killings of mothers and fathers by their offspring in Africa, North America, South America, Asia, Australia/Oceania, and Europe. The term parricide actually refers to the killing of a close relative, but has increasingly become identified in the professional and popular literature with the murder of an individual's mother (*matricide*) or father (*patricide*).

When these incidents occur, they often result in widespread media coverage because the killing of parents is considered taboo in all cultures and is in direct opposition to the two Biblical commandments: "Honor thy father and mother" and "thou shall not kill" (Heide 2013). The public's fascination with parricide dates back thousands of years, as evidenced by it being a recurrent theme in Greek and Roman literature and mythology. Parricidal thoughts were major themes in the works of Sigmund Freud, the founder of psychoanalysis (Freud 1919; Wertham 1941). Analyses of databases of the *New York Times* and the *Chicago Tribune* provide convincing data that parricides have been newsworthy events in the United States for more than 150 years (Shon and Roberts 2008).

An extensive search of news coverage of parricide cases occurring worldwide, using multiple online databases in 2003, found 226 online news accounts of children killing their parents. In 222 of these cases, the country where the incident occurred could be identified. Of these reported cases, 68 percent occurred in the United States. The percentage distribution was as follows: 71 percent in the North America (United States and Canada), 17 percent in Asia, 9 percent in Europe, 2 percent in Australia, and the remaining 1 percent in South America and Africa. This analysis found that the media give excessive coverage to the most disturbing

The Handbook of Homicide, First Edition. Edited by Fiona Brookman, Edward R. Maguire, and Mike Maguire.

cases of parricides, those committed by children and adolescents, perpetrated by females, and incidents involving multiple victims (Boots and Heide 2006; Heide and Boots 2007). Killings involving three or more victims in one incident are referred to as *multicides or mass murders*; when those slain are family members, the events are referred to as *familicide* (Malmquist 1980).

Parricide in Perspective

Despite the interest these cases generate, parricides are rare events in countries where this phenomenon has been investigated. Fathers and mothers comprise about 2 percent of all murder victims in Australia, Japan, and the United States, between 2 and 3 percent of homicide victims in France, less than 4 percent of those killed in Serbia and Canada, and between 1 and 5 percent of all homicides in Tunisia. Although most parricide incidents involve biological parents, victims also include adoptive parents and stepparents (Heide 2013).

The United States maintains a national homicide data base that makes investigation of parricide cases over many years possible. Analyses of 32 years of data (1976–2007) involving nearly 9,800 parricide and stepparricide incidents (Heide 2013) were consistent with earlier analyses (Heide 1993a, 1993b) and revealed that this phenomenon is remarkably stable over time. These data clearly indicated that most parents and stepparents in the United States were slain in single victim, single offender incidents. Of individuals arrested for parricide from 1976 to 2007, 84 percent acted alone when they killed a single parent or stepparent. Nine percent of the remaining 16 percent had accomplices assist them during the murder. The final 7 percent of those arrested for parricide during the period killed two or more victims, whether acting alone (6.3%) or with the help of others (0.8%) (Heide 2013).

In the United States, from a legal perspective, many of the "children" who killed parents in single victim, single offender situations during the study period were 18 years old or older and technically adults. More than one in five of those who killed their parents or stepparents, however, were under age 18 and more than 30 percent were under 20 years old. The percentages of youths through age 19 involved in parricide incidents was higher when victims were stepparents. Over the 32 year period examined, youths under age 20 comprised 45 percent of those who killed stepmothers, 44 percent of stepfathers (44%), 33 percent of biological fathers, and 20 percent of biological mothers (Heide 2013).

Males predominated as the killers in parricide incidents overall: 85 percent of parents and 85 percent of stepparents were slain by sons or stepsons. Among juvenile offenders, males comprised 81 percent of those who killed parents and 84 percent of those who killed stepparents. Among adult offenders, males comprised 86 percent of those who killed both parents and stepparents. When incidents involved multiple victims (MV), males were the killers in 88 percent and 94 percent of incidents involving parents and stepparents, respectively. The very high involvement of males (86% or more) involved in MV parricides held for both juvenile and adult offenders (Heide 2013).

The constellation of offender characteristics in multiple offender (MO) parricide incidents differed from those identified in parricide incidents overall and in MV parricide incidents. The involvement of females was noticeably higher in MO incidents. Females comprised 33 percent and 21 percent of those arrested for killing parents and stepparents in MO situations, respectively. Also noteworthy, a significantly higher percentage of juveniles were involved in MO parricides than adults (18% vs 7%). Interestingly, relative to male juveniles, a significantly higher percentage of female juveniles were involved in MO incidents involving the killing of parents (36% vs 14%) and stepparents (21% vs 12%). Similarly, a significantly higher percentage of female adults, when compared with male adults, acted with others in killing parents (14% vs 5%) and stepparents (21% vs 13%) (Heide 2013).

Age: Critical Legal and Developmental Issues

Age is an important consideration in evaluating offspring who kill their parents. Although most parricide offenders are teenagers and adults, cases exist of young children killing parents. In the United States, for example, 33 children under age 12 were arrested for killing parents during the period 1976–2007. Six of these offenders were under age 10; the remaining 27 were 10 and 11 years old (Heide 2013).

Younger children differ significantly from older children, often referred to as adolescents, who kill parents. Younger children do not typically understand the finality of death and are not capable of forming intent to kill. They often act impulsively and can be easily influenced to engage in lethal behavior by others (Bender 1959; Bender and Curran 1940; Cornell 1989). Younger children who kill are much more likely to be severely disturbed than adolescents and are often dealt with by child protective services or referred for intensive mental health treatment (Bender 1959; Zenoff and Zients 1979).

Adolescence and juvenile status, although often used interchangeably, are not the same. The term juvenile is an age-based legal designation that is set at 18 by federal law in the United States. In contrast, the period of adolescence is a more fluid term. It is generally defined as starting at puberty and is a period marked by significant physiological, physical, psychological, and cognitive changes. The onset of puberty varies by individual, but now typically starts at about age 10 to 12 years. From a biological and psychological perspective, in contrast to the legal definition of juvenile, adolescence lasts until the individual becomes a young adult at about age 20 to 24 (Solomon, Berg, and Martin 2015).

Adolescents, in contrast to younger children, are more likely to kill in response to environmental constraints or situational demands that they perceive parents or others have placed upon them or because of the lifestyle that they have adopted. In the United States, adolescent parricide offenders, unlike children 10 and under, are typically charged when they kill parents. When they are 12 and older, serious consideration is given in almost all of the 50 states in the United States and the District of Columbia (Washington, DC) to transferring them to adult court, given the severity of the crime.

Many, if not most, teen parricide offenders are prosecuted in adult court where, under today's laws, they can be sentenced to long sentences, including life without parole under certain circumstances (Heide 2013; *Miller v Alabama* 2012).

Although adolescents and adults who kill parents may receive similar legal treatment and punishment, there are important developmental differences between the two groups. Adolescents, unlike adults, are at a higher risk of killing their parents when conditions in the home are unfavorable because they have limited options and alternatives. They often cannot legally leave their homes ("runaway"), quit school, secure full-time employment, buy a house, or rent an apartment. Even if they could, surviving on their own is not a realistic alternative for youths due to their lack of financial resources, limited job skills, and incomplete education.

As a group, adolescents have less experience than adults in coping with deplorable environmental conditions. They are less likely to see alternatives and evaluate different courses of action. Research has established that the prefrontal cortex, the area of the brain associated with thinking and judgment, is not completely developed until individuals are in their mid-twenties (Heide and Solomon 2006). Given that adults as a class are developmentally more mature than juveniles and have more resources and alternatives, the motivations that propel adults to kill are often different from their younger counterparts, as reflected in my typology of parricide offenders.

Typology of Parricide Offenders

In my 1992 book entitled *Why Kids Kill Parents: Child Abuse and Adolescent Homicide,* I proposed a typology of parricide offenders based on my review of the professional literature and my own clinical evaluations. The typology consisted of three types of parricide offenders: the *severely abused child* who kills to end the abuse, the *severely mentally ill child*, and the *dangerously antisocial child.* Over the last two decades, the typology has been used and referenced by other clinicians and researchers (see, e.g., Ewing 1997, 2001; Hillbrand *et al.* 1999; Kashani *et al.* 1997; Lennings 2002; Palermo 2007). Children and adolescents who kill parents typically fit into two of the categories: severely abused or dangerously antisocial. Adult parricide offenders generally fall into the severely mentally ill or dangerously antisocial categories. In my 2013 book *Parricide: Understanding Sons and Daughters Who Kill Parents,* I retained these three types and proposed a fourth type: the *enraged* parricide offender who kills out of deep-seated anger. To avoid confusion and in recognition that offspring who kill parents can be adults as well as juveniles, I now refer to the four categories as parricide offender types. The case illustrations used below to explicate the parricide offender types adopt pseudonyms.

The severely abused parricide offender

The severely abused parricide offender is the most common type identified among adolescents. An extensive and long-standing history of child maltreatment is typically easily verified through interviews with family members, friends, and neighbors; previous complaints to child protective agencies are not uncommon in these cases. Over time, these youths come to believe that their physical safety or the lives of other family members are in danger; sometimes they feel as though their psychological survival is at risk. These individuals kill for two fundamental reasons: (1) they are terrified that they or others in the home will be seriously injured or killed, and/or (2) they are desperate to end the abuse and see no other way out. *They are not killing to get back at the parent or to seek revenge.* These youths generally have attempted unsuccessfully to get help from others. Many have tried to run away; some have considered, and even attempted, to kill themselves. From their viewpoint, killing the abusive parent is their only recourse.

Many case reports of severely abused parricide offenders exist (see Heide 2013). These accounts provide convincing evidence that these individuals, typically adolescents, killed their parents because they could no longer cope with conditions in the home. These youths were psychologically abused by one or both parents. In addition, they either endured physical, sexual, and verbal abuse or watched other family members, typically mothers and siblings, being severely maltreated by the abusive parent(s). These youths rarely had histories of serious or extensive delinquent behavior or debilitating mental illness that is typically associated with psychotic disorders. My review of these case studies, as well as my own clinical evaluations of many adolescents who fit this type, indicates that these youths frequently had been severely depressed for months, and sometimes longer, and met the diagnostic criteria of *post-traumatic stress disorder* (*PTSD*).

PTSD is a stress-related disorder that some individuals develop as a result of their exposure to actual or threatened death, serious injury, and/or sexual violence. Individuals with PTSD continually re-experience the traumatic event through intrusive images, flashbacks, thoughts, nightmares, or physical and psychological reactivity to reminders of the traumatic event. They attempt to avoid thoughts, feelings, events, or people associated with the traumatic event. They experience negative changes in their mood or thoughts, such as feeling isolated or disconnected from others, blaming themselves for the event, or being unable to remember aspects of the event. They also tend to be easily startled and on guard for changes that might alert them to danger. These symptoms have been ongoing for at least a month and seriously affect the individual's ability to function (American Psychiatric Association 2013).

The case of Peter Jones is an excellent illustration of a severely abused parricide offender whom I evaluated (Heide 2013). Peter was the older of two boys born to his parents. From the time Peter was a young boy, he watched his father beat and berate his mother. Peter was also physically and verbally abused by his father from a young age.

When Peter became a teenager, he took a protective stance toward his mother and told his father to leave his mother alone. Mr Jones continued to beat Peter. Over time, Mrs Jones became more physically and psychologically debilitated, used Valium to cope, and was unable to parent either of her children. Mr Jones had been on social security disability due to serious mental illness for five years prior to the killing. He was reportedly diagnosed as schizophrenic and, like his wife, was unable to meet the demands of parenting. As a result, Peter took on more of the tasks of running the household, including taking care of his brother, getting him to school, cleaning the house, and cooking. He took care of his mother, protected her, and became her confidante.

In the weeks before the killing, friends and relatives of Peter noticed he seemed stressed and exhausted. Mr Jones had become more explosive and made threats to kill the family. In the days preceding the killing, tension in the home escalated when Peter's mother was hospitalized and his father resumed drinking.

On the night of the homicide, Peter's father had hit him a few times. The boy left the house. When he returned, Peter took his father's rifle, loaded it for protection, and put it under his bed. When his father saw that Peter was home, he chased Peter, who ran out the back door. Shortly thereafter Peter climbed into the house through his bedroom window. Terrified that his father heard him re-enter the house, Peter grabbed the rifle and went back out the same window. As Peter stood unobserved outside the house watching his father through the living room window, he was terrified that his father was going to see him and kill him. As he pulled the rifle up to aim, Peter had flashbacks of violence that his father had inflicted on his mother, brother, and himself. He dissociated (lost conscious awareness), regaining awareness as he heard the gunshots. Although he had no memory of shooting his father, Peter knew that he must have fired the rifle. He ran into the house, cradled his father's body, told his father not to die, and asked his neighbor to call the police and the ambulance.

Peter had just about all of the 12 characteristics I identified from the literature as associated with cases of severely abused parricide offenders (Heide 1992). (1) He lived in a home in which parental brutality and cruelty had been ongoing for years. (2) Peter had tried to escape the family situation by running away, but was returned home by police. (3) Over time, the family situation became increasingly intolerable and (4) Peter felt increasingly helpless and trapped. (5) At the time of the shooting, he was isolated from others and had fewer people in his life than other adolescents his age. Peter was not attending school and spent his time taking care of his brother and the household. In addition to his parents and younger brother, his uncle and a boarder lived in the home. (6) On the night of the shooting, Peter's inability to cope with the escalating tension led to a loss of control. (7) Peter was not a criminally sophisticated youth; his prior criminal history was limited to a fist fight with a boy who called Peter's girlfriend a name, and to driving under the influence. (8) The rifle Peter used belonged to his father and was readily available. (9) Peter's father and his mother were both chemically dependent; his father was an alcoholic and his mother self-medicated with tranquilizers. (10) At the time of the shooting, Peter experienced dissociation and met the diagnostic criteria of post-traumatic stress disorder (PTSD). (11) The victim's death was initially perceived by Peter and family members as a relief. There was only one criterion not present in Peter's case. (12) Unlike many severely abused parricide offenders, Peter did not attempt to get help from others. However, many relatives and neighbors testified at Peter's trial that they knew about the abuse and did not intervene to help Peter.

Peter's lawyer raised the insanity defense at trial. Four mental health professionals, including myself, evaluated Peter's mental status at the time of the shooting. These included experts retained by the defense and the state and appointed by the court. All mental health professionals agreed that Peter was in a dissociative state at the time of the shooting; he was experiencing episodes of past trauma and terrified by the events that had transpired on the evening of the killing. All of the experts concluded that Peter was insane at the time of the killing. The police officer testified that Peter seemed out of touch with what was going on when the officer interacted with Peter shortly after the shooting.

The jury was unable to reach a verdict in Peter's trial. The judge declared a mistrial when it was clear that jurors were hopelessly deadlocked. The judge then directed a verdict of acquittal on the grounds of insanity, indicating that the prosecution had introduced no evidence to rebut the defense's assertion that Peter was insane when he killed his father. The judge ordered Peter to be transferred to a local hospital for evaluation and treatment to be followed by therapy with a psychiatrist who had previously treated Peter and his parents.

The severely mentally ill parricide offender

Adults who kill their parents, particularly their mothers, are frequently diagnosed as severely mentally ill. Occasionally, younger children and adolescents who kill parents are also identified as seriously mentally disturbed. These individuals characteristically have a long and documented medical history of serious mental illness, which is known to family members (Heide 2013). Many are diagnosed with *schizophrenia, schizoaffective disorder*, or other psychotic conditions on the schizophrenia spectrum. Occasionally, these individuals are diagnosed with *bipolar disorder with psychotic features* or *major depression with psychotic features* at the time of the killing (American Psychiatric Association 2013).

The reason that these individuals kill their parents is directly related to their mental illness, which is often debilitating and severely interferes with their ability to function in social situations and work settings. They may experience *hallucinations* (false sensory perceptions, such as hearing or seeing things that are not happening). For example, they may hear God telling them that "You must kill your mother now." They may also experience *delusions* (false beliefs that have no basis in reality), such as their mother is a Russian spy who is going to kill the president unless she is stopped. Severely mentally ill parricide offenders often have been prescribed psychotropic medication to manage their symptoms and may have been hospitalized in a psychiatric facility. These killings frequently happen when these individuals stop taking their medication and their behavior becomes noticeably bizarre. For example, severely mentally ill parricide offenders may use extreme violence (e.g., dismembering of the corpse, decapitation of victims) or select unusual weapons to kill, such as swords or machetes.

Sometimes the mental illness is so debilitating that prosecution is stopped until the parricide offender is treated and restored to competency. *Competency* is a legal term used to denote that a defendant has the ability to understand the nature of the criminal charges and to assist in his or her defense. In rare instances, prosecution may be dropped if a judge finds, after reviewing the evaluations of mental health professionals, that it is unlikely that the defendant will become legally competent. In a situation of this nature, the parricide offender will be civilly committed to a mental hospital where he will stay until he is no longer perceived as mentally ill and a danger to himself or others.

The case of Jason is an excellent example of a severely mentally ill parricide offender whom I evaluated. Jason was arrested at age 21 for killing his mother by thrusting two kamas (martial arts weapons similar to a sickle with a sharp knife-like edge and point) into her abdomen while she slept. Jason had a documented history of severe mental illness dating back to age 13. Over the years, Jason was given several diagnoses of serious mental illness indicative of a thought disorder. These included paranoid schizophrenia and schizoaffective disorder (mood and thought disorder). Prior to the killing, Jason had been admitted and detained twice for several weeks in psychiatric hospitals. He had a long history of being prescribed psychotropic medication and had been receiving social security disability checks for years.

Although early testing revealed that he was gifted, Jason had difficulties in school and was placed in special education classes as he got older due to his difficulties in functioning in a normal classroom. Largely as a result of the commitment of one of his special education teachers, Jason was able to meet the requirements to be graduated from high school. Upon graduation, Jason was unable to work due to the severity of his mental illness and he continued to live at home with his mother.

Jason was fascinated by the medieval period of history. He was very involved in "massively multiplayer online role play games" (MMORPG). He spent hours every day playing these war games in which participants moved units under their control to secure areas and attempted to destroy their opponents' assets. Jason took great pleasure in playing these games. He preferred absorption in these games to living in the real world of adult responsibilities.

Jason liked the weaponry used during medieval times. Contrary to advice from mental health professionals, school authorities, and relatives, Jason's mother helped him purchase more than a dozen swords. The swords were not stage props; they were razor sharp weapons. Jason liked to posture using these swords; he enjoyed making some basic exercise moves and pretending he was fencing with others. In his fantasy games, he was thrusting his swords into imaginary villains.

Jason remembered very little of the events that resulted in the death of his mother. He remembered that he played for hours being a hunter with a bow and arrow in a widely popular MMORPG. He remembered going back to his room, wrapping his fingers, wrists, and hands with material to make fingerless gloves, and lifting weights. The next thing he remembered was being in his mother's room with a kama and making a motion with this weapon. He vaguely recalled hitting his mother one time with the sharp instrument; he did not remember hitting her multiple times and exiting his mother's bedroom.

Later, Jason recalled that he went into his mother's room and saw two kamas protruding from her stomach. He knew from looking at her body that she was dead. Although he had no memory of stabbing her repeatedly and thrusting the two sharp weapons into her abdomen, Jason knew that he must have done this, because the doors were locked, preventing anyone else from entering the home.

Jason was overcome with grief and attempted to kill himself. When he failed, he stayed in his mother's home, knowing eventually the police would be alerted by one of his sisters that something was wrong and come to the residence. When the officers arrived, Jason, dressed only in his underwear, emerged from a closet in which he was hiding, wielding a sword and pleading with law enforcement to kill him.

Jason was initially found incompetent to stand trial and was placed in the mental hospital run by the state (jurisdiction in which he lived). After several months of treatment, he was restored to competency. He was subsequently found not guilty by reason of insanity at a bench trial (trial by judge, no jury) and committed to a mental hospital.

In some instances, severely mentally ill parricide offenders do not have a history of psychosis. Instead these individuals may be diagnosed as having a brief psychotic disorder, brought on by acute stress and possibly intensified by excessive substance abuse. Marcus Sanchez, for example, had a history of severe depression that included multiple failed suicide attempts. He drank alcohol excessively and used extreme amounts of drugs, particularly crystal methamphetamine, LSD, and marijuana. Shortly before he shot his father to death, Marcus got in trouble with the law again and had to go back to court. At that time Marcus was living with his mother who had become a stable and hard-working parent. The judge, unaware that Marcus's father was an alcoholic and drug abuser and had abused Marcus in the past, allowed the boy to leave the state to live with his father.

During the 10 days that Marcus lived with his father, the two smoked marijuana a lot, got drunk, and got along reasonably well. On the day of the killing, Marcus, plagued by voices commanding him to kill his father, prayed to God to help him. Marcus maintained that the gun went off, hitting his father in the head, as he desperately tried to resist the voice that was controlling his body (Heide 2013).

On occasion, some adults kill their parents because they are mentally disturbed or overwhelmed by the excessive demands placed upon them as caretakers for aging parents. These adult parricide offenders do not have severe and long-standing mental illnesses. However, their homicidal behavior is caused by mental illness brought on by the enormous stress placed upon them. Some of these individuals will be diagnosed with severe depression that may include psychotic features. These individuals may have killed their parents while "under the influence of extreme mental or emotional disturbance," a statutorily defined mitigating factor in sentencing in many of the 50 states in the United States (see, e.g., Florida Statutes 2014: ch. 921.141(6)(b)). In rare cases, adult children who are thrust in the caretaking role are unable to provide the level of care needed for their aging and infirm parents with tragic outcomes. If their inability to meet these obligations leads to the parent's death, the caretaker may be charged with criminally negligent homicide (Heide 2013).

The dangerously antisocial parricide offender

This type of parricide offender is represented among both adolescents and adults. These individuals kill their parents for selfish reasons. They see their parents as obstacles preventing them from getting what they want. For example, these individuals may kill a parent to obtain more freedom, to take the family car, or to get money. I have had several cases of female adolescents, for example, who killed or attempted to kill their parents so they could date the boyfriend of their choice. In one of these cases, a 16-year-old girl appeared to murder her wealthy parents because they disapproved of her boyfriend. The young man, who had no involvement in the murders, had dropped out of school, had limited financial resources, and was reportedly selling drugs.

Middle-aged sons in two of my recent cases were charged in separate incidents with killing their parents for their money. Both men were having financial difficulties at the time of the murders. Their parents, who had come to their sons' rescue with money several times in the past, had refused to provide additional funds prior to their deaths.

Dangerously antisocial parricide offenders typically have an established history of antisocial and criminal behavior. When these parricide offenders are under 18, diagnoses of *conduct disorder* (*CD*) are not uncommon. When they are 18 years of age or older, they frequently meet the diagnostic criteria for *antisocial personality disorder* (*APD*). Individuals diagnosed with CD and APD have an established pattern of violating other people's rights (American Psychiatric Association 2013). Some of them would also meet the diagnostic criteria of a *psychopath*, meaning that they lack a sense of emotional connection to other people, in addition to having a history of antisocial behavior. Psychopaths do not perceive themselves as responsible for the consequences of their behavior, are self-absorbed, and lack empathy (Hare 1999).

Individuals who are diagnosed as having CD, APD, or psychopathy frequently appear to behave in an irrational manner. They often demonstrate poor judgment and do not learn from experience. These parricide offenders, unlike those who are psychotic, however, know what they are doing. Psychopaths, in particular, may present as charming and poised, mainly because they do not experience anxiety, guilt, and remorse about breaking laws and violating the rights of others (Hare 1999).

Daniel Culbreath presented as a dangerously antisocial parricide offender when I evaluated him (Heide 2013). Daniel, age 20, was arrested soon after his parents were found shot to death. Suspicion focused on Daniel largely because several of his friends told the police that Daniel had talked repeatedly about killing his parents. Daniel denied that he intentionally killed his parents to get access to his parents' estate, which was quite substantial, and to be free of their demands and expectations. He insisted he did not intend to kill his parents when he opened fire. He did acknowledge, however, that he repeatedly thought about killing them. It was clear from his statements that parricidal thoughts were a source of pleasure for Daniel and made him feel powerful. He was quite upfront that he enjoyed talking about killing people to others and watching their reactions.

Daniel had a history of antisocial behavior that dated back to childhood and he would likely have been diagnosed as having conduct disorder had he been evaluated as a juvenile. Although he had not been arrested as a juvenile or adult prior to the killings, Daniel admitted that he broke into houses, engaged in theft from homes and cars, initiated fights, participated in vandalism, was truant from school, and frequently lied to his parents.

At the time of the evaluation, Daniel met the diagnostic criteria for antisocial personality disorder. Daniel repeatedly drove while intoxicated, evincing an unwillingness to obey the law, as well as showing a reckless disregard for others' safety. Daniel repeatedly lied to his parents, embellished stories apparently to impress others, and was frequently deceitful. Despite being paid by the government to attend school so he could learn a trade, Daniel repeatedly failed to attend, demonstrating consistent irresponsibility. Daniel had no remorse for any antisocial behavior in which he engaged prior to the murder of his parents. This illegal conduct included destroying property, stealing, and subjecting others to physical danger.

Although Daniel did not meet the threshold to be diagnosed as a psychopath, he had a number of psychopathic traits. These included pathological lying, shallow affect, callousness and lack of empathy, impulsivity, irresponsibility, failure to accept responsibility, lack of realistic, long-term goals, and promiscuous sexual behavior (Hare 1999). I was particularly concerned that Daniel enjoyed fantasies about acts of destructiveness. As noted above, he enjoyed thinking about and discussing parricidal and homicidal thoughts. In addition, Daniel related that he watched the film *Natural Born Killers* on several occasions. He intentionally ran over a fox and returned later to photograph it. Daniel's childhood history of antisocial behavior, the diagnosis of antisocial personality disorder, the presence of many psychopathic traits, particularly those considered personality traits, and the enjoyment of homicidal thoughts were unfavorable prognostic indicators (Heide 2013).

The enraged parricide offender

Most parricide offenders fit into the three categories described above. Over the years, however, I have evaluated some parricide offenders who appeared to kill because they were enraged with their parents. For example, in a few cases individuals killed their mothers or fathers when their deep-rooted rage linked to past parental abuse and/or neglect was unleashed by an external event. In some of these cases, the offender's rage was fueled by alcohol and drugs.

Karl Roberts, age 16, is an excellent example of the enraged parricide offender (Heide 2013). Karl and his half-sister were raised by two chemically dependent parents. The two siblings had a very close bond. Their lives changed significantly when Karl's sister told the family that Mr Roberts, her stepfather (Karl's father) had sexually abused her for years. Charges were not pursued because Mr Roberts agreed to move out. Due to financial reasons, Karl went to live with his father while his sister stayed with her mother.

Karl hated his father for what the man did to his sister. After he moved in with his father, Karl became very rebellious and got into trouble frequently at school, dropping out in the 8th grade. He smoked marijuana daily, experimented with other drugs, and had accumulated an extensive array of delinquency charges. Mr Roberts could not control Karl and eventually stopped trying.

On the day of the shooting, Karl and two of his friends were planning to leave town and go to another state to live. They needed money and a car. Karl broke into a house and stole jewelry and a couple of guns. After realizing that none of them knew how to steal a car, they went back to Karl's house to smoke marijuana and figure something out. Karl's father and his fiancé were asleep in bed when the idea struck the boys to take Mr Robert's car.

Twice Karl tried to sneak into his father's bedroom to get the keys, but his father woke up and Karl left the room. The third time he attempted to enter the bedroom, he saw the dog sitting on his dad's bed. Karl shut the door and told his friends that he was abandoning the plan. At this point, one of his friends suggested that Karl kill his father and take his car. Karl told this boy he could not kill his father and his fiancé. The boy replied (corroborated by the third boy), "Remember what he did to your sister."

Karl's memory as to what happened was blurry; he remembered bits and pieces of what happened, which was consistent with dissociation. His accounts to me, the police, the detention deputy, his mother, and his friends all suggested that he was "on automatic pilot" when he pivoted around and kicked open the door to his father's bedroom. One of Karl's friends described him prior to the shooting as "disturbed and confused." Karl opened fire while his father and the man's fiancé were sleeping, hitting both of them. Mr Roberts, survived the bullet wounds; Mr Roberts's fiancé did not. After the shooting, Karl took his father's car keys and his wallet and drove hundreds of miles away with his two friends.

Within 24 hours of the incident, Karl was arrested and subsequently charged with murder and attempted murder. Karl felt badly that he had shot and killed his father's fiancé, seeing her as an innocent bystander. In contract, he was not remorseful for shooting his father and was pleased that the shooting left his father with some disability (Heide 2013).

The Need for a Thorough Forensic Assessment

Karl's case is an excellent case to illustrate the importance of a thorough forensic assessment by a mental health professional with experience in evaluating violent offenders. The four categories described appear cut and dry. In reality, some cases contain facts that cross categories and underscore the importance of unraveling the motivational dynamics behind the killing. The question that must be answered to correctly classify the individual who has killed his or her parent is *what propelled the killing* (Heide 1992, 2013).

Frequently defense attorneys note that there was abuse in the family and erroneously conclude that the offender would be classified as a severely abused parricide offender.

Karl's shooting of his father was propelled by being reminded of his father's abuse of his sister. The sexual abuse, however, was not ongoing. Simply put, Karl did not shoot his father in a desperate attempt to end the abuse of his sister.

In contrast, prosecutors often see that a parricide offender, such as Karl, has a significant juvenile or criminal history and mistakenly believe that the killer would be classified as a dangerously antisocial parricide offender. Although Karl was a conduct disordered juvenile, he did not attempt to kill his father to serve a selfish, instrumental reason, such as stealing his father's car. Rather, the reminder of his father's sexual abuse of his sister by his friend at that instant unleashed the rage that Karl had been carrying toward his father for years. Rage was the driving factor behind the attempted murder of his father and the unforeseen killing of his father's fiancé. Hence, Karl did not meet the requirement to be classified as a dangerously antisocial parricide offender.

It is important to note that mental disorders can be found among each of the parricide offender types. For example, as noted earlier, the severely abused parricide offender often suffers from PTSD or depression; the accumulation of stress and terror can result in dissociation during the killing. The dangerously antisocial parricide offender, depending on age, frequently meets the diagnostic criteria of either conduct disorder or antisocial personality disorder, which are mental disorders also listed in DSM-5. These disorders are to be distinguished from disorders that are associated with the severely mentally ill parricide offender. The severely mentally ill parricide offender typically suffers from a long-standing mental illness, such as schizophrenia, that impairs his or her grasp of reality and ability to meet the requirements of daily functioning with respect to self-care, family and social situations, and work. The severely mentally ill parricide offender kills because of mental illness, which impairs his or her ability to function across societal domains.

In contrast to the severely mentally parricide offender type, the severely abused and the dangerously antisocial parricide offender types generally have a good hold on reality and are able to function in myriad situations as they go about their daily lives. Neither of these types kills directly as a result of a mental disorder. Instead, the severely abused parricide offender kills either out of desperation or terror; the goal is to end the abuse. The dangerously antisocial parricide offender kills a parent because the parent is perceived as an obstacle in his or her path; the goal is to get what the parricide offender wants, such as freedom, money, or power.

Understanding why a particular individual killed a parent involves knowledge of that person, the other family members involved, and the home environment. An in-depth clinical interview with the parricide offender is essential. Review of records, including the offender's statements to the police, police reports, witness statements, autopsies, and crime scene photos should be carefully reviewed prior to reaching any conclusions. Collateral interviews with surviving family members, other relatives, neighbors, and friends are critically important to corroborate statements made by the killer. Consultations with professionals who have had involvement with the parricide offender prior to the incident, such as mental health professionals, social service providers, and teachers, often can provide invaluable data. Psychological and neuropsychological testing is recommended to firm up diagnoses, assess the offender's abilities and possible deficiencies, and measure personality traits.

A comprehensive forensic evaluation can be valuable in several ways in addition to helping the lawyers and the court understand what propelled the individual to kill his or her parent(s). It can help defense attorneys identify if there is a viable legal defense, such as insanity or self-defense. A thorough report discussing social history, family dynamics, child maltreatment, and motivational factors behind the crime, when buttressed with corroborative data, can provide the foundation to establish a battered child defense, although this defense is not formally recognized in many of the 50 states in the United States (Heide 2013). In addition, discussion of the case dynamics and the offender background characteristics may help to identify factors in mitigation that might persuade the court to be more lenient than it otherwise might be and to consider making treatment a major focus of the sentencing decision. Alternatively, an in-depth assessment by a mental health expert knowledgeable about parricide cases might identify risk factors that need to be addressed before the parricide offender can be released back into society.

Processing of parricide cases through the criminal justice system is to some degree affected by the type of parricide offender. The state of mind of the offender is likely to be raised with respect to both severely abused and severely mentally ill parricide offenders. In cases of dangerously antisocial offenders, denial of involvement is a more likely defense strategy unless physical evidence tying the offender to the crime is present and implicates them in the killing. In such situations, an alibi is not a good defense strategy.

Treatment should be tailored to the specific type of parricide offender. In cases of severely abused parricide offenders, the extensive history of trauma must be processed and resolved in treatment for the offender to adopt a more healthy way of coping. In case of severely mentally ill parricide offenders, the mental illness must be addressed first and the offender stabilized before other issues can be examined. The treatment for dangerously antisocial offenders needs to take into account to what degree the offender has psychopathic traits, particularly those identified as personality traits. Offenders whose pattern of offending is more reflective of behavioral problems rather than personality traits are far more likely to be helped by cognitive and behavioral programs, vocational training, education, social skills training, anger management, and empathy training that individuals who possess callous and unemotional traits seen in psychopaths. In cases of enraged parricide offenders, the offender must process and resolve the suppressed anger that is often rooted in traumatic experiences. In addition, substance abuse and dependence must be addressed in cases where enraged parricide offenders have self-medicated with alcohol and/or drugs (Heide 2013).

Directions for Future Research

The parricide literature to date has largely been limited to case studies, analyses of characteristics of hospitalized patients, and correlates of parricide victims, offenders, and incidents. The field of parricide would benefit from studies focusing on the incidence of parricide types and then examining what happens to these different types of offenders. For example, do the charges, verdicts, and sentences vary by parricide offender type? What treatments are used with the various types and how successful are these interventions? How do the different types of offenders cope when released from a juvenile facility, an adult prison, or a mental hospital? What factors are associated with success and with failure at follow-up? Can risk and protective factors be developed that would increase the likelihood that each type of parricide offender could be successfully returned to the community? Finally, and most importantly, could the insights gleaned from working with these offender types provide a blueprint for preventing parricide in the first place by more clearly delineating risk factors and harnessing protective factors before a tragedy occurs?

References

American Psychiatric Association (2013) *Diagnostic and Statistical Manual of Mental Disorders: DSM-5* (5th edn). Washington, DC: APA.

Bender, L. (1959) Children and adolescents who have killed. *American Journal of Psychiatry*, 116: 510–513.

Bender, L. and Curran, F.J. (1940) Children and adolescents who kill. *Criminal Psychopathology*, 1: 297–321.

Boots, D.P. and Heide, K.M. (2006) Parricides in the media: A content analysis of available reports across cultures. *International Journal of Offender Therapy and Comparative Criminology*, 50(4): 418–445. doi: 10.1177/0306624X05285103.

Cornell, D.G. (1989) Causes of juvenile homicide: A review of the literature. In E. P. Benedek and D. Cornell (eds), *Juvenile Homicide* (pp. 3–36). Washington, DC: American Psychiatric Press.

Ewing, C.P. (1997) *Fatal Families: The Dynamics of Intrafamilial Homicide*. Thousand Oaks, CA: SAGE.

Ewing, C.P. (2001) Parricide. In G.-F. Pinard and L. Pagani (eds), *Clinical Assessment of Dangerousness: Empirical Contributions*. New York: Cambridge University Press.

Florida Statutes (2014) 921.141 Sentence of death or life imprisonment for capital felonies. Available online at http://www.leg.state.fl.us/statutes/index.cfm?mode=View%20Statutes&SubMenu=1&App_mode=Display_Statute&Search_String=921.141&URL=0900-0999/0921/Sections/0921.141.html (accessed September 2, 2016).

Freud, S. (1919) *Totem and Taboo* (trans. A.A. Brill). London: George Routledge & Sons.

Hare, R.D. (1999) *Without Conscience: The Disturbing World of the Psychopaths among Us*. New York: Guilford Press.

Heide, K.M. (1992) *Why Kids Kill Parents: Child Abuse and Adolescent Homicide*. Columbus: Ohio State University Press.

Heide, K.M. (1993a) Parents who get killed and the children who kill them. *Journal of Interpersonal Violence*, 8(4): 531–544. doi: 10.1177/088626093008004008.

Heide, K.M. (1993b) Weapons used by juveniles and adults to kill parents. *Behavioral Sciences and the Law*, 11: 397–405. doi: 10.1002/bsl.2370110407.

Heide, K.M. (2013) *Understanding Parricide: When Sons and Daughters Kill Parents*. New York: Oxford University Press.

Heide, K.M. and Boots, D.P. (2007) A comparative analysis of media reports of US parricide cases with officially reported national crime data and the psychiatric and psychological literature. *International Journal of Offender Therapy and Comparative Criminology*, 51(6): 646–675. doi: 10.1177/0306624X07302053.

Heide, K.M. and Solomon, E.P. (2006) Biology, childhood trauma, and murder: Rethinking justice. *International Journal of Law and Psychiatry*, 29(3): 220–233. doi: 10.1177/0886260504268119.

Hillbrand, M., Alexandre, J.W., Young, J.L., and Spitz, R.T. (1999) Parricides: Characteristics of offenders and victims, legal factors, and treatment issues. *Aggression and Violent Behavior*, 4(2): 179–190. DOI: 10.1016/S 1359-1789(97)00056-6.

Kashani, J.H., Darby, P.J., Allan, W.D., *et al.* (1997) Intrafamilial homicide committed by juveniles: Examination of a sample with recommendations for prevention. *Journal of Forensic Sciences*, 42(5): 873–878.

Lennings, C.J. (2002) Children who kill family members: Three cases from Australia. *Journal of Threat Assessment*, 2(2): 57–72. doi: 10.1300/J177v02n02_04.

Malmquist, C.P. (1980) Psychiatric aspects of familicide. *Bulletin of the American Academy of Psychiatry & Law*, 13: 221–231. Available online at http://www.jaapl.org/content/8/3/298.full.pdf (accessed September 2, 2016).

Miller v Alabama (2012). 132 S. Ct. 2455. Retrieved from http://scholar.google.com/scholar_case?case=6291421178853922648&hl=en&as_sdt=6&as_vis=1&oi=scholar (accessed September 2, 2016).

Palermo, G.P. (2007) Homicidal syndromes: A clinical psychiatric perspective. In Richard N. Kocsis (ed.), *Criminal Profiling: International Theory, Research, and Practice* (pp. 3–26). Totowa, NJ: Human Press.

Shon, P.C. and Roberts, M.A. (2008) Post-offence characteristics of 19th century American parricides: An archival exploration. *Journal of Investigative Psychology and Offender Profiling*, 5: 147–169. doi: 10.1002/jip.85.

Solomon, E.P., Berg, L.R., and Martin, D.W. (2015) *Biology* (10th edn). Belmont, CA: Brooks/Cole/Cengage.

Wertham, F. (1941) The matricidal impulse. *Journal of Criminal Psychology*, 2: 455–464.

Zenoff, E. and Zients, A.B. (1979) Juvenile murderers: Should the punishment fit the crime? *International Journal of Law and Psychiatry*, 2: 53–55.

13

Corporate Homicide, Corporate Social Responsibility, and Human Rights

Gary Slapper

Historically, the criminal law was very much concerned with individuals who do wrong and with notions of personal responsibility. The exponential growth of corporations over the last 150 years, and their immeasurable impact on humanity, was not followed by a rapid development of the criminal law to cope with the way that corporations can commit some crimes and inflict harm upon citizens on an industrial scale.

Where an individual commits a form of culpable but unintentional homicide—for example, by drunkenly driving a car—he might kill several people. If a corporation acts recklessly by, for example, putting a car or a pharmaceutical product on to the market knowing it is dangerous, or operates a ferry or a train in a grossly negligent way, hundreds or thousands of people might be killed. The degree of moral wrongdoing where corporate conduct is homicidal—albeit committed by an aggregate of directors—is not significantly different from where an individual does something reckless that kills another.

Public tolerance of corporate misconduct has sunk notably in recent times. Crime committed by companies hurts, kills, misappropriates, pollutes, deceives, defrauds, and despoils to a far greater extent than ordinary crime. Suite crime is more socially inimical than street crime. Corporate fraud, commercial pollution of the air and water, crimes relating to food hygiene, trade descriptions, pensions, securities, and health and safety all widely affect the public.

The Handbook of Homicide, First Edition. Edited by Fiona Brookman, Edward R. Maguire, and Mike Maguire.

Corporate Homicide

Corporate homicide can be broadly defined as a crime in which a person or people are killed as the result of corporate conduct—actions or omissions—which fall far below what can reasonably be expected of the corporation in the circumstances.

If a motor company sells unsafe cars, the victims are many and across a wide geography. As the German sociologist Ulrich Beck has argued (Beck 1992), in the modern world, the eventuation of commercial risk (in cases involving things like chemical explosions or pesticides) can injure people across a wide geographical area and over history as the harms last for many years.

I turn now to put this type of homicide in a wider social and legal context, to explore legal approaches to this type of killing, and to consider the various merits and demerits of the relevant legal policies.

The term "global village" is usually attributed to Marshall McLuhan. He gave it a wide currency in the 1960s (McLuhan 1962, 1964). The more the world becomes a global village, and society becomes more globally integrated, the greater the need for certain types of law to have global effect. Such law includes human rights law and the law of corporate crime.

A fundamental human right, enshrined in most human rights codes and conventions, is the "right to life." In countries like the United Kingdom that have embedded human rights law into their domestic law, this right is generally enforceable only against *public* or *governmental* authorities or organizations performing public functions. Commercial companies are not generally governed by human rights law. It is, however, arguably important that the application of the right to life should extend into the commercial world because more people are killed worldwide by industrial accidents and industrial diseases each year (2.3 million) than are killed in wars (ILO 2015; Work and Pensions Committee 2004: para 16; Takala 2005).

The phrase "industrial accident" has a dry, obscure quality to it. In cases of corporate homicide, what we are concerned with, however, are circumstances in which men and women who go to work one day do not come home because they have been impaled, burned alive, electrocuted, fallen in acid, crushed by machinery, drowned, decapitated, frozen, gorged, suffocated, smashed in high-altitude drops, or poisoned with noxious gas. Most of these deaths are avoidable.

Worldwide, commercial activity kills many people each year. For example, the International Labour Organization figures (Takala 2005: 6) show that for 2001, India (with an economically active population of 443,860,000) had an estimated 40,133 deaths from fatal accidents and 261,891 deaths from industrial diseases. The figures for China (with an economically active population of 740,703,800) were 90,295 industrial accident deaths and 368,645 deaths from work-related industrial diseases. One important theme and argument of this chapter is that as commercial activity kills so many people each year, and as human rights laws do not cover most commercial activity, criminal law dealing specifically with corporate crime can help improve the corporate social responsibility of many commercial organizations.

The law of manslaughter, designed for individual alleged perpetrators does not work well where the body accused of being grossly negligent is a corporate body. This has led to crimes of comparable iniquity (individual and corporate homicide) being treated differently with greater lenience being shown toward corporate culprits.

Each year in England and Wales, about 200 people are killed at work or through commercially related disasters (Health and Safety Executive 2014). This figure rises to several thousand if we include chronic deaths from conditions like asbestosis and mesothelioma which people get while they are working but which take many years to kill them (Slapper 1999). In recent history, there have been about 5,500 fatal work-related incidents a year in the United States (USA Bureau of Labor Statistics 2009), that is approximately 27 times the annual work-related death toll for England and Wales though the United States is not 27 times larger in population but only six times larger (estimated US population in 2015: 320,990,000, www.census.gov/popclock; estimated England and Wales population in 2015: 56,948,200, Office of National Statistics 2015).

The United Kingdom consistently has one of the lowest rates of fatal injury across the European Union's EU-15.[1] In 2011, the standardized rate of fatal incidents per 1,000 of the UK workforce was 0.74 per 100,000 workers, which compared favorably with other large economies such as France (2.74 per 100,000 workers), Germany (0.94 per 100,000 workers), Italy (1.5 per 100,000 workers), and Spain (2.16 per 100,000 workers) (Eurostat 2011).

These deaths are for the most part preventable and unnecessary. Most result from the direct and indirect impacts of commercial pressures on work practices. Culturally, however, they have been coded as unfortunate and almost inevitable corollaries of commerce and the profit system.

Let us consider two dramatic instances of death at work from Britain.

Glanville Evans, a 27-year old welder, was killed when the bridge he was working on collapsed and he fell into the river Wye on the border between England and Wales. The company that employed him had been grossly negligent in instructing him to work in a perilous way but an attempt to convict it for common law manslaughter failed.[2]

Jason Pennington, a 42-year old construction worker, was killed when he fell through a skylight on the roof on which he had been instructed to work. The company that employed him had been grossly negligent in instructing him to work in a perilous way, and an attempt to convict it for manslaughter under the Corporate Manslaughter and Corporate Homicide Act 2007 succeeded at Preston Crown Court.[3]

The first case was in February 1965. The second was in February 2015. Between the two cases, over 40,000 people in England and Wales were killed at work or in commercially related disasters like train crashes. Management failures are responsible in most cases of work-related death (Slapper 1999), yet only 20 companies have ever been convicted of common law manslaughter, and another four have been convicted under the Corporate Manslaughter and Corporate Homicide Act 2007 (Slapper 1999, 2009; Sentencing Council 2014: 6; Health and Safety Executive 2014).

Commercially related deaths are almost always immediately reported in the news as "accidents." Such a label prejudges how the victim met his or her death. Downplaying a train disaster as an "accident" is right in the sense that it was an unintended event. But people and companies can be inculpated in "accidents." Many people are in prison for having unintentionally killed someone—the crime of manslaughter. The fact that a killing was unintended does not stop it being treated as a serious crime if the killer acted in a grossly negligent way with someone else's life.

The History of the Criminalization of Corporate Homicide

Since the early part of its history, the company lay outside of the criminal law. Lord Thurlow, the eighteenth-century English Lord Chancellor, said "Corporations have neither bodies to be punished, nor souls to be condemned; they therefore do as they like" (Poynder 1844: 268). Certainly, the practice of excommunicating corporations had been pronounced contrary to Canon law by Pope Innocent IV at the Council of Lyons in 1245 (excommunication is the process of banishing a member of a church from the communion of believers and the privileges of the church). The company was brought within the jurisdiction of the criminal law for various purposes, for example, concerning financial irregularity, but not explicitly for the purposes of crimes of violence.

In 1990, the prosecution in London for corporate manslaughter of P & O Ferries (Dover) Ltd collapsed after Mr Justice Turner ruled that the evidence which the Crown intended to produce would be insufficient to prove the indictment. The prosecution had followed the capsizing of *The Herald of Free Enterprise* on March 7, 1987 when 192 people died. The vessel had set sail with its bow doors open and had been flooded. There was evidence that the company had been previously informed that there was serious danger of precisely such an incident occurring. Mr Justice Turner ruled that the Crown were not in a position to satisfy "the doctrine of identification," that is, the principle by which the actions or omissions of someone at directorial level in the company are legally recognized as being those of the company itself. The court agreed that the offense of corporate manslaughter was one that existed in law but only if all the necessary faults could be found to exist in at least one director or "controlling mind" of the company. The partial knowledge of several directors—what is very common in corporate affairs—was not enough to convict the company.

As a result of factors like a law commission report on the subject in 1996—and its recognition of a deepening public intolerance about commercially related death—it was announced in 1997 that there was to be new legislation specifically criminalizing corporate killing in the United Kingdom. The Corporate Manslaughter and Corporate Homicide Act 2007 is designed to criminalize "corporate manslaughter," an offense broadly comparable to "killing by gross negligence" on the part of an individual. Instead of having to identify a person who is tantamount to the "controlling mind" of the company, and to prove that in him or her resided all the necessary fault, the 2007 law says that the crime is committed when someone is killed as the result of a senior management failure involving a gross breach of the duty of care to others.

In 2010, *R v Cotswold Geotechnical Holdings Ltd* became the first case brought under the Corporate Manslaughter and Corporate Homicide Act 2007. It arose from the death of Alexander Wright, a 27 year old geologist, who was taking soil samples from a pit which had been excavated as part of a site survey when the sides of the pit collapsed crushing him. The case marked the beginning of a new chapter in English law (Slapper 2016).

Corporate Social Responsibility

Although there is a prodigious and rapidly growing literature on corporate social responsibility, and although tens of thousands of companies across the world have already adopted corporate social responsibility undertakings, there is no single agreed template or index of the principles or precepts which are at the core of corporate social responsibility. A company could therefore put in its official documents or on its website a declaration of, say, six key aims of its corporate social responsibility but, however odd these choices looked to some experts in this field, they would not be classifiable as officially "wrong" under any universally adopted code. So company experts, academics, and members of the general public could in fact quarrel for months or years about the tenets of corporate social responsibility.

Whatever else might be included in an organization's corporate social responsibility obligations, reasonableness will dictate that the list should include the undertaking not, by negligence, to endanger life and limb. There are over 26,000 books in English about business ethics[4] and an enormous range of ideas about what should be included among the core principles of ethical business. One point, though, is incontestable: a *sine qua non* (an indispensable condition) of ethical business is that its conduct should not subject its customers or members of the public to unwarranted risk of injury or death.

The Global Nature of Corporate Risk-taking and Technology

Law within many national jurisdictions is already changing to accommodate the commercial and human rights demands for greater international uniformity. Such change has occurred because lawyers in private practice and government service have been educated in a way that allows them to see the world and its legal challenges from international perspectives.

Of the world's 100 largest economic entities, 51 are companies and 49 are countries (Anderson and Cavanagh 2000). This is a world in which the power and reach of large transnational corporations is something requiring the development of a jurisprudence different from that which emerged in an earlier era with a different landscape of legal subjects.

The principles of modern state sovereignty developed in the seventeenth century in Europe (Gross 1948), and begot the hegemony of *national law*, albeit with some concessions to international treaties. Globalization[5] can and will beget laws that apply on a *global* basis. It is clear that this immediately raises questions about what one means by "laws," what transnational enforcement mechanisms are possible and practicable, how such a phenomenon can be made compatible with the autonomy of nation states, and many more similar points. None of these points, however, poses an insuperable obstacle to some form of global law.

Comparable objections were made at various stages in the development of European Union law from the 1960s (particularly in the United Kingdom after it joined the European Economic Community in 1972) but European law now has a substantial and demonstrable impact across a European population of over 500 million people in 28 culturally and economically diverse nations.

As corporate globalization progresses (by which hundreds of separate companies each become operational across the world), the effectiveness of individual jurisdictional safeguards against crime, financial malpractice, and health and safety dangers becomes much attenuated because risk can be simply shifted to the jurisdiction of least resistance. In effect, this means that the most hazardous risks hurt developing communities—the very countries least able to cope with the disasters when they do materialize. There was some evidence, for example, that the defective chemical plant in Bhopal (where over 5,000 people were killed)[6] had been established in India having been declined authorization in Canada (Jones 1988). In the modern world, the eventuation of commercial risk (in cases involving things like chemical explosions or pesticides) can injure people across a wide geographical area and over history as the harms last for many years.

When Does a Risk Become Unlawful?

The law does not, and should not, prohibit all forms of risk-taking. It should, however, encourage corporate decision-makers to get right the balance between excessive caution and excessive imperilment of workers and the public at large. As Lord Justice Asquith said in 1946:

> if all the trains in this country were restricted to a speed of five miles an hour, there would be fewer accidents, but our national life would be intolerably slowed down. The purpose to be served, if sufficiently important, justifies the assumption of abnormal risk.[7]

Under English law, exposing someone to an *unjustified* risk will be the basis for a manslaughter charge if death results. Sometimes, of course, we subject ourselves to a *justified* lethal risk, as in surgery or if we work as emergency rescuers; if death results in those sorts of situations it will not normally be a crime provided there has been no gross negligence in the surgery or by the emergency service employer. So, part of working out whether a death has resulted from a crime entails looking at why the person doing something dangerous was doing it. The more socially useful and necessary it is to do, the less likely it will be seen as unlawful if death results.

The principle that "the more socially useful something is, the less likely it will be seen as unlawful" is an important part of criminal jurisprudence (Ormerod and Laird 2015: 116–161). If you throw a piece of concrete from a high-rise car park there is no possible good that can come from such conduct. It will amount to an *unjustified* risk, and thus be indictable as manslaughter if someone is hit and killed. Cutting someone open carries an even higher risk of death but if the incision is made by a surgeon as part of emergency medical treatment, the conduct can easily be seen as a justified risk. This ingredient of culpability is an elemental part of unlawful homicide. In most jurisdictions some forms of homicide, under particular circumstances, are lawful; these include self-defense, killing in war, and capital punishment in states where that is lawful. At the core of the crime of manslaughter is the idea that the defendant has taken an unjustified risk with the life of his victim or victims.

Beck (1992) argues that the social nature of risk has radically changed in our times. Unlike nineteenth-century society, where members of the ruling class lived geographically apart from workers, and the catastrophes (although often causing great carnage) were limited to "contained" destruction and injury (poisoned food, factory deaths, etc.), today's risks put huge swathes of the *general population* in peril. Chemical disasters like Chernobyl (Culbert 2003)[8] or Bhopal kill thousands of people in the short term, and then, as the atmosphere absorbs and redistributes the poison, another longer wave of deaths occurs. The toxic flow does not discriminate between rich and poor. If poisonous gas clouds contaminate a city, they contaminate both wealthy and impoverished districts. The toxic flow does not respect national boundaries, nor does it evaporate in a matter of hours.

Oddly, however, the law has not really reflected this social and technological change and the increased magnitude of many modern corporate risks. As we move further into the twenty-first century, the way these sorts of industrial risks are policed and occasionally punished is still a largely nineteenth-century affair.

The Legal Implications of the Global Nature of Risk

As so many corporations are large, powerful, and transnational, they can easily locate operations or commercial activity in any given jurisdiction. There will thus be an incentive for some to choose jurisdictions that offer the least legal control. The danger in any country easing the tightness of its control can be seen in relation to avoidable financial disasters that have occurred recently in the United Kingdom. This was highlighted by Sir Ken Macdonald QC, the former director of Public Prosecutions. He observed that:

> financial deregulation undoubtedly released great energy and wealth into the markets and did so in part by giving bankers and financiers more space. But this space had another effect. It created a growing distance between wealthy and powerful individuals and the agencies designed to police their behavior. Not sensing the danger in this, our two main political parties supported looser regulation over many years … the

> scale of failure is laid bare by one inevitable consequence clear for all to see: too many people and too many institutions function as though they are beyond the reach of the criminal law. (MacDonald 2009)

It is therefore desirable that in respect of conduct that has transnational dimensions (such as international trade or corporate crime), as far as possible, jurisdictions across the world acquire uniform law or legal principles. The current state of play concerning the law related to corporate homicide across the countries of the world is that it is highly varied.

There is a growing global acceptance that the criminal law is an appropriate instrument with which companies can be encouraged to become compliant with the provisions of human rights law—in particular those precepts that protect the right to life. Professor John Ruggie is the United Nations Special Representative of the Secretary General on human rights and transnational corporations and other business enterprises. In 2009, he and his team published a report (Ruggie 2009) that in part underlines the need for the criminal law to play a part in the enhancement of human rights in the context of corporate social responsibility. The report expounds a three-pillar framework for corporate accountability for human rights outlined in an earlier report (Ruggie 2008). The three main components on which the achievement of responsibility is posited are: the state duty to protect against human rights violations by or involving corporations; the corporate responsibility to respect human rights; and effective access to legal remedies (Černič 2009; Ruggie 2009).

Ruggie has noted:

> Recent legal and policy developments begin to address some of the challenges. In previous reports, the Special Representative noted four significant legal developments: the growing international harmonization of standards for international crimes that apply to corporations under domestic law, largely as a by-product of converging standards applicable to individuals; an emerging standard of corporate complicity in human rights abuses; *the consideration by some States of "corporate culture" in deciding criminal responsibility or punishment*; and an increase in civil cases brought against parent companies for their acts and omissions in relation to harm involving their foreign subsidiaries. (2008: para 20; emphasis added)

The law, though, to work well must be properly resourced and this is not always the case. As Ruggie notes (2009: para 96): "As regards criminal proceedings, even where a legal basis exists, if State authorities are unwilling or unable to dedicate the resources to pursue allegations, currently there may be little that victims can do." I now turn to consider the law in the United Kingdom.

The Corporate Manslaughter and Corporate Homicide Act 2007

To examine and explore the issues related to prosecuting organizations for homicide, I focus on a law in the United Kingdom which came into effect in 2008. It is the most recent type of dedicated legislation on this theme in the world. Other countries, however, have introduced laws enabling companies to be prosecuted but these have mostly been general laws, for example, in Finland in 1995, in South Africa in 1995, in Australia (some states) from 1995, in Romania, Austria, and France from 2006.

A corporation was prosecuted in the United States as far back as 1904. A New York court held that a corporation could be indicted for manslaughter. The case arose from an incident in which 900 people traveling on the steamboat, *General Slocum*, drowned in an attempt to escape the flames when a fire erupted on the ship. The issue before the court was whether the Knickerbocker Steamboat Company, the corporate owner of the *Slocum*, was liable for manslaughter. The court decided that it was liable, holding that "[t]he corporation navigated without [life preservers], and caused death thereby." The court stated that under the relevant law it was "not necessary to show intention to kill" (*United States v Van Schaick* 1904).

The UK legislation criminalizes corporate killing without the need to demonstrate that the entire guilt could be found in at least one individual. If a company can enjoy benefits by virtue of being an aggregate of people, it should be able to take the blame, in aggregate, if its corporate conduct causes death by gross negligence. This principle is generally recognized in law, and expressed in the maxim *Qui sensit commodum debet sentire et onus* (he who has obtained an advantage ought to bear the disadvantage as well).

In national research I conducted for four years across a variety of cities and towns, a detailed examination of evidence and case materials indicated that 20 percent of all work-related deaths afforded a strong prima facie case of corporate manslaughter (Slapper 1999). That now equates to about 40 corporate manslaughter prosecutions a year, or about one a week. In fact, there are annually only about three such prosecutions.

The Corporate Manslaughter and Corporate Homicide Act 2007 created a new offense of corporate manslaughter (called "corporate homicide" in Scotland, which explains the double-barreled legislative title) which applies to companies and other incorporated bodies, government departments, police forces, and certain unincorporated associations. The gist of the Act can be apprehended from its main sections.[9]

Who Should Be Open to Be Prosecuted?

Historically, in Britain, the criminal law developed to recognize only individuals as persons appropriate to "stand in the dock" when facing general criminal charges (as opposed to charges under companies legislation). Today it is recognized that organizations are capable of committing crimes. This raises the question of which sorts of organization should be within the purview of a law on homicide. The UK law addresses this in section 1 of the 2007 legislation. It is drawn quite widely and includes government departments and charities.

The offense which is set out in section 1(3) is not contingent on the personal guilt of one or more individuals. Liability depends on a finding of gross negligence in the way in which the activities of the organization are run. The offense is committed where, in particular circumstances, an organization owes a duty to take reasonable care for a person's safety, and the way in which activities of the organization have been managed or organized amounts to a gross breach of that duty and causes the person's death. How the activities were managed or organized by "senior management" must be a "substantial element" of the gross breach.

The term "senior management" is defined in section 1(4) to mean those persons "who play significant roles" in (a) deciding how the whole or a substantial part of the organization's activities are to be managed or organized, or (b) the actual managing or organizing of the whole or a substantial part of those activities. This covers both those in strategic or regulatory compliance roles and those in the direct chain of management.

The Sanctions on Convicted Corporate Defendants

Upon conviction, the sanction is an unlimited fine (section 1(6)), although the court is empowered to impose a "remedial order" (a court order to remedy whatever organizational fault caused the death or deaths) (section 9) and a publicity order (section 10) on a convicted organization.

In general, the amount of the fine must reflect the seriousness of the offense and the court must take into account the financial circumstances of the offender.[10] The court stated in one case that the fine should "reflect public disquiet at the unnecessary loss of life"[11] where a death has occurred, although it is not possible to incorporate a financial measure of the value of human life in the fine imposed for an offense.[12]

Aggravating and mitigating factors are taken into account in sentencing in the normal way. For example, offenses will be most serious where a number of deaths occur and that would have been reasonably foreseeable as likely to follow as a result of the breach of duty. If the relevant standard of care has been breached deliberately with a view to profit, this will be a seriously aggravating feature.[13] For example, in 2004 Keymark Services, a haulage company, pleaded guilty to common law manslaughter after one of its lorry drivers fell asleep on the motorway and collided with seven vehicles, killing himself and two other drivers. The subsequent investigation revealed that employees regularly tampered with tachographs and falsified records in order to work grossly excessive hours—something the firm either knew was taking place or should have known. This conduct appeared to be financially motivated. The company was fined a total of £50,000 for both manslaughter and health and safety offenses. Alongside the prosecution of the company, the managing director was also prosecuted for manslaughter under the common law in his personal capacity, convicted, and sentenced to seven years imprisonment. This was one of the longest sentences imposed for the common law (i.e., historic judge-made law) offense of manslaughter, reflecting the gravity of risking death in order to profit financially.[14]

In 2015, a period of public consultation closed on a set of draft guidelines from the Sentencing Council of England and Wales which proposed, among other things, more severe sentences for companies convicted of corporate manslaughter. The general aim of the guidelines (Sentencing Council 2014) is to ensure a more comprehensive guidance for sentencers in relation to a variety of corporate offenses and to improve the extent to which sentences not only punish the offender but deter them and others from committing these crimes in future. The draft guidelines suggest that judges should impose fines in relation to the size of the convicted organization, and that a fine of up to £20 million could be imposed on the firms who have an annual turnover of more than £50 million.

What Can a Jury Consider when Deciding whether an Organization has Committed Manslaughter?

It is relatively easy to measure the conduct of an individual against that of a notional "reasonable person"; it is considerably harder to judge the conduct of an organization like a commercial company against a relevant standard. Section 8 of the 2007 Act is a very innovative provision. Before turning to that section, it is important to put it in its legal context. Earlier in the Act, section 1(4)(b) sets out the test for assessing whether the breach of duty involved in a management failure was "gross." The test asks whether the conduct that constitutes this failure "falls far below what can reasonably be expected of the organization in the circumstances." Whether the standard has been so breached will be an issue for the jury to determine. The old common law offense of gross negligence manslaughter (the one still used where individuals are prosecuted for gross negligence manslaughter) asks simply whether the conduct in question was "so negligent as to be criminal." When, historically, the common law was used to prosecute companies for manslaughter, it was the jury who had to decide whether the corporate carelessness in question went:

> beyond a mere matter of compensation between subjects and showed such a disregard for the life and safety of others as to amount to a crime against the State and conduct deserving of punishment.[15]

Lord Mackay said that to decide whether negligence is culpable at a criminal level is "supremely a jury question."[16] It was, in other words, something a jury just had to use its common sense to decide.

Now, however, to assist in the determination of an organization's culpability, section 8 of the 2007 Act sets out a number of matters for the jury to consider. These put the management of an activity into the context of the organization's obligations under health and safety legislation in general, the extent to which the organization was in breach of such laws, and the risk to life that was involved. First, section 8(2) says that the jury *must* consider whether the evidence shows that the organization failed to comply with any health and safety legislation that relates to the alleged breach, and if so,

(a) how serious that failure was;
(b) how much of a risk of death it posed.

Section 8 also provides for the jury to consider the wider context in which these health and safety breaches occurred. It states:

> 8 (3) The jury may also—
>
> (a) consider the extent to which the evidence shows that there were *attitudes, policies, systems or accepted practices within the organization* that were likely to have encouraged any such failure as is mentioned in subsection (2), or to have produced tolerance of it;
> (b) have regard to any health and safety guidance that relates to the alleged breach. (emphasis added)

This is a most interesting development. Section 8(3)(a) means that the attention of juries is being focused upon what might be called the "corporate culture" of the organization standing trial for homicide, with the particular question of whether this culture was conducive of the unsafe practices that resulted in death. The significance of this element of "corporate culture" is that it will enable courts to evaluate a defendant corporation's conduct in a more general and reliable way than, as previously, when the moments of alleged corporate wrongdoing were examined in a very telescopic close-up magnification. That older system was very often rather like trying to comprehend a wall-sized, ornate oil painting by examining it only through a straw without ever having seen the larger picture. The 2007 Act, by contrast, invites the jury, when considering whether the defendant corporation is guilty of manslaughter, to consider the whole picture of how its business was run.

For example, suppose 50 people have been killed in a train crash. After the incident, the train's defective braking system is in question. If a jury focuses alone on whether a particular director did or did not open and read a particular email about the brakes one day, a week before the carnage, the jury might arrive at a "not guilty" verdict as it cannot be sure what to make of that one failure to read an email. If, however, that email not being read or acted upon was the latest example among very many examples of endemic indifference to safety on the corporation's part, the jury might more easily come to a "guilty" verdict.

Supposing a ferry capsizes, killing hundreds of people. Imagine this happens in circumstances where a special safety device for alerting the captain to the danger that materialized, and that would have averted the deaths had it been installed, was not installed because of the indifference of the board of directors. Suppose that the company was very happy to continue making profits while being indifferent to the safety of its passengers. In such circumstances, it might be an impossible challenge to pin particular blame for the catastrophic incident on one director or even to show that the board at any one moment consciously and deliberatively took a significant risk. If, however, the prosecution in a case of corporate homicide of this kind (corporate manslaughter) has evidence to show that there were scores of relevant emails pinging to, and among, senior directors but these emails were consistently ignored, and, further, that the general culture of the company was one where matters of safety were routinely treated within difference (postponed meetings, badly written meeting minutes and agendas, and lack of action following resolutions) then these matters relating to the surrounding "corporate culture" of inertia could be adduced in evidence to support argument that the company had fallen far below the standard of what could be reasonably expected.

Critical Evaluation of the Corporate Manslaughter and Corporate Homicide Act 2007

At the heart of the legislation is the replacement of an old common law principle called the "identification doctrine" with a new test of liability. To convict an organization or corporation, the 2007 test does not, as previously in law, require the identification of a particular individual director or senior manager *prosecutable* personally for manslaughter before consideration of the prosecution of the organization. This can be seen as an advance as it assists in the process of the law being able to visit criminal culpability on an organization *qua* organization. Removal of the element of individual liability from the test of corporate culpability is a positive step and makes it easier to prosecute organizations whose corporate conduct, looked at as a whole, has resulted in death.

It should, however, be noted that the use of the criminal law in reducing the extent of potentially lethal risk-taking in a corporate setting is only one of a number of social strategies that can be utilized to help save life. A culture promoting "whistle-blowing" (i.e., employees going to relevant authorities to report unlawful or potentially dangerous conduct or processes at their place of work) by legally protecting employees who report corporate misconduct is one relevant plank of policy engendering a safety culture. Another policy plank is that of encouraging stakeholders, such as shareholders (also called stockholders), to exercise vigilance over the policies of their company.

In the United Kingdom, section 172 of the Companies Act 2006 imposes clear duties on directors, and this imposition, in combination with the power of shareholders also confirmed in the Act, serves to focus directorial minds more sharply on health and safety issues. The section states:

> Duty to promote the success of the company
>
> 1. A director of a company must act in the way he considers, in good faith, would be most likely to promote the success of the company for the benefit of its members as a whole, and in doing so have regard (among other matters) to—
>
> (a) the likely consequences of any decision in the long term,
> (b) the interests of the company's employees …

(c) the desirability of the company maintaining a reputation for high standards of business conduct.

Thus shareholders (i.e., stockholders) might raise objections if they think the directors are not acting in a way that ensures the safety of the company's employees are being properly considered or defective safety issues are not conducive to "a reputation for high standards of business conduct" (section 172(1)(e)).

The Corporate Homicide and Corporate Manslaughter Act's test of liability for corporate manslaughter does require (section 1 (3)) that for a corporation to be convicted, a "substantial" element of the gross failure resulting in the death must have been found at a senior management level. This test thus still contains a flavor of the old "identification principle." This is odd as it was that very principle which was key to the reason why the old law was widely seen as inadequate (Centre for Corporate Accountability 2007).

Conclusions

In its Regulatory Impact Assessment for the legislation, the UK government estimated that the offense created in 2007 would only result in 10–13 additional prosecutions for corporate manslaughter each year (Home Office 2006). Whether one regards that number as regrettably high or low, or apparently about right, it should not be *hoped* that any number of companies get convicted of the new crime. A better hope would be that, over time, the 2007 legislation so discourages commercial recklessness that there are no cases to be prosecuted. It should be that as a result of the legislation companies at large take better care than they do now.

It must be noted that by 2015, after the Corporate Manslaughter and Corporate Homicide Act 2007 had been operative for seven years, there had still been no appreciable decline in the number of annual commercially related deaths. During the first seven years of the Act's operation there were in excess of 1,000 deaths of workers and members of the public at work or in commercial incidents but only four companies were convicted of the crime (Sentencing Council 2014: 6; Health and Safety Executive 2014).

One major question in many jurisdictions will be whether there is sufficient political will to bring corporations within the criminal law of homicide. Are governments and legislators sufficiently independent of commercial interests? A Bureau of Corporations was set up by Theodore Roosevelt in the United States in 1903 with the purpose of being able to identify corporate malpractices. The Bureau was to investigate companies and also to monitor practices on an industry wide level. It seemed like it would be an agency effective in the reduction of corporate delinquency. It did not, however, last for very long. It was shut down in 1914 without having exercised much influence over corporations. There was even evidence that Roosevelt had obtained election funds from some of the largest corporations during a period when the full force of the law was not used against them (Johnson 1959; Weisman 2004: 197) so there was at least the appearance of a suspicious leniency.

I began by noting that the more the world becomes a global village, the greater the need for certain types of law to have global effect. Corporate social responsibility and the commercial recognition of human rights principles such as "the right to life" can only really be achieved on a global basis. The "human" in "human rights," after all, refers to a species not to a nationality. The role of the criminal law in prompting corporations to treat all human life with appropriate care is of elemental importance in twenty-first-century jurisprudence.

Notes

1 The EU-15 comprises Austria, Belgium, Denmark, Finland, France, Germany, Greece, Ireland, Italy, Luxembourg, the Netherlands, Portugal, Spain, Sweden, and the United Kingdom.

2 *The Times*, February 2, 4, 5, 1965.

3 Health and Safety Executive Press Release, February 3, 2015 (http://press.hse.gov.uk/2015/building-firm-sentenced-for-corporate-manslaughter/).

4 Library databases and Amazon.com search on June 2, 2015.

5 By this I mean the phenomenon whereby (through international travel, international telephony, and preeminently the Internet), companies trade, and customers buy from sources across the planet unmindful of national boundaries; human rights becomes a pan-global jurisprudence, and the art, sport, culture, news, and politics of any nation becomes accessible to people from all nations.

6 The true number of dead is disputed. The Indian government counted 5,370. However, one organization believes the total was about 8,000, a figure based on the number of shrouds sold to cover the dead (*The Times*, November 21, 2004).

7 *Daborn v Bath Tramways Motor Co Ltd and Trevor Smithey* 1946-2 All ER 333 at 336.

8 The major nuclear reactor disaster in the Ukraine. See *The Times*, April 29, 1986, April 10, 1996. In the 11 days following the Chernobyl catastrophe on April 26, 1986, more than 116,000 people were permanently evacuated from the area surrounding the nuclear power plant.

9 A full version of the Act can be found on this website: http://www.uk-legislation.hmso.gov.uk/acts/acts2007a (accessed June 5, 2015).

10 Criminal Justice Act, 2003: s164 (http://www.legislation.gov.uk/ukpga/2003/44/section/164).

11 *R v Howe and Son (Engineers) Ltd* 1999-2 All ER 249 at 254.

12 *R v Howe and Son (Engineers) Ltd* 1999-2 Cr App R (S) 37; and see *R v Friskies Petcare UK Ltd* 2000 Cr App R (S).

13 *R v Howe and Son (Engineers) Ltd* per Scott Baker J. 1999-2 All ER 249 at 254.

14 Sentencing Guidelines Panel report (2007: para 25). The following case (although prosecuted as manslaughter against a director and an employee personally) is also cited in fn. 35, to para 35. Following the Tebay rail deaths in 2004, the owner and operator of the machinery company responsible was sentenced to nine years, reduced to seven on appeal: *R v Connolly* 2007 EWCA Crim 790. The jury found that the defendant had deliberately disabled the trailer braking system and then concealed the disablement. The motive for this perilous conduct was said by Holland J. to be "solely profit," and this was the first aggravating factor mentioned by the judge when sentencing the defendant at first instance. The sometimes homicidally reckless drive for profit is captured in the D.H. Lawrence poem *The Mosquito*:

The mosquito knows full well, small as he is
he's a beast of prey
but after all
He takes only his bellyful
He doesn't put my blood in the bank.

15 According to Lord Hewart CJ in *R v Bateman*, quoted with approval by Lord Mackay in *R v Adomako* 1994-2 All ER 79 at 84d; both cases were indictments against individual doctors.

16 *R v Adomako* 1994: 87c, note 19.

References

Anderson, S. and Cavanagh, J. (2000) *The Top 200 Corporations*. Institute for Policy Studies report, December 2000. Available online at www.corporations.org/system/top100.html (accessed June 5, 2015).

Beck, U. (1992) *Risk Society: Towards a New Modernity*. London: SAGE.

Centre for Corporate Accountability (2007) Is the Corporate Manslaughter and Homicide Bill 2006 worth it? Statement by the Centre for Corporate Accountability, May 14. Available online at http://www.corporateaccountability.org.uk/manslaughter/reformprops/2007/howgood.htm (accessed June 5, 2015).

Černič, J. (2009) John Ruggie's 2009 report on Business and Human Rights. *International Law Observer*, May 28. Available online at http://internationallawobserver.eu/2009/05/28/john-ruggies-2009-report-on-business-and-human-rights/(accessed at June 5, 2015).

Culbert, E. (2003) *Zones of Exclusion: Pripyat and Chernobyl*. New York: Steidl.

Eurostat (European Statistical Office) (2011) Accidents at work by sex and age (NACE Rev. 2, A, C-N). Available online at http://appsso.eurostat.ec.europa.eu/nui/show.do?dataset=hsw_mi01&lang=en (accessed September 29, 2016).

Gross, L. (1948) The peace of Westphalia 1648–1948. *American Journal of International Law*, 42(1): 20–41.

Health and Safety Executive (2014) *Statistics on Fatal Injuries in the Workplace in Great Britain 2014*. London: Health and Safety Executive.

Home Office (2006) *Corporate Manslaughter and Corporate Homicide: A Regulatory Impact Assessment of the Government's Bill*, July 20. London: Home Office.

ILO (International Labour Organization) (2015) *Occupational Injuries 2014*. Geneva: ILOSTAT.

Johnson, A.M. (1959) Theodore Roosevelt and the Bureau of Corporations. *The Mississippi Valley Historical Review*, 45(4): 571–590.

Jones, T. (1988) *Corporate Killing: Bhopals will happen*. London: Free Association Books.

Macdonald, K. (2009) Give us laws that the city will respect and fear. *The Times*, February 23.

McLuhan, M. (1962) *The Gutenberg Galaxy: The Making of Typographic Man*. Toronto: University of Toronto Press.

McLuhan, M. (1964) *Understanding Media*. Abingdon, UK: Routledge.

Office of National Statistics (2015) *Population Estimates for United Kingdom, England and Wales, Scotland and Northern Ireland, Mid-2013*. London: Office of National Statistics.

Ormerod, D. and Laird, K. (2015) *Smith and Hogan's Criminal Law* (14th edn). Oxford: Oxford University Press.

Poynder, J. (1844) *Literary Extracts from English and other Works Collected Together during Half a Century with Some Original Matter* (Vol. 1). London: John Hatchard & Son.

Ruggie, J. (2008) Protect, respect and remedy: A framework for business and human rights, UN Doc. A/HRC/8/5, April 7. Business & Human Rights Resource Centre.

Ruggie, J. (2009) Business and Human Rights: Towards operationalizing the "protect, respect and remedy" framework, UN Doc. A/HRC/11/13/, April 22. Available online at http://www2.ohchr.org/english/bodies/hrcouncil/docs/11session/A.HRC.11.13.pdf (accessed June 15, 2015).

Sentencing Council (2014) Health and safety offences, corporate manslaughter and food safety and hygiene offences guidelines, Consultation paper, November, Sentencing Council, London.

Sentencing Guidelines Panel (2007) Consultation paper on sentencing for corporate manslaughter. London: Sentencing Guidelines Panel.

Slapper, G. (1999) *Blood in the Bank.* Aldershot, UK: Ashgate.

Slapper, G. (2009) Corporate crime in a global business environment. *Asia Pacific Law Review*, 17(2): 149–166.

Slapper, G. (2016) *How the Law Works.* Abingdon, UK: Routledge.

Takala, J. (2005) *Introductory Report: Decent Work—Safe Work*, Geneva: International Labour Organization.

United States v Van Schaick (1904). 134 Fed. 592.

US Bureau of Labor Statistics (2009) Census of Fatal Occupational Injuries Charts, 1992–2007. US Department of Labor.

Weisman, S. (2004) *The Great Tax Wars: Lincoln, Teddy Roosevelt, Wilson—How the Income Tax Transformed America.* New York: Simon & Schuster.

Work and Pensions Committee (2004) *The Work of the Health and Safety Commission and Executive*, House of Commons, Fourth Report of Session 2003–4, Vol III, Written Evidence, House of Commons, July 14, Ev219.

Further Reading

Brehony, P. and Daniels, I. (2009) Kill Bill 2? *New Law Journal*, January 23.

Catan, T. (2008) Pilots' union warned "chaotic" Spanair passengers were at risk. *The Times*, August 23.

Centre for Corporate Accountability (2008) *The Relationship between the Levels of Fines Imposed upon Companies Convicted of Health and Safety Offences Resulting from Deaths, and the Turnover and Gross Profits of these Companies*, Research report, CCA, London.

Clarkson, C. (2007) Corporate manslaughter: Need for a special offence? Paper delivered to the Society of Legal Scholars conference on Criminal Liability for Non-Aggressive Death, University of Leicester, April 19.

Crane, A. and Matten, D. (2003) *Business Ethics.* Oxford: Oxford University Press.

Crane, A. and Matten, D. (2006) *Business Ethics: Managing Corporate Citizenship and Sustainability in the Age of Globalization.* Oxford: Oxford University Press.

Cullen, F., Maakestad, W., and Cavender, G. (1987) *Corporate Crime under Attack.* New York: Anderson.

Eurostat (European Statistical Office) (2015) European statistics on accidents at work (ESAW). http://ec.europa.eu/eurostat/statistics-explained/index.php/Accidents_at_work_statistics (accessed September 29, 2016).

Fisher, C. and Lovell, A. (2008) *Business Ethics and Values: Individual, Corporate and International Perspectives*. London: Pearson.

Gumbel, A. (2002) US firm sued after mine union leaders' deaths. *The Independent*, March 25.

Health and Safety Executive (1988) *Blackspot Construction*. London: HSE.

Health and Safety Executive (2004) *The Work of the Health and Safety Commission and Executive, House of Commons, Work and Pensions Committee*, Fourth Report of Session 2003–4, vol. III, Written Evidence, House of Commons, July 14, Ev219.

Health and Safety Executive (2012) *Annual Report 2011/12*. London: Health and Safety Commission.

Health and Safety Executive (2013) *Annual Report 2012/13*. London: Health and Safety Commission.

Health and Safety Executive (2014) *Annual Report 2013/14*. London: Health and Safety Commission.

Health and Safety Executive (2014) *European Comparisons, Summary of UK Performance*. London: Health and Safety Executive

Home Office (2000) *Reforming the Law on Involuntary Manslaughter: The Government's Proposals*. London: Home Office.

Home Office (2005) *Corporate Manslaughter: The Government's Draft Bill for Reform, Cm 6497*. London: Home Office.

House of Commons Home Affairs and Work and Pensions Committees (2005) *Draft Corporate Manslaughter Bill, First Joint Report of Session 2005–06, vols I–III*, London: House of Commons.

HSC (Health and Safety Commission) (2005) *Statistics of Fatal Injuries, 2004/05*. London: HSC.

Ministry of Justice (2007) A guide to the Corporate Manslaughter and Corporate Homicide Act 2007. Available online at http://www.hseni.gov.uk/guidetomanslaughterhomicide07.pdf (accessed June 15, 2015).

Office of Fair Trading (2004) Guidance as to the appropriate amount of a penalty. Available online at https://www.gov.uk/government/uploads/system/uploads/attachment_data/file/284393/oft423.pdf (accessed June 15, 2015).

Robbins, S., Odendaal, A., and Roodt, G. (2003) *Organizational Behaviour*. Cape Town: Pearson Education South Africa.

Takala, J. (2005) Global estimates of traditional occupational risks. *Scandinavian Journal of Work, Environment and Health*, 1(suppl.): 62–67.

Work-Related Road Safety Task Group (2001) Reducing at-work road traffic incidents, November. Available online at http://www.hse.gov.uk/roadsafety/experience/traffic1.pdf (accessed June 15, 2015).

14

Empirical Challenges to Studying Terrorism and Homicide

Joseph K. Young and Erin M. Kearns

Introduction

The study of terrorism has bridged multiple scholarly domains. Terrorism is discussed within political science as a form of political violence (Crenshaw 1981) related to civil conflict (Findley and Young 2012) and interstate war (Findley, Piazza, and Young 2012). Terrorism is studied within criminology as a form of criminal violence along with homicide and assault, and under political crime as a form of oppositional action put alongside sedition and treason (J.I. Ross 2006). In scholarly work, it is becoming increasingly more common to see works on terrorism connected to political violence (e.g., Thomas 2014) or political crimes (e.g., Chermak, Freilich, and Suttmoeller 2013), but less so with other forms of crime (e.g., Mullins and Young 2012).[1]

How is studying homicide different from studying terrorism? And how is it similar? The term *terrorism* evokes images of 9/11, the Boston Bombing, or other grizzly attacks committed for an ideological reason. Conversely, the term *homicide* brings to mind shootings on the streets or in one's home, generally for personal reasons. At first glance, these two concepts may not appear connected to one another. LaFree and Dugan (2004), for instance, explore the relationship between terrorism and crime, including homicide, and suggest a long list of affinities and differences. While their investigation is theoretical, this chapter provides an empirical approach.

We use standard modeling approaches from the homicide and terrorism literatures to predict each outcome cross-nationally. Potentially surprising to some who feel these are wholly distinct phenomena, we find more similarities than differences between the factors that predict each.

The Handbook of Homicide, First Edition. Edited by Fiona Brookman, Edward R. Maguire, and Mike Maguire.

In what follows, we discuss the issues with defining, operationalizing, and measuring both terrorism and homicide, and challenges with finding valid and reliable cross-national data on both. We discuss the cross-national study of both terrorism and homicide, including their similarities, differences, and what lessons could be learned from the study of other cross-national forms of political violence. We then use cross-national data to see if models of homicide can predict terrorist attacks and vice versa. We conclude with a discussion of the replication results, research that blends violence types, and future research directions.

Definitions

Given the often-politicized nature of defining terrorism, it is unsurprising that there are many scholarly pieces on the topic (e.g., Weinberg, Pedahzur, and Hirsch-Hoefler 2004; Hoffman 2006; Schmid 2011; Young and Findley 2011). More recently, a scholarly consensus is emerging (Schmid 2012) that terrorism is violence or threats thereof[2] against noncombatants[3] to coerce a target for political[4] goals.[5] Fear generated by the violence is often a component of this definition. Most academic work views terrorism as a tactic that actors use and can be combined with or as a substitute for other tactics (Findley and Young 2012). This is in stark contrast to popular descriptions of terrorism as an ideology or philosophy. The language of the Bush Administration's Global War on Terrorism (GWT) suggests such a belief in terrorism. Since nearly all major religions (Juergensmeyer 2003), and diverse ideologies, such as racism, atheism, environmentalism, communism, and others have produced groups that use the tactic, scholars have generally shied away from conflating tactics with ideology.

Homicide, like most social science concepts, has also been contested. Homicide, however, as a concept and measure has faced less scholarly examination as compared to terrorism. Homicide is a legal category of offenses that involve purposeful infliction of harm that leads to death, which is neither sanctioned by the state nor occurring in conflict (Eisner 2012). Specific legal definitions, however, vary by country (LaFree 1999). Additionally, there are different categories of homicide by country. Lastly, the final charge can vary by jury, plea deal, and other circumstances. The nuance of this is not fully captured in any cross-national data source. Despite these limitations, as LaFree (1999) and others like Archer and Gartner (1984) note, homicide and the data that proxy the concept are the most valid and reliable cross-national crime data to which scholars have access.

Like terrorism, homicide is a socially constructed phenomenon (Brookman 2005). In each case, what constitutes an example of the violence is dependent on time period and context.[6] With all forms of violence, criminal and political, the slippery nature of definition is present. At the level of understanding and theorizing, however, this should not be a call to abandon defining the concept. Instead, as a consensus definition develops, this might indicate scientific progress as the concept is proving useful in explaining some aspect of the empirical world.

Measurement

There are issues with operationalizing and measuring both terrorism and homicide. Some of these issues are similar between the two forms of violence, while others diverge. Categorization allows us to consider appropriate measurement strategies.

There are many ways to divide both terrorism and homicide. Terrorism can be categorical or selective (Goodwin 2006), similarly homicide can be expressive or instrumental (Block and Block 1992). Terrorism can be perpetrated by an individual or by a group (Sambanis 2008), similarly homicide can be perpetrated by individuals or as part of organized crime such as gangs (Rosenfeld, Bray, and Egley 1999). Both homicide and terrorism can involve suicide. Terrorism can also occur domestically or transnationally (Enders, Sandler, and Gaibulloev 2011).[7] Domestic homicide, however, has a different denotation and refers to killing one's partner or relative. Homicide can also occur in the course of committing another crime or as part of a series, to name a few. Additionally, both terrorism and homicide may be spatially concentrated by region (Baller *et al.* 2001; Braithwaite and Li 2007).

Theory

Theoretical explanations of variations in cross-national homicide rates include modernization and social disorganization, relative and absolute deprivation, social and cultural factors, and situational perspectives (Nivette 2011). Explanations of homicide have generally been divided between structural and cultural, though there is a movement to study them in tandem (Pridemore 2002; Trent and Pridemore 2012). Most studies find a negative relationship between homicide and economic development, meaning that economic inequality leads to more homicide (i.e., LaFree 1999; Nivette 2011; Pratt and Godsey 2003). Pridemore (2002), however, finds that this relationship is less consistent than social disorganization as a predictor of the spatial distribution of homicides rates. Additionally, Pratt and Godsey (2003) as well as Rogers and Pridemore (2013) found that greater social support and protections help to mitigate the relationship between poverty and homicide. In a meta-analysis of homicide, Nivette (2011) found that inequality, decommodification, and a Latin America dummy variable are the strongest cross-national predictors while population, democracy, and economic development were the weakest. Additionally, divorce rates, population growth, female labor force participation, infant mortality, and ethnic heterogeneity were positively associated with homicide rates while social welfare programs, ethnic homogeneity, and modernization were negatively associated with it (Nivette 2011). Other hypothesized factors such as urbanization, unemployment rates, and demographic structure (LaFree 1999) have not been found to predict homicide rates.

LaFree and Dugan (2004) note that terrorism and crime in general are highly relevant to one another. While they discuss the similarities and differences between terrorism and crime, they state that homicide itself is conceptually more dissimilar to terrorism than other crimes like gang violence and organized crime. Though homicide may be more different than terrorism as compared with other crimes, homicide and terrorism still share a number of similarities. For example, the study of both is inherently interdisciplinary, both are social constructs, there are differences between definitions and how they are applied, both are generally committed by young men, and both damage social trust. Like crime, terrorism may involve organizations and people who are variously committed to the group, may be part of more prolonged violence, and may involve selective target selection. Also like terrorism, there is substantial variation in patterns of homicide across countries. For example, Eisner (2012) found that more violent societies have higher percentages of male homicide victims. Interestingly, some of these countries also have more gang violence (e.g., Honduras) or terrorism (e.g., Sri Lanka).

There is variance in the patterns of both homicide and terrorism across regions and countries. For example, homicide victims in the United States tend to be male. By contrast, in South Africa homicide victims tend to be female whereas serial homicide victims are more male, females seeking employment, or couples attacked together (Salfati *et al.* 2015). Additionally, single homicide victims tend to be someone known to the offender whereas known serial homicide victims are more likely to be people on the margins of society (i.e., sex workers, runways, homeless) who are less likely to be reported missing. Spatial variance in terrorism is most evident in tactics used. For example, suicide attacks are more common in parts of the Middle East while relatively unheard of in the West.

LaFree and Dugan (2004) also offer a number of conceptual differences between terrorism and crime in general. For example, compared to crime in general, terrorism is generally a constellation of other crimes (sometimes including murder), has a broader scope of response, involves a greater desire for attention, generally involves a larger goal than the crime itself, is perpetrated by people who think their actions are altruistic, and are more likely to innovate.

Terrorism has likely been around since at least biblical times (Rapoport 1983), but it has been made easier by modernization, urbanization, and social facilitation (Crenshaw 1981). While some have argued the same for homicide, the data may not support these claims (LaFree 1999).

Strain theory, a general set of arguments about how individual or societal grievance can induce violence, has been used to explain general crime, homicide, and terrorism (Agnew 1992, 2010) suggesting some support for the notion of commonality in explanation for these forms of violence.

How to Differentiate

When is it terrorism and when is it homicide? Consider the cases of the man with alleged affinity for ISIS who beheaded a coworker in Oklahoma in 2014,[8] or the violence in Mexico committed by drug gangs who sometimes are referred to as narco-terrorists. Given the debate over motives and varying definitions of both homicide and terrorism, it may not be clear how to classify these instances. Additionally, they may not be classified consistently across datasets.

Questions about how different datasets classify and measure events are particularly an issue when studying terrorism. For example, in a recent study comparing Global Terrorism Database (GTD) data to official terrorism data from Turkey, there were many attacks not included in the GTD and a few not included in the official data (Cubucku and Forst 2014). Additionally, terrorism research generally uses count of attacks (Li 2005; Enders, Sandler, and Gaibulloev 2011) whereas homicide research more commonly uses rate of homicides per 100,000 people. Are the results dependent upon these operational choices? What if we measure terrorism as a rate and homicide as a count? Would changing the unit of measurement impact results? Would predictors of terrorism and homicide converge?

Perpetrators and targets of both terrorism and homicide vary. For terrorism, perpetrators can be non-state actors, state actors, or semi-state actors, and can be part of an organization or not (Sambanis 2008). For homicide on the other hand, the offenders are only non-state actors, as being connected with the state would change the classification of the crime.[9] Similar to terrorism, homicide offenders can be part of an organization—such as a gang or organized crime—or can act alone. Targets of violence can differ as well depending on the type of homicide or terrorism. Homicide is often described as either expressive (interpersonal) or instrumental (to achieve a material goal), whereas terrorism is often described as either selective or indiscriminate.

Terrorism is generally thought to speak to a larger audience than just the victim. While this can be the case for some forms of homicide, like those that are gang related, sending a message to a larger audience is usually not a part of homicide. However, terrorism and homicide can have some similar goals such as financial gain. Similarly, both can be either symbolic or strategic. There are also gray zones, such as hate crimes, where it is not always clear how to classify an incident. For both terrorism (Kearns, Conlon, and Young 2014) and homicide, we frequently do not know the identity of the perpetrator(s). If we do not know who perpetrated an attack and why they did it, then how do classify lethal attacks as either homicide or terrorism? This may be particularly the case in domestic or lone-wolf attacks with a low fatality rate.

Cross-National Data

The World Health Organization (WHO) homicide data are probably the most reliable. Homicide data report the number of victims, not the number of events (UNODC 2014). For example, one event with two homicide victims would be recorded as two homicides. This contrasts terrorism data, which is generally reported as the number of events not the number of casualties or fatalities. Only about one-quarter of countries report their statistics, however, and it generally only includes *successful* homicide.[10] A major strength is that these data are disaggregated by victim age and gender (LaFree 1999). Other data that have been commonly used for cross-national studies of homicide include Interpol and the Comparative Crime Data File (CCDF). As LaFree (1999) discusses, the Interpol data use broad definitions, are largely not validated, many countries do not report, and the data are aggregated so researchers cannot explore within-state variation. The CCDF data, on the other hand, report different variations of homicide and were compiled by academic researchers. More recently, the United Nations Office on Drugs and Crime (UNODC) data have been used more widely. The UNODC data are a combination of primarily two sources: the WHO homicide data based on national mortality statistics and the United Nations Survey of Crime Trends and Operations of Criminal Justice Systems derived from reports of police recorded homicides (Eisner 2012). UNODC also expands the data to include additional contextual factors such as weapon type, relationship between perpetrator and victim, and whether or not the homicide occurred in the context of either gang/organized crime or a robbery.

Within terrorism research, the most commonly used data are the Global Terrorism Database (GTD) (LaFree and Dugan 2007) and the International Terrorism: Attributes of Terror Events data (ITERATE) (Mickolus *et al.* 2003).[11] The GTD defines *terrorism* as "the threatened or actual use of illegal force and violence by a non-state actor to attain a political, economic, religious, or social goal through fear, coercion, or intimidation." According to the codebook,[12] to be included in the GTD, an incident must be intentional, involve violence or the threat of violence, and the perpetrators must not be state actors.[13] Additionally, an incident must meet two of the following three criteria: (1) have a political, economic, religious, or social goal; (2) be intended to coerce, intimidate, or convey a message to a larger audience; and (3) occur outside the perimeter of legitimate warfare activities. The GTD includes both domestic and transnational terrorist incidents. On the other hand, the ITERATE data only include transnational incidents. ITERATE contains two different types of files: quantitatively coded data on international terrorist incidents and a qualitative component (LaFree and Dugan 2004).

By nature, crime data are fraught with issues of validity and reliability due to underreporting and differing definitions. Homicide data are regarded as the most reliable and valid of all cross-national crime data (LaFree 1999), yet there are still plenty of concerns related to its construction and use. While not inherently an issue, homicide data counts the number of victims, not the number of events. As discussed above, this differs from how terrorism data is constructed and may impact empirical comparisons of these two phenomena.

There is little to no cross-national data on the individual perpetrators of either terrorism or homicide. Additionally, there are selection effects with the data that do exist. Most cross-national data on homicide are collected by the states that report, and thus some parts of the world—like Europe—are overrepresented in the sample while other regions are virtually excluded (LaFree 1999). This is particularly problematic for low-income countries and places with higher levels of political conflict and war (Eisner 2012). Political conflict and war may also impact the validity and reliability of terrorism data. In LaFree (1999), Israel had one of the lowest reported homicide rates, yet it is not clear how much of this is classified as terrorism instead. Similarly, there is some discussion about rates of terrorism and reporting issues. As Eisner (2012) points out, the homicide data from Iraq in 2008 would indicate that it was one of the most peaceful places on earth, which we know not to be the case. At the same time, LaFree (2012) questioned whether terrorism rates in Iraq really spiked in the mid-2000s or if it was just the reporting that spiked due to Western media presence. Taken together, perhaps what would have once been classified as homicide was later being classified as terrorism.

While there are many similarities between cross-national homicide and cross-national terrorism data, there are a few important differences. Terrorism data are coded at the event level so researchers can aggregate up. This allows scholars to have a good deal more information about each event. Homicide data, on the other hand, are generally aggregated already based on the number of victims, not events. As Pridemore (2002) discusses, homicide data should be disaggregated by type. This would allow researchers to provide a more nuanced understanding of variants of homicide. Additionally, homicide data usually only provide a count of incidents for the country-year so we have no information about each event.[14] In comparing the cross-national study of these two forms of violence, what lessons could be learned from the study of other cross-national forms of violence?

Data Analysis

Can similar predictors of each of the violent phenomena explain terrorism and homicide? Pridemore, Chamlin, and Trahan (2008) found that major terrorist attacks (Oklahoma City Bombing and 9/11) did not impact homicide rates. Their study, however, looks at the direct impact of terrorism on homicide in the United States after only just two attacks. In this chapter, we are looking to see if the cross-national predictors of terrorism can also predict homicide rates and vice versa. To do so, we need to collect a core set of predictors and operationalize both terrorism and homicide.

In terrorism research, counts of terrorism events are typically used (Young 2015) to operationalize the concept. In homicide research, on the other hand, it has been more common to use homicide rates.[15] Since population is a consistent predictor of political violence across studies that examine its intensity or development (e.g., Fearon and Laitin 2003; Li 2005; Young and Dugan 2011), using a rate of terrorism—as is common in homicide studies—may help unpack whether rates of terrorism change unrelated to simple increases in population.

We examine counts, as this is the norm in terrorism research, and rates, as this is the norm in homicide research, for both terrorism and homicide. Our aim is to identify what the terrorism literature can learn from the homicide literature, what the homicide literature can learn from the terrorism literature, and where they provide similar results.

Sambanis (2008) used a host of explanatory and control variables to examine the similarities and differences between terrorism and civil war cross-nationally. In this piece, Sambanis used indicators, such as the level of *democracy*, *GDP* (gross domestic product) *per capita*, *population*, *ethnolinguistic fractionalization*, and *oil dependence*. LaFree and Tseloni (2006) used a number of variables to predict rates of homicide cross-nationally. We will borrow from each of these modeling approaches to examine the differences and affinities.

Like Sambanis (2008), we use a binary measure for *democracy* (1 if Polity IV score is higher than 5, and 0 if not). Democracy can encourage active nonviolent participation in society thus reducing all forms of violence by reducing strain or grievances. By contrast, democracy may lead to either groups being able to mobilize for violence or democracies have a softer hand when it comes to policing thus encouraging violence. In terrorism studies, democracy has been associated with greater likelihood of violence (Eubank and Weinberg 1994), while others demonstrate a more complicated relationship (Li 2005; Young and Dugan 2011). Similarly, democracy has been hypothesized to impact homicide rates in multiple ways (LaFree and Tseloni 2006).

We also use *GDP per capita* (1 if higher than the median for the sample, and 0 if not) from Sambanis's model. Studies of political violence often relate this measure to the capacity of the state (Fearon and Laitin 2003) or the development level of the country. Similarly, this measure could proxy the capacity of the police to reduce homicides. Stronger states should thus be able to deter violence or police it when needed (Hendrix 2010).

Like Sambanis (2008), we also include *ethnolinguistic fractionalization* and *oil dependence* in our models. We take measures of *ethnolinguistic fractionalization* and *oil dependence* from Fearon and Laitin (2003). Ethnolinguistic fractionalization is a measure of how diverse a society is in terms of ethnicity. It is measured as the probability that if you randomly sample two individuals, they are not from the same ethnicity (higher values mean more fractionalization). Where societies are ethnically divided, violence may be more likely. Oil dependence is a measure of fuel export revenue. Using World Bank data, a state is coded as oil dependent if fuel exports are at least one-third of their export revenue in a given year (see Fearon and Laitin 2003 for full discussion of coding). Oil has been linked to violence as it offers opportunities for predation as well as weakens links between the state and society (M. Ross 2006).

Population data are from the World Bank (2008). Most studies of political violence find a positive impact of population on terrorism, civil war, genocide, and other phenomena. This could be because increased populations create more opportunity for violence. It could be that this is an association that exists by definition. More people leads to more violence. As discussed above, we create a rate measure of each dependent variable to deal with this issue. Like LaFree and Tseloni (2006), we also measure *democracy* using the Polity IV scale, the *log of GDP per capita*, the *Gini coefficient*,[16] and dummies for *Eastern Europe*, *Latin America/Caribbean*, and *United States* (see Table 14.1). The Gini coefficient is a common indicator for inequality in society and a potential measure of strain.

LaFree and Tseloni (2006) used World Health Organization data for the percentage of the population in each country-year that was between 15 and 25 years of age. We used

Table 14.1 Homicide models—replication of LaFree and Tseloni (2006).

	Homicide count	*Terrorism count*	*Homicide rate*	*Terrorism rate*
Democracy	−0.12***	−0.23*	0.02	−0.007**
	(0.03)	(0.10)	(0.12)	(0.002)
GDP per capita (log)	0.12	0.10	0.08	0.06
	(0.10)	(0.17)	(1.02)	(0.03)
Percent of population	−0.008	−0.08	0.91	0.003
between 15 and 24	(0.05)	(0.10)	(0.43)	(0.02)
Gini	0.06***	0.03	0.72	−0.0001
	(0.013)	(0.03)	(0.15)	(0.005)
Eastern Europe	−2.07***	−1.54***	5.45	−0.12
	(0.23)	(0.41)	(2.20)	(0.08)
Latin American/	−0.66*	−1.63*	6.42	−0.15
Caribbean	(0.30)	(0.70)	(2.87)	(0.11)
United States	1.20	−1.22	2.23	−0.28
	(1.21)	(1.65)	(12.71)	(0.39)
Constant	5.95***	4.03	−39.91	−0.26
	(1.50)	(2.99)	(15.38)	(0.55)
N	273	165	284	165

*p < 0.05; **p < 0.01; ***p < 0.001.
Count models use negative binomial regression. Rate models use ordinary least squares regression. Standard errors are in parentheses below coefficient estimates. Source: LaFree and Tseloni (2006). Reproduced with permission of SAGE Publications.

census data that gave the percentage between 15 and 24. We know that criminal (Piquero 2008) and violent (Urdal 2006) actions are most often the domain of young people.

To reiterate, we are taking the models used by Sambanis (2008) and LaFree and Tseloni (2006) then swapping the dependent variables to see if a model for terrorism can be used to explain homicide and vice versa. Traditionally, models of terrorism have used counts as the outcome variable whereas models of homicide use rates. For this reason, we are using both counts and rates of terrorism and homicide per country-year from 2000 to 2012. Models in which the dependent variable is expressed as a count will be estimated using negative binomial regression. Models in which the dependent variable is expressed as a rate per unit population will be estimated using ordinary least squares regression. Terrorism data come from the GTD whereas homicide data come from UNODC, which is a created using WHO data and UN survey data as discussion above.

As shown in Table 14.2, we replicate Sambanis's (2008) model of civil war and terrorism to predict homicide and terrorism using both count and rate for each dependent variable. This generated some expected results, and some interesting ones that are worth further exploration.

In the terrorism literature, there is an assumption that higher levels of democracy will lead to better reporting of attacks and thus more attacks. What we see

Table 14.2 Terrorism models—replication of Sambanis (2008).

	Homicide count	*Terrorism count*	*Homicide rate*	*Terrorism rate*
High democracy	0.89***	0.29*	18.51***	0.05
	(0.13)	(0.12)	(1.78)	(0.03)
High GDP per capita	−0.85***	−0.30*	−9.05***	−0.05
	(0.09)	(0.13)	(1.31)	(0.03)
Population (log)	0.89***	0.64***	−0.38	−0.03**
	(0.03)	(0.05)	(0.38)	(0.01)
Ethnolinguistic fractionalization	0.04	−0.46	5.44*	−0.09
	(0.16)	(0.28)	(2.41)	(0.06)
Oil dependence	0.64***	1.08***	8.26***	0.17***
	(0.14)	(0.15)	(1.99)	(0.04)
Constant	−8.23***	−7.60***	7.94	0.60***
	(0.50)	(0.73)	(6.54)	(0.16)
N	1034	872	1058	872

*$p<0.05$; **$p<0.01$; ***$p<0.001$.
Count models use negative binomial regression. Rate models use ordinary least squares regression.
Standard errors are in parentheses below coefficient estimates.

here, however, is that higher democracy is positively associated with terrorism counts, but it is not significant for predicting the terrorism rate. States with higher levels of democracy experience a larger number of terrorism events, but this relationship disappears when controlling for population. In sum, how we measure the dependent variable impacts our inference about the relationship between democracy and terrorism. For homicide, on the other hand, higher levels of democracy are positively associated for both counts and rates. States with higher levels of democracy experience a larger number of homicides and more homicides when controlling for population, which may be reflective of reporting and not the actual phenomenon. This underreporting bias is a pernicious problem well known to terrorism researchers (Drakos and Gofas 2006). Creating a rate of the variable may help somewhat. However, issues of underreporting might be just as problematic—or even worse—for homicide studies since homicide is more likely to go undetected.

Similarly, states with a high GDP have lower homicide counts and rates. Yet, for terrorism, states with a high GDP have lower terrorism counts, but not terrorism rates. States with greater capacity may have fewer homicides, but the results for terrorism are less conclusive. States with greater ethnolinguistic fractionalization have higher homicide rates only. Other independent variables seem unrelated to this measure.

Unsurprisingly, states with larger populations have higher counts of both terrorism and homicide. Interestingly though, states with larger populations have lower terrorism rates. This is a bit of evidence to suggest that using a rate may be a more theoretically useful measure as counts may go up just because actors have more opportunity for violence.

Table 14.3 Homicide models—replication of LaFree and Tseloni (2006).

	Homicide count	*Terrorism count*	*Homicide rate*	*Terrorism rate*
Democracy	0.005	−0.02***	0.17*	−0.004**
	(0.01)	(0.004)	(0.07)	(0.001)
GDP per capita (log)	−0.47***	−0.04	0.28	0.04**
	(0.06)	(0.06)	(0.39)	(0.01)
Percent of population	0.09***	0.003	1.02***	0.01*
between 15 and 24	(0.03)	(0.04)	(0.18)	(0.007)
Eastern Europe	−1.29***	−0.91***	2.55	−0.03
	(0.13)	(0.20)	(0.93)	(0.05)
Latin American/	0.79***	−0.89***	14.92***	−0.11*
Caribbean	(0.14)	(0.19)	(0.96)	(0.05)
United States	3.52***	−0.18	3.01	−0.17
	(0.47)	(0.54)	(3.31)	(0.13)
Constant	9.82***	3.85***	−16.52**	−0.43
	(0.84)	(1.04)	(6.16)	(0.22)
N	726	605	744	605

*$p < 0.05$; **$p < 0.01$; ***$p < 0.001$.
Count models use negative binomial regression. Rate models use ordinary least squares regression. Standard errors are in parentheses below coefficient estimates. Source: LaFree and Tseloni (2006). Reproduced with permission of SAGE Publications.

From the study of political violence, it should not be surprising that oil dependent states experience more terrorism as it is positively related to human rights violations (DeMeritt and Young 2013), international conflict (Colgan 2010), and a host of other unpleasant human problems (Karl 1997). This is true regardless of whether terrorism is a count or rate. There is not much discussion of oil dependence in the homicide literature. Yet, oil dependent states have higher homicide rates and counts. As Karl (1997) notes, oil can create a host of unfortunate problems that range from political to interpersonal violence. Venezuela, Nigeria, and other petro-states are unfortunately currently familiar with these problems.

In sum, from Sambanis's (2008) model, there are a number of similarities in the cross-national study of both homicide and terrorism. For both terrorism and homicide, it is not clear whether a higher level of democracy is linked to more violence or just more reporting of these phenomena. Oil dependence is also a positive predictor of both terrorism and homicide regardless of whether they are measured as a count or a rate. The impact of population depends on whether the dependent variable is a count or rate, and suggests that rate is more theoretically useful. State capacity may reduce homicide, yet the relationship to terrorism is still unclear. Similarly, ethnolinguistic fractionalization is only predictive of higher homicide rates.

As shown in Table 14.3, we replicate LaFree and Tseloni's (2006) cross-national model of homicide. We model homicide and terrorism using both counts and rates for each dependent variable. In this model, more democratic states had lower levels of terrorism, regardless of whether we used a count or rate. This contrasts with the

Sambanis model, where more democratic states had higher counts of terrorism. In Sambanis's model, high democracy is binary whereas LaFree and Tseloni use Polity IV scores. This sensitivity to measurement calls into question the widely held notion that democracies seem to have more terrorism because there is better reporting. More democratic states had higher rates of homicide only. These inconsistent results suggest that more extensive conceptual and measurement work is needed to relate democracy to both forms of violence.

When using the log of GDP in LaFree and Tseloni's model as compared to a binary measure for high GDP from Sambanis, only the relationship with homicide counts remains negative, and the relationship with terrorism rates becomes significant and positive. Higher logged GDP is associated with a higher count of homicide, but a lower rate of terrorism. This is consistent with the homicide literature where poverty is strongly associated with homicide. The finding for terrorism and GDP is more interesting and may indicate a nonlinear relationship. States with a larger percentage of the population between 15 and 24 have a higher homicide rate and count, and a higher terrorism rate. For homicide, this result is unsurprising as such violence is more common than terrorism and generally associated with young men. Since the measure for youth is also a proportion, it is not surprising that this is associated with the terrorism rate only.

Eastern Europe countries have a lower count of both terrorism and homicide, yet this relationship disappeared for rate models. Latin America and Caribbean countries have a higher homicide count and rate, and a lower terrorism count and rate, which is what we would expect. The United States has a higher homicide count, as we would also expect. These results map onto expectations. Eastern European countries experience lower numbers of homicide and terrorism, and also have smaller populations so the count models alone are significant. Latin American and Caribbean countries experience high homicide and low terrorism. In the United States, there are a high number of homicides but also a large population.

In sum, from LaFree and Tseloni's (2006) model, there are a number of differences and inconsistencies in the cross-national study of both homicide and terrorism. The relationship between democracy and both terrorism and homicide varies depending on how the outcome variable is measured. GDP, percentage of the population between 15 and 24, and the Latin America/Caribbean dummy variable are strong predictors of homicide, but inconsistent for terrorism. The Eastern European dummy is inconsistent by type of outcome variable measurement, and the United States dummy only predicts homicide count.

For homicide, factors like gun ownership may impact national rates, but other factors may be more likely to impact at the local level. For terrorism, political rights tend to be significant (Sambanis 2004), which could partially account for homicide as well. For both homicide and terrorism, national-level income statistics in cross-country studies do not capture local-level phenomena. These macrolevel data do not tell the story of variation within a country. Future work should consider looking at these same phenomena at a more microlevel, possibly within single countries to begin the comparison.

Conclusion

Studies of homicides and terrorism are often done in isolation of each other. We find here though that there are some consistencies in predictions of each of these variables warranting future work investigating these affinities. Recent work has shown that terrorism and civil war are related and often co-occur at highly disaggregated micro-levels (Findley and Young 2012). Future work could examine spatial clustering of both terrorism and homicides and see if there are positive spatial correlations between the two, whether they co-occur or whether they follow similar temporal patterns.

Our work here has been largely empirical. Future work could examine whether there are stronger theoretical reasons to keep these phenomena together or apart. While some view one form of violence (terrorism) as political and the other as not (homicide), current violence in Latin America is challenging this conventional wisdom. Brutal homicides in Mexico, for example, seem to cross these boundaries and beg for a unified explanation.

Accordingly, we did not disaggregate terrorism nor homicides into smaller pieces. It may well be that domestic terrorism and say hate crime homicides are similar, but not to transnational terrorism. Domestic intimate partner homicides may be similar to suicide terrorism, but not to gang homicides. Beyond looking at a more micro-level, these data could also be disaggregated into types to examine these sorts of questions.

While ours is an initial foray into thinking about these questions, we hope that future work will develop and refine our understanding of these kinds of violence. That task will be made easier if we can find commonalities and differences that aid in our understanding of each of these destructive elements of human society.

Notes

1 Terrorism studies as a field has its own journals, which are interdisciplinary and include articles on geography to narrative to politics. See, for example, *Terrorism and Political Violence*, *Studies in Conflict and Terrorism*, *Critical Studies on Terrorism*, *Perspectives on Terrorism*, and *Behavioral Sciences of Terrorism and Political Aggression*.

2 Adding threats include events like hijacking that may not include actual violence, but the threat is key for coercion.

3 This may be the most contentious element of defining terrorism. Can attacks on the military be considered terrorism? The Beirut Marine barracks bombing in 1983 is a prime example. United States and French military forces were killed by a group calling itself the Islamic Jihad. These soldiers were killed to coerce this multinational force to leave Lebanon. The military were not engaged in active combat at the moment of the attack. Moreover, they were serving a peacekeeping role in the country. Most scholars would consider this act terrorism. The term noncombatant then allows us separate events such as this with killing a soldier in theater by a nonuniformed militant, more accurately described as an insurgent or guerrilla attack. The purpose of this attack is to degrade the opponent's forces not to terrorize.

4 Political means that one person or group is trying to influence another. Those political goals then can have religious, ideological, ethnic, or other motivations but at the end they are political as the goals are relational not individual.
5 This consensus is emerging in more empirical approaches to the study of terrorism. Critical scholars are the most vocal dissenters regarding this consensus. See, for example, Jackson, Breen Smyth, and Gunning (2009).
6 See Hoffman (2006: 32–33) for a discussion related to this point on terrorism.
7 Domestic terrorism often refers to the fact that the victim and the perpetrator are from the same country or the action is against a national of the territory where the act took place. Transnational terrorism often refers to either an attack that has a perpetrator attacking a person of a different nationality or an attack spilling across national boundaries (Sandler *et al.* 1983).
8 Available online at http://www.cnn.com/2014/09/29/justice/oklahoma-beheading-suspect/.
9 The United Nations Office on Drugs and Crime (UNODC) data only count intentional nonconflict deaths. State-sponsored or state-ordered killings can occur outside of conflict (i.e., capital punishment, death squads such as those in El Salvador or Brazil, genocide). However, these state-sponsored forms of killing are conceptually distinct from homicide and thus would likely not be picked up in these official data.
10 See Neapolitan (1998) for a discussion about including attempts as well as successful homicide, the issues with adjusting the data, and the differing importance of explanatory variables using adjusted and unadjusted data. We are not suggesting that cross-national homicide data should include attempts, as this would add additional uncertainty and error. We bring up this distinction between homicide and terrorism data to illustrate the differences in how these two phenomena are counted and analyzed.
11 Other databases include TWEED, which has just data from Western Europe, the Rand/MIPT data, and the now defunct US State Department sponsored WITS database.
12 Available online at http://www.start.umd.edu/gtd/downloads/Codebook.pdf (START 2012).
13 We state above that the definition of terrorism does not *have to* include perpetrators being non-state actors. States can and do use this tactic in pursuance of their goals. The GTD, however, requires that perpetrators be non-state actors for inclusion in their data. All other publically available data also exclude states from their collected events. The Political Terror Scale (http://www.politicalterrorscale.org) is a notable exception, but it only collects yearly information on state terror and for highly aggregated actions.
14 The recent European Homicide Monitor project is one notable exception. This dataset includes detailed case information for solved and unsolved homicides starting with Finland, Sweden, and the Netherlands and the goal expand to all of Europe. See Granath *et al.* (2011) for a full discussion of these data.
15 More recently, criminologists have started to utilize count models as well (i.e., Kubrin's (2003) study of homicide counts, and Osgood's (2000) study of juvenile robbery arrest counts).
16 We estimated the models with and without the Gini coefficient. When including Gini, the sample size drops dramatically (605 to 165 for terrorism, 726 and 744 to 273 and 284 for homicide count and rate, respectively). Thus, we report the models without the Gini coefficient and acknowledge that keeping Gini in the models changes the results dramatically. See Table 14.1.

References

Agnew, R. (1992) Foundation for a general strain theory of crime and delinquency. *Criminology*, 30(1): 47–88.

Agnew, R. (2010) A general strain theory of terrorism. *Theoretical Criminology*, 14(2): 131–153.

Archer, D. and Gartner R. (1984) *Violence and Crime in Cross-cultural Perspective*. New Haven, CT: Yale University Press.

Baller, R.D., Anselin, L., Messner, S.F., *et al.* (2001) Structural covariates of us county homicide rates: Incorporating spatial effects. *Criminology*, 39(3): 561–588.

Block, R. and Block, C.R. (1992) Homicide syndromes and vulnerability: Violence in Chicago community areas over 25 years. *Studies on Crime & Crime Prevention*, 1: 61–87.

Braithwaite, A. and Li, Q. (2007) Transnational terrorism hot spots: Identification and impact evaluation. *Conflict Management and Peace Science*, 24(4): 281–296.

Brookman, F. (2005) *Understanding Homicide*. London: SAGE.

Chermak, S., Freilich, J., and Suttmoeller, M. (2013) The organizational dynamics of far-right hate groups in the United States: Comparing violent to nonviolent organizations. *Studies in Conflict & Terrorism*, 36(3): 193–218.

Colgan, J.D. (2010) Oil and revolutionary governments: Fuel for international conflict. *International Organization*, 64(4): 661–694.

Crenshaw, M. (1981) The causes of terrorism. *Comparative Politics*, 13(4): 379–399.

Cubucku, S. and Forst, B. (2014) Discrepancies between open source and official terrorism data: Evidence from Turkey. Paper presented at the Annual American Society of Criminology Conference, San Francisco, CA.

DeMeritt, J.H.R. and Young, J.K. (2013) A political economy of human rights: Oil, natural gas, and state incentives to repress. *Conflict Management and Peace Science*, 30(2): 99–120.

Drakos, K. and Gofas, A. (2006) The devil you know but are afraid to face underreporting bias and its distorting effects on the study of terrorism. *Journal of Conflict Resolution*, 50(5): 714–735.

Eisner, M. (2012) What causes large-scale variation in homicide rates? In H.-H. Kortüm and J. Heinze (eds), *Aggression in Humans and Other Primates: Biology, Psychology, Sociology* (137–162). Boston: De Gruyter.

Enders, W., Sandler, T., and Gaibulloev, K. (2011) Domestic versus transnational terrorism: Data, decomposition, and dynamics. *Journal of Peace Research*, 48(3): 319–337.

Eubank, W.L. and Weinberg, L. (1994) Does democracy encourage terrorism? *Terrorism and Political Violence*, 6(4): 417–435.

Fearon, J.D. and Laitin, D.D. (2003) Ethnicity, insurgency, and civil war. *American Political Science Review*, 97(1): 75–90.

Findley, M.G., Piazza, J.A., and Young, J.K. (2012) Games rivals play: Terrorism in international rivalries. *The Journal of Politics*, 74(1): 235–248.

Findley, M.G. and Young, J.K. (2012) Terrorism and civil war: A spatial and temporal approach to a conceptual problem. *Perspectives on Politics*, 10(2): 285–305.

Goodwin, J. (2006) A theory of categorical terrorism. *Social Forces*, 84(4): 2027–2046.

Granath, S., Hagstedt, J., Kivivuori, J., *et al.* (2011) *Homicide in Finland, the Netherlands and Sweden: A First Study on the European Homicide Monitor Data*. Stockholm: The Swedish National Council for Crime Prevention.

Hendrix, C.S. (2010) Measuring state capacity: Theoretical and empirical implications for the study of civil conflict. *Journal of Peace Research*, 47(3): 273–285.

Hoffman, B. (2006) *Inside Terrorism*. New York: Columbia University Press.

Jackson, R., Breen Smyth, M., and Gunning, J. (eds) (2009) *Critical Terrorism Studies: A New Research Agenda*. New York: Routledge.

Juergensmeyer, M. (2003) *Terror in the Mind of God: The Global Rise of Religious Violence*. Berkeley: University of California Press.

Karl, T.L. (1997) *The Paradox of Plenty: Oil Booms and Petro-states* (vol. 26). Berkeley: University of California Press.

Kearns, E.M., Conlon, B., and Young, J.K. (2014) Lying about terrorism. *Studies in Conflict & Terrorism*, 37(5): 422–439.

Kubrin, C. (2003) Structural covariates of homicide rates: Does type of homicide matter? *Journal of Research in Crime and Delinquency*, 40(2): 139–170.

LaFree, G. (1999) A summary and review of cross-national comparative studies of homicide. In M.D. Smith and M.A. Zahn (eds), *Homicide: A Sourcebook of Social Research* (pp. 125–145). Thousand Oaks, CA: SAGE.

LaFree, G. (2012) Countering myths about terrorism: Some lessons learned from the global terrorism database. In B.A. Radin and J.M. Chanin (eds), *What Do We Expect from Our Government?* (pp. 71–98). London: Lexington Books.

LaFree, G. and Dugan, L. (2004) How does studying terrorism compare to studying crime? In M. Deflem (ed.), *Terrorism and counter-terrorism: Criminological perspectives* (pp. 53–74). Bingley, UK: Emerald.

LaFree, G. and Dugan, L. (2007) Introducing the global terrorism database. *Terrorism and Political Violence*, 19(2): 181–204.

LaFree, G. and Tseloni, A. (2006) Democracy and crime: A multilevel analysis of homicide trends in forty-four countries, 1950–2000. *The Annals of the American Academy of Political and Social Science*, 605(1): 25–49.

Li, Q. (2005) Does democracy promote or reduce transnational terrorist incidents? *Journal of Conflict Resolution*, 49(2): 278–297.

Mickolus, E.F., Sandler, T., Murdock, J.M., and Flemming, P.A. (2003) *International Terrorism: Attributes of Terrorist Events (ITERATE) Data Code Book*. Ann Arbor, MI: Inter-University Consortium for Political and Social Research.

Mullins, C.W. and Young, J.K. (2012) Cultures of violence and acts of terror: Applying a legitimation–habituation model to terrorism. *Crime & Delinquency*, 58(1): 28–56.

National Consortium for the Study of Terrorism and Responses to Terrorism (START) (2012). Global terrorism database. Available online at www.start.umd.edu/gtd (accessed February 1, 2015).

Neapolitan, J.L. (1998) Cross-national variation in homicides: Is race a factor? *Criminology*, 36(1): 139–156.

Nivette, A.E. (2011) Cross-national predictors of crime: A meta-analysis. *Homicide Studies*, 15(2): 103–131.

Osgood, D.W. (2000) Poisson-based regression analysis of aggregate crime rates. *Journal of Quantitative Criminology*, 16(1): 21–43.

Piquero, A.R. (2008) Taking stock of developmental trajectories of criminal activity over the life course. In A. Liberman (ed.), *The Long View of Crime: A Synthesis of Longitudinal Research* (pp. 23–78). New York: Springer.

Pratt, T.C. and Godsey, T.W. (2003) Social support, inequality, and homicide: A cross-national test of an integrated theoretical model. *Criminology*, 41(3): 611–644.

Pridemore, W.A. (2002) What we know about social structure and homicide: A review of the theoretical and empirical literature. *Violence and Victims*, 17(2): 127–156.

Pridemore, W.A., Chamlin, M.B., and Trahan, A. (2008) A test of competing hypotheses about homicide following terrorist attacks: An interrupted time series analysis of September 11 and Oklahoma City. *Journal of Quantitative Criminology*, 24(4): 381–396.

Rapoport, D.C. (1983) Fear and trembling: Terrorism in three religious traditions. *American Political Science Review*, 78(3): 658–677.

Rogers, M.L. and Pridemore, W.A. (2013) The effect of poverty and social protection on national homicide rates: Direct and moderating effects. *Social Science Research*, 42(3): 584–595.

Rosenfeld, R., Bray, T.M., and Egley, A. (1999) Facilitating violence: A comparison of gang-motivated, gang-affiliated, and nongang youth homicides. *Journal of Quantitative Criminology*, 15(4): 495–516.

Ross, J.I. (2006) *Political Terrorism: An Interdisciplinary Approach*. New York: Peter Lang.

Ross, M. (2006) A closer look at oil, diamonds, and civil war. *Annual Review of Political Science*, 9(1): 265–300.

Salfati, C.G., Labuschagne, G.N., Horning, A.M., *et al.* (2015). South African serial homicide: Offender and victim demographics and crime scene actions. *Journal of Investigative Psychology and Offender Profiling*, 12(1): 18–43.

Sambanis, N. (2004) What is civil war? Conceptual and empirical complexities of an operational definition. *Journal of Conflict Resolution*, 48(6): 814–858.

Sambanis, N. (2008) Terrorism and civil war. In P. Keefer and N. Loayza (eds), *Terrorism, Economic Development, and Political Openness* (pp. 174–206). New York: Cambridge University Press.

Sandler, T., Tschirhart, J.T., and Cauley, J. (1983) A theoretical analysis of transnational terrorism. *American Political Science Review*, 77(1): 36–54.

Schmid, A.P. (ed.) (2011) *The Routledge Handbook of Terrorism Research*. New York: Routledge.

Schmid, A.P. (2012) The revised academic consensus definition of terrorism. *Perspectives on Terrorism*, 6(2).

Thomas, J. (2014) Rewarding bad behavior: How governments respond to terrorism in civil war. *American Journal of Political Science*, 58(4): 804–818.

Trent, C.L.S. and Pridemore, W.A. (2012) A review of the cross-national empirical literature on social structure and homicide. In M.C.A. Liem and W.A. Pridemore (eds), *Handbook of European Homicide Research* (pp. 111–135). New York: Springer.

UNODC (United Nations Office on Drugs, and Crime) (2014) *Global Study on Homicide 2013: Trends, Contexts, Data*. UNODC. doi: http://dx.doi.org/10.18356/c1241a80-en.

Urdal, H. (2006) A clash of generations? Youth bulges and political violence. *International Studies Quarterly*, 50(3): 607–629.

Weinberg, L., Pedahzur, A., and Hirsch-Hoefler, S. (2004) The challenges of conceptualizing terrorism. *Terrorism and Political Violence*, 16(4): 777–794.

World Bank (2008) *World Development Indicators*. Washington, DC: World Bank.

Young, J.K. (2015) What is terrorism? American University School of Public Affairs Research Paper 2014-0007, School of Public Affairs, American University, Washington, DC.

Young, J.K. and Dugan, L. (2011) Veto players and terror. *Journal of Peace Research*, 48(1): 19–33.

Young, J.K. and Findley, M.G. (2011) Promise and pitfalls of terrorism research. *International Studies Review*, 13(3): 411–431.

Further Reading

UNODC (United Nations Office on Drugs and Crime) (2004) *World Drug Report 2004* (vol. 1). United Nations Publications.

15

Multiple Homicide
Understanding Serial and Mass Murder

Jack Levin and James Alan Fox

Introduction

Multiple homicide has long been a source of fascination and intrigue for large segments of the population. Such questions as "Who was Jack the Ripper?," "Was the Texas Tower shooting a byproduct of Charles Whitman's brain tumor?," "How could Charles Manson have manipulated so many young people into killing on his behalf?," and "What would possess Jeffrey Dahmer to devour human organs" have spirited lively debate for generations.

Individuals who murder large numbers of victims, be it one-by-one or in the course of a single rampage, have also drawn the attention of psychologists and psychiatrists. The behavioral science literature features a plethora of case studies analyzing the backgrounds and mindsets of sadistic slashers, delusional maniacs, and cold-blooded psychopaths (see, for example, Macdonald and Mead 1968; Abrahamsen 1973; Lunde 1976). Indeed, much of the conventional wisdom concerning multiple murder was grounded in some of the most extreme and bizarre cases, especially those for which mental health professionals were consulted or asked to testify in criminal trials invoking the insanity defense.

Interest among criminologists, particularly those with a social science perspective, has only emerged in recent decades. Prior to the 1980s, scholars in the disciplines of criminology and criminal justice all but ignored the subject matter (see Levin and Fox 1985). Some may have assumed that such incidents were not only rare, but aberrational enough to be unworthy of extensive research, at least empirical work. Others may have regarded multiple murder as merely a special form of homicide generally, explainable by the same criminological theories applied to more

The Handbook of Homicide, First Edition. Edited by Fiona Brookman,
Edward R. Maguire, and Mike Maguire.

commonplace single-victim incidents, and deserving of no special treatment. Still others may have conceded multiple homicide to be largely a psychiatric phenomenon, perpetrated by individuals who suffer from profound mental disorders (e.g., psychosis) and, therefore, best understood with theories of psychopathology.

During the 1980s, however, criminologists began to take notice of at least one type of multiple homicide—serial murder—when a number of high profile repeat killers became transformed into international celebrities for being prolific predators. It wasn't just the victim count that sparked interest; the veneer of respectability exuded by such killers as Theodore Bundy, John Wayne Gacy, and Harold Shipman was especially noteworthy and curious. It wasn't just the popular press and true crime writers who applied their craft to serial murder, but the academic literature in criminology and criminal justice began to offer theoretical and empirical contributions to help make sense of crimes that seemed so senseless (see Egger 1990; Hickey 1997).

While the salacious nature of serial murder drew a good number of practicing and aspiring criminologists to concentrate on the topic, still little interest was shown to massacres, even episodes involving double-digit death tolls. All that changed in 2011 and 2012, however, when a string of particularly heart-wrenching mass murders generated widespread concern from politicians, the public, and academics from several disciplines, including criminology. In July 2011, 77 victims, the majority of whom were teenagers, were killed in Norway by a marginalized 32-year-old armed assailant on a hate-inspired mission. Devastating massacres at a Colorado cinema and a Connecticut elementary school made mass shootings the top news story of 2012 in the United States (*USA Today* 2012), eclipsing a hotly contested presidential race and a massive storm along the East Coast. After decades of relative disinterest, the topic suddenly had the full attention of countless scholars.

Defining Multiple Murder

In advance of any attempt to measure the reported growth in multiple homicide, both serial killing and mass murder, we must settle on a working definition of these events. Regrettably there has been considerable disagreement over the inclusion criteria, leading to significant confusion concerning patterns and trends.

Not long ago, all forms of multiple murder were considered mass killing. In the early 1980s, however, when the FBI (Federal Bureau of Investigation) launched a large-scale initiative at its training academy in Quantico, Virginia, to document, study, and investigate repeat killers, it established a working trichotomy of multiple murder: mass (victims killed in a single event at the same general location), spree (victims killed in different places and time in a continuing event), and serial (victims killed over time with a "cooling off" period in between).

Unfortunately, the classification of multiple homicides into mass, spree, and serial subtypes based on the timing of events has sometimes been more a distraction than a helpful distinction. There are many cases that cross over these definitional boundaries, such as assailants who may commit multiple homicides on multiple occasions.

More important, there are disagreements among practitioners and scholars about the criteria for what constitutes multiple murder. For example, some practitioners narrowly limited their view of serial murder to the "classic" lust murder (see Ressler, Burgess, and Douglas 1988). Although the most publicized and prominent form of serial killing consists of a power-hungry sadist who preys upon strangers to satisfy his sexual fantasies, the motivations for, and patterns of, serial homicide are quite diverse. Included within an expanded definition of the perpetrators of serial homicide are, for example, a medical practitioner who poisons patients in order to "play God," a disturbed man who kills prostitutes to punish them for their sins and to eradicate filth, a team of armed robbers who execute store clerks after taking money from their cash registers, and a satanic cult whose members commit a string of human sacrifices as an important initiation ritual (Fox and Levin 2014).

Similarly, many researchers have narrowly defined mass murder as those events that occur in public places by an assailant who selects his targets completely at random. As a result, these scholars eliminate from consideration gang-related killings and robberies, even though their victims are every bit as dead as those whose lives are taken while shopping, sitting in a classroom, or going to a cinema. In effect, marginalized Americans who are victimized in large numbers do not seem to count as much as their more affluent counterparts.

Several studies of mass murder (e.g., Follman, Aronsen, and Pan 2013; Cohen, Azrael, and Miller 2014) have also excluded family annihilations, even those with double-digit death tolls, ostensibly because they occur in a private setting where the general public can feel safe from violence. Many people believe they can anticipate and control what happens in their own homes and thus are more unnerved about crimes committed by strangers than by intimates (Gelles and Straus 1988).

There has even been disagreement about the extent of carnage in defining multiple murder. For decades, a four-victim minimum was used by the FBI and the handful of scholars researching the phenomenon of mass murder. In December 2012, however, the US Congress passed legislation (Investigative Assistance for Violent Crimes Act of 2012) redefining mass shootings as three or more killed, compelling the FBI to modify its long-standing definition of mass murder. At the same time, the growing use of the term "active shooter" as someone intent on committing mass murder in a public place added further confusion as most who fell within this definition failed to kill even three, whatever their plan (see Blair and Schweit 2014).

There has also been disagreement about the minimum victim tally to establish a repetition of killing as serial—some defined serial murder as at least four murders separated in time, whereas others preferred a body count of three. But then in 2005, the FBI's renamed Behavioral Analysis Unit forged a discussion of the definition of serial murder—both in terms of victim count and motivational scope—during a 5-day conference that brought together more than 100 law enforcement officials and academics who specialize in homicide research. Despite a lack of consensus, the FBI adopted the broadest possible definition in terms of both motivation and victimization: "Serial murder is the unlawful killing of two or more victims by the same offender(s) in separate events" (FBI 2008: 12).

It is difficult to say for certain why such a broad approach was favored by the FBI's behavioral analysts; it may simply be a matter of resources and funding priorities. Broadening the scope of the problem, even artificially, may help law enforcement secure additional resources for investigating homicides.

Another possible justification for lowering the minimum victim count is that an individual who repeats murder has shown the potential to commit more, even if circumstances, such as apprehension, curtail his criminal career. Nevertheless, we reject this broader definition. Quite apart from the subject of repeat killing, a pair of events usually is not considered a series. The problem with such a general and broad definition is that it loses the important qualitative distinction between someone for whom murder is a significant feature of his lifestyle and someone who happens to have committed murder on a couple of occasions. Without a stricter definition, there is little reason to study serial murder as a separate phenomenon from homicide generally.

Although it may have been an arbitrarily chosen threshold, we prefer to maintain the once standard four-victim minimum for defining multiple murder, whether these homicides occur in sequence (with or without a so-called "cooling off period") or all at once. In addition, we strive to minimize the distinctions among the three subforms of multiple homicide, preferring to emphasize similarities in motivation rather than differences based on timing. For the sake of avoiding confusion, however, we shall follow the common practice in both the popular and professional literatures of discussing mass and serial killings as somewhat distinct types. Nevertheless, our focus on motivation rather than timing eliminates the need for the "spree killer" designation—a category sometimes used to identify cases of multiple homicide that do not fit neatly into either the serial or mass murder types.

Trends in Multiple Murder

Judging from the increasing number of criminologists who have been drawn to the study of serial murder (not to mention students hoping to pursue a career investigating such crimes), it might seem that the United States is in the throes of an epidemic. The scientific evidence to substantiate or deny the presence of such an upsurge is, however, limited. Indeed, it is not possible to trace, with a high degree of precision, recent or long-term trends in the prevalence and incidence of serial murder in the United States (see Egger 1990; Jenkins 1994; Kiger 1990). Moreover, even though they have operated in many other countries—especially in Australia, Germany, Russia, Mexico, and the United Kingdom—no country in the world has experienced the presence of so many serial killers as the United States (Egger 1990).

Using a variety of sources—newspaper reports, books on the topic, and Internet profiles—we have pieced together a list of 660 serial killers operating in the United States since 1900 in order to develop a sense, albeit imperfect, of the trends and patterns in serial killing (Fox and Levin 2014). The group represents known perpetrators who are believed to have murdered at least four victims. Some killers work as pairs or teams in their predatory activity; overall, this collection of 660 assailants represents 592 unique individuals or partnerships.

Determining the number of victims killed by these offenders is, unfortunately, next to impossible. Often, the full extent of their murder tolls can only be suspected, and the documented cases for which they are convicted or linked with a high degree of certainty may understate the extent of carnage. On the other hand, some offenders, grandiose in their self-image as killing machines, exaggerate their victim tallies as they boast to the press and even the police about how powerful and superior they are. Using conservative estimates of victim counts, the 592 offenders, as a group, are responsible for at least 3,915 homicides, and almost certainly many more. In fact, using more speculative upper estimates, the offenders may account for nearly twice that figure.

In addition to these known serial killers, a number of unsolved cases across the country continue to stump investigators. Furthermore, despite recent advances in technology and communication, law enforcement may still be unaware of the presence of many other serial killers. In what Egger (1984) termed linkage blindness, investigators are not always able to connect homicides, separated over time and space, to the activities of a single perpetrator, particularly murder sprees that cross jurisdictional boundaries (see Levin and Fox 1985). The unsolved or open cases and the undetected cases, taken together, would account for hundreds of additional victims.

The data on 592 known killers or killing teams can be used to examine long-term trends in serial homicide, subject to important methodological caveats concerning the completeness of the database. Not only do these data exclude unsolved and undetected cases, but it is further possible that some more obscure killing sprees have escaped the attention of those who have chronicled such events. Notwithstanding these cautions, Figure 15.1 displays counts of serial killers, partnerships, and teams each decade since the beginning of the twentieth century, using the midpoint of a killer's career as a reference point.

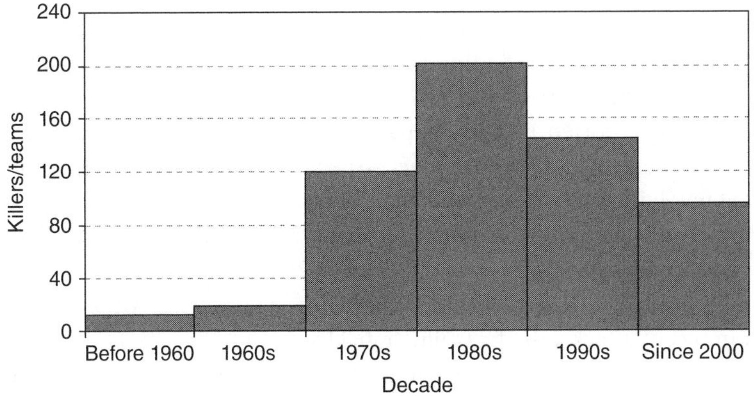

Figure 15.1 Serial killers/teams, 1900 through 2010. Source: *Extreme Killings*, 2015. Reproduced with the permission of SAGE Publications.

There were relatively few known cases of serial murder during the first half of the twentieth century. The pattern emerging during the past few decades is radically different. The number of serial killers/teams grew rapidly from the 1960s into the 1980s. Following the 1980s peak, the number of cases slipped somewhat in the 1990s and then declined even more during the first decade of the twenty-first century.

Although rapid growth into the 1980s clearly suggests significant shifts in the prevalence of serial murder, these results are vulnerable, at least in part, to alternative explanations related to changes in data accessibility and quality of record keeping. As interest in serial murder increased, so did the likelihood that case histories would be published in some fashion. Additionally, as law enforcement became better equipped to identify linkages between victims slain by the same killer or killers, the detection of serial crimes and criminals became more likely. Notwithstanding these caveats, the trend in serial killings into the 1980s is quite consistent with a more general rise in violent crime, including homicide, as well as in the resident population, strongly suggesting that the surge in serial murder is more than just an artifact of increased reporting and improved detection.

The 1980s were an unusual era in terms of the serial murder phenomenon. Not only was the term itself coined at the beginning of the decade, and the prevalence of serial killing surely peaked during that time, but both fear and fascination surrounding serial killers were widespread. Even as the attention from the popular media and the academic community remained strong, however, the prevalence of serial homicide appears to have diminished over the past decade or two. To a large extent, this decline parallels a sharp downturn in all forms of murder during the 1990s and is to some extent probably due to many of the same factors (e.g., high rates of incarceration of violent felons).

Whereas the concern surrounding serial murder has diminished in recent years, the moral panic and sense of urgency surrounding mass murder, and mass shootings in particular, have been fueled by various claims that are reaching epidemic proportions. For example, the *Mother Jones* news organization, having assembled a database of public mass shootings from 1982 through 2012, reported a recent surge in incidents and fatalities, including a spike and record number of casualties in the year 2012 (Follman, Aronsen, and Pan 2013).

However, this reported increase apparently only holds for the highly restricted class of cases identified by *Mother Jones*—specifically, random shootings in public places not involving robbery. As reflected in Figure 15.2, analysis of the mass shootings drawn from the Supplementary Homicide Reports (SHR) from 1976 to 2012 fails to show an increase (see Fox and DeLateur 2014).

Without minimizing the pain and suffering of the hundreds who have been victimized in recent attacks, the facts illustrate clearly that there has been no increase in mass shootings and certainly no epidemic. What is abundantly clear from the full array of mass shootings is the largely random variability in the annual counts. There have been several points in time when journalists and others have speculated about

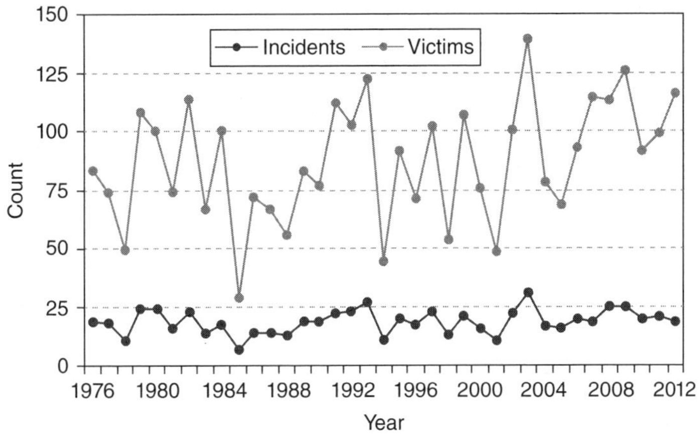

Figure 15.2 Mass shooting incidents and victims, 1976–2012.

a possible epidemic in response to a flurry of high profile shootings. Yet, these speculations have always proven to be incorrect when subsequent years reveal more moderate levels.

The year 1991, for example, saw a 35-year-old gunman kill 23 people at a cafeteria in Killeen, Texas, and a disgruntled graduate student murder five people at the University of Iowa, along with other sensationalized incidents. The surge in mass killings was so frightening that a rumor spread throughout the nation that there would be a mass murder at a college in the Northeast on Halloween (Farrish 1991). Fortunately, October 31 came and went without anything close to a massacre taking place.

With the attention on mass shootings largely driven by the debate over gun control and availability, it is important not to lose sight of the many incidents—nearly one-third of the mass murders reflected in the Supplementary Homicide Reports—that involve weapons other than firearms. In fact, some of the largest incidents have been perpetrated by fire or explosives (e.g., the Oklahoma City bombing). Moreover, in March 2015, 149 passengers lost their lives when the suicidal co-pilot aboard a Germanwings commercial jet crashed the plane into the side of a mountain.

Although the SHR is the most consistent and long-term source of data on multiple victim homicide, it certainly has its issues in terms of accuracy. Some cases are missing because of a few noncompliant reporting agencies. Also, some small jurisdictions have inappropriately included all their homicides for the year in one record, making it appear as if there had been one incident with multiple victims.

With great care, a team of analysts at *USA Today* verified each and every SHR mass murder incident from 2006 onward and filled in missing cases based on news reports. Unfortunately, extending the data verification and augmentation further back would have been especially challenging. As shown in Figure 15.3, there has been absolutely no increase, at least over the past eight years, in the incidence of mass murder, those involving a gun and otherwise (see Overberg *et al.* 2013).

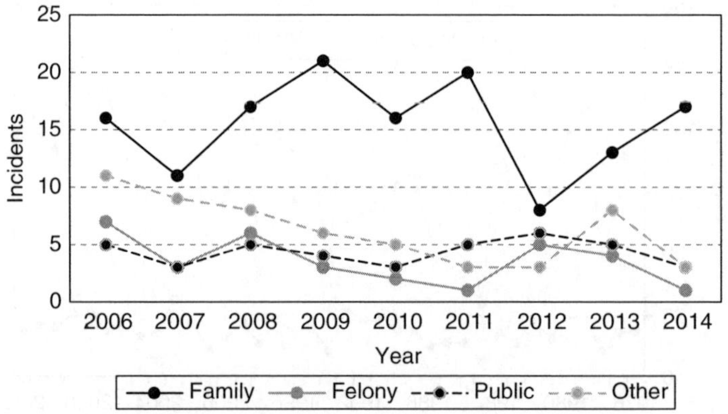

Figure 15.3 Mass murders by type, 2006–2014.

A Unified Typology of Multiple Murder

As in most social and behavioral sciences, criminologists often struggle to create typologies or taxonomies that help them to understand behavior. When a heterogeneous phenomenon, such as multiple murder, is addressed as a singular concept, it can be difficult to make sense of widely differing patterns of behavior.

Of course, the goal of creating mutually exclusive classifications is virtually impossible. The motivation-based typology we propose (see Table 15.1), not unlike other typologies before it, contains an unavoidable degree of overlap among its categories (e.g., serial killers who at one level seek to exterminate marginal victims yet also enjoy the thrill of conquest, or pseudo-commandos who massacre their coworkers). The potential for dual motivation is particularly likely in multiple murders committed by a team or group of offenders.

In addition, there is a substantial yet often unrecognized overlap between types of serial murder and mass killings. A number of serial murder cases better fit a mass killer type, and certain mass killers reflect motives common to serial offenders. For example, Richard Speck, who in 1966 raped and murdered eight Chicago nursing students in their dormitory, may have had robbery as a secondary motive, but his primary objective was, by his own admission, thrill-seeking or hell-raising. Likewise, Theodore Kaczynski, the infamous Unabomber whose fatal mail bombings spanned nearly two decades, was technically a serial killer yet resembles the "set and run" mass killer type characterized in Dietz's (1986) typology of mass murder.

Incorporating many elements of earlier classification schemes (e.g., Dietz 1986; Holmes and Holmes 1994), our unified typology of multiple murder contains five categories of motivation applicable to both serial and mass killing: power, revenge, loyalty, profit, and terror. In seeking to understand multiple murder, differences in motivation seem to be far more important than the issue of timing. Moreover, the large area of commonality among typologies developed by a number of different criminologists at different times and places strongly suggests the construct validity of their categories generally (Miller 2014).

Table 15.1 Multiple homicide typology.

Motivation	*Type of multiple murder*	
	Serial murder	*Mass murder*
Power	Inspired by sadistic fantasies, a man tortures and kills a series of strangers to satisfy his need for control and dominance	A pseudo-commando, dressed in battle fatigues and armed with a semi-automatic weapon, turns a shopping mall into a "war zone"
Revenge	Grossly mistreated as a child, a man avenges his past by brutally murdering women who remind him of his mother	After being fired from his job, a gunman returns to his former work site and opens fire on his former boss and coworkers
Loyalty	A team of killers turns murder into a ritual for proving their dedication and commitment to one another	A depressed husband/father kills his family and himself to spare them from a miserable existence and bring them to a better life in the hereafter
Profit	A middle-age woman poisons to death a series of husbands in order to collect on their life insurance policies	A band of armed robbers executes the employees of a fast food restaurant in order to eliminate all witnesses to their crime
Terror	A profoundly paranoid man methodically commits a series of deadly bombings to warn the world of impending doom	A group of antigovernment extremists blows up a commercial airplane to send a political message and advance their extremist agenda

Source: *Extreme Killings*, 2015. Reproduced with the permission of SAGE Publications.

Of course, it is not always possible to identify unambiguously the motivation for a multiple murder, to determine with certainty whether it was inspired by profit, revenge, or some other objective. The motives for multiple murder are not always mutually exclusive. In 1982, for example, seven residents of the Chicago area were fatally poisoned when they unknowingly ingested cyanide-laced Tylenol capsules. The killer responsible for placing the poisoned analgesics on the shelves of area drugstores and supermarkets was never tried and convicted. If the killer's motivation was to exact a measure of revenge against society at large, then the victim selection was, in all likelihood, entirely indiscriminate or random. If, however, the motivation involved collecting insurance money or an inheritance, the killer may have targeted a particular victim for death and then randomly planted other tainted Tylenol packages to conceal the true intention.

Power

The majority of serial killings, as well as a substantial number of mass killings, express a theme in which power and control are clearly dominant. Many serial murders can be classified as thrill killings in which the assailant's sadistic need is satisfied through inflicting pain and suffering on his victim, and then deciding who lives and who dies. Although sexually motivated murder is the most common form of torture, a significant number of homicides committed by hospital caretakers have been exposed in recent years. Although not using sex as a vehicle, these acts of murder are perpetrated for the sake of power and control nevertheless.

For example, 25-year-old Benjamin Geen, who in 2003 and 2004 worked as a hospital nurse in Oxfordshire, England, injected 17 patients with lethal doses of drugs, causing them to stop breathing. Then, he would "play God" with the lives of his victims by attempting to resuscitate them.

The thirst for power and control also inspired many mass murderers, particularly the so-called pseudo-commando killers who often dress in battle fatigues and have a passion for symbols of power, including semi-automatic firearms and knives (see Dietz 1986). Yet the motive of power and control also encompasses what earlier typologies have termed the "mission-oriented killer" (Holmes and De Burger 1988) whose crimes are designed to further a cause. Through killing, the offender claims an attempt to rid the world of filth and evil, such as by killing prostitutes or the homeless. However, most self-proclaimed "reformists" are also motivated—perhaps more so—by thrill-seeking and power, but try to rationalize their murderous behavior. Theodore Kaczynski alleged in his lengthy Unabomber manifesto (http://www.washingtonpost.com/wp-srv/national/longterm/unabomber/manifesto.text.htm) that his objective in killing was to save humanity from enslavement by technology. However, his attention-grabbing efforts to publish in the nation's most prominent newspapers, his threatening hoax that shut down the Los Angeles airport, and his obsessive library visits to read about himself in the news suggest a more controlling purpose.

Revenge

Many multiple murders, especially mass killings, are motivated by revenge against either specific individuals, particular categories or groups of people, or society at large. Most commonly, the murderer seeks to get even with people he knows—with his estranged wife and all of her children or the boss and all of his employees.

In discussing family homicide, psychiatrist Shervert Frazier (1975) identified the concept of "murder by proxy," in which victims are chosen because they are identified with a primary target against whom revenge is sought. Thus, a man might slaughter all of his children because he sees them as an extension of his wife, and he seeks to get even with her. In 1987, for example, Ronald Gene Simmons massacred his entire family, including his grandchildren, to avenge rejection by his wife and an older daughter with whom he had had an incestuous relationship.

Frazier's concept of "murder by proxy" can be generalized to crimes outside the family setting, particularly in the workplace or in schools. In 1986, for example, Patrick Sherrill murdered 14 fellow postal workers in Edmond, Oklahoma, after being reprimanded and threatened with dismissal by his supervisor. He apparently sought to eliminate everyone identified with the boss and the post office generally.

Similarly, during the 1990s, a number of disgruntled students, feeling bullied or socially ostracized by classmates, launched murderous rampages in their schools. For the most part, the students and teachers were targeted at random in an attack against the institution.

More recently, in December 2012, the killer of 20 first graders and six staff members at Sandy Hook Elementary School in Newtown, Connecticut, was apparently motivated by revenge. Twenty-year-old Adam Lanza had nothing against the first graders whose lives he took, but they seem to have been proxies for his classmates at Sandy Hook who had tormented him years earlier when he was a student there.

These crimes involve specific victims (or proxies) who are chosen for specific reasons. Some revenge multiple killings, however, are motivated by a grudge against an entire category of individuals, typically defined by race or gender if not all of humankind, who are viewed as responsible for the killer's difficulties in life (Levin and McDevitt 2002).

In June 2010, Derrick Bird, a cab driver in northern England who was angry about the size of his inheritance, drove his car from location to location, searching for victims to shoot. Seeking revenge, his first three murder victims were his twin brother, his lawyer, and a fellow cabbie, but then he went after total strangers as they walked in proximity to his cab. When his rampage ended, Bird had taken his own life, but not before killing 12 and injuring another 25.

In May 2014, 22-year-old Elliot Rodger killed six people and injured another 13 near the campus of the University of California, Santa Barbara. Then, he committed suicide. Rodger's motive for what he called his "day of retribution" was explicit. In a YouTube video as well as his 107,000 word "manifesto," he complained bitterly about "experiencing loneliness, rejection, and unfulfilled desires" all because women were never attracted to him. He talked about seeking revenge by killing as many as possible.

Loyalty

At least a few multiple murderers are inspired to kill by a confused sense of love and loyalty—a desire to save their loved ones from misery and hardship. Certain family massacres involve what Frazier (1975) describes as "suicide by proxy." Typically, a husband/father is despondent over the fate of the family unit and takes not only his own life but also those of his children and sometimes his wife, in order to protect them all from the pain and suffering in their lives.

In January 2009, for example, Ervin Lupoe and his wife Ana lost their jobs as medical technicians at a local hospital in West Los Angeles. Unable to pay their mortgage and deeply in debt, they gave up any hope of finding another job that would allow them to take care of their five children all under the age of eight. Out of desperation and a misguided sense of love, Ervin shot to death his wife and children. His suicide note indicated that death was preferable to leaving their children with a stranger.

Some cases of family mass murder appear to involve at least some degree of ambivalence between revenge and loyalty. Such mixed feelings can be seen in the

1999 case of a 44-year-old Atlanta man, Mark Barton, who murdered his wife and two children and then, waiting two days, shot to death nine people at two day trading firms located across the street from one another in Buckhead, Georgia. Over a period of days, Barton had lost more than $100,000 in stock market day trading and blamed the employees of the firms for which he had worked. According to Barton's suicide note, left at the scene of the family annihilation, the murder of his wife and children was motivated by love as well as anger. By taking their lives, he had hoped to spare them the humiliation of his murderous and suicidal behavior and to prevent them from being raised by strangers. He asked God to take care of them.

Multiple murders committed by cults reflect, at least in part, the desire of loyal disciples to be seen as obedient to their charismatic leader. In an extreme case, more than 80 Branch Davidians died in 1993 in a fiery conflagration at their Waco, Texas, compound. As devoted followers of David Koresh, they were willing to die for their radical religious cause and their beloved leader who had "inspired" them. Similarly, members of the Manson family, who on their own were more focused on love than death, were nevertheless prepared to do anything that their "messiah" dictated, including innocent strangers whose only "crime" was to be wealthy.

Loyalty has also been a motive in certain cases of serial murder, where killers operate in tandem as lovers, friends, cousins, or brothers. For example, in the "Sunset Strip" serial killing spree committed in 1980 by Douglas Clark and Carol Bundy, Clark was a sexual sadist who killed for power and control, whereas Bundy joined in the murders to express her loyalty to her boyfriend/accomplice.

Profit

Some serial and mass murders are committed purely or partially for the sake of financial gain. They are designed to eliminate victims and witnesses to a crime, often a robbery. For example, in 1983, three men "gate-crashed" the Wah Mee Club in Seattle's Chinatown, robbed each patron, and then methodically executed all 13 victims by shooting them in the head.

More recently, the so-called DC snipers who in October 2002 shot to death ten residents of the Washington DC area had hoped to negotiate with the authorities for $10 million in return for suspending their killing spree. But when law enforcement failed to respond to their phone calls to the task force's hotline, their murderous acts continued, leading finally to their apprehension and conviction but also to the death of five additional victims.

Terror

Some multiple homicides are, in fact, terrorist acts in which the perpetrators hope to send a message through violence. In 1969, for example, the Manson family left the message "Death to Pigs" written in blood following their assault on two homes in affluent areas of Los Angeles that left seven people dead. The family hoped that the vicious murders would be attributed to revolutionary black Americans and that a resultant race war would be won by blacks who—lacking in leadership experience—would select Manson as their leader.

Hate crimes are often also acts of terrorism in which a particular category of people is targeted. In August 2012, white supremacist Wade Michael Page invaded a Sikh temple outside Milwaukee and opened fire on the congregation inside. When the dust had settled, seven people were shot to death including the killer. Not unlike many other Americans, Page might have mistaken Sikh Indians—based on their beards, turbans, and skin color—for Muslims. It is just as possible, however, that Page hated all non-white members of society.

Explaining Multiple Murder

It has long been popular among laypeople and professionals alike to seek the genesis of multiple murder within the psyche of the assailant. The more extreme the bloodshed and the more bizarre or senseless the motivation, the more apt we are to assume that the murderer is driven by compulsions symptomatic of some profound mental illness. However, theories and concepts developed by criminologists and other social scientists to explain aspects of multiple homicide have emphasized the influence of environmental factors located in the family, economy, and society. Searching for variables associated with the most violent criminal behavior, researchers have investigated such factors as social learning, structural strain and frustration, everyday opportunities for victimization, as well as elements of social and self-control.

Social learning

Some individuals develop a propensity to kill from what they learn during their interactions with others. Early on, Sutherland (1939) proposed that criminal behavior is a result of differential association with a group of intimates—close friends and family members—who reinforces positive attitudes toward and teach the skills associated with criminality (as opposed to associations with those promoting more conventional attitudes). Decades later, Akers (2000) expanded the original version of the differential association explanation by recognizing that the impact of interacting with people who hold positive attitudes toward criminality varies depending on the frequency, duration, intensity, and priority of the interaction. Moreover, social learning is stronger when individuals perceive they are likely to be rewarded rather than punished for their criminal behavior. Akers also suggested that respected friends and family often serve as role models for the imitation of criminality. He recognized as well that well-publicized crimes reported in the mass media might also serve as a source of models for criminal behavior. From an early age, multiple murderer Charles Manson had many role models for violent crime.

He moved from one reform school to another, where he interacted with other crime-prone young people, received brutal punishments, and may also have been influenced by his mother who was serving a prison sentence by the time that Manson was barely out of diapers.

Strain theory

In 1957, Robert Merton suggested that American culture emphasizes economic success without also emphasizing the necessary opportunities for attaining it. Members of society are urged to succeed economically even though many of them lack access to the structural means for improving their socioeconomic status. As a result, some Americans "innovate"; they act outside of conventional society and seek to "get ahead" by engaging in criminal behavior, for example, robbery or embezzlement.

Between 1982 and 1988, landlady Dorothea Puente who ran a boarding house in Sacramento took the lives of nine of her tenants, burying their bodies in the garden. Her purpose was to steal the social security checks of her elderly victims. The strain in Puente's life began in childhood. Her abusive parents couldn't make ends meet. Both parents died within a year of one another while Dorothea was only six years old. She then spent much of her childhood in an orphanage.

Taking a broader view than Merton's conception of socioeconomic strain, Robert Agnew (1992) proposed his general strain theory whereby a range of negative experiences in social relationships at home, school, work, or in the neighborhood can lead to frustration, anger, and, ultimately, to criminal behavior. Agnew identified several sources of strain in addition to material success including the failure to achieve positively valued goals, the loss of social status, and the gap between aspirations and achievements.

Agnew's view of strain can be used to explain why certain middle and high school students would go on a rampage, gunning down many of their schoolmates. Their successes are typically evaluated by them based not on the accumulation of money or excellent grades but on their popularity with peers. Rather than being accepted, however, almost all of them had been routinely bullied, humiliated, or ignored by their fellow schoolmates (Kimmel and Mahler 2003; Larkin 2007; Newman 2007; Vossekuil *et al.* 2002). Leary and his colleagues (2003) determined that chronic rejection of the shooters was present in at least 13 of the 15 school shooting cases they examined (see also Levin and Madfis 2009).

Strain was certainly represented in the biography of Seung-Hui Cho, the student at Virginia Tech who, in April 2007, shot to death 32 people on campus and then committed suicide. After arriving in the United States from his home in South Korea, Cho was diagnosed with a severe anxiety disorder as well as major depression. Into the 8th grade, he was ignored by most students and bullied by others. His sense of rejection grew throughout his youth leading up to his decision while a senior at Virginia Tech to get his revenge.

Similarly, in January 2003, 18-year-old Edmar Freitas committed suicide after shooting eight people, mostly students, at his former school, the Colonel Benedito Ortiz High School in Taiuva, Brazil. It turned out that Freitas had been routinely teased and humiliated by his classmates since the age of seven for being overweight. Before killing himself, he decided to get revenge through the barrel of a .38 caliber pistol.

In September 2008, Matti Juhani Saari entered the Kauhajoki School of Hospitality in Kauhajoki, Finland, where he massacred nine students and then took his own life. For years, Saari reportedly had been a victim of bullying and humiliation by his classmates and later by his military peers. His fellow high school students regarded him as weird and unsociable, targeted him for scornful name-calling, hurtful pranks, and even assaulted and spat on him; his torment continued after graduation as other recruits urinated on his bed during his military service.

Hickey's (1997) trauma control model focuses on strain in the biography of a serial killer, but—at the same time—emphasizes the importance of societal values and customs with respect to disinhibiting or activating criminality. In a society where violence is glorified, a frustrated individual's aggressive urges might easily be translated into violent behavior. In a supportive and compassion-oriented society, however, the same aggressive predispositions are more likely to be expressed in some form of productive activity.

Routine activity theory

Cohen and Felson's (1979) routine activity theory suggests that everyday situations which provide opportunities for being victimized present more important causal factors than such socioeconomic conditions as poverty and inequality. In order to understand multiple homicide, this aspect of routine activity may be particularly important. According to Cohen and Felson, appropriate targets must be available, effective guardians must be absent, and the perpetrators must be motivated to commit the offense.

Serial killers often select their victims based on the presence of routine opportunities in their victims' lifestyles to lure them into vulnerable positions. The frequent choice by serial murderers to attack prostitutes may be based less on any longstanding hatred toward women and more on the ease with which a street walker can be lured into an assailant's vehicle where she is totally at his mercy.

Rampage shooters may also be influenced in their choice of victims by elements of routine activity. They may be drawn to lecture halls, classrooms, theaters, and auditoriums in which large numbers of potential victims are congregated and literally under their gun. At Northern Illinois University in February 2008, for example, former student Steven Kazmierczak was familiar with the auditorium-style lecture hall in Cole Hall where he had taken classes as an undergraduate. He entered from the stage while a class was in progress, opening fire on the 120 students in attendance, fatally shooting five people and injuring another twenty-one.

By the summer of 2012, James Holmes's performance as a graduate student in neuroscience at the University of Colorado had deteriorated so sharply that he decided to leave school. Apparently wanting to maximize his body count in response to what must have been a profoundly frustrating academic experience, Holmes chose to open fire at a crowded midnight showing of a Batman film at the local Cinemark Century cinema. According to Lott (2012), Holmes may also have been attracted to this particular venue because it was the only cinema in the state of Colorado in which firearms were explicitly banned, assuring him of being the only one packing heat.

Control theory

According to Hirschi's (1969) control theory, attachment to conventional individuals and institutions tends to immunize human beings from committing violent offenses. Freud (1910) long ago argued that the presence of a superego ensures that an individual will grow up having enough self-control to refrain from committing acts of extreme violence, including murder, even if he or she feels capable of avoiding punishment by the state. The absence of a strong superego indicates the presence of an antisocial personality type whose disorder predisposes the individual to commit hideous crimes with moral impunity.

In either case, few multiple murderers are psychotic. Some researchers argue instead that individuals who commit multiple homicide are psychopaths, representing an extreme version of antisocial personality syndrome in which lack of empathy and sadism are constituent characteristics (Hare 1999). Serial killers tend to show complete disregard for social norms as they engage in selfish and violent behavior (Hickey 1997). Mass killers are more apt to suffer from chronic depression stemming from repeated frustration. Very few possess a profound mental illness consisting of delusional thinking, hallucinations, paranoia, and a profound thought disorder (Newman 2007).

When an individual lacks the internal controls by virtue of a personality disorder, it becomes even more important that he reside in a network of significant others who are able to limit his propensity for violence, Many people refrain from engaging in violent behavior because they fear losing their relationships with significant others—with family, friends, and peers. However, members of society who lack strong social ties may also lack the motivation to become law-abiding citizens. It is the person who has nothing to lose—who lacks attachments to others, doesn't make commitments to conventional behavior, and fails to adopt a belief in the moral appropriateness of the law—who is most likely to commit murderous acts.

Gottfredson and Hirschi (2003) have emphasized the importance of parental love, supervision, and consistent discipline in the formation of self-control. Moreover, as noted by Sampson and Laub (1993), the ability of young people to develop connections through stable informal bonds as well as job and career relationships may protect them from committing criminal acts including the most violent.

Certain mass murderers have exhibited a profound deficit with respect to social control. In April, 2012, for example, 43-year-old One Goh, a former student at Oikos University in Oakland, California, opened fire on campus, killing seven and injuring another three. A native of South Korea, Goh had relocated to the United States as a child. At the time of the attack, he was living in Oakland apart from his family members. Goh's mother had died a year earlier; one of his brothers remained in Virginia, and in 2011 his second brother was killed in an automobile accident. When he was expelled from the college, Goh found himself to be alone in what he saw as an exceptionally hostile environment.

Conclusion

Whatever the short- and long-term trends in multiple murder, the public perception is that these incidents are on the rise. To a great degree, this widespread belief is based on the extensive and expanded media exposure devoted to multiple murder. Aided by modern satellite technology, cable networks are able to provide marathon coverage of mass shootings even as the drama is still unfolding. Moreover, televised news and entertainment shows often feature biographical sketches of serial and mass murderers, capitalizing on the public's fascination with these high profile criminals. Because of media overexposure, the multiple murder can easily seem ubiquitous.

Fueled by dubious claims of an epidemic, the excessive and undue attention given to multiple murderers is often defended by citing a desire to understand the genesis of multiple homicide in order to identify would-be killers and intervene preventively. Although laudable, the expectation that we can indeed avert carnage through scientifically guided prediction is misguided.

There are, of course, certain characteristics that are fairly typical among multiple murderers, including the demographic profile of white males often of middle age. Moreover, supported by the theories on causation, there are common patterns in the backgrounds of multiple murders, such as head injury and childhood trauma (see Allely *et al.* 2014), and key indicators, such as animal abuse and obsession with violent entertainment. However, as all of these characteristics are somewhat prevalent in the general population, early identification is as challenging as finding a few needles in a massive haystack.

In the aftermath of multiple murder, it is easy to isolate warning signs that were apparently overlooked or ignored by family, friends, and even mandated reporters. These presumed telltale warning signs are actually yellow flags that turn red only after the blood has spilled. Hindsight is 20/20, whereas prediction is plagued by the exceptionally low base rate of multiple murder.

References

Abrahamsen, D. (1973) *The Murdering Mind*. New York: Harper & Row.

Agnew, R. (1992) Foundation for a general strain theory of crime and delinquency. *Criminology*, 30: 47–88.

Akers, R.L. (2000) *Criminological Theories: Introduction, Evaluation, and Application*. Los Angeles: Roxbury.

Allely, C.S., Minnis, H., Thompson, L., *et al.* (2014) Neurodevelopmental and psychosocial risk factors in serial killers and mass murderers. *Aggression and Violent Behavior*, 19: 288–301.

Blair, J.P. and Schweit, K.W. (2014) A study of active shooter incidents, 2000–2013. Texas State University and the Federal Bureau of Investigation, US Department of Justice, Washington DC.

Cohen, A.P., Azrael, D., and Miller, M. (2014) Rate of mass shootings has tripled since 2011, Harvard research shows. *Mother Jones*, October 15.

Cohen, L.E. and Felson, M. (1979) Social change and crime rate trends: A routine activity approach. *American Sociological Review*, 44: 588–608.

Dietz, P.E. (1986) Mass, serial, and sensational homicides. *Bulletin of the New York Academy of Medicine*, 62: 477–491.

Egger, S.A. (1984) A working definition of serial murder and the reduction of linkage blindness. *Journal of Police Science and Administration*, 12: 348–357.

Egger, S.A. (1990) *Serial Murder: An Elusive Phenomenon*. New York: Praeger.

Farrish, K. (1991) Rumor of Halloween mass murder no threat. *Hartford Courant*, October 30. Available online at http://articles.courant.com/1991-10-30/news/0000210189_1_rumor-halloween-night-mass-murders (accessed October 30, 1991).

FBI (Federal Bureau of Investigation) (2008) *Serial Murder: Multi-disciplinary Perspectives for Investigators*. Washington, DC: Behavioral Analysis Unit, National Center for the Analysis of Violent Crimes.

Follman, M., Aronsen, G., and Pan, D. (2013) A guide to mass shootings in America. *Mother Jones*, February 27.

Fox, J.A. and DeLateur, M.J. (2014) Mass shootings in America: Moving beyond Newtown. *Homicide Studies*, 18: 125–145.

Fox, J.A. and Levin, J. (2014) *Extreme Killing: Understanding Serial and Mass Murder*. Thousand Oaks, CA: SAGE.

Frazier, S. (1975) Violence and social impact. In J.C. Schoolar and C.M. Gaitz (eds), *Research and the Psychiatric Patient*. New York: Brunner/Mazel.

Freud, S. (1910) The origin and development of psychoanalysis. *American Journal of Psychology*, 21: 196–218.

Gelles, R. and Straus, M.A. (1988) *Intimate Violence: The Causes and Consequences of Abuse in the American Family*. New York: Simon & Schuster.

Gottfredson, M.R. and Hirschi, T. (2003) A general theory of crime. In F.T. Cullen and R. Agnew (eds), *Criminological Theory: Past to Present*. Los Angeles: Roxbury.

Hare, R.D. (1999) *Without Conscience*. New York: Guilford Press.

Hickey, E.W. (1997) *Serial Killers and Their Victims*. Belmont, CA: Brooks/Cole.

Hirschi, T. (1969) *Causes of Delinquency*. Berkeley: University of California Press.

Holmes, R.M. and De Burger, J. (1988) *Serial Murder*. Newbury Park, CA: SAGE.

Holmes, R.M. and Holmes, S. (1994) *Murder in America*. Newbury Park, CA: SAGE.

Kiger, K. (1990) The darker figure of crime: The serial murder enigma. In S.A. Egger (ed), *Serial Murder: An Elusive Phenomenon*. New York: Praeger.

Kimmel, M.S. and Mahler, M. (2003) Adolescent masculinity, homophobia, and violence random school shootings, 1982–2001. *American Behavioral Scientist*, 46: 1439–1458.

Jenkins, P. (1994) *Using Murder: The Social Construction of Serial Homicide*. New York: Walter de Gruyter.

Larkin, R.W. (2007) The Columbine legacy: Rampage shootings as political acts. *American Behavioral Scientist*, 52: 1309–1326.
Leary, M.R., Kowalski, R.M., Smith, L., and Phillips, S. (2003) Teasing, rejection, and violence: Case studies of the school shootings. *Aggressive Behavior*, 29: 202–214.
Levin, J. and Fox, J.A. (1985) *Mass Murder: America's Growing Menace*. New York: Plenum.
Levin, J. and Madfis, E. (2009) Mass murder at school and cumulative strain: A sequential model. *American Behavioral Scientist*, 52: 1227–1245.
Levin, J. and McDevitt, J. (2002) *Hate Crimes Revisited*. Boulder, CO: Westview.
Lott, J.R. (2012) Did Colorado shooter single out Cinemark theater because it banned guns? FoxNews.com, September 10. Available online at http://www.foxnews.com/opinion/2012/09/10/did-colorado-shooter-single-out-cinemark-theater/print#ixzz2dOIrXblT (accessed September 11, 2012).
Lunde, D.P. (1976) *Murder and Madness*. San Francisco: San Francisco Book Company.
Macdonald, J.M. and Mead, M. (1968) *Homicidal Threats*. Springfield, IL: C.C. Thomas.
Merton, R.K. (1957) *Social Theory and Social Structure*. Glencoe, IL: Free Press.
Miller, L. (2014) Serial killers: I. Subtypes, patterns, and motives. *Aggression and Violent Behavior*, 19: 1–11.
Newman, K.S. (2007) *Rampage: The Social Roots of School Shootings*. New York: Basic Books.
Overberg, P., Hoyer, M., Hannan, M., *et al.* (2013) Behind the bloodshed: The untold story of America's mass killings. *USA Today*, December 3.
Ressler, R.K., Burgess, A.W., and Douglas, J.E. (eds) (1988) *Sexual Homicide: Patterns and Motives*. New York: Simon & Schuster.
Sampson, R.J. and Laub, J.H. (1993) *Crime in the Making: Pathways and Turning Points through Life*. Cambridge, MA: Harvard University Press.
Sutherland, E.H. (1939) *Principles of Criminology* (3rd edn). Philadelphia: Lippincott.
USA Today (2012) Poll ranks top 10 news stories of 2012, December 20.
Vossekuil, B., Reddy, M., Fein, R., *et al.* (2002) *The final report and findings of the Safe School Initiative: Implications for the prevention of school attacks in the United States*. Washington, DC: US Secret Service and US Department of Education.

Further Reading

Douglas, J.E., Burgess, A.W., Burgess, A.G., and Ressler, R.K. (1992) *Crime Classification Manual*. New York: Macmillan.

16

Genocide and State-Sponsored Killing

Andy Aydın-Aitchison

> *Among the grievous crimes this Tribunal has the duty to punish, the crime of genocide is singled out for special condemnation and opprobrium. The crime is horrific in its scope; its perpetrators identify entire human groups for extinction. Those who devise and implement genocide seek to deprive humanity of the manifold richness its nationalities, races, ethnicities and religions provide. This is a crime against all of humankind, its harm being felt not only by the group targeted for destruction, but by all of humanity.*
>
> *Prosecutor v Krstić* 2004: para. 36

While the human death in homicide is clear, the "death" of a group is more ill-defined. Genocide differs from many other acts of homicide in this book in that killing is not a necessary element of the crime: preventing births or creating conditions in which a group cannot sustain itself would suffice. The word genocide, coined to define the widespread extermination of Jews and attacks on other groups in World War II, draws political and emotional charge from its origins. Outside the courtroom the word carries "unmatched rhetorical power" (Kirsch 2013: 8), while courts declare the need for special condemnation (above). In this chapter, the meaning ascribed to genocide, generally a form of state-sponsored killing but not the only form in that category,[1] is explored through law and other disciplines which treat it as a social or political phenomenon. The chapter analyzes ways of measuring the prevalence of genocide, recognizing that given differing interpretations of the concept, this will always be open to contestation. A brief account of victim groups, perpetrators, and contexts is given and feeds into a section on explanations of how and why genocide happens. Finally, the chapter examines responses to genocide and the threat of genocide since the introduction of an international convention in 1948.

The Handbook of Homicide, First Edition. Edited by Fiona Brookman, Edward R. Maguire, and Mike Maguire.

Deconstructing Genocide

The term genocide is employed in a range of contexts. First, in international criminal law; second, a broad area of scholarship, including political science, history, and sociology, utilizes the term, developing it through analysis of empirical material; third, the term may be employed in political, moral, and lay discourse. Here I start by identifying the basic legal definition of genocide and interpretive issues around it. Subsequently, I examine employment of the term in social sciences including history.

Genocide and law

In 1946, two years after the term was created by Raphael Lemkin, genocide was recognized as a crime by the United Nations. Subsequently, in 1948 the *Convention on the Prevention and Punishment of Genocide* was adopted by the UN. The definition of genocide in Article 2 forms the basis of those of the ad hoc tribunals for the former Yugoslavia and Rwanda, the international criminal court and definitions of genocide in domestic jurisdictions.[2]

Acts listed in Article 2(a) through to Article 2(e) may be covered by existing criminal law concerning homicide, assault, kidnapping, and other offenses. Genocide is first and foremost defined not by the individual acts, but by the preceding text on group destruction. Here, this is broken down in terms of the purpose (*intent to destroy*), the extent (*in whole or in part*), and the nature of collectives (*a national, ethnical, racial, or religious group, as such*).

Box 16.1 1948 Convention on the Prevention and Punishment of Genocide, Article 2

In the present Convention, genocide means any of the following acts committed with intent to destroy, in whole or in part, a national, ethnical, racial, or religious group, as such:

(a) Killing members of the group;
(b) Causing serious bodily or mental harm to members of the group;
(c) Deliberately inflicting on the group conditions of life calculated to bring about its physical destruction in whole or in part;
(d) Imposing measures intended to prevent births within the group;
(e) Forcibly transferring children of the group to another group.

Intent to destroy Genocide requires two levels of intentionality. First, any of the acts covered by Article 2 (a) through (e) must be committed with a clear intent to kill, cause serious harm, prevent births, and so on. Second, acts must be committed with the intent, referred to as *special* or *specific intent*, that they are not only completed, but they make a contribution to group destruction.[3] While there may be occasions when statements indicate such genocidal intent,[4] it may also be inferred from indirect evidence. The case against *Popović and others* gives examples. Not all determine intent on their own, but taken together support such a finding. They include sustained or repetitive action of a systematic nature, coordination, evidence of preparation, individual knowledge of a plan, and use of discriminatory and derogatory terms for victims.[5]

Behrens (2012: 509) offers an analysis of the relationship between intent and motive in genocide, one of the most hotly debated issues in the field. He notes that mainstream thinking in international tribunals goes beyond understanding intent as evident in a suspect's awareness of a campaign or risk leading to destruction, but includes a volitional element closer to motive (the underlying individual purpose of an offender). This fits with Greenwalt's interpretation of a narrow reading of special intent as purposive (1999: 2279 ff.). He argues for a broader reading, where intent is based on an offender's knowledge of the destructive goals or effects of a set of actions in which he or she participates (Greenwalt 1999: 2288). Behrens concludes that the effect of the *Genocide Convention* is to translate "specific genocidal intent" into a "codified primary motive," in turn demanding particular evidence.

In whole or in part Intent is defined in relation to destruction of a group in whole or in part, requiring courts to analyze, in quantitative and qualitative terms, when the intent to destroy part of a group constitutes genocide.[6] The quantitative dimension focuses on the extent of destruction in absolute terms and in relation to the size of the group as a whole. The Rwandan tribunal judged that the numbers of Tutsi killed in individual communes, the widespread and systematic nature of killings, and the "undeniable scale" of massacres point toward "complete disappearance" of the victim group.[7] The frequently cited *Semanza* judgment makes it clear that there is no specific numeric threshold, but following *Kayishema* suggests that the part targeted for destruction must be "substantial."[8]

Qualitatively, subsets of a population, defined by social position or function, are of special significance to group continuity. A key element of genocide as defined by Lemkin is the "destruction of the national pattern of the oppressed group" (1944: 79). Attacks on intellectuals and leadership who bear "national ideals" featured in German occupation of Poland, Bohemia-Moravia, and Slovenia (Lemkin 1944: 88–89). In *Krstić*, the trial chamber identified a campaign to kill all military-age Bosnian men in the Srebrenica enclave, evidenced by mass executions, a disregard for civilian or military status of those killed, and a "relentless" hunt for men trying to escape the area (*Prosecutor v Krstić* 2001: para. 546). In a patriarchal community, this was deemed to be of special significance and indicative of the intent to eliminate the Bosnian Muslim community in Srebrenica.[9]

The nature of the collective Although genocide and homicide may overlap somewhat in individual killings of group members (Article 2(a)), the destruction of the collective gives genocide its specific meaning. The significance of the crime is rooted in the loss of the group felt at the level of humanity rather than the loss of any number of individuals (UNGA 1946). The groups protected by the convention are strictly limited under Article 2 ("a national, ethnical, racial or religious group"). The definition of the group has been considered by the international tribunals,[10] but it is also worth considering what it means to intend to destroy a group *as a group*. In *Akayesu*, the chamber considered the possibility of expanding the range of groups covered, and in doing so identified a key dimension of "groupness," the *stability* and *permanence* of a social formation.[11] Judge Shahabuddeen, in an opinion attached to the *Krstić* appeal, goes further and seeks to isolate the physical or biological form implied by the Article 2 acts from the intent with which these are carried out on a group which is more than physical or biological in its nature.[12] He infers that groups can be destroyed in ways other than physically or biologically, undermining intangible characteristics which bind the group. While cautious about endorsing concepts of cultural genocide, he recognizes that attempts to destroy culture may be indicative of intent "to destroy the group as such."[13] This by no means exhausts the ways in which provisions of the Genocide Convention and the subsequent statutes of international tribunals construct the concept of genocide, but taken together the understanding of intent, extent, and the nature of collectives gives a firm starting point. These issues continue to inform scholarship in history and in the political and social sciences.

Genocide in historical, political science, and social science scholarship

Although the meaning of genocide is not settled in the courtroom, as a term it is designed primarily for legal rather than historical purposes (Bloxham 2003: 189). In other disciplines, efforts to define the term proliferate and no single widely accepted definition exists (Mennecke and Markusen 2003: 295). Jones (2006a: 15–18) gathers together definitions of genocide, partly replicated in Table 16.1. They range from the short open statement from Henry Huttenbach (1988: 297), "any act that puts the very existence of a group in jeopardy," to others which delineate the nature of the perpetrators, victims, acts, intentionality or relationship between victim and perpetrator. Some of these features follow the concerns of legal scholars, but show significant differences emerging within nonlegal scholarship and between legal and nonlegal scholarship. For example, while the interpretation of intent is still an open question in international criminal law, it remains an essential element of the crime. Jones's sources range from those disregarding intent (Huttenbach, 1988: 297) to a number identifying acts as deliberate, planned,

Table 16.1 Definitions of genocide (extracted from Jones 2006a, 15–18).

Author(s)	*Definition*
Bauer	The planned destruction, since the mid-nineteenth century, of a racial, national, or ethnic group as such, by the following means: (a) selective mass murder of elites or parts of the population; (b) elimination of national (racial, ethnic) culture and religious life with the intent of "denationalization"; (c) enslavement, with the same intent; (d) destruction of national (racial, ethnic) economic life, with the same intent; (e) biological decimation through the kidnapping of children, or the prevention of normal family life, with the same intent.
Chalk and Jonassohn	One-sided mass killing in which a state or other authority intends to destroy a group, as that group and membership are defined in it by the perpetrator.
Charny	The mass killing of substantial numbers of human beings, when not in the course of military action against the military forces of an avowed enemy, under conditions of the essential defenselessness of the victim.
Dadrian	The successful attempt by a dominant group, vested with formal authority and/or with preponderant access to the overall resources of power, to reduce by coercion or lethal violence the number of a minority group whose ultimate extermination is held desirable and useful and whose respective vulnerability is a major factor contributing to the decision for genocide.
Drost	The deliberate destruction of individual human beings by reason of their membership of any human collectivity as such.
Fein	A sustained purposeful action by a perpetrator to physically destroy a collectivity directly or indirectly, through interdiction of the biological and social reproduction of group members, sustained regardless of the surrender or lack of threat offered by the victim.
Horowitz 1976	A structural and systematic destruction of innocent people by a state bureaucratic apparatus … a systematic effort over time to liquidate a national population, usually a minority … [functioning as] a fundamental political policy to assure conformity and participation of the citizenry.
Horowitz 1996	A structural and systematic destruction of innocent people by a state bureaucratic apparatus … the physical dismemberment and liquidation of people on large scales, an attempt by those who rule to achieve the total elimination of a subject people.
Huttenbach	Genocide is any act that puts the very existence of a group in jeopardy.
Katz	The actualization of the intent, however successfully carried out, to murder in its totality any national, ethnic, racial, religious, political, social, gender, or economic group, as these groups are defined by the perpetrator, by whatever means.
Porter	The deliberate destruction, in whole or in part, by a government or its agents, of a racial, sexual, religious, tribal, or political minority. It can involve not only mass murder, but also starvation, forced deportation, and political, economic, and biological subjugation. Genocide involves three major components: ideology, technology, and bureaucracy/organization.

intended, or purposeful. There is variation in relating the intent to individual acts targeting victims on the basis of group membership, but without an overall aim of group destruction (Drost), or to the planned destruction or total murder of groups (Bauer, Chalk and Jonassohn, Katz).

Regarding victim groups, further differences emerge. Charny and Horowitz's later work make no mention of a group, focusing on the scale of killing and the defenselessness or innocence of victims. Others state that the target is a group or a collectivity, without further specifying (e.g., Drost, Fein), but this may be qualified as a minority (Dadrian, Horowitz's earlier definition). A number specify the types of groups that are targeted, again with some specifying minority status. Variously these include economic, gender, ethnic, national, political, racial, religious, sexual, social or tribal groups (e.g., Porter, Bauer, Katz). Finally, a number of authors note that what matters is how the collective is defined by the perpetrator (Chalk and Jonassohn, Katz).

As the legal definition of genocide shapes prosecutorial and defense strategies, and decisions on guilt, definitions employed in historical, social science, and political scholarship impact upon analyses. Through the various features included, episodes are defined in or out of the genocide category. If the target group must be a minority, the 1972 mass killing of the Hutu majority by the Tutsi-dominated army in Burundi is excluded. Yet Lemarchand and Martin described the events as "systematic," composed of a mixture of indiscriminate killings of Hutu along with particular elite groups (1974: 15), and ultimately leading to the aim of "the physical liquidation of nearly every educated or semi-educated Hutu" (Lemarchand and Martin 1974: 18).

Different rationales inform working definitions of genocide. Bauer values fidelity to the linguistic origins of the term, particularly as categories such as ethnicity, race, or nationality offer little theoretical avenue of escape (1999: 35). Yet the perpetrator's power to define group membership equally denies a lack of escape (e.g., Chalk and Jonassohn 1990). Campbell includes a limited number of elements in his definition and provides a framework allowing for variation and contradiction in genocidal episodes. For him, the ideal-typical genocide is "unilateral, ethnically based mass killing" (Campbell 2011: 589). His explanation focuses on differences in the intensiveness, the proportion of the target group killed, and scope, the temporal and geographical extent of killing. He associates the intensiveness of killing with the mobility of victim groups (2011: 592). In Bosnia, where transfer of Bosnian Muslims to government territory was possible, genocidal killing was more selective. The Srebrenica massacres of July 1995 concentrated on men, while women along with elderly and younger community members were expelled (2011: 592–593). The Holocaust shows variation over time, with expulsion and concentration of the Jewish population in early stages shifting toward extermination as options for separation became limited (Bloxham 2010). Campbell further associates scope with inequalities in organization between perpetrators and victims (2011: 593). By providing categorical flexibility, implied by ideal types, or by including associated phenomena in analysis,[14] scholars recognize that genocide stands at the extreme end of a continuum of collective violence. Ultimately, definitions are working tools and are formulated in line with research goals and questions, shifting as these develop.

Prevalence and Distribution of Genocide

Kuper suggests that genocide is "all too common" (1981: 9). Yet absent a formal body to investigate charges of genocide in 1981, he acknowledged problems with measurement. While homicides are measured through records held in national law enforcement agencies, there is no comparable system for reported genocides or other international crimes. A number of alternative approaches exist. The most simple might be a snapshot of ongoing genocidal processes. Genocide Watch (2014) currently lists 11 countries that have reached the exterminatory phase[15] of genocide (see Table 16.2). A narrow interpretation reduces this to four or five involving a group or groups within the protected categories under the 1948 convention and adds a recent "alert" on the Central African Republic, where Genocide Watch identify exterminatory attacks by both Christian and Muslim forces.

Harff and Gurr (1988; 1989) provide a historical survey of the period for 1945 through to 1988, subsequently reanalyzed by Fein (1993). This illustrates changes in the distribution and prevalence of genocide. Fein groups episodes as genocides and other state-sponsored massacres, and lists 16 genocides, some contained within one or two years, and others running across two or three decades.[16]

Fein's list shows a number of things. First, there is not one year between 1945 and 1988 without at least one government involved in genocide. The peak value is 6, and occurs in both 1983 and 1984. The data shows a general upward trend (Figure 16.1), supporting Greenfield's claim that genocide has become more common since the

Table 16.2 Countries at exterminatory phase of genocide, adapted from Genocide Watch (2014).

Country	*Victim group(s)*
Burma/Myanmar	Shan, Kachin, Karen, Rohinga
Central African Republic	Muslims, Christians
Iraq	Kurds, Shia, Sunni, Christians, Yazidis
Nigeria (Borno)	Christians
Somalia	Opposing clans
Sudan	Darfurese, Abyei, Nuba
Afghanistan	Government supporters
Ethiopia	Government opponents
North Korea	Government opponents
Pakistan	Government supporters
South Sudan	Civilians, women, children
Syria	Antigovernment rebels

Shading indicates a victim group not covered by the 1948 convention.

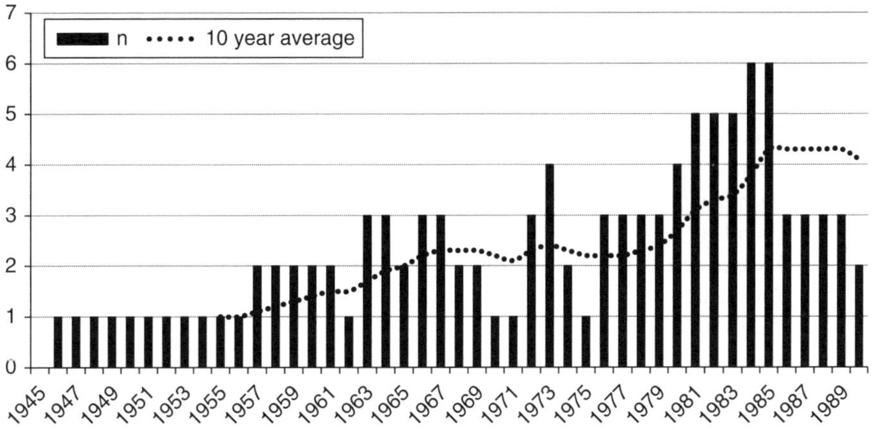

Figure 16.1 Governments involved in genocides 1945–1988 (Fein 1993, after Harff and Gurr).

convention (2008: 923). To Fein's list, we might add another 17 governments listed by Charny for genocides against indigenous people in the same period (Charny 1999: 350, table 1). Harff and Gurr suggest a "typical year" during the period would feature six episodes of politicide or genocidal violence. As is evident from Table 16.2, since 1988 mutliple genocidal processes continue to unfold. In terms of distribution, the events cover most continents, the exclusion being Australasia.[17] Finally, it is worth noting that there are certain countries that appear repeatedly.[18]

Rather than counting episodes, some estimate the numbers dying from organized state violence. Harff and Gurr (1988: 370) cautiously suggest that, since 1945, genocides and politicides combined probably cost as many lives as "all organized combat." Reanalyzing their data, Fein (1993: 81) suggests that the figure may be as much as double that of wars and natural disasters. Rudolph Rummel estimates state-sponsored killings. He identifies the twentieth century as a period in which states have developed greater capacity to act arbitrarily toward their own and other populations, and introduces the terms megamurder, the killing of more than one million, and democide, encompassing genocide, politicide and mass murder (Rummel 1992: 47). He claims that democide accounted for nearly 151 million deaths between 1900 and 1987, and that 11 megamurderers account for over 142 million deaths, of which 86 percent took place in states with absolute power (1992: 48). His argument that democracy is a bulwark against genocide is supported by the selection of countries in Table 16.2 and Table 16.3.

The snapshot, historical survey, and efforts to quantify the number of victims reflect different ways of understanding the impact of genocide and other mass killing. The first two fit with a focus on the lost contribution of a group to humanity. The last is closer to homicide, albeit on a massive scale. The focus on the period from 1945 onward makes sense in terms of when the concept of genocide was introduced, and also gives a sense of modern genocides directed by states at their own citizens. This form is apparent earlier in the twentieth century in the genocide of Armenians in 1915 (Bloxham 2003). It nonetheless hides different forms of genocide

Table 16.3 Genocides 1945–1988, Fein (1993) after Harff and Gurr.

Country	*Victim group(s)*	*Period*
Burundi	Hutu	1972–1973
Ethiopia	Tigris/Eritrea	1983–1984
Rwanda	Tutsi	1962–1963
Uganda (1)	Multiple	1971–1979
Uganda (2)	Multiple	1979–1986
Afghanistan	Afghans	1980–1989
Cambodia	Minorities, Khmer	1975–1979
China	Tibetans	1956–1960
Indonesia (1)	Communists, Chinese	1965–1966
Indonesia (2)	East Timorese	1975–1999*
Pakistan	Bengalis	1971–1972
Guatemala	Mayan tribes	1980–1984
USSR	7 nationalities	1943–1968
Paraguay	Ache	1960s and 1970s
Iran	Baha'is	1979–1984
Iraq	Kurds	1987–1988

* The situation was resolved in 1999 with a UN sponsored peacekeeping mission.

from ancient and colonial periods (Chalk and Jonassohn 1990). While the logic of genocide may change over time, it is a longstanding phenomenon.

Victims, Genocidaires, and Contexts

Victims

Legal and extra-legal definitions of genocide identify specific social collectives as victims of genocide. There are two key ways in which the questions of victimhood might be examined. First, features which make genocidal victimization of a group more or less likely. Second, within a group, characteristics likely to lead to particular subgroups being victimized. It stands to reason that a victim group must be identifiable to its perpetrators (Kuper 1981: 53). This may involve visual cues such as skin color (e.g., Darfur), cultural cues such as names (e.g., Bosnia and Herzegovina), official identification (e.g., Rwanda), or other forms of differentiation. Differentiation may be encouraged by state practices. The separation of German Jews from the rest of the population was achieved through law (Garner 1936: 96), ultimately undermining their social relations with other Germans (Stowell 1936: 103). This contributed to the exclusion of victims from a "universe of obligation" making their unopposed victimization more likely (Fein 1990: 34). Rafter and Walklate (2012) identify group features pertinent to victimization: the lack of the protection afforded by national statehood, lower legal protections through different forms of citizenship, and attempts to secure some form of autonomy.

Within the target group, Article 2 acts of genocide may be directed at subgroups in different ways. Jones writes on the risk to noncombatant battle-age males originating in a heteronormativity which casts them as a danger (2006b: 452). MacKinnon identifies that women are "violated in ways men are not, or that are exceptional for men," primarily through rape and sexual murder (1994: 6). She goes on to show how state-sponsored rape contributes to genocide (1994: 11). In *Akayesu*, the chamber included rape in its deliberations on genocide under the heading of causing serious bodily or mental harm (*Prosecutor v Akayesu* 1998: para. 731):

> These rapes resulted in physical and psychological destruction of Tutsi women, their families and their communities. Sexual violence was an integral part of the process of destruction, specifically targeting Tutsi women and specifically contributing to their destruction and to the destruction of the Tutsi group as a whole.

Perpetrators

As with victims it is possible to think of perpetrators at the level of the collective (for example, the state or a state-like body) and individual. Gerlach has suggested that the focus on state-crime has been driven by a European model of totalitarian state bureaucracy, diverting attention from the complexity of extremely violent societies and the breadth of participation (Gerlach 2006: 458–460, 465). The extent of participation is underscored by Drumbl (2000: 1252) suggesting that roughly one third of adult Hutu participated in the Rwandan genocide. Thus, analyses of genocide involve accounting for conformity, albeit within the context of a "deviant normative order" (Maier-Katkin, Mears, and Bernard 2009: 237). Schabas criticizes current case law for focusing too much on individuals at the expense of understanding their action "on behalf of a state and in accordance with a state policy" (2008: 954). Between the state and the individual lie other structures playing a supporting role in genocides. For example, Huisman (2010) identifies 70 corporations involved in crimes under international law, including genocide, either directly or as contributors or beneficiaries. Equally, a number of studies of semi-autonomous "subalterns" suggest that groups pursuing their own agenda contribute to the overarching genocidal aims of states (see Weiss-Wendt and Üngör 2011; Tanner and Mulone 2013). The role of intermediary organizations will be further explored under explanatory frameworks.

Contexts

The contexts in which genocide takes place bring together an empowered perpetrator and a vulnerable victim group in a suitable opportunity structure. Chalk and Jonassohn (1990) provide a historical survey of genocides dating back to antiquity, identifying various contexts including war and colonization. Modern genocides are often located in contexts of social and political instability. Elias (1998: 23) examines the structural change and attendant status uncertainty in Germany following World War I. Bloxham points to unstable and contested border zones as key contexts of genocides and mass anti-civilian violence in the three generations preceding the Holocaust, and within the Holocaust notes the vulnerability of populations in territory changing hands (2010: 320, 323). Harff and Gurr's historical review suggests that the instability associated with decolonization is correlated with a spike in genocides and politicides in the period 1961–1966 (1988: 367; see also Kuper 1981: 46). Many of the decolonizing territories were plural societies with enduring cleavages, exacerbated by colonial policy. Kuper identifies this as a structural base for genocide (1981: 54–57). Local contextual factors also need to be accounted for, as is evident from Korb's (2010) work on Ustaša violence in the Independent State of Croatia during World War II. Conversely the cases such as South Africa and Northern Ireland show apparently permissive factors such as cleavages, but without genocide (Kuper 1981: 191 ff.).

Explanatory Frameworks

Explanatory frameworks for genocide address various questions: under what circumstances does genocide take place (Kuper 1981)? How do processes unfold in the short and long term (Klusemann 2012; Bloxham 2010)? How do seemingly "ordinary" individuals come to participate in genocidal activity (Browning 2001)? Others treat genocide as an independent variable, asking how genocide impacts upon post-genocidal societies or exploring manifest and latent functions of genocide (Doubt 2000). Different disciplinary perspectives operate at a range of different levels. Political science tends to focus on the features of states in which genocide occurs (Rummel 1992), while psychological explanations focus on individual motivations (Wilson 2010) and the interactions of individual and context (Haslam and Reicher 2007). Recent work in history (Bloxham 2008) and criminology (Van Baar and Huisman 2012) has also sought to locate the individual in a social and political context, introducing mid-level phenomena such as groups and organizations into multilevel explanations of genocide. A further international level can be factored into analyses. Each level of analysis will be discussed, before showing how they may be integrated.

State (macro) level analyses

States with deep, longstanding cleavages are contextually conducive to genocide, but not all divided societies are genocidal and the nature of state power may be a further explanatory factor. Writing on state aggression, Durkheim linked this to an overly powerful unified state dominating civil society (1915: 30, 34). State power, unconstrained by democratic controls, is a common explanation of state involvement in genocide.

Fein notes that genocidal states are most likely to be authoritarian, one party states (1999: 159). While no democratic state was directly involved in genocide from 1945 to 1988 (Fein 1999: 159), democratizing states may experience instability conducive to emerging genocidal regimes. In Bosnia and Herzegovina, free elections and multiparty rule preceded the 1992–1995 war. The process by which the Serb republic in Bosnia and Herzegovina was created and came to be dominated by one party shows the interplay of democracy and authoritarian legacies in processes running up to genocide.

The international environment

Karstedt underscores the importance of "connectivity within the international system and 'world politics'" (2013: 386). Two key aspects of the international environment are directly relevant to the occurrence of genocide. First, international relations that emphasize state sovereignty are more permissive of genocide within state borders. During the Cold War, intervention was most likely when genocidal actions threatened to spill over borders (e.g., East Pakistan, Uganda). Second, international political economy plays a role. Verhoeven (2011) analyzes Sudan's shift from colonial to postcolonial agricultural exploitation in a globalizing economy. This favors riverain elites and marginalizes Darfuri subsistence farmers disconnected from global markets, a factor in their vulnerability to victimization.

Individual (micro) level analyses

A review of the literature on perpetrators shows variation in terms of level of participation and role, suggesting that some explanation utilizing individual characteristics is necessary (Hollows and Fritzon 2012: 459). Some studies pay close attention to a single perpetrator (e.g., Arendt 2006 on Eichmann; Wilson 2010 on Duch), trading off depth against generalization. Hollows and Fritzon adopt a larger convenience sample of 80 perpetrators tried in international courts (2012: 460). This sampling strategy is hostage to prosecutorial choices, but the International Criminal Tribunal for the former Yugoslavia (ICTY) has tried suspects from the front line, up through regional and organizational hierarchies to top leaders, providing a cross-section of offenders. They identify four models of functioning (adaptive, conservative, expressive, and integrative) and find statistically significant relationships between these and the offending patterns of individuals (Hollows and Fritzon 2012: 462–465). For example, the expressive model includes harassment, denigration, and dehumanization and is associated with individuals with a "poorly constructed emotional system," internal instability, and a dysfunctional manner of communicating (Hollows and Fritzon 2012: 465).

Organizational (meso) level analyses and integrated frameworks

Integrated analyses recognize that states and organizations depend on individuals to execute specific tasks (Collins 2009: 17) and that individuals exist in, and interact with, contexts structured by states and intermediate organizations (Haslam and Reicher 2007: 620). Alvarez locates impetus, ideology, and resources in the state; bureaucracies translate this into structured practices enacted by individuals (2001: 8). Other forms exist between state and individual. Van Baar and Huisman (2012) describe one firm involved in producing ovens for use in Nazi death camps. Tanner and Mulone (2013) identify informal groupings in the gray area covering private security and paramilitarism. Studies like these allow comparison and go some way toward providing differentiation between different types of administrator and administration (Bloxham 2010: 211).

The medical profession in Nazi Germany provides an example (Browning 1988; Haque *et al.* 2012). Browning gives a detailed account of public health officials' support and rationalization of exterminatory policies in occupied Poland. This included concentrating Jews in overcrowded and insanitary ghettoes with insufficient food, shooting Jews found outside the ghettoes, and, ultimately, the mass murder of Jews in death camps. The enthusiastic participation of doctors is presented as a puzzle by Haque and colleagues. Around half of German physicians were "early joiners" of the party, a figure exceeding that of any other profession (Haque *et al.* 2012: 473–474). Aside from the clash of values in a profession geared toward preserving life, Haque and colleagues observe that German Jews were prevalent in the medical profession, so it was likely that many of the non-Jewish German doctors would have trained and worked with Jewish colleagues (Haque *et al.* 2012: 473). The authors propose a range of explanations that tie together individual characteristics, professional structures, and state. First, an authoritarian personality was common among doctors (2012: 474). Haslam and Reicher suggest that this may not be a product of the organizational environment, but that individuals with certain characteristics are more likely to enter particular situations (2007: 615). Nonetheless, Haslam and Reicher see that both person and situation are altered by the interplay. The strict rules of practice in medicine may strengthen tendencies toward conformity and authoritarianism (Haslam and Reicher 2007: 615; Haque *et al.* 2012: 475).

In terms of the profession's position in society, Haque and colleagues note that, in a time of demoralization in the turbulent economic and political climate following Germany's defeat in war, the profession was overcrowded and suffered relative economic decline as well as the aftereffects of wartime de-professionalization. The Nazi party's penetration of state and profession offered a way to remove competitive colleagues and a path toward upward social mobility (Haque *et al.* 2012: 476–477). In the *Generalgouvernement*, by 1941 these factors combined with anti-Semitic stereotypes and a mission to preserve the German people, justifying "any means" to prevent their endangerment (Browning 1988: 22, 26). Organizations and professions select their members, but specialists are drawn from a limited pool leading to compromises on ideological criteria. The Warsaw public health official Dr Hagen was "politically unreliable" on account of his involvement in Weimar's leftist politics. Although he sought to counter the spread of disease within the ghetto, he did not oppose ghettoization and continued to believe into the 1970s that spotted fever was endemic among Jews (Browning 1988: 25). Hagen, once considered as a candidate to be imprisoned in a concentration camp, resigned on the grounds of conscience and took up a posting in Russia (Browning 1988: 30–31).

Historical and sociological studies show that any explanation of genocide needs to show multilevel processes over the short term (Klusemann 2012; Tanner and Mulone 2013) and the long term (Bloxham 2010). In the short term, concentration, starvation, and denial of hygiene and other public health measures created a self-fulfilling prophecy of disease among Jews. This threatened the spread of disease as those detained in the ghetto sought to escape their deaths. In turn, this boosted medical support and legitimation for radical responses, escalating from shooting Jews found outside the ghettoes to killing them in huge numbers. Against a background of ideological sympathy, the case of the medical profession is an example of the Nazi state using professional structures to do what they are best suited to: "the harnessing of different individual dispositions and ambitions to the achievement of common goals by the provision of various incentives" (Bloxham 2008: 204).

Prevention and Reduction

States party to the 1948 *Genocide Convention* undertake to prevent and punish genocide (Article 1). Weighing the genocides in Table 16.3 against the limited number of preventive interventions, the convention's success is questionable. A number of reasons have been posited, including the lack of institutionalized coercive power to back up the law (Hagan and Levi 2005: 1500). Waxman notes a number of coercive interventions, with and without UN Security Council backing (2009: 8–9; contrast Haiti and Kosovo), but his cases include Bosnia, where the Srebrenica genocide followed UN intervention from the start of the conflict. Waxman's interventions all follow the Cold War, a period in which support for different client regimes and protection of regional interests blocked the consensus required for intervention (Sumner 1982: 2; Totten 2005: 6). This has lessened to some extent, but Waxman notes that veto holders with ideological objections to intervention in internal affairs, or interest-driven objections to particular interventions, still act to obstruct UN Security Council consent for military intervention (Waxman 2009: 12).

The punishment envisaged by the convention may serve preventive ends. This is the most common justification of international criminal law, even if supporting evidence is sketchy (Tallgren 2002: 565, 569). Tallgren cites deterrence as one preventive model, but also highlights the internalization of norms and integration into a system of common values. Deterrence may develop over time, inasmuch as classical features of deterrence theory are attained by the institutions of international criminal justice. In the short term, the credible threat of prosecutions[19] is unlikely to stop crimes in a context already deeply affected by hatred and violence (Akhavan 2001: 9), but from the 1990s international criminal law extended to include a permanent international criminal court, special courts combining international and domestic elements,[20] domestic trials following regime change, and the use of universal jurisdiction over international crimes such as genocide. Rikhof identifies 13 European states exercising such jurisdiction to investigate or prosecute crimes from 19 countries (2009: 26–37). This takes place against a background of the thickening of institutions of global governance, and the growth of regional and international bodies monitoring, regulating, or governing states (Cronin 2005: 315; Falk 2001: 118).

Final Remarks

The chapter does not exhaustively cover the developing field of genocide studies. As it continues to develop, we can anticipate a wider range of mid-level studies, the greater possibility of comparative work, and, through journals such as *Holocaust and Genocide Studies*, the continued application of different disciplinary frameworks to describe, analyze, and explain the phenomenon.

Notes

1 A number of forms of state-sponsored killings exist short of genocide, ranging from individual assassinations through to mass killings that do not fit all the required elements of the crime.

2 Individual states differ in terms of how they define genocide. Ethiopia, for example, went beyond the convention to include attacks on political groups (see Tiba 2007: 517n12).

3 *Prosecutor v Tolimir* (2012: para. 744).

4 See *Prosecutor v Karadžić* (Rule 98 *bis* Appeal, July 11, 2013: 78, ll. 17ff).

5 *Prosecutor v Popović et al.* (2010: paras 823, 830, 856–860, and 1177); on the importance of knowledge of a plan in the Eichmann conviction, see also Schabas (2008: 962).

6 For example, *Prosecutor v Blagojević and Jokić* (2005: 668).

7 *Prosecutor v Akayesu* (1998: paras 118, 704, 730).

8 *Prosecutor v Kayishema* (1999: para. 89); *Prosecutor v Semanza* (2003: para. 316).

9 *Prosecutor v Krstić* (2001: paras 594-5); reiterated in *Prosecutor v Krstić* (2004: para 19); see also Buss (2014) for a discussion of how women's testimony was interpreted in relation to patriarchy.

10 For instance, in *Prosecutor v Akayesu* (1998: para. 702) the court identified the Tutsi as a protected *ethnic* group on the basis of ethnic categorization on Rwandan identity cards and on witnesses' ready identification as Hutu or Tutsi when asked their ethnicity.

11 *Prosecutor v Akayesu* (1998: para. 701).

12 *Prosecutor v Krstić* (2004: paras 48ff).

13 *Prosecutor v Krstić* (2004: para. 53).

14 See, for example, Fein (1990: 18) on including more sporadic "genocidal massacres" alongside genocides.

15 Extermination is stage 9 of a ten stage process, the final stage being denial of a genocide.

16 On the latter, attacks against multiple nationalities in the USSR between 1943 and 1968 and attacks on the Ache in Paraguay in the 1960s and 1970s.

17 But on a "continuing genocide" against indigenous Australians, see Short (2010).

18 Uganda, Indonesia,and, going back to Harff and Gurr's original list, the USSR, which is listed for three separate episodes (Harff and Gurr 1989: 26, table 1).

19 By the time of the genocidal massacre at Srebrenica in July 1995, the ICTY had been established (May 1993), had issued its first indictment (Dragan Nikolić, November 1994) and received its first arrestee (Duško Tadić, April 1995).

20 Examples include the Special Court in Sierra Leone, the Cambodian Extraordinary Chambers, and the State Court of Bosnia and Herzegovina.

References

Akhavan, P. (2001) Beyond impunity: Can international criminal justice prevent future atrocities? *American Journal of International Law*, 95: 7–31. doi: 10.2307/2642034.

Alvarez, A. (2001) *Governments, Citizens and Genocide: A Comparative and Interdisciplinary Approach*. Bloomington: University of Indiana Press.

Arendt, H. (2006) *Eichmann in Jerusalem: A Report on the Banality of Evil*. London: Penguin Books.

Bauer, Y. (1999) Comparison of genocides. In L. Chorbajian and G. Shirinian (eds), *Studies in Comparative Genocide* (pp. 31–43). London: Macmillan.

Behrens, P. (2012) Genocide and the question of motives. *Journal of International Criminal Justice*, 10: 501–523. doi: 10.1093/jicj/mqs038.

Bloxham, D. (2003) The Armenian genocide of 1915–1916: Cumulative radicalization and the development of a destruction policy. *Past and Present*, 181: 141–191. doi: 10.1093/past/181.1.141.

Bloxham, D. (2008) Organized mass murder: Structure, participation, and motivation in comparative perspective. *Holocaust and Genocide Studies*, 22: 203–245. doi: 10.1093/hgs/dcn026.

Bloxham, D. (2010) Europe, the final solution and the dynamics of intent. *Patterns of Prejudice*, 44: 317–335. doi: 10.1080/0031322X.2010.510711.

Browning, C. (1988) Genocide and public health: German doctors and Polish Jews, 1939–41. *Holocaust and Genocide Studies*, 3: 21–36. doi: 10.1093/hgs/3.1.21.

Browning, C. (2001) *Ordinary Men: Reserve Police Battalion 101 and the Final Solution in Poland*. Harmondsworth, UK: Penguin Books.

Buss, D.E. (2014) Knowing women: Translating patriarchy in international criminal law. *Social and Legal Studies*, 23: 73–92. doi: 10.1177/0964663913487398.

Campbell, B. (2011) Genocide as a matter of degree. *British Journal of Sociology*, 62: 586–612. doi: 10–1111/j.1468-446.2011.01382.x.

Chalk, F. and Jonassohn, K. (1990) *The History and Sociology of Genocide: Analyses and Case Studies*. New Haven, CT: Yale University Press.

Charny, I. (1999) *Encyclopedia of Genocide [e-book]*. Santa Barbara, CA: ABC-CLIO.

Collins, R. (2009) Micro and macro causes of violence. *International Journal of Conflict and Violence*, 3: 9–22. doi: 0070-ijcv-2009120.

Cronin, B. (2005) International legal consensus and the control of excess state violence. *Global Governance*, 11: 311–330. doi: 10.5555/ggov.2005.11.3.311.

Doubt, K. (2000) *Sociology after Bosnia and Kosovo: Recovering Justice*. Lanham, MD: Rowman & Littlefield.

Drumbl, M. (2000) Punishment postgenocide: From guilt to shame to *Civis* in Rwanda. *New York University Law Review*, 75: 1221–1326.

Durkheim, É. (1915) *Germany above All: German Mentality and War*. Paris: Librarie Armand Colin.

Elias, N. (1998) *The Germans: Power Struggles and the Development of Habitus in the 19th and 20th Centuries*. New York: Columbia University Press.

Falk, R. (2001) Accountability for war crimes and the legacy of Nuremberg. In A. Jokić (ed.), *War Crimes and Collective Wrongdoing: A Reader* (pp. 113–136). Oxford: Blackwell.

Fein, H. (1990) Genocide: A sociological perspective. *Current Sociology*, 38(1): 1–126.

Fein, H. (1993) Accounting for genocide after 1945: Some theories and findings. *International Journal on Group Rights*, 1: 79–106. doi: 10.1163/157181193X00013.

Fein, H. (1999) Testing theories brutally: Armenia (1915), Bosnia (1992) and Rwanda (1994). In L. Chorbajian and G. Shirinian (eds), *Studies in Comparative Genocide* (pp. 157–164). London: Macmillan.

Garner, J. (1936) Recent German nationality legislation. *American Journal of International Law*, 30: 96–99. doi: 10.2307/21290563.

Genocide Watch. (2014) Countries at risk. Available online at www.genocidewatch.net/alerts-2/new-alerts (accessed October 20, 2014).

Gerlach, C. (2006) Extremely violent societies: An alternative concept to genocide. *Journal of Genocide Research*, 8: 455–471. doi: 10.1080/14623520601056299.

Greenfield, D. (2008) The crime of complicity in genocide: How the international criminal tribunals for Rwanda and Yugoslavia got it wrong, and why it matters. *Journal of Criminal Law and Criminology*, 98: 921–952. doi: 0091-4169/08/9803-0921.

Greenwalt, A. (1999) Rethinking genocidal intent: The case for a knowledge-based interpretation. *Columbia Law Review*, 99: 2259–2294. doi: 10.2307/1123611.

Hagan, J. and Levi, R. (2005) Crimes of war and the force of law. *Social Forces*, 83: 1499–1534. doi: 10.1353/sof.2005.0066.

Haque, O.S., De Freitas, J., Viani, I., *et al.* (2012) Why Did so many German doctors join the Nazi party early? *International Journal of Law and Psychiatry*, 35: 473–479. doi: 10.1016/j.ijlp.2012.09.022.

Harff, B. and Gurr, T.R. (1988) Toward empirical theory of genocides and politicides: Identification and measurement of cases since 1945. *International Studies Quarterly*, 32: 359–371. doi: 10.2307/2600447.

Harff, B. and Gurr, T.R. (1989) Victims of the state: Genocides, politicides and group repression since 1945. *International Review of Victimology*, 1: 23–41. doi: 10.1177/026975808900100103.

Haslam, S.A. and Reicher, S. (2007) Beyond the banality of evil: Three dynamics of an interactionist social psychology of tyranny. *Personality and Social Psychology Bulletin*, 33: 615–622. doi: 10.1177/0146167206298570.

Hollows, K. and Fritzon, K. (2012) "Ordinary men" or "evil monsters"? An action systems model of genocidal actions and characteristics of perpetrators. *Law and Human Behavior*, 36: 458–467. doi: 10.1037/h0093987.

Huisman, W. (2010) *Business as Usual: Corporate Involvement in International Crimes*. The Hague: Eleven International.

Huttenbach, H. (1988) Locating the Holocaust on the Genocide Spectrum: Towards a Methodology of Definition and Categorization. *Holocaust and Genocide Studies*, 3: 289–303. doi: 10.1093/hgs/3.3.289.

Jones, A. (2006a) *Genocide: A Comprehensive Introduction*. Abingdon, UK: Routledge.

Jones, A. (2006b) Straight as a rule: Heteronormativity, gendercide, and the noncombatant male. *Men and Masculinities*, 8: 451–469. doi: 10.1177/1097184X04268797.

Karstedt, S. (2013) Contextualizing mass atrocity crimes: Moving toward a relational approach. *Annual Review of Law and Social Science*, 9: 383–404. doi: 10.1146/annurev-lawsocsci-102612-134016.

Kirsch, S. (2013) The social and the legal concept of genocide. In P. Behrens and R. Henham (eds), *Elements of Genocide* (pp. 7–19). Abingdon, UK: Routledge.

Klusemann, S. (2012) Massacres as process: A micro-sociological theory of internal patterns of mass atrocities. *European Journal of Criminology*, 9: 468–480. doi: 10.1177/1477370812450825.

Korb, A. (2010) Understanding Ustaša violence. *Journal of Genocide Research*, 12: 1–18. DOI: 10.1080/14623528.2010.508273.

Kuper, L. (1981) *Genocide: Its Political Use in the 20th Century*. New Haven, CT: Yale University Press.

Lemarchand, R. and Martin, D. (1974) *Selective Genocide in Burundi*. London: Minority Rights Group.

Lemkin, R. (1944) *Axis Rule in Occupied Europe: Laws of Occupation, Analysis of Government, Proposals for Redress*. Washington DC: Carnegie Endowment for International Peace.

MacKinnon, C. (1994) Rape, genocide and women's human rights. *Harvard Women's Law Journal*, 17: 5–16.

Maier-Katkin, D., Mears, D., and Bernard, T. (2009) Towards a criminology of crimes against humanity. *Theoretical Criminology*, 13: 227–255. doi: 10.1177/1362480609102880.

Mennecke, M. and Markusen, E. (2003) The international criminal tribunal for the former yugoslavia and the crime of genocide. In S. Jensen (ed.), *Genocide: Cases, Comparisons and Contemporary Debates* (pp. 293–360). Copenhagen: Danish Centre for Holocaust and Genocide Studies.

Rafter, N. and Walklate, S. (2012) Genocide and the dynamics of victimization: Some Observations on Armenia. *European Journal of Criminology*, 9: 514–526. doi: 10.1177/1477370812450824.

Rikhof, J. (2009) Fewer PLACES TO HIDE? The impact of domestic war crime prosecutions on international impunity. *Criminal Law Forum*, 20: 1–51. doi: 10.1007/s10609-008-9092-7.

Rummel, R.J. (1992) Megamurders. *Society*, 29: 47–52. doi: 10.1007/BF02695268.

Schabas, W. (2008) State policy as an element of international crimes. *Journal of Criminal Law and Criminology*, 98: 953–982. doi: 0091-4169/08/9803-0953.

Short, D. (2010) Australia: A continuing genocide. *Journal of Genocide Research*, 12: 45–68. doi: 10.1080/14623528.2010.508647.

Stowell, E. (1936) Intercession against the persecution of Jews. *American Journal of International Law*, 30: 102–106. doi: 10.2307/2190565.

Sumner, C. (1982) Crime, justice and underdevelopment: Beyond modernization theory. In C. Sumner (ed.), *Crime, Justice and Underdevelopment* (pp. 1–39). London: Heinemann.

Tallgren, I. (2002) The sensibility and sense of international criminal law. *European Journal of International Law*, 13: 561–595. doi: 10.1093/ejil/13.3.561.

Tanner, S. and Mulone, M. (2013) Private security and armed conflict: A case study of the Scorpions during the mass killings in Yugoslavia. *British Journal of Criminology*, 53: 41–58. doi: 10.1093/bjc/azs053.

Tiba, F. (2007) The Mengistu genocide trial in Ethiopia. *Journal of International Criminal Justice*, 5: 513–528. doi: 10.1093/jicj/mqm021.

Totten, S. (2005) The UN and genocide. *Society*, 42: 6–13. doi: 10.1007/BF02687423.

UNGA (United Nations General Assembly) (1946) Resolution 96(1), 55th Plenary Meeting, December 11.

Van Baar, A. and Huisman, W. (2012) The oven builders of the Holocaust: A case study of corporate complicity in international crimes. *British Journal of Criminology*, 52: 1033–1050. doi: 10.1093/bjc/azs044.

Verhoeven, H. (2011) Climate change, conflict and development in Sudan: Global neo-Malthusian narratives and local power struggles. *Development and Change*, 42: 679–707. doi 10.1111/j.1467-7660.2011.01707.x.

Waxman, M. (2009) *Intervention to Stop Genocide and Mass Atrocities*, Special Report 49. New York: Council on Foreign Relations. Available online at http://www.cfr.org/genocide/intervention-stop-genocide-mass-atrocities/p20379 (accessed October 28, 2014).

Weiss-Wendt, A. and Üngor, U.Ü. (2011) Collaboration in genocide: The Ottoman Empire 1915–1916, the German occupied Baltic 1941–1944 and Rwanda 1994. *Holocaust and Genocide Studies*, 25: 404–437. doi: 10.1093/hqs/dci507.

Wilson, P. (2010) Do normal people commit genocide? Observations from the Cambodian trial of "Duch." *Psychiatry, Psychology and Law*, 17: 495–502. doi 10.10800/1321871103739060.

Further Reading

Carrier, N. and Park, A. (2013) On an entrepreneurial criminology of mass violence. *Crime, Law and Social Change*, 60: 297–317. doi: 10.1007/s10611-013-9452-z.

Hagan, J. and Rymond-Richmond, W. (2008) The collective dynamics of racial dehumanization and genocidal victimization in Darfur. *American Sociological Review*, 73: 875–902. doi: 10.1177/000312240807300601.

Hinton, A. (2011) Genocide, categorical certainty, and the truth: Questions from the Khmer Rouge tribunal. *Journal of Analytical Psychology*, 56: 390–394. doi: 0021-8774/2011/5603/375.

Komar, D.A. (2008) Variables influencing victim selection in genocide. *Journal of Forensic Sciences*, 53: 172–717. doi: 10.1111/j.1556-4029.2008.00590.x.

Osiel, M. (2010) Ascribing individual liability within a bureaucracy of murder. In Alette Smeulers (ed.), *Collective Violence and International Criminal Justice* (pp. 105–130). Antwerp: Intersentia.

Cases

International Criminal Tribunal for Rwanda, *Prosecutor v Akayesu*, ICTR-96-4, September 2, 1998.

International Criminal Tribunal for Rwanda, *Prosecutor v Kayishema*, ICTR-95-1, May 21, 1999.

International Criminal Tribunal for Rwanda, *Prosecutor v Semanza*, ICTR-97-20, May 15, 2003.
International Criminal Tribunal for the former Yugoslavia, *Prosecutor v Krstić*, IT-98-33, August 2, 2001.
International Criminal Tribunal for the former Yugoslavia, *Prosecutor v Krstić*, IT-98-33-A, April 19, 2004.
International Criminal Tribunal for the former Yugoslavia, *Prosecutor v Blagojevžić and Jokić*, IT-02-60, January 17, 2005.
International Criminal Tribunal for the former Yugoslavia, *Prosecutor v Popović and others*, IT-05-88, June 10, 2010.
International Criminal Tribunal for the former Yugoslavia, *Prosecutor v Tolimir*, IT-05-88/2, December 12, 2012.
International Criminal Tribunal for the former Yugoslavia, *Prosecutor v Karadžić*, IT-95-5/18-AR98bis.1, July 11, 2013.

Part III

Homicide around the Globe

International Perspectives

17

Homicide in Europe

Marieke Liem

Introduction

For a long time, European comparative homicide research has remained a relatively marginal field. Relative to the United States and several commonwealth countries, Europe[1] does not have a long tradition of studying the trends, patterns, and explanations of homicide. This is perhaps not surprising given the large differences that exist between European countries in legal definitions of and data sources on homicide. In addition, the overwhelming presence of the United States as the point of reference in studies on European homicide may have impeded comparative analysis within Europe (Granath *et al.* 2011). Recent initiatives, however, have begun to systematically address homicide and homicide research in Europe.

First, the construction of the European Homicide Monitor (EHM) is enabling comparisons and analyses among European countries. So far, three countries constitute the basis of the database: Finland, the Netherlands, and Sweden (Granath *et al.* 2011; Liem *et al.* 2013). Other European countries, including Norway and Switzerland, are now in the process of joining this initiative, filling a long-existing lacuna. A homicide measurement project like this is fundamental for further research that will provide evidence-based knowledge on topics such as the social factors that foster lethal violence, effective violence prevention, and setting rational punishment, sentencing policy, and treatment of offenders. A second initiative includes the publication of the *Handbook of European Homicide Research: Patterns, Explanations, and Country Studies*, which provides the first large-scale systematic collection of information on homicide research in Europe and serves as a foundation for research on the topic moving forward. Third, the increased activity of the

The Handbook of Homicide, First Edition. Edited by Fiona Brookman, Edward R. Maguire, and Mike Maguire.

European Homicide Research Group, part of the European Society of Criminology, reveals an indication of the growing interest in this field. A recent special issue on homicide in Europe of the *European Journal of Criminology* featured the diverse and exciting work of our research group members. In short: Research on homicide in Europe is rapidly expanding, giving rise to new initiatives and collaborations.

This chapter builds on these new developments, providing an overview of contemporary homicide research in Europe. The chapter is organized in three sections. Section I presents an overview of prior and current research on homicide in Europe.[2] Section II provides a description of the geographical and historical variation of homicide throughout Europe, and draws from current theories to explain these spatial and temporal variations. Finally, Section III explores ways in which future research may contribute in moving forward the field of European homicide research.

Section I: An Overview of Research on Homicide in Europe

Research on homicide in Europe can roughly be divided into four approaches: Sociological, historical, psychological, and descriptive (the last mainly exploring specific subtypes of homicide). Next, I will provide a brief overview of each of these approaches.

Sociological approaches to homicide in Europe

One of the earliest accounts of sociological approaches to homicide in Europe can be traced back to the 1920s when the Finnish scholar Verkko (1951) observed that the proportion of female homicide victims was higher when the overall homicide rate was low, and vice versa. Homicides involving unrelated young males as offender and victim tended to be the most variable part. In other words, increases and decreases of homicide are typically explained by the prevalence of such male-to-male encounters (Kivivuori, Savolainen, and Danielsson 2012). Today, these laws are also known as "Verkko's laws" and can still be applied to explain regional and historical variations in homicide.

Contemporary sociological approaches to homicide in Europe tend to focus on how the causes of homicide are located in the sociodemographic structure of society as well as in the recurring temporal and spatial dimensions and rhythms of everyday life (for an overview, see Granath *et al.* 2011). Much of this European research is inspired by US colleagues, as scholars have examined whether US-based findings hold in Europe as well (Kivivuori, Suonpää, and Lehti 2014).

Three major themes can be identified in these sociological approaches. The first is the role of alcohol in lethal violence. It is estimated that in the European Union, over 2,000 homicide deaths per year are attributable to alcohol use. This implies that four out of every ten homicides that occur in the European Union are alcohol-related (Bye 2012). The role of alcohol is particularly pronounced in male-on-male homicides in the context of a fight or conflict. Data from the United Kingdom, Sweden, and Finland show that in these male-to-male homicides, a significant proportion of offenders, victims, or both have consumed alcohol, oftentimes to excess (Brookman 2003; Brookman and Maguire 2004; Granath *et al.* 2011). There are at least three possible mechanisms for the alcohol–violence association (Bye 2008, 2012): First, people who have been drinking may feel less inhibited from using violence to achieve their ends in interactions. A second perspective holds that alcohol may not only enhance or trigger aggressive behavior and increase the risk of violent victimization, but may reduce the likelihood of any bystanders intervening when a violent encounter takes place. Third, the association between alcohol consumption and homicide may depend on other factors associated with violence; for example, alcohol consumption may be greater in times or regions of high unemployment or poverty. Recent studies show that the association between alcohol consumption and homicide rates is stronger in Northern and Eastern Europe than in Southern Europe. The reason for this discrepancy can be found in different drinking patterns. Southern European countries are characterized by frequent daily drinking, mainly during meals. In these countries there is less acceptance of drunkenness in public. In contrast, the main drinking pattern in Northern Europe, and in several East European countries, consists of irregular and intoxication-oriented drinking (sometimes referred to as "binge" drinking), combined with societal acceptance of drunkenness in public (Bye 2012).

A second important string of sociological approaches to homicide focuses on the link between economic deprivation and homicide. In this light, economic deprivation may result in individuals striking out against the sources of economic strain or produce diffused aggression that stimulates violent behavior. On a macro level, McCall and Nieuwbeerta (2007) suggested that in areas suffering an economic decline, criminally predisposed individuals may become further marginalized and the social bonds and networks that might otherwise support law-abiding behavior may be compromised. In using data from over 100 European cities, McCall and Nieuwbeerta (2007) found that economic hardship was a robust predictor of urban homicide rates. The relationship between relative deprivation and homicide has also been found in cross-national comparisons assessing nationwide homicide rates (Bjerregaard and Cochran 2008a, 2008b; Chamlin and Cochran 2006; Savolainen 2000). It should be noted, however, that the last comparisons relied on global, crude data, rather than zooming in on the relationship between economic deprivation and homicide in Europe specifically.

The third major strand of sociological perspectives in homicide research focuses on the relationship between firearms and homicide. The notion of guns facilitating violence is the key assumption behind the strict regulation of gun ownership in most European countries. Even though the percentage of the European population possessing a firearm is lower than other Western countries, particularly the United States, there are considerable variations between European countries when it comes to gun ownership. Finland and Switzerland, for example, have very high rates of firearm possession compared to other Western European countries such as the

Netherlands and England and Wales. The reasons for firearm possession, however, differ markedly. For example, in Finland guns (particularly rifles) are mostly used in hunting and sports, but the dominant reason among the Swiss is having a gun as part of military equipment (Killias and Markwalder 2012). European studies consistently find positive correlations between the rates of household gun ownership and the national rates of homicide as well as the proportions of homicides committed with a firearm (Killias 1993). The correlation is particularly strong between firearm possession and female firearm homicide (Killias, Van Kesteren, and Rindlisbacher 2001). In these analyses, there was no negative correlation between the rates of ownership and the rates of homicide committed by other means; in other words, other means are not used to "compensate" for the absence of guns in countries with a lower rate of gun ownership and victimization. In their recent analyses on 50 (mostly European) countries, Van Kesteren (2014) focused on the individual level of gun ownership. They found that high availability of guns in a country increases the risk of being victimized by gun-related violence or homicide, suggesting that gun availability offers potential offenders the opportunity to be more intimidating in their threats or attacks. Alternatively, it may be argued that ownership, and especially the habit of carrying a concealed gun around, may generate the "illusion of invincibility." This could result in risk-taking or provocative behavior, which in turn increases the risk of becoming a victim of lethal violence (Van Kesteren 2014).

Historical approaches to homicide in Europe

Through historical analyses, various researchers have been able to trace homicide figures in Europe back to the thirteenth century. These show that serious interpersonal violence decreased remarkably throughout Europe between the mid-sixteenth and early twentieth centuries (Eisner 2003). While in the fifteenth century, about 50 people per 100,000 were victimized in a homicide, in the nineteenth century this figure had decreased to about one per 100,000. The transition to declining homicide rates appears to have started earliest in the northwestern parts of Europe and then to have gradually diffused to more peripheral regions of the continent (Eisner 2003). In combining various data sources in a historical dataset, Manuel Eisner (2003) found that the long-term decline was particularly associated with a disproportionate decline in elite homicide and a drop in male-to-male conflicts in public space. In such confrontations the role of honor seemed to have played an important role: in medieval and early modern society, insults constituted a frequently cited motive for knife fighting if efforts at reconciliation failed. The decline of the duel, the vendetta, and other forms of private revenge went hand in hand with the overall drop in homicide rates. Declines in homicide rates, in short, primarily resulted from some degree of pacification of encounters in public space, a reluctance to engage in physical confrontation over conflicts, and the waning of honor as a cultural code regulating everyday behavior (Eisner 2003).

Strongly associated with this line of reasoning is the work by Norbert Elias (2000[1939])—particularly his civilization theory (Spierenburg 2012). In this major work, Elias assumed that an interplay between the expansion of the state's monopoly of power and increasing economic interdependence would lead to the growth of pacified social spaces and restraint from violent behavior through increased self-control (Eisner 2003).

The downward trend of homicide rates in Western Europe continued well into the twentieth century. Homicide rates remained low (below 2 per 100,000) until approximately the late 1960s. Starting in the early 1970s, homicide rates showed a slight increase throughout Europe, before decreasing again in the 1990s. Eisner (2008) has argued that this increase can be attributed to an increase in homicides between young men in public places, who are often strangers to one another. In this light, the "swinging sixties" brought along a loosening of social control and a relaxation of the norms that regulated the relationships between youths. In the same period, others point out, homicide peaks were recorded by individual countries such as France, which waged the Algerian war around 1960, and Italy, where years of terrorism and Mafia-related violence continued until the early 1990s (UNODC 2014). The overall European decrease in homicide rate in the early 1990s, in turn, could be explained by pan-Western cultural changes: to a new emphasis on self-control and more conservative cultural values. In their latest analysis of Western European homicide rates, Aebi and Linde (2014) found that male and female victims from different age categories followed the same trend from the 1960s through the 1990s, not only the young generations. This throws into doubt the Eliasian idea that the homicide rate is merely a reflection of the presence of young men in public space. Instead, Aebi and Linde (2014) hold that the increases and decreases in homicide are reflections of a change in lifestyle. They attribute the parallel trends in male and female victimization since the 1960s to the integration of women in the labor market, and the sharing of similar lifestyles by men and women. As a result, both men and women are exposed to similar risks outside their homes. From a lifestyle theory perspective, the decrease of homicide in the late 1990s could be attributed to the rapid development of computer technologies and the Internet, leading to an increase in time spent at home, especially for young people, and in turn, a lowered risk of homicide victimization.

It is important to note that not all European countries followed this pattern. The homicide drop was particularly noticeable in Western European countries. Homicide levels in Eastern Europe remained high, while rates in Southern European countries have converged to levels typically found in Northern and Western Europe (Eisner 2003). We will take a closer look at these regional variations shortly.

Psychological approaches to homicide

A third line of research on homicide in Europe involves psychological approaches, particularly those that focus on the role of mental illness in homicide. Several population-based studies in England (Flynn *et al.* 2011; Nielssen and Large 2010; Swinson *et al.* 2011), Denmark (Brennan, Mednick, and Hodgins 2000), Sweden

(Fazel and Grann 2006), and Finland (Eronen, Hakola, and Tiihonen 1996; Tiihonen *et al.* 1997) revealed a higher prevalence of mental illness among homicide offenders compared to the general population. Similar findings have been reported on the relationship between mental illness and victims of homicide in studies in Sweden (Crump *et al.* 2013) and Denmark (Hiroeh *et al.* 2001). One of the explanations for these associations lies in the relationship between mental illness, drug use, and alcoholism. Individuals suffering from mental illness and substance abuse are more likely to live in, and contribute to, a violent (inner-city) subculture where there is a higher likelihood that they will become involved in violent encounters (Hiroeh *et al.* 2001). Alternatively, they may have behavioral characteristics, such as alcohol or drug misuse, that increase their risk of becoming involved in violent conflict. Further, they may be less aware of their safety needs, or may provoke the hostility of others through the symptoms of illness, such as irritability or paranoia (Hiroeh *et al.* 2001).

Within the (forensic) psychological approach to homicidal behavior, numerous European studies have focused on specific subtypes of mental illness. Here, the focus lies on the association between psychotic disorders, such as schizophrenia, and homicidal behavior (Fazel *et al.* 2010; Sturup and Lindqvist 2014; Vinkers and Liem 2011). These studies all take a national perspective, describing the nature and incidence of the relationship between severe mental illness and homicide in separate countries. With the exception of several meta-analyses (Fazel *et al.* 2009; Nielssen and Large 2010) that include several European countries among other Western countries, studies based on pan-European data are virtually absent.

Descriptive approaches to subtypes of homicide

The fourth set of studies on homicide in Europe is also the most voluminous and the most rapidly increasing (Kivivuori, Suonpää, and Lehti 2014). These studies focus on specific subtypes of homicide, in which research on domestic homicides is well represented. This includes research on spousal homicide based on national data, such as conducted in Russia (Gondolf and Shestakov 1997), England (Dobash, Dobash, and Cavanagh 2009), Sweden (Belfrage and Rying 2004), and Denmark (Leth 2009). In their meta-analysis on spousal homicide worldwide, Stöckl and colleagues (2013) were able to include data on the majority of European countries, indicating that figures on this type of homicide are obtainable and suitable for comparisons. This development is underscored by a recent Europe-wide initiative, the COST Action on Femicide, which seeks to combine already existing national research efforts into a pan-European coalition of research on intimate partner homicide.

Another branch of research focuses on event and perpetrator characteristics of child homicide. The majority of these studies tend to rely on forensic-psychiatric data, stemming from forensic hospitals and connected universities, and are conducted in countries such as England and Wales (Wilczynski 1997), Finland (Vanamo *et al.* 2001), the Netherlands (Liem and Koenraadt 2008), and Denmark (Laursen *et al.* 2011). Again, similar to psychotic homicide and intimate partner homicide, there is an absence of studies that include data from multiple countries that allow for comparisons. One exception constitutes a comparison between child homicide in Austria and Finland (Putkonen *et al.* 2009, 2011).

Homicide-suicides constitute another homicide subtype that has been studied in European countries separately (Barraclough and Harris 2002; Flynn *et al.* 2009; Kivivuori and Lehti 2003; Liem and Koenraadt 2007; Shiferaw *et al.* 2010) as well as several countries combined (*Liem et al.* 2011; Liem and Oberwittler 2012).

Other subtypes of nondomestic homicide include stranger murder, which has been studied in the United Kingdom (Salfati and Canter 1999; Hall and Wilson 2014) and Germany (Harbort and Mokros 2001) in particular. A more common type includes confrontational and revenge homicides, which have been examined extensively by Brookman (2003). Based on Home Office data and police murder files, she showed that homicides among unrelated men are often characterized by either confrontational "honor contests" that erupt spontaneously, or by preplanned assaults in which the offender seeks out the victim because of a grudge or the need for revenge (Brookman 2003; Brookman and Maguire 2004). Finally, due to their low prevalence in Europe, studies on other subtypes of homicide such as sexual homicides (Greenall and Richardson 2014; Häkkänen-Nyholm *et al.* 2009) are relatively rare and limited to anecdotal accounts.

Section II: Patterns of Homicide in Europe

Spatial and temporal variation

First, it should be noted that precise definitions of homicide throughout Europe are diffuse; some European nations combine incomplete homicides with completed homicide as a singular legal entity and include infanticide and aggravated assaults, while others offer a variety of distinctions based on the severity of the crime, age of the offender, mental state, and other mitigating factors (Aebi and Delgrande 2010). In spite of the discrepancies in definitions and the scope of data collection, some general patterns throughout Europe can be observed.

If measured by crude homicide rates, Europe is one of the most peaceful regions in the world (Granath *et al.* 2011): In their recent report on global homicide rates, the United Nations Office on Drugs and Crime (UNODC 2014) reported that Europe and Oceania shared the lowest homicide rate among the regions of the world. The estimated homicide rate in Europe is 3.0 per 100,000, compared to 6.2 per 100,000 worldwide (UNODC 2014). It is important to note, however, that although homicide rates in Europe in general are low compared to global standards, there is a considerable variation in homicide rates between European countries (Granath *et al.* 2011). This is particularly noticeable when comparing Eastern Europe to its counterparts (see Figure 17.1 and Figure 17.2).

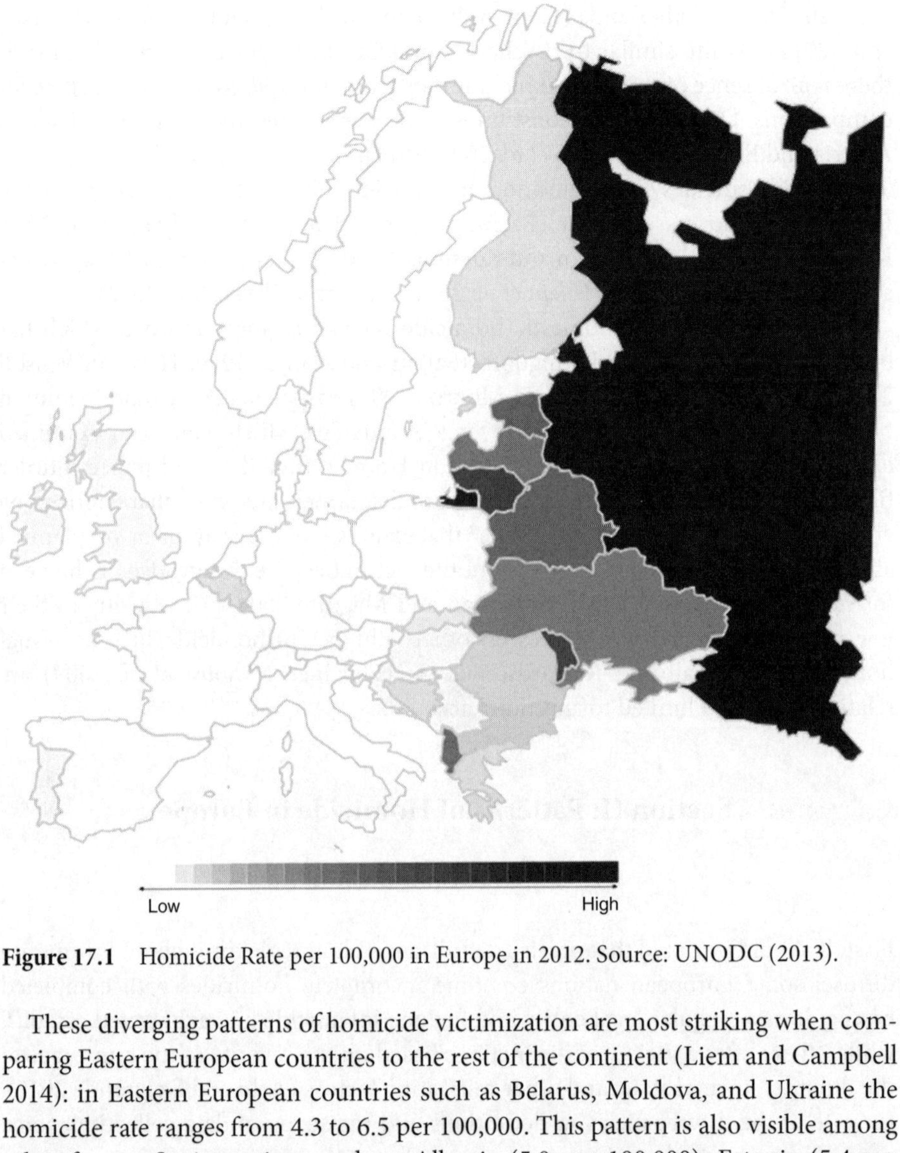

Figure 17.1 Homicide Rate per 100,000 in Europe in 2012. Source: UNODC (2013).

These diverging patterns of homicide victimization are most striking when comparing Eastern European countries to the rest of the continent (Liem and Campbell 2014): in Eastern European countries such as Belarus, Moldova, and Ukraine the homicide rate ranges from 4.3 to 6.5 per 100,000. This pattern is also visible among other former Soviet nations such as Albania (5.0 per 100,000), Estonia (5.4 per 100,000), Latvia (4.7 per 100,000), and Lithuania (6.7 per 100,000). Russia appears to be a notable outlier with 9.2 homicide deaths per 100,000. It should be noted that, as Stamatel (2009) points out, former communist Eastern European countries are often treated as a monolithic bloc by Westerners. However, they are quite different in terms of pre-communist political configurations, state formation, the adoption and implementation of communism, and extent of political and economic reforms embraced after the fall of communism. East-central European countries such as Bulgaria, Croatia, Czech Republic, Hungary, Macedonia, Poland, Romania, Slovakia, and Slovenia have quickly assimilated with Western Europe, as witnessed by early accessions into the European Union—as opposed to the newly independent states such as Ukraine, Belarus, and Moldova. The quick adaptation of democratization

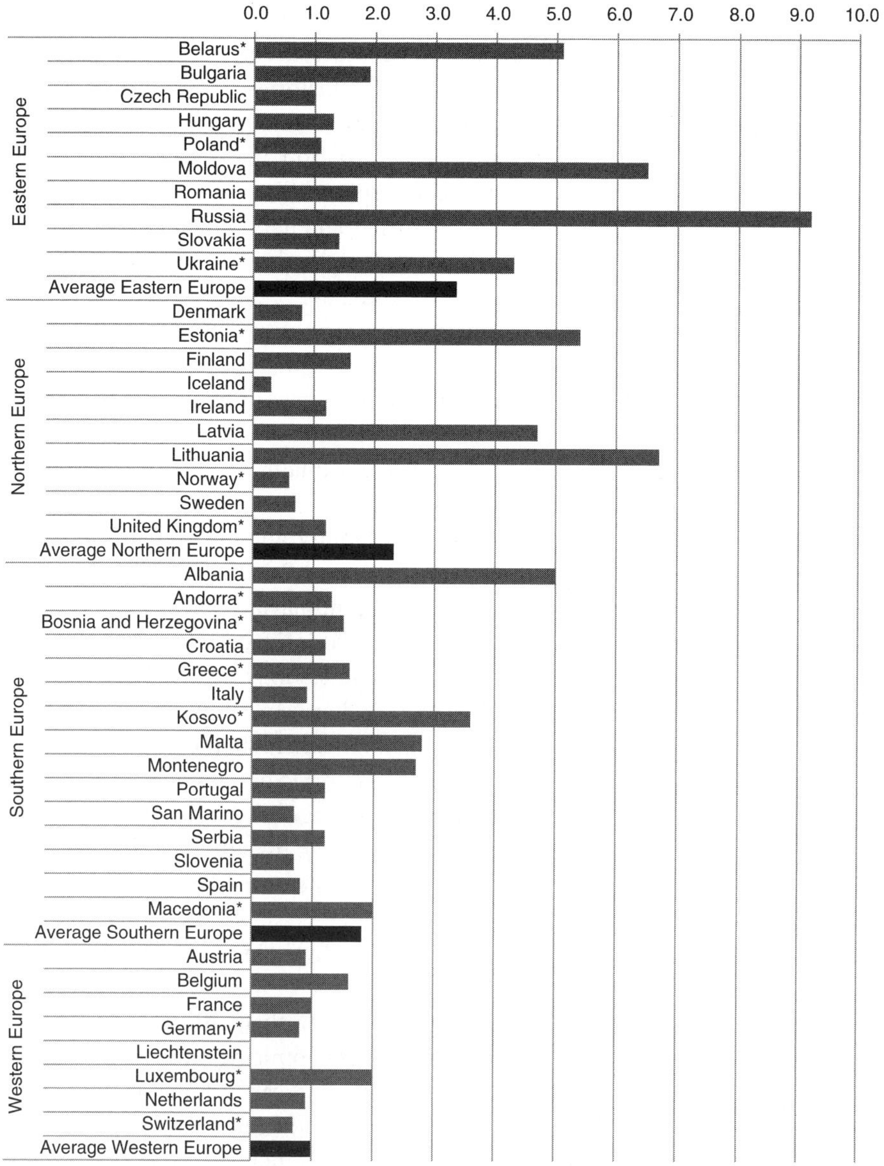

Figure 17.2 Homicide Rate per 100,000 by region and country in 2012. Source: UNODC (2013). Note: For countries with an asterisk (*) rates are based on 2010 as data for 2012 was unavailable.

and economic reforms toward marketization among East-central European countries are associated with relatively low contemporary homicide rates, ranging from 0.7 per 100,000 in Slovenia to 2 per 100,000 in Macedonia. Arguably, these rates are expected to decline even further: Following the years after the fall of communism in 1989, the homicide rates in countries such as Poland and East Germany doubled (Stamatel 2012) before showing a steady decline at the turn of this century.

The reasons for present-day high homicide rates in former Soviet states, such as Belarus, Ukraine, Lithuania, and Russia, can be found, according to Pridemore and Kim (2006), in these countries' sheer size and histories of authoritarian rule. Continuing high levels of violence may be regarded as a result of swift political change following the transition toward democratization and marketization, which stress individual freedoms, goals, rights, and responsibilities. This has arguably led to societal deregulation and anomie and, in turn, to higher homicide rates. Another reason can be found in the relationship between alcohol and homicide. In this regard, Russia—with widespread alcohol use and a high homicide rate—appears to be a case in point. Intoxication-oriented, heavy drinking episodes dominate the drinking pattern in Russia. Rapid intoxication in unregulated private or semiprivate settings, and thus a lack of regulatory mechanisms, could explain why a simple argument could lead to a homicide when alcohol is involved (Pridemore 2002, 2004; Pridemore and Chamlin 2006). Other factors that explain the relatively high homicide rate in former Soviet countries include specific historical conditions, social structural factors such as poverty and family instability, and individual-level factors such as education and marriage (Lysova, Shchitov, and Pridemore 2012).

Shifting our attention to Western Europe and Scandinavia, relatively low homicide rates can be observed, ranging from 2.0 per 100,000 in Luxembourg to even lower rates in Scandinavia (0.3 per 100,000 in Iceland and 0.6 in Norway). The overall low homicide figures can be ascribed to the fact that these countries are rather alike in terms of the variables commonly used to explain differences in the levels of homicide on a pan-European level (Nivette 2011). High economic development, a high standard of living, a high level of education, and high average life expectancy characterize all these nations (Granath *et al.* 2011; Liem *et al.* 2013). In addition, it has been suggested that what Western European countries have in common are functioning and stable state structures that are accountable to their citizens, relatively effective public health, education, and criminal justice systems, relatively low social inequality, and substantial proportions of citizens that actively engage in matters of shared concern (Eisner and Nivette 2012). It should be noted, however, that nationally low levels of homicide can obscure subnational "hotspots," where homicide rates are consistently higher compared to their direct surroundings. Such spots can be found in the Algarve, the southernmost part of Portugal, which has a homicide rate of 2.5 per 100,000; in the southern tip of Italy, whose homicide rate is attributable to the prevalence of Mafia-related killings; on the French island of Corsica; and in certain more densely populated urban areas that have higher homicide rates than the rest of their respective countries, such as Amsterdam, Brussels, Prague, and Vienna (UNODC 2014).

The demographic and situational context of homicide

Similar to other types of violence, homicides are not randomly distributed. Perpetrators—and, to a lesser extent, victims as well—of homicide and sublethal violence are disproportionately represented in the lower socioeconomic strata

(Brookman and Maguire 2004; Granath *et al.* 2011). This pattern is also reflected on a geographical level by McCall *et al.* (2012), who found that European homicide rates are highest in cities with highest economic deprivation as measured in percentage of low-income households, percentage of households reliant on social security, percentage of households with one-half of national mean income, and median disposable annual income. In their study based on 117 European cities they did not find support, however, for the relationship between unemployment and homicide rates. The absence of such a direct relationship may be explained by the fact that many European countries provide unemployment and other social benefits that cushion the economic hardship that citizens face in financially depressed periods.

In terms of gender, following long-term historical trends, men are still more likely to become victimized in homicide compared to women, although the gender gap is decreasing over time, particularly in recent years. In terms of age, recent figures based on the *Global Study on Homicide* (UNODC 2014), indicate that men between the ages of 30 and 44 run the highest risk of falling victim to homicide (6.4 per 100,000) compared to women of all ages and compared to men in other age categories[3]. The pattern of female homicide victims has remained fairly stable throughout age groups in Europe in recent years, although women aged 30 through 59 and above are at slightly higher risk (1.9 per 100,000) than younger women aged 15 through 29 (1.5 per 100,000) and at higher risk than older women (over 60 years of age). This could be explained by their exposure to intimate partner homicide, which disproportionately affects women compared to men (UNODC 2014). In Europe overall, the homicide rate of children under the age of 14 is 0.5. Among this youngest age group, gender differences are not as pronounced as in older age groups. Insofar as detailed data is available, throughout Europe children in general constitute a low-risk group, although the risk for babies under one is often higher than among any other single-year age group (see also Brookman and Maguire 2004).

Compared to other types of homicide, interpersonal homicide is still the most prevalent. Throughout Europe, the largest component of interpersonal homicides consists of family related homicides, accounting for 28 percent of all homicides. By contrast, homicides related to criminal activity, such as gang-related homicides or organized crime, are rare. A slight exception to this is homicides related to robbery or burglary, accounting for about 5 percent of homicides. In such cases, even though homicide may be considered a possible outcome of criminal action, it does not represent the primary goal of the perpetrator (Brookman and Maguire 2004). It should also be noted that although sociopolitical homicides generate much media attention, they are so far relatively rare in the European context.

Finally, regarding the modus operandi in homicides throughout Europe, data from 42 countries indicates that physical violence (hitting, kicking, pushing, strangling) and so-called "other" methods such as drowning, poisoning, et cetera, are used in over half (54%) of all homicides. The use of firearms is relatively rare (at approximately 13%), especially compared to other Western countries such as the United States. Sharp objects such as knives are used in about one-third of all homicides. As mentioned earlier, there are notable exceptions to this rule, particularly concerning areas such as Finland and Eastern Europe, where the use of firearms in homicide is more widespread than elsewhere. Other exceptions include Scotland, England and Wales, where knives constitute the most prevalent type of modus operandi (Brookman and Maguire 2004; UNODC 2014), both in "domestic" and "street" homicides. These findings suggest that carrying a knife is by no means unusual, especially among young men who carry knives as a weapon or as a "means of self-defense" when they go out (Brookman and Maguire 2004).

Section III: Directions for Future Research

In this contribution, my aim has been to provide a brief overview of the current status of research on homicide in Europe, and to identify fruitful directions for future research. As outlined earlier, for many EU countries there is no systematic knowledge on lethal violence. Again, despite the central need for sound knowledge on lethal violence, the majority of EU countries lack well-developed data of the kind that is required for reliable assessments. As this overview shows, detailed data that allows for in-depth analyses on homicide patterns is available in only a handful of countries. The national databases that do exist are not compatible with one another, and reports such as supplied by the UNODC are helpful for rough statistics, but lack detail that enables the study of specific dynamics underlying homicides. Moving forward, we should join efforts in creating a data clearinghouse that would facilitate more sophisticated analyses. Further developing the European Homicide Monitor can fill these voids (Liem 2013). Future collaborations forged through the European Society of Criminology, the European Homicide Research Group or other professional forums might help overcome the extreme variation in linguistic, legal, administrative, and institutional norms and processes across Europe.

The European Homicide Monitor (Granath *et al.* 2011; Liem *et al.* 2013), in its present state, including three European countries (Finland, the Netherlands, and Sweden), may provide a suitable platform to meet this aim. This Monitor promises to be an even richer data source in the future to be used by researchers and policy makers. In its present form, the European Homicide Monitor spans four years (2003–2006). We aspire to continue data collection, allowing for more detailed trend analyses, while at the same time allowing other countries to join this initiative. Expanding the temporal and geographical scope of the monitor would provide unique opportunities to follow and make assessments of trends in and factors that foster lethal violence from a pan-European perspective. This would greatly improve the opportunities for EU-level initiatives to work in different ways to prevent and reduce lethal violence and to follow up the measures that are introduced. With combined efforts, we can reach its full potential in the future.

If such an endeavor could be completed, several areas of homicide research warrant particular attention. One of these areas consists of the criminal justice response to homicide. Even though Europe is increasingly becoming legally, politically, and economically unified, there is still a large discrepancy as to how we deal with those who commit violent offenses. Preliminary analyses show that punishments for homicide vary widely throughout Europe, ranging from life imprisonment to several years' confinement (Liem and Campbell 2014). To conduct a pan-European comparison of the types of punishments given, accurate and reliable data collection is required that captures data on the main law enforcement, judicial, and correctional institutions involved, including the police, prosecution, courts, and prisons. Data on individual offenses and suspects should be collected at each stage of the process, so that criminal justice responses can be measured and compared across European countries (UNODC 2014).

Another area of attention constitutes the evaluation of policies aimed at violence reduction, including homicide reduction. These include evaluations of specific policies designed to impact violence, such as domestic violence prevention schemes, parenting programs, alcohol and drug programs, firearm reduction programs, violence awareness programs, and policing strategies. Given that there is little knowledge and reliable data on such programs, research on the impact of these interventions has the potential to generate evidence-based policy to further reduce the burden of homicide throughout the continent.

Notes

1 I should note that in this contribution, I consider Europe as the Council of Europe member states (which includes 47 member states spanning from the Russian Federation in the east to the United Kingdom, Ireland, and Iceland in the west) together with Belarus.

2 In assembling this overview, I relied on articles and book contributions that were written in English. The reader should be aware that there is an abundance of literature on region-specific and type-specific homicide available in French, German, Dutch, Finnish, Swedish, Danish, Portuguese, Spanish, Russian, Italian, et cetera. Given the readership of this book, however, I chose to include scholarly work that would be accessible for all.

3 Other age categories include 0–14, 15–29, 45–59, and 60+.

References

Aebi, M. and Delgrande, N. (2010) *Council of Europe Annual Penal Statistics: SPACE I*. Strasbourg: Council of Europe.

Aebi, M. and Linde, A. (2014) The persistence of lifestyles: Rates and correlates of homicide in Western Europe from 1960 to 2010. *European Journal of Criminology*, 11(5): 552–577.

Barraclough, B. and Harris, E.C. (2002) Suicide preceded by murder: The epidemiology of homicide-suicide in England and Wales 1988–92. *Psychological Medicine*, 32(04): 577–584.

Belfrage, H. and Rying, M. (2004) Characteristics of spousal homicide perpetrators: A study of all cases of spousal homicide in Sweden 1990–1999. *Criminal Behaviour and Mental Health*, 14(2): 121–133.

Bjerregaard, B. and Cochran, J.K. (2008a) Cross-national test of institutional anomie theory: Do the strength of other social institutions mediate or moderate the effects of the economy on the rate of crime? *Western Criminology Review*, 9(1): 31–48.

Bjerregaard, B. and Cochran, J.K. (2008b) Want amid plenty: Developing and testing a cross-national measure of anomie. *International Journal of Conflict and Violence*, 2(2): 182–193.

Brennan, P.A., Mednick, S.A., and Hodgins, S. (2000) *Major Mental Disorders and Criminal Violence in a Danish Birth Cohort. Archives of General Psychiatry*, 57(5): 494–500.

Brookman, F. (2003) Confrontational and revenge homicides among men in England and Wales. *Australian and New Zealand Journal of Criminology*, 36(1): 34–59.

Brookman, F. and Maguire, M. (2004) Reducing homicide. *Crime, Law, and Social Change*, 42(4): 325–403.

Bye, E.K. (2008) Alcohol and homicide in Eastern Europe a time series analysis of six countries. *Homicide Studies*, 12(1): 7–27.

Bye, E.K. (2012) Alcohol and homicide in Europe. In M. Liem and W. Pridemore (eds), *Handbook of European Homicide Research: Patterns, Explanations, and Country Studies* (pp. 231–245): New York: Springer.

Chamlin, M.B. and Cochran, J.K. (2006) Economic inequality, legitimacy, and cross-national homicide rates. *Homicide Studies*, 10(4): 231–252.

Crump, C., Sundquist, K., Winkleby, M.A., and Sundquist, J. (2013) Mental disorders and vulnerability to homicidal death: Swedish nationwide cohort study. *British Medical Journal*, 346: 1–8.

Dobash, R.E., Dobash, R.P., and Cavanagh, K. (2009) "Out of the blue": Men who murder an intimate partner. *Feminist Criminology*, 4(3): 194–225.

Eisner, M. (2003) Long-term historical trends in violent crime. *Crime and Justice*, 30: 83–142.

Eisner, M. (2008) Modernity strikes back? A historical perspective on the latest increase in interpersonal violence (1960–1990). *International Journal of Conflict and Violence*, 2(2): 288–316.

Eisner, M. and Nivette, A. (2012) How to reduce the global homicide rate to 2 per 100,000 by 2060. In R. Loeber and B.C. Walsh (eds), *The Future of Criminology* (pp. 219–228). New York: Oxford University Press.

Elias, N. (2000[1939]) *The Civilizing Process: Psychogenetic and Sociogenetic Investigations*. Oxford: Blackwell.

Eronen, M., Hakola, P., and Tiihonen, J. (1996) mental disorders and homicidal behavior in Finland. *Archives of General Psychiatry*, 53(6): 497–501.

Fazel, S., Buxrud, P., Ruchkin, V., and Grann, M. (2010) Homicide in discharged patients with schizophrenia and other psychoses: A national case-control study. *Schizophrenia Research*, 123(2): 263–269.

Fazel, S. and Grann, M. (2006) The population impact of severe mental illness on violent crime. *American Journal of Psychiatry*, 163(8): 1397–1403.

Fazel, S., Gulati, G., Linsell, L., *et al.* (2009) Schizophrenia and violence: Systematic review and meta-analysis. *PLoS Medicine*, 6(8): e1000120.

Flynn, S., Abel, K.M., While, D., *et al.* (2011) Mental illness, gender and homicide: A population-based descriptive study. *Psychiatry Research*, 185(3): 368–375.

Flynn, S., Swinson, N., While, D., *et al.* (2009) Homicide followed by suicide: A cross-sectional study. *Journal of Forensic Psychiatry & Psychology*, 20(2): 306–321.

Granath, S., Hagstedt, J., Kivivuori, J., *et al.* (2011) *Homicide in Finland, the Netherlands and Sweden: A First Study on the European Homicide Monitor Data.* Stockholm: Brottsförebyggande rådet/The Swedish National Council for Crime Prevention.

Gondolf, E.W. and Shestakov, D. (1997) Spousal homicide in Russia: Gender inequality in a multifactor model. *Violence Against Women*, 3(5): 533–546.

Greenall, P.V. and Richardson, C. (2014) Adult male-on-female stranger sexual homicide a descriptive (baseline) study from Great Britain. *Homicide Studies*, 19(3): 237–256. doi: 1088767914530555.

Häkkänen-Nyholm, H., Repo-Tiihonen, E., Lindberg, N., *et al.* (2009) Finnish sexual homicides: Offence and offender characteristics. *Forensic Science International*, 188(1): 125–130.

Hall, S. and Wilson, D. (2014) New foundations: Pseudo-pacification and special liberty as potential cornerstones for a multi-level theory of homicide and serial murder. *European Journal of Criminology*, 11(5): 635–655.

Harbort, S. and Mokros, A. (2001) Serial murderers in Germany from 1945 to 1995: A descriptive study. *Homicide Studies*, 5(4): 311–334.

Hiroeh, U., Appleby, L., Mortensen, P.B., and Dunn, G. (2001) Death by homicide, suicide, and other unnatural causes in people with mental illness: A population-based study. *Lancet*, 358(9299): 2110–2112.

Killias, M. (1993) International correlations between gun ownership and rates of homicide and suicide. *Canadian Medical Association Journal*, 148(10): 1721–1725.

Killias, M. and Markwalder, N. (2012) Firearms and homicide in Europe. In M. Liem and W. Pridemore (eds), *Handbook of European Homicide Research: Patterns, Explanations, and Country Studies* (pp. 261–272). New York: Springer.

Killias, M., Van Kesteren, J., and Rindlisbacher, M. (2001) Guns, violent crime, and suicide in 21 countries. *Canadian Journal of Criminology*, 43: 429–448.

Kivivuori, J. and Lehti, M. (2003) Homicide followed by suicide in Finland: Trend and social locus. *Journal of Scandinavian Studies in Criminology and Crime Prevention*, 4(2): 223–236.

Kivivuori, J., Savolainen, J., and Danielsson, P. (2012) Theory and explanation in contemporary European homicide research. In M. Liem and W. Pridemore (eds), *Handbook of European Homicide Research: Patterns, Explanations, and Country Studies* (pp. 95–109). New York: Springer.

Kivivuori, J., Suonpää, K., and Lehti, M. (2014) Patterns and theories of European homicide research. *European Journal of Criminology*, 11(5): 530–551.

Laursen, T.M., Munk-Olsen, T., Mortensen, P.B., *et al.* (2011) Filicide in offspring of parents with severe psychiatric disorders: A population-based cohort study of child homicide. *Journal of clinical psychiatry*, 72(5): 698–703.

Leth, P.M. (2009) Intimate partner homicide. *Forensic Science, Medicine, and Pathology*, 5(3): 199–203.

Liem, M. (2013) A brief history of the future of European Homicide. In A. Kuhn, P. Margot, M.F. Aebi, *et al.* (eds) *Kriminologie, Kriminalpolitik und Strafrecht aus internationaler Perspektive: Festschrift für Martin Killias* (pp. 279–286). Bern: Stämpfli.

Liem, M., Barber, C., Markwalder, N., *et al.* (2011) Homicide-suicide and other violent deaths: An international comparison. *Forensic Science International*, 207(1): 70–76.

Liem, M. and Campbell, M. (2014) Punishment of homicide in Europe: Research challenges and a roadmap for progress. *International Criminal Justice Review*, 24(3): 285–297.

Liem, M., Ganpat, S., Granath, S., *et al.* (2013) Homicide in Finland, the Netherlands, and Sweden: First findings from the European Homicide Monitor. *Homicide Studies*, 17(1): 75–95.

Liem, M. and Koenraadt, F. (2007) Homicide-suicide in the Netherlands: A study of newspaper reports, 1992–2005. *Journal of Forensic Psychiatry & Psychology*, 18(4): 482–493.

Liem, M. and Koenraadt, F. (2008) Filicide: A comparative study of maternal versus paternal child homicide. *Criminal Behaviour and Mental Health*, 18(3): 166–176.

Liem, M. and Oberwittler, D. (2012) Homicide followed by suicide in Europe. In M. Liem and W. Pridemore (eds), *Handbook of European Homicide Research: Patterns, Explanations, and Country Studies* (pp. 197–215). New York: Springer.

Liem, M., Postulart, M., and Nieuwbeerta, P. (2009) Homicide-suicide in the Netherlands an epidemiology. *Homicide Studies*, 13(2): 99–123.

Lysova, A.V., Shchitov, N.G., and Pridemore, W.A. (2012) Homicide in Russia, Ukraine, and Belarus. In M. Liem and W. Pridemore (eds), *Handbook of European Homicide Research: Patterns, Explanations, and Country Studies* (pp. 451–469). New York: Springer.

McCall, P.L. and Nieuwbeerta, P. (2007) Structural covariates of homicide rates: A European city cross-national comparative analysis. *Homicide Studies*, 11: 167–188.

McCall, P.L., Nieuwbeerta, P., Engen, R.L., and Thames, K.M. (2012) Explaining variation in homicide rates across Eastern and Western European cities: The effects of social, political, and economic forces. In M. Liem and W. Pridemore (eds), *Handbook of European Homicide Research: Patterns, Explanations, and Country Studies* (pp. 137–154). New York: Springer.

Nielssen, O. and Large, M. (2010) Rates of homicide during the first episode of psychosis and after treatment: A systematic review and meta-analysis. *Schizophrenia Bulletin*, 36(4): 702–712.

Nivette, A.E. (2011) Cross-national predictors of crime: A meta-analysis. *Homicide Studies*, 15(2): 103–131.

Pridemore, W.A. (2002) Vodka and violence: Alcohol consumption and homicide rates in Russia. *American Journal of Public Health*, 92(12): 1921–1930.

Pridemore, W.A. (2004) Weekend effects on binge drinking and homicide: The social connection between alcohol and violence in Russia. *Addiction*, 99(8): 1034–1041.

Pridemore, W.A. and Chamlin, M.B. (2006) A time-series analysis of the impact of heavy drinking on homicide and suicide mortality in Russia, 1956–2002. *Addiction*, 101(12): 1719–1729.

Pridemore, W.A. and Kim, S.-W. (2006) Democratization and political change as threats to collective sentiments: Testing Durkheim in Russia. *Annals of the American Academy of Political and Social Science*, 605(1): 82–103.

Putkonen, H., Amon, S., Almiron, M.P., *et al.* (2009) Filicide in Austria and Finland: A register-based study on all filicide cases in Austria and Finland 1995–2005. *BMC Psychiatry*, 9(1): 74.

Putkonen, H., Amon, S., Eronen, C., *et al.* (2011) Gender differences in filicide offense characteristics—a comprehensive register-based study of child murder in two European countries. *Child Abuse & Neglect*, 35(5): 319–328.

Salfati, C.G. and Canter, D.V. (1999) Differentiating stranger murders: Profiling offender characteristics from behavioral styles. *Behavioral Sciences & the Law*, 17(3): 391–406.

Savolainen, J. (2000) Inequality, welfare state, and homicide: Further support for the institutional anomie theory. *Criminology*, 38(4): 1021–1042.

Shiferaw, K., Burkhardt, S., Lardi, C., *et al.* (2010) A half century retrospective study of homicide-suicide in Geneva—Switzerland: 1956–2005. *Journal of Forensic and Legal Medicine*, 17(2): 62–66.

Spierenburg, P. (2012) Long-term historical trends of homicide in Europe. In M. Liem and W. Pridemore (eds), *Handbook of European Homicide Research: Patterns, Explanations, and Country Studies* (pp. 25–38). New York: Springer.

Stamatel, J.P. (2009) Correlates of national-level homicide variation in post-communist East-Central Europe. *Social Forces*, 87(3): 1423–1448.

Stamatel, J.P. (2012) The effects of political, economic, and social changes on homicide. In M. Liem and W. Pridemore (eds), *Handbook of European Homicide Research: Patterns, Explanations, and Country Studies* (pp. 155–170). New York: Springer.

Stöckl, H., Devries, K., Rotstein, A., *et al.* (2013) The global prevalence of intimate partner homicide: A systematic review. *Lancet*, 382(9895): 859–865.

Sturup, J. and Lindqvist, P. (2014) Psychosis and homicide in Sweden—a time trend analysis 1987–2006. *International Journal of Forensic Mental Health*, 13(1): 1–7.

Swinson, N., Flynn, S.M., While, D., *et al.* (2011) Trends in rates of mental illness in homicide perpetrators. *The British Journal of Psychiatry*, 198(6): 485–489.

Tiihonen, J., Isohanni, M., Rasanen, P., *et al.* (1997) Specific major mental disorders and criminality: A 26-year prospective study of the 1966 northern Finland birth cohort. *American Journal of Psychiatry*, 154(6): 840–845.

UNODC (2013) *Global Study on Homicide*. Vienna: United Nations Office on Drugs and Crime.

UNODC (2014). *The Global Study on Homicide 2013*. Vienna: United Nations Office on Drugs and Crime.

Vanamo, T., Kauppi, A., Karkola, K., *et al.* (2001) Intra-familial child homicide in Finland 1970–1994: Incidence, causes of death and demographic characteristics. *Forensic Science International*, 117(3): 199–204.

Van Kesteren, J.N. (2014) Revisiting the gun ownership and violence link: A multilevel analysis of victimization survey data. *British Journal of Criminology*, 54: 53–72.

Verkko, V. (1951) *Homicides and Suicides in Finland and Their Dependence on National Character*. Copenhagen: C.F.C. Gads Forlag.

Vinkers, D. and Liem, M. (2011) Psychosis and homicide. *Psychiatric Services*, 62(10): 1234.

Wilczynski, A. (1997) *Child Homicide*. London: Greenwich Medical Media.

Further Reading

Brookman, F. and Maguire, M. (2005) Reducing homicide: A review of the possibilities. *Crime, Law and Social Change*, 42(4–5): 325–403.

Liem, M. and Pridemore, W.A. (2012) *Handbook of European Homicide Research: Patterns, Explanations, and Country Studies*. New York: Springer.

Liem, M. and Pridemore, W. (2014) Introduction. In Homicide in Europe. *European Journal of Criminology*, special issue, 11(5): 527—529.

Smit, P.R., De Jong, R.R., and Bijleveld, C.C.J.H. (2012) Homicide data in Europe: Definitions, sources, and statistics. In M. Liem and W. Pridemore (eds), *Handbook of European Homicide Research: Patterns, Explanations, and Country Studies* (pp. 5–23). New York: Springer.

18

Comparing Characteristics of Homicides in Finland, the Netherlands, and Sweden

Soenita M. Ganpat

Introduction

This chapter provides a cross-national comparison of homicide characteristics in three European countries,[1] based on data from the European Homicide Monitor (EHM)—the first joint database on homicide in Europe.[2] Earlier in this book, Liem has provided a valuable general outline of the current situation regarding homicide research in Europe. As pointed out by Liem, the EHM is a recent initiative that has great potential to stimulate further cross-national homicide research in Europe. This chapter therefore devotes full attention to the EHM and its first results. More specifically, it examines the characteristics of homicide cases in Finland, Sweden, and the Netherlands. First, I will briefly discuss why and how the joint database was created. After that, and based on the EHM, I will discuss the main results of the first comparative analysis to create a first descriptive overview of characteristics of homicide in Finland, Sweden, and the Netherlands concerning: (a) homicide incidents (rates, location, modus operandi, homicide subtype, victim–offender relationship, and alcohol use); (b) homicide victims (age, sex, and country of birth); and (c) homicide offenders (age, sex, country of birth, and employment status).

Background and Aim of this Study

Violence resulting in the killing of a human being is commonly considered the most serious form of violence, both in and outside Europe. However, compared especially to the United States, there is relatively limited systematic cross-national knowledge

The Handbook of Homicide, First Edition. Edited by Fiona Brookman, Edward R. Maguire, and Mike Maguire.

on lethal violence in Europe (Liem and Pridemore 2012). The main reason for this is that the comparability of national homicide data among European countries is extremely limited. This is largely due to the fact that existing national sources commonly differ in their approach: for example, some only contain homicide data on either the offenders or the victims whereas others contain data at incident level (Smit, De Jong, and Bijleveld 2012). This means that these sources commonly do not include combined data on offenders, victims, and incidents. In addition, differences in (legal) definitions have also contributed to this rather unsatisfactory situation (Smit, De Jong, and Bijleveld 2012). For example, in terms of the legal elements in the definition of homicide, countries differ in what they consider a homicide, resulting in the inclusion or exclusion of nonintentional homicide, such as assault leading to death. Also, in some homicide statistics attempted homicide is counted under the category homicide, thwarting comparability between European countries (Smit, De Jong, and Bijleveld 2012). Nevertheless, systematic cross-national knowledge on lethal violence in Europe is crucial, especially because it provides insight into trends and patterns and may contribute to the prevention of and fight against the most serious crime in Europe.

To overcome this important limitation, the EHM project has taken a first critical step toward creating a joint database for European countries. More specifically, through a three-year project (2009–2011),[3] the EHM dataset was set up to create a comparable homicide database between Finland, Sweden, and the Netherlands, describing main similarities and differences in certain characteristics of lethal violence between these countries.

Data and Method

Data sources used in this study

The EHM contains all homicides that were committed during the period 2003–2006 in Finland, Sweden, and the Netherlands which were known to the police or other law enforcement authorities, comprising data on characteristics of homicide incidents, victims, and offenders. This timeframe was chosen, because all three countries had data available for these four years.

Definitions

In this research project, homicide is defined as "an intentional criminal act of violence by one or more human beings resulting in the death of one or more human beings" (Ganpat *et al.* 2011: 32). In the three countries, this definition roughly covers the country's legal codes of homicide including murder, manslaughter, infanticide, or assault leading to death; however, in contrast to the Nordic countries, the Dutch legal definition of homicide does not include assault leading to death. Furthermore, excluded in all three countries were attempted homicide, suicide, abortion, euthanasia, assistance with suicide, involuntary manslaughter (e.g., drunk driving) and legally justified killings (e.g., killings by police).

National homicide data per country

By combining separate national homicide data already collected in Finland, Sweden, and the Netherlands, we were able to construct the EHM database, which will be discussed further below.

The first dataset covers national data from Finland, maintained by the National Research Institute of Legal Policy, the Police Department of the Ministry of the Interior, and the Finnish Police College (Lehti and Kivivuori 2012). Based on the Finnish Homicide Monitoring System (FHMS), this database contains all cases of lethal violence—covering the legal definition of murder, manslaughter, infanticide, and assault leading to death—which were committed in the period 2003–2006 and were known to the police (for more information, see also Ganpat *et al.* 2011).

The second dataset contains national data from Sweden, maintained by the Swedish National Council for Crime Prevention (Brottsförebyggande rådet, Brå) (see also Granath 2012; Rying 2007). The Swedish homicide data comprise all cases of lethal violence in the country in the period 1990–2008, covering the legal definition of murder, manslaughter, and assault leading to death which were known to the police or to other law enforcement authorities (Ganpat *et al.* 2011).

The third dataset includes national data from the Netherlands, jointly maintained by Leiden University and the Netherlands Institute for the Study of Crime and Law Enforcement (NSCR). The Dutch data stem from the Dutch Homicide Monitor, which is an ongoing monitor based on multiple (partially overlapping) sources, containing all homicide cases in the Netherlands committed in the period 1992–2009 and covering the legal definitions of murder and manslaughter (for more information about the Dutch Homicide Monitor, see also: Ganpat *et al.* 2011, 2014; Ganpat and Liem 2012; Ganpat, Van der Leun, and Nieuwbeerta 2013a, 2013b; Leistra and Nieuwbeerta 2003; Nieuwbeerta and Leistra 2007; Van Os, Ganpat, and Nieuwbeerta 2010).

To lay a foundation for the joint dataset, common variables were selected by thoroughly comparing the variables in the three datasets. Most of these common variables required recoding for which a guidebook and a coding manual especially created for this study were used (for more information, see also Ganpat *et al.* 2011). Each of the three national datasets was then merged into one joint dataset, after which the dataset was rigorously checked for inconsistencies. As such, the joint database—referred to as EHM—consists of 85 variables concerning characteristics of the incidents, victims, and offenders. In total, it comprises data on 1,577 homicide cases, involving 1,666 victims and 1,917 offenders. A selection of these variables is discussed below.

Results

Characteristics of homicide incidents in Finland, the Netherlands, and Sweden

In 2010, the total population in the Netherlands was estimated at 16.6 million; Finland counted 5.4 million inhabitants, and Sweden 9.3 million inhabitants. Of the total 1,577 homicide cases committed in the period 2003–2006, nearly half of all homicide cases (N = 760) were committed in the Netherlands; a third of the cases (N = 475) occurred in Finland, and approximately a fifth in Sweden (N = 342) (Table 18.1). However, taking into account the population size of each country, the average annual homicide rate during this period was highest in Finland (2.34 per 100,000 population) and lowest in Sweden (0.98). The Netherlands was placed in the middle with a homicide rate of 1.26 per 100,000 inhabitants.

The vast majority of all homicides involved one offender and one victim and occurred in the evening or at night (Figure 18.1). Furthermore, comparing the homicide location between the countries revealed that in the Nordic countries it was more common for the event to take place in a private setting (both countries 75%), whereas in the Netherlands it was more common that the homicide occurred in a public place (50%). When it comes to offenders' modus operandi (MO), a sharp instrument was the most commonly used weapon in Finland (42%) and Sweden (45%), whereas a firearm was the most commonly used weapon in the Netherlands (35%, which was more than double the rate of the other two countries; see Table 18.2). Noteworthy here is that previous research has shown that the firearm ownership in the three countries was lowest in the Netherlands (5%) when compared to Sweden (19%) and Finland (38%) (Van Dijk, Van Kesteren, and Smit 2007).

Domestic homicide was the most common type of homicide to occur in all three countries—especially intimate-partner homicide (Table 18.2). However, domestic homicide made up a higher proportion of cases in Sweden (45%) than in Finland (36%) and the Netherlands (39%). Homicides in the criminal milieu were more often committed in the Netherlands (19%) than in Sweden (12%) and Finland (3%).

Table 18.1 Total number of homicide cases, victims and offenders and homicide rates in Finland, the Netherlands, and Sweden (2003–2006).

	Finland	*The Netherlands*	*Sweden*	*All*
	N	*N*	*N*	*N*
Total number of homicide cases	475	760	342	1,577
Total number of homicide victims	491	820	355	1,666
Total number of homicide offenders	475	1,022	420	1,917
Average annual homicide rate	2.34	1.26	0.98	—

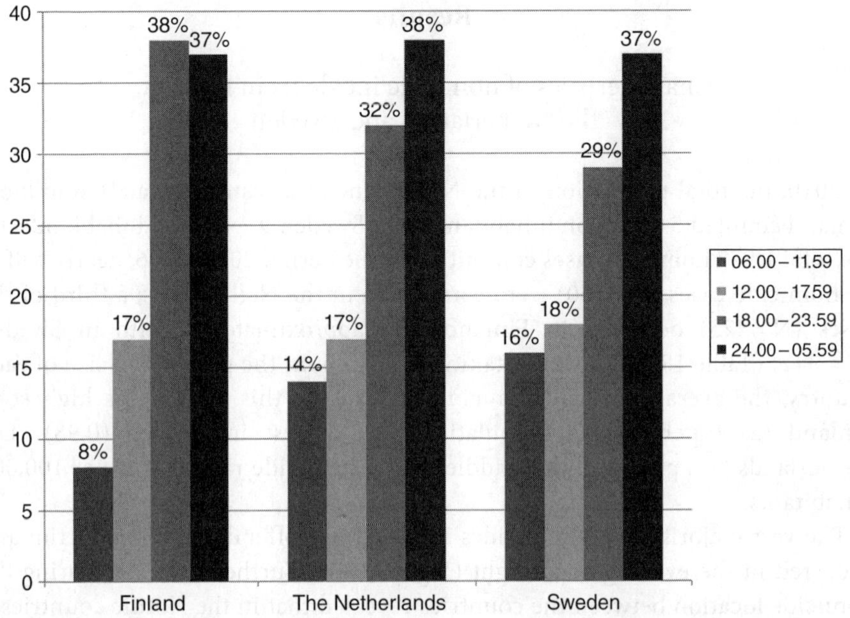

Figure 18.1 The daily distribution of homicides in Finland, the Netherlands, and Sweden (2003–2006).

Likewise, sexual homicides were much more prevalent in the Netherlands (3%) than in both Finland (0.2%) and Sweden (0.3%), while robbery homicides were more prevalent in the Netherlands (9%) and Sweden (8%) than in Finland (3%).

Also, comparing the victim–offender relationship between the countries demonstrates that, in the overwhelming majority of cases, the victim and the offender knew each other (Table 18.3). However, the data reveals that Dutch and Swedish homicide victims more often had an intimate or family relationship with the offenders (49% and 45%, respectively), whereas most Finnish victims and offenders were acquaintances (54%). In addition, although data on substance use was not available for the Netherlands, in most Swedish homicides (58%) and certainly in Finnish homicides (83%) at least one of the involved parties was found to be under the influence of alcohol during the incident. Whereas data on alcohol use by victims are missing for the Netherlands, Finnish victims (77%) were far more often under the influence of alcohol during the offense than their Swedish counterparts (45%). In addition, similar to what was found for victims, Finnish offenders (82%) were far more often under the influence of alcohol during the incident than Swedish offenders (52%) suggesting that in the majority of Finnish cases both parties were under the influence of alcohol. Again, comparisons with Dutch offenders could not be made as these data were missing from the Netherlands. Correspondently, the alcohol consumption level in the countries was highest in Finland (10.7 liters of alcohol per capita in adult population) compared to Sweden (6.9) and the Netherlands (9.6) (OECD Health Data 2010).

Table 18.2 Characteristics of homicide incidents in Finland, the Netherlands, and Sweden (2003–2006).

Characteristics	*Finland*		*The Netherlands*		*Sweden*	
	N	*Percentage*	*N*	*Percentage*	*N*	*Percentage*
Location:						
Public	115	25	373	50	83	25
Private	355	75	374	50	244	75
Total	470		747		327	
Modus operandi (by victim):						
Firearm	77	16	256	35	56	17
Blunt instrument	41	8	47	6	34	10
Sharp instrument	202	42	250	34	154	45
Strangulation	45	9	63	9	31	9
Hitting/kicking	80	18	76	11	40	12
Other	40	8	33	5	24	7
Total	485		725		339	
Type of homicide (by incident):						
Domestic homicide						
Intimate-partner homicide	112	24	152	24	92	29
Child homicide	24	5	39	6	15	5
Other domestic	31	7	59	9	35	11
Criminal milieu	13	3	123	19	38	12
Robbery	12	3	58	9	23	8
Nonfelony related homicide						
Nightlife violence	23	5	22	3	31	10
Mental illness: Nonfamily	25	5	12	2	19	6
Sexual motive	1	0.2	18	3	1	0.3
Other	211	46	148	23	64	20
Total	458		631		318	

Table 18.3 Victim–offender relationship in homicides in Finland, the Netherlands, and Sweden in 2003–2006 (by victim).

Victim–offender relation	*Finland*		*The Netherlands*		*Sweden*	
	N	*Percentage*	*N*	*Percentage*	*N*	*Percentage*
Intimate partner/Ex-partner	109	23	124	28	87	28
Homosexual partner	3	1	5	1	1	0.3
Child	27	6	42	9	16	5
Parent	18	4	19	4	24	8
Sibling	4	1	8	2	5	2
Other relative	6	1	22	5	6	2
Acquaintance	257	54	191	43	129	41
Stranger	51	11	32	7	43	14
All valid cases	475	100	443	100	311	100
All cases	491		820		355	

Background characteristics of homicide victims in Finland, the Netherlands, and Sweden

During the period 2003–2006, a total of 1,666 victims were killed in the three countries, of which 820 were killed in the Netherlands, 491 in Finland, and 355 in Sweden. On average, the Netherlands has the highest number of homicide victims per year with 205 victims; Finland is second with 123 victims a year, whereas Sweden has the lowest number of homicide victims with an average of 89 a year. In all three countries over 60 percent of all homicide victims were male (Table 18.4). Over two-thirds of homicide victims were between the ages of 25 and 40 years, but the mean age of homicide victims in the Netherlands (37.4) was lower than those in Finland (42.1) and Sweden (41.5). Furthermore, although in all three countries most victims were born in the country where the homicide took place, Dutch victims were far more often born in a foreign country (43%) (especially in the Dutch Antilles, Surinam, Turkey, and Morocco) compared to Finland (4%) and Sweden (20%). In particular, this suggests an overrepresentation of foreign-born individuals among Dutch victims. The over-representation becomes more apparent when the population makeup of the countries is considered: in 2010, 11 percent of the Dutch population was born in a foreign country compared to 5 percent in Finland and 15 percent in Sweden (OECD 2016). However, given that the birth country of a relatively high percentage of the Dutch victims was unknown (45%), this finding should be treated with caution (Table 18.4).

Table 18.4 Background characteristics of homicide victims in Finland, the Netherlands, and Sweden (2003–2006).

Characteristics	*Finland*		*The Netherlands*		*Sweden*	
	N	*Percentage*	*N*	*Percentage*	*N*	*Percentage*
Sex						
Male	355	72	548	68	222	63
Female	136	28	260	32	133	38
Age						
≤17	30	6	82	10	23	7
18–24	38	8	91	11	41	13
25–39	139	29	301	38	92	28
40–64	249	51	265	33	133	40
≥65	35	7	61	8	40	12
Mean	42.1 (SD = 16.4)		37.4 (SD = 18.2)		41.5 (SD = 18.5)	
Birth country						
Native	461	96	256	57	229	80
Foreign-born	20	4	193	43	59	20

Background characteristics of homicide offenders in Finland, the Netherlands, and Sweden

In the period 2003–2006, a total of 1,917 homicide offenders were registered in the three countries; more than half of all offenders were Dutch (N = 1,022), a quarter were Finnish (N = 475), and approximately one-fifth were Swedish (N = 420). On average, with 256 offenders the Netherlands has the highest number of homicide offenders per year, followed by 119 in Finland and 105 in Sweden. As Table 18.5 shows, homicide offenders in all three countries were mainly male (approximately 90% in these countries). As regards age, Dutch offenders (31.9) were on average younger than Finnish (37.5) and Swedish offenders (34.7). Furthermore, in all three countries perpetrators of robbery homicide and nightlife violence were on average the youngest, while perpetrators of intimate-partner homicide were the oldest. In all three countries, the majority of homicide offenders were born in the same country as where the crime took place. However, as with victims, homicide offenders in the Netherlands were much more often (48%) born in a foreign country (especially in the Dutch Antilles, Surinam, Turkey, and Morocco) compared to Finnish (5%) and Swedish offenders (25%). Accordingly, an overrepresentation of foreign-born individuals also exists among Dutch offenders. But again, given that the birth country of a relatively high percentage of the Dutch offenders was unknown (38%), this finding should also be treated with caution.

Finally, Finnish homicide offenders were more often unemployed than Swedish offenders (51% vs 43%). However, care needs to be taken in interpreting these results, as the employment status was unknown for a relatively high percentage of Swedish offenders (35%) and is wholly lacking in the Dutch data.

Table 18.5 Background characteristics of homicide offenders in Finland, the Netherlands, and Sweden (2003–2006).

Characteristics	*Finland*		*The Netherlands*		*Sweden*	
	N	*Percentage*	*N*	*Percentage*	*N*	*Percentage*
Sex						
Male	413	89	778	90	340	89
Female	52	11	91	10	40	11
Age						
≤17	8	2	33	4	22	6
18–24	78	17	215	27	92	25
25–39	188	40	369	46	137	37
40–64	175	38	182	23	103	28
≥65	16	3	10	1	17	5
Mean	37.5 (SD = 13.0)		31.9 (SD = 11.3)		34.7 (SD = 14.8)	
Birth country						
Native	435	95	332	53	232	75
Foreign-born	23	5	301	48	78	25

Conclusion and Discussion

The aim of the EHM was to produce a first cross-national description of main similarities and differences in characteristics of homicides in Finland, Sweden, and the Netherlands. We found several differences and similarities. First of all, of the three countries studied, and for the period 2003–2006, Finland had the highest homicide rate whereas Sweden had the lowest with the Netherlands placed second. Further, the most common type of homicide in all three countries was domestic homicide, in particular intimate-partner homicide. However, homicides committed in the criminal milieu and sexual homicides were more common in the Netherlands than in the Nordic countries, and more robbery homicides took place in the Netherlands and in Sweden than in Finland. Most homicides in the Nordic countries occurred in a private setting whereas Dutch homicides more often took place in a public setting. In addition, in the Nordic countries, the most commonly used weapon to kill the victim was a sharp instrument whereas a firearm was the most commonly used weapon in the Netherlands. This result is remarkable in light of the fact that, at 5 percent, Dutch firearm ownership is among the lowest in Europe, with firearm ownership being far higher in Sweden (19%) and certainly in Finland (38%) compared to the Netherlands. In fact, Finnish firearm ownership is among the highest in the European Union (Van Dijk, Van Kesteren, and Smit 2007). The higher proportion of firearms in Dutch homicides may possibly relate to the fact that, in the Netherlands, homicides occurred more frequently in the criminal milieu than in the Nordic countries. Especially relevant in light of this result is a recent study by Ganpat, Van der Leun and Nieuwbeerta (2015) showing that certain immediate situational characteristics are particularly conducive to a lethal outcome, including firearm use by the offender and alcohol use by the victim. These findings make it all the more relevant to gather national data on the role of alcohol use in homicide cases, which is currently unavailable in the Netherlands, and to further invest in hindering access to (illegal) firearms in the Netherlands (Ganpat 2014). Furthermore, in the Netherlands and Sweden a much greater proportion of victims had an intimate or family relationship with the offender, whereas most homicide victims in Finland were acquaintances of the offender. Dutch homicide victims as well as offenders were on average younger than victims and offenders in the Nordic countries, and were also far more often born in a foreign country than their Finnish and Swedish counterparts. Finally, while no comparison was possible with the Netherlands, in homicide cases in the Nordic countries—most strikingly in Finland—the great majority of victims and/or offenders were under the influence of alcohol. The Finnish finding may be related to the country's exceptionally high alcohol consumption level, which is above the European Union average (OECD Heath Data 2010).

All in all, this study highlights the relevance of cross-national comparisons on lethal violence in Europe. Evidently, the EHM provides an important tool for improving systematic knowledge on the subject. Such comparisons help to distinguish important similarities and differences in homicide patterns between European countries and might help contribute in future to the prevention of and fight against the most serious crimes in Europe.

Although the EHM has made an important step forward in European cross-national research, this chapter also showed that some methodological issues still exist hampering cross-national comparison to some extent. In particular, the relatively large amount of missing and unknown values is an important issue to consider when improving the monitor. Another issue to take into account is that the legal definition of homicide was not completely identical given that assault leading to death is counted as homicide in both Finland and Sweden while disregarded under the homicide category of the Dutch Criminal Code (though this affects only a small percentage of cases). Also, as a consequence of recoding existing national categories, in some countries a relatively large proportion of the data was recorded under the category "other," causing diffusion of the figures when analyzing cross-national data. This was especially the case when coding the homicide subtype variable.

The EHM obviously does not preclude at all the possibility that it could be further expanded, refined, and improved. In fact, since this could further enhance the quality of the data, it is highly recommended. Seeing as only a small selection of the EHM variables were discussed here, the EHM offers rich potential for future research to address various issues of interest in the area of lethal violence. Filling an important void in European homicide research (which is striking when compared to the volume of cross-state comparative research in the USA), this effort has proven that constructing a joint European homicide database is possible, opening new doors for research in various domains of homicide. In order to understand cross-national differences in homicide patterns better, we therefore call for more cross-national homicide research in Europe, preferably using a unique internationally comparable homicide database similar to the EHM. Joining forces in this way should generate more systematic knowledge on lethal violence in Europe, which in turn may well contribute to reducing this most serious crime.

Notes

1 This chapter is largely based on two publications of the EHM research team, Ganpat *et al.* (2011) and Liem *et al.* (2013).

2 The EHM research team consists of Sven Granath and Johanna Hagstedt from the National Council for Crime Prevention in Sweden; Janne Kivivuori and Martti Lehti from the National Research Institute of Legal Policy in Finland; and Soenita Ganpat, Marieke Liem, and Paul Nieuwbeerta from the Institute for Criminal Law and Criminology at Leiden University in the Netherlands. The author would like to thank Sven Granath, Johanna Hagstedt, Janne Kivivuori, Martti Lehti, Marieke Liem, and Paul Nieuwbeerta for their efforts, collaboration, and dedication in making the EHM possible.

3 The work presented in this study has been funded and supported by the European Union.

References

Ganpat, S.M. (2014) Dead or alive? The role of personal characteristics and immediate situational factors in the outcome of serious violence. PhD thesis, Leiden University, Amsterdam: Ipskamp.

Ganpat, S.M., Granath, S., Hagstedt, J., *et al.* (2011) *Homicide in Finland, the Netherlands and Sweden: A First Study on the European Homicide Monitor Data.* Stockholm: Brottsförebyggande rådet/The Swedish National Council for Crime Prevention.

Ganpat, S.M. and Liem, M.C.A. (2012) Homicide in the Netherlands. In M.C.A. Liem and W.A. Pridemore (eds), *Handbook of European Homicide Research: Patterns, Explanations, and Country Studies* (pp. 329–342). New York: Springer.

Ganpat, S.M., Liem, M., Van der Leun, J., and Nieuwbeerta, P. (2014) The influence of criminal history on the likelihood of committing lethal versus nonlethal violence. *Homicide Studies*, 18: 221–240.

Ganpat, S.M., Van der Leun, J.P., and Nieuwbeerta, P. (2013a) The influence of event characteristics and actors' behaviour on the outcome of violent events: Comparing lethal with non-lethal events. *British Journal of Criminology*, 53: 685–704.

Ganpat, S.M., Van der Leun, J.P., and Nieuwbeerta, P. (2013b) Dead or alive? De invloed van incidentkenmerken en gedragingen van actoren op fatale versus niet-fatale uitkomsten van geweld. *Tijdschrift voor Criminologie*, 55: 259–277.

Ganpat, S.M., Van der Leun, J.P., and Nieuwbeerta, P. (2015) The relationship between a person's criminal history, immediate situational factors, and lethal versus non-lethal events. *Journal of Interpersonal Violence*. doi: 10.1177/0886260515593297.

Granath, S. (2012) Homicide in Sweden. In M.C.A. Liem and W.A. Pridemore (eds), *Handbook of European Homicide Research: Patterns, Explanations, and Country Studies* (pp. 405–420). New York: Springer.

Lehti, M. and Kivivuori, J. (2012) Homicide in Finland. In M.C.A. Liem and W.A. Pridemore (eds), *Handbook of European Homicide Research: Patterns, Explanations, and Country Studies* (pp. 391–404). New York: Springer.

Leistra, G., and Nieuwbeerta, P. (2003) *Moord en Doodslag in Nederland 1992–2001.* Amsterdam: Prometheus.

Liem, M.C.A., Ganpat, S.M., Granath, S., *et al.* (2013) Homicide in Finland, the Netherlands and Sweden: First findings from the European Homicide Monitor. *Homicide Studies*, 17: 75–95.

Liem, M.C.A. and Pridemore, W.A. (2012) Introduction. In M.C.A. Liem and W.A. Pridemore (eds), *Handbook of European Homicide Research: Patterns, Explanations, and Country Studies* (pp. 3–4). New York: Springer.

Nieuwbeerta, P. and Leistra, G. (2007) *Dodelijk Geweld: Moord en Doodslag in Nederland.* Amsterdam: Balans.

OECD (2016) Foreign-born population (indicator). OECD Data. Available online at https://data.oecd.org/migration/foreign-born-population.htm#indicator-chart (accessed September 13, 2016).

OECD Health Data (2010) www.ecosante.org/oecd.ht (accessed January 2, 2011).

Rying, M. (2007) *Trends in Lethal Violence against Women in Intimate Relationships* (vol. 6). Stockholm: Brå.

Smit, P.R., De Jong, R.R., and Bijleveld, C.C.J.H. (2012) Homicide data in Europe: Definitions, sources, and statistics. In M.C.A. Liem and W.A. Pridemore (eds), *Handbook of European*

Homicide Research: Patterns, Explanations, and Country Studies (pp. 5–23). New York: Springer.

Van Dijk, J., Van Kesteren, J., and Smit, P. (2007) *Criminal Victimisation in International Perspective: Key Findings from the 2004–2005 ICVS and EU ICS*. The Hague: WODC.

Van Os, R., Ganpat, S.M., and Nieuwbeerta, P. (2010) Moord en Doodslag in Nederland. In E.R. Muller, J.P. van der Leun, M. Moerings, and P. van Calster (eds), *Criminaliteit* (pp. 181–193). Deventer, Netherlands: Kluwer.

19

Homicide in Britain

Fiona Brookman, Helen Jones, and Sophie Pike

Introduction

Placed in the global context, homicide rates in Britain are among the lowest in the world. To illustrate, in 2014/2015 there were 9 offenses of homicide per million population in England and Wales and 11 offenses per million population in Scotland (Office for National Statistics (ONS) 2016; Scottish Government 2016), placing Britain well below many other industrialized nations, such as the United States (a rate of 47 per million) and many Eastern European Countries (where the rates generally range from 43 to 65 per million population; see Chapter 17, this volume). The British rate is comparable to other Western European countries such as France and Germany and similar to that experienced in Canada and Australia. Moreover, the homicide rate has been steadily declining since the early 2000s. Nevertheless, Britain experiences a diverse range of homicides including serial killing, terrorist attacks, gang shootings, masculine lethal confrontations, domestic homicide, and infanticide. In fact, the most prolific modern day serial killer ever identified operated in Britain: namely Dr Harold Shipman, responsible for the murder of over 200 of his patients over a 23 year period.

After a brief description of the British context, the legal framework of unlawful homicide and available data sources, the chapter describes historical and contemporary homicide trends, the characteristics of British homicide (offender, victim, and event characteristics), as well as explanations for, and responses to, this uniquely harmful crime. We end with some reflections on the state of knowledge of homicide in Britain and directions for future research.

The Handbook of Homicide, First Edition. Edited by Fiona Brookman, Edward R. Maguire, and Mike Maguire.

Understanding the British context

Great Britain is comprised of three countries, England, Wales, and Scotland and, together with Northern Ireland, forms the United Kingdom. In mid-2014, Britain's estimated population was 62.7 million, with significantly more people living in England (54.3 million) than Wales (3.1 million) or Scotland (5.3 million) and slightly more females (50.8%) than males (49.2%) (ONS 2015a). In 2011 the majority of people living in Britain (86.7%) described themselves as belonging to a white ethnic group, with a further 5.7 percent of the population describing themselves as Asian/Asian British (including Indian, Pakistani, Bangladeshi, or Chinese) and 3.1 percent describing themselves as black/African Caribbean/black British (ONS 2012).

The legal framework of homicide in Britain

In Britain the legal framework distinguishes between different types of homicide by virtue of their apparent seriousness. England and Wales share a common legal system, whereas Scotland has a somewhat different system based on Roman law. We deal here mainly with the law relating to England and Wales, highlighting any important distinctions in Scotland. Unlawful homicide is legally classified, in England and Wales, as murder, manslaughter, or infanticide. Each of these categories share a common *actus reus* (guilty act) but are distinguished by the extent to which the offender is deemed to have intended to cause the victim's death, that is, their *mens rea* (guilty mind). Unlawful homicide is covered by the Homicide Act 1957 and more recently by amendments under the Coroners and Justice Act 2009. Scottish law makes a similar distinction between murder and culpable homicide but does not make any special provision for infanticide.

The classic definition of murder is provided by Lord Chief Justice Coke from the early seventeenth century, "when a man of sound memory, and of the age of discretion, unlawfully killeth within any county of the realm any reasonable creature *in rerum natura* [i.e., in existence] under the King's peace, with malice aforethought" (Card 2014: 231).[1] The phrase "malice aforethought" is somewhat misleading though as a conviction for murder does not require ill-will or premeditation; although it can involve an intention to kill, it also includes an intention to cause grievous bodily harm. As the most serious category of unlawful homicide, murder carries a mandatory penalty of life imprisonment.

Manslaughter is commonly divided into the subgroups of "voluntary" and "involuntary," based on the defendant's intention at the time of the killing. Voluntary manslaughter comprises cases where the defendant had the intention to kill or cause grievous bodily harm but because of some defined mitigating circumstance (e.g., loss of self-control or diminished responsibility) the conviction is reduced to manslaughter. Alternatively, involuntary manslaughter refers to cases where there is no intention to kill or cause grievous bodily harm (Ormerod and Laird 2015) but the death was caused by the defendant's gross negligence or involvement in an unlawful or dangerous act (Crown Prosecution Service 2015). Scottish law makes a similar distinction between voluntary and involuntary culpable homicide.

Lastly, infanticide applies when a woman kills her own biological child, who is less than a year old, while suffering from some kind of psychological imbalance linked to childbirth (for example, postnatal depression). It includes a willful act or omission on behalf of the mother and is covered by the Infanticide Act 1938 as amended by the Coroners and Justice Act 2009. Infanticide is both a partial defense to murder (reducing it to voluntary manslaughter) and an offense in its own right, both carrying a maximum penalty of life imprisonment though often a noncustodial sentence is given. Scottish law makes no such provision for infanticide and women who kill their babies are charged with either murder or culpable homicide.

Although the legal categories of homicide are presented here as distinct entities, in reality "a very fine line divides 'murder' from 'accidents,' 'licensed killings' by law enforcers or euthanasia" (Croall 2011: 240). As Brookman has noted elsewhere (2005, 2010), the divide between acceptable and unacceptable killings is socially, historically, and culturally constructed and the laws governing homicide in Britain are the product of a complex legislative history, which some have argued are in need of complete reform (e.g., Law Commission 2006).

British homicide data sources

Most of what is known about the overall patterns, trends, and characteristics of homicide in Britain comes from government statistical publications. The Home Office collects and collates homicide data for England and Wales (based on police reported data for the 43 police forces across England and Wales) and maintain it in their Homicide Index database.[2] In a similar manner the Scottish Government collate details of homicides that occur in Scotland.[3] We draw upon each of these sources in this chapter in order to provide an overview of the extent and nature of homicide in Britain. In addition, when considering explanations for, and responses to homicide, we draw upon research conducted by academics in Britain and beyond, in order to illuminate the complexity of homicide and the nuanced responses that have evolved over the years.

Historical and Contemporary Trends in Homicide

As illustrated in Figure 19.1 below, there was a steady increase in the number of homicides recorded by police in England and Wales from the mid-1960s, with this increase accelerating in the mid-1990s. This was then followed by a downward trend from the early 2000s. The data show a dramatic spike in 2002/2003, with over 950 homicides recorded. However, this peak is almost wholly artificial—the result of 172 homicides attributed to the serial killer Harold Shipman being coded to this one-year period. Shipman was convicted in January 2000 of murdering 15 of his patients

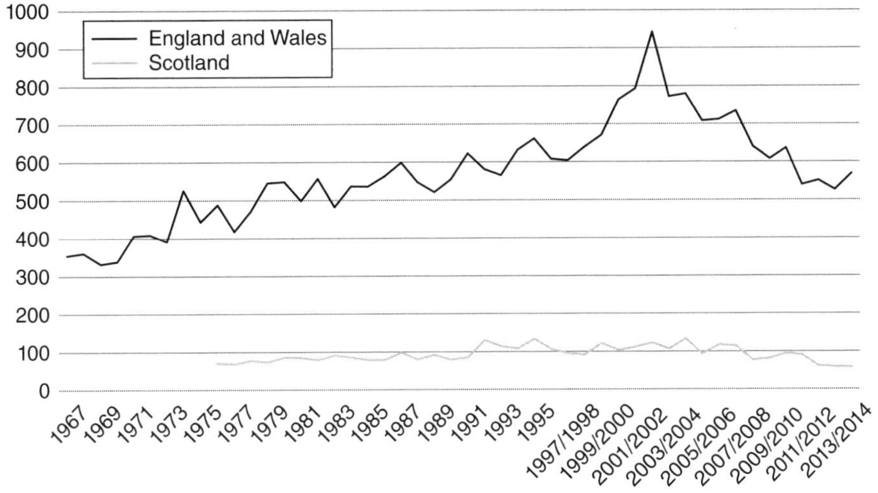

Figure 19.1 Number of homicides in Britain, 1967–2014. Sources: These figures were compiled from Home Office and Scottish Government Homicide statistics and personal communication with the Scottish Government (Scottish data were only available from 1976).

while he was a general practitioner in Greater Manchester but the independent public inquiry identified a total of 215 victims believed to have been killed over an estimated 23-year period (Smith 2002). Most of these additional homicides were recorded by Greater Manchester Police in 2002/2003 and thus appear in the 2002/2003 homicide figures (see Smith 2002). The vast majority of Shipman's victims were elderly females whom he mainly killed by administering lethal doses of morphine and diamorphine and so, for 2002/2003 the proportion of female homicide victims is unusually elevated, as is death by poisoning (Cotton and Bibi 2005). Overall, the offenses attributable to Shipman artificially inflated the homicide rate by 20 percent during 2002/2003. Other events of note include 58 Chinese nationals who collectively suffocated in a lorry en route to the United Kingdom (recorded 2000/2001), 20 cockle pickers who drowned in Morecambe Bay (recorded 2003/2004) and 52 victims of the July 7th London bombings (recorded in 2005/2006).

Although the number of homicides experienced in Scotland is much lower than in England and Wales (due to its comparative size) the overall pattern of increases and decreases is broadly similar. Homicide in Scotland has fallen by one third in the past ten years (Scottish Government 2016).

Homicide rates provide a clearer picture of patterns over time and regional differences in exposure to homicide. As illustrated in Figure 19.2 below, Scotland persistently has a higher rate of homicide than England and Wales (i.e., note that the graph lines have now reversed when compared to Figure 19.1 above). Since the early 2000s the homicide rate has been on a continual declining trajectory in England and Wales with rates now close to those as far back as the mid-1970s. The picture in Scotland is a little more uneven, with several peaks and troughs. The most dramatic of these

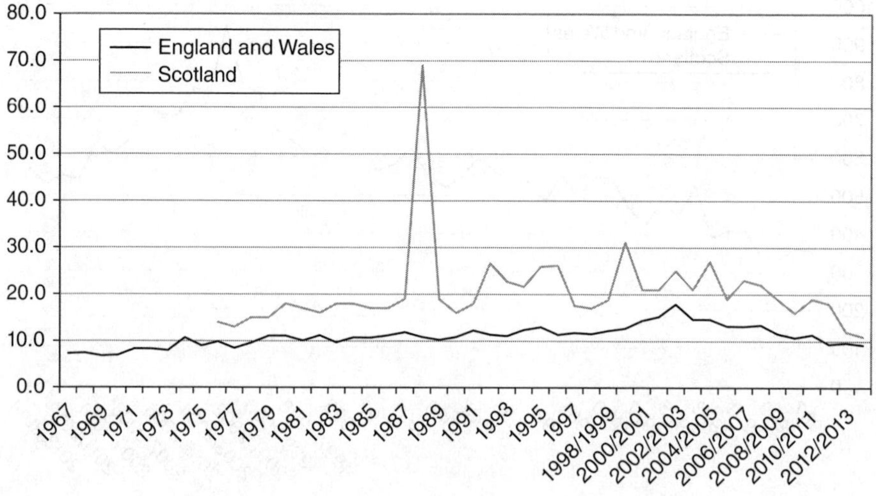

Figure 19.2 Homicide victimization rates in Britain per million population, 1967–2015.

is the large spike in 1988. This peak is attributable to the large number of victims (270) who were killed during the *Lockerbie bombing* when Pan Am flight 103 was destroyed by a terrorist bomb over the town of Lockerbie, Scotland, killing 243 passengers, 16 crew, and 11 people on the ground (AAIB 1990). Nevertheless, the general trend observed elsewhere in Britain, of increases in homicide up to the early 2000s, followed by decreases, is also found in Scotland.

Certain parts of Britain experience much greater exposure to homicide than others. It is generally the case that urban areas experience higher rates of homicide than rural areas and some of the larger conurbations experience rates up to four times higher than more rural areas. For example, higher homicide rates are found in Merseyside (18.7), Greater Manchester (12.4), and London (11.8) compared with Durham (3.2), Wiltshire (4.3), and Devon and Cornwall (7) (see ONS 2016, appendix, table 2.20). In Scotland, Glasgow City has the highest proportion of all homicide cases (24% of the Scottish total in 2014/2015), which is more than double its share of the population (11% of the Scottish population) (Scottish Government 2016).

International comparisons

Comparative analysis of homicide statistics needs to be approached cautiously due to differences in legal definitions of homicide across countries and differences in the criteria adopted to collect and record homicide. There is some evidence that variations in crime reporting rates are strongly related to measures of institutional stability and police presence (Soares 2004) and the political will to accurately present such statistics (see Chapter 25, on the misrepresentation of homicide statistics in Russia, and Chapter 26 for a similar discussion on China, both in this volume).

Table 19.1 Homicide Rates per 100,000 population, selected countries of the world, 2012 or latest data (ranked in order high to low).

Country	*Rate*	*Country*	*Rate*
El Salvador	66.0	Iraq	2.0
Jamaica	52.1	Canada	1.8
Zambia	38.0	Cyprus	1.7
South Africa	33.8	Hungary	1.4
Colombia	33.4	France	1.4
Bahamas	28.0	United Kingdom	1.2
Mexico	18.1	China	1.1
Russian Federation	11.2	Germany	0.8
USA	5.0	Switzerland	0.7
Sri Lanka	4.6	Austria	0.5
Turkey	3.3	Japan	0.5
Afghanistan	2.4	Iceland	0.3

Source: Adapted from Eurostat Homicide statistics (http://ec.europa.eu/eurostat), ONS (2015b: 25) and global homicide study (UNODC 2014: 24). The global average homicide rate stood at 6.2 per 100,000 at 2012 (UNODC 2014: 12).

There are also numerous difficulties in explaining homicide trends. For example, despite a proliferation of lethal weapons in developing countries since the 1960s, the lethality of assaults has decreased due to developments in medical technology and care (Krause, Muggah, and Wennmann 2008). With these caveats in mind, Table 19.1 above provides an overview of homicide rates for selected countries of the world. The British rate is less than one-fifth of the global average (1.2 per 100,000 population, compared to 6.2) and only a small fraction of the rate in some African and Central or South American countries.

Characteristics of British Homicide

This section will outline the defining characteristics of homicide in Britain. The sociodemographic characteristics of offenders and victims will be presented before the features of the homicide event are explored.

Sociodemographic characteristics of offenders and victims

Gender In Britain, as in many other countries, males dominate as offenders and victims of homicide. Figures for the year ending March 2015 indicate that 90 percent of homicide suspects in England and Wales were male and 9 percent were female (ONS 2016).[4] Males also dominate as victims of homicide, comprising 64 percent of the total and females making up the remaining 36 percent. Interestingly, the number of male victims reported in the current statistics is the lowest since 1996 (ONS 2016).

In Scotland, the gender of homicide suspects is virtually identical to that in the rest of Britain; 91 percent of homicide suspects were male and 9 percent were female in 2014/2015. However, in Scotland males comprise a greater proportion of victims than in England and Wales with over three quarters of victims being male and the remaining 24 percent female (Scottish Government 2016).

Age Infants aged below one year face the highest levels of victimization in Britain of any one-year age group. In England and Wales their victimization rate was 35.8 offenses per million population in 2015 (ONS 2016). Thus, despite comprising just 1 percent of the population, 4 percent of homicide victims were under the age of one (ONS 2016). The equivalent victimization rate in Scotland was 53 offenses per million population (Scottish Government 2016).

With the exception of those aged under one year it is young adults that generally experience the highest levels of victimization. The latest statistics reveal that in England and Wales those aged 20–49 years old constituted a disproportionately large number of victims when compared to their presence in the population (ONS 2016). Particularly, adults aged 20–24 were the five-year age group most likely to fall victim to homicide in 2015, comprising 11 percent of victims, followed by those aged 40–44 and 45–49, each comprising 10 percent of victims (ONS 2016). The statistics also reveal that young males are at the greatest risk: although the proportion of males in the population aged 20–24 was 7 percent, they accounted for 12 percent of homicide victims (ONS 2016). By comparison, females aged 20–24 comprised 7 percent of the population and 8 percent of victims (ONS 2016). Similarities are evident in Scotland where the victimization rate for males peaks for those aged 21–30 (Scottish Government 2016).

Race/ethnicity Black people and Asians are overrepresented as victims of homicide in England and Wales when compared to their numbers in the population. Data are not available on ethnicity and homicide for Scotland.

Between 2011/2012 and 2013/2014 the rate of homicide for black victims was four times higher than it was for white victims and the rate for Asian victims was 1.5 times higher than for white victims (Ministry of Justice 2015). Offenders most often kill those belonging to the same ethnic group (see Table 19.2). For example, during this time period, 94 percent of white suspects killed someone belonging to the same

Table 19.2 Ethnic appearance of suspects by ethnicity of principal suspect in England and Wales 2011/2012 to 2013/2014.

Ethnic appearance of victim	*Ethnicity of principal suspect*			
	White	*Black*	*Asian*	*Other*
White	94%	33%	25%	30%
Black	2%	53%	10%	12%
Asian	3%	10%	60%	9%
Other	1%	4%	5%	48%

Source: Adapted from Ministry of Justice (2015).

ethnic group, 60 percent of Asian suspects killed an Asian victim, and 53 percent of black suspects killed a black victim (Ministry of Justice 2015).

Victim–offender relationship In Britain, individuals are more likely to be killed by someone known to them than by a stranger, which contrasts with popular media portrayals of homicide. However, there are significant gender differences here (see Figure 19.3). Women are most likely to be killed by a partner or former partner: in 2014/2015, 44 percent of female homicide victims in England and Wales were killed by a partner or ex-partner. This compares to just 6 percent of all male victims of homicide (ONS 2016). Conversely, 32 percent of males were killed by a friend or acquaintance and 31 percent by a stranger, whereas just 8 percent of females were killed by a friend or acquaintance and 12 percent by a stranger (ONS 2016).

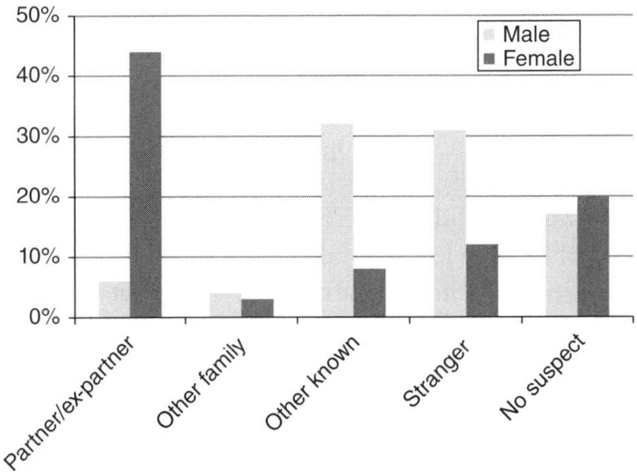

Figure 19.3 Victim–offender relationships for England and Wales year ending March 2015. Adapted from ONS (2016).

A similar pattern is evident in Scotland. In 2014/2015, 78 percent of homicides involved individuals who were known to one another (Scottish Government 2016). Figures for the last ten years show that over half of female victims in Scotland were killed by either a partner or ex-partner (53%). The proportion of females killed by an acquaintance or stranger was considerably lower, 26 percent and 8 percent respectively. The picture in respect of males is also comparable to England and Wales: 62 percent were killed by an acquaintance, 18 percent by a stranger, and just 7 percent by a partner or ex-partner (Scottish Government 2016).

Features of the homicide event

Temporal and spatial patterns Most homicides in Britain occur within a home or dwelling. Unlike Scotland, England and Wales only recently began to record information about location. The data reveal that 56 percent of homicides occurred within a home or dwelling, followed by 19 percent that took place on a street, footpath, or alleyway and 6 percent in other outdoor spaces (ONS 2016). Females are more likely to be killed within the home, that is, 82 percent compared to 49 percent of males (ONS 2016)—perhaps unsurprising given that we know that the majority of female victims are killed in the context of intimate-partner homicide. In Scotland also the majority of homicides take place within the home and females are more likely to be killed here. Notably, the recent homicide statistics for Scotland show that the number of homicides that take place within the home has increased and the number occurring outside has decreased (Scottish Government 2016).

Information pertaining to temporal patterns of homicide is unfortunately not recorded in official data in Britain. Brookman (2000) found that of 95 homicides in England and Wales, almost one third (31%) occurred between midnight and 4 a.m. with a further 29 percent taking place between 8 p.m. and midnight. Evidence suggests that these patterns are connected, in part at least, to spontaneous violence that occurs on "a night out" where the consumption of alcohol and/or drugs forms part of the context of the growing British night-time economy (Tomsen 1997; Winlow 2010).

Drugs and alcohol Information on drug and alcohol-related homicide was released for the first time in England and Wales in statistics published in 2016. The publication cautions that this particular data "have not been subject to the same level of quality assurance with police forces as other variables" (ONS 2016: 27).

For the two year period ending March 2015, a third of homicide victims were reported to have been under the influence of alcohol and/or illicit drugs at the time of the homicide: 24 percent had been drinking alcohol, 3 percent had been taking an illicit drug, and 7 percent were under the influence of both (ONS 2016). The number of male victims under the influence of drugs and/or alcohol outweighed the number of females: 44 percent of male victims were under the influence of alcohol and/or drugs compared to 14 percent of female victims (ONS 2016). Scotland, by contrast, has recorded the drug and alcohol levels for suspects and victims since 2000. In 2014/2015, 38 percent of homicide suspects had consumed alcohol and/or drugs at the time that the offense was committed: of these 14 percent had consumed alcohol, 3 percent had taken drugs, and 21 percent were under the influence of both substances (Scottish Government 2016).

Other independent research studies have revealed significantly higher levels of drug and/or alcohol-related homicide in Britain. For example, Miles (2012) examined drug and alcohol-related homicides in England and Wales combining Homicide Index (HI) data, police murder files, and offender interview data. She discovered that 67 percent of the 60 cases examined through police file analysis and interviews were categorized as intoxication-related, compared to just 18 percent of the HI cases. Of these, 48 percent involved alcohol intoxication, 45 per cent involved alcohol and drug intoxication, and 7 per cent involved drug-only intoxication, implicating alcohol as a fundamental factor in fatal violence.

Method of homicide The dominant methods of killings in Britain have remained consistent over many decades, with a sharp instrument being the most prevalent means (ONS 2016; see Figure 19.4). In England and Wales a sharp instrument was

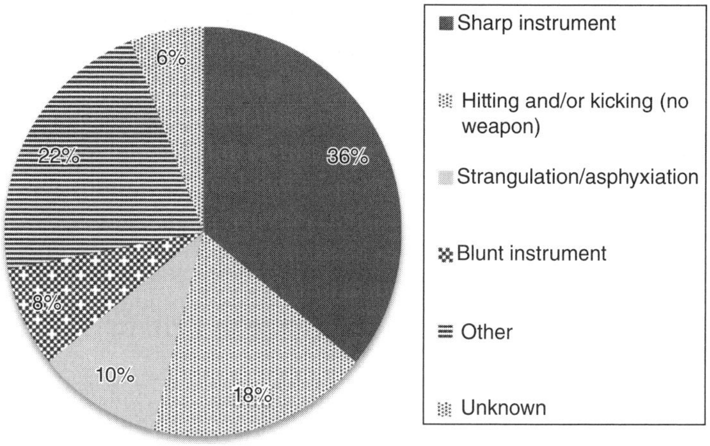

Figure 19.4 Method of killing for England and Wales, year ending March 2015. Adapted from ONS (2016).

used in 36 percent of all homicide cases in 2014/2015. The second most common method was hitting and/or kicking without a weapon (18%). Just 4 percent of victims were killed as a result of a shooting, a figure which was the lowest since 1980. Other methods recorded included strangulation or asphyxiation (10%), blunt instrument (8%), poisons or drugs (5%), motor vehicle (2%), burning (2%), drowning (1%), and in 6 percent of cases the method was unknown (ONS 2016). The second most common method differs when gender is considered. Specifically, after stabbings, males in England and Wales are most likely to be killed by hitting and/or kicking, whereas females are most likely to be killed by strangulation or asphyxiation (ONS 2016).

In Scotland the number of homicides perpetrated using a sharp instrument has persistently been higher than across the rest of Britain. In 2014/2015 the figure stood at 56 percent. Hitting and/or kicking was the second most prevalent method at 17 percent. Once again, very few homicides were carried out with a firearm (less than 5%) (Scottish Government 2016). The more prevalent use of sharp instruments in Scottish homicides links to longstanding concerns around the so-called knife-carrying culture in Scotland. In a study examining homicide in Scotland between 1981 and 2003, Leyland (2006) found that the increases during this period were largely attributable to an increase in homicides using knives and other sharp objects.

Circumstances or motive for homicide Official data on offense circumstances or motive for homicide provide only a rudimentary sense of the circumstances surrounding these lethal events or the factors that may have motivated offenders to act violently. Data for Britain reveal that around 50 percent of homicides occurred following a fight or quarrel as a result of a revenge attack or following a loss of temper (ONS 2016; Scottish Government 2016). In England and Wales, 7 percent of homicides were categorized as "irrational" acts, 4 percent were committed during the commission of a theft or other gain, and the motive was unknown in 17 percent of cases (ONS 2016).

In reality, homicide is rather more complex in terms of the range of motives involved and how it unfolds in the moment, as will become apparent when we explore explanations of homicide and, later, responses to different forms of homicide.

Understanding Homicide in Britain

It is not possible, in one chapter, to consider all potential explanations for homicide—given its diversity and the different levels at which theories operate (see Chapter 1, this volume). Here we focus upon theories that (1) are particularly pertinent to understanding two of the most prevalent forms of homicide in Britain (masculine lethal confrontations and domestic homicide) and (2) have not been covered in detail elsewhere in this *Handbook*. To these ends we focus upon cultural and situational explanations (with particular attention, in the latter, to recent research on the role of emotion and violence). We, of course, recognize the importance of the broader structural factors that can set the conditions for (lethal) violence to emerge and, in some cases, flourish, that is, structural disadvantage, poverty, discrimination, and so forth (see Brookman 2010; see also Chapter 1, Chapter 5, Chapter 21, and Chapter 24, all in this volume).

Cultural explanations

Cultural theorists focus upon the ideas and values that particular groups hold and how these can generate involvement in crime. The basic premise of such theories is that violent individuals share beliefs that are conducive to the use of force and violence when insulted or challenged due to an exaggerated sense of honor, courage, and manliness (Wolfgang and Ferracuti 1967). Research in this area has flourished with various criminologists exploring "codes of the street" (Anderson 1999) and how these codes demand violent responses to interpersonal confrontation and retaliation for certain (often trivial) infractions (Brookman *et al.* 2011; Garot 2010). These accounts provide rich descriptions of the circumstances under which such violence is approved or even demanded and, to varying degrees, acknowledge that such cultures are formed as a result of the marginalization of certain sections of society—hence the critical link between structural factors and the development of violent street cultures (e.g., see Bernard 1990).

There is evidence in Britain that a sizable proportion of homicides among young males can be explained by the existence of such cultural codes. For example, Brookman (2003) found that many of the men in her study of homicide in England and Wales killed in defense of masculine honor (whether during spontaneous confrontations or planned revenge killings). In keeping with Polk's (1994) Australian based research, she observed that these men tended to be young and relatively powerless (i.e., working class and often unemployed) and that their displays of masculine power in defense of honor seemed to be related to their marginalized status. As Lindegaard discovered in South Africa, men who killed other men who had challenged them in public gained street capital and status among peers involved in street culture (see Chapter 28, this volume). In the United States, Wilkinson (2001) found that among young people involved in street culture, excessive forms of violence such as homicides were found to provide more street capital than less excessive forms such as assaults and robberies. Of course, violent subcultures come in various forms, some being closely tied to specific activities such as drug taking or distribution or the consumption of alcohol (e.g., see Chapter 25, this volume, on drinking cultures and homicide in Russia).

Cultural explanations are also relevant for understanding domestic homicide and, perhaps most especially, so-called honor killings. As Gill (Chapter 9, this volume) notes, in honor cultures, aggression is an acceptable reaction to insults and threats to honor, and intra-familial honor killings embody the most extreme form of such aggression. To illustrate, Arin (2001) studied femicide in Turkey and discovered that the most trivial of acts, such as strolling alone in town or requesting a love song on the radio could tarnish a female's "virgin" status rendering them "unclean" and leading their whole family to be dishonored. As Arin (2001: 823) explains: "these beliefs are so powerful that families are prepared to sacrifice the life of one of their female members to restore their honour and standing in the eyes of others."

The murder of Banaz Mahmod in England in 2006 exemplifies the persistence of such powerful cultural beliefs across time and international borders. Originally born in Iraqi Kurdistan in 1985, Banaz and her family moved to the United Kingdom in 1995. Banaz married in 2003 following arrangements made by her father, but two years later she left her husband and returned to her family. She subsequently formed a new relationship which was deemed unsuitable and was considered to have brought shame on her family. On January 25, 2006 her boyfriend reported her missing and on April 29, 2006 her body was discovered in a suitcase buried in a garden in Birmingham. In June 2007, Banaz's father, uncle, and another distant male relative were convicted of her murder.

Although honor killings are less prevalent in Britain than many other countries (figures suggest there are around 12 honor killings each year, though it is acknowledged that this is likely to be an underestimate; House of Commons 2008), the broad ideology that supports such extreme views and behaviors can be found, in watered down form, in other domestic homicides.

Research on domestic homicide more generally has consistently found that the themes of separation, possessiveness, and jealousy characterize many situations of intimate-partner femicide (see Websdale 2010; James and Daly 2012). Dobash and Dobash (2011) examined the case files of 104 men convicted of murdering an intimate partner in Britain and found that the relationships were characterized by conflict, abuse, and controlling behavior as well as jealousy and possessiveness in which men used violence to enforce rigid standards based on their beliefs about relationships between intimate partners. Dobash, Dobash, and Cavanagh (2009) found that even so-called conventional British men (with no prior criminal records and who were often in employment) held negative views about the victim, were possessive and jealous, and failed to feel empathy for the victim. Their research challenged the notion that such killings came "out of the blue."

In summary, research in Britain has illustrated that violence against women, including homicide, is almost invariably underpinned by patriarchal belief systems (see Dobash and Dobash 2015; see also Chapter 8, this volume). As Britain becomes ever more culturally diverse, it is quite possible that we will need to attune our cultural theories further in order to provide more nuanced understandings of how different groups acquire subcultural codes of violence and how these are enacted in different situations.

Situational explanations

Wolfgang's (1958) classic study of homicide in Philadelphia, and notably his assertion that over a quarter of the homicides he examined were victim-precipitated, paved the way for a body of work within criminology that focused upon the interactional dynamics of violent situations. This work has been partly guided by symbolic interactionism that stresses the role of situational identities or self-images in interaction (e.g., Becker 1962; Toch 1969; Athens 1997) as well as a broader body of criminological research on the micro-environment of crime. The latter, for example, includes studies of the interactional dynamics of offenders, victims, and third parties (Luckenbill 1977; Polk 1994; Collins 2008), the lethality of situations dependent upon the availability of weapons (Felson and Steadman 1983), the role of temporal and spatial factors (Ganpat, Van der Leun, and Nieuwbeerta 2013), and work on adversary effects (the perceived threat of the opposition; see Felson and Painter-Davis 2012). What the two approaches (interactionist and situational) acknowledge is that homicide is (often) a dynamic and evolving event where the "actors" involved interpret and mold each other's decision-making and behavior.

One recent Dutch study serves as a useful illustration as the authors compared several event characteristics and actors' behavior in lethal versus nonlethal events and examined the extent to which these factors influenced the likelihood of a lethal outcome. In terms of event characteristics, Ganpat, Van der Leun, and Nieuwbeerta (2013) found that in lethal events it was more likely that offenders carried a firearm, that there were no third parties present or, if present, third parties had no ties with either offender or victim, and that victims were under the influence of alcohol. Alcohol use by offenders did not influence the likelihood of a lethal versus nonlethal outcome. In terms of actors' behavior, they discovered that offenders of lethal events were more likely to have displayed or used a firearm and that victims who died were more likely to have precipitated the event than those who survived. These findings, while useful, do not allow us to understand why particular factors impacted in particular ways. Research of a qualitative nature has helped to illuminate these issues. For example, Stretesky and Pogrebin (2014) conducted in-depth interviews with inmates in the United States convicted of gang-related gun violence and discovered that all 22 viewed "the streets" as fraught with danger. This fear, combined with a desire to display power, ensured that they armed themselves and were willing to use their weapons. It is to a further consideration of the role of emotions, such as fear, in the etiology of (lethal) violence that we now turn.

Emotion and the homicide moment What is telling from the aforementioned discussion is the extent to which various powerful emotions feature in different kinds of homicides. Yet the role of emotion within homicide has rarely been explored by criminologists. There are, however, some notable exceptions, that we explore below. Although none of this research specifically relates to Britain, the lessons drawn from it are undoubtedly relevant to the British context.

Researchers have distinguished between expected emotions (i.e., predictions about the emotional consequences of one's actions/behavior) and immediate emotions (experienced at the time of the event) (see Loewenstein and Lerner 2003) as well as a broad range of emotions (for a review see Brookman 2015).

In addition to primary emotions such as anger and fear (to which we return shortly) moral emotions such as shame and humiliation have been identified as predominant features in violent offenders' accounts of their behavior. For example, Gilligan (2000) found that homicide and violent offenders identified being "disrespected" or "ridiculed" as a key trigger for their violence as it engendered feelings of shame and humiliation. Shame has also been identified as the dominant emotion propelling offenders to commit familicide (Websdale 2010) and multiple homicide (Scheff 2011). For example, Scheff (2011) suggests that, together with social isolation, shame, embarrassment, and humiliation result in an emotional chain reaction that leads individuals to decide to commit multiple murder.

Hull (2001) conducted in-depth interviews with 12 men who had planned to commit an act of workplace homicide (or serious violence),[5] but then decided against this course of action. Her work reveals how a range of primary and moral emotions impact upon offenders' behavior. Hull discerned five disinhibitor themes (i.e., cognitive or emotional factors) that moved the would-be perpetrators toward the decision to commit fatal or serious violence. The most frequently described of these was what Hull termed "*victim stance/restorative revenge*" described as feelings of shame, disrespect, or embarrassment due to the provocateur's words or actions and a belief that the only way to restore a sense of power or respect is to avenge the individual.

Five inhibitors were also identified: (1) "*fear of consequences to self*" (e.g., a shift away from the belief that they will not get caught); (2) "*fear of consequences to others*" (extend their consideration of consequences to how others will be hurt by their proposed actions—mainly family or friends); (3) "*viewed self as better*" (after consideration, come to conclude that they were above or beyond such behavior—a moral engagement mechanism that allowed the individual to refrain from violence and still feel intact emotionally); (4) "*found safer, lesser form of revenge*" (this lesser form of revenge still allowed them to know that they had taken action toward reinstating self-respect and power); (5) "*forgave or reinterpreted*" (actively decided not to take revenge or decided that the provocateur did not mean to be as insulting as previously assessed). Time appeared to play an important function in that some respondents were able to feel less enraged as time distanced them from the incident.

In a similar manner, Athens (1980, 1997) analyzed the accounts of violent offenders, focusing upon the interpretations they made of situations in which they committed violent acts as well as those situations in which they *almost* committed such acts. The emotions of fear, anger, and hatred played an important role in these offenders' violent actions. For example, some offenders (labeled as "*physically defensive*") interpreted the victim's behavior as constituting a physical attack, generating a grave sense of fear for self or other. On those occasions when these same individuals *almost* resorted to violence they formed a "restraining judgment," escaping the tunnel vision that characterized the violent events and redefining the situation as not requiring violence. There were various reasons for the change of interpretation, such as perceiving that the attack would fail, fear of jeopardizing an important intimate or social relationship, deference to the other person, or fear of legal sanctions.

It is notable that the emotion of fear, while more prevalent in restraining both Hull's and Athens's violent offenders, also led some to commit violent acts (i.e., Athens's physically defensive category). Collins (2008) argues that "confrontational tension and fear" are the emotional states from which violence stems. Specifically, he suggests that tension and fear have to be overcome in order for violence to unfold, as he puts it: "no matter how motivated someone may be, if the situation does not unfold so that confrontational tension/fear is overcome, violence will not proceed" (Collins 2008: 20).

Most recently, Lindegaard (2010) unraveled how fear and thrill influenced young male killers in South Africa, before, during, and after the homicide. Through her ethnographic research in Cape Town she discovered that the young men who had killed interpreted the emotions of excitement and fear as occurring at different times in the process of killing. None of the youngsters described being afraid of their opponent either before or during the killing. In fact, the only kind of fear described during these two stages was the (ultimate) victims' fear of the killer; and this fear from the opposition was described as thrilling. Excitement was also associated with committing ruthless acts and crossing moral boundaries. The role of these two emotions was, however, far from clear cut. For example, while the killers did not fear their victims, they felt indifferent toward them and experienced an overwhelming bodily feeling of "being warm" and "in love with oneself" when enacting the violence, this state of moving to the "dark side" was described as both thrilling and terrifying. After committing the violent act, all of the young men were overwhelmed by confusion and other people's fear of their proven ability to kill was experienced as traumatic. Lindegaard's detailed work perfectly illustrates the complex and shifting nature of emotions in and around the homicide moment.

In conclusion, recent years have seen the emergence of research on emotion and violence that has injected renewed energy into our understanding of the foreground of homicide. As Brookman (2015) has suggested previously, there is much work still to be done within criminology to unpack more carefully how a range of positive and negative emotions (experienced at the time of the crime or anticipated beforehand) propel or repel would-be-offenders in the direction of lethal violence.

Responding to Homicide

Given the diverse nature of homicide, space does not permit a detailed discussion of all strategies implemented in Britain to prevent or reduce it, or a full evaluation of their effectiveness. Instead, this section will focus briefly on three homicide types that were identified earlier as contributing significantly to the overall homicide figures in Britain: domestic homicide, infanticide, and alcohol-related homicide in the context of the night-time economy (NTE).

Domestic homicide

Domestic homicide includes a broad range of relationships (see ONS 2016). However, the focus here will be limited to homicides committed against females by a current or former spouse, cohabitant, or sexual partner. This section will include responses to domestic violence in general but will be limited to criminal justice and multi-agency responses.

In March 2016 the British government produced its strategy "Ending violence against women and girls" (HM Government 2016). Since its previous strategy, set in 2010, a number of new legislative measures were introduced: that is, stalking became a specific offense, coercive and controlling behavior became recognized as a form of domestic abuse, and domestic violence protection orders (DVPO) and the domestic violence disclosure scheme (Clare's Law) were introduced. There have also been shifts in how the police respond to domestic violence, with the adoption of policies that require officers to take "positive action" and conduct risk assessments with victims utilizing the DASH (Domestic Abuse, Stalking and Honour Based Violence) risk identification tool (Maguire, Brookman, and Robinson, in press). However, there are still opportunities for improvements. In their review of police forces, HMIC (2015) found there were difficulties in identifying repeat victims, inconsistent awareness of coercive and controlling behavior, and limited application of DVPOs.

Central to the response to domestic violence in the British context has been the development of a multi-agency approach. For example, over the last ten years, SafeLives (2015) have trained more than 1800 independent domestic violence advisors (IDVAs) and set up 288 multi-agency risk assessment conference (MARAC) teams. IDVAs work with victims to provide advice and support, and can have a measurable improvement on victims' safety (Howarth and Robinson 2016). MARACs are multi-agency meetings where information is shared between statutory and voluntary agencies (such as the police, probation, IDVAs, children's services, health, and housing) about high-risk victims of domestic abuse, and a coordinated action plan is produced with the aim of improving victim safety. A national review by Steel, Blakeborough, and Nicholas (2011) found that 97 percent of practitioners and stakeholders believed MARACs to be effective. Specialist domestic violence courts (SVDCs) have also been introduced and have improved support for victims, made information-sharing easier, and improved victim participation and satisfaction (Cook *et al.* 2004).

One specific response to domestic homicide has been the introduction of domestic homicide reviews (DHRs) in England and Wales, mandated under the Domestic Violence, Crime and Victims Act 2004 (see Payton, Robinson and Brookman, in press). The purpose of a DHR is to identify lessons that can be learned following a domestic homicide and in doing so prevent domestic homicides and improve services for all domestic violence victims and children (Home Office 2013). Although a reduction in deaths is one of the stated aims of many DHRs, no review has yet reported any actual reduction (Bugeja *et al.* 2015). Recently, HMIC (2015) noted that opportunities to learn from DHRs are still being missed and that learning needs to be disseminated more swiftly and effectively.

The British Government's 2016–2020 domestic violence strategy is based on four areas and draws many of the above themes together: preventing violence and abuse, provision of services, partnership working, and pursuing perpetrators (HM Government 2016). To prevent violence and abuse, professionals will be supported to identify and deal with signs of abuse at the earliest opportunity. Alongside this, the strategy aims to educate, inform, and challenge young people; the new campaign "Disrespect Nobody" (www.disrespectnobody.co.uk) builds teenagers' awareness of healthy relationships, abuse, and consent with the aim of preventing the onset of domestic violence in adults. The government aims to deliver a secure future for services such as rape support centers and refuges, with the aim of early intervention and prevention rather than crisis response. Perpetrators will also be pursued by harnessing new technology, for example, police officers using body-worn cameras to collect best evidence.

Infanticide

The term "infanticide" is used here to include the killing of an infant less than one year old regardless of the perpetrator. Brookman and Maguire (2005) identified four preventative strategies that were most prevalent in Britain: parental education, improvements in diagnoses and identification of infant and child abuse, more coordinated responses to suspected abuse cases, and improved services to parents both before and after childbirth. Some of these strategies will be discussed here.

Education programs are based on the premise that deaths may be reduced by lowering the incidence of infant maltreatment. The World Health Organization (2014) notes that parenting education programs and home visiting programs can prevent or reduce child maltreatment. To illustrate, the NSPCC campaign, "Coping with Crying," acknowledges that brain damage caused by shaking is a major cause of death for abused children and recognizes the importance of educating parents about the risks of head injuries and providing them with practical advice. The focus of the campaign is a short film shown to parents during pregnancy or just after they have returned home with their new baby. The film is shown by professionals who work with babies, including midwives, health visitors, and children's center workers. Parents also receive a leaflet with further information. Following promising results of a pilot version of this scheme in 2011, this campaign will be rolled out nationally in 2016 (Richards 2015).

By identifying and diagnosing child abuse early, and ensuring a coordinated response, further harm may be mitigated. In 2015, Her Majesty's Government (HM Government) published guidance around safeguarding and promoting the welfare of children, highlighting the need for all professionals who come into contact with children and families to be involved in the process and to adopt a coordinated approach. The importance of effective multi-agency working is highlighted by Ofsted (2010) who evaluated 147 serious case reviews (SCRs)[6] from 2009–2010 and noted inadequate practice related to poor communication, failure to include key professionals or agencies, and ineffective meetings.

The importance of early identification, management, and treatment of perinatal mental illness has also been recognized (see, for example, Hogg 2013). NICE (2014) provides guidance for healthcare professionals in relation to antenatal and postnatal mental health, and recommends that a series of depression identification questions are asked at a woman's first contact with primary care and during the early postnatal period.

Lastly, preventing or reducing neonaticides (where pregnancies are often denied and hidden from view) is particularly challenging. Ali and Paddick (2009: 647) note that "There is a paucity of quality research addressing undetected pregnancy, which has resulted in the problems associated with this issue being unrecognized and unaddressed in policy statements." Similar concerns were raised by the SCR into the death of Baby W, which highlights that there is no prescribed typology of women most at risk of concealed/denied pregnancies (Davies 2015). Baby W was killed by a tissue blocking his airway. His mother, who was 16 years old at the time, had concealed/denied her pregnancy and given birth alone in her bedroom. She pleaded guilty to infanticide but the SCR highlighted that, unusually, no concerns had been raised about her or her family and she did not present as a vulnerable young person.

Alcohol-related homicide and the night-time economy

There is little research that focuses on preventing alcohol-related *homicide* but strategies which reduce or prevent alcohol-related *violence* are likely to be of relevance (Brookman and Maguire 2005). The focus here will be on targeting "at-risk" premises and managing city centers, reducing alcohol consumption, and minimizing the level of harm that results from violent incidents.

It is not the case that all pubs and clubs attract violence, rather towns and cities contain a number of "hot spots" where establishments are associated with a disproportionate number of violent incidents, together with a larger number of relatively unproblematic premises (Brookman and Maguire 2005). Many towns and cities in Britain now have initiatives like the pioneering Tackling Alcohol-Related Street Crime (TASC) project in Cardiff (Maguire and Nettleton 2003), which involve partnership-working between the police, county council, local hospital and representatives of pub and club owners and managers. In 2014, 20 areas across England and Wales were established as local alcohol action areas, where different agencies work together to reduce alcohol-related crime and disorder and the negative health impacts caused by alcohol (Home Office 2014). There are also industry-led initiatives that tackle crime and disorder, and underage sales, including partnerships, like Pubwatch and Best Bar None (Portman Group 2015), and voluntary groups, like Street Pastors, who provide assistance to people on an evening out (www.streetpastors.org.uk). Although these initiatives have not been formally evaluated, there is evidence that multi-agency programs which include the community, staff training, and law enforcement, can reduce harms (Boiler *et al.* 2011).

Alongside multi-agency initiatives, there has been a move toward statutory regulation. Guidance has been revised under the Licensing Act 2003 that permits licensing authorities to issue early morning alcohol restriction orders to prohibit the sale of alcohol for a specified time period between 12 a.m. and 6 a.m., and to use public spaces protection orders (as part of the Anti-Social Behaviour Crime and Policing Act 2014) to restrict the drinking of alcohol in a public space (Home Office 2015). The guidance also acknowledges "cumulative impact," the impact that a significant number of licensed premises may have on an area, and lists mechanisms for controlling this including: provision of CCTV, planning control, confiscation of alcohol, issuing fixed penalty notices for disorder and anti-social behavior, and prosecutions for the offense of selling alcohol to a person who is drunk. However, the Alcohol Health Alliance (2013) argues that although licensing has focused on pubs and clubs, it has overlooked shops and supermarkets and the problem of "preloading," where customers get drunk on cheap, shop-bought alcohol before going out at night.

A number of approaches have been taken to reduce alcohol consumption. Based on the premise that affordability is related to increased consumption, the WHO (2009) and the Alcohol Health Alliance (2013) argue that raising alcohol prices will lower consumption and its associated harms. However, neither group advocate this strategy alone and identify other measures such as regulating the availability of alcohol, community interventions to improve drinking environments, the prohibition of alcohol advertising, and early identification and support for people with alcohol problems. Maguire, Brookman, and Robinson (in press) also point to broader preventative approaches that target the social and cultural roots of alcohol-related harms. For example, Alcohol Concern (www.alcoholconcern.gov.uk)

and DrinkAware (www.drinkaware.co.uk) offer advice and support with the aim of changing problematic drinking habits.

Given that not all violent incidents are likely to be prevented, it is appropriate to consider measures which minimize the level of harm from such incidents. One strategy is to use safer drinking vessels. Research conducted in Lancashire, England found that the introduction of polycarbonate glasses within licensed venues reduced the number of glass-related injuries (Anderson *et al.* 2009). Similar findings were also reported by Forsyth (2008) who conducted an observational study in Glasgow, Scotland, and found that the severity of injuries can be greatly reduced by a 100 percent glass-free environment.

A final strategy for reducing homicide concerns the response by emergency services and applies not only to alcohol-related violence but to any violent incident where the victim does not die immediately. Although very little research has explored the role of emergency medical treatment in preventing serious assaults becoming homicides in Britain, research from other countries (see, for example, Harris *et al.* 2002) suggests this warrants further attention.

Homicide is a difficult offense to prevent, not least because of its relative infrequency, diversity, and apparently low predictability (Brookman and Maguire 2005). For example, there are still no statistically reliable risk factor tools to identify which victims of domestic violence will become victims of domestic homicide. The same is true for child victims of abuse in the home. Hopefully future research will help to refine risk factor tools and ultimately our ability to prevent such lethal events.

Conclusions

Homicide rates in Britain are relatively low in global perspective and have been decreasing since the early 2000s. It is not clear why the homicide rate has been in decline though this is a trend evident across many other countries of the world including the United States, Canada, Japan, and many parts of Western Europe. Certainly it is feasible that improvements in medical care combined with the growth of various multi-agency initiatives to prevent and reduce (lethal) violence may have contributed to the downward trends.

Many of the basic patterns that characterize British homicide have remained consistent over recent history. For example, males have consistently comprised over 90 percent of offenders and the majority of victims (around 70%) are also male. Sharp instruments continue to be the weapon of choice, followed by physical attacks without weapons, and firearms rarely feature in homicide. Most victims (and especially females) are killed by somebody that they know.

Unlike some other countries of the world (e.g., Russia, India, China, and, to some extent, Canada), homicide statistics are routinely collected and published in Britain and researchers can sometimes gain access to the raw data (e.g., the Homicide Index) to conduct independent analyses. That said, the data are limited in various ways. Notably, no information is disseminated on the socioeconomic status of victims or offenders, information on circumstance is vague and rudimentary, and data on temporal and spatial patterns are not released in England and Wales. Further, the accuracy of the Homicide Index is questionable.

Homicide comes in numerous guises. Understanding why around 600 people die each year in Great Britain as the result of unlawful homicide (as indeed do almost half a million people worldwide, UNODC 2014) is not a simple task. At the outset, it requires disaggregating homicide into conceptually meaningful subtypes. More detailed independent research studies are required in order to illuminate the causes of homicide and the potential to prevent these events.

Notes

1 Coke's original definition referred to the individual dying from their injuries within a year and a day but this was amended by the Law Reform (Year and a Day Rule) Act 1996.
2 Since 2011/2012 the data have been passed to the Office for National Statistics (ONS) who are now responsible for producing an annual statistical bulletin—"Focus on: Violent Crime and Sexual Offences."
3 Scottish homicide statistics present the number of homicide cases. A single case of homicide is counted for each homicide event, irrespective of the number of victims or accused (Scottish Government 2016: 1). In contrast, homicide data for England and Wales is based on the number of victims.
4 The other 1 percent relates to two corporate manslaughter cases (ONS 2016).
5 Workplace homicide/violence in this context referred to a planned act (though ultimately aborted) of lethal or serious violence against one or more individuals working at, or otherwise present at, the workplace of the offender. Generally this referred to co-workers and bosses.
6 "Serious case reviews are local enquiries into the death or serious injury of a child where abuse or neglect is known or suspected to be a factor" (Ofsted 2010: 4).

References

AAIB (Air Accident Investigation Branch) (1990) *Report on the Accident to Boeing 747–121, N739PA at Lockerbie, Dumfriesshire, Scotland on 21st December 1998*. Aircraft Accident Report 2/90. Department of Transport. London: HMSO.

Alcohol Health Alliance (2013) *Health First: An Evidence-based Alcohol Strategy for the UK*. Stirling: University of Stirling. Available online at https://www.stir.ac.uk/media/schools/management/documents/Alcoholstrategy-updated.pdf (accessed April 19, 2016).

Ali, E. and Paddick, S. (2009) An exploration of the undetected or concealed pregnancy. *British Journal of Midwifery*, 17(10): 647–651.

Anderson, E. (1999) *Code of the Street: Decency, Violence and the Moral Life of the Inner City*. New York: W.W. Norton.

Anderson, Z., Whelan, G., Hughes, K., and Bellis, M. (2009) *Evaluation of the Lancashire Polycarbonate Glass Pilot Project*. Liverpool: Liverpool John Moores University. Available online at http://www.cph.org.uk/wp-content/uploads/2012/08/evaluation-of-the-lancashire-polycarbonate-glass-pilot-project.pdf (accessed April 18, 2016).

Arin, C. (2001) Femicide in the name of honour in Turkey. *Violence Against Women*, 7(7): 821–825.

Athens, L.H. (1980) *Violent Criminal Acts and Actors: A Symbolic Interactionist Study*. London: Routledge & Kegan Paul.

Athens, L.H. (1997) *Violent Criminal Acts and Actors Revisited*. Chicago: University of Illinois Press.

Becker, E. (1962) Anthropological notes on the concept of aggression. *Psychiatry*, 23: 328–338.

Bernard, T.J. (1990) Angry aggression among the truly disadvantaged. *Criminology*, 28(1): 73–96.

Boiler, L., Voorham, L., Monshouwer, K., *et al.* (2011) Alcohol and drug prevention in nightlife settings: A review of experimental studies. *Substance Use and Misuse*, 46: 1569–1591.

Brookman, F. (2000) Dying for control: Men, murder and sub-lethal violence in England and Wales. Unpublished PhD, Cardiff University.

Brookman, F. (2003) Confrontational and grudge revenge homicides in England and Wales *The Australian and New Zealand Journal of Criminology*, 36(1): 34–59.

Brookman, F. (2005) *Understanding Homicide*. London: SAGE.

Brookman, F. (2010) Homicide. In F. Brookman, M. Maguire, H. Pierpoint, and T. Bennett (eds), *Handbook on Crime* (pp. 217–244). Cullompton, England: Willan.

Brookman, F. (2015) "Killer" decisions: The role of cognition and affect and "expertise" in homicide. *Aggression and Violent Behavior*, 20: 42–52.

Brookman, F., Bennett, T., Hochstetler, A., and Copes, H. (2011) The "code of the street" and the generation of street violence in the UK. *European Journal of Criminology*, 8: 17–31. doi: 10.1177/1477370810382259.

Brookman, F. and Maguire, M. (2005) Reducing homicide: A review of the possibilities. *Crime, Law and Social Change*, 42: 325–403.

Bugeja, L., Dawson, M., McIntyre, S., and Walsh, C. (2015) Domestic/family violence death reviews: An international comparison. *Trauma, Violence and Abuse*, 16(2): 179–187.

Card, R. (2014) *Card, Cross and Jones Criminal Law*. Oxford: Oxford University Press.

Collins, R. (2008) *Violence: A Micro-sociological Theory*. Oxford: Princeton University Press.

Cook, D., Burton, M., Robinson, A., and Vallely, C. (2004) *Evaluation of Specialist Domestic Violence Courts/Fast Track Systems*. Available online at https://www.cps.gov.uk/publications/docs/specialistdvcourts.pdf (accessed April 12, 2016).

Cotton, J. and Bibi, N. (2005) Homicide. In D. Povey (ed.), *Crime in England and Wales 2003/2004. Supplementary Volume I: Homicide and Gun Crime*. London: Home Office.

Croall, H. (2011) *Crime and Society in Britain*. Harlow, England: Pearson Education.

Crown Prosecution Service (2015) Homicide: Murder and manslaughter. Available online at http://www.cps.gov.uk/legal/h_to_k/homicide_murder_and_manslaughter/(accessed March 17, 2016).

Davies, C. (2015) *Serious Case Review: Baby W Overview Report*. Available online at http://www.westsussexscb.org.uk/wp-content/uploads/SCR-W-Overview-Report.pdf (accessed April 8, 2016).

Dobash, R.E. and Dobash, R.P. (2011) What were they thinking? Men who murder an intimate partner. *Violence Against Women*, 17: 111–134.

Dobash, R.E. and Dobash, R.P. (2015) *When Men Murder Women*. New York: Oxford University Press.

Dobash, R.E., Dobash, R.P., and Cavanagh, K. (2009) "Out of the blue." Men who murder an intimate partner. *Feminist Criminology*, 4(3): 194–225.

Felson, R.B. and Painter-Davis, N. (2012) Another cost of being a young black male: Race, weaponry, and lethal outcomes in assaults. *Social Science Research*, 41: 1241–1253.

Felson, R.B. and Steadman, H.J. (1983) Situational factors in disputes leading to criminal. *Violence Criminology*, 21: 59–74.

Forsyth, A. (2008) Banning glassware from nightclubs in Glasgow (Scotland): Observed impacts, compliance and patron's views. *Alcohol and Alcoholism*, 43(1): 111–117.

Ganpat, S.M., Van der Leun, J., and Nieuwbeerta, P. (2013) The influence of event characteristics and actors' behaviour on the outcome of violent events. *British Journal of Criminology*, 53: 685–704.

Garot, R. (2010) *Who You Claim: Performing Gang Identity in Schools and on the Streets*. New York: NYU Press.

Gilligan, J. (2000) *Violence: Reflections on Our Deadliest Epidemic*. London: Jessica Kingsley.

Harris, A., Thomas, S., Fisher, G., and Hirsch, D. (2002) Murder and medicine. The lethality of criminal assault 1960–1999. *Homicide Studies*, 6(2): 128–166.

HM Government (2015) *Working Together to Safeguard Children: A Guide to Inter-Agency Working to Safeguard and Promote the Welfare of Children*. Available online at https://www.gov.uk/government/uploads/system/uploads/attachment_data/file/419595/Working_Together_to_Safeguard_Children.pdf (accessed April 12, 2016).

HM Government. (2016) *Ending Violence Against Women and Girls: Strategy 2016–2020*. Available online at https://www.gov.uk/government/uploads/system/uploads/attachment_data/file/505961/VAWG_Strategy_2016-2020.pdf (accessed April 8, 2016).

HM Inspectorate of Constabulary (2015) *Increasingly Everyone's Business: A Progress Report on the Police Response to Domestic Abuse*. Available online at http://www.justiceinspectorates.gov.uk/hmic/wp-content/uploads/increasingly everyones-business-domestic-abuse-progress-report.pdf (accessed April 13, 2016).

Hogg, S. (2013) *Prevention in Mind. All Babies Count: Spotlight on Perinatal Mental Health*. Available online at https://www.nspcc.org.uk/globalassets/documents/research-reports/all-babies-count-spotlight-perinatal-mental-health.pdf (accessed April 18, 2016).

Home Office (2013) *Multi-Agency Statutory Guidance for the Conduct of Domestic Homicide Reviews*. Available online at https://www.gov.uk/government/uploads/system/uploads/attachment_data/file/209020/DHR_Guidance_refresh_HO_final_WEB.pdf (accessed April 13, 2016).

Home Office (2014) Local alcohol action areas. Available online at https://www.gov.uk/government/uploads/system/uploads/attachment_data/file/278742/LAAAs.pdf (accessed April 18, 2016).

Home Office (2015) *Revised Guidance Issued Under Section 182 of the Licensing Act 2003*. https://www.gov.uk/government/uploads/system/uploads/attachment_data/file/418418/182-Guidance2015.pdf (accessed April 18, 2016).

House of Commons Home Affairs Committee (2008) *Domestic Violence, Forced Marriage and "Honour"-based Violence*. Sixth report of session 2007–08. London: HMSO.

Howarth, E. and Robinson, A. (2016) Responding effectively to women experiencing severe abuse: Identifying key components of a British advocacy intervention. *Violence Against Women*, 22(1): 41–63.

Hull, J. (2001) Identifying cognitions that influence decisions to engage in or refrain from acts of workplace homicide. PhD Thesis, Walden University.

James, B. and Daly, M. (2012) Cohabitation is no longer associated with elevated spousal homicide rates in the United States. *Homicide Studies*, 16(4): 393–403.

Krause, K., Muggah, R., and Wennmann, A. (2008) *Global Burden of Armed Violence*. Geneva: Geneva Declaration Secretariat.

Law Commission (2006) *Murder, Manslaughter and Infanticide*. London: TSO. Available online at http://www.lawcom.gov.uk/wp-content/uploads/2015/03/lc304_Murder_Manslaughter_and_Infanticide_Report.pdf (accessed April 7, 2016).

Leyland, A. (2006) Homicides involving knives and other sharp objects in Scotland, 1981–2003. *Journal of Public Health*, 28(2): 145–147.

Lindegaard, M.R. (2010) Moving to the "Dark side": Fears and thrills in Cape Town, South Africa. *Ethnofoor*, 21: 35–62.

Loewenstein, G. and Lerner, J.S. (2003) The role of affect in decision making. In R.J. Davidson, K.R. Scherer, and H.H. Goldsmith (eds), *Handbook of Affective Sciences*. Oxford: Oxford University Press.

Luckenbill, D.F. (1977) Criminal homicide as a situated transaction. *Social Forces*, 25: 176–186.

Maguire, M., Brookman, F., and Robinson, A. (in press) Violent crime. In N. Tilley and A. Sidebottom (eds), *Handbook of Crime Prevention and Community Safety* (2nd edn). London: Routledge.

Maguire, M. and Nettleton, H. (2003) *Reducing Alcohol-Related Violence and Disorder: An Evaluation of the "TASC" Project*. Home Office Research Study 265. London: Home Office.

Miles, C. (2012) Intoxication and homicide: A context-specific approach." *British Journal of Criminology*, 52: 870–888.

Ministry of Justice (2015) *Statistics on Race and the Criminal Justice System 2014*. Available online at https://www.gov.uk/government/uploads/system/uploads/attachment_data/file/480250/bulletin.pdf (accessed April 3, 2016).

NICE (National Institute for Health and Care Excellence) (2014) Antenatal and postnatal mental health: Clinical management and service guidance. Available online at https://www.nice.org.uk/guidance/cg192 (accessed April 12, 2016).

Office for National Statistics (2012) Statistical bulletin: 2011 Census: Key statistics for England and Wales, March 2011. Available online at http://www.ons.gov.uk/peoplepopulationandcommunity/populationandmigration/populationestimates/bulletins/2011censuskeystatisticsforenglandandwales/2012-12-11#ethnic-group (accessed April 7, 2016).

Office for National Statistics (2015a) Statistical bulletin: Annual mid-year population estimates: 2014. Available online at http://www.ons.gov.uk/peoplepopulationandcommunity/populationandmigration/populationestimates/bulletins/annualmidyearpopulationestimates/latest (accessed April 7, 2016).

Office for National Statistics (2015b) Focus on: Violent Crime and Sexual Offences, 2013/14. Available online at http://www.ons.gov.uk/peoplepopulationandcommunity/crimeandjustice/compendium/focusonviolentcrimeandsexualoffences/2015-02-12 (accessed April 17, 2016).

Office for National Statistics (2016) Focus on: Violent crime and sexual offences, year ending March 2015. Available online at https://www.ons.gov.uk/peoplepopulationandcommunity/crimeandjustice/compendium/focusonviolentcrimeandsexualoffences/yearendingmarch2015 (accessed April 3, 2016).

Ofsted (2010) Learning lessons from serious case reviews 2009–2010. Available online at https://www.gov.uk/government/publications/ofsted-learning-lessons-from-serious-case-reviews-2009-2010 (accessed April 12, 2016).

Ormerod, D. and Laird, K. (2015) *Smith and Hogan's Criminal Law*. Oxford: Oxford University Press.

Payton, J., Robinson, A., and Brookman, F. (in press). Domestic homicide reviews in the UK. In M. Dawson (ed.) *Domestic Homicide and Death Reviews: An International Perspective*. Palgrave Macmillan.

Polk, K. (1994) *When Men Kill: Scenarios of Masculine Violence*. Cambridge: Cambridge University Press.

Portman Group (2015) Local alcohol partnerships. Available online at http://www.portmangroup.org.uk/docs/default-source/recruitment-jds/local-alcohol-partnerships-.pdf?sfvrsn=0 (accessed April 18, 2016).

Richards, P. (2015) "Coping with crying": An innovative new programme to support positive parenting and prevent child abuse. *International Journal of Birth and Parent Education*, 2(4): 29–32.

SafeLives. (2015) Getting it right first time. Available online at http://www.safelives.org.uk/sites/default/files/resources/Getting%20it%20right%20first%20time%20-%20complete%20report.pdf (accessed April 13, 2016).

Scheff, T.J. (2011) Social–emotional origins of violence: A theory of multiple killing. *Aggression and Violent Behavior*, 16, 453–460.

Scottish Government. (2016) Homicide in Scotland 2014–15. Available online at http://www.gov.scot/Publications/2015/09/8172/downloads#res486224 (accessed April 22, 2016).

Smith, J. (2002) *First Report of the Shipman Inquiry. Volume One: Death Disguised*. Norwich: Crown.

Soares, R.R. (2004) Crime reporting as a measure of institutional development. *Economic Development and Cultural Change*, 52: 851–871.

Steel, N., Blakeborough, L., and Nicholas, S. (2011) *Supporting High-risk Victims of Domestic Violence: A Review of Multi-agency Risk Assessment Conferences (MARACs)*. Research Report 55. Available online at https://www.gov.uk/government/uploads/system/uploads/attachment_data/file/116537/horr55-report.pdf (accessed April 18, 2016).

Stretesky, P.B. and Pogrebin, M.B. (2014) Gang-related gun violence: Socialization, identity, and self. In P. Cromwell and M.L. Birzer (eds), *In Their Own Words: Criminals on Crime*. New York: Oxford University Press.

Toch, H. (1969) *Violent Men: An Inquiry into the Psychology of Violence*. Chicago: Aldine.

Tomsen, S. (1997) A top night: Social protest, masculinity and the culture of drinking violence. *The British Journal of Criminology*, 37(1): 90–102.

UNODC (2014) *Global Study on Homicide 2013*. Vienna: United Nations.

Websdale, N. (2010) *Familicidal Hearts: The Emotional Styles of 211 Killers*. New York: Oxford University Press.

Wilkinson, D.L. (2001) Violent events and social identity: Specifying the relationship between respect and masculinity in inner-city youth violence. *Sociological Studies of Children and Youth*, 8: 235–269.

Winlow, S. (2010) Violence in the night-time economy. In F. Brookman, M. Maguire, H. Pierpoint, and T. Bennett (eds), *Handbook on Crime* (pp. 331–350). Cullompton, England: Willan.

Wolfgang, M. (1958) *Patterns in Criminal Homicide*. Montclair, NJ: Patterson Smith.

Wolfgang, M.E. and Ferracuti, F. (1967) *The Subculture of Violence: Towards an Integrated Theory in Criminology*. London: Tavistock.

World Health Organization (2009) Preventing violence by reducing the availability and harmful use of alcohol. Available online at http://www.who.int/violence_injury_prevention/violence/alcohol.pdf (accessed April 13, 2016).

World Health Organization (2014) Child maltreatment. Fact sheet no. 150. Available online at http://www.who.int/mediacentre/factsheets/fs150/en/(accessed April 19, 2016).

20

Homicide in Canada

Myrna Dawson

Introduction

It has been argued that, compared to other Westernized countries, Canada has lower rates of violence (Gurr 2009) and, when compared to rates of violence in the United States, the "peaceable kingdom" thesis is arguably easier to believe. A brief example underscores this point. In 2013, the Canadian homicide rate was 1.44 per 100,000, its lowest point since 1966, compared to the US homicide rate which was 4.7 per 100,000—over three times higher than Canada (Cotter 2014: 4). To explain these varying rates, some have identified Canada's perceived distinct culture; that is, "Canadians supposedly have greater respect for authority than citizens of the United States, have less tolerance for individual and group deviance from community norms, and are more disposed to give the state primary responsibility for maintaining social order" (Gurr 2009: xxxii; see also Hagan 1984). In short, Canada is portrayed as the peaceable kingdom. However, when comparing Canada to countries with which it has arguably more in common than primarily proximity, this "peaceable" existence is more easily challenged. Canada's homicide rate is higher than the majority of similar countries, ranking fifth highest among those compared (see Figure 20.1). Therefore, the peaceable (or not) context in which Canadians live depends upon who is looking and from where. It also depends on whose experiences are being examined because, as will be discussed below, Aboriginal[1] Canadians and some urban black populations face homicide risks many times higher than other Canadians. Below, after a brief description of the Canadian context, its legal

The Handbook of Homicide, First Edition. Edited by Fiona Brookman, Edward R. Maguire, and Mike Maguire.

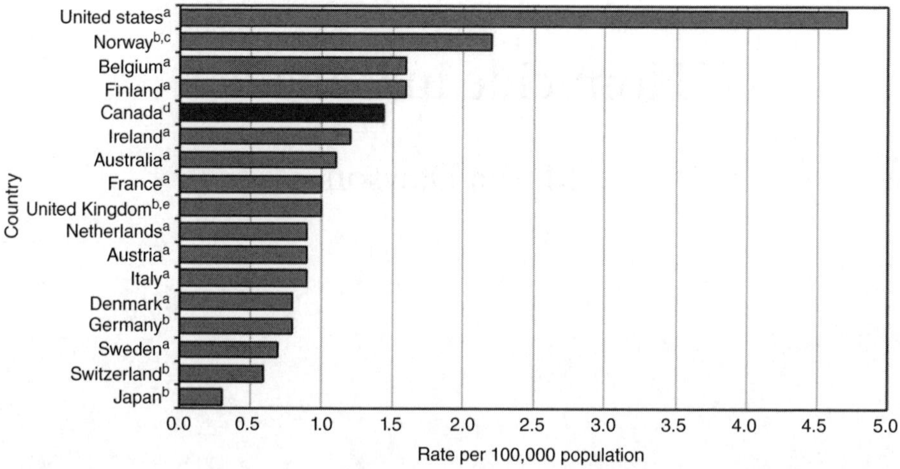

Figure 20.1 Homicides by peer countries in most recent years. (a) Figures reflect 2012 data. (b) Figures reflect 2011 data. (c) Includes homicides committed during the Utoya Island mass shooting in July 2011. From 2001 to 2010, Norway's annual homicide rate fluctuated between 0.6 and 1.1 per 100,000 population. (d) Figures reflect 2013 data. (e) Includes England and Wales. Note: Peer countries were determined using a methodology developed by the Conference Board of Canada. The Conference Board of Canada began by selecting countries deemed "high income" by the World Bank, then eliminated countries with a population less than one million, as well as countries smaller than 10,000 square kilometers. Of the remaining countries, the Conference Boards of Canada used a five-year average of real income per capita and eliminated any countries that fell below the mean. Based on these criteria, a total of 17 countries remained. Source: Statistics Canada and United Nations Office on Drugs and Crime. Reproduced with the permission of Statistics Canada.

framework surrounding homicide, and available data sources, the chapter describes historical and contemporary homicide trends and patterns as well as priorities for future research.

Understanding the Canadian Context

Canada is officially a bilingual country (English and French) comprised of 10 provinces and three territories representing four regions: Western Canada (British Columbia, Alberta, Manitoba, Saskatchewan), Central Canada (Ontario, Quebec), Atlantic Canada (Newfoundland/Labrador, New Brunswick, Nova Scotia, Prince Edward Island), and Northern Canada (Northwest Territories, Nunavut, Yukon). In 2014, Canada's estimated population was 35.5 million with slightly more women than men (Statistics Canada 2014). More than 60 percent of its residents live in the two most populous provinces (Ontario and Quebec). Slightly more than 80 percent of the population lives in urban areas (although this varies across the nation) with the three largest urban centers (e.g., Toronto, Vancouver, and Montréal) totaling about one-third of the population (35%; Statistics Canada 2014). Similar to other

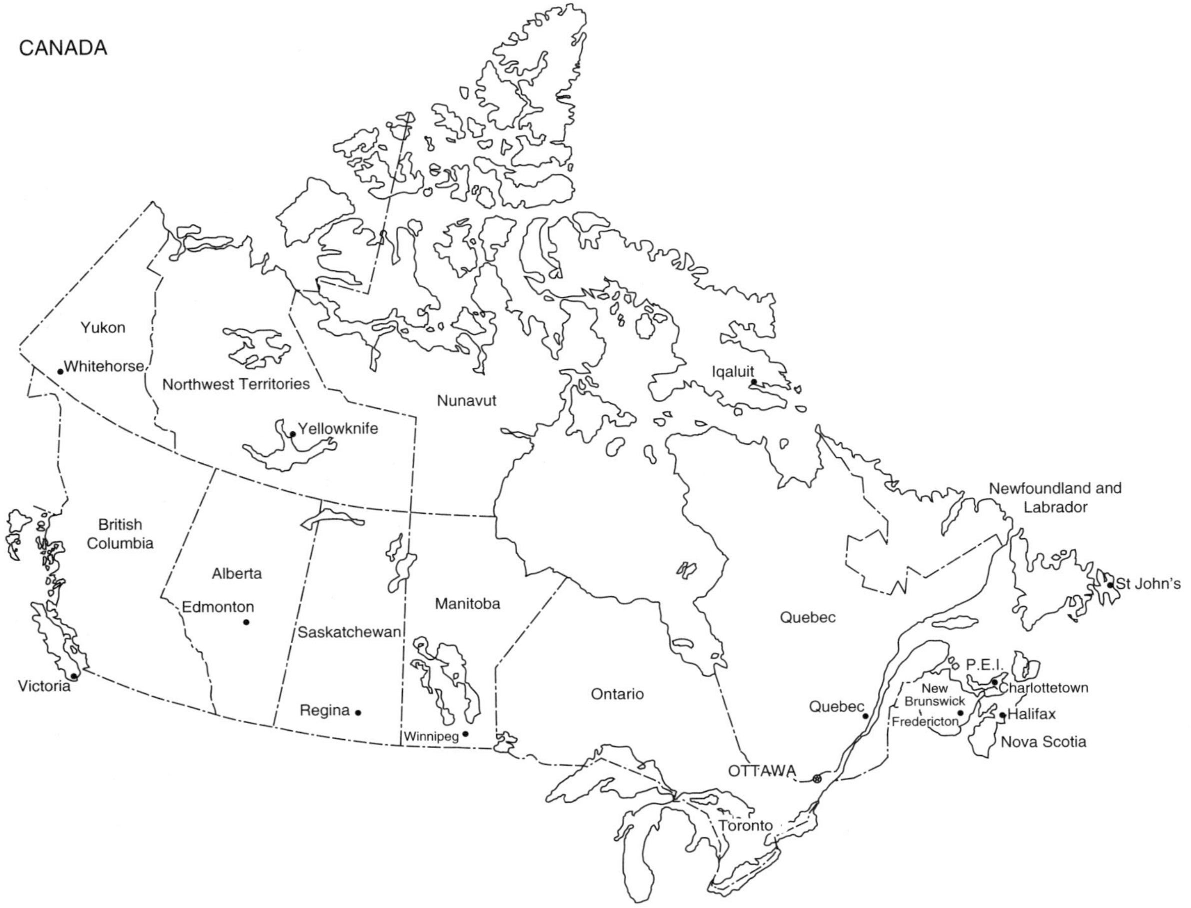

Figure 20.2 Canada. St Catharines Downtown [computer file] (no date) St Catharines, Ontario: Brock University Map, Data & GIS Library. Available: Brock University Map, Data & GIS Library Controlled Access (https://brocku.ca/maplibrary/maps/outline/local/stcathDT.jpg, accessed April 27, 2010).

developed countries, Canada has been moving toward an older population with declines in people of working age. In 2014, for example, almost 16 percent of the population was aged 65 and older compared to less than 10 percent in the early 1980s. These numbers are expected to jump to more than one-fifth of the population in less than 20 years (Statistics Canada 2014). For the first time, the proportion of those aged 55 to 64—a time when many begin to exit the workforce—now exceeds those aged 15 to 24 (Statistics Canada 2015).

In 2011, Canada had one of the highest proportions of foreign-born populations (20.6%), the largest group of new immigrants arriving from Asia (57%) and settling in the largest urban centers (Statistics Canada 2013a). As such, Canada is seen as an ethnically diverse nation with over 200 ethnic origins reported in 2011 (Statistics Canada 2013a). Aboriginal Canadians, the country's first inhabitants, represent just over four percent of the total population and include First Nations (the largest proportion), Métis, and Inuits (Statistics Canada 2013b). The Aboriginal population is growing faster than the general population, increasing by about 20 percent between 2006 and 2011. The provinces/territories with the highest proportion of Aboriginal peoples are (in order) Nunavut, the Northwest Territories, Yukon, Manitoba, and Saskatchewan (ranging from 86% to 16%). Aboriginals tend to be much younger than the overall population in Canada (46 percent are 24 years or less compared to only 29 percent in the general population). In 2011, about one in five (19%) Canadian residents identified themselves as a visible minority,[2] up from 16 percent in 2006 (Statistics Canada 2013a). This increase is largely due to the high proportion of visible minority immigrants (78%) arriving in Canada since 2006 with the three largest groups being South Asian (25%), Chinese (21%), and black (15%) (Statistics Canada 2013a), making up over 60 percent of visible minorities.

Legal Framework

In Canada, Section 222(4) of the *Criminal Code of Canada* (*CCC*) includes three types of culpable homicide: murder (first- and second-degree), manslaughter, and infanticide. First-degree murder involves one or more of the following components: (1) planning/deliberation; (2) death of a police officer(s), custodian(s), or prison personnel while on duty; or (3) occurred during commission of certain criminal acts (e.g., hijacking, kidnapping, forcible confinement, criminal harassment, or sexual assault) (Manson 2001). If one of these criteria is not met, the homicide may be classified as second-degree murder. The line separating first- and second-degree murder is often obscure, but usually at issue is how much planning/deliberation was undertaken by the accused prior to the killing (Boyle, Grant, and Chunn 1998). Section 235 stipulates that those convicted of first- or second-degree will be sentenced to life in prison. First-degree murder carries a mandatory minimum 25-year parole ineligibility period. This ranges from 10 to 25 years for second-degree murder. Capital punishment was abolished in Canada in 1976, although the last executions by hanging were actually in 1962 (Hoshowsky 2007).

Manslaughter is culpable homicide that is not murder because "the person who committed it did so in the heat of passion caused by sudden provocation" (s. 232(1) *CCC*).[3] Manslaughter is subject to a maximum of life in prison, but has no mandatory minimum. The mental element has been the crucial factor in distinguishing between murder and manslaughter, so decisions about degree of accused culpability or blameworthiness have not only been affected by the presence of provocation, but also by other factors (e.g., intoxication) (Boyle, Grant, and Chunn 1998). Finally, punishable by a maximum of five years, infanticide is the killing of a child less than one year, by willful act or omission, by the mother who had not fully recovered from the effects of childbirth (i.e., mental disturbances, postpartum disorders).

Homicide Data Sources

Official data sources on homicide have not been readily available to researchers in Canada; therefore, what is currently known about homicide comes primarily from annual reports released by Statistics Canada and a smaller, but well-established body of literature by various researchers on specific homicide-related topics. The primary data source on homicide is Statistics Canada's Homicide Survey that has collected information on police-reported homicide incidents, victims, and accused since 1961 and on manslaughter and infanticide since 1974. Two other sources of homicide data are the Uniform Crime Report (UCR) surveys and the Vital Statistics Death Database. The UCR surveys, also administered by Statistics Canada, comprise police-reported aggregated data counts of offenses and more detailed victim, accused, and incident information. The Vital Statistics Death Database collects demographic and medical cause of death information annually from each province/territory. The remainder of the chapter draws on official data and more focused Canadian research examining specific questions about homicide.

Historical and Contemporary Trends in Homicide

There have been four distinct trends in Canadian homicide rates over the past century (Cotter 2014; Dawson 2001; Gartner 1995; Silverman and Kennedy 1993): (1) from 1921 to 1930, the rate rose dramatically, peaking in 1930, exceeding two per 100,000; (2) from 1930 to mid-1960s, declined during the Depression then were stable until the mid-1960s; (3) the most dramatic rise in the homicide rate took place between 1966 and 1975 with steady increases from 1.25 in 1966 to 3.03 in 1975, the latter remaining one of the highest rates; and (4) from 1976–present, despite yearly fluctuations, Canada has seen a steady decline with the 2013 rate being less than half of the 1975 rate. Although Canadian rates remain significantly lower than the United States, both countries exhibit similar trends during the above period (Ouimet 2002). Disaggregating Canadian rates along various dimensions exposes some important variations in homicide, however. Provincial/territorial and urban/rural differences in homicide rates are consistently documented and type of homicide (e.g., intimate partner, stranger) has been shown to vary nationally and regionally, by jurisdiction size, and other sociodemographic characteristics (Kennedy, Forde, and Silverman 1989; O'Grady 2014). For example, intimate partner homicide (IPH) and firearms-related homicide have declined in the past several decades. These and other variations are essential to understanding what and how various social changes may be contributing to trends in homicide.

Regional Distribution of Homicide Rates

Throughout the twentieth century, Canada has consistently documented crime rates, including homicide, that increase from east to west (Andresen 2009, 2013; Kennedy, Silverman, and Forde 1991). When the Territories are included, the east-to-west pattern shifts to a south-to-north trend because homicide rates in the north are two to three times higher than British Columbia and over 10 times higher than Atlantic Canada (Cotter 2014: 6). However, some argue that traditional rate calculations may not portray an accurate picture of homicide patterns across the country, focusing on Nunavut—the smallest of the three territories—to illustrate this point (Andresen 2009). In 2006, Nunavut had a population of about 31,000 and two homicides, producing a reported homicide rate of 6.5 per 100,000—the highest in the country (Li 2007: 12). In contrast, in Ontario which had a population of more than 12 million in 2006, there were 196 homicides for a rate of 1.54 per 100,000. Thus, while rate calculations are accurate, such figures lack context and may contribute to misunderstandings of the everyday experiences of Nunavut residents or others in sparely populated or rural regions in Canada. However, homicide has not typically been a big-city phenomenon in Canada.

Urban and Rural Variations in Homicide Rates

It is a common perception that residents of urban areas are more likely to be victims of violence than those living in rural settings. This may be one reason why fear of crime is also typically much higher among city dwellers than those in smaller towns and rural areas in Canada (Sacco and Johnson 1990). Community size or population density can lead to varying levels of homicide, but not in the way expected. Official figures show that homicide rates in Canadian cities are often below or similar to national averages and rates in Census Metropolitan Areas (CMAs; populations of at least 100,000) are often lower than those in non-CMAs (Cotter 2014; Francisco and Chénier 2007). As such, Canadian homicide rates are not driven by urban homicides like in the United States (Trussler 2013). For example, in 2005, homicide was the only offense of the four offenses examined (robbery, motor vehicle theft, breaking/entering) for which the highest rate was recorded in rural areas—areas with the lowest reported overall crime rates (Francisco and Chénier 2007). However,

Canadian regions differ in the distribution of urban and rural populations with Atlantic Canada (which includes Nova Scotia, New Brunswick, Prince Edward Island and Newfoundland/Labrador), the Prairies (including Alberta, Manitoba, and Saskatchewan), and the Territories (including Yukon, Northwest Territories, and Nunavut) having more rural residents than Central Canada (Ontario and Quebec). Further disaggregating homicide rates by province, then, showed some regional variations in urban/rural homicide trends. The highest homicide rates were documented in rural areas in the Prairies (with higher Aboriginal populations), but Ontario, British Columbia, and Nova Scotia reported higher rates in their larger urban areas. At the national level, the proportion of homicide incidents involving family members was highest in rural areas and lower in large or small urban areas (Francisco and Chénier 2007).

Sociodemographic Characteristics of Homicide Victims and Perpetrators

Gender. Males account for the majority of homicide victims and perpetrators in Canada which has been the case historically and worldwide. In 2013, for example, men comprised 71 percent of victims and 88 percent of identified perpetrators (Cotter 2014). As such, while men are more likely to be killed than women, they are typically killed by other men (e.g., friends, acquaintances, and strangers). In contrast, while females are also more likely to be killed by men, they are at greatest risk from male partners—82 percent of IPHs involved female victims in 2013 (Cotter 2014: 3). Homicide risk has been declining for women and men in recent decades although declines may be more pronounced for male victims (Boyce and Cotter 2013).

Age. The age group at greatest risk of becoming a homicide victim or a perpetrator in Canada are between the ages of 18–24 years after which risk decreases (Cotter 2014: 16). Those identified as young offenders under the Canadian Youth Criminal Justice Act (12–17 years of age) represented one in 10 of all those accused of homicide in 2013 (Cotter 2014), the majority of whom are male. Various studies have examined how youth-perpetrated homicide might differ from homicides committed by adults and how patterns in youth-perpetrated homicides may have changed over time. This research has shown that youth-perpetrated homicides today more often involve multiple perpetrators, instrumental motivations, and strangers as victims (Meloff and Silverman 1993; Woodworth, Agar, and Coupland 2013).

Race/ethnicity. Limited Canadian research has examined the relationship between race/ethnicity and violence, including homicide, largely due to restrictions that preclude the collection of this information by researchers when accessing particular data sources. The one exception is with respect to Aboriginal Canadians whose overrepresentation both as victims and perpetrators has been well documented.

Focusing on 1962–1984, Moyer (1992) showed that Aboriginal homicide victimization rates were six times that of non-Aboriginals (12 and 2 per 100,000 respectively; p. 389). Thus, while Aboriginals comprised only 2–3 percent of the population at that time, they represented 17 percent of homicide victims. Aboriginal women and men were overrepresented equally (17% of male victims and 16% of female victims) and Aboriginal victims were younger than other victims. With respect to perpetration, Moyer (1992) found that Aboriginal Canadians reportedly represented about 20 percent of all suspects, with a higher proportion of female suspects being Aboriginal than male suspects (p. 396). More recent work shows that the situation has not improved over time as shown below.

Focusing on 1997–2000, Brzozowski, Taylor-Butts, and Johnson (2006: 7) found the average homicide rate for Aboriginal Canadians was 8.8 per 100,000, almost seven times higher than non-Aboriginal peoples (1.3 per 100,000; see Figure 20.2). This is true for both Aboriginal men and women; however, the rate for Aboriginal men (12.2 per 100,000) is twice that of Aboriginal women (5.4 per 100,000). During the same period, Aboriginals were 10 times more likely to be accused of homicide than were non-Aboriginal people (11.2 per 100,000 compared to 1.1 respectively; Brzozowski, Taylor-Butts, and Johnson 2006: 8). This overrepresentation is reflected in overall crime victimization and offending rates as well. Two primary reasons have been offered to explain these patterns: discriminatory practices, particularly in

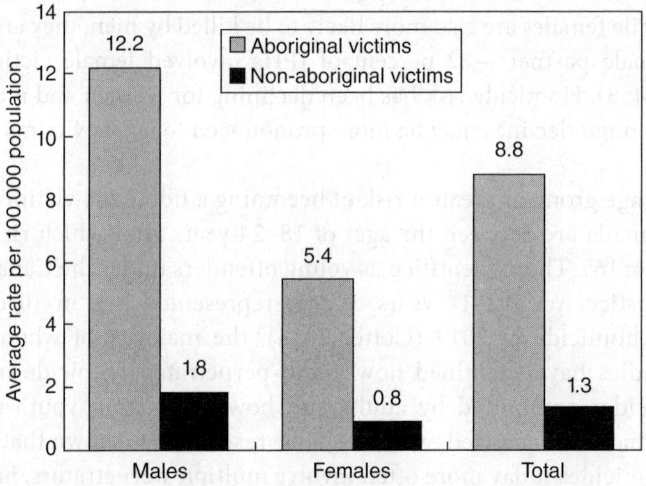

Figure 20.3 Rates of homicide much higher for Aboriginal victims, 1997–2000 (original in Brzozowski, Taylor-Butts, and Johnson 2006: fig. 4). Rates are calculated per 100,000 population and are based on the average number of homicides per year, between 1997 and 2000. It excludes homicides where the Aboriginal status of the victim was unknown. Population estimates were derived from 2001 post-censal estimates and 1996 census counts, provided by Statistics Canada, Census and Demographic Statistics, Demography Division. Source: Brzozowski, Taylor-Butts, and Johnson (2006). Reproduced with the permission of Statistics Canada.

the criminal justice system, and economic and social inequality (O'Grady 2011). Finally, research shows that Aboriginal homicides are more likely than non-Aboriginal homicides to involve stabbings and beatings; victims and perpetrators known to each other, particularly family members; to be intra-racial; and to involve alcohol and/or drugs use (Brzozowski, Taylor-Butts, and Johnson 2006; Moyer 1992) (see Box 20.1).

Box 20.1 Missing and murdered Aboriginal women as a case study

In the past decade, the vulnerability of Aboriginal women has come to the forefront of national and international attention. The Sisters in Spirit initiative launched in 2005 by the Native Women's Association of Canada (NWAC) has documented that, by 2010, over 582 Aboriginal women and girls across Canada were murdered or went missing (NWAC 2010). Key contributing factors identified are violence experienced by Aboriginal women, their families, and communities for decades due to "the intergenerational impact and resulting vulnerabilities of colonization and state policies" (e.g., residential schools, child welfare system) (NWAC 2010: i). These factors have perpetuated and maintained violence against Aboriginal women and girls along with inadequate and oftentimes absent state responses. NWAC findings have shown that: (1) the majority of missing and murdered women and girls are from Western Canada; (2) over half were under the age of 31; (3) many were mothers and grandmothers; (4) they were more often killed by an acquaintance or stranger in contrast to non-Aboriginal women more often killed by male partners; (5) the majority of cases occurred in urban areas; (6) nearly half the homicides remain unsolved and no charges have been laid in about 40 percent of the cases (see also Pearce 2013).

Stemming, in part, from inadequate state responses to the investigation of these crimes and ongoing systemic issues that lead to increased vulnerabilities for Aboriginal women, there have been repeated calls for a national inquiry. Until the newly-elected Canadian government launched an inquiry in 2016, there had been no move in this direction despite additional investigations documenting the gravity of the situation. For example, conducting their own study, the Royal Canadian Mounted Police (RCMP) found that between 1980 and 2012 there were 1,017 Aboriginal victims of homicide and another 164 Aboriginal women were identified as missing (RCMP 2014). At minimum, then, Aboriginal women account for 16 percent of all victims yet only four percent of the female population. The most recent call for an inquiry followed the 2013 investigation by the Inter-American Commission on Human Rights, an arm of the Organization of American States, which concluded that a national action plan was required to address the situation (IACHR 2014).

More systematic and recent research is limited, particularly as it relates to other Canadian racial/ethnic or visible minority groups. For example, while much research in the United States has focused on black homicide victimization and perpetration, there is little Canadian research even though they are the third largest visible minority group. Similar to US cities, recent research from Toronto shows that young, black males are overrepresented as both victims and perpetrators (Thompson 2014; Thompson and Gartner 2014). Between 1992 and 2003, for example, young blacks in Toronto reportedly accounted for about 30 percent and 36 percent of homicide victims and offenders, respectively, while comprising only about 10 percent of the population (Bania 2009). Some estimate that the homicide rate among young Toronto blacks increased from 2.4 to 10.1 per 100,000 from the 1990s to early 2000s and is now at least four times that of non-blacks (Galabuzi 2009).

Variations in Situational Characteristics of Homicide

Multiple homicides. Similar to other developed countries, only a small portion of Canadian homicides involve more than one victim or more than one accused. When multiple persons are involved, however, incident characteristics often differ from single homicide events. For example, in 2013, multiple-victim homicides were more likely to involve guns, female victims, and accused who were family members—the latter most often parents of the victim (Cotter 2014: 8). The greater likelihood of guns in multiple-victim homicides arguably stems from their use in what are often referred to as gang-related killings often committed with firearms and involving illegal criminal activity (Boyce and Cotter 2013: 15). The higher proportion of female victims and accused family members may be explained, in part, by familicide incidents which are almost exclusively committed by males against female partners and/or their children (Aston and Pottie Bunge 2005).

Other types of multiple homicides such as mass, spree, or serial killings are not as common in Canada and are rare compared to other types of homicides. However, these types of killings do occur perhaps with greater frequency than typically believed as highlighted in recent years. In June 2014, for example, a small city in Atlantic Canada experienced a two-day lockdown—schools were closed and residents told to stay inside—as the country followed media coverage of a manhunt for 24-year-old Justin Bourque who, during his killing spree, shot and killed three Royal Canadian Mounted Police (RCMP) officers and wounded two others (CBC 2014). In 2010, the arrest of now-former Canadian Forces Colonel Russell Williams for murder, sexual assault, and a host of other offenses reminded Canadians that serial killers typically live unrecognizable among us. Similarly, the trial and conviction of British Columbia's Robert Pickton for six counts of second-degree murder in 2007 drew attention to the numbers of missing and murdered women from Vancouver's Downtown Eastside, underscoring the vulnerability of these mostly poor and Aboriginal women (CBC 2007).

When it comes to Canadian serial killers, perhaps there are none more famous than the husband–wife team, Paul Bernardo and Karla Homolka, who were apprehended in the early 1990s for a series of killings in Ontario that shocked the nation (Mellor 2012). Among their young, female victims was Karla's sister. The impact of such events is far-reaching as starkly evident by the effects of a mass homicide which occurred more than 25 years ago in Quebec, leaving 14 young women dead at the hands of Marc Lepine who reportedly killed them because they were feminists and then killed himself (Mellor 2013). Referred to as the Montréal Massacre, the effects of this mass homicide continue to reverberate throughout the country, particularly on December 6 of each year when the anniversary of the event is marked as a reminder of the work yet to be done in combating violence against women.

Victim–accused relationship. Research tends to compare homicides that occur across several conceptually important victim–accused relationships, focusing primarily on intimate partners, family members, friends, acquaintances, and strangers (Silverman and Kennedy 1993). Recent Canadian figures indicate that most solved homicides continue to involve victims killed by someone they know (87%), primarily acquaintances and family members (Cotter 2014), although this varies by gender of the victim. As noted, Canadian females are most often killed by male intimate partners and, in 2013, 82 percent of IPHs involved female victims (Cotter 2014). In contrast, males are more often killed by friends, acquaintances, and strangers, often described as confrontational homicides, typically involving other males (Brookman 2003; Polk 1999). These patterns vary across the country, however. For example, more than 40 percent of homicides that occurred in Atlantic Canada, Ontario, the Prairies, and the Territories involved intimate partners or family members. In contrast, less than one-quarter of Quebec homicides and less than one-third of those in British Columbia involved intimate partners or family members which may be due to the larger proportion of homicides remaining unsolved in those two provinces, an issue that will be discussed below.

Rates of IPH have consistently been higher for female victims compared to male victims but, similar to some other countries, there have been documented declines in IPH for both women and men in Canada during the past several decades although greater declines for male victims compared to female victims. For example, recent figures show that the rate of homicide for male IPH victims in 2013 was 73 percent lower than in 1993 whereas women's was 48 percent lower for the same period (Cotter 2014: 14). Research suggests that these declines may stem from a variety of sources, including increased resources/services, enhanced policing as well as changing social and economic patterns (e.g., delayed marriage and/or childbirth, rising income levels, and increased labor force participation for women) (Dawson, Pottie Bunge, and Baldé 2009; Dugan, Nagin, and Rosenfeld 1999).

Method of homicides. For the past three decades, shootings and stabbings have been the two most common methods used in Canadian homicides (Boyce and Cotter 2013). However, after reaching its peak in the 1970s, firearms-related homicides have been declining and, in 2012, were at their lowest rate in almost half a century. The decline in firearms-related homicides can largely be explained by fewer homicides involving rifles or shotguns (Dauvergne and De Socio 2008). That is, prior to the early 1990s, homicides committed with a firearm more often involved a rifle or shotgun; however, post-1990, handguns are now more commonly used. The issue of gun control in Canada and recent changes has been the focus of attention (see Box 20.2).

Box 20.2 Firearms and homicide in Canada

Similar to many countries, the role of firearms in homicide and other violent crime has been a controversial issue in Canada, particularly so in the recent past when it again became the focus of public and government debate related to the abolition of the long-gun registry. The key precursor to the federal long-gun registry was the 1989 Montréal Massacre (discussed above). Soon after its implementation in 1995, a battle to have it abolished began and this goal was achieved in 2012. Canadians still need a license to possess a firearm and all restricted/prohibited firearms must still be registered, but there is no longer a requirement to register nonrestricted firearms and existing registration records were destroyed (http://www.rcmp-grc.gc.ca/cfp-pcaf/change-changement-eng.htm). Given the long-gun registry's origins, as well as the continued debate about the potential of gun control to impact rates of violence, particularly against women, many see the association between firearms and violence as both a public safety and a gender issue, although intensely debated (Mauser 2015; McPhedran and Mauser 2013).

Over a period of more than four decades, Canada has adopted a series of firearms laws, providing researchers an opportunity to examine their impact on rates of violence and homicide. However, despite declines in firearms-related homicides during this same period, findings have been mixed about the impact of Canadian firearms legislation. For example, in Canada, some studies have shown that the rate at which females were killed with a firearm decreased after the passage of Bill C-51 which required, among other changes, criminal record checks (Leenaars and Lester 1996).[4] In contrast, other studies have shown that various changes in legislation decreased homicide rates for both women and men (Carrington 1999) or had little to no effect on risk of homicide (Langmann 2012), particularly for women (McPhedran and Mauser 2013).

Further research focusing on Australia, Canada, and New Zealand found changes in gun control policies did not align with declining homicide rates (McPhedran, Baker, and Singh 2011). In particular, given some sharp increases in Canadian firearm homicide rates that may be associated with homicides in some cities, the authors argued that other factors such as illegal drugs, other criminal activities and socioeconomic disadvantage may be more important than gun ownership and control (McPhedran, Baker, and Singh 2011). As a result, despite noticeable declines in firearms-related violent crime, including homicide, concrete conclusions about the cause-and-effect relationship between gun control legislation and public policy and homicide are not yet possible in Canada.

Alcohol/drug use. While the collection of information on alcohol and/or drug use at the time of a killing is fraught with difficulty, research contends that there is an association between the consumption of such substances and violence, including homicide (Kuhns *et al.* 2013). The Homicide Survey began to collect this information in 2003 and, although information is unknown for over one-third of the accused and almost 30 percent of the victims, where such determinations were possible, about 70 percent of accused and almost 60 percent of victims were under the influence of a substance (Cotter 2014: 19). The majority of cases involved alcohol rather than drugs. Examining the issue at the macro-level across seven provinces and for Canada as a whole, Rossow (2004) found that there was an association between alcohol sales (and consumption) and homicide rates in Canada, but this varied by region and gender.

Understanding Homicide in Canada

As discussed in previous chapters, there is no single explanation for homicide and explanations often depend on the type of homicide being examined and at what level (e.g., individual, community, or societal). In Canada, despite several studies that have sought to explain homicide and its various subtypes as well as seemingly entrenched regional differences (Daly, Wilson, and Vasdev 2001; Hartnagel 1978, 1997; Kennedy, Silverman and Forde 1991), little consensus has been reached. Further, aggregate-level research seeking to identify associations among homicide rates and other macro-level factors such as incarceration rates, varying police practices, and enhanced medical responses has failed to explain homicide trends and, in particular, recent documented declines (Andresen 2007; Ouimet 2002). Some common factors examined, similar to other countries, are sociodemographic characteristics, varying economies, immigration/migration patterns, and sociopolitical dynamics (Brantingham and Brantingham 1984; Trussler 2013). Researchers have argued that varying levels of social disorganization among particular groups and in particular regions may be part of the explanation (Gartner and Thompson 2014; Kennedy, Silverman, and Forde 1991) as discussed below.

Sociodemographics factors

The age composition of the population as an explanation for declines in homicide has been a key focus of Canadian research similar to other countries during the past several decades. For example, using national-level data, Trussler (2013) showed that regions with larger young, male population had higher homicide rates (p. 61), arguing that this may explain national declines (i.e., total population of young males decreasing) and higher homicide rates in Western Canada (i.e., with slight increases in young males). Western Canada has consistently had higher homicide rates, however, so other factors may be important, particularly with respect to how they interact with the higher proportion of young males (and higher numbers of Aboriginals). Examining this question, Trussler (2013) found that, when the proportion of young males was considered, migration patterns remained the only significant socioeconomic factor associated with homicide rates, suggesting that it had its own role to play beyond the age-cohort effect. Supporting this argument, using aggregate data on international immigration, interprovincial migration, and homicide in Canadian provinces, Andresen (2013) found that "provinces that have increases in the in-migration of young males from other provinces have decreases in the traditional homicide rate, but provinces that have a *net* increase in young males from interprovincial migration have increases in traditional homicide rates" (p. 651). As such, similar to Trussler (2013), he concluded that increases in young males, rather than immigrant populations, are positively related to increases in homicide, challenging the public perception, perhaps exacerbated by media portrayals of crimes among particular racial/ethnic groups, that immigration is positively associated with homicide rates.

Socioeconomic factors

Poverty, income inequality, and employment rates have been common socioeconomic factors examined in theoretical literature on violence and homicide and, although such research is limited in Canada, income inequality appears to find some support. Daly, Wilson, and Vasdev (2001) found that unequal distribution of resources (measured using average income, Gini Index) was a strong predictor of homicide, but that income inequality was a more robust predictor than average income (p. 232). Western Canada, with consistently higher homicide rates, has also experienced higher levels of inequality over time (Trussler 2013). According to the Organization for Economic Cooperation and Development (OECD), however, levels of income inequality have gradually increased in Canada, now higher than in the mid-1980s and, during the same period, rates of homicide have declined. As such, further disaggregation of homicide rates by region and an examination of the conditioning effects of other factors are warranted. For example, Trussler (2013) found a positive association between inequality and homicide, but only after the proportion of the young male population reached 12 percent (p. 61). Further, focusing on the higher homicide rates for Toronto's black urban youth, Gartner and Thompson (2014) argue that this population has faced increasing inequalities as a result of policy decisions that have negatively impacted the social conditions in which they live.

In summary, Canadian research has primarily focused on factors that produce social disorganization (Sampson, Raudenbush, and Earls 1997; Sampson and Raudenbush 1999; Shaw and McKay 1931, 1942) to explain varying rates of homicide in particular regions and among particular groups who face higher homicide victimization and perpetration risks (e.g., Andresen 2013; Kennedy, Silverman, and Forde 1991; Trussler 2013). A high percentage of young males living in particular areas, their migration patterns, and levels of income inequality appear to provide a partial explanation for increased risk of homicide for residents of Western Canada, urban black youth, and Aboriginal Canadians. Of course, for the last group, the historical and continuing impact of colonization remains significant in understanding the experiences of violence among Aboriginals.

Criminal Justice Responses to Homicide

Police Clearance: When examining police clearance rates for homicides, time, geography, and type of homicide appear to be important. Overall, clearance rates for homicide tend to be higher than most other crimes. In 2013, three-quarters (76%) of police-reported homicides were cleared and charges laid in most cases (Cotter 2014). While these rates are higher than for some other countries, rates have declined from about 95 percent—almost a 20 percent decrease—in the past four decades (Hotton Mahony and Turner 2012: 5). The proportion of solved homicides also varies with rates being consistently lower in British Columbia (42%) and Quebec (69%) for which an explanation has yet to be identified (Cotter 2014: 11; Silverman and Kennedy 1997; Trussler 2010). Finally, recent research has shown that police clearance rates also tend to be lower for particular types of homicide such as gang-related killings and those involving firearms and/or the illegal drug trade (Hotton Mahony and Turner 2012; Regoeczi, Kennedy, and Silverman 2000; Trussler 2010).

In a recent examination, Trussler (2010) found that offense characteristics played a greater role in predicting homicide clearance rates: those involving handguns, occurring outside the home and in more densely populated areas had lower clearance rates. Arguably, these factors are also more common in gang- or drug-related killings which also have lower clearance rates than other homicides. In contrast, there has been less support for the role of victim factors. Early research showed that particular victim characteristics lead to higher clearance rates nationally (e.g., female, non-white, those under age 10) as did the presence of firearms (Regoeczi, Kennedy, and Silverman 2000). However, when focusing on only one province, none of these factors remained significant, underscoring the importance of regional variation (Regoeczi, Kennedy, and Silverman 2000). More recently, controlling for province/territory, Trussler (2010) found that victim age (under 10 years) was the only victim factor that increased clearance rates, arguing that this was likely attributable to the fact that children are most often killed by someone they know and their cases attract significant law enforcement resources (pp. 14–15).

Consistent with other research on clearance rates (Regoeczi and Miethe 2003), an acknowledged limitation has been the extent of missing information for unsolved homicides, particularly for victim–offender relationship and Aboriginal status. Further, the exploration of community context factors (e.g., poverty, police workload) would enhance our understanding of police clearance (Paré, Felson, and Ouimet 2007). This is supported by a recent and comprehensive analysis of crime clearance in close to 600 Canadian municipalities focusing on varying social conditions. Wong (2010) found that clearance rates for violent crime, including homicide, were affected by inequality, the percent Aboriginal population, divorce rate, employment rate, level of education, percent immigration population, amount of government transfer, the voting rate, population size, violent crime rate, and policing expenditures.

Court outcomes. In Canada, there is little information on court outcomes for homicide and crime more generally. One major reason for this is the continued absence of systematic court data that allows researchers to link case characteristics to punishment outcomes (Doob 2011). Until 1977, Statistics Canada operated a court program and, using these descriptive data, Moyer (1992) compared court outcomes for Aboriginal and non-Aboriginal accused. She demonstrated that: (1) preliminary hearing outcomes did not differ by Aboriginal status with the majority being sent to trial; (2) non-Aboriginals, and particularly women, were more likely to be found unfit to stand trial and to be found not guilty by reason of insanity (NGRI) compared to other accused; (3) female Aboriginal conviction rates (57%) were higher than non-Aboriginals (48%); (4) Aboriginals were less likely to be convicted of first- or second-degree murder and more likely to be convicted of manslaughter; and (5) Aboriginals also received shorter sentences than other offenders. Since the court program ended, court data primarily comes from federal corrections, single jurisdiction studies, and media sources, increasing challenges of missing and inconsistent data.

In the past decade, focusing on a large urban jurisdiction, research has examined court outcomes for the total population of homicide cases over a significant period of time in Toronto, Canada (Dawson 2003, 2004, 2012). From 1974 to 2002, differential treatment was documented across various victim, offender, and offense characteristics, depending on the stage of the process and time period in which the case was disposed. As expected, factors typically seen as legally relevant (e.g., prior record, particularly violent, multiple victims) increased the severity of court outcomes, such as initial charge laid, conviction severity, and sentence (Dawson 2012). Some extra-legal factors (e.g., gender, relationship) were also found to be relevant at various stages. For example, examining victim–offender relationship, homicides involving intimate partners were more likely to be resolved by guilty plea compared to non-intimate partner killings (e.g., friends, acquaintances, and strangers). When cases went to trial, however, defendants who killed intimate partners were more likely to be found guilty than those who killed non-intimates. Cases involving male accused, accused who had been drinking/using drugs, employed victims, and guns lead to more serious court outcomes. In contrast, cases involving male victims were associated with less severe punishments. The criminal justice processing of homicide appears to have changed somewhat over time, however (Dawson 2012). While cases of intimate partner homicide are still more likely than other homicides to be resolved by guilty pleas, they are more likely to be found guilty at trial today than in the past. Further, intimate partner killers are now as likely to be convicted of murder (rather than manslaughter), similar to other types of killers, in contrast to earlier years. Beyond this work, there is no national-level or multiple jurisdiction research on court outcomes in homicide cases in Canada.

Conclusion and Priorities for Future Research

Canada's peaceable existence clearly depends upon who is looking and from where, as well as whose experiences are being examined. However, given the limited access to and/or collection of national-level data, important gaps remain in understanding trends and patterns in Canadian homicides. Four key areas are identified below as priorities for future research.

Urban/rural differences in homicide

Declines in homicide in Canada have yet to be examined across urban and rural jurisdictions to determine if rural areas have experienced decreases in the same way as urban centers. US research has suggested that declines documented there have not been experienced to the same degree, if at all, in rural areas compared to urban centers (Jennings and Piquero 2008). Given that research has shown rural homicide differs along a number of important dimensions in Canada, it may be that similar patterns are evident. For example, urban homicides are more likely to involve multiple accused, handguns, crime-related activities, and strangers as victims. In contrast, rural homicides are more often single victim–single accused events, involving rifles/shotguns, and family members as victims. Further, despite some fluctuations, homicides committed with firearms have been declining in recent decades, reaching its lowest rate in four decades in 2013 (Cotter 2014). Research has yet to examine whether these declines are distributed evenly across urban and rural regions in Canada.

Youth homicide

A comparison of early and current research shows that the dynamics of youth-perpetrated homicide are changing; that is, relative to several decades ago, when young people kill today, homicides more often involve multiple perpetrators, instrumental motivations, and strangers as victims. Given that this age group is at greatest risk of both homicide victimization and perpetration, understanding how changing social factors contribute to changes in youth-perpetrated homicides can help identify appropriate intervention and prevention strategies. Further, one's age is only part of an individual's identity and, therefore, understanding how trends and patterns in youth-perpetrated homicide vary across gender and race/ethnicity is equally important in terms of developing prevention and intervention initiatives.

Race/ethnicity and homicide

As noted above, there has been a long-standing, oftentimes informal, ban on the collection and dissemination of data (primarily for researchers) that identifies the race/ethnic identity of victims and perpetrators of crime. This has precluded a systematic examination of varying risks for particular visible minority populations in Canada. The exception to this has been the attention paid to the overrepresentation of Aboriginals, both as victims and as accused. Even among Aboriginal Canadians, however, systematic examinations are limited. Whether the motivation of government and criminal justice agencies that often have access to and/or collect such data is benevolence or a fear of criticism, the outcome is the same: a dearth of research on the groups that are most vulnerable to violence, including homicide. Without the information provided by systematic data, public perceptions of the links between immigration and crime, violence and visible minority groups, and the unsubstantiated fear of the "other" will likely continue. This will, in turn, make it more difficult to improve our understanding of the risks faced by particular victims and perpetrators, identifying the origins or explanations of their risk, and the prevention and policy initiatives that might reduce their likelihood of violence in the future.

Similar to the United States, it has recently been argued that the rates of homicide among African Canadian, or black, male youth, who also represent a large percentage of gang members in Canada, can be described as a public health crisis (Khenti 2013). While these high rates are often linked to gangs, guns, and turf wars, given the conditions which reign in many Toronto neighborhoods, it is equally likely that child maltreatment, poor education, poor police–community relations, mental illness, substance abuse, concentrated poverty, and racial discrimination may be equally, if not more, important contributing factors (Khenti 2013). Without detailed, longitudinal data, however, identifying the correlates of this violence remains a challenge and real political will to rise to this challenge so far appears to be absent. Further, there is a need to focus examinations more at the local or neighborhood level to provide a better understanding of how particular social conditions impact risk of homicide victimization and perpetration (O'Grady 2014).

Criminal justice responses to violent crime

Little attention has been given to variation in court responses to crime across Canadian jurisdictions despite recognition that courts operate in distinct environments that impact how cases are processed and disposed (Ulmer 2012). However, understanding what groups are affected, where, and why is integral to ensuring consistency in access to justice for victims and defendants. While criminal justice responses to homicide are practical in terms of the need for society to respond to such acts, these responses are also symbolic—that is, they contribute to the public's knowledge about what are and are not serious crimes. In Canada, the dearth of research on the criminal justice processing of homicides, and most crimes, precludes any adequate understanding of who is or is not accessing justice, whether they are perpetrators or victims, and whether access to justice is equitable across particular groups and regions of the country.

Notes

1 Recently, the Canadian federal government has moved from using the term 'Aboriginal' to 'Indigenous' prompting the change in terminology to be adopted more broadly. For the purposes of this chapter, Aboriginal will be used given that much of the literature captures earlier work before this change was adopted; however, it is recognized and acknowledged that Indigenous Canadians is the more respectful and accurate terminology to be used as we move forward.

2 Used by Statistics Canada and defined by the Employment Equity Act, the term "visible minority" refers to "persons, other than Aboriginal peoples, who are non-Caucasian in race or non-white in colour" and consist mainly of the following groups: Chinese, South Asian, Black, Arab, West Asian, Filipino, Southeast Asian, Latin American, Japanese, and Korean (see http://www.statcan.gc.ca/eng/concepts/definitions/minority01).

3 There is no distinction between voluntary and involuntary homicide in Canadian law.

4 The legislation also introduced several provisions such as regulations surrounding the safe storage and display of firearms by businesses and collectors as well as mandatory minimum sentences in an effort to deter crimes using firearms (Pottie Bunge 2002).

References

Andresen, M.A. (2007) Homicide and medical science: Is there a relationship? *Canadian Journal of Criminology and Criminal Justice* (April): 185–204.

Andresen, M.A. (2009) Crime specialization across the Canadian provinces. *Canadian Journal of Criminology and Criminal Justice*, 51(1): 31–53.

Andresen, M.A. (2013) International immigration, internal migration, and homicide in Canadian provinces. *International Journal of Offender Therapy and Comparative Criminology*, 57: 632–657.

Aston, C. and Pottie Bunge, V. (2005) Family homicide-suicides. In K. AuCoin (ed.), *Family Violence in Canada: A Statistical Profile 2005* (pp. 60–65). Ottawa: Statistics Canada (cat. no. 85-224-XIE).

Bania, M. (2009) Gang violence among youth and young adults: (Dis)affiliation and the potential for prevention. *IPC Review*, 3: 89–116.

Boyce, J. and Cotter, A. (2013) Homicide in Canada, 2012. *Juristat*, 33 (Statistics Canada, cat. no. 85-002-X).

Boyle, C., Grant, I., and Chunn, D.E. (1998) *The Law of Homicide*. Scarborough, ON: Carswell.

Brantingham, P. and Brantingham, P. (1984) *Patterns in Crime*. New York: Macmillan.

Brookman, F. (2003) Confrontational and revenge homicides among men in England and Wales. *The Australian and New Zealand Journal of Criminology*, 36(1): 34–59.

Brzozowski, J.-A., Taylor-Butts, A., and Johnson, S. (2006) Victimization and offending among the Aboriginal population in Canada. *Juristat*, 26(3) (Statistics Canada, cat. no. 85-002-XIE).

Carrington, P.J. (1999) Gender, gun control, suicide and homicide in Canada. *Archives of Suicide Research*, 5: 71–75.

CBC (Canadian Broadcasting Corporation) (2014) Justin Bourque pleads guilty to murdering 3 Moncton Mounties. August 8. Available online at http://www.cbc.ca/news/canada/new-brunswick/justin-bourque-pleads-guilty-to-murdering-3-moncton-mounties-1.2730536 (accessed September 29, 2016).

CBC (Canadian Broadcasting Corporation) (2007). Pickton gets maximum sentence for murders. December 11. Available online at http://www.cbc.ca/news/canada/british-columbia/pickton-gets-maximum-sentence-for-murders-1.650944 (accessed September 29, 2016).

Cotter, A. (2014) Homicide in Canada, 2013. *Juristat*, 34(1) (Statistics Canada, cat. no. 85-002-X).

Daly, M., Wilson, M., and Vasdev, S. (2001) Income inequality and homicide rates in Canada and the United States. *Canadian Journal of Criminology* (April): 219–236.

Dauvergne, M. and De Socio, L. (2008) Firearms and Violent Crime. *Juristat*, 28(2) (Statistics Canada, cat. no. 85-002-XIE).

Dawson, M. (2001) *Examination Of Declining Intimate Partner Homicide Rates: A Literature Review*. Ottawa: Department of Justice Canada.

Dawson, M. (2003) The cost of "lost" intimacy: The effect of relationship state on criminal justice decision-making. *The British Journal of Criminology*, 43(4): 689–709.

Dawson, M. (2004) Rethinking the boundaries of intimacy at the end of the century: The role of victim–defendant relationship in criminal justice decision-making over time. *Law & Society Review*, 38(1): 105–138.

Dawson, M. (2012) Intimacy, homicide and punishment: Examining court outcomes over three decades. *Australian and New Zealand Journal of Criminology*, 45(3): 400–422.

Dawson, M., Pottie Bunge, V., and Baldé, T. (2009) National trends in intimate partner homicides: Explaining the decline, Canada, 1976–2001. *Violence Against Women*, 15(3): 276–306.

Doob, A. (2011) The unfinished work of the Canadian Sentencing Commission. *Canadian Journal of Criminology and Criminal Justice* (July): 279–297.

Dugan, L., Nagin, D., and Rosenfeld, R. (1999) Explaining the decline in intimate partner homicide: The effects of changing domesticity, women's status and domestic violence resources. *Homicide Studies*, 3(3): 187–214.

Francisco, J. and Chénier, C. (2007) A comparison of large urban, small urban and rural crime rates, 2005. *Juristat*, 27(3) (Statistics Canada, cat. no. 85-002-X).

Galabuzi, G. (2009) Diversity on the mean streets of Toronto. *Canada Watch*, Fall: 38–40.

Gartner, R. (1995) Homicide in Canada. In J.I. Ross (ed.), *Violence in Canada: Sociopolitical Perspectives* (pp. 186–222). Toronto: Oxford University Press.

Gurr, T.R. (2009) Foreword. In J.I. Ross (ed.), *Violence in Canada: Sociopolitical Perspectives* (2nd edn, pp. xxxi–xl). New Brunswick, NJ: Oxford University Press.

Hagan, J. (1984) Toward a structural theory of crime, race, and gender: The Canadian case. *Crime and Delinquency*, 31(1): 129–146.

Hartnagel, T. (1978) The effect of age and sex composition of provincial populations on provincial crime rates. *Canadian Journal of Criminology*, 20: 28–33.

Hartnagel, T. (1997) Crime among the provinces: The effect of geographic mobility. *Canadian Journal of Criminology*, 39: 387–402.

Hoshowsky, R.J. (2007) *The Last to Die: Ronald Turpin, Arthur Lucas, and the End of Capital Punishment in Canada*. Toronto: Dundurn.

Hotton Mahony, T. and Turner, J. (2012) Police-reported clearance rates in Canada, 2010. *Juristat* (Statistics Canada, cat. no. 85-002-X).

IACHR (Inter-American Commission on Human Rights) (2014) *Missing and Murdered Indigenous Women in British Columbia, Canada*. Ottawa: IACHR.

Jennings, W.G. and Piquero, A.R. (2008) Trajectories of non-intimate partner and intimate partner homicides, 1980–1999: The importance of rurality. *Journal of Criminal Justice*, 36: 435–443.

Kennedy, L.W., Forde, D.R., and Silverman, R.A. (1989) Understanding homicide trends: Issues in disaggregation for national and cross-national comparisons. *Canadian Journal of Sociology* 14(4): 479–486.

Kennedy, L.W., Silverman, R., and Forde, D. (1991) Homicide in urban Canada: Testing the impact of economic equality and social disorganization. *Canadian Journal of Sociology* 16(4): 397–410.

Khenti, A.A. (2013) Homicide among young black men in Toronto: An unrecognized public health crisis? *Canadian Journal of Public Health*, 104(1): 12–14.

Kuhns, J.B., Exum, M.L., Clodfelter, T.A., and Bottia, M.C. (2013) The prevalence of alcohol-involved homicide offending: A meta-analytic review. *Homicide Studies*, 18(3): 251–270.

Langmann, C. (2012) Canadian firearm legislation and effects on homicide 1974–2008. *Journal of Interpersonal Violence*, 27(12): 2303–2321.

Leenaars, A.A. and Lester, D. (1996) Gender and the impact of gun control on suicide and homicide. *Archives of Suicide Research*, 2(4): 223–224.

Li, G. (2007) Homicide in Canada, 2006. *Juristat*, 27(8) (Statistics Canada, cat. no. 85-002-X).

Manson, A. (2001) *The Law of Sentencing*. Toronto: Irwin Law.

Mauser, G. (2015) The Canadian long-gun registry: A preliminary evaluation. *Journal on Firearms and Public Policy*, March 9. Available online at SSRN: http://papers.ssrn.com/sol3/papers.cfm?abstract_id=2575866 (accessed September 29, 2016).

McPhedran, S., Baker, J., and Singh, P. (2011) Firearm homicide in Australia, Canada and New Zealand: What can we learn from long-term international comparisons? *Journal of Interpersonal Violence* 26(2): 348–359.

McPhedran, S. and Mauser, G. (2013) Lethal firearm-related violence against Canadian women: Did tightening gun laws have an impact on women's health and safety? *Violence and Victims*, 28(5): 875–883.

Mellor, L. (2012) *Cold North Killers: Canadian Serial Killers*. Toronto: Dundurn.

Mellor, L. (2013) Rampage: *Canadian Mass Murder and Spree Killing*. Toronto: Dundurn.

Meloff, W. and Silverman, R.A. (1993) Canadian kids who kill. *Canadian Journal of Criminology*, 34: 15–34.

Moyer, S. (1992) Race, gender, and homicide: Comparisons between Aboriginals and other Canadians. *Canadian Journal of Criminology* (July): 387–402.

NWAC (Native Women's Association of Canada) (2010) *What Their Stories Tell Us: Research Findings from the Sisters in Spirit Initiative*. Ottawa: NWAC.

O'Grady, B. (2011) *Crime in the Canadian Context: Debates and Controversies*. Toronto: Oxford University Press.

O'Grady, B. (2014) A comparative analysis of homicide in Canada and the United States. In B. Agger and T. Luke (eds.), *Gun Violence and Public Life*. Boulder, CO: Paradigm Publishers.

Ouimet, M. (2002) Explaining the American and Canadian crime "drop" in the 1990s. *Canadian Journal of Criminology*, 44(1): 33–50.

Paré, P.-P., Felson, R.B., and Ouimet, R.M. (2007) Community variation in crime clearance: A multilevel analysis with comments on assessing police performance. *Journal of Quantitative Criminology*, 23: 243–258.

Pearce, M. (2013) An awkward silence: Missing and murdered vulnerable women and the Canadian justice system. Dissertation, University of Ottawa.

Polk, K. (1999) Males and honor context violence. *Homicide Studies*, 3(1): 6–29.

Pottie Bunge, V. (2002) National trends in intimate partner homicides, 1974–2000. *Juristat*, 22(5) (Statistics Canada, cat. no. 85-002-X1E).

Regoeczi, W., Kennedy, L.W., and Silverman, R.A. (2000) Uncleared homicides: A Canada/United States comparison. *Homicide Studies*, 4: 135–161.

Regoeczi, W. and Miethe, T. (2003) Taking on the unknown: A qualitative comparative analysis of unknown relationship homicides. *Homicide Studies*, 7: 211–234.

Rossow, I. (2004) Alcohol consumption and homicides in Canada, 1950–1999. *Contemporary Drug Problems*, 31(3): 541–559.

Royal Canadian Mounted Police (2014). *Missing and Murdered Aboriginal Women: A National Operational Overview*. Ottawa: RCMP.

Sacco, V.F. and Johnson, H. (1990) *Patterns of Criminal Victimization in Canada*. Ottawa: Statistics Canada.

Sampson, R.J. and Raudenbush, S.W. (1999) Systematic social observation of public spaces: A new look at disorder in urban neighborhoods. *American Journal of Sociology*, 105: 603–651.

Sampson, R.J., Raudenbush, S.W., and Earls, F. (1997) Neighborhoods and violent crime: A multilevel study of collective efficacy. *Science*, 277: 918–924.

Shaw, C.R. and McKay, H.D. (1931) *Social Factors In Juvenile Delinquency*. National Commission on Law Observance and Enforcement, Report on the Causes of Crime, Volume II. Washington, DC: US Government Printing Office.

Shaw, C.R. and McKay, H.D. (1942) Juvenile Delinquency and Urban Areas: A Study of Rates of Delinquency in Relation to Differential Characteristics of Local Communities in American Cities. Chicago, IL: University of Chicago Press.

Silverman, R.A. and Kennedy, L.W. (1993) *Deadly Deeds: Murder in Canada*. Scarborough, ON: Nelson Canada.

Silverman, R.A. and Kennedy, L.W. (1997) Uncleared homicide in Canada and the United States. In M. Riedel and J. Boulahanis (eds), *Lethal Violence: Proceedings of the 1995 Meeting of the Homicide Research Working Group* (pp. 81–86). Washington, DC: Office of Justice Programs, US Department of Justice.

Statistics Canada (2013a). 2011 National household survey: Immigration, place of birth, citizenship, ethnic origin, visible minorities, language and religion. *The Daily*, May 8.

Statistics Canada (2013b) *Aboriginal Peoples in Canada: First Nations People, Métis, and Inuit*. Ottawa: Statistics Canada (cat. no. 99-011-X2011001).

Statistics Canada. (2014). Canada's population estimates: Age and sex, 2014. *The Daily*, September 26.

Thompson, S.K. (2014) Case study: Black homicide victimization in Toronto, Ontario, Canada. In S. Bucerius and M. Tonry (eds), *The Oxford Handbook of Ethnicity, Crime and Immigration* (pp. 430–456). Oxford: Oxford University Press.

Thompson, S.K. and Gartner, R. (2014) The spatial distribution and social context of homicide in Toronto's neighborhoods. *Journal of Research in Crime and Delinquency*, 51(1): 88–118.

Trussler, T. (2010) Explaining the changing nature of homicide clearance in Canada. *International Criminal Justice Review*, 20(4): 366–383.

Trussler, T. (2013) Demographics and homicide in Canada: A fixed-effects analysis of the role of young males on changing homicide rates. *Western Criminology Review*, 13(1): 53–67.

Ulmer, J.T. (2012) Recent developments and new directions in sentencing research. *Justice Quarterly*, 29(1): 1–40.

Wong, S.K. (2010) Crime clearance rates in Canadian municipalities: A test of Donald Black's theory of law. *International Journal of Law, Crime and Justice*, 38: 17–36.

Woodworth, M., Agar, A.D., and Coupland, R.B.A. (2013) Characteristics of Canadian youth-perpetrated homicides. *Criminal Justice and Behavior*, 40(9): 1009–1026.

Further Reading

Amnesty International Canada (2004) *Stolen Sisters: A Human Rights Response to Discrimination and Violence against Indigenous Women in Canada*. Ottawa: Amnesty International.

Andresen, M.A., Jenion, G.W., and Jenion, M.L. (2003) Conventional calculations of homicide rates lead to an inaccurate reflection of Canadian trends. *Canadian Journal of Criminology and Criminal Justice*, 45(1): 1–17.

Employment and Social Development Canada. 2015. Canadians in context—Population size and growth. Available online at http://www4.hrsdc.gc.ca/.3ndic.1t.4r@-eng.jsp?iid=35 (accessed September 29, 2016)

Gabor, T., Hung, K., Mihorean, S., and St-Onge, C. (2002) Canadian homicide rates: A comparison of two data sources. *Canadian Journal of Criminology*, 44: 351.

Johnson, H. (2006) *Measuring Violence Against Women: Statistical Trends* (cat. no. 85-570-X). Ottawa: Statistics Canada.

Kelly, K. and Totten, M. (2002) *When Children Kill: A Social Psychological Study of Youth Homicide*. Peterborough, ON: Broadview Press.

21

Typifying American Exceptionalism
Homicide in the USA

Amanda L. Robinson and Christopher D. Maxwell

Introduction

Alexis de Tocqueville made a well-observed comment nearly 200 years ago that aspects of American society and culture are "exceptional." While describing something as "exceptional" is usually taken as complimentary, notably the idea of "American exceptionalism" is considered a double-edged sword because it "permits pernicious and beneficial social phenomena to arise simultaneously" (Lipset 1996: 268). Notwithstanding debates about the veracity of this idea more broadly conceived, the United States is exceptional in many ways related to crime and criminal justice. Regarding American homicide, its volume, nature, and correlates are distinctive and so too are the explanations for it and responses to it that have emerged over time. Within this chapter, we give an overview of the key issues that signify the exceptional nature of American homicide.

Describing American Homicide

Homicide data in the US

In the United States, there are two major federal repositories of homicide data: the US Department of Justice's Uniform Crime Reporting (UCR) Program, and the National Vital Statistics System (NVSS) operated by the Centers for Disease Control and Prevention (CDC). In the context of homicide, these systems capture information about the same events, although the information that each collects is somewhat different.

The Handbook of Homicide, First Edition. Edited by Fiona Brookman,
Edward R. Maguire, and Mike Maguire.

First, in 1929 the UCR Program began collecting information about serious crimes, including homicide and non-negligent manslaughter, reported to law enforcement authorities. Today more than 18,000 law enforcement agencies across the United States voluntarily report data on select crimes brought to their attention. The UCR Program also collects additional information about victims, offenders, and circumstances surrounding homicides with the Supplementary Homicide Reports (SHR), where each record represents a homicide "incident" (homicides, non-negligent manslaughter, and justifiable homicides)[1] with information collected on a maximum of 11 offenders and victims for each. For this chapter, we reorganized these data for the period 1980–2012 so that each record represents an individual victim of homicide, resulting in a unique dataset covering 32 years and 618,080 victims. Second, in 1933, the NVSS began to collect uniformly birth and death records registered by state and local governments, as opposed to crimes reported to the police. The death certificate data that the NVSS compiles include decedent's age, race, ethnicity, marital status, resident status, educational attainment, residence, cause of death, and the nature of the injuries sustained (but not information on the suspected perpetrator nor the victim-perpetrator relationship).

Multiple sources of data create both opportunities and problems. Although an early comparison of UCR and NVSS found that the use of either produced the same substantive results, a more recent comparison was less optimistic. Due to their different definitions of cases, and because of failures to follow data collection procedures within each system, their estimates agree less often than might be expected.[2] For the purpose of this chapter, these measurement errors should be borne in mind for analyses below the national level.

Trends over time

Figure 21.1 displays counts and rates derived from the two federal data systems available for American homicides. Across the 62 years displayed, it is clear that homicides have both substantially increased (e.g., from 1950 to 1980) and decreased (e.g., 1991–2012). The UCR rate, which is observable over the most years, varies from a low of 4.0 in 1957 (n = 8,060) to a high of 10.2 in 1980 (n = 23,040). The most recent rate of 4.7 in 2012 is the lowest since the early 1960s. Although not producing identical estimates, the CDC data supports the same substantive conclusion drawn from the UCR data: US homicide rates have declined significantly since the 1990s. However, at time of writing, homicide rates are rising in some large American cities, prompting concern.[3]

In Figure 21.2 we compare these national trends for rural versus urban areas. The overwhelming majority of Americans live in urban areas (81% according to the 2010 census). In terms of both counts and rates, most homicides take place in urban areas, so accordingly any changes in urban homicide naturally influences the national picture. For example, both the spike in the mid-1990s and the subsequent decline are

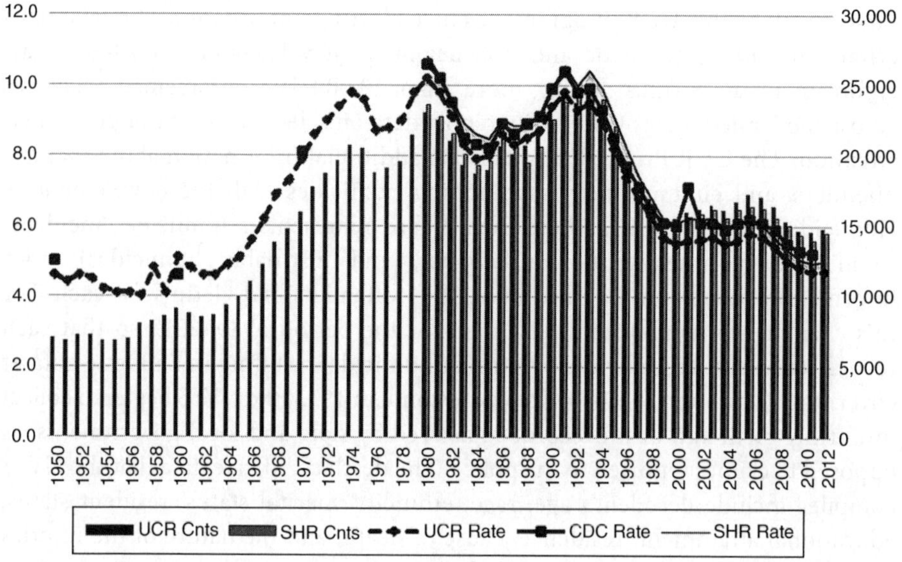

Figure 21.1 US homicide trends, 1950–2012. National totals for UCR and SHR are based on data from all reporting agencies and estimates for unreported areas. The 168 homicide and non-negligent homicides that occurred as a result of the bombing of the Federal Building in Oklahoma City in 1995 are included in the national estimate, whereas the 2,823 that occurred as a result of the events of September 11, 2001 are not included. UCR and SHR rates are based on the number of reported offenses per 100,000 population. CDC rates are reported as deaths per 100,000 resident population.

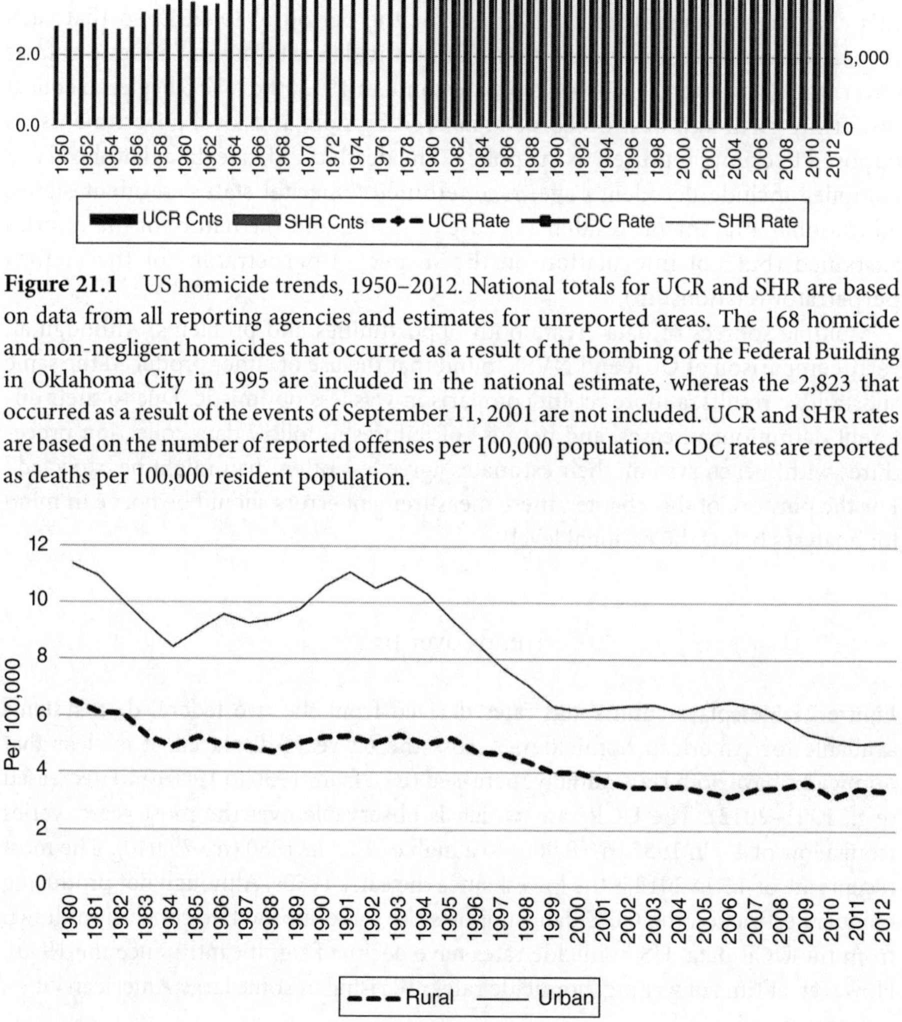

Figure 21.2 Rural and urban homicide rates, 1980–2012.

largely attributed to changes in the urban homicide rate. At its height in 1980 and the early 1990s, the urban rate was roughly twice that of the rural rate. In recent years, these differences are smaller (e.g., 5.1 compared to 3.4 in 2012).

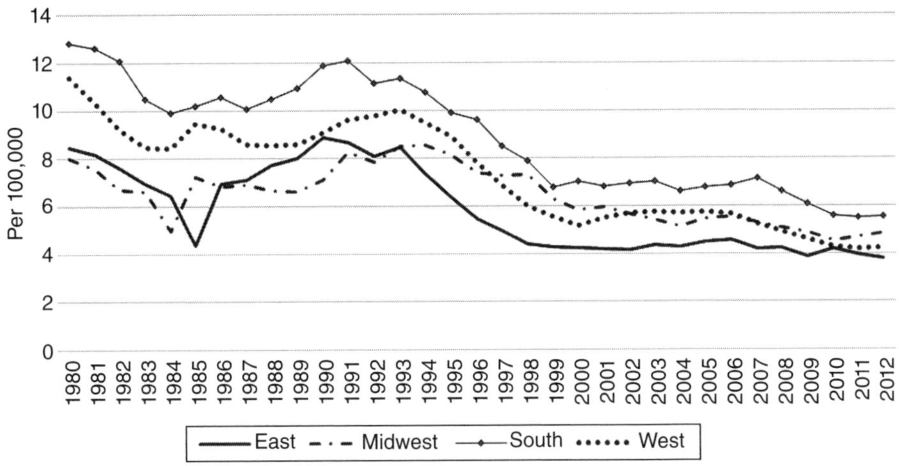

Figure 21.3 Homicide rates by US geographic region, 1980–2012.

The homicide rate also varies according to the geographic region of the United States, as Figure 21.3 shows. Some regions, such as the South, produce higher rates of violent crime, including homicide, throughout history and into the present day. Some explanations for these differences are explored later in the chapter. Although these national trends are informative, producing them requires pooling all types of homicide, which masks distinctive trends for subgroups, as the next section will show.

Victims and offenders

In the United States, as in other countries, different demographic groups experience different risks for becoming a homicide victim or offender; therefore, homicide is another way that structural inequalities according to sex, age, and race/ethnicity are revealed. Using the period 1980–2012, our analysis of data from the UCR Program reinforces well-documented trends about the demographic profile of homicide victims.

First, the majority of both homicide victims and offenders each year are male. The homicide victimization rate for males is approximately three times the female rate (11.6 compared to 3.4 per 100,000) and the homicide offending rate is also substantially higher for males than females (15.1 compared to 1.7 per 100,000) (Cooper and Smith 2011). These trends are noticeably stable over time, and reveal that men are more likely to commit murder than to be murdered, while the opposite is true for women.

Second, our age analysis indicates that, although the changes are relatively modest, over time the proportion of homicide victims that are adults (25+) has declined, whereas for the other age categories it has increased. Teens and young adults consistently have the highest victimization and offending rates when it comes to homicide. Although this is true for all racial and sex groups, there are extreme differences

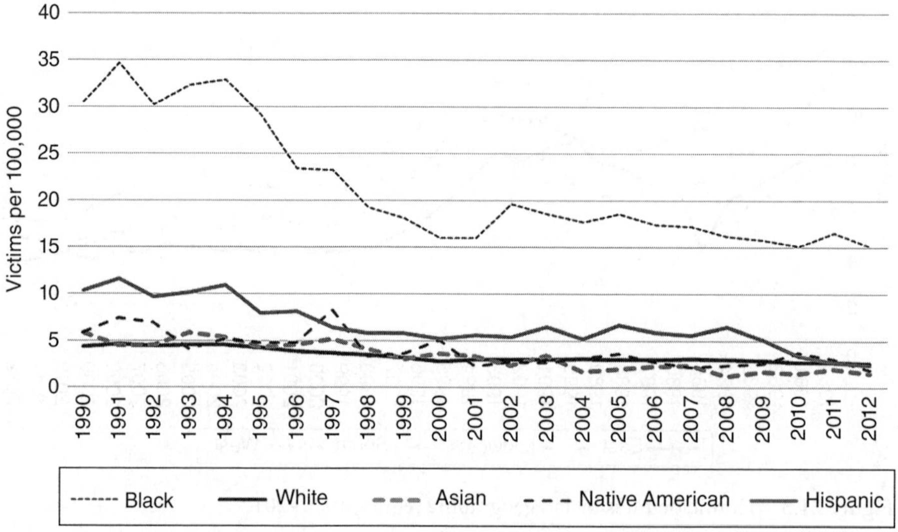

Figure 21.4 Homicide rate by victim's race and ethnicity.

according to race. For example, when the victimization rates for teens peaked in 1993, 9.4 white teens died from homicides per 100,000 whereas for black teens it was more than eight times higher at 79 per 100,000 (Cooper and Smith 2011).

Third, we compared trends over time for the main racial/ethnic categories in the United States (see Figure 21.4). In line with a multitude of other studies, our analysis shows that the average rate of homicide victimization for black people is several times higher than that for any other racial/ethnic group (21.5 per 100,000 compared to 3.5 for white people, 3.3 for Asians, 4.1 for American Indians, and 6.4 for Hispanics). This means that the majority of homicide victims are black (47% of total victims), nearly quadruple their proportion within American society generally (approximately 13%) (Cooper and Smith 2011). Victims of "other" ethnic origins constitute less than 3 percent of the total. Although this is lower than their proportion in society generally, it does mask markedly different trends for different groups (e.g., Native Americans have the highest rate of victimization and Asian Americans the lowest).

Not only do trends differ according to victim demographics, the type of homicide also plays a role. Besides the overall drop in homicide in the United States, no other rate has drawn more attention than the rate of intimate-partner homicide (IPH) (although several recent mass shootings may change this focus; see http://shootingtracker.com/; see also Chapter15, this volume). Figure 21.5 displays the overall IPH rate as well as the percentage of these incidents that involved male and female victims. Across the 32-year period displayed, IPH makes up a stable proportion of the overall total (about 10%). Yet over this period, the number of male victims declined more sharply than it did for female victims: 1,300 reduced to 400 compared to 1,500 reduced to 1,000, respectively. An alternative expression of the same finding is that the percentage of IPH victims that were female increased from 55 percent in 1980 to 75 percent in 2012. This is a growing disparity, particularly given the disproportionate amount of policies and

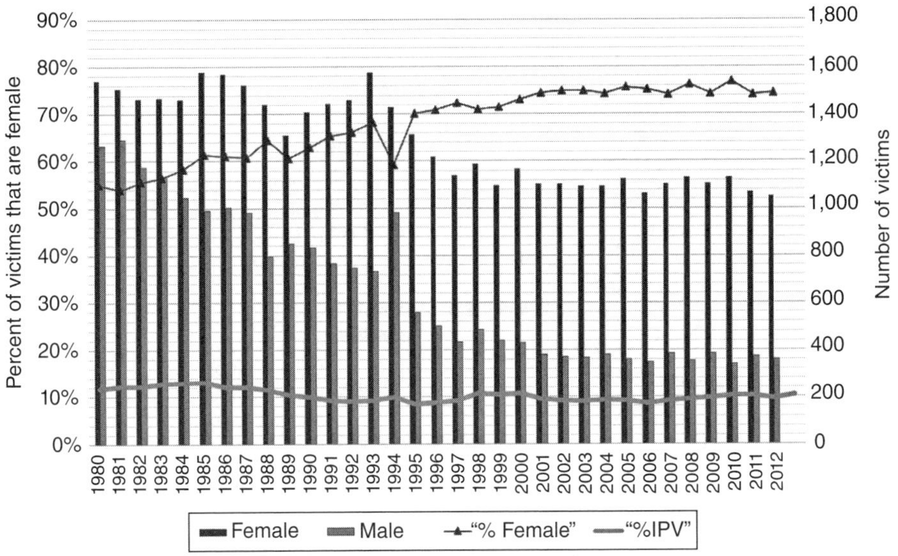

Figure 21.5 Intimate partner homicide in the United States, 1980–2012.

services directed toward protecting women experiencing abuse from their intimate partners, and has prompted a number of studies into this differential decline by gender (Dugan, Nagin, and Rosenfeld 2004).

Further analysis incorporating victims' ethnicity (not shown) revealed that white victims were more likely to be killed by intimate partners whereas both black and Hispanic victims were more likely to die from other types of homicide. This is likely a reflection of their higher risk of victimization from other types of homicide (e.g., drug-related, gang-related and those involving firearms) (Cooper and Smith 2011).

Homicidal circumstances

Homicide scholars have identified a number of circumstances that are important for explaining its occurrence. Here we will focus on three that are distinctly relevant for understanding American homicides: handguns, gangs, and illicit drugs.

Figure 21.6 indicates the type of weapon involved in homicides. Notably, the majority of homicides in the United States involve a firearm of some type (e.g., handguns, rifles, shotguns, and other types of guns). In most states more than 50 percent of homicides involved a firearm. Handguns are the most frequently identified type of firearm used in a substantial proportion, if not a majority, of homicides in nearly every state. Despite more attention and public debate than ever on the pernicious role of guns in American life, their role in serious violence is intensifying. Gun involvement in gang-related homicides and in homicides that occurred during the commission of a felony has substantially increased over time, and adolescents are still most likely to be killed with guns (Cooper and Smith 2011).

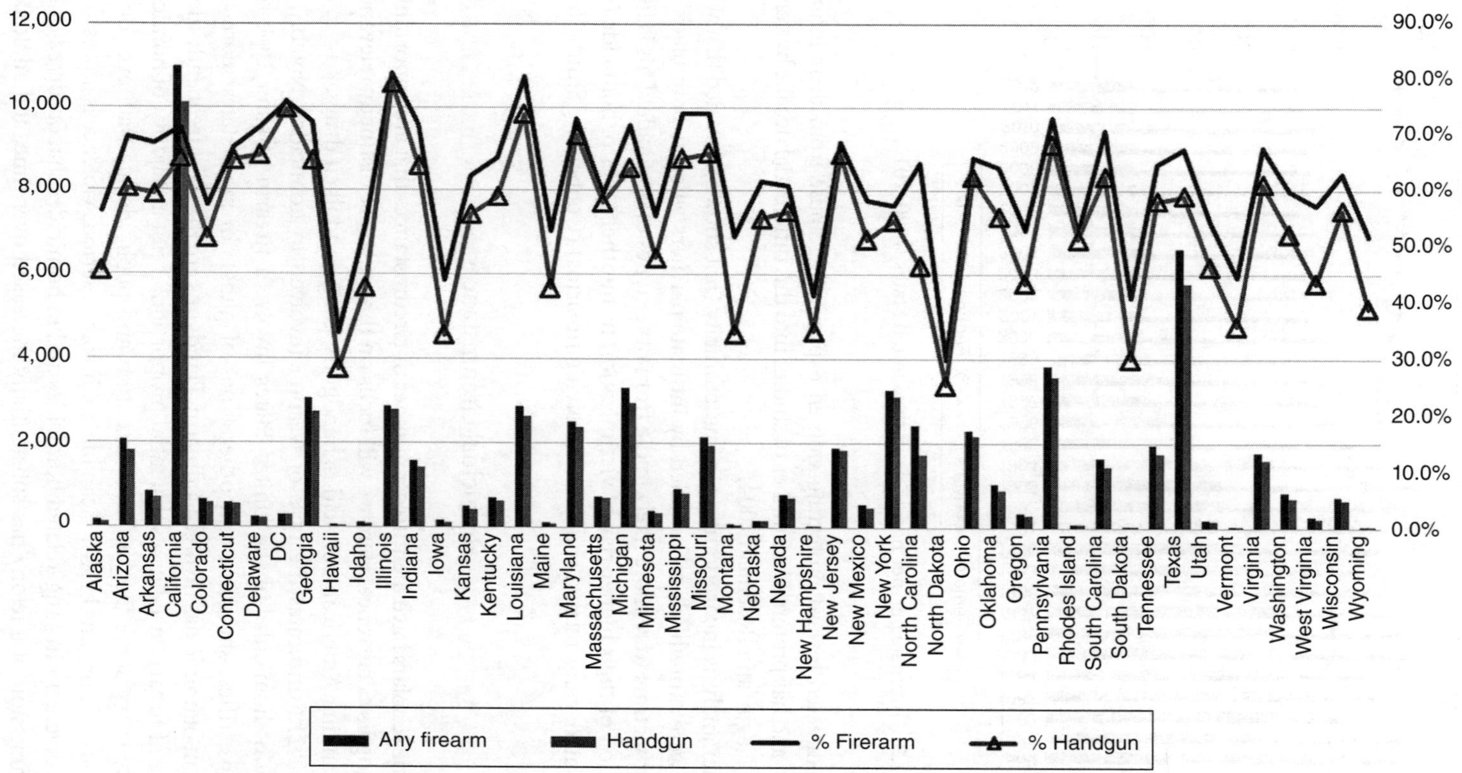

Figure 21.6 Homicides by firearm and handgun, 2006–2012.

As indicated previously, each year additional information is collected about the circumstances surrounding homicides through the UCR Program. Unfortunately, many law enforcement agencies do not specify the type of circumstance surrounding the homicide, therefore, details about the nature of the circumstances surrounding the homicidal incident are more often unknown than known. Nevertheless, the available data is instructive for painting a picture of the most prevalent circumstances surrounding homicides in the United States. During 2009–2013, the most common description of the circumstance of the homicide was "other type of arguments" (i.e., those *not* involving disputes over money or property, romantic triangles,[4] or brawls due to the influence of alcohol or drugs), followed by gangs, robberies, and narcotics as the next most prevalent types. Homicides involving gangs, robberies, and narcotics are significantly more likely to involve firearms, specifically handguns (the weapon of choice in two-thirds or more of these types of homicides). It is important to bear in mind that UCR figures underestimate the influence of gangs, and therefore guns, on homicide statistics. For example, the National Youth Gang Survey reports more than twice the number of incidents of gang-related homicides, or approximately 2,100 per year during 2008–2013. These same data also demonstrate that gang homicides are spatially concentrated events: nearly 67 percent occurred in cities with populations over 100,000 and in a typical year about one in four takes place in either Chicago or Los Angeles (National Gang Center 2015).

Explaining American Homicide

Much American scholarship has focused on explaining the "great American crime drop" and by extension the significant declines in homicide seen since the mid-1990s. Intertwined are attempts to account for distinctly American aspects of the problem, such as the high rates experienced by some racial groups, the influence of gangs and illicit drug markets, and incomparable levels of gun ownership. Accordingly, in this section we focus on two areas of theoretical enquiry that have produced long-standing and highly developed bodies of US-based research: (1) the structural conditions that make some communities more susceptible to lethal violence and (2) cultural explanations such as the "code of the street" which help explain how these play out in daily life. This section is illustrative, not exhaustive, and reading about other compelling explanations such as the availability of crack cocaine and the legalization of abortion is highly recommended (Blumstein, Rivara, and Rosenfeld 2000; Levitt 2004).

Structural conditions

Going back nearly a hundred years to the work of the Chicago School, researchers have documented the influence that positive and negative features of a community have on the chances that people in these communities will experience various forms of crime, including homicide. Importantly, this pioneering research revealed that structural conditions that affect communities matter even when the ethnic composition of the residents change (known as the "racial invariance thesis") and in so doing this research started to pinpoint why crime flourishes more in some areas than others. According to this thesis, the influence of factors, such as poverty, unemployment, and segregation, on homicide are expected to be similar across different racial and ethnic groups, assuming equivalent exposure and distribution (Sampson and Bean 2006). This thesis finds support in extant research. For example, homicide rates for both black and white Americans living in urban areas have been shown to be similarly influenced by whether these areas are socioeconomically disadvantaged with high concentrations of poverty (although the same relationships do not hold for rural areas) (Lee, Maume, and Ousey 2003; Lee, Sebold, and Uken 2003). Community level factors have even been shown to influence levels of intimate-partner homicides that tend to occur "behind closed doors" (Beyer *et al.* 2015). Studies also have elucidated *how* communities plagued by structural disadvantages can affect an individual's willingness to use violence or their susceptibility to violent victimization. For example, decreased guardianship and exposure to criminals was found to generate motivations and opportunities susceptible to offending in highly disadvantaged areas, and this was true regardless of the demographic profile of offenders and victims (Broidy *et al.* 2006).

Some researchers have employed a multilevel approach to reveal the complex and intertwined relationships between disadvantaged areas, impoverished and minority ethnic individuals, and homicide. Their results suggest both race and place matter for understanding homicide. For example, Berthelot *et al.* (2015) found that the murder of affluent black individuals living in the least deprived areas occurred at twice the rate as compared to low-income white people in highly disadvantaged areas. They concluded that "in disadvantaged communities, it is not being poor in a poor area that increases victimization risk but rather being black, poor, and residing in a disadvantaged area that substantially increases the risk of being murdered" (Berthelot *et al.* 2015: 20). How can the race of an individual remain an important correlate of whether they experience homicide as a victim or as an offender, even when structurally induced characteristics of their neighborhood are taken into account? Massey and Denton (1993) contend that, because it is rooted in purposeful actions by the majority group (e.g., segregation caused by institutional racism and discrimination within housing and banking systems), structural disadvantages experienced by black Americans are inherently more damaging to their life outcomes. Thus poor to middle-class black neighborhoods cannot fairly be compared with their white counterparts.

Building on these findings, recent research advances the notion that the painful historical legacy and persistent reality of racial segregation is quintessentially American and thus holds the key to explaining American homicide. For example, an analysis of homicide rates in New York and 171 other US cities from 1980–2010 highlights the most pernicious consequence of racial segregation is the social isolation it produces, even more so than the accompanying social deprivation, which leads to higher levels of homicide among black Americans. Consequently, the authors concluded that "the long-term reduction in the homicide victim and offender rates of young black men will require a greatly expanded movement toward a fully integrated society" (Chilton and Chambliss 2014: 14). The segregation–homicide link was tested for Hispanics by Bisciglia (2014) who found that as Hispanics become more segregated from white non-Hispanics and more isolated within their own enclaves the number of Hispanic homicides increased. This goes against the "Latino Paradox," a term coined from earlier research which found that Hispanics generally fare better with regard to violence even in the face of extreme disadvantage (Sampson 2008). This apparent contradiction may be explained by the many ethnicities covered by the term Hispanic and by the difference between self-segregation (which might foster community cohesion) compared to segregation that is due to institutionalized racism. The idea of "community" and its relationship to homicide is complex, multifaceted, and only just beginning to be systematically untangled, but its value in explaining American homicide cannot be ignored.

Cultural perspectives

Understanding the relationship between culture and violence has occupied researchers for decades (e.g., Wolfgang 1958). Much of this work originated in order to explain two of the marked and distinctly American trends we presented earlier: what is it about the South and what is it about predominantly black inner-city areas that produce violence that is more lethal? The first tends to be attributed to the particular historical and economic circumstances of Southern states (e.g., religious, poor, agrarian, slavery-based economy) which contributed to the development of what is known as a "culture of honor" (Nisbett and Cohen 1996). In effect, this cultural perspective views violence as a response to provocations, to "save face" or when family honor is in jeopardy. Consequently, violence is often used and, when guns are available, more frequently results in homicide. The second also has been subjected to a cultural analysis. For example, Anderson's (1999) influential book proposed that "codes of the street" were values which recognized violence as *the* way to achieve status and respect, when other, legitimate methods are not available. His ideas recently have been followed up and extended by Goffman's (2014) controversial ethnography that illustrated how urban black people's experience and resistance transformed their "legal entanglements" in daily life, sometimes through violence. In these contexts, violence is used to achieve a range of objectives.

Rather than contradicting structural explanations, such as those described in the previous section, cultural perspectives on homicide can be seen as complementary. In fact, recent research explicitly seeks to bridge the two literatures, in order to produce more nuanced and holistic understandings of why homicide occurs. For example, Lee (2011) uses a culture-as-action paradigm to forge awareness of the similar underpinning factors that promote high levels of lethal violence from two seemingly different groups: rural Southern white people and inner-city black people. He argues that both settings offer opportunities for violence through an absence of law (which is geographically distant for rural white people and socially distant for urban black people) combined with entrenched poverty and weak social institutions. Socialization therefore takes place through other, limited, and negative channels, such as gangs and illicit drugs markets. These inculcate a few cultural scripts that promote violence rather than a broader, more diversified set of scripts. Thus it is not only entrenched socioeconomic disadvantage that make communities more or less susceptible to violence, but the residents within them that use, reinforce, and transmit a more narrow range of strategies to navigate through society. Explaining American homicide through understanding the contours of American culture is a compelling line of enquiry and one that has produced a remarkably insightful and wide-ranging body of research.

Responding to American Homicide

In this section we describe a continuum of interventions aimed at reducing homicide ranging from those based on principles of general deterrence to those more specific in their focus. As in most other countries, the responsibility for responding to homicide in America falls mainly to criminal justice agencies and this section reflects that reality, although partnership initiatives involving other agencies are included when possible.

Incarceration and the death penalty

One of the most significant debates in criminology concerns whether criminal justice sanctions can deter offending. A large majority of studies have focused on the impact of incarceration on crime, but we found just 11 articles that examined homicide separately from other types of violent crime. Unfortunately, this body of research has produced varying, even conflicting, conclusions regarding the relationship between incarceration rates and homicide rates. On one side of the ledger, at least six studies (see DeFina and Arvanites 2002; Levitt 1996; Marvell and Moody 1994; Rosenfeld, Fornango, and Rengifo 2007; Sampson 1986; Zimring and Hawkins 1995) have not demonstrated that incarceration has a significant impact on homicide. For example, national-level research found that each additional prisoner reduced only 0.004 homicides (Levitt 1996) while each additional year of incarceration prevented just 0.007 homicides (Zimring and Hawkins 1995). Conversely, other scholars have produced results that are more consistent with Ehrlich's (1975) view about the responsiveness of even the most emotionally charged crimes to criminal sanctions. We were able to locate five studies (see Cohen and Land 1987; Devine, Sheley, and Smith 1988; Levitt 2004; Marvell and Moody 1997; McCall, Parker, and MacDonald 2008) that each produced statistically significant negative, deterrent effects between incarceration and homicide rates. For instance, Marvell and Moody (1997), analyzing the relationship between incarceration and homicide between 1930 and

1994, found that every 10 percent increase in the prison population is associated with an estimated 13 percent reduction in homicides. Further complicating the picture, more recent research found that the level of incarceration increased homicides among those aged 15–24 but was unrelated for all other age groups (Cerdá *et al.* 2010).

In addition to its high homicide and incarceration rates, America sets itself apart from most other nations by continuing to offer the death penalty as a punishment option in a majority of states. A related branch of criminological scholarship has sought to determine whether the death penalty specifically has any deterrent effect on homicide rates. One of the earliest empirical works in this area found that each execution prevented approximately eight homicides (Ehrlich 1975).[5] However, several scholars failed to replicate these results using different data, alternative statistical methods, and other modifications to address Ehrlich's techniques and data errors. More recent studies have attributed "strong deterrent effects" to the death penalty; for example, finding that executions decrease all homicides (Dezhbakhsh, Rubin, and Shepherd 2003) including those committed as "crimes of passion" (Shepherd 2004), and that commutations and removals from death row increase homicides (Mocan and Gittings 2003). Although this evidence has been described as "impressive" (Sunstein and Vermeule 2005: 713), others have expressed dissenting perspectives on the quality of these newer studies (e.g., Berk 2005), cautioning against using them to influence policy (Nagin and Pepper 2012).[6] In conclusion, research about the value of incarceration and the death penalty for deterring homicide at best yields inconclusive results.

Controlling access to firearms

As previous sections have illustrated, homicides and firearms share an enduring relationship in America. Perhaps it comes as no surprise then, that there has been spirited discussion about preventing or regulating access to firearms, particularly handguns, for nearly 100 years (Harwood 2002).[7] Over time, the federal government and many states have passed laws that limit those who can purchase a weapon. For example, by the end of twentieth century, 33 states had laws (commonly known as "shall-issue" statues) that allow adults to have permits to carry concealed weapons if they have no significant criminal history or mental illness, and have passed a training course (Donohue 2003). In this context, debates have raged about whether or how governments should regulate gun possession. Almost as controversial has been the nature of the research about the effects of control laws on homicide. Lott (1998) produced the most influential findings on this topic through his analysis of US county-level UCR data for the period 1976–1995. He estimated that 9 percent of homicides, 5 percent of rapes, and 7 percent of aggravated assaults could have been avoided if all states had adopted a right-to-carry (RTC) concealed handgun law in 1992. Furthermore, he asserted that the prevention effects of these laws was greatest in high-crime and high-population counties, even after controlling for other effects such as poverty, unemployment, and police arrest rates. Several scholars have sought to replicate these findings, with little success. For example, Black and Nagin (1998) used an alternative model that looked at year-to-year differences and found no significant impact for any type of violent crime. Further clouding the issue is other research indicating that higher rates of household firearms ownership are associated with higher rates dying from a homicide in the home and of gun suicide (Dahlberg, Ikeda, and Kresnow 2004; Miller, Azrael, and Hemenway 2002).

Since Lott (1998) and Black and Nagin's (1998) landmark debate, a great deal more published research has presented conflicting conclusions. The National Research Council's Committee to Improve Research Information and Data on Firearms "found no credible evidence that the passage of right-to-carry laws decreases or increases violent crime" (Wellford, Pepper, and Petrie 2004). Aneja, Donohue, and Zhang (2011) extended NRC's research by adding six years of county data as well as state panel data, but still concluded that RTC laws did not affect murder rates. Additional contradictory results from other studies (e.g., Gius 2013; Lanza 2014; Moody *et al.* 2014) enables only a weak conclusion that RTC laws have not reduced the incidence of firearm deaths, but "tighter controls" might produce "modest reductions." Regardless of the approaches taken to date to estimate the relationship between gun controls and violence across America, the apparent effect, whether it is statistically significant or not, must be marginal compared to other factors driving down homicide rates since 1992.

Offender-focused deterrence programs

Beginning in the mid-1990s, with homicides reaching a level not measured before in the United States, particularly among urban minority youths, a number of large cities began to develop comprehensive strategies to reduce homicides by adopting a "problem-solving" approach (Sheppard and COSMOS Corporation 1999). Each community differed in the ways that it implemented their comprehensive plan; however, each was supported by the US Department of Justice's Anti-Violent Crime Initiative effort to identify and prioritize local violent crime problems and to develop and implement coordinated approaches to address them. By the late 1990s, eight US cities were using this method to address illegal guns sales, deter illegal gun possession and use, and provide educational programs that taught alternatives to violence (Fagan 2002). The most notable of these initial programs was Boston's Gun Project, a multi-agency collaboration that included the Boston Police Department, the Massachusetts probation and parole department, Harvard University, the US Attorney's Office and other federal law enforcement agencies, and several local NGOs. Responding to analyses that estimated 1 percent of the city's youth population was responsible for 60 percent of Boston's homicides, the group developed two interventions, which they collectively entitled Operation Ceasefire (Kennedy, Piehl, and Braga 1996). The first intervention called for law enforcement agencies to use "all possible legal levers" to disrupt the illicit firearms markets that supplied Boston's youth with guns and to focus more of their attention on gang violence (Kennedy 1997). Such activities included: concentrating on low-level crimes; serving outstanding warrants; delivering strict probation and parole enforcement; seizing drug proceeds and other assets; requesting and enforcing higher bail terms following arrest; and increasing prosecutions and sanctions by using either local or federal law enforcement agencies. The second intervention called for directly contracting gang members to deliver a message that their violence "would no longer be tolerated," while also offering needed services. Notably, an evaluation of Operation Ceasefire found a statistically significant decrease of 63 percent in Boston's youth homicides, and significant reductions in gun assault incidents, shots-fired calls for service, and youth gun assaults (Braga *et al.* 2001). Although Fagan's (2002) analysis did not find as large of an effect,[8] at least ten other similar sites have evaluated "pulling levers" focused deterrence programs, with a meta-analysis concluding they are associated with an overall statistically significant crime reduction effect (Braga and Weisburd 2012). However, this conclusion is based upon studies that did not use strong research designs, and the research that assesses how offenders respond to the focused deterrence process has produced mixed results (Chermak and McGarrell 2004; Papachristos *et al.* 2013). Although stronger research is needed, offender-focused deterrence programs, by virtue of their targeted interventions and multi-agency partnership approach, may offer the most effective response yet to deal with American homicide.

Another, much touted, offender-focused homicide reduction effort is the Cure Violence program (see also Chapter 34, this volume). This program emphasizes using outreach workers, rather than police and probation officers, to address norms, decisions, and risk-taking among both its target population of 18–25-year-olds living in high-crime areas as well as the wider community. Since its inception, a few quasi-controlled evaluations of this approach have reported positive results (e.g., Picard-Fritsche and Cerniglia 2013; Webster *et al.* 2012). Skogan *et al.*'s (2009) evaluation found that areas implementing the program experienced reductions in a number of measures including fewer shootings, killings, and retaliatory homicides. The program also appeared to make shooting "hot spots" cooler in some (but not all) participating neighborhoods. However, it is not clear whether Skogan's evaluation had adequately controlled for other explanations for these declines (e.g., other homicide reduction activities taking place in the same neighborhoods). Nevertheless, the National Institute of Justice rates this program as one of many "promising" approaches (see https://www.crimesolutions.gov/).

Concluding Thoughts

There are a number of takeaways from our discussion of changing American homicide rates over the past several decades, and possible explanations for these. One fact is clear: despite significant reductions since the peak periods of the early 1980s and mid-1990s, American homicide remains exceptionally prevalent in comparison to other developed Western nations (see also Chapter 2, this volume). Furthermore, as important as this overall drop is to the health and welfare of the US population, it is also clear that many of the disparities that became known during the 1980s still exist nearly 40 years later. In our view, the most notable of these inequalities is the disturbing gap in the homicide rate that remains between black and white Americans. The sheer volume of black people losing their lives to homicides is so immense it is difficult to comprehend: 176,594 over a 20-year period (1992–2012). This number represents 49 percent of all US homicides during this period, or about 3.75 times more homicides than would have occurred if black and white Americans were equally at risk from homicide.

A second trend worth commenting upon is the number of homicides per year (roughly 16,000) that has remained quite stable over the past decade (although this stability may evaporate if the rates seen in some large American cities continue to rise). On the one hand, some may find this nearly flat annual rate surprising given the focused efforts made by many policymakers, practitioners, and scholars on homicide. For example, McGarrell *et al.* (2009) reported the US government spent an estimated three billion dollars to fund Project Safe Neighborhood programs. These investments in "smart policing" and targeted offender programs, such as those described in the previous section, might continue to pay off. However, if this were the case, we would hope the trend would be one of decline rather than stability.

On the other hand, this flat rate also overlaps with the Great Recession: a period of worldwide economic decline between 2007 and 2010.[9] US police chiefs warned that this economic downturn would produce an increase in crime that they could not respond to because of budget cuts. Yet, after the dust had settled, inexplicably neither homicide nor crime in general increased significantly anywhere in the United States. Zimring (NBC 2012) described this paradox as the "mystery meat in the recipe of recent years" and then went on to say that what did *not* happen during the recession challenged everything known about crime. Nevertheless, one possible explanation is the investments that McGarrell and others have described in targeted multi-agency homicide reduction strategies may have blunted any negative effects from foreclosures and unemployment. Maybe it is indeed this investment and other, much larger investments, such as the 2009 American Recovery and Reinvestment Act, that have prevented the homicide and crimes rates more generally from sky-rocketing. Without this infusion of cash into America's cites to expand employment opportunities, ease city budget cuts, and rebuild infrastructure, homicides rates may indeed have returned to peak levels.

Finally, we would like to comment on future developments in both policy and research. We are pleased to see more coordinated interventions to reduce homicide that are based upon a partnership approach, involving practitioners from a range of agencies both within and outside of the criminal justice system working together to develop and implement evidence-based initiatives tailored to the local landscape. Although the evidence base about the effectiveness of such initiatives could be deepened, it is reassuring that many studies from a range of disciplines and involving different policy issues support the principle of taking a more focused, problem-oriented approach over any generic, wholesale initiative. Research should continue on these initiatives, making use of both qualitative and quantitative methods to answer a broader range of research questions. American homicide research more generally would benefit from more comprehensive coverage of the National Incident-based Reporting System (NIBRS), which we hope will continue to grow, in order to support a more varied assortment of theoretically interesting projects.

Notes

1 The FBI's UCR Program defines murder and non-negligent manslaughter as "the willful (non-negligent) killing of one human being by another." Justifiable homicides are killings that are determined through law enforcement investigation to be justifiable, so they are tabulated separately from murder and non-negligent manslaughter (see https://www.fbi.gov/about-us/cjis/ucr/).

2 For example, Wiersema, Loftin, and McDowell (2000) found agreement in only 22 percent of counties for the period 1979–1988, although this rose to 68 percent using a looser definition of agreement (a difference of no more than four homicides). Furthermore, these differences are more likely to occur in large population counties (Wiersema, Loftin, and McDowell 2000) and rural counties (Baller *et al.* 2002).

3 On 7 October 2015, US Justice Department officials met with police commanders, mayors and FBI leaders to discuss rising violence (Tucker 2015; see also Davey and Smith 2015).

4 This term has been in use since the SHR was established in 1977. Over the period 1980–2012 there have been n = 8862 in total. Most involve male victims (n = 6641) and male offenders (n = 7663). Most of the female offenders (n = 995) kill male victims (n = 664).

5 This finding was particularly noteworthy because it clashed with the scholarly perspective at that time which had discarded the death penalty as a deterrent to crime even though available research was not convincing one way or the other (Bailey 1974). Even though other scholars quickly disputed Ehrlich's findings, the United States Supreme Court in 1976 used Ehrlich's data in a decision that restored capital punishment (following the moratorium imposed by the 1973 decision *Furman v Georgia*). Regrettably, the justices settled this case before the National Academy of Sciences' Panel on Research on Deterrence and Incapacitation published their review of the results produced by Ehrlich, concluding they should be ignored because they were useless for estimating the magnitude of the effects of different sanctions on various crime types (Blumstein, Cohen, and Nagin 1978).

6 The panel did offer several recommendations for addressing the shortcomings that they found in the current body of capital punishment research. These recommendations included collecting data "required for a more complete specification of both the capital and noncapital components of the sanction regime for homicide; research on how potential offenders perceive the sanction regime for homicide; and use of methods that makes less strong and more credible assumptions to identify or bound the effect of capital punishment on homicides" (Nagin and Pepper 2012: 7).

7 For instance, New York State passed its first gun control law in 1911, which required police-issued licenses for those wishing to possess a concealable firearm and made

carrying an unlicensed concealed weapon a felony. At the federal level, following the assassination of President John Kennedy, the US congress passed the Gun Control Act of 1968 to regulate interstate commerce in firearms (ironically by restricting mail-order sales of shotguns and rifles). It also defined a class of people ineligible to possess firearms. Later the Brady Law required background checks for purchases.

8 Fagan (2002) showed that firearm homicide victimization of those under age 25 began to decline the year preceding the implementation of Operation Ceasefire, and then began to rise again three years later. He also demonstrated similar declines in other Massachusetts cities during this same period and showed that in cities with populations of 75,000 to 175,000, youth firearm homicide victimization rates had declined nearly 50 percent more by 1998 than what was found in Boston.

9 During this period, the US unemployment rate doubled (from 5% to nearly 10%), the Consumer Sentiment Index and the US Dow Jones Industrial averages both dropped by more than 50 percent from their historic peaks, and the number of new property foreclosures increased from 0.6 per million in 2005 to 2 per million by 2009.

References

Anderson, E. (1999) *Code of the Street: Decency, Violence, and the Moral Life of the Inner City*. New York: W.W. Norton.

Aneja, A., Donohue, J.J., and Zhang, A. (2011) The impact of right-to-carry laws and the NRC report: Lessons for the empirical evaluation of law and policy. *American Law and Economics Review*, 13(2): 565–631.

Bailey, W.C. (1974) Murder and the death penalty. *Journal of Criminal Law and Criminology*, 65(3): 416–422.

Baller, R.D., Messner, S.F., Anselin, L., and Deane, G. (2002) The interchangeability of homicide data sources: A spatial analytical perspective. *Homicide Studies*, 6(3): 211–227.

Berk, R. (2005) New claims about executions and general deterrence: Deja vu all over again? *Journal of Empirical Legal Studies*, 2(2): 303–330.

Berthelot, E.R., Brown, T.C., Thomas, S.A., and Burgason, K.A. (2015) Racial (in)variance, disadvantage, and lethal violence: A survival analysis of black homicide victimization risk in the United States. *Homicide Studies*, 20(2): 103–128.

Beyer, K.M., Layde, P.M., Hamberger, L.K., and Laud, P.W. (2015) Does neighborhood environment differentiate intimate partner femicides from other femicides? *Violence Against Women*, 21(1): 49–64.

Bisciglia, M.G. (2014) Segregation and Hispanic homicide: An examination of two measures of segregation on rates of Hispanic homicide in major metropolitan areas. *SAGE Open*, 4(1).

Black, D.A. and Nagin, D.S. (1998) Do right-to-carry laws deter violent crime? *Journal of Legal Studies*, 27(1): 209–219.

Blumstein, A., Cohen, J., and Nagin, D. (eds) (1978) *Deterrence and Incapacitation: Estimating the Effects of Criminal Sanctions on Crime Rates*. Washington, DC: National Academy of Sciences.

Blumstein, A., Rivara, F.P., and Rosenfeld, R. (2000) The rise and decline of homicide—and why. *Annual Review of Public Health*, 21: 505–541.

Braga, A.A., Kennedy, D.M., Waring, E.J., and Piehl, A.M. (2001) Problem-oriented policing, deterrence, and youth violence: An evaluation of Boston's Operation Ceasefire. *Journal of Research in Crime and Delinquency*, 38(3): 195–225.

Braga, A.A. and Weisburd, D. (2012) *The Effects of "Pulling Levers" Focused Deterrence Strategies on Crime*. Oslo: Campbell Collaboration.

Broidy, L.M., Daday, J.K., Crandall, C.S., et al. (2006) Exploring demographic, structural, and behavioral overlap among homicide offenders and victims. *Homicide Studies*, 10(3): 155–180.

Cerdá, M., Messner, S.F., Tracy, M., et al. (2010) Investigating the effect of social changes on age-specific gun-related homicide rates in New York City during the 1990s. *American Journal of Public Health*, 100(6): 1107–1115.

Chermak, S. and McGarrell, E. (2004) Problem-solving approaches to homicide: An evaluation of the Indianapolis Violence Reduction Partnership. *Criminal Justice Policy Review*, 15(2): 161–192.

Chilton, R. and Chambliss, W.J. (2014) Urban homicide in the United States, 1980–2010: The importance of disaggregated trends. *Homicide Studies*, 19(3): 257–272.

Cohen, L.E. and Land, K.C. (1987) Age structure and crime: Symmetry versus asymmetry and the projection of crime rates through the 1990s. *American Sociological Review*, 52(2): 170–183.

Cooper, A. and Smith, E.L. (2011) *Homicide Trends in the United States, 1980–2008*. Washington, DC: National Government Publication.

Dahlberg, L.L., Ikeda, R.M., and Kresnow, M.-J. (2004) Guns in the home and risk of a violent death in the home: Findings from a national study. *American Journal of Epidemiology*, 160(10): 929–936.

Davey, M. and Smith, M. (2015) Murder rates rising sharply in many US cities. *The New York Times*, August 31. Available online at http://nyti.ms/1KACvGj (accessed August 31, 2015).

DeFina, R.H., and Arvanites, T.M. (2002) The weak effect of imprisonment on crime: 1971–1998. *Social Science Quarterly*, 83(3): 635–653.

Devine, J.A., Sheley, J.F., and Smith, M.D. (1988) Macroeconomic and social-control policy influences on crime rate changes, 1948–1985. *American Sociological Review*, 53(3): 407–420.

Dezhbakhsh, H., Rubin, P.H., and Shepherd, J.M. (2003) Does capital punishment have a deterrent effect? New evidence from postmoratorium panel data. *American Law and Economics Review*, 5(2): 344–376.

Donohue, J.J. (2003) The impact of concealed-carry laws. In J. Ludwig and P.J. Cook (eds), *Evaluating Gun Policy: Effects on Crime and Violence* (pp. 287–325). Washington, DC: Brookings Institution.

Dugan, L., Nagin, D.S., and Rosenfeld, R. (2004) *The Effects of State and Local Domestic Violence Policy on Intimate Partner Homicide*. Washington, DC: National Institute of Justice.

Ehrlich, I. (1975) The deterrent effect of capital punishment: A question of life and death. *American Economic Review*, 65(3): 397–417.

Fagan, J.A. (2002) Policing guns and youth violence. *Future Child*, 12(2): 132–151.

Gius, M. (2013) An examination of the effects of concealed weapons laws and assault weapons bans on state-level murder rates. *Applied Economics Letters*, 21(4): 265–267.

Goffman, A. (2014) *On the Run: Fugitive Life in an American City*. Chicago: University of Chicago Press.

Harwood, W.S. (2002) Gun control: State versus federal regulation of firearm. *Maine Policy Review*, 11(1): 58–73.

Kennedy, D.M. (1997) Pulling levers: Chronic offenders, high-crime settings, and a theory of prevention. *Valparaiso University Law Review*, 31(2): 449–484.

Kennedy, D.M., Piehl, A.M., and Braga, A.A. (1996) Youth violence in Boston: Gun markets, serious youth offenders, and a use-reduction strategy. *Law and Contemporary Problems*, 59(1): 147–196.

Lanza, S.P. (2014) The effect of firearm restrictions on gun-related homicides across US states. *Applied Economics Letters*, 21(13): 902–905.

Lee, M.R. (2011) Reconsidering culture and homicide. *Homicide Studies*, 15(4): 319–340.

Lee, M.R., Maume, M.O., and Ousey, G.C. (2003) Social isolation and lethal violence across the metro/nonmetro divide: The effects of socioeconomic disadvantage and poverty concentration on homicide. *Rural Sociology*, 68(1): 107–131.

Lee, M.Y., Sebold, J., and Uken, A. (2003) *Solution-Focused Treatment of Domestic Violence Offenders: Accountability for Change*. Oxford: Oxford University Press.

Levitt, S.D. (1996) The effect of prison population size on crime rates: Evidence from prison overcrowding litigation. *Quarterly Journal of Economics*, 3(2): 319–351.

Levitt, S.D. (2004) Understanding why crime fell in the 1990s: Four factors that explain the decline and six that do not. *Journal of Economic Perspectives*, 18(1): 163–190.

Lipset, S.M. (1996) *American Exceptionalism: A Double-Edged Sword*. New York: W.W. Norton.

Lott, J.R., Jr (1998) *More Guns, Less Crime: Understanding Crime and Gun Control Laws*. Chicago: University of Chicago Press.

Marvell, T.B. and Moody, C.E. (1994) Prison population growth and crime reduction. *Journal of Quantitative Criminology*, 10(2): 109–140.

Marvell, T.B. and Moody, C.E. (1997) The impact of prison growth on homicide. *Homicide Studies*, 1(3): 205–233.

Massey, D.S. and Denton, N.A. (1993) *American Apartheid: Segregation and the Making of the Underclass*. Cambridge, MA: Harvard University Press.

McCall, P.L., Parker, K.F., and MacDonald, J.M. (2008) The dynamic relationship between homicide rates and social, economic, and political factors from 1970 to 2000. *Social Science Research*, 37(3): 721–735.

McGarrell, E.F., Kroovand, N., Corsaro, N., *et al.* (2009) *Project Safe Neighborhoods—A National Program to Reduce Gun Crime: Final Project Report*. East Lansing: Michigan State University.

Miller, M., Azrael, D., and Hemenway, D. (2002) Firearm availability and unintentional firearm deaths, suicide, and homicide among 5–14 year olds. *Journal of Trauma, Injury, Infection, and Critical Care*, 52(2): 267–274.

Mocan, H.N. and Gittings, R.K. (2003) Getting off death row: Commuted sentences and the deterrent effect of capital punishment. *Journal of Law and Economics*, 46(2): 453–478.

Moody, C.E., Marvell, T.B., Zimmerman, P.R., and Alenante, F. (2014) The impact of right-to-carry laws on crime: An exercise in replication. *Review of Economics and Finance*, 4(1): 33–43.

Nagin, D.S. and Pepper, J.V. (eds) (2012) *Deterrence and the Death Penalty*. Washington, DC: National Academies Press.

National Gang Center (2015) *National Youth Gang Survey Analysis: Number of Gang-Related Homicides*. Tallahassee, FL: National Gang Center.

NBC News (2012) Jobless rate up, but crime down: What gives? January 3.

Nisbett, R. and Cohen, D. (1996) *Culture of Honor: The Psychology of Violence in the South*. Boulder, CO: Westview Press.

Papachristos, A.V., Wallace, D.M., Meares, T.L., and Fagan, J.A. (2013) *Desistance and legitimacy: The impact of offender notification meetings on recidivism among high risk offenders*. Unpublished manuscript, Yale University, New Haven, CT.

Picard-Fritsche, S. and Cerniglia, L. (2013) *Testing a Public Health Approach to Gun Violence: An Evaluation of Crown Heights Save Our Streets, a Replication of the Cure Violence Model*. New York: Center for Court Innovations.

Rosenfeld, R., Fornango, R., and Rengifo, A.F. (2007) The impact of order-maintenance policing on New York City homicide and robbery rates: 1988–2001. *Criminology*, 45(2): 355–384.

Sampson, R.J. (1986) Effects of socioeconomic context on official reaction to juvenile delinquency. *American Sociological Review*, 51: 876–885.

Sampson, R.J. (2008) Rethinking crime and immigration. *Contexts: Understanding People in Their Social Worlds*, 7(1): 28–33.

Sampson, R.J. and Bean, L. (2006) Cultural mechanisms and killing fields: A revised theory of community level racial inequality. In R.D. Peterson, L.J. Krivo,and J. Hagan (eds), *The Many Colors of Crime: Inequalities of Race, Ethnicity, and Crime in America* (pp. 8–36). New York: NYU Press.

Shepherd, J.M. (2004) Murders of passion, execution delays, and the deterrence of capital punishment. *Journal of Legal Studies*, 33(2): 283–321.

Sheppard, D. and COSMOS Corporation (1999) *Promising Strategies to Reduce Gun Violence*. Washington, DC: US Department of Justice

Skogan, W.G., Hartnett, S.M., Bump, N., and Dubois, J. (2009) *Evaluation of CeaseFire-Chicago*. Chicago: Northwestern University.

Sunstein, C.R. and Vermeule, A. (2005) Is capital punishment morally required? Acts omissions and life–life tradeoffs. *Stanford Law Review*, 58(3): 703–751.

Tucker, E. (2015) Justice department, police chiefs gather for summit on violent crime prevention strategies. *US News*, October 7. Available online at http://www.usnews.com/news/politics/articles/2015/10/07/justice-dept-police-gather-for-summit-on-violent-crime (accessed October 7, 2015).

Webster, D.W., Whitehill, J.M., Vernick, J.S., and Parker, E.M. (2012) *Evaluation of Baltimore's* Safe Streets *Program*: Baltimore, MD: Johns Hopkins Center for the Prevention of Youth Violence.

Wellford, C.F., Pepper, J.V., and Petrie, C.V. (eds.) (2004) *Firearms and Violence: A Critical Review*. Washington, DC: National Academies Press.

Wiersema, B., Loftin, C., and McDowell, D. (2000) A comparison of Supplementary Homicide reports and National Vital Statistics System Homicide estimates for US Counties. *Homicide Studies*, 4(4): 317–340.

Wolfgang, M.E. (1958) *Patterns in Criminal Homicide*. New York: John Wiley & Sons.

Zimring, F.E. and Hawkins, G. (1995) *Incapacitation: Penal Confinement and the Restraint of Crime*. New York: Oxford University Press.

22

Homicide in Japan

Tom Ellis and Koichi Hamai

Introduction

There are many types of killing and as UNODC (United Nations Office on Drugs and Crime) recognize, not all of them are intentional or unlawful. It is important, therefore, to be clear on what is included in this chapter. We have taken the UNODC (2014: 1, 2013) definition: "*unlawful death purposefully inflicted on a person by another person*," or "*intentional homicide*" (emphases added). This most closely relates to the Japanese criminal justice system's definitions of homicide. Most studies of this type are reliant on officially recorded crimes and these have their well-trodden limitations of underreporting and under-recording (e.g., Bottomley and Coleman 1981; Maguire 2012). In our case, there is the additional problem of whether the categories and recording practices used are consistent when comparing rates between different countries (Bennett and Lynch 1990; Finch 2001). However, the UNODC (2014: 9) argues that, within advanced democracies, homicide is often "*the most readily measurable, clearly defined and most comparable indicator for measuring violent deaths*" (emphasis added) and is in most cases a reasonable proxy for violent crime. Many researchers agree (Kawai 2004; Marshall and Block 2004) and add that differences in homicide trends are the most reliable way to do this (LaFree and Drass 2002; White 1995).[1]

There are also three key categories of homicide, which UNODC (2014: 11) has defined as: sociopolitical; related to other criminal activities (e.g., organized/gang-related crime); and interpersonal homicide. As the victim and the killer are related in most homicides in Japan (53.5% relatives, 34% acquaintances; Cabinet Office,

The Handbook of Homicide, First Edition. Edited by Fiona Brookman, Edward R. Maguire, and Mike Maguire.

Japan 2013: fig. 5-1-2-1), the primary focus of this chapter is, therefore, interpersonal homicide, though we also include organized/gang-related homicide.

We have organized the chapter into two sections. The first section, Profile of Homicide in Japan, outlines the global and historical context of homicide in Japan before looking at the very particular and changing combination of age and gender factors present in Japanese homicide offenders. It then moves on to outline the declining and changing profile of homicide victims which has disproportionately affected women. We then summarize the relationship between homicide offenders and victims and the changing nature of the methods used to commit homicide before providing an outline of the contribution of organized crime to the Japanese homicide picture. In the second section, Explanations for Changes in Homicide Trends in Japan, we provide a summary of the main explanations offered so far for Japan's low and declining homicide rate, along with a critique of these. The chapter ends with an outline of the areas that need further research if the changing nature of homicide in Japan is to be explained adequately.

Profile of Homicide in Japan

Japanese homicide in global and historical context

UNODC (2014: 11) notes that nearly half of all homicides take place in countries with only 10 percent of the planet's population. Globally, 95 percent of perpetrators and 80 percent of victims are male and half of all victims are under 30 years of age. The Americas skew these global homicide rates where organized crime/gang-related murder is much more prevalent (UNODC 2014: 13, 43). The male homicide rate in the Americas is consequently nearly four times the female rate (9.7 versus 2.7 per 100,000) and rises to 29.3 per 100,000 (UNODC 2014: 13) for males alone. In contrast, Asia, Europe, and Oceania have homicide rates under 4.5 per 100,000. The key to these low homicide rates in Asia, as will be outlined, is that killing is mostly through interpersonal violence, involving smaller numbers, and disproportionately affecting women. We argue therefore that while Japan has one of the lowest homicide rates in the world at 0.3 per 100,000 (UNODC 2014: 37, 54), it is not exceptional within the homicide trend that is increasingly apparent among the economically advanced nations in its geographical region.

Our analysis is limited to the post-World War II period. In the immediate aftermath of World War II, Japan shared the typical pattern of widespread offending in defeated countries, as many of their citizens fought to survive (Dower 1999: 97). Unsurprisingly, therefore, from the late 1940s to 1955, the homicide rate was relatively high (Johnson 2006: 75; Shikita and Tsuchiya 1992: 74). However, as industrialization took hold, the rate began a long decline. It reached 1 in 100,000 by 1990 and the trend was flat during that decade while property offenses, robberies, rapes, and assaults increased (Johnson 2006: 75). This trend appears counter to the general pattern of industrializing nations as homicide tends to "boom" in times of rapid industrialization (LaFree and Drass 2002).

Writing in 2006, Johnson (2006: 74) noted that the Japanese homicide rate had fallen 80 percent over the last 50 years and that "A decline of this magnitude has not been observed in any other nation" (emphasis added). Figure 22.1 shows this precipitous decline, from 1,791 just after World War II, up to 2,683 in 1958 and 1959, before declining to 1,052 in 2011, yet the clearance rate has remained impressively high at well over 90 percent.[2]

At the time he was writing, Johnson (2006: 77) also noted that the average homicide rate of other "industrialized Asian cases"—Singapore, Hong Kong, and South Korea—had more than double the Japanese homicide rate. As with most other measures, it seemed that Japan had also maintained its exceptionalism in relation to homicide. However, this view does need to be balanced in the light of more recent changes. Asia's homicide rate has declined generally since 1995. In particular, the Eastern Asia subregion has the lowest homicide rates in the world, with Japan, Hong Kong, and China all with rates below 1 per 100,000 population (UNODC 2014: 34).

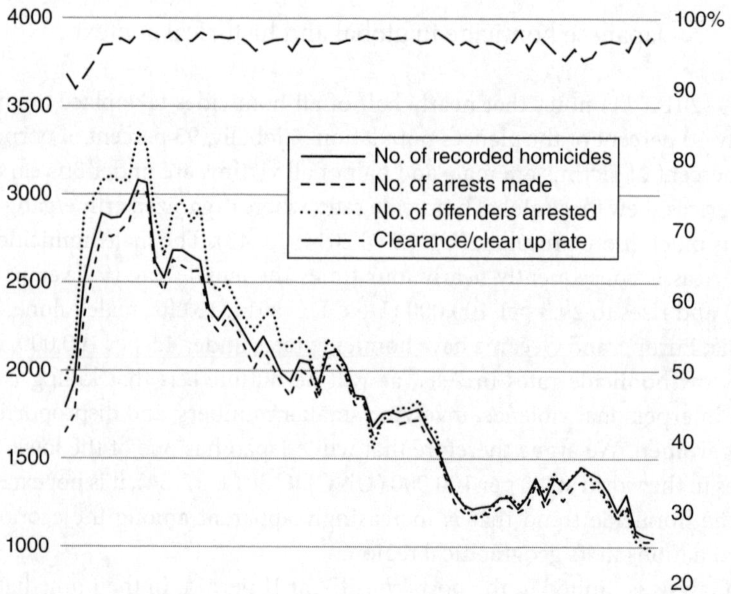

Figure 22.1 Number of recorded homicides in Japan, 1946–2011.

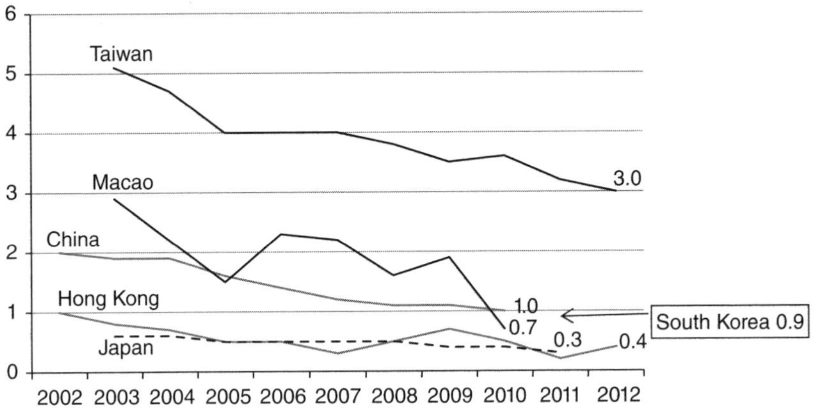

Figure 22.2 Trends in homicide rates (per 100,000) in East Asian countries, 2002–2012. Adapted using available data over this time period from UNODC (2014: 127–128).

Figure 22.2 shows how the most developed East Asian countries have converged, both on declining trends and current homicide rates (based on UNODC 2014: 127–128). While Japan has the lowest homicide rate, the rates for its closest neighbors are also now very low and only Taiwan exceeds one homicide in 100,000.[3]

Who commits homicide in Japan: Age and gender factors in the declining homicide rate

As Johnson argues (2008: 146), it is easier to explain *who* is responsible for the decline in Japanese homicide than *what* has caused it. However, he is clear that the drop has been caused by the dramatic decline of homicide among young Japanese males. Certainly, compared to 1955 rates, young men in Japan now commit only a tenth of the number of homicides (UNODC 2014: 37; Dai 2013: 18; Johnson 2006: 73).

The distinction between youth/juvenile and adult justice systems in Japan occurs at age 20. In 2001, those under 20 accounted for only 6 percent of arrests for homicide (Johnson 2006: 74). This was roughly the same as for those who were 70 plus (Miyazaki and Otani 2004: 19; Matsuda 2000). Those in their 20s accounted for more homicides than those under 20, but the homicide rate in 2000 was higher among men in their 40s and 50s than among males aged 20 to 24 (Matsuda 2000; Hasegawa 2003).

This meant that the homicide rate of 23 per 100,000 men in 1955 had dropped to 2 per 100,000 since 1990 (Hasegawa 2003), which Uchiyama (2003) saw as unprecedented. As Johnson (2006: 74) argues, this seemed, in 2006, a "*striking exception to the pattern found in other nations where young males are the demographic group most likely to kill*" (emphasis added). For instance, Johnson (2008: 149–150, 2006: 79) points out that the comparable homicide rate for the United States would be just under four times the Japanese rate.

Our analysis is consistent with Johnson's (2006: 80) argument that the Japanese profile of homicides challenges the seemingly universal positivistic notion that crime declines with age (Gottfredson and Hirschi 1990: 124; see also Chapter 3, this volume). However, this situation has moved on somewhat and Figure 22.3 shows that over the last five decades, and in tandem with the decreasing Japanese crime rate, there has been a dramatic shift in the relative proportions of homicides committed by different age groups. The first decade (1963–1972) shows a more typical global age distribution for those committing homicide (see Gottfredson and Hirschi 1990). Those classed as juveniles and in their 20s committed the majority of homicides and a lesser proportion was then committed by each successive age group. From the 1970s onward, however, those under 20 (technically juveniles in Japan) generally committed only around 5 percent of homicides, which has remained a flat trend ever since. The proportion of homicides committed by those in their 20s continually reduced over the five decades (summarized in Figure 22.3), from 47 percent to only 18 percent. To put this in perspective, since 1998, the number of homicides committed by juveniles has reduced from 115 to just 46 in 2012 (Cabinet Office, Japan 2013: fig. 1-1-2-3). In contrast, those who are age 50-plus have continued to commit a larger share of homicides into the 2000s. Perhaps the most striking feature of the final decade (2003–2012) is that, with the exception of the smaller under 20 (juveniles) age group, all other age groupings now have a very similar share of the homicides committed in that decade (a variation between only 17% and 22%).

Overall, the evidence from earlier authors, and our later analysis, suggest that concerns about delinquent youth in Japanese government and media discourses is unjustifiable, since Japanese youth are among the least likely in the world to commit homicide (Hasegawa 2005; Miyazaki and Otani 2004).[4] As identified by Hamai and Ellis (2006), in such discourses, concerns about short-term rises in relatively trivial crimes have been conflated with individually gruesome or unusual murders despite the fact that the homicide rate has been declining for so long. As Maeda (2003) has argued, the very low involvement of the young in committing homicides should be

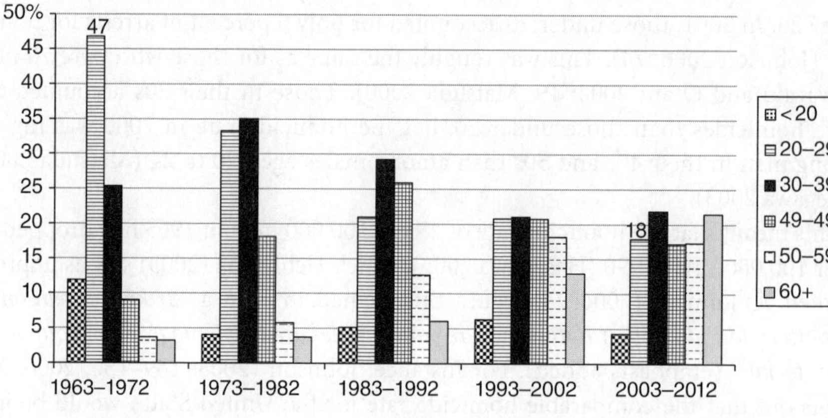

Figure 22.3 Decade averages (means) of proportion of homicides committed by each age group, 1963–2012.

recognized and perhaps celebrated, instead of being misrepresented in Japan's "law and order crisis," while Johnson (2006: 80) adds "Rather than fomenting fear ... officials and analysts ought to be searching for the causes of Japan's vanishing killer."

Gender

Consistent with most countries, most of the murders committed in Japan are by males. However, while the number and proportion of homicides by young males has declined, Japanese females now commit a larger share of their society's lethal violence than their equivalents in other comparable countries (Johnson 2006: 79, 2008: 150). Streib (2003) notes that females accounted for 18 percent of homicide arrests in Japan and stresses that this was a very high proportion on a global scale (noting, for example, that US females accounted for only around 10% of all homicide arrests). That proportion has now reached 25 percent in both 2011 and 2012.[5]

The most recent five-year trend data available suggest two clear trends for females committing homicide in Japan.[6] First, and similar to overall trends since the 1970s, females below 20 only accounted for around 2–6 percent of all homicides committed by females between 2008 and 2012. Second, women in their 30s and 40s have become the biggest single group of females committing homicide, around 45 percent on average over the period 2008–2012. Women aged 50 and over committed around a third (32%) of all homicides committed by females over the same period (see Figure 22.4).

We currently know of no published examinations of the reasons why these patterns occur, but it is clear again that, as with young men, young women appear less homicidal than their older counterparts. One possible explanation, in the past, could have

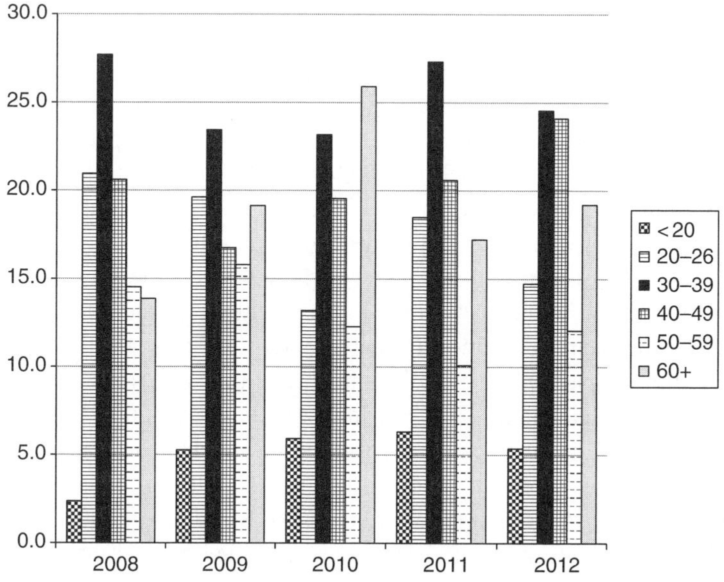

Figure 22.4 Proportion of homicides committed by females by age groups, 2008 to 2012.

been the unusually high (though declining) comparative rate of infanticide (*eijisatsu*) in Japan, 94 percent of which are committed by females (Hasegawa and Hasegawa 2000a, 2000b). Indeed, there is a long and contested history of infanticide in Japanese history, often referred to by the slang term *mabiki* (literally, thinning of the rice crop), and enforcement against it. However, recorded incidences are low and had fallen from around 130 in 1980 to just 17 by 2009 (Cabinet Office, Japan 2010a, fig. 7-1-1-5). Much of the decline is likely to be down to the 1949 revision of the 1948 Eugenic Protection Act, legalizing abortion and thereby reducing recording of detected abortions as infanticide and child killing. It is unlikely, therefore, that the rise in the proportion of women homicide offenders is explained by this factor. However, there has been little attempt to link the legalization of abortion in Japan (although, see Hamai 2011) to lower crime rates in general, and lower homicide rates in particular, in the way that Levitt (2004), for instance, has argued for the United States.

One element is clear from figures available for 2009: of the 899 homicides, men killed roughly double the number (99) of women partners than vice versa (53). This means that spousal homicide (defined as partners, irrespective of marriage) accounts for only 15 percent of homicides by men, but for nearly a quarter (24%) of all homicides by women.

Victims of homicide in Japan: The feminization of homicide victimization?

The very low homicide rate in Japan and in other East Asian countries presents new challenges. As UNODC (2014: 54) notes, in countries with very low (less than 1 per 100,000 population) and *decreasing* homicide rates (especially between males), women provide an increasing share of the proportion of remaining victims. Indeed, if interpersonal violence is assessed separately, its disproportionate impact on women as victims is "remarkably stable at the global level" (UNODC 2014: 13).

As Figure 22.5 shows, East Asia is a clear case in point. Japan and its two most comparable countries, Hong Kong and South Korea, have respective intentional homicide rates of 0.3, 0.4, and 0.9 per 100,000,[7] but show that just over half of all homicides result in women victims (UNODC 2014: 137). In contrast, Mongolia, North Korea, and Taiwan, with respective homicide rates of 9.7, 5.2, and 3.0 per 100,000, show a more typical global pattern where women comprise only between 13 and 23 percent of homicide victims. In this context, China, rather than Japan, appears to be the clearer exception in that women form only a fifth of intentional homicide victims despite China's overall homicide rate also falling to only 1 per 100,000.

This picture has changed rapidly since Johnson (2008: 150, 2006: 79) commented that females make up around 35 percent of all homicide victims in Japan and constitute 18 percent of those arrested for homicide. The UNODC now puts the proportion of female homicide victims in Japan at 52.9 percent (based on the 2009 White Paper) although this falls to 40 percent if victims were killed as a result of an offense, including robbery and causing injury.

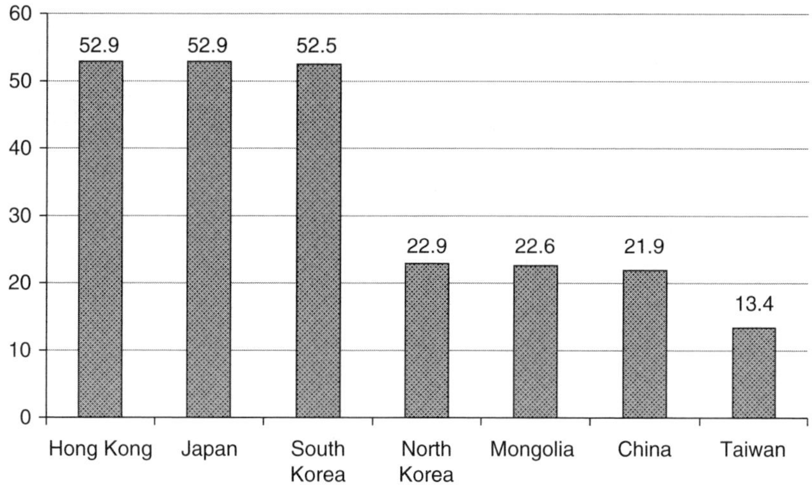

Figure 22.5 Comparison of East Asian countries by the proportion of female homicide victims, 2010–2011.

It seems that, while Japan has a lower homicide rate than the United States, the price of this is that a greater proportion of the remaining homicides are against women and women commit more of those homicides. However, the homicide pattern (as opposed to the rate) in Japan still conforms to global norm, that is, it is most likely that "men kill both men and women" (UNODC 2014: 55).

UNODC (2014: 56) have noted that, despite low levels of homicidal violence, Japanese authorities are committed to reducing precursors to homicide still further (see Messing *et al.* 2015) and this has largely focused on measuring and combating intimate-partner violence. In 2004, the Cabinet Office (2004) brought in a series of laws aimed at reducing intimate-partner/family violence: the Law on Proscribing Stalking Behavior and Assisting Victims (2000), the Act on the Prevention of Spousal Violence and Protection of Victims (2001), and the Violence Prevention Law (Act no. 31). The latter was amended for a second time in 2007 to include protection orders on serious stalking, threatening phone calls, and violence toward the victim's child or relatives (Tabin 2012).

The impact of these changes and associated services was measured by the introduction of the Cabinet Office's "Survey on Violence between Men and Women" carried out every 3 years. The 2008[8] survey (see Cabinet Office, Japan 2009: ch. 5, 34–35) found 4.4 percent of female respondents had been in fear of their lives through "spousal violence,"[9] while the 2012 survey showed that this fear had increased to 13 percent of women and 9 percent of men fearing for their lives. Other key indicators from the 2015[10] survey suggest a more positive change for women, to 33 percent of women reporting spousal violence in 2012, reducing to 24 percent in 2015, and being "punched, kicked or shoved" reduced from 26 percent to 15 percent. On the other hand, the equivalent figures for men showed very little change: 18 percent down to 17 percent and 13 percent down to 11 percent.

Responding to the 2012 survey results (and perhaps supported since by the 2015 results), Hassett (2012) criticizes the Japanese Gender Equality Bureau for only focusing on protecting women from domestic abuse. However, while the figures from the 2008 survey show that spousal murder accounts for 24 percent of all homicides committed by women, but only 15 percent of those committed by men, it is also the case that men killed many more partners and in fact committed three-quarters of all homicides, with over half of these being women.

There are dangers in interpreting short-term trends, but this is an area that clearly requires more research. Ethnographic work suggests there are competing views of Japanese women, from submissive, to "women who run men, not the other way around" (Lebra 1984: ix). While there is empirical work on domestic abuse of women in Japan (e.g., Kamimura, Bybee, and Yoshimama 2014), factors affecting inter-gender violence, and its relationship to homicide, are yet to be examined.

Methods used in Japanese homicides

UNODC (2014: 15, 65) notes that firearms account for 40 percent of global homicides, "sharp objects" 25 percent, and "other means" such as physical force and blunt objects, over a third. UNODC (2014: 141–142) do provide some more comparable figures for East Asia (2010–2012) within these categories.[11] These are presented in Table 22.1 below, along with those for the United Kingdom, United States, and Canada for appropriate points of comparison outside East Asia.

Equivalent figures for Japan (Research and Training Institute of the Ministry of Justice 2013) have been summarized in Figure 22.6 below.[12] Finch (2001: 226) notes that weapons were used in most Japanese homicides and adds that this is still the case. As Figure 22.6 shows, from 1998 to 2008, just under a quarter (23–24%) of homicides involved no weapons, but by 2011 this had dropped considerably so that 83.5 percent of all cleared[13] homicides involved some type of weapon. Knives are still the Japanese homicide weapon of choice and are now used in just over half of homicide cases (51–53%), while toxic substances and blunt instruments or cable/rope accounted for most of the remaining homicides.

Table 22.1 Differences in methods of homicide in selected countries compared to Japan.

	Firearms %	*Sharp objects %*	*Other %*	*Average gun ownership per 100 people*
Hong Kong	0	26	74	4.9 (China)
South Korea	2	DK	DK	1.1
UK	7	39	54	6.2 (England and Wales)
USA	60	11	30	88.8
Canada	29	36	34	30.8

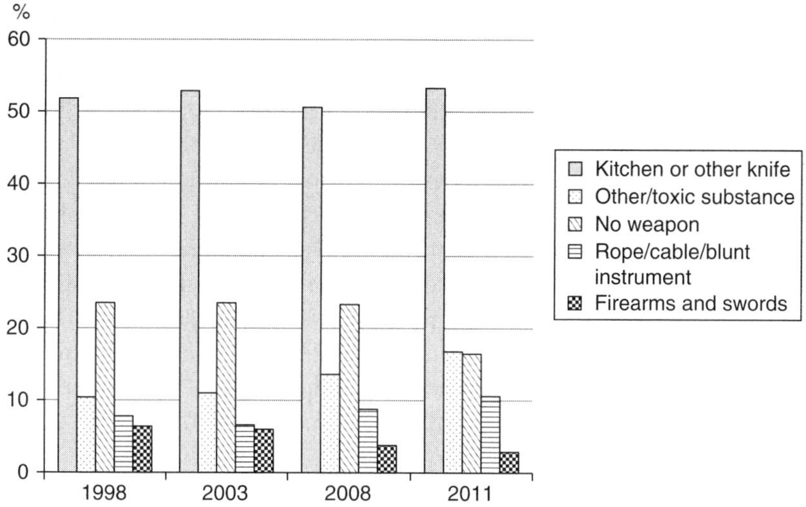

Figure 22.6 Changes in methods of homicide in Japan, 1998–2011.

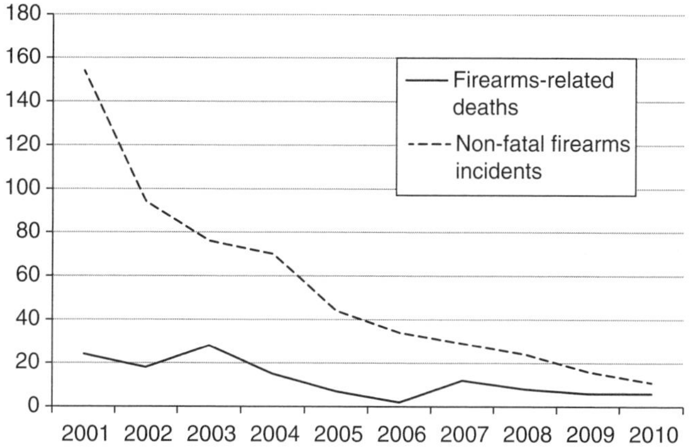

Figure 22.7 Overall trend in fatal and nonfatal firearms incidents in Japan, 2001–2010.

Japan has one of the lowest levels of gun ownership in the world at 0.6 per 100 people (Small Arms Survey 2007). While arguments continue about the relationship between gun ownership and homicide (UNODC 2011: 41–43), it is unsurprising that homicides involving firearms or swords (recorded as a single category) are rare in Japan (6% in 1998 to only 3% in 2011).

Firearms and sword use are more limited to organized crime-related homicides in Japan. The Police Policy Research Center (2010) shows that firearm-related incidents have been reduced drastically, from 178 in 2001 to only 17 in 2010 (see Figure 22.7). Paradoxically, as the numbers are reduced, a greater proportion of these incidents have resulted in death. As Figure 22.7 shows, 24 deaths from firearms in 2001 amounted to 13 percent of all firearms incidents, but the equivalent 6 deaths in 2010 amounted to 35 percent of the meager 17 incidents in that year.

Organized crime and homicide in Japan

As UNODC (2014: 15) notes, organized crime/gang-related homicide accounts for 30 percent of all homicides in the Americas, but less than 1 percent in Asia, Europe, and Oceania. Given Japan's overall homicide profile, it might be reasonable to expect that gang-related homicide would form a very small proportion of homicide cases. However, Japan is exceptional in East Asia in conforming to the global norm. Johnson (2006: 79) finds that around 20 percent of all homicides in Japan were gang-related, which is more than the equivalent proportion of homicides in the United States (15%) and way above England and Wales (1%) (Finch 2001: 228). The *yakuza* (a Japanese "mafia equivalent," referred to officially as *boryokudan*) form less than 0.1 percent of citizens and therefore have a disproportionate effect on the relatively small number of Japanese homicides. The most recent UNODC (2013: 43) figures show 22.6 percent of all intentional homicides in 2008 were carried out by gangs/organized crime, while the White Paper on Crime (Cabinet Office, Japan 2010b: fig. 3-2-2-2) found that 19.7 percent (204) of 1,036 homicides in 2009 were classified in this way. The 2007 White Paper on Crime also provided an insight on repeat offenders, which showed that of the 0.9 percent of homicide offenders who have killed before, 52.5 percent were *boryokudan* members (Cabinet Office, Japan 2007).

Space restricts us from an in-depth exploration of organized crime's contribution to the homicide rate in Japan and most of the focus will now be on explaining the bulk of interpersonal homicide in Japan that is not in this category. Before moving on, however, it is important to outline one way in which organized criminals have been prevented from killing people. Certainly, as Figure 22.8 shows, it appears that *boryokudan* have been eliminated entirely from the small number of gun incidents in 2010 while they accounted for 40 percent of the 178 firearms incidents in 2001 (Police Policy Research Center 2010).

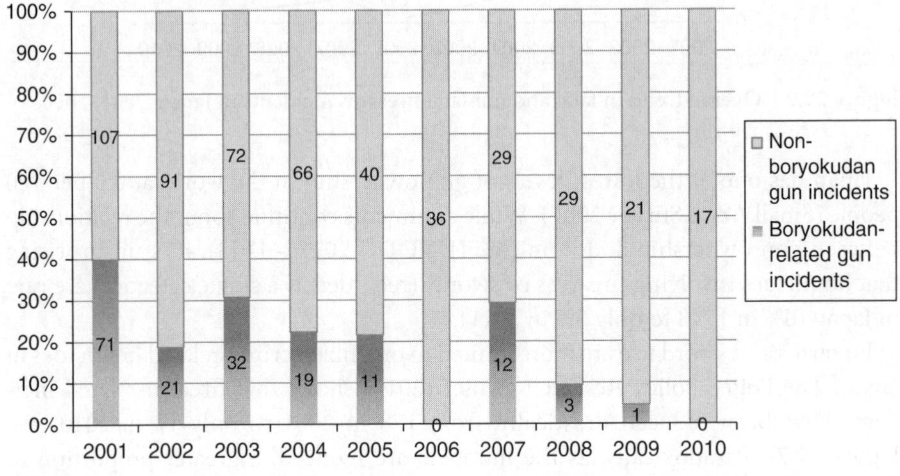

Figure 22.8 Overall changes in proportions of *boryukodan* and non-*boryukodan* firearms incidents in Japan, 2001–2010.

This pattern is also discernible in the numbers of victims of homicide by firearms. Until 2009, the majority of the small and decreasing number of such homicides were *boryukodan* related, but of the eight fatalities in 2011, only two were *boryukodan* related (Cabinet Office, Japan 2012, fig. 4-2-2-4).

Johnson (2008: 154) notes that future research should explore whether there has been a significant change in the supply of guns or in the willingness to use them in interpersonal conflicts in postwar Japan. A partial answer is that they were never prevalent in Japanese homicides, usage has declined precipitously and the known involvement of *boryukodan* has been virtually eliminated.

Explanations for Changes in Homicide Trends in Japan

As UNODC (2014: 37) notes, Japan's low homicide rate is "*associated with a stable and prosperous society*" (emphasis added). Explanations offered are the extremely low levels of gun ownership and high clear-up/clearance rates, as outlined above. Others focus on the official rejection of violence following World War II, but, as Johnson (2006: 80) notes, there is no empirical evidence.

Explanations that link the low levels of inequality and high levels of development (Park 2006; Hasegawa 2005) to Japanese cultural mores have been pursued more systematically. Johnson (2006, 2008) has summarized and critiqued these main explanations for Japan's low and decreasing homicide rate. He focuses on Roberts and LaFree's (2004) four main conclusions based on their national time-series analysis (1951–2000) and cross-sectional time-series analysis (1955–2000) of both homicide and robbery.

First, there is skepticism about the overreliance on cultural explanations, especially the role of informal controls, to explain Japan's low crime rate, and homicide in particular (see Komiya 1999; Bayley 1991; Braithwaite 1989). As Roberts and LaFree (2004: 82) note, homicide rates continued to decline while informal controls in Japan weakened. Johnson (2006: 81) argues that this approach still needs to be refined so that the aggregate quantitative measures of culture and social disorganization are combined with micro-dimensions of control (Miller and Kanazawa 2000; Rohlen 1989).

Second, Roberts and LaFree (2004: 194) argue that the high clear-up/clearance rate could affect homicide rates, although Johnson (2006: 81) points out that they used the clear-up/clearance rate for all crimes and that these rates had worsened in the period examined. However, this again illustrates the need for caution in interpreting small fluctuations in trend data. The clear-up/clearance rate for homicide was always above 90 percent throughout this period and has remained extraordinarily high. Indeed, Table 1-1-1-2 of each year's White paper[14] provides these figures which show that the rates were 101.3 percent[15] in 2013, 93.5 percent in 2012, and 97.9 percent in 2011.

Third, Roberts and LaFree argue that reduced levels of "economic stress" in Japan's postwar economy had reduced homicide. However, the downturn of the economy in the 1990s was matched with a continuing decline in murders. Roberts and LaFree's (2004: 202) prediction of a rise in violent crime in these circumstances has not happened, although Yoshikazu, Kanazawa, and Yuma (2010) did find a stable long-term relationship (1973–2006) between the unemployment rate and the homicide rate for 16–17 year-olds and 18–19 year-olds, but could not find any structural explanation for this, or for the period since 2006.

Fourth, Roberts and LaFree argue for an orthodox view that, between 1951 and 2000, a higher proportion of young men was associated with higher homicide rates. However, as outlined above, this ignores the increasingly minor role young men play in committing homicides and the growing one played by older men and women.

Johnson (2006, 2008) therefore turns to explanations offered by Mariko Hasegawa's (2003, 2005) risk-assessment model of homicide, which focused on the impact of age in homicide patterns within a social psychological paradigm. She found that motives for homicide by young men, for example, status, loss of face, and so on, were similar over time and founded her evolutionary biological approach on the hypothesis that young Japanese men needed to enhance their "resource-holding ability" to increase their "reproductive success" (Hasegawa 2005). Males with access to fewer resources (e.g., education, jobs, housing) in this scenario are more likely to "risk" violence in social confrontations as a way of obtaining self-perceived justice. Accordingly, Hasegawa argues that young Japanese men now have more to lose and have therefore become more averse to risk. This relies, in part, on declining income inequality, but also on the rapid change to single child families and the lack of competition for resources within the family.

Johnson (2006) acknowledges that Hasegawa's approach is an important advance on previous models, mainly because it addresses the age–homicide link, which had previously been ignored and because its social psychological approach, and inclusion of many behavioral spheres, also attempts to include those micro-elements of control that were absent from Roberts and LaFree's economic-factors approach.

However, there are inevitable weaknesses. First, the insistence on the primacy of "reproductive success" as the driver of homicide ignores the stronger impact of sociocultural factors that Hasegawa's own empirical work identifies (Johnson 2006: 83). Second, the reliance on a "rational actor" model of human behavior for homicide incidents is at variance with previous authors (Katz,1988; Athens 1997; Buss 2005) who stress the irrational element in homicide. Indeed, the White Paper on Crime (Cabinet Office, Japan 2010b: fig. 7-2-1-1-2, fig. 7-2-1-1-4) shows planning in only 40 percent of homicides, and much of the motivation was accounted for by "anger/violent emotion," "blind passion/conflicts in relations with the opposite gender," and even "exhaustion from nursing care/nurturing." It is easy to overstate rationality.

Third, in private correspondence with Johnson (2006: 84, 2008: 154), Hasegawa admits that her bivariate approach to examining homicide against single independent variables, such as gross domestic product (GDP), is limited and that a more sophisticated multivariate approach to contextual variables such as unemployment, divorce, availability of guns, and so on, is needed, which, to some extent, is the type of approach taken by Levitt (2004) for the United States. Perhaps the key criticism Johnson (2006: 84) levels at Hasegawa's model for this study though, is that she only calculated risk in relation to homicide, while he notes that trends for other serious crimes at that time appear not to have mirrored the continual decline of homicides. While this is a potential limitation, updated figures do show that serious and violent crimes, other than homicide, now show similar declining trends for juveniles.

As outlined in Figure 22.9, those serious offenses which might mask changes in overall homicides within the Japanese crime classification system's recording process have also declined. Robberies that resulted in death have reduced from a high point of 96 in 2001 to 31 in 2013, while injuries resulting in death have shown the equivalent figure of 202 down to only 11 over the same period.[16]

Data over a longer time period (Cabinet Office, Japan 2013: fig. 1-1-2-3) show that the other two most serious offenses of arson and rape have also shown a marked decline in recorded offenses since high points in 2003 for rape and 2004 for arson. However, if, as above, all age groups are included, then other key violent offenses prove more inconsistent with Hasegawa's theory as Johnson suggests. Assault and injury (not resulting in death) both declined from 1982 in parallel to homicide, but then showed dramatic rises. Assaults declined until 1994 and then showed a gradual increase, but between 1999 and 2007 increased by over 400 percent from 7,792 to

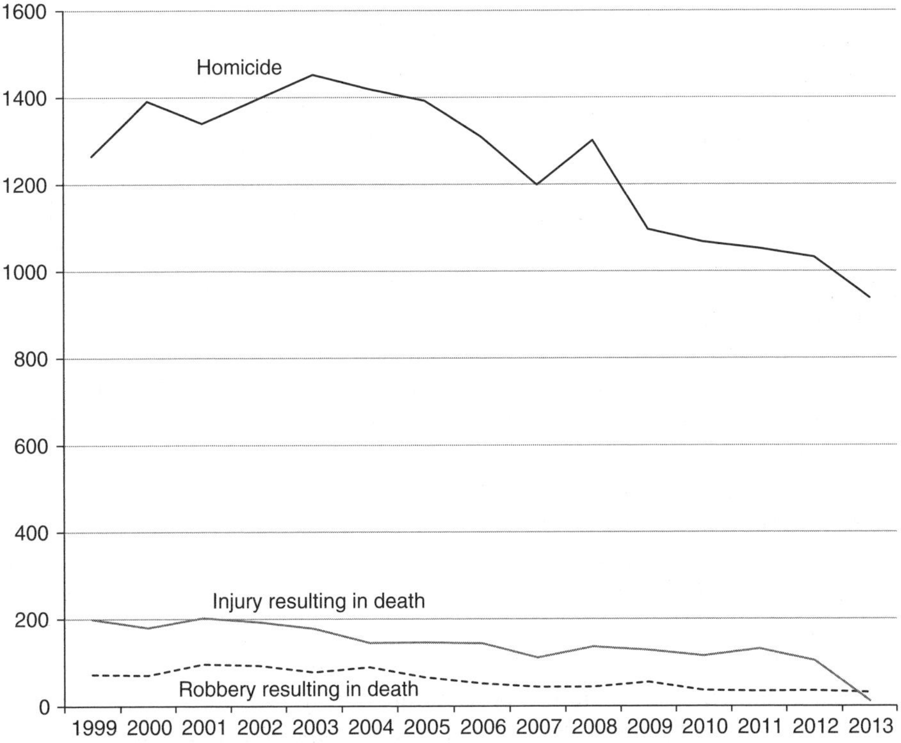

Figure 22.9 Serious offenses resulting in death and homicide, 1999–2012.

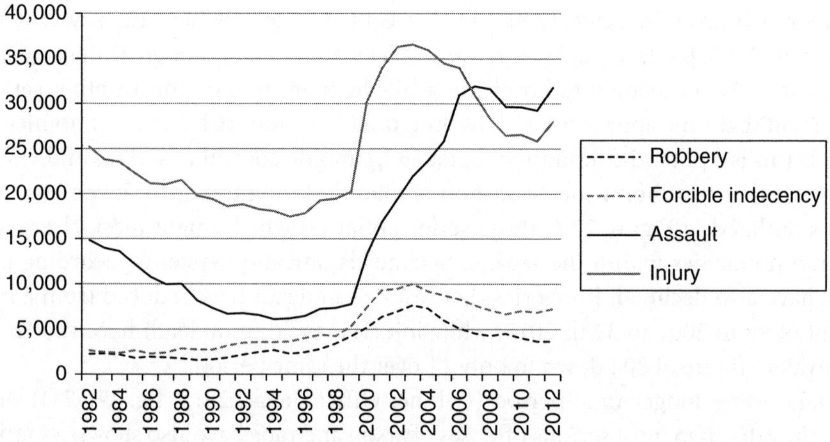

Figure 22.10 Recorded violent crimes, 1982–2012.

31,966 and have remained above 29,000 ever since. The pattern for injury is very similar, but with less dramatic changes, as evidenced in Figure 22.10. Similarly, robbery and forcible indecency show a muted but similar pattern.

These trends, which may also involve changes to policing and recording practices, suggest that there is no clear indication that males are more risk averse to using violence in confrontations as Hasegawa's current model suggests. However, we also found that if juvenile crime is looked at as a proportion of each type of violent and serious crime (Cabinet Office, Japan 2013: fig. 1-1-2-3), there has been a much clearer reduction in youth involvement compared to a relatively flat homicide rate, which only varied between 4.1 percent and 8.4 percent from 1982 to 2012. While arson has shown a gentle decline, over the same period, juveniles involved in assaults have dropped from 38 percent to 6 percent, while robbery and injury have shown similar, though less dramatic, declines. The pattern apparent in Figure 22.11 suggests that Hasegawa's model may have more explanatory power for juveniles than even she first thought.

The equivalent analysis carried out for females, however, shows a very different trend, as Figure 22.12 shows below. While rates for involvement are much lower than for juveniles, female participation in serious and violent offenses has grown at a comparatively high rate, most strikingly for arson, where the proportion of cases involving women rose from 13 percent in 1982 to 22 percent in 2012. Rises for the higher volume of offenses for robbery, injury, and assault were less dramatic, rising from low percentage points, but these represent considerable changes in the sense that a rise from 4.1 percent of assaults in 1982 to 7.7 percent in 2012 represents an overall increase of 187 percent.

While Hasegawa's explanation has more utility than expected in relation to (mostly male) juveniles, there has been no attempt to explain the rise in female offending. Men still commit the majority of crime and female criminality is still largely ignored (Leonard 1982) in Japan in the way that was historically common in

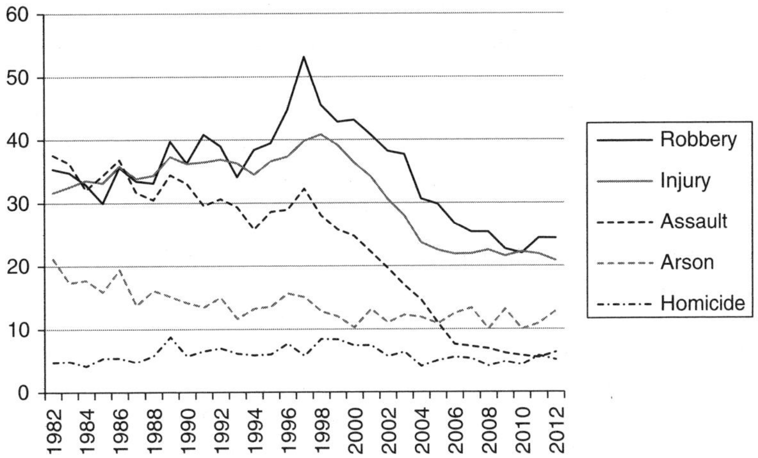

Figure 22.11 Proportion of serious/violent crimes committed by juveniles, 1982–2012.

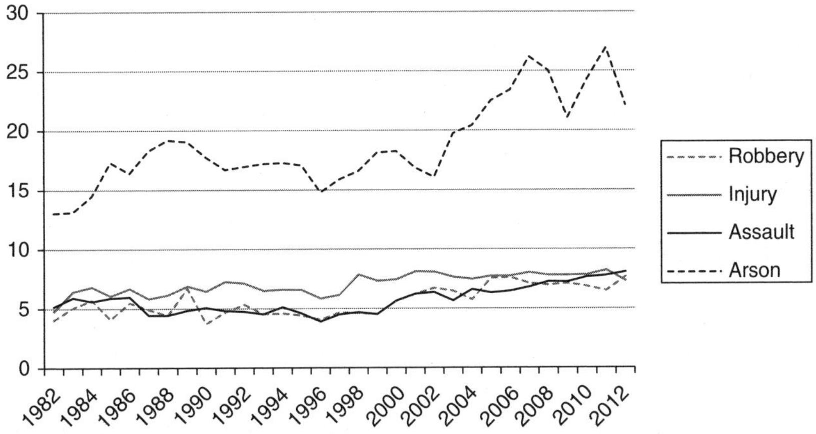

Figure 22.12 Proportion of serious/violent crimes committed by females, 1982–2012.

the United States and the United Kingdom (Heidensohn and Silvestri 2012). As with Hassett's (2012) concern that Japanese male victims are being ignored, it seems that the there is a need for more of a feminist inflected criminological approach to challenge existing theories based on male offenders in order to illuminate a gender specific explanation of female offending (Heidensohn and Silvestri 2012).

However, there is a difficult path to tread here. On the one hand, there is a danger of starting a media-led moral panic on the rise in female violence (Steffensmeier *et al.* 2005; Sharpe and Gelsthorpe 2009) in addition to the unreasonable focus on juveniles as overly criminogenic. On the other hand, the increasing arson trends or even the relatively static homicide trend for Japanese females do require explanation. This could, of course, relate to changes in policy which leads to more aggressive and efficient police tactics resulting in "net widening" and "defining deviance up" (Steffensmeier *et al.* 2005), but homicide, as argued above, is the measure most impervious to this.

Finally, since Hasegawa did not attempt to assess the risk-based explanation comparatively, Johnson (2006: 84) notes that many economically advanced countries have experienced similar "resource-enhancing" changes to Japan, but have not experienced such a clear decline in homicide rates. This situation is now clearer, and as argued above, Hong Kong, South Korea, and China have all shown similar contemporary patterns.

There are also specific social issues affecting Japan that may have had an impact on homicide rates. There is evidence of young men increasingly withdrawing from social interaction, such as, *futoko* (refusal to attend school) and *hikikomori* (effectively a hermit-like existence within the parental home). These phenomena are on the rise, with over 1 million *hikikomori* (Saito 2013) and there has to be a consideration of whether this has an incapacitation effect on homicides committed by young people in Japan.

The role of video gaming might also contribute here.[17] There is a preponderance of studies correlating violent video games to increases in aggressive assaults and homicides (Markey, Markey, and French 2014: 1). However, there is also recent counterintuitive evidence that aggressive games may have a prosocial or cathartic effect (Cunningham, Engelstätter, and Ward 2013). Indeed, Markey, Markey, and French (2014: 15) find a correlation between the release of violent video games and decreases in homicides. Perhaps more importantly though, Markey, Markey, and French (2014: 15) also argue that this has an incapacitative effect, removing potential offenders from public venues "where they might have otherwise committed a violent act."

This needs to be considered alongside evidence that violent gaming in Japan tends to take place in a more social/family setting and is more role-play (JRPG: Japanese role-playing games) oriented (Anderson *et al.* 2010) than "Western" "hack and slash" gaming (Navarro-Remesal and Loriguillo-López 2015: 9–10). These differences may have a further impact on lower levels of violence, and ultimately homicides, in Japan. As Markey, Markey, and French (2014: 15) admit, video gaming is only a single risk factor in attempting to explain violent crime, but with Japan's high level of gaming involvement,[18] it is certainly another area that requires further investigation.

A final area that has also not been explored in Japan is the role of increasingly effective medical interventions, which has been shown to reduce the murder rate in the United States (Harris *et al.* 2002), given that "nonlethal" violence has increased in Japan as the homicide rate has reduced (though not for juveniles). There are indications that since the 1991 Paramedic Law was introduced, allowing paramedics to operate under doctors' remote instructions, survival rates for cardiac arrest have gradually improved, from 7.2 percent in 2005 to 11.4 percent in 2011 (Fire and Disaster Management Agency 2014). However, the direct impact on homicides is an area that requires more research in Japan.

Conclusions

Overall, Japan does have a very low homicide rate in a global context. In the Southeast Asian region, however, when Japan is compared with its most advanced neighbors, it is less exceptional. However, the analysis of the age of Japanese offenders who commit homicide clearly questions the universal acceptance that crime reduces with age. The numbers and proportions of juveniles (under 20 years old) committing homicide have consistently decreased, as they have for young adults (20–29 years old). Conversely, older people are now committing a much larger share of Japanese homicides, although this varies by age group and by gender. The low involvement in homicide is not seen as overwhelmingly positive by some, with Johnson (2006, 2008) arguing strongly that if suicide is included in lethal violence rates, Japan's young people have a very high offending rate, but even this is now surpassed by its comparable near neighbor South Korea.

None of the explanations for the reduction in homicide in Japan is currently fully convincing, but it is also clear that such explanations would be better sought in a comparative regional context, since Hong Kong, South Korea, and China now have very similar homicide trends to Japan. While factors such as culture, changes in the economy, an aging population, and detection/deterrence have been explored, and largely dismissed, there is still room for exploration of the impact of, for instance, changes in the number of police officers/practices, increased incarceration/incapacitation, and the impact of abortion rates, as applied in other contexts (see Levitt 2004, for a summary), while also not ignoring the cathartic and incapacitation potential of gaming.

Although we cannot adequately explain the overall reduction in Japanese homicides, we do know that most of this reduction is accounted for by young men not killing other men. The concomitant of this is that Japanese women then form an increasingly larger proportion of those who are killed. While this remains unusual in a global context, it is also a very similar profile to other Southeast Asian, low homicide-rate countries such as Hong Kong and South Korea. The Japanese Gender Equality Bureau has taken steps to address domestic/intimate partner violence, with early indications of success for women victims, but this has also highlighted that there is a relatively high male victim rate. Since women in Japan also form a comparatively high proportion of homicide offenders and an increasing proportion of offenders who commit serious and violent crime, more research attention, particularly from feminist perspectives, is required to explain the circumstances in which Japanese women kill, and what else can be done to reduce this.

Notes

1 There are always anomalies. Japanese criminal statistics also include attempted homicides, which have formed half of all recorded postwar homicides (Johnson 2006: 75; Miyazaki and Otani 2004: 5; Hasegawa 2003). South Korea also includes attempted homicides in its returns, but these constitute only 17 percent of recorded

homicides (Johnson 2008: 151). Japan also excludes "robbery resulting in homicide" (*goto satsujin*), which might add about 3 percent to the average annual homicide figures (Finch 2001).

2 Heisei 23 nen no Hanzai (National Police Agency) (2011: 176, table 7). These are annual reports in Japanese only. (Because of the way these are organized, the number following Heisei plus the year following Hanzai varies according to the year of the statistics. The index for all years can be accessed and translated into English, but the related spreadsheets are in Japanese only; https://www.npa.go.jp/hakusyo/index.htm.)

3 While China and its territories have very different political systems to Japan and Taiwan, the level of infrastructure development and their proximity do provide instructive comparisons to show that Japan's low homicide rate is not exceptional. However, we have not included Mongolia (8.8 per 100,000) or North Korea (figures available only for 2012, 5.2 per 100,000) in this comparison given their very different histories and profiles. Only 2011 figures are available for South Korea.

4 UNODC (2014: 109–151) figures show the vast majority of countries, 219, now have recorded homicide statistics which continue to support this statement.

5 Heisei 24 nen no Hanzai (2012: 226, table 22).

6 Between 2008 and 2009, Cabinet Office, Japan (2009: 221, fig. 7-1-1-9). In 2010, Heisei 22 nen no Hanzai (2010: 224–225, table 22); in 2011, Heisei 23 nen no Hanzai (2011: 226–227, table 22); and in 2012, Heisei 24 nen no Hanzai (2012: 226–227, table 22).

7 Based on the latest UNODC figures available, 2011–2012.

8 The latest available in English at the time of writing.

9 This term is used in English language versions but refers to all intimate partner violence.

10 2012 and 2015 surveys only available in Japanese.

11 Though not for Japan.

12 Available only in Japanese at the time of writing.

13 Japanese criminal statistics use this measure, which may limit comparisons with other countries, but the homicide clear-up/clearance rate is very high (consistently over 90%) and is covered in detail later in this chapter.

14 These can all be accessed in English at http://hakusyo1.moj.go.jp/en/nendo_nfm.html. This is a useful general resource for the reader, but be aware that (a) later years will usually be available for the Japanese language version and (b) many of the statistics used are difficult to interpret and can offer seemingly different values for the same query in different tables as different filters have been applied.

15 This "impossible" rate for 2013 relates to homicides committed in earlier years, but resolved in 2013 and emphasizes the provisional nature of year on year changes.

16 The White Paper on Crime (Cabinet Office, Japan 2014) does not include injury resulting in death, meaning police statistics for each year must be cited: Heisei 24 nen no Hanzai (2012: 176, table 7); Heisei 23 nen no Hanzai (2011: 176, table 7); Heisei 22 nen no Hanzai (2010: 174, table 7); and so on.

17 Thanks are due here to Isaac Ellis-Nee (Havant College) in assisting with this topic.

18 At an estimate of $22.29 billion for 2013, Japan's game industry revenues are higher than those for the whole of Europe ($20 billion) or for the United States and Canada combined ($19.69 billion). Video game sales wiki, Video game industry, Regional video game industry revenues (http://vgsales.wikia.com/wiki/Video_game_industry).

References

Anderson, C.A, Shibuya, A., Ihori, N., *et al.* (2010) Violent video game effects on aggression, empathy and prosocial behavior in Eastern and Western countries: A meta-analytic review. *Psychological Bulletin*, 136(2): 151–173.

Athens, L. (1997) *Violent Criminal Acts and Actors Revisited.* Urbana: University of Illinois Press.

Bayley, D.H. (1991) *Forces of Order: Policing Modern Japan.* Berkeley: University of California Press.

Bennett, R.R. and Lynch, J.P. (1990) Does a difference make a difference? Comparing cross-national crime indicators. *Criminology*, 28(1): 153–181.

Bottomley, A.K. and Coleman, C.A. (1981) *Understanding Crime Rates: Police and Public Roles in the Production of Official Statistics.* Farnborough, UK: Saxon House.

Braithwaite, J. (1989) *Crime, Shame, and Reintegration.* Cambridge: Cambridge University Press.

Buss, D.M. (2005) *The Murderer Next Door: Why the Mind Is Designed to Kill.* New York: Penguin Books.

Cabinet Office, Japan (2004) Annual report on the state of formation of a gender-equal society and policies to be implemented in 2004 to promote the formation of a gender-equal society. Available online at http://www.gender.go.jp/english_contents/about_danjo/whitepaper/pdf/ewp2004.pdf (accessed May 15, 2014).

Cabinet Office, Japan (2007) White Paper on crime (fig. 7-3-4-1). Available online at http://hakusyo1.moj.go.jp/en/56/nfm/n_56_2_7_3_4_1.html (accessed May 15, 2014).

Cabinet Office, Japan (2009) White Paper on gender equality 2009. Available online at http://www.gender.go.jp/english_contents/about_danjo/whitepaper/pdf/ewp2009.pdf (accessed May 15, 2014).

Cabinet Office, Japan (2010a) Number of cleared cases by type of relationship to victim (1980–2009). Available online at http://hakusyo1.moj.go.jp/en/59/image/image/h007001001005e.jpg.

Cabinet Office, Japan (2010b) White Paper on crime. Available online at http://hakusyo1.moj.go.jp/en/59/nfm/mokuji.html (accessed January 4, 2015).

Cabinet Office, Japan (2012) White Paper on crime. Available online at http://hakusyo1.moj.go.jp/en/61/image/image/h004002002004e.jpg (accessed January 15, 2015).

Cabinet Office, Japan (2013) White Paper on crime. Available online at http://hakusyo1.moj.go.jp/en/62/nfm/mokuji.html (accessed May 15, 2015).

Cunningham, S., Engelstätter, B., and Ward, M.R. (2013) Understanding the effects of violent video games on violent crime. social science research network. Available online at http://papers.ssrn.com/sol3/papers.cfm?abstract_id=1804959 (accessed May 15, 2015).

Dai, M. (2013) Homicide in Asia. In L. Jianhong, S. Jou, and B. Hebenton (eds), *Handbook of Asian Criminology* (pp. 11–23). New York: Springer.

Dower, J.W. (1999) *Embracing Defeat: Japan in the Wake of World War II.* London: W.W. Norton.

Finch, A. (2001) Homicide in Contemporary Japan. *British Journal of Criminology*, 14: 219–235.

Fire and Disaster Management Agency (2014) The situation of lifesaving rates of cardiopulmonary arrest, White Paper. http://www.fdma.go.jp/html/hakusho/h24/h24/html/2-2-5-5_2.html (accessed May 3, 2016).

Gottfredson, M.R. and Hirschi, T. (1990) *A General Theory of Crime.* Palo Alto, CA: Stanford University Press.

Hamai, K. (2011) Crime in an aging society with a declining birth rate and sustainable criminal justice policy in Japan: From retribution to rehabilitation. *Japanese Journal of Sociological Criminology*, 36: 76–106.

Hamai, K. and Ellis, T. (2006) Crime and criminal justice in modern Japan: From reintegrative shaming to popular punitivism. *International Journal of the Sociology of Law*, 34(3): 157–178.

Harris, A.R, Thomas, S.H., Fisher, G.A, and Hirsch, D.J. (2002) Murder and medicine: The lethality of criminal assault 1960–1999. *Homicide Studies*, 6: 128–166.

Hasegawa, M. (2003) Nihon no wakamono wa naze sekai de mottomo hito o korosanakunatta no ka (Why have Japan's youth become the least likely killers)? *Jimon Koryu*, October: 12–22.

Hasegawa, M. (2005) Homicide by men in Japan and its relationship to age, resources, and risk-taking. *Evolution and Human Behavior*, 26: 332–343.

Hasegawa, M. and Hasegawa, T. (2000a) Senzen Nihon ni okeru Joshi Shibo no Kajo (Excess female deaths in prewar Japan). *Kagaku*, 70: 388–396.

Hasegawa, T. and Hasegawa, M. (2000b) Sengo Nihon no Satsujin no Doko: Toku ni, Eiji-Goroshi toDansei ni yoru Satsujin ni tsuite (Trends in homicide in postwar Japan, with a focus on infanticide and homicide by males). *Kagaku*, 70: 560–568.

Hassett, M. (2012) Japan's battered men suffer abuse in silence: Equality bureau turns a blind eye as growing ranks of husbands claim mistreatment at the hands of their wives. *Japan Times*, July 10. Available online at http://www.japantimes.co.jp/community/2012/07/10/issues/japans-battered-men-suffer-abuse-in-silence/#.VZud7mVwbIU (accessed June 3, 2016).

Heidensohn, F. and Silvestri, M. (2012) Gender and crime. In M. Maguire, R. Morgan, and R. Reiner (eds), *The Oxford Handbook of Criminology* (5th edn, pp. 336–369).Oxford: Oxford University Press.

Johnson, D.T. (2006) The vanishing killer: Japan's postwar homicide decline. *Social Science Japan Journal*, 9(1): 73–90.

Johnson, D.T. (2008) The homicide drop in postwar Japan. *Homicide Studies*, 12(1): 146–160.

Kamimura, A., Bybee, D., and Yoshimama, M. (2014) Factors affecting initial intimate partner violence-specific health care seeking in the Tokyo metropolitan area, Japan. *Journal of Interpersonal Violence*, 29(13): 2378–2393.

Katz, J. (1988) *Seductions of Crime: Moral and Sensual Attractions in Doing Evil*. New York: Basic Books.

Kawai, M. (2004) *Anzen Shinwa Hokai no Paradokkusu: Chian no Ho-shakaigaku* (The paradox of the shattered safety myth: A socio-legal study of order). Tokyo: Iwanami Shoten.

Komiya, N. (1999) A cultural study of the low crime rate in Japan. *British Journal of Criminology*, 39: 369–390.

LaFree, G. and Drass. K.A. (2002) Counting crime booms among nations: Evidence for homicide victimization rates, 1956 to 1998. *Criminology*, 40(4): 769–799.

Lebra, T.S. (1984) *Japanese Women: Constraint and Fulfillment*. Hawaii: University of Hawaii Press.

Leonard, E. (1982) *Women, Crime and Society: A Critique of Criminology Theory*. New York: Longman.

Levitt, S.D. (2004) Understanding why crime fell in the 1990s: Four factors that explain the decline and six that do not. *Journal of Economic Perspectives*, 18(1): 163–190.

Maeda, M. (2003) *Nihon no Chian wa Saisei Dekiru ka* (Can Japan revive public order)? Tokyo: Chikuma Shinsho.

Maguire, M. (2012) Criminal statistics and the construction of crime. In M. Maguire, R. Morgan, and R. Reiner (eds), *The Oxford Handbook of Criminology* (5th edn, pp. 206–244). Oxford: Oxford University Press.

Markey, P.M., Markey, C.N., and French, J.E. (2014) Violent video games and real-world violence: Rhetoric versus data. *Psychology of Popular Media Culture*, 4(4): 277–295.

Marshall, I.H. and Block, C.R. (2004) Maximising the availability of cross-national data on homicide. *Homicide Studies*, 8(3): 267–310.

Matsuda, T. (2000) Gendai no Wakamono wa Naze Satsujin o Shinakunatta no ka (Why have today's youth stopped committing murder)? *Japan Skeptics Newsletter*, October.

Messing, J.T., Campbell, J., Sullivan Wilson, J., *et al.* (2015) The lethality screen: The predictive validity of an intimate partner violence risk assessment for use by first responders. *Journal of Interpersonal Violence*, Online, May. doi: 10.1177/0886260515585540.

Miller, A.S. and Kanazawa, S. (2000) *Order by Accident: The Origins and Consequences of Conformity in Contemporary Japan*. Boulder, CO: Westview Press.

Miyazaki, M. and Otani, A. (2004) *Satsujinritsu: Nihonjin wa Satsujin ga Dekinai! Sekai Saitei Satsujinritsu no Nazo* (Homicide rates: Japanese people cannot commit murder! The puzzle of the world's lowest homicide rate). Tokyo: Ota Shuppan.

Navarro-Remesal, V. and Loriguillo-López, A. (2015) What makes Gêmu different? A look at the distinctive design traits of Japanese video games and their place in the Japanese media mix. *Journal of Games Criticism*, 2(1): 1–18.

Park, W.K. (2006) *Trends in Crime Rates in Postwar Japan: A Structural Perspective*. Morioka City, Japan: Shinzansha.

Police Policy Research Center (National Police Academy) (2010) Crime in Japan 2010. Alumni Association for NPA. Available online at https://www.npa.go.jp/english/seisaku/Crime_in_Japan_in_2010.pdf (accessed May 30, 2016).

Research and Training Institute of the Ministry of Justice (2013) *Research on Random Killings in Japan 2013*. Report no. 50. Available online at http://www.moj.go.jp/content/000112398.pdf (accessed May 30, 2016).

Roberts, A. and LaFree, G. (2004) Explaining Japan's postwar violent crime trends. *Criminology*, 42: 179–209.

Rohlen, T.P. (1989) Order in Japanese society: Attachment, authority, and routine. *Journal of Japanese Studies*, 15: 5–40.

Saito, T. (2013) *Hikikmori: Adolescence without End*. Minneapolis: University of Minnesota Press.

Sharpe, G. and Gelsthorpe, L. (2009) Engendering the agenda: Girls, young women and youth justice. *Youth Justice*, 9(3): 195–208.

Shikita, M. and Tsuchiya, S. (1992) *Crime and Criminal Policy in Japan: Analysis and Evaluation of the Showa Era, 1926–1988*. New York: Springer.

Small Arms Survey (2007) *Completing the Count* (ch. 2, annex 4). Geneva: Graduate Institute of International and Development Studies. Available online at http://www.smallarmssurvey.org/fileadmin/docs/A-Yearbook/2007/en/Small-Arms-Survey-2007-Chapter-02-annexe-4-EN.pdf (accessed May 15, 2014).

Steffensmeier, D.J., Schwartz, J., Zhong, H., and Ackerman, J. (2005) An assessment of recent trends in girls' violence using diverse longitudinal sources: Is the gender gap closing? *Criminology*, 43(2): 355–405.

Streib, V.L. (2003) Executing women, juveniles, and the mentally retarded: Second class citizens in capital punishment. In J.R. Acker, R.M. Bohm, and C.S. Lanier (eds),

America's Experiment With Capital Punishment: Reflections on the Past, Present, and Future of the Ultimate Penal Sanction (pp. 301–323). Durham, NC: Carolina Academic Press.

Tabin, M. (2012) Domestic violence in Japan—support services and psychosocial impact on survivors. *FOCUS*, 70. Available online at http://www.hurights.or.jp/archives/focus/section2/2012/12/domestic-violence-in-japan---support-services-and-psychosocial-impact-on-survivors.html (accessed September 19, 2016).

Uchiyama, Y. (2003) Nihon no wakamono wa korosanai: Boryoku hanzai enerugi ga gekigen (Generation gap: Japan's youth commit fewer murders than their counterparts elsewhere). *Asahi Shinbun*, April 4 (evening edn): 3.

UNODC (2011) *Global Study on Homicide 2011: Trends, Context, Data*. Vienna: United Nations Office on Drugs and Crime. Available online at http://www.unodc.org/documents/data-and-analysis/statistics/Homicide/Globa_study_on_homicide_2011_web.pdf (accessed May 15, 2015).

UNODC (2013) *Homicide Statistics 2013*. Vienna: United Nations Office on Drugs and Crime. Available online at http://www.unodc.org/gsh/en/data.html (accessed May 15, 2015).

UNODC (2014) *Global Study on Homicide 2013: Trends, Context, Data*. Vienna: United Nations Office on Drugs and Crime. Available online at http://www.unodc.org/documents/data-and-analysis/statistics/GSH2013/2014_GLOBAL_HOMICIDE_BOOK_web.pdf (accessed May 28, 2015).

White, P. (1995) Homicide. In M.A. Walker (eds), *Interpreting Crime Statistics* (pp, 130–144). Oxford: Oxford University Press.

Yoshikazu, Y., Kanazawa, Y., and Yuma, C. (2010) 少年の殺人事件発生率と完全失業率の長期的関連：日本における1974年から2006年までの時系列データの実証分析 [The relationship between the incidence of juvenile homicides and unemployment rates in Japan: A time-series analysis 1974–2006]. *Japanese Journal of Criminological Sociology* (35): 115–130.

Further Reading

Brookman, F. (2004) *Understanding Homicide*. Thousand Oaks, CA: SAGE.

Cabinet Office, Japan (2013) White Paper on crime (table 4-5-1-1). Available online at http://hakusyo1.moj.go.jp/en/62/image/image/h004005001001h.jpg (accessed May 15, 2015).

Daly, K. and Chesney-Lind, M. (1988) Feminism and criminology. *Justice Quarterly*, 5(4): 498–538.

gamespot.com (n.d.) So what's the difference between JRPGs and WRPGs? Available online at http://www.gamespot.com/forums/system-wars-314159282/so-whats-the-difference-between-jrpgs-and-wrpgs-27512048/(accessed May 23, 2016)

Heidensohn, F. (1985) *Women and Crime*. London: Macmillan.

Heidensohn, F. (1996) *Women and Crime* (2nd edn). Basingstoke, UK: Macmillan.

Kalata, K. (n.d) A Japanese RPG primer: The essential 20. Gamasutra http://www.gamasutra.com/view/feature/131985/a_japanese_rpg_primer_the_.php?print=1 (accessed May 23, 2016).

Kitsuse, J.I. and Cicourel, A.V. (1963) A note on the uses of official statistics. *Social Problems*, 11: 131–139.

LaFree, G. (1999) Homicide: Cross-national perspectives. In M.D. Smith and M.A. Zahn (eds), *Studying and Preventing Homicide: Issues and Challenges* (pp. 115–139). Thousand Oaks, CA: SAGE.

LaFree, G. (1999) A summary and review of cross-national comparative studies of homicide. In M.D. Smith and M.A. Zahn (eds), *Homicide: A Sourcebook of Social Research* (pp. 124–148). Thousand Oaks, CA: SAGE.

Sellin, T. (1938) *Culture, Conflict and Crime.* New York: Social Science Research Council.

Smart, C. (1976) *Women, Crime, and Criminology: A Feminist Critique.* London: Routledge & Kegan Paul.

Von Hirsch, A., Bottoms, A.E., Burney, E., and Wikstrom, P.O. (1999) *Criminal Deterrence and Sentence Severity: An Analysis of Recent Research.* Oxford: Hart.

Wiles, P. (1971) Criminal statistics and sociological explanations of crime. In W.G. Carson and P. Wiles (eds), *The Sociology of Crime and Delinquency in Britain.* London: Martin Robertson.

Zimring, F.E. and Hawkins, G. (1997) *Crime is Not the Problem: Lethal Violence in America.* New York: Oxford University Press.

23

Homicide in Australia and New Zealand

Precursors and Prevention

Paul Mazerolle, Li Eriksson, Richard Wortley, and Holly Johnson

Introduction

Much of what is known about homicide in Australia and New Zealand is based upon official data drawn from police, court, and coroner records. These types of data are particularly valuable in providing a broad picture of rates, trends, and demographic relationships. In this chapter, we use these data to describe the characteristics of homicide in Australia and New Zealand. Given the regional, cultural, and political similarities across Australia and New Zealand it might be assumed that the essential features of homicide are similar across both countries. Yet, very little research has examined homicide patterns and trends across both countries.

We also present findings from the Australian Homicide Project (AHP), which utilizes interviews with offenders to uncover developmental pathways, precursors, and offender motivations for homicide. This project is unique in its design and provides an opportunity to extract first-hand information from the perpetrators of these serious incidents. To illustrate, from these very detailed interviews we present data on two aspects of homicide offending not readily ascertained from official source data, namely reported mental health problems over time, and plans to kill.

The Australian and New Zealand Offence Classification

Across Australia and New Zealand, government agencies utilize the Australian and New Zealand Offence Classification to produce and analyze criminal justice statistics on criminal offenses. Various legal offense definitions exist across New Zealand and

The Handbook of Homicide, First Edition. Edited by Fiona Brookman, Edward R. Maguire, and Mike Maguire.

the Australian states and territories and the classification provides a uniform cross-jurisdictional framework for use by statistical and criminal justice agencies.

Within this classification system homicide is defined as to "unlawfully kill, attempt to unlawfully kill or conspiracy to kill another person" (Australian Bureau of Statistics 2011a: 24). Homicide is further subdivided into three categories: (1) murder, (2) attempted murder, and (3) manslaughter and driving causing death. Homicides are classified as murder if there is intent to kill or cause grievous bodily harm. Murder also includes homicides where intent was absent, but where the killing occurred in the course of another crime. Manslaughter is defined as "the unlawful killing of another person while deprived of the power of self-control by provocation, or under circumstances amounting to diminished responsibility or without intent to kill, as a result of a careless, reckless, negligent, unlawful or dangerous act (other than the act of driving)" (Australian Bureau of Statistics 2011a: 27). Infanticides are included in this category.[1] Homicides with an absence of intent, but where the killing was a result of culpable, reckless, or negligent driving are classified as driving causing death.

The focus of this chapter is on unlawful homicide and excludes homicides committed within the context of legal duties (e.g., by police). We restrict our analyses to the Australian and New Zealand Offence Classification subdivisions of murder and manslaughter (including infanticide) and exclude attempted murder and driving causing death.

Examining Homicide through Official Statistics

Criminal justice data on homicide available publicly from various local and state governments across Australia and New Zealand consist of statistics provided by police, criminal courts, and correctional agencies. In New Zealand, official statistics on recorded and resolved homicide offenses are available in reports published by New Zealand Police (e.g., New Zealand Police 2014a) and as raw data accessible through Statistics New Zealand's interactive web tool (Statistics New Zealand 2015). These data are limited to offender characteristics, however, New Zealand Police further publishes a report containing descriptive information on homicide victims, geographic location of the homicide, and weapon use (New Zealand Police 2014b). This information is taken from the national homicide database, which contains information on all homicides investigated by police. This database is maintained by New Zealand Police for operational purposes, but has also been used by researchers to study homicide patterns and contexts (e.g., Moskowitz *et al.* 2006). In addition, researchers studying homicide in New Zealand rely on coronial data, to which historically the Coronial Services of New Zealand held access, but that are currently held by the National Coronial Information System. This database covers not only New Zealand, but also Australian jurisdictions, and contains information provided in coronial files such as autopsy and toxicology reports.

In Australia, the main source of information on homicide is the National Homicide Monitoring Program (NHMP), which is held by the Australian Institute of

Criminology (AIC). The NHMP has recorded the nature and extent of homicides in Australia since 1989 and data are collated from police reports, coronial reports, and press clippings and further cross-validated with additional sources (Mouzos 2002). The AIC frequently analyzes and publishes NHMP data in comprehensive and detailed reports (e.g., Chan and Payne 2013). Thus, the collation, analysis, and reporting of homicide data is more centralized in Australia compared with New Zealand.

One of the main advantages with using official data is that they are relatively accessible and do not require fieldwork. Depending on the level of detail contained in the data, official records can provide important information relating to homicide rates, demographic and mental health characteristics of victims and offenders, victim–offender relationship, and legal aspects of homicide incidents. These data are particularly valuable for examinations of characteristics of offenders across demographic groups, correlates of homicide, historical trends, and cross-national comparisons. However, it is important to keep in mind that official data are collected for specific administrative purposes, and that these purposes may not directly align with the aims of a particular research project. For example, while official data often contain offender demographics, the prospect of examining the life histories and specific motivations of offenders is limited.

In the following sections we compare homicides in Australia and New Zealand in terms of rates, trends, regional distributions, and victim and offender characteristics.

Homicide Rates, Trends, and Regional Distribution

Homicide in Australia and New Zealand is a rare event, especially compared with international figures. According to data collated by the United Nations Office on Drugs and Crime (UNODC 2015) as part of their Global Study on Homicide, in 2012 there were 254 homicides committed in Australia and 41 homicides committed in New Zealand. Taking population estimates into account, this equates to a rate of 1.1 per 100,000 population in Australia and 0.9 per 100,000 population in New Zealand. Compared to countries such as the United States (4.7 per 100,000) and the Russian Federation (9.2 per 100,000), the rates in Australia and New Zealand are relatively low, while they are similar to the homicide rates in the United Kingdom (1.0 per 100,000) and Canada (1.6 per 100,000) (UNODC 2015). The homicide rates in Australia and New Zealand are low in comparison to the global average homicide rate of 6.9 per 100,000 (UNODC 2015).

In terms of broad trends, both countries have seen a slight decline in homicide rates over the past couple of decades. As illustrated by data from the Global Study on Homicide presented in Figure 23.1, the larger and more consistent drop is seen by Australia where the rate has declined by 35 percent since 1995. In comparison, the rate has remained steadier overall in New Zealand, declining by 9 percent between 1995 and 2013.

While some countries display higher homicide rates in urban areas compared to the national average, this does not appear to be the case in Australia and New Zealand.

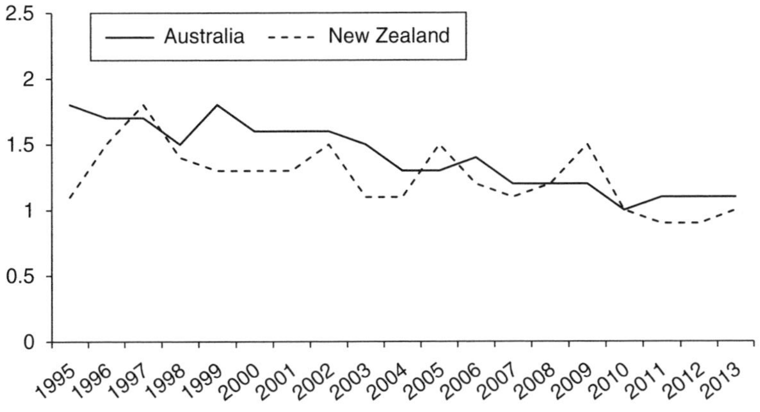

Figure 23.1 Homicide rates in Australia and New Zealand 1995–2013. Source: United Nations Office on Drugs and Crime (2011, 2015).

Table 23.1 Homicide in Australia by state/territory, 2009–2010.

	N	*Rate per 100,000*
New South Wales	76	1.1
Victoria	59	1.1
Queensland	56	1.2
Western Australia	23	1.0
South Australia	21	1.3
Tasmania	6	1.2
Northern Territory	13	5.7
Australian Capital Territory	3	0.8
National	257	1.2

Source: Australian Institute of Criminology (adapted from Chan and Payne, 2013)

In fact, the homicide rate in the most populous city is comparable, and even slightly lower, than the national average in each country. Data from the Global Study on Homicide reveal that in 2007 Sydney had a homicide rate of 1.1 compared to the Australian national average of 1.2 (UNODC 2015). Similarly, while the New Zealand national homicide rate in 2012 was 0.9, Auckland reported a homicide rate of 0.7.

Although homicide rates in the most populous cities may not differ from the national average in Australia and New Zealand, some differences across regions do exist. This is particularly evident in Australia. Table 23.1 details the recorded homicide rates across eight states and territories of Australia. The data, taken from the NHMP (Chan and Payne 2013), reveal that the homicide rate in the Northern Territory is almost five times higher than the national average, all other states, and the Australian Capital Territory. The high rate of homicide in the Northern Territory may be attributed to a complex set of interrelated dynamics, including high levels of alcohol-related assault, high incidences of domestic and family violence, and high concentrations of Aboriginal and Torres Strait Islander peoples experiencing

Table 23.2 Homicide in New Zealand by police district, 2013–2014.

	N	*Rate per 100,000*
Northland	2	1.3
Waitemata	9	1.6
Auckland	6	1.3
Counties/Manukau	2	0.4
Waikato	2	0.6
Bay Of Plenty	3	0.9
Eastern	2	1.0
Central	5	1.4
Wellington	4	0.8
Tasman	1	0.6
Canterbury	6	1.1
Southern	5	1.6
National	47	1.0

Note: Although preventing cross-country comparisons of specific years, the decision was made to use the most recently available data sources for each country (in this case 2008–2010 for Australia and 2013–2014 for New Zealand). For the purpose of this chapter, these numbers, retrieved from Statistics New Zealand (2015) exclude attempted murder, conspiracy to murder, incitement/counsel/attempt to procure murder, and homicides committed as part of legal duty. Source: Statistics New Zealand (2015).

social and economic disadvantage, dispossession, and breakdown of traditional culture (e.g., Goedegebuure 1993; James and Carcach 1997; Memmott 2010; Memmott *et al.* 2001). The Northern Territory also faces natural geographic barriers to violence prevention and accessing community services, with 43.4 percent of the population living in remote or very remote areas in comparison to the national average of 2.3 percent who live in these areas (Public Health Information Development Unit 2015).

Regional differences in homicide rates also exist in New Zealand, although not to the same extent. Table 23.2 details the recorded homicide rates in the police districts in New Zealand. The Waitemata district (on the North Island) and Southern district (on the South Island) display the highest recorded homicide rates at 60 percent higher than the national average.

Offender, Victim, and Event Characteristics

Victim–offender relationship

In Australia and New Zealand most homicide offenders knew their victims. As shown in Figure 23.2, in 2008–2010 only one in seven homicide incidents in Australia were classified as stranger homicides. Most commonly, victims and

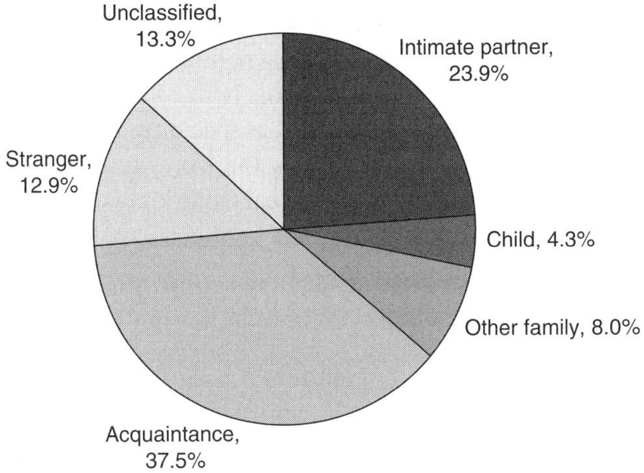

Figure 23.2 Victim–offender relationship, Australia 2008–2010. Source: adapted from Chan and Payne (2013).

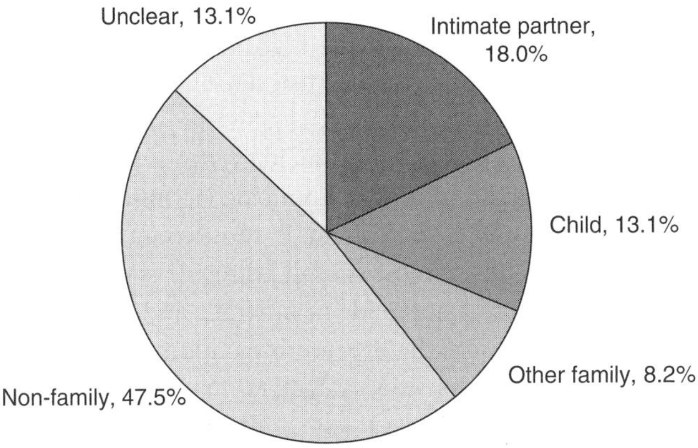

Figure 23.3 Victim–offender relationship, New Zealand 2011. Source: New Zealand Police (2014b).

offenders were known to each other but were not related or in an intimate relationship. More than one in three homicide incidents were classified as acquaintance homicides and a similar proportion were also classified as domestic-related. The most common form of domestic homicide was intimate partner homicide: in approximately one-quarter of the homicide incidents committed in 2008–2010, the victims and their offenders were current or former intimate partners. Parents who killed their children (filicide) contributed to a relatively small proportion, as did offenders who killed family members other than partners and children.

Similar to Australia, domestic homicides also contribute a relatively large proportion to the overall homicide statistics in New Zealand. As shown in Figure 23.3, current or former intimate partners commit nearly one in five homicides. A higher proportion of homicides in New Zealand involved parents killing their children, while the proportion of homicide incidents where other family members (excluding partners and children) are killed is similar across both countries.

Publicly available New Zealand data are not as specific in relation to nondomestic victim–offender relationship categories. It is therefore difficult to establish how common it is for victims of homicide in New Zealand to know the offender. However, what is clear is that in New Zealand domestic homicides are less common proportionately compared to nondomestic homicides.

Gender

The majority of homicide offenders in Australia and New Zealand are male. According to NHMP data, in Australia in 2009–2010 males represented 86 percent of recorded offenders (Chan and Payne 2013). Patterns are similar in New Zealand. Conviction data from New Zealand show that between 2000 and 2013 on average 86 percent of offenders convicted of murder and manslaughter were male and that this fluctuates over time (Statistics New Zealand 2015).[2] The lowest proportion of males was recorded in 2009 (78%) and the highest in 2003 (96%). Males are also overrepresented as victims of homicide. In Australia, 65 percent of homicide victims in 2009–2010 were male (Chan and Payne 2013). Similarly, in New Zealand between 2007 and 2011 on average 61 percent of homicide victims were male (New Zealand Police 2014b). The gender distributions in homicide victimization and perpetration are not unique to Australia and New Zealand. In most countries, males are overrepresented as victims and offenders in the overall homicide statistics (UNODC 2011).

However, while on the surface homicide in Australia and New Zealand appears to be a male-on-male phenomenon, the overrepresentation of males is not consistent across all victim–offender relationship categories. In particular, homicides within the family display unique patterns. Of all family related homicides committed between 2007 and 2013 in New Zealand, slightly over half of victims were female (56.6%) (New Zealand Family Violence Clearinghouse 2014). The overrepresentation of females as victims is particularly true in cases where intimate partners are killed. Australian NHMP data from 2002–2003 to 2011–2012 show that 75 percent of victims killed by a current of former intimate partner were female (Cussen and Bryant 2015a). Similarly, data from New Zealand Police show that females constituted 74.7 percent of homicide victims involving couple relationships between the years 2007 and 2013 (New Zealand Family Violence Clearinghouse 2014). This overrepresentation of women as victims of intimate partner homicide is part of an international pattern (Stöckl *et al.* 2013).

Another form of domestic homicide with distinct gender patterns is the killing of children by biological parents or stepparents. Here females comprise a relatively large proportion of offenders, especially compared with the overall homicide statistics. A New Zealand study of child homicides committed between 1991 and 2000 found that 40 percent of the offenders in filicide cases were mothers (Doolan 2004).

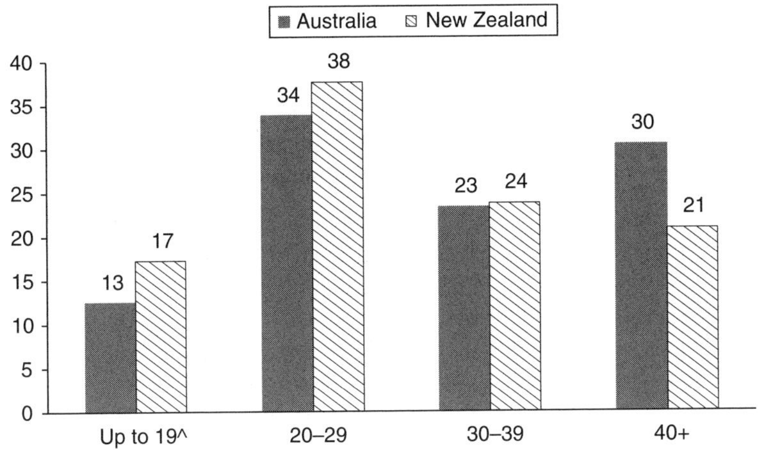

Figure 23.4 Age distribution (in percentage) of homicide offenders in Australia (2006–2007) and New Zealand (2000–2013). Although more recent Australian data are available, the report by Dearden and Jones (2008) was chosen to better match the age categories of homicide offenders and victims extracted from the New Zealand Police data. Note: ^ Australia = 15–19; New Zealand = 17–19. Sources: adapted from Dearden and Jones (2008) and Statistics New Zealand (2015).

In addition, another 6 percent of cases involved both mothers and fathers as offenders. NHMP data from 2002–2003 to 2011–2012 reveal similar gender distributions, with 52 percent of filicides in Australia perpetrated by mothers (Cussen and Bryant 2015a). Thus, it is clear that although the majority of victims and offenders of homicide are male, gender distribution varies according to victim–offender relationship.

Age distribution

In Australia and New Zealand the majority of offenders are relatively young when they commit homicide, with comparatively low prevalence rates of child/teenage and older offenders. As shown in Figure 23.4, the majority of homicide offenders in Australia and New Zealand were aged between 20 and 29 at the time of the homicide. By comparison, a smaller proportion of offenders were aged 19 or below when they committed the homicide.

According to the data presented in Figure 23.4 approximately 20–30 percent of offenders in Australia and New Zealand were aged 40 or above at the time of the homicide. At first glance, this may be interpreted as though older individuals constitute a relatively large proportion of offenders. However, this category incorporates a wide range of offender ages. Although available data from Statistics New Zealand do not readily allow for age disaggregation, the Australian NHMP data provide information useful for this specific purpose. According to these data, 19.3 percent of

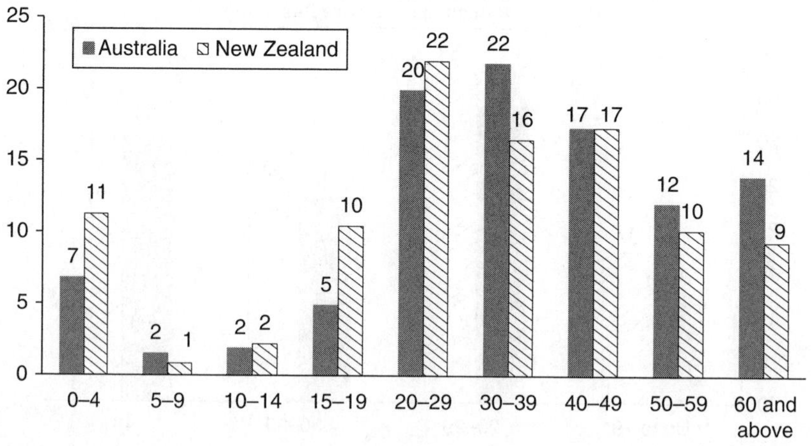

Figure 23.5 Age distribution (in percentage) of homicide victims in Australia (2006–2007) and New Zealand (2007–2011). Sources: adapted from Dearden and Jones (2008) and New Zealand Police (2014b).

all homicide offenders in 2006–2007 were aged 40–49, 7.4 percent were aged 50-59, and only 3.7 percent of offenders were over the age of 60 at the time of the offense (Dearden and Jones 2008).

The age distribution of homicide victims differs somewhat to that of offenders. Figure 23.5 presents information on the age of homicide victims. What the data show is that most homicide victims are aged in their 20s or 30s. In New Zealand, the most common age of homicide victims was 20–29, with over one-fifth of victims falling into this category. By comparison, the modal age group of victims in Australia is slightly higher, with the majority aged between 30 and 39 at the time of death.

Child victims represent a relatively large proportion of homicide victims in Australia and New Zealand: 11 percent of victims in Australia and 14 percent of victims in New Zealand were below the age of 15 (see Figure 23.5). Children are particularly at risk in the early years of childhood, with the majority of child homicide victims aged 4 or under at the time of their death. Further breakdown of NHMP data from 2010–2012 shows that 28.3 percent of child victims (aged under 15) were killed before their first birthday (Bryant and Cussen 2015). This is consistent with international figures, which show that children are the most vulnerable in the first 12 months of life (Brookman and Nolan 2006; Smith and Cooper 2013).

In terms of victim–offender relationship, most children are killed by a family member, most commonly a parent or stepparent. Of the child victims in Australia in 2006–2007, in 85 percent of cases the offender was the custodial or a noncustodial parent (Dearden and Jones 2008). Similar patterns are observed in New Zealand, where data from 1990–1999 show that 74 percent of child homicides were committed by a parent or partner/guardian (Dean 2004).

Indigenous background

Most homicides in Australia and New Zealand are intra-racial. From a review of homicides involving victims and/or offenders of Aboriginal and Torres Strait background in Australia between 1998–1990 and 2011–2012, Cussen and Bryant (2015b) found that only 5 percent were inter-racial. In numbers, most victims of homicide in Australia are of Caucasian appearance (Dearden and Jones 2008). Similarly, Europeans constitute the majority of homicide victims in New Zealand (New Zealand Police 2014b). Data show that Caucasians/Europeans comprise around three-quarters of homicide victims in Australia and New Zealand (Dearden and Jones 2008; New Zealand Police 2014b). Thus, in actual numbers, the Indigenous populations of Australia (Aboriginal and Torres Strait Islander) and New Zealand (Maori) make up a relatively small proportion of homicide victims, although they are clearly overrepresented as victims of lethal violence when population estimates are taken into account. Aboriginal and Torres Strait Islander populations account for approximately 2–3 percent of the total population in Australia (Australian Bureau of Statistics 2011b), yet 17 percent of homicide victims in 2010–2012 were of Aboriginal and Torres Strait Islander status (Bryant and Cussen 2015). Similarly, in New Zealand, approximately 15 percent of the population identify with Maori ethnicity (Statistics New Zealand 2013), yet one-third of homicide victims in 2011 were recorded as Maori (New Zealand Police 2014b).

Indigenous populations in Australia and New Zealand are also overrepresented within the offending statistics. In Australia, the rate of offending for Aboriginal and Torres Strait Islanders was 4.7 per 100,000 in 2011–2012 (Bryant and Cussen 2015). This is approximately four times higher than the rate of offending for persons of non-Aboriginal and Torres Strait Islander backgrounds. Similarly, 42.9 percent of all convicted homicide offenders in New Zealand were reported by the prosecuting authority to be of Maori background (Statistics New Zealand 2015).

Australian data show that in the majority of homicide cases involving Aboriginal and Torres Strait Islander persons the victim and offender knew each other. NHMP data from 1989–1990 to 2011–2012 reveal that only 10.6 percent of all homicide incidents involving victims and/or offenders of Aboriginal and Torres Strait Islander background were classified as stranger homicides (Cussen and Bryant 2015b). Most commonly, these homicides occurred within the family unit. This is particularly the case for female victims. Among female Aboriginal and Torres Strait Islander homicide victims in 2006–2007, a current or former intimate partner was the offender in 59 percent of cases and another family member was the offender in a further 18 percent of cases (Dearden and Jones 2008). By comparison, male Aboriginal and Torres Strait Islander victims less commonly fell victim to an intimate partner (21%) and more commonly fell victim to a family member (37%) or a friend/acquaintance (42%).

The above statistics illustrate that Indigenous homicide in Australia is often an intra-familial affair. Due to the lack of publicly available data, it is difficult to ascertain whether this is also the case among the Maori population in New Zealand. However, death review data suggest that Maori persons are overrepresented as victims of family violence deaths. Of all intimate partner violence deaths in New Zealand between 2009 and 2012, the victim was reported as Maori in 32 percent of cases (Family Violence Death Review Committee 2014). This translates to a rate of 0.75 per 100,000 people, which is 2.8 times higher than the victimization rate of other ethnicities.[3] The victimization rate is even higher for children (17 and under) of Maori background, with Maori children 5.5 times more likely to fall victim to fatal child abuse and neglect compared to children of other ethnicities.[4]

Mental illness

In Australia and New Zealand, as in other countries around the world, the media tend to over-emphasize the relationship between mental disorder and perpetration of violent acts (Coverdale, Nairn, and Claasen 2002). However, available evidence suggests that mental disorders are not particularly common among homicide offenders in Australia and New Zealand. For example, analyzing Australian NHMP data across the years 1989 to 1998, Mouzos (1999) found that only 4.4 percent of homicide offenders were recorded by police as suffering from a mental disorder. These figures are similar to New Zealand: in one of the most comprehensive studies of homicide in New Zealand to date, Simpson *et al.* (2003) found that 8.7 percent of all homicides committed between 1970 and 2000 were perpetrated by offenders with a serious mental illness. Across the time period the highest proportion observed was 22.2 percent and the lowest proportion observed was 0 percent. What was evident was a decline in the proportion of homicides committed by offenders with a serious mental illness in New Zealand at a rate of approximately 4 percent per year across the 30-year time span.

The most common diagnosis of homicide offenders with a serious mental illness was schizophrenia (Simpson *et al.* 2003) and in one-tenth of cases the diagnosis was depression (Mouzos 1999; Simpson *et al.* 2003). In addition, although the majority of homicide offenders with a mental disorder are male, the proportion of females is higher among offenders with a mental disorder than among other homicide offenders. For example, in Australia, females represent 11.4 percent of homicide offenders without mental disorders, but among offenders with mental disorders females represent 29.5 percent (Mouzos 1999). Similar figures are reported in New Zealand (9% versus 33%; Simpson *et al.* 2003).

Another discerning characteristic of homicides perpetrated by offenders with a mental illness is the victim–offender relationship. Although the concept of "stranger danger" may be particularly prevalent in media's representation of mental disorder and violence, the victims of these types of homicides often belong to the offender's family. In Australia, family members (other than intimate partners) were the victims in 49 percent of cases involving an offender with a mental disorder, compared to only 14 percent of cases involving other homicide offenders (Mouzos 1999). Similarly, in New Zealand, 58 percent of victims of offenders with a serious mental illness were family members (other than intimate partners), compared to 10 percent of victims of "mentally normal" homicide offenders (Simpson *et al.* 2003).

Weapon use

Firearm availability and ownership in Australia and New Zealand is low and this is reflected in the homicide statistics. A relatively small proportion of all homicides in Australia and New Zealand involve the use of firearms. To illustrate, Australian NHMP data from 2008–2010 show that 12.7 percent of homicide incidents involved the use of a firearm (Chan and Payne 2013). Similarly, of all victims of homicide between 2007 and 2011 in New Zealand, 9.9 percent were killed with a firearm (New Zealand Police 2014b). These proportions are considerably lower than the global average of 42 percent (UNODC 2011).

It is more common for homicide offenders in Australia and New Zealand to use knives or other sharp objects. In Australia, the majority (38.4%) of homicide victims in 2008–2010 died of stab wounds (Chan and Payne 2013). The proportion of victims killed by stabbing or cutting in New Zealand between 2007 and 2011 was slightly lower compared to Australia (22.5%; New Zealand Police 2014b).

Summary of key characteristics from official statistics

Publicly available data on homicide reveal that homicide rates in Australia and New Zealand are relatively low by international standards, although regional differences exist. In general, the relationships between key correlates of homicide are similar between Australia and New Zealand. In the main, homicide offenders and victims in Australia and New Zealand are young, non-Indigenous men (although some subregional variations can exist) who are known to each other. However, the gender distribution varies according to victim–offender relationship, with, for example, women overrepresented as victims of intimate partner homicide. The data further show that homicide offenders rarely suffer from a mental disorder or use firearms as a method of killing.

Challenges in Understanding Homicide in Australia and New Zealand

As illustrated, data obtained from police case files, court records, and similar official sources provide useful information about the nature and occurrence of homicide in Australia and New Zealand. This information is informative for uncovering trends over time, regional differences in homicide rates, as well as providing valuable demographic characteristics of the offenders of homicide and their victims. This information helps inform our understanding of homicide for policy makers, legislators, researchers, practitioners, and the general community. However, there remain gaps in our knowledge. Official sources provide only a partial representation of the characteristics and dimensions of homicide. Official sources are constrained by the information included on file, which provides a limited and static snapshot of the context for homicide. Although such data may offer detailed information about the homicide event, they are limited in their ability to provide comprehensive information on the dynamic processes that impact upon risks for homicide. This is problematic because such information fails to illuminate the dynamic nature of homicide including the conditions and unfolding events that magnify risks for homicide. Thus, there is an important need to consider a developmental approach for better understanding homicide, and how risks change over time. In addition, official data is limited in their ability to further expand understanding on the various cognitive and emotive processes that impact on homicide offending. To date, limited research has examined decision-making, motivations, and intentions of homicide offenders, and more work is needed (see Brookman 2015; Dobash and Dobash 2011).

Interviewing Homicide Offenders: The Australian Homicide Project

The AHP aims to uncover new knowledge on the causes and precursors of homicide and to identify opportunities for effective intervention. Extending the information provided by official sources, the AHP involves interviewing offenders serving custodial or community sentences for murder or manslaughter. Research projects utilizing direct interviews with homicide perpetrators remain scarce and are often, though not always, restricted to small sample sizes. The AHP is unique in that it is the first major study of homicide in Australia and one of few in the world that involves face-to-face interviews with a large sample of homicide offenders.

Between 2009 and 2013, as part of the AHP we conducted 302 interviews with homicide offenders across Australia, of which 262 were males (86.8%) and 40 were females (13.2%). The interviews were conducted at correctional centers and probation and parole offices. Eligible offenders were provided with an information sheet detailing the study and were asked to express their interest to participate on an opt-in form. The interviews were comprehensive and each took approximately 1.5–2 hours.

The interviews were divided into three sections. In the first section we collected data relating to demographic variables, childhood experiences, drug and alcohol use, attitudes, personality traits, and relationship characteristics. The second part of the interview used a life event calendar technique that has been used successfully in studies on developmental offending patterns (Roberts and Horney 2010). The AHP represents the first study to apply this technique to homicide. This approach retrospectively places events (e.g., job loss) and crimes (e.g., violence) in temporal sequences across units of time. The life event calendar used in this research covered the 12 months prior to the homicide incident. The third and last section of the interview schedule was semi-structured and allowed for short-sentence open-ended answers. In this section, we asked the offenders questions relating to the situational aspects of the homicide incident. This included, but was not limited to, emotions experienced, drug and alcohol use, weapon use, third party involvement, motivations and intentions, as well as post-event behavior and emotions.

Characteristics of Homicide: The Perpetrator View

By using interview data with offenders, the AHP is able to provide rich and contextualized information on the characteristics of homicide offenders, victims, and events. AHP data provide valuable information on offender cognitive processes and how various risks emerge over time. To illustrate, below we present selected findings as they relate to the changing nature of offender mental health problems in the year leading up to the homicide, as well as offender accounts on whether they planned to commit the homicide.

Contact with mental health professionals in the year prior

As discussed previously in this chapter, according to official data less than one in ten homicide offenders in Australia and New Zealand display mental health problems around the time of the offense. Although official data assist in combating the stereotypical media representation of mental illness and homicide, they are limited in their ability to examine the development of mental health problems over time. Using the life event calendar, the AHP represents a unique opportunity to examine how risk, in this case mental health problems, change over time. Together the interviewer and offender map out life events on a calendar that covers the year preceding the homicide. Among other details, offenders are asked to self-report whether they received treatment or assessment by a psychiatrist or a doctor for a mental health problem across each of the 12 months leading up to the offense, and, if so, what types of mental health problems.

Interestingly, the self-reported prevalence rates of mental health problems are not overly divergent from the Australian and New Zealand official data. Figure 23.6 reveals the percentage of offenders interviewed who reported receiving assessment

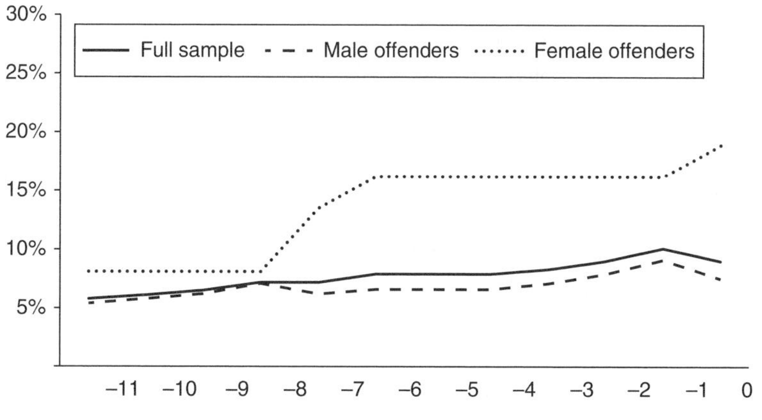

Figure 23.6 Offenders reporting receiving assessment or treatment for a mental health problem in the 12 months preceding the homicide incident (valid percent).

or treatment for depression, bipolar, schizophrenia, anxiety, PTSD, or any personality disorder across the 12 months leading up to the offense (with 0 indicating the month of the homicide). As seen in Figure 23.6, one year prior to the homicide 5.8 percent of the sample reported mental health problems. By the month of the homicide, this had increased slightly (to 9%). While the proportion of male offenders with mental health problems increased slightly across the 12 months, the proportion of females more than doubled across the same time period (from 8.1% to 18.9%).

As seen in Figure 23.7, differences also exist across victim–offender relationships. The data illustrate an increase in the proportion of offenders reporting mental health problems for those offenders who killed intimate partners or other family members. In contrast, the proportion of offenders reporting mental health problems who killed acquaintances or strangers remained relatively constant across the 12 months. Importantly, using a life event history calendar approach provides an opportunity to examine changing events and circumstances leading up to a homicide.

Offender planning

Interviews with offenders can also build knowledge around contextual aspects of the homicide event. While it is common for research to examine situational features of homicide events, such as spatial and geographical details, as well as weapon use, the official data sources that much of this research relies upon are limited in their ability to provide insights into offender cognitions and motivations. For example, although the official legal conviction (i.e., murder or manslaughter) may suggest whether an offender planned to kill the victim, in the majority of cases this is inferred from circumstantial evidence. Thus, studies using interview data with offenders (such as the AHP) are uniquely placed to supplement and extend available official data.

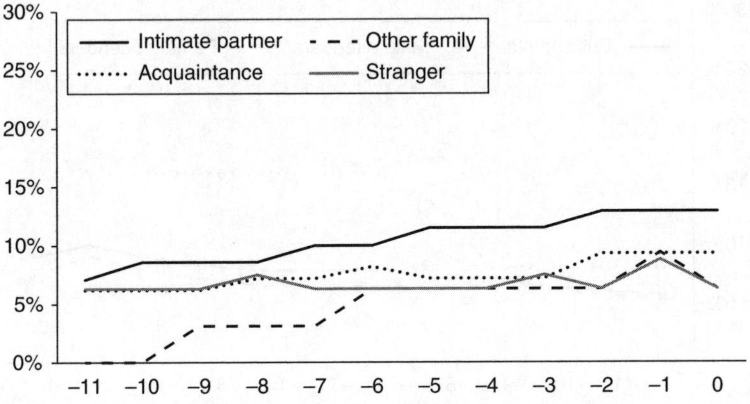

Figure 23.7 Offenders reporting receiving assessment or treatment for a mental health problem in the 12 months preceding the homicide incident (valid percent).

During the interviews, offenders were asked whether they had made plans to kill the victim and most stated that they had not. As one offender said: "It wasn't planned, happened very quickly." However, 14.1 percent stated that they had made plans to kill the victim.[5] For some, the planning had been ongoing for months, although the majority began planning a few days prior to, or on the same day as, the killing.

Again, the data reveal differences across gender and victim–offender relationship. Females more commonly reported planning to kill their victims compared to males. More than one-quarter of the female offenders interviewed reported planning the homicide compared to one in ten male offenders (27% versus 12.1%). For female offenders, plans to kill often involved family members as victims, such as children or parents. For example, one female interviewee referred to the killing of her father as "premeditated." When asked to elaborate she said her father was a "cruel man" who had "destroyed [her] emotionally during childhood." After years of emotional abuse, her planning started one week before the homicide, when she "put a plan together" to kill him.

Planning was less common among offenders who had killed a stranger (8.9%) compared with offenders who killed intimate partners (17.1%), other family members (15.6%), and acquaintances/friends (15.5%). In cases of stranger homicide, the offenders did not plan to kill the victim specifically. Instead, their plans were general, in the sense that their intent was to kill anyone as opposed to a specific victim. For example, one of the male interviewees revealed "most of that week I had been thinking about killing someone." On the evening of the homicide, he waited for a suitable victim to walk past and, as he said, he "took the first person." Although severely intoxicated while committing the crime, it was clear that his motivation was to kill someone that night.

Discussion

This chapter presented information on homicide in Australia and New Zealand. Much of what is known about homicide in Australia and New Zealand is based upon existing official data consisting of criminal justice statistics provided by police, court, and coroner records. The official data on homicide reveal that Australia and New Zealand are relative low homicide countries by international standards. However, like other countries, regional variations occur, with Australia's Northern Territory revealing the highest regional homicide rates. In general, the relationships between key correlates of homicide are similar between Australia and New Zealand. For example, key similarities are evident in terms of offender, victim, and event characteristics, including gender, victim–offender relationships, Indigenous over-representation, the prevalence of mental illness, and the low rates of homicides involving firearms.

Australia and New Zealand also share some of the same challenges in fully understanding the nature and dimensions of homicide due to the over-reliance on official statistical information. The limits of official statistics about crime are well known

(Coleman and Moynihan 1996), but in this chapter we provided an alternative illustration by seeking the views of homicide perpetrators to illuminate more detailed information about homicide, including the pathways and contextualized aspects of homicide events.

The AHP uses a unique methodology to uncover developmental pathways, precursors, and offender motivations for homicide. Such an approach has been lacking in Australia, and is generally lacking in New Zealand and many other countries despite the evident richness of the information that can be revealed through homicide perpetrator accounts. It is in this way we will be able to learn more about specific sequences and dimensions. It is well know that official data on homicide is valuable in providing a broad picture of trends and demographic relationships, but it does little to assist in understanding the complexity of homicide offending and events. The AHP is unique in its design and provides an opportunity to extract first-hand information from the perpetrators of these serious incidents. For example, selected findings from the AHP data showed that for some offenders, mental health problems develop over the 12 months preceding the homicide. This is particularly the case for females. The findings also show that although most homicides are unplanned, the planning of homicide differs across gender and who the offender killed. Of course, despite the many strengths associated with the AHP, we also acknowledge that self-report methodology relies upon perpetrators recalling events accurately and reporting truthfully, which may not always be the case.

Although our focus in this chapter has been on describing homicide in Australia and New Zealand and on illustrating an alternative methodological approach, this information has much relevance for practical responses to homicide. Findings from the AHP provide a unique opportunity to uncover new sequences and pathways to homicide that can inform preventative responses. Thus, informed by more illustrative and accurate information will reveal new opportunities for reflective interventions. The AHP findings have practical implications for police organizations and social welfare agencies, such as improving mental health interventions and detection of high-risk situations. By providing a stronger evidence base about the causes, contexts, and pathways leading to homicide, the findings have potential to better inform service delivery responses and contribute to homicide prevention. In particular, findings from the life event calendar can assist in the development of a more systematic way to assess markers for escalation of risk toward fatal incidents. Ultimately, intervention efforts informed by the latest knowledge about the precursors of homicide incidents are best placed to be effective.

In closing, although the extent and pattern of homicide in Australia and New Zealand is somewhat similar, regional variations exist. Moreover, the opportunities to learn more about the precursors for homicide by accessing perpetrator accounts bodes well for informing extant theories about homicide causation and preventative responses.

Acknowledgments

This research was supported under the Australian Research Council's Discovery Projects funding scheme (DP0878364). We wish to acknowledge the assistance of the various correctional departments across Australia for their significant support in the conduct of this research. The views expressed in this report are those of the authors and do not represent the policies or views of the correctional departments.

Notes

1 Infanticide legislations exist in the jurisdictions of New South Wales (Crimes Act 1900 s 22A), Victoria (Crimes Act 1958 s 6), Tasmania (Criminal Code Act 1924 s 165A) and New Zealand (Crimes Act 1961 s 178).
2 These calculations exclude the offense categories of attempted murder, driving causing death, and homicide and related offenses not further defined. Note that the 2012 data contains one case where the gender of the offender was classified as unknown/corporation.
3 The "other" category excludes Pacific peoples, whom the report shows are also overrepresented as victims and offenders of family violence deaths.
4 We acknowledge that there are also other definitions of child homicide, not referred to in this paragraph.
5 Excluding response refusals/response not stated (n = 18)

References

Australian Bureau of Statistics (2011a) *Australian and New Zealand Standard Offence Classification*. Canberra: Australian Bureau of Statistics.

Australian Bureau of Statistics (2011b) *Census of Population and Housing—Counts of Aboriginal and Torres Strait Islander Australians, 2011*. Canberra: Australian Bureau of Statistics.

Brookman, F. (2015) Killer decisions: The role of cognition, affect and "expertise" in homicide. *Aggression and Violent Behavior*, 20: 42–52. doi: 10.1016/j.avb.2014.12.007.

Brookman, F. and Nolan, J. (2006) The dark figure of infanticide in England and Wales: Complexities of diagnosis. *Journal of Interpersonal Violence*, 21(7): 869–889. doi: 10.1177/0886260506288935.

Bryant, W. and Cussen, T. (2015) *Homicide in Australia: 2010–11 to 2011–12: National Homicide Monitoring Program report*. Monitoring report series no. 23. Canberra: Australian Institute of Criminology.

Chan, A. and Payne, J. (2013) *Homicide in Australia: 2008–09 to 2009–10 National Homicide Monitoring Program Annual Report*. Monitoring report series. Canberra: Australian Institute of Criminology.

Coleman, C. and Moynihan, J. (1996) *Understanding Crime Data: Haunted by the Dark Figure*. Buckingham, UK: Open University Press.

Coverdale, J., Nairn, R., and Claasen, D. (2002) Depictions of mental illness in print media: A prospective national sample. *Australian & New Zealand Journal of Psychiatry*, 36(5): 697–700.

Cussen, T. and Bryant, W. (2015a) Domestic/family homicide in Australia. *Research in Practice*, 38(May). Canberra: Australian Institute of Criminology.

Cussen, T. and Bryant, W. (2015b) Indigenous and non-Indigenous homicide in Australia. *Research in Practice*, 37(May). Canberra: Australian Institute of Criminology.

Dean, P.J. (2004) Child homicide and infanticide in New Zealand. *International Journal of Law and Psychiatry*, 27(4): 339–348. doi: 10.1016/j.ijlp.2003.03.001.

Dearden, J. and Jones, W. (2008) *Homicide in Australia: 2006–2007: National Homicide Monitoring Program Annual Report*. Monitoring report series. Canberra: Australian Institute of Criminology.

Dobash, R.E. and Dobash, R.P. (2011) What were they thinking? Men who murder an intimate partner. *Violence Against Women*, 17(1): 111–134. doi: 10.1177/1077801210391219.

Doolan, M. (2004) Child death by homicide: An examination of incidence in New Zealand 1991–2000. *Te Awatea Review*, 2(1): 7–10.

Family Violence Death Review Committee (2014) *Fourth Annual Report: January 2013 to December 2013*. Wellington: Family Violence Death Review Committee.

James, M. and Carcach, C. (1997) *Homicide in Australia 1989–96*. Research and public policy series. Canberra: Australian Institute of Criminology.

Goedegebuure, W.L. (1993) Homicide: The Northern Territory perspective. In H. Strang and S.-A. Gerull (eds), *Homicide: Patterns, Prevention and Control*. Canberra: Australian Institute of Criminology.

Memmott, P. (2010) On regional and cultural approaches to Australian Indigenous violence. *Australian and New Zealand Journal of Criminology*, 43(2): 333–355. doi: 10.1375/acri.43.2.333.

Memmott, P., Stacy, R., Chambers, C., and Keys, C. (2001) *Violence in Indigenous Communities*. Canberra: Attorney-General's Department.

Moskowitz, A., Simpson, A.I.F., McKenna, B., et al. (2006) The role of mental illness in homicide-suicide in New Zealand, 1991–2000. *Journal of Forensic Psychiatry & Psychology*, 17(3): 417–430. doi: 10.1080/14789940600761410.

Mouzos, J. (1999) Mental disorder and homicide in Australia. *Trends and Issues in Crime and Criminal Justice*, 133: 1–6.

Mouzos, J. (2002) *Quality Control in the National Homicide Monitoring Program (NHMP)*. Canberra: Australian Institute of Criminology.

New Zealand Family Violence Clearinghouse (2014) *Data Summary: Family Violence Deaths*. Auckland: New Zealand Family Violence Clearinghouse.

New Zealand Police (2014a) New Zealand crime statistics 2013: A summary of recorded and resolved offence statistics. Wellington: Office of the Police Commissioner.

New Zealand Police (2014b) Police statistics on homicide victims in New Zealand for the period 2007–2011: A summary of statistics about victims of murder, manslaughter, and infanticide. Wellington: Office of the Police Commissioner.

Public Health Information Development Unit (2015) *Social Health Atlases of Australia: Remoteness in Australia: Data by Remoteness Area*. Adelaide: The University of Adelaide.

Roberts, J.J. and Horney, J. (2010) The life event calendar method in criminological research. In A. Piquero and D. Weisburd (eds), *Handbook of Quantitative Criminology* (pp. 289–312). New York: Springer.

Simpson, A., McKenna, B., Moskowitz, A., et al. (2003) *Myth and Reality: The Relationship between Mental Illness and Homicide in New Zealand*. Auckland: Health Research Council of New Zealand.

Smith, E.L. and Cooper, A. (2013) *Homicide in the US Known to Law Enforcement, 2011.* Washington, DC: US Department of Justice.

Statistics New Zealand (2013) *2013 Census QuickStats about Māori.* Wellington: Statistics New Zealand.

Statistics New Zealand (2015) NZ.Stat DataHub table viewer. Available online at http://nzdotstat.stats.govt.nz/wbos/Index.aspx (accessed January 22, 2015).

Stöckl, H., Devries, K., Rotstein, A., *et al.* (2013) The global prevalence of intimate partner homicide: A systematic review. *The Lancet,* 382(9895): 859–65. doi: http://dx.doi.org/10.1016/S0140-6736(13)61030-2.

UNODC (United Nations Office on Drugs and Crime) (2011) 2011 Global Study on Homicide: Trends, Contexts, Data. Vienna: UNODC.

UNODC (2015) UNODC Statistics. Available online at https://data.unodc.org (accessed October 27, 2015).

Further Reading

Mouzos, J. (2001) Indigenous and non-Indigenous homicides in Australia: A comparative analysis. *Trends and Issues in Crime and Criminal Justice,* 210: 1–6.

24

Drivers of Homicide in Latin America and the Caribbean

Does Relative Political Capacity Matter?

Erik Alda

Introduction

High homicide levels in Latin America and the Caribbean (LAC) have triggered a vast amount of literature trying to determine the causes of this epidemic. Scholarly literature on the drivers of homicides in LAC has been extensive (see World Bank 2010, 2011a, 2011b; Maertens and Anstey 2007; Fajnzylber, Lederman, and Loayza 1998; Cuevas and Demombynes 2009) and suggests that homicidal violence is a multifaceted problem in LAC. Empirical literature on this topic has identified a variety of causes that explain the high homicide levels, particularly inequality (Fajnzylber, Lederman, and Loayza 1998), unemployment, poverty, poor institutional quality (Tebaldi and Alda 2012), the size of the youth population, and the presence of drug trafficking and organized crime (Cuevas and Demombynes 2009).

The principal policy directions emerging from the scholarly and policy research about homicides in the region are: reducing inequality and poverty, increasing employment opportunities for youth, strengthening both the education and criminal justice system, and increasing efforts to combat organized crime.

In dealing with these myriad issues, however, more must be known about the effect of actual government performance on crime and violence, particularly homicides. Poor or weak government performance may enable conditions for homicides to emerge by not allocating enough resources to control the population, resulting in crime. Prescriptive policy approaches emphasize the importance of strengthening and improving government performance to address this problem. Thus, understanding the mechanisms under which weak government performance influences violence is essential to improve understanding of the role of government in containing and

The Handbook of Homicide, First Edition. Edited by Fiona Brookman,
Edward R. Maguire, and Mike Maguire.

reducing violence by developing long-term sustainable violence-prevention strategies.[1] Furthermore, according to World Bank data (2011a), high homicide levels are a threat to poverty reduction, economic growth, and consolidation of democracy; thus, reducing and preventing violence is imperative if LAC societies are to show sustained growth and alleviate deep structural problems.

While many researchers have investigated the causal determinants of crime and violence, little is known about the effects of government performance on the levels of violence. Departing from previous empirical examinations of violence in LAC, this chapter addresses the potential effect of the concept of relative political capacity—a key measure of government performance—on levels of violence. Essentially, this concept advances the premise that better and more efficient allocation of resources helps reduce homicides. Consequently, the chapter includes information from the scholarly literature on relative political capacity (Nishishiba *et al.* 2012; Kugler and Tammen 2012) to examine this relationship.

Levels of Homicide in Latin America and the Caribbean

The LAC region is arguably the most violent region in the world, according to international crime statistics (UNODC 2011, 2014). Although homicide levels have been consistently high in the LAC region since the mid-1950s, it was not until the 1990s, with the explosion of violence in the region, that the LAC began to be referred to as being the most violent region in the world. According to the United Nations Office on Drugs and Crime (UNODC), the homicide rate per 100,000 inhabitants in the LAC region in 2012 was 16.7 per 100,000 inhabitants, compared to the world's average of 6.7 homicides per 100,000 inhabitants (UNODC 2014). Figure 24.1 shows the average homicide rate from 1990 to 2011, and Figure 24.2 depicts the homicide rates for 1990 and 2009 at the country level. As the darker shading in Figure 24.2 indicates, homicide levels have increased significantly since the 1990s. Furthermore, in 2013, in their citizen security flagship report for the region, the United Nations Development Programme (UNDP) indicated 11 of the 18 countries assessed in their report had a homicide rate higher than 10 per 100,000 inhabitants (UNDP 2013).

It is important to note that significant differences exist at the subregional level in terms of homicides. For example, the Central American region records the highest levels of violence, with an average homicide rate of over 25 per 100,000 inhabitants. The southern cone and the Caribbean regions followed Central America with average homicide rates of 20 and 16 per 100,000 inhabitants, respectively (UNODC 2014). Even more significant disparities exist at the subnational level.

For example, in Central America, Honduras reached its highest homicide levels with a homicide rate of 90 per 100,000 inhabitants in 2011 compared to, for example, Chile, which had the lowest homicide levels in the region with 3.7 per 100,000 in 2011. Such differences in levels of homicides within the same region raise this fundamental question: what drives the high levels of homicides? Numerous answers to this question have been postulated in scholarly research focused on the socioeconomic drivers and, to a lesser extent, on the institutional drivers of homicides.

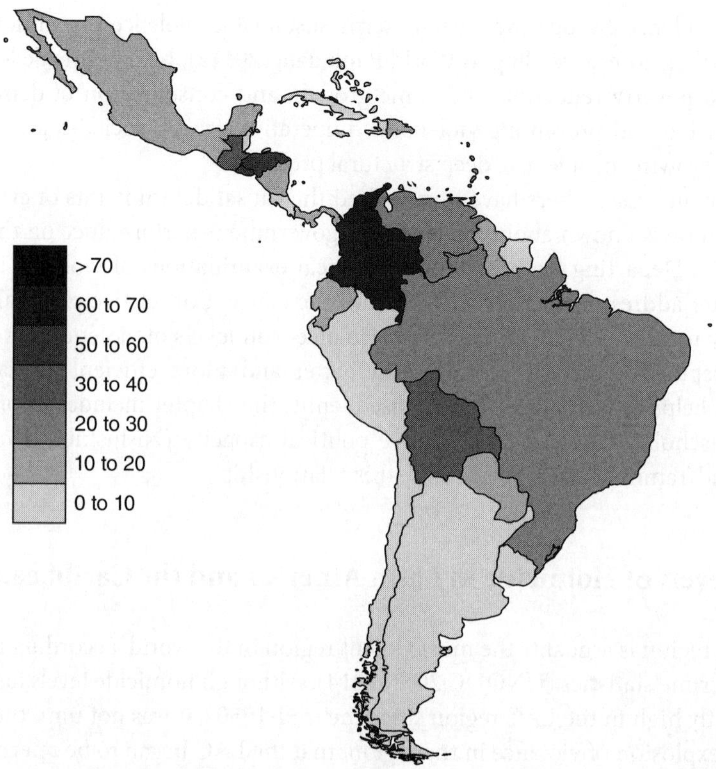

Figure 24.1 Mean homicide rates per 100, 000 inhabitants 1990 to 2011. Source: own analysis based on homicide statistics.

The next section of this chapter contains a brief review of the literature on the drivers of homicide in LAC.

Literature Review on the Drivers of Homicides

The empirical literature on the drivers of crime and violence in developing countries, especially in LAC, has taken two distinct directions: one focused on the socioeconomic factors, and the other focused on the institutional factors. Studies examining socioeconomic determinants of homicides have considered whether such important issues as poverty, inequality, unemployment, and the size of the youth cohort, for example, affect the rapid increase in homicides. Empirical results have demonstrated that issues such as income inequality have helped exacerbate homicides in the region (Loayza, Fajnzylber, and Lederman 2000; Fajnzylber, Lederman, and Loayza 1998, 2002b; World Bank 2011a). The empirical study done by Fajnzylber, Lederman, and Loayza (1998) is regarded as a definitive examination of the drivers of homicides in the region.

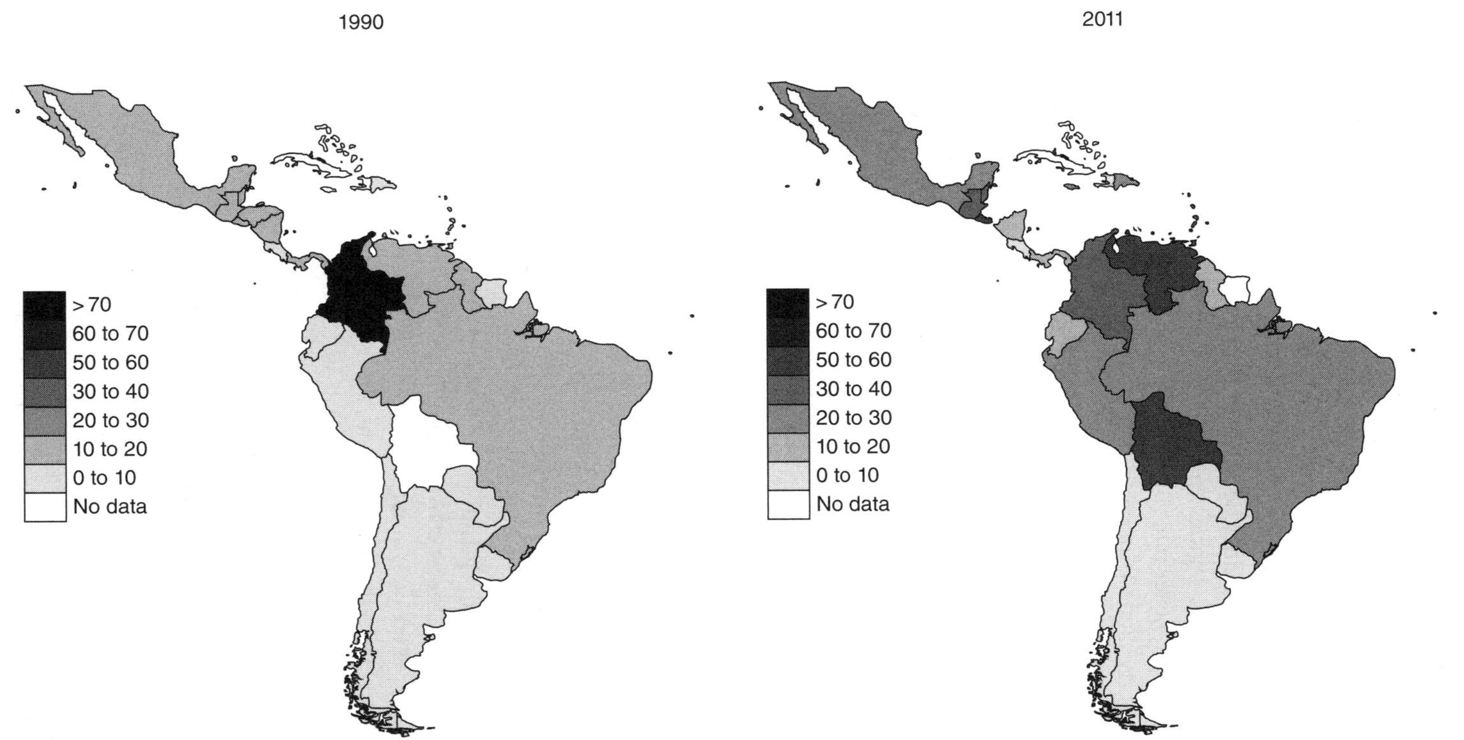

Figure 24.2 Homicide rates per 100,000 inhabitants 1990 and 2011. Source: own analysis based on homicide statistics.

Others have found that poverty also contributes to increased homicide levels. The effect of poverty on homicides, however, remains a subject of debate among scholars of the region. Some have argued, for example, that the relationship between poverty and homicides is ambiguous because there is an apparent correlation between poverty and social inequities, which some regard as the ultimate contributors to high homicides (Briceño-León, Villaveces, and Concha-Eastman 2008). Strong arguments have been made that support a weak correlation between poverty and homicides because, in fact, levels of poverty have declined significantly in the LAC region while the number of homicides has continued to increase at a much faster rate (Briceño-León *et al.* 2008). Others have argued that extreme poverty alone is one of the primary causes of homicides in the region (Kliksberg 2008). Kliksberg (2008) argues that both inequality and poverty feed off each other and help explain why homicides have increased dramatically in recent years.

Another important driver of the rapid increase in the homicide levels is the growth of the youth cohort. Empirical evidence consistently indicates that homicides are disproportionately concentrated in males aged 15 to 30 years old (Soares and Naritomi 2010; Di Tella, Edwards, and Schargrodsky 2010). Data show that youth account for almost one-fourth of all homicides in the region, a ratio four times larger than the mean global homicide rate for this age group (UNDP 2013). At subregional and country levels, the differences are even more marked. For example, Brazil's homicide rate among those aged 19 to 29 in 2012 was well above 100 compared to the overall homicide rate of 29 (Waiselfisz 2014). Similarly, Central America, El Salvador, Honduras, and Guatemala have youth homicide rates that rank among the highest globally (UNDP 2013; PNUD 2009).

More recently, research has begun to ascertain the effects of other important drivers of homicides in the region, specifically the presence of organized crime and drug trafficking and the poor quality of institutions, like those of the criminal justice system (Tebaldi and Alda 2012). For example, a World Bank report argued that the intensity of drug trafficking for territorial control in Central America explains the spikes in the levels of violence in this region (Cuevas and Demombynes 2009). Finally, there are other important drivers explored in the literature,[2] including high levels of unemployment, the availability of firearms, alcohol abuse, unemployment, and poor public education (Soares and Naritomi 2010; Small Arms Survey 2012).

Relative Political Capacity

Relative political capacity is a conceptually comprehensive measure that captures the capacity of governments to obtain resources from their population to promote effective and efficient resource allocation and policy choices for economic growth (Hendrix 2010; Arbetman and Kugler 1997; Mohiddin 2007; Arbetman and Johnson 2008; Kugler and Arbetman 1997). That is, if a government has sufficient capacity to extract resources from its population, it will be in a stronger position to make better decisions in terms of resource allocation and policy choices (Arbetman and Kugler 1997; Arbetman and Johnson 2008).

Political capacity is a relatively unexplored concept in the criminological literature. The concept emerged in an attempt to represent the performance of a country's economy in a more comprehensive way than using "total level output per capita" (Arbetman and Kugler 1997; Arbetman and Johnson 2008).[3] Proponents of using the measure of political capacity assert that measuring government performance must include ways in which a capable government can achieve its stated outcomes regardless of political ideology (Arbetman and Johnson 2008). According to Arbetman and Johnson (2008), relative political capacity comprises three different measures: (1) relative political extraction (RPE), (2) relative political reach (RPR), and (3) relative political allocation (RPA).

1. Relative political extraction measures the capacity of governments to extract resources through, for example, taxation to enact policies to improve a country's performance.
2. Relative political reach measures the capacity of governments to influence the lives of the population of a country.
3. Relative political allocation measures how public expenditures are allocated and prioritized in budgetary allocations in ways that boost the development and performance of a country (Arbetman and Johnson 2008).

The concepts described above constitute the overarching concept of political performance, which is defined as the ability of governments to mobilize their citizens so that resources can be extracted more efficiently and use them to design policies and effectively allocate resources so that a country can perform (Kugler and Tammen 2012).

Relative political capacity originated in the work of Organski and Kugler (1980) and focused on how governments with high capacity were able to wage war more effectively. The authors used Japan's military expenditures in the period before and during the early years of World War II as an example of the extractive capability resulting from high political capacity. This concept was applied in other areas to help explain countries' economic performance as well as to apply the measure of relative political capacity to subnational levels (Kugler and Arbetman 1997; Nishishiba *et al.* 2012). For example, extensions of the relative political capacity concept focused on examining government effectiveness in relationship to demographic changes related to declines in fertility and mortality (Arbetman and Kugler 1997; Arbetman, Kugler, and Organski 1997).

Furthermore, empirical studies at the subnational level found a strong correlation between government performance and development outcomes. For example, Kugler and Swaminathan (2006) and Swaminathan and Thomas (2007) examined the effect of political capacity on declines in fertility. Kugler and Swaminathan (2006) argued that governments with higher political performance are able to reduce child mortality and increase income gains in Indian states (Kugler and Swaminathan 2006; Swaminathan and Thomas 2007).

Overall, however, there has been little empirical work examining government performance and political capacity. Johnson (2007) analyzed how differences in government performance affected intrastate conflict (Arbetman and Johnson 2008: 3). More recently, Johnson, Arbetman, and Swaminathan (2012) examined the effect of relative political capacity on violence in China, concluding that relative political capacity—measured by the relative political reach—is strong and correlated with lower levels of violence. Finally, Nishishiba *et al.* (2012) analyzed the effect of relative political capacity on crime at the subnational level in the United States, and found a strong negative correlation between the political capacity measure and crime rates.

In the context of LAC's high levels of violence, the author argues that governments with more efficient and effective levels of resource allocation are better able to implement adequate policy choices geared toward long-term violence reduction. Thus, for the purposes of this chapter, the author uses relative political allocation (RPA) as the measure of relative political capacity of governments and examines its relationship with violence. The following sections describe the data sources, methodology for the analysis, and the results of the analyses.

Data and Methods

This section contributes to the literature by estimating a parsimonious model that examines the effects of RPA on violence. As noted above, the premise for this analysis is that higher government performance, as measured by the capacity to allocate available resources, will contribute effectively to reducing the levels of violence.

To conduct the analysis, RPA[4] was employed as the measure of interest because it captures the capacity of governments to allocate resources efficiently in key sectors of the economy, including the criminal justice system. Safety and security comprise a core public good offered by governments to their populations; adequate resource allocation is therefore a critical component of the actual governmental capacity to curb violence effectively and efficiently and, consequently, improve the performance of an economy. By contrast, poor or inefficient resource allocation to the criminal justice system might lead to difficulties in addressing safety and security and this may affect a country's economic performance negatively (Sutton, Cherney, and White 2013; Small Arms Survey 2013).

As far as the levels of violence in LAC are concerned, adequate resource allocation, which can both contain and reduce homicides, has become a priority for many governments in the region. These priorities, however, are often guided by ideological premises as opposed to actual performance measures (Dammert and Arias 2007). For example, the use of *mano dura* and *super mano dura*[5] policies in some countries in Central America to curb the levels of gang violence are arguably based on political ideology rather than attempts to be politically effective as a government

(Kliksberg 2008; De la Torre and Álvarez 2011). The limited success of these antiviolence policies may be a result of poor resource allocations by governments.

Data

In the analysis, a panel data set from 1990 to 2009 was used.[6] The dependent variable in the model was the homicide rate per 100,000 inhabitants. This measure was drawn from the World Bank's world development indicators (WDI), the United Nations Office for Drugs and Crime's (UNODC) international homicide database, and the Organization of American States' crime data. All these homicide measures are official statistics collected by the criminal justice system.[7] The homicide rate variable was significantly skewed[8] and therefore not normally distributed. The author log transformed the measure to normalize its distribution.

Figure 24.3 (a and b) shows how the levels of homicide are associated with the RPA measure[9]. Those countries with more effective levels of resource allocation had lower levels of homicides. Even after smoothing out the outliers by logging the homicide rate measure, the results still indicate a negative relationship between RPA and violence. It is worth noting, however, that there appears to be a nonlinear relationship between RPA and homicides that will require further exploration in the econometric analyses.

The primary working hypothesis of this chapter is that strong government performance, indicated by better resource allocation to key socioeconomic sectors in government, including law enforcement and the criminal justice system, will contribute to reducing homicides in the region. Although it may appear obvious, it is important to underscore the significance of the bivariate association shown in Figure 24.3 between government performance and lower homicides. Until now, this relationship has rarely been tested in the context of developing countries, particularly in the LAC countries.

Regression analysis

In the following equation (Tebaldi and Alda 2012),

$$C_i = \alpha + \beta \hat{Z}_i + X_i \gamma + \varepsilon_i,$$

i denotes country; C is a measure of homicides at the country i (homicide rate); $\hat{Z}$ measures the quality of resource allocation in LAC countries; X denotes other control variables previously used in the literature on the determinants of violence; α, β, and γ are parameters; and ε is the error term.

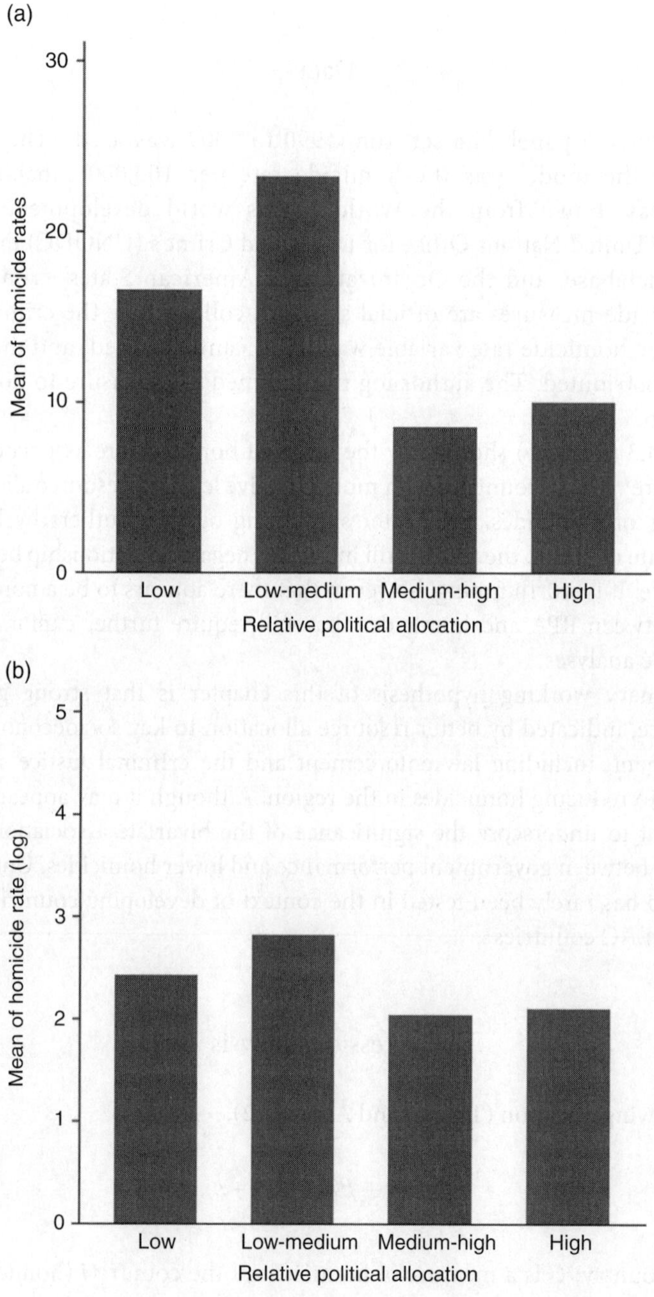

Figure 24.3 Relative political allocation and homicide. Source: own analysis.

As discussed above, the explanatory variable of interest is relative political allocation, which captures the capacity of government to allocate resources effectively. The control variables used in the analysis include the following:

Gini coefficient. The Gini coefficient of income inequality captures the vertical difference in income between the richest and the poorest in the region. It ranges from 0 (no inequality) to 1 (perfect inequality). Inequality has been found to be one of the stronger determinants of violent crime (World Bank 2011a; Fajnzylber, Lederman, and Loayza 2002a). The author predicts that higher levels of inequality will result in higher levels of violence.

GDP growth per capita. Gross domestic product growth per capita captures the total output of a country. It is calculated by dividing a country's total GDP by the total number of people in the country. Scholarly research has consistently shown that higher levels of growth are associated with lower homicides (World Bank 2006). Empirical studies demonstrate that per capita income has a significant negative effect on the homicide levels in LAC. For example, the World Bank found that higher levels of growth in per capita income reduced crime by 1 percent (World Bank 2006). Contrary to this result, Fajnzylber, Lederman, and Loayza (2002b) found the effect of GNP per capita on violence is not statistically significant. The author predicts that GDP growth per capita will be negatively correlated with homicide.

Urban population growth. Rapid, unplanned urbanization is a significant problem in the LAC region. The rapid migration patterns into large cities to seek better employment and quality of life during the 1950s led to a rapid expansion of cities, which were unprepared for large population influxes (Briceño-León 2002; Fox 2008). As a result, many slum areas emerged, characterized by poor infrastructure and a noticeable lack of government presence. Such conditions triggered an explosion of violence in many slums in the region (Briceño-León 2002). In recent years, however, urban population growth has not increased as rapidly as in previous decades. Despite this slowing of urban growth, recent research indicates that urban areas which experienced growth of 2 percent or higher also reported higher homicide rates (UNDP 2013). It is anticipated that the analysis will show that urban growth is positively correlated with higher homicide levels.

Percentage of males aged 15 to 24. There is extensive empirical evidence that young males are both the main perpetrators and victims of homicides (Briceño-León 2002; Cunningham *et al.* 2008; Dammert Guardia 2011; PNUD 2009; UNDP 2014). Data indicate that youth violence accounts for more than 50 percent of all homicides in the region (UNDP 2013). The author predicts that a higher percentage of young people in the country will be associated with higher levels of violence.

Descriptive statistics

As Table 24.1 indicates, the mean homicide rate (log) for the years in the data set—1990 to 2009—was 2.49 homicides per 100,000 inhabitants. It is important to keep in mind that for purposes of the regression analysis undertaken, a logarithmic

Table 24.1 Descriptive statistics.

Variable	*Mean*	*Std. dev.*	*Min*	*Max*
Homicide rate (log)	2.49	0.83	0.34	4.40
Percent of males 15–24	19.27	1.53	15.20	23.10
Growth in urban population (% of total)	1.80	1.42	−3.36	6.18
Growth in GDP per capita (%)	1.94	3.99	−15.40	21.60
GINI	52.06	5.44	34.80	69.20
RPC-allocation (RPA)	1.08	0.32	0.53	2.37
RPC-allocation (squared term) (RPA)	1.26	0.81	1.27	5.66

Source: own analysis.

transformation of the homicide rate was employed to smooth out the outliers; thus, the mean of the logarithmic transformation of the homicide rate (2.49) corresponds to a mean of 17 homicides per 100,000 inhabitants.

This statistic confirms that levels of violent crime in LAC are more than twice the global average. Despite experiencing reductions in homicide levels in recent years (Figure 24.2), these statistics are unacceptably high by international standards. The minimum value in the average homicide rate in Table 24.1 corresponds to Uruguay (5.55) while the maximum value corresponds to Colombia (59.6). Overall, the data show 19.3 percent of the population were males 15 to 24 years old, the mean urban growth as a percentage of the total population was about 2 percent (1.8%) for the period of study, the mean Gini coefficient for the period considered in this study was 52, and the mean growth in GDP per capita was also about 2 percent per year for the period considered. The RPA measure has a mean of about 1.1.

A preliminary OLS (ordinary least squares) model (not reported here) was utilized to gauge the overall fit of the model, and three significant issues were identified that could lead to inconsistent and biased estimates. The first was that in the OLS model it is not possible to control for time invariant, unobserved characteristics of each country that could affect homicide levels.[10] The second issue was that because panel data were employed, potential autocorrelation could occur in the model, leading to inconsistent estimates (Wooldridge 2009).[11] Finally, the data were also checked for potential multicollinearity in the model. These tests indicated that the standard errors of the OLS model did not appear to reveal any issues with multicollinearity.[12]

To address the issues noted above, two alternative econometric strategies were used to estimate a parsimonious model of the effect of relative political allocation on homicides controlling for other factors. The first strategy is a fixed effects model to account for time invariant unobserved heterogeneity, and the second model is a model that fits the structure of the data and addresses issues of serial correlation and heteroskedasticity.

Results

To estimate the regression model, several model specifications were run to test the validity and consistency of each model. The first model run—omitted from this chapter but available upon request—was an OLS model. The results showed that

Table 24.2 Fixed effects regression models.

	Model 1 *Homicide rate (log)*	*Model 2* *Homicide rate (log)*
Male (%)	0.117*	0.095*
	[0.061]	[0.055]
Urban population growth (%)	−0.035	−0.122*
	[0.076]	[0.069]
GDP	−0.020**	−0.020**
	[0.009]	[0.008]
GINI index	0.006	0.008
	[0.010]	[0.008]
Relative political capacity (allocation)	−0.338**	2.933***
	[0.158]	[0.626]
Relative political capacity (allocation)-squared term		−1.188***
		[0.222]
Constant	0.389	−1.13
	[1.358]	[1.236]
Observations	122	122

Standard errors in brackets.
* $p < 0.10$;
** $p < 0.05$;
*** $p < 0.01$.
Source: own analysis.

higher levels of RPA are associated with lower homicides. The coefficients for the control variables had the expected signs, but only the percentage of males in the population was statistically significant at the 5 percent level.

Table 24.2 shows the results of the fixed effects model conform to most of the results previously found in the literature, particularly insofar as the control variables were concerned (e.g., Tebaldi and Alda 2012; Fajnzylber, Lederman, and Loayza 1998, 2002a, 2002b). The measure of particular interest—relative political capacity—was tested using two different specifications. The first specification in Model 1 of Table 24.2 regresses the dependent variable—homicide rate—on RPA and a set of control variables, and the second specification adds the squared term of the RPA measure to examine potential nonlinearities in the relationship between RPA and homicides. In Model 1, the results show that, controlling for other factors, a higher level of RPA is statistically significant and correlates with lower homicides. The size of the coefficient is the largest and accounts for more than one-third of the variation in the model.

Figure 24.3 suggests that there is a nonlinear relationship between homicides and relative political capacity.[13] To examine the effect of this nonlinear relationship, the second model specification in Table 24.2 (Model 2) includes the squared term of the RPA measure. It is clear that the results suggest strong nonlinearity. The coefficients of both the original and the squared term of the RPA measure are very large and are

Table 24.3 Regression model corrected for autocorrelation and heteroskedasticity.

	Model 1 *Homicide rate (log)*	*Model 2* *Homicide rate (log)*
Male (%)	0.348***	0.358***
	[0.035]	[0.036]
Urban population growth (%)	−0.112**	−0.051
	[0.046]	[0.058]
GDP	−0.005	−0.009*
	[0.004]	[0.004]
GINI index	0.007	0.011**
	[0.005]	[0.005]
Relative political capacity (allocation)	−0.219**	2.294***
	[0.103]	[0.502]
Relative political capacity (allocation)-squared term		−0.999***
		[0.178]
Constant	−4.223***	−6.129***
	[0.636]	[0.773]
Observations	121	121

Standard errors in brackets.
* $p < 0.10$;
** $p < 0.05$;
*** $p < 0.01$.
Source: own analysis.

statistically significant at the 1 percent level ($p<0.01$). The point at which the relationship has its turning point equals 1.22, which corresponds to the top 25th percentile of the RPA measure.

The remainder of the control measures behaved as expected and with the expected signs except for urban population growth, which carried a negative sign that was not statistically significant. An alternative specification used the total urban population (not reported here) with this result: the sign was in the right direction (positive) and statistically significant at the 5 percent level. The estimates for the Gini coefficient of income inequality were positive, but were not statistically significant at the 5 percent level. The percentage of growth in GDP per capita was statistically significant at the 10 percent level and carried the expected negative sign.

These findings were consistent with previous studies concerning the effect of economic growth on violence in LAC and indicated an increase of one percentage point in the GDP growth per capita would predict a reduction in homicides of about 1 percent, all else being equal (e.g., World Bank 2006).

Table 24.3 shows the results of the regression model, addressing the issues of autocorrelation and heteroskedasticity identified in the initial OLS model. The results were very similar to those found in the fixed effects model. The results provide evidence that high relative political allocation is associated with lower homicides in both specifications. After correcting for heteroskedasticity and autocorrelation, the size of the coefficient is smaller, but still highly statistically significant ($p < 0.05$). These results demonstrate robustness to the analysis shown in Table 24.2 concerning the importance of effective resource allocation to reducing homicides.

The control variables also had the expected signs except for the variable capturing the percentage of urban population growth, which carried the opposite sign and was statistically significant at conventional levels. This finding was initially somewhat puzzling given that urban population growth is conceptually associated with more homicides. Declines in the speed of urban growth in recent years could explain the negative coefficient in the regression. Furthermore, because the data are aggregated at the national level, they may not have enough granularity to capture differences in the rates and levels of urban growth within countries. The results shown in Table 24.3 also indicated that the measure of growth per capita in GDP became statistically insignificant, but carried the expected negative sign; the Gini coefficient became statistically significant in the second model specification ($p < 0.05$), conforming to previous findings in the literature concerning the determinants of homicides in LAC (e.g., World Bank 2011a; Fajnzylber, Lederman, and Loayza 1998).

Reverse causality between relative political allocation and homicides

Conceptually, it could be argued that relative political allocation is correlated with the dependent variable in the analysis presented here. Because safety and security comprise a core service provided by government, it is possible that allocating resources to criminal justice may become a higher government priority when homicide levels increase rapidly. Evidence indicates that there has been increased spending in the criminal justice sector during the past decade when these trends are present (Alda 2014; Pino 2011). Such increases appear to be present in high homicide countries, such as those in the northern triangle of Central America, where additional funding has been channeled to strengthen the capacity of the police and the criminal justice system. However, if homicide levels are low or are declining, governments could achieve their policy goals by reallocating resources from the criminal justice system.

It is important to examine potential reverse causality between relative political capacity and homicide to determine if such analyses might yield inconsistent and biased estimates.[14] However, the instruments considered in this study performed poorly and did not pass any conventional tests[15] for instrumental variable regression (Kennedy 2003) and, thus, the analysis did not yield any meaningful results.

Concluding Remarks

This chapter has examined the effect of a measure of relative political capacity on homicides in LAC. Relative political allocation measures the capacity of governments to allocate resources effectively to key sectors such as the criminal justice system.

The results from these analyses indicate the importance of governments' performance in seeking to reduce homicides in LAC. Increasing governmental capacity to allocate resources efficiently can facilitate their policy choices more effectively in their efforts to reduce homicides. This finding confirms the unexplored hypothesis that there is a strong link between government performance and lower homicide levels. In addition, the findings of this chapter indicate that, controlling for other factors, the higher the government capacity is to allocate resources effectively, the higher the reduction is in the homicide levels.

In the case of what is now commonly referred to as the most violent region in the world, improving government performance, particularly that of criminal justice institutions, can contribute to containing the homicide problem in the region. The findings of this chapter indicate that differences in government performance, as indicated by better resource allocation, can help explain why countries with many similarities have different homicide rates. In conducting the analysis, the author attempted to correct for the potential endogenous relationship between relative political capacity and homicides by instrumentalizing the relative political allocation measure. However, the instruments used for the analyses were not adequate to yield any meaningful results, and, consequently, it was not possible to resolve the issue of reverse causality between homicides and relative political allocation.

The relative political allocation measure used indicated that effective and efficient governments, irrespective of political ideology, can allocate resources to key sectors in order to achieve their policy choices and goals (Arbetman and Johnson 2008). In LAC, where there are governmental priorities to contain the homicide epidemic, improving the allocation of resources to the security sector is essential, even though improved allocations alone are unlikely to be sufficient to curb homicide levels over time. To be successful, organizational and institutional reforms are needed, along with strong political leadership and national commitments and determination that have not yet been evident in many of the countries comprising this region.

Notes

1 National policy documents have emphasized the importance of having effective governments to reduce and prevent violence.

2 These other drivers are not discussed here to save space.

3 Total level output per capita is a measure that captures the level of prosperity of a country in relation to its population.

4 For more information on how relative political capacity measures are estimated, see Kugler and Arbetman (1997). The measure comes from Kugler and Arbetman (1997).

5 These terms described anti-gang policies implemented in the early 2000s in El Salvador, Honduras, and Guatemala to address the high numbers of homicides, which were attributed to gang violence. These policies employed suppressive tactics to incarcerate large numbers of youths, especially those with tattoos that identified with gangs, and increased sentences for membership in gangs and gang activity related crimes. The effectiveness of these policies has been questioned because it had no effect in reducing homicides (Donaldson 2012).

6 The author deliberately cut the sample in the year 2009 because of missing data for the explanatory variable of interest.
7 Some scholars have argued health statistics are more accurate in depicting actual homicide levels (Stamatel 2008). In this chapter, however, the author decided to use homicide statistics from the criminal justice system, which are the statistics officially reported by governments.
8 The skewness value was above the conventionally accepted threshold of −1/+1 (1.37) (Hinton 2014).
9 For illustration purposes, the author grouped the levels of RPA into four categories: low RPA if the measure was between the minimum value (0.52) and smaller than or equal to 1; low-medium RPA if the value was greater than 1 and smaller than 1.5; medium-high if the value was greater than 1.5 and smaller than or equal to 2; and high if the value was larger than 2.
10 The F-test results of the fixed effects model suggest that a fixed effects model is more adequate than OLS for the analyses ($p < 0.01$)
11 In effect, the author ran the ACTEST command (Baum and Schaffer 2014), which indicated there was serial autocorrelation.
12 The author estimated the variance inflation factor (VIF) to quantify the severity (if any) of multicollinearity. The results showed the VIF factors were not an issue. The mean VIF score was 1.17 and the highest value was for the measure of the percentage of young males (1.33) and the lowest value was for the measure of GDP per capita (1.07). The values were well below the conventionally accepted threshold of 10 (Hair *et al.* 2006; Kennedy 2003).
13 Tests confirm the presence of nonlinearity in the relationship between relative political allocation and homicides ($p < 0.10$).
14 Instrumental variable analysis would help address the potential endogeneity if the instruments used in the analysis are valid and exogenous, not correlated with the error term. The author considered the lagged values of relative political capacity for the analysis. Davidson and MacKinnon (1995) suggest using lagged values as instruments when using panel data. A parallel issue to consider is the number of lags to use to re-estimate the model. Wooldridge (2009) argued that the first lagged values of the endogenous variable could still be correlated with the error term, but the second lagged values are unlikely to be correlated with the error term. Thus, the author employed second lagged values as an instrumental variable for the analysis.
15 The first-stage estimates showed all relevant "excluded variables" in the analysis were not statistically significant. Only the lags of relative political capacity were statistically significant, indicating relative political capacity follows a persistent process and is serially correlated. Therefore, the use of lag values for relative political capacity is not adequate in the presence of serial correlation (Angrist and Krueger 2001).

References

Alda, E. (2014) How are police doing in combating crime? An exploratory study of efficiency analysis of the Policia Nacional Civil in Guatemala. *Policing: An International Journal of Police Strategies & Management*, 37(1): 87–107.

Angrist, J. and Krueger, A.B. (2001) *Instrumental Variables and the Search for Identification: From Supply and Demand to Natural Experiments*. Cambridge, MA: National Bureau of Economic Research.

Arbetman, M. and Kugler, J. (1997) *Political Capacity and Economic Behavior*. Boulder, CO: Westview Press.

Arbetman, M., Kugler, J., and Organski, A.F.K. (1997) Political capacity and demographic change. In M. Arbetman and J. Kugler (eds), *Political Capacity and Economic Behavior* (pp. 193–221) Boulder, CO: Westview Press.

Arbetman, M. and Johnson, K. (2008) Relative political capacity: Empirical and theoretical underpinnings. Annual meeting of the International Studies Association, New York.

Baum, C.F. and Schaffer, M.E. (2014) ACTEST: Stata module to perform Cumby-Huizinga general test for autocorrelation in time series. Statistical Software Components, Boston College Department of Economics.

Briceño-León, R. (2002) La nueva violencia urbana de América Latina. *Sociologías*, 8: 34–51.

Briceño-León, R., Villaveces, A., and Concha-Eastman, A. (2008) Understanding the uneven distribution of the incidence of homicide in Latin America. *International Journal of Epidemiology*, 37(4): 751–757.

Cuevas, F. and Demombynes, G. (2009) Drug trafficking, civil war, and drivers of crime in Central America. Unpublished manuscript. Washington, DC: World Bank.

Cunningham, W., McGinnis, L., García Verdú, R., et al. (2008) *Youth at Risk in Latin America and the Caribbean*. Washington, DC: The World Bank.

Dammert, L. and Arias, P. (2007) El desafío de la delincuencia en América Latina: diagnóstico y respuestas de política. In L. Dammert and L. Zúñiga (eds), *Seguridad y violencia: desafíos para la ciudadanía* (pp. 21–66). Santiago, Chile: FLACSO.

Dammert Guardia, M. (2011) Violence research in Latin America and the Caribbean: A literature review. *International Journal of Conflict and Violence*, 5(1): 87–154.

Davidson, R. and MacKinnon, J.G. (1995) Estimation and inference in econometrics. *Econometric Theory*, 11: 631–635.

De la Torre, V. and Martín Álvarez, A. (2011) Violencia, Estado de derecho y políticas punitivas en América Central. *Perfiles latinoamericanos*, 19(37): 33–50.

Di Tella, R., Edwards, S., and Schargrodsky, E. (2010) *The Economics of Crime: Lessons for and from Latin America*. Chicago: University of Chicago Press.

Donaldson, W. (2012) Gangbangers and Politicians: The effects of *mano dura* on Salvadoran politics. Tulane University, Stone Center for Latin American Studies, New Orleans.

Fajnzylber, P., Lederman, D., and Loayza, N. (1998) *Determinants of Crime Rates in Latin America and the World: An Empirical Assessment*. Washington, DC: World Bank.

Fajnzylber, P., Lederman, D., and Loayza, N. (2002a) Inequality and violent crime. *Journal of Law and Economics* 45(1): 1–39.

Fajnzylber, P., Lederman, D., and Loayza, N. (2002b) What causes violent crime? *European Economic Review*, 46(7): 1323–1357.

Fox, S. (2008) On the origins and consequences of slums. Development Studies Institute, London School of Economics and Political Science.

Hair, J.F., Black, W.C., Babin, B.J., et al. (2006) *Multivariate Data Analysis* (vol. 6). Saddle River, NJ: Pearson Prentice Hall.

Hendrix, C.S. (2010) Measuring state capacity: Theoretical and empirical implications for the study of civil conflict. *Journal of Peace Research*, 47(3): 273–285.

Hinton, P.R. (2014) *Statistics Explained*. London: Routledge.

Johnson, K. (2007) Sub national capabilities and internal conflict. Unpublished doctoral dissertation, Claremont Graduate University, Claremont, CA.

Johnson, K., Arbetman, M., and Swaminathan, S. (2012) Following the wisdom of elders: Instability in China. In J. Kugler and R.L. Tammen (eds) *The Performance of Nations* (pp. 173–190). Lanham, MD: Rowman & Littlefield.

Kennedy, P. (2003) *A Guide to Econometrics*. Cambridge, MA: MIT Press.

Kliksberg, B. (2008) ¿Cómo enfrentar la inseguridad en América Latina? *Nueva Sociedad*, 215: 4–16.

Kugler, J. and Arbetman, M. (1997) Relative political capacity: Political extraction and political reach. In M. Arbetman and J. Kugler (eds), *Political Capacity and Economic Behavior* (pp. 11–45). Boulder, CO: Westview Press.

Kugler, J. and Tammen, R.L. (eds) (2012) *The Performance of Nations*. Lanham, MD: Rowman & Littlefield.

Kugler, T. and Swaminathan, S. (2006) The politics of population. *International Studies Review*, 8(4): 581–596.

Loayza, N., Fajnzylber, P., and Lederman, D. (2000) Crime and victimization: An economic perspective. *Economia*, 1(1): 219–302.

Maertens, F. and Anstey, C. (2007) Crime, violence, and development: Trends, costs, and policy options in the Caribbean. Washington, DC: United Nations Office on Drugs and Crime Latin America and the Caribbean Region of the World Bank.

Mohiddin, A. (2007) Reinforcing capacity towards building the capable state in Africa. Concept paper for AGF VII.

Nishishiba, M., Arbetman, M., Kraner, M., and Jones, M. (2012) Do Local Governments Matter? In J. Kugler and R.L. Tammen (eds), *The Performance of Nations* (pp. 295–314). Lanham, MD: Rowman & Littlefield.

Organski, A.F.K. and Kugler, J. (1980) *The War Ledger*. Chicago: University of Chicago Press.

Pino, H.N. (2011) *Gasto público en seguridad y justicia en Centroamérica*. Mexico: CEPAL.

PNUD. (2009) Abrir espacios para la seguridad ciudadana y el desarrollo humano: Informe sobre desarrollo humano para America Central 2009–2010. United Nations Development Program (UNDP).

Small Arms Survey (2012) *Small Arms Survey 2012: Moving Targets*. Cambridge: Cambridge University Press.

Small Arms Survey (2013) Insecurity and violence in the post-2015 development agenda. Global Dialogue on Rule of Law and Post 2015 Development Agenda held in New York on September 26–27, 2013.

Soares, R.R. and Naritomi, J. (2010) Understanding high crime rates in Latin America: The role of social and policy factors. In Di Tella, R., Edwards, S., and Schargrodsky, E. (2010) *The Economics of Crime: Lessons for and from Latin America* (pp. 19–55). Chicago: University of Chicago Press.

Stamatel, J.P. (2008) Using mortality data to refine our understanding of homicide patterns in select postcommunist countries. *Homicide Studies*, 12(1): 117–135.

Sutton, A., Cherney, A., and White, R. (2013) *Crime Prevention: Principles, Perspectives and Practices*. Cambridge: Cambridge University Press.

Swaminathan, S. and Thomas, J. (2007) Saving the next generation: Political capacity and infant mortality decline in India's states. *International Interactions*, 33(3): 217–242.

Tebaldi, E. and Alda, E. (2012) Do institutions impact violence? World Bank Policy Series Working Paper (under review).

UNDP (United Nations Development Programme) (2013). Citizen security with a human face: Evidence and proposals for Latin America. New York: United Nations Development Programme.

UNODC (United Nations Office on Drugs and Crime) (2011) *Global Study on Homicide 2011*. New York: UNODC.

UNODC (2014) *Global Study on Homicide 2013*. New York: UNODC.

Waiselfisz, J.J. (2014) *Mapa da violência 2014: os jovens do Brasil*. São Paulo, Brasil: Instituto Sangari.

Wooldridge, J.M. (2009) *Introductory Econometrics: A Modern Approach*. Cincinnati, OH: South-Western College Publishers.

World Bank (2006) *Crime, Violence and Economic Development in Brazil: Elements for Effective Public Policy*. Washington, DC: World Bank.

World Bank (2010) *Violence in the City: Understanding and Supporting Community Responses to Urban Violence*. Washington, DC: World Bank. Available online at http://siteresources.worldbank.org/EXTSOCIALDEVELOPMENT/Resources/244362-1164107274725/Violence_in_the_City.pdf (accessed October 26, 2012).

World Bank (2011a) *Crime and Violence in Central America: A Development Challenge*. Washington, DC: World Bank.

World Bank (2011b) *World Development Report 2011: Conflict, Security, and Development*. Washington, DC: World Bank.

25

Homicide in Russia

Issues of Measuring and Theoretical Explanations

Alexandra Lysova and Nikolay Shchitov

Introduction

The Russian homicide rate is the highest in Europe and one of the highest in the world (UNODC 2014). Moreover, it has been gradually increasing during the twenty-first century, arguably due to the role of the Soviet state in exacerbating a cultural predisposition for violence and the survival of a "binge" drinking pattern of alcohol consumption (Stickley and Mäkinen 2005; Stickley and Pridemore 2007). In 1994, homicides in Russia peaked at over 47,000 homicide victims, a rate of approximately 33 per 100,000 population (WHO, n.d.). Widespread and profound political, economic, and social changes in the mid-1980s and the early 1990s appear to account for this dramatic increase in the homicide rate (Kim and Pridemore 2005; Walberg *et al.* 1998). In the 2000s, however, the official homicide rate has demonstrated a dramatic decrease, with estimates ranging between 10 (police data) and 13 (mortality data) per 100,000 population in 2010 (MVD, n.d.; Rosstat, n.d.).

The concept of a "criminological transition" (Pridemore 2007) suggests that some crucial changes in social structure, culture, technology, and other aspects of society are likely to be responsible for this remarkable decline in homicide in recent years. Indeed, the first decade of the twenty-first century, when Vladimir Putin came to power as president of Russia, is generally characterized by greater political and economic stability linked to high prices of oil relative to the 1990s. However, these improvements were accompanied by some negative trends. While some of these unfavorable processes seemed to be a continuation from the Soviet period (e.g., political repression and corruption), others, such as xenophobia, racism, violence against non-Slavs, predatory policing of citizens, and state violence against businesses,

The Handbook of Homicide, First Edition. Edited by Fiona Brookman, Edward R. Maguire, and Mike Maguire.

appeared to have emerged in the 2000s. Such patchy and inconsistent improvements in Russian society are unlikely to account for what official statistics suggest is a considerable decrease in the homicide rate in the 2000s.

An alternative explanation for the apparent decrease in homicide in Russia can be linked to the ways in which homicide statistics are produced. The Soviet Union has a notorious legacy of falsification and concealment of data, including data on homicide (e.g., Tolts 2012), that would put Russia in an unfavorable light. After a brief moment of greater availability of more reliable population data in the early 1990s, the quality of the Russian vital statistics data (Gavrilova *et al.* 2008; Pridemore 2003) and police data (Inshakov 2011) has deteriorated. More specifically, some researchers argue that the real homicide rate is much higher and is not declining at a pace suggested by the official sources (Andreev *et al.* 2015; Inshakov 2011).

This chapter focuses on the puzzle of rapidly declining homicide rates in Russia after 2000 (as demonstrated by official sources) under conditions that would suggest a very different trend. We first examine the quality of post-Soviet homicide statistics and attempt to determine more accurate estimates of homicide rates in Russia in the 2000s. Although issues around measuring homicide in Russia and other countries are not new and have been recently summarized in the *Global Study on Homicide 2013* (UNODC 2014), current literature lacks a consistent understanding of what the homicide rate in Russia is and how it has been changing in post-Soviet Russia. Next this chapter discusses how a "decivilizing process" (Elias 1978) and a Russian culture of drinking can provide explanations for the high and non-declining homicide rate in contemporary Russia.

Measuring the Homicide Rate

Official police data

There are two branches of executive power dealing with homicide in Russia: the Ministry of Internal Affairs (MVD) and the office of the public prosecutor (Prokuratura in Russian). The Criminal Police Department of the MVD is in charge of registering and investigating homicides. In addition to supervising the execution of the law, the office of the public prosecutor can also investigate homicide. For the public, data about crime and homicide is available from MVD through annual publications and online sources (www.mvd.ru).

There are several serious concerns about the police data that suggest these data underrepresent the true homicide rate in Russia (Inshakov 2011; Luneev 2005; Pridemore 2003). One indicator of underreporting is inconsistency in the official numbers of homicides provided by MVD. For example, a 2010 MVD crime report indicates there were 15,000 registered cases of completed and attempted homicides and almost 40,000 cases of "intentional grievous body injury" (victims died in some of these cases) in 2010. However, in its summary section, the report states that 42,000 people died as the result of "criminal assault" and 51,000 people received grievous body injuries in 2010 alone (MVD, n.d.).

Furthermore, there are some gray areas in the production of police statistics of homicides, which potentially open up the opportunity for manipulation. One of the most important is the definition of homicide in Article 105 of the Russian Criminal Code, which defines homicide as an intentional act meant to cause the death of one (part 1) or more people (part 2). The definition includes attempted homicides, however, without access to unpublished MVD data, there is no way to extract the number of attempts, though they appear to constitute between 5 and 10 percent of total homicides reported annually (Luneev 2005). At any rate, it creates a certain degree of confusion around homicide statistics.

In addition, if a person died not during an attack but later (e.g., after three days in hospital), the event would be registered as intentional grievous bodily harm leading to death (Part 4 Article 111 of the Criminal Code) and would not be included in the homicide category. This seems to differ from practices in other countries. For example, in the United States and United Kingdom, any death caused by the injuries at any time and as a result of the offense would be classified as homicide.

In addition, only cases in which there was the intent to kill, and not simply to inflict injuries that might lead to death, would be counted as homicide according to the Criminal Code definition; all other cases would be coded as intentional grievous bodily harm leading to death. Luneev (2005: 409) argues that about one-third of the latter are cases of intentional homicide. In other countries, for example in the United States, a criminal homicide is defined as "any death caused by injuries received in a fight, argument, quarrel, assault, or commission of a crime" (Federal Bureau of Investigation 2004: 15). Because it is often problematic to differentiate in real life intent to kill and intent to severely injure another person (who died from this injury), this constitutes another gray area in the production of Russian homicide statistics.

Another aspect that should be kept in mind while interpreting police homicide data in Russia is that it is an event-based rather than victim-based reporting system. In other words, homicides of tens or hundreds of people resulting from a bomb explosion would be recorded as one crime, as defined in paragraphs (a) and (e) of Part 2 of Article 105 of the Criminal Code (Luneev 2005: 409).

Vital statistics data

An alternative source of information on homicide is provided by vital statistics data, which is available at the Federal State Statistics Service website (Rosstat in Russian) (www.gks.ru). Russia classifies the causes of death according to WHO recommendations and in 1999 it began using the WHO International Classification of Diseases (ICD) codes, 10th revision. In relation to homicides, vital statistics data supply information on deaths as the result of interpersonal violence (ICD 10 codes X85-Y09, Y871), which excludes collective violence and legal interventions, self-harm, and any unintentional injuries.

Although vital statistics data in Russia seem to be more trustworthy and reliable than police data (Pridemore 2003), these also contain errors. Mortality data as well as police data in Soviet Russia were subjected to manipulations. For example, deaths due to homicide (as well as deaths resulting from suicide, occupational injuries, and various types of infectious diseases) were extracted from the original statistical tables and publicly reported in the category "other and unknown causes" (Andreev, Scherbov, and Willekens 1995). Then, during the 1990s, there was a disproportionate increase in the number of violent deaths recorded as "unspecified" (i.e., the accidental or purposeful nature of the injuries is supposedly unknown), many of which are thought to have been homicides (Gavrilova *et al.* 2008; Ivanova, Semyonova, and Dubrovina 2004; Pridemore 2003). The increase in the number of deaths at unknown ages and from unspecified causes and in the number of violent deaths of undetermined intent continued through the 2000s (Andreev *et al.* 2008, 2015; Semyonova and Antonova 2007).

Because Russia uses the summarized list of causes of death, which means that the number of items used in the classification of cause of death is considerably smaller than in the ICD-10 system, WHO cannot estimate the overall quality of mortality data provided by Russia (i.e., the proportion of so-called "garbage codes"), but can detect the most obvious cases of miscoding. For example, HIV deaths recorded in the registration data were substantially miscoded to tuberculosis, lower respiratory infections, and other diseases (WHO 2014b). This implies that similar pressure may be exerted over other "unsavory" findings, such as homicide and suicide.

The aforementioned misclassification of violent deaths to some other categories may represent the difficulty of making complete and accurate decisions given the heavy workloads and insufficient budgets of many medical examiners (Andreev *et al.* 2015), the existing practice whereby "provisional" death certificates often are not replaced by the final ones (Gavrilova *et al.* 2008) and an intention to conceal a murder (Ivanova *et al.* 2013; Pridemore 2003; Vaysman, Dubrovina, and Redko 2006). In the latter, the MVD officers can influence the cause of death determination made by medical officials in order to reduce the gap between the number of homicides reported by them and by the Ministry of Health. Such pressure may explain a decreasing gap between homicide reporting systems in recent years (Figure 25.1).

Figure 25.1 provides data on police-recorded data and mortality data for homicide and injuries for the period 1980–2010. As we can see, the trends in both police-recorded homicide and vital statistics data seem to follow each other (a sharp increase from 1992 with its peak in 1994 and then a new rise after the economic crisis in 1998 with the peak in 2001–2002), although homicide estimates from the mortality data substantially exceed those from the crime data for the same years. During the 1990s, the vital statistics data reported an average of nearly 40 percent more homicides annually than the crime reporting system (Pridemore 2003), a much greater difference than in many other countries. Figure 25.1, however, shows that the gap between the two datasets decreased after 2005.

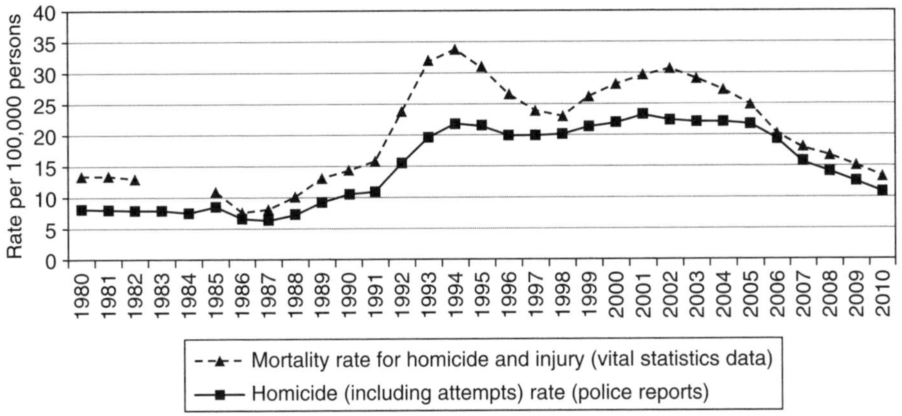

Figure 25.1 Police-recorded homicide rate (including attempts) per 100,000 residents (police reports) and mortality rate per 100,000 residents for homicide (vital statistics data), 1980–2010. Source: Police-recorded data are from Luneev (2005) for 1980–2002 and MVD (n.d.) for 2003–2010. Vital statistics data for 1980–1994 are from WHO (n.d.) and for 1995–2010 are from Rosstat (n.d.).

Computed estimates of the homicide rate

Estimates based on the police homicide data Some Russian criminologists have been skeptical about the remarkable decline in the police-recorded homicide rate in the 2000s and consider it to reflect an artificial tampering with the statistical data (Inshakov 2011; Luneev 2005). For example, professor and former colonel of militia Mikhail Babaev has openly stated that he does not believe any number published officially by the MVD, calling crime statistics in Russia "an unscrupulous lie" (*The New Times* 2009). He argues that there is no possible realistic explanation for such an unprecedented decline in the homicide rate and a simultaneous increase in the number of unidentified bodies (Figure 25.2).

A group of scholars from the Research Institute of the Academy of General Prosecutor's Office headed by Professor Sergei Inshakov conducted a comprehensive study to calculate more accurate homicide estimates from 2001 to 2009, including the "dark figure" of homicides absent from official police data (Inshakov 2011). Having direct access to the first-hand unmodified police statistics, Inshakov (2011) discovered that the total number of homicides reported to the police increasingly exceeded the number of homicides officially registered by police. Specifically, the number of reports of homicide tripled from about 14,000 to 45,000 whereas the total number of homicides registered by the police almost halved from 34,000 to 18,000 between 2001 and 2009. As a result, in 2009 police registered 2.5 times fewer homicides than were reported to them. In addition, the number of unidentified dead bodies doubled from 37,000 in 2001 to almost 78,000 in 2009 (or a 109% increase between 2001 and 2009) (Inshakov 2011); some of these people presumably were murdered (Andreev *et al.* 2008; Gavrilova *et al.* 2008). In addition,

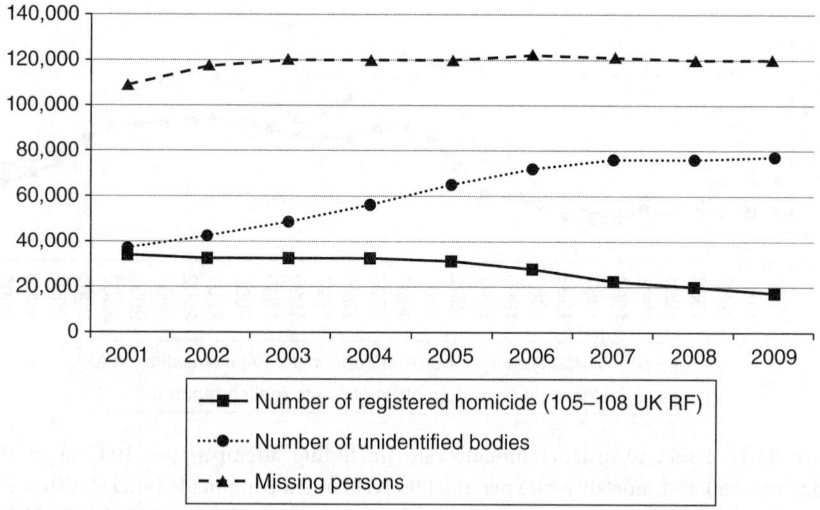

Figure 25.2 Dynamics of registered homicide in comparison with the number of unidentified dead bodies and missing persons in 2001–2009 (Inshakov 2011).

whereas the total number of missing persons appears to have grown from about 110,000 to 120,000 between 2001 and 2009 (Inshakov 2011; Zakatnova 2007), the number of people officially declared missing by the police declined from 78,000 to 71,000 over the same period. While many of these would have died from natural causes or simply started new lives, some of them met violent deaths and, as a consequence, the official homicide rate clearly fails to convey the true scale of the problem.

To produce more accurate estimates of homicide rates in Russia in 2001–2009, Inshakov (2011) used a mathematical model of homicide-related risk factors, similar in its basic principles to the estimation models used by WHO (2014). Using multivariate regression analysis, Inshakov (2011) first identified the regression coefficients for each of the 16 risk factors in the model (e.g., poverty, income disparity, unemployment, ineffective functioning of institutions of social control), which predicted the registered homicide rate in 2001, and then included these regression coefficients and the means of the risk factors to estimate the number and the rate of homicide for each year until 2009 (Figure 25.3).

Computed estimates suggest that the average annual homicide rate per 100,000 population in 2002–2009 was about 27.7, whereas the official police data reported homicide rate was about 18.7 in the same period. Moreover, computed estimates also suggest that the number of homicides did not decline and appeared to hold stable across the 2000s. At the same time, it is important to mention potential limitations of the Inshakov estimation of homicide rates. First, Inshakov (2011) provides no detailed information on the independent indicators in this model and how exactly they were measured. In addition, homicide rates tend to have nonlinear relationships with some of the independent variables in the model, which could affect Inshakov's estimates in complex ways.

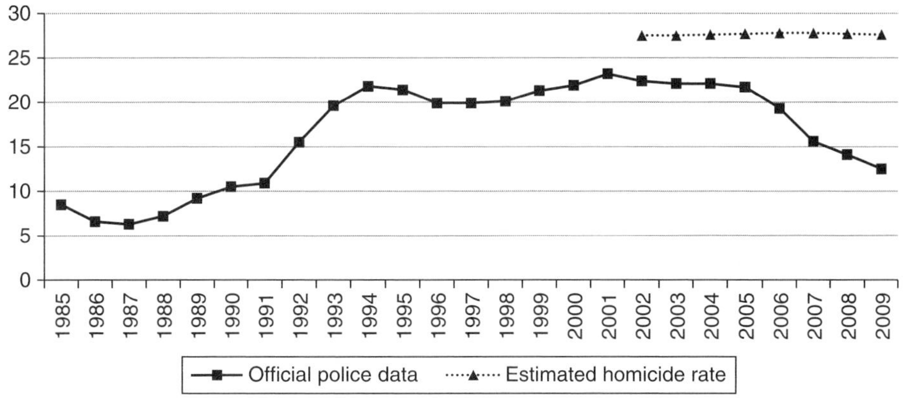

Figure 25.3 Official homicide (including attempts) rate (police reports) and estimated homicide rate per 100,000 persons (Inshakov 2011).

Homicide estimates based on the vital statistics data Recently there have been attempts to more accurately estimate the number of deaths by homicide in Russia based on official vital statistics data (e.g., Andreev *et al.* 2015; Ivanova *et al.* 2013; Semyonova and Antonova 2007). The major problems with the homicide vital statistics data tend to arise from misclassification of homicides as events of unidentified intent (EUIs). The rate of external causes of death due to EUIs is extremely high in Russia, about 28 per 100,000 residents between 2000 and 2011, and their proportion of all deaths from external causes accelerated in the years following the collapse of the Soviet Union (Andreev *et al.* 2015).

In the recent study, Andreev *et al.* (2015) modeled the relationships between three causes of death (non-transport accident, suicide, and homicide) and ten independent variables, which allowed them to predict the cause of death for EUI cases. The model tended unambiguously to assign 33 percent of EUIs to homicide. Moreover, between 2000 and 2011, the proportion of homicides that were initially classified as EUIs increased from 28 percent to 44 percent, with the most dramatic increase occurring after 2006 (Andreev *et al.* 2015). The redistribution of EUIs resulted in a substantial elevation of the official mortality figures for homicide in the 2000–2011 period. For example, based on Andreev *et al.*'s estimates, the Russian age standardized homicide rate for 2011 is 20.9 per 100,000, which is nearly double the officially recorded value of 11.5 per 100,000. Furthermore, the percent increase between Andreev *et al.*'s estimated and official rates of homicides grew substantially from 41 percent in 2000 to 82 percent in 2011 with the most rapid rise happening after 2006. This means that the level of homicide in 2000 would have been about 41 percent higher than that reported by official vital statistics data, whereas the 2011 level of homicide would have been about 82 percent higher than that reported by the official statistics. This supports the concerns of some scholars (Gavrilova *et al.* 2008; Pridemore 2003) about the quality of the Russian homicide data and the validity of the officially registered reduction in homicide mortality in Russia. According to Andreev *et al.*'s (2015) reclassification of deaths categorized as EUIs, the homicide rate in Russia appears to be 1.5 times to twice as high as the official figure and to decrease from 2002 to 2011, but at a much slower pace than suggested by the official vital statistics data.

Estimates of homicides by other researchers appear to be consistent with these findings. For example, according to Antonova's estimates (2007), the actual number of homicides at ages 20–39 years was about 1.5 times higher than that registered by official data, and at ages 40–59 the actual number of homicides was nearly twice as high as the official figure. Semyonova and Antonova (2007) examined suspiciously high rates of deaths among working people in Moscow in 2003 due to EUIs, falls, and other accidents. Detailed analysis of certificates of death and reclassification of these categories of cause of death increased the number of homicides and moved this cause of death from the fourth to the second position in the ranking of injury-related deaths.

Offering their version of EUI redistribution and focusing on the most frequent combination of the type of injury and cause, Ivanova *et al.* (2013) suggested that the 2010 level of homicides of men aged 20–59 would have been about 94 percent higher than reported by official vital statistics, that is, about 23,000 deaths rather than 12,000 deaths respectively. For women, the 2010 level of homicide would have been 66 percent higher than that from official statistics.

At the same time, it should be noted that the problem of underestimation of homicides is not specific only for Russia and is quite common to many other countries. For example, some research suggests there is substantial misclassification of female homicides, especially dowry deaths, as suicides or accidents in India (Mukherjee, Rustagi, and Krishnaji 2001; Sanghavi, Bhalla, and Das 2009; Shaha and Mohanthy 2006), which seriously challenges the accuracy of existing estimates and official police data. Moreover, the percent increase of a number of homicides reported by the police (for the latest available year) and WHO estimated number of homicides (for 2012) is 51 percent in India, 37 percent in Brazil, 30 percent in Colombia, and 22 percent in Russia (WHO 2014a). However, the degree of underestimation seems especially high in Russia comparing to the nations with reliable mortality statistics. For example, Russia's percent of deaths from external causes that were categorized as events of undetermined intent is 15.1 percent, which is 15 times more than that in Norway (0.2%), five times more than that in the United States (2.9%) and twice of that in Germany (7.1%) (Andreev *et al.* 2015).

In this section, we examined the main sources of data about homicide in Russia, that is, official police data and vital statistics data, and pointed to a number of issues that cast doubt on the accuracy of official data, especially in the 2000s. The most pronounced problems in both sources relate to a disproportionate increase in the categories with unspecified causes of death and deaths of undetermined intent in vital statistics data and a category of intentional grievous bodily harm leading to death in the police data. Although vital statistics data have appeared to be more accurate in Russia, in fact, both reporting systems seem to provide questionable data on homicide.

Potential Incentives for Misrepresenting Homicide Statistics

Clearly, there are ways to misrepresent the homicide data in Russia if there is a will for that. First, measurement of changes in the amount of crime is politically important and crime statistics are widely used to evaluate the effectiveness of strategies of crime control. In other words, there are pressures to have the crime statistics show certain things. In Russia, it appears there is political pressure to show that crime is being reduced, which would fit the "dictatorship of law" proclaimed by President Putin (Walker 2007).

Distortions of population statistics regarding homicide, suicide, child mortality, migration, prison population, hidden settlements (secret towns built to develop the nuclear industry), and other unsavory phenomena were pervasive under the Soviet regime (Tolts 2012). USSR authorities unabashedly used these statistics as a tool of political propaganda. Distortion of population statistics has been a complex multi-level process. After Soviet leaders publicly announced specific numbers or expectations about population trends, it was common for the central statistical administration to bend to pressure and adjust its numbers (Tolts 2012). In contrast, President Boris Yeltzin seemed not to have the resources and political interest to encourage the manipulation of population data. Moreover, the 1990s are often perceived as a brief period of a greater tolerance toward freedom in different segments of life, for example, the media, politics, and culture. However, under Putin's regime, there is evidence of a return to practices similar to those in Soviet Russia. Putin's messages about strengthening law and order in the 2000s may well have been perceived and interpreted by officials in the police, hospitals, and statistics departments as a direct call for action to reduce violent crime statistics.

A second potential incentive for manipulating crime statistics comes from a vested interest that police officers have in lowering homicide rates due to the so-called "stick" ("*palochnaya*") system. According to this system, police officers strive to show positive performance and are less concerned about an absolute level of criminal cases. Furthermore, police face penalties for unsolved criminal cases, so there is a tendency for them to officially register cases that can be easily solved or cases already solved at the moment of investigation (for similar problems in relation to economic crimes in Russia, see Nazrullaeva, Baranov, and Yakovlev 2013).

There are other potential factors that can explain inaccuracies with homicide data in Russia, including a lack of manpower and resources to conduct the required thorough investigation of deaths (especially of unidentified bodies and missing people), reliance on established practices of registering causes of death that are associated with underreporting of violent deaths (e.g., using provisional death certificates; Gavrilova *et al.* 2008), and a shift in priorities among police officers toward earning money through their status and away from doing their job well (this will be discussed in the next section). All these reasons seem likely to create an atmosphere conducive to the underrepresentation of homicides.

The trends depicted in the homicide estimates, which differ substantially from the official statistics of homicide, require explanation. For that, we will partly draw on the concept of a "criminological transition" (Pridemore 2007), according to which a country's crime rate and crime characteristics may change (or hold stable) over time depending on the socioeconomic changes in the society. The next section will discuss the broader conditions in Russian society in the 2000s, how they changed or remained stable relative to the 1990s and Soviet times, and the implications they may have for the homicide rate.

Potential Explanations for Homicide in Russia

Decivilizing process and violence in Russia

Norbert Elias's (1978) civilizing process framework suggests that there has been a centuries-long "civilizing process" that resulted in a major reduction in homicide since the late Middle Ages (Eisner 2001; Pinker 2011). By civilizing process he understood the emergence of centralized states that increasingly suppressed private violence by accumulating a monopoly on legitimized force and shaping the internalized self-restraint in its citizens. However, Elias was convinced that the civilizing process might be reversed and this could happen very rapidly through an abrupt change in a society. This "decivilizing process" returns a society to a previous state of insecurity and danger. Elias (1996) stated that the Holocaust and other atrocities of German Nazis were an example of a decivilizing process. Arguably, Russia has undergone a decivilizing process in the wake of the collapse of its former government twice in the twentieth century, once after the October Revolution in 1917 and again after the collapse of the Soviet Union in 1991.

The most recent dramatic increase in homicide rates occurred during the deep social-political and economic crisis of the 1990s, including the dissolution of the Soviet Union in 1991 and the economic crisis of 1998 (Figure 25.1). Russia's economy rapidly grew and the average living standards undoubtedly increased after 1999. Nevertheless, the Russian state has remained weak according to the decivilizing process framework, because "weakness" of the state refers not so much to its economic performance as to the functioning of its social institutions, such as, the courts and law enforcement.

Although promised by Putin and his administration, the "rule of law" has not been established in the 2000s in Russia. Instead of becoming a foundation of the state applicable to everybody, law has been used mainly to constrain ordinary citizens and selective politicians and businessmen with their businesses (Walker 2007). The police, as one of the central institutions intended to ensure the rule of law, turned its powers and resources to advance its members' material interests rather than to fight crime; as a consequence, policing in Russia can best be described as "predatory policing" (Gerber and Mendelson 2008). It is not surprising that in these circumstances many Russians hold negative perceptions of, and have little trust in, the police and other "power institutions" (Semukhina and Reynolds 2014; Zernova 2012). Russia's political legitimacy index—which has been associated with homicide rates (Nivette and Eisner 2013)—is one of the lowest among other countries. Some of the mechanisms that can explain the association between low legitimacy and high homicide rates are low self-control and use of violence as a means of self-help (Black 1983).

One part of Elias's civilizing process theory highlights the role of "sensibilities" in the decline of violence; that is, an increased sensitivity toward others' suffering and an aversion to the expression of raw emotions can contribute to suppression of impulsive behaviors, including violence. People in Russia have experienced substantial shifts in expressing their true feelings and behaviors. In the Soviet time, people kept their true thoughts and spontaneous emotions suppressed and hidden out of fear of being discovered by the secret police and prosecuted by the KGB. After the fall of the Soviet Union, people seemed to start expressing themselves more openly (Rosenkrans 2001). Although largely spontaneous in nature, some of these emerging attitudes, particularly those related to hatred of others and closely linked to anger, are said to have been cultivated under the influence of coordinated propaganda efforts; this kind of propaganda appears to have been a tool to unify Russian society and to further its domestic and foreign policies (Shlapentokh 2007). One of the most pervasive forms of mass consciousness in the 2000s has become xenophobia and nationalism (Pain 2007; Sevortian 2009; Verkhovsky 2007). The percentage of Russians openly expressing xenophobia increased from 20 percent in 1989 to nearly 60 percent in 2005 (Shlapentokh 2007). Hatred of Chechens, Ukrainians, Georgians, and "real foreigners," especially Americans, exacerbated after 2000 (e.g., Petersson and Persson 2011). Putin has arguably contributed to these trends by resuscitating an "all against us" attitude that included encouraging anti-American sentiments, manufacturing the enemies in and outside of Russia (Mendelson and Gerber 2008), and generating nostalgic feelings about the great Soviet past, including the World War II victory (Hutchings and Rulyova 2009). In addition to xenophobia and nationalism, other forms of hatred and intolerance appear to have grown intensely after 2000. The most notorious of these are homophobia, as evidenced by the 2013 law banning the promotion of homosexuality, and intolerance/hatred of "blasphemy" epitomized in the criminal case against "Pussy riot" (Smyth and Soboleva 2014).

These perceptions have been confirmed in a recent study of the psychological wellbeing of Russians in three periods of time, that is, the 1980s, the 1990s, and the 2000s (Urievich and Urievich 2013). Conducted by the Institute of Psychology of the Russian Academy of Sciences, this study suggests that, relative to other time periods, the 2000s are associated with an increase in negative indicators (e.g., aggressiveness, hostility, brutality, malice, rudeness, xenophobia, egoism, apathy) and a decrease in positive indicators (e.g., kindness, empathy, compassion, fairness, calmness, honesty, and humanity). Authors of the study conclude that positive economic changes in the 2000s are not necessarily associated with improvements in the psychological characteristics of society. In fact, heightened economic stability instead uncovers deep psychological issues of contemporary Russian society.

Drawing on the decivilizing process theory, Russia's currently high and relatively stable homicide rate can be explained mainly by the erosion of the state, which is associated with the lack of political legitimacy, loosened social bonds and controls within society, and people's loss of trust in political and civil society. The combination of violent emotions (such as frustration and distrust as a result of an illegitimate state and unfair distribution of services to citizens) on the one hand, and "unavailability of law" on the other hand, results in crime as a tool of social control (Black 1983). In other words, the exertion of "private justice" or "self-help" seems to prevail.

Russian drinking culture and alcohol-related homicide

Discussion of violence in Russia can hardly avoid mentioning the role of alcohol. However, alcohol-related harm in Russia is not due solely to the amount that Russians drink, but also to what, where, and how they drink. Binge drinking, preference for distilled spirits (mainly vodka) over wine and beer, drinking home-made *samogon*, surrogates, and non-beverage substances, drinking mainly in home kitchens and not bars and restaurants (for a review, see Lysova and Pridemore 2010) are distinct characteristics of the so-called "Russian drinking culture" (Stickley and Mäkinen 2005). Together with prevailing emotions of anger, hostility, and a lack of sympathy, Russian patterns of alcohol drinking appear to contribute to the perpetration of violence and homicide.

Multiple studies support the hypothesis that homicide and alcohol are closely connected in cultures where an intoxication-oriented drinking pattern prevails, and several scholars suggest that a binge drinking pattern is important in explaining the high rate of homicide in Russia (Bye 2008; Razvodovsky 2007). Pridemore (2002) found that Russian provinces with higher levels of heavy drinking had higher levels of homicide. This provincial-level association is not new, however, as Stickley and Pridemore (2007) used historical data from 1910 for western Russian provinces and found the same association. A time-series analysis by Stickley and Razvodovsky (2012) revealed that the consumption of vodka (but not beer or wine) was significantly related to homicide in Russia. They found that a one liter increase in overall alcohol sales is associated with a 5.9 percent increase in the male homicide rate and a 5.1 percent increase in the female homicide rate; the respective figures for vodka were 16.4 percent and 14.3 percent. Relatedly, a recent large-scale prospective study confirms that vodka use in Russia is strongly predictive of premature death, mainly from external causes, including homicide, and eight particular disease groupings (Zaridze *et al.* 2014). In addition, a comparative international study of the aggregate relationship between alcohol and homicide in Russia and in the United States suggests a larger role of alcohol in homicide in Russia than in the United States, that is, 73 percent and 57 percent of homicides can be attributable (explained by the changes in alcohol drinking) to alcohol in Russia and the United States respectively (Landberg and Norström 2011).

Binge drinking is one of the strongest predictors for violence even after controlling for other factors that can affect injuries and lethal violence (e.g., age, race, sex). It can trigger violent behavior among both youth and adults due to a variety of factors, including physiological and pharmacological influences (e.g., disinhibition and psychological and cognitive impairment, which results in miscommunication, misinterpretation of social cues, attention deficits, and bad judgment); individual expectations regarding the effects of alcohol use; and various situational factors, including the setting and social context in which drinking occurs (Brewer and Swahn 2005).

In recent years there appears to be a downward trend in the consumption of alcohol, driven by a decrease in spirit consumption in Russia (Neufeld and Rehm 2013).

These changes can be linked to the implementation of the 2005 federal alcohol control law in Russia (Levintova 2007). However, it is not clear whether this recent trend in alcohol consumption will be able to change the notorious drinking culture especially among the most disadvantaged and impoverished groups of population in which homicide is typically a more likely outcome of violent disagreements. Moreover, major changes aimed at liberalization of alcohol policy planned for 2015, including cheaper vodka and more available alcohol, can overturn recent achievements in decreasing spirit consumption and its association with a decline of total deaths (Zinkina *et al.* 2015).

Conclusion

This chapter examined homicide statistics in Russia, in the context of a history of falsification and concealment of population data in the Soviet and post-Soviet Russia. Recent studies, which employed sophisticated mathematical models to estimate more accurate rates of homicide, suggest that the homicide rate in the 2000s was much higher than that reported by official crime and mortality data. While official sources indicate that in 2002–2009 the homicide rate per 100,000 population ranged between 19 (official police data) and 23 (official vital statistics data), the computed estimated rates ranged between 28 and 34 respectively. Moreover, while statistics from official sources demonstrate a rapid decline in homicide in the 2000s, the computed estimates suggest that the homicide rate held relatively steady (based on crime data) or declined at a much slower pace (based on mortality data) than reported by official data. Future studies should continue to examine the validity of official homicide data and the concrete mechanisms of their falsification in order to improve the quality of homicide data. This chapter also discussed Norbert Elias's decivilizing process and Russian drinking culture as explanatory frameworks for the high and non-declining homicide rate in contemporary Russia. The concept of a decivilizing process sheds light on some nontrivial factors for homicide, such as, for instance, the general distrust of power institutions and hostile emotions associated with xenophobia and nationalism, in addition to the traditional but important ones, such as a Russian pattern of alcohol drinking.

References

Andreev, E., Pridemore, W.A., Shkolnikov, V.M., and Antonova, O.I. (2008) An investigation of the growing number of deaths of unidentified people in Russia. *European Journal of Public Health*, 18(3): 252–257.

Andreev, E., Scherbov, S., and Willekens, F. (1995) *Sources of Information on the Population of Russia*. Groningen, Netherlands: University of Groningen Press.

Andreev, E., Shkolnikov, A.M., Pridemore, W.A., and Nikitina, S.Y. (2015) A method for reclassifying cause of death in cases categorized as "event of undetermined intent." *Population Health Metrics*, 13(1): 23.

Antonova, O.I. (2007) Regional'nye osobennosti smertnosti naseleniia Rossii ot vneshnikh prichin [Regional characteristics of Russian mortality from external causes]. PhD thesis. Russian Academy of Sciences, Institute of Social and Political Studies.

Black, D. (1983) Crime as social control. *American Sociological Review*, 48: 34–45.

Brewer, R.D. and Swahn, M.H. (2005) Binge drinking and violence. *JAMA*, 294(5): 616–618.

Bye, E.K. (2008) Alcohol and homicide in Eastern Europe: A time series analysis of six countries. *Homicide Studies*, 12: 7–27.

Eisner, M. (2001) Modernization, self-control and lethal violence: The long-term dynamics of European homicide rates in theoretical perspective. *British Journal of Criminology*, 41: 618–638.

Elias, N. (1978) *The Civilizing Process* (vols 1–2). Oxford: Oxford University Press.

Elias, N. (1996) *The Germans: Power Struggles and the Development of Habitus in the Nineteenth and Twentieth Centuries*. New York: Columbia University Press.

Federal Bureau of Investigation (2004) *Uniform Crime Reporting Handbook*. Washington, DC: Federal Bureau of Investigation.

Gavrilova, N.S., Semyonova, V.G., Dubrovina, E., *et al.* (2008) Russian mortality crisis and the quality of vital statistics. *Population Research and Policy Review*, 27(5): 551–574.

Gerber, T.P. and Mendelson, S.E. (2008) Public experiences of police violence and corruption in contemporary Russia: A case of predatory policing? *Law & Society Review*, 42(1): 1–44.

Hutchings, S. and Rulyova, N. (2009) Commemorating the past/performing the present: Television coverage of the Second World War victory celebrations and the (de) construction of Russian nationhood. In B. Beumers, S. Hutchings, and N. Rulyova (eds), *The Post-Soviet Russian Media: Conflicting Signals* (pp. 137–156). New York: Routledge.

Inshakov, S.M. (ed.) (2011) *Theoretical Foundations of Research and Analysis of Latent Crime* [in Russian]. Moscow: UNITI-DANA.

Ivanova, A.E., Sabgayda, T.P., Semenova, V.G., *et al.* (2013) Factors distorting structure of death causes in working population in Russia. *Sotsial'nye aspekty zdorov'ia naseleniia* [Russian electronic edition]. Available online at http://vestnik.mednet.ru/content/view/491/27 (accessed September 1, 2014).

Ivanova, A.E., Semyonova, V.G., Dubrovina, E. (2004) Marginalization of Russian mortality. A number of violent deaths is higher than we think [In Russian]. *Demoscope Weekly* [Russian electronic edition]. Available online at http://demoscope.ru/weekly/2004/0181/tema01.php (accessed September 1, 2014).

Kim, S.-W. and Pridemore, W.A. (2005) Social change, institutional anomie, and serious property crime in transitional Russia. *British Journal of Criminology*, 45: 81–97.

Landberg, J. and Norström, T. (2011) Alcohol and homicide in Russia and the United States: A comparative analysis. *Journal of Studies on Alcohol and Drugs*, 72(5): 723.

Levintova M.V. (2007) Russian alcohol policy in the making. *Alcohol and Alcoholism*, 42(5): 500–505.

Luneev, V. (2005) *Crime in the XXth Century: Global, Regional and Russian Trends* [in Russian]. Moscow: Wolters Kluwer.

Lysova, A.V. and Pridemore, W.A. (2010) Dramatic problems and weak policy. *Nordic Studies on Alcohol and Drugs*, 27(5): 425–447.

Mendelson, S.E. and Gerber, T.P. (2008) Us and them: Anti-American views of the Putin generation. *Washington Quarterly*, 31(2): 131–150.

Mukherjee, C., Rustagi, P., and Krishnaji, N. (2001) Crimes against women in India: Analysis of official statistics. *Economic and Political Weekly*, 36(43): 4070–4080.

MVD (n.d.) Sostoyanie prestupnosti (Situation with crime) [in Russian]. Available online at http://mvd.ru/Deljatelnost/statistics/reports (accessed July 18, 2014).

Nazrullaeva, E., Baranov, A., and Yakovlev, A. (2013) Criminal persecution of business in Russia's regions: Private interests vs."Stick" system. Paper presented at the 7th Annual Conference of The International Society for New Institutional Economics in Italy. Available online at http://papers.sioe.org/paper/1034.html (accessed September 20, 2016).

Neufeld, M. and Rehm, J. (2013) Alcohol consumption and mortality in Russia since 2000: Are there any changes following the alcohol policy changes starting in 2006? *Alcohol and Alcoholism*, 48: 222–230.

Nivette, A.E. and Eisner, M. (2013) Do legitimate policies have fewer homicides? A cross-national analysis. *Homicide Studies*, 17(1): 3–26.

Pain, E.A. (2007) Xenophobia and ethnopolitical extremism in post-Soviet Russia: Dynamics and growth factors. *Nationalities Papers*, 35(5): 895–911.

Petersson, B. and Persson, E. (2011) Coveted, detested and unattainable? Images of the US superpower role and self-images of Russia in Russian print media discourse. *International Journal of Cultural Studies*, 14(1): 71–89.

Pinker, S. (2011) *The Better Angels of Our Nature: Why Violence Has Declined* (vol. 75). New York: Viking.

Pridemore, W.A. (2002) Vodka and violence: Alcohol consumption and homicide rates in Russia. *American Journal of Public Health*, 92(12): 1921–1930.

Pridemore, W.A. (2003) Measuring homicide in Russia: A comparison of estimates from the crime and vital statistics reporting systems. *Social Science & Medicine*, 57(8): 1343–1354.

Pridemore, W.A. (2007) Change and stability in the characteristics of homicide victims, offenders and incidents during rapid social change. *British Journal of Criminology*, 47(2): 331–345.

Razvodovsky, Y. (2007) Homicide and alcohol intoxication in Russia, 1956–2005. *Alcoholism*, 43: 37–49.

Rosenkrans, G. (2001) Since the end of the state-run press: Evolution of Russian newspapers from Perestroika to 1998. *Journal of Government Information*, 28(5): 549–560.

Rosstat (n.d.) Mortality classified by main causes of deaths [in Russian]. Available online at http://www.gks.ru/bgd/regl/b10_13/Main.htm (accessed September 14, 2014).

Sanghavi, P., Bhalla, K., and Das, V. (2009) Fire-related deaths in India in 2001: A retrospective analysis of data. *The Lancet*, 373(9671): 1282–1288.

Semukhina, O. and Reynolds, K.M. (2014) Russian citizens' perceptions of corruption and trust of the police. *Policing and Society*, 24(2): 158–188.

Semyonova, V.G. and Antonova, O.I. (2007) Veracity of mortality statistics (based on injury- and poisoning-related mortality in Moscow) [in Russian]. *Sotsial'nye aspekty zdorov'ia naseleniia*. Available online at http://vestnik.mednet.ru/index2.php?option=com_content &task=view&id=28&pop=1&page=0&Itemid=30 (accessed September 11, 2014).

Sevortian, A. (2009) Xenophobia in Post-Soviet Russia. *The Equal Rights Review*, 3: 19–27.

Shaha, K.K. and Mohanthy, S. (2006) Alleged dowry death: A study of homicidal burns. *Medicine, Science and the Law*, 46(2): 105–110.

Shlapentokh, V. (2007) The hatred of others: The Kremlin's powerful but risky weapon. *World Affairs*, 169(3): 134–142.

Smyth, R. and Soboleva, I. (2014) Looking beyond the economy: Pussy Riot and the Kremlin's voting coalition. *Post-Soviet Affairs*, 30(4): 257–275.

Stickley, A. and Mäkinen, I.H. (2005) Homicide in the Russian Empire and Soviet Union: Continuity or change? *British Journal of Criminology*, 45(5): 647–670.

Stickley, A. and Pridemore, W.A. (2007) The social-structural correlates of homicide in late-Tsarist Russia. *British Journal of Criminology*, 47(1): 80–99.

Stickley, A. and Razvodovsky, Y. (2012) The effects of beverage type on homicide rates in Russia, 1970–2005. *Drug and Alcohol Review*, 31(3): 257–262.

The New Times (2009) Babaev versus Veller, March 23: 11. Available online at http://newtimes.ru/articles/print/2853 (accessed May 6, 2010).

Tolts, M. (2012) The failure of demographic statistics: A Soviet response to population troubles. Paper presented at the IUSSP XXIVth General Population Conference, Salvador-Bahia, Brazil, August 18–24, 2001 (revised).

UNODC (2014) *Global Study on Homicide 2013. Trends, Context, Data.* Available online at http://www.unodc.org/gsh/(accessed July 18, 2014).

Urievich, A.V. and Urievich, M.A. (2013) Dynamics of psychological health of Russian society: Expert opinion [in Russian]. In *Morality of Modern Russian Society: Psychological Analysis*. Moscow: Institute of Psychology of the Russian Academy of Sciences. Available online at http://psyfactor.org/lib/social8.htm (accessed September 15, 2014).

Vaysman, D.A., Dubrovina, E.V., and Redko, A.N. (2006) Information support for studies of mortality in Russia. *Obschestvennoe zdorovye i profilaktika zabolevaniy* [Public Health and Disease Prevention], 6: 31–38.

Verkhovsky, A. (2007) The rise of nationalism in Putin's Russia. *Helsinki Monitor*, 18(2): 125.

Walberg, P., McKee, M., Shkolnikov, V., *et al.* (1998) Economic change, crime, and mortality crisis in Russia: Regional analysis. *British Medical Journal*, 317: 312–318.

Walker, E.W. (2007) Crime without punishment: The Litvinenko affair and Putin's culture of violence. *Georgetown Journal of International Affairs*, 8: 97.

WHO (World Health Organization) (2014a) *Global Status Report on Violence Prevention*. Geneva: World Health Organization.

WHO (2014b) WHO methods and data sources for country-level causes of death 2000–2012. Global heath estimates technical paper. Available online at http://www.who.int/healthinfo/statistics/GlobalCOD_method.pdf (accessed September 14, 2014).

WHO (n.d.) Health statistics and information systems. Available online at http://www.who.int/healthinfo/statistics/en/(accessed July 18, 2014).

Zakatnova, A. (2007) Social minimum discussed in Moscow (Sozialnyi minimum obsudili v Moscve). *Rossiskaya Gazeta*, October 15. Available online at http://www.rg.ru/2007/10/15/a182445.html (accessed September 9, 2014).

Zaridze, D., Lewington, S., Boroda, A., *et al.* (2014) Alcohol and mortality in Russia: Prospective observational study of 151,000 adults. *The Lancet*, 383(9927): 1465–1473.

Zernova, M. (2012) The public image of the contemporary Russian police: Impact of personal experiences of policing, wider social implications and the potential for change. *Policing: An International Journal of Police Strategies & Management*, 35(2): 216–230.

Zinkina, Y., Korotaev, A., Rybalchenko, S., Khalturina, D. (2015) Nadvigaushchaysya alcogolnaya katastrofa i kak ee predotvratit [Impending alcohol catastrophe and how to prevent it]. *Polit.ru*. Available online at http://polit.ru/article/2015/01/13/disaster/ (accessed January 19, 2015).

26

Understanding Homicide in China

Liqun Cao

In researching this chapter, we realized that there were no chapters or articles on homicide in China in any other publications or on the Internet. Instead, we have found many articles on the death penalty in China.

Homicide, arguably the most heinous crime of all, does not seem to be the most serious crime in China while capital punishment is widely used by the Chinese regime as a way of social control. In order to understand the contradiction, we must appreciate the nature of the Chinese politics. China has changed greatly in the past 35 years or so. In the economic arena, China has been trying to act in line with the world standard practice (*yu guoji jiegui*) while in the political and legal arenas, it maintains its status as one of the vanguards of its exceptionalism, largely outside of the world norm. Continuing economic reforms therefore seem to have placed increasing strain on the political and legal systems. In this chapter, we attempt to incorporate politics in the discussion in order to understand homicide in China, and then we examine the homicide data and the sources of data inaccuracy. This is followed by a discussion of capital punishment.

Politicization of Crime and Homicide in China

To understand crime in China, we must understand its politics, as crime is not simply an issue of quality of life, but an indicator of legal and political environment (Cao and Dai 2001). The Chinese Communist Party (CCP) took over the state power through an armed struggle. To maintain the regime's continuity and stability, it has relied on the coercive powers of both the police and the army (Fu 2005) as well as economic development (Cao, Sun, and Hebenton 2014).

The Handbook of Homicide, First Edition. Edited by Fiona Brookman, Edward R. Maguire, and Mike Maguire.

In China, the study of crime in the Western sense is relatively new. China joined the socialist camp headed by the former Soviet Union after 1949, and as with the other socialist nations, information on many issues, such as homicide, was classified as state secrets. During the 1960s when the ties with other socialist brother states, especially the Soviet Union, were broken, China became a hermetically closed universe of its own.

As China moved on its own road of socialism, counting, or recording data, which is ubiquitous in both modern and ancient societies as a way to collect social data, remained important. While ancient societies paid attention to recording the current and past events, modern societies make more use of data, extending it into the analysis of the current situations through sampling in the decision-making process, and in the estimation of future trends. As China's socialist system was based on the "planned economy" (Cao 2007), it was all the more important to have accurate information. Because of its importance in decision making and in daily life, statistical data are exceedingly significant and often sources of severe difficulty and political contention in all nations (He 2014b).

Recording data for statistical purposes is of great interest when studying social issues, not only because it is connected with various social problems, but also because the recording process often constitutes a social problem (Martin and Lynch 2009): methods of data processing often become caught up in the political and epistemic conflict that they are used to address.

The first basic principle of data recording is to put results into categories. This may sound simple and clear, but once applied in practice, all sorts of issues will emerge. The mixing of old revolutionary and new markets language in China, for example, has resulted in much distortion of the realities for foreigners (Huang 2013). For our purpose, it is required that the police force records aspects of crime in a particular place per year. So, the first question we need to ask is what was considered a crime in Mao's time (1949–1976)? Once Mao became the new ruler of China in 1949, he abolished all the previous laws and replaced them with CCP policies and principal statutes (Lewis 2014; Qi and Oberwittler 2009).

In all social democratic nations, the right to life and the right of private property are sacred. Therefore, distinction is made between the two major types of crime, that is, violent crime and property crime. Since 1949, China established a socialist system where private ownership of production was nationalized or closed down and private ownership of property for enemies of the party was not acceptable at first and then during the Great Proletarian Cultural Revolution (1966–1976), when China was considered outside the international community, private property and enterprise was haphazardly scorned and violated. There was no respect in socialist collectivism for private property and/or privacy (Dutton 1992; Lieberthal 2003).

Although there was a definition for crime in the Soviet-inspired constitution, the CCP did not obey its own constitution. They acted above the law. "The police enforced the norms of the Party, not law of the nation" (Cao 2007: 41). Total social control was achieved and maintained outside the codified laws. Following the Soviet Union, large scale labor camps began to operate around the big cities and labor farms were set up in remote provinces (Dikotter 1997; Dutton 1992).

The concept of crime was greatly inflated to include anti-CCP behavior and anti-CCP thinking. In the name of revolution, Mao replaced the old stratification with a more rigid caste-like stratification system where people were divided into friends and enemies (criminals) (Dutton 2004; Cao 2007). In this system, Mao created a world similar to the wonderland invented by English author Lewis Carroll (Dodgson 1865), so much so that even the Soviet advisors found it troublesome (Dutton 2005). In the enemy camp at the bottom of society, five new categories of crime, called black five categories (*heiwulei*), were invented in the 1950s through the process of juridical othering: landlords, rich peasants, anti-revolutionaries, bad elements, and rightists. The groups were enlarged into nine categories during the Cultural Revolution in the late 1960s with the following groups added: traitors, spies, capitalist roaders, and intellectuals. Once a person was labeled in these categories, he/she would be marginalized and periodically prosecuted. Extra-legal execution methods such as beating and starving to death were common for people in these groups during the 1950s (Dikotter 1997; Strauss 2002). In addition, the regime obfuscated their responsibility in state crime and nurtured a punitive culture to its citizens by organizing huge rallies to condemn and openly humiliate these people and their family members. Violence against class enemies was considered revolutionary (and just) behavior (Mao 1967). Mercy to enemies was considered cruel to class brothers and sisters.

Through a series of political campaigns, Mao consolidated his role as both the CCP's paramount leader and as the new regime supreme leader. The political campaigns invented by Mao were notable for the methods of Soviet-inspired thought reform first developed in Yan-an and then institutionalized and standardized throughout entire China, including the use of self-criticism and dividing people into two categories of friends and enemies (Cao 2007; Dutton 2005; Lieberthal 2003). Mao placed conspicuous stress on political ideology, personal loyalty, and coercion (Eddy 2007). Total conformity was achieved through rigorous thought-control methods rather than the enforcement of legal statutes (Cao and Dai 2001). The concept of crime was both present and retrospective: red-handed counterrevolutionary and historical counterrevolutionary. Some historical behavior was considered crime again and again in various political campaigns. For example, if a person worked for the previous government, which many people did, it was considered a historical dark point (*lishi wudian*) and would be politically humiliated (self as well as in public) every time when there was a political campaign. This is what Dutton (2004: 167) called "blood on the file." In addition, these labels had severe ramification for those related to labeled persons. Offsprings of those being labeled would not be able to live a normal life because they were born with the original sin. They were not to be treated equally. For whatever perceived bad behavior they may have had, their punishment would be doubled automatically.

The most severe category of crime was not homicide, but anti-revolution, anti-CCP, and anti-Mao. In the name of defending the new regime, about 712,000 people were sentenced to death between 1950 and 1953 during the Campaign to Suppress Counterrevolutionaries – an average of 177,500 per year. It was one of the largest killing of citizens during a peaceful time for any nation. Widespread fabrication of counterrevolutionaries became the order of the day with arbitrary arrests and executions without evidence commonplace (Trevaskes 2012). Yang (2008) notes that the actual number of being executed was likely much higher than the official acknowledged estimates of 712,000. Other scholars put the number of executed people during the Campaign to Suppress Counterrevolutionaries between 1 million and 2 million (Dikotter 2013: 83; Pye 1991: 235; Strauss 2002: 87). Whether such state behavior is state crime ("state violence" according to Zhang 2008; "state terror" according to Strauss 2002; "state killing" according to Trevaskes 2012; "political killing" according to Johnson and Miao) or not is a subject for further exploration (see Chambliss 1989; Green and Ward 2004; and Michalowski 2010, for a detailed discussion of the concept).

The most unique feature of Mao's method of social control was that Mao set the quota of killing at 1 per 1,000 population (Zhang 2008; Yang 2008). The Campaign to Suppress Counterrevolutionaries was not the only campaign during Mao's time (1949–1976), but it was his first large-scale campaign aiming at maintaining a "peaceful" political domestic environment. The campaign was soon followed by the Anti-Rightist Campaign in 1957, the Great Leap Forward in 1958, the Great Famine in 1959–1961, the Socialist Education Movement (or Four-Cleanup Campaign) in 1963–1966, and, finally, the Cultural Revolution from 1966 to his death in 1976. The scale of each campaign increased in size, the number of people in the othering categories grew larger, and the deaths were no longer limited to formal sentencing, but would include thousands of "abnormal deaths." Chen (2001) estimated that non-natural deaths occurring during the Cultural Revolution exceeded 1,700,000 people. In a more meticulous study, using the snowball sampling technique, Wang (2004) revealed that 30.5 percent of the victims died from various torture methods, 65.1 percent committed suicide in order to escape mental and physical torture, and 4.4 percent were sentenced to death for being guilty of counterrevolutionary crimes.

Therefore, it is a total misunderstanding to describe China as a society free of crime as Fairbank once did (1987). It may be true that property violations were lower in those days, but if political crimes and state crime (state execution of people) were included, crime rates were considerably higher. The retrospective crime data, published nowadays, were the result of reinterpreting the history by removing the categories of these "political enemies." If all nine categories of people, anti-Maoists, capitalist roaders, and people in the labor camps, were counted as having committed "crime," the total crime rates would shoot up significantly. Put simply, there was no utopia of a "crime free" period in China and the real story was uglier and more dreadful than anyone could imagine. To understand China under Mao, scholars must never forget the political *episteme*.

After Mao's death in 1976, China began the post-Cultural Revolution process of legal construction (Alford 1995). Within a short period of time, the nation's constitution were rewritten twice and over a hundred laws were promulgated. The nature and functions of the police have slowly shifted from single-minded suppression under the dictatorship toward law enforcement and public services

(Sun and Wu 2010; Wu and Sun 2009) as the nation moved toward becoming a normal society (Cao 2007). Crime categories have become more consistent with the international standard and gradually the right to protection of life and property has been recognized in the Chinese criminal law.

Even so, politics has never been eliminated from the control and punishment of crime (Trevaskes 2011; Wang 2008). The control of crime was repoliticized rather than depoliticized. Although economy has been moving toward the market economics, the society remains under the single-party rule. In its domestic politics, political stability, meaning any imagined or real threat to the CCP monopoly of power, is the overriding concern while crime is a byproduct of that concern. Homicide is again not considered the most heinous category of crime. Instead, economic crimes replaced the counterrevolutionary as the most serious crimes since Deng's reform (Wang 2008).

During the economic reform era, campaigns against crime have been regarded as an effective way to mobilize public support for a regime which has questionable legitimacy (Dutton and Lee 1993; Trevaskes 2004; 2012). The form of the rallies, where several dozen folks gather in a village or several thousands of people congregate in a stadium in a city, remains, but the nature has changed slightly. During Mao's time, the rally was called "Open Trial Rally" (*gongshen dahui*) while during Deng's time, it is called a "mass sentencing rally" (*gongpan dahui*): instead of passing the judgment on the spot based on the emotion of the day, the sentence is decided previously and the judges announce it at the rally – a step forward toward the rule by law.

The Extent of Homicide in China

As a general rule, an authoritarian regime is less transparent than a democratic government. A democratic regime tends to publish more information of all sorts. As with other authoritarian regimes in the world, the CCP regime tends to be secretive and guard their information tightly. The CCP is not a political actor in the state affairs; it is the only actor and it is an integral part of the apparatus of all state affairs (Trevaskes 2011).

Crime data have been considered as sensitive political information for two main reasons. First, they may reveal the reality that China is a peaceful nation. The appearance of peace and stability are maintained in the international eye but with extremely barbaric measures behind the scenes, such as liberal use of capital punishment and brainwashing methods. Second, this practice is consistent with policies of other socialist nations (Robertson 2006) as well as with the Confucian philosophy of keeping people unaware of their real situation.

The combination of its socialist nature and its Confucian tradition justifies the action of keeping crime data secretive. Reform, in this regard, will go beyond the legal arena into the educational system. Confucius (2003) says: "One can make the common people follow a course of action, but must not let them understand why they should do so." (子曰:民可使由之，不可使知之。《论语·第八章·泰伯篇》). In contrast to this Chinese tradition, democratic education aims at producing citizens that are well informed to be educated voters. While skills, another goal of education, are important, equally important is the liberal arts tradition where the development of kids' critical thinking is vital.

Ever since the idea of democracy became an aspiration rather than a fear or threat, political scientists have argued that citizens must be knowledgeable. Thomas Jefferson prescribed one measure, "without which no republic can maintain itself in strength": that of general education, "to enable every man to judge for himself what will secure or endanger his freedom" (Thomas Jefferson to John Tyler, 1810, in Jefferson 1903–1904: vol. 12, p. 393). Political scientists concur that a knowledgeable citizenry is necessary for effective and gratifying democratic governance. As Michael Delli Carpini and Scott Keeter put it in the most authoritative study on the subject,

> Factual knowledge about politics is a critical component of citizenship, one that is essential if citizens are to discern their real interests and take effective advantage of the civic opportunities afforded them .... Knowledge is a keystone to other civic requisites. In the absence of adequate information neither passion nor reason is likely to lead to decisions that reflect the real interests of the public. And democratic principles must be understood to be accepted and acted on in any meaningful way. (Delli Carpini and Keeter 1996: 3, 5)

The Chinese government has been firm in keeping crime data secretive, but it has published some "clean data" under international pressure. The "clean" homicide rates published by the Chinese government before 1979 were not to be used. The political nature and the legal nature were totally mixed up to the point of being inseparable. The lower rates of homicide were not to be believed. As Li (1978) observes, China was not a society based on formal law during Mao's time. Even without laws, social control was tighter (Li 1996) and repression of deviant thinking and behavior was severe, instant, and brutal (Cao 2007). The abolished laws of Qing Dynasty and the Republic of China were actually very sophisticated in their definitions of homicide, intentional or negligent (Neighbors 2014).

As Deng Xiaoping changed the course of China's development and decided to lead China out of its isolation, official crime data began to be more normal and great progress has been made toward more usable crime data based on criminal codes that are similar in definitions to the international standard since the 1980s. Even so, crime has been greatly underestimated in China and severely manipulated (Cao and Dai 2001; Dutton and Lee 1993; He and Marshall 1997; Yu and Zhang 1999). It is true everywhere that underreporting is related to the seriousness of offense. Serious crimes are less likely to be underreported. In China, however, even the most serious form of violent crimes – homicide – has the problem of being buried at the bottom of the bureaucratic hierarchy and being inconsistent with the international standard.

Statistical recording are always political, more so in China than elsewhere. A body is found in a place. A police officer arrives at the scene. The first decision is whether it is a victim of homicide, a victim of suicide, a victim of unintentional killing, or simply a death by heart attack, and so on. How a crime is recorded depends on who is doing the recording, what the statistic is for, and the occupational and physical location of the recorded event. When treated as a contextual performance, such as a measure of police performance, the situated work of counting is subject to practical, organizational, and political contingencies.

The number of homicides is part of statistics that is part of police work. While all police officers are subject to similar contingencies when recording the number of homicides, there are unique situations that police officers in China have to face. Legal philosophy, cultural values, and political ideology shape citizen reporting and officer recording practices in China (He and Marshall 1997).

There are four sources of inaccuracy of homicide data in China (Wang 2015). First, the definition of homicide; second, the counting of a homicide; third, the collection and recording of data; and fourth, political manipulation of data.

Most democracies use the definition of homicide by the UN (He *et al.* 2003): intentional homicide is defined as "unlawful death purposefully inflicted on a person by another person." For the sake of simplicity, the term "homicide" is used throughout as shorthand for "intentional homicide."

In China, the homicide data sent to the United Nations state that it is data of "established homicide cases" (*li-an-shu*), not cases of homicide. There is a huge difference between the two concepts. For an established homicide case, the case must first be determined as a case of homicide, then the case would have to be resolved, and would have to be prosecuted in the courts. This is similar to the concept of cleared cases in the United States, not a homicide case. If a dead body is found and nobody ended up being arrested for it, it might not be an established case in police statistics in China.

Second, an established case of homicide refers to situations of both mass murderer and series murderer. In the U.S.A., a case of homicide is based on a victim's body. If a murderer kills ten victims on a spree, there will be ten homicide cases. Similarly, if a murderer kills five victims over a period of ten years, there will be five homicide cases in the police report. In China, these hypothetical examples would have been counted as one established case each.

Third, the pressure of resolving all homicide cases have been so great that many cases are deliberately classified into other categories, such as accidents, suicide, negligence, and so on, in order to please their superiors (Dai 1994; Dutton and Lee 1993). Unless the case becomes well known, it is very easy for the police to cover it up. Geographically unbalanced development makes homicide data from the rural and remote inland incomparable with the big cities and coastal areas, where data are in general more reliable.

Fourth, the police chief could make a decision to suppress the number of cases without much consequence because all police operations are secretive, public surveillance is impossible, and the internal supervision in this regard is not strict. There is a general tendency of indifference toward the real number at every level of administration. This is different from underreporting; it is a unique situation called "burying cases." The underreporting happens when a case has not been brought to the attention of the police. Burying cases occurs when the case is filed at the lower level of the police bureau, but it does not show up in the report to the upper level of police hierarchy. It is estimated that as much as 12 percent of established homicide cases were lost because of neglecting to report to superiors (Yu and Zhang 1999). This is different from many underdeveloped societies where data were simply not collected.

All the above reasons result in an underestimation. The official homicide rate in China, therefore, is severely underestimated. While the first and second situations are systemic in nature (or they have fixed effect on data accuracy), the errors could be reasonably estimated. The third and fourth circumstances are quite variable (or they have variable effects on each year's data quality). The reported rates depend on the leadership and political environment. As a result, their effects on homicide data quality are quite unpredictable. One of the unique problems of homicide data in China is that of burying the information at the bottom of the police bureaucratic hierarchy.

The homicide number and rate reported to the United Nations are the established cases of homicides. Underestimated as they are, some data are better than no data at all. The homicide rates in China are reported in Table 26.1 (UNODC 2013). The trend of homicide seems clear: the homicide rate has been declining since 2001, and in ten years, the rate has been cut by half: from about 2 per 100,000 in 2002 to 1 per 100,000 population in 2010.

Examining the homicide rates within the region, the rates of homicide published by the Chinese government look normal. Table 26.2 lists all neighboring societies of China with an emphasis on the Confucian and Buddhism traditions (Moody 1988). The homicide rate is as high as in Mongolia (9/100,000) and as low as in Singapore (0.2/100,000). China's homicide rate sits close to the mean. The relatively

Table 26.1 Homicide number and rates in China from 2002 to 2011 (UN data: https://www.unodc.org/gsh/en/data.html).

Years	*Number of homicides*	*Rate per 100,000*
2001	27,501	2.1
2002	26,776	2.0
2003	24,393	1.9
2004	24,711	1.9
2005	20,770	1.6
2006	17,973	1.4
2007	16,119	1.2
2008	14,811	1.1
2009	14,667	1.1
2010	13,410	1.0

Table 26.2 Homicide rates in Confucian/Buddhism societies.

Country	*Rate/100,000*
China	1.0
Hong Kong	0.4
Japan	0.3
Macao	0.7
Mongolia	9.7
North Korea	5.2
South Korea	0.4
Singapore	0.2
Taiwan	2.9
Vietnam	3.3

Data from "United Nations Office on Drugs and Crime, 2013"

low rate of homicide in China cannot be attributed entirely to the communist rule. For non-communist societies, like Hong Kong, Japan, and Singapore, homicide rates are even lower. The Confucian/Buddhist societies have the homicide rates as low as Japan and Singapore (0.3/100,000 and 0.2/100,000 respectively) and as high as Mongolia and North Korea (9.7/100,000 and 5.2/100,000). Democratic regimes cannot take too much credit either because homicide rates are significantly higher in Mongolia and in Taiwan. If Mongolia remains in the democratic transition when a high crime rate is expected, Taiwan has reached the stage of democratic consolidation (Cao, Huang, and Sun 2014), when the crime rate is expected to decline, which is the case, but not closer to South Korea or Japan yet.

Two key elements of data quality are important from a statistical perspective: the accuracy of the data (i.e., how closely data represent the reality of the situation) and the international comparability of the data. Accuracy relates to how close the homicide count is to the standard definition of international homicide. Since 1979, the quality of homicide data in China has greatly improved and data have become more comparable internationally. Discrepancies with the "true value" can be due to weaknesses in data collection systems, such as incomplete coverage of the events and/or misrepresentation of the data. Both coverage and misrepresentation exist in Chinese homicide data. In addition, there is an unknown number of buried crime data, homicide included, at the bottom of the bureaucratic hierarchy. In more developed democracies, it is possible to check the accuracy through different sources of information. For instance, a homicide is often recorded by both criminal justice and public health sources. If the two sources match each other closely, then we can say the data have a high degree of accuracy. In nations like China, there has been up to now only one source of information.

Homicide and Capital Punishment: Why is China a Retentionist Nation?

Almost without exception, every political regime in the world at some point or another used the death penalty. The abolition movement is relatively new, and it began to spread after World War II as an indication that human development has reached a higher state of civilization where life is valued more than anything else. It gained worldwide momentum in the 1980s when the number of nations without the death penalty surpassed the number of nations with capital punishment.

Contrary to the global abolitionist trend, capital punishment has continued to be widely used in China. Unlike nations who retain the death penalty only for homicide with aggravated circumstances or only for exceptional crimes, such as crimes committed under military law or in wartime, there are 55 different crimes that are subject to the death penalty in China (Lewis 2014; Liang 2016; Trevaskes 2012). This is some progress because China's newly revised criminal law became effective on February 25, 2011. Before that date, the number of crimes subject to the death penalty grew from 28 in 1979 at the beginning of the reform to 68. Homicide is only one of the crimes that are subject to capital punishment. Among others are embezzlement, rape (particularly of children), fraud, bombing, people trafficking, piracy, corruption, arson, poaching, endangerment of national security, and terrorism. Xiong (2016) shows that capital punishment is largely applied to violent and drug related criminals in practice even though the majority of criminal behavior subject to capital punishment are economic in nature.

As argued previously, political stability, meaning any imagined or real threat to the CCP monopoly of power, is the overriding concern in its domestic politics while crime is a byproduct of that concern. Homicide, arguably the worst violation of criminal laws in most democratic societies (UNODC 2013), is not regarded as the most serious crime category in the minds of Chinese leaders. While rallies are held to frighten would-be criminals and to educate the general public during both Mao's time and Deng's time, there is a key difference: in the post-Mao time, law rather than solely party policy became an organizing device for the death penalty, which eliminated killing outside the law and reduced the chances of arbitrariness, fabrication, and repression of political-legal practices so commonplace during Mao's time (Trevaskes 2004).

According to Amnesty International (2014), there were 21 countries which carried out executions in 2013. The top three nations who executed its own citizens were China, Iran, and Iraq. The number of execution in China was unknown, but it is believed that the number is larger than the rest of the world's executions added together. Therefore, both in number and proportion, China is the leading state executioner of its own citizens in the world (Trevaskes 2012; Zimring and Johnson 2008). "Whatever country is in second place is not close" (Johnson and Zimring 2009: 232). Although many Chinese are proud of being considered a civilized and peaceful people, its death penalty record speaks differently and loudly. The only other nation which did not provide even an estimated number of executions in 2013 was North Korea.

The death penalty in the United States was a legal sentence in 32 states in 2013. Its application is limited by the Eighth Amendment to the US Constitution to aggravated murders committed by mentally competent adults. It is important to note that 18 states do not have the death penalty. Michigan led the nation in abolishing the death penalty as early as 1846 and it remains so despite the fact that Detroit leads the nation in its homicide rates for many years.

Hong Kong and Macau, both of which share the Chinese culture and tradition, have separate legal systems and both have abolished the death penalty (Johnson and Miao 2016). Even when they had the death penalty on their books, both colonies used it very rarely. The last time Hong Kong used the death penalty was in 1966 and it was officially abolished in 1993 under the then British colonial government. In Macau, it was last used in the nineteenth century and it was abolished in 1976 when Portugal abolished the death penalty in all its territories. Therefore, culture is not a reason to retain the death penalty.

The liberal use of capital punishment has never been a "Chinese tradition" (Cao 2012). In a comparative light, Bakken (2014: 40) observed that "The Chinese imperial tradition was by no means harsher than the regime of executions and punishments practiced in Europe at the same time." Similarly, cited by Bakken, Muhlhahn reported that "When compared to the execution of corporal punishments in early modern Europe … The executions in late imperial China were no match for the ferocious events staged in eighteenth-century Europe."

Brook, Bourgon, and Blue (2008) concluded that *lingchi* (death by a thousand cuts) was rarely practiced in China and its abolition must be seen not only as a product of adopting elements of Western law but as deeply rooted in native elite antipathy to the practice. Throughout the history of its use, it encountered strong opposition among Chinese scholars and officials who felt it undermined the ethical boundaries of the law.

According to Qian (2009), Confucius (551–479 BCE) was the only sage in the world during his time who opposed the liberal use of capital punishment as a way of social control. He argues that the state should cultivate the rites (*li*) and the ruler should set a virtuous example by his own behavior and choose virtuous men to staff his government (Cao and Cullen 2001). Rule by punishment was to be avoided at all costs, as it would lead people to obey out of fear and not the goodness in their hearts (He 2014a). Confucius (2003) also emphasizes the importance of legal procedure when he says that "Putting a man to death without giving him any judicial instruction beforehand is called cruelty." (子曰:不教而杀谓之虐。《论语·第二十章·尧曰篇2》). Wang (2006) examines the history of "careful sentencing" (*shenxing*) since the Han Dynasty and concludes that the practice of careful sentencing of the death penalty prevailed in the history of China during peaceful times. Cao (2012), therefore, argues that the liberal use of the death penalty is not a Chinese tradition per se, but a more recent revolutionary tradition started by Mao.

The liberal use of capital punishment as an effective way of social control was a new revolutionary tradition since 1949. It can be traced back to the late 1920s when Mao first began his revolutionary career (Dutton 2005; Zhang 2008). When the CCP institutionalized the binary divide between friends and enemies, when the CCP advocated to treat the enemies like "the fall wind to the fallen leaves" (merciless), and when Mao openly defied the international condemnation of executing counter-revolutionaries so recklessly without any procedural prudence, the liberal use of the death penalty symbolized the CCP's unchallenged monopoly of state power in China.

Mao is responsible for the liberal use of capital punishment (Cao 2012; Johnson and Miao 2016; Zhang 2008). Like Lenin, who saw it as an indispensable tool of proletarian power, "Mao was a fervent partisan of capital punishment, particular because he believed that it played a dissuasive function when carried out on a large scale" (Zhang 2008: 118). The law was reduced to a simple instrument of control and repression. During Mao's time, the class divide between class enemies and the people justified this liberal use of capital punishment. During Deng's economic reform, the CCP apparatus was changed from totalitarianism to "consultative authoritarianism" (Teets 2013). Even so, Mao's legacy left its indelible mark on Deng's reform era. Deng Xiaoping altered Mao's political killing to judicial execution (Johnson and Miao 2016) and continued to use similar strategies, such as public rally, and political rhetoric, such as mass line (Trevaskes 2004), for his rule. In addition, he instructed the Standing Committee of the Communist Party Political Bureau in January 1986 that it cannot be abolished (cited by Scobell 1990).

Isolated voices calling for the immediate abolition of capital punishment have been heard occasionally (He 2011; Qiu 2002). The heated debate in China regarding the death penalty, however, has not focused on whether to abolish it or not, but rather on how it should be used and reduced (Chen 2009; Trevaskes 2012; Zhang 2005). It is not an issue of whether to kill or not, but an issue of killing fewer and killing more carefully (Trevaskes 2012).

Public opinion is frequently cited as a reason in defense of using capital punishment and even as an excuse to justify its retention (Zhang 2009). Indeed, the support for the death penalty in China is comparably high with that of US citizens (Jiang and Wang 2008; Qi and Oberwittler 2009). The percentage of Americans who supported the death penalty ranged from 66 percent to 79 percent in the 1990s (Cullen, Fisher, and Applegate 2000; Stack 2004). When direct comparison is possible, the support for the death penalty is, in general, higher among Chinese than citizens of other nations (Cao and Cullen 2001; Jiang, Lambert, and Wang 2007; Jiang *et al.* 2010; Qi and Oberwittler 2009; Wu, Sun, and Wu 2011). While the results of these studies are comparable, the political environments are not. Before 2000, the death penalty was a taboo topic in China (Zhang 2009) and no meaningful national attention had been paid to its use. Furthermore, no wrongful conviction had attracted the attention of the public. The blind faith of the system's infallibility might be one of the driving forces for the higher percentage of support. More recently, high profiled cases (Jiang 2013; Liang 2016), such as Zhao Zuohai and the 18-year-old Hugjiltu (also known as Qoysiletu), raised the public awareness of the injustice and unfairness of the system (Haas 2014). These cases will surely cast doubt on the ability of the current criminal justice administration to deliver impartial sentences to everyone under its control.

In addition, the high support rates for the death penalty indicate that China is suffused with repressed criminal impulses seeking an outlet, vicarious or otherwise. Once someone is caught breaking the law, fulfilling the unconscious desires for aggression, the law breaker can be made to shoulder the guilt people refuse to accept. The CCP has been a mastermind in spreading the hatred among the masses, especially among the younger generation, attacking Confucius's idea of benevolence and the Western idea of mercy as the ruling classes' hypocrisy and deceit. The popular movies of *Little Soldier Zhang Ga* (1963, directed by Cui Wei) and *Sparkling Red Star* (1974, directed by Li Jun) inoculate hatred into peasant kids' innocent minds and encourage underage children to kill political enemies. Miao (2013) argues that the demand of the masses for revenge and justice have been translated into a fervent passion for capital punishment. The public is secure in the knowledge that they are the good people, vehement in their rejection of the criminal and attaching a high degree of importance to the feeling of security that comes with the expectation that evil meets with its just deserts. By reaching out to satisfy these public demands and sentiments, the party state hopes to enhance the political legitimacy (Dutton and Lee 1993; Trevaskes 2004). The death penalty serves as a penal populist mechanism to strengthen the resilience of the authoritarian party state by venting public anxiety and resentment toward social problems created in the process of rapid modernization and social fragmentation.

The death penalty in China is thus political at heart (Trevaskes 2012; Wang 2008). It is not a purely legal subject, nor is it a cultural issue. Capital punishment has remained important as a way for the CCP to assuage intense political and social instability and to preserve its rule.

Conclusion

As the last of the communist old guard acquiesces in the move from Mao and Marx to market economics, China is in transition, which has been characterized by emergence of a slew of private property, a more private sphere, more autonomy for intellectual life, and the attention paid to legal procedure. With the tardy progress of China's legal project, the definitions of crime have become closer to the international standard. Yet, homicide is still not regarded as the most serious violation of law that worries the regime. A substantial increase in criminal activity has taken place since the reform. Instead of saying the crime is a silent companion of economic reform in China (Bakken 2005; Hebenton and Jou 2010; Jou, Hebenton, and Cao 2014), this essay argues that crime is an inevitable consequence of the transition into the market economy as people were liberated from dreadful ideology control and are allowed to explore new opportunities in a changed environment. As the social stratification enlarges, crime of all sorts increases as a result (Cao and Dai 2001; Lo and Jiang 2006; Shi and Wu 2010; Whyte 2010; Zhang, Cao, and Vaughn 2009; Zhao and Cao 2010).

Official crime statistics, especially homicide data, are a vital part of academic inquiry. The published crime data are severely underestimated. Total counts and rates of homicide only provide an opaque insight into the nature of violent crime in China. Better data should be able to disaggregate homicide by a number of characteristics, such as gender of offenders and victims, the relationships, weapons used, motivation, geographic unit, and so on, so that the causes and correlations of homicide can be studies (see Cao, Hou, and Huang 2008; Hilal *et al.* 2014). Without disaggregated quality information, an evidence-based social policy of control cannot be proposed. Crime control through repression is not compatible with the rule of law. The submitted homicide data are not yet in line with the worldwide homicide data. Limited availability, restricted access, and underestimation of crime statistics (including homicide) identified by He and Marshall (1997) were and remain the major problems in the study of crime.

China's economic reform has unleashed the pressure on criminal justice systems for a more civilized approach to criminals as the civilization theory has suggested: as nations modernize, structural changes engender personality changes, resulting in the control of individual behavior shifting from external sanctions to internal self-control (Elias 1982; Heiland and Shelley 1992). The essence of civilization theory is consistent with Confucius' teachings on the internalization of societal norms. The outcry for abolishing capital punishment is consistent with the teachings of Confucius and the civilization theory.

Zooming in historically, China's legal construction project has made great progress from the blunt legal nihilism during Mao's time (He 2014a). Zooming out globally, China has a long way to catch up with the international prevailing criminal justice practices. The censure of corruption under the new leader of Xi Jinping is popular, but it fails to convince the world that it is different from all the previous regimes' efforts in their fights against corruption. Instead, it may be similar to all those failed efforts in Chinese history because it is seen as a political weapon for the pursuit of factional interest, and not simply as an earnest drive against widespread bureaucratic corruption. Genuine anti-corruption must rely on the rule of law, not the rule by law, or even worse, rule by man. The new guiding cases issued by the Supreme People's Court are a welcome new mechanism to improve consistency in adjudication across jurisdictions and geographical boundaries (Ahl 2014). The recent death penalty for Jia Jinglong (贾敬龙) put the policy of "Killing fewer and killing more carefully" on trial. The tighter control of the media and the educational system and targeting outspoken reform scholars and lawyers by the regime do not fare well to instill confidence in the system. China has made good progress in economic development since Deng, and is continuing its metamorphosis. Legal consciousness is rising slowly but steadily. Disenchantment with the the legal system does not lead to despondency for many Chinese, but to more critical and informed action (Gallagher 2006). Increased reliance on the legal system and a concerted attempt to replace mass campaigns and administrative rule with a thin version of "rule of law" (Peerenboom 2002) has been an indicator of China's progress. We are hopeful.

References

Ahl, B. (2014) Retaining judicial professionalism: The new guiding cases mechanism of the Supreme People's Court. *The China Quarterly*, 217: 121–139.

Alford, W.P. (1995) Tasselled loafers for barefoot lawyers: Transformation and tension in the world of Chinese legal workers. *The China Quarterly*, 141: 22–38.

Amnesty International (2014) *Death Sentences and Executions 2013*. London: Amnesty International Publications.

Bakken, B. (ed.) (2005) *Crime, Punishment and Policing in China*. Lanham, MD: Rowman and Littlefield Publishers.

Bakken, B. (2014) Punishment in China. In *The Routledge Handbook of Chinese Criminology* edited by L. Cao, I. Sun, and B. Hebention, 38–48. London: Routledge.

Brook, T., Bourgon, J., & Blue, G. (2008) *Death by a Thousand Cuts*. Cambridge, MA: Harvard University Press.

Cao, L. (2007) Returning to normality: Anomie and crime in China. *International Journal of Offender Therapy and Comparative Criminology*, 51 (1): 40–51.

Cao, L. (2012) Column editor's comments on death penalty. *Issues on Juvenile Crimes and Delinquency* (in Chinese) 182: 27–28.

Cao, L. & Cullen, F.T. (2001) Thinking about crime and control: A comparative study of Chinese and American ideology. *International Criminal Justice Review*, 11: 58–81.

Cao, L. & Dai, Y. (2001) Inequality and crime in China. In *Crime and Social Control in a Changing China*, edited by J. Liu, L. Zhang, and S.E. Messner, 73–85. Westport, CT: Greenwood Press.

Cao, L., Hou, C., & Huang, B. (2008) Correlates of victim offender relationship in homicide. *International Journal of Offender Therapy and Comparative Criminology*, 52 (6): 658–672.

Cao, L., Huang, L., & Sun, I.Y. (2014) *Policing in Taiwan: From Authoritarianism to Democracy*. London: Routledge.

Cao, L., Sun, I.Y., & Hebenton, B. (2014) Introduction: Discovering and making criminology in China. In *The Routledge Handbook of Chinese Criminology*, edited by L. Cao, I. Sun, and B. Hebenton, xvi–xxvii. London: Routledge.

Chambliss, W.J. (1989) State-organized crime. *Criminology*, 27 (2): 183–208.

Chen, X. (2009) A study on the death penalty as applied to those engaged in the transportation of drugs. *Chinese Sociology and Anthropology*, 41 (4): 48–65.

Chen, Y. (2001) *The 70 Years of the Community Revolution in China* (in Chinese). Taipei: Lianjing.

Confucius (2003) *Confucius Analects*, translated by Edward Slingerland. Indianapolis, IN: Hackett.

Cullen, F.T., Fisher, B., & Applegate, B. (2000) Public opinion about punishment and corrections. *Crime and Justice: A Review of Research*, edited by M. Tonry, 27: 1–79.

Dai, Y. (1994) *On the Policies of Public Security* (in Chinese). (Series on Studies of China's Juvenile Crime and Delinquency). Chongqing: Chongqing chubanshe.

Delli Carpini, M. and Keeter, S. (1996) *What Americans Know About Politics and Why It Matters*. New Haven CT: Yale University Press.

Dikotter, F. (1997) Crime and Punishment in Post-Liberation China: The Prisoners of a Beijing Gaol in the 1950s. *The China Quarterly*, 149: 147–159.

Dikotter, F. (2013) The Chinese Revolution and "Liberation": Whose Tragedy? London: Bloomsbury.

Dodgson, C.L. (1865) *Alice's Adventures in Wonderland*.

Dutton, M.R. (1992) *Policing and Punishment in China*. Cambridge: Cambridge University Press.

Dutton, M.R. (2004) Mango Mao: Infections of the sacred. *Public Culture*, 16 (2): 161–187.

Dutton, M.R. (2005) *Policing Chinese Politics: A History*. Durham, NC: Duke University Press.

Dutton, M.R. & Lee, T. (1993) Missing the target? Police strategies in the period of economic reform. *Crime and Delinquency*, 39 (3): 316–36.

Eddy, U. (2007) Disorganizing China: Counter-Bureaucracy and the Decline of Socialism. Stanford, CA: Stanford University Press.

Elias, N. (1982) The Civilizing Process, Volume 2: Power and civility. New York: Pantheon.

Fairbank, J.K. (1987) *The Great Chinese Revolution: 1800–1985*. New York: Harper & Row.

Fu, H. (2005) Zhou Yongkang and the recent police reform in China. *The Australian and New Zealand Journal of Criminology*, 38 (2): 241–253.

Gallagher, M.E. (2006) Mobilizing the law in China. *Law & Society Review* 40 (4): 783–816.

Green, P. & Ward, T. (2004) *State Crime: Governments, Violence and Corruption*. London: Pluto Press.

Haas, B. (2014) Executed Chinese teenager found innocent 18 years later. Available online at http://news.yahoo.com/executed-chinese-teenager-found-innocent-18-years-071629483.html;_ylt=A0LEVjQXVs5UDrcAToQnnIlQ;_ylu=X3oDMTEzcmVjM2ZsBHNlYwNzcgRwb3MDMQRjb2xvA2JmMQR2dGlkA0FDQlgwNV8x (accessed January 18, 2015).

He, N. (2014a) Chinese Criminal Trials: A Comprehensive Empirical Inquiry. New York: Springer.

He, N. (2014b) The politics of numbers: Crime statistics in China. In *The Routledge Handbook of Chinese Criminology* edited by L. Cao, I. Sun, and B. Hebenton, 147–159. London: Routledge.

He, N., Cao, L., Wells, W., and Maguire, E. (2003) Forces of production and of direction: A test of an expanded model of suicide and homicide. *Homicide Studies*, 7 (1): 36–57.

He, N. & Marshall, I. (1997) Social production of crime data: A critical examination of Chinese crime statistics. *International Criminal Justice Review*, 7: 46–63.

He, W. (2011) Return justice for evil: He Weifang discusses the death penalty (in Chinese). Available online at http://www.legaldaily.com.cn/fxy/content/2011-06/02/content_2710699_2.htm (accessed February 9, 2015).

Hebenton, B. & Jou, S. (2010) Criminology in and on China: discipline and power. *Journal of Contemporary Criminal Justice*, 26: 7–19.

Heiland, H.-G. & Shelley, L. (1992) Civilization, modernization, and the development of crime and control. In H. Heiland, L. Shelley, and H. Katoh (Eds.), *Crime, and control in comparative perspectives* (pp. 1–20). New York: Walter de Gruyter.

Hilal, S.M., Densley, J.A., Li, S.D., & Ma, Y. (2014) The routine of mass murder in China. *Homicide Studies*, 18 (1): 83–104.

Huang, P.C.C. (2013) Misleading Chinese legal and statistical categories. *Modern China*, 39 (4): 347–379.

Jefferson, T. (1903–1904). *The Writings of Thomas Jefferson, Memorial Edition, 20 Volumes*. Washington, D.C: Thomas Jefferson Memorial Association.

Jiang, N. (2013) The adequacy of China's responses to wrongful convictions. *International Journal of Law, Crime and Justice*, 41: 390–404.

Jiang, S., Lambert, E.G., & Wang, J. (2007) Capital punishment views in China and the United States: A preliminary study among college students. *International Journal of Offender Therapy and Comparative Criminology*, 51 (1): 84–97.

Jiang, S., Lambert, E.G., Wang, J., *et al.* (2010) Death penalty views in China, Japan and the US: An empirical comparison. *Journal of Criminal Justice*, 38: 862–869.

Jiang, S. and Wang, J. (2008) Correlates of support for capital punishment in China. *International Criminal Justice Review*, 18(1), 24–38.

Johnson, D.T. & Miao, M. (2016) Chinese capital punishment in comparative perspective. Pp. 300–326 in *The Death Penalty in China*, edited by B. Liang and H. Lu. New York: Columbia University Press.

Johnson, D.T. & Zimring, F.E. (2009) *The Next Frontier: National Development, Political Change, and the Death Penalty in Asia*. New York, NY: Oxford University Press.

Jou, S., Hebenton, B., & Cao, L. (2014) The development of criminology in modern China. In *The Routledge Handbook of Chinese Criminology* edited by L. Cao, I. Sun, and B. Hebenton, 16–26. London: Routledge.

Lewis, M.K. (2014) Legal systems in China. In *The Routledge Handbook of Chinese Criminology* edited by L. Cao, I. Sun, and B. Hebenton, 51–63. London: Routledge.

Li, J. (1996) The structural strains of China's socio-legal system: A transition to formal legalism?' *International Journal of the Sociology of Law*, 24:41–59.

Li, V. (1978) *Law without Lawyers*. Boulder, CO: Westview Press.

Liang, B. (2016) China's death penalty practice: Working progress, struggle, and challenges with the global abolition movement. Pp. 1–30 in *The Death Penalty in China*, edited by B. Liang and H. Lu. New York: Columbia University Press.

Lieberthal, K. (2003) *Governing China: From Revolution to Reform*. New York, NY: W.W. Norton & Co.

Lo, T.W. & Jiang, G. (2006) Inequality, crime and the floating population in China. *Asian Journal of Criminology* 1 (2): 103–118.

Mao, Z. (1967) 1927. A report of Hunan peasant movement. *Selected Works of Mao Zedong* (in Chinese), Vol. 1. Beijing: Remin chubanshe.

Martin, A. & Lynch, M. (2009) Counting things and people: The practices and politics of counting. *Social Problems*, 56 (2): 243–266.

Miao, M. (2013) Capital punishment in China: A populist instrument of social governance. *Theoretical Criminology*, 17 (2): 233–250.

Michalowski, R. (2010) In search of state and crime in state crime studies. Pp. 13–30 in W.J. Chambliss, R. Michalowski and R.C. Kramer (eds.), *State Crime in the Global Age*. Devon: Willan.

Moody, P.R., Jr (1988) *Political Opposition in Post-Confucian Society*, New York: Praeger.

Neighbors, J.M. (2014) *Guoshi* killing: The continuum of criminal intent in Qing and Republican China. *Modern China*, 40 (3): 243–281.

Peerenboom, R. (2002) *China's Long March Toward Rule of Law*. New York: Cambridge University Press.

Pye, L.W. (1991) China: An introduction. 4th edition. New York: HarperCollins Publishers Inc.

Qi, S. & Oberwittler, D. (2009) On the road of law: Crime, crime control, and public opinion in China. *European Journal on Criminal Policy Research*, 15: 137–157.

Qian, M. (2009) The three religions in the world. In *The Beginning of Chinese History* by Mu Qian, 262–273 (in Chinese). Beijing: the United Bookstore.

Qiu, X. (2002) The virtue of capital punishment. *Politics and Law* (in Chinese). 2: 51–54.

Robertson, A. (2006) The significance of language, culture, and communication in researching post-Soviet crime and policing. Journal of Contemporary Criminal Justice, 22 (2): 137–156.

Scobell, A. (1990) The death penalty in post Mao China. *The China Quarterly* 123: 503–520.

Shi, J. & Wu, X. (2010) An empirical study on China's regional income inequality, floating population and criminal offense rates. *Journal of Zhejiang University* (in Chinese), 40: 73–84.

Stack, S. (2004) Public opinion on the death penalty: Analysis of individual-level data from 17 nations. *International Criminal Justice Review*, 14 (1): 69–98.

Strauss, J.C. (2002) Paternalist terror: The campaign to suppress counterrevolutionaries and regime consolidation in the People's Republic of China, 1950–1953. *Comparative Studies in Society and History*, 44 (1); 80–105.

Sun, I. & Wu, Y. (2010) Chinese policing in a time of transition, 1978–2008. *Journal of Contemporary Criminal Justice*, 26, 20–35.

Teets, J.C. (2013) Let many civil societies bloom: The rise of consultative authoritarianism in China. *The China Quarterly*, 213: 19–38.

Trevaskes, S. (2004) Propaganda work in China courts. *Punishment and Society*, 6 (1), 5–21.

Trevaskes, S. (2011) Political ideology, the party and politicking: Justice system reform in China. *Modern China*, 37 (3): 315–344.

Trevaskes, S. (2012) *The Death Penalty in Contemporary China*. New York: Palgrave Macmillan.

UNODC (United Nations Office on Drugs and Crime) (2013) *Global Study on Homicide 2013: Trends, Contexts, Data*. Vienna: UNODC.

Wang, H. (2006) *On capital review procedure of Qing Dynasty* (in Chinese). Available online at http://jyw.znufe.edu.cn/flsxsw/articleshow.asp?id=2220 (accessed on February 9, 2015).

Wang, J. (2015) The differences in the rules in comparative studies. *Journal of People's Public Security University of China* (in Chinese) 174: 21–28.

Wang, Y. (2004) Victims of the Cultural Revolution: An investigative account of persecution, imprisonment and murder, 1966–1976 (in Chinese). Hong Kong: Kaifang zazhi chubanshe.

Wang, Y. (2008) The death penalty and society in contemporary China. *Punishment & Society*, 10: 137–151.

Whyte, M.K. (2010) The paradoxes of rural-urban inequality in contemporary China. In: Whyte, M. (Ed.), *One Country, Two Societies: Rural-urban Inequality in Contemporary China*, 1–25. Cambridge, MA: Harvard University Press.

Wu, Y. & Sun, I. (2009) Citizen trust in police: The case of China. *Police Quarterly*, 12: 170–191.

Wu, Y., Sun, I.Y., & Wu, Z. (2011) Support for the death penalty: Chinese and American college student compared. *Punishment & Society*, 13 (3): 354–376.

Xiong, M. (2016) Death penalty after the restoration of centralized review. Pp. 214–246 in *The Death Penalty in China*, edited by B. Liang and H. Lu. New York: Columbia University Press.

Yang, K. (2008) Reconsidering the Campaign to Suppress Counterrevolutionaries. *The China Quarterly*, 193:102–121.

Yu, O. & Zhang, L. (1999) The under-recording of crime by police in China. *Policing*, 22: 252–263.

Zhang, M.-K. (2005) How Criminal Scholars Should Contribute to Diminishing Death Penalty. *Contemporary Law Review* (in Chinese), 19 (1): 3–13.

Zhang, N. (2008) The political origins of death penalty exceptionalism: Mao Zedong and the practice of capital punishment in contemporary China. *Punishment & Society*, 10 (2): 117–136.

Zhang, N. (2009) The debate on the abolition of capital punishment as applied to economic crimes in China. *Chinese Sociology and Anthropology*, 41 (4): 3–13.
Zhang, Y., Cao, L., & Vaughn, M.S. (2009) Social support and corruption: Structural determinants of corruption in the world. *Australian and New Zealand Journal of Criminology*, 42 (2): 204–217.
Zhao, R. & Cao, L. (2010) Social change and anomie — A cross-national study. *Social Forces*, 88 (3): 1209–1229.
Zimring, F. & Johnson, D. (2008) Law, society, and capital punishment in Asia. *Punishment & Society*, 10 (2): 103–115.

Further Reading

Cao, L., Sun, I. Y. & Bill Hebenton, B. (editors). (2014) *The Routledge Handbook of Chinese Criminology*. London: Routledge.

27

Homicide in India
Historical and Contemporary Perspectives

K. Jaishankar and Debarati Halder

Introduction

हत्या ("Hatya"), killing or homicide, is a socially unethical act well recognized by the Indian criminal justice system since ancient times. Similar to other criminal law jurisprudences, the modern Indian criminal law jurisprudence also categorizes homicide into two categories: (1) lawful or simple homicide and (2) unlawful homicide. However, it is interesting to note that even though the modern criminal law in India, including the Indian penal code, was originally made by the colonial rulers and although legal provisions regulating traditional crimes, including culpable homicide, murder, and so on, were made in the shadow of English criminal laws, the concepts of intentional and accidental homicide were present in ancient Indian scripts dating back to 200 BCE to 100 BCE (Jaishankar and Haldar 2004).

In India, criminal justice administration has been influenced by culture, religion, and colonization, namely, the Hindu religion and culture, Muslim religion and culture, and British colonization. The recognition and categorization of homicide have developed based on the above. The penology of homicide has also undergone changes accordingly. The ancient Hindu culture introduced the theory of "sin," which played a major role in correctional administration in relation to simple homicide cases or homicides of lesser gravity. While the ancient scriptures also prescribed severe punishments for other categories of homicides, the Muslim invasion brought in different understandings regarding homicide and related punishments. The colonial rulers, on the other hand, introduced homicide laws which were partly influenced by English laws and colonial cultures of punishing the killers of members of the ruling community, and partly influenced by existing Hindu and Muslim cultures and laws regarding homicide.

The Handbook of Homicide, First Edition. Edited by Fiona Brookman,
Edward R. Maguire, and Mike Maguire.

Interestingly, some categorization of homicide has existed since ancient times and this includes killing in self-defense, killing under provocation, killing of women and unborn children, and so on. However, the penology for the same may have undergone sea changes due to different interpretations of criminal justice by the then rulers. Similarly, the methods by which homicide is committed have also undergone changes because of developments in science and sociology; for instance, the present day pattern of homicide may include murder by way of acid burns, lethal drugs, machine guns, or lethal bombs. Also, India is one of those few countries where capital punishment still exists for "rarest of rare cases" (doctrine developed by the Supreme Court of India in *Bachan Singh v State of Punjab* 1980). Such cases may include murder committed in "extremely brutal, grotesque, diabolical, revolting or dastardly manner so as to arouse intense and extreme indignation of the community" (Garg 2013: para 16). Several activists are working toward eradication of capital punishment as it may be perceived as "lawful murder" (Suresh *et al.* 2014) and some question the appropriateness of the "rarest of rare" doctrine (Venkatesan 2012; Bhadra 2014). This gives an interesting understanding of contemporary Indian criminal jurisprudence regarding treatment of homicide of the gravest nature.

In this chapter, we aim to analyze the concept of homicide in India in the historical and contemporary perspectives. The chapter will follow doctrinal methodology whereby it will develop its arguments based on the ancient scriptures, existing criminal codes, and relevant literatures on ancient, medieval, and colonial criminal justice systems, case laws, and news reports. The chapter is divided into four sections. The first section deals with ancient Hindu codes regarding homicide, the responses to homicide, and related punishments; the second section deals with the concept of homicide in the medieval period; the third section deals with a British colonial understanding of homicide in India; and the last section deals with the contemporary understanding of homicide in post-independence and contemporary India.

Homicide in Ancient India

The ancient Indus civilization gifted the world with several wonderful intellectual works; the finest of them are the ancient legal codes prepared by sages of different periods. The earliest of these codes are the "Dharma Shastra." Each of these codes, or *samhitas*, was prepared by different sages and the oldest and most authoritative of these is the Manusmriti or Manu Samhita, prepared by Sage Manu. It dates back to approximately 1500 BCE. While Manusmriti (for a detailed study on Manusmriti and crimes see Jaishankar and Haldar 2004) was the first to codify the crimes, punishments, *raja Dharma* (duties of the kings), general conduct of people, trade practices, and so on, further codes were developed by learned Brahmans of later ages who were ministers to emperors before and during the Greek invasion in India. One such code is Arthasashtra, prepared by Kautilya, Vishnugupta, or Chanakya (350–275 BCE), who was the minister in the court of Mauryan Emperor Chandragupta. Even though Arthasashtra is a verse on economics and political science, it also mentions crimes, punishments, and the criminal justice system (Shamasastry 1923). The ancient Hindu understanding of the criminal justice system is heavily influenced by these two codes (Lahiri 1986).

Manusmriti categorized homicide into three main groups: (1) legal, (2) illegal, and (3) unintentional homicide. The three types of homicides are discussed below.

Legal homicide

Legal homicide could include punishment of death handed down by the kings. Manusmriti prescribes four types of "*danda*" or punishments which are as follows: (1) *vak danda* or admonition, (2) *dhik danda* or censure, (3) *dhana danda* or pecuniary punishment, and (4) *badha danda* or physical punishment, which also includes the death penalty (Lahiri 1986: 168). *Badha danda* could include punishments such as the severance of limbs, beating and whipping, putting heated oil in the ear, imprinting marks on the visible parts of the body of the offender, and so on. But these might not result in death unless a death sentence was also given along with such punishments (Lahiri 1986: 170).

Manusmriti categorizes 21 types of offenses where capital punishment can be given, including intentional homicide caused by force, a woman killing her husband, children, or spiritual guru, a woman administering poison with the intent to kill, and so on (Lahiri 1986: 191–192). Notably, among all these crimes, killing of a Brahmin by a member of a lower caste, killing of a Brahmin woman by a Brahmin man, and causing death to an unborn child were held to be the worst kind of offenses and carried a mandatory death sentence. In cases of death sentence, Manusmriti prescribed seven basic ways of execution: beheading, causing death by pushing a sharp edged weapon called "*shula*" through the anus of the offender, causing death by drowning, cutting the limbs, pushing a red hot iron rod into the mouth of the offender, burning to death, and devouring by hunting dogs (Lahiri 1986: 170). However, these types of execution were not allowed to be carried out by ordinary civilians, not even by the members of the highest Varna, that is, the Brahmans. It may be noted that death punishments were waived for Brahmins for most offenses. In cases where Brahmins were found guilty of offenses that were punishable by death, they were given other types of sentence, including pecuniary fines or banishing (Jaishankar and Haldar 2004).

Illegal homicide

As can be seen from the above list of offenses punishable with death sentences, intentional and willful homicides were recognized as illegal and liable to be punished by the Manusmriti and the *samhitas* prepared by other sages like Katyan and Yagyabalka. Such homicides could include the following types: the intentional and willful killing of a Brahman man or woman; intentionally and willfully causing death to any man or woman or child out of rage and anger by anyone belonging to any caste; intentionally and willfully causing grievous hurt which results in subsequent death; killing and subsequently burning the body; intentional and willful feticide by a mother; killing an unborn child by harming the mother either with a sharp weapon or by slow poisoning; intentional and willful killing of a husband or children by a woman; intentional and willful killing of an upper Varna member by a member of a lower Varna, for example, the Shudra, and so on (Lahiri 1986; Jaishankar and Haldar 2004). Manusmriti does not prescribe any special punishment for any special kind of homicide, but it does mention the killing of Brahmins as the highest offense and terms the offender as "*mahapataka*," or "ultimate offender."

The essential elements that were mentioned by the Manusmriti for treating a homicide as an illegal homicide are (1) intention to kill, (2) willfulness, and (3) knowledge of the consequences of the harm. It may be noted that even though Manusmriti treated women as inferior to men belonging to any other Varna, even the Shudra, intentional and willful homicides by women offenders were recognized as offenses punishable with death; similarly, intentional homicide of women by men and others was also recognized as offenses punishable with death. It may further be noted that Manusmriti also condemns *atmahatya* or suicide, especially when it is caused by self-strangulation, use of a sharp weapon, or poisoning; when it is due to frustration in love either caused by the partner or by the society; or when it is due to anger or rage (Lahiri 1986; Jaishankar and Haldar 2004). In such cases, the punishment included dragging of the corpse (of the one who committed suicide) by means of the same rope, or other weapon, that was used in the suicide along a public road (Lahiri 1986; Jaishankar and Haldar 2004). Manusmriti also prohibited any other person to perform the formal cremation of such dead bodies. It may be assumed that these measures were adopted to show the society that *atmahatya* or suicide is no lesser offense.

Unintentional homicide

Manusmriti as well as later Hindu codes also recognized unintentional homicide. In this category the following four types of homicides are included: death caused to an *atatayee* (attacker) in the course of self-defense; death caused by a child who is under 12 years of age and does not have the maturity to understand the consequences of the harm; death caused by sudden provocation and anger and when the offender was not aware of the consequences and did not intend to kill; and death caused by the offender when under the influence of liquor or directed by someone when the offender is under "*moha*" (hallucination or infatuation) and when the offender neither intended to kill the victim nor was aware of the consequences of the harm inflicted (Lahiri 1986; Jaishankar and Haldar 2004).

In the last two circumstances the Manusmriti prescribed a procedure of penance by way of treating the wrongdoing as "sin." In the case of the first type of homicide, the person who has caused the death must provide evidence of willful, sudden attack on himself or on his kith or kin or on the community that he was protecting or was associated with (Lahiri 1986; Jaishankar and Haldar 2004). However, in such cases, both Manusmriti and Arthasashtra prescribed punishment other than physical torture or death (Shamasastry 1923). Such punishments were prescribed mainly to make the offender atone for misdeeds that were caused more by mistake than by intent. In the second type of homicide, however, both Manusmriti and Arthasashtra had exempted child offenders under seven years of age, but prescribed examination of the maturity of a child offender between seven and twelve years of age (Shamasastry 1923) (interestingly, these provisions are available in the Indian penal code introduced by the British in 1860). Notably, however, Manusmriti did not exempt a Shudra from killing a Brahmin even if such homicide was unintentional (Lahiri 1986; Jaishankar and Haldar 2004).

Also, by introducing Varna-based (caste-based) social structures, Manusmriti introduced the legalized concept of honor killing. This may be evident from cases where death sentences were given for willful and consensual inter-caste sexual relationships. Even though there were instances of mixed marriages where a woman from a higher Varna could be married to a man from a lower Varna in some later *samhitas*, this was strictly forbidden between a man and a woman from the Shudra and Brahmin communities and vice versa. It may further be noted that such honor killing was not permitted by ordinary civilians as it had to be sanctioned by the lawful authorities. It is an unfortunate fact that such traditions of honor killing, for inter-caste marriages or intra-caste marriages still exist in Indian society, even though this is no longer supported by the authorities (Vishwanath and Palakonda 2011).

Homicide in Medieval India

India started losing its "Hindu" character by the end of the eleventh century CE when foreign invaders, especially the Turks, started capturing northwestern areas of India and rolled out their own criminal justice systems to rule the captured areas. "In 712 CE, Mohammad Bin al Q'asim overran Sind. The Arabs, the Turks, the Afghans and the Mughals invaded India in hordes" (Ghosh 1987: 24) and India entered the medieval period, when Qutb-ud-din Aibak became the ruler of Delhi in 1206 with the establishment of the Sultanate of Delhi. This brought about a new era for the criminal justice system in India that was influenced by Islamic philosophy (Ahmad 1941). Over the next few centuries, until 1858 when the British took over the ruling of India from the last Mughal emperor, Bahadur Shah Zafar, the criminal justice system underwent many reforms, some of which still exist today.

Before delving into the subject of homicide in the medieval Indian criminal justice system, a brief introduction to the origin of Muslim laws is needed. Islamic law is mainly based on Quranic verses. The code of laws for people belonging to Islam is known as Sharia, which finds its sources from the Quran and also the examples set forth by the Prophet Mohammed as the code of conduct for every Muslim (Coulson 2011).

The invasions by Turks and later by Afghans, being followers of Islamic laws, brought Islamic laws to India. But it needs to be stated that the early invaders, including Aibak, the first Muslim ruler in India, did not feel the need to completely replace the existing set of laws and administration including civil and criminal legal administrations. Islamic laws were imported more to regulate the people following Islam in India than to forcefully change the existing systems for the invaded (Ahmad 1941). Rather, when the Muslim invaders made India their home, they created a mixed set of civil and criminal judicial and administrative systems which gave enough space for both Hindu and Muslim laws to govern people following the respective religions.

The Islamic criminal justice system as introduced by the Turks, the Slave dynasty, and then the Mughals, maintained a threefold typology of homicide similar to that used in ancient Hindu India, namely, legal homicide, illegal homicide, and unintentional homicide. The Sharia laws dealt with specific types of crime, which included crime against individuals, crime against property, crime against God, unethical conduct, and illicit sexual conduct. Accordingly, Sharia laws followed specific types of punishments which included *Qisas*, "blood fine," and the doctrine of "eye for an eye" (Ahmad 1941) for illegal homicides, including murder and death for disputes over property; *Hudud* (restriction) for offenses against religion, including adultery and illicit sexual relationships (Mir-Hosseini 2011), robbery, and theft; and *Diyya* (financial compensation) for bodily harm. An in-depth study of the penology of medieval India shows that legal homicides or death sentences sanctioned by the king or the judge existed in India, but the legal procedure of dealing with such homicides was different from that of the ancient Hindu period.

Legal homicide or death punishments sanctioned by laws were given in cases of murder, treason, theft from the royal treasury, adultery by married men as well as women, and grave mistakes and enmity against the ruler by officials. In cases of murder, grave bodily injury leading to death, intentionally causing death out of rage, and so on, the victim's kin could enter a demand for *Qisas* (the right of the victim's kin to kill the murderer) which could be granted by the state. *Qisas* was applicable in certain cases of unintentional homicides as well. However, it is interesting to note that *Qisas* was not awarded for non-Muslim victims. In such cases, if the non-Muslim victim or his kin could prove that he was a proper tax payer, the state was empowered to award *Diyya* to be extracted from the Muslim perpetrator. However, there was discrimination regarding the amount of *Diyya* to be paid to a non-Muslim compared to a Muslim victim (Friedmann 2006: 42–50). Painful execution procedures were prescribed for the capital offenses, mentioned above, other than homicides caused by interpersonal problems. These included stoning to death (especially in cases of adultery), systematically cutting of limbs until the offender is dead, throwing the offender from height, trampling of the body of the offender by trained elephants, and poisoning the offender (especially in cases of officials who had failed in their duties) (Ahmad 1941).

It needs to be noted that the Islamic criminal law as practiced by Muslim rulers in India, did not prescribe death sentences for some kinds of homicide in the first instance. Systems of jail term, pecuniary fines, lashing, and so on, were used to provide the offender an opportunity to learn from the mistakes. Death sentences were given as final punishments (Ahmad 1941). In such cases, there was no distinction between Hindu and Muslim subjects. Notably, many kings, including the Mughals, had a preference for public execution. This was done specifically to set an example to other people about the consequences of wrongdoing.

As can be seen from the above paragraphs, illegal homicide in the criminal justice system in medieval India included intentional and willful causing of death by one to another. However, the Muslim rulers did not disturb the existing categorization of illegal homicide to a great extent, especially for non-Muslim subjects, except in the case of *Qisas* as has been discussed earlier. But similar to the ancient Hindu system, causing death in the course of exercising the right to self-defense and causing death by children under the age of 12 were recognized by the Muslim laws in India (Ahmad 1941) as unintentional homicide, falling outside the purview of illegal homicide. It may be interesting to note that in several of these situations, as well as in cases of robbery, theft, and death caused because of such instances, the governors or the *Qazis* (priests) were liable to pay the compensation to the victims (Ahmad 1941).

Homicide in British Colonial India

The East India Company ruled certain parts of India between 1757 and 1858 and during that time they did not alter the existing Mohammedan laws (Jois 1984) and allowed the laws on homicide to be practiced by the courts. In 1858, with the defeat of India's last Mughal emperor, Bahadur Shah Jafar, began the colonial rule of the British, which lasted until India's independence in 1947. Although different parts of India were colonized by other European invaders, including the Dutch and the French, during the last few decades of Mughal rule, the British colonial rulers successfully captured the whole of India and brought major reforms to the existing penal system as well as the civil procedure system in India. Notably, the British rulers maintained the existing laws of the "natives" for succession or for other civil matters including marriage, but they created a set of uniform codes in the form of the Indian penal code (1860) under the chairmanship of Lord Macaulay and the Indian Evidence Act under the chairmanship of Sir James Fitzjames Stephen, to regulate criminal justice administration. The court system was changed to the British system. Even though the procedures for investigation, evidence, prosecution, and appeal had been present since ancient times in India, the system was revamped with the introduction of the penal code and the evidence act following British courts where the supreme judicial authority was invested in the British monarch. This introduction of the new penal code shredded some of the categories of legal homicides and introduced others.

It needs to be mentioned here that on many occasions since ancient times invaders used women and children as pawns to forcefully bring villages and cities under their control. This included raping women and using children as slaves as well as the creation of local customary laws which suppressed basic rights of women in Hindu and subsequently Muslim societies. These included child marriages, female feticide, sacrificing of children in the name of religious practices, genital mutilation of children, and burning of brides in the pyres of their husbands. By the end of the seventeenth century onwards the problems of dowry harassment and killing of young brides by physical torture also erupted in Indian society. The British colonial rulers introduced a positive penal reform by categorizing such sorts of homicides as illegal homicides. There were specific laws made to criminalize bride burning or the system of *Sati Daha*, the sacrifice of children, feticide, and infanticide. Causing death by grievous harm in the form of punishment was also condemned as illegal homicide. Similarly, rape and sexual assault on women and honor killing were condemned as heinous criminal activities. The penal code also prohibited caste/religious violence (including communal riots) by way of killing members belonging to other castes, class, religion, or creed. While these were coded under specific provisions, the Indian penal code (IPC) brought in the concept of "culpable homicide" and homicide amounting to murder through sections 299 and 300, respectively.

Culpable homicide according to section 299 of the IPC is the causing of death by acting with the intention of causing death or with the intention of causing such bodily injury as is likely to cause death, or with the knowledge to cause death by such an act. The explanations attached to the provision further clarify that (1) a person who causes bodily injury to another who is already suffering due to some disease or infirmity or disorder and the death is accelerated due to the physical condition of the victim, shall be deemed to have caused his death; (2) where death is caused by bodily injury which could have been resisted by proper medication, the person who had caused such death, would be deemed to have caused the death; (3) causing of the death of an unborn child in the mother's womb would not be considered as homicide, but when the death is caused to a living child of whom any body part is brought forth from the womb even though the child may be not be fully born or breathing, may amount to culpable homicide. Culpable homicide is categorized as one of the illegal homicides, but it was differentiated from murder on the ground of intention, willfulness, and knowledge of inevitable results. However, section 300, which defines murder, provides several exceptions that may be categorized as culpable homicide not amounting to murder and also as unintentional murder. These include homicide caused by sudden provocation or without knowledge of the grave consequences.

Unintentional homicide may also include homicide by way of private defense, homicide by children, and also homicide by way of prevention of crimes. It should be noted that some of these categorizations had remained since ancient times and they were formally recognized by the British laws. Ironically, the very British who emphasized the "rule of law" also used those laws to kill innocent people who were against their "British Raj." There were many mass murders committed by the British during their rule, for example, the Jallianwala Bagh massacre. The British also fanned the hatred between Hindus and Muslims and there were large communal riots that killed many innocent individuals. The partition of India and Pakistan caused millions of people to be uprooted from their homeland and the riots during that time killed more than 5 million people.

Homicide in Post-independence and Contemporary India

Although the laws on homicide remained the same in post-independence India, patterns of homicide have changed significantly. The Indian lawmakers preferred to keep the Indian penal code introduced by the British and the laws on homicide within this code have been, and continue to be, amply used; while there are special laws like the Dowry Prohibition Act, 1961, which also has provisions for the punishment of dowry death (also amended in the Indian penal code). This law alone has not prevented dowry deaths and a significant number (15% according to the National Crime Records Bureau 2013) of recorded cases of homicide in India is from dowry deaths (UNODC 2014). Also, communal riots continued in post-independence India, more recently being added to or replaced by terrorist attacks, including the 26/11 Mumbai attacks, which killed more than 500 people. In spite of the partition of India and Pakistan, Kashmir is still a contentious area for both countries and several hundred people have been killed there either by the armies or terrorists. Armed violence or aggression by Maoists also killed many people in many parts of India (IAVA 2011a).

Post-independence India saw an increase in murders/homicides which was again dealt with the same British laws, which have continued to be used in contemporary India, although homicide has decreased considerably over the last 15 years. The numbers of homicides rose considerably in post-independence India, although there had been a marginal decline in recorded murders since the start of the twenty-first century. The National Crime Records Bureau (NCRB) shows that murder increased fourfold from 9,802 cases in 1953 to 37,399 cases in 2000, but has since declined by over 10 percent to 33,201 cases in 2013 (National Crime Records Bureau 2013: 13; see also Marwah 2014).

Except for a few armed attacks in Kashmir and Maoist-dominated areas (IAVA 2011a), India does not have a gun culture, unlike North and South American countries, for example, where the gun culture forms the major reason for homicides. Although, there is no gun culture in India, to some extent, the use of illegal guns to commit homicide is prevalent in both rural and urban areas. A study by Kohli and Aggarwal (2006) found the prevalence of firearm fatalities in New Delhi with around 90 victims being killed by firearms. Interestingly, the number of homicides based on firearms halved between 1999 (112,147) and 2008 (6,219) (IAVA 2011b: 1).

Many reasons are used as motivation to commit murders in contemporary India and many classifications are offered to explain these reasons. Nagpaul (1985: 149–153) has developed a typology, based on causal factors, of homicides occurring in post-independence and contemporary India. They are: (1) homicides arising from property disputes, (2) family violence, (3) family violence concerning dowry, (4) situational homicides, (5) village feuds and political conflicts, (6) senseless homicides, and (7) infanticides. Alternatively, Periyar's (2009) research which intends to study the victim–offender relationship in cases of revenge murders, developed the following typology as a base for homicides that occur in rural India: (1) inter-caste issues, (2) intra-caste issues, (3) class-based issues, (4) marital-based issues, (5) communal-based issues, (6) land dispute issues, and (7) others. The National

Crime Records Bureau (2013), in its publication "Crime in India," presented its statistics on murder based on 13 typologies/motives. They are: murder for gain, property dispute, personal vendetta or enmity, love affairs/sexual causes, dowry, lunacy, witchcraft, terrorism/extreme violence, political reasons, communalism, caste conflict, class conflict, and other motives (National Crime Records Bureau 2013; Marwah 2014).

In 2013, the most common motives behind murders were shown as "personal vendetta or enmity" and "property dispute," which accounted for 10.3 percent and 8.4 percent of total murder cases, respectively. The other significant causes were "love affairs/sexual causes" (7.1%), "gain" (5.0%), and "dowry" (4.1%) (National Crime Records Bureau 2013: 55). The statistics of homicide victimization in contemporary India still show females as the major victims of murder and culpable homicide, predominantly for reasons such as dowry deaths, infanticide, and honor killing. Females and young people were the main victims of murder in 2013 according to the NCRB statistics. "The share of female victims was 27.1% of the total murder victims (9,180 out of 33,901) and the youth victims (18–30 years) was maximum at 44.0% (14,910 out of 33,901 victims)" (National Crime Records Bureau 2013: 59). However, individual empirical studies based on medical autopsies show males as major victims of homicide in India (e.g., Mohanty *et al.* 2005; Gupta, Prajapati, and Kumar 2007). The reason may be the higher exposure of males to risk-based situations outside their homes compared to females, and females are more victimized in their own homes.

In contemporary India, the dynamics of homicide have changed in both urban and rural areas. While domestic and familial ("interpersonal") attacks make up many of the homicides that occur in rural areas, it is primarily "strategic benefit" that underlies homicides in the cities. A study by Dikshit, Dogra, and Chandra (1986) revealed that homicides were committed for financial gain in urban Delhi. Thus, lack of social cohesion in the urban areas is a key factor in many homicides, while the greater level of social cohesion in rural areas continues to be the reason behind many homicides there, due to adultery, revenge, love affairs, and so on. A study by Mohanty, Mohanty, and Patnaik (2013), done in rural southern India, found previous enmity and familial disharmony as the main reasons for homicide. There is a strong victim–offender relationship in the rural-based homicides. Similar situation was found when the offender is a female and the victim is a male. Studies on female homicide offending by Rani (1983), Saxena (1994), and Kethineni (2001) found that most of the female offenders have killed either their husbands or closest family members and the majority of them were from rural areas.

Also, due to globalization, large-scale migration of rural people to urban areas has taken place. This phenomenon has created culture conflict between the urbanized people and the new migrants, which has often resulted in rapes or murders. A classic example of this is the rape and murder of a 23 year old physiotherapy student in a moving bus in 2012 in New Delhi (aka the Nirbhaya incident). A small number of American-style school shootings and cyber-based murders have been committed in contemporary India (Jaishankar and Halder 2009). In addition, sensational and unique homicides occurred in the past decade in the urban regions. For example, the recent murder of an Infosys software company employee, Swathi (June 2016) in broad daylight in Nungambakkam railway station in Chennai by Ramkumar (the accused); the killing of Sheena Bhora by her mother Indrani Mukerjea (2015); the Laila Khan case (2012), where Laila, her mother, and her siblings were killed by her stepfather; the Sandhya Pandit case (2012), where she was killed by her own son Raghuveer Singh; the Arushi Talwar–Hemraj murder case (2008), where Arushi and her domestic help Hemraj were purportedly killed by her own parents; and the Nithari killings that occurred in 2006 in a neighborhood of New Delhi, where 20 victims were raped and murdered by a rich businessman, Surender Kohli, and his domestic help (FP Staff 2015). Examples from the earlier decade, such as Naina Shani (1995), who was killed by her husband Sushil Sharma and burned in a *Tandoor* (clay oven), and Jessical Lal (1999), a model that was killed at a party by Manu Sharma, were sensational cases. Notably, most of the sensational cases that occurred in urban India involved the killing of women. This shows the conflict of patriarchy with the modern values of women, wherein modern women who resist the patriarchy ruling or try to create new value systems copying the West are killed to be silenced.

Even though the analysis might indicate a rise of homicides in contemporary India, the rates of homicide in contemporary India are comparatively lower than in many other countries (IAVA 2011a; UNODC 2014). They have also been falling for some time, as noted by UNODC (2014: 26), "India has seen its homicide rate decline by 23 percent over the last 15 years, while Pakistan and Nepal have both seen slight increases in their homicide rates." Although India's homicide rates are relatively low compared to other countries, its conviction rates for homicide are also very low. Nagpaul (1985: 152) cites reasons for this, such as the purchase of eyewitnesses by the offender or the offender's family, eyewitnesses may be one of the close relatives who may not be willing to be a witness, or offenders may create false evidence. Overall, the Indian criminal justice procedure is designed in such a way to favor the accused rather than the victim.

Conclusion

In this chapter, an attempt has been made to analyze the responses to homicide in India from historical and contemporary perspectives. Homicide in India was always treated as the most heinous crime, although the level of punishment in ancient India for the same crime varied between various Varnas. In medieval India, the Muslim laws provided harsher forms of punishment based on Islamic laws. The British later made sweeping changes in the laws during their time of rule and provided punishment for homicides following the same principle of "*lex talionis*" (retributive justice, sometimes referred to as "an eye for an eye") and these are still followed in contemporary India.

There are no clear-cut statistics regarding homicides during the ancient, medieval, and British India periods. In the post-Independence and contemporary India, the National Crime Records Bureau, which was founded in 1986, is the only authentic source of homicide-related data. Many researchers on murders/homicide have utilized the NCRB data (Dreze and Khera 2000; Marwah 2014). Apart from the NCRB statistics, there are few empirical studies on homicides, but they were mostly done from a victim's perspective (Dikshit, Dogra, and Chandra 1986; Mohanty, Mohanty, and Patnaik 2013) with fewer studies on homicide offenders (Kethineni 2001). There is a need for more empirical studies on homicide to find the patterns of homicide in India.

References

Ahmad, M.B. (1941) *The Administration of Justice in Medieval India: A study in Outline of the Judicial System under the Sultans and the Badshahs of Delhi Based Mainly upon Cases Decided by Medieval Courts in India between 1206–1750 AD*. Aligarh, India: Aligarh Historical Research Institute for Aligarh University.

Bhadra, S. (2014) Indian judiciary and the issue of capital punishment. Available online at http://cafedissensus.com/2014/01/01/indian-judiciary-and-the-issue-of-capital-punishment (accessed January 13, 2015).

Coulson, N.J. (2011) A History of Islamic law. New Brunswick, NJ: Aldine Transaction.

Dikshit, P.C., Dogra, T.D., and Chandra, J. (1986) Comprehensive study of homicides in South Delhi, 1969–79. *Medicine, Science, and the Law*, 26(3): 230–234.

Dreze, J. and Khera, R. (2000) Crime, gender, and society in India: Insights from homicide data. *Population and Development Review*, 26(2): 335–352.

FP Staff (2015) Five controversial murders that shocked India before Indrani Mukerjea's arrest. *Firstpost*, August 28. Available online at http://www.firstpost.com/india/before-indrani-mukherjeas-arrest-five-controversial-murders-that-shocked-india-2408592.html (accessed October 13, 2015).

Friedmann, Y. (2006) *Tolerance and Coercion in Islam: Interfaith Relations in the Muslim Tradition*. Cambridge: Cambridge University Press.

Garg, A. (2013) Death sentence: Extent of judicial discretion and need of guidelines. Available online at http://www.legalservicesindia.com/articles/deat.htm (accessed January 13, 2015).

Ghosh, S.K. (1987) *Communal Riots in India (Meet the Challenge Unitedly)*. New Delhi: Ashish.

Gupta, S., Prajapati, P., and Kumar, S. (2007) Victimology of homicide: A Surat (South Gujarat) based study. *Journal of Indian Academy of Forensic Medicine*, 29(3): 29–33.

IAVA (India Armed Violence Assessment) Brief (2011a) India's states of armed violence: Assessing the human cost and political priorities. Small Arms Survey Issue Brief no. 1, September 2011. Available online at http://www.india-ava.org/fileadmin/docs/pubs/IAVA-IB1-states-of-armed-violence.pdf (accessed January 14, 2015).

IAVA (India Armed Violence Assessment) Brief (2011b) Mapping murder: The geography of Indian firearm fatalities. Small Arms Survey Issue Brief no. 2, September 2011. Available online at http://www.unodc.org/documents/southasia/webstories/IndiaAVA_IB2_2011_Mapping_Murder_1.pdf (accessed January 14, 2015).

Jaishankar, K. and Haldar, D. (2004) Manusmriti: A critique of the criminal justice tenets in the ancient Indian Hindu code. Available online at http://www.erces.com/journal/articles/archives/v03/v03_05.htm (accessed January 13, 2015).

Jaishankar, K. and Halder, D. (2009) Cyber bullying among school students in India. In K. Jaishankar (ed.), *International Perspectives on Crime and Justice* (pp. 579–598). Newcastle, UK: Cambridge Scholars.

Jois, M.R. (1984) *Legal and Constitutional History of India* (vol. 1). New Delhi: Universal Law.

Kethineni, S. (2001) Female homicide offenders in India. *International Journal of Comparative and Applied Criminal Justice*, 25(1): 1–24.

Kohli, A. and Aggarwal, N.K. (2006) Firearm fatalities in Delhi, India. *Legal Medicine*, 8: 264–268.

Lahiri, T. (1986) *Crime and Punishment in Ancient India*. New Delhi: Radiant.

Marwah, S. (2014) Mapping murder: Homicide patterns and trends in India. *Journal of South Asian Studies*, 2(2): 145–163. Available online at http://escijournals.net/index.php/JSAS/article/view/571/364 (accessed January 14, 2015).

Mir-Hosseini, Z. (2011) Criminalizing sexuality: Zina laws as violence against women in Muslim contexts. *SUR-International Journal on Human Rights*, 8(15): 7–33.

Mohanty, M.K., Mohan Kumar, T.S., Mohanram, A., and Palimar, V. (2005) Victims of homicidal deaths—an analysis of variables. *Journal of Clinical Forensic Medicine*, 12: 302–304.

Mohanty, S., Mohanty, S.K., and Patnaik, K.K. (2013) Homicide in southern India—a five-year retrospective study. *Forensic Medicine and Anatomy Research*, 1(2): 18–24.

Nagpaul, H. (1985) Patterns of homicide in North India: Some sociological hypotheses. *International Journal of Offender Therapy and Comparative Criminology*, 29(2): 147–158. doi: 10.1177/0306624X8502900207.

National Crime Records Bureau (2013) Crime in India—2013. New Delhi: Government of India: National Crime Records Bureau. Available online at http://ncrb.nic.in/StatPublications/CII/CII2013/Home.asp (accessed January 14, 2015).

Periyar, E.E. (2009) Victim–offender relationship: An ethnographic study of revenge murders in Tirunelveli District. Research proposal submitted for PhD thesis to the Manonmaniam Sundaranar University, Tirunelveli, Tamil Nadu, India.

Rani, B.M. (1983) Homicides by females. *Indian Journal of Criminology*, 11(1): 8–17.

Saxena, R. (1994) *Women and Crime in India: A Study in Sociocultural Dynamics*. New Delhi: Inter-India.

Shamasastry, R. (1923) *Kautilya's Arthashastra*. Mysore: Wesleyan Mission Press.

Suresh, V., Singh, P., Bhadro, S., *et al.* (2014) Say NO to death penalty. Report of Meeting of All India Human Rights Organisations and Activists on March 8, 2014 in Chennai. Available online at http://www.indiaresists.com/say-no-to-death-penalty (accessed January 13, 2015).

UNODC (2014) *Global Study on Homicide 2013: Trends, Contexts and Data*. Vienna: United Nations Office of Drugs and Crime (UNODC). Available online at https://www.unodc.org/documents/data-and-analysis/statistics/GSH2013/2014_GLOBAL_HOMICIDE_BOOK_web.pdf (accessed January 13, 2015).

Venkatesan, V. (2012) A case against the death penalty. *Frontline*, 29(17). Available online at http://www.frontline.in/static/html/fl2917/stories/20120907291700400.htm (accessed January 13, 2015).

Vishwanath, J. and Palakonda, S.C. (2011) Patriarchal ideology of honour and honour crimes in India. *International Journal of Criminal Justice Sciences*, 6(1–2), 386–395.

28

Homicide in South Africa
Offender Perspectives on Dispute-related Killings of Men

Marie Rosenkrantz Lindegaard

Introduction

Homicide is a serious health problem in South Africa. Violence caused by crime, including homicide, is the second leading cause of death in the general population (following HIV/AIDS), irrespective of gender and age (Norman *et al.* 2007a), and the first leading cause of death among males (Donson 2008). The average number of deaths caused by violence in South Africa is almost twice as high as the global average. A prevailing characteristic of homicides in South Africa is the disproportionate role of young men as perpetrators and victims. Young men in the age group of 15 to 29 have the highest homicide victimization rates in the country (184 per 100,000), and this age group is also significantly overrepresented in the statistics on homicide suspects (CSVR 2008a). In urban disadvantaged areas (referred to as township areas), the victimization rate among young men is more than twice the average for young men in other areas. South African women are six times more likely to die from a homicide than the world average and more than half of these homicides are committed by an intimate partner (Seedat *et al.* 2009).

What is striking about homicides in South Africa is the significant difference between males and females in both offending and victimization patterns. Men tend to get killed in public; women at home. Men most often get killed by strangers; women by their intimate partner. Men tend to get killed in the context of arguments; women in the context of rapes (CSVR 2008a). Homicide offending is significantly more common among men than women. This difference has been explained as the consequence of patriarchal notions of masculinity believed to influence men to use violence as a quest for dominance and control over women (Mathews, Jewkes,

The Handbook of Homicide, First Edition. Edited by Fiona Brookman,
Edward R. Maguire, and Mike Maguire.

and Abrahams 2011). For example, Mathews, Jewkes, and Abrahams (2015) found that South African men killed their intimate partner because it made them feel like a man. But if the main motivation for killings of women is to feel like a man, why do South African men then kill other men? Do killings of other men also make them feel like a man? And if so, what kind of man do they become by killing other men?

Even though a relatively large number of South African men engage in violent crime including lethal violence compared to the global average, such crime is still a minority. Yet few studies have provided insights into the sources of variation among men who do commit these crimes compared to those who do not (Gibson and Lindegaard 2007; Graham 2014; Morrell *et al.* 2013). What is known is that there are a number of factors associated with the high rate of violent crimes in South Africa (Seedat *et al.* 2009), including the violent history of the country (Abrahams and Jewkes 2005; Kaminer *et al.* 2008), the racial and economic segregation (Lemanski 2004), the high level of poverty and inequality (Demombynes and Özler 2005; Wood 2006), the history of divided families (Mathews, Jewkes, and Abrahams 2011), and the inefficiency of state responses to crime (Steinberg 2012). How these factors play out specifically in relation to homicides and why these factors supposedly influence men differently than women are unclear.

In this chapter, I propose street culture as a framework for understanding the sources of variation among South African men, including differences among men living in the "advanced marginality" (Wacquant 2008) of the townships, characterized by poverty and racial and economic segregation. Similar to some disadvantaged urban areas of the US and Europe, some young men living in township areas engage in violent behavior as a means for social status in the alternative hierarchy of street-oriented people (Baumer *et al.* 2003; Brookman *et al.* 2011; Holligan 2015; Sandberg and Pedersen 2011; Stewart and Simons 2010; Wright, Brookman, and Bennett 2006; Wright and Decker 1997). Violent behavior provides street capital (Sandberg and Pedersen 2011), and homicide as the most extreme manifestation of violence provides the most street capital. After a review of some of the key patterns and characteristics of homicides in South Africa, this chapter focuses on the most common type of homicide: dispute-related homicides, committed in public by men against men. Based on the perspectives of 14 offenders who committed such a homicide, I propose understanding these killings in the context of street culture.

Patterns of Homicide in South Africa

Compared to Europe, Canada, and the United States, as described in this volume (Chapter 17, Chapter 21), homicides in South Africa are significant for the following reasons: there is a relatively high rate of dispute-related homicides; a significant overrepresentation of males both as victims and offenders; a relatively high risk of women getting killed by an intimate partner; a tendency for other types of crime ending in lethal violence; the relatively common killings of victims previously unknown to the offender; and the more recent type of vigilantism-related homicides, currently accounting for 7 percent of all homicides in the country.

Frequency

Despite criticism of the South African Police Services (SAPS) for not providing reliable crime statistics, SAPS provides the most comprehensive information about homicides. In 2013–2014, SAPS recorded 17,068 homicides countrywide at a rate of 32.2 per 100,000 (SAPS 2015). The homicide rate has declined by 20 percent since 2004, which translates to a reduction of 40.3 to 32.2 per 100,000 of the population between 2004 and 2014. Despite this reduction, the rate is still approximately five times the world average (Norman *et al.* 2007b). Female homicides followed the general declining trend of homicides, while intimate partner femicide and suspected rape homicide (sexual component found during investigation) rates did not follow this decrease but remained steady in the period 1999–2009 (Abrahams *et al.* 2013). None of these trends of homicides have been thoroughly explained but it has been suggested that recent gun control legislation (Firearms Control Acts) with provisions for safer firearm use and ownership, and improved policing and detective work, might cause this downward trend (Abrahams *et al.* 2013).

Motivations

More than half of all murders were related to interpersonal arguments and disputes; one quarter were committed in the course of another crime such as robbery, burglary, or rape; and 7 percent were related to vigilantism and revenge (CSVR 2008a). Although many arguments between men and women result in various forms of violent assaults, 90 percent of the arguments that end with fatal violence are between men (CSVR 2010). One study of motivations for killings of women based on offender perspectives showed that these homicides were motivated by a quest for dominance and extreme control over women (Mathews, Jewkes, and Abrahams 2015). No similar study was conducted about men who killed men. Studies of violent crime in general based on offender perspectives suggested that violence provided status within a gang, proved being a real man, and generated income (CSVR 2008b). Violent crimes were also described as a means for social mobility, belonging, and respect (Lindegaard and Jacques 2014).

Conditions

Forty percent of homicides were committed with a sharp object (stabbings), 36 percent with a firearm, and 22 percent with blunt force (CSVR 2010). A study conducted by the CSVR about the six areas in South Africa where most homicides take place showed that most homicides in these areas occur on a Saturday; December is the month with the highest number of homicides (i.e., holiday season); and 46 percent occur in public places while 26 percent occur in the home of the victim (CSVR 2008a). Compared to Europe and Canada (see Chapter 17 and Chapter 20, this volume), homicides occur relatively often in public places in South Africa. Remarkably, 46 percent of all dispute-related homicides occur in public and semi-public places, such as in streets and bars (CSVR 2008a: 54). This may be a consequence of people spending more time in the street and bars generally due to overcrowded houses and generally deprived living conditions. It may also be a consequence of street culture related ideas about not losing face and acting out violence when being challenged in public (Anderson 1999).

Victim–offender relationships

In more than half the cases of reported homicides in South Africa, the relationship between the victim and offender is unclear. In 28 percent of the cases, the victim did not know the offender. In 19 percent of the cases, the offender was an intimate partner or more or less closely related to the victim (CSVR 2008a: 28). These characteristics suggest that, compared to for example Europe and Canada (Chapter 17 and Chapter 20, this volume), a relatively high rate of homicides occur between people who know each other either vaguely or not at all. Killings that result from disputes, are driven by revenge, or are motivated by rivals between groups such as gangs, are most likely to occur between people who know each other only vaguely or not at all (CSVR 2008a: 49).

Age

People in their twenties and thirties are at highest risk of becoming a victim of homicide: 41 percent of homicide victims are aged between 20 and 29 years and 29 percent are aged between 30 and 39 years (CSVR 2008a). Forty-eight percent of homicide suspects are aged between 20 and 29 years; 32 percent are older than 30 years; and 20 percent are younger than 20 years. The well-known victim–offender overlap primarily exists among 20 to 29 year age group; older people are more likely to become victims than offenders, whereas younger people are more at risk of offending than victimization (CSVR 2008a). Compared to Europe (see Chapter 17, this volume), victims and offenders of homicide are relatively young in South Africa.

Race categories

During apartheid, South Africans were categorized as White, African/Black, Colored, or Indian/Asian. Colored was a category constructed to include people who did not fit any of the other categories (Posel 2001). Despite the official elimination of the terminology, these distinctions still matter in everyday life and therefore tend to be reproduced in scientific investigations as well. Although most victims of homicides are reported among Blacks the countrywide rate reported among

Coloreds is relatively higher (Leggett 2004; Thomson 2004). Even though some variation exists between measures of the representation of people categorized as Colored in these statistics (Altbeker 2008), there seems to be consensus that 16 percent of homicide victims are Coloreds (Donson 2008) while only 9 percent of the population is classified as such (CSVR 2008a).

The CSVR homicide study showed that in specifically high-risk areas, the distribution of race categories among victims largely follows the population distribution in those areas: 89 percent were African (85% of the population); 10 percent Colored (9% of the population); 1 percent Asian (5% of the population); and less than 1 percent were White (1% population; CSVR 2008a). Apparently the race category of victims in high-risk areas is not what determines their risk of homicide victimization. The distribution of race categories of suspects similarly follows the general distribution of the population, with Coloreds being an exception. Due to their relatively high representation in dispute-related homicides, the overall representation of the category Colored among homicide suspects is 12 percent while only representing 9 percent of the population (CSVR 2008a).

The overrepresentation of Coloreds as victims and offenders has caused extensive discussions about what it is about being Colored that makes this group extraordinarily vulnerable. Coloreds represent the largest population group in Cape Town but nationwide they are rather marginal. During apartheid, the category Colored was used to classify everyone that did not fit the categories of African/Black, White, and Indian/Asian. Their rights were better than Africans/Blacks but worse than those for Whites and Indians/Asians. Their jobs and residential areas were constructed as buffer zones between Whites and Africans/Blacks (Posel 2001). Their "in-between" type of identity has been described as causing doubt, and consequently a search for recognition through various means including criminal behavior. The relatively high figures of organized crime in Colored communities have been described as a consequence of the apartheid government that supported gangs as a means of controlling the population in non-White areas (Jensen 2008; Standing 2003). In return for acting as political informants by providing information about opponents of the apartheid government, gangs were supported financially and protected by the police (Kynoch 1999). However, it is remarkable that Coloreds are not represented particularly highly in statistics of gang-related homicides. Their relative overrepresentation is mainly related to arguments that end in lethal violence. An alternative explanation may be the dominance of street culture repertoires among young men living in Colored communities, a topic to which I return shortly.

Gender

Males are highly overrepresented in the homicide statistics both as victims and offenders. Ninety-four percent of homicide suspects are male, and almost half of these suspects are between 20 and 29 years old (CSVR 2008a: 97). The highest victimization rate of homicide is among young men aged 15–29 years (184 per 100,000). In some urban disadvantaged areas this rate is more than twice this number (Groenewald *et al.* 2008). Death of men from homicide outnumbers death of women by seven to one. Of the murders that happen under known circumstances, the largest category of male victims by far is that of homicides that develop out of arguments; the second largest is that of homicides committed in the aftermath of other crimes, such as robberies and burglaries (CSVR 2008a: 45).

Twelve percent of all homicide victims in South Africa are female. The 1999 rate among South African women was six times higher (24.7 per 100,000; Seedat *et al.* 2009: 1012) than the worldwide average of homicide among women (4.0 per 100,000). The high risk of homicide among women is related to the extraordinarily high incidences of intimate partner femicide and rape-related femicide (Mathews, Jewkes, and Abrahams 2015). More than half of the female victims of homicide were killed by an intimate partner (Seedat *et al.* 2009).

Significant differences exist between killings of men and women. For example, men tend to be killed in public and are most often killed after an argument with an offender who they previously barely knew. Women tend to get killed at home, in the context of a rape, and the offender is usually an intimate partner to the victim (CSVR 2008a).

The risk of homicide among women has been explained as being the consequence of masculine ideals of extreme control of and dominance over women (Mathews, Jewkes, and Abrahams 2015). A large variety of studies have suggested that South African men perceive it as necessary to claim a position as dominant toward women (Jewkes *et al.* 2011; Morrell 2001; Wood and Jewkes 2001). According to these studies, South African men are likely to act violently because of their inability to control women through other means. They suffer from social and economic marginalized positions, which make them incapable of being good providers (Campbell 1992). At the same time they are highly competitive about power, status, and honor (Ratele 2008; Wood, Lambert, and Jewkes 2007). This combination of lacking the means to establish dominance and an unwillingness to accept a non-dominant position has been described as causing a variety of violent crimes including killings of women.

Inequality and poverty

In a study of 63 countries, South Africa had the highest levels of inequality and homicide rates (Wood 2006). Unemployment, particularly among young men, was found to be the second most consistent correlate of homicide and major assaults after income inequality (Wilkinson, Kawachi, and Kennedy 1998). Half of the homicide victims in South Africa were unemployed; 17 percent were blue-collar workers; 9 percent were students; and 5 percent were employed by the police or private security. Almost 70 percent of the victims were unmarried at the time of their death (CSVR 2008a).

It is known that homicides in South Africa are strongly related to advanced urban marginality (Lemanski 2004). Even though two of the top six neighborhoods with the highest frequency of homicides in South Africa are former White areas, homicides in South Africa most frequently occur in former Black and Colored areas (also referred to as townships), characterized by entrenched racial segregation and economic marginalization (CSVR 2008a). In a study in Johannesburg, neighborhood-concentrated disadvantage was significantly related to higher levels of male and female adolescent homicide (Swart, Seedat, and Nel 2015). It is known that people living in township areas are significantly more at risk to homicides than people living in other urban areas. From other parts of the world, a significant positive correlation between homicide rates and income inequality, as measured by the Gini coefficient, has been documented (Daly, Wilson, and Vasdev 2001). In the South African context, the correlation between inequality and homicide was confirmed in a study comparing different districts: a one percent increase in inequality of a district is associated with an increase in the homicide rate from 2.3 to 2.5 percent (Harris and Vermaak 2014).

The relative deprivation of people living in township areas of Cape Town has been described as a generator for violent crimes. The difficulties of being confronted with the wealth of people living in the more wealthy suburbs, while having to deal with poverty and a lack of future perspectives, was described by participants in my study as one of the reasons they engaged in crime. In the context of advanced marginality, agency can be a cause of crime because crime provides social mobility and is used for income-generating purposes (Lindegaard and Jacques 2014).

In summary, homicides in South Africa relatively often occur in public, among strangers, and in the context of arguments or other crimes. Homicide of women is exceptional by being committed by intimate partners at home. Even though most homicides are committed by men against men, little is known about the motivations for these killings. In the case study that follows I will focus on illustrating the complexities and nuances regarding these killings based on offender perspectives. My analysis indicates the importance of understanding the cultural repertoires, including street culture repertoires that these offenders draw upon to make sense of their violent acts.

A Case Study: Offender Perspectives on Dispute-related Killings of Men

This study is based on a broader ethnographic investigation of offending and victimization patterns among young men in Cape Town in the period of 2005–2009 (Lindegaard 2009). Of a total of 48 participants, this specific case study focuses on 14 men who had committed a male-on-male homicide in the context of a dispute in public.[1] I will illustrate how the participants described their experiences with killing as related to a certain type of lifestyle similar to what has been described as street culture in other parts of the world.

Street-oriented people are characterized by searching for status through the means of crime, and in particular through their willingness and capability to use violence (Anderson 1999; Garot 2010). Among young people involved in street culture in the United States, excessive forms of violence such as homicides were found to provide more street capital than less excessive forms such as assaults and robberies (Wilkinson 2001). Copes and Hochstetler (2003: 286) summarized that street-oriented people use crime to prove themselves as: (1) autonomous; (2) capable of providing for themselves; and (3) action oriented. These three aspects were prominent in the descriptions of the 14 homicide offenders in this case study. Furthermore, I illustrate how the participants described killing as providing them with a feeling of dominance and control (4), as found in other contexts among homicide offenders (Brookman 2000) and in particular among heavily street-oriented young people (Wilkinson 2001).

(1) Autonomous

Participants described killing as related to a particular type of lifestyle that involved "doing crime" and being willing to go "all the way" when being challenged in public. This lifestyle of crime involvement made them autonomous in two different ways: by being independent of expectations of conventional society and of expectations of gang-involved people inside and outside prison. To illustrate, Drégan killed a man with an axe in a bar after the victim provoked him by asking for a kiss. He contrasted his interest in shootings and murders with the interest of the author in the following ways:

> With your [the author's] friends you can talk about studies that you conducted or what is on the news or your friend's baby or stuff like that. But what do we [Drégan and his friends] talk about? We talk about gang members. We talk about guns, we talk about people stabbing. We're interested in that. Those things fascinate us to hear about. You're bombarded with all of that. Those people are your idols and you, yourself, you want to inspire, to incorporate some of their characteristics into your like [character] and you also want to assume that role one day.

According to Drégan, conventionally oriented people represented by the author gain status through conventional means such as education and parental responsibilities. People in his less conventional world earn street capital by talking about crime. Crime is a way to gain social status and talking about it is a way to prove your adherence to street culture, including an alternative hierarchy that provides alternative forms of social status.

Crimes committed in the context of gangs were by some participants described as making you dependent on others, which was exactly what they wanted to avoid by adhering to a criminal lifestyle. Drégan described how gang involvement was often seen as providing security but in his perception it only offered you a boss telling you what to do without the benefits of ordinary employment:

> For me, gangsterism is stupid. I mean, I don't get paid. I don't get their wages. I don't get medical insurance. I don't get nothing. I have to rob people .... That was just the way that I like ... figured it out. I felt like independent. Like me against the world. It made me feel stronger; stronger to be ... For me the chance was, to play in the game or out there without being connected to a team. On your own.

According to the participants, operating on your own in the underground world of criminal activities required being extra tough and willing to use lethal violence when being provoked in public.

(2) Capable of providing for yourself

The participants described their homicides as a consequence of being involved in a criminal lifestyle that ensured money for their own needs and those of their families (Lindegaard and Jacques 2014). Through crimes they were able to support an excessive lifestyle that would be impossible through ordinary paid work. Kenneth had killed several people, both as calculated revenge and as immediate manifestation when being challenged in public. He described his lifestyle in the following way:

> That's how I support my family, you see? My girlfriend, have a son ... I support him also. That's why I rob. I realized if I go to work, I'm gonna get paid maybe three hundred rand a week [30 Euro]. That's not enough for me. The things I want. I'm not gonna afford, that's why I do this thing.

Kyle was not involved in a gang but often spent time with gangsters. He killed a guy in a bar after the victim challenged him in front of a girl he wanted to impress. He explained that involvement in crime was a way to obtain money for alcohol, drugs, and clothes:

> My friends, they used to steal when they came to school, they have money, they smoke, they drink, use drugs and so. I was interested in those things, you see? I also wanted money, I wanted to wear what they wear, but my mother couldn't afford to buy me clothes.

(3) Action oriented

When talking about their homicides, the participants used the expression "talking type" or "acting type." Their willingness to use violence when necessary made them the acting type, whereas people who were afraid of violence, and therefore not street-capable, tended to talk themselves out of trouble:

> I don't like to talk. I'm not a talking person ... You see if this guy's taking me for this [a talking type], I must show him. I don't mind where I am. I just do my thing [use violence]. (Kenneth)

Devron had killed two people who challenged him in public. He explained the importance of showing others your "true colors" through the use of violence:

> I just wanted to show them how I'm really snapping. So actually it's showing them your true colors. How you do stuff. My friends, they're going to say "my broer" [my brother]. It's not about *knowing*. You know, we're not kittens. Get that kitten side away. Find the hardest "broer" [brother].

Damian had killed at least ten people when operating as a hit man for a gang. He was small of posture and repeatedly explained that his talent for shooting and his willingness to use excessive violence whenever being challenged made him a "big boy" in the eyes of his peers:

> It's to show them [peers] you're a man. To do things they can do. It doesn't matter if you're small or what. But if you shoot like that they say: "You're a big boy."

(4) Homicide as expression of dominance and control

Participants described the homicide as a necessary way of claiming dominance after they had been challenged in public. Responding in excessively violent ways provided them with a feeling of superiority. Kyle described his ability to stand up for himself and kill his opponent as: "It is like you are the great one. You have succeeded in what you wanted to do." Drégan said that a provocation turned him into battle mood: "You only focus on one thing. Destroying your victim. You know you just have to do that." Even though the lethal violence used by the participants was described as being the outcome of being in affective state of anger, they described the moment of killing as being a challenge in terms of staying focused and being able to actually go as far as to kill someone. Their immediate emotion of fear was an overwhelming part of this experience and needed to be blocked out by staying focused and alert (Lindegaard 2010). This complexity of the moment of homicide decision-making contributes to existing knowledge about the restraining effect of fear and the facilitating effect of anger on the decision to kill (Brookman 2015). The importance of claiming dominance was described by the participants as making them capable of blocking out their fear and staying focused in the moment of the killing:

> I didn't think before. I just started stabbing him. I must show them when they kick me. I must show them now. I must show them that they must leave me now. I must make an example. I must stay focused. You must fight now because you're afraid that they'll kill you so you must fight now. (Byron)

Being able to respond with lethal violence was an ultimate form of dominance but the way an individual killed someone also mattered for the type of status he gained from committing a murder:

> You see, when you're scared. You express your fear. You can't shoot. But someone who can shoot, you [will] hear [about it]. When he shoots and he didn't waste his bullets. (Kenneth)

The participants in this case study described committing a homicide as a means for dominance and control over their male victim after being challenged in public. They explained their killings as related to a lifestyle that included proving themselves as autonomous, capable of providing for themselves (and their families), and of being action oriented. In other parts of the world this lifestyle was described as related to street culture (Anderson 1999; Brookman *et al.* 2007; Sandberg and Pedersen 2011).

Conclusions: Street Masculinities as a Framework for Understanding Male Homicides

Homicides in South Africa are a serious health risk. Patterns of homicides are highly gendered. Men tend to get killed in public. Male homicides most often get committed in the context of arguments and revenge related disputes, and they tend to get carried out by strangers who are previously barely known to the victim. Women are most likely to get killed at home. Female homicides tend to be committed in the context of a rape and are often carried out by an intimate partner to the victim (CSVR 2008a).

Even though men are significantly more at risk of becoming homicide victims, the majority of literature on homicides in South Africa focuses on explaining homicide against women (Abrahams, Jewkes, and Mathews 2010, 2013; Jewkes and Abrahams 2002; Mathews, Jewkes, and Abrahams 2011). These studies have provided strong evidence that men who kill their intimate partners are motivated by a quest for dominance and control over women. Based on a case study of 14 male homicide offenders who killed a relatively unknown male in the context of a dispute in public, I illustrated how their motivations for homicide are similar to the motivations described by men who killed their intimate partners. The participants described their killing as being driven by a quest for dominance and control over a male victim who challenged them in public. Whereas studies of female homicides explained this motivation as a consequence of patriarchal notions of masculinity, I suggest specifying the potential sources of variation among men with a focus on the types of cultural repertoires men use to make sense of their violence.

My analysis indicated that the homicides of these offenders formed part of a certain street-oriented lifestyle that implied: (1) being autonomous from conventional society and from gang involvement; (2) proving the ability to provide for themselves and their families; and (3) being action oriented (rather than the "talking-type-of-person"). Through killing of a challenging male victim in public the participants gained street capital, and this capital provided status among peers involved in street culture (Lindegaard, Miller, and Reynald 2013).

Rather than perceiving homicides committed by men as being inherently related to dominant notions of masculinity, I propose that the quest for dominance over and control of the victim must be understood as associated with a particular type of men engaging in street culture. Men who claim street masculinities are characterized by lacking conventional means for social status such as paid jobs and educational diplomas, and by being concerned about improving their life in a short-term capacity (Lindegaard and Jacques 2014).

Future studies need to pay closer attention to the variation of cultural repertoires, including different types of street culture repertoires, which men draw upon to make sense of their violence. More insights are needed about the way street culture makes young men vulnerable to homicide offending and to violent crime victimization more generally. Studies that provide sequential insights into the courses of actions during homicides, comparing male and female offenders, and male offenders drawing on different types of cultural repertoires, will bring the field of homicide studies further. In South Africa, more insights are needed about the radical vulnerability to homicide offending and victimization among men.

Note

1 The participants were between 17 and 25 years old at the time of the study. They all grew up in township areas of Cape Town. Four described themselves as Black and ten as Colored. Two participants finished high school and continued with further studies. Five lived in a household including both their father and mother before incarceration. Ten lived with only their mother, one with only his grandmother, and one was homeless. Five were involved in well-organized gangs. One shifted between different gang affiliations without any official commitment. Five committed various forms of crimes with a group of friends without any official name or hierarchical structure. Three committed crimes together with friends who were organized in a gang.

References

Abrahams, N. and Jewkes, R. (2005) Effects of South African men's having witnessed abuse of their mothers during childhood on their levels of violence in adulthood. *American Journal of Public Health*, 95: 1811–1116. doi: 10.2105/AJPH.2003.035006.

Abrahams, N., Jewkes, R., and Mathews, S. (2010) Guns and gender-based violence in South Africa. *South African Medical Journal*, 100(9): 586–588.

Abrahams, N., Mathews, S., Martin, L.J., *et al.* (2013) Intimate partner femicide in South Africa in 1999 and 2009. *PLOS Medicine*, 10: e1001412. doi: 10.1371/journal.pmed.1001412.

Altbeker, A. (2008) Murder and robbery in South Africa: A tale of two trends. In A. van Niekerk, S. Suffla, and M. Seedat (eds), *Crime, Violence and Injury Prevention in South Africa: Data to Action* (pp. 122–149). Tygerberg, South Africa: MRC-UNISA Crime, Violence and Injury Lead Programme.

Anderson, E. (1999) *Code of the Street: Decency, Violence and the Moral Life of the Inner City*. New York: W.W. Norton.

Baumer, E., Horney, J., Felson, R., and Lauritsen, J.L. (2003) Neighborhood disadvantage and the nature of violence. *Criminology*, 41: 39–71. doi: 10.1111/j.1745-9125.2003.tb00981.x.

Brookman, F. (2000) Dying for control: Men, murder and sub-lethal violence. *The British Criminology Conference: Selected Proceedings*, 3.

Brookman, F. (2015) Killer decisions: The role of cognition, affect, and "expertise" in homicide. *Aggression and Violent Behavior*, 20: 42–52. doi: 10.1016/j.avb.2014.12.007.

Brookman, F., Bennett, T., Hochstetler, A., and Copes, H. (2011) The "code of the street" and the generation of street violence in the UK. *European Journal of Criminology*, 8: 17–31. doi: 10.1177/1477370810382259.

Brookman, F., Mullins, C., Bennett, T., and Wright, R. (2007) Gender, motivation, and the accomplishment of street robbery in the United Kingdom. *British Journal of Criminology*, 47: 861–884. doi: 10.1093/bjc/azm029.

Campbell, C. (1992) Learning to kill? Masculinity, the family, and violence in Natal. *Journal of Southern African Studies*, 18(3): 614–628.

Copes, H. and Hochstetler, A. (2003) Situational construction of masculinity among male street thieves. *Journal of Contemporary Ethnography*, 32: 279–304. doi: 10.1177/0891241603252118.

CSVR (Centre for the Study of Violence and Reconciliation) (2008a) *Streets of Pain, Streets of Sorrow: The Circumstances of the Occurrence of Murder in Six Areas with High Murder Rates*. Report by the Centre for the Study of Violence and Reconciliation, Braamfontein, South Africa.

CSVR (2008b) *Case Study of Perpetrators of Violent Crime*. Report by the Human Science research Council on behalf of the Centre for the Study of Violence and Reconciliation, Braamfontein, South Africa.

CSVR (2010) *Tackling Armed Violence: Key Findings and Recommendations of the Study on the Violent Nature of Crime in South Africa*. Report by the Centre for the Study of Violence and Reconciliation, Braamfontein, South Africa.

Daly, M., Wilson, M., and Vasdev, S. (2001) Income inequality and homicide rates in Canada and the United States. *Canadian Journal of Criminology*, 43: 219–236.

Demombynes, G. and Özler, B. (2005) Crime and local inequality in South Africa. *Journal of Development Economics*, 76: 265–292. doi: 10.1016/j.jdeveco.2003.12.015.

Donson, H. (2008) *A Profile of Fatal Injuries in South Africa 2007*. Tygerberg, South Africa: MRC-UNISA Crime, Violence and Injury Lead Programme.

Garot, R. (2010) *Who You Claim: Performing Gang Identity in Schools and on the Streets*. New York: New York University Press.

Gibson, D. and Lindegaard, M.R. (2007) South African boys with plans for the future, and why a focus on dominant discourses only tells us a part of the story. In T. Shefer, K. Ratele, A. Strebel, *et al.* (eds), *From Boys to Men* (pp. 128–144). Cape Town: Juta Press/University of Cape Town Press.

Graham, L. (2014) "But I've got something that makes me different": Young men's negotiation of masculinities. *South African Review of Sociology*, 45: 3–19. doi: 10.1080/21528586.2014.945137.

Groenewald, P., Bradshaw, D., Daniels, J., *et al.* (2008) *Cause of Death and Premature Mortality in Cape Town, 2001-2006*. Cape Town: South African Research Council.

Harris, G. and Vermaak, C. (2014) Economic inequality as a source of interpersonal violence: Evidence from sub-Saharan Africa and South Africa. *South African Journal of Economic and Management Sciences*, 18: 45–57. doi: org/10.17159/2222-3436/2015/v18n1a4.

Holligan, C. (2015) Breaking the code of the street: Extending Elijah Anderson's encryption of violent street governance to retaliation in Scotland. *Journal of Youth Studies*, 18: 634–648. doi: 10.1080/13676261.2014.992312.

Jensen, S. (2008) *Gangs, Policy, and Dignity in Cape Town*. London: James Curey.

Jewkes, R. and Abrahams, N. (2002) The epidemiology of rape and sexual coercion in South Africa: An overview. *Social Science & Medicine*, 55(7): 1231–1244.

Jewkes, R., Sikweyiya, Y., Morrell, R., and Dunkle, K. (2011) Gender inequitable masculinity and sexual entitlement in rape perpetration South Africa: Findings of a cross-sectional study. *PLoS ONE*, 6: e29590. doi: 10.1371/journal.pone.0029590.

Kaminer, D., Grimsrud, A., Myer, L., *et al.* (2008) Risk for post-traumatic stress disorder associated with different forms of interpersonal violence in South Africa. *Social Science and Medicine*, 67: 1589–1595. doi: 10.1016/j.socscimed.2008.07.023.

Kynoch, G. (1999) From the Ninevites to the hard livings gang: Township gangsters and urban violence in twentieth-century South Africa. *African Studies*, 58: 55–85. doi: 10.1080/00020189908707905.

Leggett, T. (2004) Still marginal: Crime in the coloured community. *SA Crime Quarterly*, 7: 13–45.

Lemanski, C. (2004) A new apartheid? The spatial implications of fear and crime in Cape Town, South Africa. *Environment and Urbanization*, 16: 101–112. doi: 10.1177/095624780401600201.

Lindegaard, M.R. (2009) Coconuts, Gangsters and Rainbow Fighters: How Male Youngsters Navigate Situations of Violence in Cape Town, South Africa, PhD dissertation. Amsterdam: University of Amsterdam.

Lindegaard, M.R. (2010) Moving to the "dark side": Fears and thrills in Cape Town, South Africa. *Ethnofoor*, 21: 35–62.

Lindegaard, M.R. and Jacques, S. (2014) Agency as a cause of crime. *Deviant Behavior*, 35: 85–100. doi: 10.1080/01639625.2013.822205.

Lindegaard, M.R., Miller, J., and Reynald, D.M. (2013) Transitory mobility, cultural heterogeneity and victimization risk among young men of color: Insights from an ethnographic study in Cape Town, South Africa. *Criminology*, 51: 967–1008. doi: 10.1111/1745-9125.12025.

Mathews, S., Jewkes, R., and Abrahams, N. (2011) "I had a hard life": Exploring childhood adversity in the shaping of masculinities among men who killed an intimate partner in South Africa. *British Journal of Criminology*, 51: 960–977. doi: 10.1093/bjc/azr051.

Mathews, S., Jewkes, R., and Abrahams, N. (2015) "So now I'm the man": Intimate partner femicide and its interconnections with expressions of masculinities in South Africa. *British Journal of Criminology*, 55: 107–124. doi: 10.1093/bjc/azu076.

Morrell, R. (2001) The times of change: Men and masculinity in South Africa. In R. Morrell (ed.), *Changing Men in Southern Africa* (pp. 3–37). Scottsville: University of Natal Press.

Morrell, R., Jewkes, R., Lindegger, G., and Hamlall, V. (2013) Hegemonic masculinity: Reviewing the gendered analysis of men's power in South Africa. *South African Review of Sociology*, 44: 3–21. doi: 10.1080/21528586.2013.784445.

Norman, R., Bradshaw, D., Schneider, M., *et al.* (2007a) A comparative risk assessment for South Africa in 2000: Towards promoting health and preventing disease. *South African Medical Journal*, 97: 637–641.

Norman, R., Matzopoulos, R., Groenewald, P., and Bradshaw, D. (2007b) The high burden of injuries in South Africa. *Bull World Health Organ*, 85: 695–702. doi: org/10.1590/S0042-96862007000900015.

Posel, D. (2001) What's in a name? Racial categorisations under apartheid and in its afterlife. *Transformation*, 47: 50–74.

Ratele, K. (2008) Analysing males in Africa: Certain useful elements in considering ruling masculinities. *Asian African Studies*, 7: 515–536.

Sandberg, S. and Pedersen, W. (2011) *Street Capital: Black Cannabis Dealers in a White Welfare State*. Bristol: Policy Press.

SAPS (South African Police Service) (2015) Crime in RSA for April to March 2003/2004–2013/2014. Available online at http://www.saps.gov.za/resource_centre/publications/statistics/crimestats/2014/crime_stats.php (accessed March 31, 2015).

Seedat, M., Van Niekerk, A., Jewkes, R., *et al.* 2009. Violence and injuries in South Africa: Prioritising an agenda for prevention. *The Lancet*, 374: 1011–1022. doi: 10.1016/S0140-6736(09)60948-X.

Standing, A. (2003) The social contradictions of organized crime on the Cape Flats. *Institute for Security Studies*, 74: 1–14.

Steinberg, J. (2012) Security and disappointment: Policing, freedom and xenophobia in South Africa. *British Journal of Criminology*, 52: 345–360.

Stewart, E.A. and Simons, R.L. (2010) Race, code of the street, and violent delinquency: A multilevel investigation of neighborhood street culture and individual norms of violence. *Criminology*, 48: 569–605.

Swart, L.-A., Seedat, M., and Nel, J. (2015) Neighborhood sociostructure and adolescent homicide victimization in Johannesburg, South Africa. *Homicide Studies*, 19: 1–19.

Thomson, J.D.S. (2004) A murderous legacy: Coloured homicide trends in South Africa. *SA Crime Quarterly*, 7: 9–14.

Wacquant, L. (2008) *Urban Outcasts: A Comparative Sociology of Advanced Marginality*. London: Polity Press.

Wilkinson, D.L. (2001) Violent events and social identity: Specifying the relationship between respect and masculinity in inner-city youth violence. *Sociological Studies of Children and Youth*, 8: 235–269.

Wilkinson, R., Kawachi, I., and Kennedy, B.P. (1998) Mortality, the social environment, crime and violence. *Sociology of Health and Illness*, 20: 578–597.

Wood, A. (2006) *Correlating Violence and Socio-Economic Inequality: An Empirical Analysis*. Geneva: World Organisation Against Torture.

Wood, K., Lambert, H., and Jewkes, R. (2007) "Showing roughness in a beautiful way": Talk about love, coercion and rape in South African youth culture. *Medical Anthropology Quarterly*, 21: 277–300. doi: 10.1525/maq.2007.21.3.277.

Wood, K. and Jewkes, R. (2001) "Dangerous" love: Reflections on violence among Xhosa township youth. In R. Morrell (ed.), *Changing Men in Southern Africa* (pp. 317–336). London: University of Natal Press and Zed Press.

Wright, R., Brookman, F., and Bennett, T. (2006) The foreground dynamics of street robbery in Britain. *British Journal of Criminology*, 46: 1–15. doi: 10.1093/bjc/azi055.

Wright, R. and Decker, S.H. (1997) *Armed Robbers in Action: Stickups and Street Culture*. Boston: Northeastern University Press.

Further Reading

Serran, G. and Firestone, P. (2004) Intimate partner homicide: A review of the male proprietariness and the self-defense theories. *Aggression and Violent Behavior*, 9: 1–15. doi: 10.1016/S1359-1789(02)00107-6.

Walker, L. (2005) Men behaving differently: South African men since 1994. *Culture, Health and Sexuality*, 7: 225–238. doi: 10.1080/13691050410001713215.

Part IV

Investigating Homicide

29

Technology and Homicide Investigation

Patrick Q. Brady and William R. King

Over the last quarter century, the development and adoption of technological innovations have transformed many aspects of law enforcement operations. These advancements have increased productivity and efficiency while providing a convenient and cost-effective method to create and access information and communicate with others. Despite the growing literature on the adoption and use of technology in policing, limited information exits on the use of technology in homicide investigations.

In this chapter, we review the current literature on four contemporary uses for technology in homicide investigations, along with the impact of these technologies on the effectiveness of investigatory outcomes, such as arrest. Given the wide range of technological innovations in the twenty-first century, there are numerous possible technologies that might assist in homicide investigations. Rather than provide a broad survey of many technologies, however, we chose to delve in depth into four technologies: (1) forensic, physical evidence comparative databases (PECDs); (2) cell tower and location data; (3) social networking sites (SNS); and (4) automated license plate reader systems. We chose these four due to the emerging empirical evidence and because each illustrates important points about the nexus between homicide investigations and technology. Due to the evolving nature of technology in investigations, we are rarely able to provide definitive estimates of how often a particular technology is used and to what effect. This chapter focuses on the intersection between technology and the process of criminal investigations. Therefore, it does *not* cover techniques or technologies employed in processing crime scenes (such as ground penetrating radar or GPS location techniques), or technological analysis conducted in crime laboratories (such as gas chromatography).

The Handbook of Homicide, First Edition. Edited by Fiona Brookman, Edward R. Maguire, and Mike Maguire.

Technology

In order to describe the role of technology in homicide investigations, it is important to conceptualize the meaning of the term "technology." While varying definitions exist, policing scholars have identified two broad categories of technologies: material and information-based technologies (Byrne and Marx 2011). Material-based technologies, also known as hard technologies, relate to the equipment, tools, and/or devices that police officers use to prevent or control crime or to accomplish other objectives (Byrne and Marx 2011). Hard technologies generally include—but are not limited to—items such as weapons, closed circuit television cameras (CCTVs), cellphones, and police protective gear. Information-based technologies, also known as soft technologies, refer to the less tangible resources (e.g., information management systems, new software, social networking sites, etc.) that seek to increase police performance. Overall, the extant literature on police use of hard and soft technologies focuses primarily on crime prevention. Moreover, this chapter provides insight into a select group of hard and soft technologies that officers use in homicide investigations.

Forensic Physical Evidence Comparative Databases

We use the term *forensic physical evidence comparative databases* (PECDs) to refer to databases that are populated with information derived from individuals (such as DNA) or items of physical evidence (such as toolmarks on ballistics evidence). PECDs are searchable and the information within the databases is comparative. Thus, evidence acquired at one crime scene can be automatically compared to evidence derived from suspects or other crime scenes. PECDs include fingerprint databases, such as AFIS (Automated Fingerprint Identification Systems), DNA databases, such as CODIS (Combined DNA Identification System) in the United States and NDNAD (National DNA Database) in the United Kingdom, and ballistics imaging databases such as IBIS (Integrated Ballistics Information System), NIBIN (National Integrated Ballistics Information Network) in the United States, and RIBIN (Regional Integrated Ballistics Information Network) in the Caribbean basin.[1] These three types of PECDs allow an investigator or technician to compare evidence from one source (such as the profile of a suspect's DNA or images of tool marks impressed on a fired cartridge case) to other records in the database. If a match is identified between evidence from two crimes, or from a crime and a sample from a known suspect, that match is termed a "hit."

There is ample evidence that PECDs have improved the number of hits or matches produced by forensic analysis. For example, the use of ballistics imaging technology by the Boston Police Department produced a sixfold increase in the number of hits (Braga and Pierce 2004).

In the United States, CODIS has produced more than 270,000 hits (FBI 2014) and NIBIN has produced more than 50,000 ballistics hits (ATF 2014). In the United

Kingdom, NDNAD produced 410,589 scene-to-subject matches between 1998 and 2009 (Home Office 2009: 35, table 4).

Hits or matches identified by PECDs can potentially improve the information available to investigators, however, the effectiveness of PECDs in solving homicides is determined in great measure by a range of variables. The databases must be populated sufficiently with information from criminal cases (NRC 2008), but effectiveness may be harmed by excessively large database size, at least with ballistics imaging databases (Nennstiel and Rahm 2006). PECDs are more effective when identifying repeat offenders or firearms that are used repeatedly. Additionally, a supporting network of people and processes is crucial to ensure that databases are fed sufficient inputs, and that outputs (information on hits or matches) are quickly produced and disseminated to investigators (Gagliardi 2009, 2010; King *et al.* 2013). The process of inputting and analyzing evidence and producing reports for investigators is often time consuming, and time delays and evidence backlogs can impede the timely production of information for investigators.

With these caveats in mind, a handful of studies have investigated the role of information from PECDs in homicide investigations, with mixed results. A study of 150 successful homicide investigations in Australia (Briody 2004) concluded that DNA was helpful in moving cases into court and produced more jury convictions in homicide cases, although there are sample selection issues with the research design.[2] Research on homicide cases in the New York City Police Department revealed that the results of DNA analysis were used rarely (in only 6.7% of cases) during the pre-arrest phase of homicide investigations in Manhattan, and that overall, DNA evidence was not helpful for clearing cases (Schroeder and White 2009). Detectives appeared to request DNA analysis from the lab when they had run out of other options for solving their cases. A study of the use of ballistics imaging "hit reports" in 65 homicide cases in nine US cities revealed that investigators rarely used the hit reports to identify or arrest previously unknown suspects (King *et al.* 2013). In half (50%) of the cases, the suspect had been identified before the ballistics imaging hit was made. Investigators reported that ballistic hits helped identify a suspect in 9.7 percent of cases and the hit led to an arrest in only 1.6 percent of cases.

We think there are three reasons why research with PECDs shows mixed effects on homicide investigations. First, time matters. A considerable percentage of homicides are cleared quickly. In the United States, about half of homicide cases will be cleared by the arrest of a suspect within 17 days after the crime (Regoeczi, Jarvis, and Riedel 2008). About 80 percent of homicide arrests in Cleveland, Ohio, occurred within 20 days of the crime (McEwen and Regoeczi 2015). These quickly solved cases are sometimes called "self-solvers," slam dunks, or "dunkers" (Innes 2002). When we limit the analysis to only solved cases, the quick arrest of a suspect is even more marked—46.3 percent of cleared homicides are cleared within one day, and 77.8 percent are cleared within one week (Regoeczi, Jarvis, and Riedel 2008). In comparison to the short timeline for most homicide investigations, the processing and analysis of physical evidence used by PECDs is longer. When delays in processing exist, information from PECDs rarely contributes to suspect identification or arrest for self-solvers. There are meaningful differences in processing times across organizations and countries. For example, DNA samples submitted to the UK's NDNAD system are uploaded and compared to other samples in the database much more quickly than are DNA samples in CODIS in the United States (Goulka *et al.* 2010: 15).

Some of these delays are due to practices and procedures police agencies and laboratories use to process physical evidence. One study conducted in Trinidad and Tobago found that impediments to communicating ballistics imaging hits to the proper homicide investigators were considerable, and that at least one-third of investigators never received a hit report associated with their case (King and Wells 2015). Some police agencies hold physical evidence in storage and do not submit it to laboratories for analysis. Strom and Hickman (2010) estimate that 14 percent of unsolved homicide cases in US police agencies had physical evidence that was not submitted to crime laboratories for analysis. Crime labs may adopt procedures that increase analysis time as well. For example, half (50.5%) of NIBIN labs in the United States route all ballistics evidence to their fingerprint and DNA sections *before* the evidence is sent to the firearms section (King *et al.* 2013: 33). Such a routing process lengthens the time between the crime and input into a ballistics imaging system. Additionally, lab backlogs can increase the time delay. A study of US crime lab backlogs in 2009 revealed that DNA, latent prints, and firearms/toolmarks analyses account for three of the four most backlogged requests for services (Durose, Walsh, and Burch 2012). Together, inefficient procedures and backlogs can produce relatively long processing times. For example, the median time between a crime and the identification of ballistics imaging hits in the United States stands at 101 days (King *et al.* 2013).

Second, investigators seem unwilling to submit evidence to crime labs for analysis when they do not have a suspect in homicide cases (Schroeder and White 2009). In a nationally representative study of US police agencies, Strom and Hickman (2010) report that the single greatest reason agencies gave for not submitting evidence to labs was because a suspect had not been identified. It appears the investigators use information from PECDs to confirm or disconfirm their hunches or the identities of suspects more often than they use it to identify unknown suspects.

Third, when we expand our discussion to all physical evidence at crime scenes, and not just to evidence suitable for PECDs, additional benefits emerge. The presence and collection of evidence appears to influence investigations (including crimes other than homicides). Investigators likely learn valuable clues from evidence even when it is not analyzed by a laboratory (Peterson *et al.* 2013). For instance, a national study of ballistics imaging practices in the United States revealed that investigators liked receiving hit reports:

> Investigators like the possibility that a hit may provide useful information, background, context, some history of the gun involved, or the gangs or individuals thought to be associated with the gun. One of the most useful contributions of a hit report for investigators is the ability to confirm suspicions about the suspect or case even when a suspect has already been identified or arrested. For example, if a suspect is a known

member of a particular gang and the gun used in the crime is linked to other crimes committed by that gang, investigators take the hit as validation for their suspicion of that suspect. (King *et al.* 2013: 75)

Information from PECDs appears to contribute to charging decisions, trial outcomes, and sentencing decisions (Briody 2004; Peterson *et al.* 2013).

Cell Towers and Location Data

Wireless surveillance through cell tower data has recently become a powerful tool in criminal investigations. Within the last 15 years, cellphone (or mobile phone) ownership among US adults has grown dramatically from 53 percent in 2000, to 90 percent in 2014 (Pew Research Center 2014). Indeed, 90 percent of US adults own a cellphone, with 58 percent of cellphone users having "smartphones."[3] In fact, AT&T has seen more than a 30,000 percent increase in mobile data traffic between 2007 and 2012 (AT&T 2014). In 2013, cell phone subscriptions in the United Kingdom averaged 125 subscriptions per 100 persons, 98 per 100 in France, 121 per 100 in Germany, and 96 per 100 in the United States. Even in developing nations with high rates of violent crime, cell phone usage is considerable. For example, Guyana has 69 cell subscriptions per 100 persons, Jamaica 102 per 100, and Trinidad and Tobago (145 per 100) (World Bank 2015).

Unlike traditional landlines, mobile telephones operate by communicating and registering with cell towers via radio signals that are transmitted between a consumer's device and the carrier's network (Pell and Soghoian 2012). As mobile subscribers travel from one location to the next, cellphones automatically connect to the nearest cell site within the carrier's network, and perform a registration process to ensure that "the user has a valid cell phone service" (Pell and Soghoian 2012: 127). Moreover, cell towers register the number of every connecting cellphone, which can provide investigators with the date and time a call was made, along with the geographical location of a particular device (Carter 2013).

While advancements in mobile technology provide law enforcement agencies with several methods to retrieve cellular data, two of the more common practices involve triangulation and "pinging." Triangulation is a process by which mobile service providers can obtain the longitudinal and latitudinal coordinates of a cellphone through combining data from multiple cell towers within a specific geographical area (McAllister 2013). Triangulation can be used with analog and digital cellphones and has quickly become a popular investigative method for obtaining historical data maintained by the provider in the cell site logs. Within the last five years, US wireless carriers have reported a dramatic growth in requests for cellphone records by local, state, and federal law enforcement agencies. According to Bender (2013), major wireless carriers received over 1.3 million personal mobile data requests in 2011, and 1.1 million requests in 2012 from US law enforcement agencies. In 2014, the Interception of Communications Commissioner's Officer (ICCO) within the United

Kingdom received nearly 3,000 requests for communication content from law enforcement agencies for investigative purposes (ICCO 2015).

Pinging allows for service providers to identify the location of a cellphone in real-time through the global positioning system (GPS) features of the phone (Pell and Soghoian 2012). Pinging occurs when a service provider covertly sends a signal or "ping" to a particular cellphone in order to retrieve the current location of the device in relation to the nearest cell tower. We are unaware of any estimates concerning the frequency with which cell phone data or pinging techniques are used in homicide investigations. It appears, however, from media reports and anecdotal accounts, that cell phone data are becoming increasingly used by law enforcement. We expect that such data will play a more common role in homicide investigations.

While cell tower data may provide valuable information in a homicide investigation, there are several limitations that are important to consider. First, obtaining cell tower data can be financially and logistically challenging. Not only are there multiple wireless service providers using the same cell tower, service providers also vary in the amount of time they maintain their data (Carter 2013). Thus, the information is time sensitive and may require investigators to obtain a subpoena/warrant (depending on the jurisdiction), and/or pay a fee for the information from each individual service provider.

Second, there exists an ongoing debate regarding the admissibility of cell tower data in US courts (McQuilkin 2011; Pell and Soghoian 2012). In order to prevent juries from considering information that is not based on "scientific knowledge," the US Supreme Court has established standards regulating the admissibility of expert testimony and scientific evidence at trials (Pell and Soghoian 2012). According to these standards, which are embodied under the *Frye*[4] and *Daubert*[5] doctrines, prior to admitting evidence and/or expert witness testimony, courts must consider several factors regarding the reliability of the evidence and the method by which the information was acquired. In general, these factors relate to whether the information or techniques used to obtain the evidence are empirically supported through independent studies that employ sound scientific methodologies (McQuilkin 2011).

Despite the growing number of law enforcement agencies advocating the use of cell tower data in criminal investigations (PERF 2013), there are very few empirical evaluations of this cell phone forensic technique that employ rigorous methodologies, or result in publications in peer-reviewed journals (McQuilkin 2011). Thus, the limited empirical support on the accuracy of cell tower data, along with the lack of evidence-based standards for extracting the data, may create issues for meeting admissibility standards in legal proceedings (Pell and Soghoian 2012).

In sum, cell tower data has recently become a popular investigative tool among local, state, and federal law enforcement agencies. The use of cell tower data can assist in corroborating statements, determining the time and general location of a victim or suspect, along with establishing the route of travel to and from a location. However, this investigative practice can pose financial, logistical, and legal concerns that are important for agencies to consider. Moreover, the use of cell tower data is still in its infancy and warrants the need for future empirical evaluations to address issues of feasibility, accuracy, and impact on homicide clearance rates.

Social Networking Sites and Criminal Investigations

Social networking sites (SNS), such as Facebook and Twitter, have revolutionized the manner in which we connect, interact, and share information with others. Users can personalize their profiles by uploading photographs and updating others about their location, interests, and current and/or former activities. As of March 2015, Facebook continues to be one of the most popular SNS, with 1.44 billion monthly active users, and an average of 936 million daily and 798 million mobile daily active users worldwide (Facebook Investor Relations 2015). Additionally, the prevalence of US adult social media users has significantly increased from 8 percent in 2005, to 74 percent in 2014 (Duggan *et al.* 2014). Duggan (2013) found that 54 percent of US Internet users upload personally created content online, with 47 percent of users sharing photographs and video that they found elsewhere through e-mails and popular social media platforms. More recently, however, the widespread adoption of social media platforms by the public has now diffused into police organizations worldwide.

Given the growing number of social media users, SNS platforms provide an easily accessible and rich source of information that police organizations can use to prevent and respond to criminal behavior. Although empirical investigations of this relatively new phenomenon are limited in the policing literature, the adoption and utilization of social media is becoming increasingly mainstream across local, state, and federal law enforcement agencies. In a recent survey of 600 US law enforcement agencies by the International Association of Chiefs of Police (IACP 2015), 95 percent of agencies reported using some form of social media. Findings from previous IACP surveys show that the prevalence of US law enforcement agencies using SNS has consistently increased from 81.1 percent in 2010, to 95 percent in 2014 (IACP 2011, 2015). Additionally, the Police Executive Research Forum (PERF) found that 98 percent of US law enforcement agencies noted that they planned to expand their use of SNS within the next two to five years (PERF 2013).

While social media can be a helpful resource for community policing, recent studies have shown that law enforcement agencies primarily use social media for investigative purposes. According to the IACP (2015), 82.3 percent of US law enforcement agencies use social media in criminal investigations. Of these agencies, 87.1 percent use social media to review profiles/activities of suspects, 67.7 percent solicit assistance from the public by posting surveillance videos or images, and 62 percent use an undercover identity to monitor suspect activity and gather intelligence (58.3%), or posting surveillance content (56.5%). In an online cross-sectional study of 1,221 federal, state, and local law enforcement personnel, officers perceive social media to be a valuable tool to carry out routine investigative functions

(LexisNexis Risk Solutions 2012). Findings indicated that four out of five law enforcement personnel used social media for investigative purposes. Social media was identified as an efficient and valuable resource for criminal investigations with 67 percent reporting that it helped to solve cases more quickly.

Omand, Bartlett, and Miller (2013: 804) identified four primary uses of social media in criminal investigations: crowdsourcing, situational awareness, intelligence gathering, and collection of evidence about criminal intent or criminal elements. First, crowdsourcing occurs when an individual or group(s) solicits the efforts of a larger entity or population to obtain needed resources (e.g., help, ideas, content, etc.). Voigt, Hinz, and Jansen (2013) argue that social media platforms provide a viable option for criminal investigations because of their ability to disseminate information to a large and active audience at almost no cost. Social media platforms provide a quick and immediate access to information.

The benefits of crowdsourcing for police organizations are twofold: (1) fostering community partnerships and (2) enhancing the efficiency of executing primary police functions. First, law enforcement agencies can cultivate partnerships with the community by "tapping into the wisdom of the crowd" (Omand, Bartlett, and Miller 2013: 805). In times of immediate need, law enforcement agencies can solicit the help of the community to aid them in an investigation by sharing information (e.g., photos, videos, tips, etc.) about a particular crime or person(s) of interest. Second, social media is a fast communication medium that enables users to continuously distribute information throughout their own social circles.

In a recent report by Davis, Alves, and Sklansky (2014), the Boston Police Department's use of SNS during their investigation of a deadly bombing at the Boston Marathon in Boston Massachusetts demonstrated the powerful use of crowdsourcing for both community policing and investigative purposes. In April 2013, the BPD used SNS to keep the community updated about the investigation, obtain investigative leads through crowdsourcing requests for the public's assistance, and calm members of the community by correcting inaccurate media updates. The redistribution of information by users expands the coverage and can increase the likelihood of reaching potential witnesses/leads. By obtaining the needed information from establishing active partnerships with the community, law enforcement agencies can be more equipped to enforce the law, maintain order, and provide services. Compared to the cost of traditional media outlets (e.g., newspapers, TV broadcasts), social media sites like Facebook and Twitter are free to use. Organizational resources (e.g., personnel expenditures), however, are important budgetary considerations, and more work is needed to determine whether or not social media platforms can be identified as cost-saving alternatives.

The second strategy is referred to as near "real-time situational awareness" (Omand, Bartlett, and Miller 2013). One of the many benefits of social media platforms involves the immediate, real-time access to information. Through the use of a hashtag (e.g., #BostonBombing), individuals can create trends or follow a specific event as it unfolds. Considering the ubiquity of social media use, police organizations can gather intelligence by following and monitoring certain trends and/or groups to develop a better understanding of their community (Omand, Bartlett, and Miller 2013). Monitoring social media platforms is a proactive approach that allows police organizations to forecast potential crimes and provide more effective responses. More recently, law enforcement agencies have used this strategy during large public events to ensure that officers are better prepared to maintain order (PERF 2013).

Third, intelligence gathering can provide insight into individuals or groups of interest (Omand, Bartlett, and Miller 2013). Similar to situational awareness, monitoring and tracing the behaviors and attitudes of a particular group of interest can now occur through social networking sites. As Morselli and Décary-Hétu (2013) have found, gang members are actively using social media to promote and represent their image. Luckily for law enforcement agencies, social media technologies have recently incorporated geotagging, which embeds longitudinal and latitudinal metadata into uploaded content (Boone 2013). The location of photos, videos, tweets, and status updates can be quickly traced through geographical locator websites (e.g., Google maps). Thus, police organizations can gather intelligence from gangs or other criminal groups to use as evidence or to develop proactive strategies.

Last, police organizations can use social networking sites in the "identification of criminal intent or criminal elements in the course of an enquiry both for the prevention and prosecution of crime" (Omand, Bartlett, and Miller 2013: 806). The interception of communications between suspects or groups of interest can occur in a virtual world through intelligence gathering techniques (Bartlett *et al.* 2013). Police organizations can surveil the social media sites of persons of interest to locate them, identify accomplices or criminal networks, and systematically collect information that could be used as evidence. Additionally, it is not uncommon for investigators to monitor close friends, partners, and/or family members of potential suspects, in hopes of identifying the suspects in uploaded photos or videos.

Although the research on law enforcement's use of social media is still in its infancy, the growing literature suggests that social media is becoming a transformative tool for law enforcement agencies to improve relationships with communities and investigate crimes (IACP 2015; Lieberman, Koetzle, and Sakiyama 2013; PERF 2013). Most of the research, however, focuses on exploring how organizations use this resource, with very few studies drawing attention to the use of social media in case clearances, arrests, and convictions of offenders.

Considering the ever-evolving nature of social media and technology, law enforcement agencies may even need to create new positions that are dedicated to social media. Given that younger generations are now growing up in societies where technological advancements are ubiquitous, the use of social networking sites might be a viable resource for recruiting and retaining younger generations who are known for being increasingly technologically savvy (Zickuhr 2011). Despite the dearth of research related to law enforcement agencies, Wilson *et al.* (2010) argue that social media recruitment techniques are increasingly popular among government organizations. Thus, future evaluations of the use of social media are increasingly important to determine the financial and logistical feasibility of dedicating time and resources to monitor social media activity. In the end, through effective policy development, education, and trainings for employees, social media provides the potential to enhance relationships with the community, and improve the legitimacy of police organizations worldwide.

Automated License Plate Reader Systems

While automated license plate reader systems, also known as automated number plate recognition systems, have become commonplace in the United Kingdom (PA Consulting Group 2006), their use has, more recently, rapidly diffused into law enforcement agencies across the United States (Taylor, Koper, and Woods 2011). According to a recent survey of 70 US law enforcement agencies of varying size, 71 percent use license plate readers (LPRs), with 85 percent of responding agencies indicating that they plan to adopt or increase their use of this technology within the next five years (PERF 2012). However, due to the associated cost of LPRs ($20,000–$25,000 per unit), most police agencies usually only have them installed on one or two patrol cars (Lum *et al.* 2011).

License plate readers are an operational tool for law enforcement that consists of high-speed cameras that are equipped with optical character-recognition technology and algorithms that can be used to scan and evaluate license plates on vehicles in real-time (Lum *et al.* 2011). Generally mounted on patrol vehicles or at a fixed location (e.g., toll plazas or street lights at intersections), LPRs scan the alphanumeric information on license plates and cross-references them across local, state, and national criminal databases that contain information on stolen vehicles, license plates, and other persons of interest (e.g., State-specific and National Crime Information Centers) (Lum *et al.* 2011). Once a match is made, the automated system generates a signal to alert the officer. Compared to the tedious manual process, readers have the ability to scan and cross-reference a large number of plates at varying speeds within a short period of time.

Much of the literature on LPRs focuses on the efficiency and accuracy of the readers (PA Consulting Group 2006), with findings suggesting that LPRs enhance the abilities of officers to apprehend offenders and recover stolen vehicles (Lum *et al.* 2011). More recently, however, studies have narrowed in on the use of LPRs as a means of preventing and deterring crime (Lum *et al.* 2011; Taylor, Koper, and Woods 2011). Using an experimental design, Lum *et al.* (2011) explored the deterrent effects of LPR technology on automobile and general crime control effectiveness in 30 hot spots across two neighboring jurisdictions. Findings indicated no difference between the treatment and control hot spots, which suggests that LPR technology does not produce a general or offense-specific deterrent effect.

Additionally, Taylor, Koper, and Woods (2011) used an experimental design and found that the use of LPRs, as opposed to the manual entry of license plates, significantly enhanced the productivity of an auto theft unit in scanning and detecting stolen license plates, apprehending offenders, and recovering stolen vehicles. More specifically, the use of LPRs resulted in more than eight times as many license plate checks, four times as many positive hits, and twice as many arrests and recoveries of occupied stolen vehicles than the manual process (Taylor, Koper, and Woods 2011). This technology did not, however, have any substantial impact on reducing rates of auto theft.

Overall, while LPR technologies are limited in their ability to deter and reduce crime, they do seem to be a promising resource for increasing productivity among officers and recovering occupied stolen vehicles. These findings have substantial implications for homicide investigations, as LPRs can improve the operational efficiency of investigations by quickly identifying and locating vehicles and persons of interest. For example, one important practice in homicide investigations is to canvass the neighborhood and document license plates and information on cars in the area (Carte 2013). While this was traditionally done through a manual process, assigning patrol cars with LPRs to canvass the neighborhood may identify vehicles or potential suspects in a more efficient and timely manner (PERF 2012).

Conclusions

Technology has revolutionized policing, as numerous technological advancements have, essentially, automated strategies and tactics that were previously carried out manually. In some instances we can detail the effect of a specific technology on homicide investigations because there is sufficient research to draw tentative conclusions (e.g., PECDs and homicide investigations). But for many of the technologies described in this chapter, the state of the knowledge is unclear about their impact on homicide investigations. Despite the widespread adoption of these technological innovations, there are three issues that warrant further elaboration, especially in regard to the intersection of homicide investigations and emerging technologies. First, in order to be effective, all the technologies reviewed above (and, we contend, all technologies writ large) must be part of a three-legged stool composed of people, processes, and technologies (Gagliardi 2009, 2010). The processes ensure that the technology is deployed efficiently and the results of analysis are quickly transmitted to investigators. For example, automated license plate reader systems should be deployed near homicide scenes immediately after a homicide and physical evidence must be quickly routed to labs and acquired by physical evidence comparative databases (PECDs). People, trained personnel and key boundary spanners within organizations, must be involved in the processes associated with these technologies. After all, people are responsible for implementing the processes, and ensuring that information is routed efficiently. Finally, the technologies themselves must be robust yet accurate, user friendly, and economical.

Second, there is relatively little research on the impact of most technologies on investigations, and especially on homicide investigations. There is evidence that some types of evidence and some forensic analysis influence case processing decisions later in the system, such as trial outcomes and sentencing decisions (Peterson *et al.* 2013). Less is known about the impact of information from most technologies on homicide investigations. Some studies find limited effects with DNA (Schroeder and White 2009) and ballistics imaging (King *et al.* 2013) on investigation outcomes such as suspect identification or arrest. Other studies find some effects on prosecution, trail outcomes, and sentencing (Peterson *et al.* 2013). Clearly, there is a need for additional research on the outcomes that these technologies, people, and processes produce.

Third, there are issues beyond efficiency that must be addressed. A homicide investigation can put tremendous pressure on a police agency to apprehend the suspect and dispense justice. If the pressure to solve the crime is high, any means may appear appropriate. Before this pressure mounts, it is important for police organizations to consider the legal, legitimacy-related, and financial implications of these innovations before deciding to adopt them. For example, emerging surveillance technologies, such as social networking sites, automated license plate reader systems, or closed circuit television (CCTV) cameras may invoke privacy concerns among members of the community. Surveillance technologies have the ability to collect information on the locations of individuals who are not violating the law, nor are the subjects of a criminal investigation. Thus, these emerging technologies may pose challenges to individual civil liberties and the legitimacy of policing.

While the advancement of technology and its applicability to law enforcement occurs at a faster rate than legislation (Omand, Bartlett, and Miller 2013), police organizations can improve their legitimacy through transparency and evidence-based policy development. Overall, emerging research shows that the community is supportive of the adoption of surveillance technologies, (Merola *et al.* 2014). However, police organizations should continue to work with the public to inform them about important factors, such as the length of time agencies will store data and how the information works to improve public safety through prevention and quality responses.

Fourth, police organizations should be cognizant of the financial and operational constraints that are inherent in the adoption of technological innovations. As technology continues to evolve, the adoption of these technologies will require ongoing training of investigators, storage capacity for surveillance information, occupational resources to monitor SNS, plus the costs of maintenance and regular upgrades.

Considering the limitations of technological innovations, the development and adoption of new technologies is inevitable and will continue to occur among law enforcement agencies. That being said, this area provides ample opportunities for future quality research with rigorous methodologies to assess the effectiveness, impact on officer productivity, and the practical and financial feasibility of these emerging innovations. Overall, these findings have substantial implications for improving the effectiveness and efficiency of criminal investigations.

Notes

1 RIBIN serves countries in the Caribbean basin, including Barbados, Jamaica, and Trinidad and Tobago.

2 Briody effectively sampled on his dependent variables (the outcomes of court proceedings) by selecting 75 homicide cases where DNA testing had incriminated the suspect,

the suspect had been identified, and the case had been resolved past all court appeals. In other words, the relationship between court outcomes and DNA was almost perfect. He then compared these 75 DNA cases to a sample of 75 homicides without DNA evidence.

3 A smartphone is a mobile phone that performs similar functions to a computer (e.g., use the Internet, stream content, access social networking sites, upload photos and videos, send e-mails, play games, etc.).

4 *Frye v United States*, 239 F. 1013 (1923).

5 *Daubert v Merrell Dow Pharmaceuticals, Inc.*, 509 US 579–590 (1993).

References

ATF (Bureau of Alcohol, Tobacco, Firearms and Explosives) (2014) National integrated ballistic information network (NIBIN) fact sheet. US Department of Justice. Available online at https://www.atf.gov/file/11171/download (accessed September 30, 2016).

AT&T (2014) AT&T introduces sponsored data for mobile data subscribers and businesses. Available online at http://www.att.com/gen/pressroom?pid=25183&cdvn=news&newsarticleid=37366&mapcode= (accessed August 8, 2015).

Bartlett, J., Miller, C., Crump, J., and Middleton, L. (2013) Policing in an information age. Center for the Analysis of Social Media at Demos, March. Available online at http://www.demos.co.uk/files/DEMOS_Policing_in_an_Information_Age_v1.pdf?1364295365 (accessed August 10, 2015).

Bender, B. (2013) Cellphone firms regularly give data to law enforcement: Big providers give authorities records of calls, locations. *The Boston Globe*, December 9. Available online at http://www.bostonglobe.com/news/nation/2013/12/09/new-figures-show-growth-law-enforcement-requests-for-cellphone-data/9o1TZ1xz5VUBButjteO1jL/story.html (accessed August 8, 2015).

Boone, J. (2013) Criminal use of social media (2013). NW3C. Available online at http://www.nw3c.org/docs/whitepapers/criminal-use-of-social-media.pdf?sfvrsn=10 (accessed October 12, 2014).

Braga, A.A. and Pierce, G.L. (2004) Linking crime guns: the impact of ballistics imaging technology on the productivity of the Boston Police Department's Ballistics Unit. *Journal of Forensic Sciences*, 49(4): 701–706.

Briody, M. (2004) The effects of DNA evidence on homicide cases in court. *Australian & New Zealand Journal of Criminology*, 37(2): 231–252.

Byrne, J. and Marx, G. (2011) Technological innovations in crime prevention and policing: A sreview of the research on implementation and impact. *Journal of Police Studies*, 20(3): 17–40.

Carter, D.L. (2013) Homicide process mapping: Best practices for increasing homicide clearances, Bureau of Justice Assistance, US Department of Justice. Available online at http://www.iir.com/Documents/Homicide_Process_Mapping_September_email.pdf (accessed August 12, 2015).

Davis, E.F., Alves, A.A., and Sklansky, D.A. (2014) Social media and police leadership: Lessons from Boston. *New Perspectives in Policing*, March. Available online at http://www.hks.harvard.edu/content/download/67536/1242954/version/1/file/SocialMediaandPoliceLeadership-03-14.pdf (accessed September 4, 2015).

Duggan, M. (2013) Photo and video sharing growth online. Pew Internet and America Life Project. Available online at http://pewinternet.org/~/media//Files/Reports/2013/PIP_Photos%20and%20videos%20online_102813.pdf (accessed August 8, 2015).

Duggan, M., Ellison, N.B., Lampe, C., *et al.* (2014) Social media update. 2014 Pew Internet and America Life Project. Available online at http://www.pewinternet.org/2015/01/09/social-media-update-2014/(accessed August 12, 2015).

Durose, M., Walsh, K., and Burch, A. (2012) *Census of Publicly Funded Forensic Crime Laboratories, 2009*. Washington, DC: US Department of Justice.

Facebook Investor Relations (2015) Facebook reports first quarter 2015 results. Available online at https://investor.fb.com/investor-news/press-release-details/2015/Facebook-Reports-First-Quarter-2015-Results/default.aspx (accessed August 8, 2015).

FBI (Federal Bureau of Investigation) (2014). CODIS—NDIS statistics. Available online at http://www.fbi.gov/about-us/lab/biometric-analysis/codis/ndis-statistics (accessed August 8, 2015).

Gagliardi, P. (2009) Helping police link more crimes, guns, and suspects using regional processing protocols. *Forensic Science Policy and Management*, 1: 43–48.

Gagliardi, P. (2010) *The 13 Critical Tasks: An Inside-Out Approach to Solving More Gun Crime*. Cote St Luc, Canada: Forensic Technology.

Goulka, J., Matthies, C., Disley, E., and Steinberg, P. (2010) *Toward a Comparison of DNA Profiling and Databases in the United States and England*. Santa Monica, CA: Rand Center on Quality Policing.

Home Office (2009) *National DNA Database: Annual Report: 2007–09*. Available online at https://www.gov.uk/government/uploads/system/uploads/attachment_data/file/117784/ndnad-ann-report-2007-09.pdf (accessed September 2, 2015).

IACP (International Association of Chiefs of Police) (2011). 2010 IACP social media survey results. Available online at http://www.iacpsocialmedia.org/Portals/1/documents/2011SurveyResults.pdf (accessed November 23, 2014).

IACP (2015). 2014 IACP social media survey results. Available online at http://www.iacpsocialmedia.org/Portals/1/documents/2014SurveyResults.pdf (accessed August 10, 2015).

ICCO (Interception of Communications Commissioner's Officer) (2015) *Report of the Interception of Communications Commissioner, March 2015*. Available online at http://www.iocco-uk.info/docs/IOCCO%20Report%20March%202015%20(Web).pdf (accessed September 30, 2016).

Innes, M. (2002) The "process structures" of police homicide investigations. *British Journal of Criminology*, 42(4): 669–688.

King, W. and Wells, W. (2015) Impediments to the effective use of ballistics imaging information in criminal investigations: Lessons from the use of IBIS in a developing nation. *Forensic Science Policy & Management*, 6(1–2): 47–57.

King, W., Wells, W., Katz, C., *et al.* (2013) *Opening the Black Box of NIBIN: A Descriptive Process and Outcome Evaluation of the Use of NIBIN and Its Effects on Criminal Investigations*. Washington, DC: US Department of Justice.

LexisNexis Risk Solutions (2012) Law enforcement personnel use of social media in investigations: Summary of findings. Available online at http://www.lexisnexis.com/government/investigations/(accessed August 8, 2015).

Lieberman, J.D., Koetzle, D., and Sakiyama, M. (2013) Police departments' use of Facebook: Patterns and policy issues. *Police Quarterly*, July. doi: 10.1177/1098611113495049.

Lum, C., Hibdon, J., Cave, B., *et al.* (2011) License plate reader (LPR) police patrols in crime hot spots: An experimental evaluation in two adjacent jurisdictions. *Journal of Experimental Criminology*, 7(4): 321–345.

McAllister, M. (2013) GPS and cell phone tracking: A constitutional and empirical analysis. *University of Cincinnati Law Review*, 82(1): 207–256.

McEwen, T. and Regoeczi, W. (2015) Forensic evidence in homicide investigations and prosecutions. *Journal of Forensic Sciences*, 60(5): 1188–1198. doi: 10.1111/1556-4029.12787.

McQuilkin, A. (2011) Sleeping gate-keepers: Challenging the admissibility of cellphone forensic evidence under *Daubert*. *Journal of High Technology Law*, 11: 365–406.

Merola, L.M., Lum, C., Cave, B., and Hibdon, J. (2014)Community support for license plate recognition. *Policing: An International Journal of Police Strategies & Management*, 37(1): 30–51.

Morselli, C. and Décary-Hétu, D. (2013) Crime facilitation purposes of social networking sites: A review and analysis of the "cyberbanging" phenomenon. *Small Wars & Insurgencies* 24(1): 152–170.

Nennstiel, R. and Rahm, J. (2006) A parameter study regarding the IBIS™ correlator. *Journal of Forensic Sciences*, 51(1): 18–23.

NRC (National Research Council) (2008) *Ballistic Imaging*. Washington, DC: National Academies Press.

Omand, D., Bartlett, J., and Miller, C. (2013) Introducing social media intelligence (SOCMINT). *Intelligence and National Security*, 27(6): 801–823.

PA Consulting Group (2006) *Police Standards Unit: Thematic Review of the Use of Automatic Number Plate Recognition within Police Forces*. London: PA Consulting Group.

Pell, S.K. and Soghoian, C. (2012) Can you see me now? Toward reasonable standards for law enforcement access to location data that congress could enact. *Berkeley Technology Law Journal*, 27: 117–195.

PERF (Police Executive Research Forum) (2012) How are innovations in technology transforming policing? Available online at http://www.policeforum.org/assets/docs/Critical_Issues_Series/how%20are%20innovations%20in%20technology%20transforming%20policing%202012.pdf (accessed November 23, 2014).

PERF (2013) Social media and tactical considerations for law enforcement. Office of Community Oriented Policing Services. Available online at http://ric-zai-inc.com/Publications/cops-p261-pub.pdf (accessed August 8, 2015).

Peterson, J.L., Hickman, M.J., Strom, K.J., and Johnson, D.J. (2013) Effect of forensic evidence on criminal justice case processing. *Journal of Forensic Sciences*, 58(s1): S78–S90.

Pew Research Center (2014) The Web at 25 in the US: Digital life in 2025. March. Available online at http://www.pewinternet.org/files/2014/03/PIP_Report_Future_of_the_Internet_Predictions_031114.pdf (accessed March 11, 2015).

Regoeczi, W.C., Jarvis, J., and Riedel, M. (2008)Clearing murders is it about time? *Journal of Research in Crime and Delinquency*, 45(2): 142–162.

Schroeder, D.A., and White, M.D. (2009) Exploring the use of DNA evidence in homicide investigations: Implications for detective work and case clearance. *Police Quarterly*, 12(3): 319–342.

Strom, K.J. and Hickman, M.J. (2010) Unanalyzed evidence in law enforcement agencies: A national examination of forensic processing in police departments. *Criminology & Public Policy*, 9(2): 381–404.

Taylor, B., Koper, C., and Woods, D. (2011) Combating vehicle theft in Arizona: A randomized experiment with license plate recognition technology. *Criminal Justice Review*, 37(1): 24–50.

Voigt, S., Hinz, O., and Jansen, N. (2013) Law enforcement 2.0: The potential and the (legal) restrictions of Facebook data for police tracing and investigation. *ECIS 2013 Completed Research*, Paper 5.

Wilson, J.M., Dalton, E., Scheer, C., and Grammich, C.A. (2010) *Police Recruitment and Retention for the New Millennium*. Santa Monica, CA: RAND Corporation.

World Bank (2015) Mobile cellular subscriptions (per 100 people), data table. Available online at http://data.worldbank.org/indicator/IT.CEL.SETS.P2?order=wbapi_data_value_2013+wbapi_data_value+wbapi_data_value-last&sort=asc (accessed April 22, 2015).

Zickuhr, K. (2011) Generations and their gadgets. Pew Internet and America Life Project. Available online at http://www.pewinternet.org/2011/02/03/generations-and-their-gadgets/(accessed March 11, 2015).

Further Reading

Harrell, S.L. (2008) Locating mobile phones through pinging and triangulation. *Pursuit Magazine*, July 1. Available online at http://pursuitmag.com/locating-mobile-phones-through-pinging-and-triangulation/(accessed August 8, 2015).

Jackman, T. (2014) Experts say law enforcement's use of cellphone records can be inaccurate, *The Washington Post*, June 27. Retrieved from http://www.washingtonpost.com/local/experts-say-law-enforcements-use-of-cellphone-records-can-be-inaccurate/2014/06/27/028be93c-faf3-11e3-932c-0a55b81f48ce_story.html (accessed August 8, 2015).

Koper, C.S., Taylor, B.G. and Woods, D.J. (2013) A randomized test of initial and residual deterrence from directed patrols and use of license plate readers at crime hot spots. *Journal of Experimental Criminology*, 9(2): 213–244.

30

Solving Homicides
Trends, Causes, and Ways to Improve

Thomas S. Alexander and Charles F. Wellford

Defining Homicide Clearances: The United States and Other Countries

Defining a *homicide clearance* is the starting point for any discussion on improving clearance rates. Conceptually, a clearance occurs when a duly constituted authority declares that the person or persons involved in the crime have been identified. Since 1980, an estimated 210,000 homicides in the United States have not been cleared. Clearing a case does not always mean an actual arrest was made, and it does not mean someone was found guilty of the offense in court. In the United States, the Uniform Crime Reports (UCR) specify two categories of case clearance: arrest or exceptional means. More specifically, a homicide case would be cleared by arrest if at least one person who was involved in committing the crime has been arrested, charged with the offense, and turned over to the court for prosecution. Conversely, clearance by exceptional means applies to cases where police cannot place formal charges against an offender for some reason beyond police control (FBI 2004).

There are several specific criteria in the UCR which must all be met before an agency can clear a case by exceptional means. Specifically, (1) the police must clearly know the identity of the offender, (2) there must be sufficient information that would allow charges to be placed or prosecution to proceed, (3) and the exact location of the offender is known so he or she could be taken into custody, but (4) a specific event outside police control does not allow law enforcement to arrest, charge, and forward the offender for prosecution (FBI 2004). For example, if an offender committed suicide or gave the police a deathbed confession, the case could be closed by exceptional means.

The Handbook of Homicide, First Edition. Edited by Fiona Brookman, Edward R. Maguire, and Mike Maguire.

Adding data on homicide clearances from other English-speaking countries further complicates our examination, since different countries' laws define crimes and clearances quite differently (Liem *et al.* 2013). Furthermore, while data on homicides are available worldwide, like those reported by the United Nations Office on Drugs and Crime (UNODC), variations in governments, data gathering procedures, and definitions place limits on comparisons across countries. Comparing United States and Canadian policies offers an instructive example of how differing guidelines in classification may alter any inter-country comparisons. According to the Canadian Centre for Justice Statistics, the terminology used in the UCR is similar to, yet distinct from, that in Canada's Uniform Crime Reporting Survey. Drawing from policing data or data submitted by police agencies, in Canada the clearance rate represents the proportion of criminal incidents solved by the police. However, Canadian officials define a solved homicide differently than their US counterparts. In Canada, police can clear a case by placing or "laying" a charge, or by other means. For a specific crime to be cleared by a charge, at least one of the accused persons must have been identified and either have had a charge placed, or had a charge recommended to be placed, against him or her. For an incident to be cleared without a charge, the accused must be identified and there must be sufficient evidence to place a charge in connection with the incident, but other circumstances (e.g., death of the accused by means other than suicide) cause the accused to be processed by some other means.

Of the 505 homicides that came to the attention of Canadian police in 2013, 386 (76%) were solved. This proportion is equal to the previous ten-year average that had been reported in Canada. In 2013, nine in ten (91%) solved homicides resulted in charges being laid or recommended, while the remainder were cleared by suicide of the accused (8%) or through other means (2%). As noted in Canada's crime statistics for 2013 (Boyce, Cotter, and Perreault 2014), clearance rates may be impacted by different charging policies in different jurisdictions. Police lay charges in most provinces, but in British Columbia and Quebec, the decision to lay charges is made by the Crown, while in New Brunswick police lay charges after receiving advice from the Crown (Cotter 2014). In the United States, charges are placed by the investigating law enforcement agency and clearance data is determined at this point, regardless of the future disposition of the charges. Charges can be made on the advice of the prosecutor's office, but standards vary from jurisdiction to jurisdiction.

Crime data for England and Wales are published in a report by the Office for National Statistics, "Focus on: Violent Crime and Sexual Offences." A look at England's definitions for homicide and clearance also shows how policy differences can affect what data are collected. In England and Wales, the term homicide clearance is not a general term as it is in the United States, but refers specifically to whether or not the case was solved, a determination made by a jury. The Home Office Homicide Index provides data on the outcome of cases. The English and Welsh data could be considered a more accurate representation of cleared cases, since the data can be revised as new information is developed. By comparison, in the United States once a case is cleared by meeting one of the required UCR rules it remains cleared data-wise, regardless of future developments. Adjusting the numbers to exclude cases which do not result in conviction or where the decision is made not to prosecute can ultimately end up reducing the number of homicides.

Of the 551 cases currently recorded as homicides in 2012/2013 for England and Wales, the case outcome data prior to November 8, 2013 is broken down as follows:

- Court proceedings had resulted in homicide convictions in 219 cases (40%);
- Court proceedings were pending for 209 cases (38%);
- Proceedings had been discontinued, a proceeding was not initiated, or all suspects had been acquitted in 18 cases (3%);
- Suspects had committed suicide in 17 cases (3%); and
- No suspects had been charged in connection with 88 cases (16%) (Home Office 2012/2013).

Applying the US criteria for classifying a homicide as cleared to these cases would result in an 84 percent clearance rate. England and Wales recently changed from counting homicides based on their detection to classifying them based on their outcome. This would mean a case would not be solved until the case had concluded, and the conclusion comes from the decision made by a jury. The fact that England and Wales take the final outcome into account places them at a distinct advantage over other jurisdictions. Sources that count cases as closed prior to adjudication run the risk of counting cases as cleared where the suspect is found not guilty. The main issue is that some data capture actual clearances based on convictions, whereas others count clearances based on a set of rules, regardless of whether the actual offender has been detected. Moreover, to the extent there are errors in case processing outcome-based data may not accurately identify true offenders. In this system, a person could be found not guilty due to procedural violations, but actually meet the criteria for clearance by being the actual offender.

Australia poses a unique challenge: homicide is officially defined by the varying criminal laws of each Australian state and territory. This variance makes a true perspective on clearances difficult to obtain. In contrast to England and Wales, Australia defines a homicide as solved when an offender has been arrested and charged, or when the homicide was a murder–suicide. This definition does not take into account the outcome of the judicial process, or whether the alleged offender is consequently acquitted or convicted, as it does in England and Wales. The "National Homicide Monitoring Program Report" for 2008–2010 reported that 46 of the 510 homicides had no offender identified or case solved. This clearance rate of 91 percent is slightly higher than the 2001 reports from the National Homicide Monitoring Program, which stated that unsolved homicides in Australia had been fairly stable over the years at 12 percent, leaving the clearance rates at around 88 percent.

Scotland publishes a homicide bulletin which only covers homicides as they were recorded by the police, and they do not make a distinction between open and closed cases. Significantly, while in the United States the number of victims determines the number of homicides, officials in Scotland count one event, regardless of the number of victims, as one homicide. Their crimes are defined as solved (closed) or unsolved (open). Solved cases are cases where at least one suspect has been identified by the police. Depending upon which data are examined—homicides from the recorded crime bulletin or the annex of the homicide bulletin—there could be different numbers of homicides reported. Some cases are also initially classified as homicides, but based on criminal proceedings have their classification changed at a later date. Crime data that were recorded for 2012 and 2013 show that of the 62 murder cases recorded, 61 were solved (98%).

In Northern Ireland, clearance rates are referred to as detection rates; *detected crime* is used to describe crimes which have been "cleared up" by the police. In the crime bulletin for the Police Services of Northern Ireland, crimes of violence with injury (including homicide) have followed a flat trend over the last two years. Over a 12 month period in 2013 compared to a similar period in 2014 homicides stayed the same at 19 offenses per year. Within the same timeframes, 89.5 percent of all homicides had "outcomes" for 2012 compared to 63.2 percent for 2013.[1] Taking the definition of outcomes into account, these rates could generally be classified as clearance rates according to US rules for classification, since the offender would be known and charged, unless there were means beyond the control of the police to prevent them from placing formal charges.

A lot of attention gets focused on US homicides and their clearances due to the seriousness of the crime and its seemingly low rates of clearance. Many explanations have been offered for the declining clearance rates for the nation's homicides. While accounting for this decline is important, it's also important to ask how to increase homicide clearances. One potential avenue of increasing our ability to better clear homicides would be to study countries with high and low clearance. The differences in how these countries define homicide and homicide clearance make this very difficult. Therefore, we focus in the next sections on what we have learned about variations in homicide clearance by studying the variations across jurisdictions in the United States.

Trends and Patterns of Homicide Clearances

Homicide clearances vary by year, jurisdiction, and country. In discussing homicide clearances, it is important not only to consider the definitional differences discussed above but also to consider these other sources of varying clearance rates.[2] In this section, we explore these other correlates of homicide clearance rate variation. Better understanding of how these rates vary provides valuable context for our discussion of how to improve these important measures of police performance. Unfortunately, our knowledge of homicide clearance rate patterns is limited to a few highly industrialized democratic societies, with most of the relevant research conducted on the United States.[3] Therefore, while this section focuses on clearance rates in the United States, it is important to recognize that improving clearance rates, while still making arrests that are sustained by the courts, is needed in all parts of the world.

The UNODC's study of homicide (2013) provides comparable measures of homicide clearances in 41 countries from all regions of the world. Among the 41 countries included in their study, the mean clearance rate was 62 percent, a level almost identical to the most recent clearance rate reported for the United States. The rate for the 22 countries in Europe was 82 percent; for the six Asian countries it was 80 percent; and in the 11 countries in the Americas it was 51 percent. In the 41 countries in the UNODC compilation, there was a strong relationship between levels of clearance and levels of homicide.

In the United States and Canada, the rate of homicide clearance has decreased substantially since the 1960s.[4] Figure 30.1 shows the rates for these two countries since 1961.

Anecdotal data suggest that other industrialized Western democracies are also experiencing declines in clearance. For these two countries, it is clear that the police's ability to solve what is generally considered the most serious crime has decreased. This raises a question: why have homicide clearances declined and what can be done to improve clearances?

At least in the United States, perhaps because of its highly decentralized organization of policing, the patterns of homicide clearance during this period vary substantially across police agencies. Some jurisdictions have consistently high homicide clearance rates and others have consistently low rates. This variation gives researchers the opportunity to understand why these variations occur. To demonstrate this point, Wellford and Scott (2015) analyzed the clearance rates for the one-hundred largest cities in the United States for the period 1970 to 2013.[5] The analysis used group-based trajectory modeling, which identifies subgroups of a population based on some outcome of interest—in this case the rate of clearing homicide (Nagin 2005). Figure 30.2 shows the results of that analysis.

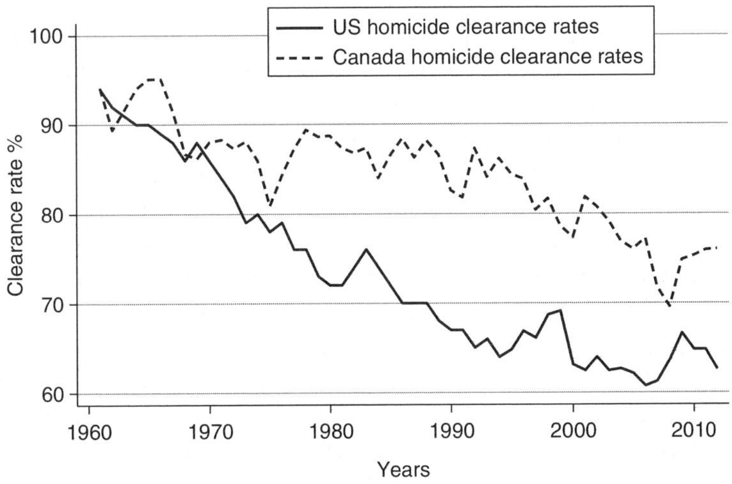

Figure 30.1 US and Canada yearly homicide clearance rates, 1961–2012.

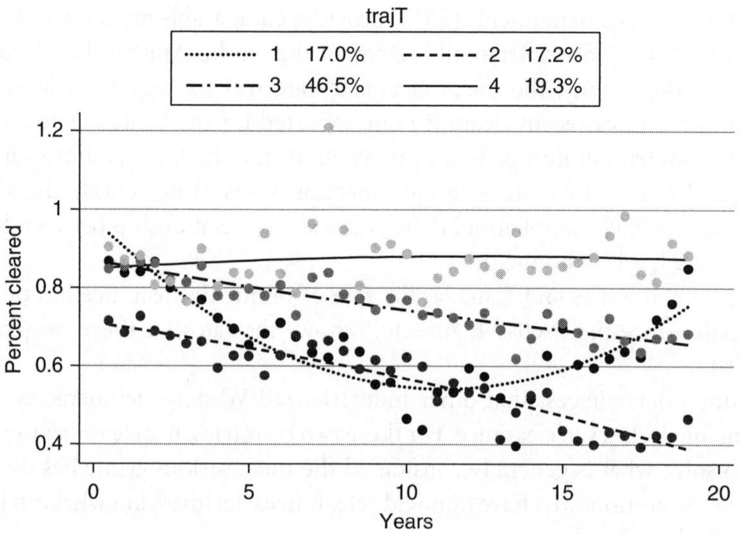

Figure 30.2 Trajectory models for homicide clearances in USA, 1980–2012.

Group four, with 19 percent of the cities, maintained high clearance rates throughout this timeframe. Group one, with 17 percent of the cities, had consistently low rates of clearance. Groups two and three, with 64 percent of the cities, showed slightly declining or flat rates of clearance. These patterns strongly suggest that at least in the United States, clearance rates vary across jurisdictions, have not declined in all jurisdictions despite the national trend, and that we may be able to improve clearance rates by better understanding why they vary.

Three broad and interrelated approaches to understanding this variation, and therefore the ability to close homicide cases, have been offered in the literature. First, some argue that variation in clearance rates across cities and/or time reflect changes in the nature of homicides. Some homicides are easier to clear than others (e.g., domestic violence homicides are easier to clear than homicides resulting from drug market disputes), so differences in clearance rates may reflect different patterns of homicides across jurisdictions. For example, the decline in clearance rates in the United States could be a result of fewer easier-to-solve homicides, with the remaining homicides being those most difficult to clear. A second approach is to focus on the organization and resources available to the police department and the priorities of the leader of the organization. These scholars argue that the variation in resources (e.g., number of detectives, crime scene support, and management of the investigation) accounts for variation in clearance rates. Finally, some suggest that the specifics of the investigation account for the observed variation. This approach places the primary focus of the explanation on the investigative process itself, including the characteristics of the investigators. In the next section, we review the research that has assessed these approaches to understanding variation in clearance rates in the Unites States, across jurisdictions and time.

The Determinants of Homicide Clearances

Since the 1990s, there has been an increase in research on homicide. Even with that increase, the scientific research on homicide clearances appears most often in *Homicide Studies*, an academic journal dedicated to the study of homicides, which was first published in 1997. Since then, the journal has published approximately 400 articles, only 15 percent of which have included the word "clearance" in the title. Perhaps little research has directly examined clearances due to the issues involved in classifying homicides as cleared. As our definitions in first section revealed, consistent definitions are required if we are to make use of others' success in clearing cases. Nonetheless, the importance of exploring homicide clearances cannot be overstated. Results can have both policy as well as theoretical implications.

The ebb and flow of crime rates as well as clearance rates brings with it the question, "Why the change?" All too often, we ignore the nexus of crime and clearance. Turning our attention to homicide, evaluating the connections between crime rates and clearances raises similar concerns about how we define clearances or solved homicides. The findings of the existing work on homicide clearance vary from study to study, but can be organized into studies that examine demographics, those that emphasize police practices, and those that consider overall case characteristics.

The clearance literature abounds with research examining demographic factors, such as race, age, gender, and ethnicity. A few studies have focused on situational factors, and even fewer look at police activities. When situational factors and police activities are examined, they are usually coupled with these same demographics. The one factor which seems to surface in the majority of the clearance research is race, typically the race of the victim, but even those studies reveal mixed results. Non-white victims have been reported to have higher rates of case clearance (Mouzos and Muller 2001; Regoeczi, Kennedy, and Silverman 2000), yet opposite results have also been reported (Litwin and Xu 2007). These last two studies report that cases with African American or Latino victims were less likely to be cleared. Lee (2005) has reported that cases that involved non-white victims as well as older victims were less likely to be solved. Other research has also reported no difference in regards to the race of the victim (Wellford and Cronin 1999; Litwin 2004; Puckett and Lundman 2003; Riedel and Rinehart 1996). Limited research has shown that the race of the offender may have a potential effect on clearance (Wellford and Cronin 1999; Jarvis and Regoeczi 2009; Roberts and Lyons 2009).

Research into police practices is lacking when it comes to the influence of the police in clearing homicides. Law enforcement is the entity that carries the burden of clearance: they are tasked with investigating a homicide and trying to determine who the perpetrator was. Naturally, then, their activities may or may not help clear a case. Research on the actual role that police practices play is very limited. Wellford and Cronin (1999) examined 251 possible predictors of clearance, and reported that 51 factors had significant effects on a case being closed. Notably, they found, the majority of characteristics that are associated with homicide clearances are related to police practice. As a result, clearance rates can be improved with a better understanding of law enforcement investigative practices. The initial response of the police to the crime, as well as the actions of detectives, play a key role in clearing the crime. Securing the crime scene and notifying detectives are both of importance, as is the swiftness of the arrival of the investigator.

Several other police activities also play key roles in clearing the homicide. The number of detectives assigned is important, and following up with witnesses also plays a vital role. Police can also make use of other sources of information like confidential informants and medical examiner reports, and use technology such as computer checks on persons, weapons, and witnesses. Factors outside the control of the police include the race of the suspect and where the homicide takes place. The involvement of gangs, drugs, and money also all play a role in whether the case gets cleared. The key findings showed that both types of factors help determine whether a case is cleared. This is important since factors outside the control of the police are enlightening, but hold little direct promise in changing clearance rates. Overall, there has been very little focus in the literature on actual police investigative practices in homicide cases. Those that do exist look at overall police practices on other crimes or build off of the Wellford and Cronin research.

For example, Jarvis and Regoeczi (2012) discuss homicide solvability. Their discussion centers on three areas: police personnel and management, investigative practices, and community factors. The investigative practices which were discussed are the staffing of detectives and others responding to the caseload, the importance of identifying witnesses, and the thorough collection and analysis of physical and electronic evidence. All are discussed as essential to clearing homicide cases. Keel, Jarvis, and Muirhead (2009) also looked at police practices. They examined factors that they thought would influence the effectiveness of an investigation. The factors under police control that were examined were the selection process of detectives, the investigative procedures used, witness processing, management of case assignments, resources used, training, and crime lab issues. While the authors could not draw solid empirical conclusions, they did report that three factors had statistically significant effects on case clearance: formal training, using sophisticated analytical tools, and the cooperation of the public in providing information.

Other areas of homicide clearances that are examined in the literature include victim–offender involvement (stranger, acquaintance, intimate partner, etc.), whether a concomitant felony is committed, and whether the killing is gang- or drug-related. Again, the results are mixed. Recent research has reported the victim's lifestyle has an effect on time to clearance (Rydberg and Pizarro 2014). The authors examined the covariates of homicide clearance through two different perspectives. They looked at event characteristics as well as victim devaluation, and reported that homicide clearances vary due to the different homicide incident characteristics rather than to various efforts by law enforcement. These findings did suggest potential strategies for investigators to use in hopes of raising clearance rates. Specifically, they recommended that investigators should use lifestyle in planning their investigative strategy. The media should be used in those cases where the persons involved have a criminal background. Examples would be notifying the media and other outlets to report the crime. Raising the public's awareness of the incident in this way may provide witnesses to the incident. As pointed out by the authors, homicides are complex sets of events that the police must investigate carefully, and future research could benefit from examining lifestyles as well as other characteristics, since they may have an effect on homicide clearance.

Other variables that have been found to have significant effects on clearances include the severity of the homicide and investigative difficulty (Roberts 2014); community characteristics, victim characteristics (race), and situational characteristics (firearm usage) (Litwin and Xu 2007); whether the killing was expressive or instrumental and whether firearms were used (Alderden and Lavery 2007); the use of police discretion based on victim characteristics (Roberts 2007); and outside influences such as the media, political figures, and prosecuting attorneys on police practices (Davies 2007). Scholars previously thought that stranger homicides were a potential reason for higher numbers of unsolved homicides (Regoeczi, Kennedy, and Silverman 2000). However, Quinet and Nunn (2014) report that decreased homicide rates are not due to an increase in stranger homicides, but agree that the relationship of the victim to the offender is important. Finally, a review of homicide characteristics by Riedel (2008) in his review of the clearance literature revealed that higher clearance rates result when weapons other than firearms are used, the location of the killing is in a residence, and the victims are intimate or killings of family member. Drug-related homicides and those involved with the crimes of rape or robbery were associated with lower case clearance rates.

In summary, when examining the existing research, we must keep in mind that although there are differing views, it's possible that specific types of homicides may have an impact on overall solvability. Homicide investigations can be very complex, and as the research has shown, many different factors can play an important part in their closure. Working on the premise that the majority of homicides are solvable, we need to look at what the research has told us. Given the mixed results on factors affecting clearance, it is especially difficult to specify the contribution of the race of the victim to understanding homicide clearance in the United States. Other factors have also been reported to influence case closure such as gang and drug involvement (Decker and Curry 2002; Alderden and Lavery 2007; Wellford and Cronin 1999). Whether or not a concomitant felony is committed has also shown promise as a predictor for homicide clearance (Riedel and Rinehart 1996; Mouzos and Muller 2001). Research on homicide clearances appear to be focused on extralegal factors, as well as situational and case-specific characteristics. The importance of police practices has been noted (Wellford and Cronin 1999; Alexander 2012). Overall, the literature has revealed promising results in the area of police practices, and there may lay the key to improving clearances.

Promising Practices for Homicide Investigations

In popular culture, homicides are solved by incredibly intelligent and perceptive individuals who see patterns in seemingly unrelated observations—think Sherlock Holmes. But at the same time, the early research literature on investigations concluded that individual detectives made little difference in case closure rates

(Greenwood and Petersilla 1975). Though the research literature summarized in the previous sections does not establish a strong foundation for identifying best practices for homicide investigations, it does suggest that homicide clearance rates vary across jurisdictions and time, and that departmental policies and practices can influence these rates. The findings from this literature have been used to encourage police departments to test the practices most likely to be successful. These findings, combined with emerging research on best practices, are leading us to a stronger scientific basis for improving homicide clearances.

Both the International Association of Chiefs of Police (IACP) and the Bureau of Justice Assistance (BJA) in the United States Department of Justice have used this approach to identify best practices for homicide investigations. The recommendations made by these organizations are based on policies and practices that are associated with relatively high clearance rates, and that have been employed in various American and international agencies. While not specifically research-based, these guides attempt to translate research into those policies and practices that are considered most useful in raising clearance rates for all types of homicides.[6]

Consistent with its focus on the role that law enforcement executives play in the success of police organizations, the IACP identifies "10 Things Law Enforcement Executives Can Do to Positively Impact Homicide Investigation Outcomes" (IACP 2013). These were identified after a review of the literature on clearances, reviews of high-performing agencies, and discussions with police leaders and researchers. The IACP encourages chiefs to: (1) invest in their relationship with their homicide unit; (2) have a system in place for the standardized and structured management of investigations; (3) mandate information sharing; (4) support investigations with appropriate resources; (5) assess current responses to victims/survivors; (6) build partnerships for information and cooperation; (7) build community cachet and give them options for cooperation; (8) manage political and public expectations of homicide investigations; (9) know the number, type, and trends for homicide and the same information for homicide clearances; and (10) measure closure and beyond. While closure is an arrest, the agency should also be concerned about the results of prosecution and especially any arrests that are later to be judged in error (exonerations and acquittals). Each of these recommendations speaks to the role that agency leadership plays in improving homicide clearances and in ensuring that homicide clearances are done with integrity, to show the public that the police are effective and just. Further testing of these recommendations is needed, but for now they represent the best ideas for improving agency management for homicide success.

The promising practices for increasing homicide clearances developed by the BJA project focus on the investigation process itself. This effort acknowledges the importance of agency leadership in setting the tone and developing oversight mechanisms, but deals more directly with the nature of the investigation. To develop these best practices, a research team led by David Carter (2013) identified seven agencies in the United States that had high clearance rates (80% or higher) and enough homicides per year to warrant their inclusion in the study (at least 24). In each of these agencies, a research team sought to understand how homicides were investigated, what seemed to make them successful, and, especially, what actions were taken in the first 48 hours after the crime, a period that past research (e.g., Wellford and Cronin 1999) has identified as critical to closure. While Carter's research design was not very strong, his work can be used to suggest areas for further, more rigorous research.

The resulting report (Carter 2013) identifies 32 specific best practices. These can be summarized into three categories: organizational, support, and investigative. The organizational section includes some items similar to those identified in the IACP report, but also suggests developing appropriate staffing levels (e.g., no more than three homicides assigned to a lead detective per year, and a minimum of three detectives for initial investigations); adequate overtime budgets and approval processes; establishing strong ties with medical examiners, forensic laboratories, prosecutor offices, the media, and the community; establishing a policy that allows on-duty officers to have take-home cars; creating victim/witness and crime stoppers programs; and providing investigators with necessary equipment. Support recommendations include crime analysts, access to centers that integrate divergent law enforcement information systems, well-trained crime scene investigators and first-responding patrol officers, access to information throughout the organization, use of specialized units to track persons of interest, and access to jail intelligence systems, especially for homicides involving gangs. Finally, best practices in the investigation process include constant training for investigators, using a team approach, video-recording all interactions and interviews with witnesses and suspects, developing good relationships with patrol officers, daily reviews of cases with peers, seeking to use federal statutes to retrieve funds acquired through the criminal act being investigated when appropriate, and maintaining well-documented case files for all cases.

The use of best practices assumes an understanding the nature and characteristics of homicides in the jurisdiction. This understanding is useful not only for developing effective prevention and investigative policies and practices, but also when assigning resources to specific investigations. This has led to an interest in developing "solvability" estimates for homicides. Such estimates would be used to select which practices are best suited for a specific homicide. We prefer to cast the issue as determining what resources are needed to solve a particular type of homicide. In the research by Wellford and Cronin (1999), one of the cities studied had clearance rates in the 90 percent range, with clearance rates for gang- and drug-related homicides in the high 70s. This agency routinely assigned 5–11 detectives to each homicide, allowed the lead investigator to keep these detectives on the case as long as they were needed, provided unlimited overtime, and allowed the lead detective to access all resources in the agency. In addition, management conducted case reviews at specified points in the investigation. This approach may not have been efficient, but it was extremely effective. In this formulation the issue is not how solvable a homicide is, but rather what level of effort is necessary to make a good arrest.

Unfortunately, as with other aspects of homicide clearances we have almost no scientific literature on this subject. While we have some idea of resource at the extremes the continuum of case complexity, for example, a homicide/suicide versus a truly random but planned homicide, in the vast majority of homicides the resources are standard at the beginning but many change as the investigators' understanding of the case develops (Jarvis and Regoeczi 2012). More large-scale, case-specific research is needed before we can offer anything more than observations on what organizations are currently doing in the area of homicide case management (Keel, Jarvis, and Muirhead 2009).

When we report on homicide clearances we understand that not all homicides are "created equally." One of the keys for understanding clearances lies in the specific types of homicide. Future research should focus on how the types of homicides are related to case closure. This focus may help explain why there are differing results for specific types of killings. Gang-related homicides, workplace and school shootings, medical/elder homicides and terroristic killings are just some different homicide types that may reveal certain factors that lead to higher clearance rates and lower rates that are type specific. Granted, specific types of homicides are only parts of the whole, but they could provide key information that is applicable to all homicides.

Future Research

In the most recent year for which data are available in the United States, there were at least 568,000 serious violent offenses that were not cleared by an arrest, including 4,933 homicides. In addition, there were over six million serious property crimes not cleared by an arrest (FBI 2014). Overall, approximately 75 percent of all serious crimes did not result in a clearance. Gradually, as we become more aware of these facts, we have begun to understand the importance of improving clearances. This is partly because we know that certainty of punishment is critical for deterrence (e.g., Nagin, Solow, and Lum 2015). More to the point, though, unsolved crimes cluster in those communities that have the lowest levels of support for law enforcement, in part because residents experience such low levels of police response to the crimes in which they are the victims. Our review of this topic has highlighted the little we know about why homicides are not cleared, and what we can do to increase clearances that result in a correct conviction. Until these questions are answered, the United States and other countries are likely to see little improvement in homicide clearances.

Notes

1 Outcomes as outlined by the recorded crime in Northern Ireland's monthly crime bulletin (Police Service of Northern Ireland 2013) are defined as charges, summonses, cautions (adult/juvenile), discretionary disposals, penalty notices for disorder, offenses taken into consideration, and indictable only offenses where no action was taken against the offender (e.g., died before proceedings or no criminal prosecution).

2 All data on clearances in this section define clearance as an arrest. But note that in almost every instance of high profile crimes like homicide, the case is reviewed by a prosecutor or other court official before an arrest is made.

3 The development of the European Homicide Monitor (http://law.leiden.edu/organisation/criminology/research/homicide/) will undoubtedly increase the availability of research on homicides and their processing in criminal justice systems outside the United States.
4 Comparable longitudinal data for other countries are not currently available.
5 Nation states with more centralized policing organizations may not feature this variation across cities, but that is an empirical question that deserves separate analysis.
6 Again, this section draws almost exclusively on police experience in the United States, only because that is where the most research has been conducted on homicide clearances. Expanding the research on clearance to other countries should be an important priority for police researchers.

References

Alderden, M.A. and Lavery, T.A. (2007) Predicting homicide clearances in Chicago: Investigating disparities in predictors across different types of homicide. *Homicide Studies*, 11(2): 115–132.

Alexander, T.S. (2012) Homicide clearances: An examination of race and police investigative effort. PhD diss., University of Maryland.

Boyce, J., Cotter, A., and Perreault, S. (2014) Police-reported crime statistics in Canada, 2013. *Juristat*, 85(2): 1–39.

Carter, D. (2013) *Homicide Process Mapping*. Washington, DC: Bureau of Justice Assistance.

Cotter, A. (2014) Homicide in Canada, 2013. *Juristat*, 85(2): 1–33.

Davies, H. (2007) Understanding variations in murder clearance rates: The influence of the political environment. *Homicide Studies*, 11(2): 133–150.

Decker, S.H. and Curry, G.D. (2002) Gangs, gang members and gang homicides: Organized crimes or disorganized criminals. *Journal of Criminal Justice*, 30: 343–352.

FBI (Federal Bureau of Investigation) (2004) *Uniform Crime Reporting Handbook*. Washington DC: US Government Printing Office.

FBI (2014) *Crime in the United States, 2014*. Washington, DC: US Government Printing Office.

Greenwood, P. and Petersilla, J. (1975) *The Criminal Investigation Process*. Santa Monica, CA: RAND Corporation.

IACP (International Association of Chiefs of Police) (2013) 10 things law enforcement executives can do to positively impact homicide investigation outcomes. Alexandria, VA: International Association of Chiefs of Police.

Jarvis, J.P. and Regoeczi, W.C. (2009) Homicide clearances: An analysis of arrest versus exceptional outcomes. *Homicide Studies*, 13(2): 174–188.

Jarvis, J.P. and Regoeczi, W.C. (2012) Homicide solvability. *The Police Chief*, 79(8): 10–11.

Keel, T., Jarvis, J., and Muirhead, Y. (2009) An exploratory analysis of factors affecting homicide investigations. *Homicide Studies*, 75(4): 22–36.

Lee, C. (2005) The value of life in death: Multiple regression and event history analyses of homicide clearance in Los Angeles County. *Journal of Criminal Justice*, 33: 527–534.

Liem, G., Ganpat, S., Granath, S., *et al.* (2013) Homicide in Finland, the Netherlands, and Sweden: First findings from the European Homicide Monitor. *Homicide Studies*, 17(1): 75–95.

Litwin, K.J. (2004) A multilevel multivariate analysis of factors affecting homicide clearances. *Journal of Research in Crime and Delinquency*, 41: 327–351.

Litwin, K.J. and Xu, Y. (2007) The dynamic nature of homicide clearances: A multilevel model comparison of three time periods. *Homicide Studies*, 11: 94–114.

Mouzos, J. and Muller, D. (2001) Solvability factors of homicides in Australia: An exploratory analysis. *Trends and Issue in Crime and Criminal Justice*, 216(October).

Nagin, D. (2005) *Group-based Modeling of Development*. Cambridge, MA: Harvard University Press.

Nagin, D., Solow, R., and Lum, C. (2015) Deterrence, criminal opportunities and the police. *Criminology*, 53(1): 74–100.

Office for National Statistics (2012/2013) Homicide: Part of crime statistics, focus on violent crime and sexual offences. Available online at http://www.ons.gov.uk/ons/rel/crime-stats/crime-statistics/focus-on-violent-crime-and-sexual-offences--2012-13/rpt---chapter-2---homicide.html (accessed June 13, 2015).

Police Service of Northern Ireland (2013) *Trends in Police Recorded Crime in Northern Ireland 1998/99 to 2012/13*. Belfast, Ireland: Police Service of Northern Ireland. Available online at http://www.psni.police.uk/police_recorded_crime_in_northern_ireland_1998-99_to_2013-14.pdf (accessed September 12, 2015).

Puckett, J.L. and Lundman, R.J. (2003) Factors affecting homicide clearances: Multivariate analysis of a more complete conceptual framework. *Journal of Research in Crime and Delinquency*, 40: 171–193.

Quinet, K. and Nunn, S. (2014) Establishing the victim–offender relationship of initially unsolved homicides: Partner, family, acquaintance, or stranger? *Homicide Studies*, 18(3): 271–297.

Regoeczi, W.C., Kennedy, L.W., and Silverman, R.A. (2000) Uncleared homicides: A Canada/United States comparison. *Homicide Studies*, 4(2): 135–161.

Riedel, M. (2008) Homicide arrest clearances: A review of the literature. *Sociology Compass*, 2(4): 1145–1164.

Riedel, M. and Rinehart, T.A. (1996) Murder clearances and missing data. *Journal of Criminal Justice*, 19: 83–102.

Roberts, A. (2007) Predictors of homicide clearance by arrest: An event history analysis of NIBRS Incidents. *Homicide Studies*, 11: 82–93.

Roberts, A. (2014) Adjusting rates of homicide clearance by arrest for investigative difficulty modeling incident- and jurisdictional-level obstacles. *Homicide Studies*, 18(3): 1–28. doi: 10.1177/1088767914536984.

Roberts, A. and Lyons, C.J. (2009) Victim–offender racial dyads and clearance of lethal and nonlethal assault. *Journal of Research in Crime and Delinquency*, 46(3): 301–326.

Rydberg, J. and Pizarro, J. (2014) Victim lifestyle as a correlate of homicide clearance. *Homicide Studies*, 18(4): 342–362.

UNODC (United Nations Office of Drugs and Crime) (2013) *Global Study of Homicide*. Vienna: UNODC.

Wellford, C. and Cronin, J. (1999) *An Analysis of Variables Affecting the Clearance of Homicides: A Multivariate Study*. Washington, DC: Justice Research Statistics Association.

Wellford, C. and Scott, T. (2015) Special analysis for this chapter. Details available from Charles Wellford at wellford@umd.edu.

Further Reading

Armstrong, J., Plecas, D.B., and Cohen, I.M. (2013) *The Value of Resources in Solving Homicides: The Difference between Gang Related and Non-gang Related Cases*. Abbotsford, British Columbia: University of the Fraser Valley.

Bryant, W. and Cussen, T. (2015) *Homicide in Australia: 2010–11 to 2011–12: National Homicide Monitoring Program Annual Report*. Canberra: Australian Institute of Criminology.

Chan, A. and Payne, J. (2013) *Homicide in Australia: 2008–09 to 2009–10: National Homicide Monitoring Program Annual Report*. Canberra: Australian Institute of Criminology.

FBI (2013) *Crime in the United States, 2012*. Washington, DC: US Government Printing Office.

Fox, J., Levin, J., and Quinet, K. (2012) *The Will To Kill: Making Sense of Senseless Murder*. Saddle River, NJ: Pearson.

Office for National Statistics (2014) *Homicide, 2014*. London: Home Office.

Scottish Government (2013) *Homicide in Scotland, 2012–13*. Statistical Bulletin Crime and Justice Series. Edinburgh, Scotland: Scottish Government Statistician Group.

Silverman, R. and Kennedy, L. (1997) Uncleared homicides in Canada and the United States. In M. Reidel and R. Boulahanis (eds), *Lethal Violence: Proceedings of the 1995 Meeting of the Homicide Research Working Group* (pp. 81–86). Washington, DC: Office of Justice Programs, US Department of Justice.

Statistics Canada (2010) *Homicide in Canada, 2010*. No. 85-002x. Ottawa: Ministry of Industry.

Trussler, T. (2010) Explaining the changing nature of homicide clearance in Canada. *International Criminal Justice Review*, 20(4): 366–383.

US Department of Labor, Bureau of Labor Statistics (2013) *National Census of Fatal Occupational Injuries in 2012 (Preliminary Results)*. Washington, DC: US Department of Labor.

Vossekuil, B., Fein, R., Reddy, M., *et al.* (2002) *The Final Report and Findings of the Safe School Initiative: Implications for the Prevention of School Attacks in the United States*. Washington, DC: US Department of Education, Office of Elementary and Secondary Education, Safe and Drug-Free Schools Program and US Secret Service, National Threat Assessment Center.

31

Using DNA in the Investigation of Homicide

Scientific, Operational, and Evidential Considerations

Robin Williams

Introduction

This chapter considers the contribution of the analysis of deoxyribonucleic acid (DNA) to the successful investigation of homicide in contemporary common-law criminal jurisdictions. It suggests that the 30 year history of developments in forensic DNA analysis comprises several distinct waves of innovation in which various kinds of forensic DNA profiles have been constructed, used, and evaluated by scientists, investigators, and courtroom actors in an increasing number of nation states. The chapter also discusses how the successful uses of DNA profiling and databasing in particular homicide investigations have provided important resources for investigative practice, and for policy claims-making by key forensic science and criminal justice stakeholders. A later section notes that the successful delivery of the criminal justice potential of DNA analysis rests on the willingness of relevant actors to commission these innovations at the appropriate stages of an investigation and also their ability to understand the significance and limitations of the scientific truths contained in the results obtained. The chapter concludes by describing the achievements and limitations of a small number of academically rigorous evaluations of the effective applications of forensic DNA technologies to homicide and serious crime investigations and prosecutions.

The Techno-scientific Trajectory of Forensic Genetics

The history of the use of genetics in support of criminal justice objectives is recent and short. It began in England in 1984 with discoveries made in one university laboratory and spread rapidly across the globe since that time. Thirty years after

The Handbook of Homicide, First Edition. Edited by Fiona Brookman, Edward R. Maguire, and Mike Maguire.

those discoveries forensic genetics is now regularly represented as the epistemic leader among all forensic science disciplines because of the strength of its underlying scientific foundations, the reliability of the laboratory and IT technologies used in its application, and its development of a robust statistical approach to the interpretation of the analytical results produced in the course of criminal casework.

However, understanding the large number of theoretical and practical accomplishments that underpin the rhetorical (and not always helpful) claim that DNA profiling now comprises the "gold standard" for forensic identification requires us to examine in more detail, the historical and organizational factors that have shaped the current repertoire of DNA profiling and databasing technologies as well as the ways in which exceptional and routine applications of these technologies have contributed to the investigation and prosecution of criminal offenses. We need to be aware of the range of new meanings that have been attached to the term "DNA profile" as new forms of forensic genetic analysis have become available. Finally, it is also important to note the troubling lack of agreement among forensic genetic practitioners about how best to interpret results obtained from the application of increasingly sensitive techniques. This has become especially problematic when analysis has produced "mixed" profiles that contain the DNA of more than one human subject. All of these intricacies are explored in the following account of three progressive waves of innovation in which the contribution of forensic genetics to successful homicide and other investigations and prosecutions first began and then subsequently expanded over the last three decades.

First wave: the establishment of biolegal credibility

Between 1900 and the early 1980s, the blood, and some other bodily fluids, of human subjects could be identified as falling into one of four inherited antigenic groups: A, B, AB, and O. Subsequently, additional red blood systems were discovered along with other polymorphic markers based on serum proteins and enzymes. A number of these were regularly used by investigators and courts to confirm or refute assertions of the involvement of individuals in crime, especially violent crime, where blood or semen had been recovered from the body of victims or elsewhere at a crime scene. However, the large number of individuals falling into each blood group meant that only limited confidence could be placed on any incriminatory inference that was made on the basis of matching samples. Since the early 1980s, the discovery of three main types of genetic markers have made it possible to replace the analysis of the protein products of DNA by the analysis of the genome itself: those based on repeat sequences of autosomal DNA, those based on sex-specific transmission regions of DNA (the Y chromosome and mitochondrial DNA), and those based on alternative alleles found at particular nucleotide sites (single nucleotide polymorphisms usually referred to as SNPs) (Jobling and Gill 2004).

Variants of the first type—repeat sequences of DNA—provided the basis for what was initially called DNA fingerprinting, and subsequently became known as DNA profiling. In the mid-1980s Jeffreys and others (Gill, Jeffreys, and Werrett 1985; Jeffreys, Wilson, and Thein 1985) showed that forensic samples from potentially crime-relevant objects could contain sufficient quantities and quality of DNA for the construction of visually distinctive profiles using restriction fragment length polymorphisms (RFLP).

The first, and highly prominent, deployment of this new technology in criminal investigations occurred only two years after Jeffreys's initial, and largely adventitious, laboratory discovery. Dawn Ashworth, a 15 year old girl, went missing from her home in Leicestershire in England on July 31, 1986. Her body was discovered two days later and blood typing of semen recovered from her revealed identical features with semen obtained from the body of Lynda Mann who had been raped and murdered by an unidentified individual three years earlier (in both cases the semen donor was a blood group A secretor). The prime suspect for the murder of Dawn Ashworth was 17 years old Richard Buckland and following his arrest on August 5, 1986 he confessed to Ashworth's murder. However, Buckland was not blood group A and could not be linked to the semen recovered from Ashworth's body. In addition, he denied involvement in Mann's death. Faced with the contradiction between the biological evidence and Buckland's confession, homicide investigators requested Jeffreys to extract DNA from both recovered semen stains and to compare them to a blood sample taken from Buckland. Jeffreys's analysis concluded that Buckland's sample did not match the crime scene semen, but the semen taken from both crime scenes matched each other. Following Buckland's exoneration, the first ever voluntary mass DNA screening of men within a given geographical area eventually resulted in the identification of Colin Pitchfork as the source of the semen. Pitchfork was convicted of the two murders on January 22, 1988 (see Lee and Tirnady 2003; McCartney 2006; Wambaugh 1989; Williams and Johnson 2008).

Very soon after Jeffreys's initial scientific success, the UK Forensic Science Service (FSS), the US Federal Bureau of Investigation (FBI), and a number of commercial biotech organizations began work to establish reliable and routine ways of constructing forensic DNA profiles from crime scene stains and from donor subjects. Although the FSS and the FBI differed somewhat in the choice and numbers of genetic loci to include in their profiles, their decisions were informed by common underlying scientific principles, knowledge of the variability of individuals at each locus, and on the preferred technologies for DNA extraction and analysis. Evidence derived from the interpretation of the results of this developing techno-science was accepted without significant opposition in English courts, whereas judicial acceptance in North America was much more halting.

The first US criminal case in which DNA evidence was presented was the trial of Tommy Lee Andrews for rape in 1987, and several other cases followed in which uncontested DNA evidence was presented to juries. However, in the trial of Joseph Castro for the double murder of Vilma and Natasha Ponce, which began in February 1989, the seemingly easy acceptance of this new technology was significantly challenged. DNA profiles developed from blood on Castro's watch were asserted by the prosecution to have come from Vilma Ponce, but in a series of pretrial hearings, the technology came under significant attack: "Castro made it clear that DNA evidence was vulnerable, and enterprising defense attorneys poked and prodded those vulnerabilities in numerous subsequent cases across the country over the next several years, leading a number of courts to reject DNA evidence altogether, something that would have been nearly unthinkable prior to Castro" (Mnookin 2007: 78). The main focus of criticism in Castro was on laboratory standards, but an additional, and rather longer-lasting, source of trouble for the early proponents of the forensic uses of DNA arose in a number of other US cases for three or four years after this case (see Kaye 2010; Lynch *et al.* 2008). This trouble concerned the adequacy of knowledge about the distribution of genetic differences among and between different population groups, knowledge on which estimates of the probability of occurrence of particular DNA profiles is based. Significant scientific and legal disagreements about this knowledge were only resolved following two US reports (National Research Council 1992, 1996) in which leading experts proposed a communal resolution of estimates of population genetics differences which eventually led to the end of what had become colloquially known in the United States as the period of the "DNA Wars." The credibility of DNA evidence was thus firmly established.

Second wave: creating and expanding forensic DNA databases

In the first wave of forensic genetics, profiling based on multiple and single locus probes were largely confined to reactive casework: laboratories directly compared DNA profiles obtained from biological material left at crime scenes with those taken from individuals already in police custody who were suspected of involvement in the specific criminal offense under investigation. The initial forensic use of DNA in the Pitchfork case had already demonstrated that the success of the technology depended upon the scope and coverage of the collection of reference profiles to which crime scene samples could be compared. However, comparison was only made possible by a long and costly process of intelligence-led screening, a technique which itself proved, through Pitchfork's initial evasion, to be a problematic method for aiding criminal detection. It is therefore not surprising that the idea of creating an "index" of DNA profiles, capable of being searched against crime scene stains, especially in cases of homicide and other serious crime cases, was very quickly considered by key stakeholders. The Home Office first recorded their interest in such a development in 1988 and began research into developing a database (Williams and Johnson 2008).

The development in the 1990s of the ability to construct digital representations of short tandem repeat (STR) profiles meant that profiles could be stored on computers and easily searched (see Kimpton *et al.* 1994). In addition, the development of the polymerase chain reaction (PCR) technique in the second half of the 1980s (Mullis *et al.* 1986) meant that small DNA fragments could be copied many times in order to increase the material available for analysis from the original sample. As PCR techniques were further improved, more degraded and smaller amounts of

DNA became amenable to analysis, and automation improved the overall efficiency of DNA profiling (e.g., Gill *et al.* 1994).

These two parallel scientific developments created the opportunities for the use of DNA profiling for a number of investigatory purposes. In England and Wales, the analysis of short tandem repeat (STR) polymorphisms was first utilized in a murder investigation in 1990, identifying 8-year old skeletal remains of missing Karen Price by matching DNA extracted from bone to that of her parents (Hagelberg, Gray, and Jeffreys 1991). Other early cases relying on STRs also focused on the identification of human remains, including the efforts to identify bodies following the events at Waco, Texas (Clayton, Whitaker, and Maguire 1995).

Since the mid-1990s the simultaneous measurement of different numbers of STR loci by commercially available multiplex assays have become the technology of choice for forensic DNA profiling and databasing around the world, being used both to exonerate and convict suspects, and also to overturn previous false convictions (for a useful summary of this history see Gill 2002). It is this technology that facilitated the establishment in 1995 of the first national forensic DNA database in England and Wales, followed three years later by the official launch of the US Federal Bureau of Investigation's Combined DNA Index System (CODIS) (although all 50 US state databases were not fully connected through CODIS until 2004). Many other nation states established their own national forensic DNA databases during the last decade of the twentieth century, and each year sees the addition of more states authorizing or creating such collections. The 2011 INTERPOL global DNA survey concluded that "129 countries use DNA analysis for criminal investigations, 62 of which have a national DNA database. Moreover, it is now estimated that, at the end of 2011, there is at least a global total of 31,870,981 DNA profiles" (INTERPOL 2012: 2).

Allowing for some simplification, the global trajectory of forensic DNA database expansion has followed a distinctive shape in which the categories and numbers of people from whom DNA samples can be taken without consent, profiled, and retained have become greater. This has most often begun by sampling only those involved in the most serious crimes against a person since it is the promise of such databases to assist in detecting homicides and serious sexual crimes that has provided the strongest case for legislation and funding to support their operation. However, once established, forensic DNA databases have usually been allowed to expand to include those involved (or suspected of being involved) in a range of property crimes. Police have also been authorized to take DNA samples at earlier points in investigative and judicial inquiries (for example, at the point of arrest rather than the point of charge, or even conviction). The period during which DNA profiles and samples can be retained has often been extended, and more DNA has been recovered from crime scenes. In addition to these developments, which together have resulted in the existence of much larger databases, the investigative applications of databased profiles have also expanded. There are increasing efforts to make possible the sharing of DNA profile information between criminal jurisdictions.

Finally it is worth noting that the capacity and utility of forensic DNA databasing has also been expanded by two additional forms of analysis. The first of these involves profiling the Y-chromosome (Y-STRs) of biological samples. Y-STRs are especially useful in establishing the male contribution to mixed samples and also in establishing paternal heritage (Jobling, Pandya, and Tyler-Smith 1997). The first criminal justice case of the use of Y-STRs contributed to the exoneration of an already sentenced rape suspect in Germany in the early 1990s (Jobling and Gill 2004), and there are an increasing number of jurisdictions that have either added Y-STRs to their national DNA databases or retain Y-STR profiles in separate databases. The second related innovation has been the establishment of mitochondrial DNA (mtDNA) databases. Non-nuclear mitochondrial DNA provides a supplementary resource to autosomal STR multiplex analysis and is used to identify the existence of maternal relationships in family lineages (Goodwin, Linacre, and Hadi 2007). This kind of genetic information is particularly helpful in identifying victims in cold/historical cases, since mitchondrial DNA is often preserved in circumstances where nuclear DNA has degraded and so cannot be successfully extracted and profiled. This type of marker was first used as part of hair analysis in a murder case in 1992 in the United Kingdom (Jobling and Gill 2004). The first forensic mtDNA used in a court featured in the US murder case of Paul Ware in 1996 (Houck and Siegel 2006).

Third wave: beyond database matches

The previous section focused on the technological and organizational innovations that made it possible to compare DNA profiles obtained from scenes of crime with the profiles of individuals already held on databases as well as the profiles of individuals sampled in the course of an investigation. However, there are many investigations in which genetic material has been recovered from a crime scene but where profiles do not match any available subject profiles. In such circumstances, and especially where no other leads are available in cases of serious crime, investigators may seek other ways to identify such individuals by using other kinds of DNA analysis. New forms of genetic knowledge, technological improvements in sample processing, novel database search methodologies, and the perceived rewards of investigative ingenuity, have all contributed to the efforts of forensic scientists to develop several new ways of analyzing unidentified genetic samples for content that can yield identifying information. It is this set of innovations that comprise the third wave of forensic genetics. Some of these innovations involve the direct examination of coding regions of the human genome—genes themselves—while others rely on new ways of using information from the non-coding STR loci included in conventional forensic genotyping.

Three of the most significant third wave innovations, and examples of their uses in particular homicide investigations, are described in the following paragraphs of this section. The first of these is "familial searching" which is based on knowledge of the probability of matches between the STR markers of two members of the same family (as opposed to the probability of matches between these markers when the individuals compared are unrelated). Familial searching can be used whenever searches of forensic DNA databases fail to establish an exact match between the DNA profile obtained from biological material collected at a crime scene and a profile obtained from a known individual. In the absence of such exact matches, "partial matches" may suggest that the crime scene sample originates from a relative of the individual(s) with whom partial matches have been made. The first application of familial searching involved the identification—in 2003—of the perpetrator of two murders that had occurred in South Wales, UK, in 1973, but this identification was only made possible by the exhumation of the perpetrators body. The first case in which intelligence derived from familial searching was used to identify an offender who was later successfully prosecuted occurred in the 2004 case of the death of Michael Little who was killed when a brick thrown from a motorway bridge smashed through the windscreen of a lorry that Little was driving at the time. DNA recovered from the brick was profiled and partly matched a databased subject profile. A familial search was then carried out which eventually led to the arrest and trial of Craig Harman who pleaded guilty to the charge of manslaughter. Since this innovation, many such searches have led to the identification of offenders, the most prominent of which in the United Kingdom was that of Jeffrey Gafoor in 2003, which brought finality to the previously bungled investigation of the murder of Lynette White in Cardiff in February 1988 (accounts of the process of familial searching as well as information about its operational outcomes can be found in a number of publications including: Bottomley and Holt 2011; Gregory and Rainbow 2011; Kruijver, Meester, and Slooten 2014; Maguire *et al.* 2014; Pham-Hoai, Crispino, and Hampikian 2014).

The second innovation in this wave is the attempt to provide intelligence for investigations based on knowledge of "ancestry informative markers" (AIMS) that can be inferred from the genetic analysis of biological material. Reliable inferences of what is variously described as the "racial origins," "ethnic origin," "ethnic affiliation," or even "ethnic appearance" of individuals can be used to focus subsequent inquiries, to determine an interview strategy, to compare with witness statements, or to design an intelligence-led mass DNA screen. These efforts largely utilize collections of single nucleotide polymorphisms (SNPs), which have been shown to vary between population groups. SNPs have a much more limited polymorphic range than STRs, but forensic interest in the promise of AIMS remains high and research is widespread and ongoing. A number of SNP panels have been developed for these purposes at varying levels of biogeographic granularity (Phillips 2015; Phillips *et al.* 2014; Syndercombe-Court *et al.* 2003) The successful use of such panels for the identification of the biogeographic origin of the North African offenders in the case of the Madrid railway train bombings in 2004 stands in stark contrast to erroneous identification of the US citizen Brandon Mayfield from fingerprints recovered from a bag that had once contained the explosive device used (Phillips *et al.* 2009). However, despite this success, significant conceptual and operational uncertainties remain surrounding such categorizations of individuals, and for some critics at least, there is a danger that "race" will be reified in the attempt to define distinctive human population groups and subgroups.

The third and final innovation has introduced into criminal justice practice the genetics of "externally visible characteristics" (EVCs) in which genetic material is examined in order to predict aspects of an individual's phenotype that make up distinctive—largely facial—appearance, in particular skin, eye, and hair color. Recent summary accounts of progress in this area of forensic genetics have been provided by several European and North American experts (Kayser 2015; Kayser and De Knijff 2011; Kayser and Schneider 2009; Shriver 2015). For the purposes of police investigations, the ability to determine directly individuals' physical characteristics from biological samples may be more appealing than assuming what those features might be on the basis of knowledge of AIMs, but despite the success of researchers in developing more robust methods for the identification of such characteristics, it remains difficult to know what has been added to particular homicide investigations by their application. At best such technology may allow investigators to develop or narrow a large number of persons of interest, but probabilistic knowledge of one or several visible characteristics will not usually provide more than a supplementary resource for the early stages of a homicide investigation. Even where the technology is used, STR profiles obtained from a crime scene will then provide the basis for evidential comparisons with STR profiles constructed from individuals whom the police seek to eliminate or incriminate later in an inquiry. For this reason it seems safer to treat this particular forensic genetic technology as emergent, and always likely to be exceptional, rather than as proven and necessarily useful even where direct STR profile matches between crime scene samples and known individuals cannot be found.

Investigations, Evidence, and the Complexity of Forensic Genetics

Innovations in forensic genetics have been strongly embraced by criminal justice agencies and by the public at large in an increasing number of nation states. It is generally asserted that the use of a range of DNA profiling and profile searching methods has provided a significant forensic science resource to many homicide investigations, although the previous section of this chapter has suggested that such assertions rest on the selection of conspicuous cases rather than a systematic research base. However, even in the absence of systematic social research, it is clear that the successful use of forensic genetics in any criminal case depends not only on the availability of a range of scientific resources but on the willingness of the police to commission the deployment of several such resources at a particular point in an investigation.

One conspicuous case which illustrates what can happen when available science is not properly deployed is that of the serial murder of (it is estimated) up to 50 women by Robert William Pickton in Canada before he was arrested on February 5, 2002. By the time that Pickton came to trial in 2007, the case was referred to in the national media as the largest DNA recovery criminal case in Canada's history. Yet the later inquiry into the failure of the police to detect these murders some years earlier uncovered a large number of investigative shortcomings, including the failure to utilize DNA profiling adequately in 1997. This conspicuous failure followed the arrest of Pickton on charges of attempted murder, assault with a weapon, forcible confinement, and aggravated assault on a victim who remains unnamed, but who is referred to in the British Columbia Missing Women Commission of Inquiry as "Ms Anderson" (Oppal 2012). The prosecution of Pickton on these charges was discontinued, and no further investigations were made of Pickton for some years, years during which he was free to murder and dispose of the bodies (on his pig farm) of Aboriginal women and girls whom he had first approached in the very deprived downtown Eastside area of Vancouver.

The Commission drew attention to the significant "delay in considering how and whether to use Pickton's DNA in relation to unsolved homicides, or to test items seized in the Anderson assault for DNA of other victims" (Oppal 2012: 79). Here the Commission referred in particular to the police decision not to act on a suggestion made by one investigator that the handcuffs used by Pickton during his attack on Ms Anderson should be sent to the laboratory in an effort to recover DNA from any other person on whom Pickton might have used this method of control. Instead, this and other items sent by investigators to laboratories in 1997 were examined only in order to identify Pickton's and Ms Anderson's DNA. However, when an analysis of Pickton's shirt that had been seized in 1997 was carried out five years later, two other profiles were found apart from Anderson's and Pickton's, and a scientist who examined the results of this and other analyses of other 1997 exhibits observed that the DNA of three murdered women (whose body parts were uncovered at Pickton's pig farm in Port Coquitlam) was found on these items. She also added that, although standard DNA extraction methods in use at the time would probably have failed to identify one of them, the profiles of two others may well have been found.[1]

Pickton was charged with 27 counts of first-degree murder; one charge was dropped at a preliminary stage for lack of evidence. The judge proceeded with six of the murder charges. Pickton was acquitted of first-degree murder but convicted of second-degree murder on all six counts. The case is a testimony to the contribution of forensic DNA profiling to the rule of law: it allowed the identification of many (but not all) of the body parts found on Pickton's farm and so was a crucial element in his successful prosecution. However, the devastating effect of earlier decisions made about DNA analysis provides a salutary reminder that its evidentiary promise remains unrealized whenever investigators fail to commission, or adequately understand, its potential uses. No degree of techno-scientific progress in forensic genetics can necessarily guarantee its successful deployment since such successes always depend on the exercise of investigative knowledge and skill at appropriate points in a criminal investigation.

In addition to decisions about what forensic genetic analysis to commission at what points in a criminal investigation, there are significant complexities surrounding its deployment that relate to sample collection, preservation, and the interpretation of analytical results of DNA profiling and profile comparison. The large technical literature on these questions are too extensive to be reviewed here, but some of the dominant themes in that literature are worthy of note.

The first issue is the contamination of the biological samples on which DNA extraction and analysis is performed. Contamination in which DNA is transferred from one object to another can occur at a number of recurrent recovery, storage, and laboratory stages in evidence collection and analysis (e.g., Champod 2013; Goray and Van Oorschot 2015; Lapointe *et al.* 2015). The increasing sensitivity of DNA extraction techniques has contributed greatly to this problem because of the ease with which DNA transfer takes place and is then detected by more sensitive techniques (e.g., Gill 2001; Jamieson 2011; Lowe *et al.* 2003; Wickenhieser 2002).[2] Realization of the many opportunities for accidental contamination has been accelerated by a number of cases in which investigations have been (temporarily) misdirected as a result of such contamination as well as by particular prosecutions where the possibility of contamination has significantly affected the disposal of the case. An example of the first occurred in the investigation of the death of Gareth Williams in London in 2010. In this case, the DNA profile of a scientist who had attended the crime scene was recovered from an item of evidence but because the scene profile results were entered incorrectly onto the computer search engine, the match with the scientist's profile was not discovered until sometime later. During that intervening period the police investigation had been significantly led astray by the development of a series of speculations about who the unknown donor might be, as well by making less credible existing alternative hypotheses of how Williams had died.

Problems of contamination and transfer lead directly to the second theme in this literature, which is the interpretation of "mixed samples." On many occasions, profiles developed from DNA testing carried out at varying degrees of sensitivity will include alleles from more than one contributor. The issue for DNA analysts is how to determine which alleles could have come from however many people are the possible source of the DNA information, a difficulty which becomes greater as the number of potential contributors grows and when reference profiles are not available for some or any of them. The development of reliable statistical methods for the determination of genetic identities from such mixed samples is a preoccupation of several groups of scientists in Europe and North America, but at present these groups have failed to reach a consensus on how best this disaggregation can be carried out (e.g., Gill *et al.* 2015; Slooten and Egeland 2015).

A third issue relates to knowledge of the source material from which DNA was extracted in any particular instance of genetic profiling. Although technologies are emerging which will make it possible to determine whether a DNA profile has been derived from blood rather than semen, or from vaginal mucosa rather than other skin cells, such differentiation is not always possible with the technologies in current use. This means, for example, that even where a sample of blood has been recovered from a scene and a DNA profile has subsequently been derived from analysis of that sample, the DNA may not have been derived from the blood itself but from another type of human cell that has been deposited in or on the surface of the blood. This particular shortcoming of DNA analysis—which experts describe as a problem of "sub-source" level is not widely recognized outside of the expert community, although it clearly can have significant implications for what can be evidentially inferred from the results obtained in many cases involving DNA evidence. There is a significant amount of research now underway to permit the attribution of the biological source material in question, but in the absence of a reliable technology for making this attribution there remains a risk that investigators, advocates, judges, and juries could be misled when considering the significance of a DNA profile (e.g., Champod, Evett, and Jackson 2004; Gill 2001).

Finally, it is widely asserted by forensic scientists that non-scientists, including police investigators, judges, advocates, and juries, lack understanding of the statistical form in which DNA findings are presented in investigations and prosecutions (e.g., Howes *et al.* 2014; Wheate 2010). One very interesting recent study by several New Zealand scholars (Grace *et al.* 2011) has explored this in detail and shown the difficulties encountered by judicial actors in efforts to grasp the typically Bayesian reasoning preferences of forensic DNA scientists. This same publication has also produced evidence on lay understandings of DNA profiling, a topic which has been of considerable interest elsewhere, but rarely the subject of rigorous empirical research. There is a growing literature on the so-called "CSI effect," to which forensic DNA is often asserted to be central (e.g., Cole 2013; Cole and Dioso-Villa 2007, 2009; Ley, Jankowski, and Brewer 2010; Ramsland 2006), however, this continues to be a controversial topic that is treated with a variable level of seriousness by different scholars.

Social Research on DNA Process and Outcomes

The earlier efforts to accumulate evidence capable of determining the value of DNA profiling to criminal investigations largely originated from the United Kingdom and were largely funded by the Home Office (e.g., Burrows *et al.* 2005; Webb *et al.* 2005; Williams 2004). However, those studies focused largely on the use of databased STR profiles in support of property crime, as did the much more ambitious United States randomized control trial study of Roman and his colleagues in the United States (Roman *et al.* 2008).

For some police stakeholders, the complexity, length, and variable circumstances that characterize homicide and major crime investigations, the variety of forensic technologies that may be deployed, their effect on one another, as well as the indeterminacy of the results of their application, all mean that it has been difficult for researchers to provide reliable accounts of the effectiveness of forensic resources applied to such investigations. Indeed, despite many UK government efforts to prove the utility of DNA profiling and the use of the NDNAD (UK National DNA Database), government spokespersons have consistently argued that detections in serious crime cases are not achieved through forensic science alone and so they do not collect data on DNA profile and database matches in homicide or rape cases. In many of the UK crimes in which DNA profiling has supported other investigative efforts (and especially in serious crime cases), it seems likely that profiles have been obtained directly from already identified suspects and has not required the speculative searching of the NDNAD. However there are no reliable official statistics against which this hypothesis can be tested.

There have been very few UK academic studies that have considered the use of forensic science in general, let alone DNA profiling in particular, in serious crime cases. The most notable of these include work by Innes, Clarke, Nicol and associates (Innes 1999, 2003; Innes and Clarke 2002; Nicol *et al.* 2004), Roycroft (2007) and Stelfox (2009). These studies have reached varied conclusions concerning the utility of forensic science support in such cases but have not systematically differentiated between different forensic technologies so that they do not directly and strongly contribute to knowledge of the contribution of DNA profiling to homicide investigations in England and Wales. The (now defunct) UK National Policing Improvement Agency surveyed the use of forensic science (especially DNA) in murder investigations in England and Wales in 2009–2010, but the results of this survey have never been publically disseminated. Beyond this jurisdiction, there has been some social science research conducted on the use of DNA in homicide investigations, one of the most interesting being the work of Briody (2004) in Queensland Australia which sampled 150 homicide cases that had occurred between 1996 and 1999. In 75 of these cases DNA profiling provided "an incriminating link … between the suspect and either the victim, the crime scene, or a weapon proven to be used by the accused," and a further 75 homicide cases investigated during the same time period in which DNA results had not been produced. In his conclusion to his study, Briody (2004: 250) asserts that "DNA evidence presented by prosecutors acted as the most significant predictor of cases reaching court," but that "there was no statistically significant association found between DNA and guilty pleas in the homicide cases sampled." He also found that "the addition of DNA evidence in particular case configurations was found to alter the predicted jury decision from an acquittal to a conviction." However, it should be noted that his assertion that "DNA evidence in homicide cases was found to exert a strong influence on jurors' decisions to convict" (Briody 2004: 247) is based on a statistical evaluation of potential determining features, and not on direct information obtained from jury members in the cases included in the study.

Research on the use of DNA in criminal investigations has been better supported in the United States, largely through the efforts of the National Institute of Justice (NIJ) and their explicit recognition of the potential contribution of social science to an understanding of the process of forensic science evidence construction and uses. Here, a program of work has been in place since 2005 and has been directed at understanding the range of policy and organizational and other social factors that affect the ways in which a range of forensic technologies are (or are not) effectively deployed in criminal investigations.

Informed by work conducted 30 years ago (Peterson, Mihajlovic, and Gilliand 1984), and before forensic genetics had entered the criminal justice system, the NIJ funded a study by Peterson and others (2010) who researched the investigations of a number of different kinds of crime (including homicide, rape, aggravated assault, robbery, and burglary) in five US jurisdictions. They focused particular attention on the ways that police officers made decisions about what evidence to send for expert analysis and particular attention was given to DNA analysis because of its ability to provide individualizing evidence capable of associating particular suspects with evidence found at crime scenes. However, the study offered a remarkably uninformative analysis of the fate of the large number of evidential items, including biological materials, recovered from the scenes of the 400 homicide investigations included in its sample of cases. The most significant (and disappointing for those interested in the effective uses of forensic DNA) finding in this study was that "only a limited amount of physical evidence linked/associated the suspect to the crime scene and/or victim. There were 54 cases with linking evidence, representing 13.5% of the 400 homicides reviewed" (Peterson *et al.* 2010: 83). The authors do not make clear exactly how much of this associative evidence was DNA, although they did note that in none of the cases was there a match between a crime scene DNA profile and a CODIS databased profile. A closely related study in the same funding stream (McEwen 2011) tracked the use of forensic evidence in five types of crime (homicide, sexual assault, aggravated assault, robbery, and burglary) in two jurisdictions. McEwen asserts the importance of DNA analysis for a large number of (both open and closed) cases studied, but the investigative utility obtained from the results of DNA analysis in the 183 homicide cases in the two jurisdictions is very difficult to determine from the data that are included in the project report. Differences between the finding of this study and that of Peterson *et al.* (2010) are however quite stark and can be illustrated by DNA processing trajectories in one of the areas studied. In Denver, homicide investigators requested DNA analysis in 80 percent of the cases, obtained matches in 36 percent of the cases with DNA evidence and exclusions in a further 22 percent of those cases. However, except in three short case narratives included in a late chapter of the report, the study methodology made it impossible to tell how any of these instances of DNA evidence were actually used by investigators or prosecutors, let alone how they combined with other forms of forensic or other evidence to detect offenders or secure prosecutions or convictions.

Although these and other studies (Schroeder and White 2009; Wilson, McClure, and Weisburd 2010) have noted that there are many investigations where DNA profiling has taken place, none of them has tested the strength of claims for the local significance of the uses of forensic DNA profiling and databasing in such cases. Most investigative authorities do not collect sufficiently robust data to make it possible to determine with an acceptable degree of certainty what any particular forensic technology contributed to the detection or prosecution of offenders in individual cases. In addition, there may appear to be too many technical and operational contingencies in the operational uses of DNA analysis (as illustrated in the previous section of this chapter) to make the measurement of the effectiveness of DNA analysis a simple matter. Many successful case narratives may suggest the usefulness of DNA profiling and databasing to homicide investigations but more intensive and detailed research is needed before the forensic genetics community are able to satisfy the demand of some civil society observers, as well as many policy and academic actors, for rigorous and systematic knowledge of DNA profiling methods and DNA databasing utility in the routine and exceptional investigation of homicide and other serious crimes.

Notes

1 Pickton's trial began on January 30, 2007. There were 235,000 items found at Pickton's farm during the course of a 20 month search and these were finally tested for DNA evidence in support of his prosecution, a number which is said to have "overwhelmed" Canada's DNA forensic capacity at that time (http://www.pressreader.com/canada/the-province/20071210/281698315407708).

2 Space does not permit consideration of the controversy over the introduction of "low template" techniques in general, but see Lawless (2012) for an elegant sociological account of this.

References

Bottomley, M. and Holt, C. (2011) Familial DNA: A relative success? *Journal of Homicide and Major Incident Investigation*, 7: 4–21.

Briody, M. (2004) The effects of DNA evidence on homicide cases in court. *Australian and New Zealand Journal of Criminology*, 37: 231–252.

Burrows, J., Tarling, R., Mackie, A., *et al.* (2005) *Forensic Science Pathfinder Project: Evaluating Increased Forensic Activity in two English Police Forces*. Report 46/05. London: Home Office.

Champod, C. (2013) DNA transfer: Informed judgment or mere guesswork? *Frontiers in Genetics*, 4: 300.

Champod, C., Evett, I., and Jackson, G. (2004) Establishing the most appropriate databases for addressing source level propositions. *Science and Justice*, 44, 153–164.

Clayton, T.M., Whitaker, J., and Maguire, C.N. (1995) Identification of bodies from a scene of a mass disaster using DNA amplification of short tandem repeat (STR) loci. *Forensic Science International*, 76: 7–15.

Cole, S.A. (2013) A surfeit of science: The "CSI effect" and the media appropriation of the public understanding of science. *Public Understanding of Science*, 24(2): 130–146.

Cole, S.A. and Dioso-Villa, R. (2007) CSI and its effects: Media, juries and the burden of proof. *New England Law Review*, 41: 435–470.

Cole, S.A. and Dioso-Villa, R. (2009) Investigating the "CSI" effect: Media and litigation crisis in criminal law. *Stanford Law Review*, 61: 1335–1373.

Gill, P. (2001) Application of low copy number DNA profiling. *Croatian Medical Journal*, 42: 229–232.

Gill, P. (2002) Role of short tandem repeats in forensic casework in the UK: Past, present and future perspectives. *Biotechniques*, 32: 366–374.

Gill, P., Haned, H., Bleka, O., *et al.* (2015) Genotyping and interpretation of STR-DNA: Low-template, mixtures and database matches—twenty years of research and development. *Forensic Science International Genetics*, 18: 100–117.

Gill, P., Ivanov, P.L., Kimpton, C., *et al.* (1994) Identification of the remains of the Romanov family by DNA analysis. *Nature Genetics*, 6: 130–135.

Gill, P., Jeffreys, A.J., and Werrett, D.J. (1985) Forensic application of DNA "fingerprints." *Nature*, 318: 577–579.

Goodwin, W., Linacre, A., and Hadi, S. (2007) *An Introduction to Forensic Genetics*. Chichester, UK: John Wiley & Sons.

Goray, M. and Van Oorschot, R.A. (2015) The complexities of DNA transfer during a social setting. *Legal Medicine* (Tokyo), 17: 82–91.

Grace, V., Midgley, G., Veth, J., and Ahuriri-Driscoll, A. (2011) *Forensic DNA Evidence on Trial: Science and Uncertainty in the Courtroom*. Litchfield Park, AZ: Emergent Publications.

Gregory, A. and Rainbow, L. (2011) Enhanced Prioritisation of Familial DNA Searches. *Journal of Homicide and Major Incident Investigation*, 7: 75–88.

Hagelberg, E., Gray, I.C., and Jeffreys, A.J. (1991) Identification of the skeletal remains of a murder victim by DNA analysis. *Nature*, 352: 427–429.

Houck, M.M. and Siegel, J.A. (2006) *Fundamentals of Forensic Science*. Burlington, MA: Elsevier.

Howes, L.M., Julian, R., Kelty, S.F., *et al.* (2014) The readability of expert reports for non-scientist report-users: Reports of DNA analysis. *Forensic Science International*, 237: 7–18.

Innes, M. (1999) Beyond the Macpherson report: Managing murder inquiries in context. *Sociological Research Online*, 4.

Innes, M. (2003) *Investigating Murder: Detective Work and the Police Response to Criminal Homicide*. Oxford: Oxford University Press.

Innes, M. and Clarke, A. (2002) *Let's Get Physical: Contact Trace Materials in the Crime Investigation Process*. London: Home Office.

INTERPOL (2012) *Global DNA Survey 2011*. Lyon, France: ICPO-Interpol.

Jamieson, A. (2011) LCN DNA analysis and opinion on transfer: *R v Reed and Reed*. *The International Journal of Evidence and Proof*, 15: 161–169.

Jeffreys, A.J., Wilson, V., and Thein, S.L. (1985) Individual-specific "fingerprints" of human DNA. *Nature*, 316: 76–79.

Jobling, M.A. and Gill, P. (2004) Encoded evidence: DNA in forensic analysis. *Nature Reviews*, 5: 739–751.

Jobling, M.A., Pandya, A., and Tyler-Smith, C. (1997) The Y chromosome in forensic analysis and paternity testing. *International Journal of Legal Medicine*, 110: 118–124.

Kaye, D.H. (2010) *The Double Helix and the Law of Evidence*. Cambridge, MA: Harvard University Press.

Kayser, M. (2015) Forensic DNA phenotyping: Predicting human appearance from crime scene material for investigative purposes. *Forensic Science International: Genetics*, 18: 33–48.

Kayser, M. and De Knijff, P. (2011) Improving human forensics through advances in genetics, genomics and molecular biology. *Nature Reviews: Genetics*, 12: 179–192.

Kayser, M. and Schneider, P.M. (2009) DNA-based prediction of human externally visible characteristics in forensics: Motivations, scientific challenges, and ethical considerations. *Forensic Science International: Genetics*, 3: 154–161.

Kimpton, C., Fisher, D., Watson, S., *et al.* (1994) Evaluation of an automated DNA profiling system employing multiplex amplification of four tetrameric STR loci. *International Journal of Legal Medicine*, 106: 302–311.

Kruijver, M., Meester, R., and Slooten, K. (2014) Optimal strategies for familial searching. *Forensic Science International: Genetics*, 13C: 90–103.

Lapointe, M., Rogic, A., Bourgoin, S., *et al.* (2015) Leading-edge forensic DNA analyses and the necessity of including crime scene investigators, police officers and technicians in a DNA elimination database. *Forensic Science International: Genetics*, 19: 50–55.

Lawless, C.J. (2012) The low template DNA profiling controversy: Biolegality and boundary work among forensic scientists. *Social Studies of Science*, 43(2): 191–214.

Lee, H.C. and Tirnady, F. (2003) Blood evidence: How DNA is revolutionizing the way we solve crimes. Cambridge, MA: Perseus.

Ley, B.L., Jankowski, N., and Brewer, P.R. (2010) Investigating CSI: Portrayals of DNA testing on a forensic crime show and their potential effects. *Public Understanding of Science*, 21: 51–67.

Lowe, A., Murray, C., Richardson, P., *et al.* (2003) Use of low copy number DNA in forensic inference. *International Congress Series*, 1239(2): 799–801.

Lynch, M., Cole, S., McNally, R., and Jordan, K. (2008) *Truth Machine: The Contentious History of DNA Fingerprinting*. Chicago: Chicago University Press.

Maguire, C., McCallum, L.A., Storey, C., and Whitaker, J. (2014) Familial searching: A specialist DNA profiling service using the NDNAD to identify unknown offenders via their relatives—the UK experience. *Forensic Science International: Genetics*, 8, 1–9.

McCartney, C. (2006) *Forensic Identification and Criminal Justice: Forensic Science, Justice and Risk*. Cullompton, UK: Willan.

McEwen, T. (2011) *The Role and Impact of Forensic Evidence in the Criminal Justice System: Final Report*. Washington, DC: US Department of Justice.

Mnookin, J.L. (2007) People v. Castro: Challenging the forensic use of DNA evidence. *Journal of Scholarly Perspectives*, 3: 77–105.

Mullis, K., Faloona, F., Scharf, S., *et al.* (1986) Specific enzymatic amplification of DNA in vitro: The polymerase chain reaction. *Cold Spring Harbor Symposia on Quantitative Biology*, 51: 263–273.

National Research Council (1992) *DNA Technology in Forensic Science*. Washington, DC: National Academy Press.

National Research Council (1996) *Evaluation of Forensic DNA Evidence—Committee on DNA Forensic Science: An Update*. Washington, DC: National Academy Press.

Nicol, C., Innes, M., Gee, D., and Feist, A. (2004) *Reviewing Murder Investigations: An Analysis of Progress Reports from Six Forces, Home Office Online Report 24/5*. London: Home Office.

Oppal, W.T. (2012) *Forsaken: The Report of the Missing Women Commission of Inquiry*. Vancouver: Missing Women Commission of Inquiry.

Peterson, J.L., Mihajlovic, S., and Gilliand, M. (1984) *Forensic Evidence and the Police: The Effects of Scientific Evidence on Criminal Investigations*. Washington, DC: Government Printing Office.

Peterson, J.L., Sommers, I., Baskin, D., and Johnson, D. (2010) *The Role and Impact of Forensic Evidence in the Criminal Justice Process*. Washington, DC: National Institute of Justice.

Pham-Hoai, E., Crispino, F., and Hampikian, G. (2014) The First Successful Use of a Low Stringency Familial Match in a French Criminal Investigation. *Journal of Forensic Sciences*, 59(3): 816–819.

Phillips, C. (2015) Forensic genetic analysis of bio-geographical ancestry. *Forensic Science International: Genetics*, 18: 49–65.

Phillips, C., Parson, W., Lundsberg, B., *et al.* (2014) Building a forensic ancestry panel from the ground up: The EUROFORGEN Global AIM-SNP set. *Forensic Science International: Genetics*, 11: 13–25.

Phillips, C., Prieto, L., Fondevila, M., *et al.* (2009) Ancestry analysis in the 11-M Madrid bomb attack investigation. *PLoS One*, 4: e6583.

Ramsland, K. (2006) *The CSI Effect*. New York: Berkley Boulevard.

Roman, J.K., Reid, S., Reid, J., *et al.* (2008) *The DNA Field Experiment: Cost-Effectiveness Analysis of the Use of DNA in the Investigation of High-Volume Crimes*. Washington, DC: Urban Institute.

Roycroft, M. (2007) What solves hard to solve murders. *Journal of Homicide and Major Incident Investigation*, 3: 93–107.

Schroeder, D.A. and White, M.D. (2009) Exploring the use of DNA evidence in homicide investigations: Implications for detective work and case clearance. *Police Quarterly*, 12(3): 319–342.

Shriver, M. (2015) *Identifying and Communicating Genetic Determinants of Facial Features: Prctical Considerations in Forensic Molecular Photofitting*. Washington, DC: US Department of Justice.

Slooten, K.J. and Egeland, T. (2015) Exclusion probabilities and likelihood ratios with applications to mixtures. *International Journal of Legal Medicine*, 130(1): 39–57.

Stelfox, P. (2009) *Criminal Investigation: An Introduction to Principles and Practice*. Cullompton, UK: Willan.

Syndercombe-Court, D., Ballard, C., Phillips, A., *et al.* (2003) Comparison of Y chromosome haplotypes in three racial groups and the possibility of predicting ethnic origin. *International Congress of Serology*, 1239: 67–69.

Wambaugh, J. (1989) *The Blooding*. London: Bantam Books.

Webb, B., Smith, C., Brock, A., and Townsley, M. (2005) DNA fast-tracking. In M.J. Smith and N. Tilley (eds), *Crime Science: New Approaches to Preventing and Detecting Crime* (pp. 167–190). Cullompton, UK: Willan.

Wheate, R. (2010) The importance of DNA evidence to juries in criminal trials. *The International Journal of Evidence and Proof*, 14: 129–145.

Wickenhieser, R.A. (2002) Trace DNA: A review, discussion of theory, and application of the transfer of trace quantities of DNA through skin contact. *Journal of Forensic Sciences*, 47: 442–450.

Williams, R. (2004) The management of crime scene examination in relation to the investigation of burglary and vehicle crime. *Home Office Online Report*, 24: 58.

Williams, R. and Johnson, P. (2008) *Genetic Policing: The Use of DNA in Criminal Investigations*. Cullompton, UK: Willan.

Wilson, D.B., McClure, D., and Weisburd, D. (2010). Does forensic DNA help to solve crime? The benefit of sophisticated answers to naive questions. *Journal of Contemporary Criminal Justice*, 26(4): 458–469.

Further Reading

Johnson, P. and Williams, R. (2004) Post-conviction DNA testing: the UK's first "exoneration" case? *Science and Justice*, 44(2): 77–83.

Lynch, M. and McNally, R. (2009) Forensic DNA databases and biolegality: The co-production of law, surveillance technology and suspect bodies. In P. Atkinson, P. Glasner, and

M. Lock (eds), *Handbook of Genetics and Society: Mapping the New Genomic Era* (pp. 283–301). London: Routledge.

Wienroth, M., Williams, R., and Morling, N. (2014) Technological innovations in forensic genetics: social, legal and ethical aspects. *Recent Advances in DNA and Gene Sequences*, 8: 98–103.

32

Cold Case Homicide Reviews

Cheryl Allsop

Introduction

This chapter provides an account of how the police seek to solve long-term undetected homicides, shining a light on the opportunities and challenges faced by cold case review teams. It will focus mainly on how cold case reviews are conducted in the United Kingdom but will also draw on examples from other countries, in particular the United States, the Netherlands, Canada, and Australia. What will become clear is that both in the United Kingdom and elsewhere it is advances in forensic techniques and technologies, along with the growth of technological databases and information from members of the public, that enable cold case homicides to be progressed. It should, however, be noted that cold case homicides are not easily detected, despite how they are portrayed in the media and in fictional accounts (Lord 2005).

This being the case, the question arises: why do the police conduct cold case homicide reviews? This question is particularly pertinent in an age of financial austerity when policing budgets are severely restricted and decisions have to be made about how best to prioritize activities and where limited resources should be spent. To that end, the chapter will begin by considering why cold case homicide reviews are conducted, before going on to outline how they are conducted, providing some examples and examining some of the opportunities and challenges which face investigators.

The Handbook of Homicide, First Edition. Edited by Fiona Brookman, Edward R. Maguire, and Mike Maguire.

Why Conduct Cold Case Homicide Reviews?

Cold case homicide investigations have captured the imagination of the media and the public. They are the ultimate "whodunnit." For detectives finally to succeed in catching an elusive offender reinforces the popular image of the crime fighting, investigative detective, unearthing and solving clues, in much the same way as popular media and dramatic accounts portray investigations. Such successes can help the police to engender a feeling of public confidence in their crime fighting abilities and quest for justice. The publicity surrounding cold case homicide successes can help the police to present themselves in a positive light.

Similarly, detecting an unsolved homicide can provide a form of community reassurance, particularly in smaller communities where the specter of an unsolved murder can loom large, including for those previously considered a suspect and who have had to live with the finger of suspicion pointing at them until the real offender(s) is caught. Additionally, of course, while the crime remains undetected an offender is still free to offend again, so the opportunity to apprehend and stop dangerous offenders cannot be underestimated. This is particularly pertinent with crimes involving sexual violence as the chances of repeat offending are high and so cold case stranger rape investigations, in particular, provide opportunities to link offenses and prevent further recidivism when advances in forensic science link crimes and offenders to crimes. Crucially, however, it is for the families of the victims who need to see justice for their loved one that a cold case review can provide the greatest benefit. Cold case review successes can also provide hope for other victims' families that they too will obtain justice for the murder of their loved one. As Rock (1998) asserted, families of homicide victims need to know what happened to their loved one and want to obtain justice for them. Seeing offenders caught and punished for the crimes committed provides an opportunity for families to gain some kind of closure. Conversely, investigating cold cases requires significant amounts of time and resources that could be invested in current crime fighting, where there are arguably greater chances of success, and so police agencies must balance the resources devoted to older and newer cases. Achieving this balance in the context of limited investigative resources is difficult particularly when close relatives of the victim and the offender might well be dead.

What Is a "Cold Case"?

Unsolved homicides are never closed, it is simply that an investigation will stop when all lines of enquiry have been explored and there appear to be no further investigative opportunities to follow at that time (Innes and Clarke 2009; Allsop 2013). As such, there is no prescribed time when an unsolved homicide "goes cold": it is generally recognized that this occurs simply when there are no viable investigative opportunities left to pursue (Jones, Grieve and Milne 2008; Innes and Clarke 2009; Allsop 2013). In the United Kingdom, in order to try to prevent homicide investigations from stalling, they will be subject to periodic progress reviews to ensure that all investigative opportunities have been explored, that all procedures have been followed correctly and to provide guidance to the investigating team (Nicol *et al.* 2004; Jones, Grieve, and Milne 2010). Cold case reviews are also conducted ideally at two year intervals on cases that remain unsolved to establish whether there are likely to be any new potential investigative opportunities to pursue (Innes and Clarke 2009). However, the robustness of this two year review cycle does depend on the police having the resources in place to do the reviews. As one might expect, both nationally and internationally, it is the availability or lack of resources that will determine the likelihood of a review team being in place to actively conduct such reviews.

In short, cold case investigation teams are not universally in existence and, as will be seen presently, there are no uniform or prescribed ways of approaching cold case reviews. Indeed, even within individual teams there are differences in how they are tackled. Likewise there are similarities and differences in how different countries approach cold case homicides, and many do not appear to have any form of systematic investigative policy in place for reviewing unsolved homicides. Those that do are, for the most part, taking advantage of advances in forensic techniques and technologies including DNA databases to progress cold case homicides. As Hulshof, Knotter, and Spoormans (2015) note, in the Netherlands the first cold case unit was established in 1999 and in 2000 a cold case pilot initiative between Amsterdam-Amstelland and Utrecht, successfully linked two crimes to one offender using new scientific techniques to re-examine DNA evidence which could then be compared to a suspect sample held on the DNA database. In 2000, the Minister of Justice advised that all homicides and sex crimes should be reinvestigated and as units were beginning to achieve successful results so it spurred on other areas to review their unsolved crimes (Hulshof, Knotter, and Spoormans 2015). In the United Kingdom and in the United States, cold case reviews have become an established component of policing, again fueled by advances in forensic techniques and technologies that potentially provide new investigative opportunities. Adcock and Stein (2015) noted that in the United States, in the absence of forensic opportunities, it is unlikely that cold cases will be reviewed. However, it should be pointed out that in the United States, in particular, new forensic techniques and technologies were not always the driver of cold case investigations, as they are now.

As Innes and Clarke (2009) illustrate, when the term cold case review originally came into parlance in the United States in the 1990s the focus was very much on witness testimony and changing allegiances. Based on the idea that as time goes on and people fall out or change loyalties, interviewing these witnesses years later might elicit new information which could subsequently be used to generate new lines of enquiry (Innes and Clarke 2009; Allsop 2013). These avenues of enquiry are, of course, still pursued but the focus now is much more on the opportunities that advances in forensic techniques and technologies present to these old cases. Now, as in the United Kingdom, forensic opportunities are exploited to identify suspects. Funding provided by the National Institute of Justice has further allowed for historic crimes to be reinvestigated (NIJ 2002; Lord 2005; Innes and Clarke 2009). Similarly, in the United Kingdom the Home Office has provided funding for forces to exploit forensic opportunities in long-term unsolved homicides and unsolved stranger rapes (Allsop 2013).

Operation Stealth

In 2007, the Home Office in the United Kingdom provided funding to support police teams keen to detect unsolved homicides. An initial budget of £250,000 was provided from which review teams had to bid for money for cases which they thought could be progressed from forensic opportunities. Over 50 unsolved homicides were reviewed by police teams across England and Wales. A second proactive phase began in 2008 which saw the Operation Stealth project team search the Homicide Index[1] for homicides they believed had the potential for progression by drawing on advances in forensic science, especially where there were suspects in the frame who could be implicated or eliminated from the investigation. The then Forensic Science Service were also asked to rate the chances of potential forensic success in each case. A further £250,000 was set aside for this, and in March 2010/2011 two million pounds was allocated to cold case homicide reviews. The Operation Stealth project team recorded a number of successes, most notably that of John William Cooper convicted of the double murders of siblings Richard and Helen Thomas in 1985 and husband and wife Peter and Gwenda Dixon in 1989. Cooper had previously been a suspect but with insufficient evidence available initially to connect him to the crimes, he was not originally prosecuted for them. It was not until the cold case review team were able to link him to the victims after DNA from the victim's blood was found on his shotgun and fibers from their clothes were found on his, that he was finally able to be prosecuted and convicted for the murders (Wilkins and Hill 2014).

Another notable conviction was that of Mark Weston, convicted of the murder of Vikki Thompson in 1995. He was originally acquitted of the murder in 1996 but subsequently convicted after the unsolved homicide was reopened in 2005. He was convicted in 2010, after microscopic traces of blood were found on his footwear which enabled him to be connected to the victim. His conviction was made possible by changes to the double jeopardy laws, which now allows for suspects to be prosecuted again for crimes of which they have previously been acquitted, if there is new and compelling evidence available. In this case the blood found on his footwear provided the new and compelling evidence which gave rise to the new prosecution (Allsop 2013).

Similar changes to the double jeopardy laws in Scotland, in 2009, allowed for the conviction of Angus Sinclair, a prolific serial sexual offender, for the murders of Helen Scott and Christine Eadie. Although the original trial in 2004 had been stopped and Sweeney acquitted of the murders, he was eventually convicted in 2011, when DNA found on one of the victims' coats was said to originate from the two victims and only two others, one being John Sweeney (Police Scotland 2014).

Canada and Australia similarly draw on forensic techniques and technologies in historic unsolved homicides, and the opportunity to progress cold cases is also solicited through the media and Crime Stopper appeals with sometimes substantial rewards offered for information, as will be noted presently. However, despite the new leads witness information can generate it is easy to see why forensic opportunities are pursued in unsolved homicide reviews. In the United Kingdom, the introduction of the National DNA Database (NDNAD) in 1995 and in the United States the Combined DNA Index System (CODIS) has enabled crime scene samples from historic crimes to be upgraded and compared with samples held on the database of offenders and other crime scenes, thereby providing investigators with a new line of enquiry to explore when a match is achieved (Harper 2015). As Adcock and Stein (2015) suggest the ability to link crimes using CODIS has been a key factor in detecting many cold cases.

Having DNA profiles enables cold case investigators to explore further lines of enquiry that would not have been available at the time the offense was committed and allows for new investigative leads and lines of enquiry to be explored. For example, mass screening was successfully used in the Netherlands to identify an offender in a 1999 rape and murder case. The investigation into the murder of 16-year-old schoolgirl Marianne Vaatstra, in fact, highlights a number of the main drivers in identifying suspects in historic homicides. The case was kept alive through media appeals and forensic techniques enabled the mass screening of local men to identify the offender. A number of "tip offs" provided by members of the public following a news broadcast suggested that a cigarette lighter identified in the victim's handbag, which contained traces of DNA matching traces of DNA found on the victim's body, was sold locally to where the victim lived in Zwaagwesteinde. A mass screening of local men identified a farmer who lived near to where the victim's body was found. He later confessed to the crime and was convicted of the rape and murder of Marianne, receiving an 18 year jail sentence (DutchNews.nl 2012).

In the United Kingdom the cold case review into the murder of Stephen Lawrence is one of the most high profile cold case investigations, and it was microscopic specks of blood on the jacket of one of the suspects that indicated his presence at the crime scene. Stephen was murdered in 1993 and although five suspects were identified at the time it was not until January 2012 when two of the five, David Norris and Gary Dobson, were convicted of the murder after DNA found on exhibits retained from the murder placed them at the crime scene (Laville and Dodd 2012).

In Canada, investigations into the cold case disappearance of Henrietta Millek, who went missing in 1982, are being progressed at the time of writing to establish whether an item belonging to the victim, her purse, which was found in a bar where she was last seen, may hold the DNA of her abductors given the improvements in forensic techniques now available including "Touch DNA" analysis. In addition, appeals have been made to the local community to come forward with information (CBC News 2009). Returning again to the Netherlands and the United Kingdom we see here how forensic techniques enabled two unsolved homicides across two continents to be linked. The cold case review by Rotterdam police in 2008 linked the two murders of Melissa Halstead in Amsterdam in 1990 and Paula Fields in London in 2000. In addition, the introduction of the missing persons database in the Netherlands in 2007 enabled the body of Melissa Halstead to be identified in 2008 through familial DNA techniques. Finding a connection between the two victims provided investigators with the opportunity to explore their connection to each other and to the potential offender. So following a joint operation by the Dutch police and the Metropolitan Police, John Sweeney was convicted of the murders of Melissa Halstead and Paula Fields (Davies 2011; Summers 2011).

Of course these successes depend on relevant items being retained and being correctly stored and labeled such that review officers can connect exhibits to the crimes. A problem not unique to the United Kingdom is the fact that many exhibits cannot be found or cannot be used because of the manner of their collection and storage. It is, therefore, the task of a review team to locate any potential exhibits to be able to establish any new forensic opportunities to identify a suspect.

Process

In the United Kingdom, while there are no uniform approaches to conducting cold case reviews there are certain tasks which must be completed. Before a review can take place the first task is to locate the documentation from the original investigation. This in itself can be problematic as documentation, paperwork, and exhibits can often be spread far and wide across the force areas in several places. Depending on the age of the case the investigation may not have been documented and stored on HOLMES[2] so all the information may be held on paper. All of the boxes containing the investigative paperwork and exhibits must be found, and once located, searched through for important documents including the closing statement report which details the senior investigating officer's (SIO) thinking at the end of the original investigation (and any subsequent reviews), and the exhibits log to establish what exhibits are held by the police. The case files can then be reviewed looking for forensic opportunities to progress, potential suspects who need to be eliminated or implicated, and considering any hypotheses as to what might have happened in the case.

An important part of the review process is to prioritize which cases to review. Decision makers have to weigh up factors such as the likely chances of success, the forensic opportunities available, whether there are any suspects previously identified who need to be eliminated from the enquiry, and how high profile the case is. The police also have to consider and manage the risk that an offender could offend again. Ultimately, however, it is the potential for a successful result which determines the priority given. Similarly, in the United States, cases are again prioritized considering the chances of solving the case, the existence of physical evidence that could be tested using new scientific techniques and whether there are likely to be witnesses and suspects still alive (Lord 2005). Likewise, cases being reviewed by the Victoria Police Cold Case and Missing Persons Squad have been prioritized based on new information being available which could lead to the identification of an offender, and advances in forensic technologies enabling forensic opportunities to be explored and again, as one would expect, focusing on those cases with the most likely chance of success (Moor 2014).

Given the focus on exploiting forensic potential, an important step in the review process is to establish what tests have already been carried out on the exhibits. A review team, often in conjunction with the scientific support team, will decide what further tests may be viable on samples held and in what order. This is important because certain tests may render the sample unsuitable for any further testing, so it is important for review teams to carefully consider the order and priority of any forensic tests being conducted.

In addition to forensic expertise, cold case review conferences can incorporate multi-disciplinary expertise, with teams drawing on psychological as well as forensic expertise (Innes and Clarke 2009). As Innes and Clarke (2009) note, further lines of enquiry can be generated when behavioral advisers can suggest a new investigative hypothesis, including suggesting the type of person who may have committed the homicide, which in turn can be used to narrow down the potential suspect population. It is open to debate how effective it can be to know the type of offender who may have committed the crime after many years. That having been said, it can help to narrow down a large suspect pool and can also be utilized in conjunction with forensic opportunities, including when familial DNA opportunities are being progressed, in particular in helping to decide upon the parameters to be explored.

Opportunities and Challenges

Forensic opportunities therefore provide the potential for identifying suspects in cold case homicides, in particular in sexually motivated crimes. However, the value of forensic science to an investigation depends on a number of important factors. It is worth remembering that historically crime scene samples were not collected as they would be today. Samples would be handled without protective gloves and crime scenes would be trampled on without officers wearing protective clothing. Samples would be collected based on what was known at the time. As such, samples could easily be contaminated. Similarly, the manner in which items and samples were collected at the time and subsequently stored can also impact on any future value. Exhibits were often thrown together in storage bags, again running the risk of cross contamination. In addition, samples can degrade over time. The ability to take advantage of new scientific techniques and technologies is also dependent on the exhibits being retained in the first place and it was not uncommon for items to be returned to victims' families, especially as detectives would not have been aware of the future potential opportunities that are now available. Ultimately though, it is the potentially prohibitive costs of forensic testing that can be the biggest obstacle for cold case review detectives, particularly in the United States where it can be difficult for police teams to gain access to expensive DNA testing thereby precluding them from exploring potential new lines of enquiry. Police teams have to decide between spending the limited resources on forensic testing in cold cases with allocating resources to current crimes. With finite resources available often the decision is made to allocate them to current cases and returning to cold cases as and when there is time available to do so.

As was alluded to earlier, in the United Kingdom as in other countries, in addition to the opportunities that advances in forensic techniques and technologies can bring to cold case investigations, as in live homicide investigations, information from the public and new witness testimony is also elicited by investigators. The passage of time provides both an opportunity and a challenge for obtaining viable witness testimony from people who haven't previously come forward with information, or who were reluctant to share with detectives what they knew about the crime. However, as time passes and people change allegiance they may be more likely to come forward to reveal what they know about the crime, albeit as time passes memories fade and witnesses may not be able to accurately recall what they saw or heard or know. The vagaries of eyewitness testimony and memory and recall processes have long been established (see, for example, Loftus 1996; Wells 1993; Williamson 2007) and these can be amplified by the continuing passing of time. Moreover, if witnesses are now proffering a different statement from the one originally provided, detectives have to consider the credibility of the information and the value of the information they can provide, given that they will have changed their account of events, at least once, from accounts they have previously given. Locating witnesses can also be difficult after a number of years; however, the media can be used to great advantage to trace witnesses and suspects, and to encourage both them and potential new witnesses to come forward.

The Media

The media play a vital role in live homicide investigations and the ability to manage the media is a key skill for senior investigating officers. In cold case investigations the media are utilized in a number of ways. The newspaper report referred to earlier, (by Keith Moor in the Herald Sun) on the newly established Cold Case and Missing Persons Squad in Victoria Australia, demonstrates how the media can be instrumental in generating new leads in cold case investigations, with the Acting Detective Inspector reporting that information from the public had given them new lines of enquiry to explore in a number of unsolved homicides. The online version of the newspaper has links to their unsolved homicide database and provides information to the public on the details of the unsolved homicides; with links to Crime Stoppers enabling members of the public to come forward anonymously with information in connection to the unsolved crimes (see Moor 2014). In other jurisdictions across Australia, Crime Stopper appeals on police websites are also utilized in an effort to encourage witnesses to come forward, again offering rewards for information leading to an arrest. Following one such "tip-off," not initially concerned with a cold case, new investigative avenues are being explored in connection to the cold case abduction of two young girls in Adelaide in 1973. Again, a substantial financial reward has been offered to encourage anyone with information to come forward and report it to the police (Littlely and Rice 2014).

In the United Kingdom, newspaper and television appeals are often made in an attempt to jog memories and encourage witnesses to come forward with information. Anniversary appeals, often many years after the murder, are seen as a timely opportunity to remind the public of the ongoing investigation and to encourage anyone with information to come forward. Unsolved homicides are regularly reported on the factual television program, Crimewatch, which focuses on showing crimes in the hopes of generating new information from the public. The program often includes reconstructions of cold case homicides to encourage people to telephone in to the television studio to talk to officers in charge of the case or to contact the police directly.

Social media has also been utilized by review teams keen to engage a wide audience. Police Twitter accounts can be used to publicize a review and request information from their followers in the hopes that their followers will retweet the information request to their followers, and so on, reaching a wide audience of Twitter users. For example, in November 2014 in the United Kingdom, West Yorkshire police coining the term "tweeconstruction" tweeted a reconstruction of a cold case to appeal for witnesses to the unsolved murder of a 13-year-old school girl in an attempt to elicit new information from an interested public. Police Facebook pages are also used to publicize cold case reviews and to appeal for information. As noted previously, cold case review successes are also publicized to remind the public that the police never give up on obtaining justice for victims. Family members will themselves set up websites, blogs, and Facebook pages to highlight the unsolved homicide of their loved one, www.whokilledmymum.com is one such site pertaining to the 1986 murder of Patricia Grainger and her son's quest to find the killer. When the media are to be utilized by the police, families will be kept informed by review officers so that they do not have to learn of the review via the media and to help minimize the impact any such publicity might have on the families. On occasions family members might also be used in these appeals to remind the public of the human side of the story in the hopes of encouraging the offender and witnesses to come forward.

The above having been said, in the United Kingdom families are often not advised of a cold case review until the investigating team start to elicit publicity about the case or if they are making enquiries that might come to the attention of the family. If there is a chance that this will happen then they will advise relatives to prepare them for it. That notwithstanding, families will contact review teams to push for a review of the unsolved murder of their loved one and this can prompt further action on a case. In live homicide investigations families can be an invaluable source of information about the victim (McGarry and Smith 2011) and so it would seem that including them in the review would be worthwhile, notwithstanding the risk of raising their hopes and then dashing them again in the event of the review coming to nothing, particularly given the regular cycle of reviews.

So, in the quest for publicity and public information the Internet provides a valuable resource to cold case reviewers. In the United States, in particular, there are numerous websites and blogs dedicated to unsolved murders, designed to publicize cases and keep them in the public eye. Often run by volunteers and family members of victims they support law enforcement officials in eliciting information from the public.

In fact, in the United States volunteers are often used in cold case investigations. Lord (2005) notes the value of deploying experienced detectives and volunteers in cold case units in the United States, where volunteers provide additional resource and expertise to the investigation team. Pettem (2013) similarly notes the value of volunteers, including, for example, college interns and retired professionals. The Vidocq Society, where members have expertise in a number of areas—including criminal investigations, forensic techniques, and technologies and the law—provides voluntary assistance to law enforcement officials tasked with investigating unsolved homicides. Their advice is given for free and is simply designed to help assist and progress unsolved homicide investigations albeit a small operation only available to review a very small number of cases (http://www.vidocq.org/). This use of volunteers in this way currently seems to be unique to America but the benefit of doing so is immediately apparent.

Conclusion

Having a dedicated cold case review team in place with the resources available to review unsolved homicides provides the greatest opportunity to detect these crimes. Advances in forensic techniques and technologies provides a good starting point for identifying suspects and eliminating others from police enquiries, notwithstanding the potential problems that may arise when relying on old crime scene samples. The potential to revisit cold cases and link current to past offending has grown exponentially through the establishment and continual growth of DNA databases and it is often the value that these databases can add to cold case investigations that is used to justify further expenditure and their continued growth (Williams and Johnson 2008). But, the costs involved can make cold case investigations a luxury that cannot be afforded when already stretched resources are allocated to current crime investigations. The ability to utilize various forms of media to encourage witnesses and suspects to come forward and the changing allegiances of those previously loyal to the offender also provides further potentially less costly opportunities to finally detect long-term unsolved homicides. These opportunities are not without the requisite challenges which need to be overcome to progress these investigations. It is often the traditional detective skills that enable investigators to bring together all of the pieces of the puzzle, drawing on all of the investigative tools at their disposal to identify and ultimately bring offenders to justice, in so doing obtaining long overdue justice for the families. But while governmental funding has been allocated to progress cold case homicide reviews it remains to be seen whether the necessary resources will continue to be available for this form of policing.

Notes

1 The Homicide Index contains details of all homicides in the United Kingdom.
2 HOLMES is the Home Office Large Major Enquiry System, a computer system used to manage and store information gathered during an investigation.

References

Adcock, J. M. and Stein, S.L. (2015) An alternative model for evaluating cold cases. In J.M. Adcock, and S.L. Stein (eds), *Cold Cases Evaluation Models with Follow-up Strategies for Investigators* (2nd edn, pp. 87–98) Boca Raton, FL: CRC Press.

Allsop, C. (2013) Motivations, money and modern policing: Accounting for cold case reviews in an age of austerity. *Policing and Society: An International Journal of Research and Policy*, 23(3): 362–375. doi: 10.1080/10439463.2013.782211.

CBC News (2009) 30-year-old St. John's cold case gets new review. Available online at http://www.cbc.ca/news/canada/newfoundland-labrador/30-year-old-st-john-s-cold-case-gets-new-review-1.1352308 (accessed January 23, 2015).

Davies, C. (2011) John Sweeney convicted of canal murders as police warn of more bodies. *The Guardian*, April 4. Available online at http://www.theguardian.com/uk/2011/apr/04/carpenter-convicted-canal-murders-more-bodies (accessed January 23, 2015).

DutchNews.nl (2012) Man arrested following dna tests to solve 1999 schoolgirl murder. November 9. Available online at http://www.dutchnews.nl/news/archives/2012/11/man_arrested_following_dna_tes.php (accessed January 23, 2015).

Harper, A.B. (2015) Applying science and technology to cold cases. In J.M. Adcock and S.L. Stein (eds), *Cold Cases Evaluation Models with Follow-up Strategies for Investigators* (2nd edn, pp. 133–150). Boca Raton, FL: CRC Press.

Hulshof, R.A.M., Knotter, J.C., and Spoormans, Y.M. (2015) Cold case investigation in an educational environment: The Dutch experience in cold cases evaluation models with follow-up strategies for investigators. In J.M. Adcock and S.L. Stein (eds), *Cold Cases Evaluation Models with Follow-up Strategies for Investigators* (2nd edn, pp. 105–132) Boca Raton, FL: CRC Press.

Innes, M. and Clarke, A. (2009) Policing the past: Cold case studies, forensic evidence and retroactive social control. *British Journal of Sociology*, 60(3): 543–563. doi: 10.1111/j.1468-4446.2009.01255.x.

Jones, D., Grieve, J., and Milne, B. (2008) A case to review murder investigations. *Policing: A Journal of Policy and Practice*, 2(4): 470–480.

Jones, D., Grieve, J., and Milne, B. (2010) Reviewing the reviewers: The review of homicides in the United Kingdom. *Investigative Sciences Journal*, 2(2): 1–31.

Laville, S. and Dodd, V. (2012) Stephen Lawrence murder: Norris and Dobson get 14 and 15 years. *The Guardian*, January 4. Available online at http://www.theguardian.com/uk/2012/jan/04/dobson-norris-murder-stephen-lawrence (accessed January 23, 2015).

Littlely, B. and Rice, S. (2014) Excavation in South Australia's mid-north for clues to 1973 abduction of Joanne Ratcliffe and Kirste Gordon from Adelaide Oval. *The Advertiser*, September 18. Available online at http://www.adelaidenow.com.au/news/south-australia/excavation-in-south-australias-midnorth-for-clues-to-1973-abduction-of-joanne-ratcliffe-and-kirste-gordon-from-adelaide-oval/news-story/65a1939c17d92399af4f05e6114ea5c3 (accessed January 23, 2015).

Loftus, E.F. (1996) *Eyewitness Testimony*. Cambridge, MA: Harvard University Press.

Lord, V.B. (2005) Implementing a cold case homicide unit. *FBI Law Enforcement Bulletin*, 74(2): 1–6.

McGarry, D. and Smith, K. (2011) *Police Family Liaison*. Oxford: Oxford University Press.

Moor, K. (2014) Cold case files: Victoria Police secretly starts fresh investigations into 63 unsolved murders. *Herald Sun*, December 7. Available online at http://www.heraldsun.com.au/news/law-order/cold-case-files-victoria-police-secretly starts-fresh-investigations-into-63-unsolved-murders/news-story/45ab429f8a2222e67fa31c31dc7e6dbe (accessed January 23, 2015).

Nicol, C., Innes, M., Gee, D., and Feist, A. (2004) Reviewing murder investigations: An analysis of progress reviews from six police forces. Home Office Online Report 25/04. Available online at http://library.college.police.uk/docs/hordsolr/rdsolr2504.pdf (accessed January 12, 2016).

NIJ (National Institute of Justice) (2002) Using DNA to solve cold cases. Special report, US Department of Justice. Available online at https://www.ncjrs.gov/pdffiles1/nij/194197.pdf (accessed January 12, 2016).

Pettem, S. (2013) *Cold Case Research Resources For Unidentified, Missing, And Cold Homicide Cases*. Boca Raton, FL: CRC Press.

Police Scotland (2014) Man convicted of World's End murders. Available online at http://www.scotland.police.uk/whats-happening/news/2014/november/man-convicted-of-world%27s-end-murders (accessed January 23, 2015).

Rock, P. (1998) *After Homicide: Practical and Political Responses to Bereavement*. Oxford: Clarendon Press.

Summers, C. (2011) Killer planted clues in misogynistic artworks BBC News, April 4. Available online at http://www.bbc.co.uk/news/uk-12749478 (accessed January 23, 2015).

Wells, G.L. (1993) What do we know about eyewitness identification? *American Psychologist*, 48: 553–571.

Wilkins, S. and Hill, J. (2014) *The Pembrokeshire Murders Catching the Bullseye Killer*. Bridgend: Seren.

Williams, R. and Johnson P. (2008) Genetic Policing: The Use of DNA in Criminal Investigations. Cullompton, UK: Willan Publishing.

Williamson, T. (2007) Psychology and criminal investigation. In T. Newburn, T. Williamson, and A. Wright (eds), *Handbook of Criminal Investigations* (1st edn, pp. 68–91) Cullompton, UK: Willan Publishing.

33

A Damning Cascade of Investigative Errors

Flaws in Homicide Investigation in the USA

Deborah Davis and Richard A. Leo

At about 9:30 a.m. on February 6, 1985, Florence Arnst found her sister Helen Wilson brutally raped and murdered in her apartment in Beatrice, Nebraska. A cascade of investigative errors followed over a period of years, eventually leading to the prosecution of six innocent defendants, now known as the "Beatrice Six." In an unusual twist of events, police initially identified the actual perpetrator, Allen Smith, but faulty forensics freed him from suspicion. A speck of blood from Wilson's panties had identified the perpetrator as a blood type B positive "non-secretor," whereas subsequent testing of Smith's blood classified him as a "secretor." His guilt was not discovered until DNA testing of the original sample was requested by defendant Joseph White subsequent to a 2001 Nebraska act mandating testing of DNA at the request of any prisoner. In 2008 the blood was tested and the three members of the Beatrice Six who were still imprisoned were freed after they had served 20 years; the other three had served 5 years and been released. All six wrongfully convicted defendants were not only exonerated by DNA, but pardoned by the governor of Nebraska.

Much of the original investigation of the murder was driven by Burdette Searcey. Searcey had been a detective in Beatrice, but had resigned to become a private investigator. He had reapplied to the police department in 1984, but had been rejected. At the time of the murder, he was not employed by the police or as a private investigator. However, he became obsessed with the case, and launched his own private investigation, convinced he could solve the murder.

Searcey was rehired by the sheriff's department in 1987, and began pressuring the sheriff to allow him to take over the Wilson investigation, which the sheriff eventually allowed in 1989. Searcey then pursued the case with single-minded purpose. Unfortunately, he targeted the wrong suspects.

The Handbook of Homicide, First Edition. Edited by Fiona Brookman,
Edward R. Maguire, and Mike Maguire.

Three of the Beatrice Six had been investigated by law enforcement in March of 1985, but after a brief investigation were not active suspects. However, Searcey had interviewed witnesses as part of his private investigation (keeping no records of his interviews). In a police report in 1989 after he took over the investigation, he claimed that two witnesses had told him four years earlier that Joann Taylor (one of the six) had told them shortly after the murder that she and Joseph White (another of the six) had committed the murder. The remaining four were known associates of these two.

Searcey used these purported claims of the two witnesses to support a warrant for the arrest of Taylor and White. A series of interrogations of Taylor and White led them to implicate themselves and others among the six, who reciprocally implicated them and others. The suspects all initially denied involvement, but over time and repeated interrogation progressively implicated themselves and others. The investigators elicited false confessions, each including false statements about the others, from four of the six: three developed false beliefs and memories of having committed the crime. They had been subjected to extended incarceration, and one reportedly experienced psychotic breaks with reality during this period, but was nevertheless interrogated. The four false confessors pled guilty, as did one of the other two they had implicated. The final defendant was convicted at trial.

A Cascade of Investigative Errors

Wrongful convictions often flow from a cascade of investigative errors and sometimes deliberate investigative and/or prosecutorial misconduct. In the United States, the websites of the National Registry of Exonerations[1] and the Innocence Project[2] present tallies of the types of flawed evidence or behavior that have contributed to the wrongful convictions of exonerated prisoners. Though not all types of errors or behaviors are represented on their websites, Figure 33.1 depicts the percent of cases entailing each factor from each group's website as of June 2015. The National Registry of Exonerations tracks these factors separately for several crime types, including murder, and Figure 33.2 presents their crime-specific numbers as of June 2015.

Among the investigative errors tracked by these websites, forensic errors are among the most prominent factors in documented wrongful convictions, as is prosecutorial misconduct. Other significant factors in wrongful conviction are not always directly caused by investigative errors, such as eyewitness misidentification, false accusation/perjury of witnesses, snitches, and false confession. However, even these can be the result of flawed police procedure (such as suggestive identification procedures and witness interviews, or coercive interrogations) or deliberate misconduct (such as failure to turn over exonerating evidence to the defense, suborning perjury, and other misconduct). Many studies have documented the roles of investigative errors and misconduct in wrongful conviction.[3]

This chapter considers several steps in the cascade of errors and misconduct that can lead to wrongful conviction. We begin with the difficulty of the process of

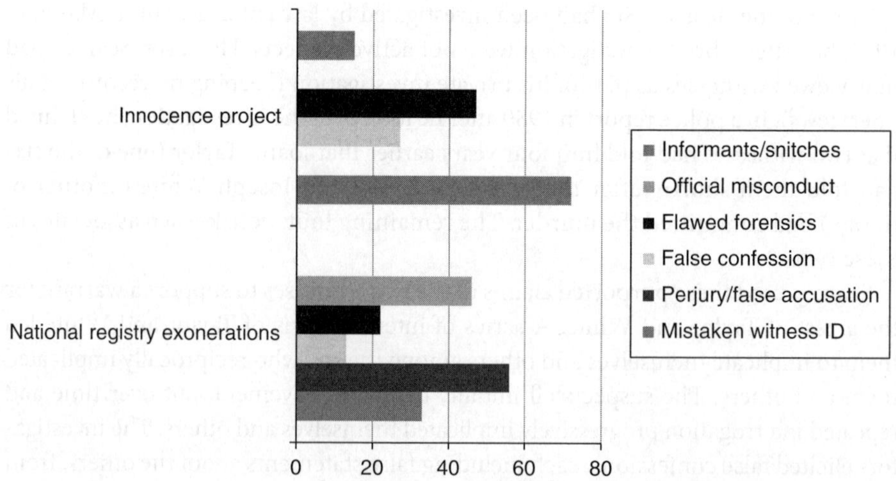

Figure 33.1 Percent of cases of wrongful conviction involving each form of flawed evidence/misconduct.

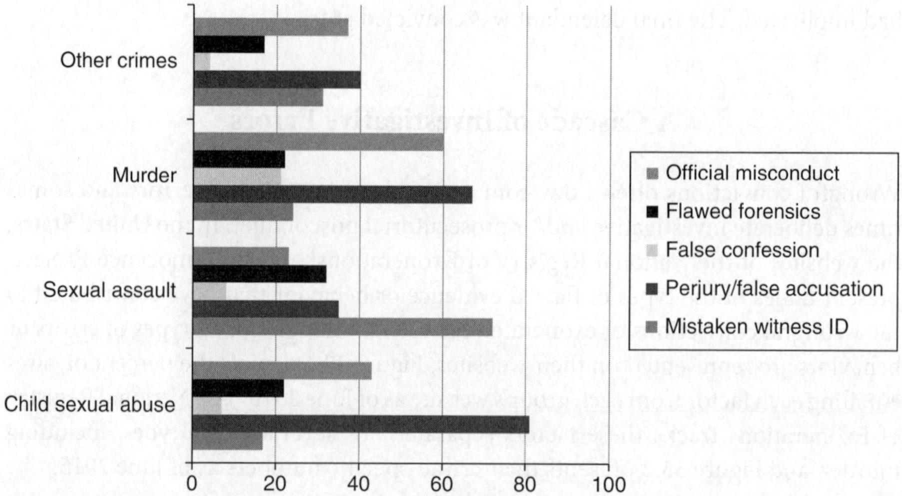

Figure 33.2 Percent of 1618 cases of wrongful conviction involving each form of flawed evidence/misconduct (National Registry of Exonerations). Note: Child sex abuse, N = 178; Sexual assault, N = 274; Murder, N = 714; Other crimes, N = 452.

investigation and the inevitable infusion of bias into it. We then consider specific errors, such as the targeting of innocent suspects. We next consider the nature and operation of confirmation and motivational biases that may infuse the investigation and trial. We consider basic problems with investigative procedures and forensic methods and their vulnerability to these biases. For procedural issues, we address primarily the United States justice system, while directing the reader to some resources addressing similar concerns in the United Kingdom and elsewhere.

The Basic Difficulty of Criminal Investigation

The many television depictions of police investigation severely underplay the difficulty law enforcement faces when investigating crimes and overstate the success of these investigations. In reality, leads are often lacking, suspects may be difficult to identify, and evidence may be scant. Sometimes, there may instead be too many possibilities to follow up. Investigators enjoy a great degree of choice: freedom to follow leads, interview witnesses, collect evidence, pursue suspects, and determine when to make an arrest or close the case. But they are also subject to a number of pressures from superiors, the public, politicians, media, and others. And they face mounting difficulties as time passes and evidence or witnesses are lost, while being constrained by available resources. If not cleared immediately, many crimes are not solved (see Simon 2012).

Faced with a situation that could prove so taxing, difficult, and prone to failure, it is not surprising that investigators may prematurely latch onto the first or seemingly most promising path of investigation. But, the earliest choices in an investigation tend to shape the investigation from that point on, including the collection and interpretation of evidence (Simon 2012). While this may prove quite functional when the early choices are correct, it may prove quite the reverse when these choices are incorrect.

Targeting the Wrong Suspect

The investigation may go wrong at the very earliest stages, when police target the wrong suspect for investigation. For most cases, the majority of investigation takes place after a suspect has been identified (Simon 2012). In each wrongful conviction, witnesses and/or investigators, of course, targeted one or more innocent suspects. In rare cases, such targeting of innocents may be deliberate, but here we consider the psychological forces among investigators that might lead them to unknowingly do so. In particular, we examine (1) the tendency to use "available" information to form initial assumptions about the crime and the perpetrator, (2) the role of investigators' assumptions and stereotypes regarding who tends to commit the type of crime in question, and (3) faulty assessments of people, in particular potential suspects.

The availability heuristic in action: shaping the initial choice of suspect

Keep in mind that there is often little to no concrete evidence to reliably identify the correct suspect, particularly early in an investigation. Sometimes there is not any that is actually probative of a particular suspect's involvement. Investigators can be faced with trying to identify suspects based on little to no evidence. Yet, they must form initial hypotheses to direct further investigation based on what they have at that point.

Too much reliance on the initial information may lead to investigative dead ends. But the more serious error occurs when something in the available information directs investigators' attention to the wrong suspect. This can be as simple as a suspect in the vicinity of the crime fitting a description given by a witness (and then being put in a witness identification procedure and possibly misidentified).[4] Or it could involve someone fitting a profile the department has offered as the likely type of offender;[5] someone connected to the victim (however tenuously);[6] or someone mentioned by another witness as having opportunity or motive.[7] The possibilities are countless. Many mistaken prosecutions could have been avoided had investigators simply collected more evidence prior to concentrating on the quickly chosen suspect, and taken care to identify other plausible suspects.

Criminal stereotypes, intuitive profiling, and the "usual" suspects

In many cases, an innocent individual may become a suspect because he or she fits common stereotypes or "intuitive profiles" (Davis and Follette 2002, 2003) of the type of person likely to commit the crime. How many times have we heard, for example, "It's always the husband!" when a woman is dead? There are many different stereotypes associating particular classes of crime with particular categories of persons. Some associate race with overall criminality, while others specifically associate drug and violent crimes with black people and Hispanics, white-collar crime with the white middle class, child sex abuse with male relatives, step-fathers, Boy Scout leaders, or gay men, and so on (see Villalobos and Davis, 2016). Such stereotypes may also associate individual characteristics, circumstances, or motives with the propensity to commit specific crimes (see Davis and Follette 2002). For example, a spouse's infidelity, the purchase of a valuable life insurance policy, or the threat of an expensive divorce might be assumed to provide a motive for the murder of a mate, and a gambling debt might seemingly provide motive for murder or theft.

Faulty assessments of persons

The reader may be familiar with television or literary detectives who seem to have the preternatural ability to instantly and accurately diagnose the guilt of those they interview upon their first encounter—even upon the investigator's arrival at the crime scene. Were it so easy! Overconfidence in the ability to make such early assessments accurately, combined with use of inappropriate indicators of deception and guilt, has contributed to several high-profile wrongful convictions.

Often, such mistakes have been based on incorrect assumptions about displays of emotion: interestingly, either too much or too little. For example, Tom Sawyer became a suspect for a Florida sexual assault and murder because his face flushed and he appeared embarrassed in an initial interview (Leo and Ofshe 1998).

Not knowing that Sawyer suffered from a social anxiety disorder that caused him to sweat profusely and blush in evaluative social situations, the detectives assumed his demeanor reflected guilt. Michael Crowe was targeted as a suspect for his sister's death because detectives believed he reacted to her death with too little emotion (Johnson 2003; Sauer 2004).

Unfortunately, mistaken beliefs about behavioral reflections of deception are widespread among police. Yet the ability to accurately detect deception is not significantly better than chance among law enforcement, attorneys, judges, jurors, and the public, particularly if other evidence of the truth is not available (see Vrij 2008; Vrij, Granhag, and Porter 2010). Law officers are widely taught discredited methods of detection of deception by prominent interrogation manuals and training organizations, such as Reid.com or W-Z.com. Their incorrect but powerful assumptions about reflections of deception can lead investigators to confidently target a person, and exert even stronger influence if other assumptions also point to that person, such as intuitive profiles of the perpetrator.

Pursuing the Investigation: The Role of Bias

It is a capital mistake to theorize before one has data. Insensibly one begins to twist facts to suit theories, instead of theories to suit facts.

Sherlock Holmes[8]

Sir Arthur Conan Doyle, the creator of Sherlock Holmes, wrote of the inherent problems of investigating with a specific hypothesis in mind. His observation presaged modern interest in "tunnel vision" and "confirmation biases" in police investigation. The rest of the chapter focuses on the operation of such biases, as well as motivational biases, in two areas of investigation heavily implicated in wrongful convictions: witness interviews/suspect interrogations and forensics.

Cognitive bias

Much research in law, psychology, and criminal justice has focused on cognitive biases that may mislead an investigation. In particular, it has examined "tunnel vision" and "confirmation biases" (or more broadly, "investigator bias") (see Findley and Scott 2006; Findley 2012; Gould *et al.* 2012; Martin 2002; Simon 2012; Snook and Cullen 2009; Stubbins and Stubbins 2009; Rossmo 2009). Findley and Scott (2006) define "tunnel vision" as consisting of common heuristics and logical fallacies that lead investigators to focus on particular suspects and investigative theories, and to select and filter the evidence that helps build a case for conviction while ignoring or suppressing evidence inconsistent with guilt (Findley and Scott 2006: 292). "Investigator biases" refer to expectations, heuristics, and logical fallacies that influence the investigation. They do so primarily through effects on the direction and activities of the investigation, the interpretation of evidence, and behavioral confirmation (or "self-fulfilling prophesies," whereby one's expectations affect behavior toward others and causes them to confirm—or appear to confirm—one's expectations).

Motivational biases

The very focus on a particular suspect, and rising confidence in his/her guilt, may increase motivation to inculpate and convict. But motivation is fueled by other factors too. The job of the investigator is to solve the crime and provide the evidence necessary to convict, and that of the prosecutor to do justice by securing incarceration through conviction or plea if they believe the suspect committed a crime and his guilt can be proved beyond a reasonable doubt. If evidence contradicts the current theory of the case, completion of the job is threatened, as may be the investigator's or prosecutor's sense of competence. This may be particularly painful in high-profile cases where failure will result in public pressure and embarrassment; the more time and resources have been invested in the pursuit of the case theory and suspect, the more painful it will be. The basic conflict between objective truth-seeking and performance of one's duties to identify and prosecute the guilty (and perhaps to advance or protect one's career) can affect police, forensic examiners, and prosecutors alike. Their professional motivations may be amplified by crime-related emotions. The latter may flow from the very nature of the crime, relationships with witnesses or victims, anger toward suspects, and other sources. They may also result from loyalty to the team of investigators, a sense of belonging, and a reluctance to contradict group sentiment. Together, these varied motivations and emotions can create an "adversarial pull" (Simon 2012) or "one sided skepticism" (Leo 2008). Police and forensic investigators and prosecutors are pulled away from the goal of strict objectivity in investigation toward the presumption of guilt and single-minded pursuit of the theory and suspect at hand.

Bias in context: interviews and interrogations of witnesses

Research across a wide range of disciplines (e.g., medicine, education, psychology, law, and other fields) and situations (formal interviews, assessments, interrogations, informal conversations, teaching) has shown that when interviewers develop hypotheses about their interviewees, they tend to ask suggestive questions that tend to elicit answers consistent with their hypotheses (e.g., Ceci and Bruck 1995; Meissner and Kassin 2004; Snyder and Stukas 1999). Thus, confirmation bias leads investigators to behave in a way that elicits apparent confirmation of their expectations from their targets. A primary task of investigators is, of course, interviews of witnesses and suspects. But suggestive or coercive interviews and interrogations have contributed to many false accusations and wrongful convictions.

Suggestion/coercion in witness interviews Modern awareness of the biasing role of suggestion and coercion in witness interviews derived in large part from two major sources. The first was the highly publicized wrongful allegations of sexual abuse in day care centers across the United States beginning in the 1980s. During this time, a number of high-profile allegations of sexual abuse also arose among adults claiming to have "recovered" "repressed" memories of sexual abuse (and sometimes satanic ritual abuse and murder) that allegedly occurred decades earlier. The many false allegations made clear the role of suggestion in distorting and fabricating witness reports. The accusers had been subject to official forensic and/or therapeutic interviews and procedures that developed and shaped the allegations, as well as some external influences from television and books focused on victimization (see Howe and Knott 2015; McNally 2003). Confirmation biases played a significant role in most such cases, as police, forensic examiners, and therapists, as well as parents, friends, and other relatives, often had very clear and strong expectations about the reality of the allegations.

A number of specific suggestive behaviors among interviewers have been shown to shape the responses of interviewees. These include use of closed-ended questions, and questions that imply facts; repeating questions despite receiving an answer; selective reinforcement (e.g., positive reactions to desired/expected answers); direct claims about what happened; providing "evidence" of the interviewer's account; using suggestive props; demanding particular responses; offering incentives for telling; indicating that the interviewee could demonstrate positive qualities by disclosing the requested information; accusing the interviewee of lying; and many others. The interviewer may also characterize the suspect in negative ways that might encourage the interviewee to interpret the suspect's behavior more negatively. Such suggestive behaviors can increase interviewees' belief in specific accounts, create imagery of them, distort memory of them, and create expectations of more approval for giving specific reports in the future.

In response to these problems, a number of recommendations, procedures, and training protocols for law enforcement and forensic interviewers have been developed in the United States and the United Kingdom to avoid suggestion while facilitating complete and accurate witness reports (see Bull 2014; Technical Working Group for Eyewitness Evidence 1999; Fisher and Geiselman 2010; Lamb *et al.* 2011).

The second source of modern awareness of suggestive witness interviewing was the rising tide of DNA exonerations of the wrongfully convicted whose cases involved mistaken eyewitness identifications. Though these mistaken identifications can be attributed in large part to faulty perception and memory, suggestion was also a significant source of error. Suggestion was inherent to some identification procedures, such as use of single-suspect show-ups rather than multi-suspect lineups; use of simultaneous lineups (showing all suspects at once) versus sequential ones (showing one suspect at a time);[9] construction of suggestive lineups (e.g., where only one suspect truly fit the description given by the witness); and allowing cross-contamination of witnesses undergoing procedures together. However, investigators sometimes overtly behaved suggestively, such as by encouraging the witness to more fully consider a specific suspect; telling the witness the investigators thought they had their guy; and through more subtle nonverbal cues, including expressing enthusiasm when witnesses mentioned the suspects or displeasure when witnesses seemed ready to identify a known foil.

Each of these practices has been shown to increase the rate of false identifications and specific recommendations have been developed to prevent or minimize such sources of bias. These include guidelines for construction of lineups (e.g., to ensure that each member fits the description of the witness) and administration of lineups (e.g., instructions given to witnesses to minimize the presumption that the perpetrator is in the lineup, avoiding influencing the witness's choice, and prevent influence between witnesses; use administrators who do not know the identity of the suspect, and others). They also include avoiding feedback to the witness that could artificially inflate confidence (e.g., "Good, that is the one we thought did it!"), among others (see Technical Working Group for Eyewitness Evidence 1999; Fitzgerald, Oriet, and Price 2015; Lindsay *et al.* 2007; Wells and Quinlivan 2009).[10]

Another important concern about law enforcement interactions with witnesses and suspects is the translation of their conversations to the notes of the interviewers and thus ultimately to trial testimony. When such interactions are not recorded, the notes are likely to be strongly affected by the expectations and interpretations of the investigator. This presents an unfortunate opportunity for confirmation biases to infect the remaining record of the interaction. When notes are not taken contemporaneously or very shortly after an interview, the investigator's memory of the interview may well drift toward his expectations as time passes. Burdette Searcey, who did not record notes of his interview with a crucial witness in the Beatrice Six case until four years later, was consequently certain to report the interview incompletely, and almost certainly in a manner distorted by his confidence in the suspects' guilt. And not all interrogations of the suspects were fully recorded, leaving their content subject to disagreement.

Finally, interviewers sometimes interrogate reluctant witnesses using many of the most suggestive techniques discussed in the next section: direct suggestion of what happened, recounting evidence that contradicts initial accounts, and threats of consequences of deception. Such coercive tactics with witnesses can promote false accounts or accusations (e.g., Loney and Cutler 2015; Moore, Cutler, and Shulman 2014).

Suggestion/coercion in suspect interrogations Little in the course of police investigation is carried out with as strong a presumption of guilt as interrogation. Indeed, interrogators are trained to proceed from interviewing a suspect to interrogation only if the suspect is considered likely guilty of the crime (see Inbau *et al.* 2013). The goal of interrogation is not to objectively assess the truth, but to induce the suspect to provide a full and detailed confession to what the investigator believes to be the truth, and to do so in a way that will leave no doubt of his guilt (see Davis 2010; Davis and O'Donohue 2004; Davis and Leo 2014; Leo 2008; Kassin *et al.* 2010). There is little to no concern with the impact of suggestion on the suspect's account.

Interrogation incorporates all forms of suggestion discussed earlier, as well as even stronger suggestive and persuasive behaviors.

As taught by prominent interrogation training manuals and organizations in America (e.g., Inbau *et al.* 2013; Zulawski and Wicklander 2002), the process begins with a strong claim that the suspect is guilty.[11] This is commonly accompanied by presentation of evidence against the suspect—which may or may not actually exist—such as claims of fingerprints, DNA, eyewitnesses, accusations of alleged co-perpetrators or victims, polygraph results, and much more. Since the suspect's perception of the strength of evidence against him strongly impacts the likelihood that he will confess, claims regarding evidence can be very effective in promoting confession. *Lies* about evidence have been particularly implicated in promoting false confessions in both laboratory studies and proven cases of false confession (see Leo 2008; Kassin *et al.* 2010).

Lies that make the suspect's guilt more plausible have been present in several documented wrongful convictions. Often, these entail false explanations of memory failures. In the case of the Beatrice Six, the psychologist/interrogator suggested that the suspects couldn't tolerate awareness of the heinous nature of the crime and their roles in it, and therefore had "repressed" their memories of it. He further told suspect Dean that he had failed the polygraph, and that this indicated subconscious awareness of his guilt. Dean became convinced that he must have committed the crime, followed recommendations as to how to "recover" his memories, later confessed his guilt, and reported his memories of the other defendants' involvement.

In one of the cases mentioned earlier of "recovered" memories of child sexual abuse, Paul Ingram, who claimed to have no memory of abusing his children, asked his pastor if Satan could make him do such things and then make him forget he had done them. Upon receiving a "yes," Ingram set out to try to remember the abuse, and developed false memories of countless alleged offenses brought up during interrogations, including some that were deliberately concocted by an interviewer (Ofshe 1992; Wright 1995). When alcohol is involved, the suspect may be told that he committed the crime during a "blackout," leaving no memory. Many suspects misled by claims about memory failures have become convinced they "must have" committed the crime by other evidence claimed by investigators. In some cases they developed false memories of having done so (see Kassin 2007; Leo 2008; Gudjonsson *et al.* 2014).

American interrogations are pervasively deceptive (Davis 2010). So long as it is not coercive, there are no restrictions against deceit in interrogations. Claims about evidence or the operation of memory may be false, and many other messages may also be deliberately false. The many deceptive tactics of interrogation promote the illusions (1) that the interrogator has much more choice over how to handle the suspect than he actually has (e.g., whether to arrest and charge him) and more impact on the later decisions of prosecutors, judges, and juries than he can actually have, (2) that the consequences of guilt are more flexible than they really are, and (3) that these issues will be primarily decided within the context of interrogation, with the suspect having much less ability to determine his fate once he leaves the interrogation room. Specific tactics are taught to promote each of these illusions (see Davis and Leo 2014).

As the interrogation proceeds from the initial accusation of guilt, it remains highly suggestive, as well as coercive. The illusion of flexibility of consequences is facilitated when the interrogator proceeds from stating his confidence in the suspect's guilt to suggestions of how and why he thought the suspect committed the crime. He suggests scenarios to the suspect that appear to minimize the seriousness of the crime: to render it understandable, less unusual or deviant, less serious, and perhaps not so criminal as it is (e.g., it happened in self-defense). Such suggestions are made to lower the perceived costs of confession, and indeed such "minimizing" has been shown to promote both true and false confessions (see Leo 2008; Kassin *et al.* 2010). Threats about the consequences of refusal to confess may also be implied, such as how judges or juries will react to a suspect who fails to "take responsibility" versus one who recognizes his mistake and expresses remorse. Such threats and promises may also be conveyed more explicitly, though this is not recommended and can result in the exclusion of the confession from trial evidence.

US interrogators are trained to interrupt the suspect if he tries to deny guilt, to maintain outward confidence in his guilt, and to persist in presentation of argument and evidence for that guilt. The interrogator may present various scenarios for the commission of the crime until the suspect appears ready to endorse one. The suspect is allowed to do little talking until he appears ready to begin making admissions. Meanwhile, he will be faced with accusations that he is lying, interruptions, and repeated questions (until the interrogator likes the answers). He may be faced with these behaviors for hours, sometimes days, until he either confesses or refuses to talk further without an attorney. The interrogator may or may not conclude at some point that further interrogation is fruitless. Defendant Dean of the Beatrice Six was confined in a 2.7 × 1.2 meter (9 × 4 feet) cell for 22 days and interrogated repeatedly, in isolation from all who might have offered support.

Not surprisingly, interrogations can be experienced as very distressing and many suspects confess simply to terminate the interrogation and get away from their interrogators. Others become convinced by the interrogation tactics that they cannot hope for exoneration, that the evidence implicates them (even if they are innocent), and that the best outcomes can be achieved through confession. Some confess because they are unable to defy the demands of the interrogator (e.g., those who are unusually conflict avoidant or compliant). Some innocents confess because they have become convinced they must have committed the crime, despite having no memories of it (see Leo and Davis 2010; Kassin *et al.* 2010). Each of these mechanisms is more likely to occur in vulnerable suspects, such as those with low IQs or mental illness, the very young, and the unusually compliant (see Gudjonsson 2014; Kassin *et al.* 2010).

Generally, false confessions are difficult to detect. They can appear very convincing and include detailed accounts of the crime, motives, expressions of remorse, apologies, and more. They may include many details that should be known only to the perpetrator, but that suspects have been exposed to during the interrogation or through publicity. Beatrice Six defendants Dean, Taylor, and Shelden, for example, were exposed extensively to crime scene videos, photos, and diagrams during interrogations, along with claims of what other defendants and witnesses allegedly reported. Given the persuasiveness of confessions, and general lack of understanding of the forces facing suspects in interrogation, most false confessors whose cases go to trial are convicted (see Davis and Leo 2012).

Bias in context: forensic errors

Once considered nearly infallible, forensic sciences have faced a number of public scandals and scathing scientific attacks in recent decades. Some have been over high-profile mistakes, such as the FBI's notorious mismatch of the fingerprint of the 2004 Madrid bomber to Brandon Mayfield (OIG 2006); others have been over inadequate scientific underpinnings of procedures, inadequate standardization and qualifications of examiners, or cognitive and motivational biases (e.g., National Academy of Sciences 2009). Still others have involved deliberate falsification of results (e.g., Thompson 2006; Trager 2013).

Perhaps the most disturbing problems facing the forensic sciences are lack of basic scientific underpinnings and validation of procedures, and lack of specific standards for the tests themselves and for qualification and certification of examiners. Some widely used tests have not been sufficiently validated (e.g., graphology; Lilienfeld and Landfield 2008), or have been shown to be invalid (e.g., matching a bullet found at the crime scene to a box of bullets possessed by the suspect; NAS 2004). Moreover, even for tests that have been shown to be reasonably valid, there are often no standards for ensuring the ability of those who perform the tests to do so correctly, including standards for qualification and hiring. And, there may be no standards for determining results, such as when determining whether two fingerprints came from the same source. Moreover, flaws in execution, such as sample contamination, may compromise the tests (see Faigman *et al.* 2014–2015; Kassin, Dror, and Kukucka 2013; National Academy of Sciences 2009; National Commission on Forensic Science 2014). Yet, despite the scandals and criticism, little has changed to address these problems (see Gabel 2014).

Forensic errors have featured prominently in many documented wrongful convictions. As shown in Figure 33.1 and Figure 33.2, such errors have been present in over 20 percent of the cases tallied by the National Registry of Exonerations, and almost 50 percent of those of the Innocence Project. One study of wrongful convictions that differentiated between types of forensic errors found that 38 percent contained errors of serology, 22 percent contained hair comparison errors, 3 percent involved bite mark comparison errors, and 2 percent had fingerprint comparison errors (Hampikian, West, and Akselrod 2011). Note that these are predominantly match evidence (matching hairs, fingerprints, and bite marks with a suspect), which has been widely criticized on virtually all grounds: including validity; standardization of training, procedures, criteria, and reporting; testing of examiners and labs:

subjectivity and bias; and sometimes for outright fraud (see Faigman *et al.* 2014–2015; Kassin, Dror, and Kukucka 2013; National Academy of Sciences 2009; National Commission on Forensic Science 2014; Risinger *et al.* 2002). These criticisms have also been directed at many other forms of forensic evidence, such as blood spatter and toxicology.

The basic problems with validity of tests, subjectivity, qualifications of examiners, and standardization (of tests, procedures, criteria for findings, and reporting of results) themselves offer opportunity for bias to infuse the findings and reports of the forensic examiners. And, indeed, a number of studies have demonstrated the operation of confirmation biases for forensic tests (see Kassin, Dror, and Kukucka 2013; Faigman *et al.* 2014–2015; Risinger *et al.* 2002 for reviews). These and other writers have pointed out the many types of contextual biases that can influence forensic judgments. They include the structural affiliation of forensic labs with police departments; examiners' sense of affiliation with the investigative team; pressure from investigators; testifying on behalf of the prosecution; awareness of the nature of the crime and other evidence; cross-communication with other forensic examiners; and requests to retest when the results don't confirm the expectations of investigators. Some biases involve simple context (expectancy) effects on judgment, whereas others may reflect motivations (e.g., to help, to solve the case, to satisfy superiors).

Fingerprint matching has been shown to have one of the lower error rates among match judgments (other than DNA and other biological tests). As Dror and Cole (2010) noted, bias in fingerprint examinations has been studied the most among match judgments, since if one of the most error-free fields involving such judgments is shown to be subject to bias, one can assume that others that are less well-tested and more prone to error will also show biases (though even DNA profiling has also been shown subject to bias; e.g., Thompson 2006).

As with other match judgments, specific criteria are not enforced for calling a fingerprint a match. The examiner himself determines whether the prints are sufficiently similar to conclude they came from the same source. Hence, concerns about both inter-rater reliability and test–retest reliability have been raised. Indeed, one study found that the same examiners reached different conclusions for 10 percent of the comparisons of the same fingerprints on different occasions (Ulery *et al.* 2012). Other studies have found inconsistencies in initial component judgments (such as specific point comparisons) as well as ultimate match decisions both by the same examiner and between examiners (Dror and Hampikian 2011).

This is not surprising, given the general difficulty of the task. Even prints from the same source are not identical, but vary based on the pressure applied, the material where the print is left, how the print is lifted, and other factors. Moreover, sources can have very similar prints, and the use of large databases to locate suspects increases the likelihood that innocent sources with similar prints may be targeted for suspicion (see Dror and Cole 2010).

Given that the available fingerprints may be of poor quality and otherwise present ambiguity, it is not surprising that fingerprint match assessments have been shown to be subject to contextual biases and effects of crime-related emotions. In one study,

80 percent of examiners who were unknowingly exposed to prints they had previous found to match changed their assessments to either inconclusive (20%) or no match (60%) when led to expect the prints did not match. Awareness of evidence suggesting guilt (such as a confession) versus innocence (an alibi) was also shown to bias judgments of experienced examiners. Even something as simple as the order in which suspects are identified by computerized systems affects the likelihood that the examiner will call a match. False positives are more likely for candidates near the top of the list and false negatives for those near the bottom, perhaps in response to greater expectations of a match for those nearer the top (see Kassin, Dror, and Kukucka 2013; Dror and Cole 2010).

Aside from inaccuracies in the findings of forensic examinations, forensic examiners may report their findings in a misleading way. Indeed, there has been widespread criticism of error, imprecision, exaggeration, and inflated confidence in the reporting of results (e.g., Garrett and Mitchell 2013; National Academy of Sciences 2009; National Commission on Forensic Science 2014). The overall effect is that investigators, prosecutors, judges, and juries can be led to draw erroneous or inappropriately strong inferences based on the test in question.

The Problem of Cross-Contamination

Our discussion has shown that a number of different but related errors can combine to lead investigators to the wrong conclusion. Some, such as a simple witness error or mistaken identification, do not flow from bias, but failures of cognition. But early evidence, however generated, tends to shape further investigation: at a minimum by directing the search for further evidence, and, more disturbingly, by creating hypotheses and expectations that can also distort the search for and interpretation of evidence. Each piece of evidence does not independently contribute to judgments; rather, judgments of evidence are both shaped by and shape judgments of other evidence. An *escalation of errors* may occur, such that initial errors lead to others that appear to reinforce the validity of the first judgment, and of one another (Simon 2012). This effect has also been referred to as "corroboration inflation" (Kassin 2012), or a "bias snowball" (Dror 2012).

The tendency of one form of evidence to alter the meaning of others has been demonstrated in several laboratory contexts. For example, knowledge of a recanted confession led participants in one study to view handwriting samples as a match more often than those who did not hear of the confession (Kukucka and Kassin 2012). And trained student examiners were more likely to conclude that a signature was forged after exposure to inculpatory evidence (Miller 1984). What's more, eyewitness identifications were affected by exposure to information that the suspect had confessed (Hasel and Kassin 2009), and findings of polygraph examiners were affected by exposure to either inculpatory or exculpatory evidence (Elaad, Ginton, and Ben-Shakhar 1994). When applied to mixed samples, even DNA analyses have been shown to be subject to contextual bias (Dror and Hampikian 2011).

Similarly, suspects' confessions can be the product of evidentiary cross-contamination, with the perceived strength of evidence against the suspect strongly affecting the likelihood that he will give either a true or false confession. When interrogators lie about evidence, or present incriminating actual evidence, confession becomes more likely. Then the confession affects the perceived strength of other evidence (see Kassin 2012). Together, these multiple forms of evidentiary cross-contamination may result in trials that possess little probative value. While the various forms of evidence are viewed as independent cumulative evidence of guilt, the evidentiary cross-contamination actually means they are each less probative than they appear (Simon 2012).

Cross-contamination of evidence clearly occurred in the case of the Beatrice Six; for example, the polygraph examiner who tested Beatrice Six defendant Dean at his attorney's request. The county prosecutor sent a letter to the examiner prior to the test asserting that a witness had identified Dean in a photo lineup. And Detective Searcey had communicated to the examiner that there was "no doubt in his mind" that Dean was involved in the murder, that he believed Dean would confess if pressured, and that there was a potential plea agreement if Dean was found deceptive. Given that Dean was actually innocent, the examiner's finding of deception may well have been a product of his presumption of guilt. Nevertheless, the result infected the subsequent investigation, as it further convinced the investigators and prosecutor of Dean's guilt, and was used against him in his interrogations to convince him that he had committed the crime (but had repressed his memory of it), and to facilitate his false confession and false memories of the crime.

Conclusions

The process of investigating crime is both difficult and fraught with opportunity for error at all stages. Yet, the integrity of such investigations is vitally important: both for protection of the public against those who would do harm and for protection of the accused. Errors can leave perpetrators free to commit future crimes or lead to the wrongful prosecution, conviction, and incarceration of the innocent.

Many investigative errors resulting from cognitive biases cannot be fully prevented, though they may be reduced by increased training and awareness. And many reforms in the United States could reduce some of the procedural errors we've discussed. But despite the prevalence of these errors, little has been done in the United States to address them. Perhaps the exceptions are improvements in forensic interviewing of children (see Lamb *et al.* 2008), which has on average become much less suggestive than in the past, and improvements in eyewitness identification procedures (see Technical Working Group 1999). But forensic testing is still affiliated with police departments, against the recommendations of the National Academy of Sciences and others, and invalid and untested procedures are still presented in court. Interrogation reforms have been few in the United States, despite many reforms in the United Kingdom and to some extent in Canada. It is our hope that our own country will catch up with the most progressive of our allies to enact more reforms to minimize miscarriages of justice.

Notes

1 https://www.law.umich.edu/special/exoneration/Pages/about.aspx.
2 http://www.innocenceproject.org.
3 Innocence projects that identify and exonerate the wrongfully convicted exist in other countries as well, some in collaboration with the US Innocence Project. The United Kingdom, for example, has several such projects run by law school faculty and staffed with law students, operating generally according to the US model (see Sarfraz Manzoor, "The Innocence Project: The Court of Last Resort." *The Guardian,* January 8, 2011: http://www.theguardian.com/law/2011/jan/09/innocence-project-conviction-hilary-swank). In Australia, a branch of the Innocence Project is run at Griffith University by attorneys and students (https://www.griffith.edu.au/criminology-law/innocence-project/about-us). Moreover, authors have documented wrongful convictions and the investigative errors leading to them in a number of publications (e.g., Naughton 2013, regarding the United Kingdom; Gudjonsson 2014, regarding United Kingdom and Iceland).
4 See Garrett (2011: ch. 3).
5 See the discussion of the false confessions of Calvin Ollins and Marcellius Bradford in Drizin and Leo (2004: 981–985).
6 Loftus and Ketcham (1991). In which suspect Timothy Hennis was targeted because he had recently bought a dog from the deceased victim of a home invasion.
7 Wells and Leo (2008). *The Wrong Guys.* Describing the targeting of Danial Williams as suspect for the murder of his neighbor because a neighbor reported that she thought he had a crush on the victim.
8 Arthur Conan Doyle (1891).
9 Though sequential lineups do come at the cost of some correct identifications, which has led some to question their utility (e.g., Clark 2012).
10 But see Clark (2012) in disagreement with recommendations for use of sequential lineups.
11 This section focuses on interrogation practices in the United States. Other countries have been much quicker to recognize the problems with American interrogation practices and to enact reforms to avoid practices most strongly implicated in increasing risks of false confession (such as more thorough warnings of the risks of self-incrimination; limits on the length of interrogations; prohibitions against lying to suspects; and reduced emphasis on accusation and confrontation). See Shawyer, Milne, and Bull (2009) regarding United Kingdom; Snook, Eastwood, and Todd 2014 regarding Canada.

References

Bull, R. (ed.) (2014) *Investigative interviewing.* New York: Springer.

Ceci, S.J. and Bruck, M. (1995) The role of interview bias. In S.J. Ceci and M. Bruck (eds), *Jeopardy in the Courtroom: A scientific Analysis of Children's Testimony* (pp 87–108). Washington, DC: American Psychological Association.

Clark, S.E. (2012) Eyewitness identification reform: Data, theory, and due process. *Perspectives on Psychological Science*, 7: 279–283.

Davis, D. (2010) Lies, *damned* lies, and the path from police interrogation to wrongful conviction. In M.H. Gonzales, C. Tavris, and J. Aronson (eds), *The Scientist and the Humanist: A Festschrift in Honor of Elliot Aronson* (pp. 211–247). New York: Psychology Press.

Davis, D. and Follette, W.C. (2002) Rethinking probative value of evidence: Base rates, intuitive profiling and the *post*diction of behavior. *Law and Human Behavior*, 26: 133–158.
Davis, D. and Follette, W.C. (2003) Toward an empirical approach to evidentiary ruling. *Law and Human Behavior*, 27(6): 661–684.
Davis, D. and Leo, R.A. (2012) To walk in their shoes: The problem of missing, misrepresented and misunderstood context in judging criminal confessions. *New England Law Review*, 46(4): 737–767.
Davis, D. and Leo, R.A. (2014) The problem of police-induced false confession: Sources of failure in prevention and detection. In S. Morewitz and M.L. Goldstein (eds), *Handbook of Forensic Sociology and Psychology* (pp. 47–75). New York: Springer.
Davis, D. and O'Donohue, W.T. (2004) The road to perdition: "Extreme influence" tactics in the interrogation room. In W.T. O'Donohue and E. Levensky (eds), *Handbook of Forensic Psychology* (pp. 897–996). New York, Elsevier Academic Press.
Doyle, A.C. (1891) *Scandal in Bohemia*. Chicago: E.A. Weeks.
Drizin, S. and Leo, R.A. (2004) The problem of false confessions in the post-DNA world. *North Carolina Law Review*, 82(3): 891–1007.
Dror, I.E. (2012) Cognitive bias in forensic science. In *McGraw-Hill Yearbook of Science & Technology* (pp. 43–45). New York: McGraw-Hill Professional.
Dror, I.E. and Cole, S.A. (2010) The vision in blind justice: Expert perception, judgment, and visual cognition in forensic pattern recognition. *Psychonomic Bulletin and Review*, 17: 161–167.
Dror, I.E. and Hampikian, G. (2011) Subjectivity and bias in forensic DNA mixture interpretation. *Science & Justice*, 51: 204–208. doi: http://dx.doi.org/10.1016/j.scijus.2011.08.004
Elaad, E., Ginton, A., and Ben-Shakhar, G. (1994) The effects of prior expectations and outcome knowledge on polygraph examiners' decisions. *Journal of Behavioral Decision Making*, 7: 279–292. doi: 10.1002/bdm.3960070405.
Faigman, D.L., Blumenthal, J.A., Cheng, E.K., *et al.* (eds) (2014–2015) *Modern Scientific Evidence* (vols 3–5). Eagan, MN: Thomson West.
Findley, K.A. (2012) Tunnel vision. In B.L. Cutler (ed.), *Conviction of the Innocent: Lessons from Psychological Research* (pp. 303–323). Washington, DC: American Psychological Association.
Findley, K.A. and Scott, M.S. (2006) The multiple dimensions of tunnel vision in criminal cases. *Wisconsin Law Review*, 2: 291–397.
Fisher, R.P. and Geiselman, R.E. (2010) The cognitive interview method of conducting police interviews: Eliciting extensive information and promoting therapeutic jurisprudence. *International Journal of Law and Psychiatry*, 33: 321–328. doi: 10.1016/j.ijlp.2010.09.004.
Fitzgerald, R.J., Oriet, C., and Price, H.L. (2015) Suspect filler similarity in eyewitness lineups: A literature review and novel methodology. *Law and Human Behavior*, 39: 62–74.
Gabel, J.D. (2014) Realizing reliability the forensic science from the ground up. *Journal of Criminal Law and Criminology*, 104: 283–352.
Garrett, B. (2011) *Convicting the Innocent: Where Criminal Prosecutions Go Wrong*. Cambridge, MA: Harvard University Press.
Garrett, B. and Mitchell, G. (2013) How jurors evaluate fingerprint evidence: The relative importance of math language, method information, and error acknowledgment. *Journal of Empirical Legal Studies*, 10: 484–511.
Gould, J.B., Carrano, J., Leo, R., and Young, J. (2012) Predicting erroneous convictions: A social science approach to miscarriages of justice. Washington, DC: National Institute of Justice.

Gudjonsson, G.H. (2014) Mental vulnerabilities and false confession. In M. St-Yves (ed.), *Investigative Interviewing: The Essentials* (pp. 191–222). Toronto: Carswell.

Gudjonsson, G.H., Sigurdsson, J.F., Sigurdardottir, A.S., *et al.* (2014) The role of memory distrust in cases of internalized false confession. *Applied Cognitive Psychology*, 28: 336–348.

Hampikian, G., West, E., and Akselrod, O. (2011) The genetics of innocence: Analysis of 194 US DNA exonerations. *Annual Review of Genomics and Human Genetics*, 12: 97–120.

Hasel, L.E. and Kassin, S.M. (2009) On the presumption of evidentiary independence: Can confessions corrupt eyewitness identifications? *Psychological Science*, 20: 122–126. doi: http://dx.doi.org/ 10.1111/j. 1467-9280.2008.02262.x.

Howe, M.L. and Knott, L.M. (2015) The fallibility of memory in judicial processes: Lessons from the past and their modern consequences. *Memory*, 23: 633–656.

Inbau, F. Reid, J., Buckley, J., and Jayne, B. (2013) *Criminal interrogation and Confessions* (5th edn). Gaithersburg, MD: Aspen.

Johnson, M.B. (2003) The interrogation of Michael Crowe: A film review focused on education and training. *American Journal of Forensic Psychology*, 21: 71–79.

Kassin, S.M. (2007) Internalized false confessions. In M.P. Toglia, J.D. Read, D.F. Ross, and R.C.L. Lindsay (eds), *The Handbook of Eyewitness Psychology. Vol.* I: *Memory for events* (pp. 175–192). Mahwah, NJ: Lawrence Erlbaum.

Kassin, S.M. (2012) Why confessions trump innocence. *American Psychologist*, 67: 431–445.

Kassin, S.M., Drizin, S.A., Grisso, T., *et al.* (2010) Police-induced confessions: Risk factors and recommendations. *Law and Human Behavior*, 34: 3–38. doi: http://dx.doi.org/ 10.1007/s10979-009-9188-6.

Kassin, S.M., Dror, I.E., and Kukucka, J. (2013) The forensic confirmation bias: Problems, perspectives, and proposed solutions. *Journal of Applied Research in Memory and Cognition*, 2: 42–52. doi: dx.doi.org/10.1016/j.jarmac.2013.01.001.

Kukucka, J. and Kassin, S.M. (2012) Do confessions taint juror perceptions of handwriting evidence? Paper presented at the Annual Meeting of the American Psychology-Law Society San Juan, Puerto Rico, March 14–17.

Lamb, M.E., Hershkowitz, I., Orbach, Y., and Esplin, P.W. (2008) *Tell Me What Happened: Structured Investigative Interviews of Child Victims and Witnesses*. New York: John Wiley & Sons.

Lamb, M.E., La Rooy, D.J., Malloy, L.C., and Katz, C. (eds) (2011) *Children's Testimony: A Handbook of Psychological Research and Forensic Practice*. New York: Wiley-Blackwell.

Leo, R.A. (2008) *Police Interrogation and American Justice* (Cambridge, MA: Harvard University Press).

Leo, R.A. and Davis, D. (2010) From false confession to wrongful conviction: Seven psychological processes. *Journal of Psychiatry and Law* (special issue on Interrogations and Confessions), 38(Spring/Summer): 9–56.

Leo, R.A. and Ofshe, R.J. (1998) The consequences of false confessions: Deprivations of liberty and miscarriages of justice in the age of psychological interrogation. *Journal of Criminal Law and Criminology*, 88: 429–496.

Lilienfeld, S. O. and Landfield, K. (2008) Science and pseudoscience in law enforcement: A user-friendly prime. *Criminal Justice and Behavior*, 35(10): 1215–1230.

Lindsay, R.C.L., Ross, D.F., Read, J.D., and Toglia, M.P. (eds) (2007) *The Handbook of Eyewitness Psychology. Vol. II: Memory for People*. Mahwah, NJ: Lawrence Erlbaum.

Loftus, E.F. and Ketcham, K. (1991) *Witness for the Defense*. New York: St Martin's Press.

Loney, D.M. and Cutler, B.L. (2015) Coercive interrogation of eyewitnesses can produce false accusations. *Journal of Police and Criminal Psychology*, Feb 21 Online.

Martin, D.L. (2002) Lessons about justice from the "laboratory" of wrongful convictions: Tunnel vision, the construction of guilt and informer evidence, *UMKC Law Review*, 70: 847–864.

McNally, R. (2003) *Remembering Trauma*. Cambridge, MA: Harvard University Press.

Meissner, C.A. and Kassin, S.M. (2004) "You're guilty, so just confess!" Cognitive and behavioral confirmation biases in the interrogation room. In G.D. Lassiter (ed.), *Interrogations, Confessions, and Entrapment* (pp. 85–106). New York: Kluwer Academic/Plenum.

Miller, L.S. (1984) Bias among forensic document examiners: A need for procedural changes. *Journal of Police Science and Administration*, 12: 407–411.

Moore, T.E., Cutler, B.L., and Shulman, D. (2014) Shaping eyewitness and alibi testimony with coercive interview practices. *Champion*, 38: 34–41.

NAS (National Academy of Sciences) (2004) Forensic Analysis: Weighing Bullet Lead Evidence. Washington, DC: National Academies Press.

NAS (2009) *Strengthening Forensic Science in the United States: A Path Forward*. Washington, DC: National Academies Press.

National Commission on Forensic Science: National Institute of Standards and Technology (2014) Presentation of expert testimony: Policy recommendations. Available online at http://www.justice.gov/sites/default/files/pages/attachments/2014/10/20/draft_on_expert_testimony.pdf (accessed September 28, 2016).

Naughton, M. (2013) *The Innocent and The Criminal Justice System*. Basingstoke, UK: Palgrave Macmillan.

Ofshe, R. (1992) Inadvertent hypnosis during interrogation: False confessions due to dissociative state; misidentified multiple personality disorder and the satanic cult hypothesis. *Journal of Clinical and Experimental Hypnosis*, 40: 125–156.

OIG (Office of the Inspector General) (2006) A review of the FBI's progress in responding to the recommendations in the office of the inspector general: Report on the fingerprint misidentification in the Brandon Mayfield case. Available online at http://www.justice.gov/oig/special/s1105.pdf (accessed September 28, 2016).

Risinger, D.M., Saks, M.J., Thompson, W.C., and Rosenthal, R. (2002) The Daubert/Kumho implications of observer effects in forensic science: Hidden problems of expectation and suggestion. *California Law Review*, 90: 1–56.

Rossmo, D.K. (ed.) (2009) *Criminal Investigative Failures*. Boca Raton, FL: CRC Press.

Sauer, M. (2004) Former detective won't say Tuite was overlooked. *San Diego Union-Tribune*, March 26: B1.

Simon, D. (2012) *In Doubt: The Psychology of the Criminal Justice Process*. Cambridge, MA: Harvard University Press.

Snook, B. and Cullen, R.M. (2009) Bounded rationality and criminal investigations: Has tunnel vision been wrongfully convicted? In D.K. Rossmo (ed.), *Criminal Investigative Failures* (pp. 71–98). Boca Raton, FL: CRC Press.

Snyder, M. and Stukas, A.A. (1999) Interpersonal processes: The interplay of cognitive, motivational, and behavioral activities in social interaction, *Annual Review of Psychology*, 36: 1202–1212.

Stubbins, D. and Stubbins, N. (2009) On the horns of a narrative: Judgment, heuristics, and biases in criminal investigation. In D.K. Rossmo (ed.), *Criminal Investigative Failures* (pp. 99–140). Boca Raton, FL: CRC Press.

Technical Working Group for Eyewitness Evidence (1999) Eyewitness evidence: A guide for law enforcement. US Department of Justice.

Thompson, W.C. (2006) Tarnish on the "gold standard": Understanding recent problems in forensic DNA testing. *The Champion*, 30: 10–16.

Trager, R. (2013) Forensic chemist imprisoned for falsifying tests. *Chemistry World*, November 27. Available online at http://www.rsc.org/chemistryworld/2013/11/forensic-lab-chemist-annie-dookhan-imprisoned-falsifying-tests (accessed September 28, 2016).

Ulery, B.T., Hicklin, R.A., Buscaglia, J., and Roberts, M.A. (2012) Repeatability and reproducibility of decisions by latent fingerprint examiners. *PLoS ONE*, 7(3): e32800.

Villalobos, J.G. and Davis, D. (2016) Interrogation and the minority suspect: Pathways to true and false confession. In M.K. Miller and B.H. Bornstein (eds) *Advances in Psychology and Law* (vol. I, pp. 1–41). New York: Springer.

Vrij, A. (2008) *Detecting Lies and Deceit: Pitfalls and Opportunities* (2nd edn), Chichester, UK: John Wiley & Sons.

Vrij, A., Granhag, P.A., and Porter, S. (2010) Pitfalls and opportunities in nonverbal and verbal lie detection. *Psychological Science in the Public Interest*, 11(3): 89–121.

Wells, G.L. and Quinlivan, D.S. (2009) The eyewitness post-identification feedback effect: What is the function of flexible confidence estimates for autobiographical events? *Applied Cognitive Psychology*, 23(8): 1153–1163. doi: 10.1002/acp.1616.

Wright, L. (1995) *Remembering Satan: A Tragic Case of Recovered Memory*. New York: Vintage Books.

Zulawski, D. and Wicklander, D. (2002) *Practical Aspects of Interview and Interrogation* (2nd edn). Boca Raton, FL: CRC Press.

Further Reading

Cole, S.A. (2001) *Suspect Identities: A History of Fingerprinting and Criminal Identification*. Cambridge, MA: Harvard University Press.

Davis, D. and Leo, R.A. (2012) "Interrogation-related regulatory decline:" Ego-depletion, self-regulation failure, and the decision to confess. *Psychology, Public Policy and Law*, 18(4): 673–704.

Davis, D. and Leo, R.A. (in press) Stereotype threat and the special vulnerabilities of sexual abuse/assault suspects to false confession. In R. Burnett (ed.) *Vilified: Wrongful Allegations of Person Abuse*. Oxford: Oxford University Press.

Hill, C., Memon, A., and McGeorge, P. (2008) The role of confirmation bias in suspect interviews: A systematic evaluation. *Legal and Criminological Psychology*, 13: 357–371. doi: http://dx.doi.org/10.1348/135532507X238682.

Kassin, S.M., Goldstein, C.C., and Savitsky, K. (2003) Behavioral confirmation in the interrogation room: On the dangers of presuming guilt. *Law and Human Behavior*, 27: 187–203. http://dx.doi.org/10.1023/A:1022599230598.

Narchet, F.M., Meissner, C.A., and Russano, M.B. (2011) Modeling the influence of investigator bias on the elicitation of true and false confessions. *Law and Human Behavior*, 35(6): 452–465.

Shawyer, A., Milne, R., and Bull, R. (2009) Investigative interviewing in the UK. In S. Savage, R. Milne, and T. Williamson (eds), *International Developments in Investigative Interviewing*. Cullompton, UK: Willan.

Snook, B., Eastwood, J., and Barron, W.T. (2014) The next stage in the evolution of interrogation: The PEACE model. *Canadian Criminal Law Review*, 18: 219–239.

Ulery, B.T., Hicklin, R.A., Buscaglia, J., and Roberts, M.A. (2011) Accuracy and reliability of forensic latent fingerprint decisions. *Proceedings of the National Academy of Science of the United States of America*, 108(19): 7733–7738.

Part V

Reducing and Preventing Homicide

34

Seeing and Treating Violence as a Health Issue

Charles Ransford and Gary Slutkin

Violence should be defined globally as primarily a health issue—and health approaches should be utilized to understand, detect, interrupt, and prevent events and outbreaks and reduce its spread. Although violence is commonly understood by the general public and mostly treated by our governmental and nongovernmental institutions as a problem of "bad" people, the health sector understands it differently. Violence is not a human universal—it does not occur in all societies (e.g., Robarchek 1980). Rather, violence is a behavior or set of behaviors that are acquired mostly through social learning (Bandura, Ross, and Ross 1961; Akers 1985). Further, relatively standard and well-tested and highly effective public health approaches are being increasingly applied to the problem of violence and are showing strong evidence of impact among individuals and communities. The active involvement of the health sector in the treatment of violence is long overdue, specifically through more operational and vigorous implementation of the means of prevention and epidemic control that the health sector knows well.

In this chapter, we make the case for viewing violence primarily as a health issue and we define the roles of the health sector in addressing violence. We also address how the health sector's response to violence fits into a larger context that also includes the community, schools, mental health, and social services. It should be noted that appropriately defining violence as a health issue should not be read as redefining or changing the role of law enforcement or other sectors, because critical roles for law enforcement are important even in more ordinarily accepted epidemic disease control situations (e.g., Patil 2014). Law enforcement and the health approach are complementary and in many ways law enforcement works toward prevention and incorporates many health-based principles and approaches as well. We will

The Handbook of Homicide, First Edition. Edited by Fiona Brookman, Edward R. Maguire, and Mike Maguire.

clarify the value of defining and understanding violence as a health issue and then describe how the health sector can quickly increase its involvement and efficacy in treating violence, to save lives, and accomplish better outcomes for individuals and communities.

Evolution of Violence as a Public Health Issue

Violence is both a health and a public health problem. It is a health problem because there is a specific health lens that helps us in science and in the application of science in getting better outcomes. By understanding violence as a health problem, we can recognize that the *people* themselves doing violence as well as those who have been affected through injury and exposure essentially *have a personal health problem*—a problem of exposure, contagion, and trauma or pain. Violence is a public health problem because it is also a serious *threat to the health of populations and* because *public health techniques* are effectively utilized to reduce the prevalence and incidence of violence and make communities safer and healthier. We will introduce some of the public health discussion first and then come back to health.

For decades, violence has been viewed as a public health issue (Dahlberg and Mercy 2009), motivated initially by the fact that violence injures and kills *many people* (Cron 1986). Internationally, it is estimated that more than 1 billion children—half of all children in the world—are exposed to violence every year (CDC 2015) and over 1 million are estimated to be killed every year as a result of all forms of violence (Krug *et al.* 2002).

Increasingly, violence has also been viewed as a public health issue because of the extremely harmful effects of exposure to violence on a wide array of other types of very serious health problems, including life threatening chronic diseases such as cancer and heart disease (Felitti *et al.* 1998), infectious diseases such as HIV (Jewkes *et al.* 2010), as well as serious mental health problems (Singer *et al.* 1995). Exposure to violence is therefore an enormous concern to both public health and health practitioners—and to all of us.

Typical public health approaches to violence involve multiple disciplines, emphasize collective action, and are based on the scientific approach—which includes gathering information, identifying causes and other factors, exploring methods of prevention, and disseminating evidence-based approaches (Krug *et al.* 2002; Mercy *et al.* 1993). Public health approaches are also frequently categorized as primary (early intervention before manifestation or problem), secondary (more immediate responses to violence), or tertiary (long-term care in the wake of violence) (Krug *et al.* 2002). Public health approaches can be further characterized by the groups that they target—general population, at risk, and actively involved (Krug *et al.* 2002).

The vision of violence as a public health issue is an important shift in the approach to addressing violence—from reactive to preventative through a focus on social, behavioral, and environmental factors (Mercy *et al.* 1993). The utilization of the scientific approach has also ensured that effective approaches are utilized and replicated. Furthermore, the public health lens has helped people to understand the problem of violence as a community problem and has led to community-level solutions (Mercy and Hammond 1998).

Why Violence Should Be Seen as a Health Issue

The health perspective on violence prevention is a much more fundamental shift in our understanding of violence and suggests a more comprehensive and deeper understanding of the people involved themselves and why violence is present. The *health* perspective is about *understanding* based in physiology, biology, neuroscience, psychology, and sociology. It is ethnic, cultural, racial, gender, class, and sexual orientation neutral, though it accounts for different influences and manifestations. There is no role for punishment in health-based solutions. Harm is to be avoided at all costs. Thinking about good and bad people is replaced by good and bad outcomes and with people viewed under contextual, biological, environmental, and social influences. Although all of our systems are imperfect, the biases of health-based solutions are prevention, behavior change, and helping those in greatest need. The health system provides education, guidance, and care. *Care* is the fundamental guiding principle of health and health systems, and prevention is a way of giving care in advance of things going too far. [1]

The emergence of the public health framing of violence is an incredibly important innovation and has been instrumental in reversing the rates of violence in many countries throughout the world (Krug *et al.* 2002; Kieselbach and Butchart 2015). Public health then is a subset of health and is an application of health principles to the community. This broader framing of violence as a health issue therefore includes applying public health methods and helps make the case for a prevention and public health approach. The health and public health ideas share the need to involve multiple disciplines, emphasize collective action, and utilize the scientific approach including using evidence-based and evidence-informed models. However, where the health approach adds the most is in the seeing and understanding of the person him/herself through the health lens—and as fundamentally having a health problem.

Violence as a Contagious Process

Violence is a health issue because it can be addressed through both personal care and broader public health approaches, but it is also a health issue because it fulfills the criteria of an epidemic and contagious disease. Not all health or public health issues do. The management of contagious or epidemic processes are a subspecialty within health and public health—as additional steps and methods are required and a full system is required for personal, family, contact, and community management.

Violence meets both the definitions of contagious and of disease, and also meets the specific individual and population criteria of contagious diseases (Slutkin 2013a).

Violence has been shown to cluster (Sherman, Gartin, and Buerger 1989; Slutkin 2013a; Buhaug and Gleditsch 2008; Gould, Wallenstein, and Kleinman 1990) and spread geographically (Zeoli *et al.* 2014; Cohen and Tita 1999) just like epidemic diseases. Violence also has been shown to transmit (cause more of itself)—and does so between individuals for many types of violence, including child abuse (Widom 1989; Egeland, Jacobvitz, and Sroufe 1988), community violence (Bingenheimer, Brennan, and Earls 2005; Kelly 2010), intimate partner violence (Ehrensaft *et al.* 2003; Black, Sussman, Unger 2010), and suicide (Gould *et al.* 2010) as well as transmit *between* syndromes. For example, those exposed to war violence have an increased risk of perpetrating community violence (MacManus *et al.* 2013) and those exposed to community violence have an increased risk of perpetrating domestic violence (Mullins *et al.* 2004).

Further, in recent years, much progress has been made in understanding *how* violent behavior is transmitted—both in terms of social psychology as well as the underlying brain. At the individual level, violence is transmitted through social learning or modeling. Many behaviors have been shown to spread in this manner (Christakis and Fowler 2009) because much of our behavior is developed through modeling (Slutkin 2013a; Bandura 1977) including, and especially, violence (Bandura, Ross, and Ross 1961; Akers 1985). People not only copy their friends, but also their friends' friends, and their friends' friends' friends (Christakis and Fowler 2009). Neuroscience researchers theorize that mirror neurons may have something to do with this unconscious learning process, as these neurons have been shown to fire both during an action and during observation (Iacoboni 2009; Iacoboni *et al.* 2005).

At the group level, violent behavior also transmits through social norms and scripts. For example, in a climate of chronic community violence, violence becomes the accepted or even expected response to conflict, including small disputes, perceived slights, or insults. Such street codes emphasize toughness and quick, violent retribution for transgressions against one's sense of self or insults to one's reputation. Failure to respond can become perceived to be or thought to be perceived to be a sign of weakness with a possible ensuing loss of status which can be thought to predispose the individual to further victimization (Anderson 2000; Wilkinson 2006). Similar norms and expectations also play a significant role in perpetuating other types of violence, including child abuse (Spinetta and Rigler 1972), intimate partner violence (Ahmad *et al.* 2004; Yoshioka, DiNoia, and Ullah 2001), bullying (Nesdale *et al.* 2008), law enforcement violence (Westley 1953; Westley 1970), and post-conflict violent communities (Ember and Ember 1994).

Through the lens of neuroscience, transmission through social norms is thought to occur because social pain associated with exclusion is experienced much like physical pain and in fact the same areas of the brain are involved in processing both types of pain (Eisenberger 2008, 2012; Kross *et al.* 2011; Eisenberger, Lieberman, and Williams 2003; Macdonald and Leary 2005). Similarly, social approval has been linked to dopamine pathways (Baumeister and Leary 1995; Izuma, Saito, Sadato 2008). In other words, social norms transmit behavior through an innate desire to avoid pain and obtain "pleasure," in this case anticipation of social acceptance, approval, or status as reward.

Violence has the added effect of being a traumatic experience, which can have a profound mental impact and physiological effects (Slutkin 2013a). Exposure to violence can lead to several adaptive responses including aggression, impulsivity, depression, stress, and exaggerated startle responses (Singer *et al.* 1995; Schuler and Nair 2001; Mead, Beauchaine, and Shannon 2010), as well as changes in our neurochemistry including degrading monoamine neurotransmitters (MAOA), a flood of neuroendocrine responses, and changes to the brain structure (such as hippocampal volume and prefrontal cortex abnormalities) (Child Welfare Information Gateway 2015; McCrory, De Brito, and Viding 2010; Mead, Beauchaine, and Shannon 2010; Wilson, Hansen, and Li 2011; Hanson *et al.* 2010; Perry 2001).

Not everyone who is exposed to violence becomes violent, just as not everyone exposed in other epidemics (for example, colds, flu, tuberculosis, etc.) contracts the problem or disease following exposure. As with diseases, many risk factors[2] help determine whether the violence contagion is more or less likely to "take"—or result in its effects being incorporated in the individual as symptoms likely to present at some time in the future. Age is a particularly important factor for violence, as it is for diseases such as influenza (Taubenberger and Morens 2006) and tuberculosis (Comstock 1982). Children and adolescents are more susceptible to picking up violent behaviors in part because their brains are more malleable (Perry *et al.* 1995) and are more prone to making risky choices, particularly when the risk is ambiguous (Van Leijenhorst *et al.* 2010; Tymula *et al.* 2012). Studies have also shown that adolescents have an elevated neurological response to gains that leads to greater reward seeking (Galvan 2010; Van Leijenhorst *et al.* 2010) and that their choices are more driven by occasional outcomes than adults (Van Duijvenvoorde *et al.* 2012). Finally, adolescents are less able to take others' perspectives into account and in general have diminished decision-making capabilities (Van Duijvenvoorde and Crone 2013).

The dose—essentially the amount or intensity of the exposure to violence—can also affect acquisition of violent behavior. Violence exposure has been shown to have a cumulative effect on trauma (Dubow *et al.* 2012) and those with chronic exposure have shown a more than 30 times greater risk of future violent behavior than low exposure (Spano, Rivera, and Bolland 2010). Context is also important; for example, the presence of peers has a clear effect on whether a person chooses to engage in risk-taking behavior (Chein *et al.* 2011). This dose responsiveness implies an acquired and biological phenomena (Nelson and Williams 2014).

It might be worthwhile to consider that *Dorland's Illustrated Medical Dictionary* (Dorland 2010) defines a disease as: "any deviation or interruption of structure or function of a part, organ, or system of the body, as manifested by characteristic symptoms and signs (causing morbidity and mortality); the etiology, pathology, and prognosis may be known or unknown."

It is known that violence does affect the structure and function of the brain, does have characteristic signs and symptoms, and does causes morbidity and mortality. Violence also shows all of the characteristics of an *epidemic* type of disease—including clustering, spread, and transmission. Further, violence has been shown to be responsive to health approaches, including epidemic control approaches (Skogan *et al.* 2009; Webster *et al.* 2012; Picard-Fritsche and Cerniglia 2013; Henry, Knoblauch, and Sigurvinsdottir 2014) and hospital-based interventions (Purtle *et al.* 2013).

Even for those not willing to accept violence as a contagious disease, its contagious nature and role as a health problem can still be recognized. There is still much to be worked out in understanding the pathogenesis of violence as a contagious health problem, as is the case for many other health problems, but enough is now known—about how violent behavior is formed, how it affects people including their brain and other systems, and how it spreads in individuals and communities—to change our perspective about how we understand and treat violence.

The Importance of the Health Perspective

The health perspective is important because it is based on a scientific understanding that reveals to us that violence is a behavior developed through exposure and is thereby transmissible, allowing us to see and understand people differently. Every response to violence should be based on this scientific understanding.

The health perspective then allows us to move away from the moralistic perspective that understands violence as caused by "bad" people and "evil." There is no science in moralistic explanations. Moralism as a perspective on violence is completely subjective. Often, perpetrators of violence believe that they are in the right or that their behavior was appropriate (Fiske and Rai 2014; Kelty, Hall, and O'Brien-Malone 2012). A young person from a violent community may believe he is right or justified in avenging his friend's killing—he may even believe that such vengeance is expected. A police officer might believe he is right or justified in acting violently with a suspected person in certain circumstances. A government might believe it is right or justified in bombing a community. For each of these cases, an opposing moralistic perspective exists. However, from a health perspective, the preferred outcome is objective and clear: to maintain and improve the physical, mental, psychological, and emotional wellbeing of each individual and of the community.

The health perspective is also important because it emphasizes preventing violence rather than simply reacting to it. We can detect and successfully treat people before they become violent by understanding the effects of exposure to violence, the symptoms (and latency) of violent ideation, and the effectiveness of particular methods of behavior change, care, or treatment. Furthermore, understanding and trying to reduce additional risk factors (and enhance protective factors) can and should be used to help persons become less susceptible and increase resistance to the transmission and progression (or pathogenesis) of violence.

Some may not understand health as preventative, instead viewing health in terms of medical treatment for a particular physical condition. However, much of what health sector professionals do is prevention and this is often done through helping people to change and supporting this change. In fact, the "prevention of the three leading causes of death in the United States—heart disease, cancer, and stroke—rests largely on behavioral modifications"—in these cases exercise, changes in diet, and cessation of smoking (Dahlberg and Mercy 2009). The same approaches used by the health sector against these causes of death can also be utilized to detect and treat violent behavior. Likewise specific community-based methods can be used to interrupt spread and change norms as for epidemic diseases.

With a new scientific understanding of violence as a contagious health problem, our approach to violence can fundamentally change. We recognize health as the proper perspective for other behaviors such as smoking behavior, sexual behavior, eating behavior, drug using behavior, and so on. In the same way, we must recognize that the health perspective is essential to properly and effectively addressing violent behavior.

The Health Approach to Reducing Violence

Many programs, models, and system changes are already being used in implementing a health approach to violence, although some may not identify their approach as such. Health approaches for preventing violence are those that are based on an understanding of how violent behaviors are formed and of the effects of exposure to violence; that apply a preventative approach; that use evidence-based or evidence-informed approaches; and that are nonjudgmental, have a commitment to do no harm, and approach people through the lens of care. Health approaches to violence typically fall into four categories, which can be implemented in combination or individually.

The first strategy centers on stopping the transmission of violence by detecting situations in the community where the risk of future violence is high and preventing these situations from becoming lethal, thus *interrupting* the contagion where it is potentially occurring. This prevents events and reduces further exposure. Preventing retaliations is one of the ways of working in this area, however, it is equally or even more important that health outreach specialists prevent "first events." One example of this approach is the violence interrupters from the Cure Violence program, who detect group or individual conflicts and mediate these conflicts before they become lethal (Skogan *et al.* 2009; Webster *et al.* 2012; Ransford, Kane, Slutkin 2013; Slutkin, Ransford, Decker 2015). This approach is now being implemented in over 60 communities in the United States as well as in Latin America and the Caribbean, South Africa, and in early forms of adaptation in the Middle East and elsewhere. An important part of the interrupter and outreach approach is a focus in the hospital in order to prevent retaliation to shooting events (Purtle *et al.* 2013; Cunningham *et al.* 2009; Zun, Downey, and Rosen 2006). It is critical that highly trusted community-based health workers provide these services and in a confidential way so as not to dissuade people from seeking care. Similar health-based outreach methods exist to interrupt ongoing violence for child abuse, intimate partner violence, and elder abuse, often through detecting the abuse and referring to intervention (US Preventive Services Task Force 2013). Interruption itself helps to stabilize communities and also helps to shift norms (Webster *et al.* 2012).

The second strategy focuses on identifying and treating those at highest risk for violent behavior. A health approach can effectively detect cases of potentially violent individuals, in the same way that disease control specialists, case workers, and other health outreach workers detect those suspected of having tuberculosis, syphilis, gonorrhea, HIV/AIDS, or even Ebola—all of which also are not obvious, frequently hide from persons with authority,[3] and are hard to reach without very high and very local credibility, access, and trust that only the right health workers can provide (e.g., Aggleton *et al.* 1994).

The public health community refers to proactive detection as "*active case finding*," which differs from "passive case finding" in that it does not rely solely on referrals, but instead actively seeks out cases that need most attention. Programs that have done this type of outreach identify those at high risk and treat them to address their needs and reduce their risk for violent behavior, including for community violence (Spergel, Grossman, and Wa 1998; Skogan *et al.* 2009), suicide (Motto 1979), and war violence (Espie *et al.* 2009).

Identification and treatment of those at risk for violence works because people can be changed and their risk for behaving violently can be diminished. Many effective treatment options exist that both treat existing trauma and help provide resistance and resilience to exposure. For some, a positive role model and mentor may be effective (Tolan *et al.* 2008), while others may need a treatment program such as cognitive behavior therapy or functional family therapy (Lipsey 2009).[4] These types of treatment are particularly important for those at high risk, but it is also important to provide treatment for everyone traumatized by exposure to violence—both direct and indirect exposure. There are many effective treatments for people with differing levels of exposure (see NCTSN 2015 for examples). While not everyone exposed will need treatment, it is important to seek out those who do need more extensive help.

The third type of health strategy addresses environmental factors to reduce the community's susceptibility or increase its resistance to the violence contagion. These approaches typically address two areas of environmental factors: community norms and social determinants of health. Working to change the norms that encourage the use of violence both reduces susceptibility by discouraging and challenging negative norms, and increase resistance by amplifying positive norms. Addressing social determinant of health also work to affect the susceptibility or resistance through other outside factors, including addressing issues related to employment, built environment, and social cohesion and support. Most programs addressing these social determinants do not specifically seek to reduce violence only, but it is one of the many positive effects. One example is the greening of vacant lots to reduce the number of areas where violent events would be likely to occur (Branas *et al.* 2011; Garvin, Cannuscio, and Branas 2013). Other programs seek to build a community's resilience through linking a network of adaptive capacities such as social capital and economic resources (Norris 2008), or through urban upgrading to improve the general conditions and quality of life in a certain communities—for example, through the provision of clean piped water, electricity, basic health care, and school facilities, or by providing parks and other public places for leisure activities (Kieselbach and Butchart 2015).

The fourth type of health strategy addresses risk factors (and protective factors) that affect an individual's susceptibility or resistance to the violence contagion, and also includes many social determinants of health. One of the primary methods of doing this is by addressing mental health issues that can increase the risk of being traumatized, such as depression, anxiety, and alcohol and drug use. Individuals can also use various approaches to increase resilience, including constructing and maintaining social support networks as well as cognitive and behavioral interventions (Southwick and Charney 2012; Luthar and Cicchetti 2000; Luthar, Cicchetti, and Becker 2000; Masten, Best, and Garmezy 1990) or developing skills in meditation or mindfulness (Farb *et al.* 2007).

All of these approaches address violence as a health issue and as a behavior and implement health methods that reduce the likelihood of that behavior occurring. Multiple approaches should have a cumulative effect and all approaches should be carefully monitored and adjusted as needed.

The Epidemic Control Approach to Reducing Violence

Epidemic control is a subspecialty of public health with specific considerations, concerns, and methods. The epidemic control requirements for reducing violence begins with clearly recognizing the existing science that violence is contagious (IOM 2013; Slutkin 2013a, 2013b) and therefore that the methods used to stop epidemics, can be successful in stopping violence. The epidemic control method specifically combines many of the elements of a health model outlined above, including stopping transmission, treating the highest risk, and addressing norms. One prominent example of the epidemic control method of violence prevention is the Cure Violence Health Model, which adapts the World Health Organization's model for addressing other epidemics (Heymann 2008). Cure Violence outlines its main components as follows.

1. Detect and interrupt the transmission of violence—by anticipating where violence may occur and intervening before it erupts.
2. Change the behavior of the highest potential transmitters—by identifying those at highest risk for violence and working to change their behavior.
3. Change community norms—by influencing social norms to discourage the use of violence.

A central characteristic of the Cure Violence model is the use of credible messengers as workers—individuals from the same communities who are trusted and have access to the people who are most at risk of perpetrating violence. Those hired can include people who have formerly been involved in violence, but have changed their behavior. Because Cure Violence workers have access and trust, they are able to talk about violent behavior credibly and persuade high-risk individuals to resist behaving violently. Intensive and very specific training is required, but hiring the right workers is essential to get the access, trust, and credibility required for the job—as for all health workers attempting to access hard to reach populations of any type (McDonnell 2011).

Changing behaviors and norms becomes profoundly easier when the change agents have credibility with the populations being served. The credibility allows access to individuals and communities that can lead to the types of conversation and participation needed to achieve positive outcomes. While it is certainly possible for people from many different backgrounds to be credible, as with other community health workers, people from the same community who have had similar experiences are most likely to be able to be credible.

The Cure Violence approach is being implemented in more than 60 communities across seven countries. The model has been externally evaluated four times, with each evaluation showing large, statistically significant reductions in gun violence. Studies by Northwestern University and Johns Hopkins University showed 41 to 73 percent reductions in shootings in neighborhoods in Chicago (Skogan *et al.* 2009)[5] and as much as a 56 percent decrease in killings in Baltimore (Webster *et al.* 2012), while an evaluation by the Center for Court Innovations showed that the area in New York City in which the program operated went one year without a killing and had 20 percent fewer shootings compared to the trend in the neighboring communities (Picard-Fritsche and Cerniglia 2013). An evaluation of the program from 2012 to 2013 in Chicago found a 31 percent reduction in killings in the two target districts (Henry, Knoblauch, and Sigurvinsdottir 2014).

The international adaptations of the Cure Violence model have also demonstrated large reductions, although formal evaluations are needed to determine causality. In three communities in San Pedro Sula, Honduras, the program implementation has coincided with 73 percent-86 percent reductions in shootings and killings.[6] In the target community in Cape Town, South Africa, there has been a reduction of 52 percent in gang-related killings. [7] In Loiza, Puerto Rico there was a 50 percent reduction in killings associated with first year of implementation of the program.[8] In Ciudad Juarez, Mexico, after implementation of Cure Violence the rate of killing dropped by 24.3 percent.[9]

Activating a Full Health Approach

The health sector can be much more fully utilized to reduce violence than we have seen utilized so far. What is needed from the health sector was identified 30 years ago by the United States Surgeon General C. Everett Koop's Workshop on Violence and Public Health: "education of the public on the causes and effects of violence, education of health professionals as to better care for victims and better approaches to violence prevention, improved reporting and data-gathering, some additional research, and increased cooperation and coordination-networking if you will among health and health-related professions and institutions" (Cron 1986). In essence, Dr Koop saw the need for a health system to respond to violence as a health problem in a much more energized and comprehensive way.

Despite Dr. Koop's call three decades ago, the health sector today remains severely underutilized. Below we outline a framework for a full health approach to violence. We will describe very briefly the roles for the institutions in the health sector, roles for different types of health professionals, and the ways in which sectors outside of the formal health sector can also utilize elements of the health perspective with the goal of reducing violence.

Ministries of health and health departments

Since it has been decades that violence has been viewed as a public health issue (Dahlberg and Mercy 2009), and since then multiple intervention have been more fully developed (WHO 2015; Krug *et al.* 2002; Skogan *et al.* 2009; David-Ferdon and Simon 2012; Weiss and Kelly 2013; Purtle *et al.* 2013), it is time for ministries of health and health departments to play a much more active and prominent role in violence. As the agency of government responsible for issues related to the health of the populations, ministries of health and health departments assume these responsibilities by assessing and analyzing data on violent events, locations, characteristics, and trends from hospitals, police, medical examiners, universities, the community, and other sources to provide improved information on violence for analysis, intervention, and for educating the public. Educating the public is a critically important role for health leaders.

Ministries of health and health departments also need to be involved in identifying, disseminating, and evaluating evidence-based strategies to prevent violence, change behaviors, and reduce susceptibility and enhance resistance to violent behavior. Depending on what the data shows a community most requires, this work may include a full epidemic approach to violence or specific targeted elements of a health approach such as marketing efforts to change norms about violence and promote health behaviors that prevent violence. Since violence always has the potential to act in an epidemic fashion, appropriate health-based strategies need to be put into place.

When there is any type of violence in a community—community violence, child abuse, intimate partner violence, elder abuse, sexual abuse, or suicide—the ministry of health or health department should be "out front." When the public wants to understand why "senseless" violence is occurring in a community, the ministries of health or health department should be offering answers that help people "make sense" of it—as a contagious issue related to exposure—to understand the scientific explanation for why violence occurs and to explain and likewise outline the response to prevent future events.

Ministries of health and health departments should coordinate community-based efforts as well as the relationship between community-based efforts and hospitals to prevent events, including the prevention of spread once events have occurred through interrupters and outreach workers based in community organizations, as well as monitor their performance and results (Ransford, Kane, Slutkin 2013).

Hospitals, trauma centers, and emergency rooms

Hospitals are an important setting for health responses to violence because victims of violence often come to hospitals to seek treatment. Hospitals need to implement measures to properly detect and treat victims of violence.

First, hospitals must make an assessment of the types, severity, and amount of violence that the hospital treats to determine what type of approaches should be implemented. At a minimum, hospitals should include violence in their community health needs assessment and implementation plan. Hospitals should also implement a screening tool to determine if a patient has been a victim of violence, and then have a set of referral options for the patient, including resources for conflict mediation, behavior change, domestic violence services, trauma treatment, and mental health care.

If a hospital treats a high volume of victims of community violence, it should implement a hospital-based program to prevent relapses, prevent retaliation, treat mental trauma, and address behavioral effects; such programs have been shown to have significant effects on reducing re-injury (Smith *et al.* 2013). If community outreach programs are available, the hospital should be connected with these programs to provide long-term treatment when needed.

Mental health centers

An important element of preventing violence is the treatment of those who are at risk for becoming violent and those who have been heavily exposed. As described above, exposure to violence is a significant risk factor. For this reason, efforts to prevent violence need to include treatment of the trauma associated with exposure. Mental health centers are an ideal venue for this type of service because of their experience in treating mental health issues generally. Mental health centers need to increase capacity so that they can treat exposure to violence and meet the need of the large amount of untreated people.

Health and mental health centers in schools and prisons

Any institution with a medical facility should adopt strategies to address violent behavior based on their need. In particular, schools and prisons need to implement health approaches to violence prevention based on the needs of the populations that they serve. Schools in all communities should be trained to detect violence exposure and refer exposed people to appropriate treatment, particularly in high violence communities but also in other communities because domestic violence is so prevalent.

Medical facilities in prison systems are a crucial part of a health system to address violence because very high percentages of persons who are incarcerated have been exposed to violence and suffer trauma from this exposure (James and Glaze 2006). Furthermore, those in prison are victims of violence at very high rates (Wolff and Shi 2009; Mendel 2011). It is well known that trauma can also occur to a person while incarcerated. Our current system is releasing highly traumatized individuals back into the community without any treatment for their serious conditions, which plays a large role in exacerbating violence in communities (IOM 2013). Equipping prisons to treat exposure to violence is a crucial element for stemming the cycle of violence.

Within other institutions, including daycare centers, corporations, government agencies, universities, medical facilities and people serving medical roles should also be trained to respond to violence exposure. At a minimum this should include training in how to screen for exposure to violence and make appropriate referrals, but could also include more proactive methods such as trainings and group meetings.

Community-based organizations implementing health programs

Many community health issues are addressed by community organizations or community health clinics. As with other medical systems, community health workers come into contact with people who have been exposed to violence; these health workers are crucial actors in identifying and referring people for treatment.

For communities with chronic and severe violence, community organizations are frequently the best entities to implement community-based health approaches to prevent violence. Community organizations, because of their knowledge of and connection to the community, are ideal because health approaches rely on having access to those most likely to commit violence; embedded community organization can often gain this access.

Primary care—pediatricians, doctors, nurses, and other health professionals

Just like hospitals, health professionals are in a position to prevent violence because they come into contact with people who are victims of violence, exposed to violence, or are at risk for becoming violent. All types of health professionals should be included, from pediatricians to family practitioners to community health workers to nurses. Health professionals working in settings like veteran clinics or in chronically violent communities should be given special training so that they are able to respond sufficiently to individuals with higher levels of exposure to violence.

All health professionals should be trained in detection of violence exposure and trauma, and standard screening tools should be universally available. These efforts should focus on identification and ensuring appropriate referral and treatment for violence exposure and risk of behaving violently. These types of screening tools have been shown to be effective in the primary care setting at reducing violence (Borowsky *et al.* 2004).

Working with Other Sectors in Applying Health Approaches

Health approaches do not only come from the health sector. Other sectors can take the principles of the health approach and apply them in different settings. For example, schools and educators can learn methods of screening students to determine if they have had exposure to violence and are at risk for becoming violent, and then make appropriate referrals for treatment. Law enforcement is currently and can benefit from even further training in peaceful mediation and de-escalation of conflict. Further, many law enforcement departments are also making real time information and referrals to health and related professionals to be used to detect conflicts and prevent violence as well as for treating trauma.

The entire justice system, including prisons and jails, probation and parole, prosecutors, defense attorneys, and attorneys general can take on a health perspective that recognizes both violence as a behavior and the impacts of exposure to violence. This perspective can result in an increased utilization of treatment services for trauma and mental health care, behavior change, and interruption of conflicts leading to less violence.

Many other agencies that come into contact with people traumatized by violence, such as child welfare agencies, are also important in detecting ongoing violence and identifying those exposed or at risk. Likewise, any agency or organization that is involved in planning or maintaining the built environment, such as parks and public areas, should, and many do, consider a health perspective to reduce risk of violence. Each of these sectors and others have been working toward prevention and incorporating many health-based and related principles and approaches already and will hopefully be continuing this trend.

How Health Fits in a Bigger Picture

We are making the case for prioritizing a health perspective as foundational to how we understand and address violence, but that does not mean that we believe that the health sector alone can solve the problem of violence, any more than the health sector alone can solve cholera or Ebola epidemics or in fact any problem. Health approaches add to, but do not replace existing efforts. Accountability for violent behaviors is still required if we as a society are ineffective at providing health-based prevention to sufficient scale coverage and effectiveness.

There are also other roles that are needed to reduce and prevent violence that fall outside usual law enforcement responsibilities, but are often expected by the general public to be performed by law enforcement officers. Violence against another person is against the law, but that does not mean that those assigned to enforce these laws should also be expected to be held fully and totally responsible for preventing violence, and expected to fill every gap in society's deficiencies. For example, even where deterrence can be shown to reduce violence (e.g., Braga and Weisburd 2012), this should not be the primary focus or limit to society's efforts to do full scale prevention. Likewise, police should not be expected by society to be behavioral scientists, clinicians, social workers, doctors, mentors, or everything to everybody—or every solution to our social problems. In fact, police are being blamed commonly for many societal problems that they did not make and have very understandably limited ability to influence. Based on what we now know about how behaviors are actually formed at home and by peers, how they are maintained, and what the modern science tells us of how behaviors are effectively changed, it is way beyond what punishment is known or could be expected to accomplish.

Therefore, although police have a role of enormous importance, risk, and responsibility, it is unrealistic for us to expect police to provide the full solutions to all of the aspects of violence. It is both unrealistic and scientifically ungrounded—and it is not fair to the police themselves or to the community. Nor is it realistic or aligned with the scientific understanding of the problem. Also, just because two or more professions may be considered connected does not mean that the same people can or should perform all functions.

The health approach helps frame the issue and helps provide an understanding that informs the approaches used, but not all approaches should come from the health sector either. Likewise, other framings of violence can also supplement this health approach. For example, the human rights and child protection framing of violence adds extremely important elements to seeing the effects of violence more fully in certain situations, and keeps us vigilant about equity. Further the women's safety and protection framings help to prioritize certain populations that may be more vulnerable or possibly affected by violence more severely, and thereby also help us guide our interventions geographically as well as in application.

Conclusion

We are proposing a new lens—one different from how much of the general public currently sees violence and how our current governmental and nongovernmental institutions respond to violent events or outbreaks of violence. We are proposing that all of us take in more of the health framing and use a health lens as much as possible. Violence is a very unhealthy and very risky behavior—both to the individual as well as to his/her family and community. It is acquired through contagious brain mechanisms and social processes and can be treated using health methods. If we want to reduce violence in our communities locally and around the globe and in all of its forms, we must acknowledge that violence is both resultant and predictable. There is no "senseless" violence. Saying it is "evil" or done by "bad" people does not help in deriving solutions and frequently makes violence worse. Violence is a behavior that is modeled, passed on and transmitted by norms and social expectations, and accelerated through mental trauma. Brain processes mediate all of this.

Numerous other factors affect violence, many of which are frequently and largely inaccurately cited as "primary" causes of violence—such as poverty, dysfunctional families, and poor schools, to name a few. These are incredibly important problems—they all need to be addressed—and they are factors that can make violence worse by increasing the likelihood of spread and increasing the susceptibility of individuals, as other factors may do for contagious diseases. These are critical risk factors that we should all aim to address.

What is currently missing and is critically needed is a health understanding of violence that offers a deeper understanding of behavior in individuals and communities. Crucially, the process through which violence spreads must itself be understood—particularly the importance of social approval and norms, both very powerful forces that are neurologically driven. The reversal of violence outbreaks requires working on these processes through the health and other sectors and involving credible health workers with access, trust and skills.

Seeing violence as a health problem does not mean rationalizing violent behavior or excusing an individual who behaves violently. The health approach fundamentally sees violence as negative to the outcomes of the persons affected, community as a whole, and the person exhibiting the behavior. The fundamental shift of the health approach is in understanding violence as resulting from exposure. Violence is the problem itself, and people who are caught up in the cycle of violence—or have "caught" violence—can and should be treated. And individuals who have this health problem need care and support to heal as well as an effective and appropriate regimen as is provided to individuals with other health problems.

Violence can be successfully diagnosed, criteria can be developed and refined to predict it, and people can be successfully and humanely treated to become less violent. People do change. There are programs that help people to stop behaving violently, and there is not an age after which it is too late (Ross *et al.* 2013). Sending persons exposed to violence home without a reliable and effective treatment plan for exposure and mental trauma is irresponsible and unhealthy.

One intention of this framework is to develop a more connected health system to reduce violence, in the same way that our society successfully addresses conditions such as AIDS, TB, diabetes, and asthma. These approaches not only work toward greatly improved health and safety outcomes but also use health methods that cause no additional harm or trauma to the individual or community. These approaches are performed in a way that supports and provides people and communities with healthier lives. Furthermore, as with all health interventions, these approaches respect confidentiality and put a very high value on trust.

This framework also emphasizes the need to focus resources on what has previously been sometimes referred to as "late" or "tertiary" prevention efforts. In reality, the individuals actively committing the violence today are the center of the spread of violence itself. Science has illuminated the role of exposure in the transmission of violent behavior and therefore we must address ongoing violence, which transmits the violent behavior and limits the effectiveness of primary and secondary approaches. In other words, you can provide increased resistance to the violence through primary and secondary approaches, but it might not be enough if ongoing violence is not addressed and the dose of violence exposure is still high. Young people are being exposed to violence in the community, in their schools, and in their homes, and modeling those who are doing it now.

We have listed some of the elements of the health system and the roles they need to play to prevent violence. However, there are many others that are critical and are part of the system, including teachers, law enforcement, several parts of the youth and social sector, and the media. These other sectors have key roles in spreading the health understanding of violence and its causes, providing effective solutions, and to the extent they are able, screening and providing appropriate referral for treatment of people heavily exposed. In many instances, each of these sectors and others have been incorporating health-based principles and approaches already and our hope is that this discussion further encourages collaboration and even more utilization and adaptations of health approaches by all sectors to help produce and an even healthier and safer society.

We might follow the wisdom laid out by the Surgeon General's Workshop of 30 years ago: "The solution to the problem of violence requires a total community effort, but health care providers can play a special role … The health care system must help to make victims whole emotionally as well as physically, and help to prevent further violence. Providers must be alert to the special needs of those most at risk of becoming repeat victims" (Cron 1986).

The issue of lethal violent behavior is much broader, deeper, and more specific than the current law enforcement, gun control, and mental health debates. If these areas represent the limit of our response, that response will be ineffective, in particular because they fall short of conveying to the public how violence is formed, maintained, and changed, that is, how violent behavior is an unconsciously acquired unhealthy state perpetuating itself. Effective solutions must be based on this more scientifically grounded understanding of the violent behavior of an individual as an acquired and preventable event which society has the responsibility to prevent. That includes reducing the exposure, transmission, and progression of violence in individuals' brains and in communities—using community-based and health system-based outreach methods used for epidemics and diseases that spread. In this case this includes using peers, outreach, modified expectations, new skills, and changing norms—all specialized skills of the health sector and their partners. Massive reductions in other serious behaviors and problems have been achieved with public health methods. Violence can be reduced to much lower levels in our communities—perhaps to even rare events—when we take the time to understand, explain, and treat violence as a health issue by activating and organizing the health lens, sector, system, and partners to prevent it better. We all look forward to and work toward this realization of safer and healthier communities.

Notes

1 The criminal justice sector has been working more and more toward prevention and incorporating many of the health-based principles and approaches. This is a positive trend that we hope to further encourage.
2 This chapter makes no attempt to list all of the major factors that modulate the risk for developing violent behavior. It is important to note that co-factors affect susceptibility in two primary periods—during exposure to the contagion and during activation of the contagion.
3 This may be particularly true for the poor and other marginalized populations, such as immigrants, refugees, or racial or ethnic minorities.
4 These methods may require that they are maintained by outreach services.
5 Statistically significant reductions specifically attributable to the program were found in six of the seven communities examined—between 16 percent and 28 percent in four communities by time series analysis and between 15 percent and 40 percent in four partially overlapping communities by hot spot analysis.
6 Data source: Honduras site program data.
7 Data source: *Argus*, Thursday October 8, 2015 (Cape Town newspaper article based on official Cape Town Police data).
8 Data source: University of Puerto Rico, official police data.
9 Data source: Mesa De Seguridad Y Justicia De Ciudad Juarez.

References

Aggleton, P., O'Reilly, K., Slutkin, G., and Davies, P. (1994) Risking everything? Risk behavior, behavior change, and AIDS. *Science*, 265(5170): 341–345.

Ahmad, F., Riaz, S., Barata, P., and Stewart, D. (2004) Patriarchal beliefs and perceptions of abuse among South Asian immigrant women. *Violence Against Women*, 10: 262–282.

Akers, R.L. (1985) *Deviant Behavior: A Social Learning Approach* (3rd edn). Belmont, CA: Wadsworth.

Anderson, E. (2000) *Code of the Street: Decency, Violence, and the Moral Life of the Inner City*. New York: W.W. Norton.

Bandura, A. (1977) *Social Learning Theory*. Englewood Cliffs, NJ: Prentice-Hall.

Bandura, A., Ross, D., and Ross, S. (1961) Transmission of aggression through imitation of aggressive models. *Journal of Abnormal and Social Psychology*, 63: 575–582.

Baumeister, R.F. and Leary, M.R. (1995) The need to belong: Desire for interpersonal attachments as a fundamental human motivation. *Psychological Bulletin*, 117: 497–529.

Bingenheimer, J., Brennan, R., and Earls, F. (2005) Firearm violence exposure and serious violent behavior. *Science*, 308(5726): 1323–1326.

Black, D.S., Sussman, S., Unger, J.B. (2010) A further look at the intergenerational transmission of violence: Witnessing interparental violence in emerging adulthood. *Journal of Interpersonal Violence*, 25(6): 1022–1042.

Borowsky, I.W., Mozayeny, S., Stuenkel, K., and Ireland, M. (2004) Effects of a primary care-based intervention on violent behavior and injury in children. *Pediatrics*, 114(4): e392–e399.

Braga, A.A. and Weisburd, D.L. (2012) *The Effects Of "Pulling Levers" Focused Deterrence Strategies On Crime*. Oslo: Campbell Systematic Reviews.

Branas, C.C., Cheney, R.A., MacDonald, J.M., *et al.* (2011) A difference-in-differences analysis of health, safety, and greening vacant urban space. *American Journal of Epidemiology*, 174(11): 1296–1306.

Buhaug, H. and Gleditsch, K.S. (2008) Contagion or confusion? Why conflicts cluster in space. *International Studies Quarterly*, 52(2): 215–233.

Chein, J., Albert, D., O'Brien, L., *et al.* (2011) Peers increase adolescent risk taking by enhancing activity in the brain's reward circuitry. *Developmental Science*, 14: F1–F10.

Child Welfare Information Gateway (2015) *Understanding the Effects of Maltreatment on Brain Development.* Washington, DC: US Department of Health and Human Services, Children's Bureau.

Christakis, N.A. and Fowler, J.H. (2009) *Connected: The Surprising Power of Our Social Networks and How They Shape Our Lives.* New York: Little, Brown.

Cohen, J. and Tita, G. (1999) Diffusion in homicide: Exploring a general method for detecting spatial diffusion processes. *Journal of Quantitative Criminology*, 15(4): 451–493.

Comstock, G.W. (1982) Epidemiology of tuberculosis. *American Review of Respiratory Disease*, 125: 8–15.

Cron, T. (1986) The Surgeon General's Workshop on violence and public health: Review of the recommendations. *Public Health Reports*, 101: 8–14.

Cunningham, R., Knox, L., Fein, J., *et al.* (2009) Before and after the trauma bay: The prevention of violent injury among youth. *Annals of Emergency Medicine*, 53(4): 490–500.

Dahlberg, L.L. and Mercy, J.A. (2009) History of violence as a public health issue. *Virtual Mentor*, 11(2): 167–172. Available online at http://virtualmentor.ama-assn.org/2009/02/mhst1-0902.html (accessed September 26, 2016).

David-Ferdon, C. and Simon, T.R. (2012) *Striving To Reduce Youth Violence Everywhere (STRYVE): The Centers for Disease Control and Prevention's National Initiative to Prevent Youth Violence Foundational Resource.* Atlanta, GA: Centers for Disease Control and Prevention.

Dorland, W.A.N. (2010) *Dorland's Illustrated Medical Dictionary* (32nd edn). Philadelphia, PA: Elsevier/Saunders.

Dubow, E.F., Boxer, P., Huesmann, L.R., *et al.* (2012) Cumulative Effects of Exposure to Violence on Posttraumatic Stress in Palestinian and Israeli Youth. *Journal of Clinical Child and Adolescent Psychology*, 41(6), 837–844.

Egeland, B., Jacobvitz, D., and Sroufe, A. (1988) Breaking the cycle of abuse. *Child Development*, 59: 1080–1088.

Ehrensaft, M.K., Cohen, P., Brown, J., *et al.* (2003) Intergenerational transmission of partner violence: A 20-year prospective study. *Journal of Consulting and Clinical Psychology*, 71: 741–753.

Eisenberger, N.I. (2008) Understanding the moderators of physical and emotional pain: A neural systems-based approach. *Psychological Inquiry*, 19(3–4): 189–195.

Eisenberger, N.I. (2012) The pain of social disconnection: Examining the shared neural underpinnings of physical and social pain. *Nature Reviews Neuroscience*, 13(6): 421–434.

Eisenberger, N.I., Lieberman, M.D, and Williams, K.D. (2003) Does rejection hurt? An fMRI study of social exclusion. *Science*, 302: 290–292.

Ember, C.R. and Ember, M. (1994) War, socialization, and interpersonal violence: A cross-cultural study. *Journal of Conflict Resolution*, 38(4): 620–646.

Espie, E., Gaboulaud, V., Baubet, T., *et al.* (2009) Trauma-related psychological disorders among Palestinian children and adults in Gaza and West Bank, 2005–2008. *International Journal of Mental Health Systems*, 3(21).

Farb, N.A.S., Segal, Z.V., Mayberg, H., *et al.* (2007) Attending to the present: Mindfulness meditation reveals distinct neural modes of self-reference. *Social Cognitive and Affective Neuroscience*, 2: 313–322.

Felitti, V.J., Anda, R.F., Nordenberg, D., *et al.* (1998) Relationship of childhood abuse and household dysfunction to many of the leading causes of death in adults—The adverse childhood experiences (ACE) study. *American Journal of Preventive Medicine*, 14(4): 245–258. doi: 10.1016/s0749-3797(98)00017-8.

Fiske, A.P. and Rai, T.S. (2014) *Virtuous Violence: Hurting and Killing to Create, Sustain, End, and Honor Social Relationships*. Cambridge: Cambridge University Press.

Galvan, A. (2010) Adolescent development of the reward system. *Frontiers in Human Neuroscience*, 4: 1–9.

Garvin, E.C., Cannuscio, C.C., and Branas, C.C. (2013) Greening vacant lots to reduce violent crime: A randomised controlled trial. *Injury Prevention*, 19(3): 198–203.

Gould, M.S., Greenberg, T., Velting, D.M., Shaffer, D. (2010) Youth suicide risk and preventive interventions: A review of the past 10 years. *Journal of the Academy of Child and Adolescent Psychiatry*, 42: 386–405.

Gould, M.S., Wallenstein, S., and Kleinman, M. (1990) Time-space clustering of teenage suicide. *American Journal of Epidemiology*, 131(1): 71–78.

Hanson, J.L., Chung, M.K., Avants, B.B., *et al.* (2010) Early stress is associated with alterations in the orbitofrontal cortex: A tensor-based morphometry investigation of brain structure and behavioral risk. *Journal of Neuroscience*, 30: 7466–7472.

Henry, D., Knoblauch, S., and Sigurvinsdottir, R. (2014) *The Effect of Intensive CeaseFire Intervention on Crime in Four Chicago Police Beats: Quantitative Assessment*. Chicago: Robert R. McCormick Foundation.

Heymann, D. (2008) *Control of Communicable Diseases Manual*. Washington, DC: American Public Health Association.

Iacoboni, M. (2009) Imitation, empathy, and mirror neurons. *Annual Review of Psychology*, 60: 653–670.

Iacoboni, M., Molnar-Szakacs, I., Gallese, V., *et al.* (2005) Grasping the intentions of others with one's own mirror neuron system. *PLoS Biology*, 3(3): e79.

IOM (Institute of Medicine) (2013) *Contagion of Violence: Forum on Global Violence Prevention*. Fairford, UK: National Academies Press.

Izuma, K., Saito, D.N., Sadato, N. (2008) Processing of social and monetary rewards in the human striatum. *Neuron*, 58: 284–294.

James, D.J. and Glaze, L.E. (2006) *Mental Health Problems of Prison and Jail Inmates*. Washington, DC: US Department of Justice.

Jewkes, R.K., Dunkle, K., Nduna, M., and Shai, N. (2010) Intimate partner violence, relationship power inequity, and incidence of HIV infection in young women in South Africa: A cohort study. *The Lancet*, 376(9734), 41–48.

Kelly, S. (2010) Exposure to gang violence in the community: An integrated review of the literature. *Journal of Child and Adolescent Psychiatric Nursing*, 23: 61–73.

Kelty, S.F., Hall, G., and O'Brien-Malone, A. (2012) You have to hit some people! Endorsing violent sentiments and the experience of grievance escalation in Australia. *Psychiatry, Psychology and Law*, 19(3): 299–313.

Kieselbach, B. and Butchart, A. (2015) *Preventing Youth Violence: An Overview of the Evidence*. Geneva: World Health Organization.

Kross, E., Berman, M.G., Mischel, W., *et al.* (2011) Social rejection shares somatosensory representations with physical pain. *Proceedings of the National Academy of Sciences*, 108(15): 6270–6275.

Krug, E.G., Dahlberg, L.L., Mercy, J.A., *et al.* (eds) (2002) *World Report on Violence and Health*. Geneva: World Health Organization.

Lipsey, M.W. (2009) The primary factors that characterize effective interventions with juvenile offenders: A meta-analytic overview. *Victims and Offenders*, 4(2): 124–147.

Luthar, S.S. and Cicchetti, D. (2000) The construct of resilience: Implications for interventions and social policies. *Development and Psychopathology*, 12: 857–885.

Luthar, S.S., Cicchetti, D., and Becker, B. (2000) The construct of resilience: A critical evaluation and guidelines for future work. *Child Development*, 71(3): 543–562.

Macdonald, G. and Leary, M.R. (2005) Why does social exclusion hurt? The relationship between social and physical pain. *Psychological Bulletin*, 131: 202–223.

MacManus, D., Dean, K., Jones, M., *et al.* (2013) Violent offending by UK military personnel deployed to Iraq and Afghanistan: A data linkage cohort study. *The Lancet*, 381: 907–917.

Masten, A.S., Best, K.M., and Garmezy, N. (1990) Resilience and development: Contributions from the study of children who overcome adversity. *Development and Psychopathology*, 2(4): 425–444.

McCrory, E., De Brito, S.A., and Viding, E. (2010) Research review: The neurobiology and genetics of maltreatment and adversity. *Journal of Psychology and Psychiatry*, 51: 1079–1095.

McDonnell, J. (2011) CeaseFire employs public health methodology to fight urban violence [Audio Podcast], August 24. Available online at http://www.wbez.org/episode-segments/2011-08-24/ceasefire-employs-public-health-methodology-fight-urban-violence-90962 (accessed September 26, 2016).

Mead, H.K., Beauchaine, T.P., and Shannon, K.E. (2010) Neurobiological adaptations to violence across development. *Development and Psychopathology*, 22: 1–22.

Mendel, R.A. (2011) *No Place for Kids: The Case for Reducing Juvenile Incarceration*. Baltimore, MD: Annie E. Casey Foundation.

Mercy, J.A. and Hammond, W.R. (1998) Combining action and analysis to prevent homicide: A public health perspective. In M.D. Smith and M.A. Zahn (eds), *Homicide: A Sourcebook of Social Research* (pp. 297–310) Thousand Oaks, CA: Sage.

Mercy, J.A., Rosenberg, M.L., Powell, K.E., *et al.* (1993) Public health policy for preventing violence. *Health Affairs Winter*, 12(4): 7–29.

Motto, J.A. (1979) New approaches to crisis intervention. *Suicide and Life-Threatening Behavior*, 9(3), 173–184.

Mullins, C.W., Wright, R., Jacobs, B.A. (2004) Gender, streetlife and criminal retaliation. *Criminology*, 42: 911–940.

NCTSN (National Child Traumatic Stress Network) (2015) Empirically supported treatments and promising practices. Available online at http://www.nctsnet.org/resources/topics/treatments-that-work/promising-practices (accessed September 26, 2016).

Nelson, K.E. and Williams, C.M. (2014) *Infectious Disease Epidemiology: Theory and Practice*. Sudbury, MA: Jones & Bartlett.

Nesdale, D., Durkin, K., Maass, A., and Kiesner, J. (2008) Effects of group norms on children's intentions to bully. *Social Development*, 17(4).

Norris, F.H., Stevens, S.P., Pfefferbaum, B., *et al.* (2008) Community resilience as a metaphor, theory, set of capacities, and strategy for disaster readiness. *American Journal of Community Psychology*, 41(1–2): 127–150.

Patil, S. (2014) Police and HIV prevention: A crucial partnership. Open Society Foundations, July 18. Available online at http://www.opensocietyfoundations.org/voices/police-and-hiv-prevention-crucial-partnership (accessed September 26, 2016).

Perry, B.D. (2001) The neurodevelopmental impact of violence in childhood. In D.H. Schetky and E.P. Benedek (eds), *Textbook of Child and Adolescent Forensic Psychiatry* (pp. 221–238). Washington, DC: American Psychiatric Press.

Perry, B.D., Pollard, R.A., Blakley, T.L., *et al.* (1995) Childhood trauma, the neurobiology of adaptation, and "use-dependent" development of the brain: How "states" become "traits." *Infant Mental Health Journal*, 16(4): 271–291.

Picard-Fritsche, S. and Cerniglia, L. (2013) *Testing a Public Health Approach to Gun Violence*. New York: Center for Court Innovation.

Purtle, J., Dicker, R., Cooper, C., *et al.* (2013) Hospital-based violence intervention programs save lives and money. *Journal Of Trauma and Acute Care Surgery*, 75(2): 331–333.

Ransford, C.L., Kane, C., Slutkin, G. (2013) Cure violence: A disease control approach to reduce violence and change behavior. In E. Waltermauer and T. Akers (eds), *Epidemiological Criminology*. London: Routledge.

Robarchek, C.A. (1980) The image of nonviolence: World view of the Semai Senoi. *Federated Museums Journal*, 25: 103–117.

Ross, J., Quayle, E., Newman, E., and Tansey, L. (2013) The impact of psychological therapies on violent behavior in clinical and forensic settings: A systematic review. *Aggression and Violent Behavior*, 18(6): 761–773.

Schuler, M.E. and Nair, P. (2001) Witnessing violence among inner-city children of substance-abusing and non-substance-abusing women. *Archives of Pediatrics & Adolescent Medicine*, 155(3): 342–346.

Sherman, L.W., Gartin, P.R., and Buerger, M.E. (1989) Hot spots of predatory crime: Routine activities and the criminology of place. *Criminology*, 27:27–55.

Singer, M.I., Anglin, T.M., Song, L.Y., and Lunghofer, L. (1995) Adolescents' exposure to violence and associated symptoms of psychological trauma. *Journal of the American Medical Association*, 273: 477–482.

Skogan, W., Harnett, S.M., Bump, N., and DuBois, J. (2009) *Evaluation of CeaseFire-Chicago*. Chicago: Northwestern University Institute for Policy Research.

Slutkin, G. (2013a) Violence Is a contagious disease. In Institute of Medicine (ed.), *Contagion of Violence: Forum on Global Violence Prevention*. Fairford, UK: National Academies Press. Available online at www.cureviolence.org/wp-content/uploads/2014/01/iom.pdf (accessed September 26, 2016).

Slutkin, G. (2013b) "Treatment of violence as an epidemic disease." In John Snow's *Legacy, Epidemiology Without Borders. The Lancet*, 381(9874): 1302–1311.

Slutkin, G., Ransford, C.L., and Decker, R.B. (2015) Cure violence—treating violent behavior as a contagious disease. In M. Maltz and S. Rice (eds), *Envisioning Criminology: Researchers on Research as a Process of Discovery* (pp. 43–56). New York: Springer.

Smith, R., Dobbins, S., Evans, A., *et al.* (2013) Hospital-based violence intervention: Risk reduction resources that are essential for success. *Journal of Trauma and Acute Care Surgery*, 74(4): 976–982.

Southwick, S.M. and Charney, D.S. (2012) The science of resilience: Implications for the prevention and treatment of depression. *Science*, 338: 79–82.

Spano, R., Rivera, C., and Bolland, J. (2010) Are chronic exposure to violence and chronic violent behavior closely related developmental processes during adolescence? *Criminal Justice and Behavior*, 37(10): 1160–1179.

Spergel, I.A., Grossman, S.F., and Wa, K.M. (1998) *Evaluation of the Little Village Gang Violence Reduction Project: The First Three Years*. Chicago: University of Chicago.

Spinetta, J. and Rigler, D. (1972) The child-abusing parent: A psychological review. *Psychological Bulletin*, 77, 4: 296–304.

Taubenberger, J.K. and Morens, D.M. (2006) 1918 influenza: the mother of all pandemics. *Emerging Infectious Diseases*, 12(1): 15–22.

Tolan, P., Henry, D., Schoeny, M., and Bass, A. (2008) *Mentoring Interventions to Affect Juvenile Delinquency and Associated Problems*. Oslo: Campbell Systematic Reviews.

Tymula, A., Rosenberg Belmaker, L.A., Roy, A.K., *et al.* (2012) Adolescents risk taking behavior is explained by a tolerance to ambiguity. *Proceedings of the National Academy of Sciences, USA*, 109: 17135–17140.

US Preventive Services Task Force (2013) Primary care interventions to prevent child maltreatment: US Preventive Services Task Force recommendation statement. Annals of Internal Medicine, 159(4): 289–295.

Van Duijvenvoorde, A.C. and Crone, E.A. (2013) The teenage brain: A neuroeconomic approach to adolescent decision making. *Current Directions in Psychological Science*, 22(2): 108–113.

Van Duijvenvoorde, A.C., Jansen, B.R., Bredman, J.C., and Huizenga, H.M. (2012) Age-related changes in decision making: Comparing informed and noninformed situations. *Developmental Psychology*, 48: 192–203.

Van Leijenhorst, L., Gunther Moor, B., Op de Macks, Z.A., *et al.* (2010) Adolescent risky decision-making: Neurocognitive development of reward and control regions. *NeuroImage*, 51: 345–355.

Webster, D.W., Whitehill, J.M., Vernick, J.S., and Parker, E.M. (2012) *Evaluation of Baltimore's Safe Streets Program: Effects on Attitudes, Participants' Experiences, and Gun Violence*. Baltimore, MD: Johns Hopkins Center for the Prevention of Youth Violence.

Weiss, B. and Kelly, M.M. (2013) UNITY assessment II: Results of an innovative initiative to improve the urban response to youth violence. Available online at http://www.preventioninstitute.org/component/jlibrary/article/id-343/127.html (accessed September 26, 2016).

Westley, W.A. (1953) Violence and the police. *American Journal of Sociology*, 59(1).

Westley, W.A. (1970) *Violence And The Police—A Sociological Study Of Law, Custom, And Morality*. Cambridge, MA: MIT Press.

WHO (World Health Organization) (2015) Preventing youth violence: An overview of the evidence. Preamble to the Constitution of the World Health Organization as adopted by the International Health Conference, New York, June 19–22, 1946; signed on July 22, 1946 by the representatives of 61 states (Official Records of the World Health Organization, no. 2, p. 100) and entered into force on April 7,1948.

Widom, C.S. (1989) The cycle of violence. *Science*, 244: 160–166.

Wilkinson, D.A. (2006) Close examination of the social worlds of intentionally injured Philadelphia youth: Survey results from a hospital-based sample. Prepared for the William Penn Foundation.

Wilson, K.R., Hansen, D.J., and Li, M. (2011) The traumatic stress response in child maltreatment and resultant neuropsychological effects. *Aggression and Violent Behavior*, 16(2): 87–97.

Wolff, N. and Shi, J. (2009) Contextualization of physical and sexual assault in male prisons: Incidents and their aftermath. *Journal of Correctional Health Care*, 15(1): 58–77, 80–82.

Yoshioka, M.R., DiNoia, J., and Ullah, K. (2001) Attitudes towards marital violence: An examination of four Asian communities. *Violence Against Women*, 7: 900–926.

Zeoli, A.M., Pizarro, J.M., Grady, S.C., and Melde, C. (2014) Homicide as infectious disease: Using public health methods to investigate the diffusion of homicide. *Justice Quarterly*, 31(3): 609–632.

Zun, L.S., Downey, L. and Rosen, J. (2006) The effectiveness of an ED-based violence prevention program. *American Journal of Emergency Medicine*, 24(1): 8–13.

Further Reading

Centers for Disease Control and Prevention (2010) Web-based Injury Statistics Query and Reporting System (WISQARS). National Center for Injury Prevention and Control, Centers for Disease Control and Prevention (June 14, 2010). Available online at www.cdc.gov/injury (accessed September 26, 2016).

Centers for Disease Control and Prevention (2010) Youth violence: Facts at a glance, 42. Available online at http://www.cdc.gov/violenceprevention/pdf/YV-DataSheet-a.pdf (accessed September 26, 2016).

Centers for Disease Control and Prevention (2015) Violence Against Children Survey (VACS). National Center for Injury Prevention and Control. Centers for Disease Control and Prevention (2007) Available online at http://www.cdc.gov/violenceprevention/vacs/index.html (accessed September 26, 2016).

Fetsch, R.J. and Silliman, B. (2002) Which Youth Violence Prevention Programs Work? *The Forum for Family and Consumer Issues*, 7(1).

Finkelhor, D. (2009) Children's Exposure to Violence: A Comprehensive National Survey. Washington, DC: US Department of Justice.

Garbarino, J., Dubrow, N., Kostelny, K., and Pardo, C. (1992) *Children in Danger: Coping with the Consequences of Community Violence*. San Francisco: Jossey-Bass.

Huesmann, L.R. (2012) The contagion of violence: The extent, the processes, and the outcomes. In Institute of *Medicine, Social and Economic Costs of Violence: Workshop Summary* (pp. 63–69). Washington, DC: IOM and NRC.

Koop, C.E. and Lundberg, G.B. (1992) Violence in America: A public health emergency. *JAMA*, 267(22): 3075–3076.

Mercy, J.A., Hillis, S., Butchart, A., *et al.* (2013) Interpersonal violence: Global burden and paths to prevention. Disease Control Priorities in Developing Countries (3rd edn), Working paper. Centre for Global Health Research.

Pridemore, W.A. (2003) Demographic, temporal, and spatial patterns of homicide rates in Russia. *European Sociological Review*, 19(1): 41–59.

Rosenberg, M.L. and Fenley, M.A. (eds) (1991) *Violence in America: A Public Health Approach*. New York: Oxford University Press.

Schwab-Stone, M., Ayers, T., Kasprow, W., *et al.* (1995) No safe haven: A study of violence exposure in an urban community. *Journal of the American Academy of Child and Adolescent Psychiatry*, 10: 1343–1352.

Slutkin, G., Okware, S., Naamara, W., *et al.* (2006) How Uganda reversed its HIV epidemic. *AIDS Behavior*, 10(4): 351–360.

UN General Assembly, Declaration on the Elimination of Violence against Women, December 20, 1993, A/RES/48/104, available online at http://www.un.org/documents/ga/res/48/a48r104.htm (accessed September 26, 2016).

Ury, W.L. (ed.) (2002) *Must We Fight? From the Battlefield to the Schoolyard, a New Perspective on Violent Conflict and its Prevention*. San Francisco: Jossey-Bass.

US Public Health Service (1980) *Promoting Health/Preventing Disease: Objectives for the Nation*. Washington DC: US Public Health Service.

WHO (World Health Organization) (2014) Definition and typology of violence. Available online at http://www.who.int/violenceprevention/approach/definition/en/ (accessed September 26, 2016).

Wolf, A.M., Del Prado Lippman, A., Glesmann, C., and Castro, E. (2015) *Process Evaluation for the Office of Neighborhood Safety*. Oakland, CA: National Council on Crime and Delinquency.

35

Identifying and Intervening in Homicide Networks

Andrew M. Fox and Olivia R. Allen

Social network analysis (SNA) provides a framework for understanding how humans are connected with, relate to, and influence one another individually, in groups, and in organizations. It also allows us to map the social systems or networks that are formed by those connections. As with other systems, an event or change occurring anywhere within a social network will almost certainly have one or more corresponding impacts elsewhere in the network. SNA is an effective research tool for identifying the members, relationships, and dynamics of social networks, including those most associated with crime and violence. That kind of knowledge can enable deliberate, precise interventions that may alter network dynamics and affect outcomes in socially beneficial ways—for example, to significantly reduce homicide rates.

Homicide rates vary widely across the world. Using data from the United Nations and the World Health Organization, Rogers and Pridemore (Chapter 2, this volume) documented trends in international homicide rates. Internationally, the authors found geographic and temporal variations in homicide rates. The average homicide rate in European nations from 1979 to 2010 was 3.8 per 100,000 residents, compared to 4.2 in Asian nations, 8.1 in North American nations, and 12.9 in South American nations. The homicide rates in Latin America are comparatively high and increasing in recent years. And while the rates in the United States have been declining, the rate is still higher than in comparable Western nations. It is clear that homicide rates in some nations are unacceptably high relative to other nations. SNA may be a particularly effective tool for gaining insight into homicide problems in places with high homicide rates and helping to develop strategies for reducing the severity of the problem.

The Handbook of Homicide, First Edition. Edited by Fiona Brookman,
Edward R. Maguire, and Mike Maguire.

This chapter reviews the literature on social network analysis and crime, specifically violent crime in the United States. Recent research on social network analysis and homicide offers insights into the nature of violence, and how it might spread, that can inform the development of focused intervention and prevention strategies. Second, this chapter shows how SNA is being used in one city (Kansas City, Missouri, United States) to guide the development and execution of a focused violence reduction strategy.

SNA as a Tool for Understanding the Context of Society

The individual units within social networks are interdependent. Human relationships, for example, transform clusters of individuals into communities and provide the context through which their activities take place (Coleman 1988; McPherson, Smith-Lovin, and Brashears 2006). Social network analysis is a process for mapping relationships and interconnections whether between individuals, neighborhoods, institutions, countries, or any other entities that have been organized, intentionally or otherwise.

Examples of two different social network maps, also called sociograms, can be found in Figure 35.1 and 35.2 below. Figure 35.1 displays a sociogram of individuals (dots) connected through police contact (lines). Figure 35.2 shows a sociogram of gangs (dots) connected through either an alliance (thin line) or conflict (dark line) between the groups as determined by the police. In both situations, the relationships are graphically displayed so that social distance corresponds to the distance between two dots on a page. Sociograms can be created to display relationships whether they are between individuals, groups, organizations, crimes, or any other unit of analysis.

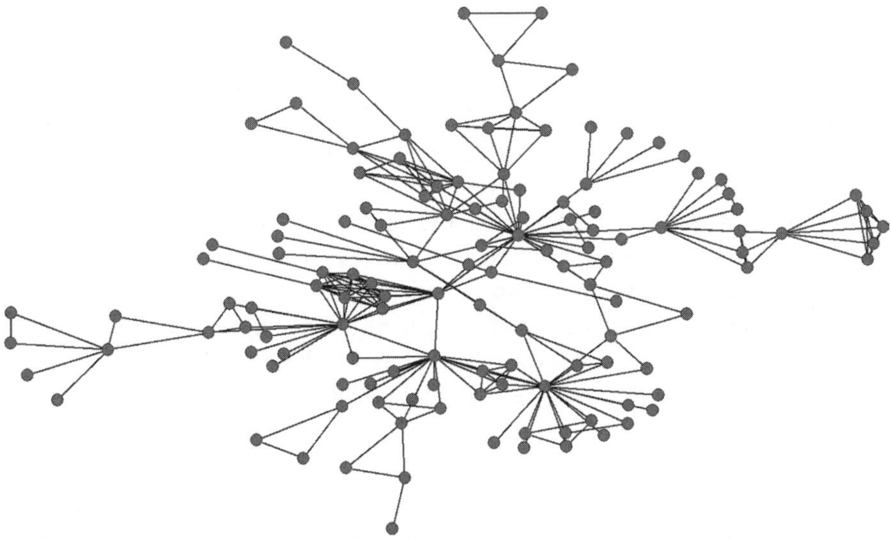

Figure 35.1 Social network of individuals liked through police contact.

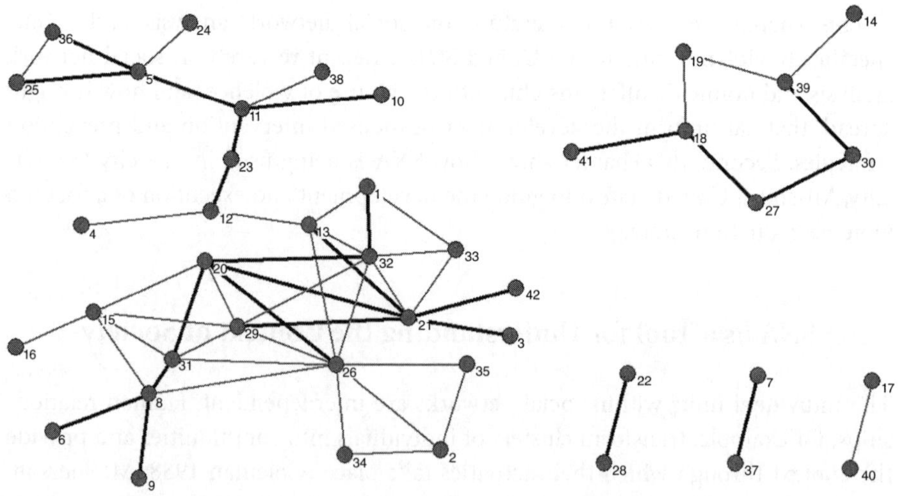

Figure 35.2 Social network of groups based on conflicts and alliances.

With social network analysis, researchers can identify relationships and assess the social positions of individual persons within any given network. One's social network strongly influences one's life. For example, it determines opportunities and access to social capital (Granovetter 1973), and it sets behavioral parameters. Social network analysis has been described as a tool for connecting microlevel interactions with macrolevel patterns, as well as for identifying relational ties and illustrating the strength (or weakness) of those ties (Granovetter 1973). The strength of ties between individuals can have serious implications. Having too many strong ties will limit one's reach (that is, maintaining strong ties absorb one's time); having more weak ties, if not redundant, allows greater social reach. To understand a particular social network, researchers examine its system of relationships and how it both constrains and permits behaviors.

Data used in mapping social networks may be drawn from various sources, including official police data, field observations, self-report surveys, and other documented lists of social participation (e.g., meeting attendance, clubs). The ultimate quality and usefulness of social network analysis relies on the completeness and quality of that data. Given quality input, the resulting graphic representation of any social structure allows researchers and practitioners to visually understand it, the individuals and relationships within it, and the nature of their connections. For mapping purposes, the people, groups, or other units being studied are viewed as a set of *nodes*, connected by the social relationships that have developed among them; the nodes with their connections represent a social network (Krohn 1986). The patterns of relations that link one node to multiple others can then be analyzed to learn how the network grants opportunities and/or constrains access to monetary, status, and informational social resources that, in turn, guide behaviors (Wellman 1983).

With this process, social network analysis has redefined both the units of analysis and the empirical importance of the web of relationships that reveals each member's peer associations and social position. We find our places in society by the relationships we maintain (Granovetter 1973; Marsden 1987). Discovering and comprehending the relationships that bind us is key to understanding how our multilayered society functions. SNA diagrams and analyzes how our relational ties form the context of society.

Thus, one can begin to see how associations shape society. A system of societal relationships will influence the kind of people its members become and the behaviors that follow as well as how those members influence and affect others with whom they interact. In short, social network analysis is a lens through which to watch how networks of individuals are influenced by and impact society generally and, of most interest to law enforcement and criminal justice professionals, how networks shape criminal behaviors specifically. Focused on that subset of the wider social structure—that is, those networks most associated with violence and other crimes—SNA advances our understanding of criminal behavior and of the nature of violent crime.

SNA's Contribution to Understanding Violent Crime

SNA has been increasing our understanding of gangs and crime since the 1960s (Klein and Crawford 1967). Recent methodological advances have led to further empirical findings, such as the probability that social networks are related to violent behavior and one's vulnerability to becoming a victim of violence (Papachristos and Wildeman 2014; Papachristos, Wildeman, and Roberto 2014). Much has been learned about the geographic and social concentration of homicides. At the macrolevel, research has shown that homicides are more likely to occur in places with socioeconomic disadvantage, higher rates of gang membership, high population density, and population heterogeneity (Pyrooz 2011; Land, McCall, and Cohen 1990; Rosenfeld, Bray, and Egley 1999). Research also suggests that gangs are one of the major facilitators of violence in cities across the United States (Decker and Curry 2002; Decker and Pyrooz 2010). A recent assessment of gang literature suggested that social network analysis is further enhancing our understanding of gang processes related to violence (Decker, Melde, and Pyrooz 2013). Researchers and practitioners need to know more about how social network analysis can refine that understanding and lead to effective strategies for disrupting of homicide networks. Researchers have established that inner-city violence is likely to be gang related, driven by the "street code," where perceived disrespect, even if it is slight, is met with violence (Anderson 1999; Decker and Pyrooz 2010; Decker 1996; Pyrooz 2011). Clearly, violence takes place within the context of social interaction. The application of social network analysis to understanding homicide patterns has revealed the concentrated nature of violence, specifically homicides (Papachristos and Wildeman 2014; Papachristos, Wildeman, and Roberto 2014; Papachristos, Braga, and Hureau 2012). Social network analysis, building on previous findings, has advanced the literature by showing how violence can spread through social networks like a contagious disease (see Chapter 34, this volume).

For some time, social network analysis has been benefiting the wider field of criminology and criminal justice theoretically and methodologically. Criminologists are concerned with how individuals learn criminal behaviors and how they internalize and pass on the related values. Research using SNA has shown the ways in which peers influence one another within their friendship networks to form delinquent groups (Haynie 2002; Haynie and Osgood 2005; Payne and Cornwell 2007; Warr 1993, 2002; Steglich, Snijders, and Pearson 2010; Haynie 2001). Individuals' social networks have been found to provide access to criminal capital, to distribute information about other individuals' reputations for trustworthiness, and to allow for contact with potential criminal cooperators (McCarthy, Hagan, and Cohen 1998). In a study of African American boys, individuals who were social bridges (i.e., those who connect otherwise disconnected clusters of people) between two or more large yet cohesive peer groups were found to be considerably less delinquent than their counterparts who were members of a single peer group (Mangino 2009). Individuals who were social bridges between groups gained access to social capital due to their open peer network in which opportunities were provided (Mangino 2009). Even one's position in a social network can further provide or constrain the type of experience one will have among other members.

Haynie (2001) found that in order to understand the impact of peer influence, fundamental structural properties of friendship networks must be considered. Adolescent delinquency has been connected with spending significant amounts of unstructured time with friends and with having delinquent friends (Haynie and Osgood 2005). Network density[1] was found to be related to delinquency where cohesive networks contained stronger delinquent peer associations than did less cohesive networks (Haynie 2001). Furthermore, the proportion of delinquent friends within an individual's network was strongly connected to the individual's subsequent involvement in delinquency (Haynie 2002).

The nature of the delinquent peer relations also matters. Weerman and Smeenk (2005) found few or no major differences between best friends and regular friends with regard to peer similarity in delinquency, while less intimate relationships actually had a stronger association with peer delinquency. Other research suggests that the balance of delinquency within one's network might explain one's own involvement in delinquency (Mcgloin 2009). The ability to grasp the nature of the peer delinquency association helps to understand peer influence on network members better. SNA can be used to understand the significance of members' social distance from one another and even the implications that such a distance can have for health-related factors.

SNA has been used to assess the importance of social distance within a network for predicting the likelihood of gunshot injury and substance abuse (Ennett *et al.* 2006; Papachristos, Braga, and Hureau 2012). Analyzing records documenting fatal and nonfatal gunshot injuries, Papachristos, Braga, and Hureau (2012) found the likelihood of gunshot victimization to be associated with an individual's network distance to other gunshot victims. The odds of becoming a gunshot victim were reduced by 25 percent for every network connection, or "handshake," away from another gunshot victim that one is (Papachristos, Braga, and Hureau 2012). Ennett *et al.* (2006) used SNA similarly to look at different domains of social networks, such as the social status, social proximity, and social embeddedness of substance users in three public schools. They found that compared with their counterparts, adolescents had higher probabilities of substance use if they were less embedded in their social network, but had greater status and closer social proximity to peers who reported substance use. The closer the social distance to a substance user, the more likely an individual would be also to use substances. Such findings exemplify the need to better understand the nature of high-risk social networks and their implications.

SNA and homicide

More recently, the SNA framework has been used to better understand the nature of homicide. Elevated levels of violence among gang members are well documented (Thornberry *et al.* 1993; Battin *et al.* 1998; Papachristos 2009). SNA is useful for understanding the street gang, but also for understanding the violent encounters between their members and between gangs (Decker 1996; Decker and Curry 2002).

Preventable losses of human life are cause for concern. The high rate of homicides concentrated in small populations, specifically among street gang members, indicates a much larger social problem (Decker and Pyrooz 2010). The high proportion of homicides that are from the deaths of gang members adds to the overall US homicide rate. Criminologists use SNA to understand the dynamics of gun violence, how shootings become part of normative social processes, and how gunshot victimizations and murder networks exhibit patterns among the connected members (Decker and Curry 2002; Decker 1996; Papachristos and Wildeman 2014; Papachristos, Braga, and Hureau 2012).

Gang homicides in US urban areas account for a considerable portion of the overall homicide numbers. During the five-year period from 2002 through 2006 in the 100 largest US cities, they averaged around 1,500 per year (Decker and Pyrooz 2010), approximately 25 percent of all homicides in those cities, raising awareness that only a small population of society is contributing to violent crime. Evidence also shows that even a slight neighborhood street gang presence can be associated with about three times more homicides per square kilometer than occur in neighborhoods without a gang presence (Decker and Pyrooz 2010: 134). The proportion of homicides attributable to street gangs merits considerable investigation into the makeup of those networks and what makes them so purposefully violent.

Gang members most often kill other gang members (Decker and Curry 2002), as the intersection of power and respect, economic gain, and conflict between races and ethnicities fuels street gang violence (Decker 1996; Decker and Curry 2002). Gangs are groups of individuals who compete for dominance, responding to threats to social status and demonstrating solidarity within the group to (re)establish status, while trying to minimize future victimizations (Papachristos 2009). The gang mentality is formulated by the very things that allow their structures to be maintained, such as the search for dominance and reputation and the use of reciprocity in retaliation.

Street gangs typically operate in disadvantaged areas (Pyrooz, Fox, and Decker 2010) where social status, authority, and rules are not as clearly defined as they are in established organizations or socially organized places (Browning, Dietz, and Feinberg 2004; Stewart and Simons 2010). Hierarchical relations, such as police and citizen, or employer and employee, have explicit, socially understood rules of engagement and authority. When social hierarchies are not defined, disputes and use of violence in pursuit of claims of dominance over another socially equitable individual are more likely (Papachristos 2009; Kubrin and Weitzer 2003). Violence being the accepted way to make a statement about who is most powerful means that a continuous cycle of reciprocity and retaliation revolves between groups.

Between gangs, reciprocal violence fulfills the expectation that once a violent act is perpetrated on another group, that violent act will be reciprocated in order to maintain social standing or honor among the other groups (Papachristos 2009; Decker 1996; Papachristos, Hureau, and Braga 2013). In order to uphold that honor, the offended party must be able to retaliate and protect the individuals within the group. Reciprocal retaliation between gangs creates a culture that embeds conflict into the structure of the gang (Papachristos 2009). The violent culture of the gang tends toward the self-destruction of the individuals within and the murder of individuals of rival gangs who choose to uphold their own honor (Decker and Curry 2002).

Street gang members typically are not out looking for random members of society to kill. The dynamics of the street gang culture creates a network conducive to the murder of other gang members for reasons that adhere to the status of the gang and the organization of the street code. Excessive use of gun violence and retaliation removes weakness from the gang and maintains its vitality over time (Papachristos 2009; Papachristos, Braga, and Hureau 2012). Understanding how and why gang-related homicides occur provides a framework within which to gain additional insight into the gang membership dynamics and the pressures and expectations that each member faces that can lead to the demise of other gang members. Those social patterns can be explained and predicted.

Understanding homicide patterns Patterns of murder between gangs persist despite membership turnover (Papachristos 2009). Social network analysis can give insight into how such murderous networks are created, the probability of one becoming a gunshot victim, or the pattern of murders within a given network; thus, violence can be better predicted and prevented.

Murder networks are created through the acceptance and spread of violence between the disputants (Papachristos 2009: 81). The consequences of violence involve further conflict and interaction between disputants and rivalries that sustain the murderous network (Papachristos, Hureau, and Braga 2013). Street gangs are involved in activities that generate conflict, such as dealing drugs, fighting, partying, and just hanging out (Decker 1996; Decker and Curry 2002). Individually, members work to meet the ideals of toughness and "being a man," including a propensity to fight, to maintain their status. As a group, collective status is directly associated with the ability to handle perceived threats from other groups or individuals (Jacobs 2004; Anderson 1999). SNA allows researchers and practitioners to identify patterns of gunshot victimization visually—literally "to see" the creation and development of murderous networks.

As with murders, most gunshot victimizations do not involve random strangers. In Boston, researchers used SNA to examine whether one's social network could predict one risk of gunshot victimization (Papachristos, Braga, and Hureau 2012). A community at high risk for crime and violence was selected for the study, using Boston Police Department's Field Intelligence Observations (FIOs) of nonfatal and fatal gunshot injuries.[2] When two or more individuals were observed together under any circumstances, that was considered a tie. Then combining FIO data and nonfatal and fatal gunshot injuries records, researchers determined which individuals were gunshot victims. The analysis showed that the majority of the individuals identified were members of the larger social network, and that on average each was about five "handshakes" away from a gunshot victim (Papachristos, Braga, and Hureau 2012). The finding that the closer an individual is to a gunshot victim, the higher the risk of that individual also becoming a victim has been consistent both in Chicago and Boston (Papachristos and Wildeman 2014; Papachristos, Wildeman, and Roberto 2014).

Patterns of gang violence and homicide persist over time, even with membership turnover. SNA reveals those patterns. For instance, Papachristos (2009) reviewed all homicide records in Chicago from 1994 to 2002 involving identified gang member victims and offenders. Each homicide was coded to construct a social network for the gang affiliation of the victims and offenders. Data collected from geographic maps of Chicago police beats were used to determine the gang size, the extent to which any two gangs' turfs overlapped, and how many pieces of turf a gang controlled. Mapping the social structure around the gang homicides, the researcher used SNA to determine its basic properties, its patterns, and its stability. The findings suggested that patterns found in the murderous exchanges were relatively stable, even as individual gang membership turned over. The gang murders had constructed a lasting culture or social structure of violence from their continuous disputes and the social contagion of those exchanges.

As we have seen, the patterns of inner-city violence persist over time, with the same groups and neighborhoods continuing to shoot and retaliate, despite membership turnover. Thus, the spread of violence is deeply embedded in the social structure of certain communities, and being socially connected to a victim of violence increases one's own chance of becoming a victim. Intervening to prevent such homicides requires that we reveal and understand the social networks in which violence is concentrated, before they occur.

Using SNA to respond to and prevent violence

Social network analysis has been used by several police departments (Mcgloin 2005; Goga, Salcedo-Albaran, and Goredema 2014), and the literature provides examples of law enforcement–academic partnerships that have involved the use of SNA to guide police strategies (Mcgloin 2005; Morselli 2010; John and Maquire 2007). In Kansas City, Missouri, SNA is institutionalized and routinely used to understand and respond to violent crimes, specifically homicides.

Institutionalizing SNA In 2012, the Kansas City, Missouri Police Department (KCMO PD) and the University of Missouri–Kansas City (UMKC) extended their partnership to increase the police department's capacity for problem-oriented policing with the addition of social network analysis. The department is comprised of roughly 1,400 sworn and 700 civilians who serve a daytime population of nearly one million individuals, including about 450,000 actual residents, in an area that extends over 829 square kilometers (320 square miles).

In early 2012, a group of policymakers pursued an innovative strategy to stop the spread of violent crime in the city. The group had become aware of a problem-oriented policing strategy known as *focused deterrence*, widely recognized for lowering violent crime rates in other large cities (see Chapter 36, this volume; Braga and Weisburd 2012). The initial working group appointed a governing board to assume leadership and decision-making authority. One of the key tenets of focused deterrence is the identification of gangs and other groups that are connected to violence, along with their associated members.

The idea is to focus narrowly and intensively on those few groups of individuals who have been associated, directly and sometimes indirectly, with the crimes most detrimental to the community—that is, to identify the social networks within which violent crime is being perpetrated. The effectiveness of a focused deterrence initiative depends in large part upon how quickly law enforcement can locate offenders. The ideal sources of the kind of intelligence most needed for this are those officers who confront violent offenders day after day. They offer the most complete and up-to-date data available; that can then be analyzed to identify the social networks of individuals who are most violence-prone. Focused deterrence initiatives commonly use techniques such as group audits and social network analysis for that purpose (Engel, Tillyer, and Corsaro 2013).

Although focused deterrence is comprised of several elements, we focus here on the incorporation and institutionalization of social network analysis into violent crime prevention and intervention—using law enforcement data to produce actionable intelligence to intervene in homicide-prone social networks. In early 2013, a UMKC faculty member trained two full-time crime analysts to conduct social network analysis. The analysts were shown the methodology for building social networks using law enforcement data such as arrest records and field interview forms. The analysts learned the implications of reaching back several years and expanding

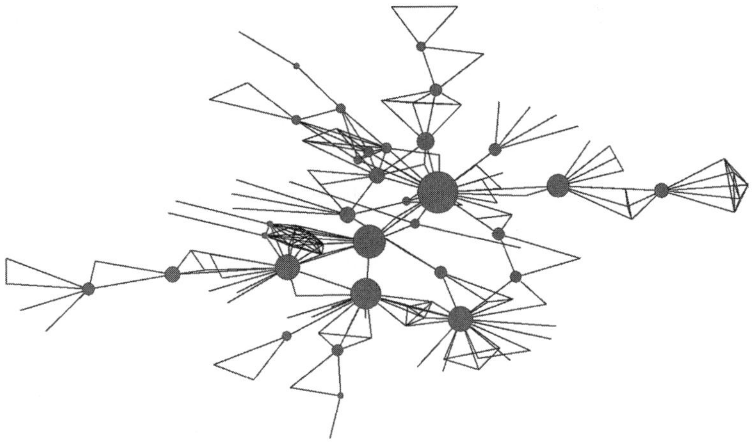

Figure 35.3 Social network of individuals, node sized based on betweenness centrality.

a network outward by one, two, or more steps. Additionally, the analysts recognized the value and learned the techniques of layering descriptive information, such as whether or not a person of interest had an outstanding warrant or was on probation or parole. Finally, the analysts were taught to determine a person's centrality to the network. Each individual in a social network occupies a unique position, and those positions differ in significant ways. In particular, some are more central than others (Morselli 2010), and therefore potentially more influential. Two KCMO PD crime analysts can now calculate *degree* and *betweenness centrality*[3] (see Figure 35.3) for every person in a criminal social network. Focusing scarce law enforcement resources on those who have high centrality gives law enforcement the best chance of disrupting criminal networks. This training had the added benefit of supporting the sustainability of the innovation; it has increased the police department's capacity to conduct actionable analyses that focus on violent crime prevention.

Integrating SNA into police responses can raise new issues for law enforcement practitioners, some of them requiring changes in longstanding practices and attitudes. SNA may require coordination among individuals and investigations that had not previously been associated. It also requires a deeper understanding of analytic reports. For example, showing up in a social network does not automatically make someone a person of interest; the network suggests a social tie, but not necessarily a criminal tie—an individual could also be a pastor, a mother, or even a loss prevention officer who showed up on a field interview form in the course of work. A social network is a place to start, a multidimensional map of the social world with which the officer is about to engage. As social networks are constructed from the data, one's preconceptions about that network will need to give way to take in what they reveal; for instance, the world of violent crime becomes much smaller than many expect. Finally, as social networks are built, departments and units across the agency will need to work together in new ways as more cases are shown to be closely connected.

The increase in relevant intelligence gathered from street-level officers is one significant indicator of the impact that SNA sociograms are having in Kansas City. Because paperwork consumes a great deal of an officer's time, the quality of the information captured in that paperwork suffers if the officer does not see its benefit. KCMO PD has begun educating officers on social network analysis, drawing the connection between the information they record on field interview forms and the quality of the sociograms of high-risk individuals and other intelligence products they receive; since then, the number of field interview forms completed has increased significantly. From July 1, 2013 to June 30, 2013, officers had completed about 3,880 field interview forms. A year later, from July 1, 2013 to June 30, 2014, they had completed about 5,258 field interview forms—an increase of over 35 percent. Creating this feedback loop with the knowledge and participation of patrol officers facilitates street-level buy-in and creates better intelligence and, as a result, more efficient policing and crime prevention.

Further, that increase in data quality gives patrol officers and detectives a social map for locating offenders and their associates. With that map, officers can more readily target those who are causing problems. Social network analysis has potential to save lives. The number of homicides in Kansas City at the end of 2014 was encouragingly low, down by about 30 percent from the previous four years. An outcome evaluation of Kansas City's focused deterrence project has not been completed as of this writing, but the increase in field interview form completion is evidence that routinely incorporating social network analysis is increasing work productivity and data quality; there are now fewer missing ties. With consistent data collection, law enforcement will have a valid and more complete social network; working with that, they can design prevention and enforcement strategies with greater precision and effectiveness.

Outcomes to date suggest that finding ways to overcome the inevitable obstacles to institutional change will be well worth the effort. This type of research and analysis can easily be incorporated by other agencies. Getting started in Kansas City was facilitated when KCMO PD analysts learned that they did not have to purchase additional software or bootstrap the learning process; up front, they were offered free software and network theory training. Having a social network analyst on board will help police departments connect information about groups, individuals, guns, and crimes in ways that agencies were unable to do in the past. The art in investigation lies in making connections that were previously unrecognized. Social network analysis helps with that process.

Responding to homicide using SNA Research has shown that more attention should be focused on criminal groups and the relationships between those groups (Mcgloin 2005, 2007). By network mapping groups of individuals—specifically those who have been found to be criminally involved—law enforcement, social service providers, and others can respond more efficiently when crimes occur. Imagine, for example, a world in which a homicide victim's name, associations, and other important information are available immediately after the homicide is discovered. Detectives would be able to quickly access social network information and integrate that into their investigation, instead of knocking on doors, hoping to glean enough random information to piece together an idea of who might have been involved and why. With SNA, they could analyze what was most likely to have happened in time to prevent retaliatory violence.

Social networks have been one of the key intelligence products of the focused deterrence project in Kansas City during its implementation in 2013 and 2014, and now the use of social network analysis has expanded to other areas. Over the past year, sociograms have been built for every known homicide victim and suspect. Understanding the social structure surrounding a homicide allows investigators to better understand its dynamics and to proceed accordingly. Sociograms are being built at the request of patrol officers when they need to become more knowledgeable about a group of individuals who are causing problems in an area; most are constructed within a few hours.

In Kansas City, the police department builds networks beginning with the suspect and victim, then adding associates two steps out.[4] The ultimate effect of this is yet to be seen, but giving the investigator a picture of even the closer social structure within which a crime has occurred will likely accelerate the process of solving it. It is not unheard of for the perpetrator to be in the victim's network; we know that homicides are likely to involve someone the victim knows (Gruenewald and Pridemore 2009).

Application of SNA to homicide prevention

Social network analysis provides practitioners with a more complete and precise knowledge of the identities of and dynamics among organized groups that are associated with violent incidents. The same holds true for loosely organized and even entirely informal social networks, the very existence of which may only be recognized through social network analysis. These are social structures that nurture and perpetuate violence; violent individuals initially operate from them and they tend to return to them after conviction and incarceration. One effective prevention strategy is to disrupt or destabilize those structures. As Papachristos and Wildeman explain:

> network analysis can guide immediate homicide reduction efforts by identifying specific points of intervention involved in crime epidemics. By mapping the terrain within high-risk social networks and analyzing shooting patterns, network analysis offers a more direct road map for intervention (2014: 149).

This leads to the realization that, rather than focusing only on individuals directly associated with a crime (suspects), practitioners should consider focusing on the group with which the suspect is associated (Braga and Weisburd 2011). Offenders tend to return to the social networks from which they were removed; thus, crime reduction strategies should consider the entire network, as well as the position of the offender within the network, as a part of re-entry planning. Although researchers frequently have discussed the role of those communities and neighborhoods to which offenders return (Clear 2007), they rarely have discussed the role of the offender's social network in re-entry. This is true even though the social network is likely to be the "community" with the greatest influence on the offender's future opportunities and behaviors.

With accurate, current data, law enforcement, and social service agencies can strategize more effective ways to disrupt violence-prone social networks. Of course, SNA will improve the targeting of suppression and intervention strategies, but disruption is an effective prevention tactic, as well. Law enforcement agencies could build and update social networks, identifying and monitoring violent individuals who are present in the network from year to year. We know that long-term members provide stability to social network and, as we have learned from the neighborhood literature, stability can translate into organization (Sampson and Groves 1989). The same kind of organization that is good for a community can also be good for making gangs more efficient as criminal enterprises (Browning, Dietz, and Feinberg 2004). Strategic interventions that contribute to high turnover in such groups should help prevent them from becoming well organized.

Social network analysis can inform structured violence prevention projects, such as Cure Violence, and focused deterrence. To date, many jurisdictions have used some form of social network analysis to identify violent groups while implementing focused deterrence projects (Engel, Tillyer, and Corsaro 2013). Expanding the use of SNA could be a cornerstone of those efforts as we refine both prevention and intervention strategies.

Future Research: SNA and Homicide

Social network analysis is already contributing to our understanding of the nature of homicide, especially inner-city homicide in the United States. Violence spreads through social networks. SNA has much more to offer in terms of understanding concentrations of violence and thus the prevention of further violence. We need additional research on this topic. Network validation studies and post hoc homicide network studies would help researchers and practitioners alike. Since most research on SNA and homicide uses police data (Papachristos and Wildeman 2014; Papachristos, Wildeman, and Roberto 2014), more research is needed on the validity of those networks (Berlusconi 2013). How closely do networks constructed from police data capture the social reality? Such studies can be conducted by combining official police data with qualitative or survey data. We need to know more about the strengths and weaknesses of network data in order to improve the quality of that data.

Second, SNA research on homicides can help us better understand homicides where the victim and suspect are known. A social network can be built, after the fact, to see whether the victim and suspect were in the same network and whether, using SNA to predict and recognize early accelerations of violence, we could have known this before the homicide occurred. This would allow researchers to examine network relationships between victim and offender beyond the conventional dichotomy of the offender being known or unknown to the victim. If we knew the percentage of time that an offender was in the victim's social network (and the most efficient network specifications), for example, updated investigative strategies could be employed immediately after a homicide, even before a suspect has been identified.

Third, SNA gives researchers an additional technique to compare groups from different countries and across different crime problems (Pyrooz *et al.* 2012). The discussion above focused mainly on the United States, however, we should begin constructing and comparing networks across contexts. For example, how do gang networks in the United States compare to those in Western Europe? And how are organized crime networks in Latin America similar or different from terrorist networks? SNA should be used to help researchers and practitioners better understand the organization of crime problems across the world and how interventions impact these networks.

Finally, researchers need to understand how violent crime networks evolve. Research in Chicago has shown the stability of violence in gang-level networks (Papachristos 2009); that research should be extended to the individual level and tracked over time. We must discover how the social processes of violent crime networks differ from and are similar to the social processes of prosocial networks. Researchers have just started to realize the possibilities for SNA to shed light on violent crime. For now, we can predict who has the highest probability of becoming a homicide victim before it happens. We can and should use that information to save lives.

Notes

1 Network density is the level to which individuals in a social network are directly connected (friends). Observed ties are compared with the number of possible ties in the group. Within a dense friendship network, each individual would be a friend to every other individual.

2 Used alone, FIO data can result in narrow measurement of social networks, because police rarely would have observed all of an individual's friends and associates.

3 *Degree centrality* is the direct number of ties, regardless of type, that each individual in the social network has that can be used to measure that individual's popularity or prominence in the group. Persons having more ties would seem to be more prominent or more involved, even if those ties are not necessarily positive. *Betweenness centrality* refers to the strategic position held by an individual from which they can act as facilitators for indirect connections throughout the network. Such an individual may have fewer direct contacts, but could facilitate contacts among other network members. This works effectively to keep the entire network connected. Such individuals may be less directly tied to the other members, but are positioned to hold a great deal of power and influence.

4 The core of a network, or the group of people we start with, are considered step 0. Individuals who are connected to those in step 0 are considered step 1. Individuals connected to those in step 1, but were not in step 0, are considered step 2, and so on.

References

Anderson, E. (1999) *Code of the Street: Decency, Violence, and the Moral Life in the Inner City* (reprint edn). New York: W.W. Norton.

Battin, S.R., Hill, K.G., Abbott, R.D., *et al.* (1998) The contribution of gang membership to delinquency beyond delinquent friends. *Criminology*, 36(1): 93–116.

Berlusconi, G. (2013) Do all the pieces matter? Assessing the reliability of law enforcement data sources for the network analysis of wire taps. *Global Crime*, 14(1): 61–81.

Braga, A.A. and Weisburd, D.L. (2011) The effects of focused deterrence strategies on crime: A systematic review and meta-analysis of the empirical evidence. *Journal of Research in Crime and Delinquency*, 49(3): 323–358.

Braga, A.A. and Weisburd, D.L. (2012) The effects of "pulling levers" focused deterrence strategies on crime. *Campbell Systematic Reviews*, 6(April): 91.

Browning, C.R., Dietz, R.D., and Feinberg, S.L. (2004) The paradox of social organization: Networks, collective efficacy, and violent crime in urban neighborhoods. *Social Forces*, 83(2): 503–534.

Clear, T.R. (2007) *Imprisoning Communities: How Mass Incarceration Makes Disadvantaged Neighborhoods Worse*. Oxford: Oxford University Press.

Coleman, J.S. (1988) Social capital in the creation of human capital. *American Journal of Sociology*, 94: S95–S120.

Decker, S.H. (1996) Collective and normative features of gang violence. *Justice Quarterly*, 13: 243–264.

Decker, S.H. and Curry, G.D. (2002) Gangs, gang homicides, and gang loyalty: Organized Crimes or disorganized criminals. *Journal of Criminal Justice*, 30: 343–352.

Decker, S.H., Melde, C., and Pyrooz, D.C. (2013) What do we know about gangs and gang members and where do we go from here? *Justice Quarterly*, 30(3): 369–402.

Decker, S.H. and Pyrooz, D.C. (2010) Gang violence worldwide: Context, culture and country. In Graduate Institute of International and Development Studies, *Small Arms Survey 2010* (pp. 129–155). Cambridge: Cambridge University Press.

Engel, R.S., Tillyer, M.S., and Corsaro, N. (2013) Reducing gang violence using focused deterrence: Evaluating the Cincinnati Initiative to Reduce Violence (CIRV). *Justice Quarterly*, 30(3): 403–439.

Ennett, S.T., Bauman, K.E., Hussong, A., *et al.* (2006) The peer context of adolescent substance use: Findings from social network analysis. *Journal of Research on Adolescence*, 16(2): 159–186.

Goga, K., Salcedo-Albaran, E., and Goredema, C. (2014) A network of violence: Mapping a criminal gang network in Cape Town. *Institute for Security Studies Papers*, 271(November).

Granovetter, M.S. (1973) The strength of weak ties. *American Journal of Sociology*, 78(6): 1360–1380.

Gruenewald, J.A. and Pridemore, W.A. (2009) Stability and change in homicide victim, offender, and event characteristics in Chicago, 1900 and 2000. *Homicide Studies*, 13(4): 355–384. doi: 10.1177/1088767909348587.

Haynie, D.L. (2001) Delinquent peers revisited: Does network structure matter? *American Journal of Sociology*, 106(4): 1013–1057.

Haynie, D.L. (2002) Friendship networks and delinquency: The relative nature of peer delinquency. *Journal of Quantitative Criminology*, 18(2): 99–133.

Haynie, D.L. and Osgood, D.W. (2005) Reconsidering peers and delinquency: How do peers matter? *Social Forces*, 84(2): 1109–1130.

Jacobs, B.A. (2004) A typology of street criminal retaliation. *Journal of Research in Crime and Delinquency*, 41(3): 295–323.

John, T. and Maquire, M. (2007) Criminal intelligence and the national intelligence model. In T. Newburn, T. Williamson, and A. Wright (eds) *Handbook of Criminal Investigation* (pp. 199–225). Cullompton, UK: Willan.

Klein, M.W. and Crawford, L.Y. (1967) Groups, gangs, and cohesiveness. *Journal of Research in Crime and Delinquency*, 4(1): 63–75.

Krohn, M.D. (1986) The web of conformity: A network approach to the explanation of delinquent behavior. *Social Problems*, 33(6): S81–S93.

Kubrin, C.E. and Weitzer, R. (2003) Retaliatory homicide: Concentrated disadvantage and neighborhood culture. *Social Problems*, 50(2): 157–180.

Land, K.C., McCall, P.L., and Cohen, L.E. (1990) Structural covariates of homicide rates: Are there any invariances across time and social space? *American Journal of Sociology*, 95(4): 922–963.

Mangino, W. (2009) The downside of social closure: Brokerage, parental influence, and delinquency among African American boys. *Sociology of Education*, 82(2): 147–172.

Marsden, P.V. (1987) Core discussion networks of Americans. *American Sociological Review*, 52(1): 122–131.

McCarthy, B., Hagan, J., and Cohen, L.E. (1998) Uncertainty, cooperation, and crime: Understanding the decision to co-offend. *Social Forces*, 77(1): 155–184.

Mcgloin, J.M. (2005) *Street Gangs and Interventions: Innovative Problem Solving with Network Analysis*. Washington, DC: US Department of Justice, Office of Community Oriented Policing Services.

Mcgloin, J.M. (2007) The continued relevance of gang membership. *Criminology & Public Policy*, 6(2): 231–240.

Mcgloin, J.M. (2009) Delinquency balance: Revisiting peer influence. *Criminology*, 47(2): 439–477.

McPherson, M., Smith-Lovin, L., and Brashears, M.E. (2006) Social isolation in America: Changes in core discussion networks over two decades. *American Sociological Review*, 1: 353–375.

Morselli, C. (2010) Assessing vulnerable and strategic positions in a criminal network. *Journal of Contemporary Criminal Justice*, 26(4): 382–392.

Papachristos, A.V. (2009) Murder by structure: Dominance relations and the social structure of gang homicide. *American Journal of Sociology*, 115(1): 74–128.

Papachristos, A.V., Braga, A.A., and Hureau, D.M. (2012) Social networks and the risk of gunshot injury. *Journal of Urban Health: Bulletin of the New York Academy of Medicine*, 89(6): 992–1003.

Papachristos, A.V., Hureau, D.M., and Braga, A.A. (2013) The corner and the crew: The influence of geography and social networks on gang violence. *American Sociological Review*, 78(3): 417–447.

Papachristos, A.V. and Wildeman, C. (2014) Network exposure and homicide victimization in an African American community. *American Journal of Public Health*, 104: 143–150.

Papachristos, A.V., Wildeman, C., and Roberto, E. (2014) Tragic, but not random: The social contagion of nonfatal gunshot injuries. *Social Science & Medicine*, 125: 139–150.

Payne, D.C. and Cornwell, B. (2007) Reconsidering peer influences on delinquency: Do less proximate contacts matter? *Journal of Quantitative Criminology*, 23(2): 127–149.

Pyrooz, D.C. (2011) Structural covariates of gang homicide in large US cities. *Journal of Research in Crime and Delinquency*, 49(4): 489–518.

Pyrooz, D.C., Fox, A.M., and Decker, S.H. (2010) Racial and ethnic heterogeneity, economic disadvantage, and gangs: A macro-level study of gang membership in urban America. *Justice Quarterly*, 27(6): 867–892.

Pyrooz, D.C., Fox, A.M., Katz, C.M., and Decker, S. (2012) Gang organization, offending and victimization: A cross national analysis. In F.-A. Esbensen and C. Maxson (eds), *Youth Gangs in International Perspective* (pp. 85–106). New York: Springer.

Rosenfeld, R., Bray, T.M., and Egley, A. (1999) Facilitating violence: A comparison of non-gang youth homicides. *Journal of Quantitative Criminology*, 15: 495–517.

Sampson, R.J. and Groves, W.B. (1989) Community structure and crime: Testing social-disorganization theory. *American Journal of Sociology*, 94(4): 774–802.

Steglich, C., Snijders, T.A.B., and Pearson, M. (2010) Dynamic networks and behavior: Separating selection from influence. *Sociological Methodology*, 40(1): 329–393.

Stewart, E.A. and Simons, R.L. (2010) Race, code of the street, and violent delinquency: A multilevel investigation of neighborhood street culture and individual norms of violence. *Criminology*, 48: 569–605.

Thornberry, T.P., Krohn, M.D., Lizotte, A.J., and Chard-Wierschem, D. (1993) The role of juvenile gangs in facilitating delinquent behavior. *Journal of Research in Crime and Delinquency*, 30(1): 55–87.

Warr, M. (1993) Age, peers, and delinquency. *Criminology*, 31(1): 17–40.

Warr, M. (2002) *Companions in Crime*. Cambridge: Cambridge University Press.

Weerman, F.M. and Smeenk, W.H. (2005) Peer similarity in delinquency for different types of friends: A comparison using two measurement methods. *Criminology*, 43: 499–524.

Wellman, B. (1983) Network analysis: Some basic principles. *Sociological Theory*, 1: 155–200.

36

Focused Deterrence and the Reduction of Gang Homicide

Anthony A. Braga

Introduction

Street gangs represent a persistent threat to public safety. Conflicts between street gangs have long been noted to fuel much of the violence in US cities. City-level studies have found gang-related motives generate large shares of homicides in Chicago (Block and Block 1993), Los Angeles (Tita, Riley, and Greenwood 2003), and Boston (Kennedy, Piehl, and Braga 1996). Moreover, relative to non-gang delinquent youth offending patterns, youth involvement in gangs leads to elevated levels of criminal behavior, especially violent offending (Thornberry *et al.* 2003). Dealing with gangs and gang-related violence is a challenge for most cities in the United States. In 2011, there were an estimated 29,900 gangs and 782,500 gang members throughout 3,300 jurisdictions with gang problems (Egley and Howell 2013). While this chapter focuses on new developments in US gang homicide reduction efforts, broadly similar street gang violence problems have been noted in countries throughout the world (Klein, Weerman, and Thornberry 2006; Gatti, Haymoz, and Schadee 2011).

Focused deterrence strategies are a relatively new addition to a growing portfolio of evidence-based crime prevention practices available to policymakers and practitioners. Briefly, focused deterrence strategies seek to change offender behavior by understanding underlying crime-producing dynamics and conditions that sustain recurring crime problems and implementing a blended strategy of law enforcement, community mobilization, and social service actions (Kennedy 1997, 2008). Direct communications of increased enforcement risks and the availability of social service assistance to target groups and individuals is a defining characteristic of focused

The Handbook of Homicide, First Edition. Edited by Fiona Brookman, Edward R. Maguire, and Mike Maguire.

deterrence programs. In response to conflicting reports on the crime control efficacy of these new prevention strategies (see e.g., Braga *et al.* 2001; Rosenfeld, Fornango, and Baumer 2005; Wellford, Pepper, and Petrie 2005), the United Kingdom's National Policing Improvement Agency (NPIA) provided funds to support a Campbell Collaboration systematic review of the available evaluation evidence on the crime control efficacy of focused deterrence strategies. The Campbell review found that focused deterrence strategies were associated with significant reductions in targeted crime problems, particularly gang homicide (Braga and Weisburd 2012).

Focused deterrence strategies were pioneered in Boston to address an epidemic of gang homicides. It is important to note here that the focus of this chapter is almost exclusively on experiences in the United States, although such strategies have been used in other countries. This chapter begins by describing Boston's experiences implementing focused deterrence strategies beginning in the mid-1990s and continuing through the 2000s. The gang homicide reduction mechanisms underpinning Boston's focused deterrence intervention are subsequently delineated. The chapter then reviews applications of focused deterrence programs to reduce gang homicide problems in other cities. The available empirical evidence suggests these strategies generate noteworthy gang homicide reduction impacts and should be part of a broader portfolio of homicide prevention strategies available to policymakers and practitioners.

Focused Deterrence Strategies

The Boston Gun Project and Operation Ceasefire in the 1990s

The Boston Gun Project was a problem-oriented policing enterprise expressly aimed at taking on a serious, large-scale crime problem—homicide victimization among young people in Boston. Like many large cities in the United States, Boston experienced a large sudden increase in youth homicide between the late 1980s and early 1990s. The project began in early 1995 and implemented what is now known as the "Operation Ceasefire" intervention, which started in the late spring of 1996 (Kennedy, Piehl, and Braga 1996). Led by the Boston Police Department's (BPD) Youth Violence Strike Force (YVSF, informally known as the "gang unit"), a working group of law enforcement personnel, youth workers, and Harvard University researchers diagnosed the youth violence problem in Boston as one of patterned, largely vendetta-like ("beef") hostility among a small population of chronic offenders, and particularly among those involved in loose, informal, mostly neighborhood-based gangs (Kennedy, Braga, and Piehl 1997). These gangs represented less than 1 percent of the city's youth between the ages of 14 and 24, but were responsible for more than 60 percent of youth homicide in Boston.

The focused deterrence strategy behind Operation Ceasefire was designed to prevent violence by reaching out directly to gangs, saying explicitly that violence would no longer be tolerated, and backing up that message by "pulling every lever" legally available when violence occurred (Kennedy 1997, 2011). The chronic involvement of gang members in a wide variety of offenses made them—and their groups—vulnerable to a coordinated criminal justice response. The YVSF and their criminal justice partners could disrupt street drug activity, focus police attention on low-level street crimes such as trespassing and public drinking, serve outstanding warrants, cultivate confidential informants for medium- and long-term investigations of gang activities, deliver strict probation and parole enforcement, seize drug proceeds and other assets, ensure stiffer plea bargains and sterner prosecutorial attention, request stronger bail terms (and enforce them), and bring potentially severe federal investigative and prosecutorial attention to gang-related drug and gun activity. Rather than simply dealing with individual offending, groups were held accountable for outbreaks of serious gun violence.

Simultaneously, youth workers, probation and parole officers, and later churches and other community groups offered gang members services and other kinds of help. These partners also delivered an explicit message that violence was unacceptable to the community and that "street" justifications for violence were mistaken. The Ceasefire Working Group delivered this message in formal meetings with gang members (known as "forums" or "call-ins"), through individual police and probation contacts with gang members, through meetings with inmates at secure juvenile facilities in the city, and through gang outreach workers. The deterrence message was not a deal with gang members to stop violence. Rather, it was a promise to gang members that violent behavior would evoke an immediate and intense response. If gangs committed other crimes but refrained from violence, the normal workings of police, prosecutors, and the rest of the criminal justice system dealt with these matters. But if gang members persisted in their violent behaviors, the working group concentrated its enforcement actions on their gangs.

The idea of the Ceasefire "crackdowns" specifically but the focused deterrence model more generally was not to eliminate gangs or stop every aspect of gang activity, but rather to control and deter serious violence among specified groups (Kennedy 1997). To do this, the working group explained its actions against targeted gangs to other gangs, as in "this gang did violence, we responded with the following actions, and here is how to prevent anything similar from happening to you." The ongoing working group process regularly watched the city for outbreaks of gang violence and framed any necessary responses in accord with the Ceasefire strategy. As the strategy unfolded, the working group continued communication with gangs and gang members to convey its determination to stop violence, to explain its actions to the target population, and to maximize both voluntary compliance and the strategy's deterrent power.

A large reduction in the yearly number of Boston youth homicides followed immediately after Operation Ceasefire was implemented in mid-1996. A US Department of Justice (DOJ)-sponsored quasi-experimental evaluation of Operation Ceasefire revealed that the intervention was associated with a 63 percent decrease in the monthly number of Boston youth homicides, a 32 percent decrease in the monthly number of shots-fired calls, a 25 percent decrease in the monthly number of gun assaults, and, in one high-risk police district given special attention in the evaluation, a 44 percent decrease in the monthly number of youth gun assault incidents (Braga *et al.* 2001). The evaluation also suggested that Boston's significant youth homicide reduction associated with Operation Ceasefire was distinct when compared to youth homicide trends in most major US and New England cities (Braga *et al.* 2001). In a companion paper to the main impact evaluation, Piehl *et al.* (2003) developed an econometric model that evaluated all possible monthly break points in the time series to identify the maximal monthly break point associated with a significant structural change in the trajectory of the time series. Controlling for trends and seasonal variations, the timing of the "optimal break" in the monthly counts of youth homicides time series was in the summer months after Ceasefire was implemented in 1996.

Given the high profile of the Boston experience, the Ceasefire evaluation has been reviewed by a number of researchers and the relationship between the implementation of Ceasefire and the trajectory of youth homicide in Boston during the 1990s has been closely scrutinized. The evaluation methodology and results were greeted both with a healthy dose of skepticism (Fagan 2002; Rosenfeld, Fornango, and Baumer 2005) and some support (Cook and Ludwig 2006; Morgan and Winship 2007). The National Academies' Panel on Improving Information and Data on Firearms (Wellford, Pepper, and Petrie 2005) concluded that the Ceasefire evaluation was compelling in associating the intervention with the subsequent decline in youth homicide. However, the panel also suggested that many complex factors affect youth homicide trends and it was difficult to specify the exact relationship between the Ceasefire intervention and subsequent changes in youth offending behaviors. The panel further observed that the Ceasefire evaluation examined aggregate citywide data and did not provide any empirical evidence that treated gangs modified their violent behaviors after being exposed to the intervention.

Operation Ceasefire in the 2000s

Despite the national acclaim, the BPD discontinued the Ceasefire strategy as its primary response to outbreaks of gang violence in January 2000 (see Braga and Winship 2006). Yearly counts of gang homicides, unfortunately, increased linearly after Ceasefire was halted in Boston (Braga, Hureau, and Winship 2008). In 1999, the last full year of Ceasefire intervention, there were only five gang-motivated homicides in Boston. By 2006, this number had increased more than sevenfold to 37 gang-motivated homicides in Boston. During this time period, the BPD experimented with alternative approaches to violence prevention by adapting certain Ceasefire tactics to a broader range of problems such as investigating unsolved shootings, facilitating the re-entry of incarcerated violent offenders back into high-risk Boston neighborhoods, and addressing criminogenic families in hot spot areas (Braga and Winship 2006). Unfortunately, the slate of new approaches seemed to diffuse the ability of the City of Boston to deal with gang violence as no one group was focused exclusively on addressing ongoing conflicts among street gangs (Braga, Hureau, and Winship 2008).

At the beginning of December 2006, newly appointed BPD commissioner, Edward F. Davis, announced that Operation Ceasefire would once again be the BPD's main response to outbreaks of serious gang violence (Braga, Hureau, and Papachristos 2014). The YVSF reinstated the Ceasefire approach as a citywide, interagency effort to disrupt ongoing cycles of gang violence and regular working group meetings soon commenced. The Lucerne Street Doggz was the first group selected for Ceasefire intervention because it was the city's most violent gang of that time period. The Doggz were a loosely organized gang based in the disadvantaged Lucerne Street area of the Mattapan section of Boston. In 2006, the Lucerne gang had roughly 50 members and was involved in violent disputes with eight rival gangs—Big Head Boys, Morse Street, Norfolk, Greenwood, Heath Street, Orchard Park, H-Block, and Winston Road. Drawing on data collected from ongoing crime incident reviews (Klofas and Hipple 2006; Braga, Hureau, and Grossman 2014), it was revealed that Lucerne was involved in 37 fatal and nonfatal shootings in 2006, representing nearly 10 percent of all shootings in Boston that year.

The YVSF partnered with the same criminal justice, social service, and community-based partners from the strategy's first incarnation on a call-in to deliver the Ceasefire antiviolence message to the Lucerne Street Doggz. However, after the call-in, Lucerne continued its torrid involvement in shootings and, by the end of May 2007, was the suspect group in another 21 gang-involved shootings and the victim group in another 6 gang-involved shootings. Consistent with the overall focused deterrence strategy, it was critical to establish the credibility of the Ceasefire antiviolence message on the streets of Boston again. Since Lucerne had been subjected to a call-in and continued on its violent path, the Ceasefire Working Group needed to make good on the promise that a strong law enforcement response would soon follow. On May 24, 2007, 25 Lucerne Street gang members were taken into custody and charged with federal and state drug and firearms offenses (Braga, Hureau, and Papachristos 2014). As Figure 36.1 reveals, the impact of the Ceasefire intervention on their gun violence behavior was noteworthy. In 2006 and 2007, Lucerne gang averaged 33.5 total shootings per year. Their yearly average plummeted by 87.2 percent to 4.3 per year between 2008 and 2010.

Between January 2007 and December 2010, 19 Boston gangs were subjected to the Ceasefire focused deterrence strategy. Braga, Hureau, and Papachristos (2014) conducted a rigorous quasi-experimental evaluation of the reconstituted Boston Ceasefire program that used statistical matching techniques to develop balanced treatment gangs and comparison gangs. Growth-curve regression models were then used to estimate the impact of Ceasefire on gun violence trends for the matched treatment gangs relative to matched comparisons gangs during the 2006 through 2010 study time period. The evaluation reported that total shootings involving directly treated Ceasefire gangs were reduced by a statistically significant 31 percent relative to total shootings involving comparison gangs. Using similar evaluation

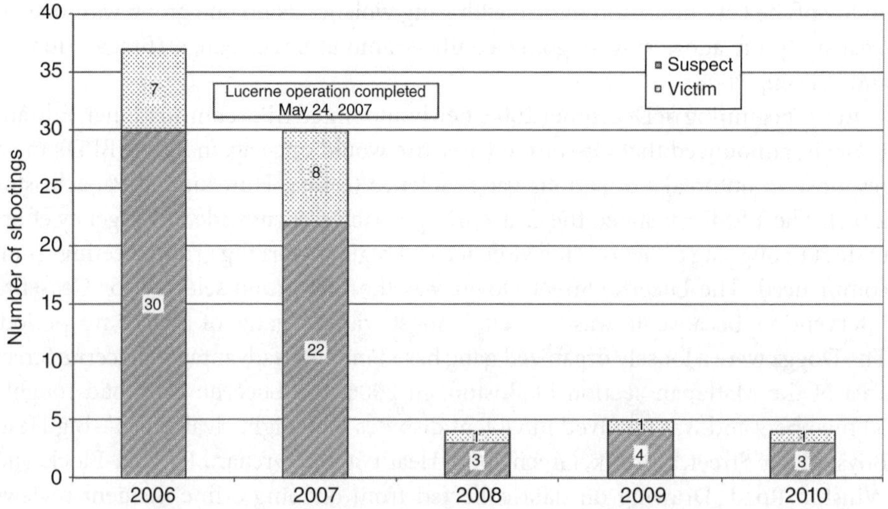

Figure 36.1 Fatal and non-fatal shootings involving the Lucerne Street Doggz, 2006–2010. Source: Braga et al., 2014. Reproduced with the permission of Springer.

methods, Braga, Apel, and Welsh (2013) found that the Ceasefire strategy also created spillover deterrent effects onto other gangs that were socially connected to targeted gangs through rivalries and alliances. Total shootings involving these "vicariously treated" gangs were also decreased by a statistically significant 24 percent relative to total shootings by matched comparison gangs.

Operation Ceasefire gang homicide reduction mechanisms

Although Operation Ceasefire was a problem-oriented policing project centered on law enforcement interventions, the other elements of Ceasefire that involved community organization, social intervention, and opportunity provision certainly supported and strengthened the ability of law enforcement to reduce gang homicide. Beyond deterring violent behavior, Ceasefire was designed to facilitate desired behaviors among gang members. As described earlier, coordinated strategies that integrate these varied domains are most likely to be effective in dealing with chronic youth gang problems. To be successful in gang homicide reduction, one lesson from the Ceasefire experience for effective law enforcement operations is the considerable value added by including an array of non-law enforcement partners in comprehensive gang strategies.

Social intervention programs encompass both social service agency-based programs and detached "streetworker" programs; opportunity provision strategies attempt to offer gang members legitimate opportunities and means to success that are at least as appealing as available illegitimate options (Curry and Decker 1998; Spergel 1995; Klein 1995). Boston street workers were key members of the Ceasefire

Working Group and, along with the juvenile corrections case workers, probation officers, and parole officers in the group, added a much needed social intervention and opportunity provision dimension to the Ceasefire strategy. Community organization strategies to cope with gang problems include attempts to create community solidarity, networking, education, and involvement (Spergel and Curry 1993). The Ten Point Coalition of activist black clergy played an important role in organizing Boston communities suffering from gang violence and evolved into an institution that provides an umbrella of legitimacy for the police to work under (Winship and Berrien 1999; Brunson *et al.* 2013). With the Ten Point's approval of and involvement in Operation Ceasefire, the community supported the approach as a legitimate youth violence prevention campaign. Ten Point clergy also provided a strong moral voice at the gang forums in the presentation of Operation Ceasefire's antiviolence message and aided in forming bridges between gang members and social services. Ten Point clergy and others involved in this faith-based organization accompanied YVSF officers on home visits to the families of gang youth and also acted as advocates for gang members in the criminal justice system.

With these resources, the Ceasefire Working Group was able to pair criminal justice sanctions, or the promise of sanctions, with help and with services. When the risk to drug dealing gang members increases, legitimate work becomes more attractive, and when legitimate work is more available, raising risks will be more effective in reducing violence. The availability of social services and opportunities were intended to increase the Ceasefire strategy's preventive power by offering gang members any assistance they may want: protection from their enemies, drug treatment, access to education, and job training programs, and the like. While these resources were important ingredients, the focused suppression actions led by the YVSF comprised the key component of the Ceasefire intervention. In essence, the Boston experience represents an exercise in getting deterrence right (Kennedy 1997).

The Operation Ceasefire Working Group recognized that, in order for the strategy to be successful, it was crucial to deliver a credible deterrence message to Boston gangs. Therefore, the Ceasefire intervention only targeted those gangs that were engaged in violent behavior rather than wasting resources on those who were not. Spergel (1995) suggests that problem-solving approaches to gang problems based on more limited goals such as gang violence reduction rather than gang destruction are more likely to be effective in controlling gang problems. Operation Ceasefire did not attempt to eliminate all gangs or eliminate all gang offending in Boston. Despite the large reductions in gun violence, Boston still has gangs and Boston gangs still commit crimes.

The Ceasefire focused deterrence approach attempted to prevent gang homicide by making gang members believe that consequences would follow on violence and gun use and choose to change their behavior (Kennedy 1997). A key element of the strategy was the delivery of a direct and explicit deterrence message to a relatively small target audience regarding what kind of behavior would provoke a special response and what that response would be. In addition to any increases in certainty, severity, and swiftness of sanctions associated with acts of violence, the Operation

Ceasefire strategy sought to gain deterrence through the advertising of the law enforcement strategy, and the personalized nature of its application. As Zimring and Hawkins (1973: 142) observe, "the deterrence threat may best be viewed as a form of advertising." It was crucial that gang youth understood the new regime that the city was imposing. Knowledge of what happened to others in the target population was intended to prevent further acts of violence by gangs in Boston.

In the communication of the deterrence message, the working group also wanted to reach a common piece of shared moral ground with gang members (Kennedy, Piehl, and Braga 1996). The group wanted the gang members to understand that most victims of gang homicide were gang members, that the strategy was designed to protect both gang members and the community in which they lived, and the working group had gang members' best interests in mind even if the gang members' own actions required resorting to coercion in order to protect them. The working group also hoped the process of communicating face-to-face with gangs and gang members would undercut any feelings of anonymity and invulnerability they might have, and that a clear demonstration of interagency solidarity would enhance offenders' sense that something new and powerful was happening.

In their recent essay on the limits of lengthy prison stays to deter crime, Durlauf and Nagin (2011: 40) suggest that "strategies that result in large and visible shifts in apprehension risk are most likely to have deterrent effects that are large enough not only to reduce crime but also apprehensions." Focused deterrence strategies, such as Boston's Operation Ceasefire, are identified by Durlauf and Nagin (2011) as having this characteristic. Moreover, they suggest that these "carrot and stick approaches" to crime prevention creatively use positive incentives, such as social services and job opportunities, to reward compliance and facilitate nonviolent behavior.

Experiences and Evaluation Evidence in Other US Jurisdictions

At first blush, the effectiveness of the Operation Ceasefire intervention in preventing gang homicide may seem unique to Boston. Operation Ceasefire was constructed largely from the assets and capacities available in Boston at the time and deliberately tailored to the city's particular gang homicide problem. Operational capacities of criminal justice agencies in other cities will be different and gang homicide problems in other cities will have important distinguishing characteristics. However, the basic working group problem-oriented policing process and the "pulling levers" approach to deterring chronic offenders are transferable to violence problems in other jurisdictions. A number of cities have experimented with these analytic frameworks and have reported noteworthy crime control gains. In this section, gang violence reduction efforts in Los Angeles (CA), Indianapolis (IN), and Lowell (MA) are highlighted. Research evidence on some promising applications of focused deterrence strategies to individual offenders and overt drug markets is also presented. Consistent with the problem-oriented policing approach (Goldstein 1990), these cities have tailored the approach to fit their violence problems and operating environments.

Operation Ceasefire in Los Angeles

In March 1998 the US National Institute of Justice (NIJ) funded the RAND Corporation to develop and test strategies for reducing gun violence among youth in Los Angeles. In part, the goal was to determine which parts of the Boston Gun Project might be replicable in Los Angeles. In designing the replication, RAND drew a clear distinction between the process governing the design and implementation of the strategy (data-driven policy development; problem solving, working groups) and the elements and design (focused deterrence, collective accountability, retailing the message) of the Boston model. Processes, in theory, can be sustained and adaptive, and as such can be utilized to address dynamic problems. By singling out process as an important component, the RAND team hoped to make clear that process can affect program effectiveness independently of the program elements or the merits of the actual design (see Tita, Riley, and Greenwood 2003).

The Los Angeles replication was unique in several important ways. First, the implementation was not citywide, but only within a single neighborhood (Boyle Heights) within a single Los Angeles Police Department Division (Hollenbeck). The project site, Boyle Heights, had a population that was relatively homogenous. Well over 80 percent of the residents were Latinos of Mexican origin. The same was true for the gangs, many of which were formed prior to World War II. These gangs were clearly "traditional" gangs, with memberships exceeding a hundred members or more. The gangs were strongly territorial, contain age-graded substructures, and are inter-generational in nature (Maxson and Klein 1995).

Unlike other cities where gang violence was a rather recent phenomenon, Los Angeles represented an attempt to reduce gun violence in a "chronic gang city" with a long history of gang violence, and equally long history of gang reduction strategies. The research team had to first convince members of the local criminal justice and at large community that the approach we were espousing differed in important ways from these previous efforts to combat gangs. And in fact it does—the RAND project was not about "doing something about gangs," but rather "doing something about gun violence" in a community where gang members committed an overwhelming proportion of gun violence. The independent analysis of homicide files confirmed the perception held by police and community alike that gangs were highly over-represented in homicidal acts. From 1995–1998, 50 percent of all homicides had a clear gang motivation. Another 25 percent of the homicides could be coded as "gang related" because they involved a gang member as a victim or offender, but were motivated for reasons other than gang rivalries.

Given the social organization of violence in Boyle Heights, the multidisciplinary working group embraced the focused deterrence strategy developed in Boston. A high-profile gang shooting that resulted in a double homicide in Boyle Heights triggered the implementation of the Operation Ceasefire intervention in October 2000. The processes of retailing the message were formally adopted, though it was mostly accomplished through personal contact rather than in a group setting. Police, probation, community advocates, street gang workers, a local hospital and local clergy were all passing along the message of collective accountability for gangs continuing to commit gang violence. However, Tita *et al.* (2003) reported that the Los Angeles pulling levers intervention was not fully implemented as planned. The implementation of the Ceasefire program in the Boyle Heights was negatively affected by the well-known Ramparts LAPD police corruption scandal and a lack of ownership of the intervention by the participating agencies.

Despite the implementation difficulties, the RAND research team was able to complete an impact evaluation of the violence prevention effects of the pulling levers focused deterrence strategy that was implemented (Tita *et al.* 2003). Using a variety of methods, the evaluation revealed consistent noteworthy short-term reductions in violent crime, gang crime, and gun crime associated with the Ceasefire program. In addition to their analyses of the main effects of the intervention, RAND researchers examined the effects of the intervention on neighboring areas and gangs. Their analyses suggested a strong diffusion of violence prevention benefits emanating from the targeted areas and targeted gangs.

Indianapolis violence reduction partnership

The Indianapolis Violence Reduction Partnership (IVRP) Working Group was comprised of Indiana University researchers and federal, state, and local law enforcement agencies (McGarrell and Chermak 2003). During the problem analysis phase, the researchers examined 258 homicides from 1997 and the first 8 months of 1998 and found that a majority of homicide victims (63%) and offenders (75%) had criminal and/or juvenile records. Those with a prior record often had a substantial number of arrests. The working group members followed the structured qualitative data gathering exercises used in Boston to gain insight on the nature of homicide incidents. The qualitative exercise revealed that 59 percent of the incidents involved "groups of known chronic offenders" and 53 percent involved drug-related motives such as settling business and turf disputes (McGarrell and Chermak 2003). It is worth noting that the terminology "groups of known chronic offenders" was initially used because, at that point in time, there was not a consensual definition of "gang" and the reality of much gang activity in Indianapolis was of a relatively loose structure (McGarrell and Chermak 2003).

The working group developed two sets of overlapping strategies (McGarrell and Chermak 2003). First, the most violent chronic offenders in Indianapolis were identified and targeted for heightened arrest, prosecution, and incarceration. Second, the working group engaged the pulling levers approach to reduce violent behavior by gangs and groups of known chronic offenders. The IVRP strategy implemented by the Indianapolis Working Group closely resembled the Boston version of pulling levers. The communications strategy, however, differed in an important way. The deterrence and social services message was delivered in meetings with high-risk probationers and parolees organized by neighborhoods. Similarly, home visits by probation and parolees were generally organized by neighborhood. As the project progressed, when a homicide or series of homicides involved certain groups or gangs, the working group attempted to target meetings, enforcement activities, and home visits on the involved groups or gangs (McGarrell and Chermak 2003).

A US Department of Justice-funded evaluation revealed that the IVRP strategy was associated with a 34 percent reduction in Indianapolis homicides (McGarrell *et al.* 2006). The evaluation further revealed that the homicide reduction in Indianapolis was distinct when compared to homicide trends in six comparable Midwestern cities during the same time period.

Project Safe Neighborhoods in Lowell, Massachusetts

Supported by funds from the US Department of Justice-sponsored Project Safe Neighborhoods initiative, an interagency task force implemented a pulling levers focused deterrence strategy to prevent gun violence among Hispanic and Asian gangs in Lowell, Massachusetts in 2002 (Braga, McDevitt, and Pierce 2006). While the Lowell authorities felt very confident about their ability to prevent violence among Hispanic gangs by pursuing a general focused deterrence strategy, they felt much less confident about their ability to prevent Asian gang violence by applying the same set of criminal justice levers to Asian gang members. As Malcolm Klein (1995) suggests, Asian gangs have some key differences from typical black, Hispanic, and white street gangs. They are more organized, have identifiable leaders, and are far more secretive. They also tend to be far less territorial and less openly visible. Therefore, their street presence is low compared to other ethnic gangs. Relationships between law enforcement agencies and the Asian community are often characterized by mistrust and a lack of communication (Chin 1996). As such, it is often difficult for the police to develop information on the participants in violent acts to hold offenders accountable for their actions.

During the intervention time period, the Lowell Police Department (LPD) had little reliable intelligence about Asian gangs in the city (Braga, McDevitt, and Pierce 2006). The LPD had attempted to develop informants in the past but most these efforts had been unsuccessful. With the increased focus on Asian gang violence, the LPD increased its efforts to develop intelligence about the structure of the city's Asian gangs and particularly the relationship between Asian gang violence and ongoing gambling that was being run by local Asian businesses. Asian street gangs are sometimes connected to adult criminal organizations and assist older criminals in extortion activities and protecting illegal gambling enterprises (Chin 1996). In many East Asian cultures, rituals and protocols guiding social interactions are well defined and reinforced through a variety of highly developed feelings of obligation, many of which are hierarchical in nature (Zhang 2002). This facilitates some control over the behavior of younger Asian gang members by elders in the gang.

In Lowell, Cambodian and Laotian gangs were comprised of youth whose street activities were influenced by "elders" of the gang (Braga, McDevitt, and Pierce 2006). Elders were generally long-time gang members in their 30s and 40s that no longer engaged in illegal activities on the street or participated in street-level violence with rival youth. Rather, these older gang members were heavily involved in running illegal gambling dens and informal casinos that were operated out of cafes, video stores, and warehouses located in the poor Asian neighborhoods of Lowell. The elders used young street gang members to protect their business interests and to collect any unpaid gambling debts. Illegal gaming was a very lucrative business that was much more important to the elders than any ongoing beefs the youth in their gang had with other youth (Braga, McDevitt, and Pierce 2006). In contrast to acquiring information on individuals responsible for gun crimes in Asian communities, it was much easier to detect the presence of gambling operations through surveillance or a simple visit to the suspected business establishment.

The importance of illegal gaming to influential members of Asian street gangs provided a potentially potent lever to law enforcement in preventing violence. The authorities in Lowell believed that they could systematically prevent street violence among gangs by targeting the gambling interests of older members. When a street gang was violent, the LPD targeted the gambling businesses run by the older members of the gang. The enforcement activities ranged from serving a search warrant on the business that houses the illegal enterprise and making arrests to simply placing a patrol car in front of the suspected gambling location to deter gamblers from entering. The LPD coupled these tactics with the delivery of a clear message, "when the gang kids associated with you act violently, we will shut down your gambling business. When violence erupts, no one makes money" (Braga, McDevitt, and Pierce 2006: 40). Between October 2002 and June 2003, the height of the focused attention on Asian gangs, the LPD conducted some 30 search warrants on illegal gambling dens that resulted in more than 100 gambling-related arrests (Braga, McDevitt, and Pierce 2006).

An impact evaluation found that the Lowell focused deterrence strategy was associated with a 43 percent decrease in the monthly number of gun homicide and gun aggravated assault incidents (Braga *et al.* 2008). A comparative analysis of gun homicide and gun aggravated assault trends in Lowell relative to other major Massachusetts cities also supports a unique program effect associated with the focused deterrence intervention.

Conclusion

The cumulative experience described above as supportive of the proposition that the basic Boston approach has now been replicated, with promising results, in a number of disparate sites in the United States. This suggests that there was nothing particularly unique about either the implementation or the impact of Operation Ceasefire in Boston. It suggests further that the fundamental focused deterrence framework behind Ceasefire can be successfully applied in other jurisdictions; with other sets of partners; with different particular activities; and in the context of different basic types of gangs and groups. Further operational experience and more refined evaluation techniques will tell us more about these questions, as experience and analysis continues to accumulate. At the moment, however, there appears to be reason for continued optimism that gang homicide problems are open to direct and powerful prevention.

The ultimate target of focused deterrence gang homicide reduction strategies is the self-sustaining dynamic of retaliation that characterizes many ongoing gang conflicts (Kennedy, Piehl, and Braga 1996; Kennedy 2008). Focused deterrence operations are not designed to eliminate gangs or stop every aspect of gang activity, but to control and deter gang homicide. The communication of the antiviolence message, coupled with meaningful examples of the consequences that will be brought to bear on gangs that break the rules, sought to weaken or eliminate the "kill or be killed" norm as individuals recognize that their enemies will be operating under the new rules as well. The social service component of focused deterrence strategies serves as an independent good and also helps to remove excuses used by offenders to explain their offending (Braga and Kennedy 2012). Social service providers present an alternative to illegal behavior by offering relevant jobs and social services. The availability of these services invalidates excuses that their violent behavior is the result of a lack of legitimate opportunities for employment, or other problems, in their neighborhood.

While the evaluations identified in their Campbell review were supportive of deterrence principles, Braga and Weisburd (2012) noted that that it was difficult to know whether observed reductions represented a true deterrent impact. Some of the identified evaluations were weaker quasi-experimental studies that didn't adequately rule out other factors in explaining the observed reductions. Focused deterrence programs can, and should, be subjected to more rigorous tests that generate more robust evidence on program impacts (Braga and Weisburd 2014). Moreover, a growing number of scholars suggest that that there seems to be additional crime control mechanisms at work in these strategies beyond straight-up deterrence (Braga 2012; Corsaro *et al.* 2012; Papachristos, Meares, and Fagan 2007). Other prevention frameworks, such as community social control and procedural fairness, might help explain the observed impacts of focused deterrence programs on crime. In addition to advocating for more rigorous evaluation designs, Braga and Weisburd (2012) recommended that the next wave of research on focused deterrence strategies needs to develop further knowledge *why* these strategies seem to work in reducing gang homicide.

Comparative research on applications of focused deterrence strategies in other countries is also needed to determine whether these violence reduction policies and practices can be transferred to settings outside US urban environments. Experiences in Glasgow, Scotland, suggest that the approach may be beneficial in addressing serious youth violence problems in other Western countries (Deuchar 2013). Police executives and other public officials in Eastern European and South American countries, such as Turkey and Brazil, have also explored the possibility of implementing focused deterrence strategies to control gang and group-related violence in their cities (National Network for Safe Communities 2013). Indeed, these environments represent strong tests for the focused deterrence approach. Many questions need to be answered. For instance, is it possible to develop a network of capacity that could mobilize communities to complement law enforcement efforts to control the violent behaviors of drug gangs in severely disadvantaged favelas of Rio de Janeiro? Drawing on the positive experiences in developing such capacities in very violent disadvantaged neighborhoods in the United States, it seems possible. Indeed, the flexible problem-solving framework undergirding focused deterrence strategies suggests that the approach can be appropriately tailored to varying urban contexts. At this point in time, the potential violence reduction efficacy of these approaches in other countries is largely based on speculation rather than empirical facts and practical experience. However, experimentation with focused deterrence strategies to control gang and group-related violence beyond US settings is clearly warranted by the available scientific evidence.

References

Block, C.R. and Block, R. (1993) *Street Gang Crime in Chicago*. Washington, DC: US National Institute of Justice.

Braga, A.A. (2012) Getting deterrence right? Evaluation evidence and complementary crime control mechanisms. *Criminology & Public Policy*, 11: 201–210.

Braga, A.A., Apel, R., and Welsh, B.C. (2013) The spillover effects of focused deterrence on gang violence. *Evaluation Review*, 37: 314–342.

Braga, A.A., Hureau, D.M., and Grossman, L. (2014) *Managing the Group Violence Intervention: Using Shooting Scorecards to Track Group Violence*. Washington, DC: Office of Community Oriented Policing Services.

Braga, A.A., Hureau, D.M., and Papachristos, A.V. (2014) Deterring gang-involved gun violence: Measuring the impact of Boston's Operation Ceasefire on street gang behavior. *Journal of Quantitative Criminology*, 30: 113–139.

Braga, A.A., Hureau, D.M., and Winship, C. (2008) Losing faith? Police, black churches, and the resurgence of youth violence in Boston. *Ohio State Journal of Criminal Law*, 6: 141–172.

Braga, A.A. and Kennedy, D.M. (2012) Linking situational crime prevention and focused deterrence strategies. In G. Farrell and N. Tilley (eds), *The Reasoning Criminologist: Essays in Honour of Ronald V. Clarke* (pp. 65–79). London: Routledge.

Braga, A.A., Kennedy, D.M., Waring, E., and Piehl, A.M. (2001) Problem-oriented policing, deterrence, and youth violence: An evaluation of Boston's Operation Ceasefire. *Journal of Research in Crime and Delinquency*, 38: 195–225.

Braga, A.A., McDevitt, J., and Pierce, G.L. (2006) Understanding and preventing gang violence: Problem analysis and response development in Lowell, Massachusetts. *Police Quarterly*, 9: 20–46.

Braga, A.A., Pierce, G.L., McDevitt, J., *et al.* (2008) The strategic prevention of gun violence among gang-involved offenders. *Justice Quarterly*, 25: 132–162.

Braga, A.A. and Weisburd, D.L. (2012) The effects of focused deterrence strategies on crime: A systematic review and meta-analysis of the empirical evidence. *Journal of Research in Crime and Delinquency*, 49: 323–358.

Braga, A.A. and Weisburd, D.L. (2014) Must we settle for less rigorous evaluations in large area-based crime prevention programs? Lessons from a Campbell review of focused deterrence. *Journal of Experimental Criminology*, 10: 573–597.

Braga, A.A. and Winship, C. (2006) Partnership, accountability, and innovation: Clarifying Boston's experience with pulling levers. In D.L. Weisburd and A.A. Braga (eds), *Police Innovation: Contrasting Perspectives* (pp. 171–190). New York: Cambridge University Press.

Brunson, R.K., Braga, A.A., Hureau, D.M., and Pegram, K. (2013) We trust you, but not that much: Examining police–black clergy partnerships to reduce youth violence. *Justice Quarterly*, 32(6).

Chin, K.-L. (1996) *Chinatown Gangs: Extortion, Enterprise, and Ethnicity*. New York: Oxford University Press.

Cook, P.J. and Ludwig, J.O. (2006) Aiming for evidence-based gun policy. *Journal of Policy Analysis and Management*, 48: 691–735.

Corsaro, N., Hunt, E., Hipple, N.K., and McGarrell, E. (2012) The impact of drug market pulling levers policing on neighborhood violence: An evaluation of the high point drug market intervention. *Criminology & Public Policy*, 11: 167–200.

Curry, G.D. and Decker, S.H. (1998) *Confronting Gangs: Crime and Community*. Los Angeles: Roxbury Press.

Deuchar, R. (2013) *Policing Youth Violence: Transatlantic Connections*. Trentham, UK: IOE Press.

Durlauf, S. and Nagin, D. (2011) Imprisonment and crime: Can both be reduced? *Criminology & Public Policy*, 10: 13–54.

Egley, A. and Howell, J.C. (2013) *Highlights of the 2011 National Youth Gang Survey*. Washington, DC: Office of Juvenile Justice and Delinquency Prevention.

Fagan, J. (2002) Policing guns and youth violence. *The Future of Children*, 12: 133–151.

Gatti, U., Haymoz, S., and Schadee, H. (2011) Deviant youth groups in 30 countries: Results from the Second International Self-Report Delinquency Study. *International Criminal Justice Review*, 21: 208–224.

Goldstein, H. (1990) *Problem-Oriented Policing*. Philadelphia: Temple University Press.

Kennedy, D.M. (1997) Pulling levers: Chronic offenders, high-crime settings, and a theory of prevention. *Valparaiso University Law Review*, 31: 449–484.

Kennedy, D.M. (2008) *Deterrence and Crime Prevention*. New York: Routledge.

Kennedy, D.M. (2011) *Don't Shoot: One Man, A Street Fellowship, and the End of Violence in Inner City America*. New York: Bloomsbury.

Kennedy, D.M., Braga, A.A., and Piehl, A.M. (1997) The (un)known universe: Mapping gangs and gang violence in Boston. In D.L. Weisburd and J.T. McEwen (eds), *Crime Mapping and Crime Prevention* (pp. 219–262). Monsey, NY: Criminal Justice Press.

Kennedy, D.M., Piehl, A.M., and Braga, A.A. (1996) Youth violence in Boston: Gun markets, serious youth offenders, and a use-reduction strategy. *Law and Contemporary Problems*, 59: 147–196.

Klein, M.W. (1995) *The American Street Gang: Its Nature, Prevalence, and Control*. New York: Oxford University Press.

Klein, M.W., Weerman, F.M., and Thornberry, T.P. (2006) Street gang violence in Europe. *European Journal of Criminology*, 3: 413–437.

Klofas, J. and Hipple, N.K. (2006) Project Safe neighborhoods: Strategic interventions. Crime incident reviews: Case study 3. Washington, DC: US Department of Justice.

Maxson, C.L. and Klein, M.W. (1995) Investigating gang structures. *Journal of Gang Research*, 3: 33–38.

McGarrell, E.F. and Chermak, S. (2003) Problem solving to reduce gang and drug-related violence in Indianapolis. In S.H. Decker (ed.), *Policing Gangs and Youth Violence* (pp. 77–101). Belmont, CA: Wadsworth.

McGarrell, E.F., Chermak, S., Wilson, J., and Corsaro, N. (2006) Reducing homicide through a "lever-pulling" strategy. *Justice Quarterly*, 23: 214–229.

Morgan, S. and Winship, C. (2007) *Counterfactuals and Causal Models*. New York: Cambridge University Press.

National Network for Safe Communities (2013) *Group Violence Intervention: An Implementation Guide*. Washington, DC: US Department of Justice, Office of Community Oriented Policing Services.

Papachristos, A.V., Meares, T., and Fagan, T.J. (2007) Attention felons: Evaluating Project Safe neighborhoods in Chicago. *Journal of Empirical Legal Studies*, 4: 223–272.

Piehl, A.M., Cooper, S.J., Braga, A.A., and Kennedy, D.M. (2003) Testing for structural breaks in the evaluation of programs. *Review of Economics and Statistics*, 85: 550–558.

Rosenfeld, R., Fornango, R., and Baumer, E. (2005) Did Ceasefire, Compstat, and Exile reduce homicide? *Criminology & Public Policy*, 4: 419–450.

Thornberry, T., Krohn, M., Lizotte, A., *et al.* (2003) *Gangs and Delinquency in Developmental Perspective*. New York: Cambridge University Press.

Spergel, I.A. (1995) *The Youth Gang Problem: A Community Approach*. New York: Oxford University Press.

Spergel, I.A. and Curry, G.D. (1993) The national youth gang survey: A research and development process. In A. Goldstein and C.R. Huff (eds), *Gang Intervention Handbook* (pp. 359–400). Champaign-Urbana, IL: Research Press.

Tita, G.E., Riley, K.J., and Greenwood, P. (2003) From Boston to Boyle Heights: The process and prospects of a "pulling levers" strategy in a Los Angeles Barrio. In S.H. Decker (ed.), *Policing Gangs and Youth Violence* (pp. 102–130). Belmont, CA: Wadsworth.

Tita, G.E., Riley, K.J., Ridgeway, G., *et al.* (2003) *Reducing Gun Violence: Results from an Intervention in East Los Angeles*. Santa Monica, CA: RAND Corporation.

Wellford, C., Pepper, J., and Petrie, C. (eds) (2005) *Firearms and Violence: A Critical Review*. Washington, DC: National Academies Press.

Winship, C. and Berrien, J. (1999) Boston cops and black churches. *The Public Interest*, 136: 52–68.

Zhang, S. (2002) Chinese gangs: Familial and cultural dynamics. In C.R. Huff (ed.), *Gangs in America* (3rd edn, pp. 219–236). Thousand Oaks, CA: SAGE.

Zimring, F. and Hawkins, G. (1973) *Deterrence: The Legal Threat in Crime Control*. Chicago: University of Chicago Press.

37

From Theory to Practice

Reducing Gun Violence and Homicide in Detroit

Eric Grommon, John D. McCluskey, and Timothy S. Bynum

Introduction

The research project reported in this chapter concluded several years ago.[1] With the benefit of hindsight, a number of valuable lessons have been learned that are useful for understanding the responsivity of local criminal justice systems to implement policy options and address homicide and violence problems. Detroit is a unique and complex setting. The history of deindustrialization, racial animosity and segregation, and controversial governance have been well documented (see Farley *et al.* 1994; LeDuff 2014; Sugrue 2005). The contemporaneous travails of the city, with former Mayor Kilpatrick serving a 28 year prison term stemming from corruption convictions and a national news focus on the bankruptcy of the city have, in some ways, overshadowed the gun violence and homicide problems there (e.g., Baldas and Schaefer 2013). These problems have not disappeared; Detroit's rate of violent crime remains one of the highest relative to most major American cities (Papachristos and Kirk 2015).

This chapter first provides an overview of the research literature on focused deterrence strategies, which have greatly contributed to our knowledge on affecting gun violence and homicide. The context of twenty-first century Detroit, with its long struggle with rates of homicide substantially above national averages, follows the initial discussion. Next we consider the theoretical frameworks for understanding local criminal justice changes with respect to action research. The specifics of the Detroit Gun Violence Reduction Initiative are then considered, as well as the analytical framework used for evaluating the implementation effort. Finally, suggestions for more careful tracking of implementation, dosage, and the quality of criminal justice initiatives is considered for directions of future research.

The Handbook of Homicide, First Edition. Edited by Fiona Brookman, Edward R. Maguire, and Mike Maguire.

The Potential Promise of Focused Deterrence Strategies

What law enforcement and the larger criminal justice system can do to effectively reduce local gun homicide rates was unclear at the turn of the twenty-first century. However, as experiments, initiatives, and evaluations accumulated across cities, promising focused deterrence strategies have emerged across the country. These problem-focused efforts blend policing, prosecution or sentencing, and community-building components to increase costs of participating in gun violence by manipulating the certainty, swiftness, and severity of punishment among specific repeat and high-risk offenders in areas known for violent crime. Direct and repeated communication of incentives and disincentives to identified offenders by criminal justice officials, community leaders, and service providers is the key mechanism underlying this type of intervention (see Kennedy 2006). Identified offenders are informed of the array of opportunities and support that can be provided by local institutions and are advised to take advantage of the available resources. Offenders are also made aware of criminal justice system sanctions to be faced if involvement in gun violence continues.

Evaluations of focused deterrence strategies have produced a strong body of evidence. In a meta-analysis of 10 quasi-experimental focused deterrence interventions across the United States, Braga and Weisburd (2012) found that such efforts produce moderate effect sizes on average leading to substantial reductions in total homicides, gun homicides, and gun victimization. Since this first systematic review, research continues to demonstrate the efficacy of focused deterrence strategies across a variety of individual or place-based targets. Violent crime decreased 17 percent in known drug market areas after the implementation of the High Point Drug Market Intervention (Corsaro *et al.* 2012). An updated analysis of Boston's Operation Ceasefire found reductions in gun victimizations committed by or experienced among gangs exposed to the intervention relative to matched comparison gangs (Braga, Hureau, and Papachristos 2014). New Orleans' Group Violence Reduction Strategy contributed to a 17 percent reduction in homicide and a 16 percent reduction in gun violence (Corsaro and Engel 2015). Gang members who received incentive and disincentive communication messages of Chicago's Group Violence Reduction Strategy experienced a 32 percent reduction in gun victimization in the year following their participation relative to a matched comparison group (Papachristos and Kirk 2015). Exporting the strategy overseas, Glasgow's Community Initiative to Reduce Violence may have contributed to reductions in the rate weapon possession even though no significant reductions in the rate of violent offending was observed (Williams *et al.* 2014).

The promise of focused deterrence strategies has led to calls for widespread implementation in urban areas with violent crime problems (see Land 2015). Questions remain, however, in how to transfer the focused deterrence model to new jurisdictions, induce local systems change, maintain fidelity to the developed model, and reap the anticipated benefits of reduced gun violence and homicide. Information on some of the underlying processes used by different jurisdictions is developing, especially in regard to the reach of focus deterrence's incentive and disincentive communication messages. Over 400 gang members representing 149 different gang factions in Chicago participated in 18 different communication meetings across a three year period (Papachristos and Kirk 2015). Across a one and a half year period, 158 gang members from 54 gangs attended one of five meetings held in New Orleans (Corsaro and Engel 2015). Over 200 parolees with histories of gun convictions or violence participated in 29 of Rockford Area Violence Elimination Network's meetings across a nearly two year period (Rydberg and McGarrell 2015). Much less is known about systems change, or how these strategies work in practice, even though system processes are much more closely affiliated with intervention outcomes (see Griffiths and Christian 2015; Tillyer, Engel, and Lovins, 2012). This chapter contributes to the knowledge on focused deterrence strategies through a systems change lens and provides insights to how this type of strategy was adopted in Detroit.

Detroit's Toll

Citywide totals and rates of homicide in Detroit tell a sobering story. In the first 10 years of the new millennium (2000–2009), 3,799 homicides were recorded. In the past five years (2010–2014) 1,677 more homicide victims were added to the ledger, but the 2014 total was tinged with optimism as the city yielded its lowest homicide total since 1967 with 304 homicides (Hunter 2015). The 304 homicides of 2014 were spread among 688,000 residents for a homicide rate of approximately 44 per 100,000 residents (Hunter 2015). The previous recorded low of 281 homicides in 1967 occurred during a period when Detroit's population shrank from 1.67 million residents in 1960 to 1.51 million residents in 1970. Depending on the population estimate used, the 1967 rate of homicide was approximately 17.5 per 100,000 residents (Hunter 2015). In all, the risk of homicide among remaining residents has increased dramatically over the past five decades producing a web of detrimental effects through families, communities, the police and justice system, and beyond.

Efforts to respond to gun violence and homicide problems fundamentally recognize that risk is not uniformly distributed across a city. Instead, this risk is concentrated by geographic and social characteristics (e.g., Morenoff, Sampson, and Raudenbush 2001) and these patterns tend to persist over time, even among American cities with the highest homicide rates. Another common characteristic of homicides are the weapons used. Typically, more than two-thirds of the annual homicides are committed with firearms in Michigan (FBI 2015) and this pattern is consistent with Detroit homicides (Bynum and McCluskey 2005). Thus much of the lethal violence in Detroit is undeniably gun violence.

Northwest Detroit has been long recognized for its high rates of gun violence and homicide, especially concentrated along major corridors. Seeking to foster reductions in these rates, local criminal justice officials implemented a focused deterrence model in Northwest Detroit. Across a two and a half year cross-section of time in which the initiative was being implemented, Northwest Detroit was the only portion

Table 37.1 Weekly fatal and nonfatal shootings across a two and a half year period by Detroit District.

	Fatal shootings mean (SD)	*Nonfatal shootings mean (SD)*	*Minimum number of shootings*	*Maximum number of shootings*	*Total shootings mean (SD)*
Eastern	1.39 (1.26)	5.21 (2.62)	0	17	6.60 (3.20)
Northwest	1.06 (0.99)	5.11 (2.59)	1	17	6.15 (2.97)
Western	1.35 (1.43)	4.49 (2.78)	0	16	5.91 (3.45)
Southwest	1.22 (1.27)	4.05 (2.61)	0	14	5.18 (2.98)
Northeast	0.88 (1.00)	3.77 (2.41)	0	13	4.64 (2.86)
Central	0.37 (.62)	1.85 (1.43)	0	9	2.29 (1.88)

of the city without a week free of shootings (see Table 37.1). The Northwest District was just behind the Eastern District in the average number of fatal or nonfatal shootings per week. At the time of the implementation the Eastern District was also undergoing its own strategic multipronged intervention involving criminal justice system resources.

Prior to describing the key principles of the focused deterrence model, we first highlight the theoretical framework used to inform innovation and systems change.

The New Criminal Justice

Understanding local criminal justice changes, obstacles to reform, and patterns of change and continuity should be informed by theory. Theorizing in criminal justice, however, has been a story of conflicting approaches to description, prediction, and even the standards on which theories might be evaluated (Kraska 2006; Crank and Bowman 2008; cf., Snipes and Maguire 2007; Bernard and Engel 2001). Below we briefly consider two theoretical traditions for understanding the changes observed in Detroit: systemic theories and individual level theories. Next a more recent synthesis of theory in criminal justice that focuses on local patterning of criminal justice is discussed. We then consider which one is the best fitting framework for current purposes.

Some theorists argue for a holistic approach to understanding criminal justice drawn from systems theory. Bernard, Paoline, and Pare (2005) argue for consideration of understanding interconnected system processes in criminal justice from this perspective and the classic criminal justice diagram of case processing (Bureau of Justice Statistics 2015) draws upon similar ideas. Observers from this perspective seek to examine patterns of behavior within organizations, desired outputs, and also locations where goal conflict may occur and be effective in prioritizing criminal justice outcomes (e.g., Feeley 1973; Wright 1981).

Individual level explanations describe sources of variation in how criminal justice actors adapt to their environment and roles. Muir (1977) and Brown (1981) have furthered this perspective with their analysis of police officers. Similar approaches have been taken with prison guards (Kauffman 1988) and prosecutors (Carter 1972). From this perspective one can predict and understand decision-making patterns carried out by individual actors in criminal justice.

An alternative approach has recently been offered by Klofas, Kroovand Hipple, and McGarrell (2010), who coined the term "The New Criminal Justice" (TNCJ). This approach crosses systemic and individual levels of theorizing and describes local criminal justice systems as primary units of analysis and understanding. The prediction from TNCJ is one of change in local function that is dependent upon data analysis and prioritizing local problems. It does not ignore larger systemic patterns (such as state level or federal penalties) but is hypothesized to adapt these to local needs. Similarly, it does not ignore that individual variations exist in how one fills a role in criminal justice, but instead it chooses to focus on criminal justice agents and stakeholders in a fashion akin to a workgroup. The analogy here might be best suited to Eisenstein and Jacob's (1978) courtroom workgroup. Specifically, when problems in criminal justice arise to the level of being recognized as in need of local attention, the workgroup coalesces, shares resources, intelligence, and expertise to generate an outcome. In an era of increasing researcher–practitioner partnerships this approach is often undertaken with university researchers functioning in analytical capacities to deliver additional layers of description to a problem and consider workgroup solutions that will serve as guiding principles (e.g., Braga, Lum, and Davis 2014; Weisburd and Neyroud 2011). Regardless of chosen outcome or guiding principles, TNCJ implicitly posits that criminal justice system processing will become more responsive and efficient as relating to the underlying problem it confronts.

This approach to criminal justice work is a departure from the compartmentalized view of both system decision-points and individual decision-making. TNCJ offers first a framework for understanding how local criminal justice might coalesce around a problem, such as gun violence, and second it offers a flexible platform from which to derive testable criminal justice hypotheses. More specifically, in this case, TNCJ anticipates that local criminal justice system will "tighten" processing of cases and the character of case processing routines may change such that resources are targeted at certain individuals for example, those who have been identified as among "the worst of the worst," and attempt to systematically change internal agency practice to reflect that effort.

Detroit Gun Violence Reduction Initiative

Detroit was selected by the Department of Justice through the US Attorney's Office, Eastern District of Michigan to participate in the Project Safe Neighborhoods initiative. Each of the 94 Federal Judicial Districts across the United States was awarded funds to implement their own version of the initiative. While these districts were given some degree of latitude about how to address gun violence and homicide problems, the program model encouraged sites to adopt five key principles. Table 37.2 documents these principles and the implementation efforts undertaken in Detroit.

Table 37.2 Project safe neighborhood principles and Detroit initiative implementation status.

Project safe neighborhood principle	*Detroit gun violence reduction initiative implementation status*
Partnerships involving other law enforcement and criminal justice agencies, social service agencies and community groups, and a research partner	Task force formed representing all principal federal, state, and local law enforcement agencies. Overall leadership and coordination provided by the US Attorney's Office, Eastern District of Michigan. Agencies participating in the initiative include: Detroit Police Department, Wayne County Prosecutor's Office, Wayne County Sheriff's Office, Michigan State Police, Michigan Department of Corrections, Bureau of Alcohol, Tobacco, and Firearms, Federal Bureau of Investigation, US Attorney's Office—Eastern District of Michigan, Detroit Community Justice Partnership, Detroit Weed and Seed, and Michigan State University School of Criminal Justice.
Strategic Plan involving problem solving process focused on identifying the most problematic individuals, groups, and areas for focused enforcement, intervention, and prevention activities.	Northwest Detroit targeted for its fatal and nonfatal shooting rates relative to the remainder of Detroit. Special attention given to arrests involving a firearm and arrests involving a felon in possession of a firearm. Case review process used to (a) augment traditional intelligence gathering and information sharing processes to identify individuals, groups, and spatial locations, (b) enhance court sentences, and (c) target resource deployments for enforcement strategies and community mobilization efforts.
Data is used to inform the plan and make revisions when such changes are needed	Data trends within the district were presented by a member of Detroit Police Department's Crime Analysis Unit. Michigan State University School of Criminal Justice provided supplemental analytics associated with monthly and quarterly trends.
Training to task forces in a variety of topics including strategic problem solving, firearm enforcement and prosecution, and community outreach	Task force members participated in an assortment of training programs designed by the Department of Justice for federal, state, and local prosecutors and law enforcement within the state of Michigan and across the country. Site visits were made semi-annually to other federal districts to observe strong program models (e.g., US Attorney's Office, Western District of Tennessee).
Outreach efforts to spread the general deterrence message of enhanced punishment to the intended audience through the use of a variety of local media	National outreach campaign materials were adapted for use in Detroit. Brochures, literature, and other materials were disseminated among criminal justice agencies, social service agencies, and community groups across the city. Public service announcements were made on local television, print media, and affiliated websites and social media.
Site accountability involving data collection of standardized measures and periodic reporting of results	Data trends presented and reviewed during the case reviews served as the primary accountability mechanism. Target resource deployments were modified as trends changed. Monthly, quarterly, and semi-annual reporting of standardized measures were submitted to the Department of Justice for review.

One of the core components of the strategic planning principle of Project Safe Neighborhoods is a case review. Here arrests and incidents are systematically assessed by prosecutors and police officers who collectively gather intelligence regarding individuals and groups and conduct prosecution and enforcement actions aimed at disrupting gun violence and homicide within a specified target area. The case review component is quite common across Project Safe Neighborhood sites (Klofas, Kroovand Hipple, and McGarrell 2010) and was an active element of Project Safe Neighborhood's predecessor Project Exile in Richmond, Virginia (Raphael and Ludwig 2002).

The Detroit Gun Violence Reduction Initiative instituted its own case review process. The case review team consisted of one federal and two state prosecutors, a Detroit Police Department (DPD) Sergeant or Squad Leader, five DPD officers, a DPD intelligence officer, a DPD crime analyst, an agent from the Bureau of Alcohol, Tobacco, and Firearms, a field office supervisor from the Michigan Department of Corrections (MDOC), and the research partner. All of the law enforcement and prosecution personnel were assigned full time to the initiative. DPD officers were selected by supervisory and management staff on the basis of the officers' street knowledge of the various individuals and groups involved in gun violence and drug sales within the target area.

The team met on a weekly basis to discuss events of the previous week. As per the collective decision-making of the case review team, arrests for offenses involving a firearm or arrestees involved in a firearm offense who possessed prior felony convictions were specified as critical cases receiving the most scrutiny. Characteristics of each of these arrests were presented by DPD officers to the team. Incident details were provided as well as the role of the arrestee in the incident and his/her links to broader gun violence, drug sales, and gangs in the area. Sources of intelligence on individuals and networks were gathered via systematic debriefings of arrestees and were used to contextualize decisions. The MDOC representative provided information on the correctional statuses of arrestees as well as any intelligence gathered while arrestees were under the supervision of MDOC. Additionally, updates on individuals currently under parole supervision and those who may either be involved with gangs or who could provide information about active gang members were provided.

The primary objective of the case review process was to identify serious offenders and assess the potential utility of federal or state prosecution. Arrestees with past felony convictions were eligible for federal prosecution. Beyond this criteria, the case review team recommended federal prosecution for specific arrestees who were predominately intertwined in the gun violence and drug sales nexus in the target area. Case processing through the federal criminal justice system would enable a sentence enhancement of imprisonment for up to five years without the possibility of early release. Fundamentally, it is the independent and united effects of incapacitation of serious offenders and the general and specific deterrence signals sent to the community about the high costs of gun violence that may affect rates of gun violence and homicide in Northwest Detroit. Case reviews also fulfilled important secondary purposes by improving efforts to share information, identify patterns and make connections between individuals, groups, and incidents, generate actionable intelligence, and build future federal or state prosecutions. Put differently, the case review process component was used to change traditional criminal justice system activities and increase system responsivity to local problems.

The Detroit Gun Violence Reduction Initiative required various criminal justice system agencies and actors to adopt principles consistent with a new work approach; transforming roles and responsibilities and functioning as a unified front as under the auspices of a case review team. Many and significant challenges in the implementation of the initiative occurred throughout the research period. Most notable were turnovers in law enforcement and prosecution line personnel assigned to the initiative as well as leadership. As a result, there was wide variation in the level of commitment to the principles of the initiative. Yet there was a time frame of approximately nine months within the research period where consistent adherence to initiative principles was observed. This included weekly meetings of a case review team with stable membership. This period allowed for an analysis of the case review process to determine whether systematic criminal justice system processing changes had occurred or if the status quo was being maintained.

Data and Methods

Three different sources of official data were gathered. First, arrest data were obtained from DPD management information systems for all carrying concealed weapon (CCW) arrests made in Northwest Detroit over a two year period. CCW arrests were ideal for this analysis as these offenses involved a firearm and captured arrestees with and without prior criminal history records. Arrest data were then merged to case prosecution filings with the state court gathered from the management information system of the Third Judicial Circuit of Michigan which had jurisdiction over the city of Detroit and Wayne County. This second source of data contained additional state court information on charges filed, case dispositions, and sentencing information when applicable. Federal court information for cases recommended for federal prosecution were not available. Initial state court filing information was used to provide insight on cases recommended for federal prosecution as state charges were filed before or in parallel with federal charging decisions. Third, Law Enforcement Information Network (LEIN) queries were used to capture criminal history record information on arrestees.

The two year data collection period allowed for the construction of one year pre-implementation and one year post-implementation time frames. It is important to note that the pre-implementation period is not a pure "no treatment" counterfactual in a traditional quasi-experimental pre-post research design framework. Instead, this period corresponds to a time when the implementation of the initiative was being attempted but could not gain enough traction to materialize. A series of starts and stops were experienced with delays lasting months between a stop and a restart. Most of the initiative principles were being explored but had not been committed to or planned for with much fidelity. The case review team added, removed, and rotated through members during this time and was unable to meet on a frequent basis. At no point in time across this period was a case review team meeting held in back-to-back weekly successions. The post-implementation period reflects the time when the initiative had been satisfactorily implemented and maintained the greatest level of stability among criminal justice agencies and actors involved in the initiative. During this period case review team meetings were held each week and attended by the same team members.

The annual time frame is used to adjust for the research design, account for the timing of criminal justice system processing, and standardize comparisons. Individuals processed by the criminal justice system in the pre-implementation year would have been arrested before attempts at implementing the initiative. Post-implementation cases reviewed by the case review team could have persisted in the criminal justice system beyond the nine month period when the initiative was most active. Extending the time frame to a year captures most of the cases reviewed by the case review team.

If the case review process and broader initiative was working as planned, evidence of differential case processing should be observed between the pre-implementation and post-implementation periods. Consistent with the TNCJ predictions the case reviews should serve to "tighten" processing of cases and at least four plausible changes in case processing routines and characteristics are expected. First, it was anticipated that fewer cases would be dismissed. The case review team's attention to arrestees and the incidents surrounding the arrest may overcome legal or evidentiary obstacles to prosecution and increase the likelihood that charges would be filed. Second, prosecutions that did move forward would involve arrestees with substantial criminal history records. As one of the primary objectives of the case review team was to identify arrestees with past felonies, there may be important differences in the criminal history backgrounds of the arrestees moving through the system. Third, case dispositions would lead to convictions and more severe sentences. In addition to improving the likelihood of charges being filed at the start of the process, stronger cases may have been developed as part of the case review team efforts resulting in improved court outcomes. Fourth, the pool of arrestees recommended for federal prosecution would have substantially more serious criminal history records. Again, identification of serious offenders is part of the case review approach and those identified for potential federal prosecution should represent serious offenders if the initiative protocol is followed.

To examine anticipated criminal justice system processing changes, pre-implementation and post-implementation differences are examined. Analyses are largely descriptive and follow the prosecutorial process of CCW arrests through the criminal justice system. Bivariate chi-square and two-way analysis of variance statistical tests are employed to examine between group differences across periods.

Results

Overall case processing

Across a two year period, 1,206 CCW arrests were made in Northwest Detroit. More CCW arrests were made in the pre-implementation period (n = 624) than the post-implementation period (n = 582). Table 37.3 displays prosecution filings for the two groups. Forty-six percent of the pre-implementation group had arrest charges filed with the court for prosecution, while the majority of the arrestees had their charges dropped. Earlier research on the Eighth Precinct (Bynum and McCluskey 2005), which represented a subpart of Northwest Detroit, indicated CCW case attrition to be a systemic issue. Among the post-implementation group, most of the arrestees had charges filed with the court. Forty-one percent of arrestees in the post-implementation group had their charges dropped. In all, arrestees in the post-implementation group were significantly more likely to have charges filed with the court, while arrestees in the pre-implementation group were likely to have their charges dropped.

Table 37.4 presents the criminal history backgrounds of arrestees with charges filed with the court for prosecution. Approximately 40 percent of the arrestees in the

Table 37.3 Comparison of prosecution filings.

	Pre-implementation *(n = 624)*	*Post-implementation* *(n = 582)*
	N (%)	N (%)
Prosecution charges filed	286 (46%)	344 (59%)
Prosecution charges dropped	338 (54%)	238 (41%)

Table 37.4 Comparison of arrestee criminal history backgrounds for prosecuted cases.

	Pre-implementation *(n = 286)*	*Post-implementation* *(n = 344)*
	N (%)	*N (%)*
At least one felony arrest	121 (42%)	146 (42%)
At least one felony conviction	91 (32%)	102 (30%)
At least one misdemeanor conviction	12 (4%)	50 (14%)
At least one prison sentence	30 (11%)	41 (12%)
At least one jail sentence	27 (9%)	52 (15%)
Weapons offense arrest	48 (17%)	72 (21%)
Weapons offense conviction	37 (13%)	34 (10%)
Drug crime arrest	40 (14%)	62 (18%)
Drug crime conviction	31 (11%)	38 (11%)

pre-implementation and post-implementation groups had at least one prior felony arrest. Approximately 30 percent of the arrestees in both groups had a prior felony conviction. There were no significant differences between the two groups on past felonies. In fact, there did not appear to be any significant differences between the two groups on any of the criminal history background indicators.

Table 37.5 and Table 37.6 detail the case dispositions and sentences for the cases that moved forward for prosecution. One of the limitations of using official data sources is the potential for missing data. This limitation has posed problems for the current research as disposition and sentence information was either pending determination, had yet to be entered into the management information system, or was missing altogether. This was especially true for the post-implementation period where approximately one-third of the case disposition and sentencing information was missing, likely due to a lag in case processing and closure. To provide insights about outcome trends, adjusted percentages are included in the tables. These adjusted percentages remove missing data from the denominator of the percentage calculation and allow for a rudimentary comparison between pre- and post-implementation periods.

Among both groups, a majority of the cases resulted in a conviction (see Table 37.5). Further examination of how these convictions were attained indicated that most were the product of a guilty plea. Among the pre-implementation group, 86 percent of the convictions were from guilty pleas, while 87 percent of the convictions for the

Table 37.5 Comparison of case dispositions for prosecuted cases.

	Pre-implementation (n = 286)	*Post-implementation (n = 344)*
	N (%)(adjusted %)	*N (%)(adjusted %)*
Convicted	216 (76%)(79%)	168 (49%)(74%)
Not convicted	59 (21%)(21%)	58 (17%)(26%)
Missing	11 (4%)	118 (34%)

Table 37.6 Comparison of sentences for prosecuted cases.

	Pre-implementation (n = 216)		*Post-implementation (n = 168)*	
	N (%)(adjusted %)	*Average sentence*	*N (%)(adjusted %)*	*Average sentence*
Prison	58 (27%)(31%)	3.35 (5.77) Years	38 (23%)(33%)	3.77 (3.65) Years
Jail	21 (10%)(11%)	79.90 (69.43) Days	20 (12%)(18%)	104.50 (79.65) Days
Probation	93 (43%)(49%)	1.51 (.70) Years	55 (33%)(48%)	1.37 (.56) Years
Fine*	18 (8%)(9%)	$745.28 (223.39)	1 (1%)(1%)	$900.00
Missing	25 (12%)		54 (32%)	

* $p < 0.05$

post-implementation group came from a plea. Disposition outcomes are largely similar between the two groups.

Table 37.6 displays the most serious sentence received for a conviction as well as the average sentence length or penalty for the most serious sentence. Rather than allowing combinations of sentences for a conviction (e.g., prison plus probation, probation plus fine), sentences are simplified to a hierarchical ordering where prison is considered the most serious sentence type and is followed by jail, probation, and fine in decreasing order of seriousness. The modal sentence category for both groups was a sentence of probation. With the exception of the proportion of cases resulting in a fine as the most serious sentence, there were no significant differences between groups on the sentence received or the average sentence length or penalty. Although caution is needed in interpreting the effects of small cell sizes, especially in combination with missing data, there is some evidence to suggest that the post-implementation group was more likely to have received a sentence more serious than a fine.

Federal case processing recommendations

As suggested by the previous set of analyses on overall case processing, Northwest Detroit processes roughly 600 arrestees each year on CCW offenses. Such volume emanating from one portion of the city places tremendous strain on the criminal justice system. One of the primary functions of the case review team was to identify high impact individuals with prior felony convictions that could be eligible for federal prosecution. This effort attempts to further system change by allocating the attention of the system to more serious offenders.

As documented in Table 37.4, 102 arrestees in the post-implementation period had at least one prior felony conviction and 34 had a prior weapons offense conviction. As a preliminary baseline, between 21 and 30 percent of those with charges filed or 6 to 18 percent of those apprehended appeared to be eligible for federal prosecution based simply on criminal history information. Overall, 34 arrestees or 6 percent of the post-implementation arrests were recommended for federal prosecution consideration.

Twenty-nine of the arrestees recommended for federal prosecution (85% of total subsample) had accessible criminal history record information or preliminary state court information available for review. Table 37.7 provides a comparison of criminal history backgrounds for arrestees with state charges filed and arrestees who were recommended for federal prosecution. Across all of the criminal history indicators, arrestees recommended for federal prosecution had more serious records of offending. Over 70 percent of those recommended for federal prosecution had at least one prior felony conviction and nearly 80 percent had at least one prior felony arrest.

State court dispositions and sentences were observed for 16 arrestees whose cases were recommended for federal prosecution. This indicates that 55 percent of federally eligible cases recommended for federal prosecution by the case review team were instead processed by the state court. The remaining 13 cases had state charges refiled at the federal level.

Table 37.7 Comparison of criminal history backgrounds for post-implementation arrestees and arrestees recommended for federal prosecution.

	Arrestees with Charges Filed (n = 315)	*Federal Recommendations (n = 29)*
	N (%)	*N (%)*
At least one felony arrest*	123 (39%)	23 (79%)
At least one felony conviction*	82 (26%)	21 (72%)
At least one misdemeanor conviction*	38 (12%)	11 (38%)
At least one prison sentence*	28 (9%)	11 (38%)
At least one jail sentence*	44 (14%)	9 (31%)
Weapons offense arrest*	60 (19%)	13 (45%)
Weapons offense conviction*	28 (9%)	7 (24%)
Drug crime arrest*	47 (15%)	17 (59%)
Drug crime conviction*	22 (7%)	15 (52%)

* $p < 0.05$

Discussion

The purpose of this research was to describe the Detroit Gun Violence Reduction Initiative and examine whether a core component of the broader Project Safe Neighborhood program model locally implemented in Northwest Detroit facilitated systematic criminal justice system processing changes, consistent with ideas drawn from The New Criminal Justice. If the case review process was operating as designed, indicators of differential case processing through the criminal justice system should be apparent. Comparison of arrest cohorts indicated that the probability of prosecution charges being filed did substantially rise once the case review team was most active in their review of cases. Formal charges were pursued in 46 percent of cases in the pre-implementation period and rose to 59 percent in the post-implementation period. At the start of the prosecution efforts there appears to be a change in the manner of processing cases under the initiative, which may correspond to increased focus and systematic review of cases along with the close working relationship between law enforcement and prosecution agencies on a case by case basis.

With arrests resulting in more prosecutorial charges being filed, net widening is possible where charges filed during the initiative would not have been filed if the initiative was not being undertaken. The findings do not provide much evidence to support the presence of a net widening effect. First, the criminal history backgrounds of the sample were similar. Less serious offenders were not being processed through the criminal justice system during the initiative relative to the pre-implementation period. Second, the overall processing of arrestees after charges were filed was relatively stable across the two year timeframe. Case dispositions and sentences were relatively similar across the entire sample of arrestees.

Consistent with the initiative model and responsibilities of the case review team, the prior record of arrestees recommended for federal prosecution were substantially more serious than the remaining pool of arrestees. These recommendations were also highly selective; only 34 of 582 arrestees were recommended for federal prosecution. The small number of cases recommended for federal prosecution reflects the rigor of the case review process as well as the notion of concentrating resources and efforts on the highest risk individuals.

Overall, it is not completely clear whether significant criminal justice system case processing changes occurred with the implementation of the case review process. On one hand, responsivity changes were detected. Cases were less likely to be dismissed during the time when the case review team was most active in reviewing cases. The case review team also fulfilled the objective of targeting serious offenders with regard to criminal history background. On the other hand, prosecuted cases involved arrestees with similar criminal history profiles. An increase in the likelihood of a conviction or more severe sentence among those convicted during the post-implementation period was not detected. Also, a majority of the cases recommended for federal prosecution were instead processed by the state court. These trends are more symbolic of traditional case processing efforts than systemic change confronting gun violence.

Much larger questions remain about the effects of the Detroit Gun Violence Reduction Initiative as a whole as the case review process was one component of a broader attempt to address gun violence and homicide problems in Northwest Detroit. Through the use of a time-series design with 117 weekly observations across four comparison districts across the city of Detroit, significant declines in fatal and nonfatal shootings occurred during the time period when the case review process was most active (see Bynum, Grommon, and McCluskey 2014). Northwest Detroit experienced a reduction of one less shooting victimization per week relative to a 39 week pre-intervention period. This decline was not observed in any of the other districts. Once the initiative ended, the rate of fatal and nonfatal shootings reverted to near pre-intervention levels, implying that once system changes were removed gun violence issues can return. While it is difficult to dissect the unique contribution of the case review process from ongoing enforcement strategies and community mobilization efforts taking place during the initiative, the Project Safe Neighborhood program model specifies that all of these elements must be working in tandem to reduce gun violence and homicide.

Directions for Future Research

Gun violence and gun homicides are salient as crime, health, and political issues in contemporary American society and the city of Detroit is a location in which their consequences are particularly acute. Criminal justice approaches to violence reduction have, as noted, recently indicated successful programmatic approaches in the area of focused deterrence (e.g., Braga and Weisburd 2012). However, concern of what constitutes the key elements leading to changes in violence levels and how the bureaucratic commitment to interventions are maintained over time are, respectively, multifaceted and unclear (Griffiths and Christian 2015; Tillyer, Engel, and Lovins 2012). The research reported here is consistent with that larger body of focused deterrence literature as it illustrates the ambiguity of why violence changed during an intervention and documents the difficulties of starting a program and maintaining a focused and vigorous working group of criminal justice practitioners.

As such, the research frames the implementation of the Detroit Gun Violence Reduction Initiative in the context of The New Criminal Justice. However, the measures adopted, as related to case processing, are only weakly tied to that framework. Refining the measurement of implementation, dosage, and program fidelity are essential for furthering our knowledge of the effectiveness of criminal justice innovations and also important for understanding criminal justice theory. The "working group" model and the academic–practitioner collaborations are areas ripe for continued investigation and the development of measures that capture the dynamics of these partnerships as vehicles for violence reduction. Such approaches will arguably lead to more systematic and generalizable findings which will assist in confronting serious problems including gun violence and homicide.

At least two advantages accrue from focusing greater attention on implementation. First, the mechanism by which violence reductions occur (e.g., incapacitation, deterrence, etc.) will be more explicitly tied to programmatic elements. Thus the "black box" of innovation will be opened for inspection to ensure reasonable and plausible linkages to criminological theories. Second, the dosage of any particular implemented project will be more easily measured as a change from "business as usual" to the new implemented program. In this study, case characteristics were traced and compared as a proxy for understanding if and how business changed. It is unclear, however, if this would be useful in a cross-site analysis or if it would (or should) encourage adoption in another jurisdiction. As we focus on local criminal justice as a unit of analysis within TNCJ it is important to reconcile that emphasis with the ability to develop measures which will allow for useful comparisons and contrasts across local systems as we seek to understand whether specific criminal justice mechanisms inhibit violence and how to maintain their vitality if they do so.

Note

1 This research was partially funded by the National Institute of Justice grant #2004-IJ-CX-0022. The points of view in this document are the authors' and are not intended to represent those of the Department of Justice or other agencies involved.

References

Baldas, T. and Schaefer, J. (2013) "Corruption no more": Judge sends a message with 28-year sentence for Kilpatrick. *Detroit Free Press,* October 10, 2013.

Bernard, T. and Engel, R. (2001) Conceptualizing criminal justice theory. *Justice Quarterly,* 18: 1–30.

Bernard, T., Paoline, E., and Pare, P.-P. (2005) General systems theory and criminal justice. *Journal of Criminal Justice*, 33: 203–211.

Braga, A.A., Hureau, D.M., and Papachristos, A.V. (2014) Deterring gang-involved gun violence: Measuring the impact of Boston's Operation Ceasefire on street gang behavior. *Journal of Quantitative Criminology*, 30: 113–139.

Braga, A., Lum, C., and Davis, E.F. (2014) Connecting police chiefs and academic researchers: The new division of policing in the American Society of Criminology. *The Police Chief*, 81: 76–77.

Braga, A.A. and Weisburd, D.L. (2012) *The Effects of "Pulling Levers" Focused Deterrence Strategies on Crime*. Oslo: Campbell Collaboration.

Brown, M.K. (1981) *Working the Street*. New York: Russell Sage.

Bureau of Justice Statistics (2015) Criminal Justice System Flowchart. Available online at http://www.bjs.gov/content/largechart.cfm (accessed June 11, 2015).

Bynum, T.S., Grommon, E., and McCluskey, J.D. (2014) *Evaluation of a Comprehensive Approach to Reducing Gun Violence in Detroit*. Washington, DC: US Department of Justice, Office of Justice Programs, National Institute of Justice.

Bynum, T.S. and McCluskey, J.D. (2005) *Strategic Approaches to Community Safety Initiative (SACSI) Detroit, Michigan*. Washington, DC: US Department of Justice, Office of Justice Programs, National Institute of Justice.

Carter, L. (1972) *The Limits of Order*. Lexington, MA: Lexington Press.

Corsaro, N. and Engel, R.S. (2015) Most challenging of contexts: Assessing the impact of focused deterrence on serious violence in New Orleans. *Criminology & Public Policy*, 14: 471–505.

Corsaro, N., Hunt, E.D., Kroovand Hipple, N., and McGarrell, E.F. (2012) The impact of drug market pulling levers policing on neighborhood violence: An evaluation of the high point drug market intervention. *Criminology & Public Policy*, 11: 167–199.

Crank, J. and Bowman, B. (2008) What is good criminal justice theory? *Journal of Criminal Justice*, 36: 563–572.

Eisenstein, J. and Jacob, H. (1978) *Felony Justice: An Organization Analysis of Criminal Courts*. Boston: Little and Brown.

Farley, R., Steeh, C., Krysan, M., *et al.* (1994) Stereotypes and segregation: Neighborhoods in the Detroit area. *American Journal of Sociology*, 100: 750–780.

FBI (Federal Bureau of Investigation) (2015) *Crime in the United States, 2014*. Washington, DC: US Department of Justice, Federal Bureau of Investigation.

Feeley, M.M. (1973) Two models of the criminal justice system: An organizational perspective. *Law & Society Review*, 7: 407–425.

Griffiths, E. and Christian, J. (2015) Considering focused deterrence in the age of Ferguson, Baltimore, North Charleston, and beyond. *Criminology & Public Policy*, 14: 573–581.

Hunter, G. (2015) 2014 Detroit homicides fewest in 47 years. *The Detroit News*, January 2. Available online at http://www.detroitnews.com/story/news/local/wayne-county/2015/01/01/detroit-homicides/21153429/(accessed June 19, 2015).

Kauffman, K. (1988) *Prison Officers and Their World*. Cambridge, MA: Harvard University Press.

Kennedy, D.M. (2006) Old wine in new bottles: Policing and the lessons of pulling levers. In D.L. Weisburd and A.A. Braga (eds) *Police Innovation: Contrasting Perspectives* (pp. 155–170). New York: Cambridge University Press.

Klofas, J.M., Kroovand Hipple, N., and McGarrell, E.F. (2010) The new criminal justice. In J. Klofas, N. Kroovand Hipple, and E.F. McGarrell (eds), *The New Criminal Justice: American Communities and the Changing World of Crime Control* (pp. 3–16). New York: Routledge.

Kraska, P. (2006) Criminal justice theory: Toward legitimacy and an infrastructure. *Justice Quarterly*, 23: 167–185.

Land, K.C. (2015) Something that works in violent crime control: Let the focused deterrence and pulling levers programs roll with eternal vigilance. *Criminology & Public Policy*, 14: 515–519.

LeDuff, C. (2014) *Detroit: An American Autopsy*. New York: Penguin Books.

Morenoff, J.D., Sampson, R.J., and Raudenbush, S.W. (2001) Neighborhood inequality, collective efficacy, and the spatial dynamics of urban violence. *Criminology*, 39: 517–558.

Muir, W.K. (1977) *Police: Streetcorner Politicians*. Chicago: University of Chicago Press.

Papachristos, A.V. and Kirk, D.S. (2015) Changing the street dynamic: Evaluating Chicago's Group Violence Reduction Strategy. *Criminology & Public Policy*, 14: 525–558.

Raphael, S. and Ludwig, J. (2002) Prison sentence enhancements: The case of project exile. In J. Ludwig and P.J. Cook (eds), *Evaluating Gun Policy: Effects on Crime and Violence* (pp. 251–286). Washington, DC: Brookings Institution Press.

Rydberg, J. and McGarrell, E.F. (2015) Evaluating the impact of the Parole Call-In interventoin on community-level violence. Paper presented at the annual meeting for the American Society of Criminology, Washington, DC, November 18–21.

Snipes, J.B. and Maguire, E.R. (2007) Foundations of criminal justice theory. In D.E. Duffee and E.R. Maguire (eds), *Criminal Justice Theory: Explaining the Nature and Behavior of Criminal Justice* (pp. 27–49). New York: Routledge.

Sugrue, T.J. (2005) *The Origins of the Urban Crisis: Race and Inequality in Postwar Detroit*. Princeton, NJ: Princeton University Press.

Tillyer, M.S., Engel, R.S., and Lovins, B. (2012) Beyond Boston: Applying theory to understand and address sustainability issues in focused deterrence initiatives for violence reduction. *Crime & Delinquency*, 58(6): 973–997.

Weisburd, D. and Neyroud, P. (2011) *Police Science: Toward a New Paradigm*. Cambridge, MA: Harvard Kennedy School Program in Criminal Justice Policy and Management.

Williams, D.J., Currie, D., Linden, W., and Donnelly, P.D. (2014) Addressing gang-related violence in Glasgow: A preliminary pragmatic quasi-experimental evaluation of the community initiative to reduce violence (CIRV). *Aggression and Violent Behavior*, 19: 686–691.

Wright, K.N. (1981) The desirability of goal conflict within the criminal justice system. *Journal of Criminal Justice*, 9: 209–218.

Further Reading

Papachristos, A.V., Meares, T.L., and Fagan, J. (2007) Attention felons: Evaluating Project Safe Neighborhoods in Chicago. *Journal of Empirical Legal Studies*, 4: 223–272. DOI: 10.1111/j.1740-1461.2007.00096.x.

38

Preventing Homicide

Edward R. Maguire

Introduction

Conventional wisdom suggests that homicide cannot be prevented. Government officials and other influential policymakers routinely lament that it will take at least a generation to reduce the number of homicides. Many critics continue to believe it is not possible to reduce homicide without solving poverty, inequality and other "root causes" of crime. Yet, researchers have now amassed a considerable body of evidence which suggests that homicides can be prevented (Brookman and Maguire 2005). Moreover, the evidence suggests that it does not have to take a generation; short term reductions in homicide are possible with the right mix of policies. This chapter summarizes a multidisciplinary body of research evidence on what works and what doesn't work in preventing homicides.

The chapter focuses primarily on what I refer to as "street" homicides (Kuhns and Maguire 2012; Maguire *et al.* 2008). These include homicides that are associated with gangs, retail drug markets, and petty disputes that are typically carried out by and against young men using guns. The use of the word "street" does not refer to the locations where homicide incidents take place; it refers to cultural systems in which violence is commonly used to preserve one's reputation, enforce boundaries, and resolve disputes (Anderson 1999; Berg *et al.* 2012; Stewart and Simons 2010). These homicides are often difficult to classify using conventional motive categories because they may involve a mix of motives. For instance, imagine that a gang leader has an altercation with a drug dealer who he perceives as behaving disrespectfully by selling drugs in his gang's territory without permission. If the gang leader kills the drug dealer, should the motive be classified as gang-related, drug-related, revenge, or an

The Handbook of Homicide, First Edition. Edited by Fiona Brookman,
Edward R. Maguire, and Mike Maguire.

altercation? In cities and countries with high homicide rates, street homicides often constitute the majority of homicide incidents. Other specific types of homicides that are beyond the scope of this chapter include those associated with genocide, terrorism and political violence, domestic violence, sexual homicide, and serial and spree homicides.

The Knowledge-base on Preventing Homicide

The knowledge-base about how to prevent, deter, control or reduce homicides is a minefield of anecdotes and opinions, unsupported claims, unbridled advocacy, and research evidence of varying levels of quality. Anecdotes and opinions about effective solutions for reducing homicide are ubiquitous, but in the absence of rigorous evidence of their validity they provide a weak foundation for designing or implementing policy. Unsupported claims are also common, with public officials routinely claiming credit for reductions in homicide on the basis of weak evidence (Bowling 1999). These same officials are typically less eager to claim credit for subsequent increases in homicide, often attributing these increases to external factors beyond their control. Zealous advocacy for certain programs and policies intended to reduce homicide is also very common, particularly for certain deeply felt policy issues like gun control. However, the research cited by advocates to support their preferred policy positions is often based on a biased reading of the evidence. There is a considerable body of research evidence on how to prevent homicide, but the quality of the research varies widely.

In short, making sense of the literature on preventing homicide is difficult because it requires the reader to be a careful consumer of the evidence. This means setting aside the anecdotes and opinions, unsupported claims, unbridled advocacy, and poorly done research in an attempt to extract only the highest-quality scientific evidence on what works to prevent homicide. That is the purpose of this chapter. Two concepts from research methodology—internal and external validity—play an important role in assessing the quality of the evidence. *Internal validity* is the extent to which a research method is capable of discerning cause and effect. Some methods (such as bivariate correlations) are only suitable for inferring that two variables (such as poverty and crime) are statistically associated, but not for concluding that one "causes" the other. This is why research methods instructors teach students that "correlation does not imply causation." Many research designs have weak internal validity and therefore do not allow for confident inferences about causation. Randomized experiments, if designed and executed well, allow for confident assertions about cause and effect because the random assignment ensures that the only difference between the treatment and control groups is the treatment. When randomized experiments are not possible, rigorous quasi-experiments can also provide strong evidence about cause and effect. Quasi-experiments resemble randomized experiments in certain ways, but do not involve random assignment to treatment and control groups. The best scientific evidence on preventing homicides is often derived from experiments and quasi-experiments.

Much of the "evidence" that people draw on when thinking about how to reduce homicide has weak internal validity. People's opinions are often based on casual observations. For example, a police agency will launch a violence reduction program and shootings will decrease. Officials will then conclude from this evidence that the program is effective. These types of unsystematic inferences have weak internal validity because they do not account for alternative explanations for changes in violence. Journalists and advocates often write compelling stories about "effective" violence reduction initiatives for which the actual evidence of effectiveness is weak or non-existent. Policymakers routinely rely on this type of impressionistic or anecdotal evidence in deciding how to expend public funds. The central idea of evidence-based crime policy is to ensure that policies intended to reduce crime are based on the strongest evidence about what works (Mears 2007; Welsh and Farrington 2011). The strength of the evidence depends in large part on the internal validity of the studies comprising the evidence base (e.g., Farrington 2003; MacKenzie 2000; Sherman 2003; for an alternative perspective, see Pawson and Tilley 1997). Studies with weaker internal validity are more likely to report that a treatment is effective and less likely to report that a treatment has harmful effects (Weisburd, Lum, and Petrosino 2001).

Another key issue in weighing the quality of the evidence is *external validity*, which is concerned with the generalizability of a research finding "across different persons, settings, and times" (Cook and Campbell 1979: 37). Suppose we found that a certain crime prevention program was successful in reducing violence in Boston. Would this same program be effective in Baltimore or Philadelphia? How about London or Sydney? How about Port-au-Prince or the favelas of Rio de Janeiro? External validity is concerned with the applicability of a study finding outside of the specific sample from which it was generated. If a cognitive behavioral intervention works on incarcerated adults, will it also work on non-incarcerated adults? How about non-incarcerated juveniles? External validity is important because we often don't know whether a program that is effective for one population will be equally effective for others (Pawson and Tilley 1997). For instance, crime reduction initiatives established in developed nations often backfire in unexpected ways when implemented in developing nations (Maguire and King 2013). A study's external validity has implications for its policy relevance. As Eck (2010: 865) notes: "Policy relevance is not simply about 'what works.' Policy relevance is also about '*what* works *where, when,* and with *whom.*'"

External validity is especially important here because most empirical research on how to reduce homicide comes from the United States, which is a unique nation by world standards. There are good reasons to question whether research carried out in this unique setting is applicable to the rest of the world, particularly low- and middle-income countries where basic governmental and social structures differ considerably from the United States. The world often turns to the United States for ideas about how to address homicide. This is an example of a broader phenomenon known as "policy transfer" (Jones and Newburn 2007; Robertson 2005). While every nation engages in policy transfer, it is especially evident in developing countries, which often borrow policy ideas from developed nations. These imported solutions may be problematic if they are not adapted to the contexts into which they are being embedded (Maguire and King 2013).

In this chapter, I examine the evidence associated with four types of initiatives that have received significant attention in recent years: focused deterrence strategies that target high-risk violent offenders; place-based policing strategies that target "hot spots" of violence; street outreach strategies that seek to prevent violent incidents, especially retaliation shootings; and gun-related strategies.

Focused Deterrence Strategies

Deterrence is a classic theory of criminology dating back to the work of eighteenth century Enlightenment philosophers. It asserts that potential offenders weigh the costs and benefits when deciding whether to commit a crime. Deterrence theory suggests that offenders can be dissuaded from committing crime, and therefore crime can be prevented, by laws and policies which ensure that the costs of committing a crime outweigh the benefits (Cook 1980; Gibbs 1975). The literature on deterrence suggests that offenders weigh three factors when deciding whether to commit an offense: the certainty, severity, and swiftness of the sanction (Paternoster 2010). Certainty refers to the likelihood of being punished; severity refers to the harshness of the punishment; and swiftness refers to the speed with which the punishment is administered. Justice systems that optimize these three factors are thought to deter crime more effectively.

According to Kennedy (2009), deterrence often fails because policymakers and practitioners focus too heavily on the *objective* characteristics of criminal sanctions (especially their severity) and not sufficiently on how these sanctions are perceived by offenders and would-be offenders. As noted by Paternoster (2010: 785): "legislators establish and modify the objective properties of punishment with the expectation that perceptual properties of punishment will be affected." Influencing these perceptions is vital. At the core of deterrence theory is a psychological process in which offenders and potential offenders weigh the costs and benefits of offending. However, these calculations are often based on imperfect, unclear, and incorrect information. Just as the rational man in classic economic theory tries to "maximize his utility" by making optimal choices that yield the greatest benefit at the lowest cost, offenders make decisions based on whatever imperfect information is available at the time. Kennedy argues that people often misunderstand the: "radical subjectivity that is at the heart of the deterrence process ... what matters in deterrence is what matters to offenders and potential offenders. It is benefits and costs as they understand them and define them, and their thinking in weighing those benefits and costs, that are dispositive" (Kennedy 2009: 23). Designing criminal justice sanctions that deter crime more effectively means developing a deeper understanding of how offenders and potential offenders perceive the costs and benefits of crime. A key aspect of deterrence is that offenders know what consequence they are likely to face as a result of their decision to commit an offense. If offenders don't know about a sanction—or if they underestimate the certainty, severity, or swiftness of a sanction—then it is likely to be an ineffective deterrent. Put in the language of criminologists, we know very little about "the formation of sanction risk perception" (Nagin 1998: 11).

Focused deterrence strategies seek to optimize the deterrent value of sanctions (or threat of sanctions) in multiple ways. First, rather than dispersing deterrent efforts broadly across a wide range of offenses and offenders, they focus on the most serious concentrations of violent offending: those people, groups, and places most responsible for violence. Second, by assembling a working group of agencies with different mechanisms for generating compliance by offenders, they widen the range of potential sanctions to include things like relentless stops and searches, enforcing probation and parole violations, taking advantage of federal law (in the US) in cases where state law is less severe, and arresting violent offenders for minor offenses. Third, by communicating directly with the offender population about the penalties that will result from continuing to engage in violence, the working groups aim to alter risk perceptions and generate a deterrent effect, in some cases without imposing an actual sanction. Fourth, when dealing with gangs, officials make it known that the entire gang will be held accountable for violence committed by any member of the gang (an approach known as "collective accountability"). Fifth, officials coordinate with service providers who can help offenders pursue alternatives to violence by offering counseling, mentoring, job training, and employment opportunities. Taken together, this collection of strategies is intended to "pull every lever" and optimize the deterrent effects of the working group's efforts (Kennedy 2009).

A growing body of high-quality research evidence suggests that well-designed focused deterrence interventions can produce dramatic reductions in gang and group-involved violence (e.g., Braga and Weisburd 2012; Kennedy 2009; Skogan and Frydl 2004). They were initially developed and tested in Boston, where they generated a 63 percent reduction in youth homicides (Braga *et al.* 2001; Piehl, Kennedy, and Braga 2000; Piehl *et al.* 2003). Since then they have been tested and found effective in several US cities, including: Chicago, IL (Papachristos, Meares, and Fagan 2007); Cincinnati, OH (Engel, Tillyer, and Corsaro 2013); Indianapolis, IN (McGarrell, Chermak, and Wilson 2006); Lowell, MA (Braga *et al.* 2008); and Stockton, CA (Braga 2008). A recent meta-analysis found "strong empirical evidence for the crime prevention effectiveness of focused deterrence strategies" (Braga and Weisburd 2012: 349). Little is known about their effectiveness outside of the US cities where they have been tested so far (for an exception, see Williams *et al.* 2014).

Place-based Policing Strategies

A significant body of research has established that crime and violence are not distributed evenly over space. Instead, they are concentrated in micro-places that are referred to as "hot spots" (Sherman, Gartin, and Buerger 1989; Weisburd, Maher, and Sherman 1992) or "pockets of crime" (St. Jean 2007). These micro-places are typically smaller locations within larger geographical units such as communities, neighborhoods, or police beats (Eck and Weisburd 1995). They usually vary in size from something as large as a block, street segment, or block face (Sherman and Weisburd 1995; Weisburd *et al.* 2004) to something as small as a single building, address, or street corner (Sherman, Gartin, and Buerger 1989). Even within very high-crime communities, crime exhibits "non-random patterns of highly localized concentration" in certain micro-places (Tita, Cohen, and Engberg 2005: 27; also see Braga, Papachristos, and Hureau 2010; Maguire *et al.* 2008). Furthermore, street gangs, which are responsible for a significant share of gun violence in certain communities, also tend to cluster "in relatively small, geographically defined areas within a neighborhood" (Tita, Cohen, and Engberg 2005: 27). Understanding the spatial concentrations of violence is very useful for designing targeted solutions.

Braga, Papachristos, and Hureau (2010) examined spatial patterning in gun assault incidents in Boston over a 29-year period from 1980 to 2008. They found that gun violence was not "spread evenly across the urban landscape" (2010: 33). Instead, it was spatially concentrated in a handful of street segments and intersections. In some hot spots, violence was stable over time, whereas others were more volatile. Braga, Papachristos, and Hureau suggest that rapid or sudden changes in gun violence may emerge as a result of "highly volatile micro-level trends at a relatively small number of places in urban environments" (2010: 33). They note that volatile hot spots "represent less than 3% of street segments and intersections, generate more than half of all gun violence incidents, and seem to be the primary drivers of overall gun violence trends in Boston" (2010: 33). These findings are consistent with those from an earlier study which found that most street segments in Seattle had stable crime patterns over a 14-year period (Weisburd *et al.* 2004). Only a small proportion of street segments exhibited increasing or decreasing crime trajectories, and these places tended to be responsible for driving citywide trends in crime (also see Weisburd, Groff, and Yang 2012).

Understanding spatial concentrations in violence enables police agencies to deploy their resources in a more targeted manner that can increase the likelihood of preventing or deterring crime. Braga, Papachristos, and Hureau (2010: 50) recommend that a city's violence prevention strategies should include place-based interventions that are "focused in very specific locations rather than diffused across larger neighborhoods." One possible approach is for police to identify hot spots of violence, especially gun violence, and then assign officers to acquire detailed knowledge about those areas. These experts can get to know residents and other local stakeholders, collect intelligence, conduct enforcement activity, and test a variety of crime prevention measures. They can also work closely with detectives to provide local knowledge that may be useful for investigations in those areas. They can anticipate impending incidents of violence, such as retaliation shootings, and take action to prevent violence. They can also anticipate other influential events in the community like changes in gang leadership or offenders returning home from prison. In short, they can serve as a valuable resource not only for the community itself, but also for other police units to ensure that they are well-informed about the area and the offenders who may be operating there (Maguire *et al.* 2008). Koper, Egge, and Lum (2015) recommend that police agencies broaden the role of criminal investigators to focus attention on criminogenic *places* instead of just individual criminal cases. This involves tracking hot spots and developing "problem-solving interventions tailored to specific places" (2015: 242). Their suggestion reinforces the idea that hot spots policing need not focus only on patrol; criminal investigators and patrol officers can work together in focusing on micro-places where crime and violence are most prevalent.

The idea of focusing on places instead of people represents "a radical departure from traditional criminological theories that focused prevention efforts on the individual and ignored the importance of place" (Braga, Papachristos, and Hureau 2012: 9). Yet there is considerable scientific evidence to support this approach. For instance, a committee of experts assembled by the US National Research Council reviewed the research and concluded: "studies that focused police resources on crime hot spots provided the strongest collective evidence of police effectiveness that is now available" (Skogan and Frydl 2004: 250). The most systematic evidence to date comes from a meta-analysis conducted by Braga, Papachristos, and Hureau (2012), whose review included 19 studies that used quasi-experimental (9 studies) or randomized experimental (10 studies) designs to test the effects of hot spots policing interventions. These studies contained 25 separate tests of hot spots policing, 20 of which reported significant reductions in crime and disorder. Braga, Papachristos, and Hureau concluded that the evaluation evidence "provides fairly robust evidence that hot spots policing is an effective crime prevention strategy. The research also suggests that focusing police efforts on high-activity crime places does not inevitably lead to crime displacement and crime control benefits may diffuse into the areas immediately surrounding the targeted locations" (2012: 6).

Street Outreach Strategies

Another well-known violence reduction strategy is the use of street outreach workers to provide counseling, mentoring, mediation, and other services within high-risk populations. These types of initiatives were especially popular in the 1950s and 1960s for dealing with youth gangs (Klein and Maxson 2006). However, the findings from research conducted during that era raised serious questions about the wisdom of these approaches (Carney, Mattick, and Callaway 1969; Gold and Mattick 1974; Klein 1969; Klein 1971; Yablonski 1962). One of the key issues was whether outreach workers may actually make things worse by validating gangs as legitimate entities and increasing gang cohesion. In reviewing this research, Klein and Maxson (2006: 260) conclude that street outreach workers *can* be successful if they are "carefully guided and monitored" to ensure that they do not generate iatrogenic (crime amplifying) effects.

In spite of the early research findings, street outreach workers have become a central component of violence reduction initiatives in many jurisdictions.[1]

For instance, street outreach is the nucleus of the Cure Violence model and related efforts that seek to interrupt and prevent violence through mediation and other forms of intervention by street outreach workers (see Chapter 34). Rather than relying on a criminal justice approach centered on arrest and prosecution, Cure Violence is based on a public health approach that focuses on prevention. The underlying premise is that violence is socially contagious and can spread like an epidemic. Cure Violence seeks to alter existing norms that view violence as an appropriate means of resolving conflict. As outlined in Chapter 35, a growing body of research evidence finds that violence is highly concentrated in certain networks of people (e.g., Papachristos, Braga, and Hureau 2012; Papachristos and Wildeman 2014; Tracy, Braga, and Papachristos 2016). Interventions that focus on stopping the spread of violence within these networks could have robust effects.

Cure Violence relies on street intelligence to identify people at greatest risk for shooting someone or being shot so the program's outreach workers and "violence interrupters" can intervene.[2] Cure Violence staff use their deep knowledge of the community to mediate disputes and interrupt the cycles of retaliation that tend to characterize gang- and group-involved violence. Many were once drug dealers or gang members and therefore they have "street" credibility. They monitor the pulse of the community, intervening in situations where violence is imminent, and seeking to alter the way people think about how to resolve conflict. Cure Violence and related interventions have now been evaluated in six US cities.[3] Although a thorough review of these evaluations is beyond the scope of this chapter, I discuss the initial evaluation that took place in Chicago and then only briefly summarize the findings from the other studies.

Cure Violence was first tested in Chicago (where it was originally known as *Chicago Ceasefire*). An evaluation examined the effects of Ceasefire on violent crime in seven of the 27 areas in which it was implemented (Skogan *et al.* 2009). The evaluators selected matched comparison areas that were similar in demographic and socioeconomic characteristics to these seven "treatment" areas. Because violent crime had already been decreasing throughout Chicago, the primary research question was whether the decrease in the Ceasefire zones was greater than the decrease in the comparison zones. The evaluation focused on three outcomes: shots fired (whether or not someone was hit), shootings (in which someone was hit), and killings. Thus there were 21 pairs of outcomes (seven pairs of treatment/comparison areas and three outcomes per area). The most basic analysis compared the percent change in each outcome before and after the implementation of Ceasefire for both the treatment and comparison areas. Of the 21 comparisons, 12 favored the comparison areas (the decrease in crime was greater in the comparison areas), eight favored the treatment areas (the decrease in crime was greater in the treatment areas), and one favored neither (the decrease in both areas was equivalent). This simplistic analysis suggests that Ceasefire did not consistently reduce violent crime because the comparison areas fared better than the treatment areas. The evaluators also carried out more sophisticated time series analyses meant to isolate the effects of Ceasefire. These analyses showed that Ceasefire was effective at reducing violence for eight of the 21 outcomes; it was not effective for another eight; and for five of them, the effects of Ceasefire were inconclusive.

Additional evidence on the effects of Ceasefire comes from an evaluation of Project Safe Neighborhoods (PSN), a focused deterrence intervention that was implemented in Chicago in some of the areas where Ceasefire was operating. The evaluators used a sophisticated quasi-experimental design to evaluate the effects of PSN on violent crime and to separate the effects of PSN from Ceasefire in those areas where both programs were operating (Papachristos, Meares, and Fagan 2007). The authors concluded that Ceasefire was not associated with the decrease in homicide rates in the PSN treatment area.

Evaluations of Cure Violence and related initiatives in other cities have found mixed results. In Baltimore, five of the ten treatment effects reported in the evaluation favored the treatment areas, one favored the comparison area, and four revealed no significant differences between treatment and comparison areas (Webster *et al.* 2012). An evaluation of a Cure Violence replication in the Crown Heights neighborhood in Brooklyn, New York found that shooting rates decreased by 6 percent in the treatment area and increased by 18 percent to 28 percent in the three comparison areas.

In Pittsburgh, an evaluation of a program partially modeled on Chicago's Ceasefire found that homicides either increased or remained stable in the treatment areas relative to the comparison areas, whereas aggravated assaults and gun assaults increased in all three treatment areas (Wilson, Chermak, and McGarrell 2010). In Newark, evaluators examined the effects of a hybrid model that represented a blend of "the law enforcement model used in Boston's Ceasefire and the public health approach adopted by Ceasefire Chicago" (Boyle *et al.* 2010: 107).[4] The evaluators found no significant differences in the number of patients admitted to a Level 1 trauma center with gunshot wounds after the program's launch. In Phoenix, an evaluation of another program modeled on Chicago's Ceasefire found that it resulted in a significant decrease in assaults and a significant increase in shootings in contrast with the comparison areas (Fox *et al.* 2015).

Taken together, these studies suggest that street outreach strategies have variable effects: they can reduce violence, have no effect on violence, or increase violence. There is some indication in the literature that communities with more conflict mediation activity may experience greater reductions in violence (Whitehill, Webster, and Vernick 2013). Unfortunately, the scientific research on the effects of street outreach has not yet matured to the point where it is possible to reach more definitive conclusions. This is one body of research in which investments in stronger research designs, especially randomized trials, are sorely needed to improve our understanding of whether (and under what conditions) the intervention is effective. Unlike some of the other initiatives reviewed in this chapter, street outreach strategies are currently being tested in cities around the world. If these efforts are rigorously evaluated using research designs with strong internal validity, the resulting body of research should provide useful insights about external validity as well.

Gun-related Strategies

Much of the public policy debate over guns focuses on regulating civilian ownership of firearms. There is a substantial body of research on the relationship between gun ownership and violent crime. This is a heavily contested and complex body of research that is beyond the scope of this chapter. Much of the debate is unfortunately influenced by emotion and ideology rather than scientific evidence (Makarios and Pratt 2012). Because some of the research is motivated by advocacy, it is crucial to question the quality and veracity of each study carefully. For many scholars, the debate over the civilian ownership of firearms misses a crucial point: that not all guns have an equal probability of being used in violence. For instance, the evidence suggests that illegal guns (those that are unlawfully obtained or possessed) are used more often in crime than legal guns.[5] Moreover, regulations controlling civilian ownership of firearms are less focused and incur more collateral costs than those that focus on illegal guns or those who use them. Research has also shown that certain types of weapons are used more often in violent crime than others (Kennedy, Piehl, and Braga 1996; Wintemute *et al.* 2004). Although much of the United States debate on solutions to gun violence focuses on banning "assault weapons," research shows that these weapons are involved in less than 2 percent of gun homicides (Kleck 2001). Finally, results from ballistic imaging research reveal that certain individual guns are used repeatedly in crime (Braga and Pierce 2004; King and Wells 2015; Maguire *et al.* 2016). Getting these so-called "hot guns" off the streets is likely to produce disproportionate impacts on violence.

Unfortunately, since much of the debate over how to address gun violence fails to focus on the highest-risk guns, the policy solutions that emerge from this debate are often similarly unfocused. For instance, research shows that voluntary[6] gun buyback programs are ineffective at reducing violence because they typically attract weapons that are not used in crime (Kuhn *et al.* 2002; Romero, Wintemute, and Vernick 1998). Systematic evaluations of gun buyback programs in Argentina (Lenis, Ronconi, and Schargrodsky 2010) and three US cities (Callahan, Rivara, and Koepsell 1995; Phillips, Kim, and Sobel 2013; Rosenfeld 1995) have all found that they had no effect on violent crime. According to Sherman (2001: 19), gun buyback programs fail because the intervention doesn't focus sufficiently on the risk: "Guns are bought from anyone, regardless of where they live or whether the gun was readily accessible to people at high risk for crime … not all guns are equal risk of being used in crime." Gun buyback programs could actually have perverse effects. For instance, since most such programs operate with a "no questions asked" policy, they could encourage offenders to steal guns and convert them to cash, or they could provide offenders with cash for trading in their old or unused weapons. Though the research evidence clearly demonstrates that gun buyback programs are ineffective, they continue to be used by well-intentioned policymakers and community activists concerned with "doing something" about gun violence. However, the resources invested in these programs could be put to better use supporting violence reduction initiatives that actually work.

If certain guns (both individual guns and *types* of guns) are used more often by offenders to commit acts of violence, then we would expect interventions that focus on these guns to be successful in reducing violence. Koper and Mayo-Wilson (2012) report findings from a systematic review of research evidence on the effectiveness of police interventions to reduce gun violence through efforts to stem the illegal possession and carrying of firearms. The underlying basis of these interventions is their primary focus on illegal guns, which are thought to be used more often in violent crime than legally owned guns. Koper and Mayo-Wilson's review includes seven rigorous studies that examine the impact of directed patrols in which police officers are assigned "to high-crime areas at high-risk times" (Koper and Mayo-Wilson 2012: 14) and they are encouraged to engage in proactive enforcement focused on seizing guns. Five of the seven studies took place in the United States with two others taking place in Colombia. The authors conclude that the intervention reduced gun violence in six of the seven studies. Moreover, they note that "crackdowns on gun carrying are more effective and efficient when they are more intensive and focused on high-risk places, times, and people" (2012: 32). This is a robust finding that derives from high-quality research.

One of the most well-known studies of police crackdowns on guns was the Kansas City Gun Experiment, which found that intensive police efforts to detect and seize concealed guns reduced violence (Sherman and Rogan 1995). Police engaged in proactive patrols in an 80 by 10 block area with a heavy concentration of gun violence. They conducted pedestrian and traffic stops in this area as a means of carrying out legally justified searches for firearms. Most (but not all) of the weapons seized were carried illegally and were later destroyed by police. The analysis found that the intervention was responsible for significant reductions in gun violence relative to an otherwise similar comparison area that did not receive the extra gun patrols. The authors concluded that enforcing existing laws prohibiting carrying concealed weapons can be an effective strategy for reducing gun crime. Similarly, Wells, Zhang, and Zhao (2012) examined the effects of gun possession arrests by a proactive patrol unit in the Houston Police Department. They found that increasing the number of illegal gun possession arrests reduced gun violence. Their findings are consistent with the conclusion that gun violence reduction strategies which focus intently on risk—including high-risk places, offenders, and guns—can be highly effective. Although the debate over civilian ownership of firearms is often highly polarized, all sides of the debate would likely find some common ground in supporting these effective initiatives.

Conclusion

This chapter has examined the research evidence on four well-known approaches to reducing violence. The research evidence on these strategies is uneven, with some notable gaps in knowledge that need to be filled. Even when there is a body of research on certain types of strategies, internal and external validity issues sometimes make it difficult to draw confident conclusions about what works and under what conditions. In spite of these issues, the research evidence reviewed in this chapter makes it clear that homicide *can* be prevented using the right mix of policies. The challenge is to continue testing and experimenting with these and other approaches to continue filling gaps in our knowledge, with the goal of building a high-quality body of research evidence on how to prevent homicide.

Notes

1 Street outreach is an important component of the Spergel model, a comprehensive approach to dealing with gangs and gang violence in the United States (Spergel 1995, 2007). Street outreach is just one part of this larger and more complex strategy for dealing with gangs. However, evaluations of the Spergel model have not isolated the effects of street outreach from the effects of other program elements.

2 Cure Violence outreach workers serve as case managers, working closely with clients on an ongoing basis, mentoring them, helping them address their problems without using violence, and working with them to find jobs. They adopt a social work-like approach (Skogan *et al.* 2009). Violence interrupters do not manage an ongoing caseload like the outreach workers. They focus more directly on anticipating and preventing violent incidents.

3 Some of these initiatives are not viewed by Cure Violence as official partners and may be missing certain elements of the Cure Violence approach.

4 Although the evaluators describe Newark's Ceasefire as a hybrid of projects in Boston and Chicago, its similarities to Boston's approach were somewhat superficial. Newark's Ceasefire appears to have adopted many of the elements of Chicago's Ceasefire. However, its outreach workers were a mix of ex-offenders and church congregants, did not maintain formal client caseloads, and appear to have been more reactive and less preventive than their peers in Chicago.

5 I use the word "suggests" because the evidence is somewhat incomplete. Due to the difficulties inherent in obtaining a representative sample of guns used in crime (because many crime guns are never seized), the best data come from asking offenders. In the United States, for instance, surveys or interviews of prisoners have clarified the sources from which offenders obtain guns (Cook *et al.* 2015; Cook, Parker, and Pollack 2015; Planty and Truman 2013; Wright and Rossi 1994). The research shows that since many offenders are prohibited from purchasing guns legally, they get them "in off-the-books transactions, often from social connections such as family and acquaintances, or from 'street' sources such as illicit brokers or drug dealers" (Cook, Parker, and Pollack 2015: 29).

6 Compulsory gun buybacks like the one implemented in Australia are beyond the scope of this chapter. For further reading, see Lee and Suardi (2010), Leigh and Neill (2010), and Reuter and Mouzos (2003).

References

Anderson, E. (1999) *Code of the Street: Decency, Violence, and the Moral Life of the Inner City*. New York: W.W. Norton.

Berg, M.T., Stewart, E.A., Schreck, C.J., and Simons, R.L. (2012) The victim–offender overlap in context: Examining the role of neighborhood street culture. *Criminology*, 50: 359–390.

Bowling, B. (1999) The rise and fall of New York murder: Zero tolerance or crack's decline? *British Journal of Criminology*, 39(4): 531–554.

Boyle, D.J., Lanterman, J.L., Pascarella, J.E., and Cheng, C.C. (2010) The impact of Newark's Operation Ceasefire on trauma center gunshot wound admissions. *Justice Research and Policy*, 12: 105–123.

Braga, A.A. (2008) Pulling levers focused deterrence strategies and the prevention of gun homicide. *Journal of Criminal Justice*, 36: 332–343.

Braga, A.A., Kennedy, D.M., Waring, E.J., and Piehl, A.M. (2001) Problem-oriented policing, deterrence, and youth violence: An evaluation of Boston's Operation Ceasefire. *Journal of Research in Crime and Delinquency*, 38: 195–225.

Braga, A.A., Papachristos, A.V., and Hureau, D. (2010) The concentration and stability of gun violence at micro places in Boston, 1980–2008. *Journal of Quantitative Criminology*, 26: 33–53.

Braga, A.A., Papachristos, A.V., and Hureau, D. (2012) Hot spots policing effects on crime. *Campbell Systematic Reviews*. doi: 10.4073/csr.2012.8.

Braga, A.A. and Pierce, G.L. (2004) Linking crime guns: The impact of ballistics imaging technology on the productivity of the Boston Police Department's Ballistics Unit. *Journal of Forensic Sciences*, 49(4): 701–706.

Braga, A.A., Pierce, G.L., McDevitt, J., *et al.* (2008) The strategic prevention of gun violence among gang-involved offenders. *Justice Quarterly*, 25: 132–162.

Braga, A.A. and Weisburd, D.L. (2012) The effects of focused deterrence strategies on crime: A systematic review and meta-analysis of the empirical evidence. *Journal of Research in Crime and Delinquency*, 49: 323–358.

Brookman, F. and Maguire, M. (2005) Reducing homicide in the UK: A review of the possibilities. *Crime, Law and Social Change*, 42(4–5): 325–403.

Callahan, C., Rivara, F., and Koepsell, T. (1995) Money for guns: Evaluation of the Seattle Gun Buyback Program. In M. Plotkin (ed.), *Under Fire: Gun Buybacks, Exchanges, and Amnesty Programs*. Washington, DC: Police Executive Research Forum.

Carney, F., Mattick, H.W., and Callaway, J.D. (1969) *Action on the Streets*. New York: Association Press.

Cook, P.J. (1980) Research in criminal deterrence: Laying the groundwork for the second decade. In N. Morris and M. Tonry (eds), *Crime and Justice: An Annual Review of Research* (vol. 2, pp. 211–268). Chicago: University of Chicago Press.

Cook, P.J., Harris, R.J., Ludwig, J., and Pollack, H. (2015) Some sources of crime guns in Chicago: Dirty dealers, straw purchasers and traffickers. *The Journal of Criminal Law & Criminology*, 104: 717–759.

Cook, P.J., Parker, S.T., and Pollack, H.A. (2015) Sources of guns to dangerous people: What we learn by asking them. *Preventive Medicine*, 79: 28–36.

Cook, T.D. and Campbell, D.T. (1979) *Quasi-Experimentation: Design & Analysis Issues for Field Settings*. Boston: Houghton Mifflin.

Eck, J.E. (2010) Policy is in the details: Using external validity to help policy makers. *Criminology & Public Policy*, 9: 859–866.

Eck, J.E. and Weisburd, D. (1995) Crime places in crime theory. In J.E. Eck and D. Weisburd (eds), *Crime and Place* (pp. 1–34). Monsey, NY: Criminal Justice Press.

Engel, R.S., Tillyer, M.S., and Corsaro, N. (2013) Reducing gang violence using focused deterrence: Evaluating the Cincinnati Initiative to Reduce Violence (CIRV). *Justice Quarterly*, 30: 403–439.

Farrington, D.P. (2003) Methodological quality standards for evaluation research. *The Annals of the American Academy of Political and Social Science*, 587: 49–68.

Fox, A.M., Katz, C.M., Choate, D.E., and Hedberg, E.C. (2015) Evaluation of the Phoenix TRUCE Project: A replication of Chicago CeaseFire. *Justice Quarterly*, 32: 85–115.

Gibbs, J.P. (1975) *Crime, Punishment, and Deterrence*. New York: Elsevier Scientific.

Gold, M. and Mattick, H.W. (1974) *Experiment in the Streets: The Chicago Youth Development Project*. Ann Arbor: University of Michigan, Institute for Social Research.

Jones, T. and Newburn, T. (2007) *Policy Transfer and Criminal Justice: Exploring US Influence over British Crime Control Policy*. Maidenhead, UK: Open University Press.

Kennedy, D.M. (2009) *Deterrence and Crime Prevention: Reconsidering the Prospect of Sanction*. New York: Routledge.

Kennedy, D.M., Piehl, A.M., and Braga, A.A. (1996) Youth violence in Boston: Gun markets, serious youth offenders, and a use-reduction strategy. *Law and Contemporary Problems*, 59: 147–196.

King, W.R. and Wells, W. (2015) Impediments to the effective use of ballistics imaging information in criminal investigations: Lessons from the use of IBIS in a developing nation. *Forensic Science Policy & Management: An International Journal*, 6: 47–57.

Kleck, G. (2001) Impossible policy evaluations and impossible conclusions: A comment on Koper and Roth. *Journal of Quantitative Criminology*, 17: 75–80.

Klein, M.W. (1969) Gang cohesiveness, delinquency, and a street-work program. *Journal of Research in Crime and Delinquency*, 6: 135–166.

Klein, M.W. (1971) *Street Gangs and Street Workers*. Englewood Cliffs, NJ: Prentice Hall.

Klein, M.W. and Maxson, C. (2006) *Street Gang Patterns and Policies*. New York: Oxford University Press.

Koper, C.S., Egge, J., and Lum, C. (2015) Institutionalizing place-based approaches: Opening "cases" on gun crime hot spots. *Policing*, 9: 242–254.

Koper, C.S. and Mayo-Wilson, E. (2012) Police strategies to reduce illegal possession and carrying of firearms: Effects on gun crime. *Campbell Systematic Reviews*. doi: 10.4073/csr.2012.11.

Kuhn, E.M., Nie, C.L., O'Brien, M.E., *et al.* (2002) Missing the target: A comparison of buyback and fatality related guns. *Injury Prevention*, 8: 143–146.

Kuhns, J.B. and Maguire, E.R. (2012) Drug and alcohol use by homicide victims in Trinidad and Tobago, 2001–2007. *Forensic Science, Medicine, and Pathology*, 8: 243–251.

Lee, W.S. and Suardi, S. (2010) The Australian firearms buyback and its effects on gun deaths. *Contemporary Economic Policy*, 28: 65–79.

Leigh, A. and Neill, C. (2010) Do gun buybacks save lives? Evidence from panel data. *American Law and Economics Review*, 12: 509–557.

Lenis, D., Ronconi, L., and Schargrodsky, E. (2010) The effect of the Argentine gun buy-back program on crime and violence. Paper presented at the IGERT Workshop, University of California at Berkeley (November 10).

MacKenzie, D.L. (2000) Evidence-based corrections: Identifying what works. *Crime & Delinquency*, 46: 457–471.

Maguire, E.R. and King, W.R. (2013) Transferring criminal investigation methods from developed to developing nations. *Policing and Society: An International Journal of Research and Policy*, 23: 346–361.

Maguire, E.R., King, W.R., Matusiak, M.C., and Campbell, B. (2016) Testing the effects of people, processes, and technology on ballistic evidence processing productivity. *Police Quarterly*, 19(2): 199–215.

Maguire, E.R., Willis, J., Snipes, J.B., and Gantley, M.T. (2008) Spatial concentrations of violence in Trinidad and Tobago. *Caribbean Journal of Criminology and Public Safety*, 13: 48–92.

Makarios, M.D. and Pratt, T.C. (2012) The effectiveness of policies and programs that attempt to reduce firearm violence: A meta-analysis. *Crime & Delinquency*, 58: 222–244.

McGarrell, E., Chermak, S., and Wilson, J. (2006) Reducing homicide through a "lever-pulling" strategy. *Justice Quarterly*, 23: 214–231.

Mears, D.P. (2007) Towards rational and evidence-based crime policy. *Journal of Criminal Justice*, 35: 667–682.

Nagin, D.S. (1998) Criminal deterrence research at the outset of the twenty-first century. In M. Tonry (ed.), *Crime and Justice: A Review of Research* (vol. 23, pp. 1–42). Chicago: University of Chicago Press.

Papachristos, A.V., Braga, A.A., and Hureau, D.M. (2012) Social networks and the risk of gunshot injury. *Journal of Urban Health*, 89: 992–1003.

Papachristos, A.V., Meares, T.L., and Fagan, J. (2007) Attention felons: Evaluating Project Safe Neighborhoods in Chicago. *Journal of Empirical Legal Studies*, 4: 223–272.

Papachristos, A.V. and Wildeman, C. (2014) Network exposure and homicide victimization in an African American community. *American Journal of Public Health*, 104: 143–150.

Paternoster, R. (2010) How much do we really know about criminal deterrence? *Journal of Criminal Law and Criminology*, 100: 765–823.

Pawson, R. and Tilley, N. (1997) *Realistic Evaluation*. London: SAGE.

Phillips, S.W., Kim, D.-Y., and Sobel, J. (2013) An evaluation of a multiyear gun buy-back programme: Re-examining the impact on violent crimes. *International Journal of Police Science and Management*, 15: 246–261.

Piehl, A.M., Cooper, S.J., Braga, A.A., and Kennedy, D.M. (2003) Testing for structural breaks in the evaluation of programs. *Review of Economics and Statistics*, 85: 550–558.

Piehl, A.M., Kennedy, D.M., and Braga, A.A. (2000) Problem solving and youth violence: An evaluation of the Boston Gun Project. *American Law and Economics Review*, 2: 58–106.

Planty, M. and Truman, J.L. (2013) *Firearm Violence, 1993–2011*. Washington, DC: Bureau of Justice Statistics.

Reuter, P. and Mouzos, J. (2003) Australia's gun control: Massive buy-back of low risk guns. In J. Ludwig and P.J. Cook (eds), *Evaluating Gun Control* (pp. 121–156). Washington, DC: Brookings Institution.

Robertson, A. (2005) Criminal justice policy transfer to post-Soviet states: Two case studies of police reform in Russia and Ukraine. *European Journal on Criminal Policy and Research*, 11: 1–28.

Romero, M.P., Wintemute, G.J., and Vernick, J.S. (1998) Characteristics of a gun exchange program, and an assessment of potential benefits. *Injury Prevention*, 4: 206–210.

Rosenfeld, R. (1995) Gun buy-backs: Crime control or community mobilization? In M. Plotkin (ed.), *Under Fire: Gun Buy-Backs, Exchanges, and Amnesty Programs* (pp. 1–28). Washington, DC: Police Executive Research Forum.

Sherman, L.W. (2001) Reducing gun violence: What works, what doesn't, what's promising. *Criminal Justice*, 1: 11–25.

Sherman, L.W. (2003) Misleading evidence and evidence-led policy: Making social science more experimental. *Annals of the American Academy of Political and Social Science*, 589: 6–19.

Sherman, L.W., Gartin, P., and Buerger, M. (1989) Hot spots of predatory crime: Routine activities and the criminology of place. *Criminology*, 27: 27–55.

Sherman, L.W. and Rogan, D.P. (1995) Effects of gun seizures on gun violence: "Hot spots" patrol in Kansas City. *Justice Quarterly*, 12: 673–693.

Sherman, L.W. and Weisburd, D. (1995) General deterrent effects of police patrol in crime "hot spots": A randomized, controlled trial. *Justice Quarterly*, 12: 625–648.

Skogan, W. and Frydl, K. (eds) (2004) *Fairness and Effectiveness in Policing: The Evidence*. Washington, DC: National Academies Press.

Skogan, W., Hartnett, S.M., Bump, N., and Dubois, J. (2009) *Evaluation of CeaseFire-Chicago*. Washington, DC: National Institute of Justice.

Spergel, I.A. (1995) *The Youth Gang Problem: A Community Approach*. New York: Oxford University Press.

Spergel, I.A. (2007) *Reducing Youth Violence: The Little Village Gang Project in Chicago*. Lanham, MD: AltaMira Press.

Stewart, E.A. and Simons, R.L. (2010) Race, code of the street, and violent delinquency: A multilevel investigation of neighborhood street culture and individual norms of violence. *Criminology*, 48: 569–605.

St Jean, P.K.B. (2007) *Pockets of Crime: A Closer Look at Neighborhood Street Crime, Broken Windows, and Collective Efficacy*. Chicago: University of Chicago Press.

Tita, G.E., Cohen, J., and Engberg, J. (2005) An ecological study of the location of gang "set space." *Social Problems*, 52: 272–299.

Tracy, M., Braga, A.A., and Papachristos, A.V. (2016) The transmission of gun and other weapon-involved violence within social networks. *Epidemiologic Reviews*, 38(1): 70–86.

Webster, D.W., Whitehill, J.M., Vernick, J.S., and Parker, E.M. (2012) *Evaluation of Baltimore's Safe Streets Program: Effects on Attitudes, Participants' Experiences, and Gun Violence*. Baltimore, MD: Johns Hopkins University.

Weisburd, D., Bushway, S., Lum, C., and Yang, S.-M. (2004) Trajectories of crime at places: A longitudinal study of street segments in the City of Seattle. *Criminology*, 42: 283–321.

Weisburd, D., Groff, E., and Yang, S.-M. (2012) *The Criminology of Place: Developmental Patterns and Risk and Preventive Factors*. New York: Oxford University Press.

Weisburd, D., Lum, C., and Petrosino, A. (2001) Does research design affect study outcomes in criminal justice? *The Annals of the American Academy of Social and Political Sciences*, 578: 50–70.

Weisburd, D., Maher, L., and Sherman, L.W. (1992) Contrasting crime general and crime specific theory: The case of hot spots of crime. In F. Adler and W.S. Laufer (eds), *Advances in Criminological Theory* (vol. 4, pp. 45–70). New Brunswick, NJ: Transaction Press.

Wells, W.H., Zhang, Y., and Zhao, J. (2012) The effects of gun possession arrests made by a proactive police patrol unit. *Policing: An International Journal of Police Strategies & Management*, 35: 253–271.

Welsh, B.C. and Farrington, D.P. (2011) Evidence-based crime policy. In M. Tonry (ed.), *The Oxford Handbook of Crime and Criminal Justice* (pp. 60–92). New York: Oxford University Press.

Whitehill, J.M., Webster, D.W., and Vernick, J.S. (2013) Street conflict mediation to prevent youth violence: Conflict characteristics and outcomes. *Injury Prevention*, 19: 204–209.

Williams, D.J., Currie, D., Linden, W., and Donnelly, P.D. (2014) Addressing gang-related violence in Glasgow: A preliminary pragmatic quasi-experimental evaluation of the Community Initiative to Reduce Violence (CIRV). *Aggression and Violent Behavior*, 19: 686–691.

Wilson, J.M., Chermak, S., and McGarrell, E.F. (2010) *Community-based Violence Prevention: An Assessment of Pittsburgh's One Vision One Life Program*. Santa Monica, CA: RAND.

Wintemute, G.J., Romero, M.P., Wright, M.A., and Grassel, K.M. (2004) The life cycle of crime guns: A description based on guns recovered from young people in California. *Annals of Emergency Medicine*, 43: 733–742.

Wright, J.D. and Rossi, P.H. (1994) *Armed and Considered Dangerous: A Survey of Felons and their Firearms*. Hawthorne, NY: Aldine de Gruyter.

Yablonski, L. (1962) *The Violent Gang*. New York: MacMillan.

Index

Note: page numbers in *italics* refer to information contained in tables, page numbers in **bold** refer to diagrams.

The Handbook of Homicide, First Edition. Edited by Fiona Brookman, Edward R. Maguire, and Mike Maguire.